THE ROYAL INSCRIPTIONS OF SARGON II, KING OF ASSYRIA (721–705 BC)

THE ROYAL INSCRIPTIONS OF THE NEO-ASSYRIAN PERIOD

Volumes Published

1 The Royal Inscriptions of Tiglath-pileser III (744–727 BC) and Shalmaneser V (726–722 BC), Kings of Assyria
HAYIM TADMOR and SHIGEO YAMADA

3/1 The Royal Inscriptions of Sennacherib, King of Assyria (704–681 BC), Part 1
A. KIRK GRAYSON and JAMIE NOVOTNY

3/2 The Royal Inscriptions of Sennacherib, King of Assyria (704–681 BC), Part 2
A. KIRK GRAYSON and JAMIE NOVOTNY

4 The Royal Inscriptions of Esarhaddon, King of Assyria (680–669 BC)
ERLE LEICHTY

5/1 The Royal Inscriptions of Ashurbanipal (668–631 BC), Aššur-etel-ilāni (630–627 BC), and Sîn-šarra-iškun (626–612 BC), Kings of Assyria, Part 1
JAMIE NOVOTNY and JOSHUA JEFFERS

THE ROYAL INSCRIPTIONS OF THE NEO-ASSYRIAN PERIOD

VOLUME 2

The Royal Inscriptions of Sargon II, King of Assyria (721–705 BC)

GRANT FRAME

with the collaboration of Andreas Fuchs
for two inscriptions

EISENBRAUNS
University Park, Pennsylvania

Printed in the United States of America on acid-free paper.

ISBN 978-1-64602-109-3

The research and publication of this volume
have been supported by the National Endowment for the Humanities,
the Alexander von Humboldt Foundation, the University of Pennsylvania, and
Ludwig-Maximilians-Universität München.

Cover illustration: Botta, Monument de Ninive 1 pl. 12
depicting the Assyrian King Sargon II
Drawing by Sabrina Nortey

The text editions in this work were produced using Oracc.
See http://oracc.org for further information.

Library of Congress Cataloging-in-Publication Data

Names: Sargon II, King of Assyria, -705 B.C., author. | Frame, Grant, editor.
Title: The royal inscriptions of Sargon II, King of Assyria (721–705 BC) / [edited by] Grant Frame ; with the collaboration of Andreas Fuchs for two inscriptions.
Other titles: Royal inscriptions of the neo-Assyrian period ; v. 2.
Description: University Park, Pennsylvania : Eisenbrauns, [2021] | Series: The royal inscriptions of the neo-Assyrian period ; volume 2 | Includes bibliographical references and indexes. | Inscriptions are in Akkadian or Sumerian; translated into English.
Summary: "A collection of English translations of all the official inscriptions of Sargon II, king of Assyria (721–705 BC), as well as those of his wife and officials"—Provided by publisher.
Identifiers: LCCN 2020034297 | ISBN 9781646021093 (cloth)
Subjects: LCSH: Sargon II, King of Assyria, -705 B.C. | Cuneiform inscriptions, Akkadian. | Cuneiform inscriptions, Sumerian. | Akkadian language—Texts. | Sumerian language—Texts. | Assyria—History—Sources. | Assyria—Kings and rulers.
Classification: LCC PJ3837.S2 F73 2021 | DDC 892/.1—dc23
LC record available at https://lccn.loc.gov/2020034297

Eisenbrauns is an imprint of The Pennsylvania State University Press.
The Pennsylvania State University Press is a member of the Association of University Presses.

The paper used in this publication meets the minimum requirements of the American National Standard for Information Sciences—Permanence of Paper for Printed Library Materials, ANSI Z39.48-1984.

To my teachers in Akkadian and Sumerian

Contents

Detailed Table of Contents

List of Figures

Contents of Scores

(the pdf is available at http://oracc.museum.upenn.edu/rinap/scores/)

Foreword

The present series of publications, Royal Inscriptions of the Neo-Assyrian Period (RINAP), is intended to present up-to-date editions of the royal inscriptions of a number of Neo-Assyrian rulers. It is modeled on the publications of the now-defunct Royal Inscriptions of Mesopotamia (RIM) series and carries on where the RIMA (Royal Inscriptions of Mesopotamia, Assyrian Periods) publications ended. The RIM Project was initiated by A. Kirk Grayson at the University of Toronto in 1979 and over the years received extensive support from the Social Sciences and Humanities Research Council of Canada, the University of Toronto, and private individuals, in particular Laurence Shiff. In all, it produced ten volumes in its various sub-series. Grayson retired from the University of Toronto in 2000 and a few years later found it necessary to cease scholarly pursuits due to personal and family illnesses. At that time, he handed over responsibility for the work of the project to me, formerly the assistant director and at times acting director of the RIM Project. When I took up a position at the University of Pennsylvania in 2006 and the last RIM volume (RIME 1 by Douglas R. Frayne) appeared in early 2008, the RIM Project officially ceased to exist. Work on several further volumes of inscriptions of Assyrian and Babylonian rulers had already begun during the time of the RIM Project and Grayson passed on responsibility for the materials and manuscripts to me. In 2007, I initiated the current project in order to continue the task of making the official inscriptions of the several important Neo-Assyrian rulers available in modern, scholarly editions. While the volumes in the new series resemble the format of the RIM volumes in most matters, the RINAP volumes include indices of proper names, and editions of the texts are also available online, in connection with the Cuneiform Digital Library Initiative (CDLI) and the Open Richly Annotated Cuneiform Corpus Initiative (Oracc).

Five volumes have already appeared in this series: RINAP 1, comprising the inscriptions of Tiglath-pileser III and Shalmaneser V (begun by Hayim Tadmor and completed by Shigeo Yamada); RINAP 3/1–2, comprising the inscriptions of Sennacherib (begun by A. Kirk Grayson and completed by his collaborator Jamie Novotny); RINAP 4, comprising the inscriptions of Esarhaddon (by Erle Leichty, with a contribution by Grant Frame); and RINAP 5/1, comprising many of the inscriptions of Ashurbanipal (by Jamie Novotny and Joshua Jeffers). The remainder of the royal inscriptions of Ashurbanipal and those of his successors Aššur-etel-ilāni and Sîn-šarra-iškun will be presented in two forthcoming volumes (RINAP 5/2 and 5/3) by Joshua Jeffers and Jamie Novotny. The present volume (RINAP 2) provides editions of the inscriptions of Sargon II and has been completed by myself, with the collaboration of Andreas Fuchs for text nos. 82 (Nineveh Prism) and 117 (Najafabad Stele).

The National Endowment for the Humanities awarded the RINAP Project research grants in 2008, 2010, 2012, 2015, and 2017, as well as supplementary funds in 2019, to help carry out its work and my sincere thanks must be expressed to it. My appreciation must also be extended to the University of Pennsylvania and to the University of Pennsylvania Museum of Archaeology and Anthropology, where the project is based, for their constant support. Additional funding for the preparation of RINAP 2 was provided by the University of Pennsylvania Research Foundation and the School of Arts and Sciences of the University of Pennsylvania, as well as by the Alexander von Humboldt Foundation (through the establishment of the Alexander von Humboldt Professorship for Ancient History of the Near and Middle East in 2015) and Ludwig-Maximilians-Universität München (Historisches Seminar – Abteilung Alte Geschichte). I am grateful to Karen Radner for providing additional financial support for the project.

Philadelphia
June 2020

Grant Frame

Preface

When A. Kirk Grayson asked me in the late 1980s to undertake the preparation of the volume of royal inscriptions of Sargon II for the Royal Inscriptions of Mesopotamia (RIM) Project, I never thought that it would take as long as it has. The delay was largely caused by three matters: the need to deal with other editorial and administrative duties related to the RIM Project, the unexpected end of the RIM Project due to funding difficulties in the early 2000s, and, most importantly, the problems preparing satisfactory editions of some of the major texts of Sargon due to the loss of the original inscriptions and the unreliability of the available sources of information on those inscriptions. After I moved from the University of Toronto to the University of Pennsylvania in 2006, I was encouraged by Erle Leichty to revive the project, or at least the section dealing with Neo-Assyrian royal inscriptions. With the support of the National Endowment for the Humanities, in 2008 I founded the Royal Inscriptions of the Neo-Assyrian Period (RINAP) Project and since that time have directed the preparation and publication of five volumes. Work on the Sargon volume continued during all of this time, although with numerous gaps as other duties and projects took priority. Two of the inscriptions presented in this volume — the Nineveh Prism and the Najafabad Stele (text nos. 82 and 117) — are the result of collaboration between the author and Andreas Fuchs (Eberhard Karls Universität Tübingen), and the author's appreciation for all his work must be stressed. Fuchs had already published an edition of the former text about twenty years ago (SAAS 8) and the edition of the latter text presented here is the result of extensive discussion and deliberation between the two of us.

Work on the present corpus of texts necessitated extensive travel for collation of previously published inscriptions and for examination of unpublished material. The author wishes to thank the various museums and museum authorities that have cooperated in the preparation of this book. In particular, he would like to thank the directors, keepers, curators, and assistants of the Louvre Museum (Paris), the Oriental Institute of the University of Chicago (Chicago), the British Museum (London), the Institut de France (Paris), the Royal Ontario Museum (Toronto), the Vorderasiatisches Museum (Berlin), and the National Museum in Tehran. Specifically, the author expresses his gratitude to Béatrice André-Salvini, John Brinkman, John Curtis, Andrew Dix, Walter Farber, Liane Jakob-Rost, Ed Keal, John Larsen, Joachim Marzahn, Kiersten Neumann, Susanne Paulus, Bill Pratt, Clemens Reichel, Jonathan Taylor, Ariane Thomas, Christopher Walker, and Michel Zink. These colleagues, and their staff, have been extremely helpful and have extended to me every courtesy and assistance.

As usual with a volume in this series, numerous individuals aided in the production of the volume in some way. Since the preparation of this book has spanned more than three decades, it is impossible to name everyone who has contributed to RINAP 2 and thus any omissions are unintentional. While the author has collated most of the texts himself, other scholars have kindly collated some texts, provided information on pieces, or aided in some way. These include Amitai Baruchi-Unna, Stephen Batiuk, Giovanni Bergamini, Eleazar Birnbaum, S. Borowski, Jean-Marie Durand, Jeanette Fincke, Kirk Grayson, Joshua Jeffers, Enrique Jiménez, Jacob Lauinger, Erle Leichty, Gianni Marchesi, Nicolò Marchetti, Michael Müller-Karpe, Jamie Novotny, Karen Radner, Julian Reade, Johannes Renger, Michael Roaf, Marcel Sigrist, Greta Van Buylaere, Chikako Watanabe, Frauke Weiershäuser, Manfred Weippert, and Joan Goodnick Westenholz. During my various periods of working in museums and collections outside of Toronto and Philadelphia, I received much gracious hospitality from numerous friends and colleagues. During a sabbatical in 2013–2014 spent in Oxford working on the manuscript, the author received much kind fellowship and support from Tim and Kathy Clayden, Jacob Dahl, Stephanie Dalley, and Frances Reynolds and Philip Binns, as well as the fellows of Wolfson College. My thanks must also to Richard Beal and JoAnne Scurlock for hospitality during a stay in Chicago, and to Denise Bolton, Jamie Novotny, Karen Radner, Michael Roaf, Walther Sallaberger, and Frans van Koppen during stays in Munich.

In Toronto, during the RIM years, several individuals contributed to the technical and editorial preparation of the volume and they deserve credit for performing at times tedious and time-consuming tasks. In particular, the author offers his gratitude to Amy Barron, Hope Grau, Diane Kriger, and Jill Ruby. For the Philadelphia stages of production, the author would like to thank various colleagues and students: Katy Blanchard, Tegan Bunsu, Michael Chapin, Ann Guinan, Andrew Knapp, Daniel Patterson, Irene Sibbing Plantholt, Steve Tinney, Richard Zettler, and Ilona Zsolnay. Last, but by no means least, special thanks must be given to Joshua Jeffers and Steve Tinney in Philadelphia and to Giulia Lentini, Nathan Morello, and Jamie Novotny in Munich for help in numerous ways, in particular for undertaking the arduous task of preparing the final, camera-ready manuscript and the fully lemmatized and searchable online version for the texts.

The penultimate manuscript of RINAP 2 was read by Ariel Bagg, Nicholas Postgate, and Martin Worthington, each of whom made numerous useful comments, corrections, and improvements. Their time, care, and generosity are greatly appreciated. Any and all errors of commission and omission are, of course, the responsibility of the author.

Since the Editor-in-Chief of the RINAP series is also the author of this volume, Karen Radner, a member of the editorial board, kindly assumed the role of Editor-in-Chief for the volume.

The author's appreciation goes out to the University of Pennsylvania, the University of Pennsylvania Museum of Archaeology and Anthropology, the National Endowment for the Humanities, the Social Sciences and Humanities Research Council of Canada, the University of Toronto, the Alexander von Humboldt Foundation, and the Ludwig-Maximilians-Universität München, as well as to several private individuals, in particular Laurence Shiff and Malcolm Horsnell, for both financial and material support in support of the work of the RIM and/or RINAP Projects and thus the preparation of this volume.

Finally, the author wishes to express his gratitude to his numerous teachers of Akkadian and Sumerian over the years as a student at the University of Toronto and the University of Chicago: R.D. Biggs, J.A. Brinkman, M. Civil†, I.J. Gelb†, G.B. Gragg, A.K. Grayson, H. Hunger, S. Parpola, E. Reiner†, J. Renger, M. Rowton†, and R.F.G. Sweet. He hopes that nothing in this volume will make them regret their encouragement, support, and advice during his training.

Philadelphia
June 2020

Grant Frame

Editorial Notes

The volumes in the RINAP series are modeled upon the publications of the now-defunct Royal Inscriptions of Mesopotamia (RIM) Project, with a few modifications, in particular the addition of indices of proper names. Like the RIM volumes, the volumes in this series are not intended to provide analytical or synthetic studies, but rather to provide basic text editions that can serve as the foundations for such studies. Thus, extensive discussions of the contents of the texts are not presented, and the core of each volume is the edition of the relevant texts.

In this volume, the order of the texts is based for the most part upon the following two criteria:

(1) The city at which the structure dealt with in the building or dedicatory portion of the text was located. If that information is not preserved on the text, the provenance of the inscribed object is the determining factor.

(2) The type of object upon which the inscription is written (prism, cylinder, tablet, etc.).

Following the practice of the RIM series, inscriptions that cannot be assigned definitely to a particular ruler are given text numbers beginning at 1001. Certain other inscriptions that provide information relevant for establishing royal names and titles (e.g., "servant seals") and any composed in the name of another member of the royal family (e.g., royal wives) have been given numbers that begin at 2001.

In the volumes of the RINAP series, the term "exemplar" is employed to designate a single inscription found on one object. The term "text" is employed to refer to an inscription that existed in antiquity and that may be represented by a number of more or less duplicate exemplars. In these editions exemplars of one text are edited together as a "master text," with a single transliteration and translation. Variants to the "master text" are provided either on page (major variants) or at the back of the volume (minor variants).

Each text edition is normally supplied with a brief introduction containing general information. This is followed by a catalogue containing basic information about all exemplars. This includes museum and excavation numbers (the symbol + is added between fragments that belong to the same object), provenance, lines preserved, and indication of whether or not the inscription has been collated (c = collated with the original, (c) = partially collated with the original, p = collated by means of a photograph, (p) = partially collated from a photograph; and n = not collated). The next section is normally a commentary containing further technical information and notes. The bibliography then follows. Items are arranged chronologically, earliest to latest, with notes in parentheses after each bibliographic entry. These notes indicate the exemplars with which the item is concerned and the nature of the publication, using the following key words: photo, copy, edition, translation, study, and provenance. Certain standard reference works (e.g., the various volumes of "Keilschriftbibliographie" and "Register Assyriologie" published in Orientalia and Archiv für Orientforschung respectively; Borger, HKL 1–3; AHw; CAD; and Seux, ERAS) are not normally cited, although they were essential in the collecting and editing of these texts. While the bibliographies should contain all major relevant items, they are not necessarily totally exhaustive; a vast amount of scattered literature exists on many of the inscriptions edited in this volume and much of this literature is of only limited scholarly interest.

As noted earlier, a distinction is made between major and minor variants to a "master text"; the major variants are placed at the bottom of the page and the minor variants at the back of the book. In brief, major variants are essentially non-orthographic in nature, while minor variants are orthographic variations. Orthographic variants of proper names may at times be significant and thus on occasion these will also appear on the page as major variants. Complete transliterations of all exemplars in the style of musical scores are found in the pdf on Oracc at http://oracc.museum.upenn.edu/rinap/scores/ and thus any reader who finds the notes on variants insufficient for his/her needs may check the full reading of any exemplar (the pdfs of the scores for previous RINAP volumes are also now available on Oracc). Such scores, however, are not normally given for bricks and seal inscriptions. Objects whose attribution to a particular text is not entirely certain are given exemplar numbers that are followed by an asterisk (*); for example, IM 18627 is regarded as text no. 41 ex. 3*, since it is uncertain that it is an exemplar of that text. Moreover, these exemplars are listed in separate catalogues (Likely Additional Exemplars), beneath the main catalogue.

Several photographs are included in this volume. These are intended to show a few of the object types upon which Sargon's inscriptions were written and to aid the reader in understanding the current state of preservation of some of the inscriptions.

As is the normal practice for transliterating cuneiform inscriptions, lower case Roman is used for Sumerian and lower case italics for Akkadian; logograms in Akkadian texts appear in capitals. The system of sign values in Borger, Mesopotamisches Zeichenlexikon (MZ), is generally followed. A number of inscriptions use at times Babylonian sign forms in a text written mainly with Assyrian sign forms and vice versa; this has not been indicated in the editions. As in previous volumes, certain variant sign forms are not specifically indicated in the transliterations. For example, no attempt is normally made to indicate when a sign taken to be DUB was actually written with a standard UM form (and vice versa); the same generally holds true for reading such signs as EZEN/SAR, GAB/TAḪ, and DUL/DU$_6$. Italics in the English translation indicate either an uncertain translation or a word in the original language. In general, the rendering of geographical names follows the Répertoire Géographique des Textes Cunéiformes (Rép. Géogr.) and personal names follows The Prosopography of the Neo-Assyrian Empire (PNA); however, the names of Babylonian rulers follow the spelling used in RIMB 2.

There are several differences between the RIM and RINAP styles. Among these, the most notable is that all partially preserved or damaged signs, regardless of how they are broken, now appear between half brackets (⸢ and ⸣). Thus, no partially preserved sign has square brackets ([and]) inserted in its transliteration; for example, [DINGI]R and LUGA[L KU]R appear in the transliteration as ⸢DINGIR⸣ and ⸢LUGAL KUR⸣ respectively. This change was made to ensure compatibility of the online RINAP editions with the standards of the Open Richly Annotated Cuneiform Corpus (Oracc), the parent site and project where RINAP Online is housed. This change was implemented in the print version in order to present identical editions in RINAP 2 and RINAP Online. Note, however, that the translations may appear more damaged than their corresponding transliterations indicate, as the translations were prepared according to standard Assyriological practices; for example, ⸢DINGIR⸣ (= [DINGI]R) and ⸢LUGAL KUR⸣ (= LUGA[L KU]R) are translated as "[the go]d" and "king [of the lan]d," and not "the god" and "king of the land."

Since some of the most important inscriptions of Sargon either no longer exist, having been lost in the Tigris in 1855, or were reburied at the site, and thus are only attested via copies made by their excavator P.E. Botta at the site of Khorsabad (ancient Dūr-Šarrukīn) or at times also by poorly preserved squeezes of the inscriptions, it has been found necessary to edit some texts in a different manner than is normally the case in the RIM and RINAP volumes and to make use of some additional sigla. This is described more fully in the Introduction to the volume and/or at the relevant inscriptions, but a brief summary is also provided here. For texts 1–4 and 8, although there is only one actual exemplar of the inscription, it has been thought best to provide a score for each inscription, providing either full or partial transliterations of the various sources for a lost original (e.g., Botta's copy published in Monument de Ninive, a copy made by H. Winckler after examination of a squeeze of the inscription, a copy made by Ch.-F. Jean following an examination of a squeeze, a copy made by Botta at Khorsabad and preserved in the Institut de France or published in Journal asiatique in the 1840s, or a squeeze currently preserved in the Louvre). With regard to additional sigla, a superscript dagger (†) is placed after a sign that has an abnormal/incorrect form in a copy by Botta that cannot be verified or corrected from collation of the original or a squeeze, or from an earlier copy made by Botta (normally one preserved in the Institut de France and/or published in the Journal asiatique). A superscript right-facing triangular bullet (‣) is employed in the scores to note where a copy by H. Winckler specifically indicates that he began to collate the inscription from a squeeze. A superscript circular bullet (•) is similarly employed to note where Winckler specifically indicates that his collations from a squeeze ended. This latter siglum (•) is also used in the transliteration of text no. 117 (Najafabad Stele) to indicate where the lines of the inscription on the squeezes preserved in the Royal Ontario Museum end. At times Botta's copies misalign fragments of a wall slab; a double dagger (‡) is employed in the scores to indicate the point in the line of a Botta copy where one must either go up or down a line in his copy in order to continue reading the relevant line.

The reader should note that there is some inconsistency in the use of Roman versus Arabic numerals for the room numbers of the palace of Sargon at Khorsabad in publications. It has been thought best to cite the rooms from which inscribed wall slabs come (basically rooms I–XIV) using roman numerals, following the practice initiated by the first excavator of the site, Paul-Emile Botta, and used in most publications of the texts (e.g., Winckler, Sar.; Lie, Sar.; and Fuchs, Khorsabad), but to use Arabic numerals for the other rooms (mostly in connection with texts found during the later excavations of the Oriental Institute of the University of Chicago and following its practice [e.g., Loud, Khorsabad 1; and Loud and Altman, Khorsabad 2]). See the Introduction for a fuller explanation of the matter.

In addition to the indices of museum and excavation numbers and selected publications found in RIM volumes, the RINAP volumes also contain indices of proper names (personal names, topographical names, and divine names). Concordances to correlate the line numbers used for the Khorsabad Annals in this volume and those given in the previous major editions by H. Winckler and A. Fuchs are also provided. Searchable online versions of the manuscripts are maintained on Oracc by MOCCI (Munich Open-access Cuneiform Corpus Initiative). Web versions of the editions are also hosted on CDLI (Cuneiform Digital Library Initiative).

Philadelphia Grant Frame
June 2020

Bibliographical Abbreviations

AAA	Annals of Archaeology and Anthropology. Liverpool, 1908–48
AAT	J.A. Craig, Astrological-Astronomical Texts (=Assyriologische Bibliothek 14). Leipzig 1899
Aegyptus	Aegyptus: Rivista Italiana di Egittologia e di Papirologia. Milan, 1920–
AfK	Archiv für Keilschriftforschung, vols. 1–2. Berlin, 1923–25
AfO	Archiv für Orientforschung, vol. 3– (vols. 1–2 = AfK). Berlin, Graz, and Horn, 1926–
AHw	W. von Soden, Akkadisches Handwörterbuch, 3 vols. Wiesbaden, 1965–81
AJSL	The American Journal of Semitic Languages and Literatures. Chicago, 1895–1941
Akkadica	Akkadica. Brussels, 1977–
Albenda, Palace of Sargon	P. Albenda, The Palace of Sargon, King of Assyria / Le palais de Sargon d'Assyrie. Paris, 1986
AMI NF	Archaeologische Mitteilungen aus Iran. Neue Folge. Berlin, 1968–
Anadolu Araştırmaları	Anadolu Araştırmaları. Istanbul, 1955–
Andrae, AAT	W. Andrae, Der Anu-Adad-Tempel in Assur (=WVDOG 10). Leipzig, 1909
Andrae, Coloured Ceramics	W. Andrae, Coloured Ceramics from Ashur, and Earlier Ancient Assyrian Wall-Paintings, from Photographs and Water-Colours by Members of the Ashur Expedition Organised by the Deutsche Orient-Gesellschaft. London, 1925
Andrae, Festungswerke	W. Andrae, Die Festungswerke von Assur (=WVDOG 23). Leipzig, 1913
Andrae, FKA	W. Andrae, Farbige Keramik aus Assur und ihre Vorstufen in altassyrischen Wandmalereien: nach Aquarellen von Mitgliedern der Assur-Expedition und nach photographischen Aufnahmen von Originalen im Auftrage der Deutschen Orient-Gesellschaft. Berlin, 1923
André-Leicknam, Naissance de l'écriture	B. André-Leicknam and N. Ziegler, Naissance de l'écriture: cunéiformes et hiéroglyphes. Paris, 1982
ANEP[2]	J.B. Pritchard (ed.), The Ancient Near East in Pictures Relating to the Old Testament, 2nd edition. Princeton, 1969
ANET[3]	J.B. Pritchard (ed.), Ancient Near Eastern Texts Relating to the Old Testament, 3rd edition. Princeton, 1969
Annales de Philosophie chrétienne	Annales de Philosophie chrétienne. Paris, 1830–
AnSt	Anatolian Studies: Journal of the British Institute of Archaeology in Ankara. London 1951–
Anthonioz, L'eau	S. Anthonioz, L'eau, enjeux politiques et théologiques, de Sumer à la Bible. Leiden, 2009
Antike Welt	Antike Welt. Zurich, 1970–
AO	Der Alte Orient, 43 vols. Leipzig, 1899–1945
AOAT	Alter Orient und Altes Testament. Neukirchen-Vluyn, Kevelaer, and Münster, 1968–
AoF	Altorientalische Forschungen. Berlin, 1974–
Aramazd	Aramazd: Armenian Journal of Near Eastern Studies. Yerevan, 2006–
Arch.	Archaeologia, or, Miscellaneous Tracts Relating to Antiquity. London, 1770–1992
Archaeology	Archaeology. New York, 1948–
ARRIM	Annual Review of the Royal Inscriptions of Mesopotamia Project. Toronto, 1983–91
Assur	Assur. Malibu, 1974–
Assyria to Iberia	J. Aruz, S.B. Graff, and Y. Rakic (eds.), Assyria to Iberia at the Dawn of the Classical Age. New York, 2014
Atiqot, English Series	ʿAtiqot, English Series. Jerusalem, 1955–
Augustinianum	Augustinianum. Rome, 1961–
AUWE	Ausgrabungen in Uruk-Warka Endberichte. Deutsches Archäologisches Institut, Abteilung Baghdad. Mainz am Rhein, 1987–

Aviram, Eretz Shomron	J. Aviram (ed.), Eretz Shomron: The Thirtieth Archaeological Convention, September 1972. Jerusalem, 1973
Bagg, Assyrer und das Westland	A.M. Bagg, Die Assyrer und das Westland: Studien zur historischen Geographie und Herrschaftspraxis in der Levante im 1. Jt. v. u. Z. (=Orientalia Lovaniensia Analecta 216). Leuven, 2011
Bagg, Assyrische Wasserbauten	A.M. Bagg, Assyrische Wässerbauten: Landwirtschaftliche Wasserbauten im Kernland Assyriens zwischen der 2. Hälfte des 2. und der 1. Hälfte des 1. Jahrtausends v. Chr. (=Baghdader Forschungen 24). Mainz am Rhein, 2000
Bagg, Rép. Géogr. 7	A.M. Bagg, Die Orts- und Gewässernamen der neuassyrischen Zeit, 5 parts (=Répertoire Géographique des Textes Cunéiformes 7). Wiesbaden, 2007–2020
Bagh. Mitt.	Baghdader Mitteilungen. Berlin, 1960–
Ball, Light	C.J. Ball, Light from the East or the Witness of the Monuments: An Introduction to the Study of Biblical Archaeology. London, 1899
Barag, Catalogue	D. Barag, Catalogue of Western Asiatic Glass in the British Museum. London, 1985
Basmachi, Treasures	F. Basmachi, Treasures of the Iraq Museum. Baghdad, 1976
BASOR	Bulletin of the American Schools of Oriental Research. New Haven and Boston, 1919–
Bauer, Lesestücke	T. Bauer, Akkadische Lesestücke, 3 vols. Rome, 1953
BCSMS	Bulletin of the Canadian Society for Mesopotamian Studies, 40 vols. Toronto, 1981–2005
Becking, Fall of Samaria	B. Becking, The Fall of Samaria: An Historical and Archaeological Study (=Studies in the History of the Ancient Near East 2). Leiden, 1992
Berlejung, Theologie	A. Berlejung, Die Theologie der Bilder: Herstellung und Einweihung von Kultbildern in Mesopotamien und die alttestamentliche Bilderpolemik (=Biblicus et Orientalis 162). Freiburg, 1998
Berlejung and Streck, Arameans, Chaldeans, and Arabs	A. Berlejung and M.P. Streck (eds.), Arameans, Chaldeans and Arabs in Babylonia and Palestine in the First Millennium B.C. (=Leipziger Altorientalistische Studien 3). Wiesbaden, 2013
Bezold, Cat.	C. Bezold, Catalogue of the Cuneiform Tablets in the Kouyunjik Collection of the British Museum, 5 vols. London, 1889–1899
Bezold, HKA	C. Bezold, Historische Keilschrifttexte aus Assur (=Sitzungberichte der Heidelberger Akademie der Wissenschaften, philosophisch-historische Klasse 8). Heidelberg, 1915
Bezold, Literatur	C. Bezold, Kurzgefasster Überblick über die babylonisch-assyrische Literatur, nebst einem chronologischen Excurs, zwei Registern und einem Index zu 1700 Thontafeln des British-Museum's. Leipzig, 1886
Biainili-Urartu	S. Kroll et al. (eds.), Biainili-Urartu: The Proceedings of the Symposium held in Munich 12–14 October 2007 / Tagungsbericht des Münchner Symposiums 12.–14. Oktober 2007 (=Acta Iranica 51). Leuven, 2012
BiAr	The Biblical Archaeologist, New Haven and Atlanta, 1938–97
Biblica	Biblica. Rome, 1920–
Biblical Archaeology Review	Biblical Archaeology Review. Washington, DC, 1975–
Biblische Notizen	Biblische Notizen. Bamberg, 1976–
BibMes	Bibliotheca Mesopotamica. Malibu, 1975–
BiOr	Bibliotheca Orientalis. Leiden, 1943–
Blanchard, Royaumes oubliés	V. Blanchard (ed), Royaumes oubliés: De l'Empire hittite aux Araméens. Paris, 2019
BM Guide	British Museum. A Guide to the Babylonian and Assyrian Antiquities, 3rd edition. London, 1922
BMQ	British Museum Quarterly. London, 1926–73
Böhl, Chrestomathy 1	F.M.T. Böhl, Akkadian Chrestomathy, Volume 1: Selected Cuneiform Texts. Leiden, 1947
Böhl, MLVS	F.M.T. Böhl, Mededeelingen uit de Leidsche verzameling van spijkerschrift-inscripties, 3 parts. Amsterdam, 1933–36
Börker-Klähn, Bildstelen	J. Börker-Klähn, Altvorderasiatische Bildstelen und vergleichbare Felsreliefs, 2 vols (=Baghdader Forschungen 4). Mainz am Rhein, 1982
Borger, Asarh.	R. Borger, Die Inschriften Asarhaddons, Königs von Assyrien (=AfO Beiheft 9). Graz, 1956
Borger, BAL^{2}	R. Borger, Babylonisch-assyrische Lesestücke, 2nd edition, 2 vols (=AnOr 54). Rome, 1979
Borger, EAK 1	R. Borger, Einleitung in die assyrischen Königsinschriften, Erster Tell: Das zweite Jahrtausend v. Chr. (=Handbuch der Orientalistik Ergänzungsband V/1/1). Leiden, 1961
Borger, HKL	R. Borger, Handbuch der Keilschriftliteratur, 3 vols. Berlin, 1967–75
Borger, MZ	R. Borger, Mesopotamisches Zeichenlexikon (=AOAT 305). Münster, 2004

Borger, WAO^2	R. Borger et al., Die Welt des Alten Orients. Keilschrift – Grabungen – Gelehrte, 2nd edition. Göttingen, 1975
Botta, Monument de Ninive	P.E. Botta and E. Flandin, Monument de Ninive, 5 vols. Paris, 1849–50; new impression, Osnabrück, 1972
Braun-Holzinger, Bronzen	E.A. Braun-Holzinger, Figürliche Bronzen aus Mesopotamien (=Prähistorische Bronzefunde 1/4). Munich, 1984
Brereton, Ashurbanipal	G. Brereton (ed.), I am Ashurbanipal, King of the World, King of Assyria. London, 2018
Briend and Seux, TPOA	J. Briend and M.-J. Seux, Textes du Proche-Orient ancien et histoire d'Israel. Paris, 1977
Brinkman, Prelude	J.A. Brinkman, Prelude to Empire: Babylonian Society and Politics, 747–626 B.C. (=Occasional Publications of the Babylonian Fund 7). Philadelphia, 1984
CAD	The Assyrian Dictionary of the Oriental Institute of the University of Chicago, 21 vols. Chicago, 1956–2010
Cagni, Crestomazia	L Cagni, Crestomazia accadica. Rome, 1971
CAH^2 3/1	J. Boardman et al. (eds.), The Cambridge Ancient History, 2nd edition, vol. 3, part 1: The Prehistory of the Balkans; and the Middle East and the Aegean world, Tenth to Eighth Centuries B.C. and Other States of the Near East, from the Eighth to the Sixth Centuries B.C. Cambridge, 1982
CAH^2 3/2	J. Boardman et al. (eds.), The Cambridge Ancient History, 2nd edition, vol. 3, part 2: The Assyrian and Babylonian Empires and Other States of the Near East, from the Eighth to the Sixth Centuries B.C. Cambridge, 1991
Calmeyer, Datierbare Bronzen	P. Calmeyer, Datierbare Bronzen aus Luristan und Kirmanshah (=Untersuchungen zur Assyriologie und vorderasiatischen Archäologie 5). Berlin, 1969
Calmeyer, Reliefbronzen	P. Calmeyer, Reliefbronzen in babylonischen Stil: Eine westiranische Werkstatt des 10. Jahrhunderts v. Chr. Munich, 1973
Cameron, Iran	G.C. Cameron, History of Early Iran. Chicago, 1936
Caubet, Khorsabad	A. Caubet (ed.), Khorsabad, le palais de Sargon II, roi d'Assyrie: Actes du colloque organisé au musée du Louvre par le Service culturel les 21 et 22 janvier 1994. Paris, 1995
CBQ	Catholic Biblical Quarterly. Washingon, 1939–
CDA	J. Black, A. George, and N. Postgate (eds.), A Concise Dictionary of Akkadian. Wiesbaden, 1999
Chavalas, ANE	M.W. Chavalas (ed.), The Ancient Near East: Historical Sources in Translation. Oxford, 2006
Chavalas and Younger, Mesopotamia and the Bible	M.W. Chavalas and K.L. Younger, Jr. (eds.), Mesopotamia and the Bible: Comparative Explorations. New York, 2002
Clay, YOS 1	A.T. Clay, Miscellaneous Inscriptions in the Yale Babylonian Collection (=YOS 1). New Haven, 1915
Cogan, Bound for Exile	M. Cogan. Bound for Exile: Israelites and Judeans under Imperial Yoke: Documents from Assyria and Babylonia. Jerusalem, 2013
Cogan, Raging Torrent	M. Cogan, The Raging Torrent: Historical Inscriptions from Assyria and Babylonia Relating to Ancient Israel. Jerusalem, 2008
Cogan and Tadmor, II Kings	M. Cogan and H. Tadmor, II Kings: A New Translation with Introduction and Commenary (=Anchor Bible 11). Garden City, NY, 1988
Cole and Machinist, SAA 13	S.W. Cole and P. Machinist, Letters from Assyrian and Babylonian Priests to the Kings Esarhaddon and Assurbanipal (=SAA 13). Helsinki, 1998
Collon, Ancient Near Eastern Art	D. Collon, Ancient Near Eastern Art. London, 1995
Collon, First Impressions	D. Collon, First Impressions: Cyliner Seals in the Ancient Near East. London, 1987
Continuity of Empire	G.B. Lanfranchi, M. Roaf, and R. Rollinger (eds.), Continuity of Empire (?). Assyria, Media, Persia (=History of the Ancient Near East, Monographs 5). Padua, 2003
COS 2	W.W. Hallo (ed.), The Context of Scripture, Volume 2: Monumental Inscriptions from the Biblical World. Leiden, 2003
COS 4	K. Lawson Younger, Jr. (ed.), The Context of Scripture, Volume 4: Supplements. Leiden, 2016
CRAIB	Académie des Inscriptions et Belles Lettres, Comptes rendus. Paris, 1857–
Crawford, Regime Change	H. Crawford (ed.), Regime Change in the Ancient Near East and Egypt from Sargon of Agade to Saddam Hussein. Proceedings of the British Academy 136. Oxford, 2007
Crowfoot, Samaria-Sebaste	J.W. Crowfoot et al., Samaria-Sebaste: Reports of the Work of the Joint Expedition in 1931–1933 and of the British Expedition in 1935, 3 vols. London, 1938–57
CRRA	Compte Rendu de la Rencontre Assyriologique Internationale. [various locations], 1950–

CRRA 25	H.-J. Nissen, and J. Renger (eds.), Mesopotamien und seine Nachbarn: Politische und kulturelle Wechselbeziehungen im Alten Vorderasien vom 4. bis 1. Jahrtausend v. Chr., 2 vols. (=Berliner Beiträge zum Vorderen Orient 1). Berlin, 1982
CRRA 30	K.R. Veenhof (ed.), Cuneiform Archives and Libraries: Papers Read at the 30e Rencontre Assyriologique Internationale, Leiden, 4–8 July 1983 (=PIHANS 57). Leiden, 1986
CRRA 32	K. Hecker and W. Sommerfeld, Keilschriftliche Literaturen: Ausgewählte Vorträge der XXXII. Rencontre Assyriologique Internationale, Münster, 8.–12.7.1985 (=Berliner Beiträge zum Vorderen Orient 6). Berlin, 1986
CRRA 38	D. Charpin and F. Joannès (eds.), La circulation des biens, des personnes et des idées dans le Proche-Orient ancien: Actes de la XXXVIIIe Rencontre Assyriologique Internationale (Paris, 8-10 juillet 1991). Paris, 1992
CRRA 39	H. Waetzoldt and H. Hauptman (eds.), Assyrien im Wandel der Zeiten: XXXIXe Rencontre Assyriologique Internationale, Heidelberg 6.-10. Juli 1992 (=Heidelberger Studien zum Alten Orient 6). Heidelberg, 1997
CRRA 43	J. Prosecký (ed.), Intellectual Life in the Ancient Near East: Papers Presented at the 43rd Rencontre Assyriologique Internationale, Prague, July 1–5, 1996. Prague, 1998
CRRA 44	L. Milano et al. (eds.), Landscapes: Territories, Frontiers and Horizons in the Ancient Near East. Papers Presented to the XLIV Rencontre Assyriologique Internationale, Venezia, 7–11 July 1997 (=History of the Ancient Near East, Monographs 3), 3 vols. Padua, 1999–2000
CRRA 45/1	T. Abusch, P.-A. Beaulieu, J. Huehnergard, P. Machinist, and P. Steinkeller (eds.), Proceedings of the XLVe Rencontre Assyriologique Internationale, Part I, Harvard University: Historiography in the Cuneiform World. Bethesda, MD, 2001
CRAA 45/2	W.W. Hallo and I.J. Winter (eds.), Proceedings of the XLVe Rencontre Assyriologique Internationale, Part II, Yale University: Seals and Seal Impressions. Bethesda, MD, 2001
CRRA 52	H. Neumann et al. (eds.), Krieg und Frieden im Alten Vorderasien. 52e Rencontre Assyriologique Internationale / International Congress of Assyriology and Near Eastern Archaeology, Münster, 17. –21. Juli 2006 (=AOAT 401). Münster, 2014
CRRA 54	G. Wilhelm (ed.), Organization, Representation, and Symbols of Power in the Ancient Near East: Proceedings of the 54th Rencontre Assyriologique Internationale at Würzburg, 20–25 July 2008. Winona Lake, IN, 2012
CT	Cuneiform Texts from Babylonian Tablets in the British Museum. London, 1896–
Curtis, Bronzeworking Centres	J. Curtis (ed.), Bronzeworking Centres of Western Asia, c. 1000–539 B.C. London, 1988
Curtis, Examination of Late Assyrian Metalwork	J. Curtis, An Examination of Late Assyrian Metalwork: With Special Reference to Nimrud. Oxford, 2013
Curtis, Later Mesopotamia and Iran	J. Curtis (ed.), Later Mesopotamia and Iran: Tribes and Empires 1600-539 BC. London, 1995
Curtis and Reade, Art and Empire	J.E. Curtis and J.E. Reade, Art and Empire: Treasures from Assyria in the British Museum. New York, 1995
Curtis and Tallis, Balawat Gates	J.E. Curtis and N. Tallis (eds.), The Balawat Gates of Ashurnasirpal II. London, 2008
CUSAS 17	A.R. George (ed.), Cuneiform Royal Inscriptions and Related Texts in the Schøyen Collection (=Cornell University Studies in Assyriology and Sumerology 17). Bethesda, MD, 2011
Dalley, Hanging Garden	S. Dalley, The Mystery of the Hanging Garden of Babylon: An Elusive World Wonder Traced. Oxford, 2013
Damerji, Gräber	M.S.B. Damerji, Gräber assyrischer Königinnen aus Nimrud (=Sonderdruck aus Jahrbuch des römisch-germanischen Zentralmuseums 45/1998). Mainz am Rhein, 1999
Delaporte, Louvre	L. Delaporte, Catalogue des cylindres, cachets et pierres gravées de style oriental [du] Musée du Louvre, 2 vols. Paris, 1920
Delaporte, Malatya	L. Delaporte, Malatya, fouilles de la Mission archéologique française: Arslantepe. I: La porte des lions. Paris, 1940
Delitzsch, Sprache der Kossäer	F. Delitzsch, Die Sprache der Kossäer: linguistisch-historische Funde und Fragen. Leipzig, 1884
Delitzsch, Wo lag das Paradies	F. Delitzsch, Wo lag das Paradies? Eine biblisch-assyriologische Studie. Leipzig, 1881
Dezsö, Assyrian Army 1/1	T. Dezsö, The Assyrian Army. I: The Structure of the Neo-Assyrian Army as Reconstructed from the Assyrian Palace Reliefs and Cuneiform Sources. 1. Infantry Budapest, 2012
Dietrich, SAA 17	M. Dietrich, The Babylonian Correspondence of Sargon and Sennacherib (=SAA 17). Helsinki, 2003

DLZ	Deutsche Literaturzeitung. Berlin, 1880–
Dolce and Nota Santi, Dai Palazzi Assiri	R. Dolce and M. Nota Santi (eds.), Dai Palazzi Assiri: Immagini di potere da Assurnasirpal II ad Assurbanipal (IX-VII sec. a.C.) (=Studia Archaeologica 76). Rome, 1995
Donbaz and Grayson, RICCA	V. Donbaz and A.K. Grayson, Royal Inscriptions of Clay Cones from Ashur Now in Istanbul (=RIMS 1). Toronto, 1984
DOTT	D. Winton Thomas (ed.), Documents from Old Testament Times. Edinburgh, 1958
Dušek and Mynářnová, Aramaean Borders	J. Dušek and J. Mynářnová, Aramaean Borders: Defining Aramaean Territories in the 10th–8th Centuries B.C.E. (=Culture and History of the Ancient Near East 101). Leiden and Boston, 2019
Économie antique	J. Andreau, P. Briant, and R. Descat (eds.), Économie antique: Prix et formation des prix dans les économies antiques. Saint-Bertrand-de-Comminges, 1997
Ehelolf, Wortfolgeprinzip	H. Ehelolf, Ein Wortfolgeprinzip im Assyrisch-Babylonischen (=Leipziger Semitische Studien 6/3). Leipzig, 1916
Elayi, Sargon II	J. Elayi, Sargon II, King of Assyria. Atlanta, 2017
Ellis, Foundation Deposits	R.S. Ellis, Foundation Deposits in Ancient Mesopotamia (=Yale Near Eastern Researches 2). New Haven and London, 1968
Engel, Dämonen	B.J. Engel, Darstellungen von Dämonen und Tieren in assyrischen Palästen und Tempeln nach den schriftlichen Quellen. Mönchengladbach, 1987
Eph'al, Arabs	I. Eph'al, The Ancient Arabs: Nomads on the Borders of the Fertile Crescent 9th–5th Centuries B.C. Jerusalem, 1982
Eretz-Israel	Eretz-Israel: Archaeological, Historical and Geographical Studies. Jerusalem, 1951–
Expedition	Expedition. Philadelpha, 1958–
Fales, ARIN	F.M. Fales (ed.), Assyrian Royal Inscriptions: New Horizons in Literary, Ideological, and Historical Analysis. Papers of a Symposium Held in Cetona (Siena) June 26–28, 1980. Rome, 1981
Fales, Epigraphs	F.M. Fales, Aramaic Epigraphs on Clay Tablets of the Neo-Assyrian Period (=Studi Semitici NS 2). Rome, 1986
Fales and Postgate, SAA 7	F.M. Fales and J.N. Postgate, Imperial Administrative Records, Part I: Palace and Temple Administration (=SAA 7). Helsinki, 1992
Fales and Postgate, SAA 11	F. M. Fales and J. N. Postgate, Imperial Administrative Records, Part II: Provincial and Military Administration (=SAA 11). Helsinki, 1995
Finet, Opposition	A. Finet (ed.), La Voix de l'opposition en Mesopotamie: Colloque organisé par l'Institut des Hautes Études de Belgique, 19 et 20 mars 1973. Brussels, 1975
Finkbeiner, AUWE 4	U. Finkbeiner, Uruk, Kampagne 35-37, 1982-1984: Die archäologische Oberflächenuntersuchung (Survey) (=AUWE 4). Mainz am Rhein, 1991
Fitzmyer and Kaufman, Aramaic Bibliography	J.A. Fitzmyer and S.A. Kaufman, An Aramaic Bibliography. Baltimore, 1992–
Folia Orientalia	Folia Orientalia. Kraków, 1959–
Fontan, Khorsabad	E. Fontan, De Khorsabad à Paris. La découverte des Assyriens. Paris, 1994
Forbes, Ancient Technology^{2} 5	R.J. Forbes, Studies in Ancient Technology. Volume 5, 2nd edition. Leiden, 1966
Forrer, Provinz	E. Forrer, Die Provinzeinteilung des assyrischen Reiches. Leipzig, 1920
Forschungen und Fortschritte	Forschungen und Fortschritte: Nachrichtenblatt der deutschen Wissenschaft und Technik. Berlin, 1925–67
Foster, Before the Muses	B.R. Foster, Before the Muses: An Anthology of Akkadian Literature, 2 vols. Bethesda, 1993À
Foster, Before the Muses^{3}	B.R. Foster, Before the Muses: An Anthology of Akkadian Literature, 3rd edition. Bethesda, 2005
Frahm, KAL 3	E. Frahm, Historische und historisch-literarische Texte (=Keilschrifttexte aus Assur literarischen Inhalts 3 and WVDOG 121). Wiesbaden, 2009
Frahm, Sanherib	E. Frahm, Einleitung in die Sanherib-Inschriften (=AfO Beiheft 26). Vienna and Horn, 1997
Frame, RIMB 2	G. Frame, Rulers of Babylonia from the Second Dynasty of Isin to the End of Assyrian Domination (1157–612 BC) (=RIMB 2). Toronto, 1995
Frangipane, Alle origini	M. Frangipane (ed.), Alle origini del potere. Arslantepe, la collina dei leoni. Milan, 2004
Frankfort, OIC 16	H. Frankfort, Tell Asmar, Khafaje and Khorsabad. Second Preliminary Report of the Iraq Expedition (=OIC 16). Chicago, 1933
Frankfort, OIC 17	H. Frankfort, Iraq Excavations of the Oriental Institute 1932/33: Third Preliminary Report of the Iraq Expedition (=OIC 17). Chicago, 1934
Frankfort, OIC 19	H. Frankfort, Oriental Institute Discoveries in Iraq, 1933/34: Fourth Preliminary Report of the Iraq Expedition (=OIC 19). Chicago, 1935

Frankfort, OIC 20	H. Frankfort, Progress of the Work of the Oriental Institute in Iraq, 1934/35: Fifth Preliminary Report of the Iraq Expedition (=OIC 20). Chicago, 1936
Frayne, RIME 1	D. Frayne, Presargonic Period (2700–2350 BC) (=RIME 1). Toronto, 2008
Frayne, RIME 3/2	D. Frayne, Ur III Period (2112–2004 BC) (=RIME 3/2). Toronto, 1997
FuB	Forschungen und Berichte. Berlin, 1957–91
Fuchs, Khorsabad	A. Fuchs, Die Inschriften Sargons II. aus Khorsabad. Göttingen, 1994
Fuchs, SAAS 8	A. Fuchs, Die Annalen des Jahres 711 v. Chr. nach Prismenfragmenten aus Ninive und Assur (=SAAS 8). Helsinki, 1998
Fuchs and Parpola, SAA 15	A. Fuchs and S. Parpola, The Correspondence of Sargon II, Part III: Letters from Babylonia and the Eastern Provinces (=SAA 15). Helsinki, 2001.
Fügert and Gries, Glazed Brick Decoration	A. Fügert and H. Gries (eds.), Glazed Brick Decoration in the Ancient Near East: Proceedings of a Workshop at the 11th International Congress of the Archaeology of the Ancient Near East (Munich) in April 2018. Oxford, 2020
Gadd, Ideas of Divine Rule	C.J. Gadd, Ideas of Divine Rule in the Ancient Near East (=Schweich Lectures of the British Academy 1945). London, 1948
Gadd, Stones	C.J. Gadd, The Stones of Assyria: The Surviving Remains of Assyrian Sculpture, Their Recovery, and Their Original Positions. London, 1936
Galling, Textbuch^{2}	K. Galling, Textbuch zur Geschichte Israels, 2nd edition. Tübingen, 1968
Galter, Ea/Enki	H.D. Galter, Der Gott Ea/Enki in der akkadischen Überlieferung: Eine Bestandsaufnahme des vorhandenen Materials (=Dissertationen der Karl-Franzens-Universität Graz 58). Graz, 1983
Gaspa, Contenitori neoassiri	S. Gaspa, Contenitori neoassiri: Studi per un repertorio lessicale (=Philippika 67). Wiesbaden, 2014
Genge, Stelen	H. Genge, Stelen neuassyrischer Könige: Eine Dokumentation und philologische Vorarbeit zur Würdigung einer archäologischen Denkmälergattung. Teil 1: Die Keilinschriften. Freiburg, 1965
de Genouillac, Kich	H. de Genouillac, Premières recherches archéologiques à Kich (Fouilles françaises d'El-'Akhymer, Mission d'Henri de Genouillac, 1911–1912), 2 vols. Paris, 1924–25
Geographical Journal	The Geographical Journal. London, 1893–
George, Topographical Texts	A.R. George, Babylonian Topographical Texts (=Orientalia Lovaniensia Analecta 40). Leuven, 1992
GGA	Göttingische Gelehrte Anzeigen. Berlin, 1802–
Gibson, TSSI 2	J.C.L. Gibson, Textbook of Syrian Semitic Inscriptions, volume 2: Aramaic Inscriptions, including Inscriptions in the Dialect of Zenjirli. Oxford, 1975
Glassner, Chronicles	J.-J. Glassner, Mesopotamian Chronicles (=Writings from the Ancient World 19). Atlanta, 2004
Gopnik and Rothman, On the High Road	H. Gopnik and M.S. Rothman, On the High Road: The History of Godin Tepe, Iran. Costa Masa, CA, 2011
Goren, Finkelstein, and Na'aman, Inscribed in Clay	Y. Goren, I. Finkelstein, and N. Na'aman, Inscribed in Clay: Provenance Study of the Amarna Tablets and Other Near Eastern Texts. Tel Aviv, 2004
de Graeve, Ships	M.-C. de Graeve, The Ships of the Ancient Near East (c. 2000 to 500 B.C.) (=Orientalia Lovaniensia Analecta 7). Leuven, 1981
Grande Genova	La Grande Genova: bollettino municipale. Genova, 1921–
Grayson, Chronicles	A.K. Grayson, Assyrian and Babylonian Chronicles (=Texts from Cuneiform Sources 5). Locust Valley, NY, 1975
Grayson, RIMA 1	A.K. Grayson, Assyrian Rulers of the Third and Second Millennia BC (to 1115 BC) (=RIMA 1). Toronto, 1987
Grayson, RIMA 2	A.K. Grayson, Assyrian Rulers of the Early First Millennium BC I (1114–859 BC) (=RIMA 2). Toronto, 1991
Grayson, RIMA 3	A.K. Grayson, Assyrian Rulers ofthe Early First Millennium BC II (858-745 BC) (=RIMA 3). Toronto, 1996
Grayson and Novotny, RINAP 3/1	A.K. Grayson and J. Novotny, The Royal Inscriptions of Sennacherib, King of Assyria (704–681 BC), Part 1 (=RINAP 3/1). Winona Lake, IN, 2012
Grayson and Novotny, RINAP 3/2	A.K. Grayson and J. Novotny, The Royal Inscriptions of Sennacherib, King of Assyria (704–681 BC), Part 2 (=RINAP 3/2). Winona Lake, IN, 2014
Green, "I Undertook Great Works"	D.J. Green, "I Undertook Great Works": The Ideology of Domestic Achievements in West Semitic Royal Inscriptions. Tübingen, 2010
Greene and Griffin, Proceedings OSG 32	V. Greene and P. Griffin, Proceedings of the Objects Specialty Group Sesssion. 32nd Annual Meeting in Portland, Oregon, June 13, 2004 (=Objects Specialty Group Postprints 11). Electronic publication, 2004
Gressman, ABAT^{2}	H. Gressman, Altorientalische Bilder zum Alten Testament, 2nd edition. Berlin, 1927
Gressman, ATAT^{2}	H. Gressman, Altorientalische Texte zum Alten Testament, 2nd edition. Berlin, 1926

Gries, Assur-Tempel	H. Gries, Der Assur-Tempel in Assur: Das assyrische Hauptheiligtum im Wandel der Zeit, 2 volumes (=WVDOG 149). Wiesbaden, 2017
Gyselen, Prix	R. Gyselen (ed.), Prix, salaires, poids et mesures (Res Orientales 2). Paris, 1990
Haas, Urartu	V. Haas (ed.), Das Reich Urartu: Ein altorientalischer Staat im 1. Jahrtausend v. Chr. (=Xenia 17). Konstanz, 1986
Hall, Sculpture	H.R. Hall, Babylonian and Assyrian Sculpture in the British Museum. Paris and Brussels, 1928
Haller, Gräber	A. Haller, Die Gräber und Grüfte von Assur (=WVDOG 65). Berlin, 1954
Haller, Heiligtümer	A. Haller and W. Andrae, Die Heiligtümer des Gottes Assur und der Sin-Šamaš-Tempel in Assur (=WVDOG 67). Berlin, 1955
Harper, ABL	R.F. Harper, Assyrian and Babylonian Letters Belonging to the Kouyunjik Collection of the British Museum, 14 vols. 1892–1914
Harper, Assyrian and Babylonian Literature	R.F. Harper (ed.), Assyrian and Babylonian Literature: Selected Translations. New York, London and Chicago, 1901
Heintz, Oracles	J.-G. Heintz (ed.), Oracles et prophéties dans l'antiquité: Actes du Colloque de Strasbourg, 15-17 juin 1995. Paris, 1997
Hellenika	L. Ross (ed.), Hellenika: Archiv archäologischer, philologischer, historischer und epigraphischer Abhandlungen und Aufsätze. Halle, 1846
Herbordt, SAAS 1	S. Herbordt, Assyrische Glyptik des 8.–7. Jh. v. Chr. (=SAAS 1). Helsinki, 1992
Herzfeld, Iran in the Ancient Near East	E.E. Herzfeld, Iran in the Ancient Near East: Archaeological Studies Presented in the Lowell Lectures at Boston. London, 1941
Hill, Jones, and Morales, Experiencing Power	J.A. Hill, P. Jones, and A.J. Morales, Experiencing Power, Generating Authority: Cosmos, Politics, and the Ideology of Kingship in Ancient Egypt and Mesopotamia. Philadelphia, 2013
Holloway, Aššur is King	S.W. Holloway, Aššur is King! Aššur is King! Religion in the Exercise of Power in the Neo-Assyrian Empire (=Culture and History of the Ancient Near East 10). Boston and Leiden, 2002
Horowitz, Cosmic Geography	W. Horowitz, Mesopotamian Cosmic Geography (=Mesopotamian Civilizations 8). Winona Lake, IN, 1998
Horowitz and Oshima, Canaan	W. Horowitz and T. Oshima (with S. Sanders), Cuneiform in Canaan: Cuneiform Sources from the Land of Israel in Ancient Times. Jerusalem, 2006
HSAO 6	H. Waetzoldt and H. Hauptman (eds.), Assyrien im Wandel der Zeiten: XXXIXe Rencontre Assyriologique Internationale, Heidelberg 6.-10. Juli 1992 (=Heidelberger Studien zum Alten Orient 6). Heidelberg, 1997
HSAO 14	P.A. Miglus and S. Mühl, Between the Cultures: The Central Tigris Region from the 3rd to the 1st Millennium BC. Conference at Heidelberg, January 22nd-24th, 2009 (=Heidelberger Studien zum Alten Orient 14). Heidelberg, 2011
HUCA	Hebrew Union College Annual. Cincinnati, 1924–
Hunger, Kolophone	H. Hunger, Babylonische und assyrische Kolophone (=AOAT 2). Kevelaer and Neukirchen-Vluyn, 1968
Hunger, SAA 8	H. Hunger, Astrological Reports to Assyrian Kings (=SAA 8). Helsinki, 1992
Hurowitz, Exalted House	V. Hurowitz, I Have Built You an Exalted House: Temple Building in the Bible in Light of Mesopotamian and Northwest Semitic Writings (=Journal for the Study of the Old Testament Supplement Series 115). Sheffield, 1992
Hussein, Nimrud: Queens' Tombs	M.M. Hussein, Nimrud: The Queens' Tombs. Baghdad and Chicago, 2016
Hussein and Suleiman, Nimrud	M.M. Hussein and A. Suleiman, Nimrud: A City of Golden Treasures. Baghdad, 2000
Hutter, Offizielle Religion	M. Hutter and S. Hutter-Braunsar, Offizielle Religion, lokale Kulte und individuelle Religiosität: Akten des religionsgeschichtlichen Symposiums "Kleinasien und angrenzende Gebiete vom Beginn des 2. bis zur Mitte des 1. Jahrtausends v. Chr." (Bonn, 20.-22. Februar 2003) (=AOAT 318). Münster, 2004
IEJ	Israel Exploration Journal. Jerusalem, 1950–
IMSA	Israel Museum Studies in Archaeology. Jerusalem, 2002–
Inscriptions Reveal^{2}	R. Hestrin et al., Inscriptions Reveal: Documents from the Time of the Bible, the Mishna and the Talmud, 2nd edition. Jerusalem, 1973
Interpreting Herodotus	T. Harrison and E. Irwin, Interpreting Herodotus. Oxford, 2018
Iran	Iran. Journal of the British Institute of Persian Studies. London, 1963–
IrAnt	Iranica Antiqua. Leiden, 1961–
Iraq	Iraq. London, 1934–
Ishida, Insho-no-sekai	K. Ishida (ed.), Insho-no-sekai [The World of the Seal]. Tokyo, 1991
ISIMU	ISIMU: Revista sobre Oriente Próximo y Egipto en la antigüedad. Madrid, 1998–
JA	Journal asiatique. Paris, 1822–
JAH	Journal of Ancient History. Boston, 2013–

JAOS	Journal of the American Oriental Society. New Haven, 1893–
JARCE	Journal of the American Research Center in Egypt. Boston, 1962–
JBL	Journal of Biblical Literature. Boston, 1881–
JCS	Journal of Cuneiform Studies. New Haven and Cambridge, 1947–
Jean, Littérature	C.-F. Jean, La littérature des Babyloniens et des Assyriens. Paris, 1924
Jean, Milieu biblique	C.-F. Jean, Le milieu biblique avant Jésus-Christ, 3 vols. Paris, 1922–36
JEOL	Jaarbericht van het Vooraziatisch-Egyptisch Genootschap "Ex Oriente Lux." Leiden, 1933–
JFA	Journal of Field Archaeology. Boston, 1974–
JNES	Journal of Near Eastern Studies. Chicago, 1942–
Johns, ADD	C.H.W. Johns, Assyrian Deeds and Documents, Recording the Transfer of Property, Including the So-called Private Contracts, Legal Decisions and Proclamations Preserved in the Kouyunjik Collections of the British Museum, Chiefly of the 7th Century B.C., 4 vols. Cambridge, 1898–1923
Jordan, Uruk-Warka	J. Jordan, Uruk-Warka nach den Ausgrabungen durch die Deutsche Orient-Gesellschaft (=WVDOG 51). Leipzig, 1928
Journal for Semitics	Journal for Semitics = Tydskrif vir Semitistiek. Pretoria, 1989–
Journal of Jewish Studies	The Journal of Jewish Studies. Cambridge, 1948–
JPOS	The Journal of the Palestine Oriental Society. Jerusalem, 1920–48
JRAS	Journal of the Royal Asiatic Society. London, 1834–
JSOT	Journal for the Study of the Old Testament. Sheffield, 1976–
JSS	Journal of Semitic Studies. Manchester, 1956–
Karageorghis and Kouka, Cyprus and the East Aegean	V. Karageorghis and O. Kouka, Cyprus and the East Aegean: Intercultural Contacts from 3000 to 500 BC: An International Archaeological Symposium held at Pythagoreion, Samos, October 17th–18th 2008. Nicosia, 2009
Kaskal	Kaskal. Rivista di storia, ambiente e culture del Vicino Oriente Antico. Padua, 2004–
Kataja and Whiting, SAA 12	L. Kataja and R. Whiting, Grants, Decrees and Gifts of the Neo-Assyrian Period (=SAA 12). Helsinki, 1995
Katzenstein, Tyre	H.J. Katzenstein, The History of Tyre: From the Beginning of the Second Millenium B.C.E. Until the Fall of the Neo-Babylonian Empire in 538 B.C.E. Jerusalem, 1973
Khazai, De Sumer à Babylone	K. Khazai (ed.), De Sumer à Babylone: Collections du Louvre. Brussels, 1983
King, BBSt	L.W. King, Babylonian Boundary-Stones and Memorial-Tablets in the British Museum, 2 vols. London, 1912
King, Cat.	L.W. King, Catalogue of the Cuneiform Tablets in the Kouyunjik Collection of the British Museum, Supplement. London, 1914
King, First Steps	L.W. King, First Steps in Assyrian: A Book for Beginners. London, 1898
Kinnier Wilson, Wine Lists	J.V. Kinnier Wilson, The Nimrud Wine Lists: A Study of Men and Administration at the Assyrian Capital in the Eighth Century, B.C. (=Cuneiform Texts from Nimrud 1). London, 1972
Kinscherf, Inschriftbruchstücke	L. Kinscherf, Inschriftbruchstücke aus Assur, auf ihren Inhalt und Zusammengehörigkeit geprüft, übersetzt und erklärt. PhD dissertation, Berlin, 1918
Kitchen, Third Intermediate Period^{2}	K.A. Kitchen, The Third Intermediate Period in Egypt, 1100-650 BC, 2nd edition. Warminster, 1986
Klengel, Gesellschaft und Kultur	H. Klengel (ed.), Gesellschaft und Kultur im alten Vorderasien (=Schriften zur Geschichte und Kultur des alten Orients 15). Berlin, 1982
Koch-Westenholz, Mesopotamian Astrology	U. Koch-Westenholz, Mesopotamian Astrology: An Introduction to Babylonian and Assyrian Celestial Divination. Copenhagen, 1995
Koldewey, WEB^{4}	R. Koldewey, Das wieder erstehende Babylon: Die bisherigen Ergebnisse der deutschen Ausgrabungen, 4th edition. Leipzig, 1925
Köroğlu and Konyar, Urartu	K. Köroğlu and E. Konyar (eds.), Urartu: Doğu'da Değişim / Transformation in the East. Istanbul, 2011
Kuhrt, Ancient Near East 2	A. Kuhrt, The Ancient Near East c. 3000–330 BC, Volume 2. London and New York, 1995
Kuhrt, Persian Empire	A. Kuhrt, The Persian Empire: A Corpus of Sources from the Achaemenid Period. London and New York, 2007
Kwasman and Parpola, SAA 6	T. Kwasman and S. Parpola, Legal Transactions of the Royal Court of Nineveh, Part I: Tiglath-Pileser III through Esarhaddon (=SAA 6). Helsinki, 1991
Lambert, BWL	W.G. Lambert, Babylonian Wisdom Literature. Oxford, 1960
Lambert, Cat.	W.G. Lambert, Catalogue of the Cuneiform Tablets in the Kouyunjik Collection of the British Museum, 3rd Supplement. London, 1992
Lambert and Millard, Cat.	W.G. Lambert and A.R. Millard, Catalogue of the Cuneiform Tablets in the Kouyunjik Collection of the British Museum, 2nd Supplement. London, 1968

Land Between Two Rivers	E. Quarantelli (ed.), The Land Between Two Rivers: Twenty Years of Italian Archaeology in the Middle East. The Treasures of Mesopotamia. Turin, 1985
Landsberger, Sam'al	B. Landsberger, Sam'al: Studien zur Entdeckung der Ruinenstätte Karatepe. Erste Lieferung. Ankara, 1948
Lanfranchi and Parpola, SAA 5	G.B. Lanfranchi and S. Parpola, The Correspondence of Sargon II, Part II: Letters from the Northern and Northeastern Provinces (=SAA 5). Helsinki, 1990
Larsen, Conquest of Assyria	M.T. Larsen, The Conquest of Assyria: Excavations in an Antique Land, 1840–1860. New York, 1996
Larsen, Power and Propaganda	M.T. Larsen (ed.), Power and Propaganda: A Symposium on Ancient Empires (=Mesopotamia 7). Copenhagen, 1979
Last Days	S. Hasegawa, C. Levin, and K. Radner, The Last Days of the Kingdom of Israel (=Beiheft zur Zeitschrift für alttestamentliche Wissenschaft 511). Berlin, 2019
Layard, Discoveries	A.H. Layard, Discoveries Among the Ruins of Nineveh and Babylon; with Travels in Armenia, Kurdistan and the Desert: Being the Result of a Second Expedition Undertaken for the Trustees of the British Museum. London, 1853
Layard, ICC	A.H. Layard, Inscriptions in the Cuneiform Character, from Assyrian Monuments. London, 1851
Layard, Monuments	A.H. Layard, The Monuments of Nineveh. London, 1849
Layard, Nineveh	A.H. Layard, Nineveh and Its Remains, 2 vols. London, 1849
Lehmann-Haupt, Mat.	C.F. Lehmann-Haupt, Materialien zur älteren Geschichte Armeniens und Mesopotamiens. Berlin, 1907
Leichty, RINAP 4	E. Leichty, The Royal Inscriptions of Esarhaddon, King of Assyria (680–669 BC) (=RINAP 4). Winona Lake, IN, 2011
Lenormant, Choix	F. Lenormant, Choix de textes cunéiformes inédits ou incomplétement publiés jusqu'à ce jour, 3 vols. Paris, 1873-75
Levine, Geographical Studies	L.D. Levine, Geographical Studies in the Neo-Assyrian Zagros. Toronto, 1974
Levine, Historical Geography	L.D. Levine, Contributions to the Historical Geography of the Zagros in the Neo-Assyrian Period. PhD dissertation, University of Pennsylvania, 1969
Levine, Jerusalem	L.I. Levine (ed.), Jerusalem: Its Sanctity and Centrality to Judaism, Christianity, and Islam. New York, 1999
Levine, Stelae	L.D. Levine, Two Neo-Assyrian Stelae from Iran. Toronto, 1972
Levine and Young, Mountains and Lowlands	L.D. Levine and T.C. Young (eds.), Mountains and Lowlands: Essays in the Archaeology of Greater Mesopotamia (=BibMes 7). Malibu, 1977
Lewis, Sargon Legend	B. Lewis, The Sargon Legend: A Study of the Akkadian Text and the Tale of the Hero Who Was Exposed at Birth. Cambridge, MA, 1980
Lie, Sar.	A.G. Lie, The Inscriptions of Sargon II, King of Assyria. Part I: The Annals Transliterated and Translated with Notes. Paris, 1929
Lipiński, Itineraria Phoenicia	E. Lipiński, Itineraria Phoenicia (=Orientalia Lovaniensia Analecta 127). Leuven, 2004
Lipiński, Studies 4	E. Lipiński, Studies in Aramaic Inscriptions and Onomastics IV (=Orientalia Lovaniensia Analecta 250). Leuven, 2016
Liverani, Assyria	M. Liverania, Assyria: The Imperial Mission (=Mesopotamian Civilizations 21). Winona Lake, IN, 2017
Liverani, Neo-Assyrian Geography	M. Liverani (ed.), Neo-Assyrian Geography (=Quaderni di Geografia Storica 5). Rome, 1995
Livingstone, SAA 3	A. Livingstone, Court Poetry and Literary Miscellanea (=SAA 3). Helsinki, 1989
de Longpérier, Notice[3]	A. de Longpérier, Notice des antiquités assyriennes, bayloniennes, perses, hébraïques exposées dans les galeries du Musée du Louvre, 3rd edition. Paris, 1854
van Loon, Urartian Art	M.N. van Loon, Urartian Art: Its Distinctive Traits in the Light of New Excavations (=PIHANS 20). Istanbul, 1966
Loud, Khorsabad 1	G. Loud, Khorsabad, Part I: Excavations in the Palace and at a City Gate (=OIP 38). Chicago, 1936
Loud and Altman, Khorsabad 2	G. Loud and C.B. Altman, Khorsabad, Part II: The Citadel and the Town (=OIP 40). Chicago, 1938
Luckenbill, ARAB	D.D. Luckenbill, Ancient Records of Assyria and Babylonia, 2 vols. Chicago, 1926–27
von Luschan, Ausgrabungen in Sendschirli 1	F. von Luschan, Ausgrabungen in Sendschirli. I: Einleitung und Inschriften (=Mittheilungen aus den orientalischen Sammlungen der Köngilichen Museen zu Berlin 11). Berlin, 1893
Luukko, SAA 19	M. Luukko, The Correspondence of Tiglath-Pileser III and Sargon II from Calah/Nimrud (=SAA 19). Helsinki, 2012
Lyon, Manual	D.G. Lyon, An Assyrian Manual for the Use of Beginners in the Study of the Assyrian Language. Chicago, 1886

Lyon, Sar.	D.G. Lyon, Keilschrifttexe Sargon's, Königs von Assyrien (722–705 v. Chr.) (=Assyriologische Bibliothek 5). Leipzig, 1883
MacGinnis, Erbil	J. MacGinnis, A City from the Dawn of History: Erbil in the Cuneiform Sources, Oxford and Philadelphia, 2014
Madden, Jewish Coinage	F.W. Madden, History of Jewish Coinage, and of Money in the Old and New Testament. London, 1864
Mallowan, Nimrud	M.E.L. Mallowan, Nimrud and Its Remains, 3 vols. London, 1966
Mango, Marzahn, and Uehlinger, Könige am Tigris	E. Mango, J. Marzahn, and C. Uehlinger (eds.), Könige am Tigris: Medien assyrischer Herrschaft. Zurich, 2008
Maniori, Campagne di Sargon	F. Maniori, Le campagne babilonesi ed orientali di Sargon II d'Assiria: un'analisi topografica. Rome, 2014
MAOG	Mitteilungen der Altorientalischen Gesellschaft. Leipzig, 1925–43
Margueron, Mesopotamia	Margueron, Mesopotamia (=Archaeologia Mundi). Cleveland, 1965
Marucchi, Catalogo Vaticano	O. Marucchi, Catalogo del Museo Egizio Vaticano con la Traduzione dei Principali Testi Geroglifici. Rome, 1902
Marzahn, Könige am Tigris	J. Marzahn, Könige am Tigris: Assyrische Palastreliefs in Dresden. Katalogbuch zur Ausstellung der Skulpturensammlung im Albertinum, Dresden, 20. März–29. September 2004. Mainz am Rhein, 2004
Marzahn and Jakob-Rost, Ziegeln 1	J. Marzahn and L. Jakob-Rost, Die Inschriften der assyrischen Könige auf Ziegeln aus Assur, Teil 1. Berlin, 1984
Matthiae, I grandi imperi	Matthiae, I grandi imperi, 1000–300 a.C. Milan, 1996
May, Iconoclasm	N.N. May (ed.), Iconoclasm and Text Destruction in the Ancient Near East and Beyond (=University of Chicago Oriental Institute Seminars 8). Chicago, 2012
Mayer, Assyrien und Urarṭu	W. Mayer, Assyrien und Urarṭu, 2 vols. (=AOAT 395). Münster, 2013
Mayer, Politik und Kriegskunst	W. Mayer, Politik und Kriegskunst der Assyrer (=Abhandlungen zur Literatur Alt-Syrien-Palästinas 9). Münster, 1995
MDOG	Mitteilungen der Deutschen Orient-Gesellschaft zu Berlin. Berlin, 1898–
Meissner, BuA	B. Meissner, Babylonien und Assyrien, 2 vols. Heidelberg, 1920 and 1925
Meissner, Chrestomathie	B. Meissner, Assyrisch-babylonische Chrestomathie für Anfänger. Leiden, 1895
Melammu 1	S. Aro and R.M. Whiting (eds.), The Heirs of Assyria: Proceedings of the Opening Symposium of the Assyrian and Babylonian Intellectual Heritage Project Held in Tvärminne, Finland, October 8–11, 1998 (=Melammu Symposium 1). Helsinki, 2000
Melammu 2	R.M. Whiting (ed.), Mythology and Mythologies: Methodological Approaches to Intercultural Influences. Proceedings of the Second Annual Symposium of the Assyrian and Babylonian Intellectual Heritage Project Held in Paris, France, October 4–7, 1999 (=Melammu Symposium 2). Helsinki, 2001
Melville, Campaigns of Sargon	S.C. Meville, The Campaigns of Sargon II, King of Assyria, 721–705 B.C. Norman, OK, 2016
Ménant, Annales	J. Ménant, Annales des rois d'Assyrie. Paris, 1874
Ménant, Babylone	J. Ménant, Babylone et la Chaldée. Paris, 1875
Ménant, Manuel	J. Ménant, Manuel de la langue assyrienne. Paris, 1880
Ménant, Notice Lottin	J. Ménant, Notice sur les inscriptions en caractères cunéiformes de la collection épigraphique de M. Lottin de Laval. Caen, 1858
Ménant, Revers de plaques	J. Ménant, Inscriptions des revers de plaques du palais de Khorsabad, Paris, 1865
Menzel, Tempel	B. Menzel, Assyrische Tempel, 2 vols. (=Studia Pohl, Series Maior 10). Rome, 1981
Mesopotamia	Mesopotamia: Revista di archeologia, epigrafia e storia orientale antica. Turin, 1966–
Messerschmidt, KAH 1	L. Messerschmidt, Keilschrifttexte aus Assur historischen Inhalts, erstes Heft (=WVDOG 16). Leipzig, 1911
Millard, SAAS 2	A.R. Millard, The Eponyms of the Assyrian Empire 910–612 BC (=SAAS 2). Helsinki, 1994
Minerva	Minerva. London, 1990–
Moorey, Materials and Industries	P.R.S. Moorey, Ancient Mesopotamian Materials and Industries: The Archaeological Evidence. Oxford, 1994
Morenz and Bosshard-Nepustil, Herrscherpräsentation	L.D. Morenz and E. Bosshard-Nepustil, Herrscherpräsentation und Kulturkontakte: Ägypten, Levante, Mesopotamien: Acht Fallstudien (=AOAT 304). Münster, 2003
Muscarella, Archaeology, Artifacts and Antiquities	O.W. Muscarella, Archaeology, Artifacts and Antiquities of the Ancient Near East: Sites, Cultures, and Proveniences. Leiden, 2013

Muscarella, Ladders	O.W. Muscarella (ed.), Ladders to Heaven: Art Treasures from Lands of the Bible. A Catalogue of Some of the Objects in the Collection Presented by Elie Borowski to the Lands of the Bible Archaeology Foundation and Displayed in the Exhibition "Ladders to Heaven: Our Judeo-Christian Heritage 5000 BC-AD 500" Held at the Royal Ontario Museum June 23-October 28, 1979. Toronto, 1981
Muscarella and Elliyoun, Eighth Campaign of Sargon II	O.W. Muscarella and S. Elliyoun (eds.), The Eighth Campaign of Sargon II: Historical, Geographical, Literary, and Ideological Aspects. Tabriz, 2012
MVAG	Mitteilungen der Vorderasiatisch-Aegyptischen Gesellschaft. Leipzig and Berlin, 1896–1944
NABU	Nouvelles assyriologiques brèves et utilitaires. Paris, 1987–
New Light on Nimrud	J.E. Curtis, H. McCall, D. Collon, and L. al-Gailani Werr (eds.), New Light on Nimrud: Proceedings of the Nimrud Conference, 11th–13th March 2002. London, 2008
Novotny and Jeffers, RINAP 5/1	J. Novotny and J. Jeffers, The Royal Inscriptions of Ashurbanipal (668–631 BC), Aššur-etel-ilāni (630–627 BC), and Sîn-šarra-iškun (626–612 BC), Kings of Assyria, Part 1 (=RINAP 5/1). University Park, PA, 2018
Nunn, Knaufplatten	A. Nunn, Knaufplatten und Knäufe aus Assur (=WVDOG 112). Saarwellingen, 2006
Nunn, Wandmalerei	A. Nunn, Die Wandmalerei und der glasierte Wandschmuck im alten Orient (=Handbuch der Orientalistik 7/1/2/B/6). Leiden, 1988
J. and D. Oates, Nimrud	J. Oates and D. Oates, Nimrud: An Assyrian Imperial City Revealed. London, 2001
OIC	Oriental Institute Communications. Chicago, 1922–
OIP	Oriental Institute Publications. Chicago, 1924–
Olmstead, Historiography	A.T.E. Olmstead, Assyrian Historiography: A Source Study (=The University of Missouri Studies Social Science Series 3/1). Columbia, MT, 1916
Olmstead, Western Asia	A.T.E. Olmstead, Western Asia in the Days of Sargon 722–705 B.C.: A Study in Oriental History. Lancaster, PA 1908
OLP	Orientalia Lovaniensia Periodica. Leuven, 1970–
OLZ	Orientalistische Literaturzeitung. Berlin and Leipzig, 1898–
Oppenheim, Glass	A.L. Oppenheim et al., Glass and Glassmaking in Ancient Mesopotamia: An Edition of the Cuneiform Tests Which Contain Instructions for Glassmakers with a Catalogue of Surviving Objects. Corning, 1970
Oppert, Chronologie	J. Oppert, Chronologie des Assyriens et des Babyloniens. [Paris], 1856
Oppert, Dour-Sarkayan	J. Oppert, Les inscriptions de Dour-Sarkayan (Khorsabad) provenant des fouilles de M. Victor Place. Paris, 1870
Oppert, EM	J. Oppert, Expédition scientifique en Mésopotamie exécutée par ordre du gouvernement de 1851 à 1854 par MM. Fulgence Fresnel, Félix Thomas et Jules Oppert, 2 vols. Paris, 1859–1863
Oppert, Sargonides	J. Oppert, Les inscriptions assyriennes des Sargonides et les fastes de Ninive. Versailles, 1862
Oppert and Ménant, Fastes	J. Oppert and J. Ménant, Les fastes de Sargon, roi d'Assyrie (721 à 703 avant J.C.), traduits et publiés d'après le texte assyrien de la grande inscription des salles du palais de Khorsabad. Paris, 1863
Oppert and Ménant, Grande Inscription	J. Oppert and J. Ménant, Grande inscription du palais de Khorsabad. Paris, 1863
OrAnt	Oriens Antiquus. Rome, 1962–90
Orient	Orient: The Reports of the Society for Near Eastern Studies in Japan. Tokyo, 1960–
Orientalia NS	Orientalia. Nova Series. Rome, 1932–
Orthmann, Der alte Orient	W. Orthmann, Der alte Orient (=Propyläen Kunstgeschichte 14). Berlin, 1975
Parpola, SAA 1	S. Parpola, The Correspondence of Sargon II, Part I: Letters from Assyria and the West (=SAA 1). Helsinki, 1987
Parpola, Toponyms	S. Parpola, Neo-Assyrian Toponyms (=AOAT 6). Neukirchen-Vluyn, 1970
Parpola and Porter, Helsinki Atlas	S. Parpola and M. Porter (ed.), The Helsinki Atlas of the Near East in the Neo-Assyrian Period. [Chebeague Island, Me], 2001
Parpola and Whiting, Assyria 1995	S. Parpola and R.M. Whiting (eds.), Assyria 1995: Proceedings of the 10th Anniversary Symposium of the Neo-Assyrian Text Corpus Project, Helsinki, September 7–11, 1995. Helsinki, 1997
Parrot, Assyria	A. Parrot, The Arts of Assyria. New York, 1961
Parrot, Trésors	A. Parrot (ed.), Trésors du Musée de Bagdad des origines à l'Islam. Paris, 1966
Pecorella, Malatya 3	P.E. Pecorella, Malatya - III: Rapporto preliminare delle campagne 1963-1968. Il livello eteo imperiale e quelli neoetei (=Orientis antiqui collectio 12). Rome, 1975
Pecorella and Salvini, Tra lo Zagros	P.E. Pecorella and M. Salvini (eds.), Tra lo Zagros e l'Urmia: Ricerche storiche ed archeologiche nell'Azerbaigian iraniano (=Incunabula Graeca 78). Rome, 1984

Pedde and Lundström, Palast	F. Pedde and S. Lundström, Der Alte Palast in Assur: Architektur und Baugeschichte, mit interaktiven Architekturplänen und Fotos auf CD-ROM (=WVDOG 120). Wiesbaden, 2008
Pedersén, Archives	O. Pedersén, Archives and Libraries in the City of Assur: A Survey of the Material from the German Excavations, 2 vols. (=Studia Semitica Upsaliensia 6 and 8). Uppsala, 1985–86
Pedersén, Katalog	O. Pedersén, Katalog der beschrifteten Objekte aus Assur: Die Schriftträger mit Ausnahme der Tontafeln und ähnlicher Archivtexte (=Abhandlungen der Deutschen Orient-Gesellschaft 23). Saarbrücken, 1997
Pedersén, Libraries	O. Pedersén, Archives and Libraries in the Ancient Near East, 1500–300 B.C. Bethesda, MD, 1998
PEFQ	Quarterly Statement of the Palestine Exploration Fund. London, 1869–1936
Perrot and Chipiez, Histoire de l'art 2	G. Perrot and C. Chipiez, Chaldée et Assyrie (=Histoire de l'art dans l'antiquité 2). Paris, 1884
Persian Gulf Conference 3	Collection of Papers Presented at the Third International Biennial Conference of the Persian Gulf (History, Culture and Civilization). Tehran, 2013
Pezzoli-Olgiati, Immagini urbane	D. Pezzoli-Olgiati, Immagini urbane: Interpretazioni religiose della città antica (=Biblicus et Orientalis). Freiburg, 2002
PIHANS	Publications de l'Institut historique-archéologique néerlandais de Stamboul. Leiden, 1956–
Pillet, Khorsabad	M.E. Pillet, Khorsabad: Les découvertes de V. Place en Assyrie. Paris, 1918
Pillet, Pionnier	M.E. Pillet, Un pionnier de l'assyriologie: Victor Place, consul de France à Mossoul, explorateur du palais de Sargon II (722-705 av. J.-C.) à Khorsabad (1852-1855). Paris, 1962
Pinches, Outline	T.G. Pinches, An Outline of Assyrian Grammar, with a Short Sign-List, a List of Late Babylonian Forms of Characters, and Autographic Reproductions of Texts. London, 1910
Place, Ninive et l'Assyrie	V. Place, Ninive et l'Assyrie, 3 vols. Paris, 1867–70
PNA	H.D. Baker and K. Radner (eds.), The Prosopography of the Neo-Assyrian Empire. Helsinki, 1998–
Pomponio, Formule	F. Pomponio, Formule di maledizione della Mesopotamia preclassica. Brescia, 1990
Pongratz-Leisten, Ina Šulmi Īrub	B. Pongratz-Leisten, Ina Šulmi Īrub: Die Kulttopographische und ideologische Programmatik der akītu-Prozession in Babylonien und Assyrien im 1. Jahrtausend v. Chr. (=Baghdader Forschungen 16). Mainz am Rhein, 1994
Pongratz-Leisten, Religion and Ideology	B. Pongratz-Leisten, Religion and Ideology in Assyria (=Studies in Ancient Near Eastern Records 6). Boston, 2015
Pongratz-Leisten, SAAS 10	B. Pongratz-Leisten, Herrschaftswissen im Mesopotamien: Formen der Kommunikation zwischen Gott und König im 2. und 1. Jahrtausend v. Chr. (=SAAS 10). Helsinki, 1999
Postgate, Royal Grants	J.N. Postgate, Neo-Assyrian Royal Grants and Decrees (=Studia Pohl, Series Maior 1). Rome, 1969
Postgate, Taxation	J.N. Postgate, Taxation and Conscription in the Assyrian Empire (=Studia Pohl, Series Maior 3). Rome, 1974
Pottier, Antiquités assyriennes	E. Pottier, Catalogue des antiquités assyriennes. Paris, 1924
Potts, Arabian Gulf	D.T. Potts, The Arabian Gulf in Antiquity, 2 vols. Oxford, 1990
Presbyterian Life	Presbyterian Life. Dayton, 1948–72
Preusser, Paläste	C. Preusser, Die Paläste in Assur (=WVDOG 66). Berlin, 1955
Preusser, Wohnhäuser	C. Preusser, Die Wohnhäuser in Assur (=WVDOG 64). Berlin, 1954
PSBA	Proceedings of the Society of Biblical Archaeology, 40 vols. London, 1878–1918
1 R	H.C. Rawlinson and E. Norris, The Cuneiform Inscriptions of Western Asia, vol. 1: A Selection from the Historical Inscriptions of Chaldaea, Assyria, and Babylonia. London, 1861
3 R	H.C. Rawlinson and G. Smith, The Cuneiform Inscriptions of Western Asia, vol. 3: A Selection from the Miscellaneous Inscriptions of Assyria. London, 1870
4 R	H.C. Rawlinson and G. Smith, The Cuneiform Inscriptions of Western Asia, vol. 4: A Selection from the Miscellaneous Inscriptions of Assyria. London, 1875
5 R	H.C. Rawlinson and T.G. Pinches, The Cuneiform Inscriptions of Western Asia, vol. 5: A Selection from the Miscellaneous Inscriptions of Assyria and Babylonia. London, 1880–84
RA	Revue d'assyriologie et d'archéologie orientale. Paris, 1886–
Raaflaub, Anfänge politischen Denkens	K. Raaflaub (ed.), Anfänge politischen Denkens in der Antike: Die nahöstlichen Kulturen und die Griechen. Munich, 1993

Radner, Macht des Namens	K. Radner, Die Macht des Namens: Altorientalische Strategien zur Selbsterhaltung (=SANTAG 8). Wiesbaden, 2005
Records of the Past	S. Birch (ed.), Records of the Past: Being English Translations of the Assyrian and Egyptian Monuments [Series 1], 12 vols. London, 1873–81
Redman, Rise of Civilization	C.L. Redman, The Rise of Civilization: From Early Farmers to Urban Society in the Ancient Near East. San Francisco, 1978
Reiner and Pingree, BibMes 2/2	E. Reiner and D. Pingree, Babylonian Planetary Omens, Part Two: Enūma Anu Enlil, Tablets 50–51 (=BibMes 2/2). Malibu, 1981
Revue archéologique	Revue archéologique. Paris, 1844–
Reyes, Archaic Cyprus	A.T. Reyes, Archaic Cyprus: A Study of the Textual and Archaeological Evidence. Oxford, 1994
RHA	Revue hittite et asianique. Paris, 1930–
RIM	The Royal Inscriptions of Mesopotamia. Toronto, 1984–2008
RIMA	The Royal Inscriptions of Mesopotamia, Assyrian Periods, 3 vols. Toronto, 1987–96
RIMB	The Royal Inscriptions of Mesopotamia, Babylonian Periods, 1 vol. Toronto, 1995
RIME	The Royal Inscriptions of Mesopotamia, Early Periods, 5 vols. Toronto, 1990–2008
RIMS	The Royal Inscriptions of Mesopotamia, Supplements, 1 vol. Toronto, 1984
RINAP	The Royal Inscriptions of the Neo-Assyrian Period. Winona Lake, IN, 2011–
RLA	Reallexikon der Assyriologie und Vorderasiatischen Archäologie, 15 vols. Berlin, 1932–2018
RLV	Reallexikon der Vorgeschichte, 15 vols. Berlin, 1924–32
Rollinger, Interkulturalität	R. Rollinger et al. (eds.), Interkulturalität in der Alten Welt: Vorderasien, Hellas, Ägypten und die vielfältigen Ebenen des Kontakts (=Philippika 34). Wiesbaden, 2010
RPARA	Rendiconti. Atti della Pontificia Accademia Romana di Archeologia. Rome, 1923–
RT	Recueil de travaux relatifs à la philologie de à l'archeologie égyptiennes et assyriennes. Paris, 1870–1923
J.M. Russell, Senn.'s Palace	J.M. Russell, Sennacherib's Palace Without Rival at Nineveh. Chicago and London, 1991
J.M. Russell, Writing on the Wall	J.M. Russell, The Writing on the Wall: Studies in the Architectural Context of Late Assyrian Palace Inscriptions (=Mesopotamian Civilizations 9). Winona Lake, IN, 1999
SAA	State Archives of Assyria. Helsinki, 1987–
SAAB	State Archives of Assyria Bulletin. Padua, 1987–
SAAS	State Archives of Assyria Studies. Helsinki, 1992–
SAD	M. Streck (ed.), Supplement to the Akkadian Dictionaries (=Leipziger Altorientalische Studien 7,1–). Wiesbaden, 2018–
Sagona, Beyond the Homeland	C. Sagona (ed.), Beyond the Homeland: Markers in Phoenician Chronology. Louvain, 2008
Salonen, Vögel	A. Salonen, Vögel und Vogelfang im alten Mesopotamien. Helsinki, 1973
Salvini, Urartäer	M. Salvini, Geschichte und Kultur der Urartäer. Darmstadt, 1995
Sarsowsky, Urkundenbuch	A. Sarsowsky, Keilschriftliches Urkundenbuch zum Alten Testament. I. Teil: Historische Texte. Leiden, 1911
Schmidt, Perspolis 1	E.F. Schmidt, Persepolis I: Structures · Reliefs · Inscriptions (=OIP 68). Chicago, 1953
Schmidt, Persepolis 2	E.F. Schmidt, Persepolis II: Contents of the Treasury and Other Discoveries (=OIP 69). Chicago, 1957
Schmitt, Iranische Personnamen	R. Schmitt, Iranische Personnamen in der neuassyrischen Nebenüberlieferung (=Iranisches Personnamenbuch 7/1A). Vienna, 2009.
Schott, Vergleiche	A. Schott, Die Vergleiche in den akkadischen Königsinschriften (=MVAG 30/2). Leipzig, 1926
Schott, Vorarbeiten	A. Schott, Vorarbeiten zur Geschichte der Keilschriftliteratur. I: Die assyrischen Königsinschriften vor 722. a) Der Schreibgebrauch (=Bonner Orientalistische Studien 13). Stuttgart, 1935
Schrader, Cuneiform Inscriptions	E. Schrader, The Cuneiform Inscriptions and the Old Testament, 2 vols. London, 1885–88
Schrader, KAT^2	E. Schrader, Die Keilinschriften und das Alte Testament, 2nd edition. Giessen, 1883
Schrader, KB 2	E. Schrader, Sammlung von assyrischen und babylonischen Texten in Umschrift und Übersetzung (=Keilinschriftliche Bibliothek 2). Berlin, 1890
Schrader, Keilinschriften und Geschichtsforschung	E. Schrader, Keilinschriften und Geschichtsforschung: Ein Beitrag zur monumentalen Geographie, Geschichte und Chronologie der Assyrer. Giessen, 1878
Schrader, Sargonsstele	E. Schrader, Die Sargonsstele des Berliner Museums. Berlin, 1882
Schroeder, KAH 2	O. Schroeder, Keilschrifttexte aus Assur historischen Inhalts, Zweites Heft (=WVDOG 37). Leipzig, 1922

Schwemer, Wettergottgestalten	D. Schwemer, Die Wettergottgestalten Mesopotamiens und Nordsyriens im Zeitalter der Keilschriftkulturen. Materialien und Studien nach den schriftlichen Quellen, Wiesbaden 2001
Searight, Assyrian Stone Vessels	A. Searight, J. Reade, and I. Finkel, Assyrian Stone Vessels and Related Material in the British Museum. Oxford, 2008
Segert, Altaramäische Grammatik	S. Segert, Altaramäische Grammatik, mit Bibliographie, Chrestomathie und Glossar. Leipzig, 1975
Sennacherib at the Gates of Jerusaelm	I. Kalimi and S. Richardson (eds.), Sennacherib at the Gates of Jerusalem: Story, History and Historiography (=Culture and History of the Ancient Near East 71). Leiden and Boston, 2014
Seux, ERAS	M.-J. Seux, Épithètes royales akkadiennes et sumériennes. Paris, 1967
Seux, Hymnes	M.-J. Seux, Hymnes et prières aux dieux de Babylonie et d'Assyrie (=Littératures anciennes du Proche-Orient 8). Paris, 1976
de Sion, Forteresse Antonia	M.A. de Sion, La forteresse Antonia à Jérusalem et la question du prétoire. Jerusalem, 1956
G. Smith, Assyrian Discoveries	G. Smith, Assyrian Discoveries; An Account of Explorations and Discoveries on the Site of Nineveh, During 1873 and 1874. New York, 1875
W.S. Smith, Interconnections	W.S. Smith, Interconnections in the Ancient Near-East: A Study of the Relationships Between the Arts of Egypt, the Aegean, and Western Asia. New Haven, 1965
von Soden, Aus Sprache	W. von Soden, Aus Sprache, Geschichte und Religion Babyloniens: Gesammelte Aufsätze. Naples, 1989
von Soden, SAHG	A. Falkenstein and W. von Soden, Sumerische und akkadische Hymnen und Gebete. Zurich and Stuttgart, 1953
von Soden and Röllig, Syllabar^3	W. von Soden and W. Röllig, Das akkadische Syllabar, 3rd edition (=Analecta Orientalia 42). Rome, 1976
Sokoloff, Arameans	M. Sokoloff (ed.), Arameans, Aramaic and the Aramaic Literary Tradition. Ramat-Gan, 1983
Spieckermann, Juda unter Assur	H. Spieckermann, Juda unter Assur in der Sargonidenzeit. Göttingen, 1982
Stern, Archaeology of the Land of the Bible 2	E. Stern, Archaeology of the Land of the Bible, volume 2: The Assyrian, Babylonian, and Persian Periods, 732–332 BCE. New York, 1990
Stern, New Encyclopedia	E. Stern (ed.), The New Encyclopedia of Archaeological Excavations in the Holy Land, 5 vols. Jerusalem and New York, 1993
StOr	Studia Orientalia (Societas Orientalis Fennica). Helsinki, 1925–
Strassmaier, AV	J.N. Strassmaier, Alphabetisches Verzeichniss der assyrischen und akkadischen Wörter der Cuneiform Inscriptions of Western Asia, vol. II, sowie anderer meist unveröffentlichter Inschriften. Mit zahlreichen Ergänzungen und Verbesserungen und einem Wörterverzeichniss zu den in den Verhandlungen des VI. Orientalisten-Congresses zu Leiden veröffentlichten babylonischen Inschriften (=Assyriologische Bibliothek 4). Leipzig, 1886
Streck, Asb.	M. Streck, Assurbanipal und die letzten assyrischen Könige bis zum Untergange Niniveh's, 3 vols. (=Vorderasiatische Bibliothek 7). Leipzig, 1916
Studia Antiqua	Studia Antiqua: A Student Journal for the Study of the Ancient World. Provo, Utah, 2001–
Studia Iranica	Studia Iranica. Paris, 1972–
Studi Ciprioti e Rapporti di Scavo	Studi Ciprioti e Rapporti di Scavo, 2 vols. Rome, 1971–76
Studi e documenti	Studi e documenti di storia e diritto. Rome, 1880–1904
Studies Astour	G.D. Young, M.W. Chavalas, and R.E. Averbeck (eds.), Crossing Boundaries and Linking Horizons: Studies in Honor of Michael C. Astour on His 80th Birthday. Bethesda, 1997
Studies Bergerhof	M. Dietrich and O. Loretz (eds.), Mesopotamica – Ugaritica – Biblica: Festschrift für Kurt Bergerhof zur Vollendung seines 70. Lebensjahres am 7. Mai 1992 (=AOAT 232). Münster, 1993
Studies Boehmer	U. Finkbeiner, R. Dittmann, and H. Hauptmann (eds.), Beiträge zur Kulturgeschichte Vorderasiens: Festschrift für Rainer Michael Boehmer. Mainz am Rhein, 1995
Studies Cagni	S. Graziani, Studi sul Vicino Oriente antico dedicati alla memoria di Luigi Cagni, 4 vols. Naples, 2000
Studies Calmeyer	R. Dittmann et al. (eds.), Variatio delectat: Iran und der Westen; Gedenkschrift für Peter Calmeyer (=AOAT 272). Münster, 2000
Studies Diakonoff	N. Koslova (ed.), Proceedings of the International Conference Dedicated to the Centenary of Igor Mikhailovich Diakonoff (1915–1999) (=Transactions of the State Hermitage Museum 95). St. Petersburg, 2018.

Studies Dietrich	O. Loretz, K.A. Metzler, and H. Schaudig (eds.), Ex Mesopotamia et Syria Lux: Festschrift für Manfried Dietrich zu seinem 65. Geburtstag (=AOAT 281). Münster, 2002
Studies Donbaz	Ş. Dönmez (ed.), Veysel Donbaz'a Sunulan Yazılar. DUB.SAR É.DUB.BA.A: Studies Presented in Honour of Veysel Donbaz. Istanbul, 2010
Studies Dostal	A. Gingrich, S. Haas, G. Paleczek, and T. Fillitz (eds.), Studies in Oriental Culture and History: Festschrift for Walter Dostal. Frankfurt am Main, 1993
Studies Ellis	M.J. Boda and J. Novotny (eds.), From the Foundations to the Crenellations: Essays on Temple Building in the Ancient Near East and Hebrew Bible (=AOAT 366). Münster, 2010
Studies Ephʿal	M. Cogan and D. Kahn (eds.), Treasures on Camels' Humps: Historical and Literary Studies from the Ancient Near East Presented to Israel Ephʿal. Jerusalem, 2008
Studies Fales	G.B. Lanfranchi et al. (eds.), Leggo! Studies Presented to Frederick Mario Fales on the Occasion of his 65th Birthday (=Leipziger Altorientalistische Studien 2). Wiesbaden, 2012
Studies Foster	S.C. Melville and A.L. Slotsky (eds.), Opening the Tablet Box: Near Eastern Studies in Honor of Benjamin R. Foster (=Culture and History of the Ancient Near East 42). Leiden, 2010
Studies Grayson	G. Frame (ed.), From the Upper Sea to the Lower Sea: Studies on the History of Assyria and Babylonia in Honour of A.K. Grayson (=PIHANS 101). Leiden, 2004
Studies Haas	T. Richter, D. Prechel, and J. Klinger (eds.), Kulturgeschichten: Altorientalistische Studien für Volkert Haas zum 65. Geburtstag. Saarbrücken, 2001
Studies Haider	R. Rollinger and B. Truschnegg (eds.), Altertum und Mittelmeerraum: Die antike Welt diesseits und jenseits der Levante. Festschrift für Peter W. Haider zum 60. Geburtstag (=Oriens et Occidens 12). Stuttgart, 2006
Studies Heltzer	Y. Avishur and R. Deutsch (eds.), Michael: Historical, Epigraphical and Biblical Studies in Honor of Prof. Michael Heltzer. Tel Aviv, 1999
Studies Hermary	Hommage à Antoine Hermary: Colloque "Chypre e les grandes îles de Méditerranée," Marseille, 16-17 octobre 2015 (=Cahiers du Centre d'Études Chypriotes 46). Paris, 2016
Studies Hrouda	P. Calmeyer et al. (eds.), Beiträge zur altorientalischen Archäologie und Altertumskunde: Festschrift für Barthel Hrouda zum 65. Geburtstag. Wiesbaden, 1994
Studies Lanfranchi	S. Gaspa et al. (eds.), From Source to History: Studies on Ancient Near Eastern Worlds and Beyond. Dedicated to Giovanni Battista Lanfranchi on the Occasion of His 65th Birthday on June 23, 2014 (=AOAT 412). Münster, 2014
Studies Lehmann-Haupt	K. Regling and H. Reich (eds.), Festschrift zu C.F. Lehmann-Haupts sechzigstem Geburtstage. Vienna, 1921
Studies Lipiński	K. van Lerberghe and A. Schoors (eds.), Immigration and Emigration within the Ancient Near East: Festschrift E. Lipiński (=Orientalia Lovaniensia Analecta 65). Leuven, 1995
Studies Loretz	M. Dietrich and I. Kottsieper (eds.), "Und Mose schrieb dieses Lied auf": Studien zum Alten Testament und zum Alten Orient; Festschrift für Oswald Loretz zur Vollendung seines 70. Lebensjahres mit Beiträgen von Freunden, Schülern und Kollegen (=AOAT 250). Münster, 1998
Studies Mikasa	M. Mori, H. Ogawa, and M. Yoshikawa (eds.), Near Eastern Studies Dedicated to H. I. H. Prince Takahito Mikasa on the Occasion of His Seventy-Fifth Birthday. Wiesbaden, 1991
Studies Milano	P. Corò et al. (eds.), Libiamo ne' lieti calici: Ancient Near Eastern Studies Presented to Lucio Milano on the Occasion of his 65th Birthday by Pupils, Colleagues and Friends (=AOAT 436). Münster, 2016
Studies Moran	T. Abusch, J. Huehnergard, and P. Steinkeller (eds.), Lingering over Words: Studies in Ancient Near Eastern Literature in Honor of William L. Moran (=Harvard Semitic Studies 37). Atlanta, 1990
Studies Neumann	K. Kleber, G. Neumann, and S. Paulus (eds.), Grenzüberschreitungen. Studien zur Kulturgeschichte des Alten Orients. Festschrift für Hans Neumann zum 65. Geburtstag am 9. Mai 2018 (=Dubsar 5). Münster, 2018
Studies Oded	G. Galil, M. Geller, and A.R. Millard (eds.), Homeland and Exile: Biblical and Ancient Near Eastern Studies in Honour of Bustenay Oded (=Vetus Testamentum Supplements 130). Leiden and Boston, 2009
Studies Oppenheim	R.D. Biggs and J.A. Brinkman (eds.), Studies Presented to A. Leo Oppenheim, June 7, 1964. Chicago, 1964
Studies Palmieri	M. Frangipane et al. (eds.), Between the Rivers and Over the Mountains: Archaeologica Anatolica et Mesopotamica Alba Palmieri Dedicata. Rome, 1993

Studies Parpola	M. Luukko, S. Svärd, and R. Mattila (eds.), Of God(s), Trees, Kings, and Scholars: Neo-Assyrian and Related Studies in Honour of Simo Parpola (=StOr 106). Helsinki, 2009
Studies Postgate	Y. Heffron, A. Stone, and M. Worthington (eds.), At the Dawn of History: Ancient Near Eastern Studies in Honour of J.N. Postgate, 2 vols. Winona Lake, IN, 2017
Studies Renger	B. Böck, E. Cancik-Kirschbaum, and T. Richter (eds.), Munuscula Mesopotamica: Festschrift für Johannes Renger (=AOAT 267). Münster, 1999
Studies Salvini	P.S. Avetisyan, R. Dan, and Y.H. Grekyan (eds.), Over the Mountains and Far Away: Studies in Near Eastern History and Archaeology Presented to Mirjo Salvini on the Occasion of his 80th Birthday. Oxford, 2019
Studies Schoder	R.F. Sutton, Jr. (ed.), Daidalikon: Studies in Memory of Raymond V. Schoder, S.J. Wauconda, IL, 1989
Studies Tadmor	M. Cogan and I. Ephʿal (eds.), Ah, Assyria ... Studies in Assyrian History and Ancient Near Eastern Historiography Presented to Hayim Tadmor (=Scripta Hierosolymitana, Publications of the Hebrew University of Jerusalem 33). Jerusalem, 1991
Studies Volk	J. Baldwin, J. Matuszak, and M. Ceccarelli (eds.), mu-zu an-za$_3$-še$_3$ kur-ur$_2$-še$_3$ ḫe2-ĝal$_2$: Altorientalistische Studien zu Ehren von Konrad Volk (=Dubsar 17). Münster, 2020.
Studies Weippert	U. Hübner and E.A. Knauf (eds.), Kein Land für sich allein: Studien zum Kulturkontakt in Kanaan, Israel/Palästina und Ebirnâri für Manfred Weippert zum 65. Geburtstag (=Orbis Biblicus et Orientalis 186). Freiburg, 2002
Studies Wilcke	W. Sallaberger, K. Volk, and A. Zgoll (eds.), Literatur, Politik und Recht in Mesopotamien: Festschrift für Claus Wilcke (=Orientalia Biblica et Christiana 14). Wiesbaden, 2003
Subartu	Subartu. Turnhout, 1995–
Subartu 18	M. Fortin (ed.), Tell ʿAcharneh 1998-2004: Rapports préliminaires sur les campagnes de fouilles et saison d'études / Preliminary Reports on Excavation Campaigns and Study Season (=Subartu 18). Turnhout, 2006
Sumer	Sumer: A Journal of Archaeology in Iraq. Baghdad, 1945–
Sumeroloji Araştırmaları	Sumeroloji Araştırmaları: 1940–41. Istanbul, 1941
Swift, Pottery of the ʿAmuq	G.F. Swift, The Pottery of the ʿAmuq Phases K to O, and Its Historical Relationships. PhD dissertation. Chicago, 1958
Tadmor, Tigl, III	H. Tadmor, The Inscriptions of Tiglath-pileser III, King of Assyria: Critical Edition, with Introductions, Translations, and Commentary. Jerusalem, 1994
Tadmor and Yamada, RINAP 1	H. Tadmor and S. Yamada, The Royal Inscriptions of Tiglath-pileser III (744–727 BC) and Shalmaneser V (726–722 BC), Kings of Assyria (=RINAP 1). Winona Lake, IN, 2011
Tallon, Pierres	F. Tallon, Les pierres précieuses de l'Orient ancien des Sumériens aux Sassanides. Paris, 1995
Tallqvist, Götterepitheta	K. Tallqvist, Akkadische Götterepitheta, mit einem Götterverzeichnis und einer Liste der prädikativen Elemente der sumerischen Götternamen (=Studia Orientalia 7). Helsinki, 1938
Talon, Annales assyriennes	P. Talon, Annales assyriennes d'Assurnasirpal II à Assurbanipal, 2 vols. Brussels, 2011
Tavernier, Topography and Toponymy	J. Tavernier et al. (eds.), Topography and Toponymy in the Ancient Near East: Perspectives and Prospects. Louvain-la-Neuve, 2018
TCL	Textes cunéiformes du Louvre. Paris, 1910–
Tel Aviv	Tel Aviv. Tel Aviv, 1974–
Thompson, DACG	R. Campbell Thompson, A Dictionary of Assyrian Chemistry and Geology. Oxford, 1936
Thompson, Terror of Radiance	R.J. Thompson, Terror of the Radiance: Aššur Covenant to YHWH Covenant (= Orbis Biblicus et Orientalis 258). Fribourg, 2013
Thompson and Hutchinson, CEN	R. Campbell Thompson and R.W. Hutchinson, A Century of Exploration at Nineveh. London, 1929
Thureau-Dangin, TCL 3	F. Thureau-Dangin, Une relation de la huitième campagne de Sargon (=TCL 3). Paris, 1912
Thureau-Dangin and Dunand, Til-Barsib	F. Thureau-Dangin and M. Dunand, Til-Barsib, 2 vols (=Bibliothèque archéologique et historique 23). Paris, 1936
Timm, Moab	S. Timm, Moab zwischen den Mächten: Studien zu historischen Denkmälern und Texten (Ägypten und Altes Testament 17). Wiesbaden, 1989
TUAT	O. Kaiser (ed.), Texte aus der Umwelt des Alten Testaments. Gütersloh, 1982–2001
UF	Ugarit-Forschungen. Internationales Jahrbuch für die Altertumskunde Syrien-Palästinas. Münster, 1969–
Unger, IAMN 9	E. Unger, Tiglatpileser III-ün oğlu Asur kıralı Sargon II / Sargon II. von Assyrien der Sohn Tiglatpilesers III. (=İstanbul Asarıatika Müzeleri Neşriyatı 9). Istanbul, 1933

UVB 1	J. Jordan and A. Schott, Erster vorläufiger Bericht über die von der Notgemeinschaft der Deutschen Wissenschaft in Uruk-Warka unternommenen Ausgrabungen. Berlin, 1930
Vandenabeele and Laffineur, Cypriote Stone Sculpture	F. Vandenabeele and R. Laffineur (eds.), Cypriote Stone Sculpture: Proceedings of the Second International Conference of Cypriote Studies, Brussels-Liège, 17-19 May, 1993. Brussels, 1994
Vanden Berghe, Reliefs rupestres de l'Irān	L. Vanden Berghe, Reliefs rupestres de l'Irān ancien: Musées royaux d'art et d'histoire, Bruxelles, 26 octobre 1983 – 29 janvier 1984. Brussels, 1983
VAS	Vorderasiatische Schriftdenkmäler der Königlichen Museen zu Berlin. Leipzig and Berlin, 1907–
Vera Chamaza, Omnipotenz	G.W. Vera Chamaza, Die Omnipotenz Aššurs: Entwicklungen in der Aššur-Theologie unter den Sargoniden Sargon II., Sanherib und Asarhaddon (=AOAT 295). Münster, 2002
Vera Chamaza, Rolle Moabs	G.W. Vera Chamaza, Die Rolle Moabs in neuassyrischen Expansionspolitik (=AOAT 321). Münster, 2005
de Vogüé, CIS 2	M. de Vogüé, Corpus Inscriptionum Semiticarum 2. Paris, 1889
VT	Vetus Testamentum. Leiden, 1951–
Wachsmuth, Alten Geschichte	C. Wachsmuth, Einleitung in das Studium der Alten Geschichte. Leipzig, 1895
Wäfler, AOAT 26	M. Wäfler, Nicht-Assyrer neuassyrischer Darstellungen, 2 vols. (=AOAT 26). Kevelaer and Neukirchen-Vluyn, 1975
Walker, CBI	C.B.F. Walker, Cuneiform Brick Inscriptions in the British Museum, the Ashmolean Museum, Oxford, the City of Birmingham Museums and Art Gallery, the City of Bristol Museum and Art Gallery. London, 1981
Wartke, Urartu	R.-B. Wartke, Urartu, das Reich am Ararat. Mainz am Rhein, 1993
Watanabe, Animal Symbolism	C.E. Watanabe, Animal Symbolism in Mesopotamia: A Contextual Approach. Vienna, 2002
Weidner, IAK	E. Ebeling, B. Meissner, and E.F. Weidner, Die Inschriften der altassyrischen Könige (=Altorientalische Bibliothek 1). Leipzig, 1926
Weidner, Reliefs	E.F. Weidner, Die Reliefs der assyrischen Könige, 1: Die Reliefs in England, in der Vatikan-Stadt und in Italien (=AfO Beiheft 4). Berlin, 1939
von Weiher, SpTU 2	E. von Weiher, Spätbabylonische Texte aus Uruk, Teil II (=Ausgrabungen der Deutschen Forschungsgemeinschaft in Uruk-Warka 10). Berlin, 1983
Weippert, Edom	M. Weippert, Edom: Studien und Materialien zur Geschichte der Edomiter auf Grund schriftlicher und archäologischer Quellen. Theol. Diss., Tübingen, 1971
Wetzel, Stadtmauern	F. Wetzel, Die Stadmauern von Babylon (=WVDOG 48). Leipzig, 1930
Wilson and Brinkman, OI Featured Object 8	K.L. Wilson and J.A. Brinkman, Oriental Institute Museum, Featured Object Number 8, May 1990: Human-Headed Winged Bull from Khorsabad (OIM A7369). [Chicago, 1990]
Winckler, AOF	H. Winckler, Altorientalische Forschungen, 3 vols. Leipzig, 1893–1905
Winckler, Sammlung	H. Winckler, Sammlung von Keilschrifttexten, 3 vols. Leipzig, 1893–95
Winckler, Sar.	H. Winckler, Die Keilschrifttexte Sargons nach den Papierabklatschen und Originalen neu herausgegeben, 2 vols. Leipzig, 1889
Winckler, Textbuch^3	H. Winckler, Keilinschriftliches Textbuch zum Alten Testament, 3rd edition. Leipzig, 1909
Winckler, Untersuchungen	H. Winckler, Untersuchungen zur altorientalischen Geschichte. Leipzig, 1889
WO	Die Welt des Orients. Wuppertal, Stuttgart, and Göttingen, 1947–
Woolley and Barnett, Carchemish 3	Woolley, L. and R.D. Barnett, Carchemish, Report on the Excavations at Jerablus on Behalf of the British Museum, Part III: The Excavations in the Inner Town and the Hittite Inscriptions. London, 1952
Worthington, Textual Criticism	M. Worthington, Principles of Akkadian Textual Criticism (=Studies in Ancient Near Eastern Records 1). Berlin and Boston, 2012
WVDOG	Wissenschaftliche Veröffentlichungen der Deutschen Orient-Gesellschaft. Leipzig, Berlin, and Wiesbaden, 1900–
WZKM	Wiener Zeitschrift für die Kunde des Morgenlandes. Vienna, 1887–
Yadin, Art of Warfare	Y. Yadin, The Art of Warfare in Biblical Lands in the Light of Archaeological Study. New York, 1963
Yamada, SAAS 28	S. Yamada (ed.), Neo-Assyrian Sources in Context: Thematic Studies of Texts, History, and Culture. Helsinki, 2018
Yon, Kition dans les textes	E. Yon (ed.), Kition dans les textes: Testimonia littéraires et épigraphiques et corpus des inscriptions (=Kition-Bamboula 5). Paris, 2004
YOS	Yale Oriental Studies, Babylonian Texts. New Haven, 1915–

Younger, Conquest	K. Lawson Younger, Jr., Ancient Conquest Accounts: A Study in Ancient Near Eastern and Biblical History Writing (=Journal for the Study of the Old Testament Supplement Series 98). Sheffield, 1990
ZA	Zeitschrift für Assyriologie und Vorderasiatische Archäologie. Berlin, 1886–
ZÄS	Zeitschrift für Ägyptische Sprache und Altertumskunde. Leipzig and Berlin, 1863–
ZDMG	Zeitschrift der Deutschen Morgenländischen Gesellschaft. Leipzig and Wiesbaden, 1847-
ZDMG Suppl.	Zeitschrift der Deutschen Morgenländischen Gesellschaft, Supplement. Wiesbaden, 1969–
ZDPV	Zeitschrift des Deutschen Palästina-Vereins. Leipzig and Wiesbaden, 1878-
Zimansky, Ancient Ararat	P.E. Zimansky, Ancient Ararat: A Handbook of Urartian Studies. Delman, NY, 1998
Zimansky, Ecology and Empire	P.E. Zimansky, Ecology and Empire: The Structure of the Urartian State (=Studies in Ancient Oriental Civilization 41). Chicago, 1985
Zion	Zion. Jerusalem, 1949-
ZOrA	Zeitschrift für Orient-Archäologie. Berlin, 2008–

Other Abbreviations

Akk.	Akkadian
Asb.	Ashurbanipal
Asn.	Ashurnasirpal
Ass	Aššur
bibl.	Biblical
Bt	P.E. Botta
c	collated
ca.	circa
cf.	*confer* (lit. "compare")
cm	centimeter(s)
col(s).	column(s)
dia.	diameter
DN	divine name
ed(s).	editor(s)
Esar.	Esarhaddon
esp.	especially
et al.	*et alii* (lit. "and others")
ex(s).	exemplar(s)
fig(s).	figure(s)
fol(s).	folio(s)
frgm(s).	fragment(s)
gen.	gentilic
GN	geographical name
IdF	Institut de France
Je	Ch.-F. Jean
K	Konstantinopel
m	meter(s)
MA	Middle Assyrian
MdN	P.E. Botta, Monument de Ninive
MS	manuscript
n	not collated
n(n).	note(s)
NA	Neo-Assyrian
no(s).	number(s)
NS	Nova Series/New Series
obv.	obverse
p	collated from photo
p(p).	page(s)
ph(s).	photo(s)
pl(s).	plate(s)
PN	personal name
rev.	reverse
RN	royal name
Senn.	Sennacherib
SH	House of Sennacherib's son (Nineveh)
Sq	squeeze
Sum.	Sumerian
T-D	F. Thureau-Dangin

var(s).	variant(s)
vol(s).	volume(s)
Wi	H. Winckler

+	Between object numbers indicates physical join
(+)	Indicates fragments from same object but no physical join

Object Signatures

When the same signature is used for more than one group, the first group in this list is meant unless otherwise indicated. For example, "A" always means the Asiatic collection of the Oriental Institute unless stated otherwise.

A	1) Asiatic collection of the Oriental Institute, Chicago 2) Aššur collection of the Arkeoloji Müzeleri, Istanbul
AM	Prefix for excavation numbers at Tell Amarna, Syria
AnAr	Anadolu Medeniyetleri Müzesi, Ankara
AO	Collection of Antiquités Orientales of the Musée du Louvre, Paris
Ash	Ashmolean Museum, Oxford
Ass	Prefix for excavation numbers from the German excavations at Aššur
BCM	The City of Birmingham Museums and Art Gallery
BE	Prefix for excavation numbers from the German excavations at Babylon
BLMJ	Bible Lands Museum, Jerusalem
BM	British Museum, London
D	Prefix for excavation/registration number from the American excavations at Samaria
DŠ	Prefix for excavations numbers from the Oriental Institute (Chicago) excavations at Dūr-Šarrukīn (Khorsabad)
DT	Daily Telegraph collection of the British Museum, London
Erm	Hermitage, St. Petersburg
EŞ	Eşki Şark Eserleri Müzesi of the Arkeoloji Müzeleri, Istanbul
FMB	Bodmer Museum, Cologny
IAA	Israel Antiquities Authority, Jerusalem
IM	Iraq Museum, Baghdad
K	Kuyunjik collection of the British Museum, London
KH	Prefix for excavation numbers from the Italian excavations at Carchemish
LB	F.M.Th. de Liagre Böhl Collection, Leiden
M	National Museum, Aleppo
MAH	Musée d'Art et d'Histoire, Geneva
MMA	Metropolitan Museum of Art, New York
MS	Martin Schøyen collection, Oslo
N	1) collection number of the Louvre, Paris 2) Layard collection of the British Museum, London
Nap. III	Napoleon III; collection number of the Louvre, Paris
ND	Prefix for excavation numbers from the British excavations at Nimrud
P	Museo delle Antichità Egizie, Turin
PT	Prefix for excavation numbers for objects found on the Persepolis terrace by the Oriental Institute expedition
Rm	H. Rassam collection of the British Museum, London
ROM	Royal Ontario Museum, Toronto
Sm	G. Smith collection of the British Museum, London
T	Prefix for excavation number from the American excavations at Tell Tayinat
UM	University of Pennsylvania Museum of Archaeology and Anthropology, Philadelphia
VA	Vorderasiatisches Museum, Berlin
VA Ass	Aššur collection of the Vorderasiatisches Museum, Berlin
VAT	1) Tablets in the collection of the Vorderasiatisches Museum, Berlin 2) Prefix for objects in the Musei Vaticani, Museo Gregoriano Egizio, Rome
W	Prefix for excavations numbers from the German excavations at Uruk/Warka
YBC	Babylonian Collection of the Yale University Library, New Haven

Introduction

According to a Babylonian Chronicle, Shalmaneser V died in the month of Ṭebētu (X) during the fifth year of his reign (722) and Sargon II ascended the throne on the twelfth day of that month. Sargon was a son of Tiglath-pileser III and thus a brother of Shalmaneser. It was likely not a peaceful transition of power since Sargon soon thereafter had over six thousand Assyrians deported to Hamath, possibly because they had not supported him. Sargon was to reign over Assyria for seventeen years, being killed while on campaign in 705 and being succeeded by his son Sennacherib, who took the throne on the twelfth day of Abu (V) in that year. The Assyrians lost control over Babylonia almost immediately upon Sargon's accession, with the Chaldean Marduk-apla-iddina (II) (Merodach-baladan) taking the throne of Babylon in the first month of 721. Only in 710 was Sargon able to drive the latter out of Babylon and, in 709, capture his tribal stronghold of Dūr-Yakīn in the marshland at the head of the Persian Gulf. Babylonian King List A and the Ptolemaic Canon thus credit Sargon with a reign of five years (709–705) over Babylonia, with his first full year of reign in Babylon (709) being his thirteenth year on the throne of Assyria.

Sources for Reign

A large number and a wide variety of sources are attested for the reign of Sargon II. His inscriptions provide substantial information on both his military actions and building activities.[1] Two chronographic texts — the Assyrian Eponym Chronicle and a Babylonian Chronicle — as well as statements within some of the royal inscriptions as to the regnal year (*palû*) in which various events took place, provide the basic chronology of the period. Moreover, numerous letters and at least one astrological report date to his reign, some found at Nineveh (Parpola, SAA 1; Lanfranchi and Parpola, SAA 5; Hunger, SAA 8 no. 501; Fuchs and Parpola, SAA 15; and Dietrich, SAA 17) and others at Kalḫu (Luukko, SAA 19). While most were written to Sargon, including some from his son Sennacherib (Parpola, SAA 1 nos. 29–40; and Lanfranchi and Parpola, SAA 5 no. 281), a number were sent by Sargon himself. In addition, various legal and administrative documents (see Kwasman and Parpola, SAA 6; Fales and Postgate, SAA 7; and Fales and Postgate, SAA 11), and one renewal of a grant of land to provide offerings for the god Aššur (Kataja and Whiting, SAA 12 no. 19) are attested.[2] A few literary works refer to Sargon: two hymns — one to the goddess Nanāya and one to the goddess Ningal — that invoke blessings upon Sargon (Livingstone, SAA 3 no. 4; and Saggs, Studies Cagni pp. 905–912), a very fragmentary epic (Livingstone, SAA 3 no. 18), and the famous "Sin of Sargon" text, which most probably dates to the time of his grandson Esarhaddon (Livingstone, SAA 3 no. 33). A large number of stone wall slabs with reliefs depicting military and ceremonial actions were found in Sargon's palace at Khorsabad (ancient Dūr-Šarrukīn), as were a large number of bull-headed winged colossi with inscriptions on them. He is, however, mentioned only once in the Bible; Isaiah 20:1 states: "In the year that the field marshal, who was sent by Sargon, the king of Assyria, came to Ashdod, attacked Ashdod and took it." This likely refers to the capture of that city in Sargon's eleventh regnal year (711). He is almost totally absent from classical sources, although he does appear in the Ptolemaic Canon as Arkeanos (for which see below).

[1] For studies of the style and structure of Sargon's royal inscriptions, see Renger, CRRA 32 pp. 109–128 and Studies Moran pp. 425–437.

[2] Kataja and Whiting, SAA 12 no. 77 refers to decrees about offerings from several different reigns, including Shalmaneser IV, Adad-nārārī III, Tiglath-pileser III, and Sargon II. For a list of the few economic texts dated by the regnal years of Sargon II from Babylonia, see Brinkman and Kennedy, JCS 35 (1983) p. 13, to which add W 24405 (Kessler, Bagh. Mitt. 23 [1992] pp. 465–467). The astrological report mentioned above (Hunger, SAA 8 no. 501) was likely sent from Babylonia since it was dated in the first year of "Sargon, king of Babylon."

Texts Excluded from RINAP 2

As is the case in the other RINAP volumes, numerous inscriptions that refer to the respective Assyrian king fall outside the scope of the present volume. In the case of Sargon II, such texts include letters to or from Sargon, legal and administrative texts dated to his reign, the one land grant issued in his name, and the various literary texts that mention him. Several royal inscriptions that have sometimes been attributed to Sargon have been treated elsewhere in the RINAP series or are omitted here for other reasons.

(1) A fragmentary inscription on a statue (IM 60497B, ND 5571) found in the Ninurta Temple at Nimrud (ancient Kalḫu) has sometimes been assigned to Shalmaneser III, Tiglath-pileser III, or Sargon II. The text has been treated in Tadmor and Yamada, RINAP 1 as Tiglath-pileser no. 36.

(2) An inscription on a stone fragment in the Vatican Museum (VAT/15023) was once thought to come from Khorsabad and to belong to Sargon II (see Bezold, Literatur p. 94 §56.14.m), but it is now known to belong to Sennacherib. For this text, see Sennacherib no. 44 ex. 1 in Grayson and Novotny, RINAP 3/2.

(3) A poorly preserved inscription found on two fragments of a clay tablet (K 6205+82-3-23,131) describes an Assyrian king's campaign against Hezekiah of Judah and an attack on the latter's city of Azekah. This inscription, which is often called the Azekah Inscription, was assigned to Tiglath-pileser III by L. Jakob-Rost, but has more recently been assigned by scholars to either the time of Sargon II or Sennacherib. This text is arbitrarily assigned to Sennacherib in the RINAP series and is given as Sennacherib no. 1015 in Grayson and Novotny, RINAP 3/2.

(4) A fragment of a Neo-Assyrian stele was found at Ben Shemen in Israel and now bears the registration number 71.74.221 in the Israel Museum. H. Tadmor dated the text to the reign of Sargon II (in Aviram, Eretz Shomron [1973] p. 72 [in Hebrew]), and W. Horowitz and T. Oshima agreed with this (Canaan pp. 19 and 45), but M. Cogan suggests it may come from the reign of Esarhaddon (Studies Ephʿal pp. 66–69; Cogan, Raging Torrent p. 233 no. 4). The text is included in Leichty, RINAP 4 as Esarhaddon no. 1007.

(5) A rock relief located in the upper Tigris valley at Eğil, about 50 km from Diyarbakir in Turkey, has sometimes been ascribed to Shalmaneser III or Sargon II. The relief may depict a deity and the inscription is no longer legible. See Börker-Klähn, Bildstelen no. 154; Russell, RLA 9/3–4 (1999) p. 256.

(6) A weathered Neo-Assyrian relief that is located on Uzunoğlantepe, about 2 km north of the village of Ferhatlı in the vilayet of Adana in southern Turkey, has been assigned variously to Shalmaneser III and Sargon II (see Taşyürek, AnSt 25 [1975] pp. 169–172; Börker-Klähn, Bildstelen no. 235; Reade, IrAnt 12 [1977] p. 44); however, the relief bears no inscription.

(7) A stele with an inscription of the mother of Sennacherib, and thus a wife of Sargon, has been presented as Grayson and Novotny, RINAP 3/2 no. 2001, just as the inscriptions of Naqīʾa (Zakūtu) were presented with those of her son Esarhaddon (Leichty, RINAP 4 nos. 2003–2009).

(8) For the clay sealing Sm 2276 mentioning Sargon II and dating to the eponymy of Taklāk-ana-Bēl (715) that H. Winckler included in his work on the royal inscriptions of this king (Sar. 1 p. 196 and 2 pl. 49 no. 12) and D.D. Luckenbill in his translations of Sargon's inscriptions (ARAB 2 p. 114 §229), see Johns, ADD no. 766 and Fales and Postgate, SAA 11 no. 49 (with a photo of the sealing on p. 40). The royal stamp seal depicts the Assyrian king slaying a lion (see Figure 1). For another sealing possibly to be ascribed to Sargon II, see text no. 1002.

Figure 1. Sealing impressed with the royal seal of Sargon II (Sm 2276). © The Trustees of the British Museum.

Inscriptions of various independent and semi-independent rulers interacting with Assyria at the time are also not included. In addition to some Urartian royal inscriptions, we might note in particular the Akkadian inscription on the cylinder seal of Urzana, the king of Muṣaṣir whom Sargon forced to flee when the Assyrians attacked that city during Sargon's eighth campaign in 714 (see for example Thureau-Dangin, TCL 3 p. xii and Collon, First Impressions pp. 86–87 no. 405), and the Aramaic inscription on a stone stele found at Tepe Qalaichi, near Bukān in northwestern Iran, which may have been erected in the Mannean capital Izirtu during the reign of Sargon (see for example Lemaire, Studia Iranica 27 [1998] pp. 15–30 and Lipiński, Studies 4 pp. 19–27).

Survey of Inscribed Objects

One hundred and thirty inscriptions are assigned to Sargon II in this book, although a handful of these might be open to question. A further ten inscriptions are tentatively — and at times arbitrarily — assigned to him (text nos. 1001–1010). In addition, one inscription of his wife Ataliya (text no. 2001), two of his brother Sîn-aḫu-uṣur (text nos. 2002–2003), and eight of various individuals who held office either certainly or likely during his reign (text nos. 2004–2011) are included in the volume. These inscriptions are found on a variety of objects:

Object Type	*Text No.*
Stone wall slabs	1–8, 23–42, 73, 81
Stone paving slabs	10–22, 95, 2002
Stone colossi	9, 41, 107?, 1008
Stone altars	49
Stone tablet	47
Stone vessels	77 exs. 2–7
Stone steles	103–106, 108, 115, 117, 1009–1010, 2010–2011
Stone axe head	2008
Stone coffer	2005
Stone fragments (uncertain)	93–94, 1007
Clay prisms	63, 74–75, 82–83
Clay cylinders	43, 64, 76, 84–88, 109, 111–114, 125, 129, 1006, 2009
Clay tablets	48, 65, 72, 89–91, 101–102, 1001
Clay cones	67, 92, 1003–1004
Clay plaques	66, 1005?
Clay bowls	59–60
Bricks	50–56, 68–70, 95–98, 110, 123–124, 126–128, 1005?
Glazed bricks	57–58, 71
Metal tablets	44–46
Metal door jamb covers	99
Gold bowl	2001 ex. 1
Electrum mirror	2001 ex. 3
Bronze lion weights	78–79
Bronze macehead	62, 2003
Seals (including impressions and sealings)	1002, 2004, 2006–2007
Beads and eyestones	61, 100, 118–122, 130
Glass vessel	77 ex. 1
Rock crystal jar	2001 ex. 2
Ivory writing board	80
Rock face	116

Stone Wall Slabs

Inscriptions of Sargon II are found incised on the fronts of large sculpted wall slabs (or orthostats) that lined some of the most important rooms, corridors, and doorways in the palace at Dūr-Šarrukīn (modern Khorsabad), with each text incised in a band running across the middle of the front of the slab and with relief scenes depicted both above and below the band of inscription.[3] This arrangement follows in the tradition of the inscribed wall slabs of Ashurnasirpal II (883–859) and Sargon's own father Tiglath-pileser III (744–727), although some of the wall slabs of those rulers depicted just one scene (normally a human or semi-divine individual) with the inscription running across and over the middle of the scene. The wall slabs of Ashurnasirpal II bore a single display (or summary) inscription, which is represented by hundreds of copies,[4] while those of Tiglath-pileser III bore annalistic texts that stretched over a series of slabs.[5] The wall slabs from Sargon's palace bear both annalistic and display inscriptions.[6] In brief, the former present the king's military campaigns in chronological order, while the latter commonly present any military actions mentioned in some geographical order.[7]

The wall slabs in five or six rooms are known to have had versions of his annals and at least six rooms had display inscriptions:

Annals	Rooms II, V, XIII, XIV, throne room (=Court VII), and an unknown room (text nos. 1–6 respectively)
Display	Rooms I, IV, VII, VIII, and X (text no. 7); Room XIV (text no. 8)

It is worthy of note that Room XIV had both an annals inscription and a display inscription (text nos. 4 and 8) on its walls. Sometimes part of the inscription going around a room was found on slabs in one or more of the doorways leading into the room.[8]

These slabs were found for the most part by the work of P.E. Botta and V. Place at Khorsabad in the 1840s and 1850s, although a few were also found by the work of the Oriental Institute in 1929–1935. Regrettably, most of the items discovered by Botta and Place, and in particular the wall slabs with reliefs and copies of Sargon's annals and display inscriptions, as well as various other inscriptions and records, were either reburied at the site or lost in 1855 while being sent to Paris when the boat and rafts carrying them were attacked by local tribesmen and sank in the Tigris near Qurna. Vivid descriptions of the disaster are presented by M.T. Larsen in his Conquest of Assyria (pp. 344-349) and see also J.E. Reade's article on "Assyrian Antiquities Lost in Translation" (JCS 70 [2018] pp. 167–188). Since there were at least five exemplars of the display inscription, two or more of each of the five main paving slab inscriptions, and numerous exemplars of the bull inscription (see below), we can compare Botta's copy of one exemplar against that of another exemplar when one copy seems unreliable, and the basic text of these inscriptions is almost always certain, although the particular reading of parts of any one exemplar and its variants may be open to question. The fact that we are dependent for the most part upon Botta's copies for the various versions of the annals (except for text no. 5 which was found by the later American excavations) and for the Display Inscription from Room XIV is unfortunate, even when paper mache (*papier mâché*) impressions (squeezes) of the inscriptions made by Botta still exist (see below). For example, as far as I am aware, not one single original sign of the annals from Room II (text no. 1) — an inscription that was likely over five hundred lines long — is known to be preserved today, although some parts of the text may remain in situ at Khorsabad.

Some of the relief scenes found above and below the inscribed panels had short epigraphs (or captions) on them in order to identify the place depicted or to briefly describe the scene (text nos. 23–40), as was done on decorated relief slabs from the palaces of Tiglath-pileser III at Kalḫu and Sennacherib and Ashurbanipal at Nineveh.[9] Many of Sargon's wall slabs, as well as some of the stone colossi, also had a short inscription on the

[3] For the inscribed wall slabs of Sargon, see in particular J.M. Russell, Writing on the Wall pp. 111–115.

[4] The so-called "Standard Inscription" of Ashurnasirpal II; see Grayson, RIMA 2 pp. 268–276 A.0.101.23.

[5] See Tadmor and Yamada, RINAP 1 pp. 4–8 for the inscriptions of Tiglath-pileser III on wall slabs.

[6] E. Frahm (Sanherib pp. 42–43 and ISIMU 6 [2003] pp. 145–149 and 157–160, especially p. 159 n. 63) has suggested that Nabû-zuqup-kēnu, a royal scribe well attested in the reign of Sennacherib, might have been responsible for composing some of the royal inscriptions in the later years of Sargon's reign, especially his Khorsabad Display Inscription (text no. 7).

[7] With regard to these two types of inscriptions, see in particular Grayson, Orientalia NS 49 (1980) pp. 150–155.

[8] Text no. 1 sections 21–22 and any sections after section 37; text no. 2 sections 20–21; text no. 7 ex. 3 sections 7–8; and text no. 8 sections 5–6.

[9] Epigraphs are found on wall slabs in Room II (with the associated Door H_1; text nos. 23–28), Room V (text nos. 29–32), Room VIII (text nos. 33–35), Room XIII (text no. 36), Room XIV (text nos. 37–39), and an unknown room (text no. 40). For the epigraphs of Sargon in general, see in particular J.M. Russell, Writing on the Wall pp. 115–122. For the epigraphs on the wall slabs of Tiglath-pileser III, see Tadmor and Yamada, RINAP 1 pp. 143–146 Tiglath-pileser III nos. 55–57. For the epigraphs on the wall slabs of Sennacherib, see Grayson and Novotny, RINAP 3/2 pp. 100–121 nos. 53–77 and for those of Ashurbanipal, see Novotny and Jeffers, RINAP 5/1 pp. 311–349 nos. 24–58.

back, an inscription that was frequently written in a sloppy manner, with numerous errors (text no. 41; see also text no. 42). Sometimes the inscription on the back of a slab is written upside down, suggesting that it was incised off-site, before the slab was put in place in the palace and the front of the slab carved.[10]

Inscribed wall slabs have been found at two other sites in addition to Khorsabad. One discovered at Nebi Yunus (within ancient Nineveh) bears an annalistic inscription of Sargon II and the sculpted image of an Assyrian eunuch (text no. 81). Unlike the decorated wall slabs from Khorsabad where the inscription is in a central panel with relief scenes both above and below that panel, the image of the eunuch on this slab protrudes into the inscription, separating the beginning of the lines from their ends. Moreover, a ridge indicating the top of the slab appears to be immediately above the inscription and the head of the eunuch. As noted by E. Frahm, rather than having been erected at Nineveh in the time of Sargon, it is conceivable that this slab was brought to Nineveh from another site by one of Sargon's successors to the throne or in modern times.[11] In addition, two unsculpted stone slabs with text no. 73 were mounted on the wall of the palace at Kalḫu; however, these were relatively small slabs and were situated above larger slabs with the standard inscription of Ashurnasirpal II.

Stone Paving Slabs

Approximately thirty stone paving slabs incised with inscriptions have been found in the entryways of doors in the palace complex at Dūr-Šarrukīn. Those discovered within the main palace area bear one of five or six display inscriptions ranging from 23 to 150 lines in length (text nos. 10–14 and possibly 15). None of those found by Botta and copied by him (Monument de Ninive 3 pls. 1–21) are available for collation today, being either lost in the Tigris disaster in 1855 or left at the site.[12] Botta did make a squeeze of the inscription on one of these paving slabs and that squeeze is still extant today in the Louvre (text no. 11 ex. 2; Botta, Monument de Ninive 3 pl. 5[c]). Six inscribed paving slabs were found in what was originally thought to be the palace harem, but which was in fact the palace religious quarter, with the shrines of six deities (Ninurta, Ninšiku, Sîn, Adad, Ningal, and Šamaš). Place discovered two of these slabs (text nos. 16–17), but luckily, he did not attempt to send them to Paris and instead reburied them at the site. They were found in situ during the later work of the Oriental Institute, which also unearthed the other four slabs. Each paving slab has a 7–9 line inscription calling upon one of the deities to bless Sargon (text nos. 16–21).[13]

In addition to the palace complex, two other buildings within the citadel area had inscribed paving slabs: the temple of the god Nabû and the residence of Sargon's brother Sîn-aḫu-uṣur. Nine exemplars of a fourteen-line inscription (text no. 22) were found within the temple of Nabû during excavations by the Oriental Institute and either one of these or a tenth exemplar was discovered during more recent work by Iraqi archaeologists.[14] The inscription on these slabs calls upon the god Nabû to bless the king. Three exemplars of a seven-line text identifying Sîn-aḫu-uṣur as the builder of the house (text no. 2002) were found on stone slabs in doorways of Palace L (or Residence L), a building that was only exceeded in size within the citadel area by the palace complex itself.

At least three stone slabs were found by R. Campbell Thompson in the temple of Nabû at Nineveh that had an inscription identical to one found on bricks from Nineveh (text no. 95 exs. 4–6). The text identifies Sargon as the builder of the temple of the gods Nabû and Marduk.

Stone Colossi

A large number of stone bull colossi were discovered in the palace and city gates at Dūr-Šarrukīn that bore the same inscription (text no. 9), a text with a summary of Sargon's military achievements and a lengthy description of the construction of the city, and in particular its palace and city wall. It normally required two bull colossi to bear one copy of the text (i.e., a pair of colossi flanking one doorway), but at least two bulls appear to have each borne the whole inscription. Many of these were lost in the Tigris disaster in 1855, but fortunately Botta had made squeezes of the inscription on most of the bulls that he had found and copied. In view of the large number of exemplars of the text, the existence of these squeezes, and the fact that some of

---

[10] For the inscriptions on the backs of the slabs, see the article by B. André-Salvini in Caubet, Khorsabad pp. 15–45 and J.M. Russell, Writing on the Wall pp. 101–103.

[11] AoF 40 [2013] pp. 52–53.

[12] A paving slab with one of these inscriptions (text no. 10 ex. 4) was also found during the Oriental Institute excavations of Palace F, Dūr-Šarrukīn's military base (*ekal māšarti*).

[13] For the inscribed paving slabs of Sargon, see in particular J.M. Russell, Writing on the Wall pp. 108–111.

[14] Some of the exemplars were threshold slabs while others were on top of platforms flanking stairs or on the treads of stairs.

the stone colossi still exist today (in whole or in part), the basic text of the inscription is clear. Some of these colossi also have on the back of them the same display inscription that is found on the backs of numerous wall slabs (text no. 41).[15]

F. Thureau-Dangin identified a stone fragment with an inscription of Sargon found at Tell Ahmar (ancient Til-Barsip) as being from a bull colossus (text no. 107). In addition, Layard states that he found a pair of stone lions in the palace of Sennacherib at Nineveh that had a "nearly illegible" inscription (text no. 1008). The information on his discovery and the text on the objects are unclear and it is not impossible that the lions (or possibly bulls) actually came from Khorsabad.

Stone Steles

Sargon left a large number of stone steles recording his military achievements at various points throughout his realm and beyond, from Najafabad (near Isfahan) in the east to Cyprus in the west. The two best preserved were found in Cyprus (text no. 103) and in western Iran (text no. 117), and each has an image of the king on its front, in addition to an inscription. However, most of the steles exist today in only a fragmentary condition (text nos. 104–106, 108, and 115), possibly because local inhabitants intentionally destroyed them in ancient times when the Assyrians lost control of the areas in which they had been erected. The steles were set up at different points throughout his reign. The Acharneh Stele (text no. 106) and the Tell Tayinat Stele (text no. 108) may have been set up following Sargon's victory over Hamath in 720; the text of the former stele actually refers to the erection of at least three steles in the west. The Najafabad Stele (text no. 117) commemorates Sargon's campaign into the Zagros in his sixth regnal year and thus was likely set up in that year (716); unusually, the inscription on the stele was poorly written, perhaps the work of a less experienced scribe/carver.[16] Sargon may have had the stele from Ashdod (text no. 104) made following the capture of that city in 711. Since the so-called Beirut Stele (also known as the Borowski Stele and Hamath Stele; text no. 105) mentions the submission of kings from Cyprus, it must have been written after that occurred, likely in or around 708. The Cyprus Stele (text no. 103) refers to Sargon's third year as king of Babylon and thus must date to 707 at the earliest.[17] Too little is preserved of the stele fragment found at Qal'eh-i Imam, near Lake Zeribor in Iranian Kurdistan (text no. 115), to allow us to be certain about its date of composition, although it has been suggested that it was composed in 716.[18]

Small fragments of what may have been steles of Sargon were found at Samaria (text no. 1009) and Carchemish (text no. 1010). If they can be attributed to Sargon, the one from Samaria might have been erected after his involvement with that city in his accession year (722) or in his second regnal year (720), and the one from Carchemish might have been set up in his fifth regnal year (717), following the defeat of its ruler Pisīris.

Two steles of non-royal individuals are also included in this volume. The first has a relief depicting the goddess Ištar of Arbela and was erected at Kār-Shalmaneser, also known as Til-Barsip (modern Tell Ahmar), by the governor of that city Aššur-dūr-pāniya (text no. 2010). The second, found at Turlu-Höyük, bears an image of the storm god and was set up by one Bēl-iddin, who is given no title (text no. 2011). An Aššur-dūr-pāniya is attested in several letters from the reign of Sargon and this stele is possibly to be attributed to that individual. The exact date of the latter text remains unknown, although the scholars who initially published the piece suggest that it may come from the time of Sargon II.

Clay Prisms

Prior to the time of Sargon II, Assyrian royal inscriptions on clay prisms are only known with certainty from the reign of Tiglath-pileser I (1114–1076).[19] Five inscriptions from the reign of Sargon are found on prisms, although all of these are poorly preserved. All those prisms whose original shapes are clear or can be determined with some degree of certainty have eight columns. One inscription comes from Aššur (text no. 63), two from Kalḫu (text nos. 74–75), and two from Nineveh (text nos. 82–83), although there is some question as to whether or not one of the pieces said to come from Nineveh (text no. 83) was actually found at that site. It is possible that these five prisms represent only two distinct inscriptions, at least with regard to the text before

---

[15] For the inscription of Sargon on stone colossi, see in particular J.M. Russell, Writing on the Wall pp. 103–108.

[16] The edition of the Najafabad Stele presented here is the result of collaboration between the author and A. Fuchs.

[17] For an overview of Sargon's various steles, see Frame, Subartu 18 pp. 49–68.

[18] Radner and Masoumian, ZA 120 (2020) p. 91.

[19] Grayson, RIMA 2 pp. 7–31 A.0.87.1, pp. 38–45 A.0.87.4 ex. 7, and p. 60 A.0.87.14. Note also Grayson, RIMA 1 p. 182 commentary to A.0.77.1 with regard to Ass 875, which may be a prismatic cylinder of Shalmaneser I (1273–1244), although E. Weidner called it a prism. For a possible prism inscription of Ashurnasirpal II (883–859) from Tell Billah, see Grayson, RIMA 2 p. 191.

the building section, one inscription being text nos. 63 and 82, and the other being text nos. 74–75 and 83. The inscription on text nos. 63 and 82 is annalistic in form, dating the campaigns according to the king's regnal years (*palû*), although when preserved, these are always one or two years lower than those given in the annals found on wall slabs in the palace at Khorsabad (see below). Text no. 74 and apparently text no. 83 bear display inscriptions, while text no. 75 is so fragmentary that it is impossible to state what type of inscription it has. The building section of text no. 82 appears to commemorate the construction of a ziggurrat, possibly the one of Adad at Nineveh, and those of text nos. 74–75 the construction of the new city Dūr-Šarrukīn; the building reports are not preserved on the other pieces. Text no. 82 was composed no earlier than the king's eleventh regnal year (711) and text no. 74 no earlier than his sixteenth regnal year (706). The other inscriptions are much less well preserved, but since text no. 74 describes work on the palace at Khorsabad it also likely dates to around the completion of that city in 706. The latest event mentioned in text no. 63 took place in 713, but if this text were a duplicate of text no. 82, it would also have been written no earlier than 711. Text no. 83 mentions Sargon's campaign to Babylonia and the presentation of offerings to the gods of Babylonia, and thus must date to Sargon's twelfth regnal year (710) at the earliest.

Clay Cylinders

The inscription of Assyrian royal texts on clay cylinders really begins in the time of Sargon II, although one small exemplar of an Assyrian vassal from the time of Aššur-rēša-iši II (971–967) is attested.[20] A number of texts on cylinders of stone or semi-precious materials are known from earlier periods, although these are normally quite small in size.[21] Several of Sargon's royal inscriptions are found on barrel-shaped cylinders (text nos. 64, 84, 86–87, 111–114, 125, and 2009) and on prismatic (i.e., multi-faceted) cylinders (text nos. 43, 76, 85, 88, 109, 129, and 1006).[22] Some of the latter-type are also larger in the center than they are at the ends (in particular text no. 43), while others are mostly the same size from one end to the other (e.g., text no. 76). Clay cylinders with inscriptions from the time of Sargon have been found at a number of sites: Dūr-Šarrukīn (almost all exemplars of text no. 43), Aššur (text no. 64), Kalḫu (text nos. 76 ex. 2 and 1006), Nineveh (text nos. 43 ex. 5, 84–88, and possibly 76 ex. 1), Carchemish (text no. 109), Melid (text nos. 111–114), Tell Ḫaddad (text no. 129), Tell Baradān (text no. 76 ex. 5 and text no. 2009), and possibly Chenchi (text no. 43 ex. 55) and Uruk (text no. 125). Over fifty exemplars of the Khorsabad Cylinder inscription (text no. 43) have been found at Dūr-Šarrukīn, for the most part from within the palace area. Unusually, there are two versions of this inscription, an earlier version that has 67 lines of text, ten fewer than the later (and less common) version that has an additional passage in the middle of the inscription. Apart from text nos. 43 and 125, all the cylinder inscriptions are only partially preserved and it is possible that some actually come from duplicate inscriptions (text nos. 84 and 85, and text nos. 86 and 87) or even from the same cylinder (text nos. 111 and 112). Like typical Babylonian royal inscriptions, the two cylinder inscriptions from Babylonia — text no. 125 from Uruk and text no. 2009 from Tell Baradān (written in the name of Nabû-bēlu-ka''in, the governor of the city Arrapḫa) — do not commemorate or mention military actions, but instead concentrate on religious and building matters. Otherwise, all the cylinder inscriptions mention in some manner the king's military achievements, except perhaps text no. 1006.

Clay Tablets

Clay tablets and tablet fragments with inscriptions of Sargon have been found at a number of sites: Aššur (text nos. 65 and 72), Nineveh (text nos. 89–91 and 101–102), and probably Dūr-Šarrukīn (text no. 48; see also text no. 1001). Most of these are only fragments, but two important texts are relatively well preserved: Sargon's lengthy letter to the god Aššur (text no. 65) reporting on his campaign into Mannea, Urarṭu, and Muṣaṣir in his eighth regnal year (714), and the so-called Aššur Charter (text no. 89), recording his accession to the throne and granting of privileges to the city Aššur, as well military actions in his second regnal year (720). The other tablet fragments describe military (text nos. 72, 101–102, and likely 91), building (text no. 48), or dedicatory (text no. 90) actions.

[20] See Grayson, RIMA 2 pp. 126–128 A.0.96.2001 (inscription of Bēl-ēriš, an Assyrian vassal at Šadikanni).
[21] See for example Grayson, RIMA 1 pp. 51–55 A.0.39.2 (noting Reade, NABU 2000 pp. 86–87 no. 75) and p. 122 A.0.75.2; Grayson, RIMA 3 pp. 194–196 A.0.103.5–7.
[22] Prismatic cylinders are sometimes referred to as prisms or multi-faceted cylinders since they have several distinct faces like a prism; however, the inscription on these objects runs from one end of the object to the other, while the inscriptions on prisms run from one side of the face (or column) to the other. Thus, each face of a prismatic cylinder has only a few lines while one on a prism has many more lines, but lines that tend to be much shorter in length than those on the prismatic cylinders.

Bricks

Bricks with inscriptions of Sargon have been found at a number of places in addition to the major centers of Dūr-Šarrukīn, Aššur, Kalḫu, and Nineveh, including especially Carchemish, Babylon, and Uruk. The inscriptions may be inscribed or stamped; sometimes an inscription is found in both manners (text no. 50). At times, the text may be inscribed within an area that has been impressed, thus providing a border for the inscription, and in some scholarly literature such texts are described as stamped, rather than — more accurately — inscribed. While most of the inscriptions of Sargon are written in the Akkadian language, two of the brick inscriptions from Assyria are in Sumerian, one commemorating the construction of Dūr-Šarrukīn (text no. 53) and one work at Aššur (text no. 70). The latter inscription is also known from an Akkadian version (text no. 69). Three brick inscriptions from Babylonia are in Sumerian, one recording work at Babylon (text no. 124) and two work at Uruk (text nos. 127–128).

Bricks with the same three-line inscription stating that they came from Sargon's palace have been found at Dūr-Šarrukīn, Kalḫu, Nineveh, Karamles, Tag, and possibly Djigan (text no. 50). Since Sargon would have had more than one palace, this may not seem odd, but numerous bricks with inscriptions commemorating the building of Dūr-Šarrukīn and/or structures located there (e.g., the temple of Sîn and Šamaš) have also been discovered outside of Dūr-Šarrukīn, in particular at Kalḫu and Nineveh (text nos. 51 and 53–55). These bricks may have been taken to those places during the reign of Sargon or possibly after his death, when Dūr-Šarrukīn was basically abandoned and perhaps partially demolished.

Texts record the construction of the new capital Dūr-Šarrukīn (text nos. 51–54), its palace (text nos. 52–53, and see text nos. 50 and 56), and the temple of Sîn and Šamaš (text nos. 54–55). Numerous bricks from Aššur record the building of a structure for the god Aššur (text no. 68) and the paving of a processional way in the temple of that god (text nos. 69–70). Brick inscriptions commemorate work on the temple of the god Nabû (or the gods Nabû and Marduk) at Nineveh (text nos. 95–96 and possibly 97). The brick inscription from Carchemish is very short, merely indicating that the brick came from the palace of Sargon (text no. 110), while some of the brick inscriptions from Babylonia can be quite lengthy. Two brick inscriptions record construction at Babylon, one twenty-five lines long describing work on the quay wall and city walls and one eighteen lines long describing work on the city walls (text nos. 123 and 124 respectively). The three brick inscriptions from Uruk all refer to work on the Eanna temple (text nos. 126–128). Unusually, one of these latter inscriptions (text no. 126) is written in three columns of four lines each.

Glazed Bricks

Glazed bricks from friezes with cuneiform inscriptions of Sargon have been found at both Dūr-Šarrukīn and Aššur (text nos. 57 and 71 respectively), although all the friezes are in a poor state of preservation. Those from Dūr-Šarrukīn whose provenance is known come from the palace complex or Palace F, while those from Aššur were found in the temple of the god Aššur. Glazed brick panels are already mentioned in the texts of Tiglath-pileser I (1114–1076) and Ashurnasirpal II (883–859),[23] and individual glazed bricks with all or parts of inscriptions are attested from the reigns of Tukultī-Ninurta II (890–884), Shalmaneser II (858–824), and (possibly) Tiglath-pileser III.[24] In addition, ten glazed brick friezes from the palace at Khorsabad bear what is generally thought to be an inscription written in Assyrian 'hieroglyphs' or 'astroglyphs' (text no. 58). At times, that inscription is found in a shorter or abbreviated form (exs. 7–10). Such 'hieroglyphic' inscriptions are also attested in the time of Sargon's grandson Esarhaddon (680–669).[25]

Metal Tablets

Three of Sargon's inscriptions are inscribed on metal tablets, one of bronze (text no. 44), one of silver (text no. 45), and one of gold (text no. 46). A fourth metal tablet was apparently found, but was lost in the Tigris disaster in 1855, and no real information is known about it. These four had been placed in a stone box located within one of the walls of the royal palace at Dūr-Šarrukīn and the three preserved today all record the construction of that city.[26] Assyrian royal inscriptions on gold tablets are already attested from the time of

---

[23] Grayson, RIMA 2 pp. 54–55 A.0.78.10 lines 66–67; Grayson, RIMA 2 pp. 289–290 A.0.101.30 lines 30–32.

[24] Grayson, RIMA 2 pp. 184–185 A.0.100.15 (brick or tile); Grayson, RIMA 3 p. 157 A.0.102.100 exs. 1, 6, and 11, p. 168 A.0.102.112, and p. 169 A.0.102.114; Tadmor and Yamada, RINAP 1 p. 159 no. 1007. See also Grayson, RIMA 3 p. 250 A.0.0.1094–1096.

[25] Leichty, RINAP 4 pp. 238–243 no. 115.

[26] A stone tablet with an inscription also commemorating the construction of Dūr-Šarrukīn was found with these metal tablets (text no. 47). See Brinkman in Curtis, Bronzeworking Centres pp. 144–150 and 158–159.

Shalmaneser I (1273–1244), Tukultī-Ninurta I (1243–1207), Ashurnasirpal II (883–859), and Shalmaneser III (858–824),[27] and on silver tablets from the time of Tukultī-Ninurta I and Ashurnasirpal II,[28] as well as on lead tablets from the time of Tukultī-Ninurta I.[29]

Bronze Lion Weights

Weights with brief labels indicating that they belonged to a king have a long tradition in Mesopotamia, going all the way back to the third millennium. Most of these weights are made of stone and in the shape of a duck,[30] although one in the shape of a lion is known from the time of Shalmaneser III.[31] In 1846, Layard discovered sixteen bronze weights in the shape of lions in the North-West Palace at Kalḫu. Thirteen of these bear Akkadian proprietary inscriptions, one of Tiglath-pileser III (Tadmor and Yamada, RINAP 1 Tiglath-pileser III no. 63), nine of Shalmaneser V (Tadmor and Yamada, RINAP 1 Shalmaneser V nos. 1–9 and note no. 1003), one of Sennacherib (Grayson and Novotny, RINAP 3/2 text no. 211), and two of Sargon II (text nos. 78–79). Most, including the two of Sargon, also have brief Aramaic inscriptions on them indicating the weight of the object.

Rock Face

Three Assyrian rulers before Sargon II have left us royal inscriptions incised into rock faces, although the tradition of Mesopotamian rulers leaving inscriptions or reliefs on cliff faces goes back to the third millennium. Tiglath-pileser I and Shalmaneser III had two and five inscriptions respectively carved on rock faces in Turkey, mostly near the source of the Tigris River,[32] and Tiglath-pileser III had one made at Mila Mergi in Iraqi Kurdistan.[33] In addition to the inscription, a relief depicting the ruler is found with one of the inscriptions of Tiglath-pileser I, at least two of those of Shalmaneser III, and the inscription of Tiglath-pileser III. A relief and inscription of Sargon were carved into a cliff face at Tang-i Var in Iran in order to commemorate a campaign to Karalla led by Assyrian officials in 706 (text no. 116). Like the relief of Tiglath-pileser III at Mila Mergi, the one at Tang-i Var depicts the Assyrian king, but unlike the one of Tiglath-pileser, part of the inscription is written across the king's body.

Miscellaneous

Inscriptions of Sargon are found on a variety of other objects of stone, clay, metal, and other materials. Apart from a stone tablet from Khorsabad that bears a twenty-five-line inscription recording the construction of that city (text no. 47), the inscriptions on the other stone objects (altars, vessels, axe head, coffer, and unidentifiable objects) are either short or very fragmentary. When it is possible to determine the nature of the inscription, it often simply states to whom the object belonged (text no. 77) or had been dedicated (text nos. 49 and 2005), although it might mention the actual construction of the object or some edifice (text nos. 93, 1007, and 2008). As far as I am aware, apart from one stone altar from Kalḫu from time of Ashurnasirpal II and one from Nineveh from the time of Shalmaneser III,[34] the sixteen stone altars from the temple of the Sebetti at Dūr-Šarrukīn (text no. 49) are the only other altars with inscriptions of Assyrian kings upon them. The inscriptions on clay cones record the construction of temples at Aššur and Nineveh (text nos. 67 and 92; cf. text nos. 1003–1004), while the clay plaques bear a brief proprietary inscription (text no. 66; cf. text no. 1005). The inscriptions on clay vessels (text nos. 59–60) are poorly preserved and their nature is not clear.[35] Surprisingly, the only two inscriptions in this volume that clearly bear dates indicating when they were written are found on clay cones from Aššur (text nos. 67 and 1004), although only one of these is sufficiently well preserved to allow us to

---

[27] Grayson, RIMA 1 p. 196 A.0.77.7, pp. 253–256 A.0.78.11 exs. 2–3, pp. 256–257 A.0.78.12 ex. 1, pp. 259–260 A.0.78.14 exs. 1 and 4, pp. 260–261 A.0.78.15 ex. 1, and pp. 264–265 A.0.78.17 ex. 1; Grayson, RIMA 2 pp. 341–342 A.0.101.70 ex. 1; and Grayson, RIMA 3 pp. 99–100 A.0.102.26.

[28] Grayson, RIMA 1 pp. 253–256 A.0.78.11 exs. 5–6, pp. 256–257 A.0.78.12 ex. 2, pp. 259–260 A.0.78.14 ex. 3, pp. 260–261 A.0.78.15 ex. 2, and pp. 264–265 A.0.78.17 ex. 2. Grayson, RIMA 2 pp. 341–342 A.0.101.70 ex. 2.

[29] Grayson, RIMA 1 pp. 253–256 A.0.78.11 exs. 4 and 7–10, and pp. 259–260 A.0.78.14 exs. 5–6.

[30] For example, Frayne, RIME 3/2 pp. 154–155 E3/2.1.2.51–53; Grayson, RIMA 2 pp. 181–182 A.0.100.10 (Tukultī-Ninurta II) and pp. 358–359 A.0.101.107 (Ashurnasirpal II); and Tadmor and Yamada, RINAP 1 pp. 150–152 Tiglath-pileser III nos. 61–62.

[31] Grayson, RIMA 3 pp. 169–170 A.0.102.115.

[32] Grayson, RIMA 2 pp. 61–62 A.0.87.15–16; Grayson, RIMA 3 pp. 90–96 A.0.102.20–24. Note that M. Worthington suggests that one of the inscriptions attributed to Tiglath-pileser I (Grayson, RIMA 2 p. 61 A.0.87.15) may actually be of later date, possibly from the time of Shalmaneser III.

[33] Tadmor and Yamada, RINAP 1 pp. 89–92 Tiglath-pileser III no. 37.

[34] Grayson, RIMA 2 pp. 351–352 A.0.101.98 (from Kalḫu); Grayson, RIMA 3 pp. 153–154 A.0.102.95 (from Nineveh).

[35] It is not impossible that one or both of the clay bowls are actually clay cones (*sikkatu*).

identify the year (text no. 67).[36] A number of metal objects (copper covers for door jambs, gold bowl, electrum mirror, and bronze macehead) also bear short proprietary (text nos. 99, 2001 exs. 1 and 3, and 2003) or dedicatory (text no. 99) inscriptions.

With regard to stamp and cylinder seals and impressions, a clay sealing with a stamped impression of what may be a royal seal (text no. 1002) appears to have been found at Khorsabad in the mid-1800s, but its present location is not known and it is thus unavailable for collation. A cylinder seal of unknown provenance and a clay bulla from Nimrud with the impression of a cylinder seal bear proprietary inscriptions of governors (text nos. 2006–2007); a stamp seal impression with a proprietary Aramaic inscription of one of Sargon's eunuchs was also found at Khorsabad (text no. 2004). The brief inscriptions on a glass vessel (text no. 77 ex. 1) and a rock crystal jar (text no. 2001 ex. 2) are also proprietary in nature. One of the most interesting objects bearing an inscription of Sargon's is an ivory writing board found at Kalḫu (text no. 80). The inscription states that it belonged to the palace of Sargon and that that king had had the astrological series *Enūma Anu Enlil* written upon it and the board deposited at Dūr-Šarrukīn.

Overview of Previous Publications / Editions / Scholarship

In view of Sargon's involvement with Israel and the "Ten Lost Tribes of Israel" and his successful military campaigns throughout the Near East, from Philistia in the Southwest to Urarṭu in the North and Babylonia in the Southeast, every general history of ancient Assyria or Mesopotamia includes some treatment of his reign. In 1908, the American Assyriologist and historian A.T.E. Olmstead published his 1906 Cornell University dissertation Western Asia in the Days of Sargon of Assyria 722–705 B.C.: A Study in Oriental History. Surprisingly, this was to be the only monographic length study of his reign for over a century, although useful chapters on his reign appeared by A.K. Grayson in CAH[2] 3/2 in 1991 and by W. Mayer in his Politik und Kriegskunst der Assyrer in 1995. In 2001 R.A. Gabriel even had a chapter on Sargon in his book Great Captains of Antiquity (part of the series Contributions in Military Studies); Sargon was the only Mesopotamian ruler included in the volume. A. Fuchs has presented important biographical overviews of the king within the past decade in RLA 12/1–2 (2009) pp. 51–61 and PNA 3/2 (2011) pp. 1239–1247. Recently, three books on Sargon appeared in almost successive years: Le campagne babilonesi ed orientali di Sargon II d'Assiria: un'analisi topografica (a revision of a 2007 doctoral dissertation presented at the Università di Roma La Sapienza) by F. Maniori in 2014, The Campaigns of Sargon II, King of Assyria, 721–705 B.C (in the series Campaigns and Commanders) by S.C. Melville in 2016, and Sargon II, King of Assyria (in the series Archaeology and Biblical Studies) by J. Elayi in 2017. The first author provides a detailed study of Sargon's southern and eastern campaigns, while each of the latter two authors provides a study of all Sargon's campaigns, although the authors do not always see things in the same way.

Translations of individual inscriptions of his or of selective passages from them — generally those dealing with Biblical matters — often appear in compendiums of translations of ancient Near Eastern texts, for example, Gressmann, ATAT[2] (translations by E. Ebeling); Pritchard, ANET[3] (translations by A.L. Oppenheim); Briend and Seux, TPOA (translations by M.-J. Seux); Galling, Textbuch[2] (translations by R. Borger); TUAT 1/4 (translations by Borger); and COS 2 and 4 (translations by K.L. Younger and F.M. Fales).

Before discussing the major previous editions and studies of this text corpus, I would like to cite here briefly some other important works in which Sargon II texts have been published. For editions/transliterations of a single text, or a very small group of texts, often accompanied by a copy and/or a photograph, see especially: Schrader, Sargonsstele (1882); Nassouhi, MAOG 3/1 (1927); Thureau-Dangin, RA 30 (1933); Unger, IAMN 9 (1933); Weidner, AfO 14 (1941–44); Barnett in Woolley and Barnett, Carchemish 3 (1952); Gadd, Iraq 16 (1954); Wiseman, Iraq 17 (1955); Gadd in Crowfoot, Samaria-Sebaste 3 (1957); Tadmor, Eretz-Israel 8 (1967); Levine, Stelae (1972); Saggs, Iraq 37 (1975); Al-Rawi, Iraq 56 (1994); Frame, Orientalia 68 (1999); Kessler, AfO 50 (2003–4); Niederreiter, RA 99 (2005); Frame, Subartu 18 (2006); Akdoğan and Fuchs, ZA 99 (2009); Frahm, KAL 3 (2009); Frame, Studies Parpola (2009); Frame, CUSAS 17 (2011); Frahm, AoF 40 (2013); Lauinger and Batiuk, ZA 105 (2015); Baruchi-Unna and Cogan, IMSA 9 (2018–19); and Marchesi, JNES 78 (2019).

According to the noted French archaeologist J.-C. Margueron, "Mesopotamian archaeology was born at the end of March 1843, on the day when P.E. Botta, the consular agent at Mosul, brought to light a group of buildings with bas-reliefs and inscriptions on the mound of Khorsabad (Dur-Sharrukin)."[37] The buildings that

[36] At least one exemplar of a text on prismatic cylinders (text no. 76 ex. 2) has a date written on the left end of the piece, but only the day is preserved and the eponymy was clearly not given.
[37] Margueron, Mesopotamia p. 13.

Botta (1802–1870) brought to light were the palace of Sargon II at his capital of Dūr-Šarrukīn ("Fortress/Wall of Sargon"), located next to the Khosr River about fifteen km northeast of the Iraqi city of Mosul. He carried out work there only until the following year, 1844, and in 1845 returned to France. However, he had unearthed numerous magnificent stone wall panels decorated with carved reliefs and massive stone sculptures of winged bulls, among other items. He sent a series of five letters about his discoveries back to Jules Mohl in Paris and these were published in the Journal asiatique[38] while Botta was still in Iraq. These reports encouraged the French government to send the artist E. Flandin to make drawings of the reliefs. The few items that Botta brought back to Paris caused a great sensation when they were displayed in the Louvre in 1847 and V. Place was thus sent out to continue the work at Khorsabad, where he, aided by F. Thomas, excavated in 1852-1854, finding more fabulous items. In numbering the rooms and courtyards in the palace that were excavated, Botta used Arabic numerals for rooms and Roman numerals for courts; however, some of the spaces initially thought by him to have been open areas (i.e., courts) were later realized to be rooms. Thus, for example, Court VII on his plan was actually the throne room, and Courts II, V, X, XIII, and XIV were also rooms. He did however refer to areas II, V, X, XIII, and XIV as rooms in connection with his copies, but continued to cite them with Roman numerals. Place corrected most of these in his plan of the palace (replacing the Roman numerals with Arabic ones), but he did not correct all of them (e.g., the throne room remained Court VII). As mentioned in the Editorial Notes, it has been thought best to maintain Botta's numbering (i.e., using Roman numerals) when citing rooms with inscribed wall slabs since that is how they are noted on his copies and in most recent publications of the texts, but to use Arabic numerals for rooms mentioned in connection with other texts, texts mostly found during the later excavations by the Oriental Institute of the University of Chicago, which cited the rooms with Arabic numerals. Botta thought that he had found the Nineveh of the Bible and so his and Flandin's publication claimed in its title: Monument de Ninive, 5 volumes published in 1849–1850 (Paris). The first two volumes of Monument de Ninive contained plans of the individual rooms excavated and Flandin's drawings of the reliefs, as well as drawings of some individual objects and of some details on the reliefs. Volumes 3 and 4 contained Botta's typeset copies of inscriptions on the bulls, paving slabs, and wall slabs, as well as on a few other items; and volume 5 recorded the discovery of the site and a description of the excavations, as well as having chapters on writing and decipherment. Botta, and later Place, found numerous inscribed materials. Botta's initial copies of some of the texts that he found were published with his reports in Journal asiatique and the copies are preserved today in the archives of the Institut de France in Paris. He also made squeezes of many of the texts, which he used to correct his initial copies before they were published in typeset characters in Monument de Ninive. In the table of contents of volumes 3–4, a small "c" is placed with the plate number for each copy that had been collated from a squeeze or from the original in the Louvre (e.g., "99^{c}") and this is also done in this volume when a Botta plate number is cited in a text catalogue and usually in text introductions and commentaries, but it is not normally indicated in the bibliography sections of the individual texts, footnotes, or in runs of consecutive numbers.[39]

Place, who had worked at Khorsabad in 1852-1854, entitled the publication of his work Ninive et l'Assyrie (3 volumes published in 1867–1870; Paris), although he recognized that Khorsabad was not ancient Nineveh.

---

[38] JA 4/2 (1843) pp. 61–72 and pls. I–XII; and pp. 201–214 and pls. XIII–XXI. JA 4/3 (1844) pp. 91–103 and pls. XXII–XXXI; and pp. 424–435 and pls. XXXII–XXXVIII. JA 4/4 (1844) pp. 301–314 and pls. XXXIX–XLIX. These include at times notes and comments by J. Mohl. For English translations of these letters, see Botta's Letters on the Discoveries at Nineveh (London, 1850) and Illustrations of the Discoveries at Nineveh; Consisting of Forty-Nine Plates of the Sculpture and Inscriptions on Ancient Assyrian Monuments, with Descriptions, being a Translations of M. Botta's Letters on the First Discoveries at Nineveh (London, 1850). Note also JA 4/5 (1845) pp. 201–207 and pls. L–LV, a report by Botta to the Minister of the Interior.

[39] The squeezes that are still extant are preserved in the Louvre and were jointly given the museum number AO 7382 when they were accessioned into the Louvre. Although P.E. Botta indicates that he made squeezes of Monument de Ninive 3–4 pls. 32–35, 40, 47, 51, 73, 76, 79 (top), 117, 125, 135 (bottom) 139, 143 (top), 160 (bottom), 173, and 181–183, these were either destroyed or lost many years ago. The Louvre accession records indicate that squeezes of pls. 40, 47, 51, and 125 were among those acquired by the Louvre about a century ago when they moved there from the Bibliothèque Nationale, but the ones of pls. 40, 47, and 125 cannot be located today and for pl. 51, see below. Actually, there appears to be some uncertainty in the records whether squeezes of pls. 40 and 47 did indeed enter the Louvre. In addition, there may in fact never have been squeezes of the slabs presented on the top of pls. 79 and 143 (Room II, slab 2 [text no. 1 section 1] and Room VIII, slab 23 [text no. 7 ex. 5 section 12]) and bottom of pls. 135 and 160 (Room VIII, slab 16 [text no. 7 ex. 5 section 6] and Room XIV, slab 7 [text no. 8 section 3]), with Botta's indication that this plate had been collated only referring to the other slab on the plate, for which a squeeze does exist. Winckler indicates that he did not see squeezes of the inscriptions presented on the top of Botta's pl. 79 and bottom of pl. 160; the other two slabs have parts of the Display Inscription, for which Winckler only provided a copy of the text in Room X (with variants from the other exemplars). Squeezes of only ten of the fourteen epigraphs on pl. 180 are currently preserved in the Louvre and that is all that were extant at the time they entered the Louvre. There is a squeeze in the Louvre labeled as being pl. 51, but it is actually an impression of the inscription on the back of the bull colossus in question (text no. 41 ex. 21), and not of part of the inscription between the bull's legs (text no. 9 ex. 2).

The first volume included, among other matters, descriptions of the various buildings and structures found and a discussion of the manner of construction used by the Assyrians. In addition to chapters on attempts at determining what the structures would have looked like and how they were decorated, on the excavation and transport of the antiquities discovered, and on numerous other topics (e.g., glyptics, painting, and ceramics), the second volume had a chapter on cuneiform inscriptions and an almost forty-page appendix (pp. 281–319) by J. Oppert on the inscriptions on the winged bulls, clay cylinders, and gold, silver, and 'antimony' tablets (text nos. 9, 43, 46, 45, and 47 respectively), with typeset copies of the texts, interlinear transliterations and Latin translations, as well as French translations.[40] Oppert also presented a translation of the annals based on the material from Rooms II, V, XIII, and XIV of the palace (text nos. 1–4), although this translation also incorporated parts of the Display Inscription from Room XIV (text no. 8). His were the first real published editions of texts from Khorsabad, but he had previously published translations of all or part of some of them elsewhere (e.g., bull: Oppert, Chronologie [1856] pp. 35–39 = Annales de Philosophie chrétienne 53 [1856] pp. 346–350; cylinder: Annales de Philosophie chrétienne 65 [1862] p. 45 no. 5 and pp. 183–188 [with a partial translation already back in 1856]). The third volume contained plans of the site and buildings, reconstructions of various structures, drawings of various reliefs and other finds, and heliogravures of the gold, silver, bronze and 'antimony' tablets, as well as of two exemplars of the Khorsabad Cylinder inscription (pls. 77–78). Some drawings of items from other sites (in particular Kuyunjik) are also found in volume 3.

Botta's publication Monument de Ninive came out quite quickly after his work at the site, in only about five years, while Place's took about fifteen years. Among the most active scholars working at this time on the decipherment of cuneiform was the aforementioned German-French scholar Julius (Jules) Oppert (1825–1905). Situated in Paris, he produced the most important early works on the texts from Khorsabad in a series of articles and books, beginning already in 1855–1856 with a partial translation of the Khorsabad Cylinder inscription (text no. 43) in the Transactions of the Historic Society of Lancashire and Cheshire (vol. 8) and a translation of the Khorsabad Bull inscription (text no. 9) in the Annales de Philosophie chrétienne (vol. 53). Among his publications are Les inscriptions assyriennes des Sargonides et les fastes de Ninive (1862; text nos. 7, 43, and 73); Les fastes de Sargon, roi d'Assyrie (721 à 703 avant J.C.), traduits et publiés d'après le texte assyrien de la grande inscription des salles du palais de Khorsabad, with J. Ménant (1863; text no. 7); Grande inscription du palais de Khorsabad, with Ménant (1863; text no. 7); and Les inscriptions de Dour-Sarkayan (Khorsabad) provenant des fouilles de M. Victor Place (1870; text nos. 1–4, 9, 43, and 45–47). Sometimes his works were published in two different places (e.g., Sargonides also appeared in the periodical Annales de Philosophie chrétienne vol. 65, and his section in Place's Ninive et l'Assyrie volume 2 also appeared as Dour-Sarkayan). In addition to working with Oppert on two books on Sargon's Khorsabad Display inscription, Joachim Ménant (1820–1899) published French translations of all or parts of several inscriptions of Sargon in his works Annales des rois d'Assyrie (1874; text nos. 1–4, 7, 9, 12, 16–17, 41, 43, 46, 50, 55, 73, 92, 95, and 103) and Babylone et la Chaldée (1875; text nos. 1–2).

David Gordon Lyon (1852–1935) produced his book Keilschrifttexte Sargon's, Königs von Assyrien (722–705 v. Chr.) (Leipzig) in 1883 as the fifth volume in the series Assyriologische Bibliothek. This had been his doctoral thesis at the University of Leipzig, where he had been a student of Friedrich Delitzsch. The volume includes copies, transliterations, translations, and commentary of several inscriptions from Khorsabad, those on clay cylinders (text no. 43), on winged bulls (text no. 9), and on tablets of bronze, silver, gold, and 'antimony' (text nos. 44–47). The volume concludes with a glossary arranged according to the root letters in Hebraic script and a combined index of geographical, personal, and divine names. The edition of the cylinder was based on four exemplars (two in Paris and two in London) and that of the winged bulls on two exemplars in Paris, although with some variants from additional exemplars. He had also been able to examine the four tablets in the Louvre. D.D. Luckenbill later described his work as "a model of accurate, painstaking scholarship" (ARAB 2 p. 1 §2).

In 1889, Hugo Winckler (1863–1913) published an edition of the official inscriptions of Sargon II and it remained the most important and extensive publication of this ruler's inscriptions for over a century.[41] In two volumes, his Die Keilschrifttexte Sargons nach den Papierabklatschen und Originalen neu herausgegeben (Leipzig) included copies and editions of basically all the inscriptions known up until that time. Following an introduction to Sargon's official inscriptions and the historical information in them, volume 1 presents editions of Sargon's official inscriptions and concludes with an index of Akkadian words and a combined index

---

[40] Editions of some dockets dated to the reign of Merodach-Baladan (Marduk-apla-iddina II) and of a clay cone inscription of Adad-apla-iddina (see Frame RIMB 2 pp. 56–57 B.2.8.6) are also presented.

[41] Three years earlier, in 1886, Winckler had published his thesis, written in Latin at the University of Berlin, on the annals of Sargon II (De inscriptione Sargonis, regis Assyriae, quae vocatur Annalium).

of geographical, personal, and divine names. Although the editions are now outdated, they represented a great advance on what had been available up until the time of their publication. Hand copies of almost all the texts edited in volume 1 are found in volume 2. These copies were made by L. Abel; however, Winckler had clearly been involved in their preparation and they are generally referred to as his copies. Volume 2 has copies of the Khorsabad Annals (pls. 1–28 nos. 1–52, 55, and 58–60 [text nos. 1–4 and 6]), the Display Inscription of Room XIV (pls. 25–27 and 29 nos. 53–54, 56–57, and 61–62 [text no. 8]), the Display Inscription (pls. 30–36 nos. 63–78 [text no. 7]), five pavement slabs (pls. 37–40 [text nos. 10–14]), the inscription on the back of wall slabs (pl. 40 [text no. 41]), the inscription on winged bulls (pls. 41–42 [text no. 9]), the inscriptions on four metal and stone tablets (pls. 42–44 [text nos. 44–47]), the Khorsabad Cylinder inscription (pl. 43 [text no. 43]), the Nineveh Prism (pls. 44–46; referred to as "Das zerbrochene Prisma [A and B]" and "Der Bericht über den Zug gegen Asdod nach S." [text no. 82]), the Cyprus Stele (pls. 46–47 [text no. 103]), the Nimrud wall slabs (pl. 48 [text no. 73]), and various other short inscriptions (pl. 49: Khorsabad altar [text no. 49], epigraphs [text nos. 23–28, 30–32, 34–35, and 37–39], two so-called "harem" inscriptions [text nos. 16–17], inscriptions on glass and stone vessels [text no. 77], bricks [text nos. 50–51, 53–55, and 95], an eyestone [referred to as a "Siegelabdruck"; text no. 61], and clay cones [text no. 92]).[42] These copies comprise ones for which he was able to examine the originals (relatively few), ones for which he was able to collate Botta's copies from squeezes (a large part of the volume), and ones for which his copies are totally based on Botta's copies and his views of what should have been on them. The third group thus provides no independent evidence for exactly what was on the inscriptions, and, for the most part, they are not normally used in this volume, although they are cited in the text bibliographies. With regard to the second group, it is often difficult to determine whether improvements to Botta's copies were based upon what he could actually see on the squeezes or if they were based on what he believed must have been on the inscription. F. Thureau-Dangin has said with regard to Winckler's copies:

> "Il est à noter que ses copies contiennent beaucoup de restitutions, qui ne sont pas toujours signalées comme telles. Il est donc prudent de ne les utiliser qu'en les contrôlant par celles de Botta qui ont simplement pour objet de reproduire l'état réel du texte."[43]

A.T.E. Olmstead has stated:

> "Winckler ... corrected many of Botta's misreadings, and he made numerous and excellent restorations. Unfortunately, it is too often uncertain whether Winckler actually read the correct sign on the squeeze or whether it was his own correction, while the brackets which should have indicated a restoration were often misplaced or even omitted ... If Winckler's cuneiform text was to be used with caution, his transliteration and translation formed a veritable trap for those who trustingly quoted them without reference to the original text."[44]

While my own examination of the squeezes often does support or allow Winckler's corrected readings, it more often indicates that signs copied by him as being fully preserved were damaged on the original, are unclear (at times perhaps due to an imperfectly made squeeze), or are even not (or no longer$^?$) visible on the squeezes. While Winckler was an excellent scholar and his corrected copies normally make good sense, they cannot be relied upon. As already noted by Fuchs (Khorsabad p. 6), the most important of Winckler's copies are those that he made having collated the squeezes in Paris, but even here it is not possible to rely on his copies without question.[45] In sum, it is often not clear from the copies whether something was actually seen by him or has been restored/corrected in the copy, and his editions do not always clarify matters. As a result, it is likely that on occasion the editions presented in the present volume have interpreted his copies erroneously. In the text catalogues in this volume, a small "c" is placed after a Winckler text number that was collated by him from a squeeze (e.g., "Winckler, Sar. 2 pl. 16 no. 34^c" in the catalogue for text no. 2 section 5). At times his copies specifically state where a squeeze began or ended. If this does not match his square brackets, this is indicated in the transliteration based upon Winckler's copy in the score by superscript "▸" and "•" bullets, for the beginning and end of the squeeze respectively.[46]

---

[42] Note that apart from the Annals texts and the Display Inscription from Room XIV (text nos. 1–4, 6, and 8) many of these copies are composite copies, made from two or more exemplars. This is the case in particular for the Khorsabad Display Inscription (text no. 7), the five pavement slab inscriptions (text nos. 10–14), the inscription on the backs of wall slabs (text no. 41), the inscription on the winged bulls (text no. 9), and the cylinder inscription (text no. 43), but also for some of the shorter inscriptions (e.g., those on bricks).

[43] Thureau-Dangin, RA 24 (1927) p. 75.

[44] Olmstead, AJSL 47 (1930–31) p. 259.

[45] Although some of the squeezes made by P.E. Botta are no longer extant or have been lost, all of those that H. Winckler claims to have used are still preserved in the Louvre.

[46] See for example Winckler, Sar. 2 pl. 4 no. 8, which is his copy for Botta, Monument de Ninive plate 75^c (text no. 1 lines 118–130). When his indication of the beginning or end of the squeeze runs through a sign, the "▸" or "•" are given before and after the sign respectively.

The publication in 1912 of Une relation de la huitième campagne de Sargon (714 av. J.-C.) (Textes cunéiformes du Louvre 3) (Paris) by the great French Assyriologist François Thureau-Dangin (1872–1944) presented an extremely important new inscription of Sargon's, a report (or letter) from the king to the god Aššur describing the campaign in his eighth regnal year (714) against Urarṭu and Muṣaṣir (text no. 65). Although the large tablet had been purchased by the Louvre from an antiquities dealer, the piece had clearly been found at Aššur since several additional small fragments of the tablet discovered by German archaeologists at that city were later published by O. Schroeder in 1922 (KAH 2 no. 141) and by E. Weidner in 1937–39 (AfO 12 pp. 144–148 and pl. XI). In addition to a copy, photographs, and an edition of the text, Thureau-Dangin's volume also includes an edition (aided in part by collation of squeezes) of a section of the Annals from Room II that basically duplicated part of the new text and an edition of a section from the Nineveh Prism that also described the campaign against Muṣaṣir.[47]

The article "Zu den Inschriften der Säle im Palaste Sargon's II. von Assyrien" published by Franz Heinrich Weissbach (1865–1944) in 1918 (ZDMG 72 pp. 161–185 and plate before p. 161) proved to be of great importance for our understanding of Sargon's inscriptions on the walls of his palace at Khorsabad. In particular, he recognized that room XIV preserved parts of two different inscriptions, part of the king's annals (text no. 4) and a separate display inscription (text no. 8), and he provided an edition of the latter text. He also improved our understanding of the various versions and copies of the annals and main display inscription in the various rooms of the palace. His study laid an important foundation for work on these texts.

As a result of work producing editions of the corpus of Assyrian royal inscriptions for the files of the Chicago Assyrian Dictionary, in 1926–1927 Daniel David Luckenbill (1881–1927) published English translations of the entire corpus available up until that time in his two-volume work Ancient Records of Assyria and Babylonia (ARAB). For the reign of Sargon, volume two includes approximately fifty inscriptions written on stone wall slabs, winged bulls, paving slabs, and steles, on metal tablets, on clay prisms, tablets, cylinders, and cones, and on mud bricks, as well as on several other minor objects. The inscriptions from Khorsabad are presented first, followed by those from Aššur, Calah (Kalḫu), and Nineveh. Luckenbill's work was based entirely on published material, without any additional collation, and he maintained Winckler's line numbering for the annals. ARAB has remained the main English translation of the royal inscriptions of Sargon up until the present time.

Winckler, like Oppert, had combined the versions of the annals from the different rooms of Sargon's palace into one recension, which while useful in many ways, also makes it difficult at times to determine exactly what comes from which room and exactly what is based on restoration as opposed to being actually preserved in the version from one or the other room. Thus, in 1929 the Norwegian scholar Arthur Godfred Lie (1887-1932) presented The Inscriptions of Sargon II, King of Assyria. Part I: The Annals Transliterated and Translated with Notes (Paris). This volume actually only gives an edition of the version of the annals from Room II, although where sections from that room were missing, he includes an edition of the sections in Room V. In addition, numerous footnotes give variants from Rooms V, XIII, and XIV to what is found in Room II. The line numbering of the Annals is based on the text in Room II, and, where it was thought necessary to include material from Room V, the lines are numbered separately, according to the line number on the relevant slab from Room V. Like Winckler, Lie had examined the squeezes in Paris, although he does not indicate exactly which ones he was able to see and it is difficult to determine which readings in the volume are based upon examination of the squeezes. Regrettably, Lie only published Part I of Sargon's inscriptions. Useful reviews of his work were presented by Thureau-Dangin (RA 27 [1930] pp. 159–160) and Olmstead (AJSL 47 [1930–31] pp. 259–280).

Following Botta's and Place's work at Khorsabad, no further major archaeological exploration of the site took place until 1929-1935, when the Oriental Institute of the University of Chicago sent out a team led in turn by Edward Chiera (in 1928–1929), Henri Frankfort (in 1929–1932), and Gordon Loud (in 1932–1935), with Thorkild Jacobsen as the epigraphist. Two volumes in the series Oriental Institute Publications resulted: Khorsabad, Part I: Excavations in the Palace and at a City Gate, by Loud, with chapters by Frankfort and Jacobsen (OIP 38) in 1936; and Khorsabad, Part II: The Citadel and the Town, by Loud and Charles B. Altman (OIP 40) in 1938.[48] Jacobsen's chapter in Khorsabad 1 included copies and editions of the inscriptions on five pavement slabs from the palace chapels (earlier thought to be the "harem" section of the palace [text nos. 16–21]) and two inscriptions found in the throne room (one on a fragment of a wall slab with part of Sargon's

[47] It is useful to note here the article by Thureau-Dangin in RA 24 (1927) pp. 75–80 that includes important collations of the version of Sargon's Annals from Room II (text no. 1) based upon his examination of the squeezes then held in the Bibliothèque Nationale (Paris) and in particular new copies of slabs 13 and 14 that were made by Ch.-F. Jean based upon the squeezes (text no. 1 sections 12–13).
[48] Note also the four preliminary reports produced by H. Frankfort (OIC 16–17 and 19–20).

annals and one on a brick [text nos. 5 and 52 ex. 1 respectively]). The chapter on the inscriptions in Khorsabad 2 included copies and editions of three inscriptions by Jacobsen (one on threshold and stair slabs from the temple of the god Nabû, one on threshold slabs from residence L, and one on a stone altar found in the town area; text nos. 22, 2002, and 49 ex. 3 respectively), as well as a list of moveable inscriptions (those found on tablets, prisms, pottery, etc.).[49] Photos showing several inscriptions are found in these two volumes. The information given in the current volume for the findspots and excavation numbers for some of the items found by the Oriental Institute excavations may include some uncertain information, although attempts have been made to prevent this. There are various reasons for this. As noted by Loud in Khorsabad 2 p. ix, "room numbers assigned in the field have been altered in publication" and "Place's numbering of the palace rooms and courts has been retained." (See ibid. pp. 109–110 for a concordance of the publication and field numbers for the rooms.) At times information on a piece may only come from the original excavation records or from a published volume (Khorsabad 1 or 2); thus, pieces that are stated to come from different rooms may in fact have come from the same room. J. Larson has also determined that on at least three separate occasions, the excavators began the DŠ (at times DS and D.S.) series with a new no. 1.[50] As a consequence, the lower numbers in these series are shared, without explicit differentiation, by three different finds. By consulting the original field ledgers, ambiguities can be resolved in most cases.[51] In addition, the designations for various places differed from those used by Botta and Place. The most important differences between how locations are cited are given below:

Façade L	=	Court I	=	palace terrace (NW)
Façade N	=	Court III	=	palace terrace (NE)
Façade m	=	Court VI	=	third major palace courtyard
Façade n	=	Court VIII	=	second largest palace courtyard
		Court VII	=	throne room
		Court XV	=	largest palace courtyard

In 1958, Hayim Tadmor (1923–2005) published a two-part article on "The Campaigns of Sargon II of Assur: A Chronological-Historical Study" in the Journal of Cuneiform Studies (volume 12 pp. 22–40 and 77–100). Although the article published only one small new inscription (A 16947; text no. 102) and two new fragments of the Nineveh Prism (Rm 2,92 and Sm 2049; text no. 82), his careful study of the chronology of Sargon's reign has remained important for all later studies of the royal inscriptions and campaigns of Sargon. He examined in particular the information on the fall of Samaria (pp. 33–40), using information from the Annals of Room II and from the Nimrud Prism (text nos. 1 and 73), and on the campaigns to Philistia and the border of Egypt (pp. 77–84), using in particular the Aššur Prism and the Nineveh Prism (text nos. 63 and 82).

Although it only included editions (by C.B.F. Walker) of some of Sargon's epigraphs and the inscription on the altars from Khorsabad (text nos. 23, 26, 28–30, 36–39, and 49), Pauline Albenda's 1986 study The Palace of Sargon, King of Assyria / Le palais de Sargon d'Assyrie (French translation by A. Caubet) presents a detailed study of the wall reliefs and stone objects found at Khorsabad, making particular use of the original drawings produced by Botta and Flandin in the 1840s and cataloguing all the pieces known to exist today.

In 1993, Andreas Fuchs presented his doctoral dissertation, a new edition of the royal inscriptions of Sargon II from Khorsabad, at the Georg-August-Universität in Göttingen, a work completed under the supervision of R. Borger. The dissertation was published the following year as Die Inschriften Sargons II. aus Khorsabad. In August 1991, he had been able to examine original documents in the Louvre and to make use of photographs of Botta's squeezes. In addition, Borger provided him with transliterations and/or collations of seven exemplars of the Khorsabad Cylinder preserved in London and Chicago. In Fuchs' work, the various versions of the Annals were presented as one text, using the "score" method. This used a different set of line numbers for the Annals than those used by Winckler (only the first twenty-five line numbers were the same) or Lie (only the first 234 line numbers were the same). In addition to these editions, the volume concluded with four appendices — the textual building blocks of the inscriptions from the palace, notes on the Annals and the Display Inscription, the geographical lists in the texts, and a reconstruction of the campaign in the king's twelfth regnal year — and indices (with very useful commentaries) of personal, geographical, and divine names. The work is an excellent piece of scholarship, although the separation of the transliterations (pp. 29–

[49] For Jacobsen's nos. 4 and 5, see text no. 10 ex. 4 and the commentary to text no. 11 in this volume.

[50] This has to do with numbers similar to DS 22, D.S. 113, and DŠ 48, and not to those where there is an indication of the field season (e.g., DŠ 32-47). In the present volume, DŠ is used in every case, even though DS or D.S. may appear in the actual field record.

[51] My thanks must be expressed to J. Larson and J.A. Brinkman for sharing information from their work on the provenances of the materials from Khorsabad.

287) from the translations (pp. 289–372) is at times awkward, particularly with regard to the different versions of the Annals.

In November 1993, the Louvre opened "De Khorsabad à Paris," a special exhibition to commemorate the one hundred and fiftieth anniversary of Botta's opening of excavations at Khorsabad. The exhibition ran until February 1994 and resulted in two useful publications: E. Fontan (ed.), De Khorsabad à Paris: La découverte des Assyriens (1994); and A. Caubet (ed.), Khorsabad, le palais de Sargon II, roi d'Assyrie (1995). The former volume includes chapters dealing with the discovery of Khorsabad and its excavators, as well as their discoveries and publications, and how the public received them. The latter is composed of presentations given at a conference held on January 21–22, 1994 to commemorate the occasion and exhibition; it contains articles dealing with such matters as the inscriptions on the back of Khorsabad relief slabs (text no. 41), Sargon's Cyprus Stele (text no. 103), and the glazed brick panels at Khorsabad (text no. 58), as well as the construction of the city, the Oriental Institute of the University of Chicago's work at the site, and other matters.

As part of the Royal Inscriptions of Mesopotamia project, in 1995 G. Frame published the royal inscriptions of the rulers of Babylonia from 1157 to 612 BC (RIMB 2), including those from Babylonia written in the name of its Assyrian overlords. These included six inscriptions of Sargon II: two brick inscriptions from Babylon (text nos. 123–124), and one clay cylinder inscription and three brick inscriptions from Uruk (text nos. 125–128). These record him sponsoring work on the city walls of Babylon and on the Eanna temple at Uruk. The editions of these texts presented in the current volume (text nos. 123–128) are essentially duplicates of those published in RIMB 2.

A few years later, in 1998, A. Fuchs presented a study of Sargon's fragmentary Nineveh Prism, combined with the even more fragmentary texts on the Aššur Prism and a clay tablet (text nos. 82, 63, and 102 respectively). In addition to a careful edition of the texts based on an examination of the originals in London and Berlin, the volume (Die Annalen des Jahres 711 v. Chr. [SAAS 8]) includes new copies of the cuneiform texts and several appendices — dating according to regnal years in Assyria, the *sikkatu*-lock, Ursâ's companion, Daltâ and the anger of the gods, and Iāmānī and Pir'û — as well as indices of personal, geographical, and divine names. Based on the material mentioned in the text, Fuchs states that the inscription likely dates to 711, the king's eleventh regnal year. The edition of the Nineveh Prism presented by Fuchs is the basis for the one published here (text no. 82), which is the result of collaboration between G. Frame and A. Fuchs.

Editing the Lost Inscriptions from Khorsabad

As a result of the unavailability of so many of the original inscriptions on stone wall slabs, paving slabs, and bull colossi from Khorsabad (in particular text nos. 1–4, 6–14, and 23–41) because of their loss in the Tigris River in 1855 or their reburial at the site of Khorsabad, the unreliability of Botta's copies of these inscriptions, and the uncertainty about the reliability of Winckler's newer copies of the texts, editing these texts presents many problems and challenges, in particular for text nos. 1–4, 6, and 8 (Annals from Rooms II, V, XIII, XIV, and an unknown room of the palace, and the Display Inscription of Room XIV), for which only one exemplar each is known, but also for text no. 7, for which five exemplars are known. As is well known, Botta's copies contain numerous anomalous/unexpected sign forms, which is not surprising since he made no claim to be able to read cuneiform — indeed philologists were still in the process of deciphering Akkadian cuneiform texts at the time — since he was working under non-optimal conditions, and since the originals were clearly found at times in a damaged condition.[52] In addition, as was mentioned earlier, even though Winckler's copies generally make excellent sense, they are not reliable, even when he claims to have collated the squeezes.

The poor state of preservation of the squeezes that Botta made and that are still extant in the Louvre and the difficulty in working with them means they are not as useful as one might hope. The original squeezes are frequently in a fragile condition and, having been rolled up for decades, do not lie totally flat on a surface; they are unwieldy to work with and require good lighting in order to facilitate the identification of signs and traces versus damage. Fortunately, the squeezes underwent conservation work in the 1990s; all but a few of the squeezes were photographed at that time and the author was able to obtain copies of these photographs with the permission of B. André-Salvini. It is generally both easier and more productive to work from the Louvre photos than the original squeezes since the photos were taken by an excellent photographer under ideal lighting conditions and then printed in reverse; the squeezes themselves of course show a mirror image of the

[52] As has been noted by earlier scholars, on occasion Botta's copies misalign fragments of a wall slab (e.g., Room II slab 35 [Monument de Ninive 4 pl. 91]); a double dagger (‡) is employed in the scores to indicate the point in the line of Botta's copy where one must either go up or down a line in his copy in order to continue reading the relevant line.

inscription. With the permission of A. Thomas, the author made photographs of those squeezes not photographed in the 1990s.

Regrettably, while examination of the squeezes (either directly or via photos) does allow one to improve or correct Botta's copies at times, the squeezes are often unhelpful, either being damaged or unclear themselves at a critical point. (See Figure 2 below for a photo of section of a squeeze in a moderate stage of preservation.) They often suggest that the original text was damaged at the point where Botta copied an anomalous or unexpected form. They do, however, often reveal traces of signs not copied by Botta, traces that were often, but not always, noted by Winckler. It is likely (and at times proven by squeezes) that signs or parts of signs not indicated on Botta's copies were hidden/not present due to damage to the text even where Botta's copies give no indication that the text was damaged. Thus, numerous signs indicated as being abnormal or incorrect in form or omitted were likely only partially preserved or totally missing due to damage on the original.

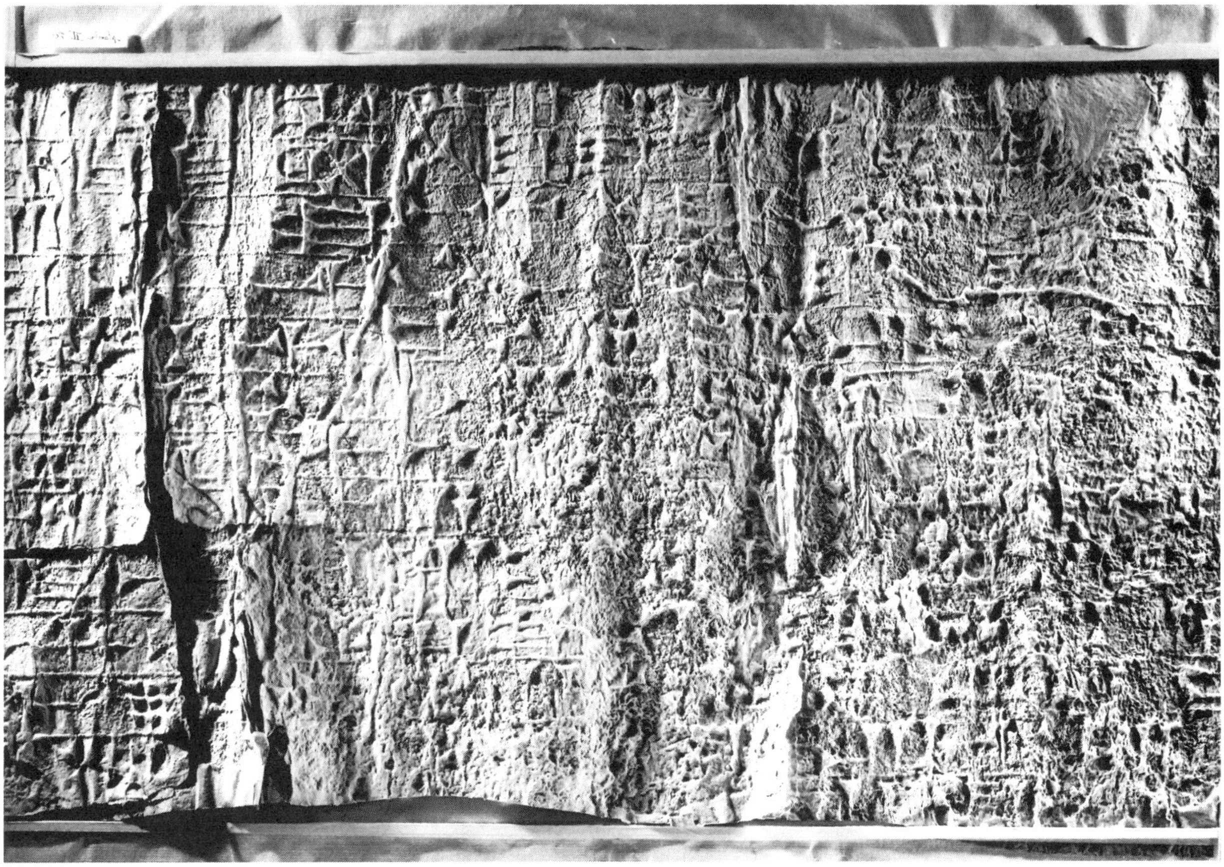

Figure 2. Squeeze of Botta, Monument de Ninive 4 pl. 80, middle (text no. 1 section 15). © Musée du Louvre, dist. RMN - Grand Palais / Christian Larrieu.

At times, lengthy discussions would be needed to justify the reading of numerous signs in a single line of a single slab; however, this would make this volume inordinately lengthy and difficult to use. After much consideration and discussion with colleagues, it has been decided that for text nos. 1–4 and 8 a score edition would be prepared and made available online with a simplified notation scheme.[53] No score is given for text no. 6 since there are no other sources of information on that text apart from Botta's copy in Monument de Ninive (i.e., no original, no earlier copy in Journal asiatique or the Institut de France, and no squeeze). In the scores, one line (indicated by the siglum Bt) indicates the reading based on Botta's copy in Monument de

[53] Note the author's article "Lost in the Tigris: The Trials and Tribulations in Editing the Royal Inscriptions of Sargon II of Assyria" in Yamada, SAAS 28 pp. 215–237; some examples of problems with Botta's copies are given ibid. p. 221. For text no. 7, see below.

Ninive, with the siglum † used here and elsewhere to indicate an abnormal sign form;[54] one line (Wi) is based on Winckler's copy, but this line is only present when Winckler claims to have collated the text from a squeeze;[55] one line (Sq) is based on collation of a squeeze still preserved in the Louvre (mostly examined by means of photographs, but at times from the original squeeze); one line (JA) gives information from Botta's copies published in Journal asiatique when a copy differs from his later one in Monument de Ninive; one line (IdF) gives information from Botta's original copy preserved in the Institut de France when it differs from his copy in Monument de Ninive;[56] one line (Je) is based on copies by Ch.-F. Jean published in Revue d'assyriologie 24 (1927) pp. 79–80 (only for two slabs in Room II [text no. 1 sections 12–13]); and one line (T-D) gives Thureau-Dangin's collations of individual words and signs on the squeezes published in RA 24 (1927) pp. 76–78 (only for slabs in Room II [text no. 1]). In most cases only one or a few of these lines will appear since the others do not exist for a line (or slab in general). On a few occasions, part of a particular wall slab still exists (see for example text no. 2 section 6 and text no. 3 section 1′) or a squeeze exists outside the Institut de France (see text no. 1 section 5) and lines in the score will be given for them, with the line siglum indicated in the commentary to that text. The dagger siglum (†) is used in the scores to indicate an abnormal sign form in Botta's copy: e.g., *i-ta*†; this may be omitted if the sign is only slightly abnormal. However, if the unexpected form is an actual sign, that form is indicated in the score: e.g., *a-di**(copy: RU).

The master line is based upon the author's best assessment of the sum total of information, although the siglum † is generally placed after the reading of any sign that is less than certain and/or has conflicting information about it that seemed worthy of note.[57] The reader then needs to look at the score to see the conflicting information on/reading of the sign. This reduces the number of on-page notes arguing about the reading of any one sign. However, where the author felt information about the reading of a sign (or group of signs) was particularly useful, an on-page note on the matter is given. The author is fully aware this is not a perfectly satisfactory manner to deal with uncertain readings, but has decided that it is the most suitable manner to present a manuscript both easily usable by non-specialists and yet able to indicate to the specialist where uncertainty remains about a reading without over-burdening him/her with numerous lengthy discussions that would in many/most cases result in no definite answer.

With regard to the master lines and scores for these texts, it may be useful to explain a number of general procedures:

a) Normally, † will be placed after a sign in the master line if Botta's Monument de Ninive copy has an abnormal or incorrect sign even if a squeeze would allow the correct reading, but cannot confirm it. For example, the score may have *a-lid**(copy: TAB) for Bt and *a-*⸢*lid*⸣ for Sq, but have *a-lid*† in the master line; this would mean that the squeeze indicates the second sign is so damaged (or that the squeeze is so damaged at that point) that although it might well be LID one cannot rule out the possibility of it being TAB. Since Winckler's copies cannot be relied upon (see above), † may still appear in the master line even if *a-lid* is given in the line for Wi.

b) If Botta's copy has a sign fully preserved, while the squeeze shows it damaged, Botta's copy is followed in the master line.

c) When Botta's copy is only slightly abnormal (e.g., MA for LA, KAL for UN, or IZ for PA), while Winckler's copy has the correct form and the squeeze while indicating that the sign is damaged, supports the correct reading, then the correct reading is given in the master line with an indication that the sign is damaged (e.g., ⸢UN⸣).

d) If Botta's copy in the Journal asiatique and/or Institut de France has the correct/desired sign form of a sign while the later copy in Monument de Ninive has an incorrect/abnormal form, preference is given to

---

54 The siglum † is given after the expected/desired reading of the sign. Such abnormal signs are not normally indicated in the lists of variants at the back of this volume, particularly when there is more than one exemplar for an inscription (text nos. 7 and 9–14 and 41).

55 At times Winckler has a line on his copies indicating either where the squeeze he had examined for collation purposes began or where it ended (e.g., his copies of Room II slabs 3 and 9 [Winckler, Sar. 2 pl. 1 no. 2 and pl. 3 no. 6]). In such cases, a superscript right-facing triangular bullet (‣) is employed in the scores to note where Winckler indicates that he began to collate the inscription from a squeeze and a superscript circular bullet (•) is similarly employed to note where he indicates that his collations ended. This latter siglum is also used in the transliteration of text no. 117 (Najafabad Stele) to indicate where the lines of the inscription on the squeezes preserved in the Royal Ontario Museum end.

56 For the most part, the copies in the Institut de France are identical to those published in Journal asiatique, but there are occasional differences between the two. My thanks must be expressed to M. Zink (now secrétaire perpetuel de l'Académie des inscriptions et belles-lettres) through whose support I was able to access the materials in the Institut de France in the summer of 2011 and also to J.-M. Durand for facilitating my visit there.

57 For texts with only one exemplar (e.g., text nos. 1–4, 6, and 8) this will generally mean that P.E. Botta's copy has an abnormal or incorrect sign form and that there is no contradictory information from an original or from a squeeze.

the former in the master line and no indication is normally given in the master line that the copy in Monument de Ninive is abnormal, although this will of course be noted in the score.

e) If the master line has † with a sign being fully restored, this means that Winckler's copy shows the sign as fully present, while Botta's copy and the current state of the squeeze do not have any indication of it being there. For example, [*a*†]-*na* in the master line, [x]-*na* in Bt, *a-na* in Wi, and [x]-*na* or [x x] in Sq. However, if Winckler only indicates that part of the sign is preserved, then his reading is sometimes accepted. For example, if Bt has [x x], Wi has [*ki*]-⸢*ma*⸣, and Sq has [x x], then [*ki*]-⸢*ma*⸣ may appear in the master line.

f) As is the case elsewhere in this series, if the unexpected sign is an actual sign, then that sign is given in parentheses following the expected reading of the sign in the score. However, † will normally be given in the master line. For example, if we expect *ia-a-ti* while Botta's copy has AD-*a-ti* and the squeeze is not preserved at that point, then the score will have *ia**(copy: AD)-*a-ti* for Bt and the master line *ia*†-*a-ti.*

g) Frequently, even if there is a squeeze of an inscription, it may not cover the whole area copied by Botta, thus not all of the copy has really been collated. In addition, the edges of the squeezes are generally the most damaged parts of them. Thus, the reader will sometimes find more signs with the siglum † in these areas.[58]

h) Squeezes and/or originals often show that a damaged area is greater or smaller in size than is indicated on Botta's copies. Thus, where we have only Botta's copy as evidence for a text or exemplar, the amount of restoration given at times in the master line may differ from what Botta's copy would suggest, although for the most part this only amounts to one or two additional or fewer signs.

In sum, unless we can confirm from a squeeze the accuracy of Winckler's copy of a sign against Botta's copy, Winckler's copy is not normally accepted in the master line. In addition, most of the signs in the master line indicated with † or as being totally omitted, were probably damaged on the original (e.g., *i*†-<*na*> should be ⸢*i*⸣-[*na*]), but of course this cannot be proven unless the originals are recovered. It must be admitted that some tiny traces (or apparent traces) on the squeezes have not been noted in the scores. This occurs when the author was uncertain if they were or were not actual traces as opposed to damage on the original or to the squeeze.

Since there are five exemplars of text no. 7 (Khorsabad Display Inscription), a score edition of that inscription is presented online; however, only one line is given for each exemplar in that score even though information on each exemplar can come from a variety of sources in addition to Botta's copies in Monument de Ninive: Winckler's copies collated from squeezes, squeezes still in existence in the Louvre, and fragments of the original slabs preserved in various museums (in particular the British Museum, Louvre, Oriental Institute [Chicago], and Museo delle Antichità Egizie [Turin]). The transliteration of each exemplar in the score is thus a conflation of information from all of the sources available for it and has been made to the best of the ability of the author, although he would admit that matters of uncertainty remain over numerous individual signs and words on any one exemplar. Even though the exact reading of the individual exemplars is a matter of uncertainty at numerous places, and the siglum † is thus frequently found in the scores, because there are five exemplars of the inscription, the overall reading of the text (i.e., the master line) is basically secure.

For the inscriptions or exemplars that use more than one wall slab (text nos. 1–4 and 7–8),[59] the catalogues list each slab separately, calling it a "section" and numbering the sections in consecutive order. For example, text no. 8 is split up into six sections numbered 1–6 to represent each of the six slabs needed for the inscription.

Name

In the past, the name of the king was often thought to mean "legitimate king" or "the king is legitimate" — *šarru-kēn*(*u*) or *šarru-kīn*(*u*) — and to have been taken by him following the death/murder of his brother in order to stress the new king's right to the throne and to remind people of the earlier great ruler Sargon of Akkad. These assumptions are open to question. The king's name is almost invariably written with logograms — $^{(m)(d)}$LUGAL/MAN-GI.NA/GIN — which allows various different interpretations of the meaning of the name. On no occasion is the first element of his name written syllabically in cuneiform texts and on only a few occasions is the second element done so, some written in Assyria (A) and some in Babylonia (B); these are listed below:

---

[58] These were probably also the most damaged areas on the originals.

[59] Text nos. 5 and 6 would have required more than one wall slab, but information only on all or part of one slab is known for either text. As noted with text no. 6, it is possible that that text comes from the same room as text no. 5, the palace throne room (Court VII).

LUGAL-*ú-kin*	text no. 69 exs. 10 and 14 line 2 (A); text no. 70 line 2 (A); text no. 125 i 26 (B); Dietrich, SAA 17 no. 22 line 2 (=Harper, ABL no. 542) (B) and no. 39 lines 1 and 3 (=Harper, ABL no. 1016+CT 54 no. 470) (B)
^{m}LUGAL-*ú-kin*	3 R pl. 2 no. 1 rev. 10′ (=AAT pl. 29) (A); AAT pl. 47a (A)
^{d}LUGAL-*ú-kin*	text no. 126 line 1 (B); text no. 128 line 4 (B)
^{aš}LUGAL-*ú-kin*	3 R pl. 2 no. 5 line 9′ (A)
^{m}LUGAL-*ú-*[*kin*]	3 R pl. 2 no. 8 line 3′ (A)
[LUGAL]-*ú-kin*	Dietrich, SAA 17 no. 46 line 1 (=CT 54 no. 109) (B) and no. 88 line 2 (=CT 54 no. 331) (B)
[^{m}LUGAL]-*ú-*[*kin*]	CT 30 pl. 28 K. 8014 rev. 14′ (A)
^{m}LUGAL-*ú-kín*	Cole and Machinist, SAA 13 no. 134 line 10′ (=Harper, ABL no. 951; time of Esarhaddon or Ashurbanipal) (A)
^{m}MAN-*ú-ki-in*	text no. 66 line 1 (A)
[LUGAL-*ke*]-*e-nu*	text no. 12 ex. 5 line 1 (variant) (A)

While the spelling Šarru-kīn is attested for Sargon I of Assyria, it is thus not clearly attested for Sargon II. As noted by Fuchs, the writers of the letters to Sargon listed above "would certainly have addressed their master in the most correct way."[60] In addition, a few of the texts using the writing *-ú-kin* were written by the well-known royal scribe Nabû-zuqup-kēnu, who would surely not have written the name of the king incorrectly.[61] Therefore, the name of Sargon II should most probably be understood to be Šarru-ukīn and to mean "He (the god) made the king firm," with only one (partially preserved) example indicating the reading Šarru-kēnu, "the legitimate/righteous/just/true king."[62] Since the name was not reserved only for rulers as has sometimes been thought,[63] it may well have been Sargon's birth name and not one that he took upon ascending the throne, although the latter possibility cannot be ruled out. The "king" originally referred to in the name would have been the ruler at the time of Sargon's birth (possibly Aššur-dān III).[64] However, once Sargon had ascended the throne, the "king" might well have been re-interpreted to refer to him and encouraged the byform Šarru-kēnu, with its respective meaning(s). This new understanding of the name may be reflected in the following statement in the Khorsabad Cylinder: "In accordance with the saying of my name (*kīma zikir šumiya*) that the great gods had given to me — to protect truth and justice, to guide the powerless, (and) to prevent the wrongful harming of the weak" (text no. 43 line 50). In this connection, it must be noted that in his inscriptions, Sargon II was sometimes given the epithets *rē'û kēnu*, "the legitimate/righteous/just/true shepherd" (text no. 9 line 3, text no. 43 line 3, text no. 44 line 4 [partially restored], text no. 73 line 2, text no. 89 line 13, and probably text no. 117 i 22, as well as a few cases where it is likely to be restored), *šarru kīnu*, "the legitimate/righteous/just/true king" (text no. 65 line 114; Kataja and Whiting, SAA 12 no. 19 line 5′; see also the note to text no. 89 line 34), and *rubû kēnu*, "the legitimate/righteous/just/true prince" (text no. 82 vii 33′′), stressing his legitimacy/righteousness/justness/trueness to be king and reminding one of his name.[65] A. Fuchs has argued that "Only a king who had won his throne by usurpation was in need of such epithets,"[66] although this may simply indicate that his accession was in some way irregular or unexpected, and not that he had violently overthrown Shalmaneser V.

The king's name is written once in Aramaic as *srgn* on an impression of a seal belonging to one of Sargon's eunuchs that was found at Khorsabad (text no. 2004 line 3) and once as *shrkn* on the Assur Ostracon.[67] In the Hebrew scriptures, the name appears as *sargōn* (var. *sarggōn*) in Isaiah 20:1.[68] The name is rendered in the

---

[60] PNA 3/2 p. 1239.

[61] 3 R pl. 2 nos. 1 and 5; AAT pl. 47a; and CT 30 pl. 28 K. 8014 (mostly restored). See also May, Studies Diakonoff pp. 110–164, especially pp. 124–125 and 127–129 nos. 1–2, 6, and 9; and Fuchs, Studies Volk pp. 75–77.

[62] Some other translations that have also been proposed are "the truthful king" (Hurowitz, Studies Eph'al pp. 114–115 and n. 28) and "the king is just" (see Frahm, Sennacherib at the Gates of Jerusalem p. 205).

[63] See PNA 3/2 p. 1247 sub Šarru-kēnu 3 for an official by this name — ^{m}LUGAL-*ki-nu* — in the time of Ashurbanipal.

[64] Fuchs, PNA 3/2 p. 1239.

[65] In the present volume *kīnu/kēnu* is arbitrarily translated as "just" in these cases. With regard to Sargon's name, see in particular Fuchs, PNA 3/2 pp. 1239–1240 sub Šarru-kēnu 2.I; Fuchs, RLA 12/1–2 (2009) pp. 51–53; Frahm, NABU 2005 pp. 46–50 no. 44; and Fuchs, Studies Volk pp. 71–75.

[66] Fuchs, PNA 3/2 p. 1239.

[67] Gibson, TSSI 2 p. 104 no. 20 line 15.

[68] R. Kittel and P. Kahle, Biblia Hebraica, 3rd ed. (Stuttgart, 1945) p. 635.

Septuagint by editorial conjecture as Σαρναν, with the various manuscripts having σαρνα, αρνας, αρναβα, αρναι, or αρνα; later Greek translations give it variously as σαραγων, σαργων, and σαργουν.[69]

Although it has at times been stated that Sargon II's name was a throne name taken by him in order to connect himself with Sargon of Akkad, a famous earlier ruler who did not come from a royal line and yet came to rule a major kingdom and found a new dynasty, it should be noted, as pointed out by Frahm (NABU 2005 p. 50 n. 30), that none of Sargon II's inscriptions ever mentions Sargon of Akkad. While he is called "the later (*arkû*) Sargon" in the date formulae of a few colophons and while the Ptolemaic canon does refer to him as Arkeanos (Ἀρκεανοῦ genitive), which may be derived from *arkû*, in theory this could simply be an indication of the existence of the (admittedly not-well-known and less significant) Old Assyrian king Sargon I instead of Sargon of Akkad.[70] There have been attempts to date the Sargon Legend and Sargon Geography to the reign of Sargon II and to consider them to reflect that ruler's political ideology.[71] While these texts may very well come from the time of Sargon II, this has not yet been proven conclusively.

The length of the wall of Sargon's new capital Dūr-Šarrukīn[72] is stated to be 16,280 cubits in four texts: ŠÁR ŠÁR ŠÁR ŠÁR GÉŠ.U GÉŠ.U GÉŠ.U 1 UŠ 1½ NINDA 2 KÙŠ in text no. 9 lines 79–80 and text no. 8 line 40 (partially restored) and ŠÁR ŠÁR ŠÁR ŠÁR GÉŠ.U GÉŠ.U GÉŠ.U 1 UŠ 3 *qa-ni* 2 KÙŠ in text no. 43 line 65 and text no. 44 line 47 (mostly restored).[73] In texts 43 and 44, the number is said to be *ni-bit* MU-*ia* "(corresponding to) the rendering of my name," or more literally "(corresponding to) the saying/pronunciation of my name."[74] Although various proposals have been made by scholars over the years to explain how this would work,[75] none has been convincing, although, as noted by Fuchs and other scholars, a connection between the sign ŠÁR and the first part of Sargon's name (*šarru*) would seem likely.[76]

Family

It has frequently been stated that Sargon was either not a son of Tiglath-pileser III or only an illegitimate one. This was based on the view that his name was a throne name meaning "legitimate king" — suggesting that he was not in fact one — that he usually never mentioned the name of his father in his royal inscriptions, and that his accession to the throne did not take place in a smooth manner. As already noted, the actual writings of his name indicate a different meaning for his name. While it is true that Sargon almost never mentions the name of his father in his royal inscriptions, text no. 66, found on several wall plaques from Aššur, does refer to him as the son of Tiglath-pileser (A ^{m}*tukul-ti*-A-*é-šár-ra* MAN KUR *aš-šur-ma*). Tiglath-pileser and Sennacherib also rarely mention the name of their respective fathers (likely Adad-nārārī III and Sargon II respectively) in their royal inscriptions[77] and it has never been suggested that they were illegitimate.[78] Moreover, a Babylonian letter

---

[69] J. Ziegler, Septuaginta: Vetus Testamentum Graecum Auctoritate Academiae Scientiarum Gottingensis editum, volume 14: Isaias, 3d ed. (Göttingen, 1983) p. 192.

[70] See Hunger, Kolophone nos. 294, 297, and 313; May, Studies Diakonoff pp. 110–164, especially pp. 116–117 and Appendix 2 nos. 1–2, 5, 6, 20, 32, 35–37, 40, 42, 45–46, and 50–51; and Fuchs, Studies Volk pp. 69–86, especially pp. 75–77. The colophons are primarily on texts written by the royal scribe Nabû-zuqup-kēnu, For the writing Ἀρκεανοῦ in the Ptolemaic Canon, see below.

[71] E.g., Lewis, Sargon Legend pp. 97–107; Horowitz, Cosmic Geography pp. 92–93; Van De Mieroop, Studies Renger pp. 327–339; Galter, Studies Haider pp. 279–302.

[72] The name of the city is always written with logograms in Sargon's royal inscriptions and thus we should perhaps give its name as Dūr-Šarru-ukīn rather than Dūr-Šarrukīn. A number of economic texts and letters write the last element of the place name syllabically or partially syllabically; however, it is often uncertain if these texts are referring to Sargon's city or to the city Dūr-Šarrukku in northern Babylonia. Note in particular Kwasman and Parpola, SAA 6 no. 106 rev. 8 [URU.BÀD-LUGA]L-*ú-k*[*in*], in connection with the eponym for 693. Two instances, for example, which might refer to Khorsabad are URU.BÀD-*sa-ru-uk-ka* and BÀD-MAN-*ka* (Fales and Postgate, SAA 11 no. 94 rev. 4 and no. 133 ii 18′ respectively); suggestion courtesy M. Worthington. See also Fuchs, Studies Volk p. 71 n. 15.

[73] Text no. 8 line 40 has ŠÁR ŠÁR ŠÁR ŠÁR GÉŠ.U GÉŠ.U GÉŠ.U [1 UŠ 1 1/2 NINDA 2 KÙŠ] and text no. 44 line 47 has [ŠÁR ŠÁR ŠÁR ŠÁR GÉŠ.U GÉŠ.U] GÉ[Š.U 1 UŠ] ⸢3⸣ *qa-ni* 2 KÙŠ.

[74] CAD N/2 p. 202 translates *nibīt šumiya* as "(corresponding to) the spelling of my name."

[75] For example, W. von Soden (Aus Sprache pp. 334–335 n. 33) suggested that the number might reflect the number of days Sargon had been alive (ca. 44.6 years) at the time.

[76] Fuchs, Khorsabad pp. 294–295 n. 88. For other recent discussions of this riddle, see Pearce, JAOS 116 (1996) 462; De Odorico, Numbers pp. 140–141; Morenz in Morenz and Bosshard-Nepustil, Herrscherpräsentation pp. 200–201; and Radner, Macht des Namens pp. 130–131. M. Roaf and M. Worthington are both preparing detailed studies of the problem with possible solutions.

[77] For Tiglath-pileser III, see Tadmor and Yamada, RINAP 1 p. 148 Tiglath-pileser no. 58 line 2. For Sennacherib, see Grayson and Novotny, RINAP 3/2 pp. 170 no. 135 line 2 (restored) and p. 232 no. 163 line 5′. See also Frahm, Sanherib pp. 194–195 and Frahm in Sennacherib at the Gates of Jerusalem p. 175. Esarhaddon, Ashurbanipal, Šamaš-šuma-ukīn, and Sîn-šarru-iškun did refer to Sargon as being their ancestor (see Fuchs, PNA 3/2 pp. 1246–1247) and Ashurbanipal affirms that he, and thus also Sargon, was a descendant of Bēl-bāni son of Adāsi (e.g., Novotny and Jeffers, RINAP 5/1 p. 220 no. 10 v 38–40). Therefore, Sargon was also a member of the long-established Assyrian royal family.

to Sargon ([*a-na* LUGAL]-*ú-kin* LUGAL [KUR.KUR], Dietrich, SAA 17 no. 46 line 1 [=CT 54 no. 109]) refers to Tiglath-pileser as the king's father (*tukul-ti*-IBILA-⌜*é*⌝-[*šár-ra*] / ⌜LUGAL AD⌝-*ka*, ibid. rev. 10–11),[79] which would seem to settle the issue. Certainly, his accession to the throne may not have taken place in a normal manner. Based upon the Aššur Charter (text no. 89), the chief god had brought about the end of Shalmaneser V's brief reign because of the latter's impious actions against the citizens of the city of Aššur and the god had then made Sargon the new king; however, this does not prove that he was not a son of Tiglath-pileser or a member of the royal family. It is not known who Sargon's mother was, although it seems unlikely that it was Tiglath-pileser's wife Yabâ.[80] A Late Babylonian literary letter likely from Nabopolassar to Sîn-šarru-iškun threatens the latter for Sennacherib's actions against Babylonia (Akkad) and refers to "Sennacherib, son of Sargon, offspring of a houseborn slave (*dušmû*) from Babylon." Lambert says that this shows that Sargon was the son of a Babylonian slave, although he does also note that the whole letter may be an ancient work of fiction.[81] However, this statement might well be simply a piece of Babylonian invective towards the Assyrian royal family and, in any case, might be intended to refer to Sennacherib as the son of a slave, not Sargon.[82]

There is no evidence to support the idea proposed by Campbell Thompson that Sargon had served as governor of the city Aššur during the time of his brother Shalmaneser V.[83] In fact, there is no evidence to show that he had held any office under his father or brother.

It is not known if Sargon was a full brother or a half-brother of Shalmaneser V. Another brother of Sargon's was Sîn-aḫu-uṣur, who served as his grand vizier (*sukkalmaḫḫu* and *sukkallu rabû*), had a large palace within the citadel area at Khorsabad (Residence L), and claimed to be Sargon's *favorite* brother (*ta-lim*).[84] The Sîn-aḫu-uṣur whose cavalry contingent accompanied Sargon in the fight against the Urarṭian Rusâ (text no. 65 lines 132–133) is likely to be identified with Sargon's brother.

According to Babylonian King List A, Shalmaneser V was a member of the dynasty Baltil, while Sargon's son and successor Sennacherib was a member of the Ḫabigal (presumably for Ḫanigalbat) dynasty. Sargon himself is given no dynastic affiliation, which could mean that he was considered by whatever Babylonians compiled the king list to be from the previously mentioned Assyrian dynasty (Baltil) or possibly from the same one as his son.[85]

Ataliya (text no. 2001), a wife of Sargon II, was buried at Kalḫu, possibly suggesting that she died before the completion of the palace at Khorsabad.[86] Her name may suggest that she was of Northwest Semitic or Arab origin.[87] If read correctly, Grayson and Novotny, RINAP 3/2 p. 364 no. 2001, may refer to another wife of Sargon, one Ra'īmâ, who appears to have been the mother of his son and successor Sennacherib.[88]

As noted by Frahm, Sargon must have been born "not much later than around 765" since his son Sennacherib, who was not the first of Sargon's sons, must have been born around 745 in order to have been made crown prince during Sargon's lifetime and to have installed his own heir (Aššur-nādin-šumi) as ruler of Babylon in 700.[89]

---

[78] E. Frahm (NABU 2005 no. 44 pp. 47–48) points out that there is a different pattern of royal name giving after Sargon than the one that had existed up until then and he suggests that the shift "may reflect an awareness on the part of the Late Assyrian rulers that they had entered a new political age."

[79] Thomas, Studies Bergerhof pp. 465–470.

[80] For Yabâ, see Tadmor and Yamada, RINAP 1 pp. 164–167 Tiglath-pileser nos. 2003–2005. For the case against Yabâ being the mother of Sargon, see Frahm in Sennacherib at the Gates of Jerusalem p. 185.

[81] Gerardi, AfO 33 (1986) pp. 30–38 BM 55467 rev. 7; Lambert, Studies Grayson p. 202 (note his collation to the end of the line in his n. 14).

[82] If it is Sargon who is meant by "offspring of a houseborn slave," this would seem to mean that Tiglath-pileser III had been a slave. Since the form *dušmû* (*du-uš-mu-ú*) is used, not *dušmītu*, it should refer to the individual's father, not his mother, as having been a slave. On the matter of Sargon's parentage, see also Frahm in Sennacherib at the Gates p. 176.

[83] Thompson, Iraq 4 (1937) pp. 40–42.

[84] See text nos. 2002–2003.

[85] See n. 156 below.

[86] E. Frahm (in Sennacherib at the Gates of Jerusalem pp. 185–186) raises the possibility that the reason Ataliya's body had apparently been conserved by some process prior to its burial might be that Ataliya accompanied Sargon on his final campaign in 705 and been killed in Tabal along with her husband; her body had then been treated to conserve it during transport back to Assyria. He also raises the possibility that the fact that the burial took place "in a somewhat haphazard way" might be the result of "the unstable political situation (and Sennacherib's unfriendly feelings towards her?)." Frahm also notes, however, that this scenario may be "nothing but speculation." It is worth wondering how likely it would be that Ataliya's body would have been recovered by the Assyrians for burial but not Sargon's (see below), although of course the enemy may well have made greater efforts to prevent the king's body being recovered than that of a woman, even if she was the king's wife.

[87] On the question of the origin and meaning of the name Ataliya, see the introduction to text no. 2001.

[88] With regard to Ra'īmâ, see Frahm in Sennacherib at the Gates of Jerusalem pp. 179–182. He suggests that she may have come from Ḫarrān or somewhere near there.

[89] NABU 2005 pp. 46–50 no. 44, especially p. 47.

At least two children of Sargon's are clearly attested: his heir Sennacherib and a daughter who made a political marriage; however, Sennacherib's name — "The god Sîn has replaced the brothers" — indicates that Sargon had had at least two previous sons who died before Sennacherib's birth. Moreover, a letter to Sargon from one Ḫunnî refers to "Sennacherib, the crown prince ... [and all] the princes/children of the king (DUMU.MEŠ MAN) (who are) [in] Assyria" (Parpola, SAA 1 no. 133 lines 9–11 [=Harper, ABL no. 216]), indicating that Sennacherib had more than one brother/sibling. While Sargon was likely off on campaign, Sennacherib remained in Assyria and sent a number of reports to his father (Parpola, SAA 1 nos. 29–40). These reports concentrate on matters to the north of Assyria, in particular events in Urarṭu, Kummu, and Ukku, but they also involve domestic matters, the receipt of tribute from Ashdod, and the arrival of emissaries from Kummuḫu (Commagene), as well as various other matters. Fuchs has argued that the earliest of these letters must date no later than 710, which would suggest that Sennacherib had been appointed crown prince by that year.[90]

In order to gain the support of Ḫullî, the king of Tabal, a daughter of Sargon's was given in marriage to Ambaris, Ḫullî's son. Ambaris was also made ruler of the city/land Ḫilakku (e.g., text no. 1 lines 194–198 and text no. 2 lines 226–230). Following the death of Ḫullî, however, Ambaris conspired with the rulers of Musku and Urarṭu and was overthrown by Sargon in 713. It is not known what happened to his wife. A letter to Sargon from his son Sennacherib refers to a message of the major-domo (*rab bīti*) of Aḫāt-abīša arriving from Tabal (Parpola, SAA 1 no. 31 rev. 26–29 [=Harper, ABL 197]) and this Aḫāt-abīša has often been assumed to be Sargon's daughter; however, this remains uncertain.[91]

Accession to the Throne

The Babylonian Chronicle states: "The fifth year (722): Shalmaneser (V) died in the month Ṭebētu (X). Shalmaneser (V) ruled Akkad and Assyria for five years. On the twelfth day of the month Ṭebētu, Sargon (II) ascended the throne in Assyria. In the month Nisannu (I), Marduk-apla-iddina (II) (Merodach-baladan) ascended the throne in Babylon." It is not known how Shalmaneser died, whether as the result of natural causes or an accident, or whether killed, either on the battlefield or as the result of some palace conspiracy.[92] There is some evidence, however, that would suggest that the change in rule did not take place in a smooth manner. In the Aššur Charter (text no. 89), one of Sargon's earliest royal inscriptions, Sargon states that Shalmaneser had "with evil intent ... *imposed oppressively* (state) service (and) corvée-duty" upon the people of the city of Aššur and "treated (them) as if they were of low rank" and that it was because of this that the chief god had overthrown him and appointed Sargon to be ruler. Sargon then claims that he restored the city of Aššur's privileges.[93] This direct criticism of the preceding ruler, a close relative of the new ruler, is unprecedented in Assyrian royal inscriptions and may well suggest that something untoward had occurred at the time of the change of rulership. Sargon may have been involved in deposing Shalmaneser, but there is no other indication of this beyond the fact that he benefited from Shalmaneser's death by becoming the new ruler. Shalmaneser's actions with regard to the city of Aššur (assuming that Sargon's statements are accurate) may or may not have been connected with the change in rule, but Sargon was likely attempting to gain the support of the citizens of that important city by granting/renewing their privileges. Early in his reign, Sargon had mercy on 6,300 Assyrian criminals (*bēl ḫiṭṭi*) and settled them in the land Hamath. Exactly what their crime(s) had been is not stated, but it is possible that they had not supported Sargon's accession to the throne.[94] It was likely uncertainty/problems in Assyria at the time of the change of ruler that encouraged the Chaldean Marduk-apla-iddina (II), likely the grandson of the earlier ruler of Babylon Erība-Marduk, to seize the throne in Babylon and remove Babylonia from Assyrian control.

Military Campaigns

The chronology for the reign of Sargon and the dating of his various campaigns is based for the most part upon the Assyrian Eponym Chronicle, a Babylonian chronicle, and statements in his royal inscriptions assigning

[90] Fuchs in Biainili-Urarṭu p. 137 no. 1.7 and pp. 155–157. For a discussion of Sennacherib's actions and life as crown prince, see Frahm in Sennacherib at the Gates of Jerusalem pp. 197–201.

[91] See Fuchs in Biainili-Urarṭu p. 155.

[92] See Mayer, Studies Loretz pp. 545–547. With regard to the accession of Sargon, see Vera Chamaza SAAB 6 (1992) pp. 21–33.

[93] G. Vera Chamaza (SAAB 6 [1992] pp. 25–29) raised the possibility that the taxation policies of Shalmaneser V and his predecessors may have been in place for some time, but had resulted in discontent among the temple elites.

[94] Text no. 84 line 20′, text no. 103 ii 61–65, text no. 105 ii′ 5–12, and text no. 108 Frgm. E. See for example Fuchs, PNA 3/2 p. 1240.

campaigns to particular regnal years (*palû*).[95] It must be noted that the dating of the campaigns in the Khorsabad Annals (in particular text nos. 1–4) and the Najafabad Stele (text no. 117) is different to that in the Aššur Prism (text no. 63), the Nineveh Prism (text no. 82), and a tablet fragment (text no. 102), with the former sources in general citing the campaigns one regnal year later than the latter and with the former's assignments better fitting the information found in the Assyrian Eponym Chronicle and Babylonian chronicle than does that of the latter.[96]

According to his annals, at the beginning of his reign Sargon defeated the city Samaria, deported a large number of its inhabitants, and then resettled the city and annexed it to Assyria proper, appointing one of his eunuchs as governor. Exactly when Samaria fell to the Assyrians — whether in the time of Shalmaneser V or Sargon II — and how many campaigns there were against Samaria have been matters of intense scholarly discussion and will not be treated here.[97] However, it is quite reasonable to assume that the deportation of the Israelites occurred at least in part during the reign of Sargon. Several actions carried out early in his reign may have been intended to reverse actions taken by his predecessor and set his own stamp on affairs. Among these may be the reopening of trade with Egypt and the reinstallation of Ḫullî as ruler of Tabal.[98]

During his first regnal year (721) Sargon does not appear to have carried out a major military campaign, likely because he needed to remain in the Assyrian heartland and consolidate his hold on the throne.[99] In Babylonia, the Chaldean Marduk-apla-iddina (II) used the uncertainty in Assyria to ascend the throne in Babylon and regain Babylonia's independence that had been lost in the time of Tiglath-pileser III.[100] The Khorsabad Annals do attribute two military actions to Sargon's first regnal year (721), a battle against the Elamites at Dēr and an action against the Aramean Tu'umuna tribe, who lived in northern Babylonia.[101] However, the Aššur Charter (text no. 89 lines 16–17a) and the Babylonian Chronicle state that the battle at Dēr actually took place in his second regnal year (720), and it is possible that the Tu'umuna were attacked in connection with that battle. The Assyrians had presumably moved south to deal with Marduk-apla-iddina's rebellion in Babylonia and were opposed by the latter's Elamite allies led by Ummanigaš (Ḫumban-nikaš I). The composer(s) of the annals may not have wanted to suggest that Sargon had been dilatory in dealing with Marduk-apla-iddina's rebellion in Babylonia and thus ascribed the battle to the previous year. According to the Babylonian chronicle the Elamite king inflicted a major defeat upon the Assyrians and forced them to retreat. Marduk-apla-iddina (II) and his troops are said to have arrived too late for the battle. Although Assyrian inscriptions state that the battle resulted in an Assyrian victory, it was clearly at best a stalemate since Babylonia remained independent for ten more years.[102] Interestingly, Marduk-apla-iddina, whose army does

---

[95] Translations of the relevant sections of the Assyrian Eponym Chronicle and the Babylonian chronicle that deal with the reign of Sargon are found at the end of this chapter. For good overviews of Sargon's campaigns, see Fuchs, RLA 12/1–2 (2009) pp. 53–58 and PNA 3/2 pp. 1240–1244. The recent books by F. Maniori (Campagne di Sargon), S. Melville (Campaigns of Sargon) and J. Elayi (Sargon II) present more detailed studies of these campaigns. Note also G.B. Lanfranchi's article on Sargon's foreign policy in CRRA 39 pp. 81–87, T. Dezsö's article on Sargon's army (SAAB 15 [2006] pp. 93–140), S. Ponchia's study of mountain routes in Sargon's campaigns (SAAB 15 [2006] pp. 231–245), and A. Bagg's study of Sargon's western campaigns (Bagg, Assyrer und das Westland pp. 233–244 and maps 4.26–4.30.

[96] The Aššur Prism, the Nineveh Prism, and the tablet fragment are all damaged and actually preserve specific mentions of only a few regnal years (Aššur Prism: 6th and 8th regnal years; Nineveh Prism: 8th and 9th regnal years; tablet fragment: 5th regnal year). While the Nineveh Prism dates the campaign against Karalla and Ellipi to the eighth regnal year, as opposed to the ninth regnal year in the Khorsabad Annals, it assigns the campaigns to Gurgum and against Iāmānī of Ashdod to Sargon's ninth regnal year (text no. 82 vii 13′–4′′′′), rather than to his eleventh regnal year as in the Annals. For the use of the term *palû* in Assyrian royal inscriptions and in those of Sargon in particular, see Tadmor, JCS 12 (1958) pp. 22–33 and Fuchs, SAAS 8 pp. 81–96.

[97] For the various theories and for bibliographical references for them, see for example Elayi, Sargon II pp. 48–50 and note also various articles in the recent book Last Days (in particular the article by Frahm on pp. 55–86).

[98] Text no. 1 lines 12b–18a (heavily restored from the following texts), text no. 7 lines 23b–25a, and text no. 74 iv 25–49. Text no. 1 lines 17b–18a assign the reopening of a sealed harbor in Egypt and the subsequent trading between Assyrians and Egyptians to Sargon's accession year (722), but this may have occurred later, possibly after the campaign to Gaza in his second year (Elayi, Sargon II p. 56) or in his sixth regnal year (Melville, Campaigns of Sargon pp. xv, 93 and 196). With regard to this trading post, see Ephʿal, Arabs pp. 101–104. For the reinstallation of Ḫullî, see text no. 1 lines 194a–198a and text no. 2 lines 226b–230a, where it is mentioned as having happened in the past. Note also May, SAAB 21 (2015) pp. 79–116 with regard to administrative changes in the reign of Sargon II (and also that of Tiglath-pileser III).

[99] Note however Tadmor's suggestion that the line for 721 in the Assyrian Eponym Chronicle read "[Against the land Ḫatt]i"; however, he had assumed that that line was for 720, not 721 (see below).

[100] See for example, text no. 1 lines 262b–268a, text no. 2 lines 287b–297a, text no. 3 lines 13′b–15′, and text no. 7 lines 121b–124a.

[101] Text no. 1 lines 18b–23a. See also text no. 81 lines 1–4a, text no. 43 line 18, and text no. 76 line 11′, which also mention actions against a second tribe, the Tēša. Text no. 81 (Mosul Annals) places the episode involving the Tēša in the regnal year before the one in which the campaign against Hamath took place, although the regnal year number is not preserved for either event.

[102] A Babylonian chronicle likely states that Assyria (or Sargon) was hostile towards Marduk-apla-iddina from his accession year until his tenth year (see below).

Table 1: Inscriptions Citing Events by Regnal and Eponym Years[103]

Year	Regnal Year	Event	Text													
			1	2	3	4	5	6	63	81	82	89	102	117	AEC	BC
722	Acc.	Accession														Acc.
		Samaria	Acc.													
		Opening of a harbor in Egypt	Acc.													
721	1															
720	2	Dēr	[1]									2				2
		Tu'umuna, (Tēša)	[1]							[1]						
		Hamath	2							[2]		2		[2]		
		Gaza, Raphia	2													
719	3	Mannea, Zikirtu	3			[3]								3		
718	4	Šinuḫtu/Tabal	4			4								4	[4]	
717	5	Carchemish	5			5							[4]	5		
		Mannea, Pāpa, Lallukna	5	[5]		5										
		Founding of Dūr-Šarrukīn													[5]	
		Death of Ummanigaš and accession of Šutruk-Naḫḫunte II in Elam														5
716	6	Mannea, Karalla, Allabria. Ḫarḫar	[6]	[6]		6			[5]		[5]		5	[6]	[6]	
		Gift from Šilkanni of Egypt							[5]		[5]					
715	7	Urarṭu, Mannea, Andia, Media	7	7					6		[6]					
		Ionians, Que	7													
		Arabs	7													
		Tribute from Pir'û, Samsi, and It'amar	7													
		Provincial governors appointed													[7]	
714	8	Mannea, Urarṭu, Muṣaṣir	8	[8]					[7]		[7]				[8]	
713	9	Karalla, Ellipi, Ḫabḫu, Media	[9]	9					8		8				[9]	
		Muṣaṣir													[9]	

[103] Text nos.: 1 = Annals of Room II; 2 = Annals of Room V; 3 = Annals of Room XIII; 4 = Annals of Room XIV; 5 = Annals of the Throne Room; 6 = Annals of an Unknown Room; 63 = Aššur Prism; 81 = Mosul Annals; 82 = Nineveh Prism; 89 = Aššur Charter; 102 = Tablet Fragment A 16947; 117 = Najafabad Stele; AEC = Assyrian Eponym Chronicle; and BC = Babylonian Chronicle (Grayson, Chronicles no. 1).

If the regnal year in which an event occurred is mentioned in the text, the number of the regnal year is given. If the regnal year is not preserved but can be determined reliably due to the mention of a preceding or subsequent regnal year in the text, the number of the regnal year is given in square brackets. If the text preserves all or part of the account of the event (but does not mention the regnal year), it is given a check mark (✓). The Assyrian Eponym Chronicle assigns the indicated events to particular eponymies and these have been converted into regnal years.

An asterisk (*) means that the event is described after the account of Sargon's campaign in his thirteenth regnal year (709), with the first event thus indicated (military actions by the Assyria governor of Que against Musku) said to have been conducted while the king was occupied defeating the Chaldeans and Arameans of the Eastern Sea and fighting Elam (text no 1 lines 444b–445a and text no. 2 line 428a). For the most part, the year to which they are assigned here follows the views proposed by other recent scholars (in particular Fuchs), although some scholars have differing views. For example, Elayi (Sargon II p. 243) places the Que/Musku and Tyre/Cyprus events in 710–709 and 709 respectively, rather than in 708. The episode in the annals involving Kummuḫu, which is in the same section in the Khorsabad Annals, can be assigned to Sargon's fourteenth regnal year (708) because the Assyrian Eponym Chronicle states that that city was captured in that year.

Year	Regnal Year	Event	Text														
			1	2	3	4	5	6	63	81	82	89	102	117	AEC	BC
		Tabal/Bīt-Purutaš	[9]	9							8					
		[*DN*] entered his new temple														
712	10	Melid, Kammanu	10	[10]							9					
		Anatolian metallic resources	10	[10]							9					
		King stayed in the land													[10]	
711	11	Gurgum/Marqasa	11	[11]	[11]						9				[11]	
		Ashdod	11	[11]	[11]						9					
710	12	Dūr-Abi-ḫāra, Babylonia	12	12	12		[12]									12
		Bīt-zēri; king stayed in Kish													[12]	
709	13	Babylonia, Dūr-Yakīn	[13]	[13]				[13]								13
		Gift from Upēri of Dilmun	[13]	[13]												
		King took the hands of Bēl													[13]	13
708	14	*Que, Musku	✓	✓												
		*Tyre, Cyprus	✓	✓												
		Kummuḫu	✓	✓											[14]	
		King stayed in the land (Babylonia)														14
707	15	*Ellipi		✓												
		King returned from Babylon													15	
		Dūr-Yakīn looted and destroyed													15	
		Gods entered Dūr-Šarrukīn		✓											15	
		Return of gods of the Sealand														15
		Plague in Assyria														15
706	16	King stayed in the land													16	
		Karalla													16	
		Dūr-Šarrukīn inaugurated		✓											16	
705	17	Tabal													17	[17]
		Death of Sargon													17	
		Accession of Sennacherib													17	

not appear to have taken part in the battle, seems to claim for himself the victory over the Assyrians in one of his inscriptions.[104]

During Sargon's second regnal year (720), the Assyrians did put down a rebellion at Qarqar in the west led by Ilu-bi'dī (Iaū-bi'dī) of Hamath, who had incited the important cities of Arpad, Ṣimirra, Damascus, and Samaria against Assyria. Ḫanūnu (Ḫanno), the vassal ruler of Gaza, made an alliance with Egypt and also

[104] Frame, RIMB 2 p. 137 B.6.21.1 lines 16–18; note Brinkman in Studies Oppenheim pp. 14–15. See also text no. 7 line 23b.

rebelled against Assyria. Their forces were defeated at the city Raphia (modern Rafaḥ). The Egyptian commander, Rēʾe, fled and Raphia was looted and then demolished.[105]

The campaigns in Sargon's third and fourth regnal years (719 and 718) were directed at the east and northwest respectively. In 719, he provided help to the Mannean ruler Iranzi. Two of the latter's cities had allied with Mitatti of the land Zikirtu and rebelled. In addition to demolishing the two cities, Sargon deported people from three other cities that had allied with the Urarṭian king Rusâ.[106] In the northwest, the various cities and states were under pressure from both Musku (Phrygia) and Urarṭu to oppose Assyria. Because Kiakki, king of the city Šinuḫtu in the land Tabal, had allied with Mitâ of Musku and withheld his tribute, in 718 Sargon devastated his city, took him and his family captive, and granted the city to Kurtî of the land Atuna.[107]

In Sargon's fifth regnal year (717), campaigns were directed both to the northwest and to the east. Pisīris of Carchemish attempted to ally with Mitâ of Musku and rebelled, but was defeated. Assyrians were settled in Carchemish and the yoke of the god Aššur imposed on them. People of the Mannean cities Papa and Lallukna who had allied with the land Kakmê against Assyria were deported and resettled in Damascus.[108] One version of a Babylonian chronicle has an entry for 717 stating that someone or some country, likely Sargon or Assyria, was hostile to the Babylonian king Marduk-apla-iddina (II) from his accession year until his tenth year, i.e., from 722 until 712. Another version of the chronicle puts this entry in the following year, the sixth regnal year (716). It is not clear why such a statement would be recorded under the fifth or sixth regnal year and not earlier, at the time Marduk-apla-iddina took control of Babylon, or why it refers to the hostility ending in 712 when Sargon invaded Babylonia in 710.

The campaigns in Sargon's sixth through ninth regnal years (716–713) were mainly directed to the north and east, against the Urarṭian ruler Rusâ and his allies. Rusâ had presumably been involved in the overthrow and murder of Azâ, the king of Mannea, by two of the latter's governors, and with the appointment of Aza's brother Ullusunu to be the new ruler of Mannea. In 716, Sargon defeated those two Mannean governors and, as a result, Ullusunu submitted to Sargon and was left in office. Sargon also dealt with Aššur-lēʾi of Karalla and Ittî of Allabria, the rulers of two lands to the south of Mannea, who had listened to Ullusunu and also allied with Rusâ. The cities Kišesim and Ḫarḫar were annexed to Assyria and renamed Kār-Nergal and Kār-Šarrukīn respectively. At this time, Sargon claims to have received tribute from twenty-eight city lords of the powerful Medes.[109] The Assyrians erected the Najafabad Stele (text no. 117) during the course this campaign in order to commemorate it. In the same year, some action may have taken place in the Palestinian area. Although nothing about this is reported in the Khorsabad Annals for that year, the end of the account for the year in the Aššur and Nineveh Prism inscriptions refers to people being settled near the Brook of Egypt under the authority of the sheikh of Laban and to the king of Egypt Šilkanni bringing an audience gift to Sargon.[110]

In 715, Sargon's seventh regnal year, twenty-two Mannean fortresses that Rusâ had seized from Ullusunu were recovered and annexed to Assyria. Dayukku, a Mannean governor who had been incited to rebel against Ullusunu by Rusâ, was captured and deported. Various other places in the lands on the borders of Urarṭu, including in the land Andia, were conquered. Sargon claims to have erected an image of himself in the Mannean capital Izirtu and to have received tribute from twenty-two Median city rulers. According to Sargon's Annals, in the same year the Assyrians also defeated some Ionians who had been raiding Que (Cilicia) and Tyre, recovered several cities of Que that the Muskian Mitâ had taken away, and defeated some Arab tribes who lived in the desert, resettling them in Samaria; these campaigns were likely led by Assyrian officials and not by the king himself. Sargon then boasts of having received tribute from the Egyptian Pirʾû (i.e., pharaoh), the Arabian queen Samsi, and Itʾamar, the ruler of the land of the Sabaeans.[111] According to the Assyrian Eponym Chronicle,

---

[105] Text no. 1 lines 23b–57, text no. 7 lines 25b–26 and 33–36a, text no. 73 line 8, text no. 81 lines 4b–20, text no. 84 lines 18′–20′, text no. 89 lines 17b–29, text no. 103 ii 51–65, text no. 105 ii′ 1′–12′, text no. 108 Frgm. D 1′–9′, and text no. 117 ii 4–13a. Likely also text no. 106. With regard to the Assyrian campaign in this year, see most recently Cogan, IEJ 67 (2017) pp. 151–167.

[106] Text no. 1 lines 58–68a, text no. 4 lines 1′–6′a, text no. 7 lines 48 and 57, and text no. 117 ii 13b–16.

[107] Text no. 1 lines 68b–71, text no. 4 lines 6′b–12′, text no. 7 lines 28–29a, text no. 74 iv 50–58, and text no. 117 ii 17–19.

[108] Text no. 1 lines 72–78a, text no. 2 lines 69–70a, text no. 4 lines 13′–20′a, text no. 73, text no. 74 iv 13–24, text no. 102 line 2′–14′, text no. 109, and text no. 117 ii 20–22a. Note also text no. 1010.

[109] Text no. 1 lines 78b–100, text no. 2 lines 70b–95a, text no. 4 lines 20′b–45′, text no. 7 lines 36b–42a, 49a, 50–51, 55–56 and 58–64a, text no. 63 i′ 1′–22′, text no. 74 ii 1–20′, text no. 82 iii 1′–12′′, text no. 102 line 15′, and text no. 117 ii 22b–71. See also text no. 72.

[110] Text no. 63 ii′ 1′–11′ and no. 82 iii 1′′′–8′′′. It is not impossible that the people settled near the Brook of Egypt were people deported from Mannea and the Zagros region. Šilkanni may be Osorkon IV, the last ruler of Egypt's twenty-second dynasty; see Schwemer, PNA 3/2 pp. 1421–1422 sub Usilkanu 1.

[111] Text no. 1 lines 101–126, text no. 2 lines 95b–101, text no. 7 lines 27, 44–45a, 49b, 52–54 and 64b–67a, text no. 63 ii′ 12′–25′, text no. 74 v 34–40, and text no. 82 iii 9′′′–17′′′.

provincial governors were appointed in this year, but nothing further is known about that action or if it was connected to Assyrian campaigns in some way.

In Sargon's eighth regnal year (714), he conducted his best documented campaign, heading east into the Zagros, traversing Mannea, defeating Mitatti of Zikirtu, and then proceeding north into Urarṭu itself, where he defeated the Urarṭian king Rusâ on Mount Uauš. While he may or may not have gone all the way around Lake Urmia during the course of the campaign, he certainly claims to have ravaged several Urarṭian districts. On the way home, and in response to omens, he marched to the religious center Muṣaṣir, and then captured and thoroughly looted it, making its ruler Urzana flee in order to save his life. Details of this campaign were reported to the god Aššur in a formal letter (text no. 65).[112]

In the following year (713), Sargon continued to consolidate his rule in the Zagros region, campaigning in Ellipi, Media, and Karalla, receiving tribute from the rulers of Mannea, Ellipi, and Allabria, as well as forty-five Median city rulers, and annexing the land Ḫabḫu. Although it is not mentioned in any royal inscription, Assyrian forces presumably also attacked Muṣaṣir during this campaign since the Assyrian Eponym Chronicle states "[again]st the city Muṣaṣir" as part of its entry for 713.[113] In the same year, Ambaris, king of Bīt-Purutaš in the land Tabal, an individual who had been granted the great honor of receiving a daughter of Sargon's in marriage, allied with the kings of Urarṭu and Musku, Rusâ and Mitâ, as well as with rulers of other principalities within Tabal, and rebelled. Assyrian troops that were presumably led by local governors defeated him. Ambaris and his family were carried off to Assyria, and the area was resettled and annexed to Assyria. Kurtî, the ruler of Atuna, to whom Sargon had given the city Šinuḫtu during his fourth campaign (719), had apparently joined the rebellion, trusting in the support of Mitâ; however, learning of the defeat of Ambaris, he immediately submitted to Sargon.[114]

According to the Assyrian Eponym Chronicle, in Sargon's tenth regnal year (712) the king remained in the land (i.e., Assyria). Sargon's Khorsabad Annals, however, recount a campaign (presumably not led by the king himself) to the northwest against Tarḫun-azi of the city Melid and the land Kammanu, whom Sargon had made ruler instead of Gunzinānu in the past but who had allied with Mitâ of Musku against Assyria. Melid and the city of Til-Garimme were captured, and Tarḫun-azi and his family were taken prisoner to Assyria. The area was annexed to Assyria and Til-Garimme was resettled with people from other lands. Several cities in the region were strengthened in order to defend against Urarṭian and Muskian actions and the city Melid was given to Mutallu of the land Kummuḫu.[115] Sargon's Annals describe the rich metallic resources found in the region that were brought to his new capital Dūr-Šarrukīn.[116]

In the following year, Sargon's eleventh regnal year (711), Assyrian attention was again drawn to the northwest and west. Tarḫu-lara of the land Gurgum, who had been defeated by Tiglath-pileser III and made an Assyrian vassal, was killed by his own son Mutallu. The Assyrians marched to Gurgum's capital Marqasa and carried off Mutallu and his family as booty. According to the Khorsabad Annals, Gurgum was then annexed to Assyria, but two other inscription of Sargon's state that that had happened earlier in his reign.[117] Desirous of no longer having to send tribute to Assyria, Azūri, the ruler of Ashdod, had rebelled against Assyria and sought to win support from other vassal rulers in the area (kings of Philistia, Judah, Edom, and Moab) and from the Egyptian pharaoh. Because of this, Sargon had removed him from the throne and made his brother Aḫī-Mīti the new ruler. The latter, however, was deposed by the inhabitants of the city and replaced by Iāmānī (or Iadna). Assyrian troops moved south, and hearing of this, Iāmānī fled to Egypt for refuge. Ashdod, as well as the nearby cities of Gath and Ashdod-Yam, were captured by the Assyrians, looted, and annexed to Assyria.[118]

The campaigns during Sargon's twelfth and thirteenth regnal years (710–709) were concentrated on the south, to deal with the Chaldean Marduk-apla-iddina (II) (Merodach-baladan) and to recover Babylonia for the

---

[112] See also text no. 1 lines 127–165a, text no. 2 lines 188–195a, text no. 7 lines 42b–43, 45b–47, 72b–78a (the suicide of Rusâ likely took place later, in 713), text no. 63 iii′ 1′–12′, text no. 74 iii 1–41, text no. 82 iv 1–v 6, and text no. 103 ii 39–50.

[113] With regard to the Assyrian conquest of, and control over, Muṣaṣir, in particular after the eighth campaign, see Dubovsky, SAAB 15 (2006) pp. 141–146.

[114] Text no. 1 lines 165b–204a, text no. 2 lines 195b–235, text no. 7 lines 29b–32 and 67b–72a, text no. 63 iii′ 13′–14′, text no. 74 iii 42–56 and v 13–33, text no. 82 v 7–vii 12′, and text no. 112.

[115] Text no. 1 lines 204b–221, text no. 2 lines 236–259a, text no. 7 lines 78b–83a, text no. 74 v 41–75, and text no. 82 vii 1′′′′′–viii 15′. Mutallu of Kummuḫu must be distinguished from Mutallu son of Tarḫu-lara, who ruled Gurgum (see the eleventh regnal year [711]).

[116] Text no. 1 lines 222–234a, text no. 2 lines 259b–267a, and text no. 82 viii 16′–17′.

[117] Text no. 8 lines 10b–11a and text no. 74 v 41–75.

[118] Text no. 1 lines 234b–262a, text no. 2 lines 267b–287a, text no. 3 lines 1′–13′a, text no. 7 lines 83b–109a, text no. 8 lines 11b–14, text no. 82 vii 13′–48′′ and possibly vii 1′′′–6′′′′, and no. 83 ii′ 1′–11′; note also text no. 104. The capture of Ashdod in 711 is likely the one mentioned in Isaiah 20:1, where it is stated that the Assyrian army was led by the field marshal (*tartan*) and not by the king himself. With regard to the eventual return of Iāmānī, see n. 126 below.

Assyrian empire. According to the Assyrian Eponym Chronicle, the campaign in the twelfth regnal year (710) was against Bīt-zēri (location unknown), with the king staying in Kish and then taking the hand of Bēl (Marduk) in the New Year's festival (at Babylon) at the beginning of his thirteenth regnal year (709). According to the Babylonian Chronicle, in the former year, Sargon invaded Babylonia and did battle with Marduk-apla-iddina, causing the latter to flee to Elam, and in the latter year, Sargon took the hand of Bēl and captured Marduk-apla-iddina's tribal capital Dūr-Yakīn. The Khorsabad Annals provide much additional information on the conquest of Babylonia. They inform us that in 710 Sargon began his campaign by first dealing with the Arameans living east of the Tigris. Marduk-apla-iddina had strengthened Dūr-Abi-ḫāra in the area of the Gambulu tribe against the Assyrian forces, but Sargon took that fortress, defeated several other Aramean tribes in the area, and annexed the region. Beginning the campaign in this area had the advantage of cutting off Babylonia's easiest access to Elam, from whose ruler Marduk-apla-iddina had hoped to receive aid in opposing the Assyrians. When the Elamite king Šutur-Naḫūndi (Šutruk-Naḫḫunte II) refused to send military support, Marduk-apla-iddina fled from Babylon, going first to Iqbi-Bēl and then to Dūr-Yakīn, his tribal stronghold in the southern marshes. As a result, Sargon was supposedly welcomed into Babylon and Borsippa. He ascended the throne of Babylon, taking the role of the king of Babylon in the New Year's festival at the beginning of the following year (709). Thus, 709 was his first regnal year as king of Babylonia and his thirteenth as king of Assyria. He then proceeded to besiege Marduk-apla-iddina in Dūr-Yakīn. Although Sargon took the city, Marduk-apla-iddina managed to flee and take refuge in Elam.[119] Hearing of Sargon's military successes, Upēri and later Aḫundāra, kings of Dilmun in the Persian Gulf, sent him gifts in order to win his favor.[120] It was likely at some point after he ascended the throne of Babylon that Sargon granted special privileges to numerous Babylonian cities, likely in an attempt to win their support.[121]

Sargon remained in Babylonia until his fifteenth regnal year (707), when he returned to Assyria. According to Sargon's annals, while he was occupied in Babylonia, the governor of the land Que invaded the territory of Mitâ of Musku three times, capturing and demolishing two fortresses. As a result of these actions, and learning of Sargon's military successes in Babylonia, Mitâ sent gifts to Sargon and offered submission to him.[122] At about the same time, the ruler of Tyre, Silṭa, appears to have requested aid from Sargon to put down a rebellion in Yadnana (Cyprus). An Assyrian official with a military contingent (perhaps just a military escort) was provided to him and as a result the rebels became afraid and brought presents to Sargon in Babylon. It was undoubtedly in connection with this episode that the stele of Sargon found on Cyprus (text no. 103) was sent or created there.[123]

---

[119] Text no. 1 lines 262b–390 (year 12) and 404–416 (year 13), text no. 2 lines 287b–371 (year 12) and 372–426a (year 13), text no. 3 lines 13′b–60′ (year 12), text no. 5 lines 2′–3′ (year 12), text no. 6 lines 1′–14′ (year 13), text no. 7 lines 121b–144a (years 12–13), text no. 8 lines 18b–20a, text no. 9 lines 30b–34a, text no. 13 lines 45b–54a, text no. 64 lines 1′–12′, text no. 74 vi 14–85 and vii 7–19 (years 12–13 [also down to 707?]), text no. 83 ii′ 12–iii′ 13 (years 12–13), text no. 86 lines 2′–18′ (year 13), text no. 87 lines 3′–16′ (year 13), text no. 91 (year 12 and possibly year 13), text no. 103 iv 1–22 (year 13), text no. 111 lines 1′–9′ (year 13), text no. 113 lines 6′–27′ (years 12–13), and text no. 114 lines 1′–14′ (year 13). While some texts state that Marduk-apla-iddina was captured (text no. 7 lines 133–134a and text no. 74 vi 45–46; note also text no. 8 lines 18b–19a, text no. 9 lines 31b–32a, and text no. 13 lines 48b–49a, where the verb *kašādu* can mean both "conquer/defeat" and "capture"), the Khorsabad Annals of Room V (text no. 2 lines 402b–403) and the Babylonian chronicle say that he fled. The Annals version from an unknown room of the Khorsabad palace records that he submitted to Sargon's messenger and apparently gave tribute (text no. 6 lines 11′b–14′); this may indicate that this text was composed before the truth was known, and thus before text no. 2. These differing accounts were noted already back in 1916 by A.T.E. Olmstead (Historiography p. 57); see most recently Fuchs, Khorsabad p. 351 n. 479. Marduk-apla-iddina will reappear in opposition to Assyria in the reign of Sennacherib.

[120] Text no. 1 lines 442b–444a, text no. 2 lines 426b–427, text no. 7 lines 144b–145a, text no. 8 lines 20b–21, text no. 9 lines 34b–35, text no. 13 lines 54b–59a, text no. 64 line 13′, text no. 74 vii 20–24a (Aḫundāra), text no. 87 line 17′, text no. 103 iv 23–27, and text no. 116 line 27 (Aḫundāra). Upēri may have brought his gifts in 710 (Sargon's twelfth regnal year) rather than 709 (Fuchs, Khorsabad p. 410) and Aḫundāra (presumably Upēri's successor as king) in or by 706 (Sargon's sixteenth regnal year), when text no. 74 was likely composed.

[121] The granting of the privileges (e.g., *šubarrû* and *andurāru*) is mentioned in numerous texts of Sargon, often soon after the mention of his titles and epithets and in association with the mention of privileges also being granted to Aššur, Ḫarrān, and at times Dēr, or as part of descriptions of the defeat of Marduk-apla-iddina and conquest of Babylonia (e.g., text no. 7 lines 5b–12a and 136b–137a, and text no. 43 lines 4–6). With regard to the granting of *andurāru* by Neo-Assyrian kings, including Sargon, see Villard, RA 101 (2007) pp. 107–124.

[122] Text no. 1 lines 444b–456a, text no. 2 lines 428–436a, and text no. 7 lines 149b–153a. The governor's actions and subsequent submission of Mitâ may have taken place in or around 710–709 and 708 respectively.

[123] Text no. 1 lines 456b–467a, text no. 2 lines 436b–441a, text no. 7 lines 145b–149a, text no. 64 lines 14′–17′, text no. 74 vii 24b–44, text no. 87 lines 18′–21′, and text no. 103 iv 28–57. The gifts likely reached Sargon in Babylon in 708, although it is not impossible this happened in 709 or early in 707 before he returned to Assyria. Josephus (Jewish Antiquities 9.283–287) describes a five-year siege of Tyre during the reign of the Assyrian king who besieged and captured Samaria. The name of the king credited with these actions is written several ways in Josephus' Greek account (one way being Salmanassēs), but it is normally understood to refer to Shalmaneser (V). J. Elayi argues that the siege took place during the reign of Sargon, probably beginning in 709 and ending in 705, and that it was supervised by one of Sargon's officials (Sargon II pp. 67–72, 237–238, and 243). I am aware of no real evidence of such a siege in the cuneiform sources for either the reign of Shalmaneser V or that of Sargon II, although the Khorsabad Cylinder inscription does state somewhat ambiguously that Sargon

While Sargon remained in Babylonia, Mutallu of the city Kummuḫu, to whom Sargon had given the city Melid in his tenth regnal year (712), rebelled, putting his trust in the Urarṭian king Argišti (II), who had ascended the throne following the suicide of his father Rusâ, an event which likely took place in 713. However, when he heard of the advance of an Assyrian army led by Assyrian officials in 708, Mutallu fled. His city was looted and his family taken prisoner to Assyria. Sargon annexed the area and resettled there some of the people whom he had captured in Bīt-Yakīn.[124]

Sargon returned to Assyria from Babylon in his fifteenth regnal year (707) and in that year Dūr-Yakīn was looted by Sargon's officials and destroyed according to the Assyrian Eponym Chronicle. A Babylonian chronicle informs us that there was plague in Assyria in that year and that the gods of the Sealand returned to their shrines. It was likely in that same year or the preceding one that Daltâ, the king of Ellipi whom Sargon had confirmed as ruler of that land in 713, died. Two of his nephews fought over the kingship, with one, Nibê, seeking aid from the Elamite king, and the other, Ašpa-bara, turning to Sargon. Assyrian officials led an army to help Ašpa-bara and captured Nibê, ending the dispute.[125] About the same time, Šapataku' (Shebitko), the Nubian ruler (king of Meluḫḫa) of Egypt's Twenty-Fifth Dynasty, extradited Iāmānī to Assyria; Iāmānī had briefly seized the throne of Ashdod and then fled to Egypt, away from Assyrian troops, in 711.[126]

In his sixteenth regnal year (706), Sargon again did not lead any campaign, staying in Assyria, where the inauguration of his new capital Dūr-Šarrukīn took place. Officials of his, however, campaigned against Karalla in the central Zagros and subdued it. This was the third time that the Assyrians had had to campaign in that region, the earlier campaigns being in Sargon's sixth and ninth regnal years (716 and 713). The campaign is briefly mentioned in the Assyrian Eponym Chronicle, but an Assyrian rock relief and inscription in the central Zagros at Tang-i Var commemorate the campaign (text no. 116).[127]

Sargon campaigned for a last time in his seventeenth regnal year (705). A Babylonian chronicle appears to state that he marched to the land Tabal. The Assyrian Eponym Chronicle informs us that he fought Gurdî, the Kulummian,[128] and was killed, but no details about the battle are given beyond the statement that the enemy seized the Assyrian camp. A later text informs us that Sargon's body was not recovered (see below).[129]

Building Activities

Just like other rulers of Mesopotamia, Sargon II carried out numerous building projects throughout his realm, in particular in Assyria and Babylonia, and especially at his new capital city Dūr-Šarrukīn.[130]

Khorsabad (Dūr-Šarrukīn)

The founding and construction of Dūr-Šarrukīn ("Wall of Sargon" or "Fortress of Sargon") to be the new royal center of Assyria is the most important building activity carried out during the reign of Sargon and is recorded in a large number of his royal inscriptions. Most of these texts come from Khorsabad (see in particular text nos. 2, 7–9, 11–14, 41, 43–48, and 51–56), but a number come from other cities, in particular from Nineveh (see text nos. 84–85) and Arslantepe (ancient Melid; text no. 111). Moreover, bricks stating that they were from the palace of Sargon or mentioning the building of the city Dūr-Šarrukīn and its palace have been found at

---

"pacified" (*ušapšiḫu*) Tyre (text no. 43 line 21). While there are few contemporary sources for events during the reign of Shalmaneser V, there are a large number for the reign of Sargon and thus the lack of any mention of a siege of Tyre in them is worthy of note, even though the scribes of Sargon's official inscriptions might not have wished to mention an episode (siege) that had not been completed or that had failed in its objective. It must also be noted that Josephus was writing his account over seven hundred years after the time of Sargon and thus his version of events may not always be accurate. He does, however, state that he used information from Tyrian archives (via Menander) for his description of this episode.

[124] Text no. 1 lines 467b–468, text no. 2 lines 441b–454, text no. 7 lines 112b–117a, text no. 74 iv 1–12 and text no. 84 lines 21′–27′; note also the Assyrian Eponym Chronicle entry for 708. Text no. 74 vii 45–76 describes the poor state of the road to Babylon and likely refers to the time in or around 708.

[125] Text no. 2 lines 455–467a and text no. 7 lines 117b–121a.

[126] The extradition of Iāmānī by the Nubian ruler Shebitko is mentioned as already having happened in an inscription composed in the following year (text no. 116 lines 19–21; note also text no. 113 lines 1′–5′). For the return of Iāmānī, see also text no. 7 lines 109b–112a, text no. 8 lines 11b–14, and text no. 83 ii′ 1–11. Note A. Fuchs' discussion of this episode in SAAS 8 pp. 124–131.

[127] See in particular lines 37–44.

[128] As noted by previous scholars, "Gurdî, the Kulummian," may be the same person as Kurtî of Atuna, who is mentioned in accounts of events in Sargon's fourth and eleventh regnal years.

[129] Livingstone, SAA 3 no. 33, especially lines 8′-9′ and 19′-20′.

[130] With regard to Sargon's building activities, see also Fuchs, RLA 12/1–2 (2009) p. 59 and PNA 3/2 p. 1244. The Assyrian Eponym Chronicle appears to state that a deity entered his/her new temple in 713. That temple may or may not be mentioned in this section. Note also the possible restoration of the entries for 720 and 719 in that chronicle (see below).

numerous locations outside of the city itself: Nimrud, Nineveh, Karamles, Tag, Tepe Gawra and possibly Djigan (see text nos. 50 and 53).

Sargon states that he founded the new city in order to make the land of Assyria prosper and that rather than expropriate land for the city he purchased it from its previous owners, paying them either in silver and bronze according to the original purchase prices for the land or with equivalent land elsewhere.[131] The new city was located about fifteen km upstream from Nineveh, at the site of a town called Maganuba and "at the foot of Mount Muṣri." Archaeological work has shown that the new city was approximately square in shape (1800×1700m) and covered an area of about 300 hectares. The Assyrian Eponym Chronicle (see below) states that the city was founded in 717 and Assyrian inscriptions tell us that individuals captured during Sargon's various campaigns were used as laborers on the massive building project[132] According to the Assyrian Eponym Chronicle, various gods entered their temples in the city on the twenty-second day of Tašrītu (VII) in 707 and the city was inaugurated on the sixth day of Ayyāru (II) in 706.[133] Thus, the construction of the city had taken about ten years and been concluded only about a year before the king's death. To celebrate the completion of the city and palace, Aššur and the other deities of Assyria (presumably their statues) were invited to the city, where the king made sumptuous offerings to them.[134] After the deities returned to their own cities, the king took up residence in his palace and held a great festival, one to which numerous foreign rulers, officials, nobles, and important Assyrians were invited. These 'guests' presented to the king substantial tribute, including among other things precious metals, garments, aromatics, ivory, ebony, horses, and oxen.[135] Among the people settled in the new city were the foreign captives who had been employed in building it, along with their Assyrian overseers and commanders.[136]

In preparation for commencing work on the city, bricks were made at an auspicious time, in the month Ṣitaš/Simānu (III), and the foundations of the city were laid in the month Abu (V).[137] The texts record in particular work on the city wall, with its gates, and the palace, with its chapels to the deities Ea, Sîn, Ningal, Adad, Šamaš, and Ninurta. The city wall is said to be 16,280 cubits long and to comprise two separate walls, an outer wall with a name honoring the state god Aššur ("The God Aššur Is the One Who Prolongs the Reign of Its Royal Builder (and) Protects His Troops [var.: Offspring]") and an inner wall with one honoring the warrior god Ninurta ("The God Ninurta Is the One Who Establishes the Foundation of His City [var.: the Wall] for (All) Days to Come"). Three texts state that there were eight gates in the city wall: two gates in each of the four sides of the city and each gate having a name honoring one of the gods. The published plan of the city (see Figure 3) has only one gate in its north(west) side. However, J.E. Reade has noted that at the point where the royal palace platform projects from the citadel, the line of the city wall was clearly eroded and the published ground plans are partly hypothetical. He thus suggests that there may have been a postern gate below the ziggurrat on the palace platform, just as there was one below the South-West Palace of Sennacherib at Nineveh. Since the gates

---

[131] Text no. 43 lines 34–52; see also text no. 8 lines 29b–31a. Note also Sargon's renewal of a land grant originally made by Adad-nārārī III to three individuals in order to ensure offerings to the god Aššur (Kataja and Whiting, SAA 12 no. 19). Sargon gave the original grantees of the land (or their sons) "field for field" in another location so that they could continue to provide the offerings while he could take the land originally granted to them for the construction of Dūr-Šarrukīn. The text was composed at Nineveh in Sargon's ninth year (713). While Sargon states that he built the new city in order to make Assyria prosper, K. Radner argues that his "decision to move the court and the central administration to a new centre was in part motivated by the lack of acceptance and the active and fierce resistance his rule had met with in the Assyrian heartland" (HSAO 14 p. 325). Radner may well be correct in this matter; however, it is not really clear who actually did oppose Sargon and how they had done so, even though it seems probable that some or all of 6,300 Assyrian "criminals" deported to Hamath early in his reign had opposed his accession. For the movement of the capital from Kalḫu to Dūr-Šarrukīn, see Radner, HSAO 14 pp. 325–327.

[132] For references in the texts to the initial work, including the making of bricks, the laying of foundation deposits, and the use of deportees, see in particular text nos. 2 lines 467b–469a and 473b–474a, 7 lines 153b–155a and 159b–160a, 8 lines 27b–28a and 31b–34a, 9 lines 49b–57a, 12 lines 23b–29, 13 lines 90–97a, 14 lines 28b–33a, 43 lines 57–61, 45 lines 40–44a, 46 lines 32b–36, and 47 lines 18–21. Samarians were among the people employed in the construction of the new city; see Cogan, Bound for Exile pp. 45–49 nos. 2.03–5. For information from contemporary letters on the actual building of the city, see S. Parpola in Caubet, Khorsabad pp. 47–77.

[133] The word used for "inaugurated" is SAR-*ru*, an Assyrian stative form from the verb *šurrû*, "to begin; to inaugurate a building, to kindle a censor; to start, originate (said of eclipses and other natural phenomenon), to erupt, grow" (CAD Š/3 p. 358), and "to begin, start; inaugurate" (CDA p. 388).

[134] One exemplar of text no. 9 informs us that these gods were invited to come to Dūr-Šarrukīn for a celebration (*tašīltu*) in the month Tašrītu (VII), i.e., in 707; see the on-page note to text no. 9 line 98. This celebration is distinct from the festival (*nigûtu*) in Ayyāru (II) of 706 to which numerous foreign rulers and important Assyrians were invited.

[135] See in particular text nos. 2 lines 483b–494, 7 lines 167–186a, 8 lines 54–69a, 9 lines 97b–100, 12 lines 34–45, 13 lines 123b–130, and 15 lines 1′–5′. Mention of this festival in a text indicates that that text was composed no earlier than 706, unless we assume that they were recording an event that was planned, but that had not yet taken place.

[136] See in particular text nos. 8 lines 49b–53, 9 lines 92b–97a, 41 lines 25b–26a, 43 lines 72–74, 44 lines 49b–54, 75 lines 10′–14′, and 84 line 11′.

[137] See for example text nos. 8 lines 31b–34a, and 9 lines 49b–57a, and 43 lines 57–61.

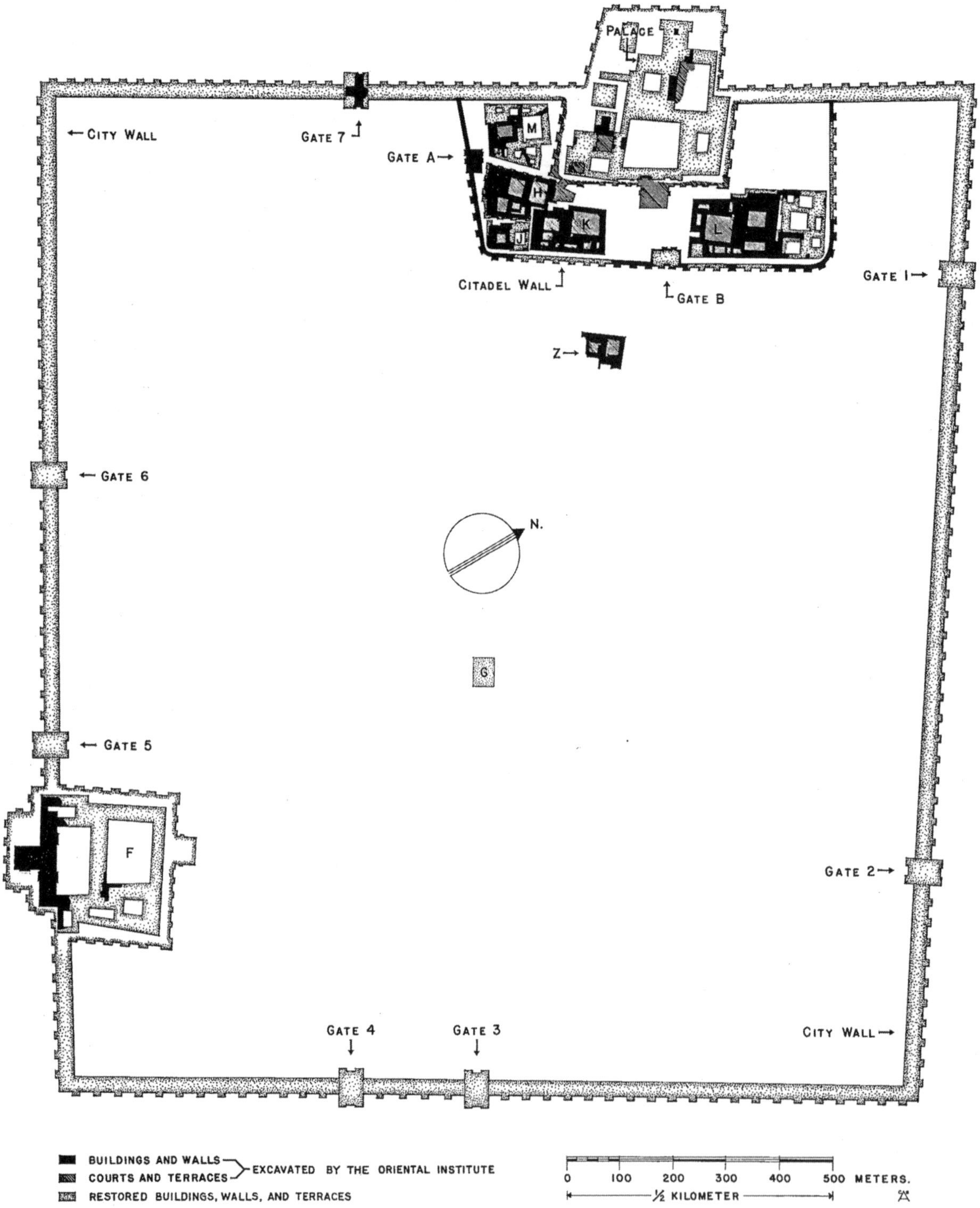

Figure 3. Plan of the city of Khorsabad. Reprinted from Loud and Altman, Khorsabad 2 pl. 69 courtesy of the Oriental Institute of the University of Chicago.

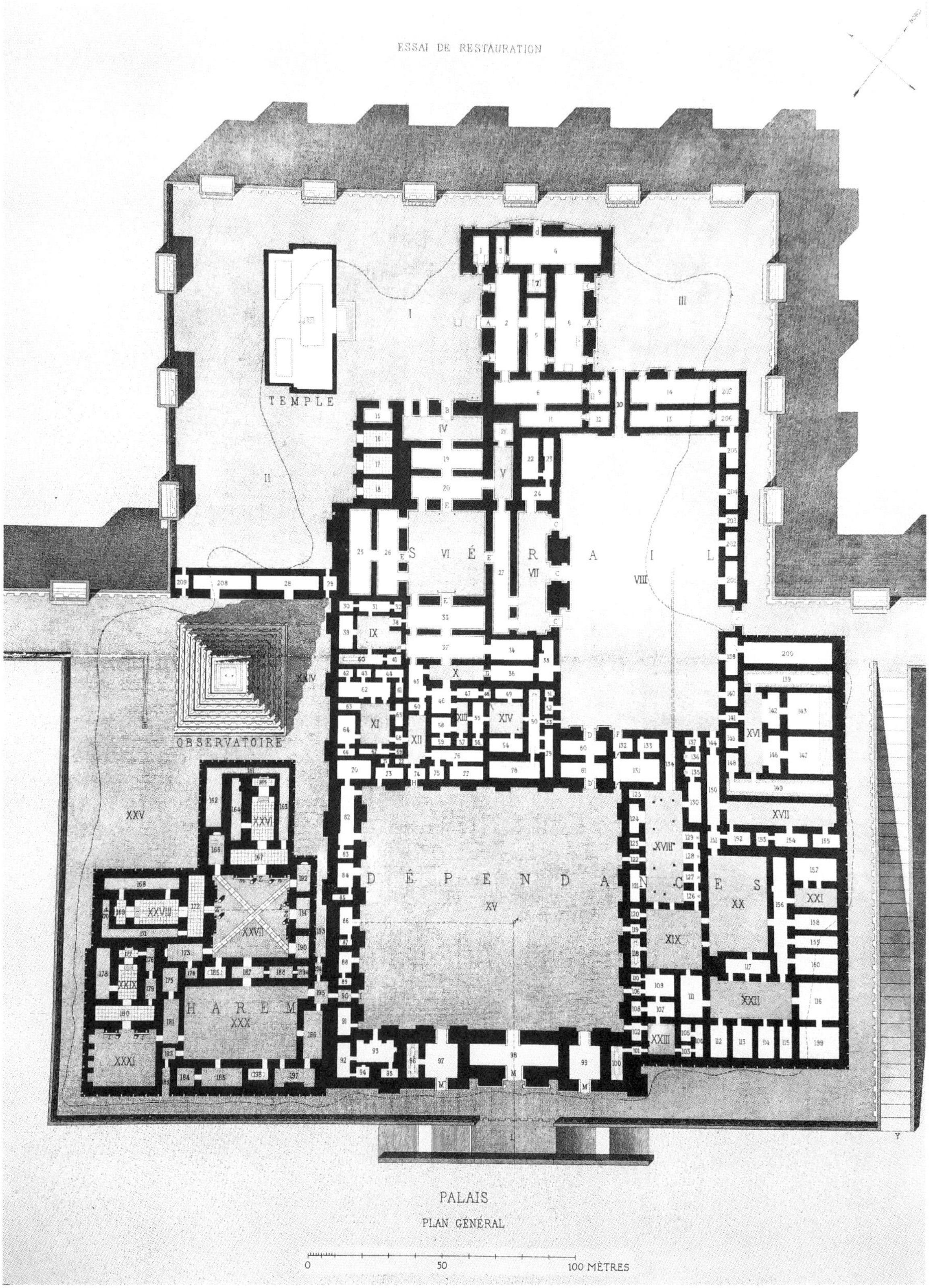

Figure 4. Plan of the palace at Khorsabad, as restored by V. Place. Reprinted from Loud and Altman, Khorsabad 2 pl. 76 courtesy of the Oriental Institute of the University of Chicago.

are listed in a counterclockwise order (east > north > west > south), the presumed postern gate would have been the one called "The God Enlil is the One Who Establishes the Foundation of My City."[138]

The palace complex (see Figure 4) and the adjoining temple of Nabû were located on raised platforms connected by a bridge within the city's 'citadel' located against the northwestern city wall; the palace partially protruded beyond the regular plan of the city wall. The palace complex consisted of over two hundred rooms and courtyards, as well as a ziggurrat. The palace was given the name *égalgabarinutukua*, "Palace That Has No Equal," and all types of luxurious materials were used in its construction. In one part of the palace was a *bīt ḫilāni* structure in imitation of a Hittite palace.[139] Pavement inscriptions have been found identifying the chapels of Ninšiku (Ea), Sîn, Ningal, Adad, Šamaš, and Ninurta within the palace complex (text nos. 16–21),[140] as well as the temple of Nabû (text no. 22).

Although the temple of Nabû was the largest religious structure at the city, no inscriptions appear to record its construction apart from a brief mention on inscribed stone slabs used as thresholds or on or near steps in the temple itself (text no. 22). The Khorsabad Cylinder inscription (text no. 43 line 43) states that Sargon ordered that a *simakku*-shrine of Šamaš be constructed in the city, but nothing further is known about it. Brick inscriptions (text nos. 54–55) record the construction of the temple of Sîn and Šamaš in the city, but it is not clear if this refers to the chapels of these gods within the palace complex, the *simakku*-shrine, or some other independent temple (or temples).[141] Archaeologists discovered a temple in the lower city in which there were numerous stone altars. The inscription on the altars only refers to them being set up for the Sebetti by Sargon, and not to the construction of the temple itself (text no. 49). No inscription refers to the ziggurrat constructed behind the palace chapels on the palace terrace.

Within the citadel were located at least four large residences (J, K, L, and M), the largest of which being the residence of the king's brother and grand vizier Sîn-aḫu-uṣur. Three pavement slabs from Sîn-aḫu-uṣur's residence (L) state that he had constructed the building (text no. 2002). In the lower city, adjacent to the southern city wall was located the city's *ekal māšarti* (Palace F), but no royal inscription mentions its construction,[142] although several inscriptions of Sargon were found there.[143] Around the city Sargon had a botanical garden (or great park, *kirimaḫḫu*) created, one that was to be a replica of Mount Amanus and to have every kind of aromatic plant and fruit-bearing mountain tree.[144]

Aššur

At the city of Aššur, work was carried out on Eḫursaggalkurkurra, the main cella within the temple of the god Aššur, in particular on the processional way in the temple courtyard (text nos. 69–70) and on a glazed brick frieze from the temple (text no. 71), but also on the towers (text no. 67). A cylinder inscription from Nineveh refers to "shining *zaḫalû*-silver for the work on Eḫursaggalkurkurra ("House, the Great Mountain of the Lands"), the sanctuary of the god Aššur [...] ... the goddesses Queen-of-Nineveh and Lady-of-Arbela."[145] In addition, one letter from the governor of the city (Parpola, SAA 1 no. 77 [=Harper, ABL no. 91]) describes work

---

[138] See Reade, SAAB 25 (2019) pp. 85–86. For the building of the city walls and its gates, see in particular text nos. 8 lines 40b–49a, 9 lines 79b–92a, 43 lines 65–71, and 44 lines 47–49a. Note also Battini, CRRA 43 pp. 41–55 and RA 94 (2000) pp. 33–56. With regard to the building of the city wall, note Cogan, IEJ 56 (2006) pp. 84–95. For the connection of the length of the city wall and the king's name, see the earlier section on the name of the king.

[139] For the building and decoration of the palace, including its gates, see in particular text nos. 2 lines 472b–483a, 7 lines 158b–166, 8 lines 35–40a, 9 lines 60b–79a, 11 lines 21b–46, 12 lines 30–33, 13 lines 97b–123a, 14 lines 33b–47, 41 lines 18b–25a, 43 lines 63–64, 44 lines 33–45, 45 lines 19–39, 46 lines 22–32a, 47 lines 14–17, 48 lines 6´b–7´, 74 viii 1´´–6´´, 75 lines 6´–9´, 84 line 10´, 85 line 6´, and 111 line 13. With regard to the *bīt ḫilāni*, see most recently Reade, Iraq 70 (2008) pp. 13–40; Erarslan, Akkadica 135 (2014) pp. 173–195; and Kertai, Iraq 79 (2017) pp. 85–104, especially pp. 97–101; see also the note to text no. 2 line 476. For the use of the term É.GAL.MEŠ, literally "palaces" but translated here as "palatial halls," for the palace complex, see the note to text no. 2 line 472.

[140] For the construction of the temples, in particular the palace chapels, and the entry of the deities into them, see in particular text nos. 2 lines 469b–472a, 7 lines 155b–158a, 8 line 34b, 9 lines 57b–60a, 41 lines 17–18a, 43 line 62, 44 lines 28b–30, 45 lines 12b–18, 46 lines 14–21, 47 lines 11b–13, 48 lines 1´b–6´a, 75 lines 1´–5´, 84 line 9´, 85 line 5´, and 111 line 12. The deities are sometimes stated to have been born within Eḫursaggalkurkurra, the cella of the god Aššur within that god's temple Ešarra at the city Aššur; see text nos. 2 lines 469b–470a, 7 lines 155b–156a, and 111 line 12a (totally restored).

[141] Bricks with these inscriptions have been found at Kalḫu and Nineveh, as well as Khorsabad. One of those from Khorsabad was found in the throne room of the palace.

[142] With regard to this structure, see in particular Loud and Altman, Khorsabad 2 and note also Matthiae in Studies Donbaz pp. 197–203.

[143] See text no. 10 ex. 4, text no. 11 commentary, text no. 43 exs. 13–21, 28, and 31–32, and text no. 57 Frgms. L and M.

[144] See in particular text nos. 8 lines 28b–29a, 9 lines 41b–42, and 74 viii 7´´–9´´.

[145] Text no. 84 line 3´–4´; cf. text no. 74 i 25–27.

on the palace of the inner city. Work may also have been carried out on the temple of the gods Sîn and Šamaš.[146]

Kalḫu

Sargon had the Juniper Palace at Kalḫu (modern Nimrud), which had previously been built by Ashurnasirpal (II), completely renovated, from its foundations to its crenellations. Upon its completion, he invited Nergal, Adad, and the other gods dwelling in the city, to come inside and he then held a festival. Silver and gold that had been taken as booty from Pisīris, king of Carchemish, were stored there (text no. 73). Very little of the end of the Nimrud Prism inscription (text no. 74) is preserved and what little there is refers to work at Dūr-Šarrukīn, but it is not impossible that some work at Kalḫu had also been mentioned.

Nineveh

Two bricks from the temple of Nabû at Nineveh record that Sargon completely (re)built that temple (text no. 96 and cf. text nos. 93 and 97), while several other bricks, pavement slabs, and cones found at Nineveh state that the king had completely (re)built the temple of the gods Nabû and Marduk (text nos. 92 and 95). The inscription on the cones states that Adad-nārārī III (810–783) had previously restored the temple.[147] Inscribed copper coverings for doorjambs in the temple of Nabû have also been recovered (text no. 99).[148] Although the passage is damaged, the Nineveh Prism likely indicates that Sargon had carried out work on a ziggurrat, possibly the one of Adad at Nineveh (text no. 82 viii 4′′′b–8′′′).

One inscribed wall slab of Sargon's is said to have been found at Nebi Yunus, the secondary mound (likely the *ekal māšarti*) at Nineveh (text no. 81), but it is not impossible that it was actually brought there by one of Sargon's successors or in modern times.[149] In addition, a later inscription of Ashurbanipal (Novotny and Jeffers, RINAP 5/1 p. 220 no. 10 v 33–42) states that Sargon had been the builder of the *akītu*-house of the goddess Ištar that was inside Nineveh.

Ḫarrān

A broken passage in a cylinder inscription from Nineveh (text no. 84 line 6′) refers to "seven and a half minas of shining silver for the work of Eḫulḫul ("House which Gives Joy"), the abode of the god Sîn who dwells in the city Ḫarrān." This presumably refers to some construction work on the temple or on some item associated with it.

Dēr

According to one letter (Fuchs and Parpola, SAA 15 no. 113 [=CT 54 no. 89+]), work was carried out on the fort and outer city wall at Dēr.

Tabal

The Khorsabad Annals (text no. 1 lines 202b–204a; cf. text no. 2 lines 234b–235a) may refer to some construction in the land Tabal, and in particular the construction of an enclosure wall (*kerḫu*), in connection with the settlement of people there and the appointment of one of Sargon's eunuchs as governor over them. As noted by Fuchs,[150] it is possible that this work was never completed.

Til-Barsip

A poorly preserved inscription from Til-Barsip (modern Tell Ahmar), possibly on part of a bull colossus (text no. 107), appears to refer to a temple of Adad, possibly one that Ashurnasirpal (II) had originally constructed, but it is not clear in which city that structure was located.

---

[146] See Haller, Heiligtümer pp. 89–92.
[147] For an inscription of Adad-nārārī III recording work on the temple of Nabû at Nineveh, see Grayson, RIMA 3 pp. 219–220 A.0.104.14.
[148] Text no. 92 states that Adad-nārārī III had carried out his work on the temple seventy-five years earlier and Reade suggests that Sargon may have restored it in 713 (Iraq 67 [2005] p. 380).
[149] See Frahm, AoF 40 (2013) pp. 52–53. Note also Reade in Studies Calmeyer p. 612. Some bricks with inscriptions of Sargon II were found at Nebi Yunus (e.g., text no. 53 ex. 24 and text no. 54 ex. 4).
[150] RLA 12/1–2 (2009) p. 59 and PNA 3/2 p. 1244.

Carchemish

A brief brick inscription (text no. 110) that refers to the palace of Sargon has been discovered at Carchemish and a nearby site (Tell Amarna), and this could suggest that there was a royal palace there. Three copies of a clay cylinder inscription of the king found at Carchemish (text no. 109) mention building activities carried out there by Sargon and the expansion of irrigation in the area of the city.

Melid

Although four texts on clay cylinders come from Melid (modern Arslantepe, near Malatya), they are all in fragmentary condition (text nos. 111–114). Only one (text no. 111) preserves part of the end of its inscription and no reference to any building work can be detected. The curse at the end of the text invokes the god Marduk, which might suggest that any structure or object whose construction or dedication was mentioned at the end of the inscription would have been associated with that deity.

Ḫarḫar and Iran

The Najafabad Stele states that following the king's conquest of the Iranian city of Ḫarḫar during his sixth regnal year (716), he renamed it Kār-Šarrukīn. In addition, as well as rebuilding a temple, he constructed something else there.[151] It is not known what that other structure was, although a later letter to the king from that city (Fuchs and Parpola, SAA 15 no. 94 [=Harper, ABL no. 126]) refers to the building of a "grand hall" (É *dan-nu*) with glazed bricks. Sargon's Khorsabad Annals also state that during the campaign of the following year (715) he rebuilt the cities Kišešlu, Kindayu, Anzaria, and Bīt-Gabaya and renamed them Kār-Nabû, Kār-Sîn, Kār-Adad, and Kār-Ištar (text no. 1 lines 113b–114a).

Babylonia

Following his defeat of Marduk-apla-iddina II (Merodach-Baladan) in 710–709, Sargon had work carried out at Babylon, Uruk, and likely Kish and Tell Haddad. Most of the texts mentioning this work are written in the Akkadian language, but three were composed in Sumerian (text nos. 124 and 127–128).

Bricks with inscriptions recording Sargon's restoration of Babylon's city walls, Imgur-Enlil and Nēmet-Enlil, for the god Marduk have been found at both Babylon and Kish (text nos. 123–124). Presumably the bricks found at Kish had been used for some work at the same time at that city or been taken there for reuse later. One of the inscriptions (text no. 123) also mentions that work had been carried out with baked bricks along the bank of the Euphrates River (presumably inside Babylon). Of the two texts, one is written in Akkadian and one in Sumerian. According to Sargon's annals from Khorsabad, the king had a new canal dug from Borsippa to Babylon for the procession of the god Nabû.[152]

One clay cylinder and several brick inscriptions testify to work carried out at the city of Uruk in southern Babylonia. The one cylinder records the restoration of Eanna, and in particular its outer enclosure wall in the lower courtyard (text no. 125), for the goddess Ištar. Numerous bricks found at Uruk record work on various parts of the Eanna temple, including the outer enclosure wall, the courtyard, the narrow gate, the regular gate, and the processional way (text nos. 126–128).

A clay cylinder of Sargon's was found at Tell Haddad in the Hamrin region (text no. 129). Although none of the building section of the text is preserved, it may have been intended to record work at that city, and in view of the fact that it was found not far from the temple of Nergal (Ešaḫula) at that site, it may well have mentioned work on that temple. A fragmentary axe head of one of Sargon's eunuchs was also found at Tell Haddad and the text on it recorded the dedication of the object to the god who dwelled in Ešaḫul(a) located inside the city Mēturna (Mê-Turnat) (text no. 2008). A clay cylinder (text no. 2009) from Tell Baradān, a neighboring site, appears to refer to the governor of Arrapḫa Nabû-bēlu-ka''in doing something because Sargon wanted to rebuild the wall of Sirara (a literary term for Mê-Turnat). The cylinder was likely created to commemorate the governor's work on that wall.

---

151 Text no. 117 ii 41b–45a; see also text no. 1 lines 114–115.
152 Text no. 1 lines 377b–379a and text no. 2 lines 359b–360.

Death

Assuming that Sargon had been born by 765 (see above), he would have been at least sixty years old at the time of his death in 705. In that year he led his troops to the land of Tabal to deal with Gurdî, the Kulummian (presumably the ruler of the city Til-Garimme).[153] Although damaged, the Assyrian Eponym Chronicle states that "the king was killed; the camp of the king of Assyria [*was*] *sei*[*zed* ...]; Sennacherib [*ascended the throne*] on the 12th day of the month Abu (V)." Thus, Sargon was likely killed early in 705 while on campaign against Tabal. The later "Sin of Sargon" text states: "the death of Sargon, [my father, who was killed in enemy country and] not buried in his house" and "[... Sargon, my father], was killed [in enemy country] and not b[uried] in his house" (Livingstone, SAA 3 no. 33 lines 8′–9′ and 19′–20′). It appears that his body had not been recovered after the battle and could not be brought back to Assyria for burial. This was a great disaster since a proper burial was essential for an individual to have a good afterlife and, as an angry ghost, Sargon might haunt his living descendants until they provided him with one. It was likely because of this disaster and in an attempt to distance himself from it that Sennacherib abandoned Sargon's capital of Dūr-Šarrukīn[154] and created a new one at Nineveh. It is not known if Sennacherib ever tried to discover the reason the gods allowed this tragedy to occur, but it is likely that Sargon's grandson Esarhaddon did and that it was under his reign that the "Sin of Sargon" text was composed. Although damaged, this text appears to be trying to determine if Sargon had met his sad fate because he had not treated the gods of Babylonia as well as those of Assyria and had not kept a treaty sworn by the "king of the gods."[155]

Dating and Chronology

Texts edited in this volume occasionally mention contemporary dates and the charts in this section are intended to aid the reader in understanding those dates.

The month names in Neo-Assyrian inscriptions and their modern equivalents are:

I	Nisannu	March–April	VII	Tašrītu	September–October
II	Ayyāru	April–May	VIII	Araḫsamna	October–November
III	Simānu	May–June	IX	Kislīmu	November–December
IV	Du'ūzu	June–July	X	Ṭebētu, Kinūnu	December–January
V	Abu	July–August	XI	Šabāṭu	January–February
VI	Ulūlu	August–September	XII	Addaru	February–March
VI_2	Intercalary Ulūlu		XII_2	Intercalary Addaru	

Unless stated otherwise, the dates given in this volume (excluding those in bibliographical citations) are all BC. Each ancient Mesopotamian year has been given a single Julian year equivalent even though the ancient year actually encompassed parts of two Julian years, with the ancient year beginning around the time of the vernal equinox. For example, Sargon ascended the throne of Assyria on the twelfth day of Ṭebētu of his accession year, which is indicated to be 722, although that event may have taken place in January 721. Thus, events that occurred late in the ancient year "722" actually happened early in the Julian year 721.

King Lists

Unfortunately, no list of Assyrian kings preserves a mention of Sargon II. The Assyrian King List ends with Sargon's predecessor Shalmaneser V, and both the Synchronistic King List and Assyrian King List fragment KAV no. 182 have lacunae immediately before their mention of Sennacherib. Sargon II is listed as a ruler of Babylonia in Babylonian King List A and the Ptolemaic Canon immediately following Marduk-apla-iddina II (Merodach-baladan), who seized control of Babylonia from Assyria upon the death of Shalmaneser V and ruled

[153] See below for translations of the Assyrian Eponym Chronicle and the Babylonian chronicle (recension B) for 705.
[154] There is in fact evidence that Dūr-Šarrukīn was not totally abandoned following the death of Sargon; see Brinkman, Prelude p. 54 n. 254 and Dalley, Kaskal 11 (2014) pp. 176–179. A prism inscription of Esarhaddon and several economic texts dated to post-canonical eponyms were found during the Oriental Institute excavations at Khorsabad; these will be published by J.A. Brinkman and S. Parpola.
[155] With regard to the death of Sargon, note Frahm, JCS 51 (1999) pp. 73–90, in particular pp. 74–76. Part of the motivation in determining if the tragedy had been connected with the Assyrian king's not having honored Babylonian gods sufficiently may have been in connection with Esarhaddon's decision to rebuild Babylon and Marduk's temple Esagila, following their destruction in the time of Sennacherib.

that land until defeated by Sargon in 710. Thus, those two lists only assign him a reign of five years (709–705). For the convenience of the user of this volume, it has been thought useful to present translations of the relevant passages here. In this section, the entries immediately preceding and following those of the king whose inscriptions are edited in this volume are given when they are preserved.

1. *Babylonian King List A*
(CT 36 pls. 24–25; Grayson, RLA 6/1–2 [1980] pp. 90–96 §3.3)

iv 9)	5 (years)	Ulūlāyu (Shalmaneser V), Dynasty of Baltil (Aššur)
iv 10)	12 (years)	Marduk-apla-iddina (II), Dynasty of the Sealand
iv 11)	5 (years)	Sargon (II)
iv 12)	2 (years)	Sennacherib, Ḫabigal (Ḫanigalbat) Dynasty[156]

2. *Ptolemaic Canon*
(Wachsmuth, Alten Geschichte p. 305; Grayson, RLA 6/1–2 [1980] p. 101 §3.8)

Ἰλουλαίου	ε	Iloulaios (Ulūlāyu) (Shalmaneser V)	5 (years)
Μαρδοκεμπάδου	ιβ	Mardokempados (Marduk-apla-iddina II)	12 (years)
Ἀρκεανοῦ	ε	Arkeanos (Sargon II)[157]	5 (years)
ἀβασίλευτα	β	Kingless[158]	2 (years)

Eponym Dates

In Assyria, each year was named after a high official, called a *limmu* or *līmu*, and lists of these officials (eponyms) were compiled by the Assyrian scribes. The following list of the eponym officials for the reign of Sargon is based upon Millard, SAAS 2, especially pp. 46–48 and 59–60. Dated inscriptions that are included in the present volume are also noted below. A number of inscriptions whose dates may possibly be determined with some degree of confidence (e.g., instances with a clear *terminus post quem* for the inscription) are given in bold. Line rulings are found before the eponym for 722 and after the eponyms for 720, 706, and 705 in one or more exemplars of the eponym lists.[159]

Year	*Regnal Year in Assyria*	*Regnal Year in Babylonia*	*Eponym*	*Dated Texts*
722	Accession year		Ninurta-ilāya, (governor of Naṣībīna)	
721	1		Nabû-tāriṣ	

[156] As noted in Grayson and Novotny, RINAP 3/1 p. 23 n. 1, see Brinkman in Studies Oppenheim pp. 35–37 and Frame, RIMB 2 pp. 90–91 for an explanation of BALA *ḫa-bi-gal* (iv 12). M. Valério (Journal of Language Relationship 6 [2011] pp. 173–183) has argued that the Semitic name of Mitanni (Ḫanigalbat) should be read as Ḫani-Rabbat, a West-Semitic (Amorite) name meaning "Great Ḫani." If this understanding of the name is correct, then one should read BALA *ḫa-bi-gal* as BALA *ḫa-bi*-GAL "Habi-Rabbat dynasty." As pointed out by G. Frame (RIMB 2 pp. 90–91), it is unclear why some Assyrian kings are given dynastic affiliation (Sennacherib and Aššur-nādin-šumi to the Ḫabigal dynasty, and Shalmaneser V to the Baltil dynasty) while others are not (Tiglath-pileser III, Sargon II, and Esarhaddon), unless we are to assume that only changes in dynasty were mentioned and thus Sargon II was of the same dynasty as his predecessor Shalmaneser V, the Baltil dynasty. It is also curious that King List A describes Marduk-apla-iddina II during his first regnal period (721–710) as being from the Sealand dynasty (KUR *tam*-<*tim*>), but as a soldier of Ḫabi (presumably for Ḫabigal) during his second regnal period (703). N. May (BiOr 74 [2017] p. 516) suggests that "[i]t seems possible that King List A considered every collateral Assyrian royal branch that came to the throne as a new dynasty. Thus, the collateral branch of Sargon is in King List A referred to as the 'Dynasty of Habi-GAL' and that of Tiglath-pileser as the 'Dynasty of Assur.'" See also Fales in Studies Lanfranchi p. 205 for the idea that BALA *ḫa-bi*-GAL refers to Sargon as well as Sennacherib. For the suggestion that Baltil and Ḫabigal may allude to the birth places of the respective king's mother and not his father, see E. Frahm in Sennacherib at the Gates of Jerusalem pp. 180–181. Frahm also raises the possibility that the reference to the dynasty of Ḫabigal for Sennacherib might be that "Sargon, Sennacherib's father, held a high military office in the west before he became king of Assyria, a position similar to that of the Middle Assyrian 'King of Ḫanigalbat'" (ibid. p. 181).

[157] Sargon II was sometimes called Sargon *arkû*, "the later Sargon" (see above) and Arkeanos may be a late reflection of *arkû* instead of Sargon's actual name (see, for example, CAD A/2 p. 286).

[158] Sennacherib is not mentioned by name in the Ptolemaic Canon and the periods when he ruled it directly at the beginning and end of his reign were recorded as being "kingless."

[159] See Ungnad, RLA 2/5 (1938) pp. 415–416 for texts with double dates, giving the equivalencies between some of the eponym years and regnal years, including some giving the equivalencies between Sargon's Assyrian regnal years and his Babylonian ones; note also Millard, SAAS 2 pp. 70–71.

Year	*Regnal Year in Assyria*	*Regnal Year in Babylonia*	*Eponym*	*Dated Texts*
720	2		Aššur-nirka-da''in	**89, 106**[?]
719	3		Sargon, king of Assyria	
718	4		Zēru-ibni,[160] governor of Raṣappa	
717	5		Ṭāb-šar-Aššur, treasurer (*masennu*)	**73**
716	6		Ṭāb-ṣil-Ešarra, governor of the Inner City (Aššur)	**117**
715	7		Taklāk-ana-bēli, governor of Naṣībīna	
714	8		Ištar-dūrī, governor of Arrapḫa	65
713	9		Aššur-bāni, governor of Kalḫu	**43**
712	10		Šarru-ēmuranni, governor of Zamua[161]	
711	11		Ninurta-ālik-pāni, governor of Si'me	**76, 82**[162]
710	12	Accession year	Šamaš-bēlu-uṣur, governor of Arzuḫina[163]	
709	13	1	Mannu-kī-Aššur-lē'i, governor of Tillê	
708	14	2	Šamaš-upaḫḫir, governor of Ḫabruri	**105**[164]
707	15	3	Ša-Aššur-dubbu, governor of Tušḫan	**13, 84, 103, 111**
706	16	4	Mutakkil-Aššur, governor of Guzāna	**2,**[165] **7–9, 12, 15, 74,**[166] **116**
705	17	5	Nasḫur-Bēl, governor of Amedi[167]	67

Chronicles

The Assyrian Eponym Chronicle and two recensions of one Mesopotamian chronicle provide useful information both on events of the reign of Sargon II and on the order of those events. The standard edition of the Assyrian Eponym Chronicle is that of A.R. Millard (Millard, SAAS 2) and the one of Mesopotamian chronicles is that of A.K. Grayson (Grayson, Chronicles), but note also the recent editions by J.-J. Glassner (Glassner, Chronicles) and the on-going online work by I. Finkel and R.J. van der Spek (see https://www.livius.org/sources/about/mesopotamian-chronicles/ [2020]). For the convenience of the user of this volume, it has been thought useful to present translations of the relevant passages here; these translations are adapted from the aforementioned works.

1. *The Eponym Chronicle*
   (Millard, SAAS 2, in particular pp. 46–48 and 59–60; Glassner, Chronicles pp. 164–177 no. 9, especially pp. 174–175; Weissert, CRRA 38 pp. 273–282, especially pp. 279–280; and Finkel and Reade, Orientalia NS 67 [1998] p. 252)

[In the eponymy of Ninurta-ilāya ...] (722):[168] [...]

[160] One copy of the eponym list (exemplar A5) has Aššur-mātu-*upaḫḫir* (^{m}*aš-šur*-KUR-*ú*[?]-*paḫ*[?]-*ḫir*[?]; see Millard, SAAS 2 p. 46) or Aššur-mātka-tēra (^{m}*aš-šur*-KUR-⸢*ka*⸣-GUR!!-⸢*ra*⸣; see Finkel and Reade, Orientalia NS 67 [1998] p. 252) instead of Zēru-ibni. I. Finkel and J.E. Reade (ibid.) suggest that he may have been field marshal (*turtānu*) and that having died or been removed from office, he was replaced by Zēru-ibni as eponym.

[161] He is at times also given the title governor of the land of the Lullumu; see Millard, SAAS 2 p. 120.

[162] Also, text nos. 63 and 102 if they prove to be duplicates of the Nineveh Prism (text no. 82).

[163] Šamaš-bēlu-uṣur was transferred to the governorship of Dēr possibly sometime in 710 or shortly thereafter (see Baker, PNA 3/2 p. 1193 sub Šamaš-bēlu-uṣur 4).

[164] Fuchs (Khorsabad p. 387) tentatively assigns this text to Sargon's fifteenth regnal year (707).

[165] Likely also the other versions of the Khorsabad Annals (text nos. 1 and 3–6).

[166] Perhaps also text no. 83 if it proves to be a duplicate of text no. 74.

[167] Or Nasḫir-Bēl; see Streck, PNA 2/2 p. 932. He is at times also given the title governor of the city Sinabu (e.g., text no. 67 line 9; see also Millard, SAAS 2 p. 109).

[168] Possibly "[In the eponymy of Ninurta-ilāya, field marsh]al"; see Finkel and Reade, Orientalia NS 67 (1998) p. 252 for a possible reading [... *tur*]-⸢*tan*⸣.

[In the eponymy of Nabû-tāriṣ ...] (721):	[...][169]
[In the eponymy of Aššur-nirka-da''in ...] (720):	[...] ...[170]
[In the eponymy of Sargon ...] (719):	[... ent]ered.[171]
[In the eponymy of Zēru-ibni ...] (718):	[Against the land Ta]bal.
[In the eponymy of Ṭāb-šar-Aššur ...] (717):	[The city Dūr-Šarru]kīn was founded.
[In the eponymy of Ṭāb-ṣil-Ešarra ...] (716):	[Against the ci]ty of the Manneans.
[In the eponymy of Taklāk-ana-bēli ...] (715):	[...] provincial governors were appointed.
[In the eponymy of Ištar-dūrī ...] (714):	[Against the land Ur]arṭu, the city Muṣaṣir, (and the god) Ḫaldi.
[In the eponymy Aššur-bāni ...] (713):	[... the no]bles in Ellipi; [*the god/goddess ...*] entered (his/her) new [tem]ple; [again]st the city Muṣaṣir.
[In the eponymy of Šamaš-ēmuranni ...] (712):	(The king stayed) in the land (Assyria).
[In the eponymy of Ninurta-ālik-pāni ...] (711):	Against the city Marqasa.
[In the eponymy of Šamaš-bēlu-uṣur ...] (710):	Against Bīt-zēri; the king stayed in Kish.
[In the eponymy of Mannu-kī-Aššur-lē'i, governor of the city Till]ê (709):	Sargon (II) took the hands of the god Bēl.
In the eponymy of [Šamaš-u]pa[ḫḫir, governor of the city Ḫabru]ri (708):	The city Kummuḫu was captured; a provincial governor was appointed. Variant: The nobles ... [(...)] against the city Kummuḫu [(...)].
In the eponymy of Ša-Aššur-dubbu, governor of the city Tušḫan (707):	The king returned fr[om Ba]bylon; the (chief) vizier (*sukkallu*) (and) the nobles carried off the booty of Dūr-Yakīn; the city Dūr-Yakīn was destroyed; on the twenty-second day of Tašrītu (VII) the gods of the city Dūr-Šarrukīn entered their temples.
In the eponymy of Mutakkil-Aššur, governor of the city Guzāna (706):	The king (stayed) in the land (Assyria); the nobles (were) in Karalla; on the sixth day of Ayyāru (II), the city Dūr-Šarrukīn was inaugurated; [...] received.

In the eponymy of Nasḫur-Bēl, governor of the city Amedi (705):	The ki[ng ... *to the land Tabal*] against Gurdî, the Kulummian ... [(...)]; the king was killed; the camp of the king of Assyria [*was*] *sei*[*zed* ...]; Sennacherib [*ascended the throne*] on the twelfth day of the month Abu (V).[172]

2. *Chronicle Concerning the Period from Nabû-nāṣir to Šamaš-šuma-ukīn*
(Grayson, Chronicles pp. 69–87 no. 1; Glassner, Chronicles pp. 193–203 no. 16 and pp. 202–207 no. 17; CT 34 pls. 43–50; note also Brinkman in Studies Moran pp. 73–104, especially p. 101 for recension B; and Weissert, CRRA 38 pp. 273–282, especially p. 282)[173]

(i) Recension A (BM 92502 [84-2-11,356]) (CT 34 pls. 46–50)
i 29–32) The fifth year (722): Shalmaneser (V) died in the month Ṭebētu (X). Shalmaneser (V) ruled Akkad

[169] H. Tadmor (JCS 12 [1958] p. 85) suggests restoring "[To the land Ḫatt]i" ([... *ana* KUR *Ḫat*]-⌈*ti*⌉) for this line (see Millard, SAAS 2 p. 46 version B4), but he assumed that both this line and the following one were for 720.

[170] H. Tadmor (JCS 12 [1958] p. 85, following Forrer, MVAG 20/3 [1915] p. 17) suggests restoring "[The foundations of the temple of the god(dess) DN of the city GN were la]id" ([*uššū ša bīt* ^{d}X *ša* URU X Y *kar*]-*ru*); cf. the entry for 788 (Millard, SAAS 2 p. 36).

[171] H. Tadmor (JCS 12 [1958] p. 85, following Forrer, MVAG 20/3 [1915] p. 17) suggests restoring "[The god(dess) en]tered [(his/her) new temple]" ([^{d}Y *a-na bīte ešše e*]-*ta-rab*); cf. the entry for 787 (Millard, SAAS 2 pp. 36–37).

[172] See Weissert, CRRA 38 pp. 279–280 and Frahm, JCS 51 (1999) pp. 75 and 83–84.

[173] J.A. Brinkman (Studies Moran pp. 73–104) prefers to treat this chronographic text as made up of three separate recensions rather than three duplicates of one text, as was done by A.K. Grayson. J-J. Glassner (Chronicles pp. 193–203 no. 16 and pp. 202–207 no. 17) treats this text as having two separate recensions, taking BM 75977 (AH 83-1-18,1339) with recension A. See also Weissert, CRRA 38 p. 273 n. 1. BM 75977 does not preserve any part of the relevant section and so it not taken into consideration here.

and Assyria for five years. On the twelfth day of the month Ṭebētu, Sargon (II) ascended the throne in Assyria. In the month Nisannu (I), Marduk-apla-iddina (II) (Merodach-baladan) ascended the throne in Babylon.

i 33–37) The second year of Marduk-apla-iddina (II) (720): Ummanigaš (Ḫumban-nikaš I), king of Elam, did battle against Sargon (II), king of Assyria, in the district of Dēr and brought about an Assyrian retreat; he inflicted a major defeat upon them. Marduk-apla-iddina (II) and his army, who had gone to aid the king of Elam, did not arrive (in time for) the battle (and so) he (Marduk-apla-iddina) withdrew.

i 38–42) The fifth year of Marduk-apla-iddina (II) (717): Ummanigaš, king of Elam, died. [For twenty-six ye]ars Ummanigaš ruled Elam. [Ištar-ḫu]ndu (Šutruk-Naḫḫunte II), his sister's son, ascended the throne in Elam. [From the accession year] of Marduk-apla-iddina (II) until the tenth year, [Assyria/Sargon] was hostile [to]ward [Marduk-apla-id]dina.

i 43–44) [The tenth year (712): Marduk-apla-idd]ina (II) [ravaged *Bīt-...*] ... [(and) plunder]ed [i]t.

ii 1–5) The [twelfth] year [of Marduk-apla-iddina (II) (710): Sargon (II) came down to the land Akkad and did] battl[e against Marduk-apla-iddina (II)]. Mard[uk-apla-iddina (II) then retreated before him (and) fled to Elam. Marduk-apla-iddina (II) ruled Babylon for] twelve y[ears]. Sargo[n (II) ascended the throne in Babylon].

(The following lines are either not preserved or too poorly preserved to allow translation. When the text is again legible, it is dealing with the reign of Sennacherib.)

(ii) Recension B (BM 75976 [AH 83-1-18,1338]) (CT 34 pls. 44–45)

(Lacuna)

ii 1′–2′) rul[ed Elam. Ištar-ḫundu (Šutruk-Naḫḫunte II), his] sist[er's] son, [ascended the throne in Elam].

ii 3′–6′) The sixth year (716): Ass[yria ...]. From the accession ye[ar of Marduk-apla-iddina (II)] until the tenth year, [Assyria/Sargon was hostile] toward Mar[duk-apla-iddina].

ii 7′–8′) The tenth year (712): Marduk-apla-iddina (II) ravaged *Bīt-...* (and) plu[nd]ered it.

ii 9′–14′) The *twelfth* year of Marduk-apla-iddina (II) (710): Sargo[n] (II) came down [*to the land Akkad*] and did battle against [Marduk-apla]-iddina (II). Marduk-apla-iddina (II) then [retreated] before [him] (and) fled to Elam. For twelve years [Marduk-apla-*idd*]*ina* (II) rul[ed] Babylon. Sargon (II) ascended the throne in Babylon.

ii 15′–16′) The thirteenth year (709): Sargon (II) to[ok] the hand of Bēl. He (also) captu[red] Dūr-Yakīn.

ii 17′) The fourteenth year (708): The king (stayed) in [the land (Babylonia)].

ii 18′–19′) The fifteenth [yea]r (707): On the twenty-second day of the month Tašrītu (VII), the gods of the Se[a]land returned [*to*] their [*shr*]*ines*. There was plague in Assyria.

ii 20′-21′) [The *seventeenth* year (705): Sarg]on (II) [*marched*] *to* the land Tabal [...] ... [...].

(Lacuna)

1–8

On the stone slabs lining the walls of several rooms and at least one corridor in the inner part the palace of Sargon II at Dūr-Šarrukīn (Khorsabad) were incised versions of the king's Annals (text nos. 1–6) and two different display (or summary) inscriptions (text nos. 7–8), as well as sculpted reliefs depicting mostly military events, but also hunting, feasting, and the bringing of tribute. The Annals come from Rooms II, V, XIII, XIV, the throne room (=Court VII), and an unknown room (text nos. 1–6 respectively). Copies of Sargon's main Display Inscription were found in Rooms I, IV, VII, VIII, and X (the last actually a corridor leading from Court VIII to the northeastern terrace). Room XIV unusually had both a version of the Annals (text no. 4) and a display inscription (text no. 8) that was about half as long as the main Display Inscription. (For a plan of the palace indicating the various rooms, see Figure 4, although note that the room numbers are given as Arabic numerals.)

No version of the Annals is fully preserved, but the best-preserved versions are those from Rooms II and V (text nos. 1 and 2 respectively). Parts of the beginning of the Annals are preserved only in Room II and parts of the end only in Room V. Events are assigned from Sargon's accession year (722) through to his thirteenth regnal year (709). Following an account of Sargon's reconquest of Babylonia in his twelfth and thirteenth regnal years (710–709), the version of the Annals in Room V recounts events in Que (Cilicia) and Musku (Phrygia), Tyre and Yadnana (Cyprus), Kummuḫu (Commagene) and Melid, and Ellipi and Marubištu; the events in Kummuḫu are likely to be associated with events recorded in the Assyrian Eponym Chronicle for 708. The inscription in Room V then describes the building of the city Dūr-Šarrukīn and a festival that the king held when he took up residence there (text no. 2 lines 467b–494). This should indicate that the text was composed no earlier than 706, since the city's inaugration took place in Ayyāru (II) of 706 according to the Assyrian Eponym Chronicle. Both display inscriptions refer to the festival held after the king took up residence in Dūr-Šarrukīn (text no. 7 lines 177b–186a and text no. 8 lines 59b–69a), indicating that they were also composed after that event, unless they were all recording an event that was planned, but that had not yet taken place.

1

The version of Sargon's Annals in Room II, a large room measuring 35.5×9 m in size, probably extended over at least thirty-seven wall slabs — thirty-five in the room itself and two in Entrance H. P.E. Botta prepared copies of the inscriptions on twenty-eight of these slabs, twenty-six from the room itself and the two in Entrance H. It is likely that the end of the inscription continued onto two or possibly four slabs in Entrance C, although we might not have expected the text to end in a doorway rather than on a slab within the room itself (see below). As far as one can tell, each slab appears to have had thirteen lines, for a total of at least four hundred and eighty-one lines and a maximum of five hundred and thirty-three lines. Regrettably, not one single original sign of this inscription is known to be preserved today, although some parts may remain in situ at Khorsabad. In the edition of this text and the other texts where the inscription requires more than one stone wall slab, the slabs are given consecutive "section" numbers in order to facilitate use of the edtions.

This is the only version of the Annals for which the beginning is preserved, albeit in a fragmentary state. As currently known, the text breaks off shortly after the beginning of the description of events in Sargon's second regnal year (720; lines 1–26) and, after a gap of twenty-six lines (sections 3–4 = lines 27–52), recommences a few lines before the end of the account for that year (lines 53–57). Following accounts of the third through tenth regnal years (719–712; lines 58–234a), the text breaks off again at the very beginning of the eleventh regnal year (711; line 234b), and, after a gap of thirteen lines (section 19 = lines 235–247), recommences within the account of that same year (lines 248–261a). The account of the twelfth year (710) is particularly lengthy (lines 262b–299 and 313–390) although there is a gap of thirteen lines within it (section 24 = lines 300–312) and the end of the account and beginning of the account of the thirteenth year (709) are also missing (section 31 = lines 391–403). After twenty-six lines (two slabs) dealing with year thirteen (709; lines 404–416), the text breaks off again, still within the account of that regnal year, for a gap of twenty-six lines (sections 33–34 = lines 417–442). When the text recommences, it is still dealing with the thirteenth regnal year, or more accurately Upēri of Dilmun who, having heard of Sargon's victories, sent a gift to the Assyrian king (lines 443–444a). It then proceeds to describe events involving Mitâ of Musku, Silṭa of Tyre, and finally Mutallu of Kummuḫu, ending just after beginning the passage about Mutallu (lines 444b–468). The account about Mutallu of Kummuḫu is probably to be dated to Sargon's fourteenth regnal year (708) in view of the mention of the capture of the city Kummuḫu in the Assyrian Eponym Chronicle's account for that year. The inscription would presumably have continued onto slab II,1 (section 37) and possibly also onto slabs in Entrance C, none of which were copied by Botta. The lines are to be associated with Winckler, Sar. Annals lines 1–208, 214–261, 266–274, 280–284, 290–314, 319–340, and 370–389, and with Fuchs, Khorsabad Annals lines 1–26, 53–234, 240–279n, 283–286c, 288–291, 297–301, 307–321e, 331–351, and 384–399. (Note that A. Fuchs' line numbering is the same as that used for this inscription for lines 1–234, after which it diverges.) Since the scheme used for numbering the lines in this room is the same as that used by A.G. Lie (Sar.), the line numbers here are the same as those used in his edition (although see the commentary below for differences with regard to lines 1–13); Lie used separate line numbers for the individual sections not preserved in Room II.

F.H. Weissbach (ZDMG 72 [1918] pp. 171–172) originally thought that the inscription was also found on two slabs in Entrance G, two slabs in Entrance B, and perhaps two or four slabs in Entrance C, but according to F. Thureau-Dangin (RA 24 [1927] p. 75 n. 4), he later abandoned this view. J.E. Reade (JNES 35 [1976] p. 96) has noted that Botta stated that the slabs in Entrances B and C were inscribed and that E. Flandin drew line delineations on his depictions of the slabs in Entrance G. It is assumed here that any inscription in Entrance B and Entrance G was different to that in Room II. It is thought, however, that Entrance C likely did have part of the inscription (the very end of the text).

For a plan of the room, with the slabs numbered, and for sketch drawings of the slabs, see Figure 5; Botta, Monument de Ninive 1 pls. 51–52; and Albenda, Palace of Sargon pls. 109–110. Drawings of the reliefs found in this room are given in Botta, Monument de Ninive 1 on pls. 53–71, and on pls. 76–77 for Entrance H_1 and H_2. With regard to the reliefs in the room, which are thought to depict Sargon's campaign to the east in his sixth regnal year (716), see Reade, JNES 35 (1976) pp. 96 and 102–104; and Reade, Bagh. Mitt. 10 (1979) pp. 78–81.

CATALOGUE

Section	Ex.	Source	Provenance	Botta, MdN	Fuchs, Khorsabad line	Lines Preserved	cpn
1	Bt	Botta, Monument de Ninive 4 pl. 79(c) top	Khorsabad, Palace, Room II, slab 2	1 pl. 53	1–13	1–13	n
	JA	Botta, JA 4/2 (1843) pl. XVIII					n
	IdF	Institut de France sheet 313					n
2	Bt	Botta, Monument de Ninive 4 pl. 70c	Khorsabad, Palace, Room II, slab 3	1 pl. 54	14–26	14–26	n
	Wi	Winckler, Sar. 2 pl. 1 no. 2c					n
	Sq	Louvre squeeze					p
	JA	Botta, JA 4/3 (1844) pl. XXIII					n
	IdF	Institut de France sheet 322					n
[3]	—	—	[Khorsabad, Palace, Room II, slab 4]	—	[27–39]	[27–39]	—
[4]	—	—	[Khorsabad, Palace, Room II, slab 5]	1 pl. 55	[40–52]	[40–52]	—
5	Bt	Botta, Monument de Ninive 4 pl. 71c	Khorsabad, Palace, Room II, slab 6	1 pl. 55	53–65	53–65	n
	Wi	Winckler, Sar. 2 pl. 2 no. 3c					n
	Sq	Louvre squeeze					p
	JA	Botta, JA 4/3 (1844) pl. XXV					n
	IdF	Institut de France sheet 321					n
	BM	BM ADD. Ms. 15441					c
6	Bt	Botta, Monument de Ninive 4 pl. 72c	Khorsabad, Palace, Room II, slab 7	1 pl. 55	66–78	66–78	n
	Wi	Winckler, Sar. 2 pl. 3 no. 4c					n
	Sq	Louvre squeeze					p
	JA	Botta, JA 4/3 (1844) pl. XXVI					n
	IdF	Institut de France sheet 329					n
7	Bt	Botta, Monument de Ninive 4 pl. 73c	Khorsabad, Palace, Room II, slab 8	1 pl. 56	79–91	79–91	n
	JA	Botta, JA 4/3 (1844) pl. XXXIII					n
	IdF	Institut de France sheet 317					n
8	Bt	Botta, Monument de Ninive 4 pl. 74c	Khorsabad, Palace, Room II, slab 9	1 pl. 57	92–104	92–104	n
	Wi	Winckler, Sar. 2 pl. 3 no. 6c					n
	Sq	Louvre squeeze					p
	JA	Botta, JA 4/3 (1844) pl. XXXIV					n
	IdF	Institut de France sheet 319					n

	T-D	Thureau-Dangin, RA 24 p. 76					n
9	Bt	Botta, Monument de Ninive 4 pl. 74$^{bis\ c}$	Khorsabad, Palace, Room II, slab 10	1 pl. 58	105–117	105–117	n
	Wi	Winckler, Sar. 2 pl. 4 no. 7^{c}					n
	Sq	Louvre squeeze					p
	T-D	Thureau-Dangin, RA 24 p. 76					n
10	Bt	Botta, Monument de Ninive 4 pl. 75^{c}	Khorsabad, Palace, Room II, slab 11	1 pl. 59	118–130	118–130	n
	Wi	Winckler, Sar. 2 pl. 4 no. 8^{c}					n
	Sq	Louvre squeeze					p
	JA	Botta, JA 4/5 (1845) pl. LV					n
	Idf	Institut de France sheet 323					n
	T-D	Thureau-Dangin, RA 24 p. 76					n
11	Bt	Botta, Monument de Ninive 4 pl. 76^{c}	Khorsabad, Palace, Room II, slab 12	1 pl. 59bis	131–143	131–143	n
	JA	Botta, JA 4/4 (1844) pl. XLV					n
	IdF	Institut de France sheet 333					n
12	Bt	Botta, Monument de Ninive 4 pl. 77^{c}	Khorsabad, Palace, Room II, slab 13	1 pl. 60	144–156	144–156	n
	Wi	Winckler, Sar. 2 pl. 5 no. 10^{c}					n
	Sq	Louvre squeeze					p
	Je	Jean in T-D, RA 24 p. 79					n
13	Bt	Botta, Monument de Ninive 4 pl. 78^{c}	Khorsabad, Palace, Room II, slab 14	1 pl. 61	157–169	157–169	n
	Wi	Winckler, Sar. 2 pl. 6 no. 11^{c}					n
	Sq	Louvre squeeze					c
	Je	Jean in T-D, RA 24 p. 80					n
14	Bt	Botta, Monument de Ninive 4 pl. 79^{c} bottom	Khorsabad, Palace, Room II, slab 15	1 pl. 62	170–182	170–182	n
	Wi	Winckler, Sar. 2 pl. 6 no. 12^{c}					n
	Sq	Louvre squeeze					p
15	Bt	Botta, Monument de Ninive 4 pl. 80^{c}	Khorsabad, Palace, Room II, slab 16	1 pl. 63	183–195	183–195	n
	Wi	Winckler, Sar. 2 pl. 7 no. 13c					n
	Sq	Louvre squeeze					p
	T-D	Thureau-Dangin, RA 24 p. 76					n
16	Bt	Botta, Monument de Ninive 4 pl. 81^{c}	Khorsabad, Palace, Room II, slab 17	1 pl. 64	196–208	196–208	n
	Wi	Winckler, Sar. 2 pl. 7 no. 14^{c}					n
	Sq	Louvre squeeze					p
	T-D	Thureau-Dangin, RA 24 pp. 76–77					n
17	Bt	Botta, Monument de Ninive 4 pl. 82^{c}	Khorsabad, Palace, Room II, slab 18	1 pl. 65	209–221	209–221	n
	Wi	Winckler, Sar. 2 pl. 8 no. 15^{c}					n
	Sq	Louvre squeeze					p
	T-D	Thureau-Dangin, RA 24 p. 77					n
18	Bt	Botta, Monument de Ninive 4 pl. 83^{c}	Khorsabad, Palace, Room II, slab 19	1 pl. 66	222–234	222–234	n
	Wi	Winckler, Sar. 2 pl. 8 no. 16^{c}					n

	Sq	Louvre squeeze					p
	T-D	Thureau-Dangin, RA 24 p. 77					n
[19]	—	—	[Khorsabad, Palace, Room II, slab 20]	1 pl. 67	[235–239]	[235–247]	—
20	Bt	Botta, Monument de Ninive 4 pl. 84[c]	Khorsabad, Palace, Room II slab 21	1 pl. 67	240–252	248–260	n
	Wi	Winckler, Sar.2 pl. 9 no. 17[c]					n
	Sq	Louvre squeeze					p
	T-D	Thureau-Dangin, RA 24 p. 77					n
21	Bt	Botta, Monument de Ninive 3 pl. 65[c]	Khorsabad, Palace, Room II, Entrance H_1	1 pl. 76	253–265	261–273	n
	Wi	Winckler, Sar. 2 pl. 14 no. 30[c]					n
	Sq	Louvre squeeze					p
22	Bt	Botta, Monument de Ninive 3 pl. 65[bis c]	Khorsabad, Palace, Room II, Entrance H_2	1 pl. 77	266–279a	274–286	n
	Wi	Winckler, Sar. 2 pl. 15 no. 31[c]					n
	Sq	Louvre squeeze					p
	T-D	Thureau-Dangin, RA 24 p. 78					n
23	Bt	Botta, Monument de Ninive 4 pl. 85[c]	Khorsabad, Palace, Room II, slab 22	1 pls. 68, 68bis	279b–279n	287–299	n
	Wi	Winckler, Sar. 2 pl. 9 no. 18[c]					n
	Sq	Louvre squeeze					c
	T-D	Thureau-Dangin, RA 24 p. 77					n
[24]	—	—	[Khorsabad, Palace, Room II, slab 23]	1 pl. 68	[280–282]	[300–312]	—
25	Bt	Botta, Monument de Ninive 4 pl. 92 top	Khorsabad, Palace, Room II, slab 24	1 pl. 69	283–286	313–325	n
26	Bt	Botta, Monument de Ninive 4 pl. 86[c]	Khorsabad, Palace, Room II, slab 25	—	286–290	326–338	n
	Wi	Winckler, Sar. 2 pl. 10 no. 20[c]					n
	Sq	Louvre squeeze					p
27	Bt	Botta, Monument de Ninive 4 pl. 92 bottom, part[?]	Khorsabad, Palace, Room II, slab 26	—	291–297	339–351	n
28	Bt	Botta, Monument de Ninive 4 pl. 92 bottom, part[?]	Khorsabad, Palace, Room II, slab 27	—	298–306?	352–364	n
29	Bt	Botta, Monument de Ninive 4 pl. 87[c]	Khorsabad, Palace, Room II, slab 28	1 pl. 70	307–316	365–377	n
	Wi	Winckler, Sar. 2 pl. 10 no. 22[c]					n
	Sq	Louvre squeeze					p
	T-D	Thureau-Dangin, RA 24 p. 77					n
30	Bt	Botta, Monument de Ninive 4 pl. 88[c]	Khorsabad, Palace, Room II, slab 29	1 pl. 70	316–321e	378–390	n
	Wi	Winckler, Sar. 2 pl. 11 no. 23[c]					n
	Sq	Louvre squeeze					p
[31]	—	—	[Khorsabad, Palace, Room II, slab 30]	—	[ca. 322–330]	[391–403]	—
32	Bt	Botta, Monument de Ninive 4 pl. 89[c]	Khorsabad, Palace, Room II, slab 31	—	331–351/2	404–416	n
	Wi	Winckler, Sar. 2 pl. 11 no. 24[c]					n
	Sq	Louvre squeeze					p

	T-D	Thureau-Dangin, RA 24 p. 77					n
[33]	—	—	[Khorsabad, Palace, Room II, slab 32]	—	[352/3-?]	[417–429]	—
[34]	—	—	[Khorsabad, Palace, Room II, slab 33]	—	[?-383]	[430–442]	—
35	Bt	Botta, Monument de Ninive 4 pl. 90[c]	Khorsabad, Palace, Room II, slab 34	1 pl. 71	384–392	443–455	n
	Wi	Winckler, Sar. 2 pl. 12 no. 25[c]					n
	Sq	Louvre squeeze					p
	JA	Botta, JA 4/4 (1844) pl. XLVI					n
	IdF	Institut de France sheet 332					n
	T-D	Thureau-Dangin, RA 24 pp. 77–78					n
36	Bt	Botta, Monument de Ninive 4 pl. 91	Khorsabad, Palace, Room II, slab 35	—	392–399	456–468	n
	JA	Botta, JA 4/5 (1845) pl. LIV					n
	IdF	Institut de France sheet 328					n
[37]	—	—	[Khorsabad, Palace, Room II, slab 1]	—	[400-?]	[469–481]	—
[(+)]							

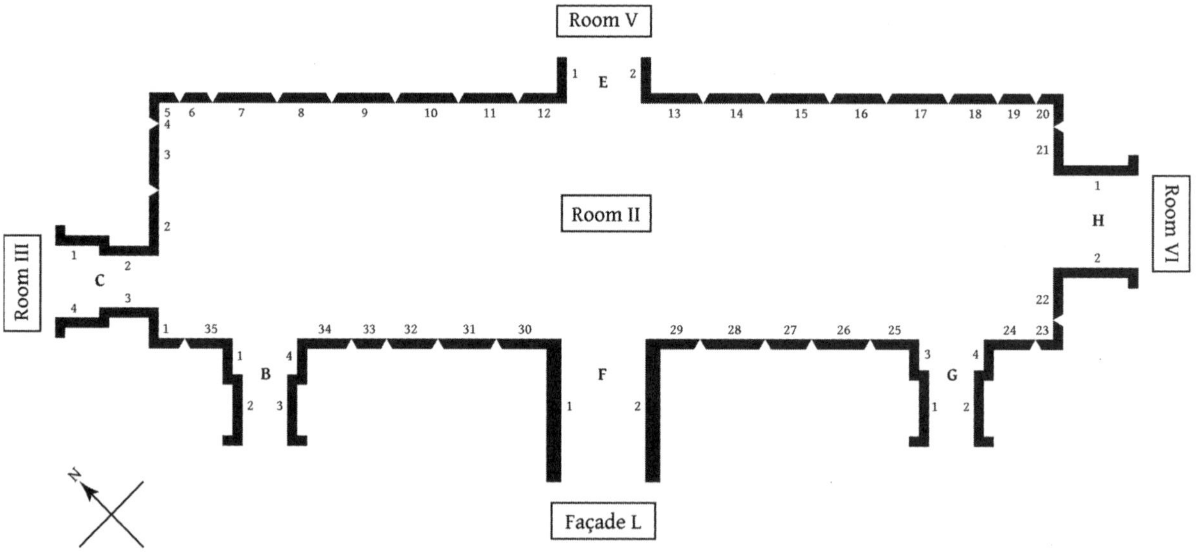

Figure 5. Plan of Room II of the palace at Khorsabad, whose wall slabs had a version of Sargon's Annals (text no. 1). Plan after Botta, Monument de Ninive 1 pl. 51.

COMMENTARY

Before publishing the copies that he had made in the field in Monument de Ninive, P.E. Botta collated most of them from *papier mâché* squeezes that he had made of the originals. These are marked with [c] after the Botta, Monument de Ninive 3–4 plate number in the catalogue; the same is done with the text numbers which Winckler is supposed to have collated from squeezes or originals. Botta did not make copies or squeezes of sections 3–4, 19, 24, 31, 33–34, and 37 (Room II slabs 4–5, 20, 23, 30, 32–33, and 1 respectively), or of any inscribed slabs that may have existed in Entrance C. Although he made copies of the inscriptions on sections 25, 27, and 36 (Room II slabs 24, 26 and 35 respectively), squeezes of these were not made. Squeezes were supposedly made by Botta of sections 1, 7, and 11 (Room II slabs 2, 8, and 12 respectively) and used by him when he prepared the final copies for Monument de Ninive, but these were already not available or extant in the time of H. Winckler. Thus, Winckler's copies of those three sections were totally based on those of Botta and provide no independent information on what was on those slabs. Botta, Monument de Ninive 4 pl. 79[c] has copies of two slabs, sections 1 and 14 (Room II, slabs 2 and 15), and Botta indicates in his table of contents that he collated what was on that plate; however, a squeeze of only the latter piece is preserved today and it is possible that he did not have one of the former piece (slab 2) to check. A new copy of section 13 (II,14) was made in the 1920s by Ch.-F. Jean based upon an examination of the squeeze.

Since the inscription crossed over a large number of slabs and since none of the original inscription is preserved today due to the loss of most of P.E. Botta's and V. Place's finds in the Tigris in 1855, it has been thought necessary to divide up the text by slab (section) in the catalogue, provide information on the sources of information for each separate slab, and create a score edition for the text based on the different sources of information, even though there was only one original text. In the catalogue and in the score, these sources are presented in the following order and with the following notations:

Bt = copy by Botta published in Monument de Ninive.

Wi = copy by Winckler, Sar. 2 (when he states that he collated a squeeze of the original).

Sq = squeeze in the Louvre (examined primarily via photographs, but also via the original squeeze in places).

JA = copy by Botta published in Journal asiatique (1843–1845). Generally these copies are exact duplicates of the ones preserved in the Institut de France (see the next entry), but there are occasional differences.

IdF = copy by Botta made while at Khorsabad, sent to Jules Mohl (secretary of the Société asiatique), and preserved in the Institut de France in the file Botta-Cotta II 2976.

Je = copy by Jean published on pp. 79–80 of Thureau-Dangin, RA 24 (1927) pp. 75–80; these are copies of sections 12 and 13 (slabs 13 and 14 respectively).

T-D = copies and transliterations of selected individual words and passages by Thureu-Dangin in RA 24 (1927) pp. 76–78. For a detailed listing of which lines are mentioned, see the bibliography below.

BM = rubbing in British Museum (only for section 5 [slab 6]).

Botta states that some of the copies made by him at Khorsabad and published in Monument de Ninive had been collated by him from the squeezes and/or originals in the Louvre (including much of this text: Monument de Ninive 3–4 pls. 65–65[bis] and 70–90 = sections 1–2, 5–18, 20–23, 26, 29–30, 32, and 35). Thus, those copies should be improvements upon those published in Journal asiatique and those preserved in the Institut de France, and it has not been thought necessary to include in the scores complete transliterations of the copies in Journal asiatique and the Institut de France, but only to note useful differences from the copies in Monument de Ninive, in particular when one or both of the copies has a correct form of a sign and the copy in Monument de Ninive is abnormal or when one or the other has major traces of a sign omitted in Monument de Ninive.

Section 1 (lines 1–13): As copied by Botta, lines 2–10 of the first section of the inscription (slab II,2) clearly duplicate parts of lines 6–16 of the Khorsabad Cylinder Inscription (text no. 43), and line 1, as far as it is preserved, could duplicate part of the third line of that inscription, but with insufficient room at the beginning of the line to restore what would be expected before that, namely the name of the king and several titles and epithets, even if that passage was a greatly abbreviated version of what was in lines 1–2 of the cylinder inscription. It is most unlikely that the inscription had begun on a previous, unpreserved slab, since slab 2 was located immediately to the left of Door C when entering Room II and the slab to the right of the doorway (Room II, slab 1), would have contained the very end of the inscription. The slabs in this room regularly have thirteen lines of text; however, Botta copied only eleven lines for slab II,2, indicating that nothing of lines 12 and 13 was preserved and that the depiction of a royal parasol protruded up into the inscribed area, taking up parts of what would have been the last four lines (lines 10–13 of the slab); see Figure 6 and Botta, Monument de Ninive 4 pl. 79[c] top and note 1 pl. 53. (Winckler's copy follows Botta's in the arrangement of the lines.) A.T.E. Olmstead assumed that line 1 of Botta's copy was actually the second line of the inscription, thus presumably assuming that nothing was preserved of only the last line of the slab, i.e., Botta's lines 1–11 are actually lines 2–12 of the original thirteen lines. Olmstead then restored his lines 1–2 based on the cylinder inscription lines 1–3, although he added the god Nabû between the gods Aššur and Marduk in line 2 (line 3 of text no. 43). A. Fuchs (Khorsabad p. 19) also considers the problem and suggests that what Botta copied for line 1 was an isolated fragment that he placed wrongly and that it was the first and third lines of the text that were completely unpreserved, i.e., what is on Botta's line 1 was actually on line 2 and Botta's lines 2–11 were actually lines 4–13. However, Fuchs also notes that the parasol intrudes well into the inscription on both Botta, Monument de Ninive 1 pl. 53 and 4 pl. 79c (top), suggesting that Botta's copy might have been accurate, and thus in his edition follows Botta's line arrangement. One should note, however, the drawing of the relief on Monument de Ninive 1 pl. 53 shows the parasol protruding into only two or at most three lines of text (assuming that the line rulings indicated by E. Flandin are correct) and that the parasols on Room II slabs 16 and 34 (sections 15 and 35) protrude into only the bottom two lines of the text, with only the top end of the stick of the parasol going just into the third line from the bottom (on both Botta's copies [ibid. 4 pls. 80 and 90] and squeezes). Flandin's drawings of those reliefs show the parasols protruding the same distance into the inscription as the one on slab 2 (see ibid. 1 pls. 63, 71 and 53 respectively). Botta's initial copy of the text preserved in the Institut de France has just eleven lines, with no indication of any damaged lines either above or below the eleven lines copied (i.e., the lines with no preserved text), and the same is true for the copy published in Journal asiatique (4/2 [1843] pl. 18). Thus, it is possible that in making the typeset copy and knowing that the slabs in this room always had thirteen lines of text he erroneously placed the two missing lines at the end of the text. Since nothing of slab II,2 is preserved today and no squeeze of it was made by Botta, no final conclusion can be made about the matter, although Fuchs' suggestion (one which he did not follow in his edition) that Botta's copies represent parts of lines 2 and 4–13 makes the best sense for the text, fits well with the drawings of the reliefs, and is followed here. Thus, lines 1 and 2–11 in Winckler's, A.G. Lie's, and Fuchs' editions are here lines 2 and 4–13 respectively. It should be noted that in his original handcopy of this slab and in the copy published in JA, there are traces of two or three unidentifiable signs to the right of the first line. Since these traces were not included in the copy published in Monument de Ninive and since it is not clear which line they would come from (presumably either what is considered here as line 2 or line 3) they are not included in the present edition. The author presented a more detailed paper on the first thirteen lines of the Annals from Room II at the 65e Rencontre Assyriologique Internationale in Paris on July 10, 2019 and this will published in the Proceedings volume of that conference.

Sections 3 (lines 27–39) and 4 (lines 40–52): Botta (followed by F.H. Weissbach) has two slabs (II,4–5) in the northwest corner of the room, unlike the other three corners where there is one corner slab; however, he provides no copies for the inscriptions upon these slabs. N. Na'aman (Tel Aviv 34/2 [2007] pp. 165–170) argues that there was likely only one slab there, based partially upon what would have been recorded on those slabs. Thus line 40 would have begun on slab II,6 (section 5) and our lines 53-481 would be 40–468 (i.e., each line number being 13 lines less). His reasoning has merit, although it is not impossible that there were two slabs there, rather than one, with each slab being much narrower than the other slabs in the room. It has been thought best to maintain the traditional slab and line numbering for this area, which is also the same line numbering used by Lie.

Section 5 (lines 53–65): A rubbing of slab II,6 was presented to the British Museum on January 23, 1845 by Rev. G.P. Badger and has the designation ADD. Ms. 15441. This occasionally shows a bit more at the beginning of a line than Botta's copy and indicates that some areas of damage on Botta's copy do not exist.

Section 9 (lines 105–117): With regard to slab II,10, Botta's copy does not include a section at the right side of the slab (lines 107–113) that is visible on the squeeze and that was copied by Winckler.

Section 10 (lines 118–130): The squeeze of slab II,11 only has approximately the first sixty percent of each line; this was also the case when Winckler saw the squeeze and made his copy.

Sections 12 (lines 144–156) and 13 (lines 157–169): The copies of these two slabs (II,13–14) done by Jean (RA 24 [1927] pp. 79–80) are in general given preference in the edition over those of Botta when they are supported by an examination of the squeezes (although at times the current state of a squeeze might suggest the addition of half brackets to indicate a certain level of damage).

Section 20 (lines 248–260): Botta's copy for slab II,21 indicates a damaged area sufficient for several (ca. 4–6) signs immediately before the final sign(s) on a line; however, the squeeze indicates that there is room for far fewer signs per line in the damaged area.

Section 25 (lines 313–325): Botta's copy for slab II,24; (Monument de Ninive 4 pl. 92 top) has parts of nine lines and indicates damage both before and after those lines. Winckler's copy (Sar. 2 pl. 9 no. 19) presents those lines as the last nine lines of the slab and that view is followed here, as it was by Fuchs (see Fuchs, Khorsabad pp. 145–147), although this must remain uncertain.

Sections 27 (lines 339–351) and 28 (lines 352–364: As already noted by Fuchs (Khorsabad pp. 20–21),

Botta's copy for Room II slab 26 (Monument de Ninive 4 pl. 92 bottom = Winckler, Sar. 2 pl. 10 no. 21; section 27), which has parts of twelve lines, presents problems if one attempts to edit it as one passage and in the order that the lines are presented. Botta provides no separate copy for slab 27 (section 28) and Fuchs proposes that the copy for slab 26 represents four fragments from the two slabs. Although there is no proof that this is correct, this suggestio is reasonable and is followed here. The text on Botta's copy is assigned to section 27 lines 339–340 and 350–351 (Botta lines 4′–5′and 2′–3′ respectively) and to section 28 lines 352–355 (Botta lines 8′–12′). Nevertheless, the exact line numbers for the fragment(s) must remain uncertain and parts of three lines copied by Botta have remained unplaced: 1′ ([...] AN [...]), 6′ ([...] A I MUNUS [...]), and 7′ ([...] *x i-na* [...]), although 6′–7′ could conceivably be from lines 341–342. See the on-page notes to lines 339–340 and 350–355.

Section 32 (lines 404–416): The squeeze for slab II,31 is faint and illegible for the most part; many of the legible signs are in the lower righthand section of the squeeze. Thus, only a few signs are noted in the score for the squeeze and it is particularly uncertain whether Winckler's copies can be relied upon or not when they deviate from Botta's copy.

Section 36 (lines 456–468): As already noted by Winckler, Botta's copy of slab II,35 is unreliable, with the right side of the copy indicated a line higher than it should be; Winckler corrected this in his own copy (Sar. 2 pl. 12 no. 26). Fuchs (Khorsabad p. 20) suggests that Botta had found the slab in two pieces and that he put them together wrongly, misaligning the lines. Thus, for example line 459 is made up of Botta's II,35 lines 4a and 3b. In the score, a double dagger (‡) indicates where the line shifts on Botta's copy. (This misalignment is found on Botta's copies in Journal asiatique and in the Institut de France Archives, as well as on the one in Monument de Ninive.)

Section 37 (lines 469–481): It is thought likely that the inscription continued after this unpreserved section (slab II,1) by going into Entrance C and continuing on two (C_3 and C_2) or four (C_3, C_4, C_1, and C_2) slabs there, for an additional 26 or 52 lines which would likely have been similar to text no. 2 lines 443–510. This would mean that the text would have ended within a doorway, rather than within the room itself, which would be most unusual; however, if it did not do so, the inscription would likely either not have had a final building section or only a much abbreviated one compared to that in Room V (text no. 2), since the end of slab II,2 is still dealing with political/military matters.

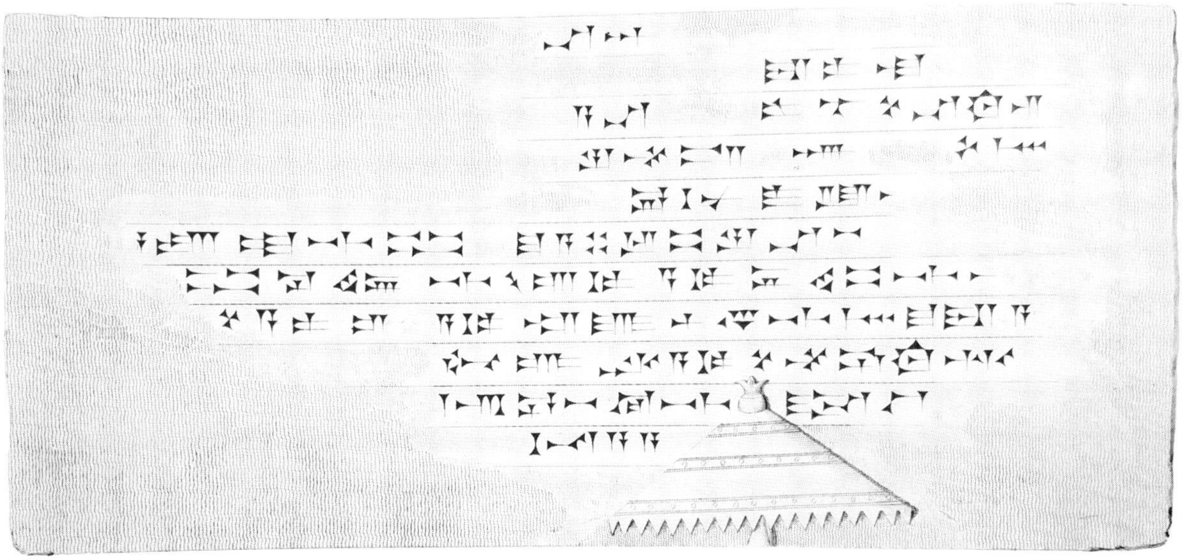

Figure 6. Copy of the inscription on Room II, slab 2, published by P.E. Botta in Monument de Ninive 4 pl. 79^{c} top (text no. 1, section 1).

BIBLIOGRAPHY

1843 Botta, JA 4/2 pl. XVIII (section 1, copy)

1844 Botta, JA 4/3 pls. XXIII, XXV–XXVI and XXXIII–XXXIV (sections 2, 5–8, copy)

1844 Botta, JA 4/4 pls. XLV–XLVI (sections 11, 35, copy)

1845 Botta, JA 4/5 pls. LIV–LV (sections 10 and 36, copy)

1849 Botta, Monument de Ninive 1 pls. 51–71 and 76–77 (drawing of reliefs, provenance); and 3–4 pls. 65, 65bis, and 70–92 (copy)

1870 Oppert in Place, Ninive et l'Assyrie 2 pp. 309–319 (translation, combined with inscriptions in Rooms V, XIII, XIV)

1870 Oppert, Dour-Sarkayan pp. 29–39 (translation, combined with inscriptions in Rooms V, XIII, XIV) (identical to preceding)

1874 Ménant, Annales pp. 158–179 (translation, combined with inscriptions in Rooms I, IV, V, XIII, XIV)

1875 Ménant, Babylone pp. 151–157 (lines 262bff., partial translation, combined with Room V)

1876 Oppert, Records of the Past 7 pp. 21–56 (translation, combined with inscriptions in Rooms V, XIII, XIV)

1883 Schrader, KAT^2 pp. 273–278 (lines 12–17, 21–23, 120–123, edition, study)

1885 Schrader, Cuneiform Inscriptions 1 pp. 265–270 (lines 12–17, 21–23, 120–123, edition, study)

1886 Bezold, Literatur p. 92 §54.10 (study)

1889 Winckler, Sar. 1 pp. VII–IX (study) and 2–79 (edition, combined with inscriptions in Rooms V, XIII, XIV, and an unknown room); and 2 pls. 1–12 and 14–15, nos. 1–26 and 30–31 (copy)

1895 Meissner, Chrestomathie p. 13 (lines 72–78a, 249b–262a, copy, combines with inscriptions in Rooms V and XIII)

1898 King, First Steps pp. 48–51 (lines 249b–262a, copy, edition, combined with inscription in Room V)

1909 Winckler, Textbuch^3 pp. 38–39 (lines 12b–17a and 23b–57, edition)

1911 Sarsowsky, Urkundenbuch p. 30 (lines 12b–17a, 23b–25, 53–57, copy)

1912 Thureau-Dangin, TCL 3 pp. 68–75 (lines 127–165a, edition)

1918 Weissbach, ZDMG 72 pp. 170–172 (study)

1926 Ebeling in Gressmann, ATAT^2 pp. 348–349 (12b–17a, 23b–25, 53–57, translation)

1927 Luckenbill, ARAB 2 pp. 2–25 §§3–51 (translation, combined with inscriptions in Rooms V, XIII)

1927 Thureau-Dangin, RA 24 pp. 75–80 (lines 144–169 [II,13–14], copy [by Jean]; miscellaneous collations [copies and/or transliterations] for lines 95, 103–104, 107, 111, 128, 145, 183, 188–189, 194, 205–206, 211, 232, 252, 279, 291, 293, 297, 372, 379, 411, 413–414, 446–451)

1929 Lie, Sar. (edition, combined at times with inscriptions in Rooms V, XIII, XIV)

1930 Thureau-Dangin, RA 27 pp. 159–60 (lines 15, 84, 94, 99, 150, 198, 199, 366, 405, 467, study)

1930–31 Olmstead, AJSL 47 pp. 259–280 (partial edition, study [as review of Lie, Sar.])

1941 Kalaç, Sumeroloji Araştırmaları pp. 982–987 (partial translation, combined with inscription from Room V)

1958 Tadmor, JCS 12 pp. 33–35 (lines 12b–18a, edition)

1958 Wiseman, DOTT pp. 59 and 61 (lines 12b–18a, 23b–25, 53–57, translation)

1964 Brinkman, Studies Oppenheim p. 44 no. 44.2.20.a (study)

1968 Borger in Galling, Textbuch^2 p. 63 no. 34 (lines 120b–123a, translation)

1969 Oppenheim, ANET^3 pp. 284–286 (lines 12b–17a, 23b–57, 72–76a, 120b–126, 249b–262a, translation)

1976 Saporetti, Studi Ciprioti e Rapporti di Scavo 2 pp. 83 and 85 (lines 457b–467a, translation, study)

1977 Briend and Seux, TPOA nos. 35A and 39A (lines 53–57 and 120b–125a, translation)

1982 Ephʿal, Arabs pp. 37–38 (lines 120–127, study)

1982 Spieckermann, Juda unter Assur p. 331 (lines 331b–332a, edition)

1984 Borger, TUAT 1/4 pp. 378–381 (lines 12b–18a, 23b–25, 53–57, 72–78a, 120b–125a, 249b–262a, translation, combined at times with inscription in Room V)

1986 Renger, CRRA 32 pp. 114–118 (lines 68b–71, 72b–76a, 198b–204a, 204b–216a, transcription, study)

1988 Cogan and Tadmor, II Kings p. 337 no. 6B (lines 120b–125a, translation)

1990 Potts, Arabian Gulf 1 p. 334 nos. 1–2 (lines 443–444a and 454b–456a, translation, combined with inscription in Room V)

1992 Becking, Fall of Assyria p. 37 (lines 13b–17a, edition)

1993 Galter, Studies Dostal p. 33 (lines 123b–125a, edition)

1994 Fuchs, Khorsabad pp. 82–188 and 313–342 no. 2.3 (edition, combined with inscriptions in Rooms V, XIII, XIV, as well as the throne room and an unknown room), and pp. 386 and 396–405 (study)

1996 Mayer, UF 28 p. 470 (lines 117–119a, edition)

1997 Tadmor in Parpola and Whiting, Assyria 1995 p. 333 (lines 262b–273a, translation, combined with Rooms V, XIII)

1998 Na'aman, Orientalia NS 67 pp. 243–244 (lines 456b–467a, edition)

1998 Younger, JBL 117 p. 226 (120b–123a, edition)

2000 Bagg, Assyrische Wasserbauten pp. 159–162 (lines 276–279a, 317–320a, 377b–379a, 406b–407a, edition, combined with Rooms V, XIII)

2000 Lanfranchi, Melammu 1 p. 14 (lines 117b–119a, edition)

2000 Younger, COS 2 pp. 293–294 no. 2.118A (lines 13–18a, 23b–25, 53–57, 72–78a, 120b–123a, 249b–262a, translation, partially combined with Rooms V, XIII, XIV)

2001 Holloway, CRRA 45/1 pp. 247–249 (lines 94b–95a, edition, study)

2001 Na'aman, CRRA 45/1 pp. 359–361 (lines 456b–467a, study, combined with Room V)

2001 Rollinger, Melammu 2 pp. 240 and 246 (lines 117b–119a, translation; lines 249b–262a, translation, combined with Rooms V, XIII)

2002 Holloway, Aššur is King pp. 157–158 n. 251 (94b–95a, edition, study)

2002 Vera Chamaza, Omnipotenz pp. 260–264 nos. 11–13 (lines 262b–273a, 371b–374a, 384b–389, edition, combined at times with Room V)

2002 Younger in Chavalas and Younger, Mesopotamia and the Bible p. 310 (lines 120b–123a, translation)

2006 Yamada, AoF 33 pp. 230–31 (204b–221, partially with Room V, translation)

2007 Kuhrt, Persian Empire p. 25 no. 2.A.2.ii (lines 114b–116, translation) and no. 2.A.2.iv (lines 191b–194a, with Room V, translation)

2008 Cogan, Raging Torrent pp. 93–96 no. 20 (lines 12b–18a, 23b–57, 101a, 120b–125a, 234b, 249b–262a, translation, study, combined at times with Rooms V, XIII)

2010 Barbato, Kaskal 7 p. 178 (lines 442b–443a, translation)

2013 Thompson, Terror of Radiance pp. 134–135, 220, 224, and 227 (lines 2b, 12–17, 20, 22–23, 54, 67–70, 72, 85, 164, partial edition, combined at times with Rooms V, XIV)

2014 Maniori, Campagne di Sargon pp. 36–37 A1, passim (study) and p. 57 fig. 1 (plan of room)
2017 Fales, SAAB 23 p. 235 (lines 117b–119a, translation)
2017 Liverani, Assyria p. 17 and passim (translation of numerous passages, combined at times with Rooms V, XIII, XIV)
2018 Frahm, Last Days pp. 70–71 no. 7 and p. 76 no. 10 (lines 12b–17, 23b–25, edition, study)
2018 Frame in Yamada, SAAS 28 pp. 234–235 figs. 17–18 (section 5, copy [by Botta])
2019 Aster, JAOS 139 pp. 594–602 (line 16, edition, study)
2019 Edmonds in Dušek and Mynářová, Aramaean Borders p. 46 (lines 404b–413a, translation, combined with Room V)
2019 Marchesi, JNES 78 p. 22 (lines 72–76a, edition)
— Frame, CRRA 65 (lines 1–13, copy, edition, study)

TEXT

1) [^{m}LUGAL-GI.NA *šá-ak-nu* ^{d}EN.LÍL NU.ÈŠ *ba-ʾi-it* ^{d}*a-šur ni-šit* IGI.II ^{d}*a-nim ù* ^{d}*da-gan* LUGAL GAL-*ú* LUGAL *dan-nu* LUGAL KIŠ LUGAL KUR *aš-šur*.KI LUGAL *kib-rat ar-ba-ʾi*]

2) [*mi-gir* DINGIR.MEŠ GAL.MEŠ RE.É.UM *ke-e-nu ša* ^{d}*a-šur* ^{d}AMAR.UTU LUGAL-*ut la šá*]-*na-an* [*ú-šat-li-mu-šu-ma zi-kir* MU-*šu ú-še-(eṣ)-ṣu-ú a-na re-še-e-te*]

3) [*šá-kin šu-ba-re-e* ZIMBIR.KI NIBRU.KI KÁ.DINGIR.RA.KI *ḫa-a-tin en-šu-te-šú-nu mu-šal-li-mu ḫi-bil-ti-šu-un ka-ṣir ki-din-nu-tu bal-til*.KI *ba-ṭi-il-tu mu-šá-áš-ši-ik tup-šik-ki* BÀD.AN.KI]

4) [*mu-šap-ši-ḫu* UN.MEŠ-*šu-un le-ʾi* DÙ *mal-ki ša* UGU URU.*ḫar-ra-na* AN].DÙL†-*la*-[*šu it-ru-ṣu-ma ki-i ṣa-ab*]

5) [^{d}*a-nim u* ^{d}*da-gan iš-ṭu-ru za-kut-su zi-ka-ru dan-nu ḫa-lip na-mur-ra-ti ša*] *a-na* ⸢*šum*⸣-*qut na-ki*-⸢*ri*⸣ [*šu-ut-bu-ú* GIŠ.TUKUL.MEŠ-*šu*]

6) [LUGAL *ša ul-tu* u_4-*um be-lu-ti-šu mal-ku gaba-ra-a-šu la ib-šu-ma i-na qab-li ù ta-ḫa-zi la e-mu*]-*ru mu-né*†-⸢*eḫ*⸣-[*ḫu*] KUR.MEŠ [DÙ-*ši-na ki-ma ḫaṣ-bat-ti ú-daq-qi-qu-ma*]

7) [*ḫa-am-ma-mi ša ar-ba-ʾi id-du-ú ṣer-re-e-tu ḫur-šá-a-ni bé-ru-ú-ti ša né*]-*reb-šú-nu áš-ṭu* ⸢*la*⸣-[*a mi-na ip-tu-ma e-mu-ru du-ru-ug-šu-un*]

1–2a) [Sargon (II), appointee of the god Enlil, nešakku-priest (and) desired object of the god Aššur, chosen of the gods Anu and Dagān, great king, strong king, king of the world, king of Assyria, king of the four quarters (of the world), favorite of the great gods];

2b) [just shepherd, (one) to whom the gods Aššur (and) Marduk granted a reign without eq]ual [and whose reputation (these gods) exalt/exalted to the heights];

3–5a) [who (re)-established the šubarrû-privileges of (the cities) Sippar, Nippur, (and) Babylon, protects the weak among them (lit.: "their weak ones"), (and) made restitution for the wrongful damage suffered by them; who (re)-established the privileged status of (the city) Baltil (Aššur) that had lapsed, who abolished corvée duty for the city Dēr (and) gave relief to their people; (most) capable of all rulers, who extended his prote]ction [over the city Ḫarrān and recorded its exemption (from obligations) as if (its people were) people of the gods Anu and Dagān];

5b–8a) [the strong man who is clad in awesome splendor (and) whose weapons are raised] to strike down (his) enemies; [the king who since the (first) day of his reign has had no ruler who could equal him and has me]t [no one] who could overpo[wer (him) in war or battle; (who) smashed all] (enemy) lands [as if (they were) pots and put halters on (all) rebels in the four (quarters of the world); (who) opened up] in[numerable distant mountainous areas who]se [pa]ss(es) are difficult [and visited their remotest region(s)]; (who) traversed [inaccessible, difficult paths

---

Section 1 = lines 1–13 = II,2:1–13. See Winckler, Sar. Annals lines 1–13; Lie, Sar. lines 1–13; and Fuchs, Khorsabad Annals lines 1–13. Cf. text no. 43 lines 1–16.

1–13 For the line arrangement and tentative restorations, see the commentary to this section and Frame, CRRA 65 (forthcoming). In brief, it is assumed that lines 1–11 of P.E. Botta's copy (Monument de Ninive 4 pl. 79^{c} top; see also Figure 6) were actually lines 2 and 4–13 and that all but one and a half lines on the slab (Botta's lines 10b and 11, here lines 12b and 13) duplicated almost exactly the introduction of the Khorsabad cylinder inscription (text no. 43) lines 1–13a. The line breaks in the restorations given above are at times uncertain (e.g., where line 11 ends and line 12 begins). Cf. Olmstead, AJSL 47 (1930–31) pp. 261–262, which would have the text omit line 4 and part of line 5 of text no. 43. Line 1: For NU.ÈŠ "*nešakku*-priest," see the on-page note to text no. 41 line 1.

2 Possibly add ^{d}AG, "Nabû," between Aššur and Marduk, following text no. 7 line 3. The copies in JA and IdF have [...] *x-na-an* [(*x x*)] *x* BAR *x* [...], where the first *x* is a vertical wedge, which might suggest a reading [...] ⸢*ša*⸣-*na-an* or less likely [...] ⸢*šá*⸣-*na-an*. Since the *x* before the BAR is an upside down vertical wedge and since the BAR *x* do not seem to fit into what is expected in line 2, it has been thought best to omit these traces from the main edition. It is possible that they actually come from line 3, situated immediately above the signs preserved for line 4.

5 The JA and IdF copies have the head of a vertical wedge before the *a*-, which could conceivably be the end of ŠA.

6 The JA and IdF copies have traces of the sign before the KUR, but they do not fit ḪU easily.

8–10 Since what is preserved of line 9 does not match exactly text no. 43 line 13, it is not clear that what was at the end of line 8 and the beginning of line 9 or if the end of line 9 and beginning of line 10 duplicated part of text no. 43 line 13.

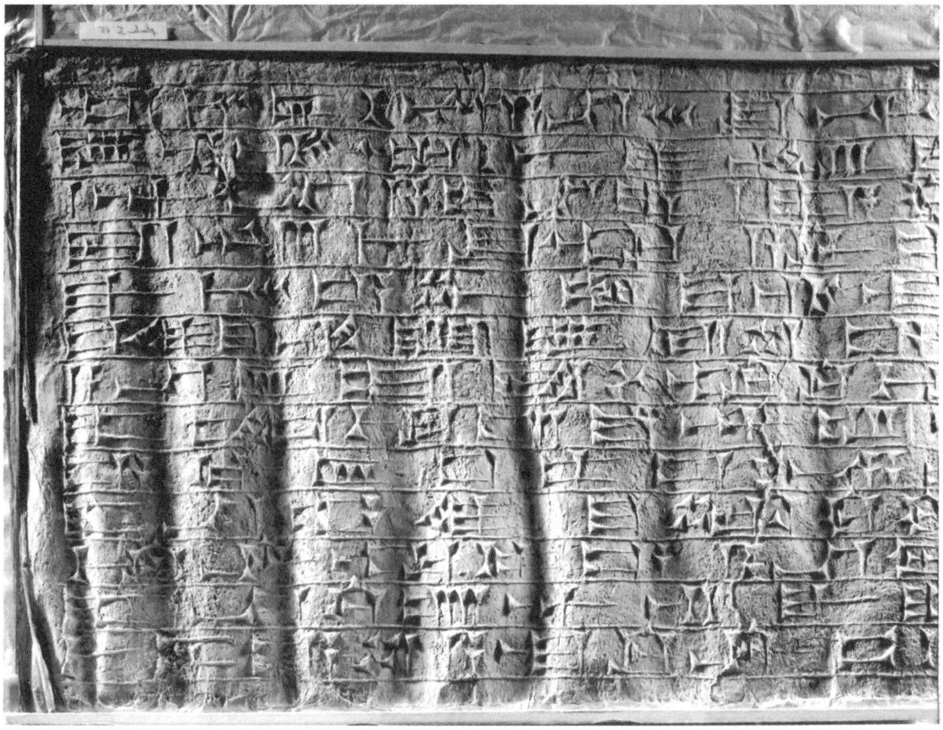

Figure 7. Squeeze of Botta, Monument de Ninive 3 pl. 65.1 (text no. 1, section 21). © Musée du Louvre, dist. RMN - Grand Palais / Christian Larrieu.

Figure 8. Squeeze of Botta, Monument de Ninive 3 pl. 65.2 (text no. 1, section 21). © Musée du Louvre, dist. RMN - Grand Palais / Christian Larrieu.

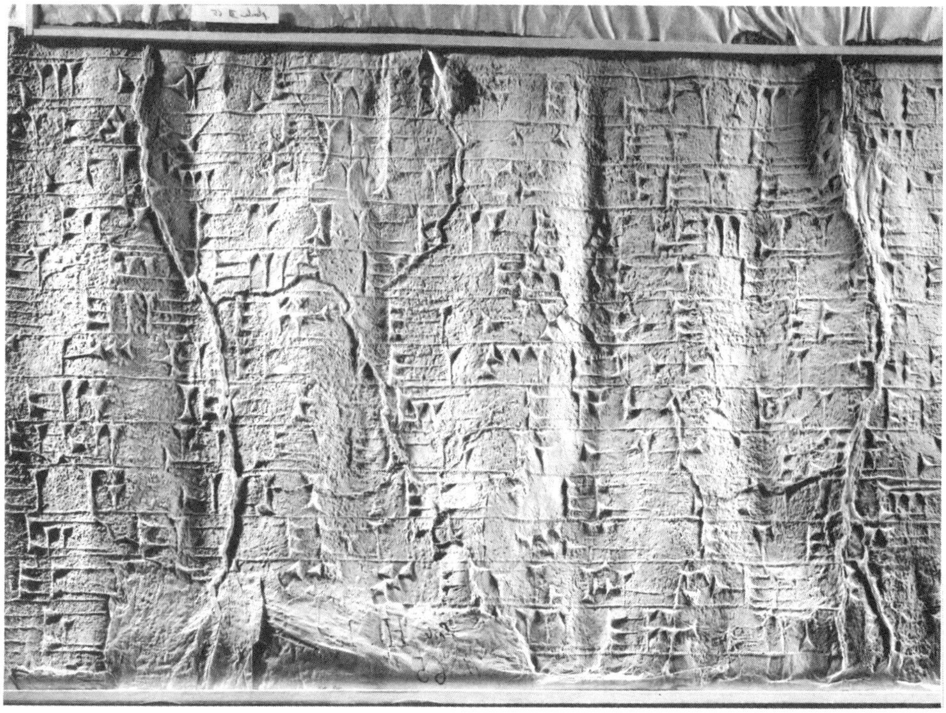

Figure 9. Squeeze of Botta, Monument de Ninive 3 pl. 65.3 (text no. 1, section 21). © Musée du Louvre, dist. RMN - Grand Palais / Christian Larrieu.

Figure 10. Squeeze of Botta, Monument de Ninive 3 pl. 65.4 (text no. 1, section 21). © Musée du Louvre, dist. RMN - Grand Palais / Christian Larrieu.

8) [ṭu-da-at la a᾽-a-ri pa-áš-qa-a-ti ša a-šar-ši-na šug-lud-du] ˹e˺-ta-at-ti-qu-ma ˹e†-te˺-eb-bi-ru na-˹gab˺ [be-ra-a-ti iš-tu? KUR.ra-a-ši? mi-ṣir?]

9) [KUR.e-lam-ti? LÚ.pu-qu-du? LÚ.da-mu-nu? URU.BÀD-ku-ri-gal-zi? URU.ra-pi]-qu si-ḫi-ir-ti KUR†.kal†-di a-di né-ber†-ti x [...]

10) [... iš-tu] KUR.ḫa†-áš†-˹mar˺ a-di URU.ṣi†-bar pat-ti KUR†.ma-da-a-[a ru-qu-ti ša ṣi-it ^{d}UTU-ši KUR.nam-ri]

11) [KUR.el-li-pí KUR.É-ḫa-am-ban KUR.par-su-a KUR.ma-an-na-a-a KUR.ur-ar-ṭu KUR.kas]-˹ku†˺ KUR†.ta†-bal a-di KUR.mu-uš-ki ik-[šu-du GAL-tum qa-a-su LÚ.šu-ut SAG.MEŠ-šú]

12) [šak-nu-ti UGU-šú-nu iš-tak-ka-nu-ma bil-tu ma-da-at-tu ki-i ša áš]-˹šu˺-ri e-mid-su-<nu>-ti i-na ˹SAG˺ [LUGAL-ti-ia šá? ina? GIŠ.GU.ZA? LUGAL-ti? ú-ši-bu-ma?]

13) [a-ge-e? be-lu-ti? an-na-ap-ru-(ma?) ... LÚ.URU.sa-me]-˹ri˺-na-a-a [...]

14) [... mu]-˹šak˺-ši-˹du˺ er-nit-ti-ia ˹it˺-[ti-šú-nu am-da-ḫi-iṣ-ma ...]

15) [27 LIM 2 ME 80 / 90 UN.MEŠ a-šib ŠÀ-šú] ˹áš˺-lu-la 50 GIŠ.GIGIR ki-ṣir šar-ru-ti-ia ˹i-na˺ [lìb-bi-šú-nu ak-ṣur-ma ...]

16) [x x x (x x) URU.sa-me-ri-na ú]-˹ter˺-ma UGU šá pa-na ú-še-me UN.MEŠ KUR.KUR.MEŠ ki-˹šit˺-[ti ŠU.II-ia i-na lìb-bi ú-še-rib LÚ.šu-ut SAG-ia]

in terrifying location(s)] and crossed eve[ry *swamp*]; 8b–12a) [(*who*) *ruled from the land Rāši on the border of the land Elam, the Puqudu (and) Damūnu (tribes), the cities Dūr-Kurigalzu* (and) Rapi]qu, all of Chaldea, as far as the other side [*of the sea* ...; (who)se great hand] con[quered from] the land Ḫašmar to the city Ṣibar — which borders on the [distant] Medes [in the east — the lands Namri, Ellipi, Bīt-Ḫamban, Parsua(š), Mannea, Urarṭu, Kask]u, (and) Tabal, as far as the land Musku; [(who) set eunuchs of his as governors over them and] imposed upon them [(the same) tribute (and) payment(s) as if (they were) Ass]yrians —

12b–17a) At the be[ginning of my reign, *having ascended the royal throne and been crowned with the crown of lordship*, ... (as for) the peo]ple [of the city Samar]ia [*who had come to an agreement with a king hostile to me not to do obeisance (to me) or to bring tribute (to me) and (who) had offered battle, with the might of the god Aššur, my lord*, who ma]kes me triumph, [I fought them and *brought about their defeat* ... I] carried off as booty [27,280/27,290 people who lived there. [I conscripted] 50 chariot(s) from [among them] into my royal (military) contingent [and (*re*)*settled the remainder of them in Assyria* ... I res]tored [the city Samaria] and *made* (it) greater than before. [I brought there] people from the lands that [I had] conquer[ed. I set a eunuch of mine as provincial governor over them and imposed upon

9–10 Following *nēberti*, we might expect something like *tam-tim* or (ÍD).*mar-ra-ti*, "other side of the sea," but the traces as copied by P.E. Botta would not seem to fit either reading; see also Fuchs, Khorsabad p. 313 and n. 223 and cf. text no. 7 lines 21–22. After URU.*ra-pi-qu* and before *iš-tu* KUR.*ḫa-áš-mar* of line 10, text no. 43 line 13 has *mad-bar* DÙ.A.BI *a-di na-ḫal* KUR.*mu-uṣ-ri* KUR.*a-mur-re-e* DAGAL-*tum* KUR.*ḫat-ti a-na si-ḫir-ti-šá i-be-lu*, "(who) ruled ... the entire desert as far as the Brook of Egypt, the wide land Amurru, (and) the land Ḫatti (Syria) in its entirety."
10–11 KUR.*ma-da-a-a* and KUR.*ma-an-na-a-a*: In this volume, it has been thought preferable to translate these terms normally as "the land Media" and "the land Mannea" (rather than more literally as "the land of the Medes" and "the land of the Manneans") unless they clearly refer to individuals (e.g., ^{m}*ul-lu-su-nu* KUR.*man-na-a-a*, "Ullusunu, the Mannean," in line 137) or are modified by a plural adjective (e.g., in line 10, where the adjective is restored based on a duplicate passage, and in line 100 where we have KUR.*ma-da-a-a dan-nu-ti*, "the powerful Medes"). The same is the case with several similar writings for other places (e.g., KUR.*zi-kir-ta-a-a*, "the land Zikirtu," rather than "the land of the Zikirtians," in text no. 37 line 2).
11 -˹*ku*†˺ KUR†: P.E. Botta's copy has [...] GU.
12 For the phrase *ki-i ša áš-šu-ri*, "as if (they were) Assyrians," see the on-page note to text no. 41 line 12. *e-mid-su-<nu>-ti*: We would expect *ēmidušunūti* since the preceding verb *ištakkanuma* (restored) is in the subjunctive; see also text nos. 10 line 23, 11 line 18, 13 line 89, 41 line 13, 42 line 19, 43 line 16, 44 line 25, 76 line 10′, 105 i′ 13′ (mostly restored), and 129 line 18 (restored).
12b–16 The tentative restorations in the translation follow for the most part text no. 89 lines 15–16 for lines 12b–13a and text no. 74 iv 25–37 (see also Tadmor, JCS 12 1958 p. 34) for lines 13b–16. It is unlikely that there was room at the end of line 13 and beginning of line 14 for the restoration of all of text no. 74 iv 25b–28 given in the translation above ("*who had come ... offered battle*"). With regard to lines 15–16, E. Frahm (Last Days pp. 70–71) suggests the possibility of also restoring at the beginning of line 15 (after *libbišu*) *adi narkabātišunu u ilāni tiklīšun*, "together with their chariots and the gods in whom they trusted," and restoring *sittātišunu* at the very end of line 15 and *ina qereb māt aššur ušaṣbit* at the beginning of line 16 (before Samaria), thus "[The rest of them I settled within Assyria]." However, while there is likely room to restore *sittātišunu* at the end of line 15, there would not be sufficient room for the additional restorations at the beginning of lines 15 and 16 based on how much is to be restored at the end of lines 16 and 17 and at beginning of lines 17 and 18, where the restorations are much more certain. It is possible that some of the actions described here should be attributed to Sargon's second regnal year (720) when he also fought against Samaria.
Section 2 = lines 14–26 = II,3:1–13: See Winckler, Sar. Annals lines 14–26; Lie, Sar. lines 14–26; and Fuchs, Khorsabad Annals lines 14–26. Since neither the beginning nor the end of any line on this slab is preserved, the line divisions in the restorations must be considered tentative.
14 -˹*du*˺: H. Winckler copied -˹*šid*˺ (note also Winckler, Sar. 1 p. 4 n. 1); Saggs, JSS 42 (1997) p. 138 read -˹*du*˺; and Fuchs, Khorsabad p. 87 line 14 has -˹*id*˺; the spacing and the traces on the squeeze fit DU better than ID.
15 27,280/27,290: Various exemplars of text no. 7 line 24 have 27,290, 27,280, and apparently 24,280 here, while the Nimrud Prism has 47,280 or 27,280 (see the on-page note to text no. 74 iv 31).
16 See the on-page note to the duplicate passage in text no. 74 iv 37–38 with regard to the restoration of Samaria.
17–18a See also text no. 74 iv 42–49.

17) [LÚ.EN.NAM UGU-*šú-nu áš-kun-ma bil-tu*] *ma-da-at-tu ki-i ša áš-šu-ri e-mid-su-nu-ti* ⌜*ka*⌝-[*a-ri* KUR.*mu-ṣur kan-gu ap-te-e-ma*]
18) [UN.MEŠ KUR *aš-šur ù* KUR.*mu-ṣur it*]-*ti a-ḫa-miš ab-lu-ul-ma ú-še-pi-šá ma-ḫi-ru* ⌜*i*⌝-[*na maḫ-re-e* BALA-*ia* ...]
19) [... *ḫi-iṭ*]-⌜*tu*$^{?}$⌝ *iḫ-ṭi-ma ig-ra-an-ni a-na qab-li a-na x* [...]
20) [...] ⌜*áš*⌝-*ku-na* [BAD$_5$].⌜BAD$_5$⌝-*šú* ⌜LÚ⌝.[KUR$^{?}$].⌜*tu*⌝-*ʾu-mu-na-a-a ni*-⌜*ir*⌝ ^{d}*aš-šur* [*iṣ-lu-ú-ma* LÚ.*na-sik-šú-nu i-pi-du-ma*]
21) [*ur-ru-ú ma-ḫar* LUGAL KUR.*kal*]-⌜*di*⌝ *ša ki-i la lìb-bi* DINGIR.MEŠ *šar-ru-ut* KÁ.DINGIR.RA.KI [*e-pu-šu* ...]
22) [...]+7 UN.MEŠ *a-di mar-ši-ti-šú-nu as-su-ḫa-am*-⌜*ma*†⌝ [...]
23) [... *i-na* KUR].*ḫa-at-ti ú-še-šib i-na* 2-*i* BALA-*ia* ^{m}*i-lu*-⌜*bi*⌝-[*iʾ-di* KUR.*a-ma-ta-a-a* ...]
24) [...] DAGAL-*tim i-na* URU.*qar-qa-ri ú*-⌜*pa*⌝-*ḫi-ir-ma ma-mit* [DINGIR.MEŠ GAL.MEŠ ...]
25) [... URU.*ar-pad-da* URU.*ṣi-mir-ra* URU].*di-maš*-⌜*qa*⌝ [URU†].⌜*sa*⌝-*me-ri*-[*na it-ti-ia*] ⌜*uš*⌝-[*bal-kit-ma* ...]
26) [...]

Lines 27–52 are not preserved

53) [*x iš/áš*$^{?}$]-⌜*kun-ma*⌝ ^{m}SIPA-*ʾe* ⌜LÚ.*tur*$^{?}$-*tan*$^{?}$-*nu*$^{?}$⌝-*šu a-na* ⌜*ki*⌝-[*it*†]-*ri-šu id*-⌜*din*$^{?}$-*šú*$^{?}$⌝-*ma a-na e-peš qab-li*
54) [*ù*] ⌜*ta*⌝-*ḫa-zi a-na* GABA-*ia it-ba-a i-na zi-kir* ^{d}⌜*aš*⌝-*šur* EN-*ia* BAD$_5$.BAD$_5$-*šú-nu am-ḫaṣ-ma*
55) [^{m}]⌜SIPA⌝-*ʾe ki-i* LÚ.SIPA* *ša ṣe-na-šu ḫab-ta e-da-nu-uš-šu ip-par-šid-ma e-li*

them (the same) tribute] (and) payment(s) as if (they were) Assyrians.

17b–18a) [I opened up *a sealed-off*] *ha*[*rbor district* of Egypt], mingled together [the people of Assyria and Egypt], and allowed (them) to engage in trade.

18b–20a) I[n my first regnal year, (...) *Ḫumbanigaš* (*Ḫumban-nikaš I*), *the Elamite*, ...] committed [a crime] and became hostile to me, (wanting) to (do) battle ... [... I] brought about his [def]eat [*on the outskirts of Dēr*].

20b–23a) The Tuʾumuna (tribe) [threw off] the yoke of the god Aššur, [arrested their sheikh, and brought (him) before the king of Chalde]a who [exercised] the kingship over Babylon against the will of the gods, [...] I deported [...]+7 people together with their property and [...] I (re)settled (them) [(...) in the land Ḫ]atti (Syria).

23b–26) In my second regnal year, Ilu-b[iʾdī of the land Hamath ...] assembled [*the troops of the*] wide [*land Amurru*] in the city Qarqar and [*transgressed against*] the oath [(sworn) by the great gods ...] he inc[ited the cities Arpad, Ṣimirra], Damascus, (and) Samaria [to rebel against me and ...]

Lines 27–52 are not preserved

53–57) [*he/I est*]*ablished* [...], he *gave him* Rēʾe, his *field marshal*, to he[l]p him, and he rose up against me to do war [and] battle. At the command of the god Aššur, my lord, I inflicted a defeat on them. [R]ēʾe then fled off by himself, like a shepherd whose flock had been stolen, and got away. I captured [Ḫ]anūnu (Ḫanno) and brought him in bondage to my city Aššur; I then

---

18b–20a Cf. text no. 7 line 23b. Although the Annals appears to date the battle of Der to Sargon's first regnal year (721), the Aššur Charter (text no. 89 lines 16–17a) and a Babylonian chronicle (see the Introduction to this volume, under the subsection "Chronicles") assign it to his second regnal year (720).

20–21 ⌜LÚ⌝.[KUR$^{?}$].⌜*tu*⌝-*u'-mu-na-a-a*: The spacing on the squeeze suggests that there was a small sign in the damaged area between the LÚ and the *tu*-. *ni*-⌜*ir*⌝: P.E. Botta's copy has *ir-ni*, while H. Winckler's copy and the squeeze have *ni*-⌜*ir*⌝. H.W.F. Saggs suggests that Botta transposed the signs when copying them (JSS 42 [1997] p. 138). 20b–21: Cf. text no 7 line 18b.

23b–26 Cf. text no. 7 lines 33–35a.

24 Among numerous other possible restorations are "[*the troops of the*] wide [*land Hamath*]" and "the vast [*troops of the land Hamath/Amurru*]" instead of "[*the troops of the*] wide [*land Amurru*]," and "[*had them take*] an oath [(sworn) by the great gods ...]" instead of "[(...) *they transgressed against*] the oath [(sworn) by the great gods ...]."

25 *di-maš*-⌜*qa*⌝ [URU†].⌜*sa*⌝-*me*-: P.E. Botta's copy has *di-maš*-[*x x* (*x*)]-*me*- and H. Winckler's copy has ... *di-maš-qi* URU.*sa-me*-.... The squeeze has *di-maš*-⌜*qa*⌝ [*x*] ⌜*sa*⌝-*me*-, where there would barely be enough room for URU in the gap.

Sections 3–5 Section 3 = lines 27–39 = II,4:1-13: See Lie, Sar. lines 27–39; and Fuchs, Khorsabad Annals lines 27–39; Winckler, Sar. Annals omits. Section 4 = lines 40–52 = II,5:1-13: See Lie, Sar. lines 40–52; and Fuchs, Khorsabad Annals lines 40–52; Winckler, Sar. Annals omits. It is possible that only one wall slab is missing and not two. Thus, only thirteen lines would be missing between our lines 26 and 53. See the commentary to this text on this matter. Section 5 = lines 53–65 = II,6:1-13: See Winckler, Sar. Annals lines 27–39; Lie, Sar. lines 53–65; and Fuchs, Khorsabad Annals lines 53–65. Cf. text no. 4 lines 1′–2′.

53 ⌜LÚ.*tur*$^{?}$-*tan*$^{?}$-*nu*$^{?}$⌝-*šu*: Text no. 7 line 25 has LÚ.*tar-tan-nu*. P.E. Botta's copy has ⌜LÚ⌝ [*x x*]-*šu*, while H. Winckler's copy has ⌜LÚ.*tur*⌝-*tan-nu-šu*; the squeeze has ⌜LÚ⌝.*x*-⌜*tan*$^{?}$-*nu*$^{?}$⌝-*šu* and the BM rubbing is not useful here. *id*-⌜*din*$^{?}$-*šú*$^{?}$⌝-*ma*: Botta's copy has *id*-[*x*-(*x*)]-*ma*. Winckler's copy has IT-*x-x-ma*, with each *x* being a Winkelhaken in a damaged area; he identified the signs as *it-mu-u-ma*. The squeeze and BM rubbing have no clear traces of the DIN and ŠÚ.

54 [*ù*]: H. Winckler's copy has ⌜*ù*⌝, but no trace of the sign is given on P.E. Botta's copy or is currently visible on the squeeze or rubbing.

55 LÚ.SIPA*: P.E. Botta's and H. Winckler's copies' LÚ.ŠAB are confirmed by the squeeze and the rubbing in the British Museum. See Frahm, CRRA 43 p. 151 for the comic wordplay between the name of the person fleeing and the Akkadian word for shepherd.

56) [^{m}*ḫa*]-⸢*a*⸣-*nu-nu i-na qa-ti aṣ-bat-ma ka-mu-us-su a-na* URU-*ia aš-šur*.KI *ú-ra-áš-šum-ma*
57) [URU.*ra*]-⸢*pi*⸣-*ḫu ap-pul aq-qur i-na* IZI *áš-ru-up* 9 LIM 33 UN.MEŠ *a-di* NÍG.GA-*šú-nu ma-aʾ-di áš-lu-la*

destroyed, demolished, (and) burned down with fire [the city Rap]ḫia. I carried off as booty 9,033 people together with their numerous possessions.

58) [*i-na*] ⸢3⸣ BALA-*ia* URU.*šu-an-da-ḫu-ul* URU.*du-ur-duk-ka* URU.MEŠ *dan-nu-ti it-ti* ^{m}*ir-an-zi*
59) [KUR.*man*]-*na-a-a* LUGAL *be-lí-šú-nu šá-di-id ni-ri-ia šit-nun-tu id-bu-bu-ú-ma*
60) [*a*]-⸢*na*⸣ ^{m}*mi-ta-at-ti* KUR.*zi-kir-ta-a-a it-tak-lu* ^{m}*mi-ta-at-ti* KUR.*zi-kir-ta-a-a*
61) LÚ.ERIM.MEŠ *ti-du-ki-šú a-di* ANŠE.*pét-ḫal-lì-šú-nu id-din-šú-nu-ti-ma iš-šá-ki-in*
62) [*re*]-*ṣu-us-su-un um-ma-na-at* ⸢^{d}⸣*aš-šur gap-šá-a-te ad-ke-e-ma a-na ka-šad*
63) [URU].⸢MEŠ⸣-*ni šu-a-tu-nu a-lik i-na* [GIŠ†].*a-ši-bi dan-ni* BÀD.MEŠ-*šú-nu dun-nu-nu-ti*
64) [*ú-par-ri*]-⸢*ir*⸣-*ma qaq-qa*-⸢*riš am-nu* UN⸣.MEŠ *a-di mar-ši-ti-šú-nu áš-lu*-⸢*la*⸣
65) [URU.MEŠ-*ni šu*]-*a*-⸢*tu*⸣-[*nu*] ⸢*ap-pul*⸣ [*aq-qur*] ⸢*i-na*⸣ IZI [*áš-ru-up*]

58–65) [In] my third regnal year, (the people of) the cities Šuandaḫul (and) Durdukka, fortified cities, plotted resistance against Iranzi, the [Man]nean, the king, their lord, one who pulls my yoke, and put their trust [i]n Mitatti of the land Zikirtu. Mitatti of the land Zikirtu gave them his combat troops, together with their cavalry and (thus) aid was provided to them. I mustered the numerous troops of the god Aššur and marched (forth) to conquer those [cit]ies. [I shatter]ed their very strong walls with a mighty battering ram, leveling (them) to the ground. I carried off as booty [the peo]ple, together with their property. [I de]stroyed, [demolished, (and) burned down th]os[e cities] with fire.

66) [LÚ.URU].⸢*su*†⸣-[*uk-ka-a-a* LÚ].URU.[*ba-la-a*]-⸢*a*†⸣ LÚ†.URU⸣.[*a-bi-ti-ik-na-a-a mi-lik*] ⸢ḪUL-*tim*†⸣ *ša na-saḫ šur*-[*še ma-ti im-tal-li-ku-ma a-na* ^{m}*ur-sa-a*]
67) [KUR.*ur*]-⸢*ar*⸣-*ṭa-a-a id-di-nu* KA-*šú-un*† *i-na ḫi-iṭ-ṭi iḫ-ṭu*†-*ú ul-tu áš-ri-šú-nu as-suḫ-šú*†-*nu-ti-ma* ⸢*i*⸣-[*na* KUR].*ḫa-at-ti ša* [KUR *a-mur-re-e*]

66–68a) [The peo]ple of the cities S[ukkia, Bāla, (and) Abitikna conceived (lit.: "deliberated") an e]vil [plan] that was to eradica[te] (lit.: "to tear out the ro[ot of]") (their own) land and g]ave their word [to Ursâ (Rusâ), the Ura]rṭian, (to do obeisance to him). Because of the crime that they had committed, I deported them from their (own) places and (re)settled them [i]n [the land] Ḫatti (Syria) *and* (lit.: "of") [the land Amurru].

68) ⸢*ú*⸣-*še-šib-šú-nu-ti i-na* 4 BALA-*ia* ^{m}*ki-ak-ki* URU.*ši-nu-uḫ-ta-a-a a-de-e* DINGIR.MEŠ GAL.MEŠ *i-miš-ma a-na la na-še*-⸢*e*⸣ GUN† *ir-šá*†-⸢*a*⸣
69) [*ni*]-*id a-ḫi a-na* DINGIR.MEŠ EN.MEŠ-*ia qa-a-ti áš-ši-ma* URU.*ši-nu-uḫ-tu* URU LUGAL-*ti-šú im-ba*†-*riš as-ḫup*†-*ma šá-a-šú a-di* LÚ.*mun*†-⸢*daḫ*⸣-[*ṣe-e-šú*]
70) 7 LIM 1+[1]+1 ME 50 UN.MEŠ DAM-*su* DUMU.MEŠ-*šú* DUMU.MUNUS.MEŠ-*šú ù* UN.MEŠ

68b–71) In my fourth regnal year, Kiakki of the city Šinuḫtu disregarded the treaty (sworn) by the great gods and became [di]latory about delivering (his) tribute. I raised my hand(s) (in supplication) to the gods, my lords, overwhelmed his royal city Šinuḫtu like a fog, and counted him as booty, together with [his] fight[ing men], 7,350 people, his wife, his sons, his daughters, and the people of his palace, together with abundant property of his. I gave his royal city

---

56 [^{m}*ḫa*]-⸢*a*⸣-*nu-nu*: H. Winckler's copy has [^{m}*ḫa*]-*nu-nu*, but the traces and spacing on the squeeze and rubbing suggests the proposed reading (see also, for example, text no. 9 line 23 and text no. 43 line 19).
58 ⸢3⸣: Although not noted on P.E. Botta's and H. Winckler's copies, there are two vertical wedges and likely a trace of a third for the number on the squeeze; the BM rubbing has [...]+2.
59 LUGAL: H. Winckler's copy has three initial horizontal wedges, but both P.E. Botta's copy and the squeeze indicate only two were present.
65 ⸢*ap-pul*⸣: The reading is based on the JA and IdF copies. P.E. Botta's copy in Monument de Ninive has ANŠE [...]; H. Winckler did not indicate any traces of the signs, although he suggested that Botta's ANŠE might stand for *al-me*. There are no discernible traces of the sign on the squeeze and A. Fuchs (Khorsabad p. 91 line 65) suggested reading *aq*-[*qur*]. The spacing on the Botta's copies would suggest, however, that there was room for several signs between the ⸢*ap-pul*⸣ and where the NA of *i-na* would begin.
Section 6 = lines 66–78 = II,7:1–13: See Winckler, Sar. Annals lines 40–52; Lie, Sar. lines 66–78; and Fuchs, Khorsabad Annals lines 66–78. Cf. no. 4 lines 3′–20′a and text no. 4 lines 3′–20′a. See also text no. 2 lines 69–70 for lines 77–78.
67 Text no. 4 line 4′ has *a-na e-peš ar-du-ti*, "to do obeisance (to him)" after [KUR.*ur*]-⸢*ar*⸣-*ṭa-a-a*. Text no. 7 refers to (re)settling people from the cities Sukkia, Bāla, Abitikna, Pappa, (and) Lalluknu "in the city Damascus and the land Ḫatti" (line 57).
68 Šinuḫtu may be Aksaray in central Anatolia (Hawkins in Liverani, Neo-Assyrian Geography p. 99 and Bagg, Rép. Géogr. 7/1 pp. 240–241).
70 H. Winckler's copy indicates that the squeeze has the last two vertical wedges of the number 3 (before ME), but the spacing on the squeeze suggests it is the final vertical wedge of the number and the beginning of the following ME. Cf. text no. 4 lines 9′b–10′a.

É.GAL-*šú a-di* NÍG.ŠU-*šú ma-a'-di a-na šal-la-ti am-nu-šú* URU.*ši-nu-uḫ-tu*
71) URU LUGAL-*ti-šú a-na* ^{m}*kur-ti-i* KUR.*a-tu-un-a-a ad-din-ma* ANŠE.KUR.RA.MEŠ ANŠE.*pa-re-e* KÙ.GI KÙ.BABBAR UGU *ša pa-na ut-tir-ma* UGU-*šú áš-kun*

Šinuḫtu to Kurtî of the land Atuna. Then, I made larger than before (the number/amount of) horses, mules, gold, (and) silver (that he had to pay as tribute) and I imposed (this) upon him.

72) *i-na* 5 BALA-*ia* ^{m}*pi-si-i-ri* URU.*gar-ga*†*-miš-a*†*-a i-na a-de-e* DINGIR.MEŠ GAL.MEŠ *iḫ-ṭi-i-ma a-na* ^{m}*mi-ta-a* ⸢LUGAL⸣ KUR.*mu-us-ki*
73) *ze-ra-a-ti* KUR *aš-šur*.KI *iš-tap-par a-na* ^{d}*aš-šur be-lí-ia* ⸢*qa*⸣*-a-ti áš-ši-*⸢*ma*⸣ *šá-a-šú ga-a-du* ⸢*qin*⸣*-ni-šú ka-*⸢*mu-su*†⸣*-nu ú-še-ṣa-šú-nu-ti-ma*
74) KÙ.GI KÙ.BABBAR *it-ti* NÍG.ŠU É.GAL-*šú ù* URU.*gar-ga-miš-a-a* EN *ḫi-iṭ-ṭi ša it-ti-šu it-ti* NÍG.GA-*šú-nu áš-lu-lam i-na qé-reb* KUR *aš-šur*.KI
75) *ú-ra-a* 50 GIŠ.GIGIR 2 ME ANŠE.*pét-ḫal-lum* 3 LIM LÚ.*zu-uk*† GÌR.II *i-na lìb-bi-šú-nu ak-ṣur-ma i-na* [UGU] *ki-ṣir šar-ru-ti-ia ú-rad-di*

72–76a) In my fifth regnal year, Pisīri(s) the city Carchemish sinned against the treaty (sworn) by the great gods and repeatedly sent (messages) hostile to Assyria to Mitâ (Midas), [k]ing of the land Musku. I raised my hand(s) (in supplication) to the god Aššur, my lord, and brought him, together with his family, out in bondage. I then carried off as booty gold (and) silver, (along) with the property of his palace and the guilty people of the city Carchemish who (had sided) with him, (along) with their possessions. (75) I brought (them) to Assyria. I conscripted 50 chariots, 200 cavalry, (and) 3,000 foot soldiers from among them and added (them) to my royal (military) contingent. I settled people of Assyria in the city Carchemish and imposed the yoke of the god Aššur, my lord, upon them.

76) UN.MEŠ KUR *aš-šur*.KI *i-na qé-reb* URU.*gar-ga-miš ú-še-šib-ma ni-ir* ^{d}*aš-šur* EN-*ia*† *e-mid-su-nu-ti* LÚ.URU.*pa-a-pa-a-a* LÚ.URU.*lal-lu-uk-na-a-a*
77) ⸢UR.GI$_{7}$.MEŠ⸣ *tar-bit* É.GAL-*ia a-na* KUR.*ka-ak-me-e id-bu-bu* [*na*]*-pa-di-iš ul-tu áš-ri-šú-nu as-su-ḫa-áš-šú-nu-ti-ma*
78) [*a-na qé*]*-*⸢*reb* URU.*di-maš-qi ša* KUR MAR.TU$^{?}$.KI⸣ [*ú-še-šib-šu-nu-ti i-na* 6 BALA-*ia* ^{m}*ur*]*-*⸢*sa*†⸣*-*[*a* KUR.*ur*]*-*⸢*ar*⸣*-ta-a*†*-a*
79) [*a-na* ^{m}*ba-ag-da-at-ti* KUR.*ú-iš-di-iš-a-a* ^{m}KAR-*x x x x* SAR KUR].⸢*zi*$^{?}$⸣*-kir*$^{?}$*-*⸢*ta*⸣*-*[*a-a* LÚ.GAR.KUR].⸢MEŠ⸣ [KUR.*man-na*]*-a-*[*a* LÚ.*rak-bu-šú ša da-ba-ab-ti sar*$_{6}$*-ra-ti iš-pur*]
80) ⸢*it*⸣*-*[*ti-(ia)* ^{m}]LUGAL-GI.NA *it-ti* ^{m}*a-za-a* DUMU EN†-*šú-nu ú-šá-an-ki-ir-šú-nu-ti-ma a-na i-*[*di-šu ú-ter-šu-nu-ti i-na* KUR].*ú-a-ú-*[*uš*]
81) KUR-*i* ⸢*mar*†*-ṣi suḫ*⸣*-ḫur*†*-ti* KUR.*man-na-a-a iš-ku-nu-ma* ⸢ADDA⸣ ^{m}*a-za-a* EN-*šú-nu id-du-ú a-na* ^{d}*a-*⸢*šur*⸣ [EN-*ia a-na tur*]*-*⸢*ri*⸣ *gi-mil*†*-li*

76b–78a) The people of the cities Pāpa (and) Lalluknu, dogs who had been brought up in my palace, conspired with the land Kakmê *for the purpose of* [*sep*]*arating* (*from Assyria*). I deported them from their (own) places and [(re)settled them i]n the city [D]a[m]ascus o[f the lan]d A[murru].

78b–83a) [In my sixth regnal year, Ur]sâ (Rusâ), [the Ura]rṭian, [sent his mounted messenger with a mendacious message to Bag-dāti of the land Uišdiš (and) KAR... of the land Z]ikirtu, governor]s [of the land Mann]e[a]. He made them hostile t[o (me)], Sargon, (and) to Azâ, the son of their (former) lord and [made them] s[ide] with [him (Rusâ)]. They brought about the rout of the Manneans [on Mount] Uau[š], a rug[ge]d mountain, and threw down the cor[pse of] Azâ, their lord, (there). I raised my hand(s) (in supplication) to the god Ašš[ur, my lord, in order to ave]nge the Manneans (and) to make (that area part of) the territory of Assyria. Then, on Mount Uauš, the

71 See Weippert, ZDMG Suppl. 1/1 (1969) pp. 213–215 and ZDPV 89 (1973) p. 50 on the reading of the personal name ^{m}*kur-ti-i*.

73b–74a Cf. text no. 4 lines 14´b–16´a. [...]-⸢*su*†⸣*-nu*: So JA and IdF copies; no trace of SU on Botta, Monument de Ninive 4 pl. 72^{c}.

76b–78a LÚ.URU.*pa-a-pa-a-a* LÚ.URU.*lal-lu-uk-na-a-a* ⸢UR.GI$_{7}$.MEŠ⸣ *tar-bit* É.GAL-*ia* "The people of the cities Pāpa (and) Lallukna, dogs who had been brought up in my palace": One should possibly understand this to refer to just the rulers of these two cities, individuals who at some point had been held hostage in Assyria, likely while their fathers were still alive and ruling those cities. However, the reference to them being deported and resettled in Damascus (lines 77b–78a) might suggest that a larger group of people are being dealt with here.

77 Text no. 2 line 69 adds *ša* after É.GAL-*ia*. Kakmê may be the Mannean name for Urarṭu (Fuchs, Khorsabad pp. 440–441).

78–83 Cf. text no. 2 lines 70–74/75 and text no. 4 lines 20´–26´.

Section 7 = lines 79–91 = II,8:1–13: See Winckler, Sar. Annals lines 53–65; Lie, Sar. lines 79–91; and Fuchs, Khorsabad Annals lines 79–91. Cf. text no. 2 lines 71–76+ and text no. 4 lines 20´b–37´a.

79 [KUR].⸢*zi*$^{?}$⸣*-kir*$^{?}$*-*⸢*ta*⸣: The tentative reading follows A. Fuchs (Khorsabad, p. 95). P.E. Botta's copy in Monument de Ninive has [...] ⸢*zi**⸣(copy:]A-ŠE)-*kir**(copy: DA)-⸢*ta*⸣-[...]. The copies in JA and IdF have [...]-⸢*a*$^{?}$⸣ ^{m}KAR DA-*x* [...], where there is a question mark inside the copy of the DA and the *x* is exactly as the trace after the DA (tentatively read *-kir-*) in Monument de Ninive and assumed to be -⸢*ta*⸣-). This could suggest the signs represent an earlier part of the restoration (note ^{m}KAR is restored from text no. 4 line 21´); however, the spacing could then be problematic for the reading after this point.

80 *-ú-*[*uš*]: P.E. Botta's copy indicates that the line ended with *-ú*, with no space to restore UŠ; thus possibly *-ú-*<*uš*>.

82) KUR.ma-an-⸢na⸣-a-a a-na mi-ṣir KUR aš-šur.KI tur-ri qa-a-ti áš-ši-ma i-na KUR.ú-a-ú-uš KUR-i a-⸢šar⸣ [ADDA ^{m}]a-za†-a id-du-ú
83) ma-šak† ^{m}ba-ag-da†-at-ti a-ku-uṣ-ma KUR.man-na-a-a ú-šab-⸢ri⸣ ^{m}ul-lu†-su†-nu ŠEŠ-šú ša i-na GIŠ.GU.ZA LUGAL†-ti ú-ši†-bu
84) šib-sa-at ^{d}[aš†-šur] UGU-šú-ma a-na ^{m}ru-<<x>>-sa-a KUR.URI-a-a it-ta-kil ^{m}aš-šur-ZU† KUR.kar-al-la-a-a ^{m}it-ti-i
85) KUR.al-lab-ra†-a-a it-ti-ia† uš-bal†-kit-ma ARAD-tu KUR.ur-ar-ṭi e-pe†-ši iz†-[kur-šu-nu]-ti i-na šu-⸢ḫu-uṭ†⸣ lìb-bi-ia KUR.KUR šá-⸢a⸣-ti-<<ŠI>>-na
86) ki-ma [ti]-⸢bu⸣-ut† a-ri-bi ak-tùm†-ma URU.i-zi-ir-tu URU šar-ru-ti-šu ša KUR.<man>-na-a-a ḫu-ḫa-riš as-ḫu†-up† di-ik-ta-šú-nu ma-⸢ʾa⸣-at-tu
87) a-duk† URU.i-zi-ir-tu i-na IZI áš†-ru-up-ma URU.zi-bi-a URU.ar†-ma-et ak-šu-⸢ud⸣ ^{m}ul-lu-su-nu KUR.ma-an-na-a-a
88) a-di kul-lat KUR-šú ki-i iš-tén ip-ḫu-ru-nim-ma GÌR.II-⸢ia⸣ [iṣ]-⸢ba⸣-tu-ma ar-[ši-šú-nu]-⸢ti⸣ re-⸢e⸣-mu ša ^{m}⸢ul⸣-lu-⸢su†⸣-nu
89) ḫi-ṭa†-ti-šu a-bu-uk i-na GIŠ.GU.ZA šar-ru-⸢ti⸣-[šú ú-še-šib-šú-ma ma-da-ta am]-ḫur-šu ^{m}it-ti-i KUR.[al-lab-ra-a-a]
90) [a-di] qin-ni-šu as-su-ḫa-⸢ma⸣ [ša ^{m}]aš-šur-ZU [KUR.kar-al-la-a-a ma-šak-šú a-ku-uṣ-ma ...]
91) [x x]-ma Ú ÁŠ [...]
92) URU.ga-nu-GIŠ [x] KUR x [... 6 URU.MEŠ šá KUR.ni-ik-sa-am]-⸢ma?⸣ na-gi⸣-i ⸢ak⸣-[šu-ud ^{m}GÌR.II-LUGAL] ⸢LÚ⸣.[EN].⸢URU⸣
93) ša URU.šur-ga-di-a i-na qa†-ti† ⸢aṣ⸣-[bat URU.MEŠ]-ni šu-a-tu-nu UGU pi-ḫa-at KUR.⸢par?⸣-[su]-⸢áš?⸣ ú⸣-[rad]-⸢di⸣

mountain wh[ere] they had thrown down [the corpse of] Azâ, I flayed the skin from Bag-dāti and (then) showed (it) to the Manneans.

83b–85a) (As for) Ullusunu, his brother, who had sat on the royal throne, the wrath of the god [Aššur] (was directed) against him. He (Ullusunu) then put his trust in Rusâ, the Urarṭian. He caused Aššur-lēʾi of the land Karalla (and) Ittî (85) of the land Allabria to rebel against me and per[suaded (lit.: "spoke to") the]m to do obeisance to the land Urarṭu.

85b–96a) Furiously, I enveloped those lands like [a swa]rm of locusts and overwhelmed the city Izirtu, the royal city of the land <Man>nea, as with a bird trap. I inflicted a major defeat on them. I burned down the city Izirtu with fire and conquered the city Zibia (and) the city Armaet. (As a result), Ullusunu, the Mannean, together with his whole land gathered together and [gras]ped hold of m[y] feet. I then h[ad] pity [on the]m (and) pardoned (lit.: "overturned") [U]llusunu's crimes. [I had him sit (again)] on [his] royal throne [and rece]ived [tribute] from him. I deported Ittî of the land [Allabria (90) together with] his family, [flayed the skin from] Aššur-lēʾi [of the land Karalla, and ...] ... [...] the city GanuGIŠ[...] ... [...] I c[onquered (in total) six cities of] the district [Niksamm]a. I s[eized Šēp-šarri], the ci[ty ruler] of the city Šurgadia, (and) [add]ed those [citie]s to the province of P[arsua]š. I personally cap[tur]ed Bēl-šarru-uṣur of the city Kiše[sim] and brought him, together with the property of his palace, to Assyria. I set a eunuch of mine as provincial governor over his city. I installed the gods who go before me inside it (the city Kišesim) and (re)named it (the city Kišesim) Kār-Ner<gal>. I erected a royal image of myself there. I conquered the lands Bīt-Sagbat, Bīt-Ḫirmami, (and) Bīt-Umargi, (and) the cities Ḫarḫubarban, Kilambāti,

83 ^{m}ul-lu†-su†-nu: The copies in JA and IdF make the suggested alternate reading ^{m}ul-⸢li⸣-[su]-nu (Fuchs, Khorsabad p. 97 line 83; Saggs, JSS 42 [1997] p. 139) unlikely; the SU is only minimally abnormal on these copies.
84 šib-sa-at: So JA and IdF copies; see also Thureau-Dangin, RA 27 (1930), p. 159.
86 In view of a possible reference to Izirtu on an Aramaic stele found at Tapeh Qalâychi (located near Bukân southeast of Lake Urmia), A. Lemaire (Studia Iranica 27 [1998] pp. 15–30, especially pp. 15 and 29) argues that that site was ancient Izirtu. H. Winckler's copy adds a RI betweeen -a-a and ḫu-ḫa-riš, although this is not included in his edition (p. 12 line 60) and is presumably a mistake since he did not have a squeeze to collate for this section.
89 ḫi-ṭa†-ti-šu: Likely ḫi-⸢ṭa⸣-ti-šu although there is no indication of damage in the area on P.E. Botta's copy. The reading ṬA as opposed to IṬ follows R. Borger (BiOr 14 [1957] p. 121 sub 211b) and A. Fuchs (Khorsabad p. 100 line 89), against H. Winckler (copy ḫi-⸢iṭ⸣-ti-šu and edition p. 14 line 63) and H.W.F. Saggs (JSS 42 [1997] p. 139).
90 For the restorations, cf. text no. 7 line 56. A.G. Lie restores the end of the line as [KUR.kar-al-la-a-a ma-šak-šu a-ku-uṣ-ma UN.MEŠ KUR.kar-al-la i-na qé-reb KUR.a-ma-at-ti ú-še-šib], i.e., "[flayed] ... [of the land Allabria, and (re)settled people of the land Karalla in the land Hamath]"; cf. Geers apud Olmstead, AJSL 47 (1930–31) p. 265.
Section 8 = lines 92–104 = II,9:1–13: See Winckler, Sar. Annals lines 66–78; Lie, Sar. lines 92–104, and Fuchs, Khorsabad Annals lines 92–104. Cf. text no. 2 lines +86–99 and text no. 4 lines 37´b–45´.
92 URU.ga-nu-GIŠ [x] KUR x [...]: This follows P.E. Botta's copy in Monument de Ninive; the exact reading of the name is unknown. The copies in JA and IdF have URU.ga-nu-GIŠ? x x x, where the -GIŠ? x could well be GA and the following x x (KUR x of Monument de Ninive) ṢU. M. El-Amin (Sumer 9 [1953] p. 53) suggested URU.ga-nu-⸢un-gu⸣-uḫ?-[tu] and connected it to the Ganguḫtu of text no. 27. As noted by A. Fuchs (Khorsabad p. 101 line 92 n. 1), A.T.E. Olmstead's suggestion that it might be compared with Qana in Sennacherib's royal inscriptions (e.g., Grayson and Novotny, RINAP 3/1 p. 117 no. 16 iv 73) and Qaniun in Harper, ABL no. 444 line 9 (= Lanfranchi and Parpola, SAA 5 no. 87) is unlikely since the former is in the vicinity of Mount Nipur and the latter in Urarṭu. There is room for ca. 10–12 signs in the gap before 6 URU.MEŠ. [KUR.ni-ik-sa-am]-⸢ma?⸣: Botta's copy has [...]-⸢a⸣; the squeeze is not clear at this point, but the sign does appear to end in one vertical wedge, not one vertical wedge on top of a second vertical wedge. Text no. 7 line 58 has KUR.ni-ik-sa-am-ma.

^{md}EN-LUGAL-*ú-ṣur* URU.⸢*ki*⸣-*še*-[*si-im*†]-⸢*a*⸣-*a*
qa-ti ⸢*ik-šu-ud*⸣-*ma*
94) *šá-a-šú a-di* NÍG.ŠU É.GAL-*šú a-na* KUR
aš-šur.KI† *ú-ra-a-šú* LÚ.*šu-ut* SAG-*ia* LÚ.EN.NAM
UGU URU-*šú áš-kun* DINGIR.MEŠ *a-li-kut*
maḫ-ri-ia i-na qer-bi-šu
95) *ú-še*-⸢*šib*⸣-*ma*† URU.*kar*-^{d}MAŠ.<MAŠ> MU-*šú*
ab-bi ṣa-lam LUGAL-*ti-ia i-na lìb-bi ul-ziz*
KUR.É-*sa-ag-bat* ⸢KUR⸣.É-*ḫi-ir-ma-mi*
KUR.É-*ú-mar-gi* URU.*ḫa*-⸢*ar*⸣-*ḫu-bar*-⸢*ban*⸣

(and) Armangu; and I added (them) to its province.

96) URU.*ki-lam-ba-a-ti* URU.*ar-ma-an-gu*
ak-šu-ud-ma UGU *pi-ḫa-ti-šú ú-rad-di*
URU.*ḫa-ar-ḫa-ra-a-a* ^{m}*ki-ba-ba*
LÚ.EN.URU-*šú-nu ir-du-du-ma*
97) *a-na* ^{m}*da-al-ta-a* KUR.*el-li-ba-a-a iš-pu-ru e-peš*
ARAD-*ti* URU *šu-a-tu ak-šu-ud-ma* ⸢*šal*⸣-*lat-su*
áš-lu-la UN.MEŠ KUR.KUR *ki-šit-ti qa-ti-ia*
98) *i-na lìb-bi ú-še-rib* LÚ.*šu-ut* SAG-⸢*ia*⸣ LÚ.EN.NAM
UGU-*šú-nu áš-kun* ÍD-*tu e-li*-⸢*tum*⸣ *ša*
KUR.*a-ra-an-ze-šú* ÍD-*tu šap-li-tu ša*
É-^{m}*ra-ma-tu-a*
99) KUR.*ú-ri-qa-tu* KUR.*si-ik-ri-is* KUR.*šá-pa-ar-da*
KUR.*ú-ri-ak-ku* 6 *na-gi-i ak-šu-ud-ma*
UGU-⸢*šú*⸣-*nu ú-rad-di* GIŠ.TUKUL ^{d}*aš-šur* EN-*ia*
a-na DINGIR-*ti-šú-un áš*-⸢*kun*⸣
100) URU.*kar*-^{m}LUGAL-GI.NA MU-*šú ab-bi ša* 28
LÚ.EN.URU.MEŠ-*ni ša* KUR.*ma-da-a-a dan-nu-ti*
ma-da-ta-šú-⸢*nu*⸣ *am-ḫur-ma ṣa-lam* LUGAL-*ti-ia*
i-na URU.*kar*-^{m}LUGAL-⸢GIN⸣ *ul*-⸢*ziz*⸣

96b–100) The people of the city Ḫarḫar drove out Kibaba, their city ruler, and sent to Daltâ of the land Ellipi to do obeisance (to him). I conquered that city and plundered it. I brought there people from the lands that I had conquered (and) set a eunuch of mi[ne] as provincial governor over them. I conquered the upper river(land) of the land Aranzêšu, the lower river(land) of Bīt-Ramatua, the land Uriqatu, the land Sikris, the land Šaparda, (and) the land Uriakku, (a total of) six districts, and added (them) to them (the people of the city Ḫarḫar). I estab[lished] the weapon of the god Aššur, my lord, to be their divinity. I (re)named it (the city Ḫarḫar) Kār-Šarrukīn. I received tribute from twenty-eight city lords of the powerful Medes and erected a royal image of myself in the city Kār-Šarrukīn.

101) *i-na* 7† BALA-*ia* ^{m}*ru-sa-a* KUR.*ur-ar-ṭa-a-a it-ti*
^{m}*ul-lu-su-nu* KUR.*man-na-a-a sar*$_{6}$-*ra-a-ti*
id-⸢*bu*⸣-*ub-ma* 22 URU.*bi-ra-a-te-šú e-kim-šú*
102) *a-mat taš-ger-ti ṭa-píl-ti* ^{m}*ul-lu-su-nu a-na*
^{m}*da-a-a-uk-ki* LÚ.GAR.KUR KUR.*man-na-a-a*
id-bu-ub-ma DUMU-*šu* ⸢*a*⸣-*na li-i-ṭi im-ḫur-šú*
a-na ^{d}*aš-šur* MAN [DINGIR.MEŠ]
103) *qa-a-ti áš-ši-ma* 22 URU.*bi-ra-a-ti šá-a-ti-na*
al-me KUR-*ud a-na mi-ṣir* ⸢KUR⸣ [*aš*†]-⸢*šur*⸣
[*ú*†]-⸢*ter-ra*⸣ $^{m⌜}$*da*⸣-*a-a-uk-ka a-di* ⸢*kim*⸣-*ti-šú*

101–104a) In my seventh regnal year, Rusâ, the Urarṭian, spoke deceitfully with Ullusunu, the Mannean, and took away from him twenty-two of his fortresses. He spoke treacherous words, libels against Ullusunu, to Dayukku, a governor of the land Mannea, and received his son as a hostage. I raised my hand(s) (in supplication) to the god Aššur, the king [of the gods], and (then) surrounded (and) conquered those twenty-two fortresses. [I ma]de (them part of) the territory of [Ass]yria. I depor[ted] Dayukku, together with

94b–95a Cf. text no. 2 lines 86b–87a and text no. 4 line 40′.

95 URU.*kar*-^{d}MAŠ.<MAŠ> "Kār-Ner<gal>: Or URU.*kar*-^{d}MAŠ "the city Kār-Ninurta". The squeeze is not preserved at this point and the reading ^{d}MAŠ.MAŠ is based on text no. 7 line 60. -*sa-ag-bat*: Note the writing -*sa-ga-bi* in text no. 117 ii 40; this could suggest that we should read -*sa-ga-be* here (as well as in text nos. 2 line 87, 4 line 41′, and 65 line 44), although it could also reflect an ancient misunderstanding. -⸢*ban*⸣: The reading is based on the squeeze; F. Thureau-Dangin (RA 24 [1927] p. 76) stated that the last sign was not NIM, as on P.E. Botta's and H. Winckler's copies (although see Winckler's note to the sign which suggests BAN instead).

97a Cf. text no. 2 lines 89b–90a and text no. 4 line 43′a.

98 ÍD-*tu e-li*-⸢*tum*⸣ and ÍD-*tu šap-li-tu* "the upper river(land)" and "the lower river(land)": Following a suggestion by G.B. Lanfranchi, S. Parpola and M. Porter (Helsinki Atlas maps 11–12 and p. 14), take these to refer to two particular rivers in Iran, while A. Bagg (personal communication) suggests they were possibly alternative names for Aranzêšu and Bīt-Ramatua respectively. *šap-li-tu*: H. Winckler's copy has *šap*$_{5}$-*li-tu*, but P.E. Botta's copy and the squeeze have *šap-li-tu*.

99 With regard to the "weapon of the god Aššur" being set up to be the god of the people of Ḫarḫar, cf. text no. 2 lines 92–93 and see Lanfranchi, SAAB 12 (1998) pp. 103–104.

100 Cf. text no. 2 lines 93–95.

101 Text no. 2 line 96 adds UD-*x-ti*-⸢*iš*⸣ before *e-kim-šú*.

102 MAN: So P.E. Botta's copy and the squeeze; H. Winckler's copy has ⸢MAN⸣, but in a note he indicates it might be the traces of EN-*ia* (thus ⸢EN⸣-[*ia*]).

103 [*ú*]-⸢*ter-ra*⸣: The reading is based on the squeeze as currently preserved. H. Winckler read *ú-tir-ra* and, based on his examination of the squeeze, F. Thureau-Dangin (RA 24 [1927] p. 76) read *ú-tir*(!)-*ra*. According to text no. 7 line 49b Dayukku and his family were deported to Hamath.

as-su-[ḫa-am-ma]

his family, [and] brought order to the disturbed land Mannea.

104) KUR.*man-na-a-a dal-ḫu ú-taq-qi-in ma-da-at-tu ša* ^{m}*ia-*⸢*an*?*-zu*?⸣*-ú* ⸢LUGAL⸣ [KUR.*na-ʾi*]-⸢*ri*⸣ [*i-na* URU].⸢*ḫu*⸣*-bu-*⸢*uš*⸣*-ki-a* URU-*šu* [*am-ḫur*] 9 URU.⸢*bi*⸣-[*ra-a-ti*]

105) [... *ša* 5] ⸢*na*⸣*-gi-*⸢*i*⸣ [*šá* ^{m}*ur*]-⸢*sa*⸣*-a* KUR.⸢*ur*⸣-[*ar-ṭa-a-a a-di*? *mar-ši-ti-šú-nu*? ...] AN [*x x*]

106) [*x x*] *x* [...] *x-ba-ni* GU$_4$.MEŠ*-šú-nu* ⸢*ṣe*⸣*-ni-šú-nu* ⸢*áš*⸣-[*lu-la* 8 URU†.*bi*†]-⸢*ra-a*?*-ti a-di*⸣ URU.MEŠ*-ni* [*ša li-me*†]-*ti-*⸢*šú*⸣-[*nu*]

107) [*ša*] ⸢KUR⸣.*tu-a-*⸢*ia*⸣-[*di na-ge-e šá* ^{m†}]⸢*te*⸣*-lu-si-na* KUR.*an-di-a-a ak-šu-ud* [4] ⸢LIM⸣ 2 [ME] ⸢UN.MEŠ *a*⸣*-di mar-ši-*⸢*ti*⸣*-šú-nu áš-lu-la* URU.⸢*bi*⸣-[*ra-a*]*-te šá-a-ti-*[*na*]

108) [*ap*]*-pul aq-qur* [*i-na* IZI *áš-ru-up ṣa*]*-lam* LUGAL*-ti-ia* DÙ*-uš-ma li-*⸢*i*⸣*-ti* ^{d}*a-šur* ⸢EN-*ia*⸣ UGU*-šú áš-ṭur i-na* ⸢URU⸣.*i-zi-ir-ti* URU *šar-ru-*[*ti*]

109) ⸢*ša*⸣ KUR.*man-na-*⸢*a*⸣-[*a ul-ziz* UN].⸢MEŠ⸣ ÍD*-ti*

104b–109a) [I received] tribute from Ia[nz]û, k[ing of the land Naʾi]ri, [in] his city [Ḫ]ubuškia. (105) [*I conquered*] nine fo[rtresses ...] I [carried off as booty *the people* of five di]stricts [of U]rsâ (Rusâ), [the] U[rarṭian, *together with their property* ...] ... their oxen, (and) their sheep and goats. I conquered [eight for]tresses, together with the settlements [in] the[ir enviro]ns, [that] belonged to the land Tuāy[adi, a district belonging to T]elusina of the land Andia. I carried off as booty [4],2[00] peo[ple], together with their property. [I des]troyed, demolished, (and) [burned down with fire] tho[se] for[tress]es. I made [a] royal [im]age of myself and wrote upon it the victor(ies) of the god Aššur, [m]y lo[rd. I (then) erected (it)] in the city Izirtu, the royal city [o]f the land Mannea.

e-li-ti ù šap-li-ti ša i-na ger-⸢*ri*⸣*-ia maḫ-*⸢*ri*⸣*-ti it-ti* ⸢UN⸣.MEŠ URU.*ḫar-ḫar am-nu-u* KUR.É-⸢*sa*⸣*-an-*⸢*gi-bu*⸣-[*ti*]

110) [KUR].*ú-*⸢*ri*⸣-[*qa-tu* KUR.*si*]-⸢*ik*⸣*-ri-is* KUR.*šá-pa-ar-da* KUR.*up-pa-ri-a a-na i-di-šú-nu ú-ter-ru-*⸢*ma*⸣ *ib-*⸢*bal*⸣*-ki-tu it-ti-*⸢*ia*⸣

111) [(*x*)] *na-*⸢*gu*⸣-[*ú šu-a-tu i*]-⸢*na*⸣ GIŠ.TUKUL *ú-šam-qit-ma šal-la-su-nu áš-lu-la* URU.*ka-x-*⸢*na*⸣ URU.*ki-in-za-*⸢*ar*⸣*-ba-*⸢*ra*⸣ URU.*ḫa-al-bu-*⸢*uk*⸣*-nu*

112) [(*x*)] ⸢URU.*šu*⸣-[*x x x x x* (*x*)] KU URU.*an-za-ri-a ša* ÍD*-ti e-li-ti šap-*⸢*li-ti ak*⸣*-šu-ud-*[*ma*† 4† LIM] *zi-*⸢*im*⸣ [*pa*†]-⸢*ni*⸣ LÚ.*qu-ra-di-šú-nu* 4 LIM 8 ME 20

113) ⸢UN⸣.[MEŠ *a-di mar-ši-ti*]*-šú-nu* ⸢*i-na*⸣ *uš-man-ni-ia am-ḫur* URU.*ki-šeš-lu*

109b–114a) [The people] of the upper and lower river(lands), whom in my previous campaign I had considered as people of the city Ḫarḫar, made the lands Bīt-Sangib[uti], Ur[iqatu, Si]kris, Šaparda, (and) Upparia side with them and (then) revolted against m[e]. I struck down [that] dis[trict wi]th the sword and plundered them. [I] conquered the cities Ka...na, Kinzarbara, Ḫalbuknu, Š[u..., ...], (and) Anzaria of the upper (and) lower river(lands) [and] received in my (military) camp [4,000] *fa*[*ce-(guards)*] of their warriors (*as trophies*) (and) 4,820 [peo]ple, [together with] their [property]. I [re]built the cities Kišešlu, Qindāu, Anzaria, (and) Bīt-Gabāya that I had conquered. I (then) (re)[na]med them Kār-Nabû, Kār-Sîn, Kār-Adad, (and) Kār-Išt[ar].

---

104 KUR.*man-na-a-a dal-ḫu* "the disturbed land Mannea": We might expect *daliḫtu* rather than *dalḫu*, but the names of lands are sometimes given masculine adjectives (e.g., text no. 43 line 31 and text no. 65 line 57). 9 URU.⸢*bi*⸣-[*ra-a-ti*]: See also F. Thureau-Dangin (RA 24 [1927] p. 76) for this reading.

Section 9 = lines 105–117 = II,10:1–13: See Winckler, Sar. Annals lines 79–91; Lie, Sar. lines 105–117; and Fuchs, Khorsabad Annals lines 105–117. Cf. text no. 2 lines 100–101+.

106 [...] *x-ba-ni*: P.E. Botta's copy has no trace of a sign before *-ba-ni*, while H. Winckler's copy has the trace of a ḪAL towards the bottom of the sign; A. Fuchs (Khorsabad p. 107 line 106 n. 1) suggests ⸢GAG⸣ or ⸢RAB⸣ based on the squeeze. [URU.*bi*]-⸢*ra-a*?*-ti*⸣: Winckler's copy has URU.*bi-ra-a-ti*, but Botta's copy has [...]-⸢*ra-ti*⸣ and the squeeze currently has [...]-⸢*ra*?*-a*?*-ti*⸣.

107 H. Winckler's copy has "[" before 4 LIM, but there is no matching "]," although square brackets are later put around [*bi-ra-a*]-. Thus, it is not clear what he saw on the squeeze for the part of the line between these markers.

110 [KUR].*ú-*⸢*ri*⸣-[*qa-tu*]: Or [KUR].*ú-*⸢*ri*⸣-[*ak-ku/ki*]; H. Winckler's copy has [KUR].*ú-ri-*[*ak-ki*]. See line 99 above and text no. 2 line 92.

111 URU.*ka-x-*⸢*na*⸣ URU.*ki-in-za-*⸢*ar*⸣*-ba-*⸢*ra*⸣: The reading is based on the squeeze. P.E. Botta's copy has URU.*ka-*[*x x x*] *x ki-in-za-*⸢*ar*⸣*-ba-x*, while H. Winckler's copy has URU.*ka-qu*?*-na-ki-in-za-ar-ba-ra*. F. Thureau-Dangin (RA 24 [1927] p. 76) copied URU.⸢*ka*⸣*-x-*⸢*na*⸣ URU.*ki-in-za-*⸢*ar-ba-ra*⸣. Winckler puts "]" at the end of the line, after *-nu*, with no matching earlier "[".

112 [(*x*)] ⸢URU.*šu*⸣-[*x x x x x* (*x*)] KU: The reading is based on the current state of the squeeze; H. Winckler's copy appears to indicate ⸢URU⸣.*šu*-[...]-⸢*al*⸣, with room for about four signs in the gap, but due to his manner of giving square brackets and indicating damage, this cannot be considered certain for the beginning of the passage, and the squeeze clearly has a KU form at the end, not ⸢AL⸣. Following the traces on Winckler's copy, A.T.E. Olmstead (AJSL 47 [1930–31] p. 266) restored URU.*šu-*[*an-da-ḫa*]-⸢*al*⸣, but as noted by A. Fuchs (Khorsabad p. 108 line 112 n. 2) that city lay in Mannea (although disputed with Zikirtu), while this passage deals with a different area. *zīm pānī*: The phrase literally means "appearance of the face," but the meaning here is not clear. The tentative translation "*face-(guards)*" for *zīm pānī* follows CDA p. 447 (cf. CAD Z p. 122) and assumes that they refer to the extensions from helmets used to protect the ears/checks. However, some Assyrian reliefs indicate that the severed heads of defeated enemies were at times collected and counted by Assyrian soldiers, and it is quite possible that this phrase refers to them instead; see also Fuchs, Khorsabad p. 319 n. 257.

113 URU.É-*ga-ba-ia*: Cf. text no. 7 line 64 URU.É-^{m}*ba-ga-ia* and text no. 28 URU.É-*ba-ga-ia*.

URU.qí-in-da-a-ú URU.an-⸢za-ri⸣-a
URU.É-ga-ba-ia ša ak-šu-⸢du⸣
114) [a-na eš-šu]-⸢ti⸣ DÙ-⸢uš URU⸣.kar-^{d}⸢AG⸣
URU.kar-^{d}EN.ZU URU.kar-^{d}⸢IŠKUR⸣
URU.kar-⸢^{d}⸣iš-⸢tar⸣ [MU†]-šú-nu ab-bi a-na
šuk-nu-uš KUR.⸢ma⸣-da-a-⸢a⸣
115) [li-me-et URU.kar-^{m}LUGAL]-⸢GI⸣.NA
⸢ú-dan⸣-ni-⸢na ri⸣-ki-si-in ša 22
LÚ.EN.⸢URU⸣.MEŠ-ni ⸢ša⸣ KUR.ma-⸢da⸣-[a†]-a
dan-nu-ti ma-da-⸢at⸣-ta-šú-nu
116) [am-ḫur x x x x x (x)] ⸢ME⸣ (x) [x x x x]
⸢URU⸣.ki-mir-ra ša KUR.É-ḫa-am-⸢ban ak⸣-šu-ud
1 LIM ⸢5+(1) ME 30 UN.MEŠ⸣ a-di
mar-ši-ti-⸢šú⸣-nu áš-lu-lam†-⸢ma⸣
117) [...] ⸢a-na⸣ [ka-šad? LÚ.ia-am-na-a-a? ša
šu-bat-sún]
118) [ina] ⸢MURUB$_{4}$? tam⸣-tim na-da-at ša ul-tu
⸢UD⸣.[MEŠ] ru-⸢ú⸣-[qu†-te†] ⸢UN†⸣.[MEŠ
URU.ṣur]-⸢ri⸣ [KUR].qu-e i-du-ku-ma ú-[x (x)] A
a-lak x [x (x)]
119) [ina? GIŠ.MÁ?].MEŠ [(x)] ⸢NA?⸣ ŠI a-na tam-di
ú-ri-da-⸢áš⸣-šú-nu-ti-ma ⸢ṣe⸣-ḫer ⸢ra⸣-bi ⸢i-na⸣
GIŠ.TUKUL ú-šam-qit URU.ḫa-⸢ar†⸣-ru-a
⸢URU†⸣.uš-na-ni-is?
120) ⸢URU.qu-um⸣-a-⸢si?⸣ ša KUR.qu-e šá ^{m}mi-ta-a
LUGAL KUR.mu-⸢us⸣-ki e-⸢ki-mu⸣ ak-šu-⸢ud⸣
[šal†]-la-su-nu áš-lu-la LÚ.ta-mu†-di
⸢LÚ⸣.[i]-ba†-a-di-di
121) ⸢LÚ⸣.mar-si-ma-[ni] LÚ.ḫa-ia-pa-a KUR.ar-ba-a-a
ru-ú-qu-ti a-ši-bu-ut mad-ba-ri ša LÚ.ak-⸢lu⸣
LÚ.šá-pi-ru la i-du-ma
122) ša a-na LUGAL ia-im-ma bi-lat-su-un la
iš-⸢šu⸣-ma i-na GIŠ.⸢TUKUL⸣ ^{d}aš-šur be-⸢lí⸣-ia

114b–117a) In order to subjugate Media [in the environs of the city Kār-Šarruk]īn, I reinforced their (the people of the riverlands) [de]fenses (lit.: "[st]uctures"). [I received tribute from twenty-two [city] rulers of the powerful Med[e]s. [...] I conquered [(...) the ci]ty Kimirra of the land Bīt-Ḫamban. I carried off as booty 1,530/1,630 people, together with their property, an[d ...]

117b–120a) In ord[er to *conquer the Ionians*, whose abode] is situated [in the] m[iddle of the s]ea (and) who from the dis[tant] pa[st] had killed pe[ople of the city Ty]re (and) [of the land] Que (Cilicia) and [...-ed] ..., I went down to the sea [*in ship*]*s* ... against them and struck (them) down with the sword, (both) young (and) old. (120) I conquer[ed] the cities Ḫa[r]rua, Ušnanis, (and) Qumas[i] of the land Que that Mitâ, king of the land Musku, had t[ak]en away, (and) I plundered them.

120b–123a) (As for) the Tamudu, [I]bādidi, Marsīma[ni], (and) Ḫayappa (tribes), faraway Arabs who live in the desert, did not know (either) overseer (or) commander, and had never brought their tribute to any king, I struck them down with the sword of the god Aššur, my lord, deported the remainder of them, and (re)settled (them) in the city Samaria.

---

114 KUR.⸢*ma*⸣-*da-a*-⸢*a*⸣: P.E. Botta's copy has ^{m}*da-a*-⸢*a*⸣ and H. Winckler's KUR.*ma-da-a*-⸢*a*⸣; KUR.⸢*ma*⸣- is clear on the squeeze.
115 For the restorations at the beginning of the line, see text no. 7 line 66, which has *maṣṣartu* instead of *rikissin*. H. Winckler puts "]" at the end of the line, after -*nu*, with no preceding matching "[" bracket.
116 1 LIM ⸢5+(1) ME 30⸣: P.E. Botta's copy has 2 LIM ⸢5+(1⸣) [x] 30, and H. Winckler's 2 LIM 5 ME ⸢30⸣, with a note indicating the 30 might be 50; however, the squeeze clearly has only 1 LIM and based on the spacing of the wedges, perhaps more likely 6 ME than 5 ME, followed by ⸢30⸣.
117 Possibly restore *šuk-nu-uš* instead of *ka-šad* (as already noted by Fuchs, Khorsabad p.109 line 117 n. 1). The restoration LÚ.*ia-am-na-a-a ša šu-bat-sún* follows Winckler, AOF 1 p. 368. The Ionians are mentioned in several of Sargon's inscriptions; see the index of geographic, ethnic, and tribal names at the back of this volume. With regard to the Akkadian words for Ionia and Ionians, see Brinkman in Studies Schoder pp. 53–71; and Muhly in Karageorghis and Kouka, Cyprus and the East Aegean pp. 23–30. W. Röllig (RLA 5/1–2 [1976] p. 150) suggests that LÚ.*ia-am-na-a-a* might be Ionian pirates on the Cilician coast; but see Lanfranchi, Melammu 1 pp. 14–22. See also Rollinger, RA 91 (1997) pp. 167–172; and Rollinger in Melammu 1 p. 13 n. 20 and Melammu 2 pp. 233–264.
Section 10 = lines 118–130 = II,11:1–13: See Winckler, Sar. Annals lines 92–104; Lie, Sar. lines 118–130; and Fuchs, Khorsabad Annals lines 118–130.
118 [*ina*] ⸢MURUB$_{4}$? *tam*⸣-*tim*: P.E. Botta's copy has [x] GIŠ [x]-*tim*, while H. Winckler copies a Winkelhaken after the GIŠ and suggests it might be the remains of a ŠA. The squeeze currently has only indistinct traces before ⸢*tam*⸣-*tim* and the copies in JA and IdF put the GIŠ in the second line of the slab. A.G. Lie reads [*i-na a-ḫi tam*]-*tim*. The proposed reading follows A. Fuchs (Khorsabad p. 109 line 118), but the spacing on the squeeze might suggest a longer restoration. [URU.*ṣur*]-⸢*ri*⸣: For the reading, see text no. 43 line 21; cf. Olmstead, AJSL 47 (1930–31) p. 266. *a-lak x* [*x* (*x*)]: Or *a-lak x x* of JA and IdF copies. Possibly *a-lak*-⸢*tu*⸣, following A.T.E. Olmstead (AJSL 47 [1930-31] p. 266) and Fuchs (Khorsabad, p. 109 line 118 n. 3); Fuchs (ibid. p. 320) tenatively translates "Handelsverkehr *unterbrachen*," which is followed by F.M. Fales (SAAB 23 [2017] p. 235) "*interrupted* commercial traffic."
119 [*ina*? GIŠ.MÁ?].MEŠ [(*x*)] ⸢NA?⸣ ŠI: The restoration [*ina* GIŠ.MÁ].MEŠ follows Fuchs, Khorsabad p. 109 line 119 (cf. Grayson, RIMA 3 p. 36 A.0.102.6 ii 12–13), who then very tentatively suggests [KUR].*ḫat*?-*ti*? based on Grayson and Novotny, RINAP 3/1 p. 222 no. 34 line 23; the traces on the squeeze do not support the latter reading. The JA and IdF copies have [*x* (*x*)] GIŠ [*x*].MEŠ [(*x*)] ⸢NA?⸣ ŠI, but the GIŠ may actually have been on the previous line (see the on-page note to line 118). A. Fuchs notes that the ŠI may have been written for ME, as in some other places.
121 -*ma*-[*ni*]: H. Winckler restores -[*nu*] rather than -[*ni*].
122 LUGAL *ia-im-ma*: As noted by H.W.F. Saggs (JSS 42 [1997]: 139), P.E. Botta's copy has a damaged area between the LUGAL and the IA which might suggest [*a*]-*ia-im-ma*. The squeeze would permit such a restoration, but does not require one.

ú-šam-qit-su-nu-ti-ma si-it-ta-te-šú-nu as-su-ḫa-am-ma

123) i-na ⸢URU⸣.sa-⸢me$^{?}$⸣-ri-na ú-še-šib ša ^{m}pi-ir-⸢ʾi⸣ LUGAL KUR.mu-ṣu-ri ^{f}sa-⸢am⸣-si šar-rat KUR.a-ri†-bi ^{m}it-⸢ʾa⸣-am-ra KUR.sa-ba-ʾa-a-a

124) LUGAL.MEŠ-ni ša a-ḫi tam-tim ù mad-⸢ba-ri KÙ.GI⸣ SAḪAR.BI KUR.RA ni-siq-ti ⸢NA$_4$⸣.MEŠ ZÚ AM.⸢SI⸣ NUMUN GIŠ.ESI ⸢ŠIM⸣.ḪI.A ka-la-ma† ANŠE.KUR.RA†.MEŠ

125) ANŠE.A.AB.BA.MEŠ ⸢ma⸣-da-ta-šú-nu ⸢am-ḫur⸣ ša ⸢^{m}mi⸣-ta-a LUGAL KUR.mu-us-ki i-na na-⸢gi⸣-šu rap-še a-di ⸢2$^{?}$⸣-šú [BAD$_5$].⸢BAD$_5$†⸣-šu aš-kun-ma URU.ḫa-ar†-ru-a

126) URU.uš-na-ni-is URU.ḪAL.ṢU.MEŠ ⸢KUR⸣.qu-e ša ul-tu UD.MEŠ ru-qu-ú-ti i-na ⸢da⸣-na-a-ni e-ki-mu áš-ru-uš-šin ú-te-er-ra

127) i-na 8 BALA-ia a-na KUR.man-na-a-a ⸢KUR⸣.ma-da-a-a ⸢al-lik⸣ ma-da-at-tu ša ⸢KUR⸣.man-na-a-a KUR.el-li-pa-a-a [x] KI [x x x (x)]

128) LÚ.EN.URU.MEŠ-ni ⸢ša⸣ KUR.MEŠ-e am-ḫur ^{m}zi-zi-i ^{m}za-la-⸢a⸣ LÚ.EN.URU.MEŠ†-ni ša URU.<<x>>-gi-⸢zi†⸣-[il-bu-un-di na-gi]-i†

129) ⸢ša⸣ LUGAL.MEŠ-ni a-li-kut maḫ-ri-ia la im-ḫu-ru bi-lat-su-⸢un⸣ ma-da-⸢at⸣-[ta-šú-nu] am-ḫur†-⸢ma⸣ [x x x (x)]

130) [(x)] x (x) [x x x x (x)] x [x x x (x)] x [x x x x x x x (x)] KUR KUR x [x x x x x x x x x (x)] ša [^{m}mi-ta-at-ti]

131) [KUR].⸢zi⸣-kir-ta-a-a di-ik-ta-šú a-duk 3 URU.MEŠ-ni dan-nu-ti a-di 24 URU.MEŠ-ni ša li-me-ti-šú†-nu [(x x x)]

132) ⸢ak⸣-šu-⸢ud šal†⸣-la-su-nu áš-lu-la URU.pa-ar-da

123b–125a) [I] received as tribute from Pirʾû (Pharaoh), king of Egypt, Sa[m]si, queen of the Arabs, (and) Itʾamar, the Sabaean, kings from the seashore and desert, gold — ore from the mountain(s) — precious stones, elephant ivory, seed(s) from ebony tree(s), every kind of aromatic, horses, (and) camels.

125b–126) For a *second* time, I brought about [the def]eat of Mitâ, king of the land Musku, in his (own) wide district and I (then) restored to their former status the cities Ḫarrua (and) Ušnanis, fortresses of the land Que (Cilicia) that he had taken away by force in the distant past.

127–133a) In my eighth regnal year, I marched to the lands Mannea and Media. I received tribute from the people of the lands Mannea, Ellipi, (and) [Media], city lords of the mountains. (As for) Zīzî (and) Zalâ, the city lords of [the distri]ct Giz[ilbunda, from wh]om the kings who preceded me had never received tribute, I received trib[ute from them] an[d ... (130) ...] lands [...] I inflicted a defeat on [Mitatti of the land Z]ikirtu. [I (surrounded and)] conquer[ed] three fortified cities, together with twenty-four settlements in their environs, [(...)]. I plundered them (and) burned down Parda, his royal city, with fire. However, that (man) (Mitatti), together with the people of [his] land, fled and their whereabouts have never been discovered.

123 ⸢URU⸣.sa-⸢me$^{?}$⸣-ri-na: P.E. Botta's copies have ŠI for ME, while H. Winckler's copy has ME and the squeeze is unclear, allowing either reading; note the commentary to line 119. KUR.a-ri†-bi: Possibly KUR.a-rib-bi, following Winckler's copy; however, Botta's copy in Monument de Ninive has a KID for the RI and his copies in JA and IdF have one long horizontal wedge cutting through three vertical wedges. ^{m}pi-ir-⸢ʾi⸣: According to A. Spalinger, Pirʾû, which stands for pharaoh, must refer to an Egyptian ruler and not one of the Kushite rulers of Egypt (JARCE 10 [1973] p. 100). For tribute from Pirʾû, Samsi, and Itʾamar, see also text no. 7 line 27. Note also text no. 82 vii 30′′ with regard to rebels in the southern Levant requesting military aid from Pirʾû in 711.

125b–126 Cf. text no. 74 v 34–40.

127 [x] KI [x x x (x)]: So the copy in Monument de Ninive and essentially that of H. Winckler; the squeeze is not helpful at this point. The JA and IdF copies have x KI† [(x)] MAN x ⸢A$^{?}$⸣. As noted by A. Fuchs (Khorsabad p. 110 line 127 n. 2), we would expect KUR.ma-da-a-a here.

128 ^{m}za-la-⸢a⸣: P.E. Botta's copy in Monument de Ninive has ^{m}za-la-ERIM, but F. Thureau-Dangin (RA 24 [1927] p. 76) read ^{m}za-⸢la⸣-a, based on the squeeze, and the squeeze currently would support the suggested reading. The copies in JA and IdF are closer to A (although with two question marks and an angled wedge at the front) than ERIM. URU.⸢MEŠ†⸣-ni: Botta's copy in Monument de Ninive has URU.ME-U-ni, without indicating the presence of any damage; the JA and IdF copies are similar but also have a small Winkelhaken attached to the beginning of the NI, which is here assumed to be the end of the MEŠ. URU.<<x>>.gi-⸢zi†⸣-[il-bu-un-di na-gi]-i†: Botta's copy has URU x gi-⸢zi*⸣(copy: MIN[]) [x x x (x)] LÚ. As noted by A. Fuchs (Khorsabad p. 111 line 128 n. 2), the traces between the URU and GI may be a copyist's (i.e., Botta's) error. Based on the spacing of Botta's copies, there is not room for the proposed restoration, but he is not always accurate with regard to the spacing on his copies.

130 The JA and IdF copies include a few more indistinct traces than appear in the copy in Monument de Ninive; they are not indicated in the score.

Section 11 = lines 131–143 = II,12:1–13: See Winckler, Sar. Annals lines 105–117; Lie, Sar. lines 131–143; and Fuchs, Khorsabad Annals lines 131–143.

131 -kir-: The copy in Monument de Ninive has MA-ḪA, but the JA and IdF copies have -kir-, with just a little space after the three horizontal wedges before the vertical wedges. [(x x x)]: P.E. Botta's copies indicate damage at the end of the line, with room for two or three signs; H. Winckler's copy indicates no damage at the end of the line, but he had not collated any squeeze. Thus, it is not clear if there was anything missing at the end of the line or not. A. Fuchs (Khorsabad p. 111 line 131 n. 1) suggests that if there was anything missing, it might be *al-me*, "I surrounded."

132 -šu-⸢ud⸣: P.E. Botta's copy in Monument de Ninive has -MA-[x], but the JA and IdF copies have an additional angled wedge-head at the beginning of the first sign and follow this sign with two angled-wedgeheads.

URU LUGAL-*ti-šu i-na* ^{d}GIBIL$_{6}$ *aq-mu ù šu-ú a-di* UN.MEŠ KUR-[*šú*]

133) *in-na-bi-du-ú-ma la in*†*-na-mir a-šar-*⸢*šu*⸣*-un di-ik*†*-tu ša* ^{m}*ur-sa-a* KUR.*ú-ra-ar-ṭa-a-*⸢*a*⸣

134) *a-na* ⸢*la*†*-a*⸣ *ma-ni a-duk* 2 ME 60 NUMUN LUGAL-*ti-šu*† LÚ.*ša pét-ḫal-lì-šu i-na qa-a-ti ú-ṣab-bit a-na šu-zu-*⸢*ub*†⸣

135) ⸢ZI.MEŠ⸣-*šu* ⸢*i-na*⸣ MUNUS.ANŠE.KUR.RA *ir-kab-ma* KUR-*a-šu e-li* 5 KASKAL.GÍD *qaq-qa-ru ul-tu* KUR.*ú-a-ú-*⸢*uš*⸣

136) [*a*]-⸢*di*†⸣ KUR.*zi-mur ar-du-us-su* KUR.*ú-iš*†*-di-iš* KUR.*na-gu-ú ša* KUR.*man-na-a-a e-ki-ma-áš-šum-*[*ma*]

137) [*a*]-⸢*na*⸣ ^{m}*ul-lu-su-nu* KUR.*man-na-a-a ad-*⸢*din*⸣ URU.*uš-qa-ia* URU.*bir-tu ša i-na né-reb* KUR.*za-ra-an-*[*da*]

138) [*na*]-⸢*gi*⸣*-i i-na* KUR.*ma-al-la-a-ú šad-di* ŠIM.LI *rak-sa-tu a-di* 1 ME 15 URU.MEŠ-*ni-šá ak-šu-*[*ud*]

139) [URU].*a-ni-áš-ta-ni-a ša mi-ṣir* KUR.É-*sa-an-gi-bu-ti* URU.*tar*†*-ú-i* URU.*tar-ma-ki-sa ša* KUR.*da-la-*⸢*a*⸣-[*a*]

140) ⸢*ta*†⸣*-mir-ti* URU.*ul-ḫu ša* GÌR KUR.*kiš-pal* KUR-*e* 21 URU.MEŠ-*ni dan-nu-ti a-di* ⸢1⸣ ME 40 URU.MEŠ-[*ni*]

141) [*ša*] *li-me*†*-ti-šu-nu ša* UGU KUR.*ar-za-bi-a* KUR-*i ak-šu-ud i-na i-šá-a-ti áš-ru-*⸢*up*⸣ [(*x*)]

142) [7] ⸢URU†⸣.MEŠ-*ni* ⸢*dan*†⸣*-nu-ti a-di* 30 URU.MEŠ-*ni ša li-me-ti-šu-nu ša* KUR.*ar-ma-ri-*[*ia*]-⸢*li*⸣-[*i*]

143) [*ša i-na* GÌR.II KUR].*ú-bi-an-da* KUR-*i ak*†*-šud* URU.*ar-bu a-šar* ^{m}*ru-sa-a* ḪI AN *x* [...]

144) [URU].⸢*ri-ia-ar* URU *ša*⸣ $^{m⸢d⸣}$INANNA-⸢BÀD⸣ *x* [*x x x*] ⸢MAḪ⸣ [(*x*) *x x x x x x x x*] *x* [*x x ak*]-⸢*šu*⸣*-ud* 30 URU.MEŠ-⸢*ni*⸣

145) ⸢*dan-nu*⸣*-ti ša* KUR.*a-ia-id na-gi-i ša a-ḫi tam-*⸢*tim*⸣ URU.*ar-*⸢*giš-ti*⸣*-ú-*⸢*na*⸣ URU.*qa-*⸢*al*⸣*-la-*⸢*ni*⸣*-a ša* UGU KUR.*ar-ṣi-*[*du*]

146) [KUR].⸢*maḫ-ḫa-un-ni-a*⸣ KUR.MEŠ-*e ru-uk-ku-sa bi-ru-*⸢*uš*⸣*-šú-un* 5 URU.*bi-ra-a-ti ša li-me-et*

133b–147a) I defeated countless (troops) of Ursâ (Rusâ), the Urarṭian. (and) captured two hundred and sixty members of his royal family (and) his cavalrymen. In order to save (135) his [li]fe, he mounted a mare and took to the hill(s). I pursued him over a distance of five leagues, from Mount Uau[š as far] as Mount Zimur. I took away from him the land Uišdiš, a district of the land Mannea, [and] gave (it) [t]o Ullusunu, the Mannean. I conque[red] the city Ušqaya — a fortress that was constructed in the pass to the [dis]trict Zaran[da] (and) on Mount Mallāu, a mountain with juniper tree(s) — together with its one hundred and fifteen settlements. I conquered (and) burned down with fire [the city] Aniaštania, which is on the border of the land Bīt-Sangibuti, the cities Tarui (and) Tarmakisa of the land Dalāy[a], (140) the environs of the city Ulḫu, which is (located) at the foot of Mount Kišpal, (and) twenty-one fortified cities, together with one hundred and forty settlements [in] their environs, which are (located) on Mount Arzabia. I conquered [seven] fortified ci[ti]es, together with thirty settlements in their environs, which belong to the land Armari[ya]l[î (and) are (located) at the foot of] Mount] Ubianda. [I ccon]quered the city Arbu, where Rusâ ... [..., the city] Riyar, a city belonging to Ištar-dūrī (Sarduri), [...]. I conquered (and) burned down with fire thirty (145) [for]tified cities of the district Ayaid (Ayādi), which is (located) on the shore of the sea, the cities Arg[išt]iun[a] (and) Qallania — which were constructed upon (and) between the mountains Arṣi[du (and)] M[a]ḫḫ[a]u[n]nia — (and) five fortresses in the environs of the land Uayi[s], [tog]et[her] with [f]orty settlements of the district Uayis.

---

135 ⸢MEŠ⸣: The JA and IdF copies have a vertical wedge followed by a Winkelhaken, although nothing of the sign is given on the Monument de Ninive copy. 5: The copies in JA and IdF have 6.

140 KUR.*kiš-pal*: Cf. KUR.*kiš-te-er* in text no. 65 line 212. 21: Or 20+[20/30]+1, but note 21 in text no. 65 line 239. ⸢1⸣ ME 40: 1 ME ⸢46$^{?}$⸣ in text no. 65 line 268.

142 For the restoration at the beginning of the line, see text no. 65 line 272. JA and IdF have [...] *x* ⸢URU⸣.MEŠ at the beginning of the line, although nothing before the MEŠ is found on the copy in Monument de Ninive. The traces before the ⸢URU⸣ may be two of the wedgeheads of the number, i.e. [5]+2.

143 For the restoration at the beginning of the line, see text no. 65 line 272. ^{m}*ru-sa-a* ḪI AN *x* [...]: P.E. Botta's copy in Monument de Ninive has ^{m}*ru-sa-*<*a*> AN *x* [...], but his copies in JA and IdF have ^{m}*ru-sa-a* ḪI AN *x* [...], where the ḪI AN could of course be A'.

Section 12 = lines 144–156 II,13:1–13: See Winckler, Sar. Annals lines 118–130; Lie, Sar. lines 144–156; and Fuchs, Khorsabad Annals lines 144–156.

144 H. Winckler's copy has MURUB$_{4}^{?}$ after BÀD.

145 KUR.*a-ia-id*: The reading follows Ch.-F. Jean's (RA 24 [1927] p. 79); the squeeze currently has ⸢KUR.*a-ia-id*⸣. Both P.E. Botta and H. Winckler's copies have KUR.*a*-RA-A-*id*; F. Thureau-Dangin initially suggested KUR.*a-*⸢*ia*⸣*-a-id* (TCL 3 p. 70 n. 5), but later retracted that reading and read KUR.*a-i-a-id* (RA 24 [1927] p. 75 n. 2). Cf. text no. 65 line 297 KUR.*a-ia-di*. URU.*qa-*⸢*al*⸣*-la-*⸢*ni*⸣*-a*: The reading follows the squeeze and Jean's copy. Cf. text no. 65 line 297 ÍD.*qa-al-la-ni-a*. Botta's copy has URU.*qa-*⸢*al*⸣-[(*x*)] and Winckler's URU.*qa-du-la-ni*$^{?}$*-a*.

146 [KUR].⸢*maḫ-ḫa-un-ni-a*⸣: The reading is based on the squeeze, Ch.-F. Jean's copy, and Thureau-Dangin, TCL 3 p. 70 line 120; H. Winckler read KUR.*ar*$^{?}$*-za-ú*$^{?}$*-ni*$^{?}$*-a*. A. Fuchs (Khorsabad p. 113 line 146) restores *ù* at the very beginning of the line, but there would not appear to be room for this.

KUR.*ú-a-ii-*⸢*is*⸣

147) [*a*]-⸢*di*⸣ [10]+30 URU.MEŠ-*ni ša* KUR.*ú-a-ii-*⸢*is*⸣ *na-gi-i ak-šu-ud i-na* IZI *áš-ru-up ša* ^{m}*ia-an-zu-*⸢*ú*⸣

148) ⸢LUGAL KUR⸣.*na-*⸢*ʾi*⸣*-ri i-na* URU.*ḫu-bu-uš-ki-a* URU *dan-nu-ti-šú* ANŠE.KUR.RA.MEŠ GU$_4$.MEŠ *ṣe-e-ni ma-da-ta-šu am-*[*ḫur*]

149) [^{m}]⸢*ur*⸣*-za-na* ⸢URU⸣.*mu-*[*ṣa*]*-ṣir-a-a ša ma-mit* ^{d}*aš-šur ù* ^{d}AMAR.UTU *e-ti-qu-ma* UGU ^{m}*ur-sa-a* KUR.*ur-ar-ṭa-a-a iš-*⸢*pú*⸣-[*ra*]

150) ⸢*ša-ru*?⸣ ^{d}*aš-*⸢*šur*⸣ *be-lí ú-ta-ki-la-an-ni-ma* ⸢*i*⸣*-na* 1 GIŠ.GIGIR-*ia ù* 1 LIM ANŠE.*pét-ḫal* GÌR.II-*ia šit-mur-ti* LÚ.*zu-uk* GÌR.II-*ia le-*[*ʾu-ut*]

151) ⸢*ta*⸣*-ḫa-zi* KUR.*ši-ia-ak* KUR.*ar-di-*⸢*ik*⸣*-ši* KUR.*ú-la-a-iu-ú* KUR.*al-lu-ri-a* KUR.MEŠ-*e mar-ṣu-ti* A.ŠÀ DÙG.⸢GA⸣

152) [*i*]-⸢*na*⸣ *ru-kub* ANŠE.KUR.RA.MEŠ *ù mar-ṣa i-na* GÌR.II-*ia e-ta-ti-iq-ma* ^{m}*ur-za-na* URU.*mu-ṣa-ṣir-a-a a-lak ger-ri-*[*ia*]

153) ⸢*iš-me*⸣*-ma iṣ-ṣu-riš ip-par-riš-ma* KUR-*ú mar-ṣu e-li* URU.*mu-ṣa-ṣi-ru šu-bat* ^{d}*ḫal-di-a ni-i-*⸢*tu*⸣

154) ⸢*al-me*⸣*-ma al-ti* ^{m}*ur-za-na* DUMU.MEŠ-*šú* DUMU.MUNUS.MEŠ-*šú* 6 LIM 1 ME 70 UN.MEŠ 6 ME 92 ANŠE.*pa-re-e* ANŠE.MEŠ 9 ME 20 [*x*]

155) ⸢GU$_4$?⸣.MEŠ 1 ME ⸢LIM⸣ 2 ME 25 UDU.MEŠ *ú-še-ṣa-a* 34 GUN 18 MA.NA KÙ.GI 1 ME 60 ⸢GUN 2⸣ 1/2 MA.⸢NA⸣ [KÙ.BABBAR] ⸢URUDU⸣ BABBAR-*ú* AN.[NA]

156) [*ni-siq*]-⸢*ti* NA$_4$.MEŠ⸣ *a-na mu-*⸢*ʾu*⸣-[*de-e x x x*] *x x x x ša iḫ-*⸢*zi*⸣*-x* [...]

157) [*x* (*x*)].MEŠ [*x x lu*]-⸢*bul-ti*⸣ *bir-me ù* GADA *a-*⸢*na*⸣ *la ma-*⸢*ni*⸣ *x x x* [...] *x x* [(*x*)]

158) ⸢*it-ti*⸣ [*x x*+4] GUN 3 MA.NA KÙ.GI ⸢1⸣ [ME] ⸢62 GUN⸣ [20] ⸢MA.NA KÙ⸣.[BABBAR† ...]+27 [*x*]

159) ⸢Ú⸣ [*x x x*].⸢MEŠ *ú*⸣*-de-*⸢*e*⸣ URUDU.⸢MEŠ⸣ AN.⸢BAR⸣ *ša ni-ba la* [*i-šu-ú* ...] *x* [*x* (*x*)]

147b–148) I rece[ived] horses, oxen, (and) sheep and goats as tribute from Ianzû, [ki]ng [of the lan]d Naʾ[i]ri, in his fortified city Ḫubuškia.

149–153a) (As for) [U]rzana of the city Mu[ṣa]ṣir who had trangressed against the oath (sworn) by the gods Aššur and Marduk and sen[t] ... to Ursâ (Rusâ), the Urarṭian, the god Ašš[ur], my lord, encouraged me and (so) I constantly moved on with (only) my (own) single chariot and one thousand of my ferocious personal cavalry (and) foot soldiers who were ski[lled in ba]ttle, (advancing over) Mounts Šiyak (Šeyak), Ardi[k]ši, Ulāyû, (and) Alluriu, rugged mountains, on horseback over easy terrain and on foot over difficult (terrain). Then, (when) Urzana of the city Muṣaṣir [he]ard of the advance of [my] expeditionary force, he flew off like a bird and took to the rugged hill(s).ê

153b–161a) [I] surrounded the city Muṣaṣir, the abode of the god Ḫaldi, and brought out Urzana's wife, his sons, his daughters, 6,170 people, 692 mules (and) donkeys, 920+[(155) ox]en, (and) 100,225 sheep. I carried off as booty 34 talents (and) 18 minas of gold, 160 tale[nts] (and) 2 1/2 min[as of silver], shining copper, ti[n, precio]us st[one]s in large qu[antitites ...] ... with mountings [..., ...]s, [..., garme]nts with multi-colored trim and linen (garments) in countless numb[ers] ... [...] ... (along) wi[th ... +4] talents (and) 3 minas of gold, 162 ta[le]nts (and) [20] m[in]a[s of si]lv[er ...]+27 [...]s, objects of copper (and) iron in cou[nt]less numbers [...] (160) ... [...] together with an ox [of copper], a cow of coppe[r, (and) a c]alf of co[pper]. I brought [his deities Ḫaldi (and) Bagbartu] into [*the temple of the god*] Aššur, [together with ... *I distributed*] the remainder of their possessions to [...]

---

147 [10]+30: The reading is based Ch.-F. Jean's copy of the number (two Winkelhaken on top of one Winkelhaken) as opposed to the copies of P.E. Botta and H. Winckler that have three Winkelhaken in a row; see also text no. 65 line 305 for the number 40. KUR.*ú-a-ii-*⸢*is*⸣: Winckler's copy has KUR.*ú-a-ii-uš*, but the reading -⸢*is*⸣ follows Jean and Thureau-Dangin, TCL 3 p. 72 line 121 (but see his n. 2).

149 *iš-*⸢*pú*⸣-[*ra*]: The reading follows Thureau-Dangin, TCL 3 p. 72 line 123, but as noted by A. Fuchs (Khorsabad p. 113), a reading *iš-*⸢*ku*⸣-[*na*] is also possible. The traces on the squeeze do not fit H. Winckler's copy *iš-*⸢*pu*?⸣-[*ru*].

150 ⸢*ša-ru*?⸣: The reading follows Thureau-Dangin, TCL 3 p. 72 line 124. While the copy by Ch.-F. Jean would allow ⸢*ša*⸣-, the reading of the second sign is less clear. The squeeze currently only has indistinct traces of the two signs, but ones which do not really fit RU. H. Winckler's copy has [...] BAR with possible earlier traces indicated by three question marks. 1 GIŠ.GIGIR-*ia*: Winckler's copy omits the 1, although it is indicated in his transliteration.

151 KUR.*ši-ia-ak*: So Ch.-F. Jean's copy (RA 24 [1927] p. 79), against P.E. Botta's and H. Winckler's copies that have E for IA; the squeeze suggests -⸢*ia*⸣-.

154 6,170: Text no. 65 line 349 has 6,110.

155 ⸢GU$_4$?⸣.MEŠ: None of the published copies shows a trace before the MEŠ, but A. Fuchs (Khorsabad p. 114 line 155) indicates a trace of the end of a GU$_4$. There is a trace on the squeeze, but it is not clear that is part of a GU$_4$, although that sign would be expected (see also Thureau-Dangin, TCL 3 p. 72 line 129). 100,225: Text no. 65 lines 349 and 424 have 1,235 and 1,285 respectively.

156 *x x x x* ⸢*ša*⸣: The reading is based on the squeeze; H. Winckler's copy has *x x* [(*x*)]-*e ša* and Ch.-F. Jean's copy *x* [*x*] *x x* ⸢*ša*⸣.

Section 13 = lines 157–169 = II,14:1–13: See Winckler, Sar. Annals lines 131–143; Lie, Sar. lines 157–169; and Fuchs, Khorsabad Annals lines 157–169. Cf. text no. 2 lines +188–202.

158 ⸢62⸣: The reading is based Ch.-F. Jean's copy; both P.E. Botta's and H. Winckler's copies have [...]+42. [...]+27: The reading is based Botta's and Jean's copies; Winckler has 37.

160) *x x* [*x x x*] *x a*-⌜*di*⌝ GU$_4$ [URUDU] ⌜GU$_4$⌝.ÁB URUDU ⌜AMAR URUDU⌝ *áš-lu-la* ⌜^{d}⌝[*ḫal-di-a* ^{d}*ba-ag-bar-tum* DINGIR.MEŠ-*šú a-di* ...] ⌜ŠU$^{?}$⌝ [*x* (*x*)]
161) [*x*] *x* [*x*] *x* [*x*] ^{d}*aš-šur ú-še*-⌜*rib*⌝ *si-ta-at* NÍG.GA-*šú-nu a*-⌜*na*⌝ [... *i-na* KUR].*ur*-[*ar-ṭi*]
162) [*rap-ši*] ⌜KUR.MEŠ-*e ka*⌝-*la-ma* ⌜*si*⌝-*pit-tu ú-šab*-⌜*ši*⌝-*i-ma* [*a*†-*na* ^{m}*ur-sa-a* LUGAL-*šú-nu ṣur-ti nag-la*]-*bi* ⌜*qu-pé-e*⌝ [*x* (*x*)]
163) [(*x*) *x x x-ti a-di*] ⌜*bal-ṭu*$^{?}$⌝ *áš-kun na-gu-ú šu*-[*a*]-*tu a*-[*na mi-ṣir* KUR *aš-šur*.KI *ú*]-⌜*ter*⌝-[*ra*]-*am*-[*ma*]
164) [*i*]-⌜*na* ŠU⌝.[II] LÚ.[*šu-ut* SAG]-⌜*ia*⌝ LÚ.NÍMGIR É.⌜GAL *am*⌝-*nu*-[*šú* ^{m}]⌜*ur*⌝-*sa-a* [KUR].⌜*ur-ar*⌝-[*ṭa-a*]-⌜*a*⌝ [*na-mur-rat*] ⌜^{d}⌝*aš-šur* ⌜*be-lí-ia*⌝
165) [*is-ḫup*]-*šu-ma* ⌜*i-na*⌝ [GIŠ.GÍR AN].⌜BAR⌝ *ra-ma-ni-šu* GIM ŠAḪ *lìb-ba*-⌜*šu is-ḫu*⌝-*ul*-⌜*ma*⌝ ZI-*šu* [*iq*]-⌜*ti*⌝ *i-na* [9 BALA]-⌜*ia*⌝ *a-na* KUR.*el*-⌜*li*⌝-[*pi*]
166) [KUR].⌜*ma*⌝-*da-a*-⌜*a*⌝ *ù* KUR.*kar-al-li a-lik* UN.MEŠ KUR.*kar-al*-⌜*li ša*⌝ LÚ.[*šu-ut*] ⌜SAG⌝.MEŠ-⌜*ia*⌝ *ir-du-du*-[*ma*]
167) [^{m}*a*]-*mi*-⌜*taš*⌝-*ši* ŠEŠ ^{m}*aš-šur*-ZU UGU-*šú-nu ú-rab-bu-ú i-na* ⌜KUR.*an-a* ŠU.SI⌝ [KUR]-*i i-na* ⌜GIŠ⌝.[TUKUL]
168) ⌜*ú-šam*⌝-*qit-su-nu-ti-ma* 2 LIM 2 ME *zi-im pa-ni-šu-nu* ⌜*i*⌝-[*na*] *uš-man-ni-ia am*-⌜*ḫur*⌝
169) ⌜EGIR$^{?}$⌝ ^{m}*a-mi-taš-ši ar-de*-⌜*ma*⌝ *šá-a*-⌜*šu ga*⌝-*du re-ṣi-šu i-na* [KUR].⌜*šu*$^{?}$-*ur-da*⌝ KUR-⌜*e*⌝ [(*x*)] *x* [(*x x*)] *x* [(*x*)]
170) [...] ⌜UN⌝.MEŠ KUR.⌜*ḫab*$^{?}$⌝-[*ḫi*$^{?}$ ...]
171) [... *iš*]-⌜*mu*⌝-*ma* ⌜*ḫat*$^{?}$⌝-*ti* ⌜*ra*⌝-[*ma-ni-šu-nu*

161b–165a) I caused there to b[e] lamenation [in the wide land] Ur[arṭu] (and in) all [the mount]ains, and I made [Ursâ (Rusâ), their king, (use) flint (blades), raz]ors, scalpels, (and) [... (to slash himself in mourning) for as long as he li]ved. [I m]a[de] that district (Muṣaṣir) [(part of) the territory of Assyria and] assigned [it t]o the auth[ority of] a [eunuch of mi]ne, the pala[ce] herald. [The awesome splendor] of the god Aššur, m[y] lord, [overwhelmed U]rsâ (Rusâ), [the U]rar[ṭi]an, and (so) with his own [iro]n [dagge]r he stabbed (himself) in the heart like a pig and [put an en]d to his life.

165b–170a) In my [ninth regnal year], I marched to the lands Elli[pi, M]edia, and Karalla. (As for) the people of the land Karalla w[ho] had driven out my [eun]uchs [and] elevated [A]mitašši, the brother of Aššur-lē'i, over them, I st[ru]ck them down with the sw[ord] on [Mou]nt Ana, [a mounta]in peak, and (then) receiv[ed] i[n] my (military) camp 2,200 of their *face-(guards)* (*as trophies*). I pursued Amitašši and [...] him, together with his allies, on Mount Šurda, [...].

170b–172a) [The peo]ple of the land Ḫ[*abḫu* (...) hear]d [*of the harsh deeds that I had done in the land Karalla;*

160 Following Fuchs, Khorsabad p. 115 line 160 n. 2, the restoration is based on text no. 7 line 76 and may be followed by [NÍG.GA É.KUR]-⌜*šu*⌝-[(*nu*)] (cf. text no. 65 line 368). ⌜ŠU$^{?}$⌝: H. Winckler's copy has ÁŠ, Ch.-F. Jean's ⌜ŠU⌝, and P.E. Botta's would allow either; the squeeze suggests possibly ⌜ŠU⌝.
161 [*x*] *x* [*x*] *x x* [*x*]: P.E. Botta has [*x x* (*x*)] MA [*x* (*x*)] and H. Winckler has *x* [*x* (*x*)] *x* MA [*x x x*]. *ú-še*-⌜*rib*⌝: The reading follows Ch.-F. Jean's copy; Botta has *ú-še*-[*x*] and Winckler *ú-še-ṣi*$^{?}$.
162 The transliteration is based on Ch.-F. Jean's copy and Thureau-Dangin, TCL 3 p. 74 line 136, as well as text no. 2 lines 189–190. P.E. Botta's and H. Winckler's copies have [*x x*] ŠÚ [*x x x*] *x-la-ma* and LUGAL-⌜*šú*⌝ [*nu-ṣur-ti-ki*] ⌜*ḫu*⌝-*la-ma* for the beginning of the line respectively. It is not clear from the Winckler's copy if the LUGAL was actually seen or is a restoration; his edition has *rap-ši* KUR for the beginning of the line (his line 136). Winckler's copy also has a trace of the A of *a-na*. ⌜*qu-pé-e*⌝: The transliteration is based on Jean's copy and the squeeze.
163 The restoration at the beginning of the line is based on text no. 2 line 191. Ch.-F. Jean's copy has a trace of the sign before *áš-kun*.
164 ⌜*be-lí-ia*⌝: The reading follows Ch.-F. Jean's copy; P.E. Botta's and H. Winckler's copies have [*x*]-⌜*lí-ia*⌝ and [EN]-⌜*ia*⌝ respectively.
165 [*is-ḫup*]-*šu-ma*: Text no. 2 line 194 has *is-ḫu-pa-šu*-[*ma*], but the spacing on all three copies (P.E. Botta, H. Winckler, and Ch.-F. Jean) and the squeeze suggests [*is-ḫup*]-*šu-ma*.
166 [KUR].⌜*ma*⌝-*da-a*-⌜*a*⌝ *ù*: The reading is based on the squeeze and Jean's copy; cf. Winckler's copy, which has [KUR.É]-*da-a*-[*a-uk*]-*ki*.
168 ⌜*i*⌝-[*na*]: Ch.-F. Jean's copy and the squeeze have space for only one sign to be restored; cf. Botta's and Winckler's copies.
169 ⌜EGIR$^{?}$⌝: Only the trace of the head of a final vertical wedge is preserved on the squeeze and indicated on Ch.-F. Jean's copy; nothing is shown on P.E. Botta's or H. Winckler's copies, although Winckler does restore EGIR. A.G. Lie (Sar. p. 30) has [*ar*]-⌜*ki*⌝ and A. Fuchs (Khorsabad p. 118 line 169) [*ar*]-⌜*ki*⌝, but the spacing on all the copies (Botta, Winckler, and Jean) and the squeeze would suggest there was not sufficient room for that restoration. [(*x*)] *x* [(*x x*)] *x* [(*x*)]: The reading is based on Jean's copy; H. Tadmor (JCS 12 [1958] p. 89) suggests restoring "killed" at the end of the line and A. Fuchs (ibid. n. 4) suggests ⌜*ú*⌝-[*šam*]-⌜*qit*⌝, "I [struck] do[wn]," noting that the preposition *i-na* speaks against restoring the verbs *nabalkutu* or *naparšudu* (⌜*ib*⌝-[*bal*]-⌜*kit*⌝ or ⌜*ip*⌝-[*par*]-⌜*šid*⌝).
Section 14 = lines 170–182 = II,15:1–13: See Winckler, Sar. Annals lines 144–156; Lie, Sar. lines 170–182; and Fuchs, Khorsabad Annals lines 170–182. Cf. text no. 2 lines 205–217a and text no. 74 iii 42–53.
170–182 Cf. text no. 2 lines 205–217a. Line 170: The tentative reading is based on text no. 82 v 31′.
171 ⌜*ḫat*$^{?}$⌝-*ti*: P.E. Botta's copy has [*x*]-*ti* and H. Winckler's -PA-*ti*; the sign before TI is indistinct on the squeeze. Winckler's copy suggests that he may have taken all the visible signs as part of a place name since he restored KUR immediately before the preserved signs [... KUR$^{?}$].*ma-pa*/*ḫat-ti*-⌜*ra*⌝, but as noted by A. Fuchs (Khorsabad p. 119 line 171 n. 2), no such place is otherwise attested. For the restoration at the end of

im-qut-su-nu-ti-(ma) ...]

172) [...] ⸢*am*⸣-*nu-šú-*[*nu*?-*ti*? ...]
173) [...]
174) [...] U [...]
175) [...]
176) [...] MIN [...]
177) [...] *mim-ma* ⸢*ma*⸣-[*la* ...]
178) [... *x x ú-šal*]-*me-šu-ma* [...]
179) [...]-*ni-šú-nu ka-mu*-⸢*su*⸣-[(*nu*?) ...]
180) [... KUR.*el*]-*li-pí áš-šu ṣa-bat* GIŠ *x* [...]
181) [... *te-me-qí iš-te-ni*]-*iš a-na* ^{m}*a-zu-uk*-[*tú* ...]
182) [... *ú-ṣal-la-an*]-*ni-ma áš-ma-a zi-kir-šu* MA [...]
183) [*e*]-⸢*peš*⸣ LUGAL-*ti-šú* ⸢*aq*⸣-*bi-ma lìb-bi* ^{m}*da-al-ta-a* ⸢*ú-ṭib*⸣-*ma* ⸢*ú*⸣-*taq-qi-na da-li-iḫ-tu*
184) [KUR]-*su* KUR.*ba-ʾi-it*-DINGIR KUR.*na-gu-ú ša* KUR.*ma-da-a-a ša* ⸢*mi*⸣-*ṣir* KUR.*el-li-pí*
185) [KUR].*ab-sa-ḫu-ut-ti* KUR.*pa-ar-nu-at-ti* KUR.*ú-tir-na* URU.*di-ri-is-ta-a-nu*
186) ⸢*ša*⸣ KUR.*ú-ri*-⸢*a*⸣-*ak-ki* KUR.*ri-ma-nu-ti* KUR.*na-gu-ú ša* KUR.*up-pu-ri-ia*
187) [KUR].*ú-ia-da-ú-e* KUR.*bu-us-ti-is* KUR.*a-ga-zi* KUR.*am-ba*-⸢*an*⸣-*da* KUR.*da-na-nu*
188) [(*x*)] KUR.*na-gi-i* [*ru*]-*qu-ti ša pat-ti* KUR.*a-ri-bi ša ni-pi-iḫ* ⸢^{d}⸣UTU-⸢*ši*⸣ *ù* KUR.*na-gi-i*
189) [*ša*] KUR.*man-da-a-a dan-nu-ti ša ni-ir* ^{d}*aš-šur* [*iṣ*†]-*lu-ma* KUR-*ú ù mad-ba-ru ir-tap-pu-du*
190) [*šar*]-*ra-qiš a-na pu-ḫur* URU.MEŠ-*ni-šú-nu a-ku-ka-a-ti ad-di-ma** *gi-mir* KUR.*na-gi-šú-nu*
191) [*ú*]-⸢*ter*⸣-*ra a-na ti-li ma-šu-ú-ti ma-da*-⸢*at*⸣-*tu ša* ⸢^{m}⸣*ul-lu-su-nu* KUR.*ma-an-na-a-a*
192) [^{m}*da*]-*al-ta-a* KUR.*el-li-pa-a-a* ^{md}⸢EN⸣-IBILA-SUM.NA ⸢KUR⸣.*al-lab-ri-a-a ša* 45 LÚ.EN.URU.MEŠ-*ni*
193) [*ša* KUR].*ma-da-a-a dan-nu-ti* 4 LIM 6 ME 9 ANŠE.[KUR†].RA.MEŠ ANŠE.*pa-re-e* GU$_4$.MEŠ ⸢US$_5$⸣.UDU.ḪI.A

their own] fear(s) (then) [fell upon them (*and*) *they sent their messenger to me to do obeisance* (*to me*). I] assigned *th*[*em* to the authority of a eunuch of mine, the governor of the land Lulumû].

172b–184a) [(*As for*) *Daltâ of the land Ellipi, a submissive subject who pulled my yoke* ... (175) ...] everythi[ng ... I had] him [surrou]nded and [...] their [... *them*] in bondage [... (180) ... the land El]lipi because of the seizure of ... [... with entreaties at the same ti]me to Azuk[tu ... he besought] me and I listened to his word(s). [...] I ordered [him (to continue) to exer]cise his kingship, made Daltâ happy, and brought order to his disturbed [land].

184b–191a) (With regard to) the land Baʾīt-ili, a district of the land Media that is on the b[o]rder of the land Ellipi; the lands Absaḫutti, Parnuatti, (and) Utirna; the city Diristānu of the land Uriakku; the land Rimanuti, a district of the land Uppuriya; the lands Uyadaue, Bustis, Agazi, Ambanda, (and) Dananu, [far]-off districts of the territory of the Arabs in the east; and the district(s) of the powerful Medes, who [had thr]own off the yoke of the god Aššur and roamed about the mountain(s) and desert like [thi]eves — I threw firebrands into all their settlements and [tu]rned all their districts into forgotten (ruin) mounds.

191b–194a) I received 4,609 ho[rs]es, mules, oxen, (and) sheep and goats, [i]n countless numbers, as tribute from Ullusunu, the Mannean, [D]altâ of the land Ellipi, Bē[l]-aplu-iddina of the la[nd] Allabria, (and) from forty-five city lords [of] the powerful Medes.

---

the line, see line 365. Fuchs (ibid. n. 1) suggests that the beginning of the line might have had [*ep-šet ma-ru-uš-ti ša i-na* KUR.*kar-al-li e-tep-pu-šu iš*]-⸢*mu*⸣-*ma* (see text no. 82 v 34′–35′) or, less likely, [*a-lak gir-ri-ia ru-qiš iš*]-⸢*mu*⸣-*ma* (see text no. 7 lines 101–102) and that *im-qut-su-nu-ti-ma* might have been followed by LÚ.DUMU *šip-ri-šú-nu/un ša e-peš ar-du-ti iš-pu-ru-nim-ma* (see text no. 82 v 35′–36′).

172 For a possible restoration, see text no. 2 line 207.

178 The restoration is based on text no. 2 line 213; H. Winckler's copy has [*i-na u*$_4$]-*me-šu-ma*.

180 P.E. Botta's and H. Winckler's copies, as well as the squeeze, would allow GIŠ.⸢TUKUL⸣, "weapon."

181 For the restoration at the beginning of the line and the reading of the name, see text no. 2 lines 216 and 209 respectively.

182 The restoration at the beginning of the line follows text no. 7 line 120.

Section 15 = lines 183–195 = II,16:1–13: See Winckler, Sar. Annals lines 157–169; Lie, Sar. lines 183–195; and Fuchs, Khorsabad Annals lines 183–195. Cf. text no. 2 lines 217b–228a. See Figure 2 for a photo of the middle section of the squeeze of Room II, slab 16.

183 ⸢*ú-ṭib*⸣: The reading follows the copy in Thureau-Dangin, RA 24 (1927) p. 76. Both P.E. Botta's and H. Winckler's copies have no trace of the Ú and an anomalous form for the DIB. The squeeze currently shows traces of what could be an Ú and indistinct traces of a sign that would fit either F. Thureau-Dangin's or Botta's and Winckler's copies.

188 H. Winckler's copy omits the -*ši* after ^{d}UTU.

190 -*ma**: P.E. Botta's copy has ÁŠ and this is supported by the squeeze, against H. Winckler's copy MA.

192b–193a See text no. 82 vi 14″–37″ for the names of some of the Median rulers who brought tribute to Sargon.

193 H. Winckler's copy has a ⸢ME⸣ following the number 9, but there are no traces of this (unwanted) sign on the squeeze. ⸢US$_5$⸣: P.E. Botta's copy has an abnormal sign form, while Winckler's is correct for US$_5$; the traces on the squeeze are indistinct and could fit either Botta's or Winckler's copies.

194) [a]-na la ma-ni am-⸢ḫur⸣ ^{m}am-ba-ri-⸢is⸣ KUR.⸢ta⸣-[bal-a-a LUGAL KUR.É-pu†]-ri-ti-⸢iš⸣ ša ⸢NUN⸣ a-⸢lik pa⸣-ni-ia

195) [kim-ti ^{m}ḫul-li-i AD-šú$^{?}$ a-di$^{?}$ šal-lat KUR]-šú [a-na KUR aš-šur.KI ú]-⸢ra⸣-[áš]-šu-nu-⸢ti⸣ i-⸢na$^{?}$⸣ GIŠ$^{?}$ UD DINGIR.MEŠ

196) [GAL.MEŠ x x] UD ku-un BALA-⸢ia⸣ [i†-na†] uz-⸢ni-ia ib⸣-šu-ú ^{m}ḫul-li-i i-na GIŠ.GU.ZA LUGAL-[ti-šú ú-še-šib]

197) [UN.MEŠ KUR.É]-pu†-ru-ta-áš ú-pa-ḫir-ma a-na qa-ti-šu ú-man-ni i-na u_4-me ^{m}ḫu-ul-⸢li⸣-[i AD-šú ...]

198) [...] ⸢áš⸣-ru-uk-šu-ma bi-in-tu it-ti URU.ḫi-lak-ki ad-di-in-šu-ma ú-⸢rap⸣-[pi-šá KUR-su u šu-ú]

199) [LÚ.ḫa]-at-tu-ú la na-ṣir kit-ti a-na ^{m}ur-sa-a LUGAL KUR.ur-⸢ar⸣-ṭi $^{m⸢}$mi-ta⸣-[a LUGAL KUR.mu-us-ki]

200) [u] ⸢MAN⸣.MEŠ-ni KUR.ta-ba-li e-⸢ke⸣-me mi-ṣir-ia iš-pur um-ma-na-at $^{⸢d?⸣}$[aš-šur ad-ke-ma KUR.ta-ba-lum a-na]

201) [paṭ gim]-⸢ri⸣-šú ú-kàt-ti-ma še-e-ti-iš ^{m}am-ba-ri-is LUGAL KUR.É-pu-ri-ti-iš ⸢a⸣-[di NUMUN É AD-šú LÚ.SAG.KAL-ut KUR-šú]

202) [ka-mu]-su-nu it-ti ⸢1⸣ ME GIŠ.GIGIR-šú a-na KUR aš-šur.KI al-qa-a KUR.É-⸢pu-ru⸣-taš KUR.ḫi-la-⸢ak⸣-[ku a-bur-riš ú-šar-bi-iṣ-ma]

203) [x x x]-re-e ker-ḫe ú-še-⸢pi⸣-šá qer-bu-uš-šú UN.MEŠ KUR.KUR ki-šit-ti ^{d}aš-šur be-⸢lí⸣-[ia ú-še-šib LÚ.šu-ut SAG-ia]

204) [LÚ.EN.NAM UGU-šú]-⸢un$^{?}$⸣ áš-kun tup-šik-ki ⸢áš⸣-šu-ri e-mid-su-nu-ti i-na 10 BALA-⸢ia⸣

194b–198a) (As for) Ambaris of the land T[abal, king of the land Bīt-Pu]rutaš, [the fam]ily of *who[se father]* Ḫull[î], a ruler, a predecessor of mine, [had bro]ught [to Assyria *together with* booty from] his [land], (*when*) ... the [great] gods [*determi*]*ned* the firm establishment of m[y] reign, they (Ḫullî and his family) were [on] my mind. [I had] Ḫullî [sit (again)] on [his] royal throne. I gathered together [the people of the land Bīt]-P[u]rutaš and assigned (them) to his authority. In the time of Ḫull[î, his father], I had granted him (Ambaris) [...], gave him a daughter (of mine), (along) with the city Ḫilakku, and (thus) ex[panded his land].

198b–204a) [However, that (man) (Ambaris), a H]ittite who did not protect justice, sent to Ursâ (Rusâ), king of the land Urarṭu, Mit[â, king of the land Musku, (200) and the ki]ngs of the land Tabal about taking away territory of mine. [I mustered] the troops of the god [Aššur and] overwhelmed [the land Tabal to] its [fu]ll [extent] as if with a net. (Then), I brought [in bond]age to Assyria Ambaris, king of the land Bīt-Purutaš, toge[ther with the (other) offspring of his father's house (and) the nobles of his land], (along) with one hundred of his chariot(s). [I had] the lands Bīt-P[ur]utaš (and) Ḫila[kku dwell (as safely) as in a meadow and ...] ... had enclosure walls built in it. [I (re)settled (there)] people from the lands that the god Aššur, [my] lor[d], had conquered. I set [a eunuch of mine as provincial governor over the]m (and) imposed upon them (the same) corvée duty (as if they were) Assyrians.

204b–208a) In [m]y tenth regnal year, (as for) Tarḫun-[azi of the city Melid, (*an evil Hittite*) who did not

---

194–196a Line 194: P.E. Botta's copy has irregular signs for the *-ḫur**(copy ḪI-PA), *-is**(copy: DI), *-iš**(copy: IB), *-lik*, and *pa**(copy GIŠ)-, and H. Winckler's copy has abnormal signes for the *-is**(copy: DI), NUN*(copy: É), *-lik**(copy: KU), and *pa**(copy: KA)-. The squeeze is currently unclear in most cases, except that it is likely -⸢*is*⸣ not DI, -⸢*iš*⸣ not IB, and clearly ⸢*pa*⸣- not KA. F. Thureau-Dangin's copy would allow -⸢*is*⸣, -⸢*lik*⸣, and -⸢*pa*⸣. Lines 194b–196a: The exact understanding of the passage is not completely clear. A. Fuchs (Khorsabad p. 323 and see his n. 283) translates "(Was) Ambaris von Tabal, [den König des Langes Bīt]-Puritiš (anlangt), so hatte mein fürstlicher Vorgänger die Familie des Ḫullī, [...] (und) die Beute aus seinem Land nach Assyrien geholt. *Als dann* ... die [großen] Götter mir eine feste Regierung *bestimmten*, da waren sie mir noch im Gedächtnis." He assumes that it was Ḫullī and his family that was on the king's mind (ibid. n. 284), and this is followed here. See also text no. 2 lines 226b–228a.

195 The tentative restoration is based in part on text no. 2 line 227 and follows A.G. Lie (p. 32); for ^{m}*ḫul-li-i* AD-*šú*, see text no. 7 line 30. [*ú*]-⸢*ra*⸣-[*áš*]-*šu-nu*-[*ti*] *i*-⸢*na*⸣: H. Winckler's copy has [...] ⸢URU.MEŠ⸣-*šu-nu-x* DUMU$^{?}$ *x*. Lie (p. 32) reads *i*-⸢*na*⸣ GIŠ.TUKUL$^{?}$ DINGIR.MEŠ for the end of the line, but Winckler states that the second sign is not TUKUL. The signs are indistinct on the squeeze, but might conceivably be ⸢*pa-ni*⸣ for GIŠ UD.

Section 16 = lines 196–208 = II,17:1–13: See Winckler, Sar. Annals lines 170–182; Lie, Sar. lines 196–208; and Fuchs, Khorsabad Annals lines 196–208. Cf. text no. 2 lines 228b–238+.

196 A.G. Lie (p. 32) restored [GAL.MEŠ *i*]-⸢*na*⸣ at the beginning of the line. Cf. *i-na uz-ni-šú-nu ib-ši-ma* in text no. 65 line 40, as noted by A. Fuchs (Khorsabad p. 123 line 196 n. 2). The restoration at the end of the line is based on text no. 74 v 16 and cf. text no. 7 line 30.

197 *-pu*†-: P.E. Botta's copy has ŠE with no indication of any damage after it; the sign is not preserved on the squeeze.

198 For the very end of the restoration, see text no. 74 v 20.

200 -⸢*ke*⸣-: P.E. Botta's copy has -⸢RIM⸣- and H. Winckler's *-ke-*; the squeeze is not clear but seems to fit -⸢*ke*⸣-. $^{⸢d?⸣}$[*aš-šur*]: Botta's copy has GIŠ and Winckler's ⸢ÁŠ$^{?}$⸣. Only the trace of the head of one horizontal wedge in the middle of the line is really visible on the squeeze.

201 LÚ.SAG.KAL-*ut*: Restored from text no. 2 line 233; written *a-šá-red-du-ti* in text no. 7 line 31.

202 -⸢*pu-ru*⸣-: P.E. Botta's copy has -ŠE-A- with no indication of any damage to the area, while H. Winckler has *-pu-ru-*; the squeeze is not clear at this point but would allow -⸢*pu-ru*⸣-.

203 It is not clear what should be restored at the beginning of the line. A.G. Lie (p. 32) and A.T.E. Olmstead (AJSL 47 [1930–31] p. 268) read [*ḫa-an-du*$^{?}$]-*re-e kir-ḫe*, while D.D. Luckenbill read [...]-*ri e-piš* DÙG (reading *ṭâbi* for DÙG), "which does good" (see ibid.).

204 -⸢*un*$^{?}$⸣: The traces as copied by P.E. Botta and H. Winckler are the ends of two horizontal wedges, one on top of the other, but these might simply be the right edges of the heads of vertical wedges, one on top of the other; no traces are visible on the squeeze. Text no. 2 line 235 has UGU-*šú-nu*. Following F.W. Geers, A.T.E. Olmstead (AJSL 47 [1930–31] p. 268) notes the possibility of adding LÚ.*ḫat-tu* ḪUL, "an evil Hittite," between URU.*me-lid-da-a-a* and *la a-dir*, but there would not seem to be room for this.

^{m}*tar-ḫu-*⸢*na*⸣-[*zi* URU.*me-lid-da-a-a* (...) *la a-dir*]

205) [*zik-ri*] ⸢DINGIR⸣.MEŠ GAL.MEŠ KUR.*kam-ma-nu rap-šú ša* ⸢*i-na*⸣ *tu-kul-ti* ^{d}*aš-šur be-lí-ia* [*e*†*-ki-mu* ^{m}*gu-un-zi-na-nu*]

206) [LUGAL-*šu*]*-nu aṭ-ru-du ka-*⸢*ma*⸣*-ti-iš* ⸢*ù*⸣ *šá-a-šú i-na* GIŠ.GU.ZA LUGAL-*ti-šú ú-še-*[*ši-bu x x x x x x x x* (*x x x*)]

207) [*ú*]*-še-pi-šá ar-du-su* ⸢*be-lut*⸣ KUR.⸢MEŠ⸣ [DAGAL].MEŠ *qa-tuš-šu ú-mal-lu-ú ú-zu-un-*[*šú x x* (*x x*) *a-na* ^{m}*mi-ta-a* LUGAL]

208) [KUR.*mus-ki*] ⸢*ze*⸣*-ra-a-ti* KUR *aš-šur*.KI ⸢*iš*⸣-[*tap-par i-na*] ⸢*ug-gat lìb-bi-ia*⸣ KUR.*kam-ma-nu a-na paṭ* [*gim-ri-šú* (*x x x x*) *ak-šu-ud*$^{?}$]

209) URU.*me-lid-du* URU LUGAL-*ti-*⸢*šu kar*⸣*-pa-niš aḫ-pi kul-lat* UN.MEŠ-*šú* ⸢*ki-i*⸣ *mar-šit ṣe-e-ni*

210) *am-nu ù šu-ú a-na šu-zu-ub* ZI.MEŠ-*šú a-na* URU.[DU$_{6}$]*-ga-ri-im-me* ⸢*e*⸣*-ru-ub* URU *šu-a-tu*

211) *ur-*⸢*pa*⸣*-niš ak-tùm ša-lum-mat* GIŠ.TUKUL.MEŠ-*ia e-du-ru-ma* ⸢*ip-tu*⸣*-ú* ⸢KÁ-*šu*⸣*-un* [^{m}]*tar-ḫu-na-zi*

212) *ma-lik-šú-nu ga-du* LÚ.*mun-daḫ-ṣe-e-šú bi-re-tu* ⸢AN⸣.BAR *ad-*⸢*di*⸣*-ma* DAM-*su* DUMU.MEŠ-*šú*

213) DUMU.MUNUS.MEŠ-*šú it-ti* 5 LIM *šal-lat* LÚ.*qu-ra-di-šu a-na* URU-*ia aš-*⸢*šur*†⸣ [*ub*]*-la* URU.DU$_{6}$*-*ga-ri-im-me*

214) *a-na eš-šu-ti* ⸢*aṣ*⸣*-bat* UN.MEŠ *ki-*⸢*šit*⸣*-ti* ŠU.II-*ia* ⸢*i*⸣*-na lìb-bi ú-še-rib* [KUR†.*kam*]*-ma-nu a-na si-ḫir-ti-šá*

215) *ú-šá-aṣ-bit-ma i-na* ŠU.II LÚ.*šu-ut* SAG-*ia am-nu il-ku tup-šik-ku* ⸢*ki*⸣-[*i ša*†] ^{m}*gu-un-zi-na-nu*

216) *e-mid-su-nu-ti* 10 URU.*bi-*⸢*ra*⸣*-a-ti dan-na-ti li-me-su ad-di-*⸢*ma*⸣ [UN].⸢MEŠ⸣*-šú šu-bat né-eḫ-ti*

217) *ú-še-šib* URU.*lu-uḫ-su* URU.⸢*pur*$^{?}$*-ṭir*⸣ URU.*an-mu-ur-ru* ⸢URU⸣.*ki-*[*a*$^{?}$*-ka*$^{?}$] URU.*an-du-ar-*⸢*sa*⸣*-li-a*

218) UGU KUR.*ur-ar-ṭi ú-*⸢*dan*⸣*-ni-na* ⸢EN⸣.NUN URU.*ú-si* URU.*ú-si-*⸢*an*$^{?}$⸣ [URU].*ú-*⸢*ar*⸣*-gi-in*

219) *pa-a-ṭi* KUR.*mu-us-ki ad-di-ma ša la mu-ṣe-e*

fear the words of the] great [go]ds, (and as for) the wide land Kammanu, which [I had taken away] with the support of the god Aššur, my lord [(and) who]se [king Gunzinānu] I had driven out and (then) had [him (Tarḫun-azi)] s[it] on his (Gunzinānu's) royal throne [... (whom) I] made do obeisance to me, to (whom) I handed over lo[rd]ship of [wide] lands, [(*and whose*)] understanding [...], he [repeatedly sent to Mitâ, king of the land Musku], (messages) hostile to Assyria.

208b–217a) Angri[ly, *I conquered*] the land Kammanu to [its full] extent [(...)]. I smashed h[is] royal city Melid like a pot (and) considered all his people as if (they were) flocks of sheep and goats. (210) However, that (man) (Tarḫun-azi) entered the city [Tīl]-Garimme in order to save his life. I overwhelmed that city like a cloud. They took fright at the awesome radiance of my weapons and op[en]ed [th]eir (city) gate. I threw in [ir]on fetters Tarḫun-azi, their ruler, together with his fighting men, and (then) [brou]ght to my city Ašš[ur] his wife, his sons, (and) his daughters, (along) with five thousand of his captured warriors. I reorganized (the administration of) the city Tīl-Garimme (and) brought there people whom I had captured. I had (them) occupy [the land Kam]manu in its entirety, (215) and assigned (them) to the authority of a eunuch of mine. I imposed upon them the (same state) service (and) corvée duty a[s (in the time) of] Gunzinānu. I erected ten strong fortresses around it (the land Kammanu) a[nd] allowed its [people] to live in peace.

217b–221) I strengthened the garrison(s) (of) the cities Luḫsu, Purṭir, Anmurru, Ki[*aka*], (and) Anduarsalia against the land Urarṭu. I erected the cities Usi, Usia[n], (and) Uargin on the border of the land Musku and seized (control of) *their* entry [point]s (lit.: "ga[te]s") so that there should be no escape (lit.:

---

205 For the restoration ^{m}*gu-un-zi-na-nu* at the end of the line, see Lie, Sar. p. 34 n. 6.

207–208a Line 207: Text no. 112 line 10′ has KUR.MEŠ-*šú-nu rap-šá-a-te*, "their wide lands." For the restoration at the end of the line, cf. text no. 74 v 49–50. Following J. Renger (CRRA 32 p. 117), perhaps restore *ú-zu-un-*[*šú a-na* ^{m}*mi-ta-a* LUGAL KUR *mus-ki* / *šá-kin-ma*], "[his] attention [was directed (lit.: "set") towards Mitâ, king of the land Musku]."

208 The tentative restoration at the end of the line follows H. Winckler (p. 32) and A.G. Lie (p. 34).

Section 17 = lines 209–221 = II,18:1–13: See Winckler, Sar. Annals lines 183–195; Lie, Sar. lines 209–221; and Fuchs, Khorsabad Annals lines 209–221. Cf. text no. 2 lines +256–259a.

210 With regard to Til-Garimme (Tilgarimmu) in Neo-Assyrian sources, and a possible location in the plain of Elbistan, see Yamada, AoF 33 (2006) pp. 223–236 and Bagg, Rép. Géogr. 7/1 pp. 256–257.

213 *aš-*⸢*šur*†⸣: P.E. Botta's copy has *aš*-BAR or AN, and H. Winckler's *aš-*⸢*šur*⸣; the squeeze has *aš-*[...]. DU$_{6}$*: The squeeze has DUL.

214 The translation "to reorganize (the administration of) GN" for GN *ana eššūti ṣabātu* is based on CAD E p. 375; see also CDA p. 83.

217 ⸢*pur*$^{?}$*-ṭir*⸣: P.E. Botta's copy has UN-SI-A and H. Winckler's *pur-ṭir*, with the PUR marked "so!"; the squeeze has ⸢*pur*$^{?}$*-ṭir*⸣, where the traces of the first sign would fit both PUR and UN. ⸢URU⸣.*ki-*[*a*$^{?}$*-ka*$^{?}$]: A.G. Lie (p. 36), following E. Forrer (Provinz. p. 75), read ⸢URU⸣.*ki-*[*ia-ka*$^{?}$] and A. Fuchs (Khorsabad p. 127 line 217) ⸢URU⸣.*ki*$^{!}$-[*a*$^{?}$*-ka*$^{?}$].

218 -⸢*an*$^{?}$⸣: P.E. Botta's copy has a horizontal wedge running into a vertical wedge, followed by a damaged area, while H. Winckler's copy has AN with a question mark. Only the head of a horizontal wedge is visible on the squeeze.

219 -⸢*šú*$^{?}$*-un*$^{?}$⸣: The reading follows the squeeze, but the traces are not clear. P.E. Botta's copy has [*x* (*x*)]; it is not clear from H. Winckler's copy if he saw -[*šú-un*] or -⸢*šú-un*⸣, although his edition has *-šu-un* (Winckler's line 193). A. Fuchs (Khorsabad p. 128 line 219) read -[*šú*]. Instead

aṣ-ba-ta ⸢KÁ⸣.MEŠ-⸢*šú*$^{?}$-*un*$^{?}$⸣ URU.*el-li-bir*
220) URU.*ši-in-da-ra-ra* UGU ⸢UN.MEŠ⸣ [KUR.*ka-as-ku*] ⸢*ar-ku-us*⸣ URU.[*me-lid*]-*du* URU LUGAL-*ti*-⸢*šu*⸣
221) ⸢*a*⸣-*di* KUR.*na-gi*-⸢*i*⸣ [*x x x x x x x x x* (*x*) ^{m}]*mut*-⸢*tal-lu*⸣ KUR.*ku-muḫ-ḫi*-⸢*a*⸣-*a* ⸢*ad*⸣-[*di-in*]
222) *i-na* u$_{4}$-*me-šu-ma ka-tim-ti* KUR.MEŠ-*e ša* KUR.*ḫat-ti ip-pe-te* [...]
223) *i-na* u$_{4}$-*me* BALA-*ia ú-bil-lu-nim-ma ak-ku-ma bu-še-e* KUR.[*ḫat-ti* ...]
224) *mé-su-ú si-mat* É.GAL KUR.*la-ri-is-ʾu* KUR.*šu-ru-ma-an* [...]
225) *bi-nu-tu* ^{d}*nu-dím*-⸢*mud*⸣ ZABAR *nam-ru i-na* KUR.*tu*-[*šá-ni-ra x* (*x*) *x-du-ri-ni*]
226) KUR.*e-li-ku-du-ri-ni ib-ba-ni par-zil-lu* KUR.*lam-mu-un šá* ⸢*bi-rit*⸣ [KUR].*ú*-(*x*)-[*x x x x x* (*x*)]
227) A.BÁR *mu-nam-mir a-ru-uš-ti-šú-nu ú*-⸢*šak*⸣-*lim* KUR.[*lam-mu*]-⸢*un*⸣ [*šá*$^{?}$] IGI [*x x x* (*x*)]
228) NA$_{4}$.GIŠ.NU$_{11}$.⸢GAL⸣ *eb-bu* KUR.*am-mu-un šá-du-ú pa-ni* Ú [*x x x* (*x*)] ⸢IM⸣ [TI] ḪI [*x x* (*x x*)]
229) *na-as-qu si-mat* LUGAL-*ti ša* ⸢GIM⸣ NA$_{4}$.ZA.GÌN.DURU$_{5}$-*i pe-ṣa*-⸢*at*⸣ [*x x x*] ⸢A⸣ [(*x*)] RA [*x* (*x*)]
230) KUR.*ba-ʾi-il-ṣa-pu-na* KUR-*ú* GAL-*ú* ZABAR ⸢*iš*⸣-[*te-niš ib-ni*]-⸢*ma*$^{?}$⸣ *ša* KUR.⸢MEŠ⸣-[*ni*]
231) *šu-nu-ti ši-pik ep-ri-šú-nu ab-lul-ma a-na ki-i*-⸢*ri*⸣ [*x x x*] ŠÚ *ú-še-ri*-[*id*$^{?}$]
232) *bu-šul*†-*šú-nu a*-⸢*mur*⸣ NÍG.GA *la ni-bi ša* AD.MEŠ-*ia la* ⸢*i*⸣-*ḫu-ru i-na qé-reb*
233) URU.BÀD-^{m}LUGAL-GI.NA URU-*ia aq-ru-un-ma*

"exit"). (220) (Finally), I constructed the cities Ellibir (and) Šindarara against the people [of the land Kasku]. I g[ave] his (Tarḫun-azi's) royal city [Meli]d, as well as the district [*in its environs*, (...) to] Mut[al]lu of the land Kummuḫu.

222–234a) At that time, (everything) that was hidden in the mountains of the land Ḫatti (Syria) was revealed (*to me*). [(...)] They brought to me during my reign [...] and I heaped up the property of the land [Ḫatti (...). *On Mount ... was produced*] refined [...], appropriate for a palace; (*on*) Mounts Larisʾu, Šuruman, [(and) ... *was produced*] (225) the creation of the god Nudimm[u]d (Ea), shining copper; on Mounts Tu[šanira, ...-durini], (and) Elikudurini was produced iron; (the part of) Mount Lammun that is (located) be[tw]een [*Mount*] U[... *and Mount* ...] produced lead, which whitens their dirty state; (the part of) Mount [Lammu]n [that is (located)] *facing* [... *produced*] pure alabaster; Mount Ammun, a mountain [that is (located)] facing [... *produced*] choice [BAR.GÙN.GÙN.NU-(stone)], fit for royalty (and) as white as pale lapis lazuli [...]; (230) (and) Mount Baʾil-ṣapūna, a great mountain, [produced at the] s[ame time] copper. I *then* mixed mound(s) of ore from those mountains, depos[ited (them)] into furnac[es ..., (and)] watch[ed] their smelting. I stored up inside my city Dūr-Šarrukīn countless possessions that my ancestors had never received; as a result, in Assyria the exchange rate for silver is fixed as if it were for bronze.

---

of the translation "seized (control of) *their* entry [point]s (lit.: "ga[te]s") so that there should be no escape (lit.: "exit")," possibly understand following Fuchs (Khorsabad p. 324) "bemächtigte ich mich seiner (Ausfall)tore, so daß (aus diesem Land nun) nichts mehr (nach Assyrien) herauskommen kann."

220 The restoration KUR.*ka-as-ku* follows Lie, Sar. p. 36, as suggested by Forrer, Provinz. p. 75.

221 A. Fuchs (Khorsabad p. 128 line 221 n. 1) suggests that in the gap we should probably restore *ša li-mì-ti-šu a-na*, for which there would certainly be room; cf. text no. 2 line 258. ⸢*ad*⸣-[*di-in*]: H. Winckler's copy has ⸢*ša*$^{?}$ KI$^{?}$⸣ [*x*], where it is not clear if he actually saw any of the KI or not. The traces on the squeeze are indistinct but would allow ⸢*ad*⸣-[...], which follows Lie, Sar. p. 36.

Section 18 = lines 222–234 = II,19:1–13: See Winckler, Sar. Annals lines 196–208; Lie, Sar. lines 222–234; and Fuchs, Khorsabad Annals lines 222–234. Cf. text no. 2 lines 259b–267a.

222–234 Since the right end of the slab is not preserved, it is not always clear how much is missing at the end of a line and the suggested numbers of signs must be considered extremely uncertain, although lines 230 and 232–234 almost certainly end as indicated.

223 The restoration follows Olmstead, AJSL 47 (1930–31) p. 268.

226–228 Line 226: KUR.*e-li-ku-du-ri-ni*: As noted by A. Fuchs (Khorsabad p. 129 line 226 n. 2), J. Lewy's (HUCA 23/1 [1950–51] p. 386 n. 99) emendation to KUR.*el-li-bìr du-ri-ni* is problematic. P.E. Botta's copy has a clear *-ku-*, while H. Winckler's copy has an abnormal form that he transliterated as *-pu* in his edition, but which looks more like KU. The sign is not clear on the squeeze, but might be KU or KI. To get Lewy's reading BIR, we would need to assume an error by the ancient scribe/stonemason. Lines 226–228: With regard to Mount Lammun and Mount Ammun, see Bagg, SAAB 15 (2006) p. 188 and Bagg, Rép. Géogr. 7/1 pp. 9 and 155–156.

227 *a-ru-uš-ti-šú-nu*: So P.E. Botta and squeeze; H. Winckler's copy has *a-ru-*DU*-ti-šú-nu*. It is not clear to what the *-šú-nu*, "their," refers; CAD A/2 p. 324 suggests it may be the buildings, while A. Fuchs (Khorsabad p. 325 n. 297) takes it to be the other metals. [*ša*/*šá*]: The spacing on the squeeze would suggest *šá* rather than *ša*.

228 Based on the squeeze, it is not clear that there is room to restore TI between ⸢IM⸣ and ḪI. For the end of the line, see text no. 2 line 263.

229 [...] ⸢A⸣: -⸢UN⸣, ⸢KAL⸣, [...] ⸢ZA⸣, etc. are also possible.

230 -⸢*ma*$^{?}$⸣: A reading *-ma* is prompted by text no. 2 line 264. P.E. Botta's and H. Winckler's copies have -ŠU, and the squeeze would seem to have -⸢ŠU⸣; A. Fuchs (Khorsabad p. 130 line 230) reads -⸢*ma*$^{!}$⸣.

231 *ú-še-ri*-[*id*$^{?}$]: Text no. 2 line 265 is restored [... *ú-še-ri-is-su*]-⸢*nu*$^{?}$⸣*-ti-ma* here, but there is room for only one or at most two signs at the end of 231.

232 *-šul*†-: P.E. Botta's copy has an extra wedge at the beginning of the sign, while H. Winckler's copy has the correct form; it is not clear from the squeeze which copy is the more accurate.

233b–234a For the translation, see Fales, SAAB 10/1 (1996) p. 20 and Radner, ZA 105 (2015) p. 193 commentary to line 5; cf. CAD S p. 298 and Š/1 p. 356.

ma-ḫi-ri KÙ.BABBAR *ki-ma si-*⸢*pár*⸣*-ri*	
234) *i-na qé-reb* KUR ^{d}*aš-šur*.KI *i-šim-mu i-*⸢*na*⸣ 11 ⸢BALA-*ia*⸣	234b) In m[y] eleventh [re]gnal year,
Lines 235–247 are not preserved	Lines 235–247 are not preserved
248) [LÚ.*šu-ut* SAG-*ia*] LÚ.EN.NAM UGU-*šu-nu áš-kun it-ti* UN.⸢MEŠ⸣ [KUR *aš*]-⸢*šur*⸣.KI	248–249a) [*I reorganized* (*the administration of*) *the people of the land Gurgum to its full extent*], set [a eunuch of mine] as provincial governor over them, (and) [considered them] as people [of Assy]ria.
249) [*am-nu-šú-nu-ti*] ^{m}*a-zu-ri* LUGAL URU.*as-du-di a-na la* ⸢*na*⸣-[*še*]-⸢*e*⸣	249b–255) Azūri, king of the city Ashdod, [pl]otted [...] (so as) to no longer (have to) de[liv]er [tribute (to me)] and sent (messages) [hostile to Assyria] to the kings in his enviro[ns]. Then, because of the e[vi]l that he had done, I di[d awa]y with [his lordship] o[ver the people of his land] and [se]t his *favorite* brother Aḫī-Mīti as king [over them. The] Hittites, who (always) speak treachery, [hated h]is rule [and] elevated over them [I]a[dn]a (Iāmānī), who had no right to the throne (and) who, like the[m], did [not] kn[o]w [how to respect (any) authority].
250) [*bíl-te* x x x *ik*]*-pu-ud-ma a-na* LUGAL.MEŠ-*ni li-me-*[*ti*]*-šu*	
251) [*ze-ra-a-ti* KUR *aš-šur*.KI†] *iš-pur-ma áš-šu* ⸢ḪUL⸣-*tu e-pu-šu* ⸢UGU⸣ [UN†].MEŠ	
252) [KUR-*šú be-lu-su*] *ú-*⸢*nak-kir*⸣*-ma* ^{m}*a-ḫi-mi-ti a-ḫu ta-lim-šú a-na* LUGAL-*ti*	
253) [UGU-*šú-nu áš*]-⸢*kun*⸣ [LÚ†].*ḫat-ti-*⸢*i*⸣ *da-bi-ib ṣa-lip-ti be-lu-*⸢*su*⸣	
254) [*i-ze-ru-ma* ^{m}*ia*†]-⸢*ad*†*-na*⸣ *la be-*⸢*el*⸣ GIŠ.GU.ZA *ša* GIM *šá-a-šu-*[*nu*†]-⸢*ma*⸣	
255) [*pa-laḫ be-lu-tim la*] *i-*⸢*du*⸣*-u ú-rab-bu-ú e-li-šu-*⸢*un*⸣	
256) [*i-na ug-gat lìb-bi-ia*] *it-ti* GIŠ.GIGIR GÌR.II-*ia ù* ANŠE.⸢*pét*⸣*-ḫal-lu*$_{4}$-⸢*ia*⸣	256–262a) [Angrily], with (only) my personal chariot and [m]y cavalry [who] never leave my [side (even) in friendly territory], I [quickly] marched to [his royal city] Ashdod. I then [surrounded (and) conq]uered the cities Ashdod, Ga[th, (and) Ashdod-Yam]. I cou[nted as bo]oty (both) the gods who d[wel]t in them (and) th[at (man) (Iāmāni), (260) together with the people of his land, gold, silver, (and) the possessions of his palace]. I reorganized (the administration of) those cities (and) settled there people from the lands that I had conquered. I set a eunuch of mi[ne] as provincial governor over them and considered them as people of Assyria; they (now) pull my yoke.
257) [*ša a-šar sa-al-me i-da*]*-a-a la ip-par-ku-ú a-na* URU.*as-du-*⸢*di*⸣	
258) [URU LUGAL-*ti-šú ḫi-it-mu-ṭiš*] *al-*⸢*lik*⸣*-ma* URU.*as-du-du* URU.*gi-*⸢*im*⸣-[*tú*]	
259) [URU.*as-du-di-im-mu al-me*] ⸢KUR⸣-*ud* DINGIR.⸢MEŠ⸣ *a-*[*ši-bu*]-⸢*ut*⸣ *lìb-bi-šu-un šá-*[*a-šú*]	
260) [*a-di* UN.MEŠ KUR-*šú* KÙ.GI KÙ.BABBAR NÍG.ŠU É.GAL-*šú a-na*] ⸢*šal*⸣*-la-ti* ⸢*am*⸣-[*nu*†]*-šú*	
261) URU.MEŠ-*ni šú-nu-ti a-na eš-šu-ti aṣ-bat* UN.MEŠ KUR.KUR *ki-šit-ti* ŠU.II-*ia i-na lìb-bi ú-še-šib* LÚ.*šu-ut* SAG-⸢*ia*⸣	
262) LÚ.EN.NAM UGU-*šú-nu áš-kun-ma it-ti* UN.MEŠ KUR *aš-šur*.KI *am-nu-šu-nu-ti-ma i-*⸢*šuṭ*⸣*-ṭu ab-šá-a-ni i-na* 12 BALA-⸢*ia*⸣	262b–271) In m[y] twelfth regnal year, Marduk-apla-iddina (II) (Merodach-Baladan), descendant of Yakīn, king of Chaldea, whose settlements are situated on the (coastal) plain of the Eastern Sea, had put his trust in the sea and (its) surging waves. He then broke (lit.: "overturned") the treaty sworn by the great gods
263) ^{md}AMAR.UTU-A-SUM.NA DUMU ^{m}*ia-ki-ni* LUGAL KUR.*kal-di ša i-na sa-pan tam-tim ṣi-*⸢*it*⸣ ^{d}UTU-*ši šit-ku-nu*	

Sections 19–20 Section 19 = lines 235–247 = II,20:1–13. See Winckler, Sar. Annals lines 209–213; Lie, Sar. lines 235–247; and Fuchs, Khorsabad Annals lines 235–239. Cf. text no. 2 lines 267b–272a and text no. 3 lines 1′–5′. Section 20 = lines 248–260 = II,21:1–13. See Winckler, Sar. Annals lines 214–226; Lie, Sar. lines 248–260; and Fuchs, Khorsabad Annals lines 240–252. Cf. text no. 2 lines 272b–284 and text no. 3 lines 6′–11′a.

248–249a The proposed restoration at the beginning of the translation assumes that the preceding line ended with UN.MEŠ KUR.*gúr-gu-me a-na paṭ gim-ri-šá a-na eš-šu-ti a-šur-ma*, for which see text no. 3 line 5′ and text no. 7 line 88.

250 H. Winckler's copy has [*bíl-te lìb-bu-šu ik*]*-pu-ud-ma* for the beginning of the line, but see text no. 2 line 274 [V,12:2] and text no. 3 lines 6′–7′.

251–252 Possibly take ⸢UGU⸣ [UN†].MEŠ [KUR-*šú*] with what goes before, rather than with what goes after, and translate instead "Thus, because of the e[vi]l that he had done ag[ainst the people of his land], I di[d awa]y with [his lordship] and ..."

252 -⸢*kir*⸣*-ma*: P.E. Botta's copy has -*x-ma* and H. Winckler's -RU-*ma*, but F. Thureau-Dangin's copy and the squeeze would allow -⸢*kir*⸣*-ma*. With regard to meaning of the word *talīmu*, see the on-page note to text no. 2002 lines 1 and 7.

254 [^{m}*ia*]-⸢*ad-na*⸣: P.E. Botta's copy has [...]-ḪAL-⸢*na*⸣, while H. Winckler's has: [^{m}]*ia-ad-na*; the squeeze currently only has -⸢*na*⸣.

Section 21 = lines 261–273 = H_1:1–13: See Winckler, Sar. Annals lines 227–246a; Lie, Sar. lines 261–273; and Fuchs, Khorsabad Annals lines 253–265. Cf. text no. 2 lines 285–306a and text no. 3 lines 11′b–15′. For photos of the squeeze from Entrance H_1 to Room II, see Figures 7–10; this is one of the best preserved squeezes.

263–264 For an alternate passage to *ša i-na sa-pan ... da-ád-me-šu*, "whose settlements ... Eastern Sea ," see text no. 3 lines 13′b–14′a and text no. 2 lines 288b–289a.

264) *da-ád-me-šu* UGU ÍD.*mar-ra-ti ù gu-pu-uš e-de-e it-ta-kil-ma a-de-e ma-mit* DINGIR.⸢MEŠ⸣
265) GAL.MEŠ *e-bu-uk-ma ik-la-a ta-mar-tuš* ^{m}*ḫu-um-ba-ni-ga-áš* LÚ.ELAM.MA.KI-*ú a-na* ⸢*re-ṣu-ti*⸣
266) *is-ḫur-ma gi-mir* LÚ.*su-te-e* ERIM.ME EDIN *it-ti-ia ú-šam-kir-ma ik-ṣu-ra ta-ḫa-zu ú-ri-dam-*[*ma*†]
267) *a-na er-ṣe-et* KUR EME.GI$_{7}$ *ù ak-ka-de-e* 12 MU.MEŠ *ki-i la lìb-bi* DINGIR.MEŠ KÁ.DINGIR.RA.KI URU ^{d}EN.LÍL.⸢LÁ DINGIR⸣.[MEŠ]
268) *i-bél ù iš-pur* ^{d}MES EN GAL-*ú ep-šet* KUR.*kal-di lem-né-e-ti ša i-zer-ru i-ṭul-*[*ma*]
269) *e-ṭe-er* GIŠ.GIDRU GIŠ.GU.ZA LUGAL-*ti-šu iš-šá-kín šap-tuš-šu ia-a-ti* ^{m}LUGAL-GI.NA LUGAL *šaḫ-*[*tu*]
270) *i-na nap-ḫar ma-li-ki ki-niš ut-ta-an-ni-ma ul-la-a* ⸢*re*⸣*-ši-ia i-na er-*⸢*ṣe*⸣*-et* KUR EME.[GI$_{7}$†]
271) *ù ak-ka-de-e a-na* GÌR.II LÚ.*kal-di* LÚ.KÚR *lem-ni pa-ra-si-im-ma ú-*⸢*šar*⸣*-ba-a* GIŠ.TUKUL.⸢MEŠ⸣-[*ia*†]
272) *i-na qí-bit* ^{d}EN GAL-*i* ^{d}MES *ṣi-in-di-*⸢*ia uš*⸣*-te-še-ra ak-ṣu-*⸢*ra uš*⸣*-ma-ni a-na* LÚ.⸢*kal*⸣-[*di* (*x x*)]
273) *lem-né-e-te a-la-ku aq-bi ù šu-ú* ^{md}AMAR.UTU-⸢IBILA⸣-[SUM.NA *a*]-⸢*lak*⸣ *ger-ri-ia iš-me-ma* URU.ḪAL.ṢU.[MEŠ†-*šú*]
274) *ú-da-an-ni-na ú-pa-aḫ-ḫi-ra ki-iṣ-re-e-šu* LÚ.*ga-am-bu-lu a-na si-ḫir-ti-šu*
275) *a-na* URU.BÀD-^{m}AD-*ḫa-ra ú-še-ri-ib-ma a-*⸢*na mé-ti*⸣*-iq ger-ri-ia ú-dan-ni-na ma-ṣar-tu*
276) 6 ME ANŠE.*pét-ḫal-lum* 4 LIM LÚ.ERIM.MEŠ *šu-lu-*⸢*ti a*⸣*-li-kut pa-an um-ma-ni-šu*
277) *i-di-in-šu-nu-ti-ma ú-šá-ar-ḫi-su-nu-ti lib-bu* BÀD-*šú-nu* UGU *šá pa-na*
278) *ú-zaq-qí-ru-ma ul-tu lìb-bi* ÍD.*su-ra-ap-pi bu-tuq-tu ib-*⸢*tu*⸣*-qu-nim-ma ki-ma* ILLU *kiš-šá-ti*
279) *ik-pu-pu li-me-es-su* URU *šú-a-tu a-di la šá-lam*

(265) and withheld his audience gift. He turned to Ḫumbanigaš (Ḫumban-nikaš I), the Elamite, for aid, made all the Sutians, the people of the steppe, hostile to me, and prepared for battle (against me). He came down to the territory of the land of Sumer and Akkad [and], against the will of the gods, ruled and governed Babylon, the city of the Enlil of the g[ods] (Marduk), for twelve years. (However), the god Marduk, the great lord, saw the evil deeds of Chaldea, which he hated. [Then], (the order for) the removal of his royal scepter (and) throne was set upon his lips. He duly chose me, Sargon, the reve[rent] king, from among all rulers and exalted me. He made [my] weapons prevail in order to bar the evil enemy Chaldeans from the territory of the land of Sumer and Akkad.

272–279a) At the command of the great divine lord, the god Marduk, I got my (chariot) teams ready, prepared my (military) camp, (and) ordered the march against the Ch[aldean, *a doer*] of evil (deeds). However, (when) that (man), Marduk-ap[la-iddina] (II) (Merodach-Baladan) heard of [the ad]vance of my expeditionary force, he strengthened [his] fortress[es] (and) assembled his (military) contingents. He brought the Gambulu (tribe) in its entirety (275) into Dūr-Abi-ḫāra and, at the approach of my expeditionary force, strengthened (its) garrison. He gave them six hundred cavalry (and) four thousand garrison soldiers, the vanguard of his army, and (thereby) made them confident. They raised their (city) wall higher than before, cut a channel from the Surappu River, and surrounded its environs as if with cresting flood (waters). I conquered that city before sunset. I carried off as booty 18,[4]30

266 Between *is-ḫur-ma* and *gi-mir*, text no. 2 line 292–293a adds LÚ.*ru-u*$_{8}$*-a* LÚ.*ḫi-in-da-ru* LÚ.KUR.*ia-ad-bu-ru* LÚ.*pu-qu-du* and text no. 3 line 15′ adds LÚ.*ru-u*$_{8}$*-a* [LÚ.*ḫi-in*]*-da-ru* KUR.*ia-ad-bu-*⸢*ri*⸣ (following line not preserved).
267 ^{d}EN.LÍL.LÁ ⸢DINGIR⸣.[MEŠ]: For the reading, see text no. 2 line 296. P.E. Botta's copy has ^{d}EN.LÍL*(copy: É) [*x*] (with presumably the final vertical wedge of the É for the vertical of the LÁ) and H. Winckler's ^{d}EN.LÍL.LÁ, but the squeeze has ⸢^{d}⸣EN.LÍL.⸢LÁ DINGIR⸣ [(*x*)].
268 *i-ṭul-*[*ma*]: H. Winckler's copy has *i-bu*$_{4}$-[*uk*].
269 *šaḫ-*[*tu*]: The restoration follows text no. 2 line 299. H. Winckler's copy has *šaḫ-tú*, but no trace of the final sign is currently preserved on the squeeze or copied by P.E. Botta. It is not clear whether some of the final signs copied by Winckler at the ends of the lines of this slab were seen by him or ever actually preserved on the squeeze.
272 LÚ.⸢*kal*⸣-[*di* (*x x*)]: The reading follows P.E. Botta's copy and the squeeze. H. Winckler's copy has LÚ.⸢*kal*⸣-[*di* LÚ.KÚR] (see text no. 2 line 304) but we would not then expect the feminine plural *lemnēte* in the following line. A. Fuchs (Khorsabad p. 138 line 264 n. 1) suggests that *ēpiš* or *kāpid* might be missing at the end of the line and the translation tentatively assumes *e-piš*, although there would be barely enough room for it. This may refer to Marduk-apla-iddina II or to the Chaldeans in general; see also text no. 2 lines 304–305 and text no. 7 line 125.
Section 22 = lines 274–286 = H$_{2}$:1–13: See Winckler, Sar. Annals lines 246b–253 and 258b–261a; Lie, Sar. lines 274–286; and Fuchs, Khorsabad Annals lines 266–279a. Cf. text no. 2 line 306b–ca. 322 and text no. 3 lines 31′–39′.
275 For the reading of the place name as Dūr-Abi-ḫāra instead of Dūr-Atḫara, see Parpola, Studies Dietrich p. 567; PNA 1/1 p. 9; and note also Van Buylaere, WO 46 (2016) pp. 140–142. The place has been tentatively identified with modern Šaiḫ-Yaʿqūb al-Yūsuf (Parpola and Porter, Helsinki Atlas map 11 and p. 8).
278 A. Fuchs (Khorsabad p. 459) identifies the Surappu River with the Rūdḫāne-ye Čangūle, while S.W. Cole and H. Gasche (Akkadica 128 [2007] pp. 34–35) identify it with the Nahr Tib [Nahr aṭ-Ṭib] (Iranian Mehmeh).
279 [LIM 4†] ⸢ME⸣ 30: P.E. Botta's copy has [*x* (*x*)] MEŠ, and H. Winckler's [LIM] 4 ME 90; the reading follows the squeeze and F. Thureau-Dangin's copy.

^{d}UTU-*ši* KUR-*ud* 18 [LIM 4†] ⸢ME⸣ 30 UN.MEŠ *a-di mar-ši-ti-*[*šú*†-*nu*†]

280) ANŠE.KUR.RA.MEŠ GU$_4$.MEŠ *ṣe-e-ni* ⸢*áš*⸣-*lu-la si-it-ta-ti-šú-nu ša* [*la-pa*]-⸢*an*⸣ GIŠ.TUKUL.MEŠ-*ia ip-par-šid-*[*du*†]-*ma*

281) ÍD.*uq-nu-ú mar-ṣu ù qa-né-e a-pi a-na ki-din-nu-*⸢*ti*⸣ [x x x (x)] x x [x x] *ka-šad* URU *šú-a-tu*

282) *iš-mu-ma it-ru-ku lib-bu-šu-un ki-ma iṣ-ṣu-ri ip-par-šu-nim-*[*ma* x x x x x (x x)] x URU *šu-a-tu*

283) ⸢*a-na*⸣ *eš-šu-ti aṣ-bat* URU.BÀD-^{d}AG MU-*šu az-kur* UN.MEŠ *šá-a-tu-nu* [x x x x x x (x x)] LÚ.*šu-ut* ⸢SAG⸣-*ia*

284) ⸢LÚ⸣.EN.NAM UGU-*šu-nu áš-kun* 1 GUN 30 MA.NA KÙ.BABBAR 2 LIM ŠE.BAR *i-na* [UGU 20 GU$_4$.MEŠ 1-*en* GU$_4$ *i*]-⸢*na* UGU⸣ 20 ⸢UDU⸣.MEŠ

285) 1-*en* UDU *na-dan* MU.AN.NA UGU-*šú-nu uk-tin* LÚ.ERIM.MEŠ *šá-a-tu-nu a-šur-ma* ⸢*i*⸣-[*na*? x x x x x x x] ERIM.MEŠ [x (x)]

286) *ú-ṣab-bit* URU.*qa-rat-*^{m}*na-an-ni* [(x)] URU *ša* ^{md}AG-*ú-ṣal-la* [x x x x x x x (x x)] MEŠ x [x (x)]

287) URU.*ma-ḫi-ru* 5 URU.MEŠ-*ni ša* KUR.*ḫu-ba-qa*†-[*nu na-gi-i*] URU.*qa-*⸢*an*⸣-^{m}*ra-a'-me*-DINGIR

288) URU *ša* ^{m}*ia-a-di* 2 URU.MEŠ-*ni dan-*[*nu-ti ša* KUR.*ti-mas*]-⸢*si*⸣-*na na-gi-i*

289) URU *ša* ^{m}*pa-ra-sa* URU *ša* ^{m}*ia-*⸢*nu*⸣-[*qu* x x x x (x) x†] 3 URU.MEŠ-*ni ša* ⸢ÍD⸣.*ḫi-ri-te*

290) *na-gi-i* URU *ša* ^{m}DÙG.GA-*a-a* URU *ša* [x x x x (x) URU] *ša* ^{m}*a-si-an* URU.*bi-ir-tu*

291) *ša* ^{m}*man-nu-ia-šá-na* URU *ša* ^{m}*ra-ḫi-*[x x x x URU *ša* ^{m}]⸢ŠEŠ⸣.MEŠ-⸢SUM⸣.NA 6 URU.MEŠ-*ni*

292) *ša* URU.*ḫi-il-ti* URU *ša* ^{m}*ḫa-za-*[DINGIR x x x x x (x x)] URU *ša* ^{m}*sab-ḫa-ar-ri*

293) URU *ša* ^{m}*ḫa-ma-da-a-ni* URU *ša* ^{m}[x x x x x (x)

people, together with [their] property, horses, oxen, (and) sheep and goats.

280b–286a) The remainder of them who had fle[d befor]e my weapons and [...] the Uqnû River, which was difficult (to ford), and reed thicket(s) for [(their)] protection, [...] heard of (my) conquest of that city and (as a result) their hearts pounded. They flew to me like a bird [and ...] I reorganized (the administration of) that city (and) (re)named it Dūr-Nabû. [*I ...-ed*] those people [...]. I set a eunuch of mine as provincial governor over them. I imposed upon them the annual payment of one talent thirty minas of silver, two thousand <*gur*> of barley, one ox out [of (every) twenty oxen (that they had), (and)] one sheep [out] of (every) twenty sh[eep] (that they had). I mustered those soldiers and took [*one soldier of theirs*] o[*ut of* (*every*) *three*] soldiers (*for my own army*).

286b–299) The city Qarat-Nanni, the city of Nabû-uṣalla [...] ... [...] (and) the city Maḫīru, (a total of) five settlements of [the district] Ḫubaqā[n]u; the city Qan-Ra'me-il (and) the city of Iādi (Iadī'), (a total of) two fort[ified] settlements [of] the district [Timass]ina; the city of Parasa, the city of Ian[nuqu, (and) ...] (a total of) three settlements of the Ḫirīte River (290) district; the city of Ṭābāya (Ṭābīya), the city of [...], the city] of Asiān, the fortress of Mannu-Iašana, the city of Raḫi[..., (and) the city of] Aḫḫē-iddina, (a total of) six settlements of the city Ḫilti; the city of Ḫazā-[il, ...], the city of Sabḫarru, the city of Ḫamadānu (Ḫamdanu), the city of [..., (and) the city] of Iašyanu, (a total) of six settlements; the city of Sa'lāni, the city of [..., the city] of Na[...], the city of Zārūtî, (295) the city of Sa'dani, the city of [..., (and) the city of ...]sal[i...], (a

281 A. Fuchs (Khorsabad p. 140 line 273 n. 1) suggests restoring *iṣ-ba-tu* or *e-ḫu-zu* in the gap after *ki-din-nu-*⸢*ti*⸣ (see line 334 versus text no. 2 line 332 and text no. 3 line 51′). H. Winckler's copy indicates that there is nothing missing between the traces *x x* and *ka-šad*, but that is not clear on the squeeze today.

284 As noted by A. Fuchs (Khorsabad p. 142 line 276 n. 1), no capacity measurement is given between 2 LIM and ŠE.BAR; A.G. Lie (p. 46) read *imêr?* after 2 LIM and before ŠE.BAR. ⸢UGU⸣ 20 ⸢UDU⸣.MEŠ: P.E. Botta's copy has UGU*(copy: KA) 10+[x].MEŠ and Winckler's UGU 10+[10 UDU].MEŠ; the squeeze has ⸢UGU⸣ 20 ⸢UDU.MEŠ⸣.

285 For the end of the line, see text no. 2 lines 321–322 and text no. 3 lines 39′–40′; however, there seems too much room in the first gap to read just ⸢*i*⸣-[*na* UGU 3 LÚ].ERIM.MEŠ and, as noted by A. Fuchs (Khorsabad p. 143 line 279 n. 1), not enough at the end for [1-*en* LÚ.ERIM-*šú-nu*].

286–299 For the places mentioned, see Zadok, WO 16 (1985) pp. 38–39. As noted by A. Fuchs (Khorsabad p. 144 line 279a n. 1), the traces after MEŠ at the end of line 286 might be ⸢BÀD⸣.

Section 23 = lines 287–299 = II,22:1–13: See Lie, Sar. lines 287–299; and Fuchs, Khorsabad Annals lines 279b–n; Winckler, Sar. Annals omits. Cf. text no. 2 lines ca. 323–324a.

287 For the reading KUR.*ḫu-ba-qa-*[*nu*], see text no. 2 line 323 and text no. 3 line 41′.

288 The restoration is based on Olmstead, AJSL 47 (1930–31) p. 271. See text no. 2 line 323 and text no. 3 line 41′.

289 Olmstead, AJSL 47 (1930–31) p. 271 reads ^{m}*ia-*⸢*nu*⸣-[*qu ša* KUR.*za-me-e*]; see text no. 2 line 327 and text no. 3 line 45′.

290 ^{m}DÙG.GA-*a-a*: For the reading Ṭābāya, see Parpola, Toponyms pp. 327–328 and Zadok, WO 16 (1985) p. 38. ^{m}*a-si-an*: Or ^{m}*a-si*-AN.

291 ŠEŠ.MEŠ-⸢SUM⸣.NA: The reading follows the squeeze and the reading of F. Thureau-Dangin.

292 URU.*ḫi-il-ti*: A.T.E. Olmstead (AJSL 47 [1930–31] p. 271; see also Fuchs, Khorsabad p. 328 n. 325) says that this is an "obvious error" for URU.*ḫi-il-mu*; KUR.*ḫi-il-mu* appears in text no. 2 line 324 and cf. line 344. ^{m}*ḫa-za-*[DINGIR]: H. Winckler's copy may indicate that he saw part of the -DINGIR on the squeeze, but it may just be a restoration from Room V (text no. 2 line 314).

293 ^{m}*ia-*⸢*aš*?⸣-*ia-nu*: The reading AŠ for the sign between the two IA signs goes back to D.D. Luckenbill (see Olmstead, AJSL 47 [1930–31] p. 271) and follows the copy of H. Winckler and (less well) that of P.E. Botta. F. Thureau-Dangin, who examined the squeeze, copied ⸢^{m}*ia*⸣-*x*-⸢*ia*⸣-*nu*, where the vague traces of the *x* would seem to fit the beginning of ÁŠ better than AŠ.

URU] ša ^{m}ia-⸢aš$^{?}$⸣-ia-nu 6 URU.MEŠ-ni
294) URU ša ^{m}sa-a'-la-a-ni URU ša [x x x x x (x)
URU] ša ^{m}na-[x (x)] x URU šá ^{m}za-ru-ti
295) URU ša ^{m}sa-a'-da-ni URU ša [x x x x x (x
x)]-sa-⸢li⸣ [(x)] x [(x)] 7 URU.MEŠ-ni
296) ša i-na bi-rit KUR.na-gi-a-[te ù ÍD.tup-li]-⸢áš⸣
ta-mir-[ta]-šú†-nu la ni-be
297) zik-ri URU.a-a-sa-mu URU.x-[x-x-(x)]-pa-qa URU
ša ^{m}di-na-ia URU šá ^{m}⸢ib⸣-na-ia
298) URU ša ba-bi-le-e URU ša [x-x]-⸢me⸣ URU [ša]
^{m}an-da-DINGIR URU.si-i'-ra-a-a
299) URU.pa-ti-ia-a-an URU.ḫu-la-[x-(x)]-su URU ša
^{m}sam-si-ia-da-a' URU.ḫa-il-a-a
Lines 300–312 are not preserved
313) [...]
314) [...]
315) [...]
316) [...]
317) [ÍD].⸢tup⸣-[li-(ia)-áš ÍD tuk-la-ti-šú-nu]
318) i-na ⸢ši†⸣-[pik SAḪAR.MEŠ ù GI.MEŠ ak-si-ir]
319) 2 URU.⸢bi⸣-[ra-a-ti a-ḫu a-na a-ḫi ad-di-ma]
320) lap-la-⸢ap⸣-[tu ú-šá-aṣ-bi-su-nu-ti-ma ul-tu
qé-reb ÍD.uq-né-e]
321) uṣ-ṣu-[nim-ma iṣ-ba-tú GÌR.II-ia ^{m}ia-nu-qu]
322) ⸢a⸣-lik pa-ni ⸢ša$^{?}$⸣ [URU.za-a-me-e
^{md}MUATI-ú-ṣal-la ša URU.a-bu-re-e]
323) [^{m}pa-áš]-šu-nu [^{m}ḫa-ú-ka-nu ša URU.nu-ḫa-a-ni
^{m}sa-'i-lu ša]
324) [URU].⸢i⸣-bu-⸢li⸣ [5 LÚ.na-si-ka-a-ti ša]
325) [LÚ.pu]-qu†-du [^{m}ab-ḫa-ta-a ša LÚ.ru-u$_{8}$-a]
326) ^{m}ḫu-ni-nu ^{m}sa-me-e' ^{m}sab-ḫa-ar-ru ^{m}ra-a-⸢pi⸣-i'
327) ⸢4⸣ LÚ.na-⸢sik⸣-ka-a-ti ša KUR.ḫi-in-da-ri a-di
LÚ.ERIM.MEŠ-⸢šú⸣-nu
328) ⸢a⸣-na URU.BÀD-^{m}AD-ḫa-ri il-li-ku-nim-ma
iṣ-ba-tu GÌR.II-⸢ia⸣
329) li-i-ṭi-šú-nu ú-ṣa-bit-ma GUN ma-da-tu ki-i ša
⸢áš⸣-šu-ri
330) e-mid-su-nu-ti i-na ŠU.II LÚ.šu-ut SAG-ia

total of) seven settlements that are (located) between the land Nagia[tu (Nagītu) and the Tupliya]š [River] (and) whose environs (are) without (special) name designation; the city Aya-Sammu, the city [...]paqa, the city of Dīnāya, the city of Ibnāya, the city of Bābilê, the city of [...]me, the city [of] Anda-il, the city Si'rāya, the city Patiyān, the city Ḫula[...]su, the city of Samsi-yada', the city Ḫa'ilāya,

Lines 300–312 are not preserved
313–316) Not preserved

317–332a) [I dammed up the] Tu[pliyaš River, a river upon which they relied], with p[ile(s) of dirt and reeds. I erected] two f[ortresses, side by side, and (320) star[ved them out. They [then came] out [from the Uqnû River and grasped hold of my feet. Iannuqu], the leader o[f the city Zāmê, Nabû-uṣalla of the city Abūrê, Paš]šunu (and) [Ḫaukānu of the city Nuḫānu, (and) Sa'īlu of the city] Ibūl[i, (a total of) five sheikhs of (325) the Pu]qudu (tribe); [Abi-ḫatâ of the Ru'u'a (tribe)]; (and) Ḫunnu, Sāme', Sabḫarru, (and) Rāpi', (a total of) four sheikhs of the Ḫindaru (tribe); together with their (tribes)men, came to me at the city Dūr-Abi-ḫāra and grasped hold of m[y] feet. I took hostages from them and (330) imposed upon them (the same) tribute and payments as if (they were) Assyrians. I assigned them to the authority of a eunuch of mine, the governor of Gambulu, and imposed the annual ṣibtu-tax on their oxen (and) their sheep for the gods Bēl (Marduk) (and) Son of Bēl (Nabû)].

294 ^{m}na-[x (x)] x: So P.E. Botta's copy; H. Winckler's copy has ^{m}na-[x] x. The traces of the final sign would fit -⸢ri⸣ or -⸢ḫu⸣ among other signs. A.T.E. Olmstead (AJSL 47 [1930–31] p. 271) suggested reading the name na-[na-aḫ]-ḫu, but the published copies and the squeeze would indicate that there was not sufficient room for this restoration.
296 For the restoration, cf. text no. 2 line 326 and text no. 3 line 43′. A. Fuchs (Khorsabad p. 465) identifies the Tupliyaš River with the Nahr al-Tib (Nahr aṭ-Ṭib), while S.W. Cole and H. Gasche (Akkadica 128 [2007] pp. 34–35) identify it with the Dawairij. -šú†-nu: P.E. Botta and H. Winckler have -ŠI-nu; it is unclear from the squeeze if the sign is ŠÚ or ŠI.
297 With regard to the reading of the city name ending in -pa-qa, see Bagg, Rép. Géogr. 7/3-2 p. 637. ^{m}⸢ib⸣-na-ia: The reading follows the squeeze and F. Thureau-Dangin's reading.
298 [ša] ^{m}an-da-DINGIR: The spacing might suggest instead [šá] ^{m}an-da-DINGIR or just ^{m}an-da-DINGIR. H. Winckler's copy has [ša] <m>an-da-DINGIR.
299 URU.pa-ti-ia-a-an: Cf. URU.pat-ti-a-nu in text no. 2 line 334 and URU.pat-ti-[...] in text no. 3 line 55′. ^{m}sam-si-ia-da-'i: The reading follows D.D. Luckenbill (apud Olmstead, AJSL 47 [1930–31] p. 271).
Sections 24–25 Section 24 = lines 300–312 = II,23:1–13: Cf. text no. 2 lines 324bff. and text no. 3 lines 34′bff. Section 25 = lines 313–325 = II,24:1–13: See Winckler, Sar. Annals lines 266–269a; Lie, Sar. lines 313–325; and Fuchs, Khorsabad Annals lines 283–286. Cf. text no. 2 lines +326–329a and text no. 3 lines +43′b–47′a.
317–325 For the restorations, see text no. 2 lines 326–329 and text no. 3 lines 43′–47′.
320 lap-la-⸢ap⸣-[tu]: Or kal-la-⸢ap⸣-[tu]; see also text no. 2 line 326.
322 ⸢a⸣-lik pa-ni: Text no. 2 line 327 has LÚ.⸢na⸣-sik-ku and text no. 3 line 45′ has LÚ.[...].
324 LÚ.na-si-ka-a-ti: Or restore instead LÚ.na-sik-ka-a-ti; see line 327.
Section 26 = lines 326–338 = II,25:1–13: See Winckler, Sar. Annals lines 269b–273a; Lie, Sar. lines 326–338; and Fuchs, Khorsabad Annals lines 286–290. Cf. text no. 2 lines 329b–333a and text no. 3 lines 47′b–54′a.

LÚ.GAR.KUR KUR.*gam-bu-li*
331) ⸢*am*⸣-*nu-šu-nu-ti-ma ṣi-bit* GU$_4$.MEŠ-*šú-nu* US$_5$.UDU.ḪI.A-*šu-nu*
332) ⸢*a*⸣-*na* ^{d}EN ^{d}DUMU EN *ú-ki-in šat-ti-šam si-ti-it* LÚ.*a-ri-me*
333) *ek-ṣu-te a-ši-bu-ut na-gi-šú-nu šá* UGU ^{md}MES-A-AŠ *u* ^{m}*šu-túr-na-ḫu-un-di* TE-*su-nu id-du-ma*
334) ⸢ÍD⸣.*uq-nu-ú e-ḫu-zu šu-bat ru-uq-ti da*-⸢*ád*⸣-[*me*†]-*šú-nu*
335) ⸢*a*⸣-*bu-biš as-pu-un-ma* GIŠ.NÍG.TUKU *tuk-lat-su-nu* GIŠ.⸢KIRI$_6$⸣.MEŠ-*ti*
336) ⸢*bal*⸣-*ti na-gi-šu-nu ak-kis-ma ù qi-ra-te-šú-nu um*-⸢*ma*⸣-*ni*
337) *ú*-[*šá*†]-⸢*kil*⸣ *a-na* ÍD.*uq-né-e a-šar ta-ap-ze-er-ti-šú-nu*
338) LÚ.[*qu*†]-⸢*ra*⸣-*di-ia ú-ma*-⸢ʾ*e-er*⸣-*ma* ⸢BAD$_5$.BAD$_5$-*šu-nu*⸣ *im-ḫaṣ-ṣu-ma*

332b–339a) (As for) the rest of the dangerous Arameans who dwell in their district (and) who had paid attention (lit.: "inclined their cheek") to Marduk-apla-iddina (II) (Merodach-Baladan) and Šutur-Naḫūndi and taken (themselves) to the Uqnû River, a far-off place to live (lit.: "a distant dwelling"), I overwhelmed their settle[ments] (335) like the Deluge, cut down *the date palm(s)* upon which they relied (and) the orchards that were the [p]ride of their district, and (then) [fe]d my army (the food in) their granaries. I sent my [war]riors to the Uqnû River, their hiding place, and they (my warriors) inflicted a defeat on [th]em. [*They* (my warriors)] then [*carried off as booty* (*those*) *people, together with their property*].

339) [... URU.*za-a-me*]-*e* URU.*a-bu*†-[*re-e* ...]
340) [...] URU.*ḫa-a-a-ma*-[*nu* ...]

339b–340) [(The people of) the cities Zām]ê, Abū[rê, Yaptiru, Maḫīṣu, Ḫilipanu, KAL-KAL, Pattiānu], Ḫayamā[nu, ...]

341) [...]
342) [...]
343) [...]
344) [...]
345) [...]
346) [...]
347) [...]
348) [...]
349) [...]

341–349) Not preserved

350) [...] ANŠE.KUR.[RA.MEŠ ...]
351) [...] *a-na eš*-[*šu-ti* ...]
352) [...] ^{m}*a-a*-[*lu-nu* ^{m}*da-iṣ-ṣa-nu šá* KUR.*la*]-*ḫi-ri* [...]
353) [... URU.*su-la*]-*ia*† 5 LÚ.*na*-⸢*sik*⸣-[*ka-a-te ša* KUR.*ia-ad-bu-ri*] ANŠE.KUR.⸢RA⸣.[MEŠ ...]

350–355) [I carried off as booty ... wagons], hors[es, mules, donkeys, (and) camels, together with their abundant property. I] re[organized (the administration of) the city Sam'ūna, changed its name, and gave it the name Enlil-iqīša. ...], Aya-[lūnu, (and) Daiṣṣānu of the land La]ḫīru [(and) ... of the city Sulā]ya — (a

332 ^{d}DUMU EN: As noted by A. Fuchs (Khorsabad p. 148 line 288b n. 1), A.G. Lie (Sar. p. 50) and K. Tallqvist (Götterepitheta p. 120) erroneously place the divine determinative before EN rather than DUMU; see also text no. 2 line 321.
335 Text no. 2 line 332 and text no. 3 line 52′ have GIŠ.GIŠIMMAR instead of GIŠ.NÍG.TUKU and place *qí-ra-a-ti-šú-nu um-ma-ni ú-šá-kil* before it; for the additional passage, cf. lines 333–334. As noted by A. Fuchs (Khorsabad p. 149 line 289 n. 2), CAD M/1 p. 387 suggests the reading of GIŠ.NÍG.TUKU to be *iṣ mašrê/î*, "tree of wealth," instead of *gišimmaru*, "date palm."
338 LÚ.[*qu*†]-⸢*ra*⸣-*di-ia*: The reading follows P.E. Botta's copy and the squeeze; H. Winckler's copy has LÚ.*qu-ra-di-ia*. -⸢*šu-nu*⸣: The reading follows the squeeze; Botta's copy has -GAL and Winckler's -*šu-nu*.
Section 27 = lines 339–351 = II,26:1–13: See Winckler, Sar. Annals lines 273b–274 and 280; Lie, Sar. lines 339–351; and Fuchs, Khorsabad Annals lines 291 and 297. Cf. text no. 2 lines 333b–340 and text no. 3 lines 54′b–55′+.
339–364 See the commentary section with regard to sections 27 and 28. Since the placement of the text on Botta, Monument de Ninive pl. 92 (bottom) is not certain, restorations in the Akkadian have been kept to a minimum, although the translation assumes that the beginning of line 339 had UN.MEŠ *a-di mar-ši-ti-šú-nu iš-lul-ú-ni* before URU.*za-a-me*; see text no. 2 lines 333b–334a and text no. 3 line 54′ for the reading. Some of the restored translation for lines 350–355 was likely at the beginning of line 356. As noted in the commentary, three lines of P.E. Botta's copy are not currently placed anywhere in the edition: Botta, Monument de Ninive 4 pl. 92 bottom lines 1′ ([...] AN [...]), 6′ ([...] A I MUNUS [...]), and 7′ ([...] *x i-na* [...]). Lines 339–340: These lines represent Botta, Monument de Ninive pl. 92 bottom lines 4′–5′ and their placement here is uncertain. Cf. text no. 2 line 334 and text no. 3 lines 54′–55′ for the restorations in the translation.
350–351 These lines represent P.E. Botta, Monument de Ninive 4 pl. 92 bottom lines 2′–3′ and their placement here is uncertain. Cf. text no. 2 line 340; the line division in the restoration is arbitrary.
Section 28 = lines 352–364 = II,27:1–13 (see the commentary section with regard to sections 27 and 28): See Winckler, Sar. Annals lines 281–284; Lie, Sar. lines 352–364; and Fuchs, Khorsabad Annals lines 298–301. Cf. text no. 2 lines 341–349.
352–355 These lines represent P.E. Botta, Monument de Ninive 4 pl. 92 bottom lines 8′ and 9′a, 9′b and 10′a, 10′b and 11′a, and 11′b and 12′a respectively, and their placement here is uncertain. Cf. text no. 2 lines 341, 342 (where it is six sheikhs, not five), 343, and 343–344 (where it is ⸢URU⸣.*a-ḫi-li-im*-⸢*mu*⸣) respectively.

354) [...] URU.*la-ḫi-*[*ra ša* KUR.*ia-a-di-bi-ri* URU].*su-la-a* ⸢URU⸣.[...]
355) [...] URU.MEŠ [KAL.MEŠ *ša* KUR.*ia-ad-bu-ri*] URU$^{?\dagger}$.*ḫi-*⸢*li*†⸣*-*[*im-mu*$^{?}$ ...]

total of) five she[ikhs of the land Yadburu — brought] horse[s, mules, oxen, and sheep and goats into my (military) camp and grasped hold of my feet in order to do obeisance. I considered] the city Laḫī[ru of the land Yadburu, the cities] Sulāya, [..., fortified] cities [of the land Yadburu], *the cities Ḫil*[*immu (and) Pillatu* that are on the border of the land Elam, together with the settlements in their environs that are (located) along the Naṭītu River, as (part) of my territory].

356) [...]
357) [...]
358) [...]
359) [...]
360) [...]
361) [...]
362) [...]
363) [...]
364) [...]

356–364) Not preserved

365) *ḫat-ti ra-ma-ni-šu im-qut-su-ma šu-ú a-di re-ṣe*†*-*[*e-šú* ERIM].⸢MEŠ⸣ MÈ-*šú mu-šiš* ⸢*uṣ*⸣*-ṣi-ma*
366) *a-na* KUR.*ia-ad-bu-ri ša* ⸢KUR.ELAM.MA⸣.KI *iš-ku-na pa-ni-šú ú-*[*nu-ut* LUGAL*-ti-šú*] ⸢GIŠ⸣.NÁ GIŠ.GU.ZA GIŠ.*né-ma-*⸢*at*⸣*-tu*
367) *nàr-ma-ak-tu* LUGAL*-ti ti-*⸢*iq*⸣*-ni* GÚ*-šú a-na tur-ri gi-mil-*⸢*li*⸣*-*[*šú a-na* ^{m}]⸢*šu*⸣*-túr-na-ḫu-un-di* ELAM.MA.KI*-i*

365–368a) [As a result, in the midst of his (own) palace] his own fear(s) fell upon him; he then went out (from Babylon) during the night together with [his] alli[es] (and) his battle [troop]s and set out for the land Yadburu, which is (part) of the land Ela[m]. He gave to [Š]utur-Naḫūndi, the Elamite, [his royal] ut[ensils], a bed, a throne, a chair, a royal washbasin, (and) his neck ornament, as gifts from him in order to get [his] revenge (on me).

368) *i-di-na kàd-ra-šú ṣe-nu* LÚ.ELAM.MA.KI *ṭa-a*ʾ*-tuš im-ḫur-ma* [*e-du-ra* GIŠ].⸢TUKUL⸣*-ia* ⸢*ip*⸣*-sil ur-ḫa-šú-ma la a-la-ka*
369) *iq-bi-šú a-mat* EN *gi-mil-li-šú* ⸢*iš*⸣*-me-ma qaq-qa-riš ip-pal-si-iḫ* [*na-aḫ-lap*]*-tuš iš-ru-ṭa nag-la-ba iš-ši-ma*
370) *ú-*⸢*šá-aṣ*⸣*-ri-ḫa bi-ki-tu šu-*⸢*ú*⸣ *a-di re-ṣe-e-šú* LÚ.ERIM.MEŠ ⸢MÈ⸣*-*[*šú* TA *qé-reb*] KUR.*ia-ad-bu-ri is-su-ḫa-am-ma*

368b–371a) (That) Elamite villain accepted his bribe, but [took fright at] my [weapon(s)]. He turned away and told him (Marduk-apla-iddina) that he would not come (to help him). (When) he (Marduk-apla-iddina II) heard the words of (the one who was to be) his avenger, he threw himself on the ground, ripped his [cloa]k, wielded (his) razor, and uttered cries of mourning. Together with his allies (and) [his] bat[tle] troops, that (man) moved away [from] the land Yadburu, entered int[o] the city Iqbi-Bēl, an[d] stayed (there) in [f]lear.

371) *a-*⸢*na*⸣ URU.*iq-bi-*^{d}EN *e-ru-*⸢*um-ma*⸣ [*a*]*-di-riš ú-šib* DUMU.MEŠ KÁ.⸢DINGIR⸣.[RA.KI *bár*]*-sípa*.KI LÚ.KU$_{4}$.MEŠ É LÚ.⸢*um*⸣*-ma-ni*
372) *mu-de-e šip-ri a-li-kut* ⸢*pa*⸣*-*[*ni*] *mu-*ʾ*e-ru-ut* KUR *ša i-*⸢*da-ag*⸣*-*[*ga-lu*$^{?}$ *pa*]*-*⸢*nu*⸣*-uš-šú re-ḫa-at* ^{d}EN ^{d}*zar-pa-ni-ti*
373) [^{d†}AG] ^{d}[*taš*]*-me-ta a-na* URU.[BÀD*-*^{m}*la*]*-*⸢*din*†*-ni*⸣ *a-di maḫ-ri-ia* ⸢*ub-lu*⸣*-*[*nim-ma e*†]*-*⸢*re*⸣*-eb* KÁ.⸢DINGIR†⸣.RA.KI *iq-bu-nim-*⸢*ma*⸣

371b–374a) The citizens of Baby[lon (and) Bor]sippa, the temple personnel, the craftsmen who know (their) trade, the lea[der]s, (and) administrators of the land, who (up till then) had been his su[bjects], bro[ught] before me in the city [Dūr-Lad]inni the leftovers of (the sacrifices to) the deities Bēl, Zarpanītu, [Nabû, (and) Taš]mētu, [and] invited (lit.: "said to") me [to en]ter into Babylon, [making] my heart [rejoice].

Section 29 = lines 365–377 = II,28:1–13: See Winckler, Sar. Annals lines 290–302; Lie, Sar. lines 365–377; and Fuchs, Khorsabad Annals lines 307–316. Cf. text no. 2 lines 350–359a.

365 The translation "[As a result, in the midst of his (own) palace]" assumes that the previous line ended with *-ma ina* MURUB$_{4}$*-ti* É.GAL*-šú* and is based on text no. 2 line 349.

368–369a A. Fuchs (Khorsabad p. 331 n. 344) notes that Šutur-Naḫūndi's refusal to come is comparable to refusals of several gods to oppose Anzû in the Anzû Epic.

369 The phrase "wield the razor" refers to using razors to slash oneself in order to indicate mourning. See also line 162.

372 *i-*⸢*da-ag*⸣*-*[*ga-lu*$^{?}$]: The reading follows F. Thureau-Dangin's collation and copy of the passage (RA 24 [1927] p. 77). P.E. Botta's copy has *i-*⸢*da*⸣*-*[...], H. Winckler's *i-da-*[*a-ga-lu*], and the squeeze currently *i-*⸢*da*⸣*-*[...]. Text no. 2 line 355 has ⸢*i-dag*†⸣*-ga-lu*.

374) [ú-šá-li-ṣu] ⸢kab⸣-ta-ti [a-na] ⸢KÁ.DINGIR†⸣.[RA†].⸢KI URU⸣ ^{d}†EN†.[LÍL.LÁ DINGIR.MEŠ] ḫa-diš e-ru-⸢um⸣-ma a-na DINGIR.MEŠ

375) [a-ši-bu-ut é-sag-íl é-zi-da am-ḫu-ur ŠÀ].⸢GI⸣.[GURU$_{6}$-e KÙ.MEŠ ma]-ḫar-šú-⸢un⸣ aq-qí i-na qé-reb É.GAL-šú

376) [mu-šab LUGAL-ti-šú ...-a]-⸢ti⸣ KUR.a-ri-me KUR.É-^{m}a-mu-ka-ni

377) [KUR.É-^{m}dak-ku-ri x x x x x x x x (x x) ka†-bit†-tu† am†-ḫur†] ÍD bár-sípa.KI maḫ-ru-ú

378) [šá†] ⸢LUGAL⸣.MEŠ-ni a-li-⸢kut⸣ pa-ni-ia e-⸢pu-šu⸣-[ma] ⸢ÍD⸣ eš-šú a-na maš-da-aḫ

379) ⸢^{d}⸣[AG] ⸢EN⸣-ia a-na qé-reb šu-an-na.KI aḫ-⸢re⸣ LÚ.ḫa-mar-a-na-a-a

380) ša la-pa-an GIŠ.TUKUL.MEŠ-ia ip-par-ši-du a-na ZIMBIR.KI

381) e-ru-bu-ma a-lak ger-⸢ri⸣ DUMU KÁ.DINGIR.RA.⸢KI iḫ⸣-ta-nab-ba-tu

382) ka-a-a-nu LÚ.šu-ut SAG.MEŠ-ia LÚ.EN.NAM.MEŠ ⸢UGU⸣-šú-nu áš-pur-ma

383) ni-i-ta il-mu-šu-nu-ti-ma ṣe-ḫer ra-bi la ip-par-ši-du i-na-ru i-na kak-⸢ki⸣

384) ik-⸢šu⸣-dam-ma ITI.⸢BÁRA⸣ [a]-ra-aḫ a-ṣe-e ^{d}⸢EN⸣ DINGIR.MEŠ ŠU.II ^{d}EN GAL-⸢i⸣

385) ^{d}⸢AMAR⸣.UTU ^{d}AG LUGAL ⸢kiš⸣-šat AN-e KI-tim aṣ-[bat]-ma ú-šal-li-ma ú-ru-⸢uḫ⸣

386) ⸢É⸣ á-ki-ti GU$_{4}$.MAḪ-ḫi bit-ru-ti šu-ʾe-e ma-ru-ú-⸢ti⸣

387) KUR.GI.⸢MUŠEN⸣.MEŠ UZ.TUR.MEŠ it-ti kàd-re-e la nar-ba-a-⸢ti⸣

388) ú-⸢šat⸣-ri-ṣa ma-ḫar-šu-un a-na DINGIR.MEŠ ma-ḫa-zi KUR EME.[GI$_{7}$]

389) ù ak-[ka-de†-e† UDU.SÍSKUR.(MEŠ)]-⸢e taš-ri⸣-[iḫ]-⸢ti⸣ aq-qi-[ma] IGI.SÁ-⸢e⸣

390) [...]

Lines 391–403 are not preserved

374b–377a) Happily, I entered Babylo[n, the c]ity of the En[lil of the gods (Marduk); I prayed] to the gods [who dwelt in Esagil (and) Ezida, (and)] offered [pure vol]u[ntary offerings bef]ore them. Inside his palace, [his royal residence, ... I received substantial ... *from* ...] the land Aram, the land Bīt-Amukāni, [the land Bīt-Dakkūri, ...].

377b–379a) (With regard to) the former Borsippa canal, [which k]ings who preceded me had co[ns]tructed, I dug a new [ca]nal into Šuanna (Babylon) for the procession of the god [Nabû], my lord.

379b–383) I sent eunuchs of mine, provincial governors, against the Ḫamarānu (tribe), who had fled from my weapons, entered Sippar, and were constantly, repeatedly robbing caravan(s) of the citizen(s) of Babylon while they were en route. They then surrounded them so that (no one), neither young (nor) old, could escape, (and) struck (them) down with the sword.

384–388a) (When) the month Nis[annu] ar[ri]ved, [the m]onth the lo[rd] of the gods goes out (from his temple), I to[ok] the hands of the great divine lord, (385) the god M[ar]duk, (and) of the god Nabû, the king of the [to]tality of heaven (and) earth, and brought (them) safely along the roa[d] to the *akītu*-house. I presented before them prize bulls in prime condition, fattened sheep, gee[se], (and) ducks, (along) with (other) innumerable gifts.

388b–390) I offered [sacrific]es of hom[ag]e to the gods of the cult centers of the land of Sum[er] and Ak[kad, and ...] presents [...]

Lines 391–403 are not preserved

374 A. Fuchs' edition (Khorsabad p. 154 line 314) ends the line with DINGIR.MEŠ [ ]-*ši*!-[ ], assuming that the following *a-ši-bu-ut* was on this line. The line actually ends with DINGIR.⸢MEŠ⸣, with a bump/flaw in the squeeze making the ⸢MEŠ⸣ appear to be ŠI.

376–377 The restorations are based on text no. 2 line 357–358. After *mu-šab* LUGAL-*ti-šú*, A.T.E. Olmstead would restore [*e-ru-um-ma bi-ra-a*]-*ti* and restore *ak-šud ma-da-ta-šu-nu* at the beginning of line 377 (AJSL 47 [1930–31] pp. 273–274), thus " [I entered] into his palace, [his royal abode. I conquered the fortress]es of the lands Aram, Bīt-Amukāni, [(and) Bīt-Dakkūri]. I received [their] substantial [tribute]." However, there would seem to be too much room for just this at the beginning of the lines and A. Fuchs (Khorsabad p. 155 line 315 n. 2) prefers to assume the tribute passage began here.

377 The restoration is based on text no. 2 lines 358–359. H. Winckler's copy indicates that *ka-bit-tu am-ḫur* is fully preserved, but there is currently no trace of this on the squeeze.

Section 30 = lines 378–390 = II,29:1–13: See Winckler, Sar. Annals lines 303–314; Lie, Sar. lines 378–390; and Fuchs, Khorsabad Annals lines 316–321 and 321a–e. Cf. text no. 2 lines 359b–371 and text no. 5 lines 1′–3′.

378 *e*-⸢*pu-šu*⸣-[*ma*]: The reading is based on the squeeze; H. Winckler's copy has *e-ḫi-ru*-[*ma*].

379 *aḫ*-⸢*re*⸣: The reading follows the squeeze. P.E. Botta's copy has *aḫ*-[*x*] and H. Winckler's *aḫ-re*-[*ma*], but as already noted by F. Thureau-Dangin (RA 24 [1927] p. 77), the squeeze indicates that there no room to restore MA.

386–389 Cf. text no. 2 lines 364b–369.

389 It is not clear from H. Winckler's copy if he saw *ak*-[*ka*]-⸢*de-e*⸣ or if the last two signs were also restored; nothing of -*de-e* is currently visible on the squeeze. The restoration and reading [UDU.SÍSKUR.(MEŠ)]-⸢*e taš-ri*⸣-[*iḫ*]-⸢*ti*⸣ is based on the squeeze; see also text no. 65 line 161 and Fuchs, Khorsabad p. 159 line 321d.

404) [*x x x x ki-sik*.KI URU.*né-med-*^{d}*la-gu-da x x x iš-lul*]*-ma* [*a-na*] URU.⸢BÀD⸣-^{m}⸢*ia*†⸣*-kin*$_7$ *ú-še-*[*rib-ma ú-dan*]*-ni-*[*na*]
405) ⸢*ker*†⸣-[*ḫe-šú*†] *áš*†*-la*.⸢TA⸣.[ÀM *la-pa-an* BÀD*-šú* GAL*-i ú-né-si-ma* 2 ME] *ina* 1.KÙŠ DAGAL *ḫa-ri-*⸢*ṣi*⸣ *iš-*⸢*ku-un*⸣*-*[*ma* 1 1/2 NINDA *ú-šap-pil-ma*]
406) [*ik-šu-da*† A†].MEŠ ⸢*nag*⸣-[*bi bu-tuq-tu ul-tu qé-reb* ÍD.*pu-rat-te ib-tú*]-⸢*qa*⸣ *ú-šar-da-a ṣe-ru-*⸢*uš*⸣*-šú ú-*[*šal-la* URU]
407) [*a*]-⸢*šar*⸣ [*naq*]*-ra-bi* A.[MEŠ *ú-mal-li*†]*-ma*† *ú-*[*bat-ti-qa ti-tur-ri šu-ú*] *a-di re-ṣi-šú* ERIM.MEŠ [MÈ†*-šú*†] *i-na bi-*[*rit*† ÍD.MEŠ†]

404–408a) [(Marduk-apla-iddina) carried off the people of (the cities) Ur, ..., Kissik, Nēmed-Laguda (and) ...], and bro[ught (them) [into] the city Dūr-Yakīn. [He then stren]gth[ened its en]clo[sure walls (and), moving back a distance of one] measuring rope [from the front of its main wall], he mad[e] a moat [two hundred] cubits wide; [he made (the moat) one and a half *nindanu* deep and reached] g[round water. He cu]t [a channel from the Euphrates River], (thereby) making (its water) flow to it (lit.: "against it"). [He (thus) filled the city's] fla[tlands, wh]e[re bat]tles (are fought), with water and [cut the bridges]. Together with his allies (and) [his battle] troops, he pitched his [royal tent] in a be[nd of the river (lit.: "bet[ween river]s") li]ke [a *cran*]*e* and [set up his] (military) cam[p].

408) [*ki*]-⸢*ma*⸣ [*ku*†*-mé*†]*-e*.[MUŠEN *kul-tar* LUGAL]*-ti-šú iš*†*-kun-ma* [*ik-ṣu-ra*] *uš-ma*†*-*[*an-šu i-na*] *qí-bit* ^{d}*aš-šur* ^{d}[UTU (*u*) ^{d}]MES† [LÚ†.*mun*†*-daḫ*†*-ṣe*†*-ia*†]
409) ⸢*na-as*⸣-[*qu*†]*-ti* UGU [ÍD.MEŠ*-šú* TI$_8$].⸢MUŠEN†⸣ SU ⸢MIR⸣ [*x ú-šap*]*-riš-*[*ma*] ⸢*iš*⸣*-ku*†*-*[*nu*] *taḫ-*⸢*ta*⸣*-šu šá-a*†*-šu* [*a-di ki-ṣir*]
410) LUGAL†-[*ti-šú*] ⸢*ni*⸣-[*i-tú al-me-šu*]-⸢*ma*⸣ *ki-ma as-*⸢*li*†⸣ [*ina pa*]*-na* GÌR.II*-šú ú-nap-*⸢*pi*⸣*-ṣa* [LÚ†].*qu-*[*ra*†*-di-šu* ANŠE.KUR.RA.MEŠ]
411) [*ṣi*†*-mit*†*-ti*† *ni*†]*-ri-*[*šu i-na*] ⸢*uṣ*⸣*-ṣi ú-*[*šaq-qir*] *ù šá-a-*[*šú i*†]*-na* ⸢*zi-qit*⸣ [*mul*†*-mul*†]-⸢*li*⸣ [*rit*†*-ta*†*-šú*† *ap*†]-⸢*ṭur*⸣-[*ma*]
412) ⸢*ki*⸣*-ma* ⸢*šik-ke-e*⸣ *ḫal-*[*la-la*]*-niš* [KÁ†.GAL†]

408b–414) [At] the command of the gods Aššur, [Šamaš, (and)] Marduk, [I had my c]ho[ice fighting men f]ly over [its water channels (like) eag]le(s) ... [and they br]oug[ht about] his defeat. [I surrounded] him [together with his] royal [(military) contingent (410) an]d slaughtered [his] wa[rriors] like shee[p a]t his feet. I [pierced the horses trained to his yo]ke [with ar]rows. Then, (as for) hi[m, I pie]r[ced (lit.: "loosened") his hand wi]th the point [of an arro]w [and] he (then) entered [the gate] of his city ste[althfu]lly, like a mongoose. [I cut] down the Puqudians, his allie(s), (and) the [Marša]nians, together with [the Sutians] who [were with him, in] fr[ont of] the gat[e (of his city) (and)] splattered his

Sections 31–32 Section 31 = lines 391–403 = II,30:1–13: Cf. text no. 2 lines 371/372–374a. The start of the account of the thirteenth regnal would have been located towards the end of this section. Section 32 = lines 404–416 = II,31:1–13: See Winckler, Sar. Annals lines 319–340/341; Lie, Sar. lines 404–416; and Fuchs, Khorsabad Annals lines 331–351/352. Cf. text no. 2 lines 374b–394+ and text no. 6 lines 1′–6′.

404–405 Following H. Winckler and A. Fuchs (Khorsabad p. 159 line 333), it is assumed here that the first sign in the first line of the slab on P.E. Botta's copy was actually on the second line (Botta's copy ḪA standing for ⸢*ker*⸣ in line 405). The restoration of line 404 follows text no. 2 lines 374–376.

405 For the passage "moving back ... main wall," see the note to text no. 74 vi 32. ⸢TA⸣: So H. Winckler's copy; no trace of the sign is found on P.E. Botta's copy or currently visible on the squeeze. Winckler restored *ú-šab* instead of *ú-né-si-ma* on his copy. Text no. 74 vi 32 has 10 NINDA.TA.ÀM, "ten *nindanu*," here instead of *áš-la*.TA.ÀM, "one measuring rope." *iš-*⸢*ku-un*⸣: The transliteration follows Winckler's copy; nothing after the IŠ is currently visible on the squeeze or on Botta's copy. A *nindanu* is 12 cubits, or about 6 m (see Powell, RLA 7/5–6 [1989] p. 459).

407 H. Winckler's copy has [...]-⸢*li*⸣*-ma* and MÈ*-šú i-na bi-rit* [ÍD].MEŠ, but the squeeze cannot confirm this, although there are traces of what might be MÈ-.

408 [*ki*]-⸢*ma*⸣ [*ku*†*-mé*†]*-e*.[MUŠEN] and [^{d}]MES† [LÚ†.*mun*†*-daḫ*†*-ṣi*†*-ia*†]: The readings are based on P.E. Botta's copy. H. Winckler's copy has [*ki*]*-ma ku**(copy: UR)*-mé-e*.[MUŠEN] and [^{d}]MES LÚ.*mun-daḫ-ṣi-ia*, but this cannot currently be confirmed by the squeeze. *uš-ma*†-: Botta's copy has *uš-*BA- and Winckler's *uš-ma-*; as noted by A. Fuchs (Khorsabad p. 160 line 340), possibly *-man-* instead of *-ma-*.

409 ⸢*na-as*⸣-[*qu*†]*-ti*: P.E. Botta's copy has ⸢*na-as*⸣-[(x)]*-ti*, while H. Winckler's copy has ⸢*na-as*⸣*-qú-ti* and the squeeze currently has ⸢*na-as*⸣-[...]. As already noted by A. Fuchs (Khorsabad p. 161 line 342) *-qú-* is less likely orthographically than *-qu-*. [TI$_8$].⸢MUŠEN†⸣ SU ⸢MIR⸣ [*x ú-šap*]*-riš-*[*ma*]: Based on text no. 2 line 385, we do not expect anything between TI$_8$.MUŠEN and *ú-šap-riš-ma*, and so Fuchs has suggested reading [TI$_8$].⸢MUŠEN⸣*-niš ú-*[*šap*]*-riš-*[*ma*] (see also text no. 6 line 1′), although he notes that this would conflict with Winckler's copy, which has ⸢MUŠEN†⸣ SU ⸢MIR⸣ [(x)] *ú-šap-riš-*[*ma*]. The squeeze is not clear at this point.

410 *ú-nap-pi*†*-ṣa* [LÚ†].*qu-*[*ra*†*-di-šu*]: P.E. Botta's copy has *ú-tap-pi**(copy: ERIM)*-ṣa* [*x x*] *qu-*[...] and H. Winckler's copy *ú-nap-pi-ṣa* LÚ.*qu-ra-*[*di-šu*]. The squeeze confirms the reading *-nap-* instead of *-tap-* (see also text no. 2 line 387), but cannot currently confirm the rest of Winckler's readings.

411 H. Winckler's copy has *ṣi-mit-ti ni-ri-*[*šu*], *uṣ-ṣi*, and *šá-a-šu i-na zi-qip mul-mul-li rit-ta-šú ap-*⸢*ṭur*⸣, but the squeeze cannot confirm the initial section. It can confirm that there is a damaged area after *šá-a-* which would allow *-*[*šú a*]*-* (as opposed to *šá-a-*<*šu i*>*-na* in P.E. Botta's copy), that it is -⸢*qit*⸣ not *-qip* (see also Thureau-Dangin, RA 24 [1927] p. 77), and that the beginning of the *-ṭur-* is present. Winckler's copy restores *ú-*[*šaq-qir-ma*]; while Botta's copy would indicate that there was room to have the *-ma*, text no. 2 line 389 does not have *-ma* here. For the translation of *rittašu apṭur*, see the note to text no. 2 lines 390–391.

412 [KÁ†.GAL†] URU*-šú e-ru*†*-ub*†: P.E. Botta's copy has [*x x*] URU*-šú e-ru**(copy: KUG)*-ub**(copy: E-AŠ-[(x)]), while H. Winckler's copy has KÁ.GAL URU*-šú e-ru-*⸢*um*⸣-[*ma*]. The squeeze is not currently useful for this passage. See text no. 6 line 3′, which has ⸢*e*⸣*-ru-ub. a-*⸢*di*⸣ [LÚ†.*su*†*-te*†*-e*†] *ša* ⸢*it*†⸣-[*ti-šú*]: Winckler's copy has *a-di* LÚ.*su-te-e ša it-*[*x*], but this cannot be currently confirmed by the squeeze, although the squeeze does allow *a-*⸢*di*⸣ rather than Botta's *a-*⸢*di*†⸣.

URU-šú e-ru†-ub† LÚ.pu-qud-da-a-a ⸢ki⸣-tar-šú LÚ.[mar-šá]-na-a-a a-⸢di⸣ [LÚ†.su†-te†-e†] ša ⸢it†⸣-[ti-šú]
413) [i†]-⸢na pa⸣-[an†] KÁ.⸢GAL⸣ [ú-nak]-⸢kis†⸣ [i†]-mat mu-ti as-lu-⸢ḫa⸣ UN.MEŠ-šú kúl-tar LUGAL-ti-šú [GIŠ.šá GIŠ].MI KÙ.[GI†] LUGAL-ti-[šú]
414) ⸢GIŠ†⸣.GIDRU [KÙ†].⸢GI⸣ GIŠ.NÁ KÙ.GI GIŠ.[né†]-med-⸢du⸣ KÙ.GI ú-de-e† KÙ.GI KÙ.BABBAR ⸢GIŠ⸣ [KUR] gan-⸢ga-ni⸣-[šu til]-⸢li⸣ ú-nu-ut† ⸢MÈ†⸣ e-kim-[šu]
415) [kul]-lat [UN].MEŠ-šú a-ši-bu-⸢ut⸣ da-ád-me ⸢si⸣-ḫir-ti KUR-šú ša TA pa†-an GIŠ†.[TUKUL†].MEŠ-⸢ia⸣ ú-še?-[x (x)] x DI AN BÀD [x x (x)]
416) [...] x [(x)] I [(x)] ŠU [x (x)]
Lines 417–442 are not preserved
443) [ša] ⸢ma⸣-lak [10]+20 KASKAL.GÍD i-na ⸢MURUB4 tam-tim⸣ ša [KUR] ⸢d⸣UTU-ši ⸢ki⸣-ma nu-ú-⸢ni⸣ šit-ku-⸢nu nar-ba-ṣu⸣ da-⸢na⸣-an? be-⸢lu⸣-ti-[(ia)]
444) [iš]-⸢me⸣-ma iš-šá-a ta-mar-⸢tuš a-di⸣ a-na-⸢ku⸣ dáb-de-e LÚ.⸢kal⸣-di LÚ.a-ri-me šá tam-tim KUR d⸢UTU⸣-ši a-⸢šak⸣-[ka-nu-ma] ⸢UGU⸣ UN.⸢MEŠ⸣
445) [KUR].⸢ELAM⸣.MA.KI ú-šam-ri-ru GIŠ.TUKUL.MEŠ-ia LÚ.šu-ut ⸢SAG⸣-ia LÚ.GAR.KUR KUR.qu-e ša i-na KUR x x x [x x (x)] TI x x [(x)]
446) [šá-lam?] ⸢d⸣UTU-ši áš-ku-nu-ma ú-ma-ʾe-ru ⸢te⸣-né-še-e-te ša mmi-ta-a KUR.mu-us-⸢ka⸣-a-a i-na ⸢na-gi⸣-[šú] a-di [1]+2-[šú]
447) [A.ŠÀ] ⸢ṭa⸣-a-bu i-na ŠÀ ⸢GIŠ⸣.GIGIR A.ŠÀ

people with deadly [ve]nom. I took away [from him] his royal tent, [his] royal go[ld para]sol, [gol]d scepter, gold bed, gold [ch]air, gold (and) silver objects, ..., [his] potstands, [equip]me[nt, (and) bat]tle gear.

415–416) [(As for) a]ll his [people], the inhabitants of the settlements of all of his land, whom *he had* [...] from before my [weapon]s, ... [...]

Lines 417–442 are not preserved

443–444a) [Upēri, king of Dilmun, who(se)] l[a]ir is situated [at a di]stance of [th]irty leagues in the middle of the [Ea]stern Sea, like (that of) a fish, [hea]rd of [(my)] lordly might and brought me his audience gift.

444b–452a) While I was br[inging about] the defeat of the Chaldeans (and) Arameans of the Eastern Sea [and] making my weapons prevail over the people of [the land El]am, a eunuch of mine, the governor of the land Que (Cilicia), whom I had established [...] in the land ... [...] ... [of the we]st and (who) governed the people (there), marched ...ly [th]ree tim[es] into the district of Mitâ (Midas) of the land Musku, (going) in a chariot over easy [terrain] (and) on foot over difficult terrain, and took away one thousand of his (Mitâ's)

413 [ú-nak]-⸢kis†⸣: For the reading, see text no. 7 line 131. P.E. Botta's and H. Winckler's copies both have [...] MEŠ; the squeeze is not clear at this point. Winckler's copy has KÙ.GI GIŠ.GU.ZA LUGAL-ti-[šú], but, as noted by F. Thureau-Dangin (RA 24 [1927] p. 77), the squeeze shows that there is not sufficient room for GIŠ.GU.ZA between KÙ.GI and LUGAL-ti-[šú].

414 ú-de-e†: Both P.E. Botta's and H. Winckler's copies have -NI for -e; the sign is not clear on the squeeze.

415 [x (x)] x DI AN BÀD [x x (x)]: Both P.E. Botta's and H. Winckler's copies copies have DI AN BÀD, but only the BÀD is clear on the squeeze. A. Fuchs (Khorsabad p. 163 line 351 n. 1) suggests possibly ⸢BÚR⸣ instead of AN.

416 ŠU: Thus the copies by P.E. Botta and H. Winckler. The squeeze would currently also allow ⸢MA⸣, ⸢ÁŠ⸣, and ⸢PA⸣ (note also Fuchs, Khorsabad p. 163 line 351).

Sections 33–35 Section 33 = lines 417–429 = II,32:1–13 and section 34 = lines 430–442 = II,33:1–13: Cf. text no. 2 lines ca. 395–426 and text no. 6 lines 7′–14′. Section 35 = lines 443–455 = II,34:1–13: See Winckler, Sar. Annals lines 370–382; Lie, Sar. lines 443–455; and Fuchs, Khorsabad Annals lines 384–392. Cf. text no. 2 lines 427–435a; note also text no. 7 lines 149b–153a.

443 The restoration at the beginning of the translation assumes that the previous line ended with mú-pe-e-ri LUGAL NI.TUK.KI; see text no. 2 line 426 and text no. 7 line 144. -ti-[(ia)]: Both P.E. Botta's and H. Winckler's copies place the TI at the end of the line, with no damage afterwards; however, the squeeze has -⸢ti⸣- and based on what is restored at the ends of some later lines, it is not clear that there would not be room for -ia at the end of the line.

445 KUR x x x [x x (x)] TI x x [(x)]: P.E. Botta's copy in Monument de Ninive has KUR LÍMMU [x] x [x x x (x)] TI [x x] IGI and H. Winckler's copy has KUR LÍMMU [(x)] ⸢LU⸣ [x x (x)] TI [x] ME. The copies in JA and IdF have KUR x [x (x)] x [x] MIN [x] ⸢TI?⸣ IGI [...]. The squeeze has KUR x x x [x x (x)] ⸢TI⸣ x x [(x)], although [...] ⸢TI⸣ x ME/⸢MEŠ⸣ [(x)] is also possible for the final few signs.

446 [šá-lam?]: The restoration follows Fuchs, Khorsabad p. 171 line 386b and is based on a proposed translation by H. Winckler (AOF 1/4 p. 365), but, as noted by A. Fuchs, other restorations (e.g., šùl-mu and e-reb) are also possible. [1]+2-[šú]: The reading is based on the squeeze, but note that F. Thureau-Dangin read 3-[šu].

446–447 It is possible that ša mmi-ta-a KUR.mu-us-⸢ka⸣-a-a should go with ⸢te⸣-né-še-e-te rather than with what follows, i.e., "... governed the people of Mitâ of the land Musku, marched ...ly [... th]ree tim[es] into his district ..."; however, this would assume that the Assyrian governor already governed some of Mitâ's subjects before these campaigns against Mitâ.

447 *šilpu illikma* "he marched ...ly ... and": The meaning of the term *šilpu* in this phrase (which also appears in text no. 2 line 429 and text no. 7 line 151, as well as text no. 117 ii 57, where *šilpu* appears with the verb *wâru* instead of *alāku*) is not clear, although it may simply mean "raid" (i.e., "he made/went on a raid ... and"), following Winckler, AOF 2 p. 133 ("hatte er einfälle gemacht") and Lie, Sar. p. 67 ("made a raiding expedition"); see CAD S p. 447 and CDA p. 373, as well as Zadok, RA 76 (1982) p. 177. 1 LIM "one thousand": So Winckler's copy and the squeeze; Botta's copy has 2 LIM, with the two vertical wedges of the 2 attached to the end of the preceding sign. The reading of the end of the line is uncertain. Fuchs (Khorsabad p. 172 line 387) reads the sign following *tidūkišu* as ⸢ša!⸣, which is possible, but not certain. Possibly GAG [(x)] instead of ⸢NI?⸣.

nam-ra-ṣi ⸢i-na⸣ GÌR.II-šu ⸢ši⸣-il-pu il-lik-ma 1
LIM ERIM.MEŠ ⸢ti-du?-ki?⸣-šú x x ⸢GAB?⸣ [x] ⸢UL?⸣
x x [(x)] Ú ⸢NI?⸣ [(x)]
448) [ANŠE.KUR].⸢RA⸣.MEŠ MÈ-šú-nu
e-kim-šú-nu-ti-ma la e-zi-bu ⸢mul⸣-taḫ-ṭu 2
URU.bi-ra-a-te tuk-lat KUR.na-⸢gi⸣-šu ša i-na
⸢KUR-i mar-ṣi⸣ i-⸢ta?-at⸣
449) [x x x] šup-šuq-qu a-šar-šin x x x ⸢ik⸣-šud-ma
LÚ.ERIM.MEŠ šu-lu-ti-šu e-piš ta-ḫa-zi i-⸢duk-ma
KÁ?⸣.GAL bi-ra-ti-šú a-na ⸢UD?⸣ [x x x]
450) [x x x] ⸢LA?⸣ ú-bal-liṭ 2 LIM 4 ME LÚ.⸢ERIM⸣.MEŠ
x ⸢GIŠ?⸣ [(x)].MEŠ ù ARAD.MEŠ ul-tu KUR-šu
iš-lu-lam-ma URU.MEŠ-[šú†] ⸢dan⸣-nu-⸢ti a⸣-di
URU.MEŠ-⸢ni⸣ ša li-me-ti-[šú-nu]
451) [ip-pul iq]-⸢qur⸣ i-na IZI iš-ru-⸢up⸣ LÚ.A KIN-šu
⸢ša⸣ a-mat MUNUS.SIG$_5$ ⸢na⸣-šu-ú 1 LIM zi-im
pa-ni LÚ.qu-⸢ra⸣-di-šú a-na URU.sa-ma-ʾu-⸢ú-na⸣
ša [pa-aṭ]
452) [KUR.ELAM].⸢MA.KI⸣ ub-lam-ma ú-šá-li-iṣ lìb-bi
u ⸢šu⸣-ú ^{m}mi-ta-a KUR.mu-us-ka-a-a ša a-na
LUGAL.MEŠ a-⸢lik⸣ pa-⸢ni?⸣-ia ⸢la⸣ ik-⸢nu-šú⸣ [la]
⸢ú?⸣-šá-[an-nu-u]
453) [ṭè-en]-šu šá-kan NÍG.È ki-šit-ti ⸢qa⸣-ti ša ^{d}aš-šur
⸢^{d}AMAR.UTU ú⸣-šat-li-mu-ni-ma i-na tam-di
⸢ṣi⸣-it ⸢^{d}⸣UTU-⸢ši e⸣-[tep]-⸢pu⸣-[šu]-ma
454) [ti-bu-ut GIŠ.TUKUL].MEŠ-ia ḫe-pe-e KUR-šú
šá-lal ⸢UN⸣.MEŠ-šú šuk-nu-⸢uš⸣ [^{m}†]ú-⸢pe⸣-[e]-⸢ri⸣
MAN NI.TUK.KI ša qa-bal tam-tim [(x x)]
⸢iš-me-ma⸣ x [(x)] MA? [x (x)] ⸢i?-na?⸣
455) [qé-reb? KUR-šú? ru-uq-ti? šá]-⸢ḫur?⸣-[ra-tú?

com[bat] troops ... (and) their war [hors]es, letting none escape. He conquered two fortresses upon which his (Mitâ's) district relied (and) which are (located) on a ru[gg]ed mountain ad[jace]nt to [... (and)] whose location is very difficult (to reach) ... He then defeated his (Mitâ's) garrison troops, those who did battle, and [...] the gate(s) of his fortresses to [...]. (450) He did [no]t allow to live [...]. He brought to me as booty two thousand four hunded soldiers ... and slaves from his (Mitâ's) land, and (then) [destroyed, demol]ished, (and) burned (them) down with fire [his fort]ified cities, together with the settlements in [their] environs. His messenger, who bore the good news, brought me one thousand *face-(guards)* (taken) from his (Mitâ's) warriors (*as trophies*) to me in the city Samaʾūna, which is (located) [on the Elami]te [border], and (thus) made my heart rejoice.

452b–456a) Moreover, that (man), Mitâ of the land Musku, who had not submitted to the kings who preceded me (and) had [never] cha[nged] his [mind (about doing so), he]ard about the accomplishment of the victori(es) (and) conquest(s) that the gods Aššur (and) Marduk had granted me and (that) I [had regularly] car[ried] out in (the region of) the Eastern Sea, as well as [of the onslaught of] my [weapon]s, the destruction of its (Bīt-Yakīn's) land, the carrying off of its [peo]ple, (and) the subjugation of U[p]ē[r]i, king of Dilmun, which is (located) in the middle of the sea [(...)]. Then, ... *in [his far-off land, dea]th[ly quiet*

448–449a 2: P.E. Botta's and H. Winckler's copies omits this, but it is present on the squeeze and noted by F. Thureau-Dangin. *na-⸢gi⸣-šu*: Winckler's copy has *na-gi-šu-nu*, but there is no trace or room for *-nu* on the squeeze; see also Thureau-Dangin, RA 24 (1927) p. 78. Lines 448b–449a: A.T.E. Olmstead (AJSL 47 [1930–31] p. 277) suggests ... *i-ta-at* [*tam-tim* KUR ^{d}UTU-*ši*] *šup-šu-qu*, which would assume that three or four signs are missing at the end of line 448. Due to damage to the squeeze, it is not clear if there was anything missing or not, but based on where the other lines on the slab end, one would assume that nothing is missing. But note line 452 might suggest there was room for the restoration.
449 *x x x*: H. Winckler describes the traces as "Unerkennbare Spuren"; A. Fuchs (Khorsabad p. 172 line 387a) suggests the third sign may be ŠE!?. *a-na* ⸢UD?⸣ [*x x x*]: A. Fuchs (ibid.) suggests *a-na* may be followed by ⸢UD!?⸣ and the squeeze would allow such a reading. The JA and IdF copies have *a*†-⸢*na*⸣ *x x* [(*x*)] *x* [(...)] where the first trace could be ⸢UD⸣.
450 ⸢LA?⸣: Various other readings are also possible, including ⸢MA⸣. LÚ.⸢ERIM⸣.MEŠ *x* ⸢GIŠ?⸣ [(*x*)] MEŠ: The reading follows the squeeze and see Thureau-Dangin, RA 24 (1927) p. 78 and Fuchs, Khorsabad p. 173 line 387b. Both P.E. Botta's Monument de Ninive copy and H. Winckler's copy have LÚ.A.MEŠ DI.MEŠ, but Winckler's copy has the following note for the A.MEŠ DI: "War auf dem Abklatsch nicht zu erkennen." The JA and IdF copies have A.MEŠ DIŠ? GIŠ? [(*x*)] MEŠ.
451 *ip-pul*: Text no. 2 line 431 has *ip-pu-*[*ul*], but the spacing would suggest the proposed restoration (following H. Winckler). URU.*sa-ma-ʾu-*⸢*ú-na*⸣: So the squeeze and F. Thureau-Dangin (RA 24 [1927] p. 78), against Winckler's URU.*sa**(copy: IR)-*ma-ʾu-mi*.
452–453a Line 452: Text no. 2 lines 432–433 add *a-di maḫ-ri-ia* before *ub-lam-ma* and have LUGAL.⸢MEŠ⸣-[*ni*†] ⸢AD⸣.MEŠ-⸢*ia*⸣ instead of LUGAL.MEŠ *a-*⸢*lik*⸣ *pa-*⸢*ni?*⸣-*ia*. Lines 452b–453a: [*la*] ⸢*ú?*⸣-*šá-*[*an-nu-u* / *ṭè-en*]-*šu*: The reading basically follows Olmstead, AJSL 47 (1930–31) p. 277; see also Meissner, MAOG 11/1–2 (1937) p. 74. Cf. text no. 2 line 433, which has ⸢*a-na*⸣ *šá-ʾa-al šul-me-šú-un la iš-*⸢*pu-ra*⸣ [*rak-bu*]-⸢*šú*⸣, "had never sent his [mounted nessenger] to inquire about their well-being."
453 ^{d}*aš-šur* ⸢^{d}AMAR.UTU⸣: H. Winckler's copy erroneously has ^{d}*aš-šur* ^{d}[x] ^{d}AMAR.UTU. As noted by A. Fuchs (Khorsabad p. 174 line 391), the error may have been inspired by text no. 2 lines 347–349 and 467.
454–456a The tentative translation is based on text no. 2 lines 435–436, but at times the traces would not seem to support this. Line 454: [*ti-bu-ut* GIŠ.TUKUL].MEŠ-*ia*: The restoration follows Olmstead, AJSL 47 (1930–31) p. 277. The *-šú* of KUR-*šú* and ⸢UN⸣.MEŠ-*šú* is assumed to refer to Bīt-Yakīn (as opposed to Marduk-apla-iddina) since the parallel passage appears to refer to the destruction of that area and the carrying off of its people (text no. 2 line 434: ⸢*ḫe?-pe?-e?*⸣ [(*x*)] ⸢É-^{m}⸣*ia-kin*$_7$ [*šá*†-*lal* UN†].⸢MEŠ-*šú*⸣). [(*x x*)] ⸢*iš-me-ma*⸣ *x* [(*x*)] MA? [*x* (*x*)] ⸢*i?-na?*⸣: The reading follows the squeeze, which is in part supported by P.E. Botta's copies in JA and IdF (as opposed to his copy in Monument de Ninive). Since the area immediately before the ⸢IŠ⸣ is taken up by the top of a parasol protruding from the relief below the inscription, it is not clear that any text is missing between *tam-tim* and ⸢*iš*⸣-. Botta's copy only indicates damage after the parasol, while H. Winckler's copy has KI [*x x x x x x* (*x*)], but there is no visible trace of a KI on the squeeze.
455 -⸢*ḫur?*⸣-: P.E. Botta's copy and H. Winckler's copy both have ŠE; only the traces of the two upper Winkelhaken are currently visible on the squeeze. *x x* [*x x*] *x* [(*x x x*)] ⸢ḪI BI?⸣ *x* [*x x* (...)]: The reading of the end of the line is not clear and based on the squeeze. Botta's copy has Ú [*x x*

it-ta-bi-ik-šu? LÚ.A? KIN-*šú*? (*x x*)] *x x* [*x x*] *x* [(*x x x*)] ⸢ḪI BI?⸣ *x* [*x x* (...)]

456) [(*x x*) IGI.SÁ-*e*? *a*?]-*na* [*tam-di*? *ša*? *ṣi-it*? ^{d}UTU-*ši*? *a-di*? *maḫ-ri-ia*? *iš-pu-ra*? ^{m}*si-il-ṭa*?]

457) [URU.*ṣur*?]-⸢*ra*?†⸣-[*a-a*?] *na*-⸢*áš*? GUN?⸣ KID [(*x*)] LA ŠE [(*x*)] ⸢*a*?-*na*?† KUR?†⸣ [^{d}*aš-šur*.KI?] ⸢7?†⸣ [LUGAL.MEŠ-*ni*?]

458) [*ša* KUR.*ia*]-*a*ʾ† *na*†-*ge*†-*e ša* KUR.*ad-na-na ša ma-lak* [7] *u*$_4$-[*me ina* MURUB$_4$ *tam-di*]

459) [*šit-ku-nu-*(*ma*)] ⸢*šu*†⸣-*bat-sún*† *ša ul*†-*tu u*$_4$-*me ul-lu*†-*ti a-na* [*x x x x x* (*x x*)]

460) [(*x*) *x x*] ŠID? *kàd*†-*ra-a-šú-un mit-ḫa-riš*† [*ú*?]-⸢*šab*?†⸣-[*ṭi-lu*?] ⸢*ik-lu*?⸣-[*ú-*(*ma*?) *bi*?]-⸢*lat*⸣-[*su-un*? *ù*?]

461) [^{m}*si-il-ṭa*?] *ma*-⸢*da*⸣-*at*-⸢*ta*†⸣-*šu*† *ka*-⸢*bit*⸣-*tu* ⸢*iš*†⸣-*šam-ma a*-⸢*na*⸣ [*šuk-nu-uš*? (*x x x*)]

462) [(*x x x*) *x*]-RI-*an-ni* ⸢*kit-ru*⸣ LÚ.*šu*-⸢*ut* SAG⸣-*ia pit-qu-du la a*-⸢*dir*⸣ [*ta-ḫa-zi it-ti*]

463) [*ki-ṣir* LUGAL-*ti*]-*ia áš-pur-šu-ma a-na tur-ri gi-mil-li-šu* [*ú-ma-*ʾ*e-ra*? (*x x*)]

464) [(...) *x*] ⸢TI?⸣ [*x*] *e-mu-qa*†-*at* ⸢^{d}⸣[*aš*]-⸢*šur gap*†⸣-*šá-a-ti iš-mu-ma a-na* ⸢*zi*⸣-[*kir šu-mì-ia iš-ḫu-tú-ma*]

465) [(...)] *ir-ma*-⸢*a*⸣ *i-da-a*-⸢*šú-un* KÙ⸣.GI KÙ.BABBAR *ú-nu-tu* GIŠ.⸢ESI⸣ [GIŠ.TÚG *né-peš-ti*]

466) ⸢KUR†⸣-*šú-un a-na*† KÁ†.DINGIR.⸢RA⸣.KI *a*-⸢*na*

overwhelmed him (*and*) *he sent his messenger before me a*]*t* [*the Eastern Sea to do obeissance* (*to me*) *and to bring* (*me*) *tribute* (*and*) *presents*].

456b–467a) [(*As for*) *Silṭa of the city Tyre*], *the brin*[*ging of tri*]*bute ... to* [*Assyria*], *seven* [*kings of* the land Y]āʾ, a region of the land Adnana (Cyprus) — whose abode(s) [are situated] at a distance of [seven] da[ys (journey) in the middle of the sea and] who from the distant past until [*now* ... (460) ...] all together [*st*]*opp*[*ed* (the delivery of)] their gifts (*and*) [*wi*]*thhe*[*ld their tri*]*bute.* [*However, Silṭa*] brought his substantial tribute to me and, in [order *to subjugate ..., he*] *asked* me for (military) aid. I sent a trustworthy eunuch of mine who was fearless [in battle, with a royal (military) contingent] of mine, and [*ordered* (*him*)] to avenge him (Silṭa). [...] they heard [(...)] of the numerous forces of the god [Ašš]ur. Then, [they became afraid] at the (mere) me[ntion of my name and (...)] their arms grew weak. They brought before me in Babylon gold, silver, (and) utensils of [eb]ony (and) [boxwood, product(s) of] their [lan]d [and (so) I considered them ...].

---

x x (*x x x*)] ḪI [*x x x x* (*x*)] and Winckler's has *x* Ú [*x x x* (*x x x*)] ḪI [*x x x* (*x*)]. A. Fuchs (Khorsabad p.175 line 392) reads ⸢*ša*!? *e*!?-*peš*!?⸣ for Botta's Monument de Ninive Ú and Winckler's *x* Ú, and this would somewhat fit Botta's copies in JA and IdF. The traces on the squeeze are unclear and a reading -⸢*peš*? *ar*?⸣-[...] might also be possible; we would expect *ar-du-ti* after *e-peš*. See text no. 2 line 435.

Section 36 = lines 456–468 = II,35:1–13: See Winckler, Sar. Annals lines 382–389; Lie, Sar. lines 456–468; and Fuchs, Khorsabad Annals lines 392–399. Cf. text no. 2 lines 435b–442.

456–468 See the commentary with regard to the line numbering. It is difficult to be sure how much is missing at the beginning or end of any one line, and what is proposed is only an educated guess. H. Winckler's copy (Sar. 2 pl. 12 no. 26) cannot be taken as proof, for example, that line 465 began with *ir-ma*-⸢*a*⸣; his copy for Room II slab 35 is totally based upon that of Botta since no squeeze of this slab was made. For the restorations, cf. in general text no. 2 lines 435–442. Lines 456b–467a: See Naʾaman, Orientalia NS 67 (1998) pp. 243–244 for the at times very tentative restorations. The name Silṭa may be derived from the root *šlṭ* or possibly be a misunderstanding for a title; see ibid. p. 242 n. 17, following A. Fuchs, and PNA 3/1 p. 1112.

457 In a communication to N. Naʾaman, A. Fuchs suggested the following alternate restoration for the latter part of the line: ÌR*(copy: KID) *kan**(copy: LA)-*še* ⸢*šá*⸣-*di**(copy: UD)-⸢*id*⸣ [*ni-ir* ^{d}*aš*]-⸢*šur*⸣ [*be-lí-ia*], "a submissive servant who pull[s the yoke of the god Ašš]ur, [my lord]"; cf. text no. 82 v 61′ and text no. 7 line 36. ⸢GUN?⸣: the copy has [*x*]-UN, thus quite possibly [GÚ].UN. ⸢KUR?†⸣ [^{d}*aš-šur*.KI?]: Cf. text no. 2 line 436.

458b–459a Based on text no. 2 line 437, H. Winckler's copy (Sar. 2 pl. 12 no. 26) has ... *ma-lak* [7 *u*$_4$-*me ina* MURUB$_4$ *tam-tim e-reb* ^{d}UTU-*ši šit-ku-nat**(copy: NU)] / *né-es-sa-at šu-bat-su-*[*un*] ..., thus "(who)s[e] dwelling(s) [are situated] far away, at distance of [seven] da[ys (journey) in the middle of the Western Sea]." As already noted by A. Fuchs (Khorsabad p. 175 line 394), it is unlikely that there was sufficient room to restore all this and it is better to follow text no. 13 lines 44–45.

459 Or restore *šit-ku-nat* following text no. 13 line 44 ex. 9 (listed in Minor Variants), rather than text no. 2 line 437 (so Fuchs, Khorsabad p. 175 line 394, for reasons of spacing). JA and IdF have *a-na x* [...] at the end of the line.

460 The tentative reading of the end of the line is partially based on text no. 7 line 113 and following Naʾaman, Orientalia NS 67 (1998) pp. 243–244, but restoring -*su-un* rather than -*sún*. JA and IdF have ⸢*ik-lu*?⸣-.

461 The tentative restoration at the beginning of the line follows Naʾaman, Orientalia NS 67 (1998) pp. 243–244. JA and IdF have [...] *x ma*-... at the beginning of the line, but the traces are too indistinct to determine if they could be -*ṭa* or not. ⸢*iš*†⸣-*šam-ma*: H. Winckler's copy has *iš-šu-ú-ma*, but as already noted by A. Fuchs (Khorsabad p. 176 line 395 n. 4), we must be dealing with a singular subject in view of the -*šu* in *madattašu*.

462 [(*x x x*) *x*]-RI-*an-ni*: Possibly [*e*]-*ri*-<*šá*>-*an-ni*, "[he] asked me for," or [*ú*]-*ṣal*†-*an-ni*, "[he] besought me for"; see text no. 2 line 461 and following N. Naʾaman (Orientalia NS 67 [1998] pp. 243–244) and H. Tadmor (Eretz-Israel 25 [1996] p. 288 n. 3 [in Hebrew]) respectively.

463 For the restorations, see text no. 2 line 439.

464 N. Naʾaman (Orientalia NS 67 [1998] pp. 243–244) suggests [*e*?]-⸢*ti*?⸣-[*qu*?-(*ma*?)], "[they] cr[ossed?]"; cf. text no. 2 lines 440. It is not clear if *išḫuṭūma* was at the end of this line (so Naʾaman, ibid. p. 243) or the beginning of the next (so Fuchs, Khorsabad p. 176 line 397).

465 JA and IdF have ...-*a*-⸢*šú-un*⸣ [...]. It is not clear if *né-peš-ti* is at the end of the this line (so Winckler and Naʾaman, Orientalia NS 67 [1998] p. 243) or the beginning of the next (so Fuchs, Khorsabad p. 177 line 398). If the latter, instead of GIŠ.TÚG we should probably restore a syllabic writing, e.g., GIŠ.*tas-ka-ri-ni*.

466 N. Naʾaman (Orientalia NS 67 [1998] p. 243) reads [KUR].⸢MEŠ⸣-*šú-un*, but see text no. 74 vii 36 and text no. 7 lines 148–149.

maḫ⸣-*ri-ia* ⸢*iš*⸣-*šu*-[*nim-ma* (*x x x*)]
467) [(...) *x x x*] ⸢*am*⸣-*nu-ú-šu-nu-ti* <m>*mut-tal-lu* [KUR].*ku-muḫ*†-*ḫa*-⸢*a*⸣-*a* LÚ.⸢*ḫat*⸣-[*tu-ú lem-nu*]
468) [*la*? *a-dir*? *zik-ri*? DINGIR.MEŠ? ...]
Lines 469–481 are not preserved

467b–468) Mutallu of [the land] Kummuḫu — an [evil] H[ittite *who did not fear the words of the gods* ...]

Lines 469–481 are not preserved

2

The version of Sargon's Annals in Room V probably extended over thirty wall slabs (twenty-eight in the room itself and two in Entrance O). P.E. Botta prepared copies of the inscriptions for twenty of these, but appears to have numbered four of his copies incorrectly, leaving the impression that the inscription did not move regularly from one slab to the next, in a clockwise manner. It was recently possible to prove that at least one of the four passages had been assigned to the wrong slab and to raise suspicions about some other assignments. (See Frame, Studies Grayson pp. 89–102 for a study of the order of the wall slabs in this room.) As far as one can tell, each slab appears to have had seventeen lines, for a total of five hundred and ten lines. The last sixty-eight lines (lines 443–510) are not preserved in any other version of the annals, as is the case for lines 403–426. Assuming that the reassignment of the inscriptions on the four slabs is correct, there are two major gaps and one minor gap in the text due to a lack of copies by Botta: The first four inscribed slabs are missing (sections 1–4 = lines 1–68), as are the seventh through eleventh slabs (sections 7–11 = lines 103–187) and the fifteenth slab (section 15 = lines 239–255).

As mentioned, the beginning of the inscription is missing (lines 1–68), with the preserved text beginning at the very end of the description of the king's fifth regnal year (717; lines 69–70a). After giving an account of the sixth regnal year (716; lines 70b–95a), the text breaks off part way through the description of the seventh regnal year (715; lines 70b–102) and recommences toward the end of the account of the eighth regnal year (714; lines 188–195a). Following an account of the ninth regnal year (713; lines 195b–235), the text breaks off again shortly after the beginning of the description of the tenth regnal year (712; lines 236–238) and then recommences part way through the description of that regnal year (lines 256–267a). The text preserves the accounts of the eleventh, twelfth, and thirteenth regnal years (711–709; lines 267b–427). Following the description of the thirteenth year's campaign in Babylonia, and in particular the conquest of Dūr-Yakīn and the sending of a gift to Sargon by Upēri of Dilmun, are sections dealing with Mitâ of Musku, Silṭa of Tyre, Mutallu of Kummuḫu, and the sons of Daltâ of Ellipi (lines 428–467a). The text then describes the construction of the city of Dūr-Šarrukīn, and in particular its palace, and the festival that took place when the city was completed (lines 467b–494), in the second month of 706, as noted in the Assyrian Eponym Chronicle. The text concludes with blessing and curse formulae (lines 495–510).

---

1 lines 467–468a Line 467: JA and IdF have [...] *x* ⸢*am*⸣-... / *x ku*-... LÚ.⸢*ḫat*⸣-[...]; the traces copied before KU do not fit KUR. Lines 467b–468a: For the tentative restoration, see text no. 2 line 442 and text no. 7 line 112.
1 lines 468 JA and IdF have traces of two signs at the end of its twelfth line, which thus should come towards the end of line 13 (see commentary).
1 Section 37 = lines 469–481 = II,1:1–3: Cf. text no. 2 lines 443ff.

Only one slab of the inscription is preserved today (section 6 = lines 86–102), on display in the Iraq Museum (Baghdad). This would have been slab 21 from the room, although Botta labeled it slab 17 on his copy (see commentary below). The rest of the inscription appears to have been lost in the Tigris disaster of 1855, unless some pieces were left in situ.

For a plan of the room and drawings of the reliefs in this room, see Figure 11 and Botta, Monument de Ninive 2 pls. 84–100. With regard to the reliefs in the room, which are thought to depict Sargon's campaign to the west in his second regnal year (720), see Reade, JNES 35 (1976) pp. 96 and 99–102; and Reade, Bagh. Mitt. 10 (1979) p. 82; cf. Tadmor, JCS 12 (1958) p. 83 n. 243.

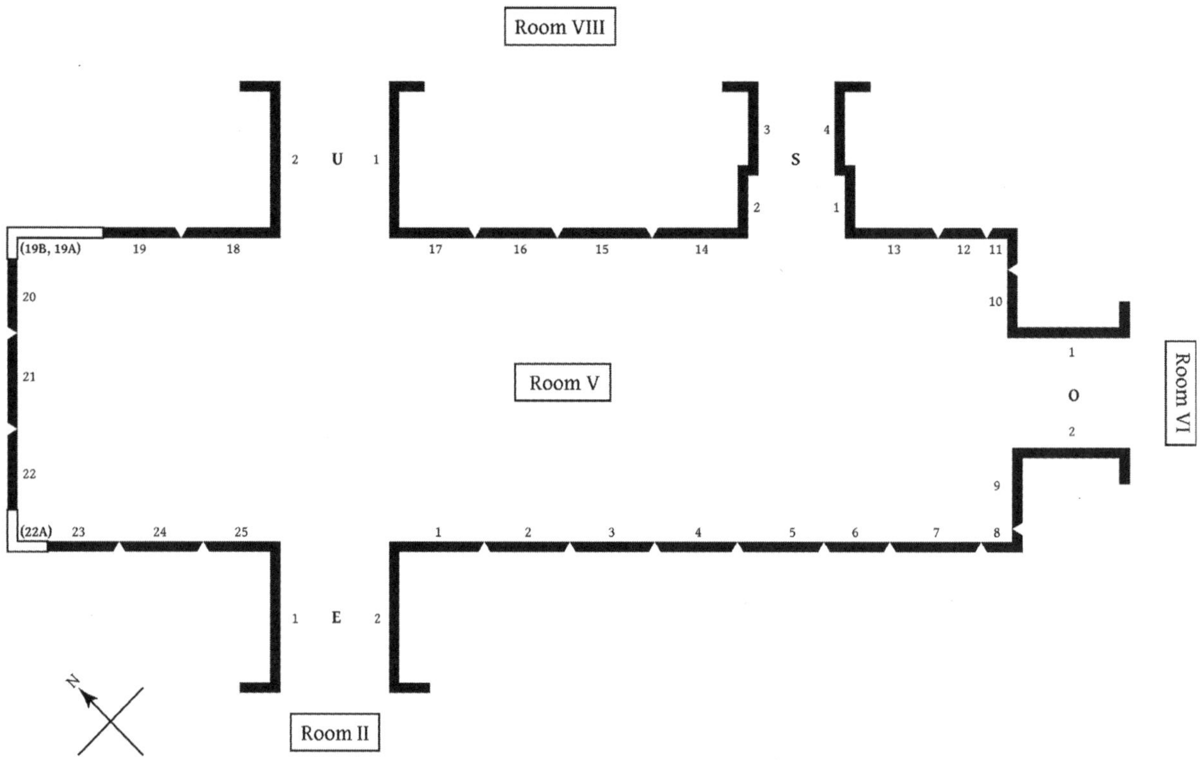

Figure 11. Plan of Room V of the palace at Khorsabad, whose wall slabs had a version of Sargon's Annals (text no. 2). Plan after Botta, Monument de Ninive 2 pl. 84.

CATALOGUE

Section	Ex.	Source	Provenance	Botta, MdN	Fuchs, Khorsabad line	Lines Preserved	cpn
[1]	—	—	[Khorsabad, Palace, Room V, slab 25	2 pl. 98	—	[1–17]	—
[2]	—	—	[Khorsabad, Palace, Room V, slab 24]	2 pl. 97	—	[18–34]	—
[3]	—	—	[Khorsabad, Palace, Room V, slab 23]	—	—	[35–51]	—
[4]	—	—	[Khorsabad, Palace, Room V, slab '22A']	—	—	[52–68]	—

5	Bt	Botta, Monument de Ninive 4 pl. 118[c] top	Khorsabad, Palace, Room V, slab '22' (Botta 16)	2 pl. 96	77–83, 83a–b, 84–94	69–85	n
	Wi	Winckler, Sar. 2 pl. 16 no. 34[c]					n
	Sq	Louvre squeeze					p
6	Bt	Botta, Monument de Ninive 4 pl. 119[c]	Khorsabad, Palace, Room V, slab '21' (Botta 17)	2 pl. 95	94, 94a, 95–96, 96a, 97–99, 99a, 100–107	86–102	n
	Wi	Winckler, Sar. 2 pl. 17 no. 35[c]					n
	Sq	Louvre squeeze					p
	IM	IM 60980					p
[7]	—	—	[Khorsabad, Palace, Room V, slab 20]	—	—	[103–119]	—
[8]	—	—	[Khorsabad, Palace, Room V, slab '19B']	—	—	[120–136]	—
[9]	—	—	[Khorsabad, Palace, Room V, slab '19A']	—	—	[137–153]	—
[10]	—	—	[Khorsabad, Palace, Room V, slab 19]	—	—	[154–170]	—
[11]	—	—	[Khorsabad, Palace, Room V, slab 18]	—	—	[171–187]	—
12	Bt	Botta, Monument de Ninive 4 pl. 120	Khorsabad, Palace, Room V, slab '17' (Botta 18)	—	161–168, 168a–168c	188–204	n
13	Bt	Botta, Monument de Ninive 4 pl. 116 bottom	Khorsabad, Palace, Room V, slab '16' (Botta 14)	—	168c/d, 170–185	205–221	n
14	Bt	Botta, Monument de Ninive 4 pl. 117[c]	Khorsabad, Palace, Room V, slab 15	—	189–206	222–238	n
[15]	—	—	[Khorsabad, Palace, Room V, slab 14]	—	—	[239–255]	—
16	Bt	Botta, Monument de Ninive 4 pl. 115[c] bottom	Khorsabad, Palace, Room V, slab 13	2 pl. 94	218–220, 220a, 222–240	256–272	n
	Wi	Winckler, Sar. 2 pl. 19 no. 39[c]					n
	Sq	Louvre squeeze					p
17	Bt	Botta, Monument de Ninive 4 pl. 115[c] top	Khorsabad, Palace, Room V, slab 12	2 pl. 94	240–255, 255a–b, 256	273–289	n
	Wi	Winckler, Sar. 2 pl. 19 no. 40[c]					n
	Sq	Louvre squeeze					p
18	Bt	Botta, Monument de Ninive 4 pl. 114[c]	Khorsabad, Palace, Room V, slab 11	2 pl. 93	256–266	290–306	p
	Wi	Winckler, Sar. 2 pl. 19 no. 41[c]					p
	Sq	Louvre squeeze					c
19	Bt	Botta, Monument de Ninive 4 pl. 113[c]	Khorsabad, Palace, Room V, slab 10	2 pl. 93	266, 266a–266b, 267–271, 271a, 272, 272a–272e, 275–280	307–323	n
	Wi	Winckler, Sar. 2 pl. 20 no. 42[c]					n
	Sq	Louvre squeeze					p
20	Bt	Botta, Monument de Ninive 4 pl. 66[c] top	Khorsabad, Palace, Room V, Entrance O_1	2 pl. 99	281–297	324–340	n
	Wi	Winckler, Sar. 2 pl. 15 no. 32[c]					n
	Sq	Louvre squeeze					p
21	Bt	Botta, Monument de Ninive 4 pl. 66[c] bottom	Khorsabad, Palace, Room V, Entrance O_2	2 pl. 100	298–314	341–357	n

	Wi	Winckler, Sar. 2 pl. 16 no. 33^{c}					n
	Sq	Louvre squeeze					p
22	Bt	Botta, Monument de Ninive 4 pl. 112^{c}	Khorsabad, Palace, Room V, slab 9	2 pl. 92	315–331	358–374	n
	Wi	Winckler, Sar. 2 pl. 20 no. 43^{c}					n
	Sq	Louvre squeeze					p
23	Bt	Botta, Monument de Ninive 4 pl. 111^{c}	Khorsabad, Palace, Room V, slab 8	2 pl. 92	332–348	375–391	n
	Wi	Winckler, Sar. 2 pl. 21 no. 44^{c}					n
	Sq	Louvre squeeze					p
24	Bt$_1$	Botta, Monument de Ninive 4 pl. 110^{c}	Khorsabad, Palace, Room V, slab 7	2 pl. 91	349–365	392–408	p
	Bt$_2$	Botta, Monument de Ninive 4 pl. 116 top				393–408	n
	Wi	Winckler, Sar. 2 pl. 21 no. 45^{c} (and pl. 22 no. 46)					n
	Sq	Louvre squeeze					p
25	Bt	Botta, Monument de Ninive 4 pl. 109^{c}	Khorsabad, Palace, Room V, slab 6	2 pl. 90	366–382	409–425	n
	Wi	Winckler, Sar. 2 pl. 22 no. 47^{c}					n
	Sq	Louvre squeeze					p
26	Bt	Botta, Monument de Ninive 4 pl. 108^{c}	Khorsabad, Palace, Room V, slab 5	2 pl. 89	383–399	426–442	n
	Wi	Winckler, Sar. 2 pl. 23 no. 48^{c}					n
	Sq	Louvre squeeze					p
27	Bt	Botta, Monument de Ninive 4 pl. 107^{c}	Khorsabad, Palace, Room V, slab 4	2 pl. 88	400–416	443–459	n
	Wi	Winckler, Sar. 2 pl. 23 no. 49^{c}					n
	Sq	Louvre squeeze					p
28	Bt	Botta, Monument de Ninive 4 pl. 106^{c}	Khorsabad, Palace, Room V, slab 3	2 pl. 87	417–433	460–476	n
	Wi	Winckler, Sar. 2 pl. 24 no. 50^{c}					n
	Sq	Louvre squeeze					p
29	Bt	Botta, Monument de Ninive 4 pl. 105^{c}	Khorsabad, Palace, Room V, slab 2	2 pl. 86	434–450	477–493	n
	Wi	Winckler, Sar. 2 pl. 24 no. 51^{c}					n
	Sq	Louvre squeeze					p
30	Bt	Botta, Monument de Ninive 4, pl. 118^{c} bottom	Khorsabad, Palace, Room V, slab 1	—	451–467	494–510	n
	Sq	Louvre squeeze					p

COMMENTARY

In the above Catalogue and in the edition below, P.E. Botta's numbering of the slabs (as indicated on the table of contents in Monument de Ninive 3 and on the plates in volume 4) for sections 5–6 and 12–13 is given in parentheses, while those proposed in Frame, Studies Grayson p. 91 are given as the primary reference, but placed within single quotes (e.g., for section 5 "Room V, slab '22' (Botta 16)." F.H. Weissbach (ZDMG 72 [1918] p. 173) assumed that there is only one slab missing in each of the two northeastern corners of the room, between his slabs V,19 and V,20 and between his slabs V,22 and V,23, but the catalogue follows Frame, Studies Grayson pp. 91–92 in assuming that there was one slab between Botta's slabs V,22 and V,23 and two slabs between Botta's slabs V,19 and V,20. Since Botta numbered the slabs in the room counterclockwise (unlike his normal procedure), these additional slabs are given the provisional numbers '22A,' '19B', and '19A' respectively (i.e., sections 4 and 8–9).

Botta did not make copies or squeezes of the inscriptions on sections 1–4, 7–11, and 15. Although he made copies of sections 12 and 13, he did not make squeezes of those sections. Squeezes of sections 14 and 30 were made and used by Botta when he prepared his copies, but these were not available in the time of H. Winckler. Thus, Winckler's copies of those two sections were solely based on those of Botta and are not taken into consideration as independent evidence of what was on those sections. The squeeze of section 30, however, is extant today and could be used here. The pieces which Botta collated either from the original or from squeezes before publishing his copies are marked with ^{c} after the Botta, Monument de Ninive 3–4 plate number in the catalogue; the same is done with the text numbers which Winckler is supposed to have collated from squeezes or originals.

Section 5 (lines 69–85): Winckler's copy of slab V,'22' (Botta 16) erroneously states that only the part of the inscription to the left of a line drawn on his copy was preserved on the squeeze (and thus collated by him); it is the section to the right of the line that is preserved. At times, however, his copy includes signs to the left of that line that are not found on Botta's copies and these have been noted in the score. In the score the point where the section collated by him begins is indicated with the siglum ▶.

Section 6 (lines 86–102): Botta's and Winckler's copies of slab V,'21' (Botta's V,17) have parts of only sixteen lines. Photos of the original in the Iraq Museum show that their copies are correct in indicating that it is the last line of the passage, and not the first line, that was not copied. The original was briefly seen in 1998, but in conditions that made careful examination of the inscription impossible. Photos of IM 60980 taken at that time are used in the score, but it must be acknowledged that they are not of high quality and combined with the fragmentary nature of the original are of only limited use. In the score only the relatively clear sections are noted, with the remaining sections indicated by "...".

Section 12 (lines 188–204): As already noted by Winckler and indicated on his copy (Sar. 2 pl. 17 no. 36), approximately the last quarter of each line on Botta's copy of slab V,'17' (Botta's V,18) (Monument de Ninive 4 pl. 120) is one line lower than it should be. (In the score, the point of the shift of line is indicated in the transliteration for Botta's copy with a double dagger [‡].) As result of this we have traces of only sixteen lines of text. It is not known whether it is the first line or the last line on the slab that is missing. Following Winckler's copy, it is arbitrarily assumed here that it is the last line (line 204) that is missing.

Section 16 (lines 256–272): Botta's copy (Monument de Ninive 4 pl. 115^{c} bottom) of slab V,13 only has parts of the right side of the slab and it is not always clear how much room for restoration is available to the left of what was copied.

Section 17 (lines 273–289): Botta's copy (Monument de Ninive 4 pl. 115^{c} top) of slab V,12 would suggest that this slab only had fifteen lines of inscription, with a gap of two lines between the first five and last eight lines. An examination of the squeeze, however, shows that the gap was four lines in length rather than just two. Thus, Botta's and Winckler's copies represent parts of lines 273–277 and 282–289. The squeeze shows traces of lines 279–281, as well as all or part of the very first sign in lines 283 and 284, which do not appear on Botta's copy; they are all situated to the left of what appears on the copy

Section 18 (lines 290–306): The squeeze of Botta, Monument de Ninive 4 pl. 114^{c}, could be checked for only a few signs, thus in the score only a limited number of collations are noted where they help the reading of the signs.

Sections 20 and 21 (lines 324–340 and 341–357) come from Entrance O and are indicated as O_1 and O_2 respectively (Botta, Monument de Ninive 3 pl. 66^{c}). Winckler, followed by A.G. Lie and A. Fuchs, refers to them as C_1 and C_2 respectively, but Winckler was using C_1 and C_2 to stand for Côte 1 and Côte 2 of Entrance O, not to indicate that they came from Entrance C (see Frame, Studies Grayson p. 91).

Section 24 (lines 392–408): Botta presents two copies of slab V,7 in Monument de Ninive 4 (pls. 110^{c} and 116 top; designated here Bt_1 and Bt_2 respectively), although he does not indicate on which slab in Room V the latter copy was found; as a result, Winckler also presents two copies (Sar. pl. 21 no. 45^{c} and pl. 22 no. 46). Botta indicates that only the first copy was checked against a squeeze, and Winckler notes that he was not able to collate his second copy (no. 46). The second copy does not include a small section on the lower left side of the slab, a section that is also not currently preserved on the squeeze. As already noted by Fuchs (Khorsabad p. 22), is it likely that the latter copy was made first, before the section on the left of the slab was discovered. In the score, transliterations of both copies are presented; pl. 110^{c} (Bt_1) is given preference in the master line.

BIBLIOGRAPHY

1849 Botta, Monument de Ninive 2 pls. 84–100 (drawing of reliefs, provenance); and 3–4 pls. 66 and 105–120 (copy)

1870 Oppert in Place, Ninive et l'Assyrie 2 pp. 309–319 (translation, combined with inscriptions in Rooms II, XIII, XIV)

1870 Oppert, Dour-Sarkayan pp. 29–39 (translation, combined with inscriptions in Rooms II, XIII, XIV) (identical to preceding)

1874 Ménant, Annales pp. 158–179 (translation, combined with inscriptions in Rooms I, II, IV, XIII, XIV)

1875 Ménant, Babylone pp. 151–157 (lines 287b–426a, partial translation, combined with Room II)

1876 Oppert, Records of the Past 7 pp. 21–56 (translation, combined with inscriptions in Rooms II, XIII, XIV)

1886 Bezold, Literatur p. 92 §54.10 (study)

1889 Peiser, ZA 4 pp. 412–413 and n. 1 (lines 399b–402, edition, combined with text no. 6)

1889 Winckler, Sar. 1 pp. VII–IX (study) and 2–79 (edition, combined with inscriptions in Rooms II, XIII, XIV, and an unknown room); and 2 pls. 15–25, nos. 32–52 (copy)

1898 King, First Steps pp. 48–51 (lines 273b–287a, copy, edition, combined with Room II)

1918 Weissbach, ZDMG 72 pp. 172–174 (study)

1927 Luckenbill, ARAB 2 pp. 2–25 §§3–51 (translation, combined with Rooms II, XIII)

1929 Lie, Sar. pp. 48–55, 58–59, 62–67, and 70–83 (lines 324–329a, 333b–349, 370–374, 396–405, 414–427, 443–510, edition), as well as numerous references in footnotes

1930 Thureau-Dangin, RA 27 pp. 159–160 (lines 481, 487, 500, study)

1941 Kalaç, Sumeroloji Araştırmaları pp. 982–987 (partial translation, combined with inscription from Room II)

1972 Kinnier Wilson, Wine Lists pp. 66–67 (lines 480b–483a, edition, study)

1977–78 van der Spek, JEOL 25 pp. 58–60 and pp. 63–64 (lines 363b–371, 399–403, edition, study)

1984 Borger, TUAT 1/4 pp. 378–381 (lines 69–70a, 273b–287a, translation, combined with inscription in Room II)

1987 Engel, Dämonen pp. 142–150 (lines 477b–480a, edition)

1990 Potts, Arabian Gulf 1 p. 334 nos. 1–2 (lines 421b–427, 434b–436a, translation, combined with room II)

1994 Fuchs, Khorsabad pp. 82–188 and 313–342 no. 2.3 lines 77–107, 161–206 and 218–467 (edition)

1997 Tadmor in Parpola and Whiting, Assyria 1995 p. 333 (lines 287b–305a, translation, combined with Rooms II, XIII)

1998 Berlejung, Theologie pp. 155–156 (lines 469b–470a, translation)

1998 Na'aman, Orientalia NS 67 pp. 242–243 (lines 436b–441a, edition)

2000 Bagg, Assyrische Wasserbauten pp. 159–162 (lines 309–312a, 326–327a, 359–360, 379b–381a, 401–402a, edition, combined with Rooms II, XIII, and an unknown room)

2000 Younger, COS 2 pp. 293–294 no. 2.118A (lines 69–70a, 273b–287a, translation, combined with Rooms II, XIII)

2001 Na'aman, CRRA 45/1 pp. 359–361 (lines 436b–441a, translation, combined with Room II; study)

2001 Rollinger, Melammu 2 p. 246 (lines 273b–287a, translation, combined with Rooms II, XIII)

2002 Vera Chamaza, Omnipotenz p. 368 no. 116b (lines 469b–470a, transliteration)

2004 Frame, Studies Grayson pp. 89–100 (lines 86–100, photos of original [IM 60980] and squeeze; study)

2006 Yamada, AoF 33 pp. 230–231 (236–238, translation, partially combined with Room II)

2007 Kuhrt, Persian Empire p. 25 no. 2.A.2.iv (lines 224b–226a, translation, combined with Room II)

2008 Cogan, Raging Torrent pp. 93–96 no. 20 (lines 95b, 283b–287a, translation, study, at times combined with Rooms II, XIII)

2010 Barbato, Kaskal 7 p. 178 (lines 426b–427a, translation)

2013 Thompson, Terror of Radiance pp. 134–135 and 227 (line 164, edition, combined with Room II)

2014 Maniori, Campagne di Sargon p. 37 A2 and passim (study)

2017 Liverani, Assyria p. 17 and passim (translation of numerous passages, combined at times with Rooms II, XIII, XIV)

2018 Frame in Yamada, SAAS 28 pp. 222–223 and 227–233 figs. 1–16 (section 6, photos of squeeze, copy [by Botta and Winckler], study)

2019 Edmonds in Dušek and Mynářová, Aramaean Borders p. 46 (lines 384–392a, translation, combined with Room II)

TEXT

Lines 1–68 are not preserved

69) [... *tar*]-*bit* ⌜É⌝.GAL-*ia ša* [*a*†]-*na* KUR.*ka-ak-me*-⌜*e*?⌝ [...]

Lines 1–68 are not preserved

69–70a) [The people of the cities Pāpa (and) Lalluknu, dogs who had been bro]ught up in my palace (and) who [had conspired wi]th the land Kakmê [*for the*

Sections 1–5 Section 1 = lines 1–17 = V, 25:1–17; section 2 = lines 18–34 = V,24:1–17; section 3 = lines 35–51 = V,23:1–17; and section 4 = lines 52–68 = 'V,22A':1–17. Cf. text no. 1 lines 1–76 and text no. 4 lines 1′–18′/19′a. Section 5 = lines 69–85 = V,'22':1–17 (Botta: V,16:1–17). See Winckler, Sar. Annals lines 51–68; Lie, Sar. lines 77–84+; and Fuchs, Khorsabad Annals lines 77–83, 83a–b, and 84–94. Cf. text no. 1 lines 77–84+ and text no. 4 lines 19′–28′+.

69–85 It is not clear how much is missing at the beginnings and ends of the lines since P.E. Botta's copy does not include either a right or left edge for the copy and the squeeze does not help in this matter. Thus, the line division for any restorations would be tentative and it has been thought best to only restore in the translation. H. Winckler assumed that for line 69 there were only four signs missing at the beginning of the line ([UR.GI$_7$.MEŠ *tar*]) and twenty-one missing at the end of the line ([*id-bu-bu na-pa-di-iš ul-tu áš-ri-šú-nu as-su-ḫa-áš-šú-nu-ti-ma*]). Line 69: Text no. 1 line 77 and text no. 4 line 19′ omit the *ša* after É.GAL-*ia*.

70 H. Winckler's copy indicates that he saw three vertical wedges — the bottom row of vertical wedges of the ÀŠ sign (= the number 6) — but the squeeze only has clear traces of two small vertical wedges — two of the three bottom wedges of the sign. Therefore, the transliteration 2+[4] indicates that only two of the six vertical wedges comprising the ÀŠ sign are preserved.

purpose of separating (from Assyria), I had deported them from their (own) places and] (re)settled them [in the city Damas]cus of the land [A]murru.

70) [... URU.*di-maš*]-*qi ša* KUR ⸢MAR⸣.TU.KI *ú*-⸢*še*⸣-*šib-šu-nu-ti* ⸢*i*⸣-[*na*†] 2+[4 ...]
71) [...] SAR KUR.*zi*†-*kir-ta-a-a* LÚ.GAR.KUR.MEŠ KUR.*man-na-a-a* [...]
72) [(...) *it-ti-(ia)* ^{m}LUGAL]-GI.NA *ù it-ti* ^{m}⸢*a*⸣-[*za-a* DUMU†] EN-*šú-nu ú*-⸢*ša*⸣-[*an-ki-ir-šú-nu-ti-ma* ...]
73) [... *suḫ-ḫur*]-*ti* [KUR†].*man-na-a-a* ⸢*iš*⸣-[*ku*†-*nu*†]-*ma* ADDA ^{m}*a-za-a* [...]
74) [... *i-na* KUR].*ú-a-ú*-⸢*uš*⸣ [KUR-*i a-šar*] ⸢ADDA⸣ ^{m}*a-za-a* ⸢*id*$^{?}$⸣-[*du-ú* ...]

70b–74) I[n my] si[xth regnal year, Ursâ (Rusâ), the Urarṭian, sent his mounted messenger with a mendacious message to Bag-dāti of the land Uišdiš (and) KAR...] of the land Zikirtu, governors of the land Mannea. He ma[de them hostile to (me), Sar]gon, (and) to A[zâ, the son] of their (former) lord, [and made them side with him (Rusâ)]. Th[ey brought about the rou]t of the Manneans [on Mount Uauš, a rugged mountain], and [threw down] the corpse of Azâ, [their lord, (there). I raised my hand(s) (in prayer) to the god Aššur, my lord, in order to avenge the Manneans (and) to make (that area part of) the territory of Assyria. Then, on Mount] Uau[š, the mountain where they had] t[hrown down the c]orpse of Azâ, [I flayed the skin from Bag-dāti and (then) showed (it) to the Manneans].

75) [...] x *šá* [*i-na* GIŠ.GU.ZA ^{m}]⸢*a-za*⸣-[*a ú-še-ši-bu*]-⸢*ma*⸣ *gi-mir* [...]
76) [... *ina* UGU]-*šu*† *ib-ši*†-*ma* [*a-na* ^{m}*ur-sa-a* KUR.*ur*]-⸢*ar-ṭa*⸣-[*a-a* ...]

75–76) [(As for) *Ullusun*]*u*, whom [they had set on the throne of] Az[â an]d [to whom they had entrusted] all [of the *wide* land Mannea, the wrath of the god Aššur] was directed [against Ullusunu, the Mannean, (ordaining) the destruction of his land. He (Ullusunu)] then [put his trust in Ursâ (Rusâ), the Ura]rṭi[an, ...]

77) [...] SIK URU UD [...]
78) [...] URU [...]
79) [...].MEŠ AD [...]
80) [... ^{m}*ul*]-*lu*-⸢*su*⸣-*nu* [...]
81) [...] LA [...]
82) [...]
83) [...] AN MIN [...]
84) [...] MIR [...]
85) [...] Ú [...]

77–85) Too fragmentary for translation.

86) [x x x x x x x x x (x x)] BAD [(x) LÚ.*šu-ut* SAG-*ia* LÚ.EN].⸢NAM⸣ [UGU†] ⸢URU⸣-*šú* ⸢*áš*†⸣-*kun* [GIŠ.TUKUL$^{?}$ DINGIR.MEŠ$^{?}$ (GAL.MEŠ$^{?}$) *a*$^{?}$]-⸢*li*$^{?}$-*kut*$^{?}$⸣ [*maḫ-ri*]-⸢*ia*⸣ *ú-še-piš*-[*ma*]
87) [*qé*]-⸢*reb*⸣-[*šu ú*]-*šar*-⸢*me* URU.*kar*⸣-[^{d†}MAŠ†.(MAŠ)] MU-*šú* ⸢*ab*⸣-*bi ṣa-lam* [LUGAL]-*ti*-[*ia i-na lìb-bi ul*]-⸢*ziz*⸣ KUR.⸢É⸣-[*sa-ag*]-⸢*bat*⸣ KUR.É-*ḫi*-⸢*ir*⸣-[*ma-mi*]

86–88) [...] I [s]et [a eunuch of mine as] provincial [governor over] his city. I had [*the weapon(s) of the (great) gods who*] *go* [before] me made [and I] install[ed (them) ins]i[de it (the city Kišesim)]. I (re)named it (the city Kišesim) Kā[r-Nergal (and) ere]cted a [royal] image [of myself there. I conquered] the lands Bīt-[Sag]bat, Bīt-Ḫi[rmami, (and)] Bīt-U[margi], (and) the cities [Ḫar]ḫubarban, Kilambāti, (and) [Ar]mang[u; and] I

---

73 ⸢*iš*⸣-[*ku*†-*nu*†]-*ma*: P.E. Botta's copy has *x* [*x x*]-*ma* and H. Winckler's copy has *iš-ku-nu-ma*, but only ⸢*iš*⸣-[*x x*]-⸢*ma*⸣ is clear on the squeeze.
75 Text no. 1 line 83 has ^{m}*ul-lu*†-*su*†-*nu* ŠEŠ-*šú ša i-na* GIŠ.GU.ZA LUGAL†-*ti*, but the trace before *šá* here does not fit -*šú*. It may be -⸢*un*⸣ and parallel to -*nu* of Ullusunu in text no. 4 line 26′, according to A. Fuchs (Khorsabad p. 97 line 83a).
77–85 P.E. Botta copied only a few signs for these lines and it is not clear if the lines would have matched all or parts of text no. 1 lines 86–95 and/or text no. 4 lines 28′–40′. See also Fuchs, Khorsabad p. 98 n. 1 to line 85. Line 77: Possibly ⸢EN⸣.URU, "city [l]ord".
79 P.E. Botta's and H. Winckler's copies both have [...].MEŠ AD [...], but the squeeze would suggest [...] *x* ⸢TA$^{?}$⸣ [...], which might allow [... *di*]-⸢*ik-ta*⸣-[*šú-nu* ...], and thus match up with *di-ik-ta-šú-nu* in text no. 1 line 86.
80 Ullusunu is mentioned in text no. 1 lines 87 and 88.
Section 6 = lines 86–102 = V,'21':1–17 (Botta: V,17:1–17). See Winckler, Sar. Annals lines 68–81; Lie, Sar. lines 94–107; and Fuchs, Khorsabad Annals lines 94, 94a, 95–96, 96a, 97–99, 99a, and 100–107. Cf. text no. 1 lines 94–107 and text no. 4 lines 40′–45′. See the commentary with regard to the line numbering.
86 H. Winckler's copy has [LÚ.EN].NAM UGU URU-*šú áš-kun*, but this is not clear from the squeeze or the original. [*a*$^{?}$]-⸢*li*$^{?}$-*kut*$^{?}$⸣ [*maḫ-ri*]-⸢*ia*⸣: P.E. Botta's and Winckler's copies have TI ŠÚ [*x x* (*x*)]-⸢*ia**⸣(copy: ZA) and TI ŠÚ [*x x x x* (*x*)]-⸢*ia**⸣(copy: ZA) respectively, while the original appears to have ...-⸢*li*$^{?}$-*kut*$^{?}$⸣ *x x*-⸢*ia*⸣; the section is not clear on the squeeze. Cf. line 92 and text no. 4 line 40′.
87 P.E. Botta's copy has [...]-*šar*-⸢*me*⸣ on the following line, but the squeeze shows that H. Winckler was correct in putting it in this line. Although Winckler's copy has URU.*kar*-^{d}MAŠ as being fully preserved, only the URU and part of the KAR are currently visible on the squeeze. It is not clear if we should restore -^{d}MAŠ, "Ninurta," or ^{d}MAŠ.MAŠ, "Nergal"; see the on-page note to text no. 1 line 95.

88) ⸢KUR⸣.É-⸢*ú*⸣-[*mar-gi*] ⸢URU⸣.[*ḫar*†]-*ḫu-bar-ban*† URU.*ki-lam-ba-*[*a*]-*ti* URU.[*ar*]-*ma-an-*⸢*gu*⸣ [*ak-šu-ud-ma*] UGU ⸢*pi*⸣-[*ḫa-ti-šú*] *ú-*⸢*rad*⸣-[*di*]

a[dded (them)] to [its] p[rovince].

89) URU.⸢*ḫar*⸣-[*ḫa-ra-a-a* ^{m†}]*ki-ba-ba* LÚ.EN.URU-*šú-nu* [*ir*]-*du-*[*du-ma*†] (*x*) *x* UD ^{m}⸢*da-al-ta*⸣-<*a*> ⸢LUGAL$^{?}$⸣ [KUR†].⸢*el*⸣-*li-*[*ba*†]-*a-a* *ú-*⸢*rab-bu*⸣-[*ú*†]

90) UGU-[*šú*]-*un* [URU† *šu-a*]-*tu ak-šu-ud-ma šal-la-su* [*áš-lu-la*] ⸢UN.MEŠ⸣ KUR.KUR *ki-*⸢*šit*⸣-[*ti*† *qa-ti*]-*ia i-na* [*lìb*]-*bi ú-še-*[*rib*]

91) LÚ.⸢*šu*⸣-[*ut*] ⸢SAG⸣-*ia* [LÚ†].EN.NAM *ina* ⸢UGU-*šú*⸣-*nu áš-kun* [ÍD-*tu e*†]-*li-tum ša* KUR.*a-*[*ra-an-ze*]-*e-šú* ÍD-*tu* [*šap*]-*li-tum ša* É-^{m}*ra-*[*ma-tu-a*]

92) ⸢KUR.*ú*⸣-[*ri-qa*]-⸢*tu*⸣ KUR.[*si*†]-*ik-ri-is* KUR.*šá-*[*pa*†]-*ar-*[*da*† KUR†].*ú-ri-ak-ki* 6 *na-gi-*[*i ak-šu*]-*ud-ma* UGU-*šú-*[*nu ú-rad*†-*di*†] GIŠ.TUKUL ⸢^{d}⸣[*aš-šur* EN-*ia*]

93) ⸢*i*$^{?}$⸣-[*na*$^{?}$ *qer*$^{?}$]-⸢*bi*$^{?\dagger}$⸣-*šu ú-šar-mi* URU.⸢*kar*⸣-[^{m}LUGAL-GIN] MU-[*šú*] ⸢*ab*⸣-*bi* NA$_{4}$.NA.RÚ.A ⸢*ab*⸣-*ni-*⸢*ma*⸣ [*x x*] Ú *x x* (*x*) ŠE [...]

94) *x* [*x x x* (*x*)] ⸢*ṣe*⸣-*ru-uš-šá ú-šá-áš-*⸢*ṭir i*$^{?}$⸣-*na qer-bi-šú* [*ul*]-*ziz ša* [26]+⸢2⸣ LÚ.[EN].⸢URU⸣.MEŠ-*ni ša* [KUR†.*ma*]-*da-*⸢*a-a dan*$^{?}$⸣-[*nu-ti*]

89–95a) [The people of] the city Ḫa[rḫar dr]ov[e out] Kibaba, their city ruler, [and] ... elevat[ed] Da[lt]â, *k*[*ing* of the land] Elli[pi] over [them]selves. I conquered [th]at [city] and [plund]ered it. [I] brou[ght th]ere peo[ple] from the lands that I had conqu[ered] (and) set a e[unuch] of mine as provincial governor ov[er] them. [I conque]red [the up]per [river(land)] of the land A[ranz]ê, the [low]er river(land) of Bīt-Ra[matua], the la[nd] U[riqat]u, the land [S]ikris, the land Ša[p]ar[da, (and) the land] Uriakku, (a total of) six distric[ts], and [added (them)] to th[em (the people of the city Ḫarḫar)]. I installed the weapon of the god [Aššur, my lord], *t*[*her*]*e*. I (re)named [it (the city Ḫarḫar)] K[ār-Šarrukīn]. I made a stele, had [...] ... [...] written upon it [(...), (and) ere]cted (it) there. I received tr[ibute] from [twenty-eig]ht city [ruler]s of the p[owerful Me]des.

95) *ma*†-[*da-at-ta*]-*šú-nu* ⸢*am*⸣-*ḫur i-na* 7 ⸢BALA⸣-*ia* ⸢^{m}⸣*ur-sa-*⸢*a*⸣ KUR.⸢*ur-ar*$^{?}$-*ṭa*⸣-[*a-a*] *it-ti* [^{m†}]*ul-lu-*[*su*†]-⸢*nu*⸣ KUR.*man-na-a*⸣-[*a sar*$_{6}$-*ra-a-ti*]

96) ⸢*id*⸣-[*bu-ub*]-⸢*ma*⸣ 22 ⸢URU⸣.ḪAL.ṢU.MEŠ-*šú* UD-*x-ti-*⸢*iš e*⸣-*kim-šú a-mat taš-ger-*[*ti*† *ṭa*†-*píl*†-*ti* ^{m†}*ul*†]-⸢*lu-su*⸣-*nu* [*a-na* ^{m}*da-a-a-uk-ki*]

97) [LÚ.GAR.KUR KUR.*man*]-⸢*na-a-a*⸣ *id-bu-ub-ma* DUMU-[*šu*] ⸢*a-na*⸣ [*li*]-⸢*ṭu*⸣-*ti im-ḫur-*⸢*šú*⸣ *a-*⸢*na*⸣

95b–98) In my seventh [regnal ye]ar, Ursâ (Rusâ), the Urart[ian], s[poke deceitfully] with Ullu[su]n[u], the Mannean, and ...ly took away from him twenty-two of his fortresses. He spoke treacher[ous] words, [libels against Ul]lusunu, [to Dayukku, a governor of the land Man]nea, and received [his] son as [a hos]tage. I rai[sed my hand(s) (in supplication)] to the god [Aššur, the king of the gods, and (then) surrounded (and)] conquered [those twenty-two fortresses. I ma]de (them

---

89 -⸢*ma*⸣ (*x*) *x* UD: The reading follows H. Winckler's copy; P.E. Botta's copy has [...] UD and the squeeze is not clear at this point. Text no. 1 line 97 has *a-na* ^{m}*da-al-ta-a* KUR.*el-li-ba-a-a iš-pu-ru e-peš* ARAD-*ti*, "sent to Daltâ of the land Ellipi to do obeisance (to him)." The *x* UD could be ⸢*a-na*⸣ but this would not make sense with the following *urabbû elišun*. ^{m}⸢*da-al-ta*⸣-<*a*> ⸢LUGAL$^{?}$⸣ [KUR†].⸢*el*⸣-*li-*[*ba*†]-*a-a ú-*⸢*rab-bu*⸣-[*ú*]: This is based on a combination of Botta's copy, the squeeze, and the original; Winckler's copy has ^{m}*da-al-ta* LUGAL KUR.*el-li-ba-a-a ú-rab-bu-ú* totally preserved. The traces following the TA on the squeeze seem closer to the beginning of LUGAL than A.

90 H. Winckler's copy has [ŠU.II]-*ia* rather than [*qa-ti*]-*ia*; the latter is based on text no. 1 line 97.

92 H. Winckler's copy has at the end of the line UGU-*šú* [*ú*]-*rad-di* GIŠ.TUKUL DINGIR.[MEŠ *a-li-kut maḫ-ri-ia*].

93–94a Line 93a: Based on text no. 4 line 40′, A. Fuchs (Khorsabad p. 105 line 99a) reads ⸢*ú*⸣-[*še-piš-ma qé*]-⸢*reb*⸣-*šu* at the beginning of the line, which would be allowed by the spacing on P.E. Botta's and H. Winckler's copies. The squeeze, however, indicates that there is not sufficient room for this. The traces at the beginning of the line could be those of numerous signs other than Ú, including I. It is not clear that there is any trace of a sign before ŠU on the squeeze, but both Botta's and Winckler's copies have a small Winkelhaken before ŠU which could fit the end of BI, or better BE, but not *reb*. -^{m}LUGAL-GIN: So Winckler's restoration. Text no. 1 line 100 has ^{m}LUGAL-GI.NA, but there is not sufficient room to restore all this here. Lines 93–94a: Text no. 1 lines 99b–100a have *a-na* DINGIR-*ti-šú-un áš-*⸢*kun*⸣ / URU.*kar-*^{m}LUGAL-GI.NA MU-*šú ab-bi*, "I estab[lished] the weapon of the god Aššur, my lord, to be their divinity. I (re)named it (the city Ḫarḫar) Kār-Šarrukīn."

94 P.E. Botta's copy has AD at the beginning of the line and H. Winckler's copy indicates nothing was visible there. A. Fuchs (Khorsabad p. 105 line 100) has ⸢GIŠ$^{!?}$⸣, which is possible but, as indicated by Fuchs, very uncertain. Winckler restored [*da-na-an* EN-*ti-ia*] at the beginning of the line, but the squeeze indicates that there is not sufficient room for this. [26]+⸢2⸣: The reading is based on the squeeze; Botta's copy has only damage here, while Winckler's copy has 28, which is also found in text no. 1 line 100.

96 UD-*x-ti-*⸢*iš*⸣: A.T.E. Olmstead (AJSL 47 [1930–31] p. 266 sub V.101) read ⸢*šal*⸣-[*la*]-*ti-iš*, but, as already noted by A. Fuchs (Khorsabad p. 105 line 101 n. 1), the first sign is clearly not ŠAL. Fuchs tentatively suggested *uṭ-*[*ṭa*]-*ti-*⸢*iš*⸣, "like grain," but examination of the original slab in the Iraq Museum showed that the second sign is smaller than *ṭa*. It could conceivably be ḪI, but we would not expect ḪI to have the value *ṭà* in this period. Could it be *tam-*⸢*ḫi*⸣-*ti-*⸢*iš*⸣, "at nightfall" or "during the dusk of evening" (derived from CAD T p. 118 *tamḫītu*, "nightfall")? *taš-qer-*[*ti*† *ṭa*†-*píl*†-*ti* ^{m}*ul*†]-⸢*lu-su*⸣-*nu*: Winckler's copy has: *taš-qer-ti ṭa-píl-*[*ti*] ^{m}*ul-lu-su-nu*, but the squeeze and original cannot support this.

97 [*li*]-⸢*ṭu*⸣-*ti*: The restoration follows Borger, BiOr 32 (1975) p. 72b. ^{d}[*aš-šur* MAN DINGIR.MEŠ *qa-a-ti*]: The restoration is based on text no. 1 lines 102–103. H. Winckler's copy has ^{d}*aš-šur* ^{d}AG ^{d}AMAR.UTU [*qa-ti*], but nothing is currently visible after the ^{d} on the squeeze or original until one gets to ⸢*áš-ši*⸣; there is room to restore seven or eight signs in the gap.

^{d}[aš†-šur† MAN DINGIR.MEŠ qa-a-ti] ⸢áš-ši⸣-[ma 22 URU.bi-ra-a-ti]
98) [šá-a-ti-na al-me] ⸢KUR⸣-ud [a]-⸢na⸣ mi-ṣir ⸢KUR⸣ aš-šur.[KI ú-ter]-ra ^{m}da-a-a-uk-⸢ku⸣ a-⸢di⸣ [kim]-⸢ti⸣-[šú†] ⸢as⸣-[su-ḫa-(am)-ma KUR.man-na-a-a] ⸢dal⸣-[ḫu ú-taq-qi-in]

part of) the territory of Assyria. I [deported] Dayukku, togeth[er with his fami]ly, [and brought order to the] dist[urbed land Mannea].

99) [ma-da-at-tu ša†] ^{m}ia-an-⸢zu⸣-ú LUGAL KUR.⸢na⸣-[ʾi-ri i]-na URU.ḫu-[bu]-uš-[ki†]-a ⸢URU⸣-[šu am]-⸢ḫur 6⸣+[3] ⸢URU†⸣.bi-[ra-a-ti (...)]
100) [x x x x (x)] x ša ⸢5⸣ na-ge-e šá ^{m}ur-sa-a KUR.URI-a-[a a-di] mar-ši-ti-šú-nu AN x [(x)] SU [... áš-lu-la (...)]
101) [8 URU].⸢bi?-ra⸣-a-ti a-di URU.⸢MEŠ⸣-ni ša ⸢li-me-ti⸣-[šú-nu ša KUR.tu-a-ia-di na]-ge-e šá ^{m}⸢te⸣-lu-[si-na KUR†.an†]-⸢di-a⸣-[a ak-šu-ud?]-ma [...]
102) [...]

99–102) [I rec]ei[ved tribute from] Ianzû, king of the land [N]a[ʾiri, i]n [his] c[ity] Ḫu[b]uš[ki]a. [*I conquered*] ni[ne] fort[resses (...) (100) ... I carried off as booty *the people*] of five districts of Ursâ (Rusâ), the Urarṭian, [together with] their property, ... [... *I conquered* eight fo]rtresses, together with the settlements in [their] environs, [that belonged to the land Tuāyadi, a dis]trict belonging to Telu[sina of the land And]ia and [...]

Lines 103–187 are not preserved

Lines 103–187 are not preserved

188) [...] NÍG [x (x)]
189) [x x i]-na KUR.[ur-ar-ṭi] rap-ši KUR.⸢MEŠ⸣-e† ka-la-ma ⸢si⸣-pit-⸢tu⸣
190) [ú-šab-ši]-i-ma a-na <<AŠ>> ^{m}ur-sa-⸢a⸣ LUGAL-šú-nu ṣur-ti nag†-la-bi qu-pé-⸢e⸣
191) GIŠ.[x x (x)]-ti a-di bal†-⸢ṭu⸣ áš-kun na-gu-ú šu-a-tú a-na mi-ṣir
192) [KUR] aš-šur.KI ú-ter-ram†-⸢ma†⸣ i-na ŠU.II [LÚ].šu†-ut SAG-ia LÚ.NÍMGIR É.GAL†
193) am-nu-šú <^{m}>ur-sa-[a] KUR.[ur]-⸢ar†⸣-ṭa-a-a na-⸢mur-rat⸣ ^{d}aš-šur be-lí†-ia
194) is-ḫu-pa-šu-[ma i-na] ⸢GIŠ.GÍR⸣ [AN].BAR [ra-ma]-ni-[šu GIM] ⸢ŠAḪ†⸣ lib-ba-šú
195) ⸢is†⸣-ḫu-ul-⸢ma†⸣ [ZI-šu] ⸢iq⸣-[ti] i-na 9 BALA-ia† ⸢a⸣-[na] KUR.[el]-li-pi†

188–195a) [... I caused there to] be lamentati[on] i]n the wide land [Urarṭu] (and) all the mountains, and I made Ursâ (Rusâ), their king, (use) flint (blades), razors, scalpels, (and) [...] (to slash himself in mourning) for as long as he lived. I made that district (Muṣaṣir) (part of) the territory of Assyria [a]nd assigned it to the authority of a eunuch of mine, the palace herald. The awes[ome] splendor of the god Aššur, my lord, overwhelmed Ursâ (Rusâ), the [Ur]a[r]ṭian, [and (so) with his o]w[n] ir[on] da[gg]er [he] stabbed (himself) in the heart [like a p]ig an[d] p[ut an end to his life].

196) ⸢KUR⸣.ma-da†-[a-a ù KUR].kar-al-li al-lik UN.[MEŠ KUR].⸢kar-al⸣-li†
197) ša ⸢LÚ⸣.šu-[ut] ⸢SAG⸣.MEŠ-ia ir†-⸢du†⸣-du†-ma
198) [^{m}]a-mi-taš-[ši] a-ḫi ^{m}aš-šur-ZU KUR.kar-al-la-a-a
199) ú-rab†-bu-<ú> UGU-šú-un ina KUR.an-a ŠU.SI KUR-i†

195b–205a) In my ninth regnal year, I marched t[o] the lands [El]lipi, Media, [and] Karalla. (As for) the peop[le of the land Ka]ra[l]la who had driven out my eu[nuc]hs and elevated Amitaš[ši] of the land Karalla, the brother of Aššur-lēʾi, over them, I struck them down with the sword on Mount Ana, a mountain peak, and (then) received in my (military) c[am]p 2,2[00] of their *face-(guards)* *(as trophies)*. Amitašši fled together with his allies [and] ... [...] ... [...] ... [...]

---

98 ⸢dal⸣-: A. Fuchs (Khorsabad p. 106 line 104) takes the traces visible on the squeeze to be the Ú of ú-taq-qi-in, but the spacing and traces fit ⸢dal⸣ better.

99 H. Winckler's copy has URU.ḫu-[bu-uš-ki-a ⸢URU⸣, thus making it uncertain if he saw any of -bu-uš-ki-a. ⸢URU†⸣.bi-: P.E. Botta's and Winckler's copies have E-bi-; the squeeze would allow ⸢URU⸣ instead of E, but cannot confirm that the sign was fully correct.

101 P.E. Botta's copy has ^{m}te*(copy: EŠ)-lu-[x x x] MA [...], while H. Winckler's copy has ^{m}te-lu-[si-na] KUR.an-di-[a-a ...]. The photos of IM 60980 indicate ⸢^{m}te-lu⸣-[x x x (x)]-⸢di-a⸣ [x x x (x)] MA [...].

102 This line may have had some or all of text no. 1 lines 107b–108a which have [4] ⸢LIM⸣ 2 [ME] ⸢UN.MEŠ a⸣-di mar-ši-⸢ti⸣-šú-nu áš-lu-la URU.⸢bi⸣-[ra-a]-te šá-a-ti-[na] / [ap]-pul aq-qur [i-na IZI áš-ru-up ṣa]-lam LUGAL-ti-ia DÙ-uš-ma li-⸢i⸣-ti ^{d}a-šur ⸢EN-ia⸣ UGU-šú áš-ṭur, "I took as booty [4],2[00] peo[ple], together with their possessions. [I des]troyed, demolished, (and) [burned down with fire] tho[se] for[tress]es. I made [a] royal [im]age of myself and wrote upon it the victor(ies) of the god Aššur, [m]y lo[rd]."

Sections 7–12 Section 7 = lines 103–119 = V,20:1–17; section 8 = lines 120–136 = 'V,19B':1–17; section 9 = lines 137–153 = 'V,19A':1–17; section 10 = lines 154–170 = V,19:1–17; and section 11 = lines 171–187 = V,18:1–17. Cf. text no. 1 lines 108–160/161? The account of the eighth regnal year would likely have begun towards the end of section 8 or the beginning of section 9. Section 12 = lines 188–204 = V,'17':1–17 (Botta: V,18:1–17). See Winckler, Sar. Annals lines 135–143; Lie, Sar. lines 161–169; and Fuchs, Khorsabad Annals lines 161–168 and 168a–c. Cf. text no. 1 lines 161–169. See also the commentary for the line numbering of this section with regard to Botta's copy. In the score, a double dagger (‡) is noted in the line for Botta's copy where the line shifts, with the end of the following line going with the current line.

191 -⸢ṭu⸣-: Or less likely -⸢ṭù⸣-, as noted by A. Fuchs (Khorsabad p. 116 line 163 n. 2).

195 It is not clear if the KUR goes in this line or with the second mention of Karalla in the following line.

200) *i-na* GIŠ†.TUKUL† *ú-šam-qit†-su-nu-ti†-ma* 2† LIM 2† [ME]
201) *zi-im*† *pa†-ni-šu-nu i-na qé-reb*† *uš-[man]-ni-⸢ia⸣*
202) *am†-ḫur*† ^{m}*a-mi-taš-ši*† *a†-di* ⸢LÚ⸣.*re-⸢ṣi⸣-šú ip-par-šid-[ma]*
203) [*x x*] E *x* [*x x*] ŠÚ IGI [*x x*] NA KUR [*x x x*] ḪU [*x x x x*]
204) [...]
205) [*x x*] IR NI [*x x x x x x* (*x*) UN.MEŠ] ⸢KUR†.*ḫab*⸣-[*ḫi*? ...]
206) [*x*] (*x*) [*x*] BU [*x x x x x x* (*x*) *iš-mu*]-*ma ḫat-*[*ti ra-ma-ni-šu-nu im-qut-su-nu-ti-*(*ma*) (...)]

205b–207a) [The people of the la]nd Ḫ[*abḫu* ... heard] [*of the harsh deeds that I had done in the land Karalla*; their own] fe[ar(s)] then fell upon them (*and they sent their messenger to me to do obeisance to me*). I assigned them] to the authority of [a] e[unuch of mine, the gove]rnor of the land L[ullumû].

207) *i-na* ŠU.II [LÚ].*šu-*[*ut* SAG-*ia* LÚ.GAR].KUR KUR.⸢*lu*⸣-[*lu-mi-i am-nu-šú-nu-ti* ...]
208) KUR.*mi-*[*x*]-KI-[*x x x* (*x*)] KUR *x* [*x x x x x* (*x*)] *x* IN [...]
209) *it-*[*ti*]-*šú ib-⸢bal⸣-ki-*[*tu x x x* (*x*) ^{m}*a-zu*?]-*uk-tú* [...]
210) URU.*ḫu-ba-aḫ-na* [URU? *dan-nu-ti-šú-un*? *a*]-⸢*di*†⸣ 24 ⸢URU⸣.[MEŠ ...]
211) *ak-⸢šu⸣-ud di-ik†-*[*ta-šú-nu a-duk x x*] PI BUR TA A [*x* ...]
212) KUR [*x*] ⸢LIM⸣ 2 ME UDU.⸢MEŠ†⸣ [(*x*) *x*] ANŠE.[*x x x* (*x*)] ANŠE.KUNGA†.MEŠ ⸢ANŠE⸣.[MEŠ ...]
213) ÁŠ [*x x*] UD *x* GIŠ [*x x*] ME MUD [*x* (*x*) *qé*]-*reb-šú ú-šal-me-*[*šu-ma* ...]
214) LAL [*x x*] *x* [*x x x*] GÌR.NÍTA MU [*x x*]-⸢*ni*†⸣-*šu†-nu ka-mu-*[*su-*(*nu*) ...]
215) GIŠ [...] TA [*x x x* KUR].*el†-li-pi* ⸢*áš*⸣-[*šu ṣa-bat* ...]
216) [*x x* (*x*)] ŠÚ [*x x x* (*x*)] KU *x* [*x x x x* (*x x*)] *te-me-qí iš-*[*te-ni*]-⸢*iš*⸣ [*a-na* ^{m}*a-zu-uk-tú* ...]
217) [*x x x*] *x* LI [*x* (*x*)] E ⸢*ú*†⸣-[*ṣal-la-an-ni*]-*ma áš-ma-*[*a zi*]-⸢*kir*⸣-[*šu* ... *e-peš* LUGAL-*ti-šú*]

207b–218a) [(*As for*) *Daltâ of the land Ellipi, a submissive subject who bore my yoke*], the lands Mi[..., (and) ..., (*a total of*) *five of his districts*], revolt[ed] aga[inst] him [... *Azu*]*ktu* [...] I conquered [(...)] the city Ḫubaḫna, [*their fortified city*, together] with twenty-four settle[ments ...] (and) [inflicted] a defe[at upon them ...] ... [...] *for*[*ty/fif*[*ty* tho]usand two hundred sheep, [...], *h*[*orses*], mules, d[onkeys ...] ... [...] ... [...] I had [him] surrounded [th]ere [and ...] governor, their [..., *them*] in bondage [... (215) ... the land] Ellipi be[cause of the seizure of ...] ... [...] with entreaties at the same [time to Azuktu ...] ... [...] he [besought me] and I listened to [his wo]rd(s). [... I ordered (him to continue) to exercise kingship. I (thus) made] Da[ltâ happy and brought order to his] dist[urbed land].

---

201 *zīm pānī face-(guards)*: See the note to text no. 1 line 112.
Section 13 = lines 205–221 = V,'16':1–17 (Botta V,14:1–17). See Winckler, Sar. Annals lines 157–162; Lie, Sar. lines 177–188; and Fuchs, Khorsabad Annals lines 168c/d and 170–185. Cf. text no. 1 lines 170–188 and text no. 74 iii 42–53.
205 The tentative restoration at the end of the line is based on text no. 82 v 31′.
206 For the restoration, cf. text no. 1 line 365. For possible additional restoration at the end of the line, see text no. 82 v 35′–36′.
207 For possible additional restoration at the end of the line, see text no. 1 line 172; cf. Olmstead, AJSL 47 (1930–31) pp. 267–268.
208 A.T.E. Olmstead (AJSL 47 [1930–31] p. 268) suggests that the land Milqia is mentioned here, but as A. Fuchs (Khorsabad p. 119 line 173 n. 1) points out, that area was part of Assyria.
209 The tentative restoration [^{m}*a-zu*?]-*uk-tú* follows A.T.E. Olmstead (AJSL 47 [1930–31 p. 268) and A. Fuchs (Khorsabad p. 120 line 174); it is based on an assumed connection with text no. 1 line 181. For a possible restoration of the end of the line, see text no. 74 iii 43–47.
210 The restoration is based on text no. 74 iii 48, although that text has 25 rather than 24. The number 24 might be an error on P.E. Botta's copy for 25.
211 Cf. text no. 74 iii 50.
212 KUR [*x*] ⸢LIM⸣: As already noted by A. Fuchs (Khorsabad p. 120 line 177 n. 1), likely 30+[10/20] ⸢LIM⸣, "for[ty tho]usand" or "fif[ty tho]usand," or KUR-[*ud x*] ⸢LIM⸣, "I conqu[ered; x tho]usand." Forty/fifty thousand would be an unusually large number of sheep.
213 As suggested by A.T.E Olmstead (AJSL 47 [1930–31] p. 268), possibly *áš-*[*lu-la*], "I car[ried off as booty]." For the restoration at the end of the line, see text no. 1 lines 178.
214 -⸢*ni*†⸣: The reading is based on text no. 1 line 179. As already noted by A. Fuchs (Khorsabad p. 120 line 179 n. 1), there is not sufficent room for A.T.E. Olmstead's suggested restoration [*ša-a-šú-nu ga-du qin*]-*ni-šu-nu* (AJSL 47 [1930–31] p. 268).
215 See text no. 1 line 180 for the restorations.
216 The restoration is based on text no. 1 line 181. Instead of -⸢*iš*⸣ [*a-na*], possibly -[*iš*] ⸢*a*⸣-[*na*], as read by A. Fuchs (Khorsabad p. 121 line 181).
217 The restoration is based on text no. 1 lines 182–183.

218) [*aq-bi*] *lìb-bi* ^{m}*da-*⸢*al*⸣*-*[*ta-a ú-ṭib-ma ú-taq-qi-na*] ⸢*da*†⸣*-*[*li-iḫ-tu* KUR-*su* KUR.*ba-ʾi-it*-DINGIR]
219) [KUR.*na-gu-ú*] *ša* KUR.*ma-da-a-*[*a ša mi*]*-ṣir* [KUR.*el-li-pí*] KUR.[*ab-sa-ḫu-ut-ti* KUR.*pa-ar-nu-at-ti*]
220) [KUR.*ú-tir-na* URU.*di-ri-is-ta-a-nu ša* KUR.*ú-ri-a-ak-ki* KUR.*ri-ma-nu-ti* KUR.*na-gu-ú ša* KUR.*up-pu-ri-ia*]
221) [KUR.*ú-ia-da-ú-e* KUR.*bu-us-ti-is* KUR.*a-ga-zi* KUR.*am-ba-an-da* KUR.*da-na-nu* KUR.*na-gi-i ru-qu-ti ša pat-ti* KUR.*a-ri-bi*]
222) [*ša ni-pi-iḫ* ^{d}UTU-*ši ù* KUR.*na-gi-i ša* KUR.*man-da-a-a dan-nu-ti ša*] *ni-ir* ⸢^{d}⸣*aš-šur* [*iṣ-lu-ma*]
223) [KUR-*ú ù mad-ba-ru ir-tap-pu-du šar-ra-qiš a-na pu-ḫur* URU.MEŠ-*ni-šú*]*-nu a-*⸢*ku*⸣*-*[*ka-a*]*-ti* [*ad*]*-di-*[*ma*] ⸢*gi-mir*⸣

218b–224a) [(With regard to) the land Baʾīt-ili, a district] of the land Media [that is on the bor]der of [the land Ellipi]; the land[s Absaḫutti, Parnuatti, (and) Utirna; the city Diristānu of the land Uriakku; the land Rimanuti, a district of the land Uppuriya; the lands Uyadaue, Bustis, Agazi, Ambanda, (and) Dananu, far-off districts of the territory of the Arabs in the east; and the district(s) of the powerful Medes, who had thrown off] the yoke of the god Aššur [and roamed about the mountain(s) and desert like thieves — I th]rew f[ir]ebrands [into all the]ir [settlements and turned a]ll [their districts into forgotten (ruin) mounds].

224) [KUR.*na-gi-šú-nu ú-ter-ra a-na ti-li ma-šu-ú-ti ma-da-at-tu ša* ^{m}]*ul-*[*lu*]*-*⸢*su*†⸣*-*[*nu*] KUR.*man-na-a-a* ^{m}[*da*]*-*⸢*al*⸣*-*[*ta-a*]
225) [KUR.*el-li-pa-a-a* ^{md}EN-IBILA-SUM.NA KUR.*al-lab-ri-a-a ša* 45 LÚ.EN.URU.MEŠ-*ni ša*] KUR.*ma-da-a-a* [*dan-nu-ti*]

224b–226a) [I] re[ceived 4,609 horses, mules], o[xe]n, [(and) sheep and goats, in countless numbers, as tribute from] Ul[lu]s[unu], the Mannean, [D]al[tâ of the land Ellipi, Bēl-aplu-iddina of the land Allabria, (and) from forty-five city lords of] the [powerful] Medes.

226) [4 LIM 6 ME 9 ANŠE.KUR.RA.MEŠ ANŠE.*pa-re-e*] ⸢GU$_{4}$.MEŠ⸣ [US$_{5}$.UDU.ḪI.A *a-na la ma-ni*] ⸢*am*⸣*-*[*ḫur* ^{m}]*am-*[*ba*]*-*⸢*ri*⸣*-is* KUR.*ta-bal-*[*a-a* LUGAL KUR.É-*pu-ri-ti-iš*]
227) [*ša* NUN *a-lik pa-ni-ia kim*]*-ti* ^{m}*ḫul-li-*[*i* AD-*šú*$^{?}$ *a-di*$^{?}$] ⸢*šal*⸣*-*[*lat*] KUR-*šú a-na* KUR *aš-šur*.KI *ú-raš-šu-*[*nu-ti*]
228) [*i-na*$^{?}$ GIŠ$^{?}$ UD$^{?}$ DINGIR.MEŠ GAL.MEŠ *x x* UD$^{?}$ *ku-un*] ⸢BALA⸣*-ia i-na* ⸢*uz*†⸣*-*[*ni-ia*] *ib-šu-ú* ^{m}*ḫul-li-i i-na* GIŠ.GU.ZA [LUGAL-*ti-šú*]
229) [*ú-še-šib* UN.MEŠ KUR.É-*pu-ru-ta-áš*] *ú-*⸢*pa*⸣*-ḫir-ma i-na* ⸢*qa*⸣*-*[*ti-šu am*]*-nu i-na u*$_{4}$*-me* ^{m}*ḫul-li-i* AD-[*šú x* (*x*)] A MA [*x x* (*x*)]

226b–230a) (As for) Am[bar]is of the land Tabal, [king of the land Bīt-Purutaš, the fam]ily of [*whose father*] Ḫullî, [a ruler, a predecessor of mine], had brought to Assyria [*together with*] bo[oty] from his land, [(*when*) ... the great gods *determined* the firm establishment of] my [re]ign, they (Ḫullî and his family) were on [my] m[ind. I had] Ḫullî [sit (again)] on [his royal] throne. I gathered together [the people of the land Bīt-Purutaš] and [assi]gned (them) to [his] a[uthority]. In the time of Ḫullî, [his] father, [I had granted him (Ambaris) ...] ... [...], gave him a dau[gh]ter of mine, (along) with [the city] Ḫilakku, and (thus) expa[nd]ed his land.

230) [... *áš-ru*]*-*⸢*uk*$^{?}$⸣*-*[*šu-ma*] *bi-*[*in*]*-ti it-ti* [URU].*ḫi-la-ak-ki ad-din-šú-ma ú-rap*†*-*[*pi*]*-šá* KUR-*su u* [*šu-ú*]
231) [LÚ.*ḫa-at-tu-ú la na*]*-ṣir* [*kit-ti a-na* ^{m}]⸢*ur*†⸣*-sa-a* ⸢LUGAL⸣ [KUR].⸢*ur*†⸣*-ar-ṭi* ^{m}*mi-ta-a* LUGAL† [KUR].⸢*mu*⸣*-us-ki* [*u* MAN.MEŠ-*ni*]
232) [KUR.*ta-ba-li e-ke*]*-*⸢*me*⸣ *mi-*[*ṣir-ia iš-pur*] *um*†*-ma-na-at*† ^{d}*aš-šur ad-ke-ma* KUR.*ta-ba-lum* [*a-na*] *paṭ gim*†*-*⸢*ri*⸣*-*[*šú*]

230b–235) However, [that (man) (Ambaris), a Hittite who did not pro]tect [justice, sent to] Ursâ (Rusâ), [ki]ng of [the land U]rarṭu, Mitâ, king of [the land M]usku, [and the kings of the land Tabal about taking aw]ay terr[itory of mine]. I mustered the troops of the god Aššur and [overwhelmed] the land Tabal [to its] full extent [as if with a net. (Then), I bro]ught in bondage [to Assyria Amba]ri[s], king [of the land Bīt-Pur]utaš, toge[ther with] the (other) offspring of

---

218–224 The restorations are based on text no. 1 lines 183–192a. The proposed division of the restorations between lines 219–222 must be considered tentative.

Section 14 = lines 222–238 = V,15:1–17. See Winckler, Sar. Annals lines 162–180; Lie, Sar. lines 188–206; and Fuchs, Khorsabad Annals lines 189–206. Cf. text no. 1 lines 188–206.

225–229 For the restorations, see text no. 1 lines 192b–197. It is possible that KUR.*na-gi-šú-nu* should go at the end of line 223 rather than at the beginning of line 224. Line 225: There is the trace of a sign (one vertical wedge on top of another) copied by P.E. Botta approximately four or five signs before KUR.*ma-da-a-a*, but it does not easily fit EN, URU, or MEŠ.

226b–228a See text no. 1 lines 194b–196a and the on-page notes to those lines.

229 Text no. 1 line 197 has *ú-man-ni* rather than [*am*]*-nu*; cf. CAD M/1 p. 227, which reads [*im*]*-nu*.

230–238 For the restorations, see text no. 1 lines 198–206/207. For line 230, see also text no. 74 v 20.

233) [*ú-kàt-ti-ma še-e-ti-iš* ^{m}*am-ba*]-*ri*-⌈*is*⌉ LUGAL† [KUR.É-*pu*]-⌈*ri*⌉-*ti-iš a*-[*di*] NUMUN É AD-*šú* LÚ.SAG.KAL†-*ut* KUR-*šú ka*-⌈*mu*⌉-*su-nu it*-[*ti*]
234) [1 ME GIŠ.GIGIR-*šú a-na* KUR *aš-šur*.KI *al*]-*qa-a* [KUR].É-*pu*-⌈*ri*⌉-[*ti*]-*iš* KUR.*ḫi-la-ak*†-⌈*ku*⌉ *a-bur-riš ú-šar*†-[*bi*]-*iṣ-ma* UN.MEŠ KUR.⌈MEŠ⌉
235) [*ki-šit-ti* ^{d}*aš-šur be-lí-ia ú*]-⌈*še*⌉-*šib* LÚ.*šu-ut* SAG-[*ia*] ⌈LÚ†⌉.EN.NAM UGU†-*šú-nu áš-kun*†-*ma ni*-[*ir*] *be*†-*lu-ti-ia e*-⌈*mid*⌉-[*su-nu-ti*]

his father's house (and) the nobles of his land, (along) wi[th one hundred of his chariot(s)]. I had the land[s] Bīt-Pur[ut]aš (and) Ḫilakku dw[e]ll (as safely) as in a meadow and [(re)se]ttled (there) people from the lands [that the god Aššur, my lord, had conquered]. I set a eunuch [of mine] as provincial governor over them and impos[ed] the yo[ke] of my lordship [upon them].

236) [*i-na* 10 BALA-*ia* ^{m}*tar*]-*ḫu-na-zi*† URU.*me*-[*lid-da*]-⌈*a*⌉-*a* SAG$^{?}$-*tu-u* x (x) *la a-dir* ⌈*zik*⌉-*ri* ⌈DINGIR⌉.[MEŠ GAL.MEŠ] KUR.[*kam*]-*ma-nu rap*†-[*šú*] ⌈*ša*⌉ [*i-na*]
237) [*tu-kul-ti* ^{d}*aš-šur be-lí-ia*] *e-ki*-[*mu* ^{m}]⌈*gu*⌉-[*un-zi-na*]-*nu* [LUGAL]-*šu*-<*nu*> *aṭ-ru*-[*du ka-ma-ti*]-*iš* [*ù*] ⌈*šá*⌉-[*a-šú i-na*]
238) [GIŠ.GU.ZA LUGAL-*ti-šú ú-še-ši-bu* ...] GIŠ [x x x x x (x)]

236–238) [In my tenth regnal year, (as for) Tar]ḫun-azi of the city Me[lid], *an evil Hittite* who did not fear the words of the [great] g[ods], (and as for) the wi[de] land [Kam]manu, which I had taken [away with the support of the god Aššur, my lord] (and) whose [king] G[unzinā]nu I had driv[en ou]t [and (then) had] h[im (Tarḫun-azi) sit on his (Gunzinānu's) royal throne ...]

Lines 239–255 are not preserved

256) [(...) UGU KUR.*ur-ar-ṭi ú-dan-ni-na* EN.NUN URU.*ú-si* URU.*ú-si-an* URU.*ú-ar*]-*gi*-⌈*in*⌉ *pa-a-ṭi*
257) [KUR.*mu-us-ki ad-di-ma ša la mu-ṣe-e aṣ-ba-ta* KÁ.MEŠ-*šú*-(*un*) URU.*el-li-bir*] URU.*ši-in-da-ra-ra*
258) [UGU UN.MEŠ KUR.*ka-as-ku ar-ku-us* URU.*me-lid-du* URU LUGAL-*ti-šu* (...)] *a-di* URU.⌈*kúm*⌉-*mu-ḫi*

256–259a) [I strengthened the garrison(s) (of) the cities Luḫsu, Purṭir, Anmurru, Kiaka, (and) Anduarsalia against the land Urarṭu. I erected the cities Usi, Usian, (and) Uar]gin on the border [of the land Musku and seized (control of) its/their entry points (lit.: "gates") so that there should be no escape (lit.: "exit"). (Finally), I constructed] the cit[ies Ellibir] (and) Šindarara [against the people of the land Kasku. *I gave his (Tarḫun-azi's) royal city Melid* (...)], as well as the city Kummuḫu, [*to Mutallu*].

259) [... *i-na* u_4-*me-šu-ma ka*]-*tim*-[*ti* KUR.MEŠ]-⌈*e*⌉ *ša* ⌈KUR.*ḫat*⌉-*ti*
260) [*ip-pe-te* ... *i-na* u_4-*me* BALA-*ia ú-bil*]-*lu*-⌈*nim*$^{?}$⌉-[*ma ak*]-*ku-ma bu-še*-[*e* KUR.*ḫat*]-*ti*
261) [(...) *mé-su-ú si-mat* É.GAL KUR.*la-ri-is-ʾu* KUR.*šu-ru-ma-an* ... *bi-nu-tu* ^{d}*nu-dím*]-⌈*mud* ZABAR⌉ [*nam-ru*†] *ina* KUR.*tu-šá-ni*-⌈*ra*⌉ [x-x]-x-*du-ri-ni*
262) [KUR.*e-li-ku-du-ri-ni ib-ba-ni par-zil-lu* KUR.*lam-mu-un šá bi-rit* x Ú ... A.BÁR

259b–267a) [At that time, (everything) that was hi]dde[n in the mountain]s of the land Ḫa[t]ti (Syria) [was revealed (*to me*). (...) They brou]ght to [me during my reign ... and I he]aped up the proper[ty of the land Ḫat]ti. [(*On*) *Mount ... was produced refined ..., appropriate for a palace; (on) Mounts Larisʾu, Šuruman, (and) ... was produced the creation of the god Nudimmu*]d (*Ea*), [shining] copper; on Mount[s] Tušanira, [...]durini, [(and) Elikudurini was produced iron; (the part of) Mount Lammun that is (located) between *Mount* U... and *Mount* ...] pro[duced lead, which whit]ens their

234 Text no. 1 line 203 adds a passage about building enclosure walls (*kerḫē*) before the resettlement of the people.
235 It is possible that *ki-šit-ti* should be restored at the end of the previous line. Text no. 1 line 204 has *tup-šik-ki* ⌈*áš*⌉-*šu-ri*, "(the same) corvée duty (as if they were) Assyrians," rather than *ni*-[*ir*] *be*†-*lu-ti-ia*, "the yo[ke] of my lordship."
236 SAG$^{?}$-*tu-u x* (*x*): F.W. Geers (apud Olmstead, AJSL 47 [1930–31] p. 268 sub line 204) reasonably suggests LÚ.*ḫat-tu* ⌈*lemnu*⌉, "an evil Hittite"; cf. text no. 1 line 204. ⌈DINGIR⌉.[MEŠ GAL.MEŠ] "[great] g[ods]": The restoration follows text no. 1 line 205. Botta's copy would suggest that there would be barely room for ⌈DINGIR⌉.[MEŠ], so GAL.MEŠ, "great," may have been omitted; however, Botta's copies are freqently not accurate with regard to the amount of damage indicated.
Sections 15–16 Section 15 = lines 239–255 = V,14:1–17. Cf. text no. 1 lines 207–217. Section 16 = lines 256–272 = V,13:1–17. See Wincker, Sar. Annals lines 192–214; Lie, Sar. lines 218–248a; and Fuchs, Khorsabad Annals lines 218–220, 220a, and 222–240. Cf. text no. 1 lines 218–248a and text no. 3 lines 1′–6′a.
256 The translation assumes that preceding UGU (either all or partially on line 255) was URU.*lu-uḫ-su* URU.*pur-ṭir* URU.*an-mu-ur-ru* URU.*ki-a*$^{?}$-*ka*$^{?}$ URU.*an-du-ar-sa-li*; see text no. 1 line 217.
259 The squeeze indicates that at the end of the line there is room for only one sign — or two signs written very close together, in contrast to the spacing of other signs — between ⌈*ḫat*⌉- and -*ti* and thus that we should read ⌈KUR.*ḫat*⌉-*ti* rather than ⌈*ḫat*⌉-[*ti ip-pe*]-*ti*, which the spacing on P.E. Botta's copy would allow.
261 H. Winckler's copy does not have a "[" to go with the "]" before -*ru*.
262 It is possible that the first word in the restoration is actually the last word of the previous line. *bi-rit* x Ú ...: Text no. 1 line 226 has ⌈*bi-rit*⌉ [KUR].*ú*-(*x*)-[x x x x x (x)].

mu-nam]-mir a-ru-[uš]-ti-šú-nu ú-šak-[lim KUR].⸢lam⸣-mu-un
263) [...] TI ḪI [(x) BAR.GÙN].GÙN.NU na-as-qu si-mat LUGAL-ti
264) [ša GIM NA$_4$.ZA.GÌN.DURU$_5$-i pe-ṣa-at x x x x A x RA x x x x KUR.ba-ʾi-il-ṣa-pu-na KUR]-ú ⸢GAL ZABAR⸣ iš-te-niš ib-ni-ma šá KUR.MEŠ-⸢ni⸣
265) [šu-nu-ti ši-pik ep-ri-šú-nu ab-lul-ma a-na ki-i-ri x x x ŠÚ ú-še-ri-is-su]-⸢nu$^{?}$⸣-ti-ma ⸢bu-šul⸣-šú-nu a-⸢mur⸣
266) [NÍG.GA la ni-bi ša AD.MEŠ-ia la i-ḫu-ru i-na qé-reb URU.BÀD-^{m}LUGAL-GI.NA URU-ia] ⸢aq⸣-[ru]-⸢un⸣-ma ma-⸢ḫi⸣-[ri KÙ.BABBAR] ⸢ki⸣-ma ⸢ZABAR⸣

dirt[y s]tate; [(the part of) Mount La]mmun [that is (located) *facing ... produced pure alabaster; Mount Ammun, a mountain that is (located) facing ... produced*] choice [BAR.GÙN].GÙN.NU-(*stone*), fit for royalty (and) [as white as pale lapis lazuli ...; (and) Mount Baʾil-ṣapūna], a great [mounta]in, produced at the same time copper. (265) [I *then* mixed mound(s) of ore] from [those] mountains, [deposited th]em [into furnaces ...], and watch[ed] their smelting. I st[or]ed up [inside my city Dūr-Šarrukīn countless possessions that my ancestors had never received]; as a result, [in Assyria] the excha[nge rate for silver is fixed] as if it were for bronze.

267) [...] x BAD I [... ^{m}mut]-tal-lu ⸢IBILA⸣-šú
268) [...]-⸢ia⸣ Ù [x x x x]-li-[x] x [x]
269) [... ^{m}tar-ḫu]-la-⸢ra$^{?}$ ^{m}mut$^{?}$⸣-[tal-lu] ⸢IBILA⸣-šu
270) [...] ⸢NA⸣ [x] TI [x x x (x)] x-šú e-pu-⸢šu⸣
271) [ŠU.II.MEŠ-šú ú-qam-me ú-kal-li-ma x (x) ^{m}mut-tal-lu IBILA-šú a-di kim-ti KUR.É-^{m}pa-ʾa-al-la mal] ba-[šu-u$^{?}$ KI$^{?}$] KÙ.GI KÙ.BABBAR
272) [NÍG.ŠU É.GAL-šú šá ni-ba la i-šu-ú a-na šal-la-ti am-nu-šú UN.MEŠ KUR.gúr-gu-me a-na paṭ gim-ri-šá a-na eš-šu-ti a-šur-ma LÚ.šu]-ut SAG-⸢ia⸣ LÚ.EN.⸢NAM⸣

267b–273a) [In my eleventh regnal year ... *Tarḫu-lara of the land Gurgum ... who*]*se* heir [Mu]tallu [had cut (him) down with the sword and taken away ... my ... *in* ... in order to avenge him (Tarḫu-lara) ... Tarḫu]-lar[a], his [he]ir M[utallu (270) *in/with* ... of the body before the god Šamaš ... *Because of*] *his* [.... *that* ...] he had done, [I/he *burned* his hands (and) showed (...). I counted as booty his heir Mutallu, together with the (royal) family of the land Bīt-Paʾalla, as many as there] we[re (of them), (along) with] gold, silver, [(and) countless property from his palace. I reorganized (the administration of) the people of the land Gurgum to its full extent, set a eu]nuch of [mi]ne as provinc[ial] governor [(...) over them, (and) consi]dered th[em as] people of [Assyria].

273) [(...) UGU-šu/šú-nu áš-kun it-ti] UN.⸢MEŠ⸣ KUR [aš-šur.KI am]-nu-šú-[nu-ti ^{m}a-zu-ri]
274) [LUGAL URU.as-du-di a-na la] na-še-⸢e⸣ [bíl-te x x] x TU [AN$^{?\dagger}$ ...]
275) [... li-me]-ti-šu ⸢ze⸣-[ra-a-ti KUR aš-šur.KI iš-pur-ma áš-šu ḪUL-tu]
276) [e-pu-šu UGU] UN.MEŠ KUR-šú [be-lu-su ú-nak-kir-ma ^{m}a-ḫi-mi-ti a-ḫu ta-lim-šú]
277) [a-na LUGAL]-ti UGU-[šú†]-⸢nu⸣ ú-[kin LÚ.ḫat-ti-i da-bi-ib ṣa-lip-ti be-lu-su]
278) [i-ze-ru-ma ^{m}ia-ad-na$^{?}$ ...]

273b–280a) [Azūri, king of the city Ashdod, *plotted* ... (so as) to no longer (have to)] deliver [tribute (to me) *and sent (messages)*] *h*[*ostile to Assyria to the kings* in] his [enviro]ns. [Thus, because of the evil that he had done, I did away with his lordship over] the people of his land [and set his *favorite* brother Aḫī-Mīti as kin]g over [th]em. [The Hittites, who (always) speak treachery, hated his rule and ... *elevated over the*]*m* [*Iadna* (Iāmānī), ...]

---

263 There is likely not sufficient room to restore all that is in text no. 1 lines 227b–229a, which have [šá$^{?}$] IGI [x x x (x)] / NA$_4$.GIŠ.NU$_{11}$.⸢GAL⸣ *eb-bu* KUR.*am-mu-un šá-du-ú pa-ni* Ú [x x x (x)] ⸢IM⸣ [TI] ḪI [x x (x x)] / *na-as-qu* "[that is (located)] *facing* [... *produced*] pure alabaster; Mount Ammun, a mountain [that is (located)] facing [...] ... [*produced*] choice [BAR.GÙN.GÙN.NU-(stone)]." [BAR.GÙN].GÙN.NU: R. Campbell Thompson (DACG pp. 169–170) assumes it is the name of a type of stone that can change its color in the sun, while E. Reiner (JNES 15 [1956] pp. 132–133 line 24) takes this to be a mountain that produced tin.

267 H. Winckler suggests in a note to his copy that instead of [...] x BAD I, one might have [^{m}*ḫul-li*]-*i*.

268 Text no. 3 line 2´a has [...]-*li-ia i*-⸢*na*$^{?}$⸣ IGI$^{?}$ TE$^{?}$ *a-na tur-ri gi-mil-li-šú* x [...], "[...] my [...] *in* ... in order to avenge him (Tarḫu-lara) [...]."

269 The reading is based on text no. 3 line 3´a.

270 Text no. 3 lines 3´b–4´a have *i-na x-ti zu-um-ri ma-ḫar* ^{d}⸢UTU$^{?}$⸣ [x x x (x)] Ú [x x x x x x x x] / [...] *x-šú e-pu*-⸢*šu*$^{?}$⸣, "in/with ... of the body before the god *Šam*[*aš ... Because of*] *his* [... *that*] he had done."

271 *ba*-[*šu-u*$^{?}$ KI$^{?}$]: The copies by Botta and Winckler, as well as the squeeze, suggest that there is not sufficient room to read the expected *ba*-[*šu-ú it-ti*]; perhaps read instead *ba*-[*šu-ú*] <*it-ti*>.

Section 17 = lines 273–289 = V,12:1–17. See Winckler, Sar. Annals lines 214–229; Lie, Sar. lines 248b–264a; and Fuchs, Khorsabad Annals lines 240–255, 255a–b, and 256. Cf. text no. 1 lines 248b–264a and text no. 3 lines 6´b–14´a. Due to the damaged state of the inscription on the slab, the exact division of words between lines is uncertain on numerous occasions.

274 Based on text no. 1 line 250 and text no. 3 line 7´ one expects *ik-pu-ud-ma a-na* LUGAL.MEŠ-*ni*.

277 The *ú*-[...] is only seen on P.E. Botta's copy; text no. 3 line 8´ has *áš-kun* and text no. 1 line 253 has [...]-⸢*kun*⸣.

278–281 For what might be in these lines, cf. text no. 1 lines 254–257 and text no. 3 lines 8´b–10´a.

279) [...] x [...]
280) [... ú-rab-bu-ú? e-li-šu?]-⸢un? i?⸣-[na? ug-gat? lìb-bi-ia? ...]
281) [x x x x x x x (x)] x [... a-na URU.as-du-di]
282) [URU LUGAL-ti-šú ḫi-it-mu-ṭiš] ⸢al?-lik?-ma? URU⸣.as-[du-du URU.gi-im-tú]
283) ⸢URU⸣.[as-du-di-im-mu al-me] KUR-ud DINGIR.[MEŠ a-ši]-⸢bu⸣-[ut lìb-bi-šu-un šá-a-šú]
284) a-[di UN.MEŠ KUR-šú KÙ.GI KÙ.BABBAR NÍG].ŠU É.⸢GAL⸣-[šú a-na šal-la-ti am-nu]-⸢šú⸣
285) [URU.MEŠ-ni šú-nu-ti a-na eš-šu]-⸢ti⸣ aṣ-[bat UN.MEŠ KUR.KUR ki-šit-ti ŠU].⸢II-ia⸣
286) [i-na lìb-bi ú-še-šib LÚ.šu-ut] ⸢SAG-ia⸣ LÚ.[EN].⸢NAM⸣ UGU-[šú-nu áš]-⸢kun⸣-ma†
287) [it-ti UN.MEŠ KUR aš-šur.KI am-nu-šu-nu-ti-ma i-šuṭ-ṭu ab]-šá-⸢ni⸣ [i]-⸢na†⸣ 12 ⸢BALA⸣-[ia ^{md}]⸢AMAR⸣.UTU-A-AŠ
288) [DUMU ^{m}ia-ki-ni LUGAL KUR.kal-di a-šib ki-šad tam]-tim [la a-dir zik-ri DINGIR.MEŠ] ⸢GAL⸣.MEŠ
289) [... UGU ÍD.mar-ra-ti ù] ⸢gu?-pu?⸣-[uš e-de-e it-ta]-kil-ma
290) [a]-⸢de⸣-[e† (ma-mit) DINGIR†].MEŠ GAL.MEŠ e-bu-uk-ma ik-la-a ta-mar-tuš
291) [^{m}]ḫu-⸢um⸣-ba-⸢ni⸣-ga-áš LÚ.ELAM.MA.⸢KI⸣ a-na re-ṣu-ti ⸢is⸣-ḫur-ma
292) LÚ.ru-u_8-a LÚ.ḫi-in-da-ru LÚ.KUR.ia-ad-bu-ru
293) LÚ.pu-qu-du gi-mir LÚ.su-ti-i ERIM.MEŠ EDIN it-ti-ia
294) ú-šam-kir-ma ik-ṣu-ra ta-ḫa-zu in-neš-ram-ma
295) [a]-na KUR EME.GI$_7$ ù URI.KI 12 MU.MEŠ ki-i la lìb-bi DINGIR.MEŠ
296) ⸢KÁ⸣.DINGIR.RA.KI URU ^{d}EN.LÍL.LÁ DINGIR.MEŠ i-be-⸢el⸣
297) ⸢ù⸣ iš-pur ^{d}AMAR.UTU EN GAL-ú ep-šet† LÚ.kal-di lem-né-ti
298) [i]-ṭul-ma e-ṭe-er† GIŠ.GIDRU ù GIŠ.GU.⸢ZA⸣ LUGAL-ti-šú iš-šá-ki†-in
299) ⸢šap†⸣-tuš-šu ia-a-ti ^{m}LUGAL-GI.NA LUGAL šaḫ-tu
300) ⸢i⸣-na ⸢nap⸣-ḫar ma-li-ki ⸢ki⸣-niš ut-ta-an-ni-ma ul-la-a
301) [re]-⸢ši⸣-ia i-na er-ṣe-et KUR EME†.GI$_7$ u ak-ka-de-e

280b–287a) [Angril]y, [... I quickly] march[ed to his royal city Ashdod. I] then [surrounded (and)] conquered the c[iti]es Ash[dod, Gath, (and) Ashdod-Yam. I counted as booty (both)] the god[s who dw]el[t in them (and) that (man) (Iāmāni)], toge[ther with the people of his land, gold, silver, (and) the prop]erty of [his] pal[ace]. (285) I [re]orga[nized (the administration of) those cities (and) settled there people from the lands that] I [had conquered. I se]t [a eunu]ch of mi[ne] as provincial [governor] over [them] and [considered them as people of Assyria; they (now) pull my y]ok[e].

287b–303a) [I]n [my] twelfth re[gnal year, Mar]duk-apla-iddina (II) (Merodach-Baladan), [descendant of Yakīn, king of Chaldea, who dwelt on the shore of the s]ea [(and) who did not fear the words of the grea]t [god]s [... had put his tr]ust [in the sea and (its) s]ur[ging waves]. (290) He then broke (lit.: "overturned") [the tr]ea[ty (sworn) by the] great [god]s and withheld his audience gift. He turned to Ḫumbanigaš (Ḫumban-nikaš I), the Elamite, for aid, made the Ru'u'a (tribe), the Ḫindaru (tribe), the Yadburu (tribe), the Puqudu (tribe), (and) all the Sutians, the people of the steppe, hostile to me, and prepared for battle against me. He proceeded (295) to the land of Sumer and Akkad and, against the will of the gods, ruled and governed [B]abylon, the city of the Enlil of the gods (Marduk), for twelve years. (However), the god Marduk, the great lord, saw the evil deeds of the Chaldeans. Then, (the order for) the removal of his royal scepter and throne was set upon his [l]ips. (300) He duly chose me, Sargon, the reverent king, from among all rulers and exalted me. He made my [weapon]s prevail [in order] to bar the e[v]il enemy Chaldeans from the territory of the land of Sumer and Akkad.

282 Cf. A. Fuchs (Khorsabad p. 134 line 249), who appears to assign these traces to the preceding line on this slab and reads ⸢ip!?-par!?⸣ rather than ⸢al?-lik?⸣.
286 -ma†: The copies by both P.E. Botta and H. Winckler have -ma*(copy ÁŠ); the sign is right at the end of the squeeze and all that is visible are the first parts of three horizontal wedges, one above the other.
287 H. Winckler's copy has a "]" toward the end of AMAR, but erroneously omits an opening bracket ("[").
288–289a The text follows text no. 3 lines 13′–14′ rather than text no. 1 lines 263–264 which have following "king of Chaldea": ša i-na sa-pan tam-tim ṣi-⸢it⸣ ^{d}UTU-ši šit-ku-nu / da-ád-me-šu, "whose settlements are situated on the (coastal) plain of the Eastern Sea."
Section 18 = lines 290–306 = V,11:1–17. See Winckler, Sar. Annals lines 230–246; Lie, Sar. lines 264b–274a; and Fuchs, Khorsabad Annals lines 256–266. Cf. text no. 1 lines 264b–274a and text no. 3 lines 14′b–15′. The edition of this section is based soley on Botta's and Winckler's copies since the squeeze used by both of them is no longer preserved. All the signs in this section marked with a dagger (†) have an incorrect/abnormal sign on Botta's copy and a perfectly correct one on Winckler's copy except as noted below. Wincker also sometimes has a sign fully preserved when Botta's copy (which is followed here) has it damaged or only partially preserved.
290 H. Winckler's copy has [a]-de-e DINGIR.MEŠ, while the squeeze has [x]-⸢de⸣-[x x (x)].MEŠ, while text no. 1 line 264 has a-de-e ma-mit DINGIR.⸢MEŠ⸣; see also text no. 3 line 14′ (partially restored).
297 Cf. text no. 1 line 268, which has ep-šet KUR.kal-di lem-né-e-ti.

302) [a]-⸢na⸣ LÚ.kal-di LÚ.KÚR ⸢lem⸣-ni pa-⸢ra⸣-si-⸢im⸣-ma ú-šar-ba-a
303) [GIŠ.TUKUL].MEŠ-ia i-[na qí]-bit EN GAL-i ^{d}AMAR.UTU ⸢ṣi⸣-in-⸢di⸣-ia
304) [uš-te]-še-ra ak-⸢ṣu⸣-[ra] uš-⸢ma⸣-ni a-na LÚ.kal-di LÚ†.KÚR
305) [ak]-⸢ṣi⸣ a-la-ku ⸢aq-bi⸣ ù šu-ú ^{md}AMAR.UTU-⸢IBILA⸣-[SUM†].NA
306) [a-lak] ger-ri-ia iš-me-ma URU.ḪAL.ṢU.MEŠ-šú ú-dan-ni-na
307) ú-paḫ-ḫi-ra ki-iṣ-⸢ri⸣-šu URU.BÀD-^{m}AD-ḫa-ra x [x x x x] x [x] SÍG-ma LÚ.gam-bu-[lu]
308) a-šib i-ti-šú qé-⸢reb⸣-[šú ú]-še-rib-ma a-na mé-⸢te⸣-[eq ger-ri†]-ia ⸢ú-dan⸣-ni-na EN.⸢NUN⸣
309) 6 ME ANŠE.⸢pét⸣-ḫal-lum 4 [LIM LÚ].ERIM.MEŠ re-ṣe-e-šu [a-li]-⸢kut⸣ pa-an um-ma-⸢ni⸣-[šú] ⸢i⸣-din-šú-[nu-ti-ma]
310) ú-⸢šar⸣-ḫi-su-nu-⸢ti⸣ [lib-bu†] BÀD-šú-nu ⸢UGU⸣ šá pa-[na] ⸢ú⸣-zaq-qí-ru-⸢ma⸣ [ul-tu] ⸢lìb?⸣-[bi?]
311) ÍD.su-⸢rap-pi⸣ bu-tuq-⸢tu⸣ [ib]-tú-qu-nim†-ma [ki-ma] ⸢ILLU⸣ kiš-šá-ti ik-pu-⸢pu⸣ [li-me-es-su] URU [šú-a-tu]
312) a-di ⸢1/2⸣ KASKAL.GÍD u_4-⸢mu⸣ la šá-⸢qé⸣-e al-me [ak†]-šud†^{tud} 18 LIM 4 [ME 30] UN.⸢MEŠ⸣ [a-di mar]-⸢ši-ti⸣-[šú-nu]
313) ⸢ANŠE⸣.[KUR].⸢RA⸣.MEŠ ⸢ANŠE⸣.KUNGA.MEŠ ANŠE.MEŠ ⸢ANŠE⸣.[A].⸢AB⸣.BA.MEŠ GU$_4$.MEŠ ù [ṣe-e-ni] áš-[lu-la]

303b–313) A[t the com]mand of the great lord, the god Marduk, [I got] my (chariot) teams ready, prep[ared] my (military) camp, (and) or[de]red the march against the Chaldean, a [danger]ous enemy. However, (when) that (man) Marduk-apla-[iddina] (II) (Merodach-Baladan) heard [of the advance] of my expeditionary force, he strengthened his fortresses (and) assembled his (military) contingents. He ...-ed the city Dūr-Abi-ḫāra [...], brought insi[de it] the Gambu[lu] (tribe) who dwell next to it, and at the appr[oach of] my [expeditionary force] strengthened (its) garrison. He gave th[em] six hundred cavalry (and) four [thousand] soldiers, his allies, [the vang]uard of [his] army, [and] (310) (thereby) [made] them confide[nt]. They raised their (city) wall higher [tha]n bef[ore, c]ut a channel [from] the Surappu River, and surrounded [its environs as if with] cresting [flo]od (waters). I surrounded (and) [con]quered [that] city before the day had proceeded half a double-hour. I carr[ied off as booty] 18,4[30] people, [together with their prop]er[ty], h[orse]s, mules, donkeys, c[am]els, oxen, and [sheep and goats].

314) ^{m}ba-[x x] IGI x [(x)] x ^{m}ḫa-⸢za⸣-DINGIR ^{m}ḫa-am-⸢da⸣-[nu ^{m}]⸢za⸣-bi-du ^{m}am-ma-i-[x x x]-⸢ia-da⸣ [x (x)]
315) ^{m}⸢ŠEŠ.MEŠ⸣-SUM.NA [^{m}]a-a-sa-am-mu 8 LÚ.⸢na⸣-[si]-ka-a-te ⸢šá⸣ [LÚ.gam-bu-li a]-⸢ši-bu⸣-[te]
316) ÍD.⸢uq⸣-né-e ⸢ka⸣-[šad] URU šú-a-tu iš-⸢mu⸣-[ma] it-ru-⸢ku lib⸣-[bu-šu-un ul]-⸢tu⸣ qé-reb ÍD.⸢uq?⸣-[né-e]
317) GU$_4$.MEŠ ù ṣe-e-⸢ni†⸣ ⸢ta⸣-mar-ta-šú-nu ⸢ka⸣-bit-tu iš-šu-⸢nim⸣-[ma] ⸢iṣ⸣-[ba-tu] GÌR.II-ia áš-šú [x x x]

314–324a) Ba[...] ..., Ḫazā-il, Hamd[anu, Z]abīdu, Ammai[(...), ...]iada[(...)], Aḫ[ḫ]ē-iddina, (and) Aya-Sammu, (a total of) eight sh[ei]khs of [the Gambulu (tribe) who dw]el[l] (along) the Uqnû River, hea[rd] of the con[quest] of that city [and (as a result) their] hea[rts] pounded. [Fro]m the U[qnû] River, they brought m[e] oxen, and sheep and goats as their substantial audience gift(s) [and] gr[asped hold of] my feet. Because [...] that land, I disregarded [their] crime(s) and stopped their deportation. I set a eunuch of mine as [provincial governor] over [th]em. (320) I imposed upon them the annual payment of one talent thirty

302 [a]-⸢na⸣ LÚ.kal-di: H. Winckler's copy has [a-na] GÌR.II LÚ.kal-di, but the GÌR.II is not on the squeeze, nor is there room to restore it at the beginning of the line (i.e., [a-na GÌR].⸢II⸣ is not possible). It is interesting that the two LÚ signs in the line are written differently, although separated by only two other signs. The first is the normal Neo-Assyrian LÚ, while the second is the abbreviated form that Borger, MZL p. 357 designates LÚ^{v} or LÚ*. In line 304, the LÚ sign has the Neo-Babylonian form. Both P.E. Botta's and Winckler's copies have -A' rather than -⸢im⸣- in parāsimma.

305 P.E. Botta's copy has -IBILA*(copy: RA-x)-<SUM>.NA (with possibly the SUM being merged into the end of the previous sign) and H. Winckler's -IBILA-SUM.NA; the squeeze has -⸢IBILA⸣-[x x].

Section 19 = lines 307–323 = V,10:17. See Winckler, Sar. Annals lines 247–263; Lie, Sar. lines 274b–280+; and Fuchs, Khorsabad Annals lines 266, 266a–b, 267–271, 271a, 272, 271a–e, and 271–280. Cf. text no. 1 lines 274b–280+ and text no. 3 lines 31′–41′a.

309 ⸢pét⸣: Both P.E. Botta's and H. Winckler's copies omit the pét, but there are very faint traces of the sign on the squeeze and certainly room for it, against the two copies.

310 ⸢lìb?⸣-[bi?]: P.E. Botta's copy and the squeeze have a trace that might fit this reading; however, H. Winckler's copy has ⸢lìb⸣-ba [x x] for the end of the line. Text no. 1 line 278 has lìb-bi, while text no. 3 line 32′ has ⸢qé⸣-[reb].

311 nim†: The squeeze appears to confirm the abnormal form of the sign copied by P.E. Botta, against the normal form on H. Winckler's copy. [ki-ma] ⸢ILLU⸣: Botta's and Winckler's copies have <ki-ma> ⸢ILLU⸣ and <ki-ma> ILLU respectively, but the squeeze shows a damaged area sufficiently large to restore ki-ma.

312 a-di ⸢1/2⸣ KASKAL.GÍD u_4-⸢mu⸣ la šá-⸢qé⸣-e "before the day had proceeded half a double-hour": I.e., within an hour of sunrise.

314 -i-[...]: Or -⸢ia⸣-[...], -⸢ad⸣-[...], or -⸢ṣi⸣-[...]. For a possible reading at the end of the line, A. Fuchs (Khorsabad p. 141 line 272a n. 2) notes ^{m}sam-si-ia-da-'i in text no. 1 line 299.

318) KUR *šu-a-tu* ⸢*gíl-la*⸣-[*sún*] ⸢*a*⸣-*miš-ma ú-šab-ṭi-la na-sa-*⸢*aḫ-šú-un*⸣ LÚ.⸢*šu*⸣-*ut* ⸢SAG⸣-*ia* ⸢LÚ⸣.[EN.NAM]
319) UGU-[*šú*†]-*nu áš-*⸢*kun*⸣ 1† ⸢GUN⸣ 30 MA.NA KÙ.BABBAR 2 LIM ŠE.BAR *ina* ⸢UGU⸣ 20 GU$_4$.MEŠ 1-*en* GU$_4$ *ina* UGU [20 UDU.MEŠ]
320) 1-⸢*en*⸣ [UDU] ⸢*na*⸣-*dan* MU.AN.NA UGU-*šú-nu uk-tin ṣi-bit* GU$_4$.MEŠ-*šú-nu ṣe-e-*⸢*ni*⸣-*šú-nu a-na* [^{d}EN]
321) ^{d}[DUMU] ⸢EN *ú*⸣-*ki-in šat-ti-šam* LÚ.⸢ERIM⸣.MEŠ *šá-tu-nu a-šur-ma i-na* UGU ⸢3⸣ [LÚ.ERIM.MEŠ]
322) 1-*en* LÚ.⸢ERIM⸣-[*šú*]-*nu aṣ-bat* URU.BÀD-^{m}AD-*ḫa-ra a-na eš-šu-ti ú-*⸢*še*⸣-*šib* [MU-*šú ú-nak-kir*]
323) URU.BÀD-⸢^{d}⸣[AG†] ⸢MU⸣-*šú* [*am*]-⸢*bi*⸣ KUR.*ḫu*-[*ba*]-*qa-nu* KUR.*tar-*⸢*bu*⸣-[*ga*]-⸢*ti*⸣ KUR.*ti-mas-su-nu* [*x x x* (*x x*)]
324) [KUR†.*pa*?]-⸢*šur*†⸣ [KUR†].*ḫi-ru-tú* KUR.*ḫi-il-mu* 6† *na-ge-e* [*ša* KUR†].*gam-bu-li a-di* 44 URU.MEŠ *dan-nu-ti ša qer-bi-šú-un a-na ku-dúr-ri* KUR *aš-šur*.KI *a-bu-uk* LÚ.*ru-u*$_8$-⸢*a*⸣
325) LÚ.*ḫi-in-da-ru* LÚ.*ia-ad-bu-ru* ⸢LÚ⸣.[*pu*]-*qu-du ki-šit-ti* LÚ.*gam-bu-li iš-mu-ma i-na šat mu-ši ip-par-šu-*⸢*ma*⸣ ÍD.*uq-nu-ú mar-ṣu iṣ-ba-tú*
326) ÍD.*tup-li-áš* ÍD *tuk-la-ti-šu-nu* ⸢*i*⸣-[*na*] ⸢*ši*⸣-*pik* SAḪAR.MEŠ *ù* GI.MEŠ *ak-si-ir* 2 URU.ḪAL.ṢU.MEŠ *a-ḫu a-na a-*⸢*ḫi*⸣ *ad-di-ma lap-lap-tu*
327) *ú-šá-aṣ-bi-su-nu-ti-ma ul-tu qé-*[*reb*] ⸢ÍD⸣.*uq-né-e* ⸢*uṣ*⸣-*ṣu-*⸢*nim*⸣-*ma* ⸢*iṣ*⸣-*ba-tú* GÌR.II-*ia* ^{m}*ia-nu-qu* LÚ.⸢*na*⸣-*sik-ku ša* URU.*za-a-me-e*
328) ^{md}MUATI-*ú-ṣal-la ša* URU.*a-bu-re-*⸢*e*⸣ ^{m}*pa-áš-šu-nu* ^{m}*ḫa-ú-ka-nu ša* URU.*nu-ḫa-a-ni* ^{m}⸢*sa*⸣-*ʾi-lu ša* URU.*i-bu-li* 5 LÚ.*na-si-ka-a-ti*
329) *ša* LÚ.*pu-qu-di* ^{m}*ab-ḫa-ta-a ša* LÚ.*ru-u*$_8$-*a* ^{m}*ḫu-*⸢*ni*⸣-*nu* ^{m}*sa-me-*⸢*eʾ*⸣ ^{m}⸢*sab*⸣-*ḫar-ru* ^{m}*ra-pi-iʾ ša* LÚ.*ḫi-in-da-ri* ANŠE.KUR.RA.MEŠ GU$_4$.MEŠ *ù ṣe-e-ni*
330) *ta-mar-ta-šú-nu ka-bit-tu a-na* URU.BÀD-^{m}AD-*ḫa-ra iš-šu-nim-ma ú-na-áš-ši-qu* GÌR.II-*ia li-ṭi-šú-nu aṣ*†-*bat il-ku tup-šik-ku ki-i ša* LÚ.*gam-bu-li*
331) *e-mid-su-nu-ti i-na* ŠU.II LÚ.*šu-ut* SAG-*ia* LÚ.GAR.KUR KUR.*gam-bu-li am-nu-šú-nu-ti si-it-*⸢*ta*⸣-*te-šú-nu ša* UGU ^{md}AMAR.UTU-A-⸢SUM⸣.NA ⸢*ù*⸣

minas of silver, two thousand <*gur*> of barley, one ox out of (every) twenty oxen (that they had), (and) one [sheep] out of (every) [twenty sheep (that they had)]. I (also) imposed the annual *ṣibtu*-tax on their oxen (and on) their sheep and goats for the god[s Bēl (Marduk) (and) Son of B]ēl (Nabû). I mustered those soldiers and took one sol[dier of theirs] out of (every) three [soldiers (for my own army)]. I resettled (them) in the city Dūr-Abi-ḫāra, [changed its (the city's) name, (and) (re)na]med it Dūr-[Nabû]. I incorporated (lit.: "led away") into the territory of Assyria the lands Ḫu[ba]qānu, Tarb[ugāt]i, Timassunu, [(...), *Pa*]*šur*, Ḫirūtu, (and) Ḫilmu, (a total of) six districts [of the land] Gambulu, together with forty-four fortified settlements that are in them.

324b–331a) (When) the Ruʾuʾa, Ḫindaru, Yadburu, (and) [Pu]qudu (tribes) heard of (my) conquest of the Gambulu (tribe), they fled during the course of the night [a]nd took (themselves to) the Uqnû River, which was difficult (to ford). I dammed up the Ṭupliyaš River, a river upon which they relied, wi[th p]ile(s) of dirt and reeds. I erected two forts, side by side, and starved them out. They then came out from the Uqnû [Ri]ver and grasped hold of my feet. Iannuqu, the [s]heikh of the city Zāmê, Nabû-uṣalla of the city Abūrê, Paššunu (and) Ḫaukānu of the city Nuḫānu, (and) Saʾīlu of the city Ibūli, (a total of) five sheikhs of the Puqudu (tribe); Abi-ḫatâ of the Ruʾuʾa (tribe); (and) Ḫunīnu, Sāmeʾ, S[a]bḫarru, (and) Rāpiʾ of the Ḫindaru (tribe) brought horses, oxen, and sheep and goats (330) as their substantial audience gift(s) to the city Dūr-Abi-ḫāra and kissed my feet. I took hostages from them (and) imposed upon them (the same state) service (and) corvée duty as (was imposed upon) the Gambulu (tribe). I assigned them to the authority of a eunuch of mine, the governor of the Gambulu (tribe).

331b–334a) (As for) the rest of those who had paid attention (lit.: "inclined their cheek") to Marduk-apla-iddina (II) (Merodach-Baladan) and Šutur-Naḫūndi and taken (themselves) to the Uqnû River, I overwhelmed

318 -⸢*šú*⸣-: So squeeze; both P.E. Botta's and H. Winckler's copies have -<*šú*>-.
322 For the restoration at the end of the line, see text no. 3 line 40′; H. Winckler's copy has *ú-še-šib-*[*šú-nu-ti*].
323 [*am*]-⸢*bi*⸣: For the restoration, see text no. 3 line 40′; H. Winckler's copy has [*aq*]-*bi*. There is room at the end of the line to restore the name of a city; however, since the following line refers to a total of six places, we do not expect the name of another place.
Section 20 = lines 324–340 = V,O$_1$:1–17. See Winckler, Sar. Annals lines 264–280; Lie, Sar. pp. 48–49 lines 1–6 and n. 5, pp. 50–51 lines 10–14, and pp. 52–53 lines 15–17; and Fuchs, Khorsabad Annals lines 281–297. Cf. text no. 1 lines +317–351 and text no. 3 lines 41′b–60′.
324 [KUR†.*pa*?]-⸢*šur*†⸣ [KUR†].*ḫi*-: P.E. Botta's copy has [*x*]-⸢*šur**⸣(copy: ⸢PAD⸣) [*x*] *ḫi*- and H. Winckler's ⸢KUR.*šur**(copy: ⸢PAD⸣) KUR⸣.*ḫi*-, while the squeeze currently has [*x x x* (*x*)] *ḫi*-. The restoration is based on text no. 3 line 41′.
326 *lap-lap-tu*: Or *kal-lap-tu*; see text no. 1 line 320.
330 *aṣ*†: The squeeze appears to support P.E. Botta's copy (as opposed to H. Winckler's copy) in having an extraneous vertical wedge after the ZA in the middle of sign, but what appears to be an extra wedge on the squeeze may conceivably instead indicate damage on the original or a flaw in making the squeeze.

^{m}šu-túr-^{d}na-ḫu-un-di

332) TE-su-nu id-du-ma iṣ-ba-⸢tu ÍD⸣.uq-nu-ú da-ád-mi-šu-nu a-bu-biš as-pu-un qí-⸢ra⸣-a-ti-šú-nu um-ma-ni ú-šá-kil GIŠ.GIŠIMMAR tuk-lat-su-nu GIŠ.KIRI$_6$.MEŠ

333) bal-ti na-gi-šú-nu ak-šiṭ ⸢a⸣-[na†] ⸢ÍD.uq⸣-né-e a-šar tap-ze-er-ti-šú-nu LÚ.qu-ra-di-ia ú-ma-ʾe-er-ma BAD$_5$.BAD$_5$-šú-nu im-ḫa-ṣu UN.MEŠ a-di mar-ši-⸢te?⸣-šú-nu

334) iš-lul-ú-ni URU.za-a-me-[e URU].a-bu-⸢re⸣-e URU.ia-ap-ti-ru ⸢URU⸣.ma-ḫi-ṣu URU.ḫi-li-pa-nu URU.KAL-KAL URU.pat-ti-a-nu URU.ḫa-a-a-ma-nu

335) URU.ga-di-ia-ti URU.[a†-ma-te] ⸢URU⸣.nu-ḫa-a-nu URU.a-ma-a URU.ḫi-ú-ru URU.sa-ʾi-lu 14 URU.MEŠ-ni dan-nu-ti a-di URU.MEŠ-ni ša li-me-ti-šú-nu

336) ša šid-di ÍD.uq-⸢né⸣-[e†] ša ti-bu-ut GIŠ.TUKUL.MEŠ-ia ⸢dan⸣-nu-ti e-du-ru-ma ú-šaḫ-ri-bu na-gu-šú-un TA qé-reb ÍD.uq-ni-i

337) ⸢a⸣-šar ru-qi il-⸢li⸣-ku-nim-⸢ma⸣ [iṣ†-ba†-tú†] ⸢GÌR⸣.II-ia na-gu-ú šu-a-tu UGU šá maḫ-ri par-ga-niš ú-šár-bi-iṣ-ma i-na ŠU.II LÚ.šu-ut SAG-ia LÚ.GAR.KUR

338) [LÚ].gam-bu-li am-nu URU.sa-am-[ʾu]-na URU.KÁ-⸢BÀD⸣ URU.ḪAL.ṢU.MEŠ ša ^{m}šu-túr-^{d}na-ḫu-un-di LÚ.ELAM.MA.KI UGU KUR.ia-ad-bu-ri ⸢ir⸣-ku-su

339) [ki-ma] ⸢ti⸣-ib me-ḫe-⸢e⸣ as-⸢ḫup⸣-ma ^{m}⸢sa⸣-[x]-nu ^{m}si-in-gam-ši-bu LÚ.GAL URU.ḪAL.ṢU.MEŠ a-di 7 LIM 5 ME 20 LÚ.⸢ELAM⸣.MA.KI-a-a ša it-ti-šú-un ù 12 LIM 62 UN.MEŠ

340) ⸢LÚ?.gu⸣-ru-mu GIŠ.ṣu-⸢um-bi ANŠE⸣.KUR.⸢RA⸣.MEŠ ⸢ANŠE⸣.KUNGA.MEŠ ANŠE.MEŠ ANŠE.A.AB.BA.MEŠ a-di NÍG.ŠU-šú-nu ma-aʾ-[di] áš-lu-la URU.sa-am-ʾu-na a-na eš-šu-ti aṣ-bat

341) MU-šá ú-nak-kir-ma URU.⸢^{d}⸣EN.LÍL-⸢BA⸣-šá az-ku-⸢ra⸣ ni-bit-sa ⸢^{m}⸣mu†-še-zi-bu ^{m}na-at-nu ^{m}a-a-lu-nu ^{m}da-iṣ-ṣa-nu šá KUR.la-ḫi-ri ^{m}a-a-ri-im-mu

342) ^{m}EN-URU ša URU.su-la-⸢ia⸣ 6 LÚ.[na†]-si-ka-a-te

their settlements like the Deluge. I (then) fed my army (the food in) their granaries (and) chopped down the date palm(s) upon which they relied (and) the orchards that were were the pride of their district. I sent my warriors t[o] the Uqnû [Ri]ver, their hiding place, and they (my warriors) inflicted a defeat on them. They (my warriors) carried off as booty (those) people, together with their property.

334b–338a) (The people of) the cities Zāmê, Abūrê, Yaptiru, Maḫīṣu, Ḫilipanu, KAL-KAL, Pattiānu, Ḫayamānu, (335) Gadiyāti, [Amate], Nuḫānu, Amâ, Ḫiuru, (and) Saʾīlu, (a total of) fourteen fortified cities, together with the settlements in their environs, (located) along the Uqnû River, who(se people) had taken fright at the onslaught of my mighty weapons and whose district I had laid waste, came to me from the Uqnû River, a faraway place, an[d grasped hold of] my [fe]et. I had that district dwell as in meadowland (in greater safety) than previously and assigned (them) to the authority of a eunuch of mine, the governor of the Gambulu (tribe).

338b–344) [Like the on]slaught of a storm, I overwhelmed the cities Sam[ʾū]na (and) Bāb-dūri, fortresses that Šutur-Naḫūndi, the Elamite, had constructed *facing* (lit.: "above") the land Yadburu, and I carried off as booty Sa...nu (and) Singamšibu, the fortress commanders, together with 7,520 Elamites who were with them and 12,062 people (340) of the [G]urumu (tribe), wago[ns, h]orses, mules, donkeys, (and) camels, together with their abund[ant] property. I reorganized (the administration of) the city Samʾūna, changed its name, and gave it the name Enlil-iqīša. Mušēzibu, Natnu, Aya-lūnu, (and) Daiṣṣānu of the land Laḫīru, (and) Aya-rimmu (and) Bēl-āli of the city Sulāya — (a total of) six [sh]eikhs of the land Yadburu — brought horses, mules, oxen, and sheep and goats into my (military) camp and grasped hold of my feet in order to do obeissance (to me). I considered the city Laḫīru of the land Yadibiri (Yadburu), the cities Sulā[ya], *G*[*ur*]muk, Samʾūna, (and) Bāb-dūri, fortified cities of the land

333 -⸢te?⸣-: P.E. Botta's copy has a partially damaged form that might represent either *ti*, *te*, or *tim* (or various other signs), while H. Winckler's copy has TI; the proposed reading is based on the squeeze, which indicates there is not sufficient space for TI or TIM.
334 URU.KAL-KAL: The reading of the name is not certain, but most likely URU.*dan-dan* or URU.*kal-kal*; see Zadok, WO 16 (1985) p. 76 no. 81.
335 Text no. 3 line 56′ has ⸢2?⸣+[2? ME† URU.MEŠ-*ni*], "(and) *fo*[*ur hundred* settlements]," instead of *a-di* URU.MEŠ-*ni*, "together with the settlements."
338 [LÚ].*gam*-: H. Winckler's copy has [*ša* KUR].*gam*-, but see text no. 3 line 59′.
339 ^{m}⸢*sa*⸣-[*x*]-*nu*: So P.E. Botta's copy. H. Winckler's copy has ^{m}*sa-ni-nu*, with a note indicating that the NI might instead be DU. No trace of the sign is currently legible on the squeeze.
340 ANŠE.A.AB.BA.MEŠ: H. Winckler's copy omits the ANŠE, which is present on both P.E. Botta's copy and the squeeze.
Section 21 = lines 341–357 = O$_2$:1–17. See Winckler, Sar. Annals lines 281–299; Lie, Sar. pp. 52–55 lines 1–9, pp. 54–55 nn. 3–6, 9, and 11–12, and p. 56 nn. 3–5 and 7; and Fuchs, Khorsabad Annals lines 298–314. Cf. text no. 1 lines 352–376a.
341 ^{m}*da-iṣ-ṣa-nu*: see Dalley and Postgate, CTN 3 p. 36 and Dezsö, SAAB 15 (2006) p. 110.
342 ^{m}EN-URU "Bēl-āli": As noted by A. Fuchs (PNA 1/2 p. 285), this may be a title ("city lord") which has been mistakenly taken for a personal name. *a†-na†*: P.E. Botta's copy has *a**(copy: DIŠ-ŠÚ)-*na**(copy: BAD) and H. Winckler's has *a†-na**(copy: BAD), where the A has a small

ša KUR.ia-ad-bu-ri ANŠE.KUR.RA.MEŠ
ANŠE.⸢KUNGA⸣.MEŠ GU$_4$.MEŠ ù ṣe-e-ni a†-na†
qé-reb uš-man-ni-ia iš-šu-nim-ma
343) a-na e-⸢peš⸣ ar-du-⸢ti⸣ iṣ-ba-⸢tu⸣ GÌR.⸢II⸣-ia
URU.la-ḫi-ra ša KUR.ia-a-di-bi-ri URU.su-la-[ia†]
URU.⸢gur$^{?}$⸣-muk URU.sa-am-ʾu-ú-na URU.KÁ-BÀD
URU.MEŠ KAL.MEŠ
344) ša KUR.ia-⸢ad⸣-bu-ri ⸢URU⸣.a-ḫi-li-im-⸢mu⸣
URU.pi-il-lu-tú ša mi-ṣir KUR.e-lam-ti a-di
URU.MEŠ-ni šá ⸢li⸣-[me†]-ti-šú-nu šá šid-di
ÍD.na-ṭi-ti a-na mi-⸢ṣir⸣-[ia] am-nu

Yadburu, the cities Aḫilimmu (Ḫilimmu) (and) Pillatu that are on the border of the land Elam, together with the settlements in their env[ir]ons that are (located) along the Naṭītu River, as (part) of [my] territory.

345) URU.DU$_6$-^{d}⸢ḫum⸣-ba ⸢URU.dun†⸣-ni-^{d}UTU
URU.bu-bé-e URU.ḫa-ma-nu ma-ḫa-zi dan-nu-ti
ša KUR.ra-a-ši ⸢ZI MÈ⸣-ia dan-ni e-du-ru-ma
a-na URU.É-^{m}im-bi-i
346) e-ru-bu ù šu-ú ^{m}⸢šu⸣-[túr]-^{d}na-ḫu-⸢un⸣-di
ma-⸢lik⸣-šú-⸢un$^{?†}$⸣ ul-tu pa-an GIŠ.TUKUL.MEŠ-ia
a-na šu-⸢zu$^{?}$-ub⸣ ZI.MEŠ-šú-nu a-na qé-reb
KUR.MEŠ-e ru-qu-ti

345–347a) (The people of) the cities Tīl-Ḫu[m]ba, D[un]ni-Šamaš, Bubê, (and) Ḫamānu, fortified cult centers of the land Rāši, took fright at my mighty battle attack and (thus) entered the city Bīt-Imbî. Moreover, that (man), Šu[tur]-Naḫūndi, the[ir] ruler, sought refuge in far-off mountains, away from my weapons, in order to save his life (lit.: "their lives").

347) šá-ḫa-tu e-mid i-na ⸢tukul†⸣-[ti] ⸢^{d}⸣aš-šur ^{d}⸢AG⸣ u
^{d}AMAR.UTU i-⸢na⸣ gi-piš um-ma-na-te-ia
⸢ÍD⸣.pu-rat-tu e-bir-ma a-na
URU.BÀD-^{m}la-din-na šá qé-reb
KUR.É-^{m}dak-ku-⸢ri⸣
348) áš-ta-kan pa-ni-ia URU.[BÀD-^{m†}]⸢la⸣-din-ni
na-⸢da⸣-a a-na eš-šu-ti ú-še-piš
LÚ.mun-daḫ-ṣe-⸢ia⸣ le-ʾu-ut ta-ḫa-zi ú-še-ri-ba
qé-reb-šú li-ta-at ^{d}aš-⸢šur⸣

347b–349a) With the suppo[rt] of the gods Aššur, Nabû, and Marduk, I crossed the Euphrates River with the main force of my army and set out for the city Dūr-Ladinni, which is in the land Bīt-Dakkūri. I had the abandoned city [Dūr-L]adinni rebuilt (and) stationed there fighting men of [mi]ne who were skilled in battle.

349) ^{d}AG u ^{d}AMAR.UTU ša UGU URU.MEŠ-ni
šá-tu-⸢nu⸣ áš-tak-ka-nu
^{md}AMAR.UTU-IBILA-⸢SUM⸣.NA ⸢MAN⸣
KUR.kár-^{d}du-ni-áš ina qé-reb KÁ.DINGIR.RA.KI
iš-me-ma ina MURUB$_4$-ti É.GAL-[šú]
350) ḫat-ti rama-ni-šu im-⸢qut⸣-su-ma šu-ú a-di
re-ṣe-⸢e⸣-šú ERIM.MEŠ ⸢MÈ⸣-šú mu-šiš uṣ-⸢ṣi⸣-ma
a-na KUR.ia-ad-⸢bu⸣-ri ša KUR.ELAM.MA.KI
iš-ku-na pa-ni-[šú]
351) GIŠ.⸢NÁ⸣ KÙ.BABBAR GIŠ.GU.ZA KÙ.BABBAR
GIŠ.né-med ⸢KÙ⸣.BABBAR GIŠ.⸢BANŠUR⸣
KÙ.BABBAR ⸢nàr-ma-ak⸣-tú KÙ.BABBAR ú-nu-ut
LUGAL-ti-⸢šú⸣ ti-iq-ni GÚ†-šú ša$^{?}$ tur-⸢ri⸣
gi-⸢mil⸣-li-šú a-na ^{m}šu-túr-na-ḫu-un-di
LÚ.ELAM.MA.KI-[i]

349b–352a) In Babylon, Marduk-apla-iddina (II) (Merodach-Baladan), king of the land Karduniaš (Babylonia), heard of the victories of the gods Ašš[ur], Nabû, and Marduk that I had repeatedly established over those cities. As a result, in the midst of [his (own)] palace (350) his own fear(s) fell upon him; he then went out (from Babylon) during the night together with his allies (and) his battle troops and set out for the land Yadburu, which is (part) of the land Elam. He gave to Šutur-Naḫūndi, the Elamite, a silver bed, a silver throne, a silver chair, a silver table, a silver wash-basin, his royal utensils, (and) his neck ornament as g[if]ts from him in order to get his revenge (on me).

352) id-⸢di-na kàd⸣-ra-a-šú ṣe-nu ⸢e⸣-la-mu-ú

352b–354a) (That) Elamite villain accepted his bribe

Winkelhaken after the first vertical wedge. The squeeze may suggest that NA was initially omitted by the stone carver and had to be added later; the trace inside the A would be the beginning of the NA and the small traces between the A and QÉ the remainder of the NA sign.

343 ⸢*gur*$^{?}$⸣- According to the squeeze, the sign is essentially as copied by H. Winckler but with slightly more damage, thus allowing for a possible GUR.

346 -⸢*un*$^{?†}$⸣: P.E. Botta's copy has BI [...], while H. Winckler's has -⸢*nu*⸣; the squeeze is not currently legible at this point. -⸢*zu*$^{?}$-*ub*⸣: Botta's copy has -BA-⸢*ub**⸣(copy: ⸢GIŠ⸣-PAP) and Winckler's -BA-*ub*. The squeeze is not clear but might allow -⸢*zu*$^{?}$-*ub*⸣, although the reading BA for the first sign cannot be excluded.

347 *tukul*: P.E. Botta's copy has *tukul**(copy: LU), while H. Winckler's has *tukul*; the squeeze is not clear, but may support Botta's copy rather than Winckler's. *u*: Winckler's copy omits this sign, but it is clear on the squeeze and Botta's copy.

349 -[*šú*]: Or -[(*x*)].

351 GIŠ.*né-med* ⸢KÙ⸣.BABBAR: So P.E. Botta's copy and squeeze; H. Winckler's copy has GIŠ.*né-med* KÙ*(copy: KUR).BABBAR, which is corrected on pl. 49 to GIŠ.*né-med-du* KÙ.BABBAR. *ša*$^{?}$: Botta's copy has MA-ŠÚ, while Winckler's copy has *a-na*; the squeeze is damaged at this point. LÚ.ELAM.MA.KI-[*i*]: Winckler's copy ends with a LÚ.ELAM.MA.KI.

ṭa-a'-tuš im-ḫur-šu-ma e-du-ra
GIŠ.TUKUL.MEŠ-ia [ip-sil ur]-ḫa-šu-ma ⸢la⸣
[a†]-⸢la-ka⸣ iq-bi-šú a-mat EN gi-mil-li-[šú]
353) iš-me-ma [qaq-qa-riš] ip-pal-si-⸢iḫ⸣
na-⸢aḫ-lap⸣-tuš ⸢iš⸣-ru-ṭa nag-la-ba iš-ši-ma
ú-šá-aṣ-ri†-ḫa ⸢bi?⸣-ki-tu šu-⸢ú⸣ a-di re-ṣi-šú
ERIM.MEŠ MÈ-[šú]

from him, but took fright at my weapons. [He turned aw]ay and told him (Marduk-apla-iddina) [that he would n]ot [co]me (to help him). (When) he (Marduk-apla-iddina) heard the words of (the one who was to be) [his] avenger, he threw himself [on the ground], ripped his cl[o]ak, wielded (his) razor, and uttered cries of mourning. Together with his allies (and) [his] battle troops, that (man) moved away from [the land Ya]dburu, entered into the city Iqbi-Bēl, and stay[ed] (there) in fear.

354) TA ⸢qé⸣-[reb KUR.ia]-⸢ad⸣-bu-ri
⸢is⸣-su-ḫa-[am†]-⸢ma a⸣-na URU.iq-bi-^{d}EN
e-ru-um-ma a-di-⸢riš⸣ ú-⸢šib DUMU⸣.MEŠ
⸢KÁ†⸣.DINGIR.RA.KI bár-sípa.KI LÚ.KU$_{4}$.MEŠ É
LÚ.um-ma-[ni]
355) mu-⸢de⸣-[e† šip†-ri† a†-li†]-⸢kut⸣ pa-ni
mu-'e-⸢ru†-ut⸣ KUR ša ⸢i-dag†⸣-ga-lu pa-nu-uš-šú
re-ḫat ^{d†}⸢EN†⸣ ^{d}[zar†]-pa-⸢ni†⸣-tum ^{d}AG
^{d}taš-me-tum a-na URU.BÀD-^{m}la-din-⸢na?⸣
356) a-di [maḫ†-ri†-ia† ub†-lu†-nim†-ma†] ⸢e-re⸣-eb
⸢KÁ⸣.[DINGIR†].⸢RA⸣.KI ⸢iq-bu†-nim⸣-ma
ú-šá-li-⸢ṣu⸣ kab-⸢ta-ti⸣ [a†-na†
KÁ†].⸢DINGIR⸣.RA.⸢KI⸣ URU ^{d}EN.LÍL.LÁ
DINGIR.MEŠ ḫa-diš e-ru-um†-[ma†]
357) a-[na DINGIR.MEŠ a-ši-bu-ut é]-sag-⸢íl é⸣-zi†-⸢da⸣
[am]-⸢ḫu⸣-[ur ŠÀ].⸢GI.GURU$_{6}$⸣-e KÙ†.MEŠ
ma-[ḫar†-šú†]-un aq-qí i-na qé-⸢reb⸣ É.GAL-[šú†]
⸢mu⸣-šab LUGAL-ti-[šú]
358) [x x x x x x x x x x (x x)] x-a-ti LÚ.a-ra-me
[KUR.É-^{m}a]-muk-ka-a-ni ⸢KUR⸣.[É-^{m}]⸢dak⸣-ku-ri

354b–356a) The citizens of Babylon (and) Borsippa, the temple personnel, the crafts[men] (355) who know [(their) trade, the lead]ers, (and) administrators of the land, who (up till then) had been his [su]bjects, [brought] be[fore me] in the city Dūr-Ladinni the leftovers of (the sacrifices to) the deities Bē[l, Zar]panītu, Nabû, (and) Tašmētu, [and i]nvit[ed (lit.: "[sa]id [to]") m]e to enter Ba[bylo]n, (thus) making [my] heart rejoice.

356b–359a) Happily, I entered [Baby]lon, the city of the Enlil of the gods (Marduk). Then, [I pra]y[ed] t[o the gods who dwelt in E]sagil (and) Ezida, (and) offered pure [vo]luntary offerings bef[ore th]em. Inside [his] palace, [his] royal residence, [...] I received substantial [... *from* ...] ... Arameans, [the land Bīt-A]mukāni, the lan[d Bīt-D]akkūri, [...].

359) [x x x x x x x x x x (x x)] ⸢ka⸣-bit-⸢tu⸣ am-ḫur
na-[ar bár†-sipa†].KI maḫ-ru-⸢ú⸣ [ša
LUGAL].MEŠ-⸢ni⸣

359b–360a) (With regard to) the former [Borsippa] can[al, which king]s [who preceded me had constructed, I d]ug [a new canal int]o Šuan[na (Babylon)] for [the process]sion of the god Nabû, [my lord].

360) [a-li-kut pa-ni-ia e-pu-šu-ma ÍD eš-šú] a-na
[maš†-da]-aḫ ⸢^{d}⸣AG [EN-ia a†-na† qé†]-reb
šu-an-[na†.KI† aḫ]-re-⸢e†⸣-[ma†]
361) [LÚ.ḫa-mar-a-na-a-a ša la-pa-an
GIŠ.TUKUL.MEŠ-ia ip-par-ši]-du ⸢a⸣-[na†]
⸢ZIMBIR⸣.[KI e-ru]-bu-[ma] ⸢a⸣-lak KASKAL
DUMU [KÁ†.DINGIR†.RA.KI]

360b–363a) [I then sent eunuchs of mine], provincial governors, against [the Ḫamarānu (tribe), who had fle]d [from my weapons, ente]red Sippar, [and were constantly, repeatedly robbing] caravan(s) of the citizen(s) [of Ba]b[ylon] while they were en route. They [then] surrounded th[e]m [so that (no one), neither young (nor) old, could escape, (and) struck (them)

---

353 ⸢*bi*?⸣-: The squeeze is not clear, but might allow this reading; P.E. Botta's and H. Winckler's copies have PA-.

355 H. Winckler's copy has *mu-de-e šip-ri a-li-kut*, but the squeeze currently has only ⸢*mu-de*⸣-[*x x x x* (*x*)] *x*. ⸢*dag*†⸣: P.E. Botta's copy has [*x*] A and Winckler's [*da*]-*a*; the squeeze is not clear, but could fit ⸢*dag*⸣-.

356 H. Winckler's copy has the whole line completely preserved, but very little of it is currently visible on the squeeze, including nothing before ⸢*e*⸣-.

357 The squeeze is not preserved for the beginning of the line. H. Winckler's copy has *a*-[*na* DINGIR.MEŠ *x x x x*]-*sag*-[*x*] GIŠ IB [*x x* (*x*)] ⸢*é*⸣-RI?-*da*?. For the restorations, cf. F.W. Geers, apud Olmstead, AJSL 47 (1930–31) p. 273. [ŠÀ].⸢GI.GURU$_{6}$⸣-*e* KÙ†.MEŠ *ma*-[*ḫar*†-*šú*†]-*un aq-qí*: Cf. text no. 8 lines 58–59.

Section 22 = lines 358–374 = V,9:1–17. See Winckler, Sar. Annals lines 299–319; Lie, Sar. lines 376b–404a and pp. 58–59 lines 13–17; and Fuchs, Khorsabad Annals lines 315–331. Cf. text no. 1 lines 376b–404a and text no. 5 lines 1′–3′.

358 *x-a-ti*: H. Winckler's copy has *-ra-a-ti*, but the traces currently visible on the squeeze are not clear for this reading. A.T.E. Olmstead (AJSL 47 [1930–31] p. 273 sub line 376) has [*bi*]-*ra-a-ti*.

359 *na*-[*ar bár*†-*sipa*†].KI: The reading is based on P.E. Botta's copy and the squeeze; H. Winckler's copy has *na*-[*a-ar*] ⸢*bár*⸣-*sipa*.KI.

360 H. Winckler's copy has *a-na qé-reb* ŠU.AN.NA.KI [*aḫ*]-*re-e-ma* for the end of the line, but this cannot be confirmed from the sqeeze today.

361 DUMU [KÁ†.DINGIR†.RA.KI]: H. Winckler's copy has DUMU.⸢MEŠ⸣ KÁ.DINGIR.[RA.KI]; the squeeze and P.E. Botta's copy have DUMU† [*x x x*] *x* [*x* (*x*)] and DUMU [*x x x*] *x* [*x* (*x*)] respectively, where the *x* could be part of DINGIR or RA, with the signs spread out.

362) [*iḫ-ta-nab-ba-tu ka-a-a-nu* LÚ.*šu-ut* SAG.MEŠ-*ia* LÚ].EN.NAM.MEŠ UGU-*šú-nu* [*áš*†*-pur-ma ni-i*†]-⸢*ta*⸣ *il-mu-šú-*[*nu*]*-ti-*[*ma ṣe*$^{?}$*-ḫer*$^{?}$]

363) [*ra-bi la ip-par-ši-du i-na-ru i-na kak*]-⸢*ki*⸣ *ik-šu-dam-ma* [ITI†.BÁRA *a-ra-aḫ a*]-⸢*ṣe-e*⸣ EN DINGIR.MEŠ ŠU†.II† [^{d}EN GAL-*i*]

364) [^{d}AMAR.UTU ^{d}AG LUGAL *kiš-šat* AN-*e* KI-*tim*] ⸢*aṣ*⸣-[*bat*†]*-ma* ⸢*ú*⸣-[*šal-li-ma ú-ru-uḫ* É] ⸢*á*⸣-[*ki*†]*-ti* ⸢1⸣ [ME 54 GUN 26 MA.NA 10 GÍN KÙ.GI *ḫuš-šu-ú*]

365) [1 LIM 6 ME 4 GUN] 20 [MA.NA KÙ.BABBAR *eb*]*-bu* ⸢NA$_4$⸣.[ZÚ *x x* NA$_4$].ZA.⸢GÌN⸣ [NA$_4$.BABBAR.DILI NA$_4$.AŠ.GÌ.GÌ] ⸢NA$_4$⸣.UGU.[AŠ.GÌ.GÌ *di-gi-li* NA$_4$.BABBAR.DILI NA$_4$.MUŠ.GÍR]

366) [*a-na mu*]-⸢*ʾu*⸣*-de-e* [SÍG.*ta-kil*]-⸢*tu*⸣ [SÍG†].⸢*ar-ga*⸣*-man-*⸢*nu*⸣ [*lu-bul-ti bir-me ù*] TÚG.GADA ⸢GIŠ⸣.[TÚG GIŠ.EREN GIŠ.ŠUR.MÌN *ka-la ri-iq-qí*]

367) [*bi-ib-lat* KUR.*ḫa-ma*]-⸢*a*⸣*-ni ša e-*⸢*ri*⸣-[*su*]-⸢*un*⸣ [*ṭa-a*]*-bu* ⸢URUDU⸣ AN.NA [AN.BAR A.BÁR *ša ni*]-⸢*ba*†⸣ *la* ⸢*i*⸣-[*šu-ú a-na* ^{d}EN ^{d}*zar-pa-ni-tum*]

368) [^{d}AG ^{d}*taš-me*]-⸢*tum*⸣ DINGIR.MEŠ *ma-ḫa-*[*zi* KUR EME.GI$_7$] ⸢*ù*†⸣ URI.⸢KI⸣ *ú-qa-*⸢*i*⸣-[*šá*† *a*]-⸢*na*⸣ *qí*$^{!}$-[*šá*]*-a-ti* GU$_4$.⸢MAḪ⸣-[*ḫi bit-ru-ti x x x x*]

369) [...] ⸢GI$^{?}$⸣ ZU [*x* (*x*)] *eb-*⸢*bu*⸣ [*x x x x* (*x*)] ⸢ḪI$^{?}$⸣.MEŠ KUR.⸢GI⸣.MUŠEN.MEŠ [UZ].TUR†.[MUŠEN].MEŠ *ma-ḫar-šú-*⸢*un*⸣ [*aq-qí áš-šú šá-kan* BAD$_5$.BAD$_5$]

370) [^{md}AMAR.UTU]-⸢A⸣-SUM.NA DUMU ⸢^{m}⸣*ia-ki-*[*ni* NUMUN LÚ.*kal-di ḫi-ri-iṣ* GAL$_5$†].⸢LÁ† *lem*⸣*-ni* ⸢*am*⸣*-ḫur-šú-*⸢*nu-ti*⸣*-ma* ⸢*ina*⸣ *su-*⸢*pe*⸣*-e* ⸢*ù te*⸣-[*me-qi*] ⸢*ma-ḫar*⸣-[*šu-un ut-nin*]

371) [*ul-tu*] ⸢*i*$^{?}$⸣*-sin-ni* EN ⸢GAL⸣*-i* ^{d}[AMAR.UTU

down with the swo]rd.

363b–364a) [(When) the month Nisannu (I)] arrived, [the month] the lord of the gods [goes] out (from his temple), I to[ok] the hands [of the great divine lord, the god Marduk, (and) of the god Nabû, the king of the totality of heaven and earth], and [brought (them) safely along the road to the] *a*[*kī*]*tu*-[house].

364b–371) I prese[nted a]s g[if]ts [to the deities Bēl (Marduk), Zarpanītu, Nabû, Tašmēt]u, (and) the (other) gods of the cult ce[nters of the land of Sumer] and Akkad 1[54 talents, 26 minas (and) 10 shekels of red gold, 1,604 talents] (and) 20 [minas of pu]re [silver, obsidian, ...], lapis laz[uli, *banded agate, blue turquoise, green*] *turq*[*uoise, ... of banded agate* (and) *muššaru*-stone in large] quantities, [blue-purple wool], red-purple wool, [garments with multi-colored trim, and] linen garments, [boxwood, cedar, cypress, (and) every kind of aromatic, the products of Mount Am]anus, who[se] sce[nt(s) are pleas]ant, copper, tin, [iron (and) lead in] imme[asurable quan]tities. [I offered] before them prize bull[s in prime condition, ...], shini[ng ..., ...]s, ge[e]se (and) [du]cks. I appealed to them (the gods) [in order to bring about the defeat of Marduk]-apla-iddina (II) (Merodach-Baladan), descendant of Yakī[n, of Chaldean extraction, the (very) image of an] evil [*gal*]*lû*-demon; [I prayed] t[o them] w[ith] supplications and en[treaties. After I had carried out] in full the festival of the great lord, the god [Marduk], ... [...] the cult centers of the land Sumer and Ak[kad] ... [...].

---

362 *-ti-*[*ma ṣe*$^{?}$*-ḫer*$^{?}$]: A. Fuchs (Khorsabad p. 156 line 319) reads *-ti-*[*ma*] *ṣe*$^{!?}$*-ḫer*$^{!?}$ with a note that the traces at the end of the squeeze are only very faint and indistinct. Any traces are most uncertain.

364b–368 For the restorations, see text no. 7 lines 141–143. ⸢*aṣ*⸣-[*bat*†]*-ma*: P.E. Botta's copy has ⸢*aṣ*⸣*-<bat>-ma*; H. Winckler's copy has [*aṣ*]*-bat-ma*; the squeeze currently has ⸢*aṣ*⸣-[*x*]-⸢*ma*⸣.

365 The squeeze shows that P.E. Botta's copy erroneously copied "[...] 20 [...]" one line too low. For the identification of the stones NA$_4$.AŠ.GÌ.GÌ (Akkadian *ašgigû/ašgikû*) and NA$_4$.UGU.AŠ.GÌ.GÌ (Akkadian reading unknown) as blue turquoise and green turquoise respectively, see Vallat, Akkadica 33 (1983) pp. 63–68. *di-gi-li* NA$_4$.BABBAR.DILI "*... of banded agate*": M. Worthington suggests that *diglī* might mean "eye-stones" here (private communication).

366 The squeeze indicates that P.E. Botta's and H. Winckler's copies erroneously place the "-⸢*u*ʾ⸣*-de-e* [...]" one line too high.

367 H. Winckler's copy has the trace of a sign before *-bu* that could conceivably be part of A. For the restoration AN.BAR A.BÁR, see text no. 74 vii 10.

368 H. Winckler's copy has *qiš-*[*šá*]*-a-ti*, while apparently indicating that the *qiš* was not on the squeeze. One expects *qí-* not *qiš-*. For the restoration at the end of the line, see text no. 1 line 386.

369 ⸢ḪI$^{?}$⸣.MEŠ: P.E. Botta's copy has [...].MEŠ and H. Winckler's copy has [...] ḪI.MEŠ; the squeeze currently has [...] ⸢ḪI$^{?}$⸣.MEŠ, where the ḪI is most uncertain. A. Fuchs (Khorsabad p. 157 line 326 n. 1) suggests possibly [GU$_4$].⸢AM⸣.MEŠ or ⸢MÁŠ⸣.MEŠ. For the restoration at the end of the line, see text no. 5 line 2′.

370 ⸢LÁ† *lem*⸣-: Botta's copy has ⸢MEŠ ME⸣; Winckler′s copy has MEŠ ME, with question marks next to each of the two signs. -⸢*ti*⸣*-ma* ⸢*ina*⸣: So P.E. Botta's copy and this is supported by the squeeze. H. Winckler's copy has -⸢*ti*⸣ *i-na* and A. Fuchs (Khorsabad p. 158 line 327) has -⸢*ti*⸣ *i*$^{!}$-⸢*na*⸣, with the *i-* partially damaged.

371 ⸢*i*$^{?}$⸣*-sin-*: Both P.E. Botta's and H. Winckler's copies have [...] MEŠ, but the squeeze has [...] *x-sin-*, where the traces before *sin* might be I. Winckler's copy has DINGIR.[MEŠ] for ^{d}[AMAR.UTU]. R.J. van der Spek (JEOL 25 [1977–78] p. 58) suggests *la a-*[*dur-ma*$^{?}$ *iš-tu*] and *at*$^{!}$-⸢*tu-muš*⸣; as noted by A. Fuchs (Khorsabad p. 158 line 328 n. 1), the latter reading is unlikely based on what is visible. Cf. text no. 1 lines 388b–389.

ú-šal]-⸢li⸣-mu LA A [*x x*] *x* ⸢*ma*⸣-*ḫa-zi* KUR EME.GI$_7$ *ù* ⸢URI.KI⸣ AB *x x* [*x x x x*]

372) [*i-na* 13†] ⸢BALA⸣-*ia i-na* ⸢ITI⸣.GU$_4$ <<GU$_4$>> [*i*†]-⸢*na*⸣ *qé*-⸢*reb*⸣ [*šu*]-*an-na*.KI [*ṣi*]-⸢*in*⸣-*di-ia uš-te-še-ra* ⸢*ak-ṣu-ra*⸣ [*uš*†]-*man*-⸢*ni*⸣ [*x x x x x*]

373) [*x x*] *x* [*x* (*x*)] PA I [*x*] KA I [*x x*] ⸢IA⸣ *el-la*-⸢*mu*⸣-[(*u*)-*a*] URU.⸢É⸣-[^{m}]⸢*za*⸣-*bi-da-ia* URU.*iq-bi*-^{d}EN URU.⸢*ḫur*⸣-[*sag*-GAL$_5$.LÁ.MEŠ *x x x x x*]

374) [*x x x x*] *x-ti-šú-nu-ma* UN.MEŠ ÚRI.KI [*x x x*].KI *ki-sik*.KI URU.*né-med*-^{d}[*la-gu-da x x x*]

375) *iš-lul-ma a-na* URU.BÀD-^{m}*ia-ki-ni ú-še-rib-ma*

376) *ú-dan-ni-na ker-ḫe-šú áš-la*.TA.ÀM *la-pa-an* BÀD-*šú*

377) GAL-*i ú*-⸢*né*⸣-*si-ma* 2 ME *ina* 1.KÙŠ DAGAL† *ḫa-ri-ṣi*

378) *iš-ku-un-ma* 1 1/2 ⸢NINDA⸣ [*ú*]-*šap-pil-ma ik-šu-da* A.MEŠ *nag-bi*

379) *bu-tuq-tú ul-tu* ⸢*qé*⸣-*reb* ÍD.*pu-rat-te ib-tú-qa ú-šar-da-a*

380) *ta-mir-tuš ú-šal-la* URU *a-šar mit-ḫu-ṣi* A.MEŠ

381) *ú-mal-li-ma ú-bat-ti-qa ti-tur-ri šu-ú a-di re-ṣi-šú*

382) ERIM.MEŠ ⸢MÈ⸣-*šú i-na bi-rit* ÍD.MEŠ *ki-ma* ⸢*ku*⸣-*mé-e*.MUŠEN

383) *kul-tar* LUGAL-*ti-šú iš-ku-un-ma ik-ṣu-ra uš-ma-an*-⸢*šu*⸣

384) *i-na qí-bit* ^{d}⸢*aš*⸣-*šur* ^{d}UTU *u* ^{d}AMAR.UTU LÚ.*mun-daḫ-ṣe*-⸢*ia*†⸣

385) UGU ÍD.MEŠ-*šú* TI$_8$.MUŠEN-*niš ú*-⸢*šap*⸣-*riš-ma iš-ku-nu*

386) *taḫ-ta-a-šú šá-a*-⸢*šu*⸣ *a-di* ⸢*ki-ṣir*⸣ LUGAL-*ti-šú* ⸢*ni*⸣-*i-tú*

387) *al-me-šu-ma ki*-⸢*ma*⸣ *as-li ina pa-an* GÌR.II-*šú ú-nap-pi-ṣa*

388) *qu-ra-di-šu* ⸢ANŠE⸣.KUR.RA.MEŠ *ṣi-mit-ti ni-ri-šu*

389) ⸢*i*⸣-*na uṣ-ṣi ú-šaq-qir* ⸢*ù*⸣ *šá-a-šú i-na zi*-⸢*qit*⸣

390) ⸢*mul*⸣-*mul-li rit*-⸢*ta*⸣-*šú ap-ṭur-ma* [*ki-ma šik-ke-e*]

391) [*ḫal*]-⸢*la*⸣-*la-niš* KÁ†.[GAL URU]-*šu* [*e-ru-ub* LÚ.*pu-qud-da-a-a*]

372–383) [In] my [thirteen re]gnal y[ear], in the month Ayyāru (II), I got my (chariot) [te]ams ready [i]n [Šu]anna (Babylon), prepared [my (military) c]amp [...] ... [...] Before [my (arrival), *he* (*Marduk-apla-iddina*) *evacuated*] the cities Bīt-[Z]abidāya, Iqbi-Bēl, Ḫu[rsaggalla, ...] ..., carried off as booty the people of (the cities) Ur, [...], Kissik, Nēmed-[Laguda, (and) ...], (375) and brought (them) into the city Dūr-Yakīn. He then strengthened its enclosure walls (and), moving back a distance of (one) measuring rope from the front of its main wall, he made a moat two hundred cubits wide; [he] made (the moat) one and a half *nindanu* deep and reached ground water. He cut a channel from the Euphrates River, (thereby) making (its water) flow (in)to its meadowland. He (thus) filled the city's flatlands, where battles (are fought), with water and cut the bridges. Together with his allies (and) his battle troops, he pitched his royal tent in a bend of the river (lit.: "between rivers") like a *crane* and set up his (military) camp.

384–394a) At the command of the gods A[š]šur, Šamaš, and Marduk, I had [m]y fighting men fly over its water channels like eagles and they brought about his defeat. I surrounded him together with his royal (military) contingent and slaughtered his warriors like sheep at his feet. I pierced the horses trained to his yoke [wi]th arrows. Then, (as for) him, (390) I pierced (lit.: "loosened") his hand with the poin[t of an a]rrow and [he (then) entered] the gat[e of] his [city ste]althfully, [like a mongoose. I cut down the Puqudians, his allie(s), (and) the Maršanians, together with the Sutians] who were wi[th him, in front of the gate (of his city) (and) splattered his people with deadly venom. I took away from him his royal tent,

---

372 [*i-na* 13†] ⸢BALA⸣-*ia*: P.E. Botta's copy has nothing before the IA, while H. Winckler's has [*i-na* 10]+3 BALA-*ia*; the squeeze currently has ⸢BALA-*ia*⸣. <<GU$_4$>> [*i*†]-⸢*na*⸣: Winckler's copy has *i-na*, but the squeeze (and Botta's copy) do not have the I and it is not clear from the squeeze that there is room to restore it, but the traces of the (second, unwanted) GU$_4$ do look more like that sign than I.

373 [*x x*] *x* [*x* (*x*)] PA I [*x*] KA I [*x x*] ⸢IA⸣: The reading mostly follows P.E. Botta's copy; H. Winckler's copy has [*x x*] *x x* ÁŠ I KA I [*x x*] IA A; the squeeze currently appears to have [...] *x* [(*x*)] *x* [(*x*)] *x* ⸢KA? I⸣ [*x x*] ⸢IA⸣. A.T.E. Olmstead (AJSL 47 [1930–31] p. 274 line 16) has ... ? .. ? *pa i ka*-⸢*ra*⸣-[*ši*]-⸢*ia*⸣ *a*. For the restoration at the end of the line, see text no. 74 vi 54.

374 As already noted by A. Fuchs (Khorsabad p. 159 line 331 n. 1), based on passages in several other texts (e.g., text no. 7 lines 8–9, text no. 8 line 4, text no. 13 lines 6–8, text no. 14 lines 6–8, and text no. 74 vi 75–76) we would expect UNUG.KI after ÚRI.KI.

Section 23 = lines 375–391 = V,8:1–17. See Winckler, Sar. Annals lines 320–337; Lie, Sar. lines 404b–412a; and Fuchs, Khorsabad Annals lines 332–348. Cf. text no. 1 lines 404b–412a and text no. 6 lines 1´–3´a.

377 DAGAL†: The squeeze appears to confirm P.E. Botta's copy that the form of the sign is slightly anomalous, MAL×BAR, against Winckler's copy of a good DAGAL(MAL×DINGIR).

389 ⸢*qit*⸣: So P.E. Botta's copy; H. Winckler's copy has KIB, but collation of the squeeze by F. Thureau-Dangin confirms Botta's copy (RA 24 [1927] p. 77). The squeeze is currently not clear but would not go against ⸢*qit*⸣.

390–391 For the restorations, see text no. 6 line 3´. Line 390: *rittašu apṭur*: The translation "I pierced his hand" follows CAD R p. 384; cf. CAD P p. 289 "I loosened (the grip of?) his hand." A. Fuchs (Khorsabad p. 334) has "ich ... lähmte ihm ... die Hand."

392) [...] *šá it-[ti-šú*? *x x x (x)]* TI [... *i-mat mu-ti as-lu-ḫa* UN.MEŠ-*šu kúl-tar* LUGAL-*ti-šu*]
393) [GIŠ.*šá* GIŠ.MI KÙ.GI LUGAL-*ti-šú* GIŠ.GIDRU KÙ.GI] GIŠ.⸢NÁ†⸣ KÙ.GI GIŠ.⸢*né*?⸣-[*med-du* KÙ.GI *ú-de-e* KÙ.GI KÙ.BABBAR GIŠ? KUR *gan-ga-ni-šu til-li*]
394) [*ú-nu-ut* MÈ *e-kim-šu kul-lat* UN.MEŠ-*šú a-ši-bu-ut*] *da-*⸢*ád*⸣*-mi si-ḫir-*⸢*ti*⸣ [KUR-*šú ša* TA *pa-an* GIŠ.TUKUL.MEŠ-*ia ú-še*?-...]
395) [*ú-šá-aṣ-bi-ta pa-ši-ru a-di su-gul-lat* GU$_{4}$.MEŠ ANŠE.GAM.MAL].⸢MEŠ ANŠE?⸣.MEŠ *u ṣe-e-*[*ni*†] *ša* [*x x (x)*] KID/ŠID/⸢Ú?⸣ [...]
396) [*šu-a-tu um-ma-nat* ^{d}*aš-šur gap-šá*]*-a-*⸢*ti* 2⸣+[1† *u*$_{4}$†*-me*†] *mu-ši-tu šal-lat la ni-bi iš-*⸢*lul-lam*⸣*-ma* [...]
397) [...] *x* ⸢UN⸣.MEŠ [1]+1 ⸢LIM⸣ 5 ME ANŠE.KUR.RA.MEŠ 7 ME 10 ANŠE.KUNGA.MEŠ [6 LIM 54 ANŠE.A.AB.BA.MEŠ ...]
398) [...]+40 UDU.NÍTA.⸢MEŠ⸣ [*ša*] *um-ma-ni iš-lu-la i-na* ⸢*qé*⸣*-reb uš-ma-*[*ni-ia am-ḫur* ...]
399) [... GU$_{4}$?].⸢MEŠ⸣ *ù* ⸢*ṣe*⸣*-e-ni ša i-na ra-ma-ni-šú-nu in-né-*⸢*ez*⸣*-*[*bu* ... *áš-šu*? *la*? *a-ṣe-e*?]
400) [URU-*šu*? *u*? *la*? *na-par-ka-a*? ...] ŠU? *x* [*x (x)*] *i-ta-at* URU-*šú ak-ṣur-ma* GIM ŠAḪ *er-*[*re-ti ina qé-reb* URU-*šu šup-šu-qiš e-si-ir-šu*]
401) [GIŠ.KIRI$_{6}$.MEŠ-*šú ak-šiṭ* GIŠ.GIŠIMMAR.MEŠ-*šú*] ⸢*ak*⸣*-kis* [*a-na* A?].MEŠ *dan-nu-ti ša ḫa-ri-ṣi* URU-*šú* [... GAL-*ti a-ram-mu*]
402) [UGU-*šu ak-bu*]*-*⸢*us*⸣*-ma*† ⸢UGU⸣ [BÀD-*šu*] ⸢*ú-šaq*⸣*-*[*qi ù šu*]*-ú ḫat-tu rama-ni-šú im-qut-*[*su-ma* ...]

his royal gold parasol, gold scepter], gold bed, [gold] ch[air, gold (and) silver objects, ..., his potstands, equipment, (and) battle gear].

394b–402a) (As for) all his people, the inhabitants] of the settlements of all [of his land, whom *he had* ... from before my weapons *and* (395) *settled in a secret place*, together with herds of cattle, camel]s, *d*[*onkey*]s, and sheep and go[ats], which [... *that* (*man*), the numer]ou[s troops of the god Aššur] (required) thr[ee days] (and) night(s) to carry (them) off as (their) countless booty and [... I received] inside [my] (military) cam[p ... *90,580*] people, 2,500 horses, 710 mules, [6,054 camels ... (and)] 40+[x] sheep [that] my troops had carried off as booty. [... *oxen*], and sheep and goats that had been le[ft] by themselves [... *In order to prevent* (*anyone*) *going out from* (400) *his city or leaving* (*it*) ...], I constructed ... around his city and [shut him up inside his city in dire circumstances], like a pig in a pig[sty. I chopped down his orchards (and)] cut down [his date palms. To *the*] *mighty* [*water*]s of the moat of his city [... *with a great* ... I construct]ed (lit.: "trod down") [a (siege) ramp against it] and r[aised (the ramp) up] a[gainst its (city) wall].

402b–416a) [Moreover, (as for) h]im (Marduk-apla-iddina II), his own fear(s) fell upon [him and ...] ... [... he f]led and his whereabouts have never been

---

Section 24 = lines 392–408 = V,7:1–17. See Winckler, Sar. Annals lines 337–349; Lie, Sar. lines 412b–416, and pp. 62–63 lines 5–14 and nn. 1 and 6; and Fuchs, Khorsabad Annals lines 349–365. Cf. text no. 1 lines 412b–415+ and text no. 6 lines 3′b–13′/14′.

392 The reading of the line follows Bt$_{1}$. For the beginning of the line, H. Winckler's copy has instead [... KÙ].GI, or less likely [...] KÙ.GI. Nothing for this line is currently preserved on the squeeze.

393 The restoration is based on text no. 1 lines 413–414 and text no. 6 lines 4′–5′. GIŠ.⸢NÁ⸣: Bt$_{1}$ has GIŠ followed by ḪAL in the middle of an area of damage. H. Winckler's copy has GIŠ followed by ḪAL [(x)] ḪI U, all in an area of damage. The squeeze shows damage with only a few traces for the area.

395 ⸢MEŠ ANŠE?⸣.MEŠ: H. Winckler's copy has [...].MEŠ GU$_{4}$.MEŠ. Only the head of a horizontal wedge for the beginning of the middle sign is currently visible on the squeeze.

396 H. Winckler's copy has [...]-*a-ti* 3 *u*$_{4}$*-me*, while the squeeze currently has [...]-⸢*a-ti* 2⸣+[*x x*].

397 Based on text no. 6 line 8′ we expect 90 LIM 5 ME 80 UN.MEŠ at the beginning of the line, but the trace on the squeeze before UN looks more like ⸢RIM⸣, [...]+⸢20 ME⸣, or just possibly ⸢LIM⸣ rather than 80. [1]+1: So squeeze; H. Winckler's copy (pl. 21 no. 45) has 2, while Bt$_{1}$ has an anomalous form (a horizontal wedge running into the bottom of a vertical wedge). 7 ME: Bt$_{2}$ has 6 ME while Bt$_{1}$ has 7 ME (as does the squeeze).

398 *iš-lu-la*: So squeeze and Bt$_{2}$; Bt$_{1}$ and Winckler have *uš-lu-la*.

399 *in-né-*⸢*ez*⸣*-*[*bu*]: The restoration was already proposed by A. Fuchs (Khorsabad p. 165 line 356); F.W. Geers (apud Olmstead, AJSL 47 [1930–31] p. 275) suggested *in-ni-*[*zib*].

400 ŠU?: Possibly KI (so Fuchs, Khorsabad p. 165 line 357). Bt$_{1}$ (not on Bt$_{2}$) and H. Winckler's copy (pl. 2 no. 45) both have ŠU; the squeeze appears to show a ŠU with a small Winkelhaken above the beginning of the extended lower horizontal wedge. *er-*[*re-ti*]: Or simply *er-*[*ri*]; see AHw p. 244 and Fuchs, Khorsabad p. 165 note 1 to line 357.

401 [*a-na* A].MEŠ: Against F.W. Geer's reading (apud Olmstead, AJSL 47 [1930–31] p. 275) *a-na* ⸢*e*⸣*-*[*ber* A].MEŠ, for which the squeeze indicates there are no traces of the *a-na* or *e-* and not sufficient room for the reading; see also Fuchs, Khorsabad p. 165 line 358 n. 1. As noted by A. Fuchs (ibid. n. 1), we should possibly restore something like *ú-ri-da-am-ma* in the gap following URU-*šú*.

402–403a Line 402: *-ma*†: Likely -⸢*ma*⸣; Bt$_{1}$ (not on Bt$_{2}$) and H. Winckler's copy both have three horizontal wedges, one above the other, with no final vertical wedge or any indication of damage there; the sign is not preserved on the squeeze. Lines 402b–403a: A.T.E. Olmstead (AJSL 47 [1930–31] pp. 275–276) would read [*šú-ú a-di re-ṣe-e-šu mu-šiš uṣ-ṣi*]*-ma a-*[*na* KUR.ELAM.MA.KI] between *im-qut-*[*su-ma*] and [*in*]*-*⸢*na*⸣*-bit-ma*, which is presumably based on line 350, but we would expect a longer passage and, as already noted by A. Fuchs (Khorsabad p. 166 line 360 n. 1), this is "allzu frei." For the different accounts of what happened to Marduk-apla-iddina, see the Introduction to this volume, under the section "Military Campaigns."

403) [...] *x* MA A [*x x x x x x* (*x*)] ⸢TIM$^{?}$⸣ [*x x in*]-⸢*na*⸣-*bit-ma la in-na-mir a-šar-šú* [...]
404) [...] ZA *x* [*x x x x x*] *x* GAG [*x x x* KÙ].⸢GI KÙ⸣.BABBAR GIŠ.⸢*tup*⸣-*nin-na-te* NA$_4$.ZÚ [...]
405) [...].⸢MEŠ⸣ IGI [*x x x x x* (*x*)] *x* MEŠ NA$_4$ [*x* (*x*)] A ME ⸢TI$^{?}$⸣ A *u* URUDU.MEŠ NA$_4$.ZA.GÌN.MEŠ NA$_4$.*aš*-⸢*pe*⸣-[*e* ...]
406) [...] Ú [*x x x x* (*x*)] *x* Ú (*x*) *x x* [*x*] DIRI [*gi*]-*mir* Ú.ḪI.A.MEŠ *nab-nit* A [...]
407) [...] ḪI [*x x x*].⸢MEŠ⸣ KÙ†.GI ZI A [(*x*)] KÙ.⸢GI⸣ *til-li ú-nu-*[*ut* ...]
408) [...] GIŠ.⸢GU⸣.[ZA].MEŠ KÙ.BABBAR GIŠ.⸢BANŠUR⸣.MEŠ KÙ.BABBAR *ú-*[*nu-ut*$^{?}$ ...]
409) [...]
410) [...].MEŠ [*x x x x*] ⸢GAL$^{?}$.MEŠ$^{?}$⸣ NÍG.[*x x x x x* (*x*)]
411) [*x x x x x x x* (*x*)] *x* [*x x x x x x x* (*x x*)] SIG [*x x x x x* (*x*)] GIŠ.BANŠUR*.MEŠ [*x*] GAN [*x*]
412) [*x x x x x x x* (*x*)] KÙ.BABBAR *ú-*[*nu-ut*$^{?}$ *x x x x x*] GIŠ$^{?}$ LA I [*x x x x la*] *mi-nam x* [*x x x x*]
413) [*x x x x x* (*x*) *ša a*]-⸢*aḫ*⸣ ÍD.*x* [*x x x x x x* (*x*)] *ú-ru-*⸢*uḫ*†⸣ [*x x x x x x x x x x* (*x*)]
414) [*x x x x x x x x x x* (*x x*)].MEŠ [*x x x x x x* (*x*)].MEŠ ⸢ANŠE⸣.MEŠ ANŠE†.A.AB.BA.MEŠ GU$_4$.⸢MEŠ⸣ [*ṣe*†-*e*†-*ni x x x*]
415) [*x x x x* (*x*) URU.BÀD-^{m}*ia*]-*ki-ni* [URU *dan-nu*]-*ti-*[*šú i-na* ^{d}]⸢GIBIL$_6$†⸣ *aq-mu ker-ḫe-e-šú* ⸢*zaq*⸣-*ru-*[*te*† *ap*†-*pul*† *aq*†]-⸢*qur*⸣
416) [*te-me-en-šú as*]-⸢*su-uḫ*⸣-[*ma*† GIM†] ⸢DU$_6$†⸣ *a-bu-bi* [*ú-še*]-⸢*mi*⸣ DUMU.MEŠ ⸢ZIMBIR⸣.KI NIBRU.KI KÁ.DINGIR.RA.KI *bár-sipa*.KI†
417) [*ša i-na la an-ni-šú-nu i-na*] ⸢*qer-bi*⸣-[*šú*

discovered. [...] ... [...] ... [... gol]d, [si]lver, chests (full) of obsidian, [... (405) ...]s, [...]s, [...]-stone, ..., copper, lapis lazuli, jasp[er, ...] ... [a]ll (kinds of) plants, product(s) of [...], gold [...]s, gold ..., equipment, uten[sils ...], silver th[rone]s, silver tables, ut[ensils ... (410) ...] *lar*[*ge* ...]s, [...] tables [...] silver [...], *u*[*tensils* ...] ... [... in]numerable [... on the ba]nk of the river [...] rout[e ...]s, [...]s, donkeys, camels, ox[en, sheep and goats ... (415) ...] I burned down [his fort]if[ied city Dūr-Ya]kīn [with f]ire. [I destroyed (and) demoli]shed its high enclosure walls. [I tor]e [up its foundation(s) and ma]de [(it) like a (ruin) mou]nd left by the Deluge.

416b–421a) (As for) the citizens of Sippar, Nippur, Babylon, (and) Borsippa [who through no fault of their own had been held capti]ve [t]her[e (Dūr-Yakīn)], I put an end to their imprisonment *and* let them see

403 *x* MA A: So Bt$_1$ and H. Winckler's copies; not currently legible on the squeeze. A. Fuchs (Khorsabad p. 166 line 360 n. 1) suggests possibly ⸢GÍN⸣ A. -⸢*na*⸣: The form is as copied by Winckler (i.e, the end of an archaizing form of the sign NA). [*in*]-⸢*na*⸣-*bit-ma la in-na-mir a-šar-šú*, "[he f]led and his whereabouts have never been discovered": Cf. text no. 6 line 12´a *iš-ḫu-ut-ma* GIŠ.GIDRU GIŠ.GU.ZA *id-di-ma ina pa-an* LÚ.A KIN-*ia ú-na-šíq*† *qaq-qa-ru*, "He became terrified, laid down (his) scepter (and) throne, and kissed the ground before my messenger."
405 A ME [(*x*)] ⸢TI$^{?}$⸣: The squeeze may suggest ⸢A MEŠ$^{?}$ TI$^{?}$⸣. NA$_4$.*aš*-⸢*pe*⸣-[*e*]: For the restoration, see text no. 7 line 159.
406 : Ú (*x*) *x x* [*x*]: This reading follows the squeeze. DIRI: So H. Winckler's copy; the squeeze apparently has ⸢DIRI⸣; Bt$_1$ has SI-A and Bt$_2$ SI [...]. Ú.ḪI.A.MEŠ: So Bt$_2$; Bt$_1$ has Ú.[*x* (*x*)].A.MEŠ and Winckler Ú.A.MEŠ; the squeeze has ⸢Ú.ḪI⸣.A.MEŠ. *nab-nit* A [...]: A. Fuchs (Khorsabad p. 167 line 363) suggests possibly *nab-nit* A.[AB.BA], "product(s) of the s[ea]." The reading of the sign after *nab-nit* on the squeeze is not clear.
407 ⸢MEŠ⸣: Or [...] EŠ. H. Winckler's copy does not have any indication of a sign or damage between A and KÙ.
408 ⸢BANŠUR⸣: Bt$_1$ and H. Winckler, Sar. 2 pl. 21 no. 45 have URU-UM, while Bt$_2$ and Winckler, Sar. 2 pl. 22 no. 46 have URU-URUDU$^{!?}$/UM$^{?}$ and URU-URUDU respectively; the squeeze has ⸢BANŠUR⸣ (URU-⸢URUDU⸣).
Section 25 = lines 409–425 = V,6:1–17. See Winckler, Sar. Annals lines 358–368; Lie, Sar. pp. 64–65 lines 6–17; and Fuchs, Khorsabad Annals lines 366–382. Cf. text no. 6 line(s 13´–)14´, and text no. 7 lines 132b–139.
409–425 The left end of the slab is not preserved but from line 415 onwards the passage can be restored from text no. 7 lines 134b–139, which allowed H. Winckler to determine how many signs are missing before the start of P.E. Botta's copy and the squeeze.
410 ⸢GAL$^{?}$.MEŠ$^{?}$⸣: or MA [*x*] EŠ.
411 A. Fuchs (Khorsabad p. 168 line 368 n. 1) suggests that the trace early in the line might be LÚ.BANŠUR*: Botta's and Winckler's copies have URU-URUDU and this appears to be supported by the squeeze.
412 GIŠ$^{?}$: Both P.E. Botta's and H. Winckler's copies have GIŠ, but the squeeze appears to have the end of only one horizontal wedge, running to the middle of the vertical wedge, thus higher than one would expect for GIŠ. As already noted by A. Fuchs (Khorsabad p. 168 line 369 n. 2), the *x* at the end of the line is two small Winkelhakens, one above the other.
414 H. Winckler's copy has [...].MEŠ [*x x* ANŠE.KUR.RA].MEŠ ANŠE.MEŠ ANŠE.A.AB.BA.MEŠ GU$_4$.MEŠ *ṣe-e-*[*ni*], but the squeeze has ... ⸢ANŠE.MEŠ ANŠE.A.AB.BA⸣.MEŠ [...].
415–425 For the restorations, see text no. 7 lines 134–139. At the end of line 415, H. Winckler's copy has -[*šú i-na*] GIBIL$_6$ *aq-mu ker-ḫe-e-šú zaq-ru-te ap-pul aq-qur*, but this cannot be confirmed from the squeeze today.
416 KI†: The copies by P.E. Botta and H. Winckler both have a LU with an area of damage immediately before it; this fits what is visible on the squeeze, although a trace of what may have been a Winkelhaken is visible before what appears to be a LU, as noted by A. Fuchs (Khorsabad p. 169 line 373 n. 2).
417 H. Winckler's copy has *qer-bi ka-mu-ú* (fully preserved); the squeeze currently has ⸢*qer-bi*⸣-[*x x*]-⸢*mu-ú*⸣, with room to restore *šú*. ⸢*bit*†⸣: P.E. Botta's copy has something like UD-⸢3⸣, while Winckler's copy has a good É; the squeeze is basically illegible here, but has nothing that

ka†]-⸢mu⸣-ú ṣi-⸢bit†-ta⸣-šú-nu a-bu-ut-⸢ma?⸣
ú-kal-lim-šú-nu-ti nu-ru A.ŠÀ.MEŠ-šú-nu
418) [ša ul-tu u$_4$-me ul-lu-ti i-na i-ši-ti] ma-a-te
LÚ.su-ti-i e-ki-mu-ma ra-ma-nu-uš-šú-un
ú-ter-ru LÚ.su-ti-i
419) [ERIM.MEŠ EDIN i-na GIŠ.TUKUL ú-šam-qit
ki†]-sur-ri-šú-nu ek-mu-te ú-ter áš-ru-uš-šú-un
ša ÚRI.KI
420) [UNUG.KI eridu].KI [ARARMA.KI ki†-sik†.KI†
URU.né-med]-⸢^{d}⸣la-⸢gu⸣-[da†] áš-ku-na
an-du-ra-ar-šú-un ù DINGIR.MEŠ-šú-nu

the light (of day). (With regard to) their fields, [which long ago, while] the land [was in disorder], the Sutians had taken away and appropriated for their own, [I struck down] (those) Sutians, [the people of the steppe, with the sword]. I restored to their former status the [ter]ritories that had been taken away from them (the citizens). (420) I (re)-established the freedom (from obligations) of (the cities) Ur, [Uruk, Eridu, Larsa, Kissik, (and) Nēmed]-Lag[uda]. Moreover, [I returned] their gods [that had been carried off as booty to their cult centers and] restored [their regular] offe[rings] that had been interrupted.

421) [šal-lu-ti a-na ma-ḫa]-⸢zi?⸣-[šú-nu ú-ter-ma
sat†-tuk†]-ki-[šú†-nu] ba-aṭ-lu-ti ú-ter
áš-ru-uš-šú-un KUR.É-^{m}ia-kin$_7$
422) [e-liš u šap-liš] a-⸢di⸣ [URU.sa-am-ʾu-na
URU].KÁ-BÀD URU.BÀD-^{d}te-li-te URU.bu-bé-e
⸢URU⸣.DU$_6$-^{d}ḫum-ba
423) [ša mi-ṣir KUR.ELAM].MA†.KI mit-ḫa-⸢riš⸣
a-[bel-ma UN.MEŠ KUR].⸢kúm⸣-[mu-ḫi†] šá
qé-reb KUR.ḫa-at-ti šá ina ⸢tu⸣-kul†-ti
DINGIR.[MEŠ†] ⸢GAL⸣.MEŠ
424) [EN.MEŠ-ia ik]-⸢šud⸣-da ŠU.II-[a†-a qé-reb-šú
ú]-⸢šar⸣-[me-ma†] ú-še-ši-ba ni-du-us-su UGU
⸢mi⸣-ṣir KUR.ELAM†.MA.KI
425) [i-na URU.sa-ag-bat] ^{md}⸢AG⸣-[SIG$_5$-DINGIR.MEŠ
a-na šup]-ru-us [GÌR.II] LÚ.KÚR† ELAM†.MA.KI
⸢ú-šar†⸣-kis ⸢URU⸣.bir-tu
426) [KUR] ⸢šu-a-tu mal-ma?-liš⸣ a-zu-uz†-ma [i†-na†
ŠU.II†] ⸢LÚ†.šu-ut SAG⸣-[ia LÚ.GAR.KUR
KÁ].DINGIR.⸢RA.KI⸣ [ù] ⸢LÚ†.šu†⸣-ut SAG†-ia
⸢LÚ.GAR⸣.KUR [LÚ.gam†]-bu-[li am-nu
^{m}ú]-⸢pe⸣-e-ri ⸢LUGAL NI⸣.TUK.[KI]
427) [ša ma-lak 30] ⸢KASKAL.GÍD⸣ i-na MURUB$_4$
tam-tim KUR ⸢^{d}UTU-ši⸣ šit-⸢ku⸣-[nu nar-ba†]-⸢ṣu
da⸣-na-⸢an be⸣-lu-ti-ia iš-me-ma iš-šá-a
ta-mar-⸢tuš⸣

421b–426a) I [ruled] all toget[her] the land Bīt-Yakīn, [from one end to the other (lit.: "above and below")], as far [as] the cities [Samʾūna], Bāb-dūri, Dūr-Telīte, Bubê, (and) Tīl-Ḫumba, [which are on the Ela]mite [border]; I se[ttled there people from the land] Ku[mmuḫu], which is (located) in the land Ḫatti that [I had con]quered with the support of the great gods, [my lords, and] I had (them) occupy its (Bīt-Yakīn's) abandoned regions. I had Nabû-[damiq-ilāni] construct a fortress on the Elamite border, (425) [at the city Sagbat, in order to b]ar [access to (lit.: "the feet of")] the enemy Elamite(s). I divided up that [land into equ]al parts and [assigned (them) to the authority of] a eun[uch of mine, the governor of Bab]ylon, [and] a(nother) eunuch of mine, the governor [of the Gam]bu[lu (tribe)].

426b–427) [Up]ēri, king of Dilmun, [who(se) lai]r is situ[ated at a distance of thirty] le[agues] in the middle of the Eastern Sea, heard of my lordly might and brought me [his] audience gift.

428) [a-di a†-na†-ku† dáb†-de†]-⸢e⸣ LÚ.kal-di ⸢ù†⸣
LÚ.[a†-ra†-me a-šak†-ka†]-nu-ma ⸢UGU UN⸣.MEŠ
KUR.ELAM.⸢MA⸣.KI ú-šam-ra-ru
GIŠ.TUKUL.MEŠ-ia LÚ.šu-ut SAG-ia LÚ.GAR.KUR
429) [KUR†.qu†-e x x x x x x x x x x (x x)] ⸢I?⸣ [x x x

428–432a) [While I was bringing ab]out [the defea]t of the Chaldeans and [Arameans] and making my weapons prevail over the people of the land Elam, a eunuch of mine, the governor [of the land Que (Cilicia), ...] marched ...ly three times into the district [of

would go against É. -⸢ma?⸣: Both Botta's and Winckler's copies have DU; the squeeze is not clear due to what may have been a crack or fold through the middle of the sign (see also Fuchs, Khorsabad p. 169 line 374 n. 3), but the spacing would fit MA better than DU.

423 a[bēlma] "I [ruled]": The verb here and in other similar passages (e.g., text nos. 12 line 20 and 14 line 26) may be in the present tense rather than the preterite tense. H. Winckler's copy has "[" before bel, but no "]" to go with it.

424 UGU: P.E. Botta's copy has UGU*(copy: KA), H. Winckler's copy has UGU, and the squeeze currently ⸢UGU⸣ (with the Winkelhaken at the beginning clearly present).

425 Perhaps URU.sa-ag-be; cf. KUR.É-sa-ga-bi in text no. 117 ii 40. This is the last line on the squeeze and the squeeze is much more damaged/unclear than for the earlier lines. Thus it is more difficult to determine if signs indicated as being abnormal on P.E. Botta's copy were such or not.

Section 26 = lines 426–442 = V,5:1–17. See Winckler, Sar. Annals lines 369–389; Lie, Sar. pp. 66–67 lines 1–2 and lines 443–468; and Fuchs, Khorsabad Annals lines 383–399. Cf. text no. 1 lines 443–468; note also text no. 7 lines 149b–153a.

426 See text no. 7 line 140 for restorations.

427 H. Winckler's copy has ^{d}UTU šit-ku-⸢na-at⸣ [nar]-ba-ṣu, but the squeeze currently has ⸢^{d}UTU-ši⸣ šit-⸢ku⸣-[x x x (x)]-⸢ṣu⸣.

429 H. Winckler's copy has [ša] KUR.qu-[e] at the beginning of the line, but nothing of this is currently visible on the squeeze and ša is not found in text no. 1 line 445. ⸢I?⸣: Possibly ⸢RA⸣ or MA. 3-šú: For the reading -šú, see also Thureau-Dangin, RA 24 (1927) p. 77. With regard to šilpu, see the on-page note to text no. 1 line 447.

x ša† ^{m†}mi†]-⸢ta-a⸣ LUGAL KUR.mu-us-⸢ki⸣ i-na na-gi-šú a-di 3-šú ši-il-pu il-lik-ma 1 LIM LÚ.ERIM.MEŠ

430) [ti-du-ki-šú x x x x x x x x x (x x)] ⸢ANŠE.KUR.RA⸣.MEŠ MÈ-šú-nu e-kim-šú-nu-ti 2 URU.⸢ḪAL.ṢU⸣.MEŠ tuk-lat na-gi-šú ⸢ša⸣ ina KUR-i mar-ṣi i-ta-at

431) [x x x x a-di] URU.MEŠ ⸢ša⸣ [li-me†-ti†-šú-nu ik†-šu†-ud] iš-lu-la šal-la-su-un ip-pu-[ul iq]-⸢qur⸣ ina IZI iš-ru-⸢up LÚ⸣.A ⸢KIN⸣-[šu/šú] ⸢šá⸣ a-mat MUNUS.SIG$_5$ na-šu-ú

Mi]tâ (Midas), king of the land Musku, and (430) took away one thousand of [his (Mitâ's) combat] troops [...] (and) their war horses. [He conquered] two fortresses upon which his (Mitâ's) district relied (and) which are (located) on a rugged mountain adjacent to [..., together with] the settlements in [their environs]. He plundered them, (and then) destro[yed, dem]olished, (and) burned (them) down with fire. [His] messenger, who bore the good news, brought [one] thous[and *face-(guards)*] (taken) from [his (Mita's) wa]rriors (*as trophies*) to me [in the city Sama'ū]na, which is (located) on the Elamite border, [a]nd (thus) made [my heart] rejoice.

432) [1†] ⸢LIM⸣ [zi†-im† pa†-ni†] ⸢LÚ⸣.[qu†]-⸢ra-di⸣-[šú a-na URU.sa-ma-'u-ú]-⸢na ša pa⸣-aṭ KUR.ELAM.MA.KI a-di maḫ-ri-ia ub-⸢lam-ma⸣ ú-šá-⸢li-iṣ⸣ [lìb-bi†] ⸢ù⸣ [šu†]-⸢u⸣ ^{m}mi-⸢ta-a⸣

433) KUR.mu-us-⸢ka-a-a ša$^{?}$⸣ a-na LUGAL.⸢MEŠ⸣-[ni†] ⸢AD⸣.MEŠ-⸢ia⸣ [la ik-nu-šú] ⸢a-na⸣ šá-'a-al šul-me-šú-un la iš-⸢pu-ra⸣ [rak-bu]-⸢šú šá-kan NÍG⸣.[È ki†-šit†-ti qa-ti]

434) ša ^{d}aš-šur $^{d⸢}$AMAR.UTU ú⸣-[šat†]-li-mu-⸢in-ni-ma ḫe$^{?}$-pe$^{?}$-e$^{?}$⸣ [(x)] ⸢É-^{m}⸣ia-kin$_7$ [šá†-lal UN†].⸢MEŠ-šú šuk-nu⸣-uš ^{m}ú-pe-e-ri ⸢LUGAL⸣ NI.⸢TUK⸣.[KI† ša qa-bal tam-tim iš-me-ma x x x]

435) i-na qé-reb KUR-šú [ru]-⸢uq$^{?}$⸣-ti šá-⸢ḫur⸣-ra-tú ⸢it⸣-[ta-bi-ik]-⸢šu LÚ⸣.[A] ⸢KIN†⸣-[šú ša] ⸢e⸣-peš [ar-du]-ti ù [na-še-e bil-ti] ⸢IGI⸣.SÁ-⸢e⸣ a-[na† tam†]-di [ša ṣi-it ^{d}UTU-ši]

432b–436a) Moreover, [th]at (man), Mitâ of the land Musku, *who* [had not submitted] to the kings, my ancestors, (and) had never sent his [mounted messenger] to inquire about their well-being, [heard] about the accomplishment of the victo[ri(es) (and) conquest(s)] that the gods Aššur (and) Marduk [had gr]anted me and *of the destruction of* Bīt-Yakīn, [the carrying off of] its [people], (and) the subjugation of Upēri, k[in]g of Dilm[un, which is (located) in the middle of the sea. Then, ...] in his [*far-o*]*ff* land, deathly quiet o[verwhelmed hi]m (and) [he se]nt [his mes]sen[ger] before m[e] a[t the Eastern Se]a to do [obeisa]nce (to me) and to bring (me) [tribute (and) pr]esents.

436) a-di maḫ-ri-⸢ia⸣ [iš]-⸢pu⸣-ra $^{m⸢}$si⸣-il-ṭa [(x) URU$^{?}$].⸢ṣur$^{?}$⸣-ra-a-⸢a$^{?}$⸣ [x x x (x) a-na$^{?}$ KUR$^{?}$] ^{d}aš-šur.[KI$^{?}$ (x) 7†] ⸢LUGAL⸣.MEŠ-ni [ša†] ⸢KUR⸣.ia-a' na-ge-e [ša KUR.ad-na-na]

437) ša ma-⸢lak⸣ 7 u$_4$-[me†] ⸢i⸣-na MURUB$_4$ tam-⸢di⸣ [e†-reb†] ^{d}UTU-ši šit-ku-⸢nu⸣-[ma$^{?}$ šu-bat-su-un$^{?}$

436b–441a) (As for) Silṭa [*of the city Ty*]*re* [... *to*] *Assyr*[*ia*, seven] k[ing]s [of the lan]d Yā', a district [of the land Adnana (Cyprus)] — who[se *abode*(*s*)] are situated [*far away*], at a distance of seven da[ys] (journey) in the middle of the [West]ern Sea (and) who [fr]om the dis[tant] pa[st] until *now* ... all together

---

431 H. Winckler's copy has [li]-me-ti-[šú-nu] ik-šu-[ud]; there may be a few traces of this on the squeeze, but it is not possible to confirm his reading.

432 H. Winckler's copy has 1 LIM zi-im pa-ni LÚ.qu-ra-di-[x x x x x x x (x)]-na ⸢ša$^{?}$⸣ pa-at, but not all of this is currently legible on the squeeze. His copy restores LUGAL at the end of the line, but the squeeze indicates that there was no room for it.

433 P.E. Botta's copy has ⸢AD⸣.DIŠ.MEŠ, but the extraneous DIŠ is not on the squeeze.

434 ⸢ḫe$^{?}$-pe$^{?}$-e$^{?}$⸣ [(x)] ⸢É-^{m}⸣ia-kin$_7$: The reading is uncertain; cf. text no. 1 line 454 ḫe-pe-e KUR-šú. A reading [É-^{m}]ia-kin$_7$ was already tentatively proposed by A. Fuchs (Khorsabad p. 174 line 391 n. 2).

435 See text no. 7 lines 111 and 153 for restorations. [ru]-⸢uq$^{?}$⸣-ti: As already noted by A. Fuchs (Khorsabad p. 174 line 392 n. 1) perhaps instead ⸢SUD⸣-ti.

436 [(x) URU$^{?}$].⸢ṣur$^{?}$⸣-ra-a-⸢a$^{?}$⸣: The tentative reading follows N. Na'aman (Orientalia NS 67 [1998] p. 242 line 11). H. Winckler's copy has ?-kum-ra-a-a and A. Fuchs (Khorsabad p. 175 line 393) has [x x] ⸢KUM$^{?}$⸣ RA ^{m}x. P.E. Botta's copy shows an area of damage immediately before two small Winkelhaken, one above the other, followed by -ra-a- and then a vertical wedge immediately before another area of damage. The two small Winkelhaken could be the end of various signs in addition to ṣur and kum (e.g., bi and ul). Fuchs (Khorsabad p. 175 line 393 n. 1) says that the first A appears to be rather a masculine determinative followed by unclear traces; however, the squeeze would allow -a-⸢a⸣, although admittedly there is slightly more space than usual in the first A between the initial vertical wedge and the following ones, and all one can see of the second A is the initial vertical wedge (i.e., as copied by Botta). [a-na$^{?}$ KUR$^{?}$] ^{d}aš-šur.[KI$^{?}$]: This tentative reading basically follows Na'aman (Orientalia NS 67 [1998] p. 242 line 11) and cf. text no. 1 line 457. Similar writings exist but are rare, see for example text no. 1 line 234 and Leichty, RINAP 4 p. 72 no. 25 line 1 and p. 130 no. 58 ii 12. Nothing of this is currently visible on the squeeze, thus possibly [a-na$^{?}$] ^{d}aš-šur [...], "[to/for] the god Aššur." Winckler's copy has [...] ^{d}aš-šur [ù] 7 LUGAL.MEŠ-ni. See text no. 7 line 145 for the restorations at the end of the line.

437 Following šit-ku-nu H. Winckler's copy has né-[es-sa]-at šu-[ba]-at but the squeeze seems more similar to P.E. Botta's copy. It is not clear that there is sufficient room on the squeeze to allow the restoration šit-ku-⸢nu⸣-[ma šu-bat-su-un né-sa]-at. x x x ⸢ŠU⸣ MA I$^{?}$ ⸢kàd-ra⸣-[a-šú-un]: Botta's copy has [x] TA ŠU U MA I EN MA IR-[x x (...)]; Winckler's copy has [x (x)] TA [x (x)] ŠU MA I$^{?}$ EN$^{?}$ MA$^{?}$ IR$^{?}$-[x x x x (x)]; the squeeze appears to have x x x ⸢ŠU MA I kàd-ra⸣-[x x x]. A. Fuchs (Khorsabad p. 175 line 394) suggests that before ŠU the squeeze may have UR$^{?}$ DU$^{!?}$, and correctly notes that the I might instead be ⸢AD⸣, ⸢IA⸣, or ⸢ṢI⸣. The reading ⸢kàd-ra⸣-[a-šú-un] follows Fuchs (Khorsabad p. 175 line 394); N. Na'aman (Orientalia NS 67 [1998] p. 242 line 12) reads [x]-ta$^{?}$-šu-ma i-x-ma$^{?}$ ir$^{?}$ [x (x) ŠID$^{?}$], putting kadrâšun in the following line after mitḫāriš.

né†-sa?]-at ša [ul]-˹tu˺ u_4-[me†] ˹ul˺-[lu†-ti†] ˹a˺-na x x x ŠU MA I? ˹kàd-ra˺-[a-šú-un?]
438) mit-˹ḫa-riš˺ [x x x x] x ŠU ˹MA? RA?˺ [x x x] x ik-lu-ú [x x] x [{m}si?-il?]-˹ṭa?˺ man-da-ta-˹šú˺ ka-bit-tú ˹iš˺-šam†-ma [a]-˹na šuk˺-nu-uš IL [x x x x x x]
439) ˹e?-ri?˺-[šá?-ni? kit-ru? LÚ].˹šu-ut˺ SAG-ia la ˹a-dir˺ ta-ḫa-zi [it†-ti†] ki-[ṣir LUGAL]-ti-ia a-na tur-ri† gi†-mil-li-šú ˹ú˺-ma-˹'e-ra˺ [x x x x x x x (x)]
440) [x x x (x)] x (x) [e]-mu-qa-at ˹{d}˺aš-šur ˹e-mu˺-ru-ma a-[na†] ˹zi˺-kir ˹šu˺-mì-˹ia iš-ḫu˺-tú-ma ˹ir-ma-a? i?-da?-a?˺-šú-˹un?˺ KÙ.GI ˹KÙ˺.[BABBAR† ú†-nu-tu GIŠ.ESI GIŠ.TÚG]
441) [né-peš-ti KUR†]-šú-˹un?˺ [a†]-na qé-reb KÁ.˹DINGIR.RA˺.[KI† a-na maḫ]-˹ri-ia˺ iš-[šu†-nim†]-˹ma˺ [x (x)] IL ˹KU?/MA?˺ x ˹RI? am-nu˺-[ú-šu-nu-ti† {m}†]mut-tal-˹lum KUR˺.[ku-muḫ-ḫa-a-a]
442) [LÚ.ḫat-tu-ú lem-nu la a]-dir zik†-ri [DINGIR.MEŠ x x x x x x x x x x x x x x x x (x x)] x [x (x)] ˹TA˺ [x x x x x x x x (x)]
443) [x (x)] ˹URU.me˺-lid-du URU-šú GAL-a ú-šad-gi-lu pa-nu-uš-šú UGU ḫur-šá-a-ni zaq-˹ru-ti˺ it-ta-kil-ma ŠE [x x x x x x x x x x (x x)]
444) [ma]-˹da˺-at-tu ik-la-a-ma a-na šá-'a-al šul-mì-ia a-na qé-reb KUR.É-{m}ia-ki-ni a-di maḫ-ri-˹ia˺ [la iš†]-˹pu˺-ra rak-˹ba˺-[šú ù šu-ú]
445) [a]-˹lak˺-ti ger-ri-ia ša qé-reb KUR aš-šur.KI ù

[*stopped (the delivery of)* their] gift(s) [...] ... [...] they withheld [... *However, Silṭ*]a brought his substantial tribute to me and, [in or]der to subjugate [...], *he a*[*sked me for (military) aid*]. I sent a eunuch of mine who was fe[ar]less in battle, [with a royal] (military) conti[ngent] of mine, to avenge him (Silṭa). [...] they saw [the fo]rces of the god Aššur. Then, they became afraid a[t the (mere) me]ntion of my name and the[ir] *arms grew weak*. They bro[ught bef]ore me in Babylon gold, sil[ver, (and) utensils of ebony (and) boxwood, product(s) of] the[ir land, an]d (so) I conside[red them] ...

441b–446a) Mutallu [of the lan]d [Kummuḫu — an evil Hittite who did not fe]ar the words [of the gods ... (and)] to [who]m I had entrusted [the c]ity [M]elid, his great city — put his trust in the high mountains, [...] withheld (his) [(...) tri]bute, and [did not se]nd [his] mounted mess[enger] before me in the land Bīt-Yakīn to inquire about my well-being. [However, (when) that (man)] (445) heard of [the advan]ce of my expeditionary force, which was (already) in Assyria, and of the deeds I had been doing among the Chaldeans (and in) the land Elam, [fear] overwhelmed [him]. He conferred (lit.: "confers") with his advisors day and night (lit.: "night and day") [in order to ...] and to save his (own) life, and ... to take to the rugged mountains.

---

438 [x x x x] x ŠU ˹MA? RA?˺ [x x x] x: N. Na'aman (Orientalia NS 67 [1998] p. 242 line 13) reads: [kàd?-ra?]-˹a˺-šu-˹un? ú?˺-[šab?-ṭi?-lu?-(ma)]; however, there is too much room on the squeeze for just kad-ra-a between riš and šu, and the traces following ŠU would not allow -un ú-. ˹RA?˺: Possibly ˹AD˺ or ˹TA˺ instead (so Fuchs, Khorsabad p. 176 line 395 n. 1). H. Winckler has ŠU MA TA ik-lu-ú but there is clearly room for several more signs before ik-lu-ú. [x x] x [{m}si?-il?]-˹ṭa?˺: Na'aman (Orientalia NS 67 [1998] p. 242 line 13) reads here [bi-lat-sún? ù {m}si-il]-˹ṭa˺ (cf. text no. 1 lines 460–461); while the x might conceivably be ˹sún˺, there would not be sufficient room to restore ù. Na'aman (Orientalia NS 67 [1998] pp. 242–243 line 13) suggests we restore il-[la-at x x x x x] at the end of the line. Possibly restore ú-ṣal-(la)-an-ni at the end of the line; see text no. 1 note to line 462.
439 ˹e?-ri?˺-[šá?-ni? kit-ru? LÚ]: The tentative reading basically follows N. Na'aman (Orientalia NS 67 [1998] p. 242 line 14), although his restoration is slightly modified to fit the space available better. Cf. also text no. 1 line 462. The traces at the beginning of the line visible on the squeeze could also fit ˹a-na˺. -ri† gi†-: Nothing is visible of these on the squeeze, but as read by A. Fuchs (Khorsabad p. 176 line 396), likely -˹ri gi˺-, although P.E. Botta's copy shows no damage at this spot.
440 A. Fuchs (Khorsabad p. 176 line 397) reads [x x] ˹KUM!?˺ [x x e]-mu-qa-at for the beginning of the line, while N. Na'aman (Orientalia NS 67 [1998] pp. 242–243 line 15) suggests [e?-ti?]-˹qu?˺-[ma? e]-mu-qa-at (cf. text no. 1 line 464). The squeeze indicates that there is room for three or four signs before the traces of the first sign(s), indicated here as x (x) (possibly ˹QU˺), and that there would not be room for both MA and E in the space after what could be QU and before the MU. ˹ir-ma-a? i?-da?-a?˺-šú-[un]: P.E. Botta's copy has NI ˹MA˺ ŠE [x (x)] x x ŠÚ [x x] and H. Winckler's has NI ˹MA ŠE˺ [x x] x ˹NÍG ŠÚ˺ [x (x)]; the squeeze has ˹ir˺-x-˹a?˺ x-˹da?-a?-šú-un?˺; see text no. 1 line 465.
441b–454 According to the Assyrian Eponym Chronicle, the campaign against Mutallu of Kummuḫu, which is described here and which was led by Assyrian officials while Sargon was in Babylonia, took place in Sargon's fourteenth regnal year (708). Line 441: See text no. 74 vii 36 and text no. 7 lines 148–149 for the restorations at the beginning of the line. H. Winckler's copy has [a-di maḫ]-ri-ia. IL ˹KU?/LU?˺ x ˹RI˺: P.E. Botta's copy has IL MA DIŠ ˹RI˺ and Winckler's has IL MA [x] DIŠ ˹RI˺; as already noted by A. Fuchs (Khorsabad p. 177 line 398 n. 2), the squeeze suggests KU or LU rather than MA.
442 For the restorations, see text no. 7 line 112. zik†: P.E. Botta's and H. Winckler's copies both have KIŠ, likely for ˹zik˺, but neither copy has an area of damage immediately before the KIŠ and the squeeze is not helpful at this point.
Section 27 = lines 443–458 = V,4:1–17. See Winckler, Sar. Annals lines 390–406; Lie, Sar. pp. 70–71 lines 1–7 and pp. 72–73 lines 8–17; and Fuchs, Khorsabad Annals lines 400–416. Cf. text no. 7 lines 112/113–119a. It is often not clear how much room was missing at the ends of the lines and as a result some of the proposed restorations must be considered uncertain.
443 ˹URU.me˺-lid-du: The reading follows the squeeze; the copies by Botta and Winckler both have Ú-lid-du.
444 The copies by P.E. Botta and H. Winckler do not indicate sufficient room in the gap to restore la after maḫriya, but the squeeze indicates that there was sufficient room.
445 ˹lak˺: So squeeze; H. Winckler's copy has UR, while nothing is present on P.E. Botta's copy. For the restoration -šú ḫa-at-tú, see text no. 7 line 111.

ep-še-et i-na LÚ.*kal-di* KUR.ELAM.MA.KI *e-tep-pu-šú iš-me-ma it-*⌈*ta*⌉*-bi-*⌈*ik*⌉*-*[*šú ḫa-at-tú a-na x (x)*]

446) ⌈*ù šu-zu*⌉*-ub* ZI-*šú mu-šu ù ur-ru it-ti ma-li-ki-šu i-tam-ma x a-na e-le* KUR-*i mar-ṣu-ti* ⌈LÚ.*šu*⌉*-ut* SAG.⌈MEŠ⌉-[*ia x x x (x)*]

447) ⌈*it*⌉-[*ti*] ⌈*um-ma*⌉*-na-*⌈*te-šú*⌉*-nu rap-šá-a-ti it-ti ki-ṣir* LUGAL-*ti-ia ú-ma-ʾe-ra ṣe-ru-uš-šú* 6 KASKAL.GÍD *qaq-qa-ru* ⌈IGI⌉ *a-*⌈*lak*⌉ *ger-ri-*[*ia*? *x x x x*]

448) ⌈DAM⌉-*su* ⌈DUMU.MEŠ-*šú*? DUMU.MUNUS⌉.MEŠ-*šú e-zib-ma e-den-nu-uš-šú ip-par-šid-*⌈*ma*⌉ *la in-na-mir a-šar-šú* URU *šu-a-tú il-mu-ma* DAM-*su* DUMU.[MEŠ-*šú* DUMU.MUNUS.MEŠ-*šú*]

449) [(*x*)] *it-ti* UN.MEŠ KUR-[*šú* ANŠE.KUR.RA.MEŠ] ⌈ANŠE⌉.KUNGA.MEŠ ANŠE.MEŠ ANŠE.GAM.MAL.MEŠ GU$_4$.MEŠ *ù ṣe-e-ni a-na šal-la-ti im-nu-ú* ⌈*ip*⌉*-tu-*[*ú-ma* É *ni-ṣir-ti-šú*]

450) *x* ⌈KÙ⌉.GI KÙ.BABBAR *lu-*⌈*bul*⌉*-ti* ⌈*bir-me ù* TÚG.GADA SÍG⌉.[*ta-kil*†]-⌈*tu*⌉ SÍG.*ar-ga-man-nu* KUŠ AM.SI ZÚ AM.SI GIŠ.ESI GIŠ.TÚG *ni-ṣir-ti* [É.GAL-*šú*]

451) [*iš*]*-šu-nim-ma a-na* ⌈*qé*⌉*-reb* URU.*kal-ḫa a-di* ⌈*maḫ-ri-ia*⌉ *ub-lu-ni* URU ⌈*šú*⌉*-a-*⌈*tú*⌉ *a-na eš-šu-ti* ⌈*aṣ*⌉*-bat* UN.MEŠ KUR.É-^{m}*ia*†-[*ki*†*-ni ki-šit-ti*]

452) [ŠU.II-*ia*] *ina lìb-bi ú-še-šib* LÚ.*šu-ut* SAG-*ia* LÚ.EN.NAM UGU-*šú-nu* ⌈*áš-kun* LÚ⌉.*tur-*⌈*ta*⌉*-nu* É GÙB *aq-bi-šu-ma* MI ḪI [*x x x x (x x)*]

453) [UGU *ša*] *maḫ-re-e ú-*⌈*kin*⌉ GIŠ.GU.ZA-*šú* 1 ME 50 GIŠ.GIGIR 1 LIM 5 ME ANŠE.*pét-ḫal-lu* 20 LIM ⌈ERIM.MEŠ⌉ GIŠ.PAN 10 LIM *na-*⌈*áš*⌉ GIŠ.⌈*ka*†⌉-[*ba*†*-bi u* GIŠ.*az-ma-re-e*]

454) [*i-na*] ⌈*lìb*?⌉-[*bi-šú-nu*] *ak-ṣur-ma ú-šad-gi-la pa-nu-uš-šú it-ti* [LÚ].⌈EN⌉.NAM.MEŠ KUR-*ia am-nu-šú-ma* MÁŠ *x* [...]

455) [^{m}*dal-ta-a* LUGAL] ⌈KUR⌉.*el-li-pi ša ina a-lak ger-ri-ia maḫ-re-*⌈*e*⌉ [*x x x x (x)*] ^{d}*aš-šur* ⌈Ú⌉ [(*x*)] *x* [...]

456) [(*x x x*) *ú-ṣu-rat a*]*-*⌈*dan*⌉*-ni* ⌈*ik*⌉*-šu-*⌈*dam*⌉*-ma šim-tú ú-bil-šu-ma* [Ú† *x x x x (x)*]*-šú il-li-*⌈*ka*?⌉

446b–451a) I sent against him eunuchs [of mine, *provincial governors*], wi[th] their extensive troops, (along) with my royal (military) contingent. (*When there was still*) a distance of six leagues [for *my*] expeditionary force to go, [...] he abandoned his [wi]fe, *his* sons, (and) his [daught]ers, fled away by himself, and his whereabouts have never been discovered. They (the Assyrian troops) surrounded that city (Melid) and counted as booty his wife, [his] son[s, (and) his daughters], (along) with the people of [his] land, [horses], mules, donkeys, camels, oxen, and sheep and goats. They opened [his treasure house, (450) to]ok [g]old, silver, gar[men]ts with multi-[co]lored trim and linen garments, [blue-purp]le wool, red-purple wool, elephant hide(s), elephant ivory, ebony, (and) boxwood, the treasure [of his palace], and brought (these) befor[e m]e in the city Kalḫu.

451b–454) I re[or]ganized that city (Melid) (and) settled there the people of the land Bīt-Ya[kīn that I had conquered]. I s[e]t a eunuch of mine as provincial governor over them. I named him field marshal of the left (wing of the army) (lit.: "field marshal of the house of the left") and ... [...] I made his throne firm[er than] before. I conscripted [from among them] 150 chariot(s), 1,500 cavalry, 20,000 bowm[en], (and) 10,000 shie[ld and spear] bearers, and entrusted (them) to him. I considered him as (one of) [the] provincial [gov]ernors of my land and ... [...].

455–463a) [(At that time), the appointed] moment came [for Daltâ, king of the lan]d Ellipi, who/whom during the course of my previous campaign [...] the god Aššur ... [...], and (so) (his) fate carried him off and [(...)] his [...] he wen[t the way of death]. In [or-

446 H. Winckler's copy has no trace or indication of damage between *i-tam-ma* and *a-na*. P.E. Botta's copy and the squeeze seem to indicate that there was one sign between them, but it is possible that this may simply be damage to the squeeze.

449 Winckler's copy restores DUMU.MUNUS.MEŠ-*šú* at the beginning of the line, but the squeeze indicates that there is not room for this restoration. Instead of É *ni-ṣir-ti-šú*, possibly restore É.GAL É *ni-ṣir-ti-šú* (see text no. 4 line 15′), É *na-kam-te*, or *na-kam-(a)-te/ti* (see text no. 65 lines 274 and 295, and text no. 73 line 21); see also Fuchs, Khorsabad p. 178 line 406 n. 2.

450 The trace at the beginning of the line on the squeeze appears to be somewhat similar to a TI.

451 Winckler's copy restores the *ki-šit-ti* at the beginning of the following line, but based on the squeeze there is not room for it there.

452 The restoration at the beginning of the line is based on text no. 7 line 116. *ina*: P.E. Botta's copy has BE and the squeeze could suggest the same; H. Winckler and A. Fuchs (Khorsabad p. 179 line 409) have *ina*. ⌈LÚ⌉.*tur-*⌈*ta*⌉*-nu* É GÙB "field marshal of the left (wing of the army) (lit.: "field marshal of the house of the left")": With regard to the office of *turtānu* and Sargon's institution of the new office of *turtān bīt šumēli*, see Dezsö, Assyrian Army 1/1 pp. 218–221. As already noted by Fuchs (ibid. n. 2), possibly *mi-*⌈*iḫ*⌉*-*[*rit*] is to be read at the end of the line.

453 Botta's copy has 4 ME, but Winckler's copy and the squeeze have 5 ME. The restoration at the end of the line is based on text no. 7 line 117.

454 The restoration at the beginning of the line is based on text no. 74 iv 11 and text no. 7 line 117. A. Fuchs (Khorsabad p. 179 line 411) suggests possibly DA for the last sign, which is found only on P.E. Botta's copy; H. Winckler's copy ends after *am-nu-šú-ma*.

455 For the restoration at the beginning of the line, see text no. 7 line 117. A. Fuchs (Khorsabad p. 179 line 412) suggests that the trace at the end of the line might be RI.

456 For the restorations, see text no. 7 lines 117–118. It is not clear if there is sufficient room for the full restoration at the end of the line.

[ú-ru-uḫ mu-ú-ti ^{m}ni-bé-e]
457) [^{m}iš-pa-ba-a-ra DUMU].⸢MEŠ NIN$_{9}$$^{?}$⸣.MEŠ-šú a-[na† a-šab] GIŠ.[GU†.ZA] LUGAL-⸢ti-šú it$^{?}$⸣-ti [x x x x] x IA LU [...]
458) [x x x x x x (x)] ⸢tu-qu-un⸣-[tu x x x x x] ip†-[pu†-šú† ta†-ḫa†-zu† ^{m†}ni†-bé†-e† áš†]-šú tur-ri [gi-mil-li-šú]
459) [UGU ^{m}šu-túr-^{d}na]-⸢ḫu⸣-un-⸢di⸣ [LÚ†.ELAM†.MA†.KI-i ur-ri-ḫa LÚ.DUMU†] šip-ri [kit-ru id-din-šu-(ma) x x].MEŠ [x x x x x x (x x)]
460) [... il-li-ka] re-ṣu-[us]-su ^{m}is-[pa†-ba†-a†-ra† x (x)]-šú e-⸢dúr⸣-[ma† a†]-⸢na e-ṭer ZI⸣-[šú i-na su-pe-e ù te-me-qi]
461) ⸢ú$^{?}$-ṣal$^{?}$-la$^{?}$⸣-[an-ni-ma] ⸢e-riš-an-ni kit-ru⸣ [7 LÚ.šu-ut†] SAG-ia ⸢LÚ⸣.EN.⸢NAM†⸣.MEŠ-ti a-na tur†-ri gi-mil-li-šú áš-pur-[(...) di-ik-tu$^{?}$ šá$^{?}$]
462) ⸢^{m}ni⸣-[bé]-⸢e ma-ʾa-at⸣-tú ⸢id$^{?}$-du-ku$^{?}$⸣-ma šu-ú ⸢a⸣-[di] ⸢4⸣ LIM 5 ME LÚ.ELAM.MA.KI-a-a ⸢ERIM⸣.MEŠ GIŠ.⸢PAN⸣ a-na šu-zu-ub ZI.MEŠ-šú-nu [ip†-par-ši-du-ma]
463) [x x (x)] ⸢URU.mar-ú⸣-biš-ti e-⸢lu⸣-ú ana URU.mar-ú-⸢biš⸣-tu URU.⸢ḪAL†⸣.ṢU šá UGU ŠU.SI KUR-⸢i⸣ gap-[ši] ⸢a⸣-ṣa-at-ma it-ti ši-kin ur-⸢pe-e⸣-[ti x x]
464) [x x x] A URU.bir-⸢tu⸣ šu-a-tú ḫu-ḫa-riš is-ḫu-pu-u-ma šá-a-šú a-di LÚ.⸢mun⸣-daḫ-⸢ṣe†⸣-[šú† i†-na†] ⸢ṣi⸣-iṣ-ṣi ù iz-qa-ti a-⸢di maḫ⸣-[ri-ia]
465) [ub-lu-ni URU]-šú URU.mar-ú-biš-tu ⸢a⸣-na eš-šú-⸢ti† aṣ⸣-bat LÚ.⸢ERIM⸣.MEŠ ka-a-di (x) ⸢DU$^{?}$⸣ [(x)] ⸢BA$^{?}$⸣ x [x x] BI ú-še-li UGU gi-mir [KUR].⸢ELAM⸣.[MA.KI]
466) ⸢ú⸣-[šat]-bi-ka ⸢šaḫ⸣-ra-⸢ar⸣-tú UN.MEŠ KUR.⸢el⸣-li-pi† a-na pa-aṭ [gim†]-ri-šá [šu]-⸢ub-tu†⸣ ne-⸢eḫ†⸣-tú ú-še-⸢šib⸣ ni-ir

der to ascend] his royal [throne, Nibê (and) Ašpa-bara, sons of] his [siste]rs, with [...] ... [... wa]rf[are ...] th[ey were doing battle (with one another). Nibê quickly sent a messe]nger [to Šutur-Na]ḫūnd[i, the Elamite, in or]der to get [revenge. He (Šutur-Naḫūndi) gave him (military) aid (and) ... (460) ... (and) came] to his assista[nce]. Aš[pa-bara] took fright at his [..., and in order] to save [his] li[fe], *he besought* [*me* with supplications and entreaties and] asked m[e] for (military) ai[d]. I sent [seven of] my [eun]uchs, provincial governors, to avenge him [(...)]. *They inflicted a* major [*defeat on*] Ni[b]ê. As a result, that (man), toge[ther with] four thousand five hundred Elamite bowmen, [fled] in order to save their lives [and (...)] went up [to] the city Marubištu.

463b–467a) To the city Marubištu, a fortress that rises up on the peak of a mass[ive] mountain and [(...) *reaches up*] among the cloud[s, ...]. They (the Assyrian troops) overwhelmed that fortress as with a bird trap and [they (then) brought] bef[ore me] that (man) (Nibê), together with [his] fighting men, [in m]anacles and handcuffs. (465) [I] reorganized (the administration of) his [city] Marubištu (and) stationed *garrison* troops ... [...] I [had] deathly silence [de]scend over all [the land E]lam. I allowed the people of the land Ellipi, to its [fu]ll extent, to live in peace. I impo[sed] the yoke of my lordship [upon them] (and) they (now) pull my yoke.

---

457 For the restorations, see text no. 7 line 118. ⸢NIN$_{9}$$^{?}$⸣.MEŠ: P.E. Botta's copy has DIŠ MEŠ and H. Winckler's DAM.MEŠ; all that is currently visible on the squeeze is [...] DIŠ.MEŠ.

458 Based on text no. 7 line 79, possibly restore [*iḫ-šu-ḫu-ma*] after ⸢*tu-qu-un*⸣-[*tu*$^{?}$], "wanted (to offer) battle"; see already A.T.E. Olmstead (AJSL 47 [1930–31] p. 279). The restorations in the line are based on text no. 7 line 118. H. Winckler's copy may suggest that he saw *ip-pu-šú ta-ḫa-zu* ^{m}*ni-bé-e áš-šú tur-ri* [*gi-mil*]-*li-šú* [...] for the end of the line, but he may have meant to indicate that more than just *gi-mil* was restored (cf. his transliteration in Sar. 1 p. 68 line 405 where this passage is given without any indication of restoration). Although a few traces on the squeeze might support some of this reading, for the most part nothing is clearly legible on the squeeze.

459 The restorations are based on text no. 7 line 119. H. Winckler's copy has -*di* LÚ.ELAM.MA and DUMU as fully preserved, but nothing of this is currently clear on the squeeze apart from -⸢*di*⸣.

Section 28 = lines 460–476 = V,3:1–17. See Winckler, Sar. Annals lines 407–423; Lie, Sar. pp. 74–75 lines 1–10 and pp. 76–77 lines 11–17; and Fuchs, Khorsabad Annals lines 417–433. Cf. text no. 7 lines 119b–121a and 153b–162a and text no. 8 lines 27b–28a and 35–37a.

460b–461a Text no. 7 lines 119b–120a have *e-ṭe-er na-piš-ti-šú / i-na su-pe-e ù te-me-qi ú-ṣal-la-an-ni-ma* here but it is not clear that there is sufficient room in this text to restore all this. The reading of the beginning of line 461 is uncertain. P.E. Botta's copy has [(*x*)] ⸢*ú*†⸣-[*x x x x x* (*x*)] ⸢*e*⸣-*riš*-⸢*an-ni*⸣ and H. Winckler's copy has [*x x x* (*x*)] *ú-ṣal-la-an-ni-ma e-riš-an-ni*. A. Fuchs (Khorsabad p. 180 line 418) reads [*ù*] ⸢*te*†⸣-*me*-[*qi ú-ṣal*]-⸢*la*$^{!}$⸣-[*an-ni-ma*] ⸢*e*⸣-*riš*-⸢*an-ni*⸣, but the squeeze would suggest that there is insufficient room for this and it is assumed that *ù te-me-qi* were at the end of the preceding line. On the squeeze, the traces of the ⸢*ú*$^{?}$⸣- at the beginning of line 461 are directly above the ⸢*ú*⸣ at the beginning of line 466 and are assumed to be the ⸢*ú*†⸣- of Botta. Following these, the squeeze has traces of a sign that would fit *ṣal* and the beginning of a horizontal wedge, which is assumed to be the beginning of the LA.

462 See already A. Fuchs (Khorsabad p. 180 line 419 n. 1), who tentatively proposed *ma*$^{?}$-*ʾa*-⸢*at*⸣-*tú id-du-ku-ma*. Cf. text no. 7 lines 120–121.

463 *gap*-[*ši*]: So P.E. Botta's copy and the squeeze; H. Winckler's copy has ⸢EDIN⸣. For the reading *urpē*[*ti*] following *šikin*, see Borger, BiOr 14 (1957) p. 192 (*šikin urpati*) and text no. 65 line 96.

464 H. Winckler's copy has *bir-tú*, but the spacing and traces on the squeeze suggest *bir*-⸢*tu*⸣.

465 Between *ka-a-di* and *ú-še-li*, P.E. Botta's and H. Winckler's copies have [*x*] *x* PA NU BAR [*x* (*x*)] BI; A. Fuchs (Khorsabad p. 181 line 422) has DU$^{!?}$ *x* (*x*) TUR$^{!?}$ ŠE$^{!?}$ BI; and the squeeze might have (*x*) ⸢DU$^{?}$⸣ [(*x*)] ⸢BA$^{?}$⸣ *x* [*x x*] ⸢BI$^{?}$⸣.

be-lu-⸢ti-ia e-mid⸣-[su-nu-ti]

467) ⸢i-šu-ṭu⸣ ab-šá-a-ni† i-na ⸢u$_4$-me⸣-šu-ma i-na te-⸢ne⸣-še-e-⸢ti na†⸣-[ki†]-ri ⸢ki†-šit$^{?}$-ti$^{?}$ ŠU$^{?}$⸣.[II†-ia†] ⸢ša†⸣ ^{d}aš-šur ^{d}[AG†] ⸢ù⸣ ^{d}AMAR.⸢UTU⸣ ú-⸢šak⸣-[ni†-šu]

468) ⸢a-na GÌR.II-ia⸣ i-na [GÌR†.II† KUR].mu-⸢uṣ⸣-[ri] ⸢KUR⸣-i e-⸢le⸣-nu† ⸢NINA⸣.KI [ki-i] ṭè-em ⸢DINGIR⸣-[ma i]-na bi-bil [lìb-bi]-⸢ia⸣ URU [DÙ]-⸢uš-ma URU⸣.[BÀD-^{m}]⸢MAN-GIN$^{?}$⸣

469) ⸢az†⸣-[ku]-ra ni-bit-su ^{d}⸢é-a⸣ [^{d}30] ⸢^{d}⸣UTU ^{d}⸢AG⸣ [^{d}]IŠKUR ^{d}⸢nin⸣-[urta] ⸢ù⸣ [ḫi]-⸢ra⸣-ti-šú-nu [ra-ba-a-ti] ⸢ša⸣ i-na qé-reb [é-ḫur-sag-gal-kur-kur-ra]

470) ⸢KUR⸣ a-ra-al-⸢li⸣ ki-niš iʾ-al-du ⸢eš-re⸣-e-ti [nam]-⸢ra$^{?}$⸣-ti [suk-ki nak-lu-ti i-na qé]-reb [URU.BÀD-^{m}MAN-GI].NA ṭa-biš ir†-[mu-ú sat-tuk-ki]

471) la nar-ba-a-ti is-qu-uš-šú-⸢un⸣ ú-⸢kin-na⸣ [LÚ.NU].⸢ÈŠ.MEŠ⸣ LÚ†.[ram-ki LÚ.sur-maḫ-ḫi] šu†-ut [it-ḫu-zu nin]-⸢da⸣-an-šú-[un la-mid pi-riš-ti]

472) [AN].⸢GUB⸣.BA.MEŠ na-⸢aṭ⸣-pu-ti ma-ḫar-šú-⸢un⸣ [ul-ziz] ⸢É.GAL⸣ ZÚ AM.[SI GIŠ.ESI GIŠ.TÚG GIŠ.mu-suk]-kan†-[ni GIŠ.EREN] GIŠ.ŠUR.[MÌN GIŠ.dup-ra-ni GIŠ.LI]

473) [ù GIŠ].⸢bu-uṭ⸣-ni é-gal-⸢gaba⸣-ri-nu-tuku-a a-na mu-šab LUGAL-ti-⸢ia†⸣ i†-na† ⸢qer⸣-[bi-šú ab-ni-ma e]-li MU.[SAR-re]-e [KÙ.GI KÙ.BABBAR NA$_4$.ZA.GÌN]

474) [NA$_4$.aš]-⸢pe-e⸣ NA$_4$.pa-⸢ru⸣-[tum] ⸢URUDU.MEŠ AN⸣.NA A.⸢BÁR⸣ ù ḫi-bi-iš-ti ŠIM.[MEŠ uš-ši-šin ad-di-ma li-bit-ta-šin ú-kin-na GIŠ.ÙR.MEŠ GIŠ.ere-IGI]

467b–469a) At that time, (using as laborers) en[em]y people whom [I] had ca[ptur]ed (and) [wh]om the gods Aššur, [Nabû], and Marduk had [made bow down] at my feet, (and) [in accordance with] divine will (and) [m]y [heart's] desire, [I bui]lt a city at the [foot of Mount] Muṣ[ri], a mountain upstream from Nineveh, [and] I [nam]ed it [Dūr]-Šarruk[īn].

469b–472a) The gods Ea, [Sîn], Šamaš, Nabû, Adad, N[inurta], and their [great spo]uses [wh]o were duly born inside [Eḫursaggalkurkurra ("House, the Great Mountain of the Lands")], the mountain of the netherworld, gladly took up [residence in resplend]ent [san]ctuaries (and) [artfully-built shrines in]side [the city Dūr-Šarrukī]n. I established innumerable [regular offerings] as their shares (of temple income). [I had *nešak]ku*-[priest]s, [*ramku*-priests, *surmaḫḫu*-priests], men [well versed in] the[ir (fields of) knowl]edge (and) [initiated in secret rites], (and) *naṭpu*-[*ecst*]*atics* [serve] them (lit.: "[stand] before them").

472b–477a) [I built] in[side it (the city) a pa]llace using (lit.: "of") elep[hant] ivory, [ebony, boxwood, *musuk*]*kan*[*nu*-wood, cedar], cyp[ress, *daprānu*-juniper, juniper, and] terebinth, (namely) the Egalgabarinutukua ("Palace That Has No Equal"), to be my royal residence [and laid their foundations up]on inscr[ibed object]s [(made) of gold, silver, lapis lazuli, jas]per, *par*[*ūtu*-alabaster], copper, tin, lead, and pieces of aromatic wood[s. Then I established their brickwork (and)] roofed them [with larg]e [cedar beam]s. (475) [I bound the] doors of cypress (and) *mus*[*ukkannu*-wood with band(s) of shining copper and installed (them in)

467 P.E. Botta's copy has *ab-šá-a-x*, where *x* is similar to DU, but with only one lower horizontal wedge, and H. Winckler's copy has *ab-šá-a-ni*; the squeeze appears to have DU for the last sign. Botta's copy has *te*-TAB-*še-e-*⸢*ti*⸣ and Winckler's copy has *te-né-še-e-ti*, but the squeeze indicates *te-*⸢*ne*⸣*-še-e-*⸢*ti*⸣.

468 Mount Muṣri was identified with Ǧabal Maqlūb by E. Forrer, but it is now generally though to be Ǧabal Bāšīqa; see Kessler, RLA 8/7–8 (1997) p. 497 and Bagg, Rép. Géogr. 7/2 p. 433. H. Winckler's copy has at the end of the line URU [DÙ-*uš-ma* [URU.BÀD-^{m}]MAN-[GIN], thus omitting a "]" to go with the "[" before DÙ. From the squeeze, it is not clear that the trace of the last sign is ⸢GIN⸣ or ⸢GI⸣.[NA].

469–470a Line 469: H. Winckler's copy has ^{d}⸢*é*⸣-[*a* ^{d}30 ^{d}UTU ^{d}AG [^{d}]IŠKUR, thus there is no "]" to match the "[" after ^{d}⸢*é*⸣-. Chapels of these five gods (with Ea referred to as Ninšiku), as well as the goddess Ningal, were found in the palace complex at Khorsabad (see text nos. 16–21). Lines 469b–470a: According to the Eponym Chronicle, the gods of the city Dūr-Šarrukīn entered their temples on the twenty-second day of Tašrītu (VII) of 707.

470 [*nam*]-⸢*ra*$^{?}$⸣-*ti*: So the squeeze; H. Winckler's copy has [*nam-ra-a*]-*ti*. The trace of the sign before TI on the squeeze fits the end of RA better than A and there does not appear to be sufficient room to read [*nam-ra*]-⸢*a*⸣-*ti*.

472b–477a Lines 472–473 refer to the building of a palace (⸢É.GAL⸣), but lines 474–477 refers to this structure in the plural ("their foundations," "their brickwork," "roofed them," "their entrance(s)," and "th[eir gat]es"), as is the case in some other texts (e.g., text no. 7 lines 158b–162a). In some similar passages, we have É.GAL.MEŠ instead of É.GAL (e.g., text no. 9 line 60 and text no. 14 line 33) and this is likely the reason for the lack of agreement; note also text no. 47 lines 14–21, where we have É.GAL.MEŠ and yet UŠ$_8$-*šú*, "its foundations." É.GAL.MEŠ presumably refers to various sections/rooms within the palace complex and the translation "palatial halls" is used, following Grayson and Novonty, RINAP 3/2 p. 37 no. 39 line 60 and passim. Note that in line 482 of the present text, work is described on [É†].GAL.MEŠ *šá-ti-*⸢*na*⸣, "these [pala]tial halls." It is possible that the text means to imply that one section of the palace used ivory as decoration, one ebony, one boxwood, etc., rather than that all were used in each section. In a text of Sennacherib (Grayson and Novotny, RINAP 3/2 p. 93 no. 49 lines 20b–23a [partially restored, but see the note there to lines 20b–23a]), É.GAL is placed before each of the sixteen items mentioned as being used to build/decorate the palace complex (gold, silver, alabaster, *alallu*-stone, cypress, cedar, etc.). It seems unlikely that the author of the Sennacherib text meant to suggest that sixteen different palaces were erected in the same city, but rather that the palace complex included numerous different sections. Cf. also Grayson, RIMA 2 p. 289 A.0.101.30 lines 25b–29a.

473 With regard to the name of the palace, see Battini, NABU 2002/2 p. 27 no. 27. Sennacherib built at Nineveh a palace even larger than Sargon's at Khorsabad and gave it essentially the same name, written slightly differently in Sumerian (*é-gal-zag-du-nu-tuku-a* and *é-gal-zag-di-nu-tuku-a*); see for example Grayson and Novotny, RINAP 3/1 p. 38 no. 1 line 79 and p. 46 no. 2 line 56. H. Winckler's copy has *i**(copy: GAN)-*na**(copy: ḪI) *qer-bu-uš-šú ab-ni-ma e*]-*li* but with no "[" to go with the "]."

475) ⸢GAL⸣.MEŠ *e-li-⸢šin⸣ ú-šat-⸢ri⸣-ṣa* ⸢GIŠ.IG⸣.MEŠ GIŠ.ŠUR.MÌN GIŠ.*mu-⸢suk⸣-[kan-ni me-se-er* URUDU *nam-ri ú-rak-kis-ma ú-rat-ta-a né-reb-šin]*
476) [É] ⸢*ap-pa*⸣-[*a-ti tam-šil* É.GAL KUR.*ḫat-ti ša i-na li-šá-an* KUR MAR.TU.KI É *ḫi-la-an-ni i-šá-as-su-šú*]
477) [*ú-še*]-⸢*pi*⸣-*šá mé-⸢eḫ-ret⸣* [*ba*]-⸢*bi-šin*⸣ [8†] UR†.⸢MAḪ†⸣.[MEŠ† *tu*†]-*ʾa-me šu-⸢ut* 1⸣ ŠÁR GÉŠ.U 6 UŠ 40+[10†.TA.ÀM GUN *mal-tak-ti* URUDU *nam-ri ša ina ši-pir*]
478) [^{d}*nin*]-⸢*á-gal nak-liš ip*⸣-[*pat*†]-⸢*qu*⸣-*ma* ⸢*ma-lu-ú*⸣ *nam-ri-ir-ri* 4 GIŠ.*tim-me* GIŠ.⸢EREN⸣ [*šu*]-⸢*ta-ḫu-ti*⸣ [*ša* 1 NINDA.TA].⸢ÀM⸣ [*ku*†-*bur-šú*†-*un*]
479) [*bi-ib-lat*] ⸢KUR⸣.*ḫa-ma-ni* UGU ⸢*pirig-gal*⸣-*le-e ú-⸢kin⸣-ma* GIŠ.*dáp-⸢pi⸣ ku-lul* ⸢KÁ⸣.MEŠ-*šin e-mid* ⸢UDU⸣.[MEŠ *šad-di*] $^{d?}$[LAMMA MAḪ.MEŠ *ša*] ⸢NA$_4$⸣ [KUR-*i*] *eš-qí* ⸢*nak*⸣-[*liš*† *ab-ni-ma*]
480) [*a-na*] ⸢*er*⸣-*bet*-[*ti šá*]-⸢*a-ri*⸣ *ú-šá-aṣ-bi-⸢ta* SI⸣.GAR-*ši-in as-mu* ⸢*as*⸣-[*kup*†]-*pi* NA$_4$.*pi-li* [GAL†.MEŠ *da*]-⸢*ád-me ki*⸣-[*šit*]-⸢*ti*⸣ [ŠU.II]-⸢*ia*⸣ *ṣe-⸢ru⸣*-[*uš-ši-in*]
481) [*ab*]-*šim-ma* [*a*†-*sur*†]-*ru-šin ú-šá-as-ḫi-ra a-⸢na⸣ tab-ra-a-te ú-šá-⸢lik⸣ te-ne-še-ti* [*ma*†]-*ti-tan šá ul-tú ṣi-⸢taš⸣* [*a*†]-⸢*di*⸣ *šil-⸢la⸣*-[*an*]
482) [*i*]-⸢*na e*⸣-*mu-⸢uq⸣* ^{d}*aš-šur* EN-*ia* ⸢*ak*⸣-*šud-du-ma i-na ši-pir* LÚ.*ùr-ra-ku-tú* [*i*]-⸢*na*⸣ *qé-*[*reb*† É†].GAL.MEŠ *šá-ti-⸢na áš-tak-ka⸣*-[*na*]
483) [*si*]-⸢*ma*⸣-*a-te i-⸢na⸣* [ITI] *še-mé-e* u$_4$-⸢*me mit-ga*⸣-*ri* ^{d}*aš-šur a-bu* DINGIR.MEŠ [EN† GAL†] DINGIR.MEŠ ⸢*ù*⸣ [^{d}]IŠ.TAR.MEŠ *a-ši-bu-⸢ut* KUR⸣ *aš-šur*.[KI]
484) [*qé-reb-ši-na*†] ⸢*aq*⸣-[*re-e-ma kàd*†]-*re-e ṣa-⸢ri-ri⸣ ru-uš-ši-*[*i*†] ⸢*ṣar-pi eb*⸣-*bi* ⸢IGI⸣.[SÁ]-⸢*e*⸣ *šad-lu-*[*ti*†] ⸢*ta*⸣-*mar-tu ka-bit-tú*

their entrance(s). I had bu]ilt in front of th[eir gat]es [a po]rt[ico ([*bīt*] *appāti*), a replica of a Hittite palace, which is called a *bīt ḫilāni* in the language of the land Amurru].

477b–483a) [Eight t]win [l]ion (colossi) [of shining copper] that weigh 4,6[10 full (lit.: "tested") talents (and) that were skill]fully [ca]st [by the craft of the god Nin]ag[al] and filled with radiance — upon (those) lion colossi I installed four [ma]tching cedar columns, [whose diameter(s) are one *nindanu* ea]ch, [the product of Mo]unt Amanus; and I positioned cross-beams (upon them) as a cornice for their ga[te]s. [I] skill[fully fashioned magnificent mountain] sheep [colossi of] massive [mountain] stone [and (480) in] the four [dir]ections I had (them) hold their (the gates') respective (lit.: "fitting") door bolt(s). [I dep]icted [the settle]ments that I [had] con[quered] upon [large] limestone s[la]bs and surrounded their (the palatial halls') [lower cou]rses (with them). I made (them) an object of wonder. I plac[ed in]si[de] these [pala]tial halls [represe]ntations — (made) by the craft of the sculptor — of the people of every [la]nd that [I] had conquered, from ea[st t]o wes[t, by] the strength of the god Aššur, my lord.

483b–489a) In a favorable [month], (on) an auspicious day, I inv[ited] the god Aššur, the father of the gods, [the great lord], (and) the gods and goddesses who dwell in Assyria [(to come) inside them and] I of[fe]red them (the gods) [gif]ts of red *ṣāriru*-gold (and) pure si[lv]er, extensive pr[esen]ts as (my) substantial audience gift. [I (thus) (485) made the]ir (the gods')

476 [É] ⸢*ap-pa*⸣-[*a-ti*] "portico": The translation follows CAD A/2 p. 183 and CDA p. 20; however, it is not impossible that the term refers instead to a structure with windows; see Reade, Iraq 70 (2008) pp. 34–36. É *ḫi-la-an-ni* "*bīt ḫilāni*": The term *bīt ḫilāni* has generally been thought to refer to a structure with an entry portico, but D. Kertai has recently argued that it refers instead to "the wide internal doors within the monumental suites of Assyria and the new types of ornamentation added within their midst," the new type of ornamentation being "statues with columns on top of them" and/or "columns standing on column bases" (Iraq 79 [2017] p. 101).
476–481a Cf. Grayson and Novotny, RINAP 3/1 pp. 38–39 no. 1 lines 82–86.
Section 29 = lines 477–493 = V,2:1–17. See Winckler, Sar. Annals lines 424–440; Lie, Sar. pp. 76–77 line 1, pp. 78–79 lines 2–10, and pp. 80–81 lines 11–17; and Fuchs, Khorsabad Annals lines 434–450. Cf. text no. 7 lines 162b–185a and text no. 8 lines 37b–40a and 54–68a.
477 H. Winckler's copy has [*ú-še-pi*]-*šá mé-eḫ-ret ba-bi-šin* 8 UR.MAḪ.MEŠ *tu-ʾa-me* .... The term *tūʾame* may refer to pairs of lion colossi instead of to twin (i.e., identical) colossi; see also Fuchs, Khorsabad p. 340. 4,610 full talents are approximately 140,000 kg, assuming the light, rather than the heavy, mina is being used. Despite the distributive TA.ÀM after the number, it seems more likely that this was the weight of all the lion colossi together.
478 [*ku*†-*bur-šú*†-*un*]: H. Winckler's copy has *ku-*[*bur*]-*šú-*[*un*] while nothing of this is indicated on P.E. Botta's copy and the squeeze only has some indistinct traces.
479 *ú-⸢kin⸣-ma*: So the squeeze and text no. 7 line 164, contra P.E. Botta's copy *ú-*TE-*ma*, H. Winckler's copy *ú-še-šib-ma*, and A. Fuchs' reading *ú-še-⸢šib⸣!-ma* (Khorsabad p. 183 line 436). ⸢UDU⸣.[MEŠ *šad-di*] ^{d}[LAMMA MAḪ.MEŠ] "[mountain] sheep [colossi]": See Engel, Dämonen pp. 31–36. Possibly "[mountain] rams," not "[mountain] sheep." With regard to the reading ^{d}LAMMA MAḪ.MEŠ as two words rather than one, see ibid. pp. 7–8. The phrase appears in several of Sargon's inscriptions, including one occasion when ^{d}LAMMA is written at the end of one line and MAḪ.MEŠ at the beginning of the following line (Botta, Monument de Ninive 3 pl. 57[c] lines 3–4 = text no. 9 line 75 ex. 19) and two occasions when it is written ^{d}LAMMA.MEŠ MAḪ.MEŠ (Botta, Monument de Ninive 3 pl. 16[quater] line 117 and pl. 11[quater] lines 88–89 [MAḪ.MEŠ restored on second line] = text no. 13 line 117 exs. 1 and 5 respectively).
480 [*a-na*] ⸢*er*⸣-*bet-*[*ti šá*]-⸢*a-ri*⸣ *ú-šá-aṣ-bi-⸢ta* SI⸣.GAR-*ši-in as-mu* "[in] the four [dir]ections I had (them) hold their (the gates') respective (lit.: "fitting") door bolt(s)": Or "I placed (them) facing their (the gates') respective (lit.: "fitting") door bolt(s) [in] the four [dir]ections" (cf. CAD Š/2 p. 409).

ú-⸢šam-ḫir-šú-nu⸣-[ti†-(ma)]

485) [ú-šá]-⸢li⸣-[ṣa] nu-⸢pa⸣-[ar-šú]-⸢un GU$_4$⸣.MAḪ-ḫi bit-ru-ti šu-᾿e-e [ma†]-ru-ti ⸢KUR.GI⸣.MUŠEN.MEŠ [UZ.TUR].MUŠEN.MEŠ PÉŠ.GIŠ.GI.MEŠ [iz-ḫe-et] ⸢KU$_6$.MEŠ⸣

486) [ù] MUŠEN†.[MEŠ] ⸢ḪÉ⸣.GÁL [ZU†.AB šá] ⸢la⸣ i-šu-ú mi-ṭi-ta ku-[ru-un-nu] ⸢làl?⸣-[la-ru] ⸢bi⸣-ib-lat ⸢KUR.MEŠ⸣ KÙ.MEŠ ⸢ki⸣-šit-ti ŠU.II-⸢ia šá a-na iš⸣-[qí†]

487) [LUGAL-ti-ia] ⸢uṣ⸣-ṣi-ba za-[ru]-u DINGIR.MEŠ ^{d}aš-šur it-ti ni-⸢iq⸣ [ŠÀ.IGI.GURU$_6$]-e [eb†]-⸢bu⸣-ti [qut†-rin†-ni†] šur-ru-ḫi tam-qi-ti la ⸢nar-ba-a-ti⸣

488) [ma-ḫar-šu-un] aq-qí áš-šú šá-⸢ṭa⸣-[pu†] ⸢na⸣-piš-[ti†] ⸢UD⸣.MEŠ ⸢SÙ⸣.[MEŠ† na†-da-nim†-ma† ù†] ⸢kun†⸣-[nu† BALA]-⸢ia na-a᾿⸣-di-iš ak-mì-sa [ut-nin†]

mo[ods j]oy[ful]. I offered [before them] prize b[u]lls in prime condition, [fa]ttened sheep, [ge]ese, [duc]ks, *dormice*, [strings of fish and] bird[s, the we]alth [of the Deep (*apsû*) that] never lessens, *ku*[*runnu-beer* (and)] whi[te honey, pr]oducts of the pure mountains, that I had conquered, which the pro[genit]or of the gods, the god Aššur, had added to [my royal] l[ot], (along) with [pur]e [voluntary sacrific]es, splendid [incense offerings], (and) in[nu]merable libations. Reverently, I knelt (and) [prayed before him] that he preser[ve (my)] lif[e, give (me) a] l[ong] life, [and fir]mly est[ablish] my [reign].

489) [ma-ḫar-šu] ul-tu KUR GAL-ú ^{d}⸢EN?.LÍL⸣ [EN† KUR†.MEŠ†] a-šib é-[ḫur†]-⸢sag-gal⸣-[kur†]-kur-[ra† ù†] DINGIR.MEŠ [a]-⸢ši-bu⸣-[ut†] ⸢KUR⸣ aš-šur.KI i-⸢na tam-gi-ti⸣

490) [ù za-mar tak†]-⸢né-e⸣ i-tu-⸢ru URU⸣-[uš-šú-un] ⸢it⸣-ti mal-[ki† ma†]-ti-tan LÚ.⸢EN⸣ pa-[ḫa†]-⸢ti⸣ KUR-ia LÚ.⸢ak-li⸣ LÚ.šá-⸢pi-ri⸣ LÚ.⸢NUN⸣.[MEŠ†]

491) [LÚ.šu-ut†] SAG.MEŠ ⸢ù LÚ⸣.[AB.BA.MEŠ KUR aš-šur.KI i-na†] qé-⸢reb⸣ [É†].GAL-ia ú-⸢šib⸣-ma ⸢áš⸣-[ta†]-kan ni-[gu†]-tú [KÙ†].⸢GI KÙ.BABBAR ú⸣-[nu†-ut†] ⸢KÙ.GI KÙ⸣.[BABBAR†]

492) [bi†-nu]-tu KUR†-[i kal ŠIM.MEŠ Ì DÙG.GA] ⸢lu⸣-[bul†]-⸢ti⸣ bir-me ù TÚG.GADA ⸢SÍG.ta-kil⸣-tu SÍG.⸢ar⸣-ga-⸢man-nu⸣ [KUŠ† AM†].⸢SI⸣ [ZÚ† AM.[SI†] ⸢GIŠ⸣.[ESI†]

493) [GIŠ.TÚG mim-ma aq-ru ni-ṣir-ti LUGAL-ti ANŠE.KUR.RA.MEŠ KUR.mu†]-⸢ṣu†⸣-ri ⸢ṣi-mit-ti ni⸣-i-ri GAL.MEŠ ⸢ANŠE⸣.[KUNGA.MEŠ ANŠE.MEŠ ANŠE.GAM.MAL.MEŠ GU$_4$.MEŠ]

494) [ù US$_5$.UDU.ḪI.A (...)] ⸢man-da†⸣-[at-ta-šú-nu ka-bit-tu am-ḫur]

489b–494) After the great mountain, the divine [En]lil (Aššur), [the lord of (all) lands], who dwells in E[ḫurs]agga[lkur]kur[ra, and] the (other) gods [who d]we[ll in] Assyria had returned [to their] c[ity] amid so[ngs of] joy (490) [and hymns of pra]ise, with rul[ers from] every [la]nd, provi[ncial gove]rnors of my land, overseers, commanders, nob[les, eun]uchs, and [elders of Assyria], I sat down [in]side my [pal]ace and h[e]ld a fes[ti]val. [I received as their substantial] tri[bute gol]d, s[ilv]er, ut[ensils] of gold (and) sil[ver, produ]ct(s) of the mountain[(s), every kind of aromatic, fine oil], gar[men]ts with multi-colored trim and linen garments, blue-[pur]ple wool, red-purple wool, [elepha]nt [hide(s)], elep[hant ivory, ebony, boxwood, everything valuable, royal treasure], large [Egy]ptian [horses] that are trai[ne]d to the yoke, [mules, donkeys, camels, oxen, and sheep and goats (...)].

495) [URU] ⸢i?⸣-[tu-ut ku-un lib-bi-ia u É.GAL šá-a-tu ^{d}aš-šur AD DINGIR.MEŠ]

495–506a) [May the god Aššur, the father of the gods, look steadfastly upon (this) city] that has been d[uly

485 ⸢KUR.GI⸣.MUŠEN.MEŠ [UZ.TUR].MUŠEN.MEŠ: The reading is based on the squeeze and follows text no. 7 lines 168–169. The copy of H. Winckler has ⸢GÚ⸣.MUŠEN.MEŠ [UZ].⸢TUR⸣.MUŠEN.MEŠ.

488 H. Winckler's copy has *šá-ṭa-pu na-piš-ti* UD.MEŠ SUD.MEŠ *na-[da]-⸢nim⸣-ma ù kun-nu*.

489 H. Winckler's copy has ^{d}EN.LÍL EN KUR.KUR *a-šib é-ḫur-sag-gal-kur-kur-ra ù* DINGIR.MEŠ *[a]-⸢ši⸣-bu-ut* KUR *aš-šur*.KI *i-na tam-gi-ti*.

490 H. Winckler's copy has *[ù mar] tak-né-e i-tu-ru* URU-*[uš-šú-un] it-ti mal-ki ma-ti-tan* LÚ.EN *pa-ḫa-ti* KUR-*ia* LÚ.*ak-li* LÚ.*šá-pi-ri* LÚ.NUN.MEŠ.

491 ⸢KÙ.GI KÙ⸣.[BABBAR†]: So the squeeze for the end of the line, contra P.E. Botta's copy which has nothing of this preserved, H. Winckler's copy which has KÙ.GI KÙ.BABBAR [NA$_4$ *a-qar-tum* URUDU], and A. Fuchs' edition (Khorsabad p. 186 line 448) which has [KÙ.GI] ⸢KÙ⸣.[BABBAR NA$_4$ *a-qar-tum* URUDU *par-zil-lum*]. Cf. text no. 7 line 180, which has *ú-nu-⸢ut⸣* KÙ.GI KÙ.BABBAR NA$_4$ *a-qar-tum* URUDU *par-zil-lum*.

492 For the start of the line, H. Winckler's copy has *[par-zil-lum] bi-[nu]-tu*, but the squeeze shows that there is insufficient room for all this. ⸢*lu*⸣-*[bul†]-⸢ti⸣*: Winckler's copy has TÚG.*lu-bul-ti*, but nothing of the TÚG or *bul* signs are on P.E. Botta's copy or currently visible on the squeeze. Text no. 7 line 181 and text no. 8 line 63 do not have TÚG before *lu-bul-ti*.

493 H. Winckler's copy has [GIŠ.TÚG] *mim-ma aq-ru ni-ṣir-ti* LUGAL-*ti* ANŠE.KUR.RA.MEŠ KUR].*mu-ṣu-ri*, thus there is no "[" to match the "]" between KUR and *mu-*.

Section 30 = lines 494–510 = V,1:1–17. See Winckler, Sar. Annals lines 441–460; Lie, Sar. pp. 80–81 lines 1–4 and pp. 82–83 lines 5–17; and Fuchs, Khorsabad Annals lines 451–467. Cf. text no. 7 lines 185b–194 and text no. 8 lines 68b–77a and 80b–87.

494 P.E. Botta's copy would allow for four or five signs between the restored US$_5$.UDU.ḪI.A and ⸢*man-da*†⸣-*[at-ta-šú-nu]*; however, text no. 7 line 185 immediately follows US$_5$.UDU.ḪI.A with ⸢*man-dat*⸣-*ta-šú-nu* and the squeeze indicates that the traces of the ⸢*man-da*†⸣- are much closer to the left end than the copy indicates.

496) [*i-na nu*]-˹*um*˺-[*mur*] *bu*-[*ni-šú* KÙ].MEŠ [*ki-niš lip-pa-lis-ma a-na* UD.MEŠ *ru-qu-ti*]
497) [*ud-du-su*]-˹*un lit-tas-qar i-na pi*†˺-[*i-šú*] ˹KÙ˺ *liš*-[*šá-kin-ma* ^{d}ALAD *na-ṣi-ru*]
498) [DINGIR *mu-šal*]-˹*li-mu im-mu*˺ *ù mu*-[*šá*] *qé*-˹*reb*˺-*šú-un*† ˹*liš*˺-[*tab-ru-ma*] ˹*a-a*˺ [*ip-par-ku-ú*]
499) [*i-da-šú-un qí-bi-tuš-šu*] ˹*mal*˺-[*ku*] ˹*ba*˺-*nu*-˹*šú*˺-*un* ˹*ši*˺-[*bu-ta lil*]-˹*lik*˺ [*lik-šu-ud*]
500) [*lit-tu*]-˹*tu*˺ [*a-na*] ˹*u*$_{4}$˺-[*me*] ˹*da-ru*˺-[*ti*] *li-bur* ˹*e-pi-su-un*˺ [*ina šap-ti-šu*]
501) [*el*]-˹*le*˺-[*tim*] ˹*li*˺-*ṣa*-[*a a*]-*šib* É.GAL† *šá*-˹*a*˺-*tu-nu* [*ina ṭu-ub*]
502) [UZU.MEŠ *nu-ug lib-bi ù*] ˹*na*˺-*mar ka-bat*-˹*ti*˺ *qé*†-[*reb*]-*šá*
503) ˹*li*˺-[*šá-li*]-˹*la*˺ [*liš-ba*]-*a bu-ʾa*-˹*a*˺-*ri*† ˹*i*˺-*na* [(*x*)] ZI [*x x x*] ŠU
504) [*x*] *x* [*x x x x*] GIŠ ID [(*x*)] NÍG.[ŠU KUR].MEŠ *na-ki*†-*ri* ˹*šad*˺-*lu-ti*
505) [IGI.SÁ-*e da*]-˹*ád*†˺-[*me*] *nu-ḫuš kib*-[*rat ḫi-ṣib*] KUR-˹*e ù*˺ *ta*-˹*ma-a*˺-*ti*
506) [*la-aq-ru-na*] ˹*qé*˺-*reb*-[*šá*] *a*-˹*na*˺ [*ar-kàt*] *u*$_{4}$-[*me*] NUN ˹*ar-ku*˺-*ú*
507) [*ina* LUGAL].MEŠ-˹*ni* DUMU.MEŠ-*ia*˺ [*an*]-˹*ḫu*˺-[*ut* É].˹GAL˺ *šá-a-tu* ˹*lu-ud-diš*˺
508) [MU.SAR-*a-a*] ˹*li*˺-*mur*-˹*ma* Ì˺.<GIŠ> ˹*lip*˺-*šu-uš ni*-˹*qa-a*˺ [*liq-qí*] *a-na áš*-˹*ri*˺-*šú*
509) [*lu-ter*] ˹^{d}*aš-šur ik-ri*˺-[*bi-šú*] ˹*i*˺-[*še-em-me mu-nak*]-˹*kir*˺ *šiṭ*†-˹*ri-ia*˺
510) [*ù* MU-*ia*] ˹^{d}˺*aš*-˹*šur*˺ [*be-lí* LUGAL-*su lis-kip* MU-*šú* NUMUN-*šú i-na* KUR *li-ḫal-liq-ma a-a ir-ši-šú re-e-mu*]

selected by me (lit.: "the ch[oice of the steadfastness of my heart]") and (upon) this palace with his holy, ra]dia[nt] fa[ce and] may he ordain [the]ir [renovation for future days]. May (the following command) c[ome] from (lit.: "be s[et] in") [his ho]ly [mouth]: May [the guardian spirit (and) the prot]ect[ive god stay continually] in them, d[a]y and nig[ht, and] may [they] never [leave them. At his command, may] the r[uler] who constructed them [li]ve l[ong (and) reach (500) extreme old a]ge. May [th]eir bu[ilder] remain in good health [for]ev[er]. May (this command) iss[ue from his (the god Aššur's) h]o[ly lips]. May [the one who d]wells inside these palatial hall(s) [rejoi]ce th[er]e [in physical well-being, merriment, and h]appiness, [(and) be fully satisf]ied with (his) good fortune. In [...] ... [May I store up] inside [it (the palace) (...)] extensive prop[erty (taken) from] enemy [land]s, [presents from (every) set]tl[ement], the yield of the (four) quar[ters (of the world), (and) the wealth] of (both) the mountain(s) and the seas.

506b–509a) In day[s to come], may a future ruler [among the king]s, m[y] descendants, renovate [(any) dilapi]da[ted sections of] this [pal]ace. May he (then) discover [my inscribed object, a]noint (it) with oil, [offer] a sac[rif]ice, [(and) return (it)] to its (original) place. The god Aššur [will (then) listen to his] pra[yers].
509b–510) [(As for) the one who alte]rs my inscri[ption or my name, may] the god Aššur, [my lord, overthrow his kingship. May he (the god Aššur) make his name (and) his descendant(s) disappear from the land and may he have no pity on him].

3

The texts on three wall slabs from the western end of Room XIII (slabs 4, 6, and 7) were copied by P.E. Botta and these preserve part of a version of Sargon's Annals. The room slabs were numbered in clockwise order and each of the three Annals slabs has 15 lines of text. The inscription describes events in Sargon's eleventh and twelfth regnal years (711–710): campaigns to Gurgum and Ashdod (lines 1′–13′a) and against Marduk-apla-iddina II (Merodach-Baladan) of Babylonia (lines 13′b–60′) respectively. As far as it is preserved, the Annals inscription in this room largely duplicates the version of the Annals in Room II (text no. 1 lines 248–266 and 276/277–340) and Room V (text no. 2 lines 267–292 and 309/310–338), but with some major variations.

---

2 lines 503–504 Cf. text no. 8 lines 79–80. Line 503: Possibly instead ˹*i*˺-*na* ZI-*šu* or ˹*i*˺-*na* ZI(-)[*x x x*]-*šu*; cf. *i-na šap-ti-šú* in text no. 8 line 80.
2 line 508 ˹Ì˺.<GIŠ>: Or less likely <Ì>.˹GIŠ˺; the squeeze indicates that there was not room for both signs.
2 line 509 *šiṭ*†: P.E. Botta's copy has ŠÁ, which A. Fuchs (Khorsabad p. 188 line 466) reasonably reads as ˹*šiṭ*˺-, assuming that there was damage at that point. There is a trace of the sign visible on the squeeze, but nothing identifiable.

Botta had squeezes made of the inscriptions on all three slabs and they are still extant, stored in the Louvre (Paris). In addition, a small part of slab 4 (section 1′) is preserved today in the Louvre (Paris), on display in its galleries. The forty-five lines on the three slabs are to be associated with Winckler, Sar. Annals lines 209–232 and 250–278; Lie, Sar. pp. 38–39 lines 1–5, lines 248–266 and 277–280 (see also n. 9 to line 280), p. 48 lines 1–6, line 326 (see also n. 5 to line 326), lines 333–338, and pp. 50–53 lines 11–15; and Fuchs, Khorsabad Annals lines 235–258 and 269–295. For a plan of the room, see Figure 12 and Botta, Monument de Ninive 2 pl. 139; for drawings of the reliefs on the slabs in the room, see ibid. pls. 139–143, in particular 141–143 for the three slabs with the inscription edited here. With regard to the reliefs in Room XIII, see Reade, JNES 35 (1976) pp. 96 and 98; and Reade, Bagh. Mitt. 10 (1979) p. 83. The slabs found in the room depict the campaign of Sargon's eighth regnal year (714) against Urarṭu and Muṣaṣir. Slab 4 has an epigraph upon it (text no. 36) identifying the scene depicted as being the capture of the city Muṣaṣir.

CATALOGUE

Section	Ex.	Source	Provenance	Botta, MdN	Fuchs, Khorsabad line	Lines Preserved	cpn
1′	Bt	Botta, Monument de Ninive 3 pl. 155[c]	Khorsabad, Palace, Room XIII, slab 4	2 pl. 141	235–255, 255a–b, 256–258	1′–15′	n
	Wi	Winckler, Sar. 2 pl. 13 no. 27[c]					n
	Sq	Louvre squeeze					p
	AO	AO 19892 (Nap. III 2884)					c
[2′]	—	—	[Khorsabad, Palace, Room XIII, slab 5]	—	—	[16′–30′]	—
3′	Bt	Botta, Monument de Ninive 3, pl. 156[c]	Khorsabad, Palace, Room XIII, slab 6	2 pl. 142	269–271, 271a, 272, 272a–e, 275–285	31′–45′	n
	Wi	Winckler, Sar. 2 pl. 13 no. 28[c]					n
	Sq	Louvre squeeze					p
4′	Bt	Botta, Monument de Ninive 3, pl. 157[c]	Khorsabad, Palace, Room XIII, slab 7	2 pl. 143	285–295	46′–60′	n
	Wi	Winckler, Sar. 2 pl. 14 no. 29[c]					n
	Sq	Louvre squeeze					p

COMMENTARY

If one assumes that each wall slab with the Annals inscription in this room had fifteen lines of text and that the inscription was in general similar to that in Room II and V, there would presumably have been about fifteen or sixteen inscribed wall slabs before Room XIII slab 4 and about eleven or twelve after slab 7. The drawing of the reliefs in the room by E. Flandin in Monument de Ninive 2 pl. 140 indicates that slab 3 was inscribed; it likely preserved the section of the Annals immediately before that found on slab 4.

Section 1′ (lines 1′–15′): A small section of the inscription (parts of three lines, 13′–15′) on slab 4 is preserved today in the Louvre (AO 19892). The squeeze of section 4 does not include the last approximately ten percent of each line.

Section 3′ (lines 31′–45′): Although a squeeze of this section is preserved in the Louvre, it is particularly faint and, except in a few places, unhelpful.

Restorations in lines 1′–5′ are based on text no. 2 lines 267b–272a; in lines 6′–15′ on text no. 1 lines 248–266a and text no. 2 lines 272b–292; and in lines 31′–60′ on text no. 1 lines 276/277–340+ and text no. 2 lines 309/310–338a.

BIBLIOGRAPHY

1849 Botta, Monument de Ninive 2 pls. 139–143 (drawing of reliefs, provenance); and 4 pls. 155–156 (copy)

1870 Oppert in Place, Ninive et l'Assyrie 2 pp. 309–319 (translation, combined with inscriptions in Rooms II, V, XIV)

1870 Oppert, Dour-Sarkayan pp. 29–39 (translation, combined with inscriptions in Rooms II, V, XIV, translation) (identical to preceding)

1874 Ménant, Annales pp. 169 and 171–172 (lines 1′–15′, 46′–60′, translation, combined with Rooms II, V)

1876 Oppert, Records of the Past 7 pp. 21–56 (translation, combined with inscriptions in Rooms II, V, XIV, translation)

1886 Bezold, Literatur p. 92 §54.10 (study)

1889 Winckler, Sar. 1 pp. VII–IX (study) and 34–49 lines 209–232 and 250–278 (lines 1′–15′ and 31′–60′, edition combined with Rooms II, V); and 2 pls. 13–14, nos. 27–29 (copy)

1918 Weissbach, ZDMG 72 pp. 174–175 (study)

1924 Pottier, Antiquités assyriennes pp. 88–89 no. 46bis (15′a, translation)

1927 Luckenbill, ARAB 2 pp. 13–17 §§29–33 (translation, combined with Rooms II, V)

1929 Lie, Sar. pp. 38–39 (lines 1′–5′, edition), as well as references in various footnotes

1960 Nougayrol, RA 54 pp. 203–206 (lines 13′–15′, photo of AO 19892, partial edition, study)

1982 André-Leicknam, Naissance de l'écriture p. 330 no. 275 (13′–15′, photo and translation of AO 19892)

1986 Albenda, Palace of Sargon p. 163, pl. 133, and fig. 90 (AO 19892, photo, drawing, study)

1994 Fuchs, Khorsabad pp. 82–83, 131–136, 139–150, and 325–330 no. 2.3 lines 235–258 and 269–295 (edition)

1995 Salvini in Caubet, Khorsabad p. 149 fig. 1 (drawing of XIII,3 and photo of AO 19892)

1997 Tadmor in Parpola and Whiting, Assyria 1995 p. 333 (lines 13′b–15′, translation, combined with Rooms II, V)

2000 Bagg, Assyrische Wasserbauten pp. 159–160 (lines 32′–33′a and 43′b–44′a, edition, combined with Rooms II, V)

2000 Younger, COS 2 p. 294 no. 2.118A (lines 6′b–13′a, translation, combined with Rooms II, V)

2001 Rollinger, Melammu 2 p. 246 (lines 6′b–13′a, partial translation, combined with Rooms II, V)

2008 Cogan, Raging Torrent pp. 93–96 no. 20 (lines 6′b–13′a, translation, study, at times combined with Rooms II, V)

2014 Maniori, Campagne di Sargon p. 37 A3, passim (study), and p. 60 fig. 2 (plan of room)

2017 Liverani, Assyria pp. 136, 152, 183, and 205 (lines 11′b–13′a, 14′b–15′a, 60′, translation, combined with Rooms II, V)

TEXT

Continued from several unpreserved slabs

1′) [...] AD *ša* [^{m}†*mut*†]-⸢*tal-lu*⸣ IBILA⸣-*šú i-na* GIŠ.TUKUL *ú-ra-si-bu-šu-ma e-ki-*[*mu x x*]

2′) [...]-*li-ia i-*⸢*na*?⸣ IGI? TE? *a-na tur-ri gi-mil-li-šú x* [*x x x x x x x x*]

3′) [... ^{m}*tar-ḫu*]-⸢*la*⸣-*ra* ^{m}*mut-*[*tal*]-*lu* IBILA-*šú i-na x-ti zu-um-ri ma-ḫar* ^{d}⸢UTU?⸣ [*x x x* (*x*)] Ú [*x x x x x x x x*]

4′) [...] *x-šú e-pu-*⸢*šu*?⸣ ŠU.II.MEŠ-*šú ú-qam-me ú-kal-li-ma* [*x* (*x*)] ^{m}*mut-tal-lu* IBILA-*šú a-di*

Continued from several unpreserved slabs

1′–6′a) [In my eleventh regnal year, (...) *Tarḫu-lara of the land Gurgum* ...] whose [he]ir [Mu]tallu had cut (him) down with the sword and tak[en away ...] my [...] *in* ... in order to avenge him (Tarḫu-lara) [... Tarḫu-l]ara, his heir Mut[al]lu, in/with ... of the body before the god *Šam*[*aš* ... *Because of*] *his* [... *that*] he had done, I/he *burned* his hands (and) showed [(...)]. I cou[nted] as boo[ty] his heir Mutallu, together with the (royal) family of the land [Bīt-Pa'alla, as

Section 1′ = lines 1′–15′ = XIII,4:1–15. See Winckler, Sar. Annals lines 209–232; Lie, Sar. pp. 38–39 lines 1–5 and lines 248–266; and Fuchs, Khorsabad Annals lines 235–255, 255a–b, and 256–258. Cf. text no. 1 lines 248–266a and text no. 2 lines 267b–292.

1′–6′a Cf. text no. 7 lines 83b–89. Line 1′: The translation assumes that in the previous line, or possibly at the beginning of this line, was *i-na* 11 BALA-*ia* (see text no. 1 line 234 and text no. 2 line 267 [restored]). AD: Not seen by H. Winckler or currently on the squeeze, but copied by P.E. Botta. For the tentative restoration "Tarḫu-lara of the land Gurgum," see text no. 7 lines 83–84. Possibly [... ^{m}*tar-ḫu-la*]-*ra**(copy: AD) at the beginning of the line.

2′ *i-*⸢*na*?⸣ IGI? TE?: P.E. Botta has RA? [(*x*)] IGI TE; H. Winckler has *i-*⸢*na*⸣ IGI? TE?; and the squeeze has ⸢*i-na*?⸣ *x x*.

3′ H. Winckler (Sar. 1 p. 36 line 211) and, tentatively, A. Fuchs (Khorsabad p. 131 line 237) read the damaged sign in *x-ti* as LI, but the traces on the squeeze are most uncertain. ^{d}⸢UTU?⸣: P.E. Botta's and Winckler's copies have no trace of the UTU; the reading is based on the squeeze; Fuchs (ibid.) had ^{d}⸢UTU!?⸣.

4′ -⸢*šu*?⸣: P.E. Botta's copy has DIŠ, while H. Winckler's copy has two vertical wedges which he suggests in a note may be the remains of a RA sign and which A. Fuchs (Khorsabad p. 131 line 238 n. 1) suggests may be the end of an UŠ; the squeeze just has a vertical wedge preceded by damage. -*qam*-: Botta's copy has -*qam*-, but Winckler's copy has KUR or ŠE; not currently preserved on the squeeze. As is often the case, it is not clear from Winckler's copy and edition if he saw KUR.[É-*pa-'a-al-la mal*] *ba-*[*šu-ú*] or KUR.É-[*pa-'a-al-la*] *mal ba-*[*šu-ú*] or even KUR.É-[*pa-'a-al-la*] *mal ba-šu-ú*.

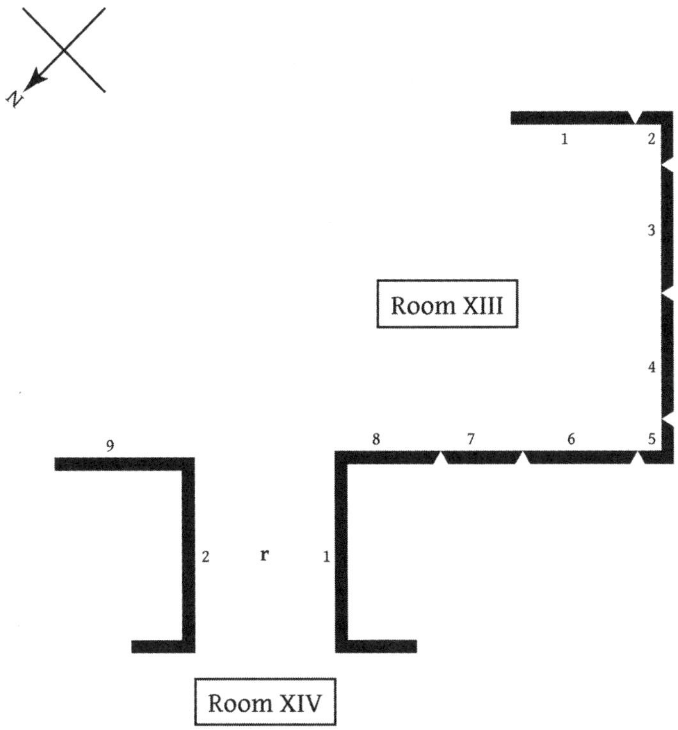

Figure 12. Plan of Room XIII of the palace at Khorsabad, whose wall slabs had a version of Sargon's Annals (text no. 3). Plan after Botta, Monument de Ninive 2 pl. 139.

kim-ti KUR.[É-^{m}*pa-ʾa-al-la mal*] *ba*-[*šu-ú*]
5′) [*it-ti* KÙ.GI KÙ.BABBAR NÍG.ŠU É].⸢GAL⸣-*šú šá ni-ba*† ⸢*la*⸣ *i-šu-*⸢*ú*⸣ *a-na šal-la-*[*ti*] *am*†-[*nu*]-*šú* UN.MEŠ KUR.*gúr*†-*gu-me a-na paṭ gim-ri-*[*šá a-na eš-šu*]-*ti a-*[*šur-ma*]
6′) [LÚ.*šu-ut* SAG-*ia* LÚ].EN.NAM UGU-*šú-nu áš-*⸢*kun it-ti*†⸣ [UN].MEŠ [KUR†] *aš-šur*.KI *am-nu-šu-*[*nu*]-*ti* ⸢^{m}⸣*a-*⸢*zu*⸣*-ri* LUGAL URU.[*as*]-*du-di a-na la na-še-e bíl-te*
7′) *x* ⸢TU$^{?}$⸣ [(*x*) *ik-pu*]-⸢*ud*⸣-*ma a-na* LUGAL.MEŠ-*ni*† *li-me-ti-šu*† [*ze-ra*]-*a-ti* KUR *aš-šur*.KI *iš-pur-ma*† ⸢*áš-šu* ḪUL⸣-*tu* [*e*]-⸢*pu*⸣-*šú* UGU UN.MEŠ KUR-*šú be-lu-su*
8′) ⸢*ú-nak*⸣-[*kir-ma* ^{m†}]*a-ḫi-mi-ti* ŠEŠ *ta-lim-šú* [*a*]-*na* LUGAL-*ti* UGU†-*šú-nu áš-kun* LÚ.*ḫat-ti-i* ⸢*da*⸣-[*bi-ib*] *ṣa-lip-ti be-lu-su i-ze-ru-ma* ^{m}*ia-ad-na* [(*x*)]
9′) *la* ⸢EN† GIŠ†⸣.GU†.ZA *ša* GIM *šá-šú-nu pa-laḫ*

many as] the[re were (of them), (along) with gold, silver, (and)] countless [property from] his [pala]ce. I [reorganized (the administration of)] the people of the land Gurgum to [its] full extent, set [a eunuch of mine as] provincial governor over them, (and) considered th[em] a[s people] of Assyria.

6′b–9′a) A[z]ūri, king of the city [Ash]dod, [plott]ed ... (so as) to no longer (have to) deliver tribute (to me) and sent (messages) [host]ile to Assyria to the kings in his environs. Thus, be[cau]se of the [ev]il [that he had do]ne, I [did] aw[ay] with his lordship over the people of his land [and] set his *favorite* brother Aḫī-Mīti [a]s king over them. The Hittites, [who (always) speak] treachery, hated his rule and elevated over them Iadna (Iāmānī), who had no rig[ht to the] throne (and) who, like them, did not know how to respect (any) authority.

9′b–13′a) [An]grily, with (only) my personal chariot

5′ *šal-la-*[*ti*]: P.E. Botta's copy would have -<*ti*> and H. Winckler's copy has -[*ti*]; the squeeze is not currently helpful as to which is correct.
6′–13′a Line 6′: [KUR†] and -[*nu*]-: P.E. Botta's copy would indicate -<KUR> and -<*nu*>-, while H. Winckler's copy has KUR and -[*nu*]; the squeeze is not currently helpful as to which is correct. Lines 6′b–13′a: Cf. text no. 7 lines 90–109a.
7′ *x* ⸢TU$^{?}$⸣: The reading follows P.E. Botta's copy, which is reproduced by H. Winckler in a manner indicating that he had not seen it on the squeeze; see also text no. 2 line 274. We expect ŠÀ-*šu ik-pu-ud-ma* at the beginning of the line; see text no. 7 line 91. ⸢*áš-šu*⸣: The reading follows Botta's copy, although ⸢*áš-šú*⸣ is also possible; Winckler's copy has *áš*-[*šú*] and the squeeze is not helpful as to which is correct.
8′ [*a*]-*na*: This follows H. Winckler's copy and the squeeze; P.E. Botta's copy has <*a*>-*na*. Text no. 7 line 95 has ^{m}*ia-ma-ni*, "Iāmānī," rather than ^{m}*ia-ad-na*, "Iadna."
9′ ⸢EN† GIŠ†⸣.GU†.ZA: This follows P.E. Botta's copy; H. Wincklers's copy has EN GIŠ.GU.ZA; the squeeze has [*x x x* (*x*)].⸢ZA⸣.

be-lu-tim la i-du-ú ú-rab-bu-ú UGU-*šú-un i-*[*na ug*]-*gat*† *lìb-bi-ia it-ti* GIŠ.GIGIR GÌR.II-*ia u* ANŠE.*pét*-⸢*ḫal*⸣-[*lu*$_{4}$-*ia*]

10′) *ša a-šar sa-al-me i-da-a-a la ip-par-ku-ú a-na* URU.*as-du-di* URU LUGAL-*ti-šú ḫi*-⸢*it-mu*⸣-*ṭiš* [*al-lik*]-⸢*ma*$^{?}$⸣ URU.*as-du-du* URU.*gi-im-tú* URU.*as-du*-[*di-im-mu*]

11′) *al*-[*me ak-šu*]-*ud* DINGIR.MEŠ *a-ši-bu-ut lìb-bi-šú-un šá-a-šú a-di* UN.MEŠ KUR-*šú* KÙ.GI KÙ.BABBAR ⸢NÍG⸣.[GA] É.GAL-[*šú*] ⸢*a*⸣-*na šal-la-ti* ⸢*am*⸣-[*nu-šú*] ⸢URU⸣.MEŠ-*šú-nu a-na* ⸢*eš*⸣-[*šu*†-*ti*†]

12′) *aṣ*-[*bat*] ⸢UN⸣.MEŠ KUR.KUR *ki-šit*-⸢*ti*⸣ ŠU.II-*ia i-na lìb-bi* [*ú*†]-*še-šib* LÚ.*šu-ut* SAG-*ia* LÚ.EN.NAM ⸢UGU⸣-[*šú-nu*] ⸢*áš*⸣-*kun-ma it-ti* UN.[MEŠ† KUR† *aš*†]-⸢*šur*⸣.KI *am*-⸢*nu*⸣-[*šu-nu-ti*]

and [my] cava[lry] (10′) who never leave my side (even) in friendly territory, [I] qu[ic]kly [marched] to his royal city Ashdod. I then surro[unded (and) conqu]ered the cities Ashdod, Gath, (and) Ashdo[d-Yam]. I consi[dered] as booty (both) the gods who dwelt in them (and) that (man) (Iāmāni), together with the people of his land, gold, silver, (and) the posses[sions] of [his] palace. I reor[ganized] (the administration of) their cities (and) settled there [peo]ple from the lands that I had conquered. I set a eunuch of mine as provincial governor over [them] and conside[red them] as people [of Assy]ria. They (now) pull my y[ok]e.

13′) *i-šu-ṭu* ⸢*ab*⸣-[*šá-a*]-⸢*ni*⸣ *i-na* ⸢12⸣ BALA†-*ia* ^{md}AMAR.UTU-⸢A⸣-SUM.NA DUMU ^{m}*ia-ki-ni* LUGAL KUR.*kal-di* [*a-šib*] *ki-šad tam-tim la* ⸢*a-dir zik*$^{?}$-*ri*$^{?}$⸣ DINGIR.[MEŠ (*x*)]

14′) [GAL$^{?}$].⸢MEŠ$^{?}$ KU⸣ BU *x* [*x* (*x*)] TAG$^{?}$ [*x* (*x*)] ⸢UGU⸣ ÍD.*mar-ra-ti ù gu-pu-uš e-de-e it-ta*-[*kil*]-⸢*ma*⸣ *a-de-e* [*ma-mit* DINGIR].MEŠ GAL.MEŠ *e-bu*-⸢*uk*⸣-[*ma*]

15′) *ik-la-a ta-mar-tuš* ^{m}*ḫum*-[*ba-ni*†-*ga*]-*áš* LÚ.ELAM†.MA.KI *a-na re-ṣu-ti is-ḫur-ma* LÚ.*ru-u*$_{8}$-*a* [LÚ.*ḫi-in*]-*da-ru* KUR.*ia-ad*-⸢*bu-ri*⸣

13′b–15′) In my twelfth regnal year, Marduk-apla-iddina (II) (Merodach-Baladan), descendant of Yakīn, king of Chaldea, [who dwelt] on the shore of the sea, who did not f[e]ar the *w*[*or*]*d*[*s*] of the [*great*] gods ... [...] put [his trust] in the sea and (its) surging waves. He then broke (lit.: "overturned") the treaty [sworn by the] great [god]s [and] withheld his audience gift. He turned to Ḫum[baniga]š (Ḫumban-nikaš I), the Elamite, for aid, [made] the Ru'u'a (tribe), [the Ḫin]daru (tribe), the land Yadburu, [the Puqudu (tribe), (and) all the Sutians, the people of the steppe, hostile to me, and prepared for battle against me].

Lines 16′-30′ not preserved

31′) [...] GIŠ [...]

32′) [UGU *šá pa-na ú-zaq-qí-ru-ma*] ⸢*ul*⸣-*tu*† ⸢*qé*⸣-[*reb* ÍD.*su-rap*]-⸢*pi*⸣ [*bu-tuq-tu ib-tú/tu-qu-nim-ma* ILLU *kiš-šá-ti ik-pu-pu li-me-es-su*]

33′) [URU *šú-a-tu a-di* 1/2] KASKAL†.GÍD *u*$_{4}$-*mu* <<NA/TAR>> *la šá-qe-e al*†-*me ak-šud*[^{ud†} 16†+2

Lines 16′-30′ not preserved

31′-34′a) [... They raised their (city) wall higher than before, cut a channel f]rom [the Surap]pu [River, and surrounded its environs with cresting flood (waters)]. I surrounded (and) conquered [that city before] the day had proceeded [half] a double-hour. I carried off as booty [18,430 people, together with their] property,

10′ [*al-lik*]-⸢*ma*$^{?}$⸣: Or [*al*]-⸢*lik*⸣. All that is visible on P.E. Botta's copy and the squeeze is a vertical wedge; H. Winckler's copy has [*al*]-*lik*, but the spacing on Botta's copy and the squeeze might suggest the proposed reading.

11′ [*ak-šu*]-*ud*: H. Winckler's copy has [*ak-šud*]^{ud} and the parallel passages in text no. 1 lines 259 and text no. 2 line 283 have ⸢KUR⸣-*ud* and KUR-*ud* respectively; the proposed restoration is based upon the spacing on P.E. Botta's copy. ⸢*eš*⸣-[*šu*†-*ti*†]: The reading follows Botta; Winckler's copy has *eš-šu-ti*, but nothing is currently visible on the squeeze.

13′–15′ Line 13′: For the restoration [*a-šib*], "[who dwelt]", see text no. 8 line 18. ⸢*zik*$^{?}$-*ri*$^{?}$⸣: P.E. Botta's copy has ⸢*zik*$^{?}$⸣-[*x*] and H. Winckler's copy has ⸢*zik*$^{?}$-*ri**⸣(copy: ⸢IZ⸣[); in both cases the traces of the first sign are similar to DÙ followed by damage. The squeeze currently seems to suggest that in the damaged area following the 'DÙ' are two small Winkelhaken. Cf. text no. 7 line 122, which has *la pa-li-ḫu zi-kir* EN EN.EN, "who does not fear the word of the lord of lords (Marduk)." Lines 13′b–14′a: Cf. J. Nougayrol (RA 54 [1960] p. 206) who suggested [*ša*] *ki-šad tam-tim la a*-⸢*dir*⸣ *kak*$^{?}$-[*ki*$^{?}$-*e*$^{?}$] ⸢DINGIR⸣.[MEŠ *a-na mi-lik*$^{?}$] ⸢*la*$^{?}$⸣ *ku-šír* ⸢*uš*$^{?}$⸣-[*ta*$^{?}$-*am*$^{?}$]-*ṣi*$^{?}$ and translated "qui est au bord de la mer, ne re[dout]ant pas les ar[mes?] di[vines,] [pri]t? [un parti i]nfortuné." Lines 13′b–15′: Cf. text no. 7 lines 121b–123a.

14′ The reading of the first part of the line is problematic. Before ÍD.*mar-ra-ti*, P.E. Botta has [*x*] KU BU *x* [*x x*] AD [*x x*] and H. Winckler [*x*] KU BU *x* [*x*] AD UGU. Based on his examination of the squeeze, A. Fuchs (Khorsabad p. 136 line 255b) read [GAL.MEŠ *x*] ŠÚ$^{!?}$ KU BU *x* [*x*] *x* TAG$^{!?}$ [*x* (*x*)] UGU, with the restoration GAL.MEŠ partially following A.T.E. Olmstead, who suggested [GAL.MEŠ *šu-bat*]-⸢*šu na-da*⸣-*at* for the beginning of the line (AJSL 47 [1930–31] p. 270 sub lines 263f.). Based on the squeeze and AO 19892, the author prefers [GAL$^{?}$].⸢MEŠ$^{?}$ KU⸣ BU *x* [*x* (*x*)] TAG$^{?}$ [*x* (*x*)] ⸢UGU⸣, although it is not clear that there is actually sufficient room to read [GAL].⸢MEŠ⸣ at the beginning of the line.

15′ The translation assumes that at the beginning of the following line was: LÚ.*pu-qu-du gi-mir* LÚ.*su-te-e/su-ti-i* ÉRIM.MEŠ EDIN *it-ti-ia ú-šam-ki-ma ik-ṣu-ra ta-ḫa-zu*; see text no. 2 lines 293–294a and cf. text no. 1 line 266.

Sections 2′–3′ Section 2′ = lines 16′–30′ = XIII,5:1–15. Cf. text no. 1 lines 266b–276/277 and text no. 2 lines 293–309/310. Section 3′ = lines 31′–45′ = XIII,6:1–15. See Winckler, Sar. Annals lines 250–268; Lie, Sar. lines 276/277–280, p. 45 n. 9, and p. 48 lines 1–5; and Fuchs, Khorsabad Annals lines 269–271, 271a, 272, 272a–e, and 275–285. Cf. text no. 1 lines 276/277–323a and text no. 2 lines 309/310–328a.

32′ The translation assumes that the preceding line ended with BÀD-*šú-nu*; see text no. 1 line 277 and text no. 2 line 310 for what may have been in line 31′. ⸢*ul*⸣-*tu*†: P.E. Botta's copy has [...] ⸢*ul*⸣-*tu**(copy: LA) and H. Winckler's copy has *ul*$^{?}$-*tu*$^{?}$; the squeeze is not helpful at this point.

33′ <<NA/TAR>>: P.E. Botta's copy has NA while H. Winckler's copy has TAR; the sign is not currently visible on the squeeze. Winckler restored 4 ME 90, rather than 4 ME 30; the former is how he read the number in text no. 1 line 279 (Sar. 2 pl. 15 no. 31 line 6), although the squeeze has [*x*] ⸢ME⸣ 30 in that place.

LIM 4 ME 30 UN.MEŠ *a-di*] *mar-ši*†-⌜*ti*⌝-[*šú-nu* ANŠE.KUR].RA.[MEŠ]

34′) [ANŠE.KUNGA.MEŠ] ANŠE.MEŠ ANŠE.A.AB.BA†.MEŠ GU$_4$.MEŠ *ù ṣe-e-ni áš*†-*lu-la*† ^{m}⌜*ba*†⌝-[*x x x x* ^{m}*ḫa*]-*za*-DINGIR ^{m}*ḫa-am-da-nu* ^{m}*za-bi*-⌜*du*†⌝

35′) [^{m}*am-ma-i-x x* (*x*) *x x* ^{m}ŠEŠ].MEŠ-SUM.NA ^{m}*a-a-sa-am-mu* 8 [LÚ].*na-si-ka-*[*a-te ša* LÚ.*gam-bu*]-*li a-ši-bu-te* ÍD.*uq-né-*[*e*]

36′) [*ka-šad* URU *šá-a-tu iš-mu-ma it-ru-ku lib*]-*bu-šú-un ul-tu qé-reb* ÍD.*uq*†-*né-*[*e* GU$_4$.MEŠ *ù*] *ṣe*-⌜*e*⌝-*ni* [*ta*]-⌜*mar-ta*⌝-*šú-nu* ⌜*ka-bit*⌝-[*tu*†]

37′) [*iš*]-⌜*šu*⌝-*nim*-⌜*ma*†⌝ [*iṣ*]-⌜*ba*†⌝-[*tu* GÌR.II]-*ia áš*†-*šu* AŠ [(*x*)] IR [(*x*)] KUR ⌜*šu*⌝-*a-tú gíl-la-*[*šún a-miš-ma ú-šab-ṭi-la*] *na-*[*sa-aḫ-šú-un* LÚ.*šu-ut* SAG-*ia*]

38′) [LÚ.EN].⌜NAM⌝ [UGU-*šú-nu áš*]-*kun* [1] GUN† 30 [MA.NA] KÙ.[BABBAR 2 LIM ŠE.BAR *i-na* UGU 20 GU$_4$.MEŠ 1]-⌜*en*†⌝ GU$_4$† *i-na* UGU [20 UDU.MEŠ 1-*en* UDU] *na-dan* MU.AN.NA

39′) [UGU-*šú*]-*nu uk*†-*tin ṣi*-⌜*bit*⌝ [GU$_4$.MEŠ-*šú*]-*nu* ⌜*ṣe*⌝-*e-ni-šú-nu a-*[*na* ^{d}EN ^{d}DUMU EN *ú-ki-in*] *šat-ti*†-⌜*šam*⌝ [LÚ.ERIM.MEŠ *šá-a-tu-nu*] *a-šur-ma* ⌜*i-na*⌝ UGU

40′) [3 ERIM].MEŠ 1†-⌜*en*†⌝ ERIM†-[*šú*]-*nu aṣ*†-[*bat*] URU.[BÀD-^{m}]AD-*ḫa-ra a-na eš*†-*šu*-⌜*ti*⌝ *ú*†-*še*†-*šib* MU-*šú ú-nak-*[*kir* URU].BÀD-^{d}AG ⌜MU⌝-*šú* ⌜*am*⌝-*bi*

41′) [KUR†.*ḫu*]-⌜*ba-qa*?⌝-*nu* KUR.*tar-bu*-⌜*ga*?⌝-*ti* [KUR.*ti-mas-su-nu*] KUR.⌜*pa*⌝-*šur* [KUR.*ḫi-ru-tú* KUR.*ḫi-il-mu*] 6 *na-gi-i* ⌜*ša*⌝ KUR.[*gam-bu-li a-di* 40†]+4 URU.MEŠ-*ni*

42′) [*dan*]-*nu-ti ša qer*-⌜*bi*⌝-[*šú-un a*]-⌜*na*⌝ *ku-dúr-ri*† [KUR†] *aš*-⌜*šur*⌝.KI [*a-bu-uk* LÚ.*ru*]-*u*$_8$†-*a* LÚ.*ḫi-in-da*-⌜*ru* LÚ.*ia-ad*⌝-[*bu*†]-*ru* LÚ.*pu*†-*qu-du*

43′) [*ki*]-⌜*šit*⌝-*ti* LÚ.*gam-bu-li* [*iš-mu-ma i-na šat mu*]-*ši ip-par-šu*-⌜*ma*⌝ [ÍD.*uq-nu-ú mar-ṣu*] *iṣ*-⌜*ba-tu*?⌝ ÍD⌝.*tup-li-ia*-⌜*áš*†⌝ [ÍD†] *tuk-la-ti-šú-nu*

44′) [*i-na ši-pik*] SAḪAR.MEŠ *ù* GI.[MEŠ *ak-si-ir* 2] ⌜URU⌝.ḪAL.⌜ṢU⌝.[MEŠ† *a-ḫu*] *a*-⌜*na*⌝ *a-*[*ḫi ad-di-ma lap-lap*]-⌜*tu*⌝ *ú-šá-aṣ-bi-su-nu-ti-ma ul-tu qé-reb* ÍD.*uq-né-e*

45′) [*uṣ*]-⌜*ṣu*⌝-*nim*-⌜*ma iṣ*⌝-*ba-tu* [GÌR.II-*ia* ^{m}*ia-nu-qu*] LÚ.[*na-sik-ku ša* URU.*za-a-me-e*

[hor]s[es, mules], donkeys, camels, oxen, and sheep and goats.

34′b–42′a) B[a..., Ḫa]zā-il, Hamdanu, Zabīd[u, Ammai(...), ..., Aḫḫē]-iddina, (and) Aya-Sammu, (a total of) eight sheikh[s of the Gambu]lu (tribe) who dwell (along) the Uqnû River, [heard of the conquest of that city and] (as a result) their [hea]rts [pounded]. From the Uqnû River, [they broug]ht me [oxen, and] sheep and goats as their subs[tantial audience g]ift(s) an[d gra]s[ped hold of] my [feet]. Because ... that land, [I disregarded their] crime(s) [and stopped their] dep[ortation. I s]et [a eunuch of mine as provincial gove]rno[r over them]. I imposed [upon th]em the annual payment [of one] talent thirty [minas of] sil[ver, two thousand <*gur*> of barley, on]e ox [out of (every) twenty oxen (that they had), (and) one sheep] out of [(every) twenty sheep (that they had). I (also) imposed] the annual *ṣibtu*-tax [on the]ir [oxen] (and) their sheep and goats f[or the god(s) Bēl (Marduk) (and) Son of Bēl (Nabû)]. I mustered [those soldiers] and (40′) to[ok] on[e] soldier of [th]eirs out of [(every) three soldier]s (for my own army). I resettled (them) in the city [Dūr]-Abi-ḫāra, chan[ged] its (the city's) name, (and) [(re)na]med it [Dūr]-Nabû. [I incorporated (lit.: "led away") int]o the territory of Ass[yria] the lands [Ḫub]aqānu, Tarbugāti, [Timassunu], Pašur, [Ḫirūtu, (and) Ḫilmu], (a total of) six districts o[f] the land [Gambulu, together with forty]-four [fort]ified settlements that are in [them].

42′b–50′a) (When) the [Ru]'u'a, Ḫindaru, Ya[dbu]ru, (and) Puqudu (tribes) [heard of (my) conqu]est of the Gambulu (tribe), they fled [during the course of the nig]ht an[d] took (themselves to) [the Uqnû River, which was difficult (to ford). I dammed up] the Ṭupliya[š Riv]er, [a river] upon which they relied, [with pile(s) of] dirt and reed[s. I erected two] fortress[ses, side] by si[de, and star]ved them out. (45′) [They] then [came o]ut from the Uqnû River an[d] grasped hold [of my feet. Iannuqu], the [sheikh of the city Zāmê, Nabû-uṣalla of the c]ity Abūrê, Paššunu [(and) Ḫaukānu] of the c[ity Nu]ḫānu, (and) Sa'[īlu of] the city Ibūli, (a to-

34′b–37′a The text follows text no. 2 lines 314–318 rather than text no. 1 lines 280–283.
38′ [1]: P.E. Botta's copy has <1>, while H. Winckler's copy has [1]; the squeeze is not helpful at this point.
40′ 1†-⌜*en*†⌝: Both P.E. Botta's and H. Winckler's copies have *x* [...] or GIŠ [...], which is assumed here to represent the first part of the ligature 1+*en*. Text no. 1 line 286 has *ú-ṣab-bit*, rather than *aṣ-bat*, and this is followed by a list of numerous cities (text no. 1 lines 286b–299), presumably the forty-four places mentioned in line 41′. Botta's copy has *a-*<<*x*>>*-na*, but Winckler's copy has just *a-na*. ⌜MU⌝-*šú* ⌜*am*⌝-*bi*: The squeeze has ⌜MU⌝-*šú* ⌜*am*⌝-[(*x*)], while Botta's copy has ⌜MU*⌝(copy:]ḪI)-*šú**(copy: DIŠ) <*am*>-*bi* and Winckler's copy has [MU-*šú*] *aq-bi*.
41′ [KUR†.*ḫu*]-⌜*ba-qa*?⌝-*nu*: P.E. Botta's copy has [...]-⌜*ba*⌝-*qa*†/*x-nu*, while H. Winckler's copy has KUR.[(*x*)]-⌜MAŠ-SI?⌝-*nu*. -*ga*?-*ti*: Botta's copy has -*ga*†/*x-ti*, while Winckler's copy has -⌜*ga*?⌝-*ti*. For the restoration KUR.*ti-mas-su-nu* (or KUR.*ti-bar-su-nu*), see text no. 2 line 323; the copies by both Botta and Winckler would suggest that there was room to restore only three or four signs. [40†]+4: Winckler's copy has [...] 44, but Botta's copy and the squeeze have [...]+4; see also text no. 2 line 324. The forty-four fortified settlements are listed by name in text no. 1 lines 286–299.
43′ *iṣ*-⌜*ba-tu*?⌝: P.E. Botta's copy has *iṣ*-[*x* (*x*)]; H. Winckler's copy has *iṣ-ba-tu*; and the squeeze has *iṣ*-⌜*ba*⌝-*x*.
44′ [*a-ḫu*] *a*-⌜*na*⌝ *a*-[*ḫi*] "[side] by si[de]": As noted by A. Fuchs (Khorsabad p. 329), this likely refers to two forts on opposite sides of the river or dam, across from one another.
45′ -*re*-[*e* m†]*pa*-: P.E. Botta's copy has -*re*-<*e* ^{m}>*pa*-, while H. Winckler's copy has -*re*-<*e*> ^{m}*pa*-; the squeeze currently has -[*x x*] ⌜*pa*⌝-.

^{md}MUATI-ú-ṣal-la ša] ⸢URU†⸣.a-bu-re-[e ^{m†}]pa-áš-šu-nu

46′) [^{m}ḫa-ú-ka-nu] ša ⸢URU⸣.[nu]-ḫa-⸢a⸣-ni† ^{m}sa-⸢ʾi⸣-[lu] ša URU.i-bu-li 5 [LÚ.na-si]-ka-[a-ti]

47′) ša LÚ.pu-⸢qu⸣-di [^{m†}ab-ḫa]-ta-a ša LÚ.ru-u$_{8}$†-⸢a⸣ [^{m}ḫu]-ni-nu ^{m}sa-me-eʾ ^{m}⸢sab⸣-ḫar-ru ^{m†}[ra†-pi-iʾ]

48′) ša LÚ.ḫi-in-[da]-ru† ANŠE.KUR.RA.MEŠ ⸢GU$_{4}$⸣.MEŠ ù ⸢ṣe⸣-[e-ni] ta-mar-ta-šú-nu ka†-[bit†]-tu a-na ⸢URU†⸣.[BÀD-^{m}AD-ḫa-ra]

49′) [iš-šu-nim-ma] ú-na-áš†-ši-⸢qu GÌR⸣.II-ia li-ṭi-šú-nu ⸢aṣ⸣-bat il-ku tup-šik-ku ki-i [ša LÚ.gam-bu-li]

50′) [e-mid-su†-nu†]-ti i-na ŠU.II LÚ.šu-ut ⸢SAG⸣-ia LÚ.[GAR.KUR] LÚ.[gam†]-bu-[li am-nu-šú†]-nu-ti si†-it-ta-[te-šú-nu]

51′) ša UGU ⸢^{m}⸣^{d}AMAR.UTU-A-SUM.NA ù ^{m}šu-[túr†-^{d}]⸢na⸣-ḫu-un-di [TE†]-⸢su⸣-[nu†] id-⸢du⸣-ma ⸢iṣ⸣-ba-tu ⸢ÍD⸣.[uq-nu-ú]

52′) da-ád†-[me†]-šú-nu a-bu-biš as-pu-⸢un⸣ [qí-ra-a]-ti-šú-[nu] um†-ma-ni† [ú†]-šá†-kil [GIŠ†].⸢GIŠIMMAR⸣ tuk-lat-su-nu [GIŠ.KIRI$_{6}$.MEŠ]

53′) bal-ti na-gi-šú-nu ak-šiṭ a-na ÍD.⸢uq⸣-[né-e] ⸢a-šar⸣ [tap]-⸢ze⸣-er-te†-šú-[nu†] LÚ.qu-ra-di-ia ú-ma-⸢ʾe⸣-[er-ma]

54′) BAD$_{5}$.BAD$_{5}$-šú-nu im-ḫa-ṣu UN.MEŠ a-di [mar-ši†-ti†-šú-nu iš-lul]-ú-⸢ni†⸣ [URU†].za-a-me-e URU.a-bu-[re-e]

55′) URU.ia-ap-ti-ru URU.ma-ḫi-ṣu URU.[ḫi-li-pa-nu URU.KAL-KAL] URU.pat-ti-[a†-nu†] ⸢URU†⸣.ḫa-[a-a]-ma-[nu† URU†.ga-di-ia-ti]

56′) URU.a-ma-te URU.nu-ḫa-a-nu URU.a-[ma†-a URU.ḫi-ú-ru] ⸢URU⸣.sa-ḫi-lu 14 URU.MEŠ-ni dan-nu-ti ⸢2$^{?}$⸣+[2$^{?}$ ME† URU.MEŠ-ni]

57′) ša li-me-ti-šú-nu ša šid-di [ÍD.pu$^{?}$]-⸢rat$^{?}$⸣-ti ša ti-bu-ut† GIŠ.⸢TUKUL⸣.MEŠ-ia e-du-ru-ma ú-⸢šaḫ⸣-[ri-bu]

58′) na-gu-šú-un TA qé-reb ÍD.[uq-ni-i a-šar ru]-qi il-li-ku-nim-ma iṣ†-ba-tu ⸢GÌR⸣.II-ia na-gu-ú

59′) ⸢šu⸣-a-tu UGU šá maḫ-ri par-⸢ga⸣-niš [ú-šar-bi-iṣ-ma] i-na ŠU.II LÚ.šu-ut SAG-ia LÚ.GAR.[KUR†] LÚ.gam-bu-li am-⸢nu⸣

tal of) five [she]ik[hs] of the Puqudu (tribe); [Abi-ḫa]tâ of the Ruʾuʾa (tribe); (and) [Ḫu]nīnu, Sāmeʾ, Sabḫarru, (and) [Rāpiʾ] of the Ḫin[da]ru (tribe) [brought] horses, oxen, and s[heep and goats] as their sub[stan]tial audience gift(s) to the cit[y Dūr-Abi-ḫāra and] kissed my [fe]et. I [t]ook hostages from them (and) [imposed upon the]m (the same state) service (and) corvée duty as [(was imposed upon) the Gambulu (tribe). I assigned th]em to the authority of a eunuch of mine, the [governor] of the [Gam]bu[lu (tribe)].

50′b–54′a) (As for) the res[t of those] who had paid [attention] (lit.: "inclined th[eir cheek]") to Marduk-apla-iddina (II) (Merodach-Baladan) and Šu[tur-N]aḫūndi and had taken (themselves) to the [Uqnû] Ri[ver], I overwhelmed their settlem[ents] like the Deluge. [I] fed my army (the food in) the[ir granari]es (and) chopped down the date palm(s) upon which they relied (and) [the orchards] that were the pride of their district. I se[nt] my warriors to the U[qnû] River, th[eir hi]ding place, [and] they (my warriors) inflicted a defeat on them. [Th]ey (my warriors) [carried off as booty] (those) people, together with [their property]. 54′b–59′) (The people of) the cities Zāmê, Abū[rê], Yaptiru, Maḫīṣu, [Ḫilipanu, KAL-KAL], Patti[ānu], Ḫa-[ya]mā[nu, Gadiyāti], Amate, Nuḫānu, A[mâ, Ḫiuru], (and) Saḫilu (Saʾīlu), (a total of) fourteen fortified cities, (and) *fo*[*ur hundred* settlements] in their environs, (located) along [the *Euphr*]*ates* [River], who(se people) had taken fright at the onslaught of my weapons and whose district I had [laid waste], came to me from the [Uqnû] River, [a far]away [place], and grasped hold of my [f]eet. [I had] that district [dwell] as in meadowland (in greater security) than previously [and] assig[ned] (them) to the authority of a eunuch of mine, the gove[rnor] of the Gambulu (tribe).

Section 4′ = lines 46′–60′ = XIII,7:1–15. See Winckler, Sar. Annals lines 268–278; Lie, Sar. pp. 48–49 lines 5–6, line 326, p. 49 n. 5, and pp. 50–53 lines 10–15; and Fuchs, Khorsabad Annals lines 285–295. Cf. text no. 1 lines 323b–340+ and text no. 2 lines 328b–338a.

47′ The reading [^{m}ḫu]-ni-nu follows text no. 1 line 326 and text no. 2 line 329.

48′ ⸢URU†⸣.[BÀD-^{m}AD-ḫa-ra]: H. Winckler's copy has ⸢URU⸣.[BÀD-^{m}AD-ḫa-ra], but P.E. Botta's copy has ⸢URU*⸣.(copy: DÙ)[x (x)], which would suggest that there was not sufficient room for Winckler's restoration; it is not clear from the squeeze whether there was room or not.

50′ P.E. Botta's copy has LÚ.<gam>-bu-, while H. Winckler's copy has LÚ.gam-[bu-...]; the squeeze is not currently helpful as to the presence or absence of GAM and BU.

56′ ⸢2$^{?}$⸣+[2$^{?}$ ME† URU.MEŠ-ni]: H. Winckler's copy has 4 ⸢ME⸣ [URU.MEŠ-ni], while P.E. Botta's copy has 1+[...] and the squeeze ⸢2$^{?}$⸣+[...]. Text no. 2 line 335 has *a-di* URU.MEŠ-*ni*, and Botta's copy, and possibly the squeeze, would allow ⸢a⸣-[di URU.MEŠ-ni] instead of the proposed reading that follows Winckler.

57′ [ÍD.pu$^{?}$]-⸢rat$^{?}$⸣-ti "[*Euphr*]*ates* [River]." P.E. Botta's copy has [*x x x x x*]-*ti*, while H. Winckler's copy restores [ÍD.uq-né-e] and omits the TI, following text no. 2 line 336, which has ÍD.uq-⸢né⸣-[e†]. The squeeze has [x x x (x)]-⸢rat$^{?}$⸣-ti, where the trace before TI is the end of a horizontal wedge in the middle of the line.

58′ H. Winckler's copy restores *uq-né-e*, but text no. 2 line 336 has *uq-ni-i*.

59′ [*ú-šar-bi-iṣ-ma*]: P.E. Botta's copy indicates there was not sufficient room for this restoration, but the squeeze indicates that there is room. LÚ.GAR.[KUR†]: Botta's copy has LÚ.GAR.<KUR>; H. Winckler's copy has LÚ.GAR.KUR; and the squeeze LÚ.⸢GAR⸣.[KUR].

60′) [URU[†]].*sa-am-ʾu-ú-na* URU.KÁ-⸢BÀD⸣ [URU.ḪAL.ṢU].⸢MEŠ⸣ *ša* [m]*šu-túr-*[(d)*na-ḫu*]*-un-di* [LÚ].ELAM.[MA.KI]

Continued on several unpreserved slabs

60′) [Like the onslaught of a storm, I overwhelmed] the cit[ies] Samʾūna (and) Bāb-dūr[i, fortress]es that Šutur-[Naḫ]ūndi, [the] Elam[ite, had constructed *facing* (lit.: "above") the land Yadburu]

Continued on several unpreserved slabs

4

Two separate inscriptions were incised on stone slabs lining the walls of Room XIV of Sargon's palace at Khorsabad: a version of Sargon's Annals (this inscription) and a summary inscription (text no. 8). Only a small portion of the version of the Annals inscription in this room is currently known, attested by P.E. Botta's copies of the texts on three wall slabs and by squeezes of two of them. Surprisingly, this inscription was not written on a continuous sequence of adjoining wall slabs, only separated by occasional doorways. The first two slabs whose Annals inscriptions are known were on adjoining slabs in the southwestern end of the room to the left of Entrance r as you enter the room from Room XIII (Room XIV slabs 1 and 2); the next several slabs had either the Display Inscription of Room XIV (slabs 3, 5, 7, and 9, as well as slabs 3 and 4 from Entrance p; text no. 8) or no inscription (slabs 4, 6, and 8) on them. The Annals text picks up again on the first wall slab (slab 10) to the left of Entrance p as you enter the room from the northeastern terrace (façade N). Parts of the next three slabs (slabs 11–13) were also found by Botta and at least the first two had inscriptions on them based on E. Flandin's drawings, but these were not copied except for an epigraph on slab 12 (text no. 39). Thus, information on only three of the slabs with the Annals text from Room XIV is known. The wall slabs in the room were numbered in clockwise order, beginning at Entrance r, and each of the three Annals slabs has 15 lines of text. As far as it is preserved, the Annals inscription in this room largely duplicates the version of the Annals in Room II (text no. 1 lines 63–99) and the version in Room V (text no. 2 lines 69–92), but with some major variations. The inscription describes events in Sargon's third through sixth regnal years (719–716): campaigns to help the Mannean ruler Iranzi against rebels in the cities Šuandaḫul and Durdukka (lines 1′–6′a), against Kiakki of the city Šinuḫtu in Tabal (lines 6′b–12′), against Pisīris of Carchemish (lines 13′–20′a), and against the Mannean ruler Ullusunu (lines 20′b–45′).

The forty-five lines on the three slabs are to be associated with Winckler, Sar. Annals lines 37–73; Lie, Sar. Annals lines 63–99; and Fuchs, Khorsabad Annals lines 63–99. For a plan of the room, see Figure 13 and Botta, Monument de Ninive 2 pl. 144; for drawings of the reliefs on slabs in this room, see Botta, Monument de Ninive 2 pls. 144–147, in particular pls. 145 and 146 (top) for the three slabs with the text edited here. With regard to the reliefs in the room, see Reade, JNES 35 (1976) pp. 96 and 98–99, and Bagh. Mitt. 10 (1979) p. 84; he believes that the reliefs in this room depict the campaign of Sargon's seventh regnal year (715) into the Zagros. At least

3 line 60′ The spacing on P.E. Botta's copy and the squeeze might suggest that the divine determinative was omitted before [*na-ḫu*]*-un-di*; H. Winckler's copy includes it in his restoration of the passage. Winckler restored [LÚ].ELAM.[MA.KI-*i*] at the end of the line, and the spacing on Botta's copy and the squeeze would allow room for -*i*, but text no. 2 line 338 does not have -*i* here. The translation assumes that the following line began with UGU KUR.*ia-ad-bu-ri ir-ku-su ki-ma ti-ib me-ḫe-e as-ḫup-ma*; see text no. 2 lines 338–339.

two or three of the wall slabs in the room with this inscription also had short epigraphs on them: slab 2 (text no. 37) and slab 10 (text no. 38); see also text no. 39 on slab 12.

CATALOGUE

Section	Ex.	Source	Provenance	Botta, MdN	Fuchs, Khorsabad line	Lines Preserved	cpn
1′	Bt	Botta, Monument de Ninive 3 pl. 158[c]	Khorsabad, Palace, Room XIV, slab 1	2 pl. 145	63–69, 69a–b, 70–72, 72a–b	1′–15′	n
	Wi	Winckler, Sar. 2 pl. 27 no. 58[c]					n
	Sq	Louvre squeeze					p
2′	Bt	Botta, Monument de Ninive 3 pl. 159[c] top	Khorsabad, Palace, Room XIV, slab 2	2 pl. 145	72c, 74–83, 83a–b, 84–85, 85a	16′–30′	n
	Wi	Winckler, Sar. 2 pl. 28 no. 59[c]					n
	Sq	Louvre squeeze					p
3′	Bt	Botta, Monument de Ninive 3 pl. 162	Khorsabad, Palace, Room XIV, slab 10	2 pl. 146	85b–c, 86–94, 94a, 95–96, 96a, 97–99	31′–45′	n

COMMENTARY

Assuming that each wall slab with the Annals inscription in Room XIV had fifteen lines of text, there would have been four to six wall slabs with this inscription before slab 1 (presumably to the right of Door r when entering the room) and twenty-five to thirty after slab 10. The drawings by Flandin in Monument de Ninive 2 pls. 144 and 146 indicate that slabs 11 and 12 were also inscribed; it is likely that they preserved the section of the Annals immediately following that on slab 10 (section 3′).

J. Oppert, followed by J. Ménant and H. Winckler, believed that all seven wall slabs copied by P.E. Botta in Room XIV preserved parts of only one inscription and edited them accordingly. F.H. Weissbach (ZDMG 72 [1918] pp. 175–177) was the first to demonstrate that three slabs preserved a version of the Annals and that the four others (slabs 3, 5, 7, and 9), as well as two slabs in Door p, had a different inscription (text no. 8, the Display Inscription from Room XIV).

In the catalogue, the pieces which Botta collated either from the original or from squeezes before publishing his copies are marked with [c] after the Botta, Monument de Ninive 3–4 plate number; the same is done with the text numbers which Winckler is suppose to have collated from squeezes or originals. No squeeze of section 3′ (slab 10) was made by Botta, and so his published copy was presumably based solely on the copy he did on the site at Khorsabad. Winckler's copy is based on Botta's copy and thus does not provide any independent information of what was on the slab; it is not taken into consideration here.

In general, restorations are based on text no. 1 lines 63b–99a, with additional help in lines 19′b–45′ from text no. 2 lines 69–92a.

BIBLIOGRAPHY

1849 Botta, Monument de Ninive 2 pls. 144–146 (drawing of reliefs, provenance); and 4 pls. 158–159 and 162 (copy)

1870 Oppert in Place, Ninive et l'Assyrie 2 pp. 309–319 (translation, combined with inscriptions in Rooms II, V, XIII)

1870 Oppert, Dour-Sarkayan pp. 29–39 (translation, combined with inscriptions in Rooms II, V, XIII) (identical to preceding)

1874 Ménant, Annales pp. 162–164 (translation, combined with inscriptions in Rooms II, V)

1876 Oppert, Records of the Past 7 pp. 21–56 (translation, combined with inscriptions in Rooms II, V, XIII)

1886 Bezold, Literatur p. 92 §54.10 (study)

1889 Winckler, Sar. 1 pp. VII–IX (study), pp. 8–17 lines 37–47 and 60–73 (lines 1′–15′ and 32′–45′, edition combined with texts in Rooms II, V), and pp. 86–89 lines 43–57 (lines 16′–30′, edition, combined with texts in Rooms II, V); 2 pls. 27–28, nos. 58–60 (copy)

1918 Weissbach, ZDMG 72 pp. 175–176 (study)
1929 Lie, Sar. pp. 10–15, references in various notes to lines 63–99 (study)
1994 Fuchs, Khorsabad pp. 82–83, 91–104, and 315–318 no. 2.3 lines 63–99 (edition)
2000 Younger, COS 2 pp. 293 no. 2.118A (lines 13′–20′a, translation, combined with Rooms II, V)
2001 Holloway, CRRA 45/1 pp. 247–249 (line 40′, edition, study)
2002 Holloway, Aššur is King pp. 157–158 n. 251 (line 40′, edition, study)
2013 Thompson, Terror of the Radiance pp. 134–135 and 224 (lines 5′–10′ and 13′, partial edition, combined with Room II)
2014 Maniori, Campagne di Sargon p. 38 A4, passim (study) and p. 60 fig. 2 (plan of room)
2017 Liverani, Assyria pp. 136, 191, 193, and 221 (lines 5′b–8′a, 13′b–14′a, 40′b–41′a, translation, combined with Rooms II, V)
2019 Marchesi, JNES 78 pp. 22–23 (lines 13′–18′a, edition)

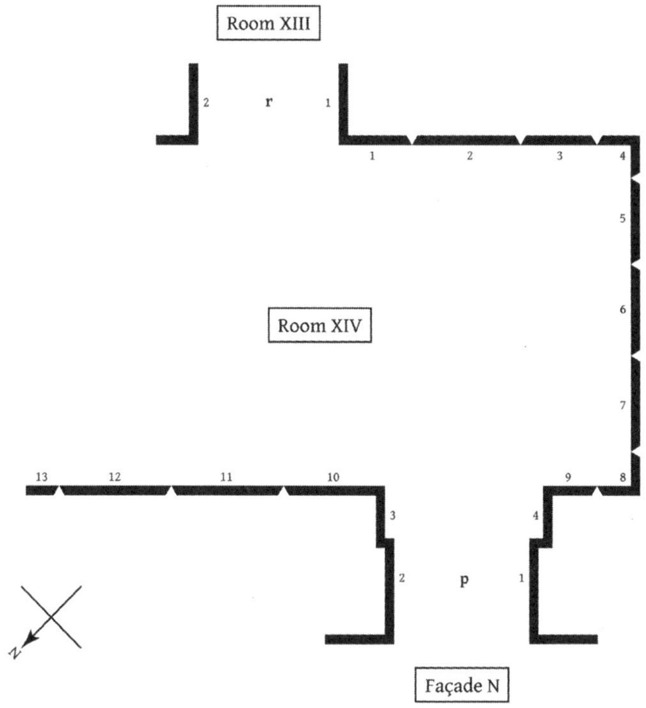

Figure 13. Plan of Room XIV of the palace at Khorsabad, whose wall slabs had a version of Sargon's Annals (text no. 4) and the Display Inscription of Room XIV (text no. 8). Plan after Botta, Monument de Ninive 2 pl. 144.

TEXT

Continued from several unpreserved slabs

1′) [*i*]-*na* GIŠ.*a-ši-bi dan-ni* ⌜BÀD.MEŠ⌝-*šú-nu*† *dun-nu-nu-ti ú-par-ri*-⌜*ir*⌝-*ma qaq*-[*qa*†]-*riš am-nu*

2′) [UN].MEŠ [*a*]-*di* ⌜*mar*⌝-*ši-ti-šú-nu áš-lu-la* URU.MEŠ-*ni šu-a-tu-nu ap-pul aq-qur ina* IZI *áš-ru-up*

3′) [LÚ].URU.*su-uk-ka-a-a* LÚ.URU.*ba-la-a-a* LÚ.⌜URU⌝.*a-bi-ti-ik-na-a-a mi-lik* ḪUL-*tim*

Continued from several unpreserved slabs

1′–2′) I shattered their very strong walls [wi]th a mighty battering ram, leveling (them) to the gr[ou]nd. I took as booty [the people], [together] with their property. I destroyed, demolished, (and) burned down those cities with fire.

3′–6′a) The people of the cities Sukkia, Bāla (and) Abitikna conceived (lit.: "deliberated") an evil plan

Section 1′ = lines 1′–15′ = XIV,1:1–15. See Winckler, Sar. Annals lines 37–47 and 1 pp. 86–87 lines 41–42; Lie, Sar. lines 63–72, with pp. 10–11 nn. 1, 3–4, 8–10, and 13–14; and Fuchs, Khorsabad Annals lines 63–69, 69a–b, 70–72, and 72a–b. Cf. text no. 1 lines 63b–74a.

1′ ⌜BÀD.MEŠ⌝-: Winckler's copy has BÀD.MEŠ-*ni*-, but Botta's copy and the squeeze suggest there was no trace of, or room for, a NI.

2′ [*a*]-*di*: P.E. Botta's copy has <*a*>-*di* and H. Winckler's copy *a-di*; the squeeze has [*x*]-⌜*di*⌝.

4′) [*ša*] *na-*⌈*saḫ*⌉ *šur-še ma-ti*† *im-tal-li-ku-ma a-*⌈*na*
ᵐ⌉*ur-sa-a* KUR.*ur-ar-ṭa-a-a a-na e-peš ar-du-ti*
5′) ⌈*id*⌉*-di-nu pi-i-*[*šú*]*-un ina ḫi-iṭ-ṭi iḫ-ṭu-ú ul-*⌈*tu*?
áš⌉*-ri-šu-nu* ⌈*as*⌉*-suḫ-šú-nu-ti-ma*
6′) [*i*]*-na* KUR.*ḫa-at-ti ša* KUR *a-mur-re-e*
ú-še-ši-ib-⌈*šu*⌉*-nu-ti i-na* 4 BALA*-ia* ᵐ*ki-ak-ki*
7′) ⌈URU⌉.*ši-nu-uḫ-ta-a-a a-de-e* DINGIR.MEŠ
GAL.MEŠ *i-mi-iš-ma a-na la na-še-e* ⌈GUN⌉
8′) [*ir*]*-šá-a* ⌈*ni*?*-id*?⌉ *a-ḫi a-na* DINGIR.MEŠ
EN.MEŠ*-ia qa-a-ti áš-ši-ma* URU.*ši-nu-uḫ-tú* URU
LUGAL*-ti-šú*
9′) [*im*]*-*⌈*ba*⌉*-riš* ⌈*as*⌉*-ḫu-*⌈*up*⌉*-ma ša-a-šu a-di*
LÚ.*mun-*⌈*daḫ*⌉*-ṣe-e-šú* DAM*-su* DUMU.MEŠ*-šú*
DUMU.MUNUS.MEŠ*-šú*
10′) [NÍG].ŠU NÍG.GA *ni-ṣir-ti* É.GAL*-šú it-ti* 7 LIM 3
ME 50 UN.MEŠ KUR*-šú a-na šal-la-ti am-nu-šú*
11′) ⌈URU⌉.*ši-nu-uḫ-tu* URU *šar-ru-ti-šú a-na*
ᵐ*kur-ti-i* KUR.*a-tu-na-a-a ad-din-ma*
12′) ⌈ANŠE†⌉.KUR.RA.MEŠ ANŠE.*pa-re-e* KÙ.GI
KÙ.BABBAR UGU *ša* ⌈*pa*⌉*-na ut-tir-ma e-li-šu*
áš-kun

[that] was to eradicate (lit.: "to tear out the root of") (their own) land and [g]ave [the]ir word to Ursâ (Rusâ), the Urarṭian, to do obeisance (to him). Because of the crime that they had committed, I deported them fr[om] their (own) places and (re)settled them [i]n the land Ḫatti (Syria) *and* (lit.: "of") the land Amurru.

6′b–12′) In my fourth regnal year, Kiakki of [the ci]ty Šinuḫtu disregarded the treaty (sworn) by the great gods and [be]came dilatory about delivering (his) tribute. I raised my hand(s) to the gods, my lords, overwhelmed his royal city Šinuḫtu like a [f]og, and counted him as booty, together with his fighting men, his wife, his sons, his daughters, (10′) [(his) pro]perty (and) possessions, the treasure of his palace, (along) with 7,350 people of his land. I gave his royal city Šinuḫtu to Kurtî of the land Atuna; I made larger than before (the number/amount of) [ho]rses, mules, gold, (and) silver (that he had to pay as tribute) and I imposed (this) upon him.

13′) [*i*]*-na* 5 BALA*-ia* ᵐ⌈*pi*⌉*-si-i-ri* URU.*gar-ga-miš-a-a*
i-na a-de-e DINGIR.MEŠ GAL.MEŠ *iḫ-ṭi-ma*
14′) [*a*]*-na* ᵐ*mi-ta-a* LUGAL KUR.⌈*mu*⌉*-us-ki*
ze-ra-a-te KUR *aš-šur*.KI *iš-*⌈*tap*⌉*-par-ma il-qa-a*
še-ṭu-tu
15′) ⌈*ša*⌉*-a-šu ga-du qin-ni-šú bi-re-tú* AN.BAR
ad-di-šú-nu-ti ap-te-e-ma É.GAL É *ni-*⌈*ṣir*⌉*-ti-šú*
10 GUN KÙ.GI ⌈*sag*⌉*-ru*
16′) [2 LIM 1] ME ⌈GUN⌉ [KÙ†.BABBAR *x x*] ⌈GUN⌉
URUDU *ar-ḫi* AN.NA AN.<BAR> KUŠ AM.SI ZÚ
AM.⌈SI⌉ [*x x x x*] *ú-nu-ut* ⌈MÈ *ù*⌉
LÚ.URU.⌈*gar*⌉*-ga-miš-*[*a*†]*-a* EN ⌈*ḫi*⌉*-*[*iṭ*†]*-ṭi*
17′) [*ša*] *it-ti-*[*šu it-ti* NÍG.GA*-šú-nu áš*]*-lu*†*-*⌈*lam*⌉*-ma*†
a†*-na qé-reb* KUR *aš-šur*.KI *ú-*⌈*ra*⌉*-a* 50†
[GIŠ†.GIGIR† 2 ME ANŠE.*pét-ḫal-lum* 3 LIM]
LÚ†.*zu-uk*† ⌈GÌR†⌉.II *ina lìb-bi-*[*šú*†]*-nu*
ak-⌈*ṣur-ma*⌉ UGU ⌈*ki*⌉*-ṣir* LUGAL*-ti-ia*

13′–18′a) [I]n my fifth regnal year, Pisīri(s) of the city Carchemish sinned against the treaty (sworn) by the great gods and repeatedly sent (messages) hostile to Assyria [t]o Mitâ (Midas), king of the land Musku; he held me in contempt. (15′) I threw him, together with his family, in iron fetters. I opened his palace, his treasure house; [I carried off] as booty 10 talents of refined gold, [2,1]00 talen[ts of silver, ... ta]lents of *arḫu*-copper, tin, ir<on>, elephant hide(s), elepha[nt] ivor[y, ...], battle gear, and the gu[il]ty people of the city Carchemish [who] (had sided) with [him, (along) with their possessions], and brought (them) to Assyria. I conscripted 50 [chariot(s), 200 cavalry, (and) 3,000 fo]ot soldiers from among [th]em and [added (them)] to my royal (military) contingent. I [settled Assyri]ans in the city Carchemish [and] imposed [the yo]ke [of the god Aššur, m]y [lord], upon them.

4′ Text no. 1 line 67 omits *a-na e-peš ar-du-ti*, "to do obeisance (to him)."
6′ Cf. text no. 7 line 57 which has *ina* URU.*di-maš-qi u* KUR.*ḫat-ti*, "in the city Damascus and the land Ḫatti" instead of [*i*]*-na* KUR.*ḫa-at-ti ša* KUR.*a-mur-re-e*, "[i]n the land Ḫatti (Syria) *and* (lit.: "of") the land Amurru."
8′ ⌈*ni*?*-id*?⌉: P.E. Botta's copy has no trace of the first sign and only a few traces of the second sign, which, however, could fit ID; H. Winckler's copy has a horizontal wedge for the first sign and the same traces as Botta for the second sign; the traces on the squeeze are not clear but would seem to allow the proposed reading. For the tentative reading, see text no. 1 line 69 and CAD N/2 p. 210.
9′b–10′a Cf. text no. 1 line 70a.
12′ ⌈ANŠE†⌉: P.E. Botta's copy has [...] AŠ; H. Winckler's copy does not have any trace of the sign, although he does restore it; the squeeze has only an indistinct trace.
14′–16′a Line 14′: *iš-*⌈*tap*⌉*-par-ma*: The reading follows the squeeze and matches text no. 1 line 73. The copies by P.E. Botta and H. Winckler both have *iš-*ID*-ma*, which was read by Winckler and A. Fuchs (Khorsabad p. 93 line 72a) as *iš-pur-ma*. Lines 14′b–16′a: Cf. text no. 1 lines 73b–74a.
15′ 10 GUN: Or possibly 10+<1> GUN. Text no. 73 line 21 has 11 GUN. P.E. Botta's copy has no traces of the number, while H. Winckler's copy has 10+[1]. The squeeze has a clear 10, but this appears to be immediately followed by the GUN.
Section 2′ = lines 16′–30′ = XIV,2:1–15. See Winckler, Sar. 1 pp. 86–89 lines 43–57; Lie, Sar. lines 73–85, with p. 11 n. 14, pp. 12–13 nn. 1, 7–9, and 11, and pp. 14–15 nn. 2–4 and 6; and Fuchs, Khorsabad Annals lines 72c, 74–83, 83a–b, 84–85, and 85a. Cf. text no. 1 lines 74b–85a and text no. 2 lines 69–76+.
16′ [2 LIM 1] ME "[2,1]00": The restoration is based on text no. 73 line 21.
17′ 50†: P.E. Botta's copy has 40+[...]; H. Winckler's copy has 50; and the squeeze currently has only indistinct traces of the number. See text no. 1 line 75. Text no.1 line 75 has *ak-ṣur-ma i-na* [UGU].

18′) ú†-[rad†-di†] LÚ.[KUR.aš]-⸢šur†⸣.KI i-na qé-reb URU.gar-ga-miš ú-[še-šib-ma ni]-ir† [^{d}aš-šur EN]-⸢ia⸣ e-mid-su-nu-ti LÚ.URU.pa-a-pa-a-a
19′) [LÚ.URU†.lal†]-lu-uk†-na-[a†-a†] UR.GI$_7$.MEŠ ⸢tar⸣-bit É.GAL-ia a-na KUR.ka-ak-[me-e] id-bu-⸢bu⸣ [na†-pa-di-iš ul]-tu [áš-ri-šú-nu as-su-ḫa-áš-šú-nu-ti]-ma a-na qé-reb URU.di-maš-qi šá KUR MAR.TU.KI
20′) ú-[še]-⸢šib⸣-[šú†]-nu-ti i-⸢na⸣ 6 BALA-ia ^{m}ur-[sa]-a KUR.[ur]-⸢ar⸣-ṭa-a-a a-[na ^{m}ba-ag-da]-⸢at⸣-ti KUR.ú-<iš>-di-⸢iš⸣-[a†]-a
21′) ^{m}KAR-[x x x (x)] x KUR.zi-kir-ta-a-[a LÚ].⸢GAR†⸣.[KUR.MEŠ KUR].⸢man⸣-na-a-[a† LÚ].⸢rak-bu⸣-[šú†] ⸢šá⸣ da-ba-ab-ti sar$_6$-ra-ti
22′) [iš-pur ú-šá-an-ni] ⸢ṭè†⸣-en-šú-un it-ti-⸢ia⸣ [^{m}LUGAL-GI.NA] ⸢ù⸣ it-ti [^{m†}a†]-za-⸢a DUMU⸣ [EN-šú]-nu ú-šam-ki-ir-šu-nu-ti-ma
23′) [a-na i-di]-šu ú-ter-šu-nu-ti i-na KUR†.⸢ú⸣-[a-ú]-uš KUR-e ⸢mar⸣-ṣi ⸢suḫ-ḫur⸣-ti KUR.man-na-a-a iš-ku-nu-ú-ma
24′) [ADDA] ^{m}⸢a⸣-[za†-a†] EN-[šú†-nu†] id-du-ú a-na ^{d}aš-šur EN†-⸢ia⸣ áš-[šú†] ⸢túr⸣-ri gi-[mil†]-⸢li†⸣ KUR.man-na-a-a qa-ti áš-ši-ma um-ma-na-at ^{d}aš-⸢šur⸣
25′) [gap]-šá-a-ti [ad-ke-e-ma i]-na KUR.ú-a-ú-uš KUR-i [a]-šar ⸢ADDA†⸣ ^{m}a-za-a id-du-⸢ú†⸣ ma-⸢šak ^{m}ba⸣-ag-da-at-ti a-ku-uṣ-[ma]
26′) UN.⸢MEŠ KUR.man⸣-[na†]-a-a ú-šab-ri ^{m}ul-⸢lu⸣-su-nu ša [i-na] GIŠ.GU.ZA ^{m}⸢a⸣-za-a ú-⸢še-ši-bu⸣-ma gi-⸢mir⸣ KUR.man-na-a-a
27′) [rap-ši?] ⸢ú⸣-šad†-⸢gi⸣-la pa-nu-uš-šú

18′b–20′a) The people of the cities Pāpa (and) [Lal]luknu, dogs who had been brought up in my palace, conspired with the land Kak[mê *for the purpose of separating* (*from Assyria*). I deported them fr]om [their (own) places] and [(re)set]tled [th]em in the city Damascus of the land Amurru.

20′b–26′a) In my sixth regnal year, Ur[s]â (Rusâ), the [Ur]arṭian, [sent his] mounted messenger [wi]th a mendacious message t[o Bag-dā]ti of the land U<iš>di[š] (and) KAR[...] of the land of Zikirtu, gov[ernors of the land] Mannea (and) [changed] their mind(s). He made them hostile to me, [Sargon], and to [A]zâ, the s[on of the]ir (former) [lord], and made them [side with] him (Rusâ). They brought about the rout of the Manneans on Mount U[a]uš, a rugged mountain, and threw down [the corpse of] A[zâ, their] lord, (there). I raised my hand(s) (in prayer) to the god Aššur, my lord, in or[der] to ave[ng]e the Manneans and [mustered the nume]rous troops of the god Aššur. [Then, o]n Mount Uauš, the mountain [wh]ere they had thrown down the corpse of Azâ, I flayed the skin from Bag-dāti [and] (then) showed (it) to the people of the land Man[ne]a.

26′b–29′a) (As for) Ullusunu, whom they had set [on] the throne of Azâ and to whom they had entrusted all of the [*wide*] land Mannea, the [wr]ath of [the god] Aššur was directed against Ullusunu, the [Man]nean,

18′ ú†-[rad†-di†] "I ... [added (them)]": H. Winckler's copy has ú-rad-di but the squeeze currently does not have any traces of this and P.E. Botta's copy only has ú*(copy: KAL)-[...]. LÚ.[KUR.aš]-⸢šur†⸣: Text no. 1 line 76 has UN.MEŠ KUR aš-šur.KI.
19′ -na-[a†-a†]: P.E. Botta's copy has -na-, followed a gap with room for the signs a-a, while H. Winckler has -na-a-a; the squeeze just shows damage or illegible traces at this point. na-pa-di-iš "*for the purpose of separating* (*from Assyria*)": The restoration is based on text no. 1 line 77; text no. 43 line 28 has na-ba-di-iš. [ul]-tu [áš]-: Winckler's copy has an opening square bracket before áš- but no closing bracket to match it in the remainder of the line, making it uncertain what he actually saw for the end of the line. a-na qé-reb URU.di-maš-qi šá KUR.MAR.TU.KI "in the city Damascus of the land Amurru": The Display Inscription (text no. 7) line 57 has ina URU.di-maš-qi u KUR.ḫat-ti, "in the city Damascus and the land Ḫatti."
20′ KUR.[ur]-⸢ar⸣-ṭa-a-a: P.E. Botta's copy has KUR.<ur>-ar*(copy: RI)-ṭa-a-a; H. Winckler's copy has KUR.[ur]-⸢ar⸣-ṭa-a-a; the squeeze currently has only indistinct traces. a-[na]: Winckler's copy omits this.
21′ H. Winckler's copy has an opening square bracket after KUR.zi-kir-ta-a-, but no closing bracket to match it, although it later puts square brackets around LÚ; thus it is unclear if he saw on the squeeze any part of LÚ.GAR.KUR.MEŠ KUR.man-na-a-a. -a-[a LÚ].⸢GAR†⸣.[KUR.MEŠ KUR].⸢man⸣-na-: The spacing on Botta' copy for this section is problematic and we should possibly read instead -a-[a LÚ.GAR.KUR].⸢MEŠ⸣ [KUR].⸢man⸣-na- (with the ⸢man⸣ coming from the squeeze, not Botta' copy).
22′ [^{m}LUGAL-GI.NA] "[Sargon]": H. Winckler's copy does not indicate that there is anything missing between ittiya and u itti, and A. Fuchs (Khorsabad p. 96 line 80) follows that view; however, both P.E. Botta's copy and the squeeze indicate that there is a damaged area between them that would provide sufficient room to restore Sargon's name.
23′ KUR†.⸢ú⸣-[a-ú]-uš: P.E. Botta's copy would suggest there was only room to restore A, and this is what Winckler's copy does; however, the squeeze clearly indicates there is room to restore both A and Ú (see also text no. 1 line 80). ⸢suḫ-ḫur⸣-ti: P.E. Botta's copy has ⸢suḫ⸣-[x-(x)]-ti; H. Winckler's copy has suḫ-⸢ḫur*⸣(copy: ḪI-[MA])-ti; and the squeeze currently has ⸢suḫ-ḫur⸣-ti.
24′–25′a Line 24′: Text no. 1 line 82 adds a-na mi-ṣir KUR aš-šur.KI tur-ri, "to make (that area part of) the territory of Assyria," after KUR.man-na-a-a. qa-ti, "my hand(s)": H. Winckler's copy has qa-a-ti, but P.E. Botta's copy and the squeeze have qa-ti. Lines 24′–25′a: Text no. 1 line 82 omits um-ma-na-at ... ad-ke-e-ma, "mustered the vast/numerous troops of the god Aššur."
25′ H. Winckler's copy has KUR.ú-a-<ú>-uš, but P.E. Botta's copy and the squeeze indicate that the -ú- is not omitted.
26′b–27′a Cf. text no. 1 lines 83b–84a.
27′ [rap-ši?] "[*wide*]": The restoration follows Fuchs, Khorsabad p. 97 line 83b, which is based on text no. 2 line 189, but there it is thought to modify Urarṭu, not the land Mannea. UGU-⸢šu?⸣: P.E. Botta's copy has UGU-[x], but H. Winckler's copy has UGU-šu*(copy: KI); the squeeze currently only has indistinct traces of a sign. -[ma (a-na)]: Although Botta's copy would indicate that there is room to restore all three signs, it is not clear from Winckler's copy or an examination of the squeeze that there was room for the a-na; however there also appears to be insufficient room to restore a-na at the beginning line 28′.

^{m}*ul-lu-su-nu* KUR.[*man*]-*na-a*-⌜*a*⌝ [*šib*]-*sa-at* [^{d†}]*aš-šur šá sa-paḫ* KUR-*šú ina* UGU-⌜*šu*$^{?}$⌝ *ib-ši*-[*ma* (*a-na*)]

28′) [^{m}]⌜*ur*⌝-*sa-a* KUR.*ur-ar-ṭa-a-a* [*x x* (*x*)] ⌜LU$^{?}$⌝ *x* [*x x* (*x*)]-*ma* ^{m}*aš-šur*-ZU KUR.⌜*kar-al-la*⌝-*a-a* [^{m†}]⌜*it*⌝-*ti-i* ⌜KUR.*al*⌝-*la*-⌜*ab*⌝-[*ra-a-a*]

29′) *it-ti-ia uš-bal-kit-ma* ⌜*ar*⌝-[*du-tu* KUR.*ur-ar-ṭi*] ⌜*e*⌝-*pe-ši iz-kur-šu-nu-ti* [*i*†]-*na* ⌜*ug*⌝-*gat lìb*-[*bi-ia*]

30′) *um-ma-na-at* ^{d}*aš-šur ga*-⌜*ap*⌝-[*šá-a-ti ad-ke*]-⌜*e*⌝-*ma a*†-*na ka-šad* KUR.*man*-[*na-a-a áš-ta-kan pa-ni-ia*]

31′) [...] AB [...]

32′) [...] I RI BI [*x x x* (*x*)] *ḫu-ḫa*-⌜*riš*⌝ [...]

33′) [... *áš-ru-up*]-*ma*† URU†.⌜*zi*⌝-[*bi-a* ...]

34′) [... *iṣ-ba*]-*tu*†-*ma* [...]

35′) [... *ma-da*]-*ta am-ḫur*-[*šu* ^{m}*it*]-*ti*-[*i* ...]

36′) [...] LA GIŠ [*x*] TI MA [*x x*] É RI UN.[MEŠ KUR].*kar-al*†-*la*-[*a-a* ...]

37′) [...] URU.É-[*x-x*]-AḪ-[*x*] URU.[*x*]-*la-ma* URU.[*ga*]-*nu*-[GIŠ *x* KUR *x* ...]

38′) [6 URU.MEŠ *šá* KUR].*ni*-⌜*ik*⌝-*sa*-[*am-ma ak-šu*]-*ud*† ^{m†}GÌR.II-LUGAL LÚ.EN.URU [(*x*) *ša*] URU.*šur*-[*ga-di-a i-na qa-ti aṣ-bat* URU.MEŠ-*ni šu-a-tu-nu*]

39′) [UGU *pi-ḫa-at* KUR.*par-su-áš ú-rad-di* ^{md}EN-LUGAL-*ú-ṣur*] ⌜URU⌝.*ki*-<*še*>-*si-im-a-a* [*qa*]-*ti ik*-[*šu*]-*ud-ma* [*šá-a-šú a-di* NÍG.ŠU É.GAL-*šú a-na*] KUR *aš*-⌜*šur*⌝.[KI]

40′) [*ú-ra-a-šú* LÚ.*šu-ut* SAG-*ia* LÚ.EN.NAM UGU URU-*šú áš-kun*] GIŠ.TUKUL DINGIR.MEŠ *a-li*-⌜*kut*†⌝ [(*x*) *maḫ*]-*ri*-[*ia*] ⌜*ú*⌝-*še-piš-ma qé*-[*reb-šú ú*]-*šar-mi*

41′) [URU.*kar*-^{d}MAŠ.MAŠ MU-*šú ab-bi ṣa-lam* LUGAL-*ti-ia i-na lìb-bi ul-ziz* KUR].É-*sa-ag-bat*

(ordaining) the dissolution of his land. [He (Ullusunu) then *put his trust in* U]rsâ (Rusâ), the Urarṭian, [...] ... [...] and caused Aššur-lē'i of the land Karalla (and) Ittî of the land Allab[ria] to rebel against me; he persuaded (lit.: "spoke to") them to do ob[eisance to the land Urarṭu].

29′b–42′a) Angr[ily, I muster]ed the num[erous] troops of the god Aššur and [set out] to conquer the land Man[nea. ...] ... [... *I overwhelmed* ... as] with a bird trap. [... *I burned down the city Izirtu with fire*] and [*conquered*] the city (Z[*ibia and the city Armaet. (As a result) Ullusunu, the Mannean, together with his whole land assembled as one and gras*]*ped* [*hold of my feet. I*] then [*had mercy on them* (*and*) *overlooked Ullusunu's crimes.* (35′) *I had him sit* (*again*) *on his royal throne* (*and*)] received [tribu]te [from him. *I deported* It]tî [*of the land Allabria, together with his family, and*] ... the peop[le of the land] Karalla [...] the city Bīt-[...], the city [...]lama, the city [Ga]nu[GIŠ... I conqu]ered [(in total) six cities of the land] Niksa[mma. I captured] Šēp-šarri, the city ruler [of] the city Šur[gadia, (and) added those cities to the province of Parsuaš]. I cap[tur]ed [Bēl-šarru-uṣur of the ci]ty Ki<še>sim and [brought him, together with the property of his palace, to] Ass[yria. (40′) I set a eunuch of mine as provincial governor over (that) city]. I had the weapon(s) of the gods who go [bef]ore [me] made and installed (them) in[side it (the city Kišesim). I (re)named it (the city Kišesim) Kār-Nergal (and) erected a royal image of myself there]. I added the lands Bīt-Sagbat, Bīt-Ḫi[rmami, (and)] Bīt-Umar[g]i, (and) the cities [Ḫarḫubarban, Kilamb]āti, (and) [A]rman[gu *to*] its [pro]vince.

28′ [*x x* (*x*)] ⌜LU$^{?}$⌝ *x* [*x x* (*x*)]-*ma*: Botta's copy has [*x x x* (*x x x*)]-*ma* and Winckler's copy has [*x x* (*x*)] KIL$^{?}$-⌜BE$^{?}$⌝-*ma*; the squeeze has [*x x* (*x*)] ⌜LU$^{?}$⌝ *x* [*x x x* (*x*)]. Text no. 1 line 84 has *it-ta-kil* here. The ⌜LU$^{?}$⌝ *x* might conceivably be ⌜*kil-ma*⌝, but the first sign looks more like LU than KIL and there is too much space between *Urarṭaya* and *Aššur-lē'i* for just *it-ta-kil-ma*.

30′ Cf. text no. 7 line 40 and text no. 1 lines 85b–86a. The restoration at the end of the line is based on text no. 7 line 40.

Section 3′ = lines 31′–45′ = XIV,10:1–15. See Winckler, Sar. Annals lines 60–73; Lie, Sar. lines 86–99; and Fuchs, Khorsabad Annals lines 85b–c, 86–94, 94a, 95–96, 96a, and 97–99. Cf. text no. 1 lines 85b–99a and text no. 2 lines +86–92a.

32′–35′ Line 32′: Assuming that the whole line duplicates text no. 1 lines 86–87 and that the gap between the two parts of the line copied by P.E. Botta was longer than the copy indicates, A. Fuchs (Khorsabad p. 99 line 86 n. 3) suggests that Botta's [...] I RI BI [...] may stand for [URU] LUGAL-*ti-šú* ⌜*ša*⌝ [...], with I for LUGAL, RI for -*ti-šú*, and BI for ⌜*ša*⌝; see text no. 1 line 86. One might then restore: "[I overwhelmed the city Izirtu, the] royal [city] o[f the land Mannea, as with] a bird trap." Lines 32′b–35′: The tentative restorations in the translation are based upon text no. 1 lines 86–89.

33′ P.E. Botta's copy has [...] MAŠ IZ *x* [...], where the *x* would fit the beginning of ZI, and the reading -*ma* URU.⌜*zi*⌝- follows Fuchs, Khorsabad p. 99 line 87.

34′ P.E. Botta's copy has [...] DA MA [...], and the reading proposed above is also assumed by Fuchs, Khorsabad p. 100 line 88.

36′ Based on text no. 7 line 56 and text no. 1 line 90 (mostly restored), we might expect in the first part of the line *ša* ^{md}*aš-šur*-ZU KUR.*kar-al-al-a-a ma-šak-šu a-ku-uṣ-ma*, "I flayed the skin from Aššur-lē'i of the land Karalla and." F.W. Geers (apud Olmstead, AJSL 47 [1930–31] p. 265) suggests that we read [*a-na*] *kit-ri*, [to] the aid of" immediately before UN.[MEŠ], "peop[le]."

37′ The reading URU.[*ga*]-*nu*-[GIŠ ...] is based on text no. 1 line 92, which has URU.*ga-nu*-GIŠ [*x*] KUR *x* [...]. Text no. 27, an epigraph on a relief, has URU.*ga-an*-⌜*gu*⌝-*uḫ-tu* and thus M. El-Amin (Sumer 9 [1953] p. 53) suggested URU.*gu-nu*-⌜*un-gu*⌝-*uḫ*$^{?}$-[*tu*] for the passage in text no. 1. See already Fuchs, Khorsabad p. 101 line 92 n. 1.

38′ For the restoration at the beginning of the line, see text no. 7 line 58 and text no. 1 line 92 (mostly restored). The restoration at the end of the line follows text no. 1 line 93.

39′ [*šá-a-šú a-di* NÍG.ŠU É.GAL-*šú a-na*]: P.E. Botta's copy would suggest that there was room for only 6–8 signs.

41′ For the tentative restoration URU.*kar*-^{d}MAŠ.MAŠ, "Kār-Nergal," instead of URU.*kar*-^{d}MAŠ, "Kār-Ninurta," see the on-page note to text no. 1 line 95.

KUR.É-*ḫi*†-[*ir-ma-mi* KUR].É-*ú*-[(*x*)]-*mar*†-⸢*gi*⸣ URU.[*ḫa-ar*?-*ḫu-bar-ban*]

42′) [URU.*ki-lam-ba*]-*a-ti* URU.⸢*ar*⸣-*ma-an*-[*gu* UGU? *pi*]-*ḫa-ti-šú* ⸢*ú-rad*⸣-*di*† URU.[*ḫa-ar*?-*ḫa-ra-a*]-*a* m*ki*-⸢*ba*⸣-[*ba*] LÚ.EN.URU-[*šú-nu*] *ir*†-⸢*du*⸣-[*du-ma*]

43′) [... m*da-al-ta*]-*a* KUR.*el*-⸢*li*†⸣-*ba-a-a* ⸢*ú*⸣-[*rab-bu*-(*ú*)] UGU-*šú-un*† URU *šu-a-tú* *ak*†-*šu-ud šal-la-su áš-lu-la* UN.[MEŠ KUR.KUR]

44′) [*ki-šit-ti qa-ti-ia i*]-*na lìb-bi* [(*x*) *ú*]-*še-rib* LÚ†.[*x x x*] EN.NAM ⸢UGU⸣-*šú-nu*† *áš*†-*kun* [(*x*)] ÍD-*tu* *e*-[*li-tum* (*x*)]

45′) [*ša* KUR.*a-ra-an-ze*-(*e*)-*šú* ÍD]-*tu šap*†-⸢*li*⸣-[*tu* (*x*)] *šá* [É-m]⸢*ra*⸣-*ma-tu-a* [KUR].⸢*ú*⸣-*ri-qa-tu* KUR.*si-ik-ri-is* KUR.[(*x*)]-*šá-pa*†-⸢*ar*⸣-[*da*]

Continued on several unpreserved slabs

42′b–45′) The pe[ople] of the city [Ḫarḫar] dro[ve out] Kiba[ba, their] city ruler, [and ... elevated Dalt]â of the land Ellipi over themselves. I conquered that city (and) plundered it. [I] brought there peop[le from the lands that I had conquered] (and) set a [*eunuch of mine*] as provincial governor [o]ver them. [I conquered] the up[per] river(land) [of the land Aranzêšu], the low[er riv]er(land) of [Bīt-R]amatua, [the land] Uriqatu, the land Sikris, the land Šapa[rda, (and) the land Uriakku, (a total of) six districts, and added (them) to them (the people of the city Ḫarḫar)].

Continued on several unpreserved slabs

5

A fragment of a wall slab with both a pictorial relief and an inscription was found in the throne room (also referred to as "Court VII") of Sargon's palace at Khorsabad. The piece is preserved in the Oriental Institute (Chicago) and the inscription appears to be a section from Sargon's Annals, in particular his actions against Marduk-apla-iddina II (Merodach-Baladan) in Sargon's twelfth regnal year (710). Restorations are based on the Annals versions in Room V (text no. 2) lines 369–371; cf. Room II (text no. 1) lines 387–389. The lines preserved are also to be associated with Winckler, Sar. Annals lines 315–316; Lie, Sar. Annals p. 58 lines 13–14; and Fuchs, Khorsabad Annals lines 326–328.

The relief shows four men towing a boat and the excavator thought that it represented a scene in Babylonia, but this remains unproven. For a study of the throne room and its reliefs, see Blocher, AoF 26 (1999) pp. 223–50, especially pp. 231–232 no. 3 for this slab; see also Reade, JNES 35 (1976) pp. 96–97 "Unknown B"; and Reade, Bagh. Mitt. 10 (1979) p. 84.

CATALOGUE

Section	Museum Number	Photograph Number	Provenance	Dimensions (cm)	Fuchs, Khorsabad line	Lines Preserved	cpn
1′	A 11258	OI 28889	Khorsabad, Palace, Throne Room (Court VII)	43×119.5	326–328	1′–3′	c

4 line 42′ Text no. 1 line 96 has ... URU.*ar-ma-an-gu ak-šu-ud-ma* UGU *pi-ḫa-ti-šú* ..., but based upon the size of the gap on the copy, there is not sufficient room for this reading.
4 line 44′ Text no. 1 line 98 has ... LÚ.*šu-ut*-SAG-⸢*ia*⸣ LÚ.EN.NAM ..., but based upon the size of the gap on the copy, there is not sufficient room for this reading.
4 line 45′ *šá* [É-m]⸢*ra*⸣-*ma-tu-a*: The reading assumes a larger damaged area between the *šá* and -*ma-tu-a* than is indicated on Botta's copy, which would suggest that both the É and the masculine determinative were omitted. The translation assumes that the following line begins with KUR.*ú-ri-ak-ku/ki* 6 *na-gi-i ak-šu-ud-ma* UGU-*šú-nu ú-rad-di*; see text no. 1 line 99 and text no. 2 line 92.

COMMENTARY

The original publication of the fragments states that it was found "loose in the debris" of the throne room "in the proximity of doorway C′′" (Loud, Khorsabad 1 pp. 58–60), but J.E. Reade states that it may have originally come from that room or from one of several other rooms that had contained wall slabs (JNES 35 [1976] pp. 96–97; see also Bagh. Mitt. 10 [1979] p. 84). Parts of the last three lines of the inscribed section on the slab are preserved. The inscription is edited both from the original and from a photograph (P28889) kindly supplied by the Oriental Institute Museum. It is not clear exactly how much is missing at the beginnings and ends of the lines. Thus, it is not known exactly where the restorations given in the transliteration should be split between the lines, and the division given below must considered extremely tentative. Since only parts of the last three lines of the inscription on the slab are preserved, it is not possible to determine how many lines of text the slab had originally.

A second inscribed fragment was found loose in the debris in the throne room, near Entrance C′. It "contains a very brief and badly damaged portion of text from the beginning of Sargon's annals." Nothing more is known of this piece; see Loud, Khorsabad 1 pp. 58–60 and Blocher, AoF 26 (1999) pp. 231–32 no. 2.

BIBLIOGRAPHY

1933 Frankfort, OIC 16 p. 90 and p. 92 fig. 58 (photo, provenance)
1936 Loud, Khorsabad 1 pp. 58–60 and fig. 72, and p. 129 no. 1 (photo, copy, edition [by Jacobsen], provenance)
1964 Brinkman, Studies Oppenheim p. 44 no. 44.2.20.a.iii (study)
1976 Reade, JNES 35 pp. 96–97 "Unknown B" (study)
1977–78 van der Spek, JEOL 25 p. 59 (transliteration)
1981 de Graeve, Ships p. 46 and pl. XVII no. 47 (photo, study)
1994 Fuchs, Khorsabad pp. 82–83, 158, and 333 no. 2.3 lines 326–328, "Thronsaal" (edition)
1995 Wilson in Caubet, Khorsabad p. 114 and p. 125 fig. 8 (photo)
1999 Blocher, AoF 26 pp. 231–232 no. 3 and p. 246 fig. 5 (photo, study)
2014 Maniori, Campagne di Sargon p. 37 A5 and passim (study)

TEXT

Continued from several unpreserved slabs

1′) [...] *x x x* [*x* (*x*)] *x x x x* [...]

2′) [KUR.GI.MUŠEN.MEŠ UZ.TUR.MUŠEN.MEŠ *ma-ḫar-šú-un aq*]-⸢*qí*⸣ *áš-šú šá-kan* BAD$_5$.BAD$_5$ <^{m}>^{d}AMAR.UTU-A-SUM.NA DUMU ^{m}*ia-ki-ni* NUMUN LÚ.⸢*kal-di*⸣ [*ḫi-ri-iṣ* GAL$_5$.LÁ *lem-ni am-ḫur-šú-nu-ti-ma*]

3′) [*i-na su-pe-e ù te*]-⸢*me*⸣-*qi* ⸢*ma*⸣-[*ḫar-šu*]-⸢*un*⸣ *ut-nin ul-tu i-sin-ni* EN GAL-*i* ^{d}AMAR.UTU *ú-šal-li-mu x* [...]

Continued on several unpreserved slabs

Continued from several unpreserved slabs

1′–3′) [... I offe]red [before them ... geese (and) ducks. I appealed to them (the gods)] in order to bring about the defeat of Marduk-apla-iddina (II) (Merodach-Baladan), descendant of Yakīn, of Chalde[an] extraction, [the (very) image of an evil *gallû*-demon;] I prayed t[o the]m [with supplications and entre]aties. After I had carried out in full the festival of the great lord, the god Marduk, [...]

Continued on several unpreserved slabs

6

The inscription on a wall slab found in Sargon's palace at Khorsabad appears to be from an edition of the king's Annals. It describes events in Sargon's thirteenth regnal year (709): a campaign to Babylonia against Marduk-apla-iddina II (Merodach-Baladan) and in particular the siege of the latter's

5 line 3′ Text no. 2 line 371 has LA A after ^{d}[AMAR.UTU *ú-šal*]-⸢*li*⸣-*mu*.

stronghold Dūr-Yakīn. As far as it is preserved, the inscription largely duplicates the versions of the Annals in Room II (text no. 1 lines 409–415) and Room V (text no. 2 lines 385–402+), but with major variations to those two versions at the end of the passage. The fourteen lines on this slab are to be associated with Winckler, Sar. Annals lines 329–348/349; Lie, Sar. Annals lines 409–415 and pp. 62–63 lines 5–10, with p. 63 n. 6; and Fuchs, Khorsabad Annals lines 342–359 and 359a–c.

CATALOGUE

Section	Source	Provenance	Fuchs, Khorsabad line	Lines Preserved	cpn
1′	Botta, Monument de Ninive 4 pl. 163	Khorsabad, Palace	342–359, 359a–c	1′–14′	n

COMMENTARY

It is not known in which room of the palace this slab was discovered. Since it duplicates (with variation) parts of the texts in Rooms II and V, it cannot come from those two rooms, nor is it likely to have come from Rooms XIII or XIV since the extant slabs with Sargon's Annals from those rooms have fifteen lines of text per slab and this one has fourteen. It may have come from the throne room (Court VII) since it is not known how many lines of text were on the slabs in that room (see text no. 5). P.E. Botta did not make a squeeze of this inscription so our knowledge of it comes solely from Botta's copy in Monument de Ninive. Since H. Winckler's copy of the text was totally based on that of Botta, it provides no independent evidence of exactly what was on the slab.

Assuming that this slab inscription comes from a version of the Annals reasonably similar to that in Rooms II and V, there would have been approximately twenty-three inscribed slabs before it and approximately eight inscribed slabs after it in the room.

As noted by J. Renger (see Borger, HKL 2 p. 322), the two short lines at the bottom of Botta's and Winckler's copies of this text are actually an epigraph that was presumably on the relief below the inscription. The epigraph is presented as text no. 40.

Restorations in lines 1′–5′a are based on text no. 1 lines 409–414 and text no. 2 lines 385–394a and those in lines 5′b–11′a are based on text no. 1 line 415 and text no. 2 lines 394b–402a. Restoration in lines 11′b–14′ receives some help from text no. 2 lines 402b–414, but text no. 2 is poorly preserved at this point and the two versions clearly are not duplicates. Since we are totally dependent upon Botta's copy for this text, all indications of † in the transliteration indicate an abnormal/incorrect sign on his copy.

BIBLIOGRAPHY

1849 Botta, Monument de Ninive 4 pl. 163 (copy)

1889 Peiser, ZA 4 pp. 412–413 and n. 1 "Unknown A" (lines 9′b–14′, edition, combined with inscriptions in Room V)

1889 Winckler, Sar. 1 pp. VII–IX (study) and 56–59 lines 329–348/349 (1′–9′, edition, combined inscriptions in Rooms II, V); and 2 pl. 26, no. 55 (copy)

1918 Weissbach, ZDMG 72 p. 175 (study)

1929 Lie, Sar. pp. X, and 60–63 various notes (partial edition, study)

1930–31 Olmstead, AJSL 47 pp. 275–276 (partial edition, study)

1976 Reade, JNES 35 pp. 96–97 (study)

1977–78 van der Spek, JEOL 25 pp. 61–63 (lines 5′b–14′, edition, study)

1994 Fuchs, Khorsabad pp. 82–83, 161–167, and 333–335 no. 2.3 lines 342–359c (edition)

2000 Bagg, Assyrische Wasserbauten p. 162 (lines 10′b–11′a, edition, combined with Room V)

2014 Maniori, Campagne di Sargon pp. 38–39 A6 and passim (study)

TEXT

Continued from several unpreserved slabs

1′) [(*x*)] ⸢*na*⸣-*as-qu-te* UGU ⸢ÍD⸣.MEŠ-[*šú*] ⸢TI$_8$⸣.MUŠEN†-*niš*† *ú-šap-riš*†-[*ma iš-ku-nu taḫ-ta-(a)-šú/šu šá-a-šu a-di ki-ṣir* LUGAL-*ti-šú ni-i-tú al-me-šu-ma ki-ma as-li*]

2′) [*i-na*] *pa*†-*na* GÌR.II-*šu ú-nap-pi*†-*ṣa* [LÚ.*qu-ra-di-šu*] ANŠE†.KUR.RA.MEŠ *ṣi-mit-ti ni*-⸢*ri*⸣-[*šu i-na uṣ-ṣi ú-šaq-qir ù šá-a-šú/šu i-na zi-qit mul-mul-li rit-ta-šú ap-ṭur-ma*]

3′) ⸢*ki*⸣-*ma šik-ke-e* <*ḫal*>-*la-la-niš* KÁ.GAL† URU-*šu* ⸢*e*⸣-*ru-ub* LÚ.*pu-qud*†-*da-a-a ki*-[*tar-šú* LÚ].⸢*mar*⸣-[*šá-na-a-a a-di* LÚ.*su-te-e ša it-ti-šú i-na pa-an* KÁ.GAL *ú-nak-kis*]

4′) ⸢*i*⸣-*mat* <<MU>> *mu-ti as-lu-ḫa* UN.MEŠ-*šu kúl-tar* LUGAL-*ti-šu* GIŠ.*šá* GIŠ.MI ⸢KÙ.GI LUGAL⸣-[*ti-šú* GIŠ.GIDRU KÙ.GI GIŠ.NÁ KÙ.GI GIŠ.*né-med-du* KÙ.GI *ú-de-e* KÙ.GI KÙ.BABBAR]

5′) ⸢GIŠ⸣ KUR *gan-ga-ni-šu til-li ú-nu-ut* MÈ *e-kim*†-*šu kul-lat* UN.MEŠ-*šú a-ši-bu-ut da*-⸢*ád*⸣-[*me si-ḫir-ti* KUR-*šú ša* TA *pa-an* GIŠ.TUKUL.MEŠ-*ia ú-še*?-...]

6′) *ú*†-*šá-aṣ-bi-ta pa-ši-ru a-di su-gul*†-*lat* GU$_4$.MEŠ ANŠE.GAM.MAL.MEŠ ANŠE.MEŠ *ṣe-e*-⸢*ni*⸣ [*ša* ...]

7′) *šu-a-tu um-ma-nat* ^{d}*aš-šur gap-šá-a-ti* 3 *u*$_4$-*me mu-ši-tu šal-lat*† *la ni-bi iš-lul-lam*†-⸢*ma*⸣ [...]

8′) 90 LIM 5 ME 80 UN†.MEŠ 2 LIM 80 ANŠE.KUR.RA.MEŠ 7 ME ANŠE.KUNGA.MEŠ 6 LIM 54 ANŠE.A.⸢AB⸣.[BA.MEŠ ...+40 UDU.NÍTA.MEŠ]

9′) *ša um*†-*ma-ni iš-lu-la ina qé-reb uš-man-ni-ia am-ḫur áš-šu la a-ṣe-e* URU-*šu u la na-par*-⸢*ka*?⸣-[*a* ... *i-ta-at* URU-*šú ak-ṣur-ma* GIM ŠAḪ *er-re-ti*]

10′) *ina qé*†-*reb* URU-*šu šup-šu-qiš e-si-ir-šu* GIŠ.KIRI$_6$.MEŠ-*šú ak-šiṭ* GIŠ.GIŠIMMAR.MEŠ-*šú*

Continued from several unpreserved slabs

1′–5′a) [At the command of the gods Aššur, Šamaš, and Marduk], I had [my] choice [fighting men] fly over [its] water [channel]s like [ea]gles [and they brought about his defeat. I surrounded him together with his royal (military) contingent and] slaughtered [his warriors like sheep a]t his feet. [I pierced] the horses trained to [his] yoke [with arrows. Then, (as for) him, I pierced (lit.: "loosened") his hand with the point of an arrow and] he (then) entered the gate of his city <ste>althfully, like a mongoose. [I cut down] the Puqudians, [his] al[lie(s), (and) the] M[aršanians, together with the Sutians who were with him, in front of the gate (of his city) (and)] splattered his people with deadly venom. I took away from him his royal tent, [his r]oya[l] g[ol]d parasol, [gold scepter, gold bed, gold chair, gold (and) silver objects], ..., his potstands, equipment, (and) battle gear.

5′b–11′a) (As for) all his people, the inhabitants of the sett[lements of all of his land, whom *he had* ... from before my weapons *and*] *settled in a secret place*, together with herds of cattle, camels, donkeys, (and) sheep and goats. [which ...] *that* (*man*), the numerous troops of the god Aššur (required) three days (and) night(s) to carry (them) off as (their) countless booty an[d ...] I received inside my military camp [(...)] 90,580 people, 2,080 horses, 700 mules, 6,054 ca[mels, ... and 40+ sheep] that my troops had carried off as booty. In order to prevent (anyone) going out from his city or *leav*[*ing* (*it*) (...) I constructed ... around his city and] (10′) shut him up inside his city in dire circumstances, [like a pig in a pigsty]. I chopped down his orchards (and) cut down his date palms. To [*the mighty waters* of the moat of his city ...] *with* a great [...] I constructed (lit.: "trod down") a (siege) ramp against it and raised

Section 1′ = lines 1′–14′ = room ?, slab ?:1–14. See Winckler, Sar. Annals lines 329b–348/349; Lie, Sar. lines 409–415, pp. 62–63 lines 5–10, and p. 63 n. 6; and Fuchs, Khorsabad Annals lines 342–359 and 359a–c. Cf. text no. 1 lines 409–415 and text no. 2 lines 385–402+.

1′–2′ Line 1′: The transliteration assumes that *i-na qí-bit* ^{d}*aš-šur* ^{d}UTU *u* ^{d}AMAR.UTU/MES LÚ.*mun-daḫ-ṣi-ia* was at the end of the preceding line (text no. 1 line 408 and text no. 2 line 384). Lines 1′–2′: Or "[I besieged him together with his royal (military) contingent and] slaughtered (them) [like lambs a]t his (own) feet. [I pierced his warriors] (and) the horses (trained to) [his] yoke [with arrows]."

2′ *i-na*: Winckler restored [*i-na*] on his copy and the spacing on Botta's copy might allow this. Text no. 2 line 387 has *ina* and if only part of NA is to be restored at the beginnning of line 1′, we would then expect *ina*, not *i-na* here. [LÚ.*qu-ra-di-šu*]: Botta's copy would suggest that the damaged area has space for only two signs.

5′ ⸢GIŠ⸣ KUR *gan-ga-ni-šu* "..., his potstands": Possibly ⸢*si*⸣-*mat gan-ga-ni-šu*, "the appropriate things for his potstands," or GIŠ.<<KUR>>.*gan-ga-ni-šu*. For the restoration at the end of the line, see text no. 1 line 415.

6′ *ú*†-*šá-aṣ-bi-ta pa-ši-ru*: The tentative translation "*settled in a secret place*" follows CAD P p. 252. Possibly restore *ša ni-ba la i-šu-ú*, "countless" (cf. text no. 1 line 159 and text no. 3 line 5′). Text no. 2 line 395 has *u*, "and," before *ṣēnī*. The ancient scribe may have omitted the sign in this passage or possibly P.E. Botta omitted copying it; note that the preceding sign MEŠ ends in three Winkelhaken so one can easily image one or the other indicating only three instead of four.

9′ *er-re-ti*: See note to text no. 2 line 400. URU-*šu u* "his city or": Or URU *šu-u*, "this city (or)," following Fuchs, Khorsabad p. 165 line 357. *na-par*-⸢*ka*?⸣-[*a*] "*leav*[*ing*]": The reading follows Fuchs, Khorsabad p. 165. Or *na-par*-⸢*šu*⸣-[*di-šu*], "esca[ping]," following van der Speck, JEOL 25 (1977–78) p. 61. The trace of the sign after *par* on Botta's copy is only slightly better for *ka* than *šu*.

10′ As noted by A. Fuchs (Khorsabad p. 334 n. 367), the felled trees would have been used in the creation of the siege ramp mentioned in the following line. ⸢A?⸣.[MEŠ *dan-nu-ti ša ḫa-ri-ṣi* URU-*šú*]: The tentative reading of the sign and the following restoration follow text no. 2 line 401. P.E. Botta's copy has a small Winkelhaken before the damaged area, which might be a miscopy by him (perhaps indicating damage to the slab) or an indication that this passage deviated from that in Room V.

ak-kis a-na ⸢A?⸣.[MEŠ *dan-nu-ti ša ḫa-ri-ṣi* URU-*šú* ...]

11′) GAL-*ti a-ram-mu* UGU-*šu ak-bu-us-ma* UGU BÀD-*šu ú-šaq-qi*† *ù šu-ú ḫat*†*-tú* ⸢*ra*⸣-[*ma-ni-šú im-qut-su-ma* ...]

12′) *iš-ḫu-ut-ma* GIŠ.GIDRU GIŠ.GU.ZA *id-di-ma ina pa-an* LÚ.A KIN-*ia ú-na-šíq*† *qaq-qa-ru* BÀD.⸢MEŠ⸣ [GAL.MEŠ? *ù*? *ker-ḫe-(e)-šú/šu*? *a-na*? *na-pa-li*? ...]

13′) *aq-bi-šu-ma im-gu-ra qí-bi-ti re-e-ma ar-ši-šu-ma* KÙ.GI KÙ.BABBAR NA$_4$.MEŠ *ni-siq-ti* KUŠ AM.SI [...]

14′) *šá ul-tú u$_4$-me pa-ni is-ki-lu a-li-kut maḫ-ri* AD.MEŠ-*šu* 1 LIM ANŠE.KUR.RA.MEŠ 8 ME ANŠE† *x* [...]

Continued on several unpreserved slabs

(the ramp) up against its (city) wall.

11′b–14′) Moreover, (as for) him (Marduk-apla-iddina II), [his] o[wn] fear(s) [fell upon him and ...] He became afraid, laid down (his) scepter (and) throne, and kissed the ground before my messenger. (When) I ordered him [*to destroy the large*] walls (of his city) [*and its enclosure wall*(s) ...], he obeyed my command. I (then) had pity upon him and [...] gold, silver, precious stones, elephant hide(s), [...] which from earlier times those who had preceded (him), his ancestors, had acquired, 1,000 horses, 800 ... [...]

Continued on several unpreserved slabs

7

This inscription, which is commonly known as the (Khorsabad) Display Inscription (Prunkinschrift), Great Display Inscription (Große Prunkinschrift), Grande inscription des salles de Khorsabad, or Fastes is inscribed on stone wall slabs lining Rooms I, IV, VII, VIII, and X of the palace of Sargon II at Khorsabad. After a brief introductory section giving the ruler's titles and epithets and mentioning the special privileges he had bestowed upon several Babylonian and Assyrian cities (lines 1–13a), the inscription describes his numerous military campaigns, which are arranged in a geographical or associative sequence, rather than in chronological order (lines 13b–153a). It then records the construction of the city of Dūr-Šarrukīn, and in particular its palace (lines 153b–186a), followed by an invocation to the god Aššur (lines 186b–194). The inscription refers to the ruler's fifteenth year (707) in line 23 and to various gods entering their sanctuaries in Dūr-Šarrukīn (lines 155b–157a), which the Assyrian Eponym Chronicle states took place in Tašrītu (VII) of that year. In addition, the text describes a great celebration that took place inside the palace that involved rulers from every land, as well as important Assyrians (lines 177b–186a); this likely refers to celebrations upon the completion of the city that the Assyrian Eponym Chronicle states happened on the sixth day of Ayyāru (II) in Sargon's sixteenth regnal year (706).

E. Frahm (Sanherib pp. 42–43 and ISIMU 6 [2003] pp. 145–149 and 157–160, especially p. 159 n. 63) notes several similarities between this text and Sennacherib's early cylinder texts (Grayson and Novotny, RINAP 3/1 pp. 29–40 no. 1) and suggests that the well-known royal scribe Nabû-zuqup-kēnu may have been the composer of all these inscriptions, as well

6 lines 11′–14′ For the different accounts of what happened to Marduk-apla-iddina, see the Introduction to this volume, under the section "Military Campaigns." Line 11′: *ḫat*†*-tú* ⸢*ra*⸣-[*ma-ni-šú*] "[his] o[wn] fear(s)": Or possibly ^{m}AMAR†.UTU-⸢IBILA⸣-[SUM.NA *ḫat-tu ra-ma-ni-šú*], "Marduk-a[pla-iddina's own fear(s)]"; see A.T.E. Olmstead (AJSL 47 [1930–31] p. 275) and R.J. van der Speck (JEOL 25 [1977–78] p. 61), but we would expect both the masculine personal determinative and the divine determinative before AMAR.UTU, not just the former.

6 line 12′ *iš-ḫu-ut-ma* "he became afraid": Or possibly *iš-ḫu-uṭ-ma*, "he removed [*his royal garment/headdress*]"; see CAD Š/1 p. 93 sub *šaḫāṭu* B.1.a. Cf. text no. 2 line 403. The restoration at the end of the line is derived from Grayson, RIMA 2 p. 25 A.0.87.1 vi 27–28 and basically follows R.J. van der Speck (JEOL 25 [1977–78] pp. 61–62) and A. Fuchs (Khorsabad p. 167 line 359a).

as possibly other royal inscriptions of Sargon, in particular his Annals from Khorsabad. With regard to the reliefs in the rooms, see Reade, JNES 35 (1976) pp. 96–98; and Reade, Bagh. Mitt. 10 (1979) pp. 78, 81, and 83. For some comments on the connection between the reliefs on the wall slabs and the inscription, see J.M. Russell, Writing on the Wall pp. 111–115.

CATALOGUE

Ex.	Section	Museum Number/ Source	Provenance	Botta, MdN	Lines Preserved	cpn
1	1	Botta, Monument de Ninive 4 pl. 144^{c}	Khorsabad, Palace, Room X, slab 1	2 pl. 123	1–12	n
		Winckler, Sar. 2 pl. 30 no. 63^{c}				n
		Louvre squeeze				p
	2	Botta, Monument de Ninive 4 pl. 145^{c} top	Khorsabad, Palace, Room X, slab 2	2 pl. 124	13–24	n
		Winckler, Sar. 2 pl. 30 no. 64^{c}				n
		Louvre squeeze				p
		47-7-2,33 (+)				p
		47-7-2,34 (+)?				p
		A 150519 (=OI unregistered 4)				p
	3	Botta, Monument de Ninive 4 pl. 145^{c} bottom	Khorsabad, Palace, Room X, slab 3	2 pl. 125	25–36	n
		Winckler, Sar. 2 pl. 31 no. 65^{c}				n
		Louvre squeeze				p
	4	Botta, Monument de Ninive 4 pl. 146^{c} top	Khorsabad, Palace, Room X, slab 4	2 pl. 126	37–48	n
		Winckler, Sar. 2 pl. 31 no. 66^{c}				n
		Louvre squeeze				p
		A 7365				p
	5	Botta, Monument de Ninive 4 pl. 146^{c} bottom	Khorsabad, Palace, Room X, slab 5	2 pl. 127	49–60	n
		Winckler, Sar. 2 pl. 32 no. 67^{c}				n
		Louvre squeeze				p
		A 7362				p
	6	Botta, Monument de Ninive 4 pl. 147^{c}	Khorsabad, Palace, Room X, slab 6	2 pl. 128 (mislabeled on pl.)	61–72	n
		Winckler, Sar. 2 pl. 32 no. 68^{c}				n
		Louvre squeeze				p
		AO 19887				c
	7	Botta, Monument de Ninive 4 pl. 148^{c}	Khorsabad, Palace, Room X, slab 7	2 pl. 129	73–84	n
		Winckler, Sar. 2 pl. 33 no. 69^{c}				n
		Louvre squeeze				p
		AO 19887 (+)				c
		OI unregistered 5 (+)				p
		A 150547				p
	8	Botta, Monument de Ninive 4 pl. 149^{c}	Khorsabad, Palace, Room X, slab 8	2 pl. 130	85–96	n
		Winckler, Sar. 2 pl. 33 no. 70^{c}				n
		Louvre squeeze				p
	9	Botta, Monument de Ninive 4 pl. 150^{c}	Khorsabad, Palace, Room X, slab 9	2 pl. 131	97–108	n
		Winckler, Sar. 2 pl. 33 no. 71^{c}				n
		Louvre squeeze				p
		OI unregistered 9				p
	10	Botta, Monument de Ninive 4 pl. 151^{c} bottom	Khorsabad, Palace, Room X, slab 10	2 pl. 131	109–120	n

		Winckler, Sar. 2 pl. 34 no. 72[c]				n
		Louvre squeeze				p
		47-7-2,43				p
	11	Botta, Monument de Ninive 4 pl. 151[c] top	Khorsabad, Palace, Room X, slab 11	2 pl. 132	121–132	n
		Winckler, Sar. 2 pl. 34 no. 73[c]				n
		Louvre squeeze				p
		BM 135992 (1973-12-8,1) (+)				c
		47-7-2,32 (+)				p
		47-7-2,42 (+)				p
		BM 118834 (47-7-2,45)				c
	12	Botta, Monument de Ninive 4 pl. 152[c] top	Khorsabad, Palace, Room X, slab 12	2 pl. 133	133–144	n
		Winckler, Sar. 2 pl. 35 no. 74[c]				n
		Louvre squeeze				p
		BM 118834 (47-7-2,22+29+30+31+35+36+37+38+40[+]39) (+)				p
		47-7-2,48 + 89-5-11,1				c
	13	Botta, Monument de Ninive 4 pl. 153[c]	Khorsabad, Palace, Room X, slab 13	2 pl. 134	145–156	n
		Winckler, Sar. 2 pl. 35 no. 75[c]				n
		Louvre squeeze				p
	14	Botta, Monument de Ninive 4 pl. 152[c] bottom	Khorsabad, Palace, Room X, slab 14	2 pl. 135	157–168	n
		Winckler, Sar. 2 pl. 36 no. 76[c]				n
		Louvre squeeze				p
	15	Botta, Monument de Ninive 4 pl. 154[c]	Khorsabad, Palace, Room X, slab 15	2 pl. 136	169–180	n
		Winckler, Sar. 2 pl. 36 no. 77[c]				n
		Louvre squeeze				p
		47-7-2,49+50 (+)				p
		Museo delle Antichità Egizie (Turin) P.2055				p
	[16]	-	[Khorsabad, Palace, Room X, slab 16]	—	[181–194]	—
2	[?]	—	[Khorsabad, Palace, Room I, slabs ?]	—	—	—
	1′	Botta, Monument de Ninive 4 pl. 69 left	Khorsabad, Palace, Room I, slab 2	1 pl. 49	57–61	n
	2′	Botta, Monument de Ninive 4 pl. 69 right	Khorsabad, Palace, Room I, slab 1	1 pl. 49	64–71	n
	[3′ff.]	—	[Khorsabad, Palace, Room I, slabs 8, 7, etc.]	—	—	—
3	1	Botta, Monument de Ninive 4 pl. 99[c]	Khorsabad, Palace, Room IV, slab 13	—	1–15	n
		Louvre squeeze				p
	2	Botta, Monument de Ninive 4 pl. 98[c]	Khorsabad, Palace, Room IV, slab 12	1 pl. 83	15–20	n
		Louvre squeeze				p
	3	Botta, Monument de Ninive 4 pl. 97[c]	Khorsabad, Palace, Room IV, slab 11	—	20–27	n
		Louvre squeeze				p
	4	Botta, Monument de Ninive 4 pl. 96	Khorsabad, Palace, Room IV, slab 10	—	27–33	n
		Institut de France sheet 327				n
	5	Botta, Monument de Ninive 4 pl. 95	Khorsabad, Palace, Room IV, slab 9	1 pl. 82	33–41	n
		Institut de France sheet 326				n
	6	Botta, Monument de Ninive 4 pl. 94	Khorsabad, Palace, Room IV, slab 8	1 pl. 82	41–48	n
		Institut de France sheet 324				n

	7	Botta, Monument de Ninive 3 pl. 63	Khorsabad, Palace, Entrance D_3	—	48–56	n
		Institut de France sheet 318				n
	8	Botta, Monument de Ninive 3 pl. 64	Khorsabad, Palace, Entrance D_4	—	56–62	n
		Botta, JA 4/3 (1844) pl. XXVIII				n
		Institut de France sheet 320				n
	[9]	—	[Khorsabad, Palace, Room IV, slab 1?]	—	[63–68]	—
	10	Botta, Monument de Ninive 3 pl. 93	Khorsabad, Palace, Room IV, slabs 2–3	1 pl. 81	68–77	n
		Botta, JA 4/4 (1844) pls. XLVII–XLVIII				n
		Institut de France sheets 330–331				n
	[11ff.]	—	[Khorsabad, Palace, Room IV, slabs 4, etc.]	—	[77–152]	n
	1′	Botta, Monument de Ninive 4 pl. 104[c]	Khorsabad, Palace, Room IV, slab 18	—	152–159	n
		Louvre squeeze				p
	2′	Botta, Monument de Ninive 4 pl. 103[c]	Khorsabad, Palace, Room IV, slab 17	—	159–166	n
		Louvre squeeze				p
	3′	Botta, Monument de Ninive 4 pl. 102	Khorsabad, Palace, Room IV, slab 16	—	166–171	n
	4′	Botta, Monument de Ninive 4 pl. 101[c]	Khorsabad, Palace, Room IV, slab 15	—	171–181	n
		Louvre squeeze				p
	5′	Botta, Monument de Ninive 4 pl. 100[c]	Khorsabad, Palace, Room IV, slab 14	—	181–194	n
		Louvre squeeze				p
4	1	Botta, Monument de Ninive 4 pl. 121[c]	Khorsabad, Palace, Room VII, slab 1	2 pl. 108	1–18	n
		Louvre squeeze				p
		A 58101 (+) A 58116 (+)				p
		IM 60971/3				p
	2	Botta, Monument de Ninive 4 pl. 122[c]	Khorsabad, Palace, Room VII, slab 2	2 pl. 108	18–25	n
		Louvre squeeze				p
	3	Botta, Monument de Ninive 4 pl. 123[c]	Khorsabad, Palace, Room VII, slab 3	—	25–40	n
		Louvre squeeze				p
	4	Botta, Monument de Ninive 4 pl. 124[c]	Khorsabad, Palace, Room VII, slab 4	2 pl. 109	40–62	n
		Louvre squeeze				p
	5	Botta, Monument de Ninive 4 pl. 125[c]	Khorsabad, Palace, Room VII, slab 5	2 pl. 109	62–73	n
		IM 60971/1 +?				p
		47-7-2,44 (+)				p
		BM 22466 (47-7-2,47)				c
	6	Botta, Monument de Ninive 4 pl. 126[c]	Khorsabad, Palace, Room VII, slab 6	2 pl. 110	73–89	n
		Louvre squeeze				p
	7	Botta, Monument de Ninive 4 pl. 127[c]	Khorsabad, Palace, Room VII, slab 7	2 pl. 111	103–115	n
		Louvre squeeze				p
	8	Botta, Monument de Ninive 4 pl. 128[c]	Khorsabad, Palace, Room VII, slab 8	2 pl. 111	116–128	n
		Louvre squeeze				p
		IM 60971/2				c

	[9]	—	[Khorsabad, Palace, Room VII, slab 9]	—	[129–137]	—
	10	Botta, Monument de Ninive 4 pl. 129[c]	Khorsabad, Palace, Room VII, slab 10	2 pl. 112	137–150	n
		Louvre squeeze				p
		A 11254				p
	11	Botta, Monument de Ninive 4 pl. 130[c]	Khorsabad, Palace, Room VII, slab 11	2 pl. 113	151–164	n
		Louvre squeeze				p
		A 11256				p
	12	Botta, Monument de Ninive 4 pl. 131[c]	Khorsabad, Palace, Room VII, slab 12	2 pl. 114	164–176	n
		Louvre squeeze				p
		A 11255				p
	13	Botta, Monument de Ninive 4 pl. 132[c]	Khorsabad, Palace, Room VII, slab 13	2 pl. 114	177–194	n
		Winckler, Sar. 2 pl. 36 no. 78[c]				n
		Louvre squeeze				p
		A 11255				p
5	1	Botta, Monument de Ninive 4 pl. 135 top	Khorsabad, Palace, Room VIII, slab 9	—	1–8	n
		Louvre squeeze				p
	2	Botta, Monument de Ninive 4 pl. 136[c]	Khorsabad, Palace, Room VIII, slab 11	2 pl. 117	8–18	n
		Louvre squeeze				p
	3	Botta, Monument de Ninive 4 pl. 137[c]	Khorsabad, Palace, Room VIII, slab 12	2 pl. 118	18–23	n
		Louvre squeeze				p
	4	Botta, Monument de Ninive 4 pl. 138[c] top	Khorsabad, Palace, Room VIII, slab 13	2 pl. 119	23–31	n
		Louvre squeeze				p
	[5]	—	[Khorsabad, Palace, Room VIII, slab 15?]	—	[31–38]	—
	6	Botta, Monument de Ninive 4 pl. 135 bottom	Khorsabad, Palace, Room VIII, slab 16	—	38–45	n
	7	Botta, Monument de Ninive 4 pl. 138[c] bottom	Khorsabad, Palace, Room VIII, slab 17	2 pl. 119bis	45–52	n
		Louvre squeeze				p
	8	Botta, Monument de Ninive 4 pl. 139[c]	Khorsabad, Palace, Room VIII, slab 18	2 pl. 119bis	52–57	n
	9	Botta, Monument de Ninive 4 pl. 140[c]	Khorsabad, Palace, Room VIII, slab 19	2 pl. 119bis	57–60	n
		Louvre squeeze				p
	[10]	—	[Khorsabad, Palace, Room VIII, slab 20/21?]	—	[60–66]	—
	11	Botta, Monument de Ninive 4 pl. 141[c]	Khorsabad, Palace, Room VIII, slab 22	—	66–74	n
		Louvre squeeze				p
	12	Botta, Monument de Ninive 4 pl. 143[c] top	Khorsabad, Palace, Room VIII, slab 23	—	75–82	n
	13	Botta, Monument de Ninive 4 pl. 142[c] bottom	Khorsabad, Palace, Room VIII, slab 24	2 pl. 120	83–95	n
		Louvre squeeze				p
	14	Botta, Monument de Ninive 4 pl. 143[c] bottom	Khorsabad, Palace, Room VIII, slab 25	2 pl. 120	95–106	n
		Louvre squeeze				p
	[15]	—	[Khorsabad, Palace, Room VIII, slab 26/28]	—	[107–112]	—
	16	Botta, Monument de Ninive 4 pl. 142[c] top	Khorsabad, Palace, Room VIII, slab 29	—	112–115	n

	Louvre squeeze				p
[17–18]	—	[Khorsabad, Palace, Room VIII, slabs 31 and 1]	—	[115–125]	—
19	Botta, Monument de Ninive 4 pl. 133 top	Khorsabad, Palace, Room VIII, slab 2	—	126–134	n
[20–21]	—	[Khorsabad, Palace, Room VIII, slabs 3–4]	—	[134–149]	—
22	Botta, Monument de Ninive 4 pl. 133 bottom	Khorsabad, Palace, Room VIII, slab 5	—	149–156	n
23	Botta, Monument de Ninive 4 pl. 134c top	Khorsabad, Palace, Room VIII, slab 6	—	157–168	n
	Louvre squeeze				p
[24]	—	[Khorsabad, Palace, Room VIII, slab 7]	—	[168–173]	—
25	Botta, Monument de Ninive 4 pl. 134c bottom	Khorsabad, Palace, Room VIII, slab 8	—	173–194	n
	Louvre squeeze				p

COMMENTARY

The pieces which P.E. Botta collated either from the original or from squeezes before publishing his copies are marked with c after the Botta, Monument de Ninive 3–4 plate number (e.g., 136c); the same is done with the text numbers which Winckler is supposed to have collated from squeezes or originals. Regrettably, some of the squeezes available to Botta are no longer extant and thus not available for consultation (ex. 4: Botta, Monument de Ninive 4 pl. 125c; ex. 5: ibid. pls. 139c and 143c top). Most of the fragments still extant of this inscription are small, representing only a tiny portion of the inscription on a particular slab. Thus, even if they have been examined in the original or by means of photographs, for the most part the edition of the text on that slab is based on Botta's copy and/or Botta's squeezes.

In the catalogue, each slab for an individual exemplar has been given a section number, just as is the case for the Khorsabad Annals (text nos. 1–4 and 6) and the Display Inscription from Room XIV (text no. 8); however, since the exemplars all bear the same inscription and have different line arrangements, these section numbers are not mentioned in the edition itself. They have been given simply to facilitate the reader's understanding of where the respective lines of the inscription on an exemplar come from and where missing sections (i.e., sections not copied by Botta) would have been located.

Ex. 1: For the plan of Room X and sketches of the wall slabs, see Botta, Monument de Ninive 2 pl. 122 and Albenda, Palace of Sargon pl. 26. The inscription began on slab 1 (section 1), to the left of Entrance c when entering the room, ran in a clockwise order around the room, and presumably ended on slab 16 (section 16), to the right of Entrance c, although no copy of the inscription on slab 16 is preserved. Botta, Monument de Ninive 2 pl. 128 (relief) is mislabeled as being Room V 25; see table of contents to ibid. 1 p. III. The two slabs on ibid. 4 pl. 145 (sections 2–3) are mislabeled as being Room X slabs 1 and 2 instead of Room X slabs 2 and 3 respectively. For the unregistered pieces in the Oriental Institute (OI), Chicago, see Albenda, Palace of Sargon pp. 174–176; the exact placement of some of these may be uncertain. Two British Museum fragments, 47-7-2,32 and 47-7-2,34 (sections 11 and 2 respectively), are shown on BM photo 56550 and two others, 47-7-2,33 and 47-7-2,42 (sections 2 and 11 respectively) on BM photo 56551. The British Museum pieces with the registration numbers 47-7-2,1ff. are part of the Hector collection, items purchased from Mr. Hector, "a merchant at Baghdad, who had himself got them, it appears, by a gleaning made after Botta's excavations had opened up the ruins of the palace" (Gadd, Stones p. 160; for this collection in general, see ibid. pp. 160–163).

Ex. 2: For the plan of Room I and sketches of the wall slabs, see Botta, Monument de Ninive 1 pl. 48 and Albenda, Palace of Sargon pl. 106. Only a small part of the inscription in this room is known, copies for two wall slabs to the right of Entrance A when entering the room from Court I (slabs 1 and 2; sections 2′ and 1′ respectively). E. Flandin's sketch drawing of the room (Monument de Ninive 1 pl. 48) indicates that slabs 7 and 8 also had inscriptions on them, and may indicate that slabs 3 and 4 in Entrance A (A_3 and A_4) were also inscribed, but these were not copied by Botta. The inscription likely began on the northeast wall of the room and ran in a clockwise order around the room, moving to slab 2 and then slab 1; after slab 1 the inscription either carried on onto the two slabs in Entrance A (A_3 > A_4) or directly across the doorway to slabs 8 and then 7.

Ex. 3: For the plan of Room IV and sketches of the wall slabs, see Botta, Monument de Ninive 1 pls. 79–80 and Albenda, Palace of Sargon pls. 79–80. The inscription began on slab 13 (section 1), to the left of Entrance T when one entered the room from Room VIII, and apparently carried on in a clockwise order, ending on slab 14 (section 5′), located to the right of Entrance T. Botta, Monument de Ninive 4 pls. 96, 95, and 94 (sections 4, 5, and 6 respectively) are mislabeled as being Room IV slabs 9, 8, and 7 respectively; see Weissbach, ZDMG 72 (1918) p. 169 and look at Botta, Monument de Ninive 1 pl. 80. Botta's hand copies of seven slabs are preserved in the Archives of the Institut de France (Botta-Cotta II 2976 folio I sheets 318 [D_3; section 7], 320 [D_4; section 8], 324 [IV,8; section 6], 326 [IV,9; section 5], 327 [IV,10; section 4], and 330–331 [IV,2–3; section 10]). These copies and the copies published in JA 4/3–4 (1844) (pls. XXVIII [D_4] and XLVII–XLVIII [IV,2–3]) are occasionally referred to in the score and list of variants when they provide a better reading or a more extensive text than the copies in Monument de Ninive. The arrangement of the text as copied on Botta, Monument de Ninive 4 pl. 99^c — section 1; lines 1–15 of the inscription — is misleading. The text is in three fragments (left = A; middle = B; right = C) which are to be read C-A-B, with C having two lines instead of just one between its first line (GAL-*ú*) and the third line of the copy (]-⌜*us*⌝-*su*). On Botta, Monument de Ninive 4 pl. 100 (section 5′; lines 181–194), the section to the extreme right of the copy is placed two lines too high. See also Fuchs, Khorsabad pp. 21–22.

Ex. 4: For the plan of Room VII and sketches of the wall slabs, see Botta, Monument de Ninive 2 pl. 107 and Albenda, Palace of Sargon pl. 84. The inscription began on slab 1 (section 1), to the left of Entrance R when entering the room from Room IV, and then ran in a clockwise order around the room, ending on slab 13 (section 13), to the right of Entrance R. The museum number for slab 8 (section 8) follows P. Albenda (Palace of Sargon p. 178), rather than E. Guralnick (Assur 1/5 [1976] p. 2 n. 5). The Oriental Institute museum numbers for Room VII slabs 11–13 (sections 11–13) follow Loud, Khorsabad 1 pp. 76–77 figs. 88–89 captions (confirmed by R.T. Tindel, against Guralnick, Assur 1/5 [1976] p. 2). The sections preserved on the two pieces in the Iraq Museum have been collated, but IM 60971/2 (sections 7–8) and IM 60971/3 (section 1) only preserve parts of 3–6 signs each. A 58101 and A 58116 (section 1) also only preserve all or parts of only a few signs (10 and 21 respectively). One BM fragment, 47-7-2,44 (part of Room VII slab 5; section 5) is shown on British Museum photo 56550.

Ex. 5: For the plan of Room VIII and sketches of the wall slabs, see Botta, Monument de Ninive 2 pls. 115–116 and Albenda, Palace of Sargon pls. 72–73. The inscription began on slab 9 (section 1), to the left of Entrance Q when entering the room from Court VIII, and ran in a clockwise order around the room, ending on slab 8 (section 25), to the right of Entrance Q. Botta, Monument de Ninive 4 pl. 137^c (section 3) shows two parts of inscription, an area on the left (lines 18b-20a) and an area on the right (lines 20b–23a); the two sections are separated by the large damaged section on the plate. Botta, Monument de Ninive 4 pl. 135 bottom (section 6) is said to be on slab 14 in the table of contents, but (correctly) on slab 16 on pl. 135. Botta, Monument de Ninive 4 pl. 141^c (section 11) appears to represent four fragments that are not properly put together. It is likely that the MEŠ of line 2 should go at the end of line 1 (line 67) or that it is a miscopy for ⌜*šat*⌝-*t*[*i*- of line 67 (a possible reading based on the squeeze). It is also likely that the MA at the end of line 3 should have more space between it and the KUR sign (line 69). Although the squeeze of pl. 141^c is almost totally illegible, it is clear that the signs at the beginnings of lines 4–7 on the copy should be moved up one line (lines 68–71), leaving a gap of one line between them and line 8, and that the new line 7 begins with *a*-⌜*di*⌝ of line 71. Botta, Monument de Ninive 4 pl. 133 bottom (section 22) shows three sections of the text (parts of lines 149–156); the section on the right should be raised by one line in relation to the other sections. Botta Monument de Ninive 4 pl. 134^c bottom (section 25) shows three sections (parts of lines 173–194); the section in the middle must be raised by one line in relation to the other two sections and the first line of this section (line with no signs preserved) must be deleted. See also Fuchs, Khorsabad pp. 24–25.

Parts of the reliefs on exemplars 1, 4, and 5 are preserved today in the British Museum, Iraq Museum, Louvre, Metropolitan Museum of Art, Musée Borely (Marseille), and Oriental Institute (Chicago). The museum numbers for these have not been included in the catalogue unless the piece also included part of the inscription.

A small stone fragment of an additional exemplar may be an item offered for sale as lot no. 660 on September 26, 1998 by Hanzel Galleries (Chicago). Information on this fragment and a photograph of its inscription were kindly provided by J.A. Brinkman. The piece measures 5(+) inches (height) × 14.5(+) inches (width) × 5.5(+) inches (thickness) and the individual signs have an average height of 1 3/8 inches. The inscription reads:

Lacuna

1′. [...] ⸢*áš-kun*⸣*-ma* GUN *ma-*[*da-at-tu* ...] (= line 32)

2′. [...] ⸢URU.*ar-pad*⸣*-da* URU.⸢*ṣi-mir*⸣-[*ra* ...] (= line 33)

3′. [... URU.*qar*]*-*⸢*qa-ri*⸣ URU *na-*⸢*ram-i*⸣-[*šú* ...] (= line 34)

Lacuna

The placement of the signs does not fit Botta's copies for exs. 1, 3, or 4. No copies of this section exist for exs. 2 and 5, but, rather than assuming that this piece comes from a new exemplar, it is possible that the fragment was so small that it was simply not copied by Botta with the other more substantial pieces that he found in Rooms I (ex. 2) and VIII (ex. 5).

Note that while [c] in the catalogue may indicate that the original of a section has been collated, the original may only preserve a tiny portion of the inscription originally on a slab (e.g., ex. 3 IM 60971/3 [Room VII,1] actually only preserves and can be relied upon for all or parts of three signs).

While the basic text of this inscription is clear, as noted in the introduction to this volume, there is no completely satisfactory way to edit this inscription and indicate the variously clear and/or possible variants (in particular possible abnormally written signs) in the various exemplars without providing lengthy notes for numerous signs. This is because most of the original slabs no longer exist (or exist in only a very fragmentary state) and there are varying (and at times contradictory) sources of information for the individual exemplars, with the reliability of some of the sources being open to question. The transliteration for each individual exemplar in the online score is based on the author's assessment of the various sources of information, although it would have been possible to produce a score for each exemplar in itself, as is done for text nos. 1–4 and 8, where, however, each text is represented by only a single exemplar. The master line is based upon ex. 1, but at times makes use of other exemplars.

BIBLIOGRAPHY

1844 Botta, JA 4/3 pp. 97–98 and pl. XXVIII (ex. 3, copy and study of Entrance D_4)

1844 Botta, JA 4/4 p. 313 and pls. XLVII–XLVIII (ex. 3, copy of Room IV,2–3)

1849 Botta, Monument de Ninive 1–2 pls. 48–50, 79–83, 107–120, and 122–136 (exs. 1–5, drawing of reliefs, provenance)

1849 Botta, Monument de Ninive 3–4 pls. 63–64, 69, 93–104, and 121–154 (exs. 1–5, copy)

1854 de Longpérier, Notice[3] nos. 30 and 616 (ex. 1, study of AO 19887)

1862 Oppert, Annales de Philosophie chrétienne 65 pp. 44–45 no. 2 and pp. 62–75 (exs. 1, 3–5, translation)

1862 Oppert, Sargonides pp. 2–3 no. 2 and 20–33 (exs. 1, 3–5, translation) (identical to the preceding)

1863 Oppert and Ménant, Fastes (exs. 1, 3–5, copy, edition)

1863 Oppert and Ménant, JA 6/1 pp. 4–26 (exs. 1, 3–5, translation)

1863 Oppert and Ménant, JA 6/2 pp. 475–517 (exs. 1, 3–5, study)

1863 Oppert and Ménant, Grande Inscription (exs. 1, 3–5, copy, edition, study)

1864 Oppert and Ménant, JA 6/3 pp. 5–62, 168–201, 209–265, and 373–415 (exs. 1, 3–5, study)

1865 Oppert, JA 6/6 pp. 289–330 (exs. 1, 3–5, study)

1865 Oppert and Ménant JA 6/6 pp. 133–179 (exs. 1, 3–5, study)

1874 Ménant, Annales pp. 179–192 (exs. 1, translation)

1877 Oppert, Records of the Past 9 pp. 1–20 (exs. 1, 3–5, translation)

1886 Bezold, Literatur p. 92 §54.11 (exs. 1, 3–5, study)

1889 Winckler, Sar. 1 pp. X and 96–135 (exs. 1, 3–5, edition); and 2 pls. 30–36 nos. 63–78 (ex. 1, copy; ex. 4, copy of lines 181–194)

1890 Peiser in Schrader, KB 2 pp. 52–81 (exs. 1, 3–5, edition)

1895 Meissner, Chrestomathie pp. 14–16 (ex. 1, copy of lines 23b–53)

1898 King, First Steps p. 47 (ex. 1, lines 23b–25a, copy, edition)

1909 Winckler, Textbuch[3] pp. 37–38 and 40–41 (lines 23b–36a, 90–112a, edition)

1911 Sarsowsky, Urkundenbuch pp. 28–29 (ex. 1, copy of lines 23b–27, 33–36a, 90–112a)

1918 Weissbach, ZDMG 72 pp. 161–170 (exs. 1–5, study)

1926 Ebeling in Gressmann, ATAT[2] pp. 349–351 (lines 23b–27, 33–36a, 90–112a, translation)

1927 Luckenbill, ARAB 2 pp. 25–39 §§52–75 (exs. 1, 3–5, translation)

1935 Boson, Aegyptus 15 p. 424 (ex. 1, photo of fragment in Museo delle Antichità Egizie [Turin])

1936 Gadd, Stones pp. 161–163 (ex. 1, transliteration of 47-7-2,22 [BM 118834])

1936 Loud, Khorsabad 1 pp. 46, 48, 72, 75–77 figs. 53, 55, 83, and 87–89 (ex. 1 [A 7365, 7362], ex. 4 [A 11254–11256], photo)

1958 Wiseman, DOTT p. 60 (lines 23b–27, translation)

1964 Brinkman, Studies Oppenheim p. 44 no. 44.2.20.c.i (study)

1968 Borger in Galling, Textbuch[2] pp. 62–64 nos. 32 and 35 (lines 25b–26, 90–112a, translation)

1968 Ellis, Foundation Deposits p. 176 no. 17 (lines 159b–160a, edition)

1969 Oppenheim, ANET[3] pp. 284–286 (lines 23b–27, 33–36a, 90–112a, translation)

1975 Orthmann, Der alte Orient pl. 224 and p. 320 (ex. 1 [AO 19887], photo)

1976 Basmachi, Treasures p. 237 and fig. 134 (ex. 4 [IM 60971/2], photo)

1976 Guralnick, Assur 1/5 (ex. 4 [IM 60971/1–3, A 11254–11256], photo, study of reliefs)

1976 Saporetti, Studi Ciprioti e Rapporti di Scavo 2 pp. 83–85 (lines 16b–17a, 145b–149b, translation, study)

1977 Briend and Seux, TPOA nos. 34, 35B, and 40A (lines 23b–26, 33–36a, 90–112a, translation)

1984 Borger, TUAT 1/4 pp. 383–385 (lines 23b–27, 33–36a, 90–112a, translation)

1985 Dalley, Iraq 47 pp. 34–35 (lines 23–25, translation)
1986 Albenda, Palace of Sargon pp. 67–71, 74–81, 87, 123–125, 135–139, 143–144, and 174–182; pls. 26–34, 72–90, and 106–108; and figs. 45–46 and 48 (ex. 1 [A 7362, A 7365, AO 19887], photo; exs. 1–5, drawings of reliefs, provenance)
1986 Renger, CRRA 32 pp. 112–114 and 116–118 (lines 1–12, 28–32, 78–83, transcription, study)
1987 Engel, Dämonen p. 47 (lines 189b–190, edition) and pp. 142–150 (lines 162b–164, edition of exs. 1, 3–5)
1990 Potts, Arabian Gulf 1 p. 334 no. 3 (lines 140b–145a, translation)
1990 Renger, Studies Moran p. 434 (ex. 1, edition of lines 1–15)
1992 Becking, Fall of Samaria pp. 25–26 (lines 23–25, edition)
1994 Fuchs, Khorsabad pp. 189–248 and 343–355 no. 2.4, and pp. 386 and 394–395 (exs. 1–5, edition; study)
1995 André-Salvini in Caubet, Khorsabad p. 32 fig. 3 (ex. 1, photo of lines 61–72)
1995 Biga in Dolce and Nota Santi, Dai Palazzi Assiri pp. 278–279 no. 61 and fig. 130 (ex. 1 [P.2055], photo, study)
1996 Matthiae, I grandi imperi p. 23 (ex. 1 [AO 19887], photo)
1996 Mayer, UF 28 pp. 475–476 and 480–481 (lines 95–96, 101–104a, 112, 145–149, edition, study)
1998 Uehlinger, Studies Loretz p. 767 (lines 33–36a, translation)
1998 Younger, JBL 117 p. 216 (lines 23b–25a, edition)
1999 Frame, Orientalia 68 p. 49 and p. 53 (lines 55–56, 109b–112a, edition)
1999 Younger, CBQ 61 p. 469 (lines 23b–25a, edition)
2000 Bagg, Assyrische Wasserbauten p. 159 n. 338 and pp. 161–162 and 327 (lines 127b–130a, 142b–143a, edition; lines 127-129, variants to text no. 74 vi 32–42)
2000 Younger, COS 2 pp. 296–297 no. 2.118E (lines 23b–27, 33–36a, 90–112a, edition)
2001 Na'aman, CRRA 45/1 p. 358 (lines 145–149, translation)
2001 Rollinger, Melammu 2 p. 246 (lines 90–111, translation)
2002 Berlejung, Studies Weippert p. 208 (lines 76–78a, edition)
2002 Vera Chamaza, Omnipotenz p. 367 no. 116a (lines 155b–156a, edition)
2002 Younger in Chavalas and Younger, Mesopotamia and the Bible p. 291 (lines 23b–25a, translation)
2005 Vera Chamaza, Rolle Moabs p. 79 n. 557 and pp. 146–147 no. 7c (lines 23b, 105–109a, edition)
2006 Cogan, IEJ 56 p. 86 (lines 153b–155a, edition)
2006 Melville in Chavalas, ANE pp. 340–342 no. 129 (lines 1–23a, 121b–144a, translation)
2006 Ponchia, SAAB 15 p. 232 (study)
2008 Cogan, Raging Torrent pp. 82–89 no. 18 (lines 23b–27, 33–36a, 90–112a, translation, study)
2010 Barbato, Kaskal 7 p. 178 (line 132, translation, study)
2012 Worthington, Textual Criticism pp. 78, 152, 157, and 237 (study)
2013 Frame in Berlejung and Streck, Arameans, Chaldeans, and Arabs pp. 106–107 (lines 121–137, translation)
2014 Maniori, Campagne di Sargon pp. 43–46 G1–G5 and passim (study)
2016 Van De Mieroop, JAH 4 p. 21 (lines 77–78, translation)
2017 Liverani, Assyria pp. 18, 38, 49, 73, 83, 145, 152, 212, and 222–224 (lines 50–51, 61b–63a, 64b–65a, 74b–76a, 105b–107a, 109b–111, 121b–124, 144b–149a, 153b–155a, 158b–166, translation)
2018 Frahm, Last Days pp. 75–76 no. 9 and p. 78 no. 12 (lines 23b–25a, 33–36a, edition, study)
2018 Zamazalová in Yamada, SAAS 28 p. 196 (lines 14b–15, translation)
2019 Aster, JAOS 139 pp. 602–609 (lines 23b–25a, edition, study)
2019 Edmonds in Dušek and Mynářová, Aramaean Borders p. 46 (vi 45–49, translation)

TEXT

1) É.⌈GAL⌉ ^{m}LUGAL-GI.NA LUGAL GAL MAN *dan-nu* MAN *kiš-šá-tim*
2) LUGAL KUR *aš-šur*.KI GÌR.NÍTA KÁ.DINGIR.RA.KI MAN KUR *šu-me-ri*
3) *ù* ⌈URI⌉.KI *mi-gir* DINGIR.MEŠ GAL.MEŠ ^{d}*aš-šur* ^{d}AG ^{d}AMAR.UTU
4) *šar-⌈ru⌉-ut la šá-na-an ú-šat-li-mu-ni-ma zi-kir* MU-*ia*
5) *dam-qu ú-še-ṣu-ú a-na re-še-e-ti ša* ZIMBIR.KI
6) NIBRU.KI KÁ.DINGIR.RA.KI *ù bár-sipa*.KI *za-nin-us-su-un*
7) *e-tep-pu-šá ša* ERIM.MEŠ *ki-din-ni mal ba-šu-ú ḫi-bil-ta-šú-nu a-rib-ma*
8) *ú-šá-áš-šík tup-šik-ki* BÀD.AN.KI ÚRI.KI UNUG.KI *eridu*.KI
9) ARARMA.KI *kul-aba$_4$*.KI *ki-sik*.KI URU.*né-med-^{d}la-gu-da ú-šap-ši-ḫa*
10) UN.MEŠ-*šú-un za-kut bal-til*.KI *ù* URU.*ḫar-ra-ni šá ul-tu u$_4$-me*
11) *ma-a'-du-ti im-ma-šu-ma ki-din-nu-us-su-un*

1–3a) Pal[ac]e of Sargon (II), great king, strong king, king of the world, king of Assyria, governor of Babylon, king of the land of Sumer and Ak[k]ad, favorite of the great gods.

3b–5a) The gods Aššur, Nabû (and) Marduk granted me a reign without equal and exalted my good reputation to the heights.

5b–12a) I continually acted as provider for (the cities) Sippar, Nippur, Babylon, and Borsippa (and) I made restitution for the wrongful damage suffered by the people of privileged status, as many as there were (of them); I abolished corvée duty for (the cities) Dēr, Ur, Uruk, Eridu, Larsa, Kullaba, Kissik, (and) Nēmed-Laguda, (and) gave relief to (10) their people. I restored the exemption (from obligations) of (the city) Baltil (Aššur) and the city Ḫarrān, which had fallen into oblivion in the distant past, and their privileged status that had lapsed.

---

6 Exs. 4–5 omit *ù*, "and."

ba-ṭil-ta ú-⌜*ter*⌝

12) *áš-ru-uš-šá* DINGIR.MEŠ GAL.MEŠ *ina ku-un lìb-bi-šú-nu ip-pal-su-ni-ma*

12b–13a) The great gods looked upon me, among all rulers, with their steadfast hearts, granted manly strength to me, and made my stature exceedingly great.

13) *i-na nap-ḫar ma-li-ki dun-nu zik-ru-ti iš-ru-ku-nim-ma ú-šá-te-ru ši-kit-ti ina u*$_{4}$*-um be-lu-ti-ia mal-ku gaba-ra-a-a ul ib-ši-ma ina e-peš* MURUB$_{4}$ *u* MÈ *ul a-mu-ra mu-né-ḫu*

14) KUR.MEŠ *na-ki-ri ka-li-šin kar-pa-niš ú-ḫap-pi-ma ḫa-am-ma-mi ša ar-ba-ʾi ad-da-a ṣer-re-e-ti ḫur-šá-a-ni bé-ru-ti šá né-reb-šú-nu áš-ṭu la mi-nam*

15) *ú-pat-ti-ma a-mu-ra du-ru-ug-šú-un ṭu-da-at la aʾ-a-ri pa-áš-qa-a-ti ša a-šar-ši-na šug-lud-du ra-biš e-te-et-ti-qa e-teb-bi-ra na-gab be-ra-a-ti*

13b–15) Since the (first) day of my reign, there has been no ruler who could equal me and I have met no one who could overpower (me) in war or battle. I smashed all the enemy lands like pots and put halters on (all) rebels in the four (quarters of the world). I opened up innumerable distant mountainous areas whose pass(es) are difficult and I visited their remotest region(s). In a grandiose manner, I traversed inaccessible, difficult paths in terrifying location(s) (and) crossed every *swamp*.

16) *i-na li-i-ti u da-na-ni šá* DINGIR.MEŠ GAL.MEŠ EN.MEŠ-*ia ša* GIŠ.TUKUL.MEŠ-*ia ú-šat-bu-ma ú-ra-as-si-ba na-gab ga-re-ia iš-tu* KUR.*ia-ad-na-na ša* MURUB$_{4}$ *tam-tim*

17) *šá-lam* ^{d}UTU-*ši a-di pa-aṭ* KUR.*mu-ṣu-ri u* KUR.*mu-uš-ki* KUR MAR.TU.KI DAGAL-*tum* KUR.*ḫat-ti a-na si-ḫir-ti-šá nap-ḫa-ar gu-ti-um*.KI KUR.*ma-da-a-a ru-qu-ú-ti*

18) *ša pa-aṭ* KUR.*bi-ik-ni a-di* KUR.*el-li-pí* KUR.*ra-a-ši šá i-te-e* KUR.ELAM.MA.KI *ša a-aḫ* ÍD.IDIGNA LÚ.*i-tu-ʾu* LÚ.*ru-bu-ʾu* LÚ.*ḫa-ṭal-lum* LÚ.*lab-du-du* LÚ.*ḫa-am-ra-nu*

19) LÚ.*ú-bu-lum* LÚ.*ru-ʾu-u*$_{8}$*-a* LÚ.*li-iʾ-ta-a-a ša a-aḫ* ÍD.*su-rap-pi* ÍD.*uq-né-e* LÚ.*gam-bu-lu* LÚ.*ḫi-in-da-ru* LÚ.*pu-qu-du* LÚ.*su-te-e ṣa-ab* ⌜EDIN⌝

20) *ša* KUR.*ia-ad-bu-ri ma-la ba-šu-ú a-di* URU.*sa-am-ʾu-ú-na* URU.KÁ-BÀD URU.BÀD-^{d}*te-li-ti* URU.*ḫi-li-im-mu* URU.*pil-la-tum* URU.*dun-ni*-^{d}UTU URU.*bu-bé-e* URU.DU$_{6}$-^{d}*ḫum-ba*

21) *ša mi-ṣir* KUR.ELAM.MA.KI KUR.*kár-dun-ía-áš e-liš u šap-liš* KUR.É-^{m}*a-muk-ka-ni* KUR.É-^{m}*dak-ku-ri* KUR.É-^{m}*šil-a-ni* KUR.É-^{m}*sa-ʾa-al-la si-ḫir-ti* KUR.*kal-di ma-la ba-šu-ú*

22) KUR.É-^{m}*ia-kin*$_{7}$ *šá ki-šad* ÍD.*mar-ra-ti a-di pa-aṭ* NI.TUK.KI *mit-ḫa-riš a-bel-ma* LÚ.*šu-ut* SAG.MEŠ-*ia* LÚ.EN *pa-ḫa-a-ti* UGU-*šú-nu áš-tak-kan-ma ni-ir be-lu-ti-ia*

16–23a) With the power and might (granted me) by the great gods, my lords, who mobilized my weapons, I cut down all my foes. I ruled all together from the land Yadnana (Cyprus), which is in the middle of the Western Sea, as far as the border(s) of Egypt and the land Musku, the wide land Amurru, the land Ḫatti (Syria) in its entirety, all of (the land) Gutium, the distant Medes (who live) on the border of Mount Bikni, as far as the land Ellipi (and) the land Rāši on the border of the land Elam, those who (live) beside the Tigris River — the Ituʾu, Rubuʾu, Ḫaṭallu, Labdudu, Ḫamrānu, Ubulu, Ruʾuʾa, (and) Liʾtaʾu (tribes) — those who (live) beside the Surappu River (and) the Uqnû River — the Gambulu, Ḫindaru, (and) Puqudu (tribes) — the Sutians, the people of the steppe of (20) the land Yadburu, as many as there are, as far as the cities Samʾūna, Bāb-dūri, Dūr-Telīte, Ḫilimmu, Pillatu, Dunni-Šamaš, Bubê, (and) Tīl-Ḫumba, which are on the border of the land Elam, the land Karduniaš (Babylonia) from one end to the other (lit.: "above and below"), the lands Bīt-Amukāni, Bīt-Dakkūri, Bīt-Šilāni, (and) Bīt-Saʾalli, all of Chaldea, as much as there is (of it), (and) the land Bīt-Yakīn, which is on the shore of the sea, as far as the border of Dilmun. I then set eunuchs of mine as provincial governors over them and I imposed the yoke of my lordship upon them.

23) *e-mid-su-nu-ti ul-tu* SAG LUGAL-*ti-ia a-di* 15

23b–25a) From the beginning of my reign until my

15 Possibly *miṭ-ra-a-ti* (*miṭirtu*, a type of canal or ditch) rather than *be-ra-a-ti* (*berâtu*, *swamp*). See also text no. 43 line 11.
17 Ex. 5 omits KUR before *ḫat-ti*.
21 Exs. 4 and 5 have LÚ.KUR and ⌜LÚ⌝.[KUR] before *kal-di* respectively.
23–25a Line 23a: Ex. 4 has LÚ before ELAM.MA.KI. Sargon's defeat of the Elamite Ḫumbanigaš (Ḫumban-nikaš I) took place in Sargon's second regnal year (720), although text no. 1 lines 18b–20a assigns it to his first regnal year; see the introduction to the volume. *re-bit "outskirts"*: The basic meaning of *rebītu/ribītu* is "street, main street, thoroughfare" (CAD R p. 317) and "square, piazza, open space" (CDA p. 300), but this meaning does not fit this passage (also found in text nos. 43 line 17, 73 line 7, 105 i′ 14′, and 129 line 18) or in passages dealing with Sargon's building of Dūr-Šarrukīn in the *re-bit* of Nineveh (text nos. 41 line 16, 43 line 44, 44 line 27, 45 line 9, and 47 line 8). The CAD gives "mng. uncert." for these passages (CAD R p. 320) and the CDA a secondary meaning "district, precincts" (CDA p. 300). Some prefer to read *tal-bit*, rather than

BALA-*ia šá* ^{md}*ḫum-ba-ni-ga-áš* ELAM.MA.KI-*i ina re-bit* BÀD.AN.KI *áš-ku-na taḫ-ta-šú* URU.*sa-me-ri-na al-me ak-šud*
24) 27 LIM 2 ME 90 UN.MEŠ *a-šib* ŠÀ-*šú áš-lu-la* 50 GIŠ.GIGIR.MEŠ *ina* ŠÀ-*šú-nu ak-ṣur-ma ù si-it-tu-ti i-nu-šú-nu ú-šá-ḫi-iz* LÚ.*šu-ut* SAG-*ia* UGU-*šú-nu áš-kun-ma* GUN LUGAL *maḫ-re-e*

fifteenth regnal year: I brought about the defeat of Ḫumbanigaš (Ḫumban-nikaš I), the Elamite, on the *outskirts* of (the city) Dēr. I surrounded (and) conquered the city Samaria. I carried off as booty 27,290 of its inhabitants, conscripted fifty chariots from among them, and *allowed* the remainder *to practice* their (normal) *occupations*. I set a eunuch of mine over them and imposed upon them (the same) tribute (as) the former king (had paid).

25) *e-mid-su-nu-ti* ^{m}*ḫa-nu-nu* MAN URU.*ḫa-zi-ti it-ti* ^{m}SIPA-*ʾe-e* LÚ.*tar-tan-nu* KUR.*mu-ṣu-ri ina* URU.*ra-pi-ḫi a-na e-peš* MURUB$_{4}$ *u* MÈ *a-na* GABA-*ia it-bu-ni*
26) BAD$_{5}$.BAD$_{5}$-*šú-nu am-ḫa-aṣ* ^{m}SIPA-*ʾe-e ri-gim* GIŠ.TUKUL.MEŠ-*ia e-dúr-ma in-na-bit-ma la in-na-mir a-šar-šú* ^{m}*ḫa-nu-nu* LUGAL URU.*ḫa-zi-ti ina qa-ti aṣ-bat*

25b–26) Ḫanūnu (Hanno), king of the city Gaza, with Rēʾe, the field marshal of Egypt, rose up to do war and battle against me at the city Rapḫia. I brought about their defeat. Rēʾe took fright at the clangor of my weapons and fled; his whereabouts have never been discovered. I captured Hanūnu, king of the city Gaza.

27) *ma-da-at-tu ša* ^{m}*pi-ir-ʾu-ú* MAN KUR.*mu-ṣu-ri* ^{f}*sa-am-si šar-rat* KUR.*a-ri-bi* ^{m}*it-ʾa-am-a-ra* KUR.*sa-ba-ʾa-a-a* KÙ.GI SAḪAR.BI KUR.RA ANŠE.KUR.RA.MEŠ ANŠE.GAM.MAL *am-ḫur*

27) I received tribute from Pirʾû (Pharaoh), king of Egypt, Samsi, queen of the Arabs, (and) Itʾamar, the Sabaean, (namely) gold ore from the mountain(s), horses, (and) camels.

28) ^{m}*ki-ak-ki* URU.*ši-nu-uḫ-ta-a-a ša ni-ir* ^{d}*aš-šur iṣ-lu-ú-ma ik-lu-ú ta-mar-tuš šá-a-šú ga-du* 30 GIŠ.GIGIR.MEŠ-*šú* 7 LIM 3 ME 50 LÚ.*mun-daḫ-ṣe-šú a-na šal-la-ti am-nu-šu*

28–29a) (As for) Kiakki of the city Šinuḫtu, who had thrown off the yoke of the god Aššur and withheld his audience gift, I counted him as booty, together with thirty of his chariots (and) 7,350 of his fighting men. I gave his royal city Šinuḫtu to Kurtî of the land (A)tuna and imposed upon him (Kurtî) (the payment of a tribute in) horses (and) mules that was higher than his previous tribute.

29) URU.*ši-nu-uḫ-tu* URU MAN-*ti-šú a-na* ^{m}*kur-ti-i* KUR.*tu-un-na-a-a ad-din-ma* ANŠE.KUR.RA.MEŠ ANŠE.*pa-re-e* UGU *man-da-at-ti-šú maḫ-ri-ti uṣ-ṣib-ma* UGU-*šú áš-kun* ^{m}*am-ri-is*
30) KUR.*ta-bal-a-a ša ina* GIŠ.GU.ZA ^{m}*ḫul-li-i* AD-*šú ú-še-ši-bu-šú bi-in-ti it-ti* KUR.*ḫi-lak-ki la mi-ṣir* AD.MEŠ-*šú ad-din-šú-ma ú-rap-piš* KUR-*su ù šu-ú la na-ṣir kit-ti*
31) *a-na* ^{m}*ur-sa-a* KUR.URI-*a-a ù* ^{m}*mi-ta-a* MAN KUR.*mu-us-ki šá e-ke-me mi-iṣ-ri-ia iš-pu-ra* LÚ.A *šip-ri* ^{m}*am-ri-is it-ti kim-ti ni-šu-ti* NUMUN É AD-*šú a-šá-red-du-ti* KUR-*šú*
32) *it-ti* 1 ME GIŠ.GIGIR.MEŠ-*šú a-na* KUR *aš-šur*.KI *al-qa-áš-šú* LÚ.*aš-šur*.KI-*ú pa-liḫ be-lu-ti-ia ina* ŠÀ *ú-še-šib* LÚ.*šu-ut* SAG-*ia* LÚ.EN.NAM

29b–32) I gave to Amris (Ambaris) of the land Tabal, whom I had seated upon the throne of his father Ḫullî, a daughter of mine, (along) with the land Ḫilakku, which had not been part of his ancestors' territory, and I (thus) expanded his land. However, that (man), who did not protect justice, sent a messenger to Ursâ (Rusâ), the Urarṭian, and Mitâ, king of the land Musku, about taking away territory of mine. I took Amris (Ambaris) to Assyria, (along) with (his) family, (his) relatives, the (other) offspring of his father's house, (and) the nobles of his land, (along) with one hundred of his chariots. I settled there Assyrians who respect my authority. I set a eunuch of mine as provincial governor over them and I imposed tribute and payment(s) upon them.

---

re-bit, and to derive the noun from the verb *lamû/lawû*, "to move in a circle, surround" (e.g., Postgate, Royal Grants pp. 117–118). Lines 23b–25a: Text no. 1 lines 12b–17a assigns Sargon's conquest of Samaria to his accession year (722).

24 27,290: So ex. 1 — 27 LIM 2 ME ⌜90*⌝(copy: MEŠ; original: ⌜90⌝). Ex. 4 has 27,280 — 27 LIM 2 ME 80 — and ex. 5 appears to have 24,280 — 24 [*x*] ⌜2⌝ ME 90. The translation of the word *inūšunu*, "their (normal) *occupations*" is uncertain; see Dalley, Iraq 47 (1985) p. 35 "their own skills." M. Cogan (Raging Torrent pp. 82 and 84) translates the passage *si-it-tu-ti i-nu-šú-nu ú-šá-ḫi-iz* as "I instructed the rest of them in correct procedure" and S.Z. Aster (JAOS 139 [2019] p. 602) as "I trained the remnant in their crafts." The current tentative translation of the verb in the passage is based on CAD A/1 p. 182.

25b–26 This took place in Sargon's second regnal year (720); see text no. 1 lines 53–57.

27 According to text no. 1 lines 123b–125a, this occurred in the seventh regnal year (715). Exs. 3 and 5 have LÚ instead of KUR before *a-ri-bi*. Ex. 3 has LÚ instead of KUR before *sa-ba-ʾa-a-a*. Ex. 5 has ANŠE.A.AB.BA.MEŠ instead of ANŠE.GAM.MAL.

28–29a See the account of Sargon's fourth regnal year (718) in text no. 1 lines 68b–71 and text no. 117 ii 17–19.

29b–32 Ambaris was defeated during Sargon's ninth regnal year (713) in text no. 1 (lines 194b–204a) and text no. 2 (lines 226b–235).

31 Ex. 3 adds *u*, "and," after *kim-ti*, "(his) family."

UGU-*šú-nu áš-kun-ma* GUN *ma-da-at-tu ú-kin e-li-šú-un*

33) ^{md}*ia-ú-bi-i'-di* KUR.*a-ma-ta-a-a ṣa-ab ḫup*†*-ši la* EN GIŠ.GU.ZA LÚ.*ḫat-tu-ú lem-nu a-na* LUGAL-*ut* KUR.*a-ma-at-ti* ŠÀ-*šú ik-pu-ud-ma* URU.*ar-pad-da* URU.*ṣi-mir-ra* URU.*di-maš-qa* URU.*sa-me-ri-na*

34) *it-ti-ia uš-bal-kit-ma pa-a e-da ú-šá-áš-kin-ma ik-ṣu-ra* MÈ *um-ma-na-at* ^{d}*a-šur gap-šá-a-ti ad-ke-ma ina* URU.*qar-qa-ri* URU *na-ram-i-šú šá-a-šú a-di* LÚ.*mun-daḫ-ṣe-šú*

35) *al-me ak-šud-su* URU.*qar-qa-ru ina* ^{d}GIŠ.BAR *aq-mu šá-a-šú ma-šak-šú a-ku-uṣ ina qé-reb* URU.MEŠ *šú-nu-ti* EN *ḫi-iṭ-ṭi a-duk-ma su-lum-mu-u ú-šá-áš-kin* 2 ME GIŠ.GIGIR 6 ME ANŠE.*pét-ḫal-lum*

33–36a) Iaū-bi'dī (Ilu-bi'dī) of the land Hamath, a member of the lower class who had no right to the throne, an evil Hittite, plotted to become king of the land Hamath. He then incited the cities Arpad, Ṣimirra, Damascus, (and) Samaria to rebel against me, made (them) act in unison, and prepared for battle. I mustered the numerous troops of the god Aššur; I surrounded him, together with his fighting men, in Qarqar, the city where he resided (lit.: "the city of his dwelling"), (and) I captured him. I burned the city Qarqar down with fire (and) I flayed the skin from him. I killed the guilty people inside those cities and imposed peace. I conscripted 200 chariots (and) 600 cavalry from among the people of the land Hamath and added them to my royal (military) contingent.

36) *i-na* ŠÀ UN.MEŠ KUR.*a-ma-at-ti ak-ṣur-ma* UGU *ki-ṣir* LUGAL-*ti-ia ú-rad-di ina* u_4*-me* ^{m}*ir-an-zu* KUR.*man-na-a-a* ARAD *kan-šu šá-di-id ni-ri-ia šim-tu ú-bi-lu-šu-ma*

37) ^{m}*a-za-a* DUMU-*šú ina* GIŠ.GU.ZA-*šú ú-še-ši-bu* ^{m}*ur-sa-a* KUR.*ur-ar-ṭa-a-a a-na* LÚ.KUR.*ú-iš-di-iš-a-a* LÚ.KUR.*zi-kir-ta-a-a* LÚ.KUR.*mi-si-an-di-a-a* LÚ.GAR.KUR.MEŠ

38) KUR.*man-na-a-a* GAL.MEŠ *a-mat su-ul-le-e u* sar_6*-ra-a-ti id-bu-ub-šú-nu-ti-ma ina* KUR.*ú-a-uš* KUR-*i mar-ṣi* ADDA ^{m}*a-za-a* DUMU EN-*šu-nu id-du-ú* ^{m}*ul-lu-su-nu*

39) KUR.*man-na-a-a ša i-na* GIŠ.GU.ZA AD-*šú ú-še-ši-bu a-na* ^{m}*ur-sa-a* KUR.*ur-ar-ṭa-a-a it-ta-kil-ma* 22 URU.ḪAL.ṢU.MEŠ-*šú ki-i ṭa-a'-tu-ú-ti id-din-šú*

36b–39) When fate carried off Iranzi, the Mannean, a submissive subject who pulled my yoke, and (after) I had seated his son Azâ on his throne, Ursâ (Rusâ), the Urarṭian, spoke treacherous and mendacious words to (the rulers of) the lands of Uišdiš, Zikirtu, Missi, (and) Andia, (and to) the governors of the land Mannea, the important men, and (as a result) they threw down the corpse of Azâ, the son of their lord, on Mount Uauš, a rugged mountain. Ullusunu, the Mannean, whom they had seated on the throne of his father (Azâ), put his trust in Ursâ (Rusâ), the Urarṭian, and gave him twenty-two of his fortresses as a gift.

40) *i-na ug-gat* ŠÀ-*ia um-ma-na-at* ^{d}*aš-šur gap-šá-a-ti ad-ke-ma lab-biš an-na-dir-ma a-na ka-šad* KUR.MEŠ *šá-ti-na áš-ta-kan pa-ni-ia* ^{m}*ul-lu-su-nu* KUR.*man-na-a-a*

41) *a-ka-mu ger-ri-ia e-mur-ma* URU-*uš-šú uṣ-ṣi-ma ina pu-uz-rat* KUR-*i mar-ṣi a-di-riš ú-šib* URU.*i-zir-tu* URU LUGAL-*ti-šú* URU.*i-zi-bi-a* URU.*ar-me-et*

42) URU.ḪAL.ṢU.MEŠ-*šú dan-na-a-ti ak-šud-ma ina* ^{d}GIŠ.BAR *aq-mu di-ik-tu šá* ^{m}*ur-sa-a*

40–42a) Angrily, I mustered the numerous troops of the god Aššur, became enraged like a lion, and set out to conquer those lands. Having seen the cloud of dust (kicked up) by my expeditionary force, Ullusunu, the Mannean, went out from his city and in fear stayed in hiding on a rugged mountain. I conquered his royal city Izirtu (and) the cities of Izibia and Armaet, his strong fortresses, and I burned (them) down with fire.

42b–44a) I inflicted a defeat upon Ursâ (Rusâ), the Urarṭian, at Mount Uauš, a rugged mountain, and

33–36a The campaign against Iaū-bi'dī took place during Sargon's second regnal year (720); see text no. 1 lines 23b–26, text no 81 lines 4b–20, and text no. 117 lines ii 4–13a. Also, ex. 3 has LUGAL-<*ut* KUR>.

34 URU *na-ram-i-šú* "the city where he resided (lit.: "the city of his dwelling)": This assumes that *na-ram-i-šú* comes from the noun *narmû* as opposed to the noun *narāmu*, which would result in the translation "his beloved city" (see CAD N/1 p. 345).

35 *su-lum-mu-u ú-šá-áš-kin* "I imposed peace": Or "I imposed a peace treaty" following CAD S p. 372, but see Fuchs, Khorsabad p. 345 n. 438.

36b–53 Sargon's campaigns involved Ullusunu and Mannea in his sixth through eighth regnal years (716–714), with prominence given to the sixth campaign; see for example text no. 1 lines 78b–96a, 101–109a, and 127–137, text no. 2 lines 70b–76, 86–102, and 188–195a, text no. 4 lines 20´b–45´, and text no. 117 ii 22b–70a. Only those events mentioned in these lines that are clearly not dated to the sixth regnal year (716) are normally indicated in the on-page notes. Line 48 also refers to events in the third regnal year (719), see below.

37 LÚ.KUR.*mi-si-an-di-a-a* is assumed to be an error, running together the names of the two countries Misi and Andia; see Gadd, Iraq 16 (1954) p. 177.

42b–43 Assyrian forces won victories on Mount Uauš during two different campaigns. They battled the troops of Azâ (Ullusunu's father and predecessor as king of Mannea) and his Urarṭian allies in Sargon's sixth regnal year (716) and those of the Urarṭian ruler Rusâ in his eighth regnal year (714); see for example text no. 1 lines 78b–83a and 133b–136a, text no. 2 lines 70b–74, and text no. 65 lines 96–145. This passage seems to refer to the latter battle.

KUR.*ur-ar-ṭa-a-a i-na* KUR.*ú-a-uš* KUR-*i mar-ṣi a-duk-ma* 2 ME 50 NUMUN MAN-*ti-šú*
43) *i-na qa-ti ú-ṣab-bit* 55 URU.MEŠ KAL.MEŠ É BÀD.MEŠ *ša* 8 *na-ge-e-šú a-di* 11 URU.ḪAL.ṢU.MEŠ-*šú mar-ṣa-a-ti ak-šud-ma i-na* ^{d}GIŠ.BAR *aq-mu*

captured two hundred and fifty members of his royal family. I conquered fifty-five fortified cities (and) fortresses in eight of his districts, together with eleven fortresses that were difficult (to conquer), and I burned (them) down with fire. I took away from him (Rusâ) the twenty-two fortresses of Ullusunu, the Mannean, and made (them part of) the territory of Assyria.

44) 22 URU.ḪAL.ṢU.MEŠ *šá* ^{m}*ul-lu-su-nu* KUR.*man-na-a-a e-ki-ma-áš-šum-ma a-na mi-ṣir* KUR *aš-šur*.KI *ú-ter-ra* 8 URU.ḪAL.ṢU.MEŠ *ša* KUR.*tu-a-ia-di na-ge-e*
45) *ša* ^{m}*te-lu-si-na* KUR.*an-di-a-a ak-šud* 4 LIM 2 ME UN.MEŠ *a-di mar-ši-ti-šú-nu áš-lu-la* ^{m}*mi-ta-at-ti* KUR.*zi-kir-ta-a-a*
46) GIŠ.TUKUL.MEŠ-*ia e-dúr-ma šu-ú a-di* UN.MEŠ KUR-*šú a-na qé-reb ḫur-šá-a-ni in-na-bit-ma la in-na-mir a-šar-šu*
47) URU.*pa-ar-da* URU LUGAL-*ti-šú ina* ^{d}GIŠ.BAR *aq-mu* 23 URU.MEŠ KAL.MEŠ *ša li-me-ti-šú ak-šud-ma áš-lu-la šal-la-su-un*
48) URU.*šu-an-da-ḫu-ul* URU.*zu-ur-zu-uk-ka* URU.MEŠ *ša* KUR.*man-na-a-a ša* UGU ^{m}*mi-ta-at-ti it-tak-lu ak-šud-ma šal-lat-su-nu áš-lu-la*
49) *ša* ^{m}*ba-ag-da-at-ti* KUR.*ú-iš-di-iš-a-a ma-šak-šú a-ku-uṣ* ^{m}*da-a-a-uk-ku a-di kim-ti-šú as-su-ḫa-am-ma qé-reb* KUR.*a-ma-at-ti ú-še-šib*

44b–49) I conquered eight fortresses of the land Tuāyadi, a district belonging to Telusina of the land Andia; I carried off as booty 4,200 people, together with their property. Mitatti of the land Zikirtu took fright at my weapons and he, together wih the people of his land, fled into the mountains; his whereabouts have never been discovered. I burned his royal city Parda down with fire. I conquered twenty-three fortified settlements in its environs and carried off booty from them. I conquered the Mannean cities Šuandaḫul (and) Zurzukka that had put their trust in Mitatti and I took booty from them. I flayed the skin from Bag-dāti of the land Uišdiš. I deported Dayukku together with his family and settled (them) in the land Hamath.

50) ^{m}*ul-lu-su-nu* KUR.*man-na-a-a ep-še-et e-tep-pu-šu qé-reb* KUR-*i mar-ṣi iš-me-ma iṣ-ṣu-riš ip-par-šam-ma iṣ-bat* GÌR.II-*ia*
51) *ḫi-ṭa-ti-šu la mi-na a-bu-uk-ma a-mi-iš gíl-lat-su re-e-ma ar-ši-šu-ma i-na* GIŠ.GU.ZA LUGAL-*ti-šú ú-še-šib-šú*
52) 22 URU.ḪAL.ṢU.MEŠ *a-di* 2 URU.MEŠ-*šú dan-nu-ti ša ul-tu* ŠU.II ^{m}*ur-sa-a ù* ^{m}*mi-ta-at-ti e-ki-ma ad-din-šú-ma ú-taq-qi-na da-li-iḫ-tu* KUR-*su*
53) *ṣa-lam* LUGAL-*ti-ia* DÙ-*uš-ma li-i-ti* ^{d}*aš-šur be-lí-ia* UGU-*šu áš-ṭur i-na* URU.*i-zir-ti* URU LUGAL-*ti-šú ul-ziz aḫ-ra-taš*

50–53) In (his) rugged mountain (region), Ullusunu, the Mannean, heard of the deeds I had been doing, flew to me like a bird, and grasped hold of my feet. I pardoned (lit.: "overturned") his innumerable sins and disregarded his crime. I had pity on him and had him sit on his royal throne. I gave (back) to him the twenty-two fortresses, together with two of his fortified cities, which I had taken away from the hands of Ursâ (Rusâ) and Mitatti, and I brought order to his disturbed land. I made a royal image of myself and inscribed upon it the victorious deed(s) of the god Aššur, my lord. I erected it for all time in his royal city Izirtu.

54) *ša* ^{m}*ia-an-zu-ú* MAN KUR.*na-ʾi-i-ri ina*

54) I received tribute from Ianzû, king of the land

---

43 Ex. 3 has [*x*]+6 for 55.

44–45a Line 44a: Sargon claims to have annexed these twenty-two cities during his seventh regnal year (715) in the Khorsabad Annals (text no. 1 line 103 and text no. 2 lines 97b–98a). Lines 44b–45a: The conquest and looting of the land Tuāyadi is mentioned in Sargon's account of his seventh regnal year (715); see text no. 1 lines 106b–107a and text no. 2 line 101.

45b–47 The flight of Mitatti, king of Zikirtu, from Assyrian troops and the burning down of the city Parda took place during Sargon's eighth regnal year (714); see for example text no. 1 lines 132b–133a and text no. 65 lines 84–90 and 141–142.

48 The capture of the cities Šuandaḫul and Zurzukka took place in Sargon's third regnal year (719); see text no. 1 lines 58–65 (with Zurzukka called Durdukka), text no. 4 lines 1′–2′, and text no. 117 ii 13b–16 (with Zurzukka called Durdukka).

49b The deportation of Daiukku and his family took place during Sargon's seventh regnal year (715); see text no. 1 lines 101–104a and text no. 2 lines 95b–98. *ú-še-šib* comes from ex. 5. P.E. Botta's and H. Winckler's copies of ex. 1 appear to have *ú-šar*?*-me*, with the ŠAR consisting of 6 Winkelhaken (3 on top of 3) followed by two horizontal wedges, one on top of the other; the squeeze appears to support these copies. Ex. 3 has *ú-še-*[x], but the ŠE could conceivably be the beginning of ŠAR.

52 These twenty-two cities were mentioned in lines 39 and 44; see also the account of Sargon's seventh campaign (715) in text no. 1 lines 101–103a and text no. 2 lines 95b–98a.

53 The royal image was erected in Izirtu during Sargon's seventh regnal year (715); see text no. 1 lines 108b–109a.

54 The receipt of tribute from Ianzû is recorded in Sargon's seventh and eighth regnal years (715 and 714); see text no. 1 lines 104b and 146–148 and text no. 2 line 99.

URU.*ḫu-bu-uš-ki-a* URU *dan-nu-ti-šú* ANŠE.KUR.RA.MEŠ GU$_4$.MEŠ *ù ṣe-e-ni man-da-at-ta-šú am-ḫur*

Na'iri, in his fortified city Ḫubuškia, (namely) horses, oxen, and sheep and goats.

55) ^{md}*aš-šur-le-'i* KUR.*kar-al-la-a-a* ^{m}*it-ti-i* KUR.*al-la-ab-ra-a-a ša ni-ir* ^{d}*aš-šur iṣ-lu-ú il-qu-ú še-ṭu-ti*
56) *ma-šak* ^{md}*aš-šur*-ZU *a-ku-uṣ-ma* UN.MEŠ KUR.*kar-al-la mal ba-šu-ú ù* ^{m}*it-ti-i a-di qin-ni-šú as-su-ḫa-am-ma ina qé-reb* KUR.*a-ma-at-ti ú-še-šib*

55–56) (As for) Aššur-lē'i of the land Karalla, (and) Ittī of the land Allabria who had thrown off the yoke of the god Aššur (and) held me in contempt, I flayed the skin from Aššur-lē'i, deported the people of the land Karalla, as many as there were, and Ittî together with his family, and settled (them) in the land Hamath.

57) UN.MEŠ URU.*su-uk-ki-a* URU.*ba-a-la* URU.*a-bi-ti-ik-na* URU.*pa-ap-pa* URU.*lal-lu-uk-nu ul-tu áš-ri-šú-nu as-suḫ-šú-nu-ti-ma ina* URU.*di-maš-qi u* KUR.*ḫat-ti ú-še-šib-šú-nu-ti*

57) I deported the people of the cities Sukkia, Bāla, Abitikna, Pappa, (and) Lalluknu from their (own) places and (re)settled them in the city Damascus and the land Ḫatti (Syria).

58) 6 URU.MEŠ *šá* KUR.*ni-ik-sa-am-ma na-gi-i ak-šu-ud* ^{m}GÌR.II-LUGAL LÚ.EN.URU *ša* URU.*šur-ga-di-a ina qa-ti aṣ-bat* URU.MEŠ *šú-a-tú-nu* UGU *pi-ḫa-at* KUR.*par-su-áš ú-rad-di*

58) I conquered six cities of the land Niksamma (and) captured Šēp-šarri, the city ruler of Šurgadia. I added those cities to the province of the land Parsuaš.

59) ^{m}EN-LUGAL-*ú-ṣur ša* URU.*ki-še-si-im šá-a-šú a-di* NÍG.ŠU NÍG.GA *ni-ṣir-ti* É.GAL-*šú a-na* KUR *aš-šur*.KI *ú-raš-šú* LÚ.*šu-ut* SAG-*ia* LÚ.EN.NAM UGU URU-*šú áš-kun*
60) URU.*kar*-^{d}MAŠ.MAŠ MU-*šú ab-bi ṣa-lam* LUGAL-*ti-ia* [*e*]-⌜*pu*⌝-*uš-ma ina qer-bi-šú ul-ziz* 6 URU.MEŠ *pa-ṭi-šú ak-šud-ma* UGU *pi-ḫa-ti-šu ú-rad-di*

59–60) (As for) Bēl-šarru-uṣur of the city Kišesim, I brought him, together with (his) property (and) possessions, the treasure of his palace, to Assyria. I set a eunuch of mine as provincial governor over his city (and) (re)named it Kār-Nergal. [I m]ade a royal image of myself and erected it inside (that city). I conquered six settlements in its neighborhood and added (them) to its province.

61) ^{m}*ki-ba-ba* LÚ.EN.URU *ša* URU.*ḫar-ḫa-ar al-me ak-šud*^{ud} *šá-a-šú a-di* UN.MEŠ KUR-*šú a-na šal-la-ti am-nu-šu*
62) URU *šu-a-tu a-na eš-šu-ti aṣ-bat* UN.MEŠ KUR.MEŠ *ki-šit-ti* ŠU.II-*ia ina* ŠÀ *ú-še-šib* LÚ.*šu-ut* SAG-*ia* LÚ.EN.NAM UGU-*šú-nu áš-kun*
63) URU.*kar*-^{m}MAN-GI.NA MU-*šú az-kur* GIŠ.TUKUL ^{d}*aš-šur* EN-*ia i-na* ŠÀ *ú-še-šib ṣa-lam* LUGAL-*ti-ia ina qer-bi-šú ul-ziz* 6 *na-gi-i pa-ṭi-šu*
64) *ak-šu-ud-ma* UGU *pi-ḫa-ti-šú ú-rad-di*

61–64a) I surrounded Kibaba, the city ruler of Ḫarḫar, (and) conquered (that city). I counted him as booty together with the people of his land. I reorganized (the administration of) that city. I settled there people from the lands that I had conquered (and) set a eunuch of mine as provincial governor over them. I (re)named (that city) Kār-Šarrukīn, set up the weapon of the god Aššur, my lord, there, (and) erected a royal image of myself inside (that city). I conquered six districts neighboring it and added (them) to his (or: its) province.

URU.*ki-šeš-lu* URU.*qí-in-da-a-ú* URU.É-^{m}*ba-ga-ia* URU.*an-za-ri-a al-me ak-šu-ud*

64b–65a) I surrounded (and) conquered the cities of Kišešlu, Qindāu, Bīt-Bagāya, (and) Anzaria. I restored (them) and reorganized (their administration). I (re)named them the cities of Kār-Nabû, Kār-Sîn, Kār-Adad, (and) Kār-Ištar (respectively).

65) *ú-ter-ma a-na eš-šu-ti aṣ-bat* URU.*kar*-^{d}AG URU.*kar*-^{d}30 URU.*kar*-^{d}IŠKUR URU.*kar*-^{d}*iš-tar* MU-*šú-nu ab-bi a-na šuk-nu-uš* KUR.*ma-da-a-a*

65b–67a) In order to subjugate the land Media in the environs of the city Kār-Šarrukīn, I strengthened (its) garrison. I conquered thirty-four districts of the land

55–56 Aššur-lē'i and Ittî were captured and punished during Sargon's sixth regnal year (716); see text no. 1 lines 83b–90, text no. 4 lines 28′–ca. 35′ and text no. 117 lines 23–32a.

57 It was during Sargon's third regnal year (719) that the people of these cities were deported; see text no. 1 lines 66–68a and text no. 4 lines 3′–6′a.

58–64a These lines refer to events dated to Sargon's sixth regnal year (716). For the capture of Šēp-šarri and the cities of Niksamma (line 58), see text no. 1 lines 92–93a and text no. 4 lines 37–39′a; for the capture of Kišesim (lines 59–60), see text no.1 l lines 93b–95, text no. 2 lines 86–87a, text no. 4 lines 39′b–42′a, and text no. 117 ii 35b–41a; and for the episode involving Kibaba and Ḫarḫar (lines 61–64a), cf. text no. 1 lines 96b–100 and text no. 117 ii 41b–46a.

64b–67a According to the Khorsabad Annals, these episodes took place in the seventh regnal year (715); see text no. 1 lines 113b–117a.

65 *ú-ter-ma a-na eš-šu-ti aṣ-bat* "I restored (them) and reorganized (their administration)": Possibly translate instead "I again reorganized (their administration)"; see also the note to text no. 64 line 6′.

66) *li-me-et* URU.*kar*-^{m}LUGAL-GI.NA *ú-dan-ni-na ma-ṣar-tu* 34 *na-ge-e ša* KUR.*ma-da-a-a ak-šu-ud-ma*
67) *a-na mi-ṣir* KUR *aš-šur*.KI *ú-ter-ra na-dan* ANŠE.KUR.RA.MEŠ *šat-ti-šam* UGU-*šú-nu uk-tin* URU.*e-ri-iš-ta-na*
68) *a-di* URU.MEŠ-*ni ša li-me-ti-šú ša* KUR.*ba-ʾi-it-i-li na-gi-i al-me* KUR-*ud áš-lu-la šal-la-su-un*
69) KUR.*a-ga-zi* KUR.*am-ba-an-da* KUR.*ma-da-a-a ša pa-ti* LÚ.*a-ri-bi ni-pi-iḫ* ^{d}UTU-*ši ša man-da-at-ta-šú-nu ik-lu-ú*
70) *ap-pul aq-qur i-na* IZI *áš-ru-up* ^{m}*dal-ta-a* KUR.*el-li-pa-a-a* ARAD *kan-šu šá-di-id ni-ir* ^{d}*aš-šur* 5 *na-gi-i šá pa-ṭi-šu*
71) *ib-bal-ki-tu-šu-ma la im-gu-ru be-lut-su a-na ni-ra-ru-ti-šú al-lik na-gi-i šu-a-tu-nu al-me ak-šud*^{ud} UN.MEŠ *a-di mar-ši-ti-šú-nu*
72) *it-ti* ANŠE.KUR.RA.MEŠ *la mi-nam šal-la-tu ka-bit-tu a-na qé-reb* KUR *aš-šur*.KI *áš-lu-la* ^{m}*ur-za-na* URU.*mu-ṣa-ṣir-a-a ša a-na* ^{m}*ur-sa-a*
73) KUR.*ur-ar-ṭa-a-a it-tak-lu-ma i-mi-šu ar-du-tu i-na gi-piš um-ma-ni-ia* URU.*mu-ṣa-ṣi-ru a-ri-biš ak-tùm*†-*ma*
74) *ù šu-ú a-na šu-zu-ub* ZI-*šú e-den-nu-uš-šú ip-par-šid-ma* KUR-*šu e-li a-na* URU.*mu-ṣa-ṣi-ri šit-lu-ṭiš e-ru-um-ma*
75) DAM-*su* DUMU.MEŠ-*šú* DUMU.MUNUS.MEŠ-*šú* NÍG.ŠU NÍG.GA *ni-ṣir-ti* É.GAL-*šú ma-la ba-šu-ú it-ti* 20 LIM 1 ME 70 UN.MEŠ *a-di mar-ši-ti-šú-nu*
76) ^{d}*ḫal-di-a* ^{d}*ba-ag-bar-tum* DINGIR.MEŠ-*šú a-di* NÍG.GA-*šú-nu ma-ʾa-at-ti šal-la-ti-iš am-nu* ^{m}*ur-sa-a* LUGAL KUR.*ur-ar-ṭi*
77) *ḫe-pe-e* URU.*mu-ṣa-ṣir šá-lal* ^{d}*ḫal-di-a* DINGIR-*šu iš-me-ma i-na* ŠU.II *ra-ma-ni-šú ina* GÍR AN.BAR *šib-bi-šú na-piš-ta-šú ú-qat-ti*
78) UGU KUR.*ur-ar-ṭi a-na paṭ gim-ri-šá ki-ḫul-lu-ú ú-šab-ši* UN.MEŠ *a-ši-ib lìb-bi-šá e-mì-da si-pit-tu ù ṣer-ḫa* ^{m}*tar-ḫu-na-zi*
79) URU.*me-lid-da-a-a tu-qu-un-tu iḫ-šu-uḫ-ma a-de-e* DINGIR.MEŠ GAL.MEŠ *e-bu-uk-ma ik-la-a ta-mar-tuš ina ug-gat* ŠÀ-*ia* URU.*me-lid-du*
80) URU LUGAL-*ti-šú a-di* URU.MEŠ *ša li-*⌜*mi*⌝*-ti-šú*

Media and made (them part of) the territory of Assyria. I imposed upon them the annual payment of horses (as tribute).

67b–70a) I surrounded (and) conquered the city Erištana, together with the settlements in its environs, belonging to the district of Baʾīt-ili. I carried off booty from them. I destroyed, demolished, (and) burnt down with fire the lands Agazi, Ambanda, (and) Media, which border on the Arabs in the east, who had withheld their tribute.

70b–72a) (As for) Daltâ of the land Ellipi, a submissive subject who pulled the yoke of the god Aššur, five districts in his neighborhood revolted against him and no longer obeyed him as (their) lord. I went to his aid and surrounded (and) conquered those districts. I carried off to Assyria as substantial booty the people, together with their property, (along) with innumerable horses.

72b–76a) (As for) Urzana of the city Muṣaṣir, who had put his trust in Ursâ (Rusâ), the Urarṭian, and disregarded (his) position as vassal (to me), I enveloped the city Muṣaṣir with the main force of my army like locusts. However, that (man) fled away by himself to save his life and took to the hill(s). I entered the city Muṣaṣir in triumph and counted as booty his wife, his sons, his daughters, (his) property (and) possessions, the treasure of his palace, as much as there was (of it), (along) with 20,170 people, together with their property, (and) his deities Ḫaldi (and) Bagbartu, along with their numerous possessions.

76b–78a) Ursâ (Rusâ), king of the land Urarṭu, heard of the destruction of the city Muṣaṣir (and) the carrying off of his god Ḫaldi and by his own hands brought an end to his life with the iron dagger from his belt. I caused there to be mourning over the land Urarṭu, to its full extent. I imposed lamentation and dirge (singing) upon the people who lived there.

78b–83a) Tarhun-azi of the city Melid wanted (to offer) battle, broke (lit.: "overturned") the treaty (sworn) by the great gods, and withheld his audience gift. Angrily, I smashed his royal city Melid, together with the settlements in its environs, like pots. I brought him out of his fortified city Tīl-Garimme, together with his wife, his sons, his daughters, the

67b–70a The capture of territory belonging to Baʾīt-ili and the burning of several cities took place during Sargon's ninth regnal year; see text no. 1 lines 184b–191a and text no. 2 lines 218b–224a.
70b–72a The campaign to help Daltâ of Ellipi is dated to Sargon's ninth regnal year (713); see text no. 1 lines 172b–184a and text no. 2 lines 207b–218a.
72b–78a The capture and looting of Muṣaṣir took place during Sargon's eighth regnal year (714); see in particular text no. 1 lines 149–165a, text no. 2 lines 188–195a, text no. 63 iii 1′–12′, text no. 65 lines 309–414, and text no. 82 iv 1′–v 6.
78b–83a The Assyrian campaign against Tarḫun-azi of Melid occurred during Sargon's tenth regnal year (712); see text no. 1 lines 204b–221 and text no. 2 lines 236–259a. According to the Assyrian Eponym Chronicle, Sargon stayed "in the land" that year, so the campaign must have been led by officials of his despite the statements in this text.

kar-pa-niš aḫ-pi šá-a-šú a-di DAM-*šú* DUMU.MEŠ-*šú* DUMU.MUNUS.MEŠ-*šú ni-ṣir-ti* É.GAL-*šú ma-la ba-šu-ú*
81) *it-ti* 5 LIM *šal-lat* LÚ.*qu-ra-di-šú ul-tu qé-reb* URU.DU$_6$-*ga-rim-me* URU *dan-nu-ti-šú ú-še-ṣa-áš-šum-ma šal-la-ti-iš am-nu-šu*
82) URU.DU$_6$-*ga-rim-me a-na eš-šu-ti aṣ-bat* LÚ.*su-te-e ṣa-ab* GIŠ.PAN KUR-*ti* ŠU.II-*ia* KUR.*kam-ma-nu a-na si-ḫir-ti-šú ú-šá-aṣ-bit-ma ú-rap-pi-šá ki-sur-ri*
83) KUR *šu-a-tu ina* ŠU.II LÚ.*šu-ut* SAG-*ia am-nu-ma il-ku tup-šik-ku ki-i ša* ^{m}*kun-zi-na-nu* LUGAL *maḫ-ri ú-kin* UGU-*šú* ^{m}*tar-ḫu-la-ra* KUR.*gúr-gu-ma-a-a*
84) *ša* ^{m}*mut-tal-lum* IBILA-*šú i-na* GIŠ.TUKUL *ú-ra-as-si-bu-šu-ma ba-lum ṭè-me-ia i-na* GIŠ.GU.ZA-*šú ú-ši-bu-ma ú-ma-ʾe-ru* KUR-*su i-na šu-ḫu-uṭ lib-bi-*⸢*ia*⸣
85) *it-ti* GIŠ.GIGIR GÌR.II-*ia u* ANŠE.*pét-ḫal-lì-ia ša a-šar sal-me* ⸢Á⸣.II-*a-a la ip-par-ku-ú*
86) *a-na* URU.*mar-qa-si ḫi-it-mu-ṭiš al-lik* ^{m}*mut-tal-lu* IBILA-*šú a-di kim-ti* KUR.É-^{m}*pa-ʾa-al-la*
87) *mal ba-šu-ú it-ti* KÙ.GI KÙ.BABBAR NÍG.ŠU É.GAL-*šú ša ni-ba la i-šu-ú šal-la-ti-iš am-nu-šú*
88) UN.MEŠ KUR.*gúr-gu-me a-na paṭ gim-ri-šá a-na eš-šu-ti a-šur* LÚ.*šu-ut* SAG-*ia*
89) LÚ.EN.NAM UGU-*šú-nu áš-kun-ma it-ti* UN.MEŠ KUR *aš-šur*.KI *am-nu-šú-nu-ti*

treasure of his palace, as much as there was (of it), (along) with five thousand of his captured warriors, and I considered him as booty. I reorganized (the administration of) the city Tīl-Garimme. I had Sutians — bowmen whom I had captured — occupy the land Kammanu in its entirety and I (thus) expanded my territory. I assigned that land to the authority of a eunuch of mine and imposed upon him (the same state) service (and) corvée duty as (in the time) of Kunzinānu (Gunzinānu), the previous king.

83b–89) (As for) Tarḫu-lara of the land Gurgum, whose heir Mutallu had cut him down with the sword, sat upon his (Tarḫu-lara's) throne without my permission, and governed his land — furiously, I quickly marched to the city Marqasa with (only) my personal chariot and my cavalry who never leave my side (even) in friendly territory. I counted his heir Mutallu as booty, together with the (ruling) family of the land Bīt-Pa'alla, as many as there were, (along) with gold, silver, (and) the countless property of his palace. I reorganized (the administration of) the people of the land Gurgum, to its full extent. I set a eunuch of mine as provincial governor over them and considered them as people of Assyria.

90) ^{m}*a-zu-ri* LUGAL URU.*as-du-di a-na la na-še-e bil-ti*
91) ŠÀ-*šu ik-pu-ud-ma a-na* LUGAL.MEŠ-*ni li-me-ti-šu*
92) *ze-ra-a-ti* ⸢KUR⸣ *aš-šur*.KI *iš-pur áš-šu* ḪUL-*tum e-pu-šu*
93) UGU UN.MEŠ [*ma*]-⸢*ti*⸣-*šu be-lut-su ú-nak-kir*
94) ^{m}*a-ḫi-mi-*⸢*ti*⸣ [ŠEŠ] *ta-lim-šu a-na* LUGAL-*ti* UGU-*šú-nu áš-kun-ma*
95) LÚ.*ḫa-at-te* ⸢*da*⸣-*bi-ib ṣa-lip-ti be-lut-su i-ze-ru-ma* ^{m}*ia-ma-ni la* EN GIŠ.GU.ZA
96) *šá ki-ma šá-a-šú-nu-ma pa-laḫ be-lu-ti la i-du-ú ú-rab-bu-ú* UGU-*šú-un*

90–96) Azūri, king of the city Ashdod, plotted (so as) to no longer (have to) deliver tribute (to me) and sent (messages) hostile to Assyria to the kings in his environs. Because of the evil that he had done, I did away with his lordship over the people of his [lan]d. I set his *favorite* [brother] Aḫī-Mīti as king over them, but (95) the Hittites, who (always) speak treachery, hated his rule and elevated over them Iāmānī, who had no right to the throne (and) who, like them, did not know how to respect (any) authority.

97) *i-na šu-ḫu-uṭ lib-bi-ia gi-piš* ERIM.ḪI.A-*ia*
98) *ul ú-paḫ-ḫir-ma ul ak-ṣu-ra ka-ra-ši*
99) *it-ti* LÚ.*qu-ra-di-ia šá a-*⸢*šar*⸣ [*sa*]-*al-me*
100) Á.II-*a-a la ip-par-ku-ú a-na* URU.*as-du-di*
101) ⸢*al*⸣-*lik-ma ù šu-ú* ^{m}*ia-ma-ni a-lak*† *ger-ri-ia*
102) *ru-qiš iš-me-ma a-na i-te-e* KUR.*mu-ṣu-ri*
103) *ša pa-aṭ* KUR.*me-luḫ-ḫa in-na-*⸢*bit*⸣*-ma la in-na-mir*

97–109a) Furiously, I neither assembled the main force of my army nor organized my (military) camp. I marched to the city Ashdod with (only) my warriors who (100) never leave my side (even) in [fri]endly territory. However, that Iāmānī heard from afar of the approach of my expeditionary force and fled to the (far) edge of Egypt, on the border with the land Meluḫḫa; his whereabouts have never been discovered. (105) I

83–89 Line 83: Ex. 4 inserts *ù*, "and," after *il-ku*, "corvée duty." Lines 83b–89: The campaign against Tarḫu-lara of Gurgum is dated to Sargon's eleventh regnal year (711); see the Khorsabad Annals (text no. 1 lines 248–249a, text no. 2 lines 267b–273a, and text no. 3 lines 1´–6´a).

90–109a The campaign to Ashdod took place in Sargon's eleven regnal year (711); see the Khorsabad Annals (text no. 1 lines 249b–262a, text no. 2 lines 273b–287a, and text no. 3 lines 6´b–13´a).

102–103 With regard to the translation of *a-na i-te-e* KUR.*mu-ṣu-ri ša pa-aṭ* KUR.*me-luḫ-ḫa* (also found in text no. 8 line 12), see Frame, Orientalia NS 68 (1999) p. 52 n. 24. W. Mayer (UF 28 [1996] p. 480) translates it as "in das benachbarte Ägypten, das zu Nubien gehört."

104) *a-šar-šú* URU.*as-du-du* URU.*gi-im-tu* URU.*as-du-di-im-mu*
105) *al-me ak-šud* DINGIR.MEŠ-*šú* DAM-*su* DUMU.MEŠ-*šú* DUMU†.MUNUS.MEŠ-*šú*
106) NÍG.ŠU NÍG.GA *ni-ṣir-ti* É.GAL-*šú it-ti* UN.MEŠ KUR-*šú*
107) *a-na šal-la-ti am-nu* URU.MEŠ *šu-a-⸢tu⸣-nu a-na eš-šu-ti*
108) *aṣ-[bat]* UN.MEŠ KUR.KUR.MEŠ *ki-šit-ti qa-ti-ia*

surrounded (and) conquered the cities Ashdod, Gath (and) Ashdod-Yam. I counted as booty his gods, his wife, his sons, his daughters, (his) property (and) possessions, the treasure of his palace, (along) with the people of his land. I reor[ganized] (the administration of) those cities, [settled] there people from the lands that I had conquered ... [... in the e]ast, [and set a eunuch of mine as [pro]vincial [governor] over [them]. I considered them [a]s people of Assyria and they (now) pull my yoke.

109) *ša qé-reb* x [x x *ni-pi]-iḫ* ^{d}UTU-*ši* ⸢*ina*⸣ *lìb-bi* ⸢*ú*⸣-[*še-šib-ma* LÚ.*šu-ut* SAG-*ia* LÚ.EN].⸢NAM⸣ UGU-[*šú-nu áš-kun it*]-*ti* ⸢UN⸣.MEŠ KUR *aš-šur*.KI *am-nu-šú-nu-ti*-⸢*ma*⸣ *i-šu-ṭu ab-šá-ni* LUGAL KUR.*me-luḫ-[ḫa]*
110) *ša i-na qé-reb* ⸢LUM⸣ x [x] KUR.*ú*-⸢*ri*?⸣-IZ-ZU *a-šar la a᾿-a-ri ú-ru-uḫ* [x x x x x x x (x x)] SU [*ša ul-tu* UD].⸢MEŠ⸣ *ru-qu-ti a-di i*-^{d}*nanna* AD.MEŠ-*šú a-na* LUGAL.MEŠ-*ni* AD.MEŠ-*ia*
111) *rak-bu-šú-un* ⸢*la*⸣ [*iš*]-*pu-ru a-na šá-᾿a-al šul-me-šú-un da-na-an* ⸢^{d}*aš-šur*⸣ ^{d}[AG] ⸢^{d}⸣AMAR.UTU *a-na ru-[qi?]* ⸢*iš?-me?*⸣-[*ma? pul*]-*ḫi me-lam-me* LUGAL-*ti-ia ik-tu-mu-šu-ma it-ta-bi-ik-šú ḫa-at-tú*

109b–112a) The king of the land Meluḫ[ḫa] — who in ... the land *U[r]izzu*, an inaccessible place, (whose) route [... who]se ancestors [from the] distant [past] until now had nev[er s]ent their mounted messenger(s) to the kings, my ancestors, in order to inquire about their well-being — *[h]e[ar]d from af[ar]* of the might of the gods Aššur, [Nabû], (and) Marduk. [*Then*, fe]ar of (my) royal brilliance overwhelmed him and terror overcame him. He threw him (Iāmānī) in manacles and handcu[ffs], (in other words in) iron [fe]tters, and they brou[ght] (him) the long journey to Assyria, into my presence.

112) *i-na ṣi-iṣ-ṣi ù iz-qa-[ti bi]-re-tú* AN.BAR *id-di-šum-ma a-na qé-reb* KUR *aš-šur*.KI *ḫar-ra-ni ru*-⸢*uq?-ti*⸣ *a-di maḫ-ri-ia ub-[lu-ni* ^{m}]⸢*mut*⸣-*tal-lum* ⸢LÚ⸣.*kúm-mu-ḫa-a-a* LÚ.*ḫat-tu-ú lem-nu la a-dir zik-ri* DINGIR.MEŠ *ka-pi-du*
113) *lem-né-e-ti da-bi-bu ṣa*-⸢*lip*⸣-*ti* UGU ^{m}*ar-giš-ti* LUGAL KUR.*ur-ar-ṭi ne-ra-ri la mu-še-zi-bi-šú it-ta-kil-ma bil-tu man-da-at-tú na-dan šat-ti-šú ú*-⸢*šab*⸣-*ṭil-ma ik-la-a ta-mar-tuš i-na ug-gat lìb-bi-ia*
114) *it-ti* GIŠ.GIGIR GÌR.II-*ia ù* ANŠE.*pét-ḫal-li-ia šá a-šar sa-al-me* Á.II-*a-a la ip-par-ku-ú aṣ-ṣa-bat ú-ru-uḫ-šú a-ka-mu ger-ri-ia e-mur-ma* URU-*uš-šú uṣ-ṣi-ma la in-na-mir a-šar-šú* URU *šú-a-tu*
115) *a-di* 62 URU.MEŠ KAL.MEŠ *ša li-me-ti-šú al-me ak-šud* DAM-*su* DUMU.MEŠ-*šú* DUMU.MUNUS.MEŠ-*šú* NÍG.ŠU NÍG.GA *mim-ma aq-ru ni*-⸢*ṣir-ti*⸣ [É.GAL]-*šú it-ti* UN.MEŠ KUR-*šú* ⸢*áš-lu*⸣-*lam-ma la e-zi-ba ma-nam-ma na-gu-ú šú-a-tú a-na eš-šu-ti*

112b–117a) Mutallu of the land Kummuḫu — an evil Hittite who did not fear the words of the gods, plotted evil, (and always) spoke treachery — put his trust in Argišti, king of the land Urarṭu, (his) ally, who (nevertheless) could not save him, stopped his annual delivery of tribute (and) payment(s), and withheld his audience gift. Angrily, I set out against him with (only) my personal chariot and my cavalry who never leave my side (even) in friendly territory. He saw the cloud of dust (kicked up) by my expeditionary force, went out from his city, and his whereabouts have never been discovered. (115) I surrounded (and) conquered that city, together with 62 fortified settlements in its environs. I carried off as booty his wife, his sons, his daughters, (his) property (and) possessions, everything valuable, the treasure of his [palace], (along) with the people of his land; I did not spare anyone. I reorganized (the administration of) that district. I settled there people of the land Bīt-Yakīn that I had conquered. I set a eunuch of mine as provincial [gove]rnor over them. I imposed the yoke of my lordship upon them. I conscripted from among them

109–112 Line 109: As suggested by A. Fuchs (Khorsabad p. 221), the traces after *qé-reb* on ex. 1 might suggest ⸢*šid*⸣-[*di*]. Lines 109b–112: Iāmānī was extradited by Šapataka᾿ (Shebitko), a member of Egypt's Twenty-Fifth Dynasty, at some point between 711 and 706; see the Introduction to the volume and text no. 116.
110 -⸢*reb* LUM⸣: This is only found on P.E. Botta's copy for ex. 4. Comparing it to *a*-⸢*lu*$_{4}$⸣-*uš-šú* in line 132, possibly read [...] *a*-⸢*lu*$_{4}$⸣-[...] here, as suggested by A. Fuchs (Khorsabad p. 221). KUR.*ú*-⸢*ri*?⸣-IZ-ZU: Ex. 4 has KUR.*ú*-[...] and ex. 1 has [...]-⸢*ri*?⸣-IZ-ZU (with the trace before IZ being visible on the squeeze but not indicated on Botta's copy). With regard to the land Urizzu (or Urişşu) as possibly deriving from the Egyptian term for Upper Egypt, see Fuchs, Khorsabad p. 469.
112b–117a The Assyrian Eponym Chronicle states that Kummuḫu was captured and a governor appointed over it in Sargon's fourteenth regnal year (708). Note that the Khorsabad Annals indicates that the actions against Mutallu were led by officials of Sargon and not by the king himself; see text no. 1 lines 467b–468 and text no. 2 lines 441b–454.

116) *aṣ-bat* UN.MEŠ KUR.É-^{m}*ia-kin*$_{7}$ *ki-šit-ti* ŠU.II-*ia ina lìb-bi ú-še-šib* LÚ.*šu-ut* SAG-*ia* ⸢LÚ.EN⸣.NAM UGU-*šú-nu* ⸢*áš*⸣-*kun ni*-⸢*ir*⸣ *be-lu-ti-ia ú-kin* UGU-*šú-un* 1 ME 50 GIŠ.GIGIR 1 LIM 5 ME ANŠE.*pét-ḫal-lum* 20 LIM ERIM.MEŠ GIŠ.PAN

117) 1 LIM *na-áš* GIŠ.*ka-ba-bi u* GIŠ.⸢*az*⸣-*ma-re-e i-na lìb-bi-šú-nu ak-ṣur-ma ú-šad-gi-la pa-nu-uš-šú i-na u*$_{4}$-*me* ^{m}*dal-ta-a*† LUGAL KUR.⸢*el*⸣-*li-pi*† ARAD *kan-še šá-di-id ni-ri-ia ú-ṣu-rat a-dan-ni ik-šu-da-áš-šum-ma*

118) *il-li-ka ú*†-*ru*-⸢*uḫ*⸣ *mu-ú-ti* ^{m}*ni-bé-e* ^{m}*iš-pa-ba-a-ra* DUMU.MEŠ NIN$_{9}$.MEŠ-⸢*šú*⸣ [*a*]-⸢*na*⸣ *a-šab* GIŠ.GU.ZA LUGAL-*ti-šú* KUR-*su* DAGAL-*tum iš-te-niš i-zu-zu-ma ip-pu-šú ta-ḫa-zu* ^{m}*ni-bé-e áš-šú túr-ri gi-mil-li-šú*

119) UGU ^{m}*šu-túr*-^{d}*na-ḫu-un-di* LÚ.ELAM.MA.KI-*i ur-ri-ḫa* DUMU *šip-ri kit-ru id-din-šu-ma il-li-ka re*-⸢*ṣu*⸣-*us-su*† ^{m}*iš*-⸢*pa*⸣-*ba-a-ra a-na túr-ri gi-mil-li ù e-ṭe-er na-piš-ti-šú*

120) *i-na su-pe-e ù te-me-qi ú-ṣal-la-an-ni-ma e-riš-an-ni kit-ru* 7 LÚ.*šu-ut* SAG.MEŠ-*ia a-di um-ma-na-te-šú-nu a-na tur-ri gi-mil-li-šú áš-pur ša* ^{m}*ni-bé-e a-di um-ma-an e-la-mi*†-*i*

121) *re-ṣi-i-šú i-na* URU.*mar-ú-bi-iš-ti iš-ku-nu taḫ-ta-a-šú* ^{m}*iš-pa-ba-a-ra i-na* GIŠ.GU.ZA-*šú ú-še-šib-ma* KUR.*el-li-pi da-li-iḫ-tú ú-taq-qin-ma ú-šad-gi-la pa-nu-uš-šú* ^{md}AMAR.UTU-IBILA-SUM.NA

122) DUMU ^{m}*ia-kin*$_{7}$ LUGAL KUR.*kal-di ze-er né-er-ti ḫi-ri-iṣ* GAL$_{5}$.LÁ *lem-ni la pa-li-ḫu zi-kir* EN EN.EN UGU ÍD.*mar-ra-ti gu-pu-uš e-di-i it-ta-kil-ma a-de-e* DINGIR.MEŠ GAL.MEŠ *i-bu-uk-ma ik-la-a*

123) *ta-mar-tuš* ^{md}*ḫum-ba-ni-ga-áš* LÚ.ELAM.MA.KI-*ú a-na re-ṣu-ti is-ḫur-ma gi-mir* LÚ.*su-te-e ṣa-ab* EDIN *it-ti-ia uš-bal-kit-ma ik-ṣu-ra ta-ḫa-zu in-neš-ram-ma a-na* KUR EME.GI$_{7}$ *u* URI.KI

124) 12 MU.AN.NA.MEŠ *ki-i la lìb-bi* DINGIR.MEŠ KÁ.DINGIR.RA.KI URU ^{d}EN.LÍL.LÁ DINGIR.MEŠ *i-bel ù iš-pur i-na qí-bit* ^{d}*aš-šur* AD DINGIR.MEŠ *ù* EN GAL-*i* ^{d}AMAR.UTU *uš-te-še-ra ṣi-in-di-ia ak-ṣu-ra uš-ma-ni*

125) *a-na* LÚ.*kal-di* LÚ.KÚR *ak-ṣi a-la-ku aq-bi ù šu-ú* ^{md}MES-A-SUM.NA *a-lak ger-ri-ia iš-me-ma ḫat-tu rama-ni-šú im-qut-su-ma ul-tu qé-reb* KÁ.DINGIR.RA.KI *a-na* URU.*iq-bi*-^{d}EN *ki-ma su-tin-ni*

150 chariots, 1,500 cavalry, 20,000 bowmen, (and) 1,000 shield and spear bearers and made (them) subject to him (the new governor).

117b–121a) At that time, the appointed moment came for Daltâ, king of the land Ellipi, a submissive subject who pulled my yoke, and he went the way of death. Nibê (and) Ašpa-bara, sons of h[is] sisters, jointly divided up his wide land (with regard to the right) to sit on his royal throne and (then) were doing battle (with one another). Nibê quickly sent a messenger to Šutur-Naḫūndi, the Elamite, in order to get revenge. He (Šutur-Naḫūndi) gave him aid and came to his assistance. In order to get revenge and to save his life, Ašpa-bara (120) besought me with supplications and entreaties and asked me for (military) aid. I sent seven of my eunuchs, together with their troops, to avenge him. They brought about the defeat of Nibê, together with the Elamite army, his allies, at the city Marubištu. I seated Ašpa-bara on his throne, brought order to the disturbed land Ellipi, and made (it) subject to him.

121b–124a) Marduk-apla-iddina (II) (Merodach-Baladan), descendant of Yakīn, king of Chaldea, a murderer (lit.: "seed of murder") (and) the (very) image of a *gallû*-demon, who does not fear the word of the lord of lords (Marduk), put his trust in the sea (and its) surging waves, broke (lit.: "overturned") the treaty (sworn) by the great gods, and withheld his audience gift. He turned to Ḫumbanigaš (Ḫumban-nikaš I), the Elamite, for aid, caused all the Sutians, the people of the steppe, to rebel against me, and prepared for battle. He proceeded to the land of Sumer and Akkad and for twelve years he ruled and governed Babylon, the city of the Enlil of the gods (Marduk), against the will of the gods.

124b–129a) At the command of the god Aššur, the father of the gods, and of the great lord, the god Marduk, I got my (chariot) teams ready (and) prepared my (military) camp. I ordered the march against the Chaldean, a dangerous enemy. However, that Marduk-apla-iddina heard of the approach of my expeditionary force. His own fear(s) then fell upon him and he flew away from Babylon to the city Iqbi-Bēl during the night like a bat. He gathered together the inhabitants of his cities (lit.: "his inhabited cities") and the

117–121a Line 117: 1 LIM, "1,000," is likely an error for 10 LIM, "10,000," as in text no. 2 line 453 (see also Fuchs, Khorsabad p. 349 n. 465). The 1 is only found on ex. 4. P.E. Botta's copy of ex. 1 has <1> LIM, while H. Winckler's has 1 LIM; the squeeze would seem to allow [1] LIM. Lines 117b–121a: The campaign against Nibê of Ellipi took place during Sargon's fifteenth regnal year (707), or just possibly in the preceding year; see text no. 2 lines 455–467a.

118 -⸢*šú*⸣ [*a*]-⸢*na*⸣ is based on the squeeze of ex. 1, as opposed to the Monument de Nineve copy which has [*x* (*x*)]; H. Winckler's copy for this exemplar has simply -*šú* (fully preserved). The passage is not preserved on any other exemplar.

121b–145a The conquest of Babylonia took place in Sargon's twelfth and thirteenth regnal years (710–709), although Sargon did not return to Assyria until 707. See in particular text no. 1 lines 262b–444a, text no. 2 lines 287b–427, text no. 3 lines 13′b–60′, text no. 5 lines 1′–3′, and text no. 6 lines 1′–14′.

126) *ip-pa-riš mu-šiš* URU.MEŠ-*šú aš-bu-te ù* DINGIR.MEŠ *a-šib* ŠÀ-*šú-un ki-i iš-tén ú-paḫ-ḫir-ma a-na* URU.BÀD-^{m}*ia-kin*$_7$ *ú-še-rib-ma ú-dan-ni-na ker-ḫe-e-šú* LÚ.*gam-bu-lum* LÚ.⸢*pu-qu*⸣*-du* LÚ.*da-mu-nu*

127) LÚ.*ru-ʾu-u*$_8$*-a* LÚ.*ḫi-in-da-ru ik-te-ram-ma a-na qer-bi-šú ú-še-rib-ma ú-šá-aṣ-ri-ḫa* MÈ *áš-la*.TA.ÀM *la-pa-an* BÀD-*šú* GAL-*i ú-né-es-si-ma* 2 ME *ina* 1.KÙŠ DAGAL *ḫa-ri-ṣi iš-kun-ma*

128) 1 1/2 NINDA *ú-šap-pil-ma ik-šu-da* A.MEŠ *nag-bi bu-tuq-tu ul-tu qé-reb* ÍD.*pu-rat-ti ib-tu-qa ú-šar-da-a ta-mir-tuš ú-šal-lu*$_4$ URU *a-šar naq-ra-bi* A.MEŠ *ú-mal-li-ma ú-bat-ti-qa*

gods dwelling in them (his cities), and he brought them into the city Dūr-Yakīn. Then, he strengthened its enclosure walls. He formed the Gambulu, Puqudu, Damūnu, Ruʾuʾa (and) Ḫindaru (tribes) into bands, brought (them) inside it (Dūr-Yakīn), and *made preparations* for battle. Moving back a distance of one measuring rope from in front of its main wall, he made a moat two hundred cubits wide; he made (the moat) one and a half *nindanu* deep and reached ground water. He cut a channel from the Euphrates River, (thereby) making (its water) flow (in)to its meadowland. He filled the city's flatlands, where battles (are fought), with water and cut the bridges. Together with his allies (and) his battle troops, he pitched his royal tent in a bend of the river (lit.: "between rivers") like a *crane* and set up his (military) camp.

129) *ti-tur-ri šu-ú a-di re-ṣi-šú* ERIM.MEŠ MÈ-*šú i-na bi-rit* ÍD.MEŠ *ki-ma* MUŠEN.*ku-mi-i kul-tar* LUGAL-*ti-šú iš-kun-ma ik-ṣu-ra uš-ma-an-šú* LÚ.⸢*mun*⸣*-daḫ-ṣe-ia* ⸢UGU⸣ ÍD.MEŠ-*šú a-ra-niš ú-šap-riš-ma*

130) *iš-ku-nu taḫ-ta-a-šú* A.MEŠ ÍD.MEŠ-*šú i-na* ÚŠ.MEŠ LÚ.*qu-ra-di-šú iṣ-ru-pu na-ba-si-iš* LÚ.*su-te-e ki-tar-šú ša i-*⸢*da*⸣*-a-šú is-ḫu-ru-ma il-li-ku re-ṣu-us-su a-di* LÚ.*mar-šá-na-a-a*

131) *as-li-iš ú-nak-kis-ma i-mat mu-ú-ti as-lu-ḫa si-it-ta-at* UN.MEŠ *mul-taḫ-ṭu ù šu-ú kul-tar* LUGAL-[*ti-šú*] GIŠ.NÁ KÙ.GI GIŠ.GU.ZA KÙ.GI GIŠ†.*né-mat-ti* KÙ.GI GIŠ.GIDRU KÙ.GI GIŠ.GIGIR ⸢KÙ⸣.BABBAR

129b–132a) I had my fighters fly [o]ver his canals like eagles and they brought about his defeat. With the blood of his warriors, they dyed the water of his canals as red as red wool. I cut down like sheep the Sutians, his allies, who had gone over to his side and come to his aid, together with the Maršanians, and I splattered the remainder of the people who survived with deadly venom. However, that (man) abandoned [his] royal tent, gold bed, gold throne, gold chair, gold scepter, silver chariot, gold parasol, and his neck ornament inside his (military) ca[m]p and fled off by himself; like a cat, he hugged the side of his (city's) wall and entered his city.

132) GIŠ.*šá ṣil-li* KÙ.GI *ù ti-iq-ni* GÚ-*šú qé-reb* ⸢KARAŠ⸣-*šú e-zib-ma e-di-iš ip-par-šid-ma ki-ma šu-ra-ni ṭe-ḫi* BÀD-*šú iṣ-bat-ma e-ru-ba a-*⸢*lu*$_4$⸣*-uš-šú* URU.BÀD-^{m}*ia-kin*$_7$ *al-me ak-šud*

133) *šá-a-šú a-di* DAM-*šú* DUMU.MEŠ-*šú* DUMU.MUNUS.MEŠ-*šú* KÙ.GI KÙ.BABBAR NÍG.ŠU [NÍG].⸢GA⸣ *ni-ṣir-ti* É.GAL-*šú ma-la ba-šu-ú it-ti šal-lat* URU-*šú ka-bit-ti ù mul-taḫ-ṭu si-it-ta-at* UN.MEŠ-*šú ša la-pa-an* GIŠ.TUKUL.MEŠ-*ia ip-par-šid-du*

132b–134a) I surrounded (and) conquered the city Dūr-Yakīn. I rounded up that man, together with his wife, his sons, his daughters, gold, silver, property (and) [possess]ions, the treasure of his palace, as much as there was (of it), (along) with substantial booty from his city and the survivor(s), the remainder of his people who had fled before my weapons, and I counted them as booty. I burned his fortified city Dūr-Yakīn down with fire. I destroyed (and) demolished its high enclosure walls; I tore out its foundation. I made it like a (ruin) mound left by the Deluge.

134) *ki-i iš-tén ú-ter-ram-ma a-na šal-la-ti am-nu-šú-nu-ti* URU.BÀD-^{m}*ia-kin*$_7$ URU *dan-nu-ti-šú ina* ^{d}GIŠ.BAR *aq-mu ker-ḫe-šú zaq-ru-te ap-pul aq-qur te-me-en-šú as-su-ḫa ki-ma* DU$_6$ *a-bu-bi ú-še-me-šú* DUMU.MEŠ ZIMBIR.KI NIBRU.KI

135) KÁ.DINGIR.RA.KI *u bár-sipa*.KI *ša i-na la an-ni-šú-nu i-na qer-bi-šú ka-mu-ú ṣi-bit-ta-šú-nu a-bu-ut-ma ú-kal-lim-šú-nu-ti*

134b–137a) (As for) the citizens of (the cities) Sippar, Nippur, Babylon, and Borsippa who through no fault of their own had been held captive in it (Dūr-Yakīn), I put an end to their imprisonment and let them see the light (of day). (With regard to) their fields, which long ago, while the land was in disorder, the Sutians had taken away and appropriated for their own, I struck down (those) Sutians, the people of the steppe, with the sword. I (re)assigned to them

---

126b–127a Due to lack of space, it appears that exemplar 4 omitted *ú-dan-ni-na ... ú-še-rib-ma*, "He strengthened its enclosure walls. He formed the Gambulu, Puqudu, Damūnu, Ruʾuʾa (and) Ḫindaru (tribes) into bands and brought (them) inside it (Dūr-Yakīn)."

132 Or *ki-ma šu-ra-ni ṭe-ḫi* BÀD-*šú iz-ziz-ma*, "Like a cat, he kept (lit.: "stood") beside his (city's) wall."

133–134a For differing accounts of what happened to Marduk-apla-iddina, see the Introduction to this volume, under the section "Military Campaigns."

nu-ru A.ŠÀ.MEŠ-šú-nu ša ul-tu u_4-me ul-lu-ti
i-na i-ši-ti ma-a-ti LÚ.su-ti-i
136) e-ki-mu-ú-ma ra-ma-nu-uš-šú-un ú-ter-ru
LÚ.su-ti-i ERIM.MEŠ EDIN i-na GIŠ.TUKUL
ú-šam-qit ki-sur-ri-šú-nu ma-šu-ú-ti ša ina
di-li-iḫ KUR ib-baṭ-lu ú-šad-gi-la pa-nu-uš-šú-un
ša ÚRI.KI UNUG.KI eridu.KI

(the citizens) their territories, (whose boundaries) had been forgotten (and) fallen into disuse during the troubled period in the land. I (re)-established the freedom (from obligations) of (the cities) Ur, Uruk, Eridu, Larsa, Kullaba, Kissik, (and) Nēmed-Laguda. Moreover, I returned their gods that had been carried off as booty to their cult centers and restored their regular offerings that had been discontinued.

137) ARARMA.KI kul-aba_4.KI ki-sik.KI
URU.né-med-^{d}la-gu-da áš-ku-na
an-du-ra-ar-šú-un ù DINGIR.MEŠ-šú-nu šal-lu-ti
a-na ma-ḫa-zi-šú-nu ú-ter-ma sat-tuk-ki-šú-nu
ba-aṭ-lu-ú-ti ú-ter áš-ru-uš-šú-un
KUR.É-^{m}ia-kin_7
138) e-liš u šap-liš a-di URU.sa-am-ʾu-ú-na
URU.KÁ-BÀD URU.BÀD-^{d}te-li-tim URU.bu-bé-e
URU.DU_6-^{d}ḫum-ba ša mi-ṣir KUR.ELAM.MA.KI
mit-ḫa-riš a-bel-ma UN.MEŠ KUR.kúm-mu-ḫi ša
qé-reb KUR.ḫat-ti ša ina tu-kul-ti
139) DINGIR.MEŠ GAL.MEŠ EN.MEŠ-ia ik-šu-da
ŠU.II-a-a qé-reb-šú ú-šar-me-ma ú-še-ši-ba
ni-du-us-su UGU mi-ṣir KUR.ELAM.MA.KI ina
URU.sa-ag-bat ^{md}AG-SIG_5-DINGIR.MEŠ a-na
šup-ru-us GÌR.II LÚ.KÚR KUR.ELAM.MA.KI-i
ú-šar-kis URU.bir-tú

137b–140a) I ruled all together the land Bīt-Yakīn, from one end to the other end (lit.: "above and below"), as far as the cities Samʾūna, Bāb-dūri, Dūr-Telīte, Bubê, (and) Tīl-Ḫumba, which are on the Elamite border; I settled there people from the land Kummuḫu, which is (located) in the land Ḫatti, that I had conquered with the support of the great gods, my lords, and I had (them) occupy its (Bīt-Yakīn's) abandoned regions. I had Nabû-damiq-ilāni construct a fortress on the Elamite border, at the city Sagbat, in order to bar access to (lit.: "the feet of") the enemy Elamite(s). (140) I divided up that land into equal parts and assigned (them) to the authority of a eunuch of mine, the governor of Babylon, and a(nother) eunuch of mine, the governor of the Gambulu (tribe).

140) KUR šu-a-tu mal-ma-liš a-zu-uz-ma ina ŠU.II
LÚ.šu-ut SAG-ia LÚ.GAR.KUR KÁ.DINGIR.RA.KI ù
LÚ.šu-ut SAG-ia LÚ.GAR.KUR LÚ.gam-bu-li
am-nu a-na KÁ.DINGIR.RA.KI ma-ḫa-zi
^{d}EN.LÍL.LÁ DINGIR.MEŠ i-na e-le-eṣ lib-bi
141) nu-um-mur pa-ni ḫa-diš e-ru-um-ma ŠU.II EN
GAL-i ^{d}AMAR.UTU aṣ-bat-ma ú-šal-li-ma ú-ru-uḫ
É á-ki-ti 1 ME 54 GUN 26 MA.NA 10 GÍN KÙ.GI
ḫuš-šu-ú 1 LIM 6 ME 4 GUN 20 MA.NA
KÙ.BABBAR eb-bu URUDU.ḪI.A
142) par-zil-la ša ni-ba la i-šu-ú NA_4.ZÚ NA_4.ZA.GÌN
NA_4.BABBAR.DILI NA_4.AŠ.GÌ.GÌ NA_4.UGU.AŠ.GÌ.GÌ
di-gi-li NA_4.BABBAR.DILI NA_4.MUŠ.GÍR a-na
mu-ʾu-de-e SÍG.ta-kil-tú SÍG.ar-ga-man-nu
lu-bul-ti bir-me ù TÚG.GADA GIŠ.TÚG
143) GIŠ.EREN GIŠ.ŠUR.MÌN ka-la ri-iq-qí bi-ib-lat
KUR.ḫa-ma-a-ni ša e-ri-su-un ṭa-a-bu a-na ^{d}EN
^{d}zar-pa-ni-tum ^{d}AG ^{d}taš-me-tum ù DINGIR.MEŠ
a-ši-bu-ut ma-ḫa-zi KUR ⌜šu⌝-me-ri ù URI.KI

140b–144a) Happily, with a joyful heart (and) a radiant face, I entered Babylon, the cult center of the Enlil of the gods (Marduk); I grasped hold of the hands of the great lord, the god Marduk, and brought (him) safely along the the road to the *akītu*-house. (With regard to) 154 talents, 26 minas, (and) 10 shekels of red gold, 1,604 talents (and) 20 minas of pure silver, copper (and) iron in immeasurable quantities, obsidian, lapis lazuli, *banded agate, blue turquoise, green turquoise, ... of banded agate* (and) *muššaru*-stone in large quantities, blue-purple wool, red-purple wool, garments with multi-colored trim and linen garments, boxwood, cedar, cypress, (and) every kind of aromatic, the products of Mount Amanus, whose scent(s) are pleasant — from the beginning of my kingship until (my) third year, I presented (these things) as gifts to the deities Bēl, Zarpanītu, Nabû, Tašmētu, and the (other) gods who dwell in the cult centers of the land of Sumer and Akkad.

144) ul-tu SAG LUGAL-ti-ia a-di MU.3.KÁM ú-qa-i-šá
qí-šá-a-ti ^{m}ú-pe-e-ri LUGAL dil-mun.KI ša 30
KASKAL.GÍD ina $MURUB_4$ tam-tim ni-pi-iḫ
^{d}UTU-ši ki-ma nu-ú-ni šit-ku-nu nar-ba-⌜ṣu⌝

144b–145a) Upēri, king of Dilmun, who(se) lair is situated (at a distance of) thirty leagues in the middle of the Eastern Sea, like (that of) a fish, heard of the might of the gods Aššur, Nabû, (and) Marduk and brought me his gift.

---

141 Ex. 4 has 1 ME 64 GUN, "164 talents," for 1 ME 54 GUN, "154 talents," and 1 LIM 8 ME 4 GUN, "1,804 talents," for 1 LIM 6 ME 4 GUN, "1,604 talents." Text no. 64 line 9′ and text no. 103 iv 7 also have 1,804 talents.
144 Text no. 74 vii 19 has MU.4.KÁM, "(my) fourth year."
145b–149a This episode is connected with the sending of help to Silṭa, king of Tyre, against these rulers in the Khorsabad Annals; see text no. 1 lines 456b–467a and text no. 2 lines 436b–441a. The gifts likely reached Sargon in Babylon in 709, in 708, or in 707 before he returned to Assyria.

145) *da-na-an* ^{d}*aš-šur* ^{d}AG ^{d}AMAR.UTU *iš-me-ma ú-šá-bi-la kàd-ra-šu ù* 7 LUGAL.MEŠ-*ni ša* KUR.*ia-a'* *na-gi-i ša* KUR.*ia-ad-na-na*
146) *ša ma-lak* 7 *u*$_4$*-me i-na* MURUB$_4$ *tam-tim e-reb* ^{d}UTU-*ši šit-ku-nu-ma né-es-sa-at šu-bat-su-un ša ul-tu u*$_4$*-me ru-qu-ti a-di i-*^{d}*nanna*
147) *a-na* LUGAL.MEŠ-*ni* AD.MEŠ-*ia ša* KUR *aš-šur*.KI *u* KUR.*kar-*^{d}*du-ni-áš ma-nam-ma la iš-mu-ú zi-kir* KUR-*šú-un ep-šet i-na qé-reb* KUR.*kal-di u* KUR.*ḫat-ti*
148) *e-tep-pu-šu i-na* MURUB$_4$ *tam-tim ru-qiš iš-mu-ma lib-bu-šú-un it-ru-ku-ma im-qut-su-nu-ti ḫat-tu* KÙ.GI KÙ.BABBAR *ú-nu-ut* GIŠ.ESI GIŠ.TÚG *né-peš-ti*
149) KUR-*šú-un a-na qé-reb* KÁ.DINGIR.RA.KI *a-di maḫ-ri-ia ú-bi-lu-nim-ma ú-na-áš-ši-qu* GÌR.II-*ia a-di a-na-ku dáb-de-e* KUR.É-^{m}*ia-kin*$_7$ *ù na-gab*
150) LÚ.*a-ri-me a-šak-ka-nu-ma* UGU KUR.*ia-ad-bu-ri ša i-te-e* KUR.ELAM.MA.KI *ú-šam-ra-ru* GIŠ.TUKUL.MEŠ-*ia* LÚ.*šu-ut* SAG-*ia* LÚ.GAR.KUR KUR.*qu-e ša* ^{m}*mi-ta-a*
151) KUR.*mu-us-ka-a-a a-di* 3-*šú ina na-gi-šú ši-il-pu il-lik-ma* URU.MEŠ-*ni-šú ip-pul iq-qur ina* IZI *iš-ru-up šal-la-su-nu ka-bit-tu iš-lu-lam*
152) *ù šu-ú* ^{m}*mi-ta-a* KUR.*mu-us-ka-a-a ša a-na* LUGAL.MEŠ-*ni a-lik pa-ni-ia la ik-nu-šu-ma la ú-šá-an-nu-ú ṭè-en-šú* LÚ.A KIN-*šú ša e-peš*
153) *ar-du-ti ù na-še-e bil-ti* IGI.SÁ-*e a-na tam-tim ša ṣi-it* ^{d}UTU-*ši a-di maḫ-ri-ia iš-pu-ra i-na u*$_4$*-me-šu-ma i-na* UN.MEŠ KUR.MEŠ
154) *ki-šit-ti* ŠU.II-*ia ša* ^{d}*aš-šur* ^{d}AG ^{d}AMAR.UTU *a-na* GÌR.II-*ia ú-šak-ni-šu-ma i-šu-ṭu ab-šá-ni ina* GÌR.II KUR.*mu-uṣ-ri e-le-na* NINA.KI
155) *ki-i ṭè-em* DINGIR-*ma i-na bi-bil lìb-bi-ia* URU DÙ-*uš-ma* URU.BÀD-^{m}MAN-GIN *az-ku-ra ni-bit-su* ^{d}*é-a* ^{d}30 ^{d}UTU ^{d}AG ^{d}IŠKUR
156) ^{d}*nin-urta ù ḫi-ra-ti-šú-nu ra-ba-a-ti ša i-na qé-reb é-ḫur-sag-gal-kur-kur-ra* KUR *a-ra-al-li ki-niš i'-al-du eš-re-ti nam-ra-a-ti*
157) *suk-ki nak-lu-ti ina qé-reb* URU.BÀD-^{m}MAN-GIN *ṭa-biš ir-mu-ú sat-tuk-ki la nar-ba-a-te is-qu-šú-un ú-kin-na* ⸢LÚ⸣.NU.⸢ÈŠ⸣.MEŠ LÚ.*ram-ki* LÚ.*sur-maḫ-ḫi*
158) *šu-ut it-ḫu-zu nin-da-an-šú-un la-mid pi-riš-ti* AN.GUB.BA.MEŠ *na-aṭ-pu-ti ma-ḫar-šu-un* [*ul-ziz*] É.GAL ZÚ AM.SI GIŠ.ESI GIŠ.TÚG

145b–149a) Moreover, seven kings of the land Yā', a region of the land Yadnana (Cyprus) — whose abode(s) are situated far away, at a distance of seven days (journey) in the middle of the Western Sea (and) the name of whose land, from the distant past until now, none of the kings, my ancestors, neither in Assyria nor in the land Karduniaš (Babylonia), had ever heard — heard from afar, in the middle of the sea, of the deeds I had been doing in Chaldea and the land Ḫatti (Syria). Their hearts then pounded and fear fell upon them. They brought before me in Babylon gold, silver, (and) utensils of ebony (and) boxwood, products of their land, and they kissed my feet.

149b–153a) While I was bringing about the defeat of the land Bīt-Yakīn and all of the Arameans and of making my weapon prevail over the land Yadburu on the border of the land Elam, a eunuch of mine, the governor of the land Que (Cilicia), marched ...ly three times into the territory of Mitâ (Midas) of the land Musku. He destroyed, demolished, (and) burned down his cities with fire. He carried off substantial booty from them. Moreover, that (man), Mitâ of the land Musku, who had not submitted to the kings who preceded me and had never changed his mind (about doing so), sent his messenger before me at the Eastern Sea to do obeisance (to me) and to bring (me) tribute (and) presents.

153b–155a) At that time, using (as laborers) people from the lands that I had conquered, whom the gods Aššur, Nabû, (and) Marduk had made bow down at my feet, and who (now) pull my yoke, (and) in accordance with divine will (and) my heart's desire, I built a city at the foot of Mount Muṣri, upstream from Nineveh, and I named it Dūr-Šarrukīn.

155b–158a) The gods Ea, Sîn, Šamaš, Nabû, Adad, Ninurta, and their great spouses who were duly born inside Eḫursaggalkurkurra ("House, the Great Mountain of the Lands"), the mountain of the netherworld, gladly took up residence in resplendent sanctuaries (and) artfully-built shrines inside the city Dūr-Šarrukīn. I established innumerable regular offerings as their shares (of temple income). I had *nešakku*-priests, *ramku*-priests, *surmaḫḫu*-priests, men well versed in their (fields of) knowledge (and) initiated in secret rites, (and) *naṭpu-ecstatics* serve them (lit.: "stand before them").

158b–162a) I built inside [it (the city)] a palace using (lit.: "of") elephant ivory, ebony, boxwood, *musukkannu*-wood, cedar, cypress, *daprānu*-juniper, juniper

147 P.E. Botta's copy of ex. 4 copy omits the *u*, "nor," after *aš-šur*.KI, "Assyria," but the photo of the squeeze suggests that it is present. Botta's copy of ex. 4 also omits the *u*, "and," after *kal-di*, "Chaldea," but the squeeze is not clear if his copy is correct or not.
149b–153 For this episode, which the Khorsabad Annals indicate took place while Sargon was active in Babylonia (710–708), see also text no. 1 lines 444b–456a and text no. 2 lines 428–436a.
155b–158a Cf. text no. 2 lines 469b–472a.
158b–162a See the on-page note to text no. 2 lines 472b–477a.

GIŠ.*mu-suk-kan-ni* GIŠ.EREN GIŠ.ŠUR.MÌN
159) GIŠ.*dup-ra-ni* GIŠ.LI *ù* GIŠ.*bu-uṭ-ni*
é-gal-gaba-ri-nu-tuku-a a-na mu-šab be-lu-ti-ia
qer-bu-uš-[šú] ab-ni-ma e-li MU.SAR-*re-e* KÙ.GI
KÙ.BABBAR NA$_4$.ZA.GÌN NA$_4$.*aš-pe-e*
160) NA$_4$.*pa-ru-tum* URUDU.MEŠ AN.NA AN.BAR
A.BÁR *ù ḫi-biš-ti* ŠIM.MEŠ *uš-ši-šin ad-di-ma*
li-bit-ta-šin ú-kin-na GIŠ.ÙR.MEŠ GIŠ.*ere*-IGI
GAL.MEŠ *e-li-šin ú-šat-ri-ṣa*
161) GIŠ.IG.MEŠ GIŠ.ŠUR.MÌN GIŠ.*mu-suk-kan-ni*
me-se-er URUDU *nam-ri ú-rak-kis-ma ú-rat-ta-a*
né-reb-šin É *ap-pa-a-ti tam-šil* É.GAL KUR.*ḫat-ti*
ša i-⸢na⸣ li-šá-an KUR MAR.TU.KI
162) É *ḫi-la-an-ni i-šá-as-su-šú ú-še-pi-šá mé-eḫ-ret*
ba-bi-šin 8 UR.MAḪ.MEŠ *tu-ʾa-a-me šu-ut* ⸢1⸣
ŠÁR GÉŠ.U 6 UŠ 50.TA.ÀM GUN *mal-tak-ti*
URUDU *nam-⸢ri⸣*
163) *ša ina ši-pir* ^{d}*nin-á-gal ip-pat-qu-ú-ma ma-lu-ú*
nam-ri-ri 4 GIŠ.*tim-me* GIŠ.*ere*-IGI *šu-ta-ḫu-ti ša*
1 NINDA.TA.ÀM *ku-bur-šú-un bi-ib-lat*
KUR.*ḫa-ma-ni* UGU PIRIG.GAL-*e*
164) *ú-kin-ma* GIŠ.*dáp-pi ku-lul* KÁ.MEŠ-*šin e-mid*
UDU.MEŠ *šad-di* ^{d}LAMMA MAḪ.MEŠ *ša*† NA$_4$
KUR-*i eš-qí nak-liš ab-ni-ma a-na er-bet-ti*
šá-a-ri ú-šá-aṣ-bi-ta SI.GAR-*šin as-mu*
165) *as-kup-pi* NA$_4$.*pi-i-li* GAL.MEŠ *da-ád-me ki-šit-ti*
ŠU.II-*ia ṣe-ru-uš-⸢ši⸣-in ab-šim-ma a-sur-ši-in*
ú-šá-as-ḫi-ra a-na tab-ra-a-ti ú-šá-lik da-ád-me
ma-ti-tan
166) *ša ul-tu ṣi-taš a-di šil-la-an i-na e-mu-uq*
^{d}*aš-šur* EN-*ia ak-šud-du-ma ina ši-pir*
LÚ.*ùr-ra-ku-ti ina qé-reb* É.GAL.MEŠ *šá-ti-na*
áš-tak-ka-na si-ma-a-ti
167) *i-na* ITI *še-me-e* *u*$_4$-*mu mit-ga-ri* ^{d}*aš-šur a-bu*
DINGIR.MEŠ EN GAL DINGIR.MEŠ *u* ^{d}IŠ.TAR.MEŠ
a-ši-bu-ut KUR *aš-šur*.KI *qé-reb-ši-na aq-re-ma*
kàd-re-e ṣa-ri-ri ru-uš-še$_{20}$-*e*
168) KÙ.BABBAR *eb-bi* IGI.SÁ-*e šad-lu-ti ta-mar-tu*
ka-bit-tu GAL-*iš ú-šam-ḫir-šu-nu-ti-ma*
ú-šá-li-ṣa nu-pa-ar-šú-un GU$_4$.MAḪ-*ḫi bit-ru-ti*
šu-ʾe-e ma-ru-ú-ti KUR.GI.MUŠEN.MEŠ
169) UZ.TUR.MUŠEN.MEŠ *šu-um-me iz-ḫe-et* KU$_6$.MEŠ
u MUŠEN.MEŠ ḪÉ.GÁL ZU.AB *ša la i-šu-ú*
170) *mi-ṭi-ta ku-ru-un-nu làl-la-ru bi-ib-lat* KUR.MEŠ
KÙ.MEŠ *re-še-et* KUR.KUR.MEŠ
171) *ki-šit-ti* ŠU.II-*ia ša a-na iš-qí* LUGAL-*ti-ia*
uṣ-ṣi-ba za-ru-ú DINGIR.MEŠ
172) ^{d}*aš-šur it-ti ni-iq* ŠÀ.IGI.GURU$_6$-*e eb-bu-ti zi-i-bi*
el-lu-ti qut-rin-ni
173) *šur-ru-ḫi tam-qi-ti la nar-ba-a-ti ma-ḫar-šú-un*
aq-qí áš-šú šá-ṭa-pu na-piš-ti
174) UD.MEŠ SÙ.MEŠ *na-da-nim-ma ù kun-nu*
BALA-*ia na-aʾ-di-iš ak-mì-sa*

and terebinth, (namely) Egalgabarinutukua ("Palace That Has No Equal"), to be my lordly residence, and I laid their foundations upon inscribed objects (made) of gold, silver, lapis lazuli, jasper, *parūtu*-alabaster, copper, tin, iron, lead, and pieces of aromatic woods. Then, I established their brickwork (and) roofed them with large cedar beams. I bound the doors of cypress (and) *musukkannu*-wood with band(s) of shining copper and installed (them in) their entrance(s). I had built in front of their gates a portico (*bīt appāti*), a replica of a Hittite palace, which is called a *bīt ḫilāni* in the language of the land Amurru.

162b–166) Eight twin lion (colossi) of shining copper that weigh 4,610 full (lit.: "tested") talents (and) that were cast by the craft of the god Ninagal and filled with radiance — upon (those) lion colossi I installed four matching cedar columns, whose diameter(s) are one *nindanu* each, the product of Mount Amanus, and I positioned cross-beams (upon them) as a cornice for their gates. I skillfully fashioned magnificent mountain sheep colossi of massive mountain stone and in the four directions I had (them) hold their (the gates') respective (lit.: "fitting") door bolt(s). I depicted the settlements that I had conquered upon large limestone slabs and surrounded their (the palatial halls') lower courses (with them). I made (them) an object of wonder. I placed inside these palatial halls representations — (made) by the craft of the sculptor — of the settlements of every land that I had conquered, from east to west, by the strength of the god Aššur, my lord.

167–175a) In a favorable month, (on) an auspicious day, I invited the god Aššur, the father of the gods, the great lord, (and) the (other) gods and goddesses who dwell in Assyria (to come) inside them and, in a grandiose manner, I offered them (the gods) gifts of red *ṣāriru*-gold (and) pure silver, extensive presents as (my) substantial audience gift. I thus made their (the gods') moods joyful. I offered before them prize bulls in prime condition, fattened sheep, geese, ducks, *dormice*, strings of fish and birds, the wealth of the Deep (*apsû*) that never (170) lessens, *kurunnu-beer* (and) white honey, products of the pure mountains, the best of the lands that I had conquered, which the progenitor of the gods, the god Aššur, had added to my royal share, (along) with pure voluntary sacrifices, pure food offerings, splendid incense offerings, (and) innumerable libations. Reverently, I knelt (and) prayed before him that he preserve (my) life, grant (me) a long life, and firmly establish my reign.

162 Ex. 4 has <1>, or less likely [1].
168 Ex. 4 has <GAL>-*iš*, or possibly [GAL]-*iš* based on squeeze.

175) *ut-nin ma-ḫar-šu* KUR GAL-*ú* ^{d}EN.LÍL EN KUR.MEŠ *a-šib é-ḫur-sag-gal-kur-kur-ra*
176) DINGIR.MEŠ *ù* ^{d}IŠ.TAR.MEŠ *a-ši-bu-ti* KUR *aš-šur*.KI *i-na tam-gi-ti*

175–177a) The great mountain, the god Enlil, the lord of (all) lands, who dwells in Eḫursaggalkurkurra, (and) the (other) gods and goddesses who dwell in Assyria returned to their city amid songs of joy and hymns of praise.

177) *ù* ⸢*za*⸣*-mar tak-né-e i-tu-ru* URU-*uš-šú-un it-ti mal-ki ma-ti-tan*
178) LÚ.EN? *pa-ḫa-ti* KUR-*ia ak-li šá-pi-ri* NUN.MEŠ LÚ.*šu-ut* SAG.MEŠ
179) *ù* LÚ.AB.BA.MEŠ KUR *aš-šur*.KI *ina qé-reb* É.GAL-*ia ú-šib-ma áš-ta-kan ni-gu-tú*
180) KÙ.GI KÙ.BABBAR *ú-nu-*⸢*ut*⸣ KÙ.GI KÙ.BABBAR NA$_4$ *a-qar-tum* URUDU *par-zil-lum*
181) *ú-nu-ut* ⸢URUDU⸣ *par-*[*zil*]*-lum*† *kal* ŠIM.MEŠ Ì DÙG.GA *lu-bul-ti bir-me* ⸢*ù*⸣ [TÚG].GADA†
182) SÍG.*ta-kil-tú* SÍG.*ar-ga-man-nu* KUŠ AM.SI ZÚ AM.SI
183) *gu-uḫ-lum* GIŠ.ESI GIŠ.[TÚG] ANŠE.KUR.RA.MEŠ KUR.*mu-ṣu-ri*
184) *ṣi-*⸢*mit*⸣*-ti* ⸢*ni*⸣*-i-ri* [*ra*]*-bu-ti* ANŠE.KUNGA.MEŠ ANŠE.MEŠ
185) ANŠE.GAM.MAL.MEŠ GU$_4$.[MEŠ (*ù*) US$_5$.UDU.ḪI].A ⸢*man-da*⸣*-at-ta-šú-nu ka-bit-tu*

177b–186a) With rulers from every land, provincial governors of my land, overseers, commanders, nobles, eunuchs, and elders of Assyria, I sat down inside my palace and held a festival. [I recei]ved as their substantial tribute (180) gold, silver, utensils of gold (and) silver, valuable stone(s), copper, iron, untensils of co[pper] (and) ir[o]n, every kind of aromatic, fine oil, garments with multi-colored trim and linen garments, blue-purple wool, red-purple wool, elephant hide(s), elephant ivory, antimony, ebony, [box]wood, [la]rge Egyptian horses that are tr[ai]ned to the yoke, mules, donkeys, camels, ox[en, (and) sheep and goats].

186) [*am*]*-*⸢*ḫur*⸣ URU *i-tu-ut ku-un lib-*[*bi-ia u*] É.GAL *šá-a-tu*
187) ⸢^{d}⸣[*aš*]*-*⸢*šur*⸣ AD DINGIR.MEŠ *i-na nu-*⸢*um*⸣*-mur bu-ni-šú* KÙ.MEŠ
188) *ki-niš lip-pa-*[*lis*]*-ma a-*⸢*na*⸣ UD†.MEŠ *ru-qu-ti ud-du-su-un lit-tas-qar*
189) ⸢*i*⸣*-*[*na*] ⸢*pi*⸣*-i-šú* KÙ *liš-šá-kin-ma* ^{d}ALAD *na-ṣi-ru* DINGIR *mu-šal-li-mu*
190) *im-mu u mu-šá qé-reb-šú-un liš-*⸢*tab*⸣*-ru-ma a-a ip-par-ku-ú i-da-šú-un*
191) *qí-*⸢*bi*⸣*-*[*tuš-šu*] *mal*†*-*⸢*ku*⸣ *ba-nu-šú-un ši-bu-ta lil-lik lik-šu*†*-ud lit-tu-tu*
192) *a-na u$_4$-*⸢*mi da*⸣*-ru-ú-ti li-bur e-pi-su-un ina šap-ti-šu*
193) *el-le-tim li-ṣa-a a-ši-ib lib-bi-šú-un ina ṭu-ub* UZU.MEŠ
194) *nu-ug lìb-bi* ⸢*ù*⸣ [*na-mar*] *ka-bat-ti qé-reb-šú-un li-šá-li-la liš-ba-a bu-ʾa-a-ri*

186b–194) May the god [Aš]šur, the father of the gods, lo[ok] steadfastly upon (this) city that has been duly selected [by me] (lit.: "the choice of the steadfastness of [my] hea[rt]") [and] (upon) this palace with his holy, radiant face and may he ordain their renovation for future days. May (the following commands) come from (lit.: "be set in") his holy mouth: May the guardian spirit (and) the protective god (190) stay continually in them, day and night, and may they never leave them. [At his] comma[nd], may the ruler who constructed them live long (and) reach extreme old age. May their builder remain in good health forever. May (this command) issue from his (the god Aššur's) holy lips. May the one who dwells inside them rejoice there in physical well-being, merriment, and [hap]piness, (and) be fully satisfied with (his) good fortune.

8

This inscription is found on a series of wall slabs from the southwest end of Room XIV and Entrance p in the palace at Khorsabad. (A version of Sargon's Khorsabad Annals is found on other wall slabs in the room [text no. 4].) The number of lines of text on an individual slab with this inscription varies from twelve to eighteen. After the introduction with the king's titles and epithets, and the mention of his grant of special privileges to selected Babylonian and Assyrian cities (lines 1–5) and a summary description of his numerous military successes (lines 6–27a), the inscription describes the construction of the city Dūr-Šarrukīn, and in particular its palace and city wall (lines 27b–69a). The text then concludes with blessing and curse formulae (lines 69b–87). Since the text mentions the celebration held upon the completion of the city (lines 59b–69a), it must have been composed after that event, which took place in the second month of the king's sixteenth regnal year (706) according to the Assyrian Eponym Chronicle. The inscription is sometimes referred to as the Display Inscription of Room XIV (Die Prunkinschrift des Saales XIV), the Small Display Inscription (Die Kleine Prunkinschrift), the Small Summary Inscription, and the Annals of Room XIV. With regard to the reliefs on the slabs in the room, which are thought to depict events in the king's seventh regnal year (715), see Reade, Bagh. Mitt. 10 (1979) p. 84.

CATALOGUE

Section	Ex.	Source	Provenance	Lines Preserved	cpn
1	Bt	Botta, Monument de Ninive 4 pl. 159[c] bottom	Khorsabad, Palace, Room XIV, slab 3	1–13	n
	Wi	Winckler, Sar. 2 pl. 26 no. 56[c]			n
	Sq	Louvre squeeze			p
	BM	BM 115034 (47-7-2,41)			c
2	Bt	Botta, Monument de Ninive 4 pl. 160[c] top	Khorsabad, Palace, Room XIV, slab 5	14–27	n
	Wi	Winckler, Sar. 2 p. 27 no. 57[c]			n
	Sq	Louvre squeeze			p
	BM	47-7-2,46 + 47-7-2,51			c
3	Bt	Botta, Monument de Ninive 4 pl. 160[c] bottom	Khorsabad, Palace, Room XIV, slab 7	28–40	n
4	Bt	Botta, Monument de Ninive 4 pl. 161	Khorsabad, Palace, Room XIV, slab 9	41–52	n
5	Bt	Botta, Monument de Ninive 3 pl. 67[c]	Khorsabad, Palace, Entrance p, slab 4 (= p, montant 1)	53–69	n
	Wi	Winckler, Sar. 2 pl. 25 no. 53[c]			n
	Sq	Louvre squeeze			p
6	Bt	Botta, Monument de Ninive 3 pl. 68[c]	Khorsabad, Palace, Entrance p, slab 3 (= p, montant 2)	70–87	n
	Wi	Winckler, Sar. 2 pl. 25 no. 54[c]			
	Sq	Louvre squeeze			p

COMMENTARY

For a plan of Room XIV and Door p, see Figure 13, as well as Botta, Monument de Ninive 2 pl. 144; and Albenda, Palace of Sargon pl. 135; the latter two also have drawings of the reliefs on the relevant slabs. H. Winckler thought that all of the wall slabs in Room XIV preserved parts of only one inscription and edited them accordingly (Sar. 1 pp. 80–95). F.H. Weissbach (ZDMG 72 [1918] pp. 175–177) was the first to demonstrate that the slabs represented two different inscriptions (this text and text no. 4) and he divided the slabs correctly between the two.

Two fragments of this inscription are found in the British Museum: BM 115034 (47-7-2,41; 34.3×21.3 cm), which preserves a small part of the first slab (XIV,3; parts of lines 1–8, and a trace from line 9), and 47-7-2,46+51 (15×15 cm), which preserves a small part of the second slab (XIV,5; parts of lines 18–24 and traces of line 25). These pieces are part of the Hector collection in the British Museum and were apparently found by an English merchant in Baghdad by the name of Hector, who carried out some digging at Khorsabad, likely after P.E. Botta had finished work at the site in November 1844 and before A.H. Layard began work in November

1845 (see Reade in Fontan, Khorsabad pp. 121–122). The fragments have been collated in the British Museum and are also shown on BM photos 56549 and 56545. (Background information on these pieces was furnished by C.B.F. Walker.)

Botta indicates that he either collated his copies of the passages on five of the slabs (sections 1–3 and 5–6) from squeezes or from the originals. Squeezes of sections 1–2 and 5–6 are preserved in the Louvre and photographs of these squeezes have been examined. Some spot-checking of the original squeezes was also carried out. These squeezes are at times damaged or unclear and they do not always cover the whole section copied by Botta, in particular the edges. Winckler indicates that he examined squeezes of sections 1–2 and 5–6 when he made his copies of these; he also states that the right end of section 1 is not preserved on the squeeze. Since he could not collate sections 3–4, his copies of these sections (Sar. 2 pl. 29 nos. 61–62) are solely reliant upon Botta's copies and Winckler's personal judgment of what should have been on those sections, and therefore they provide no independent evidence of what was actually on those slabs.

It has been thought advisable to provide a score for this text on Oracc, with the sigla "Bt" (Botta, Monument de Ninive copy), "Wi" (Winckler, Sar. 2 copy), "Sq" (Louvre squeeze), and "BM" (original fragments in the British Museum) being used to denote the various sources of information. Since there are no squeezes or originals available for the text on wall slabs 7 and 9 of the room, the master line for that section (lines 28–52) is totally based on Botta's copies.

Unusually, the slabs with this inscription do not all have the same number of lines; they may have 12 (XIV,9), 13 (XIV,3 and XIV, 7), 14 (XIV,5), 17 (p,4), or 18 (p,3) lines each. The slabs in this room with a version of the Annals all have fifteen lines each (see text no. 4). Restorations are based primarily upon text nos. 9 and 43 and, for the most part, mirror those given by Weissbach.

BIBLIOGRAPHY

1849 Botta, Monument de Ninive 2 pl. 144 (provenance); and 3–4 pls. 67–68, 159 bottom, 160, and 161 (copy)

1876 Oppert, Records of the Past 7 pp. 21–56 (translation, combined with inscriptions in Rooms II, V, XIII)

1889 Winckler, Sar. 1 pp. 76–79 lines 441–460 (lines 68–87, edition), pp. 80–87 lines 1–27 (lines 1–27, edition), and 88–95 lines 65–89 (lines 28–52a, edition); and 2 pls. 25–27 and 29, nos. 53–54, 56–57, and 61–62 (copy)

1918 Weissbach, ZDMG 72 pp. 175–185 (edition)

1926 Ebeling in Gressmann, ATAT[2] p. 352 (lines 11b–17a, translation)

1927 Luckenbill, ARAB 2 pp. 39–45 §§76–90 (translation)

1958 Wiseman, DOTT pp. 61–62 (lines 11b–15, translation)

1964 Brinkman, Studies Oppenheim p. 44 no. 44.2.20.c.iii (study)

1969 Oppenheim, ANET[3] p. 285 (lines 11b–15, translation)

1976 Saporetti, Studi Ciprioti e Rapporti di Scavo 2 pp. 84–85 (lines 17b–18a, translation, study)

1982 Spieckermann, Juda unter Assur pp. 317–318 (lines 49b–53, edition)

1984 Borger, TUAT 1/4 p. 385 (lines 11b–17a, translation)

1986 Albenda, Palace of Sargon pp. 63, 92, and 149–150; and pls. 135–138 (drawing, study of reliefs, provenance)

1986 Renger, CRRA 32 pp. 112–113 and 120–122 (lines 1–5, 7–10, and 15, partial transcription, study)

1987 Engel, Dämonen pp. 47 and 142–150 (lines 37b–39a and 73b–75a, edition)

1990 Potts, Arabian Gulf 1 pp. 334–335 no. 4 (lines 18b–21a, translation)

1992 Becking, Fall of Samaria pp. 27–28 (line 15, edition)

1992 Hurowitz, Exalted House p. 72 (lines 27b–28a, edition; study)

1994 Fuchs, Khorsabad pp. 75–81 and 307–312 no. 2.2 (edition), and pp. 392–395 (study)

1999 Frame, Orientalia NS 68 pp. 52–53 (line 14, edition)

2000 Younger, COS 2 p. 297 no. 2.118F (lines 11b–18a, translation)

2001 Rollinger, Melammu 2 pp. 239 and 246 (lines 11–14, translation; line 15b, edition)

2006 Ponchia, SAAB 15 p. 233 (study)

2010 Barbato, Kaskal 7 pp. 178–179 (lines 27b–32a, translation, study)

2012 Worthington, Textual Criticism pp. 79, 179–180, 185, 195, 237, and 285 (study)

2014 Maniori, Campagne di Sargon p. 49 g1 and passim (study)

2017 Liverani, Assyria pp. 68, 83, 162, 168–169, and 205–206 (lines 26–31a, 39–53, translation)

2018 Frahm, Last Days pp. 80–81 no. 16 (line 15a, edition, study)

2019 Marchesi, JNES 78 p. 23 (lines 9b–10a, edition)

TEXT

1) É.GAL [m]LUGAL-GI.NA LUGAL GAL-*ú* LUGAL

1) Palace of Sargon, great king, strong king, king of

Section 1 = lines 1–13 = XIV,3:1–13.

1 M. Worthington (Textual Criticism p. 195) calls the unexpected nominative forms here (LUGAL GAL-*ú* LUGAL *dan-nu*) "honorific nominative[s]"; these occur in several texts of Sargon (e.g., text no. 7 line 1, text no. 10 lines 1–2, and text no. 44 line 2). H. Winckler's copy omits the unwanted *u* found on P.E. Botta's copy after *mi-gir*; however, as Winckler's own copy indicates, the squeeze seen by him did not cover that section of the line. Thus, he had no independent evidence as to whether or not the sign was actually on the original.

dan-nu LUGAL *kiš-šá-ti* LUGAL KUR *aš-šur*.KI GÌR.⸢NÍTA⸣ KÁ.DINGIR.RA.KI LUGAL KUR EME.GI$_{7}$ *ù* URI.⸢KI⸣ LUGAL *kib-rat* LÍMMU-*i mi-gir* <<*u*>> DINGIR.[MEŠ GAL.MEŠ]

2) ^{d}*aš-šur* ^{d}AG ^{d}AMAR.UTU DINGIR.MEŠ *ti-ik-le-ia* ⸢*šar*⸣*-ru-ut la šá-na-an ú-šat-li-mu-in-ni-ma zi-kir* MU-⸢*ia*⸣ [*dam*†]*-qu ú-še-ṣu-ú a-na* ⸢*re*⸣*-*[*še-e-ti*]

3) *ša* ZIMBIR.KI NIBRU.KI KÁ.DINGIR.RA.KI *ù bár-sipa*.KI *za-nin-us-su-un e-tep-pu-šá ša* ERIM.MEŠ ⸢*ki*⸣*-din-ni mal ba-šu-ú ḫi-bíl-ta-šu-nu* [*a-rib-ma*]

4) *ša* BÀD.AN.KI ÚRI*.KI UNUG*.KI *eridu*.KI ARARMA*.KI *kul-aba$_{4}$**.KI *ki-is-sik*.KI URU.*né-med-*⸢$^{d?}$*la*$^{?}$*-gu*$^{?}$*-da*$^{?}$⸣ [*šu-ba*]*-ra-šu-un áš-kun-ma ú-*[*šap-ši-ḫa*]

5) UN.MEŠ*-šú-un za-ku-ut bal-til*.KI *ù* URU.*ḫar-ra-na šá ul-tu u$_{4}$-me ul-lu-ú-ti* ⸢*im-ma*⸣*-*[*šu-ma ki-din*†]*-nu-us-su-un ba-ṭil-ta ú-ter* ⸢*áš*⸣*-*[*ru-uš-šá*]

6) *i-na tu-kul-ti* DINGIR.MEŠ GAL.MEŠ *lu at-tal-lak-ma* KUR.MEŠ *la ma-gi-ri ḫur-šá-a-ni la* ⸢*kan-šu*⸣*-ti a-na* GÌR.II*-ia ú-šak-ni-šá e-pu-šá* x [x x]

7) *ú-par-ri-ir el-lat* ^{md}*ḫum-ba-ni-*⸢*ga-áš*⸣ LÚ⸣.ELAM.MA.KI *ú-ab-*⸢*bit*⸣ KUR.*kar-al-lum* KUR.*šur-da* URU.*ki-še-si-im* URU.*ḫar-ḫar* KUR.*ma-da-a-a a-di pa-aṭ* [KUR.*bi-ik-ni*]

8) ⸢KUR⸣.*el-li-pi e-mì-du ni-ir* ^{d}*aš-šur* [*ú*]*-*⸢*šaḫ-rib*⸣ KUR.*ur-ar-*⸢*ṭu*⸣ *áš-*⸢*lul*⸣ URU.*mu-ṣa-ṣir áš-giš* KUR.*an-di-a* KUR.*zi-kir-tú* UN.MEŠ KUR.*man-na-a-a dal-ḫu*†*-*[*ú-te*]

9) *šu-bat ne-eḫ-tu ú-*⸢*še*⸣*-šib a-na-*⸢*ar*⸣ *mal*†*-ki* KUR.[*a*]*-*⸢*ma*⸣*-at-te* URU.⸢*gar*⸣*-ga-miš* URU.*kúm-mu-ḫi* ^{m}*gu-un-zi-na-nu* KUR.*kam-ma-nu-u-a iš-tu qé-reb* URU.*me-lid-*[*di*]

10) URU LUGAL*-ti-*⸢*šú*$^{?}$⸣ *as-*⸢*suḫ*⸣*-*[*ma*† UGU† *gi*†]*-*⸢*mir*⸣ KUR.MEŠ *šá-*⸢*ti*$^{?}$*-na*$^{?}$⸣ *áš-tak-ka-na*

the world, king of Assyria, governor of Babylon, king of the land of Sumer and Akkad, king of the four quarters (of the world), favorite of the [great] god[s].

2) The gods Aššur, Nabû, (and) Marduk, the gods, my helpers, granted me a reign without equal and exalted my [go]od reputation to the h[eights].

3–5) I continually acted as provider for (the cities) Sippar, Nippur, Babylon, and Borsippa (and) [I made restitution for] the wrongful damage suffered by the people of privileged status, as many as there were (of them); I (re)-established the [*šuba*]*rrû*-privileges of (the cities) Dēr, Ur, Uruk, Eridu, Larsa, Kullaba, Kissik, (and) Nēmed-L[ag]uda and [gave relief to] their people. I resto[red] the exemption (from obligations) of (the city) Baltil (Aššur) and the city Ḫarrān, which had fallen [into oblivion] in the distant past, [and] their [privil]eged status that had lapsed.

6–11a) With the support of the great gods, I regularly advanced and made uncompliant lands (and) insubmissive mountain regions bow down at my feet; I *made* [...]. I dispersed the forces of Ḫumbanigaš (Ḫumban-nikaš I), the Elamite. I destroyed the land Karalla, the land Šurda, the city Kišesim, the city Ḫarḫar, the land Media as far as the border of [Mount Bikni], (and) the land Ellipi, (and) imposed the yoke of the god Aššur (upon them). [I laid] waste to the land Urarṭu, plundered the city Muṣaṣir, slaughtered the lands Andia (and) Zikirtu, (and) allowed the distur[bed] people of the land Mannea to live in peace. I struck down the rulers of the land [Ha]math, the city [Ca]rchemish, (and) the city Kummuḫu. I depor[ted] Gunzinānu of the land Kammanu from the city Melid, (10) his royal city, [and] set officials [over all] *these* lands. I did away with the kingship of Tarḫu-lara of the city Marqasa (and) at the sa[me time] made the wide land Gurgu[m],

4 ÚRI*, UNUG*, ARARMA*, and *-aba$_{4}$**: The squeeze has ŠEŠ.MURUB$_{4}$, MURUB$_{4}$, UD.MURUB$_{4}$, and -MURUB$_{4}$ respectively. H. Winckler's copy has *-*^{d}⸢*la-gu*⸣*-da* [*an-du*]*-ra-šu-un*. Based upon text no. 14 line 9, one might expect *andurāršun* rather than *šubarrâšun*, but no AR is present on the squeeze after the RA. Or possibly [*an-du*]*-ra-*<*ar*>*-šu-un*.

6 H. Winckler's copy has *la pa-du-ti*, "merciless," rather than *la* ⸢*kan-šu*⸣*-ti*, "insubmissive," but the squeeze supports the latter reading. Possibly *e-pu-šá* ⸢*kiš*⸣*-*[*šu-tu*], "I exercised wo[rld dominion]," at the end of the line (Fuchs, Khorsabad p. 75), although this phrase is not otherwised attested in the inscriptions of Sargon II.

7–8 While it is clear that Karalla must go with *u'abbit*, "I destroyed," it is not clear if any or all of the immediately following places (Šurda, Kišesim, Ḫarḫar, Media, and Ellipi) should also go with that verb as opposed to being restricted to the following phrase *ēmidu nīr aššur*, "I imposed the yoke of the god Aššur" (see also text no. 13 lines 15–18 and text no. 104 Frgm. B lines 2–4). F.H. Weissbach and D.D. Luckenbill understand all the places except Ellipi to go with "I destroyed." A. Fuchs (Khorsabad p. 308 and n. 181) states that of all the cities mentioned in the passage only Karalla was really destroyed, as known from other texts; thus, he would prefer "I destroyed the land Karalla. I imposed the yoke of the god Aššur upon the land Šurda ... Ellipi." However, in a similar passage, text no. 116 line 16 omits the phrase about imposing the god's yoke, thus stating that Sargon destroyed all the places following "I destroyed." Note also text no. 84 line 13′ and text no. 103 ii 29–32 which replace the phrase about imposing the god's yoke with one about not leaving (alive) any of the people of the cities (*lā ēziba pirḫīšun/piri*[*'šunu*]); in the former case the presence of a *šá* before KUR.*ma-da-a-a* could indicate that only the Median land and Ellipi were to be connected with the second phrase. Line 7b: The squeeze supports H. Wincker's copy (against P.E. Botta's copy) that all three A signs in *ma-da-a-a a-di* were found on the text.

8 One expects *ēmid* rather than *ēmidu*. Possibly *dal-pa*$^{?}$*-*⸢*a*$^{?}$⸣*-*[*te*], "the troub[led] people of the land Mannea" (see text no. 65 line 61).

9 P.E. Botta's copy has KUR.[x]*-at-te* and H. Winckler's copy has KUR.*ḫa-at-te*, "the land Ḫatti," but the squeeze supports the reading KUR.[*a*]*-*⸢*ma*⸣*-at-te*.

10 H. Winckler's copy has *as-suḫ-ma* UGU *gi-mir* KUR.MEŠ *šá-ti-na* fully preserved.

LÚ.*šá-ak-nu-ti ú-nak-kir* LUGAL-*ti* ^{m}*tar-ḫu-la-ra* URU.*mar-qa-sa-a-a pa-aṭ gi-⸢mir⸣*

to (its) full extent, (part of) the terr[itory of Assy]ria.

11) KUR.*gúr-gu-[me]* DAGAL-*[tim] iš-⸢te⸣-[ni-iš]* ⸢*a*⸣-*na mi-[ṣir* KUR *aš]-⸢šur⸣*.KI *ú-ter-ra* ^{m}*ia-ma-ni* URU.*as-du-da-a-a* GIŠ.TUKUL.MEŠ-*ia e-dúr-ma* DAM-*su* DUMU.MEŠ-*šú* DUMU.MUNUS.MEŠ-*šú*
12) *e-zib-ma a-na i-te-e* KUR.⸢*mu-uṣ-ri*⸣ *šá pa-aṭ* KUR.⸢*me*⸣-*[luḫ]-⸢ḫa in⸣-na-bit-ma šar-ra-qiš ú-šib* UGU *gi-mir* KUR-*šú* DAGAL-*tim ù* UN.MEŠ-*šú šam-ḫa-a-ti* LÚ.*šu-ut* SAG†-*ia*
13) *a-na* LÚ.EN.NAM-*ti áš-kun-ma ša* ^{d}*aš-šur* LUGAL DINGIR.[MEŠ] *ú-rap-pi-šá ki-sur-ru-uš*
14) [LUGAL KUR].⸢*me*⸣-*luḫ-ḫa pul-ḫi me-lam-me šá* ^{d}*aš-šur* EN-*ia* ⸢*is*⸣-*ḫu-⸢pu⸣-šu-ma* ŠU *u* GÌR†.II *bi-re-tú* AN.BAR *id-du-šu-ma a-na qé-reb* KUR *aš-šur*.KI *a-di maḫ-ri-ia ú-še-bi-la-áš†-šú†*

11b–14) Iāmānī of the city Ashdod took fright at my weapons, abandoned his wife, his sons, (and) his daughters, fled to the (far) edge of Egypt, on the border with the land [M]e[luḫ]ḫa, and lived (there) stealthfully (lit.: "like a thief"). I set a eunuch of mine as provincial governor over all of his wide land and his prosperous people, and (thereby) expanded the territory of the god Aššur, the king of the god[s]. Fear of the brilliance of the god Aššur, my lord, overwhelmed [the king of the land M]eluḫḫa; they put iron fetters on his (Iāmāni's) hand(s) and feet and he (the king of Meluḫḫa) had him (Iāmāni) brought to Assyria (and) into my presence.

15) [*ù*$^{?}$] ⸢*áš*⸣-*lul* ⸢URU⸣.*ši-nu-uḫ-tú* URU.*sa-mir-i-na ù gi-mir* KUR.É-*ḫu-um-ri-a* LÚ.*ia-am-na-a-a ša* MURUB$_4$ *tam-tim e-reb* ^{d}UTU-*ši* GIM *nu-ú-ni a-bar-ma*
16) [*as*]-⸢*suḫ*⸣ KUR.*ka-as-ku* KUR.*ta-ba-lum* KUR.*ḫi-lak-ku aṭ-ru-ud* ^{m}*mi-ta-a* LUGAL KUR.*mu-us-ki ina* URU.*ra-pi-ḫi* BAD$_5$.BAD$_5$ KUR.*mu-ṣu-ri áš-kun-ma* ^{m}*ḫa-nu-nu*
17) [LUGAL URU].⸢*ḫa*⸣-*zi-ti šal-la-ti-iš* ⸢*am*⸣-*nu ú-šak-ni-iš* 7 LUGAL.MEŠ *ša* KUR.*ia-a' na-gi-i ša* KUR.*ia-ad-na-na ša ma-lak* 7 *u*$_4$-*mi i-na* ⸢*qa*⸣-*bal tam-tim e-reb* ^{d}UTU-*ši*

15–18a) [*Moreover*], I plundered the city Šinuḫtu, the city Samaria, and all of the land Bīt-Ḫumria (Israel). I caught the Ionians who (live in) the middle of the Western Sea like fish and [depo]rted (the people of) the lands Kasku, Tabal, (and) Ḫilakku. I drove out Mitâ (Midas), king of the land Musku. I brought about the defeat of Egypt at the city Raphia and counted Ḫanūnu (Ḫanno), [king of the city G]aza, as booty. I subjugated seven kings of the land Yā', a region of the land Yadnana (Cyprus) — whose abode [is situ]ated at a distance of seven days (journey) in the middle of the Western Sea.

18) [*šit-ku*]-*na-at šu-bat-sún ù* ^{md}AMAR.UTU-A-SUM.⸢NA LUGAL⸣ KUR.*kal-di a-šib ki-šad* ÍD.*mar-ra-ti ša ki-i la lìb-bi* DINGIR.MEŠ LUGAL-*ut* KÁ.DINGIR.RA.⸢KI *e*⸣-*pu-uš-ma ik-šu-[da*†*]* ⸢GAL⸣-[*tu*†]
19) [*qa-(a)-ti*] *gi-mir* KUR-*šú* DAGAL-*tim mal-ma-liš a-zu-uz-ma i-na* ŠU.II LÚ.*šu-ut* SAG.MEŠ-*ia* LÚ.GAR KUR KÁ.DINGIR.RA.KI *ù* LÚ.*šu-ut* SAG.MEŠ-*ia* LÚ.GAR KUR [LÚ$^{?}$].*gam-bu-li am-⸢nu⸣-[ma*†*]*

18b–20a) Moreover, [my] great [hand] conque[red] Marduk-apla-iddina (II) (Merodach-Baladan), king of Chaldea, who dwelt on the shore of the sea (and) who exercised kingship over Babylon against the will of the gods. I divided up all of his (Marduk-apla-iddina's) wide land into equal parts, assi[gned] (them) to the authority of a eunuch of mine, the governor of the land of Babylon, and a(nother) eunuch of mine, the governor of [the] Gambulu, [and I imposed] the yoke of the god Aššur (upon them).

20) [*e-mid*] *ni-ir* ^{d}*aš-šur* ^{m}*ú-pe-e-ri* LUGAL *dil-mun*.KI *ša ma-lak* 30 KASKAL.GÍD *ina* MURUB$_4$ *tam-tim* GIM *nu-ú-ni šit-ku-nu nar-ba-⸢ṣu*$^{?}$ *da⸣-[na]-an be-lu-ti-ia [iš-me-ma]*

20b–21a) Upēri, king of Dilmun, who(se) lair is situated at a distance of thirty leagues in the middle of the sea, like (that of) a fish, [heard] of my lordly mi[gh]t [and brought me] his audience gift.

21) [*iš-šá-a*] ⸢*ta*⸣-*mar-tuš i-na e-muq* ^{d}*aš-šur* ^{d}AG

21b–27a) With the strength of the gods Aššur, Nabû,

Section 2 = lines 14–27 = XIV,5:1–14.

14 ŠU *u*: We expect ŠU.II *u*; P.E. Botta's and H. Winckler's copies have ŠU *u* and ŠU.II *u* respectively, while the squeeze currently has ... ŠU (*x*) [...]. *id-du-šu-ma*: The squeeze supports Wincker's copy in indicating that the text has *id-du-šu-ma*, not the *id-du-šu* of Botta's copy. The ruler who sent Iāmānī back to Sargon was Šapataku' (Shebitko); see text no. 116 lines 20–21.

15 The squeeze indicates that there was room for one or two signs at the beginning of the line; see line 18 for one example of *ù* beginning a passage. In view of the mention of Samaria and Bīt-Ḫumria (Israel) here and of the known deportation of the "ten lost tribes of Israel," it is worth noting that the verb *ašlul*, translated here as "I plundered," can also mean "I carried off as booty/captives."

18 Instead of translating *ik-šu-[da]* as "defea[ted]" one might translate "captu[red]" (also text no. 7 lines 133–134 and text no. 74 vi 45–46). For differing accounts of what happened to Marduk-apla-iddina II, see the Introduction to this volume, under the section "Military Campaigns."

19 [*qa-(a)-ti*]: The restoration follows text no. 116 line 25; text no. 13 line 49 has *qa-as-su*; H. Winckler's copy has [ŠU.II-*ia*]. [LÚ$^{?}$].*gam-bu-li*: Winckler's copy has KUR.*gam-bu-li*, but nothing of the KUR was seen by Botta or is currently visible on the squeeze, where the spacing would seem to fit LÚ better than KUR; parallel passages (e.g., text no. 7 line 140 and text no. 87 line 11′) have LÚ here.

20 [*e-mid*]: H. Winckler's copy has [*e-mì-du*].

^{d}AMAR.UTU DINGIR.MEŠ GAL.MEŠ EN.MEŠ-*ia ša* GIŠ.TUKUL.MEŠ-*ia ú-šat-bu-ma ú-ra-si-*⸢*ba*⸣ *na-*[*gab*] ⸢*ga*⸣-[*re-ia*]
22) [*iš-tu* KUR].*ia-ad-na-na ša* MURUB$_4$ *tam-tim a-di pa-aṭ* KUR.*mu-ṣu-ri ù* KUR.*mu-us-*[*ki*] KUR.*kúm-*⸢*mu*⸣*-ḫa* URU.*me-lid-du* ⸢KUR⸣ MAR.TU.KI DAGAL-*tú* KUR.⸢*ḫat-ti*⸣ [*a-na si-ḫir-ti-šá*]
23) [*nap-ḫar* KUR].⸢*gu*⸣*-ti-um* KUR.*ma-da-a-a ru-qu-ti ša pa-aṭ* KUR.*bi-ik-ni* KUR.*ra-a-ši* [KUR].⸢*el*⸣-[*li*]-⸢*pi*⸣ *šá i-te-e* ⸢KUR⸣.ELAM.MA.KI LÚ.⸢*a*⸣-[*ri-me a-ši-ib a-aḫ* ÍD.IDIGNA]
24) [ÍD.*su*]-⸢*rap*⸣*-pi* ÍD.*uq-né-e a-di* LÚ.*su-ti-i* ERIM.MEŠ EDIN *šá* KUR.*ia-*[*ad-bu-ri ma-la*] *ba-*[*šu-ú ul-tu* URU$^{?}$.*sa-am-ʾu-ú-na a-di*]
25) [URU.*bu-bé*]-⸢*e*⸣ URU.DU$_6$-^{d}*ḫum-ba šá mi-ṣir* KUR.ELAM.MA.KI KUR.⸢*kár*⸣*-dun-ía*†-⸢*áš*⸣ *e-liš* [*ù šap-liš gi-mir* KUR.*kal-di mal ba-šu-ú* KUR.É-^{m}*ia-kin$_7$ ša ki-šad* ÍD.*mar-ra-ti*]
26) [*a-di pa-aṭ dil*]-*mun*.KI *ki-i iš-tén a-bél-ma a-na* [*mi*]-⸢*ṣir*⸣ [(KUR)] *aš-šur*.KI *ú-*[*ter* LÚ.*šu-ut* SAG.MEŠ-*ia* LÚ.EN.NAM.MEŠ UGU-*šú-nu áš-tak-kan-ma*]
27) [*ni-ir be-lu-ti*]-⸢*ia*$^{?}$⸣ *e-mid-su-nu-ti i-na u$_4$-me-šu-ma i-na te-*[*né-še-e-ti*] *na-*⸢*ki-ri*⸣ KA [...]

(and) Marduk, the great gods, my lords, who mobilized my weapons, I cut down a[ll my] f[oes. I ruled as if (they were) one (people) from the land] Yadnana (Cyprus), which is in the middle of the sea, as far as the border(s) of Egypt and the land Mus[ku], the land Kummuḫu, the city Melid, the wide land Amurru, the land Ḫatt[i (Syria) in its entirety, all of the land G]utium, the distant Medes (who live) on the border of Mount Bikni, the land Rāši (and) [the land E]l[lip]i on the border of the land Elam, the A[rameans who live beside the Tigris, Sur]appu, (and) Uqnû rivers, together with the Sutians, the people of the steppe of the land Ya[dburu, as many as] th[ere are, from the *city* Samʾūna, as far as (25) the city Bub]ê (and) the city Tīl-Ḫumba, which are on the border of the land Elam, the land Karduniaš (Babylonia) from one end [to the other (lit.: "above [and below]"), all of Chaldea, as much as there is (of it), the land Bīt-Yakīn, which is on the shore of the sea, as far as the border of Dil]mun, and I [made (them part of) the ter]ri[tory] of Assyria. [I set eunuchs of mine as provincial governors over them and] imposed [the yoke of m]y [lordship] upon them.

27b–28a) At that time, using (as laborers) enemy pe[ople *whom I had captured, whom the gods Aššur, Nabû, and Marduk had made bow down at my feet, and* who] (now) pull my yoke, (and) in accordance with [divine] will [(and) my heart's desire, I built a city] at the foot of Mount <M>uṣri, upstream from Nineveh, [and I na]med it [Dūr-Šarrukīn].

28) *i-šu-ṭu ab-šá*†*-ni i-na* GÌR.II KUR.<*mu*>*-uṣ-ri e-le-nu* NINA.KI *ki-i ṭè-em* [DINGIR-*ma i-na bi-bil lìb-bi-ia* URU *e-pu-uš-ma* URU.BÀD-^{m}MAN-GIN *az-ku*]-*ra ni-bit-su* GIŠ.[KIRI$_6$].MAḪ-*ḫu tam-*[*šil*]

28b–29a) [I created around it] a [botanical] garden, a repl[ica] of Mount Amanus, [in] which [were gathered] every kind of aromatic plant from the land Ḫatti (Syria) (and) every type of fruit-bearing mountain tree.

29) KUR.*ḫa*†*-ma-ni šá gi-mir*† ŠIM.MEŠ *ḫi-biš-ti* KUR.*ḫat-ti* GURUN† KUR-*i* DÙ†*-šú-un* [*qé-reb-šú ḫu-ur-ru-šu ab-ta-ni i-ta-tuš ša* 3 ME 50.ÀM *mal-ki la-bi-ru*]-*ti šá el*†*-la-mu-u-*⸢*a*⸣ [*be*]-*lut*† KUR *aš-šur*.[KI]
30) *e*†*-pu-*⸢*šu-ma*⸣ [*il*]-⸢*ta*⸣*-nap-pa*†*-ru ba-*[*ʾu-lat* ^{d}]⸢EN⸣.[LÍL *a-a*]-⸢*um*⸣*-ma ina lìb-bi-šú-nu a-*⸢*šar*⸣-[*šú ul ú-maš-ši-ma šu-šu-ub-šú ul il-ma-du ḫe-re-e* ÍD-*šú*] *ù za-qip ṣip-pa-ti lib-*[*bu*]-*uš ul* [*iz-kur*]

29b–31a) Not [o]ne of [the three hundred and fifty previo]us [rulers] who had exercised [lor]dship over Assyria before my time and had [go]verned the subj[ects of the god E]n[lil had noted its (the city's)] site [or come to know how to make it habitable]; nor [had one ordered] the digging of its canal] or the planting of orchards there. [Day (and) night I planned earnestly how to settle that city] (and) to have built [a great shrine — a cella] for the great gods — and palatial [halls to be my lordly abode], and I (then) ordered its construction.

31) [*a-na šu-šu-ub* URU *šá-a-šú*] *šu-pu-uš* [BÁRA.MAḪ-*ḫi at-ma-an*] DINGIR.MEŠ GAL.MEŠ *ù*† É.⸢GAL⸣.[MEŠ *šu-bat be-lu-ti-ia ur-ru mu-šu ak-pu-ud aṣ-rim-ma*] ⸢*e*⸣*-pe-su aq-bi i-na* ITI

31b–32a) In a favorable month, (on) an [auspicious] day — [in the month of the god Ku]lla, (on) the day of an *eššēšu*-festival [...] — I had (workmen) [wiel]d [ho]e(s) an[d make bricks].

27 Based upon text no. 14 lines 29–30, the translation assumes that the end of the line reads *ki-*[*šit-ti* ŠU.II-*ia ša* ^{d}*aš-šur* ^{d}AG *ù* ^{d}AMAR.UTU *a-na* GÌR.II-*ia ú-šak-ni-šú-ma*].
Section 3 = lines 28–40 = XIV,7:1–13.
28 Probably the original had KUR.[*mu*]*-uṣ-ri*, as indicated on H. Winckler's copy (Sar. 2 pl. 29 no. 61); however, P.E. Botta's copy indicates no damage at this point and Winckler was not able to consult a squeeze for this section when making his copy.
30 Instead of restoring *il-ma-du* (following text no. 9 line 46), possibly restore *i-de-ma* (following text no. 43 line 46).

še-mé†-[(x-x)]-e ⸢u$_4$⸣-[mu]

32) [mit-ga-ri i-na ITI ^{d}]⸢kulla⸣ UD†.⸢ÈŠ⸣.ÈŠ† [(x)] NI [x x GIŠ.al]-lum ⸢ú⸣-[šat-ri]-⸢ik†-ma ú⸣-[šal-bi-na li-bit-tu i-na ITI.NE a-ra-aḫ mu]-⸢kin⸣ te-me-en URU ù É ša [(x x x)] gi-[mir]

33) [ṣal-mat SAG.DU a-na ri-mì]-ti-ši-[na i-pat-ti-qa] ⸢ṣu⸣-lu-⸢lu⸣ e-li KÙ†.⸢GI⸣ [KÙ.BABBAR] URUDU ni-[siq-ti NA$_4$].MEŠ [ḫi-bi-iš-ti KUR.ḫa-ma-ni pe-el-šú] ú-šat-⸢ri⸣-[ṣa] uš-še-šú ad-di-⸢ma⸣ [(x x)] ⸢ú⸣-[kin]

34) [lib-na-as-su pa-rak-ki ra-áš-bu-ti ša ki-ma ki-ṣir gi-né-e] šur-šu-du [a-na ^{d}é-[a] ^{d}[30 ^{d}nin-gal ^{d}]UTU ^{d}[AG ^{d}IŠKUR ^{d}MAŠ ù ḫi]-⸢ra†⸣-ti-šú-nu GAL.MEŠ ú-še-pi-šá [qer]-bu-[uš-šú]

35) [É.GAL.MEŠ ZÚ AM.SI GIŠ.ESI GIŠ.TÚG GIŠ.mu-suk-kan-ni GIŠ].⸢ere⸣-IGI GIŠ.ŠUR.MÌN GIŠ.dup-ra-⸢ni⸣ [GIŠ].⸢ŠIM†⸣.[LI u GIŠ.bu-uṭ-ni i-na qí-bi-ti-šú-nu ṣir-ti a-na mu-šab šar-ru-ti-ia] ab-ni-⸢ma⸣ GIŠ.ÙR.MEŠ GIŠ.ere-[IGI] ⸢GAL⸣.[MEŠ]

36) [e-li-šin ú-šat-ri-ṣa GIŠ.IG.MEŠ GIŠ.ŠUR.MÌN GIŠ.mu-suk-kan-ni] mé-se†-er† ⸢URUDU nam⸣-ri† ⸢ú⸣-[rak]-kis†-ma ú†-[rat-ta-a] né-[reb-šin É ap-pa-a-ti tam-šil É.GAL KUR].ḫat-ti šá i-na li-šá-an [KUR MAR].TU.[KI]

37) [É ḫi-la-ni i-šá-as-su-šú ú-še-pi-šá mé-eḫ-ret] KÁ.MEŠ-ši-⸢in⸣ 8 UR.⸢MAḪ⸣.[MEŠ tu]-ʾa-me šu-ut 1 ŠÁR GÉŠ.U 6 UŠ 50.[ÀM GUN mal-tak-ti URUDU nam]-ri šá ina ši-[pir] ^{d}nin-á-⸢gal⸣ [ip]-⸢pat-qu⸣-[ma]

38) [ma-lu-ú nam-ri-ri 4 tim-me GIŠ.ere-IGI šu-ta]-ḫu-ti ša [1 NINDA].TA.⸢ÀM⸣ [ku-bur-šu]-⸢un†⸣ bi-ib-lat KUR.ḫa-ma-ni UGU [ur-maḫ-ḫe-e ú-kin-ma dáp]-⸢pi⸣ [ku-lul] KÁ.MEŠ-ši-in [(x x)] e-[mid]

39) [UDU.MEŠ šad-di ^{d}LAMMA MAḪ.MEŠ šá NA$_4$ KUR-i eš]-qí nak-liš ab-ni-ma a-na er-bet-ti šá†-[a]-ri ú-šá-aṣ†-bi-ta SI.GAR-ši-⸢in⸣ [as-kup-pi NA$_4$.pi]-li GAL.MEŠ da-ád†-me [ki]-šit-[ti]

40) [qa-ti-ia ṣe-ru-uš-šin ab-šim-ma] ⸢a⸣-sur-ru†-šin [ú]-šá-as†-ḫi-ra [a-na tab]-⸢ra†⸣-a-ti ú†-šá-lik ŠÁR ŠÁR ŠÁR ŠÁR GÉŠ.U GÉŠ.U GÉŠ.U [1 UŠ 1 1/2 NINDA 2 KÙŠ mi-še]-⸢eḫ⸣-ti BÀD-šú áš-kun-ma ⸢UGU⸣ [NA$_4$] KUR-[i]

41) [zaq-ri ú-šar-ši-da] te-[em-me-en-šú i-na re-e-ši

32b–34a) [In the month of Abu (V) — the month for the one who lay]s the foundation of citi(es) and house(s) (and in) which a[ll the black-headed people construct] shelter(s) [for] the[ir dwelli]ng(s) — I plac[ed its limestone masonry] on top of (foundation deposits of) gold, [silver], copper, pre[cious stone]s, (and) [pieces (of aromatic woods) from Mount Amanus]. I laid its foundations and [established its brickwork].

34b) I had built [ins]ide [it (the city) for] the gods E[a, Sîn, Ningal], Šamaš, [Nabû, Adad, Ninurta, and] their great [spou]ses [awe-inspiring daises which] were made as firm [as the mountains].

35–37a) [At their august command], I built [palatial halls using (lit.: "of") elephant ivory, ebony, boxwood, *musukkannu*-wood, ce]dar, cypress, *daprānu*-juniper, [juniper, and terebinth to be my royal residence and I roofed them] with large ce[dar] beams. I [bou]nd [the doors of cypress (and) *musukkannu*-wood] with band(s) of [shi]ning [cop]per and [installed (them in) their] entr[ance(s). I had built in front of] their gates [a portico (*bīt appāti*), a replica of a] Hittite [palace], which [is called a *bīt ḫilāni*] in the language of the land [Amur]ru.

37b–40a) Eight [tw]in lion (colossi) [of shin]ing [copper] that weigh 4,610 [full (lit.: "tested") talents] (and) that [were c]ast by the cr[aft] of the god Ninaga[l and filled with radiance — upon (those) [lion colossi] I installed four mat]ching [cedar columns], whose [diameter(s) are one *nindanu*] each, the product of Mount Amanus; and] I [positioned cross]-beams (upon them) [as a cornice] for their gates. I skillfully fashioned [magnificent mountain sheep colossi of mass]ive [mountain stone] and in the four directions I had (them) hold their (the gates') door bolt(s). [I depicted] the settlements that [I had con]quer[ed upon] large lime[stone slabs and] surrounded their (the palatial halls') lower courses (with them). I made (them) [an object of wo]nder.

40b–49a) I made [the leng]th of its wall 16,2[80 cubits] and [I made its] fo[undation secure] u[pon (blocks of) massive] mountain [stone. In front (and) in ba]ck, on both sides, [facing the four directions, I opened] eight [gates (in the city wall). I named the gate(s) of the gods Šamaš and Adad that face the east "The God Šamaš

32 Based upon text no. 43 line 59, one would expect "an *eššešu*-festival for the god Nabû" or "an *eššešu*-festival for the son of the god Bēl"; however, the traces following do not appear to support either reading.

33 The passage "[construct] shelter(s) (in the fields) [for] the[ir dwelli]ng(s)" presumably refers to the erection of temporary shelters for protection against the summer sun.

34 Possibly restore *pa-rak-ki ra-áš-du-ti*, "firmly-founded daises" (following text no. 43 line 62), instead of *pa-rak-ki ra-áš-bu-ti*, "awe-inspiring daises" (following text no. 9 line 57).

39 With regard to UDU.MEŠ *šad-di* ^{d}LAMMA MAḪ.MEŠ, "mountain sheep colossi," see the note to text no. 2 line 479.

40 The restoration of the number follows text no. 9 lines 79–80; see the on-page note to text no. 9 lines 79–80.

Section 4 = lines 41–52 = XIV,5:1–12.

(ù) *ar]-ka-a-ti ina ṣe-li ki-[lal]-la-an*
42) [*mé-eḫ-ret* 4 IM.MEŠ] 8 [KÁ.GAL.MEŠ *ap-te-e-ma* ^{d}UTU *mu-šak-šid er]-nit-ti-ia* ^{d}IŠKUR *mu-kin* ḪÉ.GÁL-*ia*
43) [*šu-mu* KÁ.GAL ^{d}UTU *ù* ^{d}IŠKUR *ša* IGI-*et* IM.KUR.RA *az-kur* ^{d}]EN.LÍL *mu-kin iš-di* URU-*ia*
44) [^{d}NIN.LÍL *mu-di-šá-at ḫi-iṣ-bi zík-ri* KÁ.GAL ^{d}BAD *ù* ^{d}NIN.LÍL *ša*] ⸢IGI⸣-*et* IM†.SI.SÁ *am-bi*
45) [^{d}*a-nu mu-šal-lim ep-šet qa-ti-ia* ^{d}*iš-tar mu-šam-me-ḫa-at* UN].MEŠ-*šú ni*-[*bit* KÁ.GAL] ^{d}*a-nim*
46) [*ù* ^{d}*iš-tar ša* IGI-*et* IM.MAR].TU [*áš-kun* ^{d}*é-a muš-te-šir nag-bi-šú* ^{d}*be-let*-DINGIR.MEŠ] *mu-[rap]-pi-šat*
47) [*ta-lit-ti-šú šu-mu*] ⸢KÁ.GAL⸣ [^{d}]*é-[a ù* ^{d}*be-let*-DINGIR.MEŠ *šá* IGI-*et* IM.U$_{18}$.LU *aq-bi-ma* ^{d}*aš-šur*] ⸢*mu*⸣-*šal-bir*
48) [*pa-le-e* LUGAL *e-pi*]-⸢*ši-šu*⸣ *na-ṣir* [*um-ma-ni-šu* BÀD-*šú* ^{d}*nin-urta mu-kin te-me-en a-li-šu a-na la-bar*] UD†.⸢MEŠ⸣

Is the One Who Makes] Me [Triu]mph" (and) "The God Adad Is the One Who Establishes My Prosperity" (respectively). I called [the gate(s) of the god Enlil and the goddess Mullissu that fa]ce the north "[The God] Enlil Is the One Who Establishes the Foundation of My City" (and) ["The Goddess Mullissu Is the One Who Restores Abundance" (respectively). I made] the na[me(s) of the gate(s)] of the god Anu [and the goddess Ištar that face the we]st (45) ["The God Anu Is the One Who Makes My Undertakings Successful" (and) "The Goddess Ištar Is the One Who Makes] Its [People Flourish" (respectively). I pronounced the names of the] gate(s) [of the god] E[a and the goddess Bēlet-ilī that face the south (to be) "The God Ea Is the One Who Keeps Its Spring(s) in Good Order" (and) "The Goddess Bēlet-Ilī] Is the One Who [Incr]eases [Its (Animals') Offspring" (respectively). Its (city) wall was (called) "The God Aššur Is the One] Who Prolongs [the Reign of] Its [Royal Build]er (and) Protects [His Troops]." Its [outer] wall was (called) ["The God Ninurta Is the One Who Establishes the Foundation of His City for (All)] Days to Come."

49) [*ru-qu-ú-ti šal*]-⸢*ḫu*⸣-*ú*†-*šu ba-ʾu-[lat ar-ba-ʾi li-šá-nu a-ḫi-tu at-me-e la mit-ḫur-ti*]
50) [*a-ši-bu-ut* KUR-*i*] *ù ma-ti ma-la* [*ir-te-ʾu-u* ZÁLAG DINGIR.MEŠ EN *gim-ri ša i-na zi-kir* ^{d}*aš-šur* EN-*ia*]
51) [*ina me-tel ši-bir-ri-ia áš-lu*]-⸢*la*†⸣ *pa*†-*a*† [1-*en*] *ú-[šá-áš-kin-ma ú-šar-ma-a qé-reb-šú*]
52) [DUMU.MEŠ] KUR *aš-šur*.KI [*mu-du-ut i-ni*] *ka-[la-ma a-na šu-ḫu-uz ṣi-bit-ti pa-laḫ* DINGIR *ù* LUGAL]
53) [LÚ].*ak*-⸢*li* LÚ⸣.[*šá*]-⸢*pi*⸣-*ru-tum ú-ma-ʾe-er-šú-nu-ti*
54) ⸢*ul*?⸣-*tu ši-pir* URU-*šú*-⸢*nu*⸣ [(*u*)] ⸢É⸣.GAL-*ia ú-qat-tu-ú* ^{d}*aš-šur*
55) [AD] DINGIR.MEŠ *be-lum* GAL-*ú* DINGIR.MEŠ *u* ^{d}*iš-ta-ri a-ši-bu-ut*
56) [KUR *aš*]-⸢*šur*⸣.KI *ina* ⸢*qer*⸣-*bi-šá aq-re* IGI.SÁ-*e šad-lu-ti*
57) [*ta*]-⸢*mar*⸣-*tu ka-bit-tu kàd*†-*re-e la nar-ba-a-ti*
58) [*ú*]-⸢*šam*⸣-*ḫir**-*šú-nu-ti-ma* UDU.SISKUR.MEŠ ŠÀ.IGI.GURU$_{6}$-*e* KÙ.MEŠ

49b–53) Peop[le from the four (quarters of the world), (speaking) foreign language(s) (and of) diverse speech, those who had dwelt in (both) mountain(s)] and (low)land(s), as many as [the "Light of the Gods" (Šamaš), the lord of all, shepherded, whom I had carr]ied off [as booty by the power of my staff at the command of the god Aššur, my lord], I [made act] in con[cert and I (re)settled (them) inside it (the city)]. I commissioned [native] Assyria[ns, masters of] ev[ery craft, as] over[seers (and) comm]anders [to instruct (the settlers) in correct behavior (and how) to revere god and king].

54–59a) [Af]ter I had completed work on their city [(and)] my palace, I invited the god Aššur, [the father of the] gods, the great lord, (and) the (other) gods and goddesses who dwell [in Assy]ria (to come) inside it. [I] offered them (the gods) extensive presents, substantial [audi]ence gift(s), (and) innumerable gifts, and I offered [befor]e them sacrifices as pure voluntary offerings.

42–47 With regard to the city gates, and in particular those on the northern side of the city, see the section on Sargon's building activities at Khorsabad in the Introduction to this volume.

42 -*mu-kin*- "Establishes": See the on-page note to text no. 9 line 83.

47 ⸢*mu*⸣-*šal-bir* "Who Prolongs": See the on-page note to text no. 9 line 90.

48 With regard to the restorations *um-ma-ni-šu* "His Troops" and *a-li-šu* "His City," see the on-page note to text no. 9 line 91.

51 [*áš-lu*]-⸢*la*†⸣ *pa*†-*a*†: The reading is based on text no. 9 lines 94–95; P.E. Botta's copy has [...] UD AM. Instead of *me-tel*, "power," possibly *me-zez*, "fury"; see CAD M/2 pp. 43 and 46.

52 *a-na šu-ḫu-uz ṣi-bit-ti pa-laḫ* DINGIR *ù* LUGAL "to instruct (the settlers) in correct behavior (and how) to revere god and king": A less literal translation would be "to instruct (the settlers) in (their) correct behavior (and) reverence toward god and king."

Section 5 = lines 53–69 = p,4:1–16.

53 Text no. 9 line 97 and text no. 43 line 74 have LÚ.*šá-pi-ri* after LÚ.*ak-li* in similar passages (cf. also text no. 7 line 178 and other texts of Sargon). There is not sufficient room to allow the reading [LÚ].*ak*-⸢*li* LÚ⸣.[*šá-pi-ri mu-ma*]-⸢*ʾe*⸣-*ru-tum* suggested by H. Spieckermann (Juda unter Assur p. 318).

55 H. Winckler's copy omits the *u* after DINGIR.MEŠ, but the squeeze confirms its presence.

58 -*ḫir**-: The squeeze has- SAR-.

59) [*ma*]-⸢*ḫar*⸣-*šu-un aq-qí it-ti mal-ki kib-rat* LÍMMU-*i*
60) LÚ.EN.NAM.MEŠ KUR-*ia* LÚ.NUN.MEŠ LÚ.*šu-ut* SAG.MEŠ
61) ⸢*ù*⸣ LÚ.AB.BA.MEŠ KUR *aš-šur*.KI *ina qé-reb* É.GAL-*ia*
62) *ú-šib-ma áš-ta-kan ni-gu-tu* KÙ.GI KÙ.BABBAR *ú-nu-ut*
63) KÙ.GI KÙ.⸢BABBAR⸣ NA$_4$.MEŠ *a-qar-tú* URUDU AN.BAR *lu-bul-ti bir-me*
64) TÚG.GADA SÍG.*ta-kil-tu* SÍG.*ar-ga-ma-nu gu-uḫ-lum*
65) KUŠ AM.SI ZÚ AM.SI GIŠ.ESI GIŠ.TÚG *mim-ma aq-ru*
66) *ni-ṣir-ti* LUGAL-⸢*ti*⸣ ANŠE.KUR.RA.MEŠ KUR.*mu*-⸢*uṣ*⸣-*ri*
67) *ṣi-mit-ti ni-i-ri* ⸢GAL⸣.MEŠ ANŠE.KUNGA.MEŠ ANŠE.MEŠ
68) ANŠE.⸢A$^{?}$.AB$^{?}$.BA$^{?}$.MEŠ$^{?}$ GU$_4$$^{?}$⸣.MEŠ ⸢*ṣe-e-ni*$^{?}$⸣ *x* [*x ma*†]-*da-ta-šú-nu*

59b–69a) With rulers from the four quarters (of the world), provincial governors of my land, nobles, eunuchs, and elders of Assyria, I sat down inside my palace and held a festival. I received as their substantial [tr]ibute gold, silver, utensils of gold (and) silver, valuable stones, *copper*, iron, garments with multi-colored trim, (and) linen garments, blue-purple wool, red-purple wool, antimony, (65) elephant hides, elephant ivory, ebony, boxwood, everything valuable, royal treasure, large horses from Egypt trained to the yoke, mules, donkeys, *camels, oxen*, (and) sheep and goats, [...].

69) *ka-bit-tum am-ḫur* URU *u* É.GAL ⸢*šá*$^{?}$⸣-*a*-⸢*tu i*$^{?}$-*tu*⸣-*ut*
70) *kun lìb-bi-ia* ^{d}*aš-šur* AD DINGIR.MEŠ *i-na nu-um-mur*
71) *bu-ni-šú* KÙ.MEŠ *ki-niš lip-pa-lis-ma a-na u*$_4$-*me ru-qu-ti*
72) *liq-ba-a a-šab-šú-un i-na pi-i-šú el-li*
73) *liš*-⸢*šá*⸣-*kín-ma* ^{d}ALAD *na-ṣi-ru* DINGIR *mu-šal-li-mu im-mu*
74) *ù mu-šu qé-reb-šú-un liš-tab-ru-ma a-a ip-par*-⸢*ku*⸣-*ú*
75) *i-da-šú-un qí-bi*-⸢*tuš*⸣-*šu mal-ku ba-nu-šú-un ši-bu-tam lil-lik*
76) ⸢*lik*⸣-*šu-ud-da lit-tú-tu a-na u*$_4$-*me da-ru-ti li-bur*
77) *e-pi-su-un ia-a-ti* ^{m}LUGAL-GI.NA *a-šib qé-reb* É.GAL
78) *šá-a-šá ba-laṭ* ZI-*tì u*$_4$-*me ru-qu-ú-ti* ⸢*ṭu*⸣-*ub* UZU
79) *ḫu-ud lìb-bi* ⸢*ù na-mar*⸣ *ka-bat-ti li-šim ši-ma-ti*
80) *i-na šap-ti-šú el-le*-⸢*ti*⸣ *li-ṣa-a* NÍG.⸢ŠU$^{?}$⸣.MEŠ *na*-⸢*ki*$^{?}$-*ri*$^{?}$⸣
81) *šad-lu-ti* IGI.SÁ-*e da-ád-me nu-ḫuš kib*-⸢*rat*⸣ *ḫi-ṣib* KUR-*i*

69b–81a) May the god Aššur, the father of the gods, look steadfastly upon (this) city and this palace that have been du[ly] selected by me (lit.: "the choice of the steadfastness of my heart") with his holy, radiant face and may he ordain that it be inhabited for future days. May (the following commands) come from (lit.: "be set in") his holy mouth: May the guardian spirit (and) the protective god stay continually in them, day and night, and may they never leave (75) them. At his command, may the ruler who constructed them live long (and) reach extreme old age. May their builder remain in good health forever. (As for) me, Sargon, the one who dwells inside this palace, may he (the god Aššur) determine as my fate good health, a long life (lit.: "distant days"), physical well-being, joy of heart, and happiness. (80) May (the following command) issue from his holy lips. May I store up inside it (the city) extensive property (taken) from the enemy, presents from (every) settlement, the yield of the (four) quarters (of the world), (and) the wealth of (both) the mountain(s) and the seas.

82) *ù* A.AB.BA.MEŠ *la-aq-ru-na qé-reb-šá a-na ar*-⸢*kàt*⸣

82b–85) In days to come, may a future ruler among the kings, my descendants, renovate (any) dilapidated

---

63 NA$_4$.MEŠ *a-qar-tú*: For the use of MEŠ to mark a sumerogram, as opposed to the plural, see Worthington, Textual Criticism pp. 284–287; he also cites three other examples in text no. 65 (lines 189, 219, and 274).
68 Collation of the squeeze indicates that H. Winckler's copy of the first part of the line, which has ANŠE.A.AB.BA.MEŠ GU$_4$.MEŠ *ṣe-e-ni*, "camels, oxen, (and) sheep and goats," is likely, but not certain.
69 For the end of the line, H. Winckler's copy has *šá-a-tu* [*x*]-*tu-ut*.
Section 6 = lines 70–87 = p,3:1–18.
75 Or *ši-bu-tú*, but, as noted by A. Fuchs (Khorsabad p. 81), text no. 7 line 191 and text no. 13 line 142 have *ši-bu-ta* in similar passages.
80 For the end of the line P.E. Botta's copy has NÍG.[*x*].MEŠ NA [*x*] and H. Winckler's copy has NÍG.ŠU [*x*].MEŠ NA *x*, where the final traces suggest ⸢KU-*ri*⸣ written close together and thus possibly ⸢*ki*$^{!?}$-*ri*⸣. This passage has generally been read NÍG.[ŠU KUR].MEŠ *na*-[*ki-ri*], "prop[erty from the land]s of ... en[emies]"; see Weissbach, ZDMG 72 (1918) p. 184 and Fuchs, Khorsabad p. 81 (who also refers to text no. 2 line 504, a very poorly preserved passage). The squeeze suggests that there was only one sign (possibly ŠU) between NÍG and MEŠ. The traces after NA on the squeeze are not clear, but are not incompatible with KI-RI written closely together. Cf. also text no. 65 line 178.

83) *u$_4$-me* NUN *ar-ku-ú ina* LUGAL.MEŠ-*ni* DUMU.MEŠ-*ia an-ḫu-ut* É.⸢GAL⸣
84) ⸢*šá-a-šú*⸣ *lu-ud-diš* MU.SAR-*a-a* ⸢*li*⸣*-mur-ma* Ì.GIŠ *lip-šu-uš ni-qa-a*
85) *liq-qí a-na áš-ri-šú lu-ter* ^{d}*aš-šur ik-ri-bi-šú i-še-em-me*

sections of this palace. May he (then) discover my inscribed object, anoint (it) with oil, offer a sacrifice, (and) return (it) to its (original) place. The god Aššur will (then) listen to his prayers.

86) *mu-nak-kir šiṭ-ri-ia ù* MU-*ia* ^{d}*aš-šur* ⸢*be*⸣*-lí* LUGAL-*su lis-kip*
87) MU-*šú* NUMUN-*šú i-na* KUR *li-ḫal-liq-*⸢*ma*⸣ *a-a ir-ši-šú re-e-mu*

86–87) (As for) the one who alters my inscription or my name, may the god Aššur, my lord, overthrow his kingship. May he (the god Aššur) make his name (and) his descendant(s) disappear from the land and may he not have pity on him.

9

Numerous bull colossi from Khorsabad bear an inscription recording the construction of that city by Sargon II. In most cases the inscription is found split between two bulls, one bull placed on either side of the same doorway, but the two bulls (exs. 4–5) from Entrance M (the middle doorway leading from the northeast terrace at the back of the palace into Room VIII) each appears to have had (at least originally) the full inscription. After a brief section giving the ruler's titles and epithets (lines 1–5a) and mentioning the various Babylonian and Assyrian cities to which he had granted special privileges (lines 5b–10), the inscription gives a summary of his conquests, arranged in a geographical rather than chronological sequence (lines 11–39a). It then describes at length the construction of the new city Dūr-Šarrūkīn, and in particular its palace and city wall (lines 39b–97a), and records a celebration that took place when the gods came to the city in the seventh month of 707 (lines 97b–99a) and the king's receiving gifts from various (vassal) rulers (lines 99b–100), which occurred during the festival when the city was inaugurated in the second month of Sargon's sixteenth regnal year (706). The inscripton ends with a brief section giving blessings and curses (lines 101–106). With regard to bull inscriptions in Sargon's palace and in Assyria in general, see J.M. Russell, Writing on the Wall pp. 103–108 and Senn.'s Palace pp. 10–16.

CATALOGUE

Ex.	Museum Number	Provenance	Lines Preserved	Botta, MdN	Louvre Squeeze	cpn
1	AO 19857 (N 8032; Nap. III 2856)	Khorsabad, Palace, SW side of Entrance k (k,2)	1–52	3 pls. 48^{c}–49^{c}	yes, yes	c, c
2	AO 19858 (N 8033; Nap. III 2857)	Khorsabad, Palace, NE side of Entrance k (k,1)	53–106	3 pls. 50^{c}–51^{c}	yes, no	c, c
3	—	Khorsabad, Palace, NW side of Entrance F (F,1)	55–106	3 pls. 22^{c}–23^{c}	yes, yes	p, p
4	—	Khorsabad, Palace, NW side of Entrance M (M,1)	15–106	3 pls. 24^{c}–25^{c}	yes, yes	p, p
5	—	Khorsabad, Palace, SE side of Entrance M (M,2)	1–106	3 pls. 26^{c}–27^{c}	yes, yes	p, p
6	—	Khorsabad, Palace, NE side of Entrance c (c,2)	1–53	3 pls. 28^{c}–29^{c}	yes, yes	p, p

7	—	Khorsabad, Palace, SW side of Entrance c (c,1)	54–106	3 pls. 30^{c}–31^{c}	yes, yes	p, p
8	—	Khorsabad, Palace, NE side of Entrance d (d,2)	1–53a	3 pls. 32^{c}–33^{c}	no, no	n, n
9	—	Khorsabad, Palace, SW side of Entrance d (d,1)	53b–106	3 pls. 34^{c}–35^{c}	no, no	n, n
10	Erm 3946 and 3947	Khorsabad, Palace, Entrance f (f,1)	1–54a	3 pls. 36^{c}–37^{c}	yes, yes	p, p
11	Museo Gregoriano Egizio (Vatican) 15027 and —	Khorsabad, Palace, Entrance f (f,2)	54b–106	3 pls. 38^{c}–39^{c}	yes, yes	p, p
12	—	Khorsabad, Palace, NE side of Entrance g (g,1)	1–44a	3 pls. 40^{c}–41^{c}	no, yes	n, p
13	—	Khorsabad, Palace, SW side of Entrance g (g,2)	44b–106	3 pls. 42^{c}–43^{c}	yes, yes	p, p
14	— and Erm 3949	Khorsabad, Palace, NW side of Entrance j (j,2)	1–48a	3 pls. 44^{c}–45^{c}	yes, yes	p, p
15	Erm 3948 and Museo Gregoriano Egizio (Vatican) 15028 + Museo Archeologico di Genova 532 (+) LB 1309 (+) a piece formerly in the Convent of Les Dames de Sion (Jerusalem)	Khorsabad, Palace, SE side of Entrance j (j,1)	48b–106	3 pls. 46^{c}–47^{c}	yes, no	p, p
16	—	Khorsabad, Palace, Entrance δ (δ,1)	1–35	3 pl. 52	no	n
17	—	Khorsabad, Palace, Entrance δ (δ,2)	82–101	3 pl. 53	no	n
18	—	Khorsabad, Palace, Façade N, 10	1–50	3 pls. 54^{c}–55^{c}	yes, yes	p, p
19	—	Khorsabad, Palace, Façade N, 9	51–106	3 pls. 56^{c}–57^{c}	yes, yes	p, p
20	—	Khorsabad, Palace, Façade N, 18	1–48	3 pls. 58^{c}–59^{c}	yes, yes	p, p
21	—	Khorsabad, Palace, Façade N, 17	49–106	3 pls. 60^{c}–61^{c}	yes, yes	p, p
22	—	Khorsabad, Palace, Façade n, 47	1–29	3 pl. 62	no	n
23	A 7369	Khorsabad, Palace, Façade n, 45	47–106	—	no	c
24	BM 118809 (50-12-28,4)	Khorsabad, Left side of an inner gate (probably gate B of inner city wall)	illegible	—	no	n
25	BM 118808 (50-12-28,3)	Khorsabad, Right side of an inner gate (probably gate B of inner city wall)	55–106	—	no	c, c
26	Museo delle Antichità Egizie (Turin) P.2054	Khorsabad	9, 11–12	—	no	p
27	AO 19859 (Nap. III 2858)	Khorsabad, Right side of inner entrance in city gate 3	57b–106	—	no	c
28	AO 23012	Khorsabad	90b–106	—	no	p
29	Archbishop's palace (Florence)	As ex. 26	12–14	—	no	p
30	Archbishop's palace (Florence)	As ex. 26	35–37	—	no	p
31	MAH 0.22	As ex. 26	43–45	—	no	c

COMMENTARY

Each bull had two rectangular inscribed panels, one below the bull's belly and the other between its two hind legs. Two bulls were normally required for each inscription, with each bull having one half of the inscription and being placed on one side of a doorway. Each bull has been given a separate exemplar number, but the various pairs have been cited one after the other when they can be identified (exs. 1–2, 6–7, 8–9, 10–11, 12–13, 14–15, 16–17, 18–19, 20–21, and 24–25). For the bull that would have been paired with ex. 3, see Albenda, Palace of Sargon p. 130 and pl. 51. Two bulls (exs. 4 and 5) would have each had the complete inscription and these were placed opposite one another in Entrance M of the palace. For a plan of the palace showing the original emplacement of most of the exemplars, see Botta, Monument de Ninive 1 pls. 6 and 6bis. Flandin's drawings indicate that several bulls had inscriptions not copied by Botta (e.g., façade n, 54 and 56; see ibid., pl. 1 pl. 30); some of these may be exs. 26 and 29–31.

When making his copies for exs. 1–15 and 18–21 (Monument de Ninive 3 pls. 22–51 and 54–61), P.E. Botta states that he collated them either from the originals or from paper squeezes ("estampages"). There are at present in the Louvre squeezes for the following exemplars: 1, 2 (first section), 3–7, 10–11, 12 (second section), 13–14, 15 (first section), and 18–21; these are Botta, Monument de Ninive 3 pls. 22–31, 36–39, 41–46, 48–50, and 54–61. As with most of Botta's squeezes, they often do not cover all the inscription copied by Botta or are so damaged in places as to be unreadable; as a result, the transliterations in the score must often rely on Botta's copy.

As was mentioned, the inscription on any one bull was divided into two sections, a larger one placed under the belly of the bull and a smaller one placed between the hind-legs of the bull. In the scores for this text, // has been indicated in the scores where the inscription on an exemplar begins a new section. When the inscription required two bulls, the inscription began on the bull on the left side of the doorway (the bull facing into the room) with the first section located under the belly of the bull and the second section between the hind legs of that bull. The inscription then moved to the section between the hind legs of the bull on the right side of the doorway and ended in the section under the belly of that bull.

Under the column "cpn" in the catalogue, p indicates that the exemplar was collated from a photo of a squeeze; however, it must be noted that a squeeze may not be fully preserved today or cover all of an inscription copied by Botta. Since the inscription on each exemplar is generally split up into two sections, this column often has two entries. For example, ex. 12 has "n, p"; this indicates that the first section (Botta, Monument de Ninive 3 pl. 40^{c}) has not been collated, while the second (ibid. pl. 41^{c}) has been collated from a photograph of the squeeze. The second section of ex. 15 (Botta, Monument de Ninive 3 pl. 47^{c}) has the indication "p". Pieces comprising about eighty percent of this section are preserved in various museums and the pieces in Geneva, the Vatican, and (formerly) Jerusalem have been collated by means of published photographs. The transliteration of the remaining parts of the section is based on Botta's copy.

Ex. 2: The squeeze in the Louvre identified as being Botta, Monument de Ninive 3 pl. 51^{c} (i.e., the second section on this bull) is actually a squeeze of the inscription on the back of the bull (see text no. 41 ex. 21).

Exs. 4 and 21–22: As noted by Fuchs, Khorsabad pp. 16–17 and 60, Botta's copies of exs. 4 and 21–22 are wrongly put together. The left and middle portions of the 16th–34th lines on Botta, Monument de Ninive 3 pl. 25^{c} (ex. 4) must be moved one line down. On Botta, Monument de Ninive 3 pl. 60^{c} (ex. 21), the lower portion of the copy (the last four lines) must be moved up five lines; thus, for example, the line marked 85 on the copy is actually the right-hand portion of the line numbered 80. On Botta, Monument de Ninive 3 pl. 62 (ex. 22), the lower portion of the copy must be moved up one line.

Ex. 5: The squeeze for the first section of ex. 5 (Botta, Monument de Ninive 3 pl. 26^{c}) is torn in several places and the photo shows that parts of the squeeze are misaligned. The upper right portion is positioned one line lower than the upper left portion.

Exs. 10 and 14–15: Photographs of the four pieces in St. Petersburg were kindly supplied by the State Hermitage Museum. C. Bezold published collations of the inscription on ex. 10 (Literatur pp. 86–88), but examination of the squeeze and of a photograph of the original indicates that at times Botta's copy must be accepted over Bezold's readings. The section of ex. 15 once belonging to the Convent of Les Dames de Sion (Jerusalem) was stolen and thus its current location is not known (information courtesy M. Sigrist). R. de Vaux reports that the piece had supposedly been found in 1859 (or possibly 1857) "au cours des travaux du Père Ratisbonne à l'Ecce Homo" (JPOS 16 [1936] p. 129; cf. Lewis, PEFQ [1890] p. 266).

Ex. 12–13: J. Oppert's copies of exs. 12–13 are based upon Botta's copies; thus, Botta's copies are used here and no references are made to differences between the two sets of copies.

Ex. 22: Botta, Monument de Ninive 3 p. II (table of contents) indicates that ex. 22 is Façade n, 48, but on pl. 62 of that work it is said to be Room N, bull 47; the piece must be Façade n, 47 since there is no Room N, since Façade N has no slabs or bulls 47 or 48 (see Botta, Monument de Ninive 1 pls. 24–28), and since Façade n, 48 is not a bull, while Façade n, 47 is (see Botta, Monument de Ninive 1 pl. 30).

Exs. 24–25: The museum numbers for these two

exemplars given on Albenda, Palace of Sargon figs. 3 and 4 must be interchanged. The pieces were "obtained from Khorsabad by Sir H.C. Rawlinson in 1849" (BM Guide p. 41).

Exs. 29–30: In Borger, HKL 2 p. 7, the two fragments of this inscription in Florence published by A. Archi (OrAnt 11 [1972] pl. X nos. 10a and b) are identified with parts of Botta, Monument de Ninive 3 pls. 44^{c}–45^{c} (ex. 14), following a suggestion by J. Renger. A comparison of the published photos of these pieces to the photos of the squeezes of the Botta piece in the Louvre (see also the photos of the squeeze published by Ménant in Notice Lottin, pl. 3 and by Fontan in Khorsabad p. 179) indicates that this identification cannot be maintained. The signs on the pieces in Florence are spaced in a different manner to those on the bull seen by Botta. Thus, these fragments are kept separate and presented as exs. 29–30.

Ex. 31, now in the Musées d'Art et d'Histoire in Geneva was purchased in Paris in 1897.

V. Place (Ninive et l'Assyrie 2 pp. 266 and 268) states that the bull colossi from city gate 6 had the inscription painted on them in black paint and he proposes that this was a preliminary step to having the inscription incised in the stone and thus that the work on these bulls had never been finished. No further information is known about these exemplars of this inscription.

As is the case with most of the inscriptions found upon wall slabs in the palace at Khorsabad, many of the exemplars of this inscription found and copied by Botta either no longer exist or their whereabouts are unknown (exs. 3–9, 12–13, and 16–22). Thus, they are unavailable for collation. Although squeezes of some of these (as well as some of those exemplars still existing) made by Botta can be examined in the Louvre (exs. 3–7, 10, 13, and 18–21, as well parts of exs. 12 and 15), the exact reading of the text on these exemplars is at times in question due to the unreliability of Botta's copies and due to the poor state of preservation of the squeezes and/or the originals from which the squeezes were made. Nevertheless, the basic text of the inscription is clear due to the large number exemplars and it is really just a matter of the variants on the individual exemplars that remains at times uncertain.

The line arrangement is based upon exs. 1 and 2. The master line is, for the most part, based upon exs. 1 and 2, though there are slight deviations from these in lines 1, 19, 21, 23–24, 26, 28, 32, 38, 41, 44, 62, 67, 70–73, 75, 81, 92–93 98–99, and 105–106. The signs are generally Neo-Assyrian, but at times Babylonian or archaizing forms appear.

Large portions of this inscription either duplicate or are very similar to passages in other inscriptions of Sargon II. For example, lines 39b–98a are similar to text no. 8 lines 28b–54a.

BIBLIOGRAPHY

1849 Botta, Monument de Ninive 1–2 pls. 6–9, 24, 26, 30, 45, 52, and 122 (drawing of reliefs, provenance); and 3 pls. 22–62 (exs. 1–22, copy)

1850 Botta, Monument de Ninive 5 pp. 296–360 (exs. 1–2, copy, study)

1853 Layard, Nineveh and Babylon pp. 131–132 and 640 (exs. 24–25, provenance)

1854 de Longpérier, Notice^{3} nos. 1–2 and 598–599 (exs. 1–2, study)

1856 Oppert, Annales de Philosophie chrétienne 53 pp. 346–350 (exs. 1–2$^{?}$, translation)

1856 Oppert, Chronologie pp. 35–39 (exs. 1–2$^{?}$, translation) (identical to preceding)

1858 Ménant, Notice Lottin pp. 42–43 and pl. 3 (ex. 14, partial photo of squeeze)

1870 Oppert in Place, Ninive et l'Assyrie 2 pp. 282–291 (exs. 12–13, copy, edition)

1870 Oppert, Dour-Sarkayan pp. 2–11 (exs. 12–13, copy, edition) (identical to preceding)

1874 Ménant, Annales pp. 192–195 (exs. 12–13, translation)

1878 Oppert, Records of the Past 11 pp. 15–26 (translation)

1883 Descemet, Studi e documenti 4 pp. 99–100 (ex. 11 [Vatican 15027], translation, study)

1883 Lyon, Sar. no. 2 (exs. 1–2, composite copy, edition, with variants from exs. 12–13, 27–28)

1886 Bezold, Literatur pp. 85–88 §51.2 and p. 94 §56.14n (exs. 1–2, 10–11, 27–28, study)

1886 Bezold, ZA 1 p. 229 (exs. 15 [Vatican 15028], study)

1889 Winckler, Sar. 1 pp. x–xi and 2 pls. 41–42 (composite copy)

1890 Lewis, PEFQ pp. 265–266 (exs. 15 [section in Jerusalem], photo of squeeze, edition [by Budge])

1890 Ménant, RT 13 pp. 194-197 (ex. 15 lines 77–84 [section in Jerusalem], copy, transliteration)

1902 Marucchi, Catalogo Vaticano pp. 337–338 nos. 18–19 (ex. 11 [Vatican 15027], 15 [Vatican 15028], translation, study)

1904 Peiser, OLZ 7 col. 9 nos. 18–19 (exs. 11 [Vatican 15027], 15 [Vatican 15028], study)

1918 Pillet, Khorsabad pp. 53, 89, and 96–97 (ex. 27, study)

1922 BM Guide p. 41 no. 1 and pls. V and XIII (exs. 24–25, photo [inscription not legible], study)

1924 Pottier, Antiquités assyriennes pp. 64–67 nos. 12–14 and pls. VI–VII (exs. 1, 27 photo [inscription not legible]; exs. 1–2, 27, study)

1927 Landsberger and Bauer, ZA 37 p. 219 n. 2 (line 75, study)

1927 Luckenbill, ARAB 2 pp. 45–47 §§91–94 (translation)

1928 Hall, Sculpture p. 40 and pl. XXVIII (exs. 24, photo [inscription not legible; misidentified as BM 118909])

1929 Grosso, Grande Genova 9/12 pp. 10–12 (ex. 15 [Genova 532], photo, translation, study)

1935 Boson, Aegyptus 15 p. 424 no. 6 (ex. 26, photo)

1936 Böhl, MLVS 3 pp. 5–6 (ex. 15 [LB 1309], edition)

1936 Gadd, Stones pp. 159–160 (exs. 24–25, study)

1936 Loud, Khorsabad 1 pp. 42–55 and fig. 56 (ex. 23, photo [inscription not legible], provenance, study)

1936 de Vaux, JPOS 16 pp. 128–130 (exs. 15 [section in Jerusalem], 26, edition)

1942–43 Pohl, RPARA 19 pp. 247–249 and 252–254, and figs. 5–6 nos. 19–20 (exs. 11 [Vatican 15027] and 15 [Vatican 15028], copy, edition)

1956 de Sion, Forteresse Antonia p. 275 and pl. 69 no. 1 (exs. 15 [section in Jerusalem], photo, study)

1961 Parrot, Assyria p. 30 figs. 34a–b (exs. 2, 23, photos [inscriptions not legible])

1964 Brinkman, Studies Oppenheim p. 44 no. 44.2.20.c.v (study)

1968 Borger in Galling, Textbuch^{2} p. 61 no. 31.3 (ex. 15 [section in Jerusalem], study)

1968 Ellis, Foundation Deposits pp. 175–176 no. 15 (lines 55–57a, edition)

1972 Archi, OrAnt 11 pp. 271–272 and pl. X nos. 10a–b (exs. 29–30, photo)

1975 Orthmann, Der alte Orient pl. 176 and p. 297 (ex. 23, photo [inscription not legible], study)

1976 Saporetti, Studi Ciprioti e Rapporti di Scavo 2 pp. 84–85 (lines 28–29a, translation, study)

1979 Biga, Orientalia NS 48 pp. 476–477 and pl. XXXII (ex. 15 [Genova 532], photo, transliteration)

1982 André-Leicknam, Naissance de l'écriture pp. 257–258 (lines 1–6, 9–12, 30–31, 39–41, 97–106, translation)

1983 Khazai, De Sumer à Babylone p. 133 no. 211 (ex. 28, photo, partial translation, study)

1986 Albenda, Palace of Sargon pp. 49–51, 130–132 137, 144, 157, 166, and 173–174, figs. 1–5, and pls. 14, 17, 19, 26, 35–37, 40–43, 51–52, 55–58, 80, and 110 (exs. 1, 23–25, 27, photo [inscriptions not legible]; study, provenance)

1986 Renger, CRRA 32 pp. 112–13, 120, and 122 (lines 1–10, 12–13, 15, 17–18, 21, 26, partial transcription, study)

1987 Engel, Dämonen pp. 35 and 142–150 (lines 70–77a, edition of exs. 2–3, 5, 7, 9, 11, 13, 15, 19, 21)

1987 Heimpel, ZA 77 pp. 88–89 no. 74 (lines 32–36, study)

1990 Potts, Arabian Gulf 1 p. 335 no. 5 (lines 1–5a, 30b–36a, translation)

1990 Wilson and Brinkman, OI Featured Object 8 (ex. 23, photo [inscription not legible], provenance; lines 39b–106, translation)

1992 Becking, Fall of Assyria p. 33 (line 21, edition)

1992 Hurowitz, Exalted House p. 71 (lines 36–39, edition; study)

1994 André-Salvini in Fontan, Khorsabad p. 171 fig. 3 and p. 282 (ex. 1, photo of squeeze)

1994 Fontan, Khorsabad p. 179 fig. 2 and p. 283 (ex. 14, photo of squeeze)

1994 Fuchs, Khorsabad pp. 60–74 and 303–307 no. 2.1 (exs. 1–30, edition), and pp. 386 and 390–391 (study)

1995 André-Salvini in Caubet, Khorsabad p. 37 fig. 10 (ex. 2, photo of lines 53–74)

1995 Biga and Cagni in Dolce and Nota Santi, Dai Palazzi Assiri pp. 276–277 no. 60 and fig. 129, pp. 280–285 nos. 62–64 and figs. 131–133, and pp. 286–289 nos. 65–66 and figs. 134–135 (exs. 11, 15 [Genova 532, Vatican 15028], 26, 29–30, photo, study)

1999 J.M. Russell, Writing on the Wall pp. 103–108 (exs. 1–25, 27, study)

2000 Bagg, Assyrische Wasserbauten pp. 149 and 155 (lines 36b–46a, edition)

2001 Rollinger, Melammu 2 p. 240 (line 25b, edition)

2006 Ponchia, SAAB 15 p. 234 (study)

2008 Mango, Marzahn, and Uehlinger, Könige am Tigris p. 201 Abb. 126 and p. 205 Kat. 52 (ex. 31, photo, translation, study)

2012 Worthington, Textual Criticism p. 185 (line 48, study)

2013 Dalley, Hanging Gardens p. 89 (lines 36–42, translation)

2014 Maniori, Campagne di Sargon pp. 49–50 g2 and passim (exs. 1–2, study)

2017 Liverani, Assyria pp. 163, and 206 (lines 26–27a, 92b–97a, translation)

2018 Frahm, Last Days pp. 80–81 no. 17 (line 21b, edition, study)

2019 Aster, JAOS 139 pp. 603–604 (lines 95b–97a, edition, study)

2019 Marchesi, JNES 78 p. 24 (lines 17b–21a, edition)

TEXT

1) É.GAL ^{m}LUGAL-GI.NA LUGAL GAL-*ú* LUGAL *dan-nu* LUGAL KIŠ LUGAL KUR *aš-šur*.KI

2) GÌR.NÍTA KÁ.DINGIR.RA.KI LUGAL KUR EME.GI$_{7}$ *ù* URI.KI *mi-gir* DINGIR.MEŠ GAL.MEŠ

3) RE.É.UM *ke-e-nu ša* ^{d}*aš-šur* ^{d}AG ^{d}AMAR.UTU LUGAL-*ut la šá-na-an*

4) *ú-šat-li-mu-šu-ma zi-kir šu-mì-šu ú-še-ṣu-ú*

5) *a-na re-še-e-ti šá-kin šu-ba-re-e* ZIMBIR.KI NIBRU.KI

6) KÁ.DINGIR.RA.KI *mu-šá-áš-šík tup-šik-ki* BÀD.AN.KI ÚRI.KI *eridu*.KI

7) ARARMA.KI *kul-la-ba*.KI *ki-sik*.KI *né-med-*^{d}*la-gu-da*.KI

8) *mu-šap-ši-ḫu* UN.MEŠ-*šú-un ka-ṣir ki-din-nu-ut bal-til*.KI *ba-ṭil-ta*

9) *ša* UGU URU.*ḫar-ra-na* AN.DÙL-*la-šú it-ru-ṣu-ú-ma*

10) *ki-i ṣa-ab* ^{d}*a-nim ù* ^{d}*da-gan iš-ṭu-ru za-kut-su-un*

11) *zi-ka-ru dan-nu ḫa-lip na-mur-ra-ti ša a-na*

1–2) Palace of Sargon (II), great king, strong king, king of the world, king of Assyria, governor of Babylon, king of the land of Sumer and Akkad, favorite of the great gods;

3–5a) just shepherd, (one) to whom the gods Aššur, Nabû, (and) Marduk granted a reign without equal and whose reputation (these gods) exalted to the heights;

5b–10) who (re)-established the *šubarrû*-privileges of (the cities) Sippar, Nippur, (and) Babylon; who abolished corvée duty for (the cities) Dēr, Ur, Eridu, Larsa, Kullaba, Kissik, (and) Nēmed-Laguda, (and) gave relief to their people; who (re)-established the privileged status of (the city) Baltil (Aššur) that had lapsed; who extended his protection over the city Ḫarrān and recorded their exemption (from obligations) as if (their people were) people of the gods Anu and Dagān;

11–23) the strong man who is clad in awesome

Figure 14. A 7369 (text no. 9 ex. 23), inscription between the legs of a winged bull colossus found in the palace at Khorsabad. Courtesy of the Oriental Institute of the University of Chicago.

šum-qut
12) *na-ki-ri šu-ut-bu-u* GIŠ.TUKUL.MEŠ-*šú šá-kin taḫ-te-e* ^{md}*ḫum-ba-ni-ga-áš*
13) LÚ.ELAM.MA.KI *mu-šak-niš* KUR.*man-na-a-a* KUR.*kar-al-lu* KUR.*an-di-a*
14) KUR.*zi-kir-tú* URU.*ki-še-si-im* URU.*ḫar-ḫar* KUR.*ma-da-a-a* KUR.*el-li-pi*
15) *e-mid-du ni-ir aš-šur mu-šaḫ-rib* KUR.*ur-ar-ṭi* URU.*mu-ṣa-ṣir šá* ^{m}*ur-sa-a*
16) KUR.*ur-ar-ṭa-a-a i-na pu-luḫ-ti-šú* GAL-*ti i-na* GIŠ.TUKUL
17) *ra-ma-ni-šú ú-qat-ta-a na-piš-tuš šá-lil ma-li-ki* URU.*gar-ga-miš*
18) KUR.*a-ma-at-ti* KUR.*kúm-mu-ḫi* URU.*as-du-du* LÚ.*ḫa-at-te-e lem-nu-ti*
19) *la a-dir zik-ri* DINGIR.MEŠ *da-bi-bu ṣa-lip-ti ša* UGU *gi-mir* KUR.MEŠ-*šú-nu*
20) LÚ.*šu-ut* SAG.MEŠ-*šú a-na* LÚ.NAM-*ú-ti iš-tak-ka-nu-ma it-ti* UN.MEŠ KUR *aš-šur*.KI
21) *im-nu-šu-nu-ti sa-pi-in* URU.*sa-me-ri-na ka-la* KUR.É-^{m}*ḫu-um-ri-a* KUR.*kas-ku*
22) *ka-šid* KUR.*ta-ba-lu gi-mir* KUR.É-^{m}*pu-ru-ta-áš* KUR.*ḫi-lak-ku ša ina* URU.*ra-pi-ḫi*

splendor (and) whose weapons are raised to strike down (his) enemies; who brought about the defeat of Ḫumbanigaš (Ḫumban-nikaš I), the Elamite; who subjugated the lands Mannea, Karalla, Andia, (and) Zikirtu, the cities of Kišesim (and) Ḫarḫar, (and) the lands Media (and) Ellipi; (15) who imposed the yoke of (the god) Aššur (upon them); who laid waste to the land Urarṭu (and) the city Muṣaṣir; in great fear of whom Ursâ (Rusâ), the Urarṭian, brought an end to his life with his own weapon; who carried off as booty the rulers of the city Carchemish, the land Hamath, the land Kummuḫu, (and) the city Ashdod — evil Hittites, who do not fear the words of the gods (and always) speak treachery; who (20) set eunuchs of his as provincial governors over all their lands and considered them as people of Assyria; who overwhelmed the city Samaria, all of the land Bīt-Ḫumria (Israel), (and) the land Kasku; who conquered the land Tabal, all of the land Bīt-Purutaš, (and) the land Ḫilakku; who brought about the defeat of Egypt at the city Raphia and counted Ḫanūnu (Hanno), the king of the city Gaza, as booty;

13–15 See the on-page note to text no. 8 lines 7–8. In this case, A. Fuchs (Khorsabad p. 303 and n. 142) keeps the lands Mannea, Karalla, Andia, and Zikirtu with *mušakniš*, "who subjugated," and Kišesim, Ḫarḫar, Media, and Ellipi with *ēmidu nīr aššur*, "who imposed the yoke of the god Aššur," basing the division upon geographical reasons.
19 Exs. 10 and 14 have *e-pi-šú* and exs. 16 and 22 (mostly restored) *e-pi-šu* for *da-bi-du*, "practice" instead of "speak." Ex. 1 omits UGU.
21 Exs. 10 and 16 omit KUR.*kas-ku* "(and) the land Kasku."
22 Exs. 10 and 16 omit KUR.*ḫi-lak-ku*, "(and) the land Ḫilakku."

23) BAD$_5$.BAD$_5$ KUR.*mu-uṣ-ri iš-ku-nu-ma* ^{m}*ḫa-a-nu-nu* LUGAL URU.*ḫa-zi-ti im-nu-ú šal-la-ti-iš*

24) *na-pi-i'* URU.*ši-nu-uḫ-ti ṭa-rid* ^{m}*mi-ta-a* LUGAL KUR.*mu-us-ki mu-ter ḫal-ṣi* KUR.*qu-e*

25) *ek-mu-ti ša* URU.*ia-am-na-a-a ša* MURUB$_4$ *tam-tim ki-ma nu-ú-ni i-ba-ru*

26) *na-si-iḫ* ^{m}*gu-un-zi-na-nu* KUR.*kam-ma-nu-u-a ù* ^{m}*tar-ḫu-la-ra* KUR.*gúr-gu-ma-a-a*

27) *ša gi-mir* KUR.MEŠ-*šú-nu e-ki-mu-ma a-na mi-ṣir* KUR *aš-šur*.KI *ú-ter-ra mu-šak-niš*

28) 7 LUGAL.MEŠ-*ni ša* KUR.*ia-a' na-ge-e ša* KUR.*ad-na-na ša ma-lak* 7 *u$_4$-me i-na* MURUB$_4$ *tam-ti*

29) *ša šùl-mu* ^{d}UTU-*ši šit-ku-nat šu-bat-sún ka-šid* KUR.*ra-a-ši mu-šak-niš* LÚ.*pu-qud-du* LÚ.*da-mu-nu*

30) *a-di* URU.*la-ḫi-ri šá* KUR.*ia-ad-bu-ri e-mid-du ab-šá-an-šu šá-kin dáb-de-e* ^{md}AMAR.UTU-IBILA-SUM.NA

31) LUGAL KUR.*kal-di a-a-bu lem-nu ša ki-i la lìb-bi* DINGIR.MEŠ *šar-ru-ut* KÁ.DINGIR.RA.KI *e-pu-šu-ma tak-šu-du*

32) GAL-*tú qa-as-su na-si-iḫ šur-uš* URU.BÀD-^{m}*ia-ki-in-ni*

33) URU *tuk-la-ti-šú* GAL-*a ša* ADDA.MEŠ LÚ.*mun-daḫ-ṣe-šú i-na sa-pan*

34) *tam-ti ú-gar-ri-nu gu-ru-un-niš iš-me-ma* ^{m}*ú-pe-ri* LUGAL *dil-mun*.KI

35) *ša ma-lak* 30 KASKAL.GÍD *i-na* MURUB$_4$ *tam-tim šá ṣi-it* ^{d}UTU-*ši ki-ma nu-ú-ni*

36) *nar-ba-ṣu šit-ku-nu-ma iš-šá-a ta-mar-tuš* LUGAL *it-pe-šu*

37) *muš-ta-bil a-mat da-mì-iq-ti ša a-na šu-šu-ub na-me-e*

38) *na-du-ti ù pe-te-e ki-šub-bé-e za-qáp ṣip-pa-a-ti iš-ku-nu*

39) *ú-zu-un-šu i-na u$_4$-me-šu-ma i-na* UGU *nam-ba-'i šá* GÌR.II

40) KUR.*mu-uṣ-ri* KUR-*e e-le-nu ni-na-a*.KI URU *e-pu-uš-ma* URU.BÀD-^{m}MAN-GIN

41) *az-ku-ra ni-bit-su* GIŠ.KIRI$_6$.MAḪ-*ḫu tam-šil* KUR.*ḫa-ma-ni ša gi-mir ḫi-bi-iš-ti*

42) KUR.*ḫat-ti* GURUN KUR-*e* DÙ-*šú-un qé-reb-šú ḫu-ur-ru-šu ab-ta-ni i-ta-tuš*

24–30a) who plundered the city Šinuḫtu; who drove out Mitâ (Midas), king of the land Musku; who brought back (to Assyrian control) the fortress(es) of the land Que (Cilicia) (25) that had been taken away (by the enemy); who caught the Ionians who (live in) the middle of the sea like fish; who deported Gunzinānu of the land Kammanu and Tarḫu-lara of the land Gurgum, who took away all of their lands, and made (them part of) the territory of Assyria; who subjugated seven kings of the land Yā' — a region of the land Adnana (Cyprus) — whose abode is situated at a distance of seven days (journey) in the middle of the Western Sea; who conquered the land Rāši; who subjugated the Puqudu (and) Damūnu (tribes) as far as the city Laḫīru of the land Yadburu (and) imposed his yoke (upon them);

30b–36a) who brought about the defeat of Marduk-apla-iddina (II) (Merodach-Baladan) — king of Chaldea, an evil enemy who exercised kingship over Babylon against the will of the gods — and whose great hand conquered (him); who eradicated the city Dūr-Yakīn, the great city upon which he (Marduk-apla-iddina) relied; who heaped up the corpses of his (Marduk-apla-iddina's) fighting men in piles on the coastal plain — Upēri, king of Dilmun (35) who(se) lair is situated at a distance of thirty leagues in the middle of the Eastern Sea, like that of a fish, heard (of this) and brought me his audience gift;

36b–39a) the wise king who occupies himself with good matters (and) who turned his attention to (re)settling abandoned pasture lands, opening up unused land, (and) planting orchards.

39b–41a) At that time I built a city above the spring at the foot of Mount Muṣri, a mountain upstream from (the city) Nineveh, and I named it Dūr-Šarrukīn.

41b–42) I created around it a botanical garden, a replica of Mount Amanus, in which were gathered every kind of aromatic plant from the land Ḫatti (Syria) (and) every type of fruit-bearing mountain tree.

23 Exs. 10 and 22 have KUR "land" instead of URU "city" before Gaza."
24 Ex. 14 has URU "city" instead of KUR "land" before "Que."
25 Ex. 22 has KUR "land" instead of URU "city" before "Ionians."
28 Ex. 6 has URU "city" instead of KUR "land" before "Adnana."
29 Ex. 5 omits KUR "land" before "Rāši." Exs. 10, 22 have KUR "land" instead of LÚ before Puqudu.
30 Ex. 14 has KUR "land" instead of URU "city" before Laḫīru.
33–34 W. Heimpel (ZA 77 [1987] p. 88) argues that *ina sapān tâmti* (currently translated "coastal plain") refers instead to the extent of the region (i.e., "along the sea").
35 P.E. Botta's copy of ex. 16 has 20, not 30; no photo or squeeze of the original exists in order to check this.

43) *ša* 3 ME 50.ÀM *mal-ki la-bi-ru-ti ša el-la-mu-u-a be-lu-ut*
44) KUR *aš-šur*.KI *e-pu-šu-ma il-ta-nap-pa-ru ba-ʾu-lat* ^{d}EN.LÍL
45) *a-a-um-ma i-na lìb-bi-šú-nu a-šar-šú ul ú-maš-ši-ma šu-šu-ub-šú*
46) *ul il-ma-du ḫe-re-e* ÍD-*šú za-qáp ṣip-pa-te-šú ul iz-kur a-na šu-šu-ub*
47) URU *šá-a-šú zuq-qú-ur* BÁRA.MAḪ-*ḫi at-ma-an* DINGIR.MEŠ GAL.MEŠ *ù* É.GAL.MEŠ
48) *šu-bat be-lu-ti-ia ur-ru mu-šu ak-pu-ud aṣ-rim-ma*
49) *e-pe-su aq-bi i-na* ITI *še-mé-e* u_4-*mu*
50) *mit-ga-ri i-na* ITI ^{d}*kulla* UD.ÈŠ.ÈŠ
51) GIŠ.*al-lu ú-šat-ri-ik-ma ú-šal-bi-na*
52) *li-bit-tu i-na* ITI.NE *a-ra-aḫ*
53) *mu-kin te-me-en* URU *ù* É *ša gi-mir ṣal-mat* SAG.DU
54) *a-na ri-mì-ti-ši-na i-pat-ti-qa ṣu-lu-lu*
55) *e-li* KÙ.GI KÙ.BABBAR URUDU *ni-siq-ti* NA_4.MEŠ *ḫi-bi-iš-ti*
56) KUR.*ḫa-ma-ni pe-el-šú ú-šat-ri-ṣa uš-še-e-šú ad-di-ma*
57) *ú-kin lib-na-as-su pa-rak-ki ra-áš-bu-ti*
58) *ša ki-ma ki-ṣir gi-né-e šur-šu-du a-na* ^{d}*é-a*
59) ^{d}30 ^{d}*nin-gal* ^{d}UTU ^{d}AG ^{d}IŠKUR ^{d}MAŠ *e-pu-šá*
60) *qer-bu-uš-šu* É.GAL.MEŠ ZÚ AM.SI GIŠ.ESI GIŠ.TÚG
61) GIŠ.*mu-suk-kan-ni* GIŠ.*ere*-IGI GIŠ.ŠUR.MÌN GIŠ.*dup-ra-ni*
62) GIŠ.ŠIM.LI *u* GIŠ.*bu-uṭ-ni i-na qí-bi-ti-šú-nu*
63) *ṣir-ti a-na mu-šab šar-ru-ti-ia ab-ni-ma*
64) GIŠ.ÙR.MEŠ GIŠ.*ere*-IGI GAL.MEŠ *e-li-šin ú-šat-ri-ṣa*
65) GIŠ.IG.MEŠ GIŠ.ŠUR.MÌN GIŠ.*mu-suk-kan-ni mé-se-er* URUDU *nam-ri*
66) *ú-rak-kis-ma ú-rat-ta-a né-reb-šin*
67) É *ap-pa-a-ti tam-šil* É.GAL KUR.*ḫat-ti ša i-na li-šá-an*
68) KUR MAR.TU.KI É *ḫi-la-ni i-šá-as-su-šu*
69) *ú-še-pi-šá mé-eḫ-ret* KÁ.MEŠ-*ši-in*
70) 8 UR.MAḪ *tu-ʾa-a-me šu-ut* 1 ŠÁR GÉŠ.U 6 UŠ 50.ÀM GUN
71) *mal-tak-ti* URUDU *nam-ri ša i-na ši-pir* ^{d}*nin-á-gal ip-pat-qu-ma*
72) *ma-lu-ú nam-ri-ri* 4 *tim-me* GIŠ.*ere*-IGI *šu-ta-ḫu-te ša* 1 NINDA.TA.ÀM
73) *ku-bur-šu-un bi-ib-lat* KUR.*ḫa-ma-ni* UGU

43–49a) Not one of the three hundred and fifty previous rulers who had exercised lordship over Assyria before my time and had governed the subjects of the god Enlil (45) had noted its (the city's) site or come to know how to make it habitable; nor had one ordered the digging of its canal (or) the planting of its orchards. Day (and) night I planned earnestly how to settle that town (and) to erect (there) a great shrine — a cella for the great gods — and palatial halls to be my lordly abode, and I (then) ordered its construction.

49b–52a) In a favorable month, (on) an auspicious day — in the month of the god Kulla, (on) the day of an *eššēšu*-festival — I had (workmen) wield hoe(s) and make bricks.

52b–57a) In the month of Abu (V) — the month for the one who lays the foundation of citi(es) and house(s) (and in) which all the black-headed people construct shelter(s) for their dwelling(s) — (55) I placed its limestone masonry on top of (foundation deposits of) gold, silver, copper, precious stones, (and) pieces (of aromatic woods) from Mount Amanus. I laid its foundation and established its brickwork.

57b–60a) I built inside it (the city) for the gods Ea, Sîn, Ningal, Šamaš, Nabû, Adad, (and) Ninurta awe-inspiring daises that were made as firm as the mountains.

60b–69) At their august command, I built palatial halls using (lit.: "of") elephant ivory, ebony, boxwood, *musukkannu*-wood, cedar, cypress, *daprānu*-juniper, juniper, and terebinth to be my royal residence and I roofed them with large cedar beams. (65) I bound the doors of cypress (and) *musukkannu*-wood with band(s) of shining copper and installed (them in) their entrance(s). I had built in front of their gates a portico (*bīt appāti*), a replica of a Hittite palace, which is called a *bīt ḫilāni* in the language of the land Amurru.

70–79a) Eight twin lion (colossi) of shining copper that weigh 4,610 full (lit.: "tested") talents (and) that were cast by the craft of the god Ninagal and filled with radiance — upon (those) lion colossi I installed four matching cedar columns, whose diameter(s) are one *nindanu* each, the product of Mount Amanus; and I positioned cross-beams (upon them) as a cornice

48 Ex. 23 omits -*ia* "my" in "my lordly abode." See Worthington, Textual Criticism p. 185 for the suggestion that "there has probably been crasis: *urru u mūšu* > /*urrumūšu*/."
59 Ex. 15 has ^{d}IŠKUR ^{d}AG "Adad, Nabû." Ex .27 inserts *ù* "and" between "Adad" and "Ninurta."
60 With regard to the translation of É.GAL.MEŠ as "palatial halls," see the on-page note to text no. 2 line 472.
70 P.E. Botta's copy of ex. 4 has 40 not 50; the number is not clear on the squeeze.
73 Ex. 2 omits KUR "Mount" before "Amanus."

ur-maḫ-ḫe-e
74) *ú-kin-ma dáp-pi ku-lul ba-bi-ši-in e-mid*
75) UDU.MEŠ *šad-di* ^{d}LAMMA MAḪ.MEŠ *šá* NA$_4$ KUR-*i eš-qí*
76) *nak-liš ap-tiq-ma a-na er-bet-ti šá-a-ri ú-šá-aṣ-bi-ta*
77) SI.GAR-*ši-in as-kup-pi* NA$_4$.*pi-li* GAL.MEŠ *da-ád-me*
78) *ki-šit-ti qa-ti-ia ṣe-ru-uš-šin ab-šim-ma a-sur-ru-ši-in*
79) *ú-šá-as-ḫi-ra a-na tab-ra-a-ti ú-šá-lik* ŠÁR ŠÁR ŠÁR ŠÁR GÉŠ.U GÉŠ.U GÉŠ.U 1 UŠ
80) 1 1/2 NINDA 2 KÙŠ *mi-še-eḫ-ti* BÀD-*šú áš-kun-ma e-li* KUR-*i zaq-ri*
81) *ú-šar-ši-da te-em-me-en-šú i-na re-e-ši ù ar-ka-a-ti*
82) *i-na ṣe-li ki-lal-la-an mé-eḫ-ret* 4 IM.MEŠ 8 KÁ.GAL.MEŠ *ap-te-e-ma*
83) ^{d}UTU *mu-šak-šid er-nit-ti-ia* ^{d}IŠKUR *mu-kin* ḪÉ.GÁL-*li-ia*
84) *šu-mu* KÁ.GAL ^{d}UTU *ù* ^{d}IŠKUR *ša* IGI-*et* IM.KUR.RA *az-kur* ^{d}EN.LÍL *mu-kin*
85) *iš-di* URU-*ia* ^{d}NIN.LÍL *mu-di-šá-at ḫi-iṣ-bi zík-ri* KÁ.GAL ^{d}BAD
86) *ù* ^{d}NIN.LÍL *ša* IGI-*et* IM.SI.SÁ *am-bi* ^{d}*a-nu mu-šal-lim ep-šet*
87) *qa-ti-ia* ^{d}*iš-tar mu-šam-me-ḫa-at* UN.MEŠ-*šú ni-bit* KÁ.GAL ^{d}*a-nim*
88) *ù* ^{d}*iš-tar ša* IGI-*et* IM.MAR.TU *áš-kun* ^{d}*é-a muš-te-šir nag-bi-šú*
89) ^{d}*be-let*-DINGIR.MEŠ *mu-rap-pi-šat ta-lit-ti-šú šu-mu* KÁ.GAL ^{d}*é-a ù* ^{d}*be-let*-DINGIR.MEŠ *šá* IGI-*et*
90) IM.U$_{18}$.LU *aq-bi-ma* ^{d}*aš-šur mu-šal-bir pa-le-e* LUGAL *e-pi-ši-šu*
91) *na-ṣir um-ma-ni-šu* BÀD-*šú* ^{d}*nin-urta mu-kin te-me-en a-li-šu*

92) *a-na la-bar* UD.MEŠ *ru-qu-ú-ti šal-ḫu-šú ba-ʾu-lat ar-ba-ʾi li-šá-nu*
93) *a-ḫi-tu at-me-e la mit-ḫur-ti a-ši-bu-ut* KUR-*i ù ma-a-ti ma-la ir-te-ʾu-ú*
94) ZÁLAG DINGIR.MEŠ EN *gim-ri ša i-na zi-kir*

for their gates. (75) I skillfully fashioned magnificent mountain sheep colossi of massive mountain stone and in the four directions I had (them) hold their (the gates') door bolt(s). I depicted the settlements that I had conquered upon large limestone slabs and surrounded their (the palatial halls') lower courses (with them). I made (them) an object of wonder.

79b–92a) I made the length of its wall 16,280 cubits and I made its foundation secure upon (blocks of) massive mountain (stone). In front and in back, on both sides, facing the four directions, I opened eight gates (in the city wall). Then, I named the gate(s) of the gods Šamaš and Adad that face the east "The God Šamaš Is the One Who Makes Me Triumph" (and) "The God Adad Is the One Who Establishes My Prosperity" (respectively). I called the gate(s) of the god Enlil and the goddess Mullissu that face the north "The God Enlil Is the One Who Establishes the Foundation of My City" (85) (and) "The Goddess Mullissu Is the One Who Restores Abundance" (respectively). I made the name(s) of the gate(s) of the god Anu and the goddess Ištar that face the west "The God Anu Is the One Who Makes My Undertakings Successful" (and) "The Goddess Ištar Is the One Who Makes Its People Flourish" (respectively). I pronounced the names of the gate(s) of the god Ea and the goddess Bēlet-ilī that face the south (to be) "The God Ea Is the One Who Keeps Its Spring(s) in Good Order" (and) "The Goddess Bēlet-Ilī Is the One Who Increases Its (Animals') Offspring" (respectively). (90) Its (city) wall was (called) "The God Aššur Is the One Who Prolongs the Reign of Its Royal Builder (and) Protects His Troops." Its outer wall was (called) "The God Ninurta Is the One Who Establishes the Foundation of His City for (All) Days to Come."

92b–97a) People from the four (quarters of the world), (speaking) foreign language(s) (and of) diverse speech, those who had dwelt in (both) mountain(s) and (low)land(s), as many as the "Light of the Gods" (Šamaš), the lord of all, shepherded, whom I had car-

75 With regard to ^{d}LAMMA MAḪ.MEŠ, see the on-page note to text no. 8 line 479.

79–80 ŠÁR ŠÁR ŠÁR ŠÁR GÉŠ.U GÉŠ.U GÉŠ.U 1 UŠ 1 1/2 NINDA 2 KÙŠ: The number also appears in text no. 8 line 40 (partially restored), text no. 43 line 65, and text no. 44 line 47 (partially restored). The latter two texts have 3 *qa-ni* instead of 1 1/2 NINDA and indicate that the number must be regarded as a cryptogram for the name Sargon, although how it is to be explained has as yet not been determined. See the Introduction to this volume, under the section "Name."

83 -*mu-kin-* "Establishes": See also text no. 8 line 42; text no. 43 line 67 has -*mu-kil-* "Maintains."

90 Ex. 13 omits the divine determinative before "Aššur." *mu-šal-bir* "Who Prolongs": See also text no. 8 line 47; text no. 43 line 71 has *mu-lab-bir* "Prolongs."

91 *um-ma-ni-šu* "His Troops" and *a-li-šu* "His City": See also text no. 8 line 48 (restored); text no. 43 line 71 has NUNUZ-*šú* "His Offspring" and *a-du-uš-ši* "the Wall" respectively. The reading *um-ma-ni* may have been based upon an ancient misreading of ERIM.ḪI.A for NUNUZ; see also Fuchs, Khorsabad p. 296 no. 95.

94 For the same passage in text no. 43 line 72, Liverani (Assyria p. 206) assumes that it is the god Aššur who is being called *nūr ilāni bēl gimri* "the 'Light of the Gods' [Liverani: 'the divine light'], the lord of all"; however, the epithet *nūr ilāni* normally refers to the sun god Šamaš (see for example CAD N/2 p. 348) and some of the exemplars having this text also have text no. 41 on their back, which in lines 25–26 refers to settling in Khorsabad "people of the lands that I had conquered — as many as the god Šamaš shepherded." Ex. 27 omits *i-na* "at." Exs. 11, 13, 15, 17, and 28 omit the divine determinative before "Aššur." *me-tel* "power": See the on-page note to a duplicate passage in text no. 43 line 73.

^{d}*aš-šur* EN-*ia ina me-tel ši-bir-ri-ia áš-lu-la*
95) *pa-a* 1-*en ú-šá-áš-kin-ma ú-šar-ma-a qé-reb-šú* DUMU.MEŠ KUR *aš-šur*.KI *mu-du-ut i-ni*
96) *ka-la-ma a-na šu-ḫu-uz ṣi-bit-ti pa-laḫ* DINGIR *ù* LUGAL LÚ.*ak-li*

ried off as booty by the power of my staff at the command of the god Aššur, my lord, (95) I made act in concert and I (re)settled (them) inside it (the city). I commissioned native Assyrians, masters of every craft, as overseers (and) commanders to instruct (the settlers) in correct behavior (and how) to revere god and king.

97) LÚ.*šá-pi-ri ú-ma-ʾe-er-šú-nu-ti ul-tu ši-pìr* URU *ù* É.GAL.MEŠ-*ia*
98) *ú-qat-tu-ú* DINGIR.MEŠ GAL.MEŠ *a-ši-bu-ut* KUR *aš-šur*.KI *i-na qer-bi-ši-na*
99) *aq-re-e-ma ta-šil-ta-ši-na áš-kun ša mal-ki ṣi-it* ^{d}UTU-*ši ù e-reb* ^{d}UTU-*ši*
100) KÙ.GI KÙ.BABBAR *mim-ma aq-ru si-mat* É.GAL.MEŠ *šá-ti-na ta-mar-ta-šú-nu ka-bit-tú am-ḫur*

97b–100) After I had completed work on the city and my palatial halls, I invited the great gods who dwell in Assyria (to come) inside them and I held a celebration for them. From rulers from the east and the west, I received as their substantial audience gift(s) gold, silver, (and) everything valuable befitting these palatial halls.

101) DINGIR.MEŠ *a-ši-bu-ut* URU *šá-a-šu mim-ma lip-ta-at* ŠU.II-*ia li-im-ma-ḫi-ir-ma pa-nu-uš-šú-un*
102) *a-šab ki-iṣ-ṣi-šú-un ù kun-nu* BALA.MEŠ-*ia liq-bu-ú du-rí da-rí*

101–102) May every work of my hands be acceptable to the gods who dwell in this city. May they then forever decree that (they will) inhabit their shrines and that my reign will be firmly established.

103) *ša ep-šet qa-ti-ia ú-nak-ka-ru-ma bu-un-na-ni-ia ú-saḫ-ḫu-ú*
104) *uṣ-ṣu-rat e-ṣe-ru ú-šam-sa-ku-ma si-ma-ti-ia ú-pa-áš-šá-ṭu* ^{d}30 ^{d}UTU
105) ^{d}IŠKUR *ù* DINGIR.MEŠ *a-šib lìb-bi-šú* MU-*šú* NUMUN-*šú i-na* KUR *lil-qu-tú-ma*
106) *i-na* KI.TA LÚ.KÚR-*šú li-še-ši-bu-uš ka-meš*

103–106) (As for) the one who alters the work of my hands, mutilates my features (on a relief), obliterates the reliefs that I have engraved, or effaces my own representation(s), may the gods Sîn, Šamaš, Adad, and the great gods who dwell there remove his name (and) his descendant(s) from the land and make him live in bondage under his enemy.

10–15

Many of the stone thresholds or pavement slabs in the main area of the palace at Khorsabad bear inscriptions of Sargon II. P.E. Botta published copies of the inscriptions found on 21 or 22 slabs (Botta, Monument de Ninive 3 pls. 1-21 and likely 4 pl. 181^{c} no. 5 [probably from Entrance P; see text no. 14 ex. 3]). J.M. Russell (Writing on the Wall p. 108) has noted that several more doorways in the main part of the palace had inscriptions on their thresholds: Entrances D, F, V, X, Z, b, e, and r (see E. Flandin's detailed plans of the palace in Botta, Monument de Ninive 1–2 pls. 11, 51, 79, 121, 137, and 139) and possibly Entrance C′′ of the throne room (see Loud, Khorsabad 1 fig. 71, p. 65, and p. 139 sub thresholds, which appears to indicate that the threshold described on p. 65 was inscribed).

Five different inscriptions (text nos. 10–14) are attested on the thresholds of the main part of the palace and a sixth such inscription may be text no. 15. The inscriptions vary in length from 23 lines (text no. 10) to 150 lines (text no. 13). In two, or more likely three, inscriptions (text no. 12, text no. 14, and likely text no. 15) the king is described in the first person,

9 line 97 Ex. 13 omits *-ia* "my" with "palatial halls."
9 line 98 Ex. 2 inserts ITI.DU$_6$ after *i-na* (i.e., "in the month of Tašrītu (VII), I invited ..."). See the section on building activities at Dūr-Šarrukīn in the Introduction to the volume with regard to this date.
9 line 99 Ex. 19 omits *ù* "and" between "the east" and "the west."

while in the other three (text nos. 10, 11, and 13) the third person is used for him. The mention of Karduniaš (Babylonia), Chaldea, and "Bīt-Yakīn, which is on the shore of the sea, as far as the border of Dilmun," in the areas ruled by Sargon in text nos. 10–14 would suggest that those inscriptions were composed after the king's Babylonian campaigns in his twelfth and thirteenth regnal years (710–709). Moreover, the mentions of the gods being invited into the city Dūr-Šarrukīn in text no. 13 and of the festival that took place when the city was completed in text nos. 12 and 15 indicate that these texts were composed no earlier than the seventh month of 707 and the second month of 706 respectively (see the Introduction, under "Building Activites" at Khorsabad).

Short inscriptions are also found on paving slabs in the entrances to several chapels within the palace (text nos. 16–21). In addition, several copies of an inscription invoking the god Nabû have been found in the nearby temple of that god (text no. 22). With regard to inscribed threshold slabs in Sargon's palace in general, see J.M. Russell, Writing on the Wall pp. 108–111; see also J.M. Russell, Senn.'s Palace pp. 17–19.

10

Four exemplars of the first threshold inscription — an inscription that simply gives the king's name, several titles, and a description of the extent of his realm — are attested. Three were found in the royal palace at Khorsabad and the fourth comes from Palace F. This is the shortest of the inscriptions found on thresholds in the main part of the palace (as opposed to the chapel area).

CATALOGUE

Ex.	Source	Provenance	Lines Preserved	cpn
1	Botta, Monument de Ninive 3 pl. 13	Khorsabad, Palace, Entrance Y	1–23	n
2	Botta, Monument de Ninive 3 pl. 1	Khorsabad, Palace, Entrance A	1–23	n
	Botta, JA 4/2 (1843) pl. IX			n
	Institut de France sheet 341			n
3	Botta, Monument de Ninive 3 pl. 3	Khorsabad, Palace, Entrance C	1–23	n
	Botta, JA 4/2 (1843) pl. XV			n
	Institut de France sheets 311 and 340			n
4	Loud and Altman, Khorsabad 2 pl. 40E	Khorsabad, Palace F, entrance between Rooms 29 and 30	1–23	p

COMMENTARY

Exs. 1–3 are edited from the copies published by P.E. Botta in Monument de Ninive; no paper squeezes of these were made by him. The copy of ex. 1 published by H. Winckler has not been used since it was based solely upon Botta's copy. It should be noted that he states (Sar. 1 p. X) that he only indicates the most important variants for the inscriptions on the paving stones, bulls, and backs of reliefs in his work. The present whereabouts of these three exemplars are not known. Presumably they were either left in situ or lost in the Tigris disaster in 1855. Botta sent initial copies of exs. 2 and 3 to J. Mohl in Paris and these were published in Journal asiatique in 1843; these original copies are currently preserved in the Institut de France (Botta-Cotta II 2976 folio I sheets 311 [ex. 3], 340 [ex. 3], and 341 [ex. 2]). References to differences between the copies in Monument de Ninive and the earlier copies are noted where it has been thought useful.

Ex. 4 was found during the Oriental Institute (Chicago) excavations at Khorsabad, but was left in situ. A high resolution scan of the original photo of ex. 4 published in Loud and Altman, Khorsabad 2 (pl. 40E) was kindly supplied to the author by K. Neumann (curator, Oriental Institute), but some parts of the inscription remain unclear; thus the edition presented for this exemplar in the score is not fully complete.

The line arrangement and master line are based upon ex. 1; however, if Botta's copy indicates that a sign on that exemplar is abnormal in form (e.g., LUGAL in line 1), suspiciously incorrect (e.g., KUR for ŠE in line 11), omitted (e.g., RA in line 3), or damaged while another exemplar has the correct sign, the latter reading is given. Ex. 2 has the inscription on 32 lines, ex. 3 on 31 lines, and ex. 4 on 17 lines. In the scores, "copy" refers to Botta's copies in Monument de Ninive, not to Winckler's later copy. Abnormal and incorrect sign forms on Botta's copies are noted with a dagger (†).

BIBLIOGRAPHY

1843 Botta, JA 4/2 pp. 68 and 203, and pls. IX and XV (exs. 2–3, copy, provenance)

1849 Botta, Monument de Ninive 3 pls. 1, 3, and 13 (exs. 1–3, copy)

1880 Ménant, Manuel pp. 316–322 (exs. 1–3, variants to text no. 12 ex. 2)

1886 Bezold, Literatur p. 93 §56.13 (study)

1889 Winckler, Sar. 1 pp. X and 136–139; and 2 pl. 37 no. I (ex. 1, copy, edition; exs. 2–3, variants)

1927 Luckenbill, ARAB 2 p. 48 §§95–96 (translation)

1938 Loud and Altman, Khorsabad 2 pp. 77–78 and 104 no. 4, and pl. 40E (ex. 4, photo, study, provenance)

1976 Saporetti, Studi Ciprioti e Rapporti di Scavo 2 pp. 84–85 (lines 1a, 5–8, translation, study)

1986 Renger, CRRA 32 pp. 112–113 (lines 1–4, partial transcription, study)

1994 Fuchs, Khorsabad pp. 249–251 and 356 no. 2.5.1 (exs. 1–4, edition), and pp. 394–395 (study)

1999 J.M. Russell, Writing on the Wall pp. 108–110 (exs. 1–4, study)

TEXT

1) É.GAL ^{m}LUGAL-GI.NA LUGAL GAL-*u*
2) LUGAL *dan-nu* LUGAL *kiš-šá-tim*
3) LUGAL KUR *aš-šur*.KI GÌR.NÍTA KÁ.DINGIR.RA.KI
4) LUGAL KUR *šu-me-ri ù* URI.KI

1–4) Palace of Sargon (II), great king, strong king, king of the world, king of Assyria, governor of Babylon, king of the land of Sumer and Akkad;

5) LUGAL *ša i-na tu-kul-ti*
6) ^{d}*aš-šur* ^{d}AG ^{d}AMAR.UTU
7) *iš-tu* KUR.*ia-ad-na-na šá* MURUB$_4$ *tam-tim*
8) *a-di pa-aṭ* KUR.*mu-ṣu-ri* KUR.*mu-uš-ki*
9) KUR MAR.TU.KI DAGAL-*tim* KUR.*ḫat-ti ana si-ḫir-ti-šá*
10) *nap-ḫar gu-ti-um*.KI KUR.*ma-da-a-a ru-qu-te*
11) *šá pa-aṭ* KUR.*bi-ik-ni* KUR.*el-li-pí* KUR.*ra-a-še*†

5–23) the king who with the support of the gods Aššur, Nabû, (and) Marduk ruled all together from the land Yadnana (Cyprus), which is in the middle of the sea, as far as the border(s) of Egypt (and) the land Musku, the wide land Amurru, the land Ḫatti (Syria) in its entirety, (10) all of (the land) Gutium, the distant Medes (who live) on the border of Mount Bikni, the lands Ellipi (and) Rāši on the border of the land Elam,

1 Ex. 2 omits LUGAL GAL-*u*, "great king."
2 Ex. 2 omits LUGAL *dan-nu*, "strong king."
6 Ex. 3 inserts *ù*, "and," after ^{d}*aš-šur*.
7 Exs. 2–4 insert <*ša šá*>-*lam*† ^{d}UTU-*ši* (ex. 2), *ša šá-lam*† ^{d}UTU-*ši* (ex. 3), and ... ^{d}⸢UTU-*ši*⸣ (ex. 4) respectively after *tam-tim*, i.e., "the Western Sea."
8 Exs. 2,4, and possibly 3 (restored) add *ù*, "and," after "Egypt."

12) *šá pa-aṭ* KUR.ELAM.MA.KI *na-gab* LÚ.*a-ri-me*
13) *a-šib a-ḫi* ÍD.IDIGNA ÍD.*su-rap-pi*
14) ÍD.*uq-né-e gi*†*-mir* LÚ.*su-te-e ṣa-ab* EDIN†
15) *šá* KUR.*ia-ad-bu-ri mal* ⸢*ba*⸣*-šu-u ul-tú*
16) URU.DU$_{6}$-^{d}*ḫum-ba šá mi-ṣir* ELAM.MA.KI
17) KUR.*kár-dun-ía-áš e-liš ù šap-liš*
18) *gi-mir* KUR.*kal-di* KUR.É-^{m}*ia-kin*$_{7}$ *šá* GÚ
19) ÍD.*mar-ra-te a-di pa-aṭ* NI.TUK.KI
20) *mit-ḫa-riš i-be-lu-ma* LÚ.*šu-ut* SAG.MEŠ-*šú*
21) *a-na* LÚ.EN.NAM-*ú-ti* UGU-*šú-nu*
22) *iš-tak-ka-nu-ú-ma ni-ir*
23) *be-lu-ti-šu e-mid-su-nu-ti*

all the Arameans who live beside the Tigris, Surappu, (and) Uqnû Rivers, all the Sutians, the people of the steppe (15) of the land Yadburu, as many as there are, from the city Tīl-Ḫumba which is on the border of Elam, the land Karduniaš (Babylonia) from one end to the other (lit.: "above and below"), all of Chaldea, (and) the land Bīt-Yakīn, which is on the shore of the sea, as far as the border of Dilmun; (20) (who) set eunuchs of his as provincial governors over them, and imposed the yoke of his lordship upon them.

11

The second of the five inscriptions on stone thresholds in doorways in the main part of the palace at Khorsabad was found on two exemplars. Following the king's name and titles, and a description of the extent of the king's realm, it records the construction of the new city Dūr-Šarrukīn and, in particular, the construction and decoration of its palace.

CATALOGUE

Ex.	Source	Provenance	Lines Preserved	Louvre Squeeze	cpn
1	Botta, Monument de Ninive 3 pl. 2	Khorsabad, Palace, Entrance B	1–46	no	n
	Botta, JA 4/2 (1843) pls. XIII–XIV				n
	Institut de France sheet 314				n
2	Botta, Monument de Ninive 3 pl. 5^{C}	Khorsabad, Palace, Entrance G	1–40, 42–46	yes	n
	Louvre squeeze				p

COMMENTARY

The exemplars come from two of the three doorways leading from the palace terrace into Room II; the third (middle) doorway also had an inscription, but nothing further is known about it (see the introduction to text nos. 10–15). The present whereabouts of these exemplars are not known. They were probably either lost in the Tigris disaster in 1855 or left in situ. Both exemplars have the inscription on 46 lines, but the line division is not the same. Ex. 1 is edited from the copy by P.E. Botta in Monument de Ninive, although differences to his earlier copy published in Journal Asiatique in 1843 and currently found in the Archives of the Institute de France (Botta-Cotta II 2976 folio I sheet 314) are noted where it has been thought useful. Botta's copy of ex. 2 in Monument de Ninive has been collated by means of photographs

10 line 12 Ex. 4 has *i-te-e* for *pa-aṭ*.
10 lines 14–15 Exs. 2–4 replace *gimir ... ultu*, "all the Sutians, the people of the steppe of the land Yadburu, as many as there are, from," with *a-di* URU.*dun-ni-*[^{d}]*šá-maš**(copy: AŠ) URU.*bu-bé-e* (ex. 2), *a-di*† URU.*dun-ni-*^{d}*šá-maš* [URU].⸢*bu*⸣*-bé-e* (ex. 3), and *a-*⸢*di*⸣ URU.*dun-ni-*^{d}⸢UTU⸣ URU.*bu-bé-e* (ex. 4), "as far as the cities Dunni-Šamaš, Bubê, (and)."
10 line 16 Exs. 2–4 have KUR.ELAM.MA.KI, "the land Elam."
10 line 18 Exs. 3–4 have LÚ.*kal-di*, "the Chaldeans," rather than "Chaldea." Exs. 2–4 insert *mal ba-šu-ú*, "as much as there is (of it)," after *kaldi*, "Chaldea."
10 line 23 *e-mid-su-nu-ti*: See the note to text no. 1 line 12.

of the squeeze in the Louvre. H. Winckler only provides a copy of ex. 1, which is solely based on Botta's copy since there was no squeeze of it to be consulted by him. He does indicate with that copy variants in ex. 2.

The line arrangement and master line are based upon ex. 1, with some minor help from ex. 2 at various places in the text. Abnormal and incorrect sign forms on Botta's copies are noted with a dagger (†) in the score, but are only indicated in the master transliteration when neither of the exemplars has the correct form.

Traces of an inscription were found upon the backs of three stone wall slabs facing the terrace outside Room 15 of Palace F at Khorsabad and T. Jacobsen, who saw the pieces, has identified the inscription as this one. As noted by G. Loud and C.B. Altman, these wall slabs may have been re-used thresholds. They are the only orthostats found by the Chicago expedition in Palace F and on the middle of the three orthostats, the lines of the inscription are vertical rather than horizontal. These slabs were left in situ and no further details are known about their inscriptions. For these additional exemplars, see Loud and Altman, Khorsabad 2 pp. 77, 104 no. 5, and pl. 41D.

BIBLIOGRAPHY

1843 Botta, JA 4/2 pp. 202–203 and pls. XIII–XIV (ex. 1, copy, provenance)
1849 Botta, Monument de Ninive 3 pls. 2 and 5 (exs. 1–2, copy)
1886 Bezold, Literatur p. 93 §56.13 (study)
1889 Winckler, Sar. 1 pp. X and 138–143, and 2 pl. 37 no. II (ex. 1, copy, edition of lines 1–44a; ex. 2, variants)
1927 Landsberger and Bauer, ZA 37 p. 219 n. 2 (line 37, study)
1927 Luckenbill, ARAB 2 pp. 48–50 §§95 and 97 (translation)
1976 Saporetti, Studi Ciprioti e Rapporti di Scavo 2 pp. 84–85 (lines 1a, 3–6a, translation, study)
1986 Renger, CRRA 32 pp. 112–113 (lines 1–2, partial transcription, study)
1987 Engel, Dämonen pp. 142–150 (lines 31–39a, edition of exs. 1–2)
1994 Bergamini in Fontan, Khorsabad p. 80 fig. 8 and p. 280 (ex. 1, copy [=Botta-Cotta II 2976 folio I sheet 314])
1994 Fuchs, Khorsabad pp. 251–254 and 356–357 no. 2.5.2 (exs. 1–2, edition), and pp. 394–395 (study)
1999 J.M. Russell, Writing on the Wall pp. 108–110 (exs. 1–2, study)
2017 Liverani, Assyria p. 83 (lines 37b–46, translation)

TEXT

1) É.GAL ^{m}LUGAL-GI.NA MAN *kiš-šá-ti* MAN KUR *aš-šur*.KI
2) GÌR.NÍTA KÁ.DINGIR.RA.KI MAN KUR ⸢EME⸣.GI$_{7}$ *ù* URI.KI
3) LUGAL *ša i-na tu-kul-ti* ^{d}*aš-šur* ^{d}AG ^{d}MES
4) *iš-tu* KUR.*ia-ad-na-na ša* MURUB$_{4}$ *tam-tim*
5) *šá-lam* ^{d}UTU-*ši a-di pa-aṭ* KUR.*mu-ṣu-ri*
6) *ù* KUR.*mu-uš-ki* KUR MAR.TU.KI DAGAL-*tim*
7) KUR.*ḫat-ti a-na si-ḫir-ti-šá nap-ḫar gu-ti-um*.KI
8) KUR.*ma-da-a-a ru-qu-ti šá pa-aṭ* KUR.*bi-ik-ni*
9) KUR.*el-li-pí* KUR.*ra-a-še šá i-te-e* KUR.ELAM.MA.KI
10) *na-gab* LÚ.*a-ri-me*† *a-ši-ib a-aḫ* ÍD.IDIGNA
11) ÍD.*su*†-*rap-pi* ÍD.*uq-né-e a-di* URU.*dun-ni*-^{d}UTU
12) URU.*bu-bé-e* URU.DU$_{6}$†-^{d}*ḫum-ba ša mi-ṣir*
13) KUR.ELAM.MA.KI KUR.*kár-dun-ía-áš e-liš ù*† *šap-liš*
14) *gi-mir* KUR.*kal-di mal ba-šu-ú* KUR.É-^{m}*ia-ki-ni*
15) *šá* GÚ† ÍD.*mar-ra-te a-di pa-aṭ* NI.TUK.KI
16) *mit-ḫa-riš i-bí-lu-ma* LÚ.*šu-ut* SAG.MEŠ-*šu*
17) LÚ.EN.NAM.MEŠ UGU-*šú-nu iš-tak-ka-nu-ma*
18) *ni-ir be-lu-ti-šú e-mid-su-nu-ti ina u*$_{4}$-*me-šú-ma*

1–2) Palace of Sargon (II), king of the world, king of Assyria, governor of Babylon, king of the land of Sumer and Akkad;

3–18a) the king who with the support of the gods Aššur, Nabû, (and) Marduk ruled all together from the land Yadnana (Cyprus), which is in the middle of the Western Sea, (5) as far as the border(s) of Egypt and the land Musku, the wide land Amurru, the land Ḫatti (Syria) in its entirety, all of (the land) Gutium, the distant Medes (who live) on the border of Mount Bikni, the lands Ellipi (and) Rāši on the border of the land Elam, (10) all the Arameans who live beside the Tigris, Surappu, (and) Uqnû Rivers, as far as the cities Dunni-Šamaš, Bubê, (and) Tīl-Ḫumba which are on the border of the land Elam, the land Karduniaš (Babylonia) from one end to the other (lit.: "above and below"), all of Chaldea, as much as there is (of it), (and) the land Bīt-Yakīn, (15) which is on the shore of the sea, as far as the border of Dilmun; (the one who) set eunuchs of his as provincial governors over them, and imposed the yoke of his lordship upon them.

18b–21a) At that time, in accordance with divine will,

16 *i-bí-lu-ma* "ruled": Or possibly *i-bil-lu-ma* "rules" here and in text nos. 13 line 87 and 42 line 17.

19) *ki-i ṭè-em* DINGIR-*ma i-na* GÌR.II KUR.*mu-uṣ-ri*
20) *e-le-nu* NINA.⸢KI⸣ URU DÙ-*uš-ma* URU.BÀD-^{m}LUGAL-GIN
21) *iz-ku-ra ni-bit-su* É.GAL ZÚ AM.SI GIŠ.ESI
22) GIŠ.TÚG GIŠ.*mu-suk-kan-ni* GIŠ.EREN GIŠ.ŠUR.MÌN
23) GIŠ.*dup-ra-ni* GIŠ†.ŠIM.LI ⸢*ù*⸣ GIŠ.*bu-uṭ-ni*
24) *a-na mu-šab* LUGAL-*ti-šú qer-bu-uš-šú*
25) *ib-ni-ma* GIŠ.ÙR.MEŠ GIŠ.EREN GAL.MEŠ *e-li*†*-šin*
26) *ú-šat-ri-ṣa* GIŠ.IG.MEŠ GIŠ.ŠUR.MÌN GIŠ.*mu*†*-suk-kan-ni*
27) *me-*⸢*se*⸣*-er* URUDU *nam-ri ú-rak-kis-ma ú-rat-ta-a*
28) *né-reb-*⸢*šin*⸣ É ⸢*ap*⸣*-pa-a-ti tam-šil* É.GAL KUR.*ḫat-ti*
29) *šá ina li-šá-an* KUR MAR.TU.KI É *ḫi-la-a-ni*
30) *i-šá-as-su-šú ú-še-pi-šá mé-eḫ-ret* KÁ.⸢MEŠ⸣*-šin*
31) 8 UR.MAḪ.MEŠ *tu-ʾa-a-me šu-ut* 1 ŠÁR GÉŠ.U 6 UŠ 50.ÀM
32) GUN *mal-tak-ti* URUDU *nam-ri šá ina ši-pir*
33) ^{d}*nin-á-gal ip-pat-qu-ma ma-lu-ú*
34) *nam-ri-ir-ri* 4 GIŠ.*tim-me* GIŠ.EREN *šu-ta-ḫu-te*†
35) *ša* 1 NINDA.TA.ÀM *ku-bur-šú-un bi-ib-lat* KUR.*ḫa-ma-ni*
36) UGU *pirig-gal-le-e ú-kin-ma* GIŠ.*dáp-pi ku-lul*
37) KÁ.MEŠ-*šin e-mid* UDU.MEŠ *šad-di* ^{d}LAMMA MAḪ.MEŠ
38) *šá* NA$_{4}$ KUR-*i eš-qí nak-liš ib-ni-ma a-na er-bet-ti*
39) *šá-a-ri ú-šá-aṣ-bi-ta* SI.GAR-*šin as-kup-pi*
40) NA$_{4}$.⸢*pi*⸣*-i-*⸢*li*⸣ GAL.MEŠ *da-ád-me ki-šit-ti*
41) *qa-ti-šu ṣe*†*-ru*†*-uš-šin ib-šim-ma*
42) *a-sur-ru-šin ú-šá-as-ḫi-ra a-na tab*†*-ra-a-ti*
43) *ú-šá-lik da-*⸢*ád*⸣*-me*† *ma-ti-tan šá iš-tu ṣi-taš*
44) *a-di šil-la-an* ⸢*ina e*⸣*-mu-uq* ^{d}*aš-šur ik-šu-du-ma*
45) *ina* ⸢*ši-pir*⸣ LÚ.⸢*ùr*†⸣*-ra-ku-ti i-*[*na*] ⸢*qé*⸣*-reb* ⸢É⸣.GAL.⸢MEŠ⸣
46) *šá-ti-na iš-*[*tak*]*-*⸢*ka*†⸣*-*[*na si-ma*]*-a-ti*

he built a city at the foot of Mount Muṣri, upstream from Nineveh, and named it Dūr-Šarrukīn.

21b–30) He built inside it a palace using (lit.: "of") elephant ivory, ebony, boxwood, *musukkannu*-wood, cedar, cypress, *daprānu*-juniper, juniper, and terebinth to be his royal residence and (25) he roofed it (lit.: "them") with large beams of cedar. He bound the doors of cypress (and) *musukkannu*-wood with band(s) of shining copper and installed (them) in its (lit.: "their") entrance(s). He had built in front of its (lit.: "their") gates a portico (*bīt appâti*), a replica of a Hittite palace, which is called a *bīt ḫilāni* in the language of Amurru.

31–46) Eight twin lion (colossi) of shining copper that (weigh) 4,610 full (lit.: "tested") talents (and) that were cast by the craft of the god Ninagal and filled with radiance — upon (those) lion colossi he installed four matching cedar columns, (35) whose diameter(s) are one *nindanu* each, the product of Mount Amanus; and he positioned cross-beams (upon them) as a cornice for its (lit. their) gates. He skillfully fashioned magnificent mountain sheep colossi of massive mountain stone and in the four directions he had (them) hold their door bolt(s). (40) He depicted the settlements that he had conquered upon large limestone slabs and surrounded its (lit. their) lower courses (with them). He made (them) an object of wonder. He pl[ac]ed inside these palatial halls [representa]tions — (made) by the craft of the sculptor — of the settlements of every land that he had conquered, from east to west, by the strength of the god Aššur.

12

The third inscription on stone thresholds in doorways of the palace at Khorsabad was found on five exemplars. After recording the name, titles, and extent of the king's realm, the text briefly records the construction of the city Dūr-Šarrukīn and its palace, as well as a festival to commemorate its completion. The reference to the festival, which is also mentioned in text no. 15, may be connected to the statement in the Assyrian Eponym Chronicle that the city of Dūr-Šarrukīn was inaugurated on the sixth day of Ayyāru (II) in the eponymy of Mutakkil-Aššur (706).

---

11 line 37 With regard to LAMMA MAḪ.MEŠ, see the on-page note to text no. 2 line 479.
11 line 39 Ex. 2 inserts *as-mu* after *sigaršin*, thus "their respective (lit.: "fitting") door bolt(s)."
11 line 44 Ex. 2 has ^{d}*a-šur be-lí-*[*ia*], "the god Aššur, [my] lord."

CATALOGUE

Ex.	Source	Provenance	Lines Preserved	cpn
1	Botta, Monument de Ninive 3 pl. 9	Khorsabad, Palace, Entrance Q	1–45	n
2	Botta, Monument de Ninive 3 pl. 8	Khorsabad, Palace, Entrance O	1–45	n
3	Botta, Monument de Ninive 3 pl. 10	Khorsabad, Palace, Entrance S	1–45	n
4	Botta, Monument de Ninive 3 pl. 15	Khorsabad, Palace, Entrance d	1–38	n
5	Botta, Monument de Ninive 3 pl. 21	Khorsabad, Palace, Entrance p	1–41, 43–44	n

COMMENTARY

The current location of these exemplars is not known. They were probably either lost in the Tigris disaster in 1855 or left in situ. No squeezes of any of the originals exist and the transliterations of the various exemplars are based upon Botta's copies in Monument de Ninive. The line arrangement and master lines come from ex. 1, with some minor help from ex. 2 in lines 21, 24, and 35–38. Exs. 2–5 have the inscription on 72, 30, 36, and 38 lines respectively.

BIBLIOGRAPHY

1849 Botta, Monument de Ninive 3 pls. 8–10, 15, and 21 (exs. 1–5, copy)

1874 Ménant, Annales pp. 195–196 (ex. 2, translation)

1880 Ménant, Manuel pp. 316–322 (ex. 2, copy, edition; variants from exs. 1, 3–5 and parts of text nos. 10 and 14)

1886 Bezold, Literatur p. 93 §56.13 (study)

1889 Winckler, Sar. 1 pp. X and 142–147; and 2 pls. 37–38 no. III (ex. 1, copy, edition; exs. 2–3, variants)

1927 Luckenbill, ARAB 2 pp. 48 and 50–51 §§95 and 98 (translation)

1976 Saporetti, Studi Ciprioti e Rapporti di Scavo 2 pp. 84–85 (lines 1a, 4–8a, translation, study)

1986 Renger, CRRA 32 pp. 112–113 (lines 1–3, partial transcription, study)

1990 Potts, Arabian Gulf 1 p. 335 no. 6 (lines 1–20a, translation)

1994 Fuchs, Khorsabad pp. 254–259 and 358 no. 2.5.3 (exs. 1–5, edition), and pp. 394–395 (study)

1999 J.M. Russell, Writing on the Wall pp. 108–110 (exs. 1–5, study)

TEXT

1) É.GAL ^{m}LUGAL-GI.NA LUGAL *kiš-šá-ti*
2) LUGAL KUR *aš-šur*.KI GÌR.NÍTA KÁ.DINGIR.RA.KI
3) LUGAL KUR EME.GI$_{7}$ *ù ak-ka-di-i*
4) LUGAL *ša i-na tu-kul-ti* ^{d}*aš-šur*
5) ^{d}AG ^{d}AMAR.UTU *iš-tu* KUR.*ia-ad-na-na*
6) *ša* MURUB$_{4}$ *tam-tim ša šá-lam* ^{d}UTU-*ši*
7) *a-di pa-aṭ* KUR.*mu-ṣu-ri*
8) *ù* KUR.*mu-uš-ki* KUR MAR.TU.KI
9) DAGAL-*tim* KUR.*ḫat-ti a-na si-ḫir-ti-šá*
10) *nap-ḫar gu-ti-um*.KI KUR.*ma-da-a-a*
11) *ru-qu-ti šá pa-aṭ* KUR.*bi-ik-ni* KUR.*el-li-pí*
12) KUR.*ra-a-ši ša pa-aṭ* KUR.ELAM.MA.KI
13) *na-gab* LÚ.*a-ri-me a-ši-ib a-aḫ*
14) ÍD.IDIGNA ÍD.*su-rap-pi* ÍD.*uq-né-e*

1–3) Palace of Sargon (II), king of the world, king of Assyria, governor of Babylon, king of the land of Sumer and Akkad;

4–23a) the king who with the support of the gods Aššur, Nabû, (and) Marduk, ruled (lit.: "I ruled") all together from the land Yadnana (Cyprus), which is in the middle of the Western Sea, as far as the border(s) of Egypt and the land Musku, the wide land Amurru, the land Ḫatti (Syria) in its entirety, (10) all of (the land) Gutium, the distant Medes (who live) on the border of Mount Bikni, the lands Ellipi (and) Rāši on the border of the land Elam, all the Arameans who live beside the Tigris, Surappu, (and) Uqnû Rivers, (15) as far as the cities Dunni-Šamaš, Bubê, (and) Tīl-Ḫumba

1 Ex. 5 has [...-*ke*]-*e-nu* for -GI.NA. Ex. 3 omits LUGAL, "king," after RN.
3 Ex. 2 omits *ù*, "and."
4 Ex. 5 omits *i-na*, "with."
5 Exs. 2, 4 insert *ù*, "and," after ^{d}AG, "Nabû."
12 Ex. 2 omits KUR before ELAM.MA.KI, thus "Elam" for "land Elam."

15) *a-di* URU.*dun-ni-*^{d}UTU URU.*bu-bé-e* URU.DU$_{6}$-^{d}*ḫum-ba*
16) *šá mi-ṣir* KUR.ELAM.MA.KI KUR.*kár-dun-ía-áš*
17) *e-liš ù šap-liš gi-mir* KUR.*kal-di*
18) *mal ba-šu-ú* KUR.É-^{m}*ia-kin*$_{7}$ *ša ki-šá-di*
19) ÍD.*mar-ra-ti a-di pa-aṭ* NI.TUK.KI
20) *mit-ḫa-riš a-be-el-ma* LÚ.*šu-ut* SAG.MEŠ-*ia*
21) *a-na* LÚ.EN.NAM-*ú-ti* UGU-*šú-nu*
22) *áš-tak-kan-ma ni-ir be-lu-ti-ia*
23) *e-mid-su-nu-ti ina u*$_{4}$*-me-šú-ma ina ba-ḫu-la-te*
24) *na-ki-ri ki-šit-ti* ŠU.II-*ia šá* ^{d}*aš-šur*
25) ^{d}AG ^{d}AMAR.UTU *a-na* GÌR.II-*ia ú-šak-ni-šú-ma*
26) *i-šu-ṭu ab-šá-a-ni ki-i ṭè-em* DINGIR-*ma*
27) *ina* GÌR.II KUR.*mu-uṣ-ri e-le-en* NINA.KI
28) *ina bi-bíl lìb-bi-ia* URU DÙ-*uš-ma*
29) URU.BÀD-^{m}MAN-GIN *az-ku-ra ni-bit-su*
30) É.GAL ZÚ AM.SI GIŠ.ESI GIŠ.TÚG
31) GIŠ.*mu-suk-kan-ni* GIŠ.*ere-ni* GIŠ.ŠUR.MÌN GIŠ.*dáp-ra-ni*
32) GIŠ.ŠIM.LI *ù* GIŠ.*bu-uṭ-ni a-na mu-šab*
33) LUGAL-*ti-ia qer-bu-uš-šú ab-ni-ma*
34) ^{d}*aš-šur* EN GAL-*ú ù* DINGIR.MEŠ *a-ši-bu-ut*
35) KUR *aš-šur*.KI *ina qer-bi-ši-in aq-re-e-ma*
36) UDU.SISKUR.MEŠ *tak-bit-ti* KÙ.MEŠ *ma-ḫar-šú-un*
37) *aq-qí ša mal-ki kib-rat* LÍMMU-*i ša a-na ni-ir*
38) *be-lu-ti-ia ik-nu-šu-ma e-tè-ru*
39) *nap-šat-sún it-ti* LÚ.EN.NAM.MEŠ *ma-ti-ia*
40) LÚ.*ak-li* LÚ.*šá-pi-ri* NUN.MEŠ
41) LÚ.*šu-ut* SAG.MEŠ *u šá-tam-me*
42) *ta-mar-ta-šu-nu*
43) *ka-bit-tu am-ḫur*
44) *i-na qé-re-ti ú-še-šib-šú-nu-ti-ma*
45) *áš-ta-kan-na ni-gu-tú*

which are on the border of the land Elam, the land Karduniaš (Babylonia) from one end to the other (lit.: "above and below"), all of Chaldea, as much as there is (of it), (and) the land Bīt-Yakīn, which is on the shore of the sea, as far as the border of Dilmun; (20) I set eunuchs of mine as provincial governors over them and imposed the yoke of my lordship upon them.

23b–29) At that time, using (as laborers) enemy people that I had conquered, whom the gods Aššur, (25) Nabû, (and) Marduk had made bow down at my feet, and (who) (now) pull my yoke, (and) in accordance with divine will (and) my heart's desire, I built a city at the foot of Mount Muṣri, upstream from Nineveh, and named it Dūr-Šarrukīn.

30–45) I built inside it (the city) a palace using (lit.: "of") elephant ivory, ebony, boxwood, *musukkannu*-wood, cedar, cypress, *daprānu*-juniper, juniper, and terebinth to be my royal residence. I then invited the god Aššur, the great lord, and the (other) gods who dwell in Assyria, (35) (to come) inside it, and I offered pure, honorific sacrifices before them. I received substantial audience gift(s) from rulers from the four quarters (of the world), who had submitted to the yoke of my lordship and (thereby) saved their lives, (along) with (gifts) from the provincial governors of my land, (40) overseers, commanders, nobles, eunuchs, and temple administrators. I had them sit down for a banquet and held a festival.

13

This is by far the longest of the five texts found upon stone thresholds in various doorways of the palace at Khorsabad. Following Sargon's name, titles, and epithets (lines 1–13a), it presents a summary of the major military accomplishments of the king's reign (lines 13b–59a) — including laying waste to the land Urarṭu and plundering the city Muṣaṣir (lines 18b–19), conquering Samaria and Israel (lines 31b–32), defeating Marduk-apla-iddina II of Babylonia (lines 45b–54a), and receiving a gift from Upēri, the ruler of Dilmun (lines 54b–59a) — as well as a description of the full extent of his realm (lines 59b–89). The text then records the building of the city Dūr-Šarrukīn, including the construction and decoration of its palace, and the entry of (the statues of) gods into the palace (lines 90–130). It concludes with an invocation to the god Aššur to look with favor upon the palace's builder

12 line 20 We would expect the verbs here and in lines 22 and 23 to be in the subjunctive in view of the *ša* in line 4.

and the one who dwells in it (lines 131–150). The reference to gods being invited into the palace and receiving offerings there may be connected to the statement in the Assyrian Eponym Chronicle that "the gods of the city Dūr-Šarrukīn entered their temples" on the twenty-second day of Tašrītu (VII) in the eponymy of Ša-Aššur-dubbu (707).

CATALOGUE

Ex.	Source	Provenance	Lines Preserved	cpn
1	Botta, Monument de Ninive 3 pls. 16–16quater	Khorsabad, Palace, Entrance g	1–150	n
2	Botta, Monument de Ninive 3 pl. 4	Khorsabad, Palace, Entrance E	1–150	n
3	Botta, Monument de Ninive 3 pl. 6	Khorsabad, Palace, Entrance H	1–70, 75, 77–82, 84–105, 123–150	n
4	Botta, Monument de Ninive 3 pls. 7–7quater	Khorsabad, Palace, Entrance M	1–64, 76–147	n
5	Botta, Monument de Ninive 3 pls. 11–11quater	Khorsabad, Palace, Entrance T	1–150	n
6	Botta, Monument de Ninive 3 pls. 12–12quater	Khorsabad, Palace, Entrance U	1–150	n
7	Botta, Monument de Ninive 3 pl. 17	Khorsabad, Palace, Entrance j	1–76, 78, 82–139	n
8	Botta, Monument de Ninive 3 pls. 18–18quater	Khorsabad, Palace, Entrance k	1–77, 82–142	n
9	Botta, Monument de Ninive 3 pls. 19–19quater	Khorsabad, Palace, Entrance l	1–68, 70–150	n

COMMENTARY

The present location of these exemplars is not known. They were likely left in situ or lost in the Tigris disaster in 1855. The exemplars are edited from the copies published by P.E. Botta and made by him at the site of Khorsabad; no squeezes of any of the exemplars were made by him. As a result, the exact reading of individual exemplars at numerous points is not certain. Since H. Winckler made his copy of the inscription directly from Botta's copies, without having access to any of the originals or to paper squeezes of them, no reference to his copy is made in the on-page notes.

The line arrangement follows ex. 1. The master line is based on ex. 1 for the most part, but preference is sometimes given to what is found in other exemplars when ex. 1 appears to be the only exemplar or one of only two exemplars to have a particular reading. Ex. 3 is actually a slightly abbreviated version of this inscription in that it omits lines 71–75a, 76, 82b–84a, and 105b–123a. According to the published copies, the exemplars use both Babylonian and Assyrian sign forms.

BIBLIOGRAPHY

1849 Botta, Monument de Ninive 3 pls. 4, 6, 7, 11, 12, and 16–19 (exs. 1–9, copy)

1849–50 de Saulcy, Révue archeólogique 6 pp. 766–772 (lines 1–86, translation)

1886 Bezold, Literatur p. 93 §56.13 (study)

1889 Winckler, Sar. 1 pp. X and 146–157 (ex. 1, edition; exs. 2–9, variants); and 2 pls. 38–40 no. IIII (ex. 1, copy; exs. 2–9, variants)

1926 Ebeling in Gressman, ATAT² p. 352 (lines 31b–41a, translation)

1927 Luckenbill, ARAB 2 pp. 48 and 51–54 §95 and §99–101 (translation)

1953 von Soden, SAHG pp. 281–282 and 390 no. 24g (lines 131–150, translation)

1958 Wiseman, DOTT p. 60 (lines 31b–45a, translation)

1964 Borger, JCS 18 p. 52 and n. 3 (line 109, study)

1964 Brinkman, Studies Oppenheim p. 44 no. 44.2.20.c.iv (study)

1969 Oppenheim, ANET³ p. 284 (lines 31b–45a, translation)

1976 Saporetti, Studi Ciprioti e Rapporti di Scavo 2 pp. 84–85 (lines 41b–45a, 63–65a, translation, study)

1977 Briend and Seux, TPOA no. 41A (lines 1–4a, 31b–33a, 38b–41a, translation)

1979 Borger, BAL^2 pp. 59–63, 131–132, and 322–336 (ex. 1, copy, transliteration, study; exs. 2–9, variants)
1984 Borger, TUAT 1/4 p. 386 (lines 31b–41a, translation)
1986 Renger, CRRA 32 pp. 112–113 and 120 (lines 1–13, 20, 22–26, 31–33, partial transcription, study)
1987 Engel, Dämonen pp. 142–150 (lines 108b–120a, edition of exs. 1–2, 4–9)
1992 Becking, Fall of Samaria p. 27 (lines 31–32, edition)
1993 Foster, Before the Muses 2 p. 706 no. IV.2.a.2 (lines 131–150, translation)
1994 Fuchs, Khorsabad pp. 259–271 and 359–362 no. 2.5.4 (exs. 1–9, edition) and pp. 386, 392–395 (study)
1999 J.M. Russell, Writing on the Wall pp. 108–110 (exs. 1–9, study)
1999 Van De Mieroop, Studies Renger p. 333 (lines 41–45, 54–59, edition)
2000 Younger, COS 2 p. 298 no. 2.118G (lines 31–41a, translation)
2001 Rollinger, Melammu 2 p. 239 (lines 34–35a, edition)
2014 Maniori, Campagne di Sargon p. 50 g3 and passim (ex. 1, study)
2017 Liverani, Assyria p. 83 (lines 117–123, translation, combined with other texts)
2018 Frahm, Last Days pp. 80–81 no. 18 (lines 31b–32, edition, study)
2019 Marchesi, JNES 78 p. 24 (22–27, edition)

TEXT

1) É.GAL ^{m}LUGAL-GI.NA LUGAL GAL-*ú*
2) LUGAL *dan-nu* LUGAL *kiš-šá-ti* LUGAL KUR *aš-šur*.KI
3) GÌR.NÍTA KÁ.DINGIR.RA.KI LUGAL KUR EME.GI$_7$
4) *ù ak-ka-de-e mi-gir* DINGIR.MEŠ GAL.MEŠ
5) *za-nin* ZIMBIR.KI NIBRU.KI KÁ.DINGIR.RA.KI
6) *mu-šá-áš-šík tup-šik-ki* BÀD.AN.KI ÚRI.KI
7) UNUG.KI *eridu*.KI ARARMA†.KI *kul-aba$_4$*.KI *ki-sik*.KI
8) URU.*né-med-*^{d}*la-gu-da mu-šap-ši-ḫu*
9) UN.MEŠ-*šú-un ka-a-ṣir ki-din-nu-ut*
10) *bal-til*.KI *ba-ṭil-ta ša* UGU URU.*ḫar-ra-na*
11) AN.DÙL-*la-šú it-ru-ṣu-ma*
12) *ki-i ṣa-ab* ^{d}*a-nim ù* ^{d}*da-gan*
13) *iš-ṭu-ru za-kut-sún eṭ-lu qar-du*
14) *šá-kin* BAD$_5$.BAD$_5$-*e* ^{md}*ḫum-ba-ni-ga-áš*
15) LÚ.ELAM.MA.KI-*i mu-ab-bit*
16) KUR.*kar-al-la* KUR.*šur-da* URU.*ki-še-su*
17) URU.*ḫar-ḫar* KUR.*ma-da-a-a* KUR.*el-li-pi*
18) *e-mid-du ni-ir* ^{d}*aš-šur mu-šaḫ-rib*
19) KUR.*ur-ar-ṭi šá-lil* URU.*mu-ṣa-ṣir*
20) *šá-giš* KUR.*an-di-a* KUR.*zi-kir-tu*
21) *mu-šap-ši-ḫu* KUR.*man-na-a-a*
22) *mu-rib mal-ki* KUR.*a-ma-at-ti* URU.*gar-ga-miš*
23) KUR.*kúm-mu-ḫi na-pi-i'* KUR.*kam-ma-ni*
24) *ša* ^{m}*gu-un-zi-na-nu ul-tu*
25) *qé-reb* URU.*me-lid-di* URU LUGAL-*ti-šú*
26) *is-su-ḫu-ma* UGU *gi-mir* KUR.MEŠ-*šú-nu*
27) *iš-tak-ka-nu* LÚ.*šá-ak-nu-ti*
28) *mu-nak-kir* LUGAL-*ut* ^{m}*tar-ḫu-la-ra*
29) LÚ.URU.*mar-qa-sa-a-a ša paṭ gi-mir*
30) KUR.*gúr-gu-me a-na mi-ṣir* KUR *aš-šur*.KI
31) *ú-ter-ru ka-šid* URU.*sa-mir-i-na*
32) *ù gi-mir* KUR.É-^{m}*ḫu-um-ri-a*
33) *šá-lil* URU.*as-du-di* URU.*ši-nu-uḫ-ti*

1–4) Palace of Sargon (II), great king, strong king, king of the world, king of Assyria, governor of Babylon, king of the land of Sumer and Akkad, favorite of the great gods;

5–13a) who provides for (the cities) Sippar, Nippur, (and) Babylon; who abolished corvée duty for (the cities) Dēr, Ur, Uruk, Eridu, Larsa, Kullaba, Kissik, (and) Nēmed-Laguda (and) who gave relief to their people; who (re)-established the privileged status (10) of (the city) Baltil (Aššur) that had lapsed; who extended his protection over the city Ḫarrān and recorded their exemption (from obligations) as if (its people were) people of the gods Anu and Dagān;
13b–31a) the valiant man who brought about the defeat of Ḫumbanigaš (Ḫumban-nikaš I), the Elamite; (15) who destroyed the land Karalla, the land Šurda, the city Kišesim, the city Ḫarḫar, the land Media, (and) the land Ellipi, (and) imposed the yoke of the god Aššur (upon them); who laid waste to the land Urarṭu, plundered the city Muṣaṣir, (20) slaughtered the lands Andia (and) Zikirtu, (and) pacified the land Mannea; who made the rulers of the land Hamath, the city Carchemish, and the land Kummuḫu tremble (and) plundered the land Kammanu; who deported Gunzinānu from (25) the city Melid, his (Gunzinānu's) royal city, and set officials over all of their lands; who did away with the kingship of Tarḫu-lara of the city Marqasa (and) who made all of the land Gurgum (part of) the territory of Assyria;

31b–45a) who conquered the city Samaria and all of the land Bīt-Ḫumria (Israel); who plundered the cities Ashdod (and) Šinuḫtu; who caught the Ionians who

8 Exs. 4 and 6 omit URU "city" before Nēmed-Laguda.
12 Ex. 2 omits *ù*, "and."
15–18 See the on-page note to text no. 8 lines 7–8.
17 Ex. 1 has KUR.*ḫar-ḫar*, thus "land Ḫarḫar" for "city Ḫarḫar."
23 Exs. 2–6 have URU before *kummuḫi* instead of KUR; thus "city Kummuḫu" for "land Kummuḫu."
25 Ex. 7 has KUR before *meliddi* instead of URU; thus "land Melid" for "city Melid."

34) ša KUR.ia-am-na-a-a ša MURUB$_4$ tam-tim
35) ki-ma nu-ú-ni i-ba-a-ru na-si-iḫ
36) KUR.ka-as-ku gi-mir KUR.ta-ba-li
37) ù KUR.ḫi-lak-ki ṭa-rid ^{m}mi-ta-a
38) LUGAL KUR.mu-us-ki ša ina KUR.ra-pi-ḫi
39) BAD$_5$.BAD$_5$-e KUR.mu-ṣu-ri iš-ku-nu-ma
40) ^{m}ḫa-a-nu-nu LUGAL URU.ḫa-zi-ti
41) im-nu-ú šal-la-ti-iš mu-šak-niš
42) 7 LUGAL.MEŠ-ni ša KUR.ia-aʾ na-ge-e
43) ša KUR.ia-ad-na-na ša ma-lak
44) 7 u$_4$-me i-na MURUB$_4$ tam-tim šit-ku-na-at
45) šu-bat-su-un ù ^{md}AMAR.UTU-IBILA-SUM.NA
46) LUGAL KUR.kal-di a-šib GÚ ÍD.mar-ra-ti
47) ša ki-i la lìb-bi DINGIR.MEŠ LUGAL-ut
48) KÁ.DINGIR.RA.KI e-pu-uš-ma tak-šu-da
49) GAL-tu qa-as-su gi-mir KUR-šú
50) DAGAL-tim mal-ma-liš i-zu-zu-ú-ma
51) i-na ŠU.II LÚ.šu-ut SAG-šú LÚ.GAR.KUR
52) KÁ.DINGIR.RA.KI ù LÚ.šu-ut SAG-šú
53) LÚ.GAR.KUR KUR.gam-bu-li im-nu-ma
54) e-mid-du ni-ru-uš-šú ^{m}ú-pe-e-ri
55) LUGAL dil-mun.KI ša ma-lak 30 KASKAL.GÍD
56) i-na MURUB$_4$ tam-tim ki-ma nu-ú-ni
57) šit-ku-nu nar-ba-ṣu da-na-an
58) be-lu-ti-šú iš-me-ma iš-šá-a
59) ta-mar-tuš i-na li-i-ti
60) ù da-na-ni ša DINGIR.MEŠ GAL.MEŠ
61) EN.MEŠ-šú ša GIŠ.TUKUL.MEŠ-šú ú-šat-bu-ma
62) ú-ra-si-bu na-gab ga-re-e-šu
63) iš-tu KUR.ia-ad-na-na ša MURUB$_4$ tam-tim
64) šá-lam ^{d}UTU-ši a-di pa-aṭ KUR.mu-ṣu-ri
65) ù KUR.mu-us-ki KUR MAR.TU.KI DAGAL-tu
66) KUR.ḫat-ti a-na si-ḫir-ti-šá nap-ḫa-ar
67) KUR.gu-ti-um.KI KUR.ma-da-a-a
68) ru-qu-ti ša pa-aṭ KUR.bi-ik-ni
69) KUR.el-li-pi KUR.ra-a-ši ša i-te-e
70) KUR.ELAM.MA.KI ša a-aḫ ÍD.IDIGNA
71) LÚ.i-tu-ʾu LÚ.ru-bu-ʾu
72) LÚ.ḫa-ṭal-lum LÚ.lab-du-du
73) LÚ.ḫa-am-ra-nu LÚ.ú-bu-lum
74) LÚ.ru-ʾu-ú-a LÚ.li-iʾ-ta-a-a
75) ša a-aḫ ÍD.su-rap-pi ÍD.uq-né-e

(live in) the middle of the sea (35) like fish; who deported (the people of) the land Kasku, all of the land Tabal, and the land Ḫilakku, (and) drove out Mitâ (Midas), king of the land Musku; who brougt about the defeat of Egypt in the land Raphia and counted (40) Ḫanūnu (Hanno), king of the city Gaza as booty; who subjugated seven kings of the land Yāʾ — a region of the land Yadnana (Cyprus) — whose abode is situated at a distance of seven days (journey) in the middle of the sea;

45b–59a) moreover, (who)se great hand defeated Marduk-apla-iddina (II) (Merodach-Baladan), king of Chaldea, who dwelt on the shore of the sea (and) who exercised kingship over Babylon against the will of the gods; (50) (who) divided up all of his (Marduk-apla-iddina's) wide land into equal parts, assigned (them) to the authority of a eunuch of his (Sargon's), the governor of Babylon, and a(nother) eunuch of his, the governor of the land Gambulu, and imposed his yoke (upon them) — Upēri, (55) king of Dilmun, who(se) lair is situated at a distance of thirty leagues in the middle of the sea, like that of a fish, heard of his (Sargon's) lordly might, and brought (him) his audience gift;

59b–89) (the one who) with the power and might (granted him by) the great gods, his lords, mobilized his weapons and cut down all his foes; (who) ruled all together from the land Yadnana (Cyprus), which is in the middle of the Western Sea, as far as the border(s) of Egypt (65) and the land Musku, the wide land Amurru, the land Ḫatti (Syria) in its entirety, all of the land Gutium, the distant Medes (who live) on the border of Mount Bikni, the lands Ellipi (and) Rāši on the border (70) of the land Elam, those who (live) beside the Tigris River — the Ituʾu, Rubuʾu, Ḫaṭallu, Labdudu, Ḫamrānu, Ubulu, Ruʾuʾa, (and) Liʾtaʾu (tribes) — (75) those who (live) beside the Surappu and Uqnû Rivers — the Gambulu, Ḫindaru, (and) Puqudu (tribes) — the Sutians, the people of the steppe of the land Yadburu, as many as there are, from the land Samʾūna (80) as far as the cities Bubê

34 Exs. 2–4 and 6 have URU instead of KUR; thus "Ionians" (lit.: "people of the city Ionia") for "Ionians" (lit.: "people of the land Ionia").
36 Ex. 7 have URU before *kasku* instead of KUR; thus "the city Kasku" for "the land Kasku."
37 Ex. 4 omits *ù*, "and."
38 Exs. 3, 4, 7, 9, and possibly 2 (mostly restored) have URU before *rapiḫi* instead of KUR; thus "city Raphia" for "land Raphia."
42 Ex. 1 has 6 for 7 (error of modern copyist?).
51 Ex. 1 has LÚ.*šu-ut* SAG-*ia*, "a eunuch of mine," for LÚ.*šu-ut* SAG-*šú*, "a eunuch of his."
52 Ex. 1 has LÚ.*šu-ut* SAG-*ia*, "a(nother) eunuch of mine," for LÚ.*šu-ut* SAG-*šú*, "a(nother) eunuch of his."
53 Ex. 6 has LÚ.*gam-bu-li*, "the people Gambulu," for KUR.*gam-bu-li*, "the land Gambulu."
58 Ex. 1 has *be-lu-ti-ia*, "my lordly" for *be-lu-ti-šú*, "his (Sargon's) lordly."
61 An alternate translation making the gods the subject of the verb *ú-šat-bu-ma* would be "the one who with the power and might (granted him by) the great gods, his lords, who raised up his weapons, cut down all his foes."
65 Ex. 7 omits *ù*, "and."
67 Exs. 2–3 and 5–6 omit KUR, "land," before "Gutium."
71–75a Ex. 3 omits LÚ.*i-tu-ʾu* ... *ša a-aḫ*, "the Ituʾu ... (those) who (live) beside."

76) LÚ.*gam-bu-lum* LÚ.*ḫi-in-da-ru*
77) LÚ.*pu-qu-du* LÚ.*su-te-e ṣa-ab* EDIN
78) *ša* KUR.*ia-ad-bu-ri ma-la ba-šu-ú*
79) *ul-tu* KUR.*sa-am-ʾu-ú-na*
80) *a-di* URU.*bu-bé-e* URU.DU$_6$-^{d}*ḫum-ba*
81) *ša mi-ṣir* KUR.ELAM.MA.KI KUR.*kár-dun-ía-áš*
82) *e-liš ù šap-liš* KUR.É-^{m}*a-muk-ka-ni*
83) KUR.É-^{m}*da-ku-ri* KUR.É-^{m}*šil-a-ni*
84) KUR.É-^{m}*sa-ʾa-al-la si-ḫir-ti*
85) KUR.*kal-di ma-la ba-šu-ú* KUR.É-^{m}*ia-ki-ni*
86) *ša ki-šad* ÍD.*mar-ra-ti a-di pa-aṭ* NI.TUK.KI
87) *mit-ḫa-riš i-bí-lu-ma* LÚ.*šu-ut* SAG.MEŠ-*šú*
88) LÚ.EN.NAM.MEŠ UGU-*šú-nu iš-tak-ka-nu-ma*
89) *ni-ir be-lu-ti-šú e-mid-su-nu-ti*
90) *i-na u$_4$-me-šu-ma i-na ba-ḫu-la-ti*
91) *na-ki-ri ki-šit-ti* ŠU.II-*šú ša* ^{d}*aš-šur*
92) ^{d}AG *ù* ^{d}AMAR.UTU DINGIR.MEŠ *ti-ik-le-šú*
93) *iš-ru-ku is-qu-uš-šú ki-i ṭè-em* DINGIR-*ma*
94) *i-na* GÌR.II KUR.*mu-uṣ-ri e-le-nu*
95) URU.NINA *i-na bi-bil lìb-bi-šú*
96) URU DÙ-*uš-ma* URU.BÀD-^{m}LUGAL-GI.NA
97) *iz-ku-ra ni-bit-su* É.GAL.MEŠ ZÚ AM.SI
98) GIŠ.ESI GIŠ.TÚG GIŠ.*mu-suk-kan-ni* GIŠ.EREN
99) GIŠ.ŠUR.MÌN GIŠ.*dup-ra-nu* ŠIM.LI *ù* GIŠ.*bu-uṭ-ni*
100) *a-na mu-šab* LUGAL-*ti-šú qer-bu-uš-šu*
101) *ib-ni-ma* GIŠ.ÙR.MEŠ GIŠ.EREN GAL.MEŠ
102) *e-li-šin ú-šat-ri-ṣa* GIŠ.IG.MEŠ
103) GIŠ.ŠUR.MÌN GIŠ.*mu-suk-kan-ni mé-se-er* URUDU
104) *nam-ri ú-rak-kis-ma ú-rat-ta-a*
105) *né-reb-šin* É *ap-pa-a-ti tam-šil* É.GAL
106) KUR.*ḫat-ti ša i-na li-šá-an* KUR MAR.TU.KI
107) É *ḫi-la-a-ni i-šá-as-su-šú ú-še-pi-šá*
108) *mé-eḫ-ret ba-bi-ši-in* 8 UR.MAḪ
109) *tu-ʾa-a-me šu-ut* 1 ŠÁR GÉŠ.U 6 UŠ 50.ÀM
110) GUN *mal-tak-ti* URUDU *nam-ri*
111) *ša i-na ši-pir* ^{d}*nin-á-gal*
112) *ip-pat-qu-ma ma-lu-ú nam-ri-ri*
113) 4 GIŠ.*tim-me* GIŠ.EREN *šu-ta-ḫu-ti*
114) *ša* 1 NINDA.TA.ÀM *ku-bur-šú-un bi-ib-lat*
115) KUR.*ḫa-ma-ni* UGU *ur-maḫ-ḫe-e ú-kin-ma*

(and) Tīl-Ḫumba which are on the border of the land Elam, the land Karduniaš (Babylonia) from one end to the other (lit.: "above and below"), the lands Bīt-Amukāni, Bīt-Dakkūri, Bīt-Šilāni, (and) Bīt-Saʾalli, all of (85) Chaldea, as much as there is (of it), the land Bīt-Yakīn, which is on the shore of the sea, as far as the border of Dilmun; (who) set eunuchs of his as provincial governors over them and imposed the yoke of his lordship upon them.

90–97a) At that time, using (as laborers) enemy people whom he had captured, whom the gods Aššur, Nabû, and Marduk, his divine helpers, had granted (to him) as his lot, in accordance with divine will (95) (and) his heart's desire, he built a city at the foot of Mount Muṣri, upstream from the city Nineveh, and named it Dūr-Šarrukīn.

97b–108a) He built inside it (the city) palatial halls using (lit.: "of") elephant ivory, ebony, boxwood, *musukkannu*-wood, cedar, cypress, *daprānu*-juniper, juniper, and terebinth (100) to be his royal residence and he roofed them with large beams of cedar. He bound the doors of cypress (and) *musukkannu*-wood with band(s) of shining copper and installed (them) in (105) their entrance(s). He had built in front of their gates a portico (*bīt appāti*), a replica of a Hittite palace, which is called a *bīt ḫilāni* in the language of Amurru.

108b–123a) Eight twin lion (colossi) of shining copper that weigh 4,610 (110) full (lit.: "tested") talents (and) that were cast by the craft of the god Ninagal and filled with radiance — upon (those) lion colossi he installed four matching cedar columns, whose diameter(s) are one *nindanu* each, the product of (115) Mount Amanus; and he positioned cross-beams (upon them) as a cornice for their gates. He had magnificent

76–77 Ex. 3 has ⌜*gi*?*-mir*?⌝ *su-te-e*, "*all* the Sutians," for LÚ.*gam-bu-lum* LÚ.*ḫi-in-da-ru* LÚ.*pu-qu-du* LÚ.*su-te-e*, "the Gambulu, Ḫindaru, (and) Puqudu (tribes) — the Sutians."
79 Only exs. 1 and 3 have KUR before *samʾuna* ("land Samʾūna"). Ex. 2, 4, 6, and 9 have URU ("city Samʾūna") and ex. 5 has LÚ ("people Samʾuna").
81 Ex. 5 omits KUR, "land," before Elam.
82–84 Ex. 3 omits KUR.É-^{m}*a-muk-ka-ni* ... KUR.É-^{m}*ša-ʾa-al-la*, "the lands Bīt-Amukāni ... (and) Bīt-Saʾalli."
83 Ex. 2 omits KUR, "land" before Bīt-Šilāni.
85 Ex. 7 omits KUR, "land," before Bīt-Yakīn.
92 Exs. 3, 6, and 8 add ^{d}UTU, "Šamaš," before ^{d}AG, "Nabû." Exs. 3–9 omit *ù*, "and," after Nabû; only ex. 1 has *ù* there. Ex. 7 has *ù* between ^{d}AMAR.UTU and DINGIR.MEŠ *ti-ik-le-šú*, thus "Marduk, and the gods, his helpers."
93 Ex. 7 has *iš-qu-uš-šin*, "their (feminine) lot," for *is-qu-uš-šú*, "his lot."
95 Exs. 2, 4, 6, and 9 have NINA.KI, "Nineveh," for URU.NINA, "city Nineveh." Exs. 3–4 have *-ia* for *-šú* ("my heart's desire" for "his heart's desire").
97 Ex. 7 has *az-ku-ra*, "I named," for *iz-ku-ra*, "he named."
99 Ex. 1 omits *ù*, "and."
100 Ex. 7 has *i-na* for *a-na*.
105–123 Ex. 3 omits É *ap-pa-a-ti* ... *ú-šá-lik*, "He had built ... object of wonder."
106 Ex. 5 omits KUR, "land," before *ḫat-ti*.
109 Instead of 4,610, some exemplars appear to have other amounts, possibly due to errors of the modern copyist: 4,600 (exs. 2 and 4), 4,620 (ex. 9), and 4,730 (ex. 8).

116) *dáp-pi ku-lul* KÁ.MEŠ-*ši-in e-mid*
117) UDU.MEŠ *šad-di* ^{d}LAMMA.MEŠ MAḪ.MEŠ
118) *ša* NA$_4$ KUR-*i eš-qí nak-liš ú-še-piš-ma*
119) *a-na er-bet-ti šá-a-ri ú-šá-aṣ-bi-ta*
120) SI.GAR-*ši-in as-kup-pi* NA$_4$.*pi-li* GAL.MEŠ
121) *da-ád-me ki-šit-ti* ŠU.II-*šú ṣe-ru-uš-šin*
122) *ib-šim-ma a-sur-ru-šin ú-šá-as-ḫi-ra*
123) *a-na tab-ra-a-ti ú-šá-lik* ^{d}*aš-šur* EN
124) GAL-*ú ù* DINGIR.MEŠ GAL.MEŠ *a-ši-bu-ut*
125) KUR *aš-šur*.KI *i-na qer-bi-šin iq-re-ma*
126) UDU.SISKUR.MEŠ KÙ.MEŠ *ma-ḫar-šú-un iq-qí*
127) *kàd-re-e ṣa-ri-ri ru-uš-še*$_{20}$-*e ṣar-pi*
128) *eb-bi ta-mar-tu ka-bit-tu*
129) *ú-šam-ḫi-ir-šú-nu-ti-ma*
130) *ú-šá-li-ṣa nu-pa-ar-šú-un*
131) É.GAL *šá-a-tu* ^{d}*aš-šur* AD DINGIR.MEŠ
132) *i-na nu-um-mur bu-ni-šú*
133) KÙ.MEŠ *ki-niš lip-pa-lis-ma*
134) *a-na u*$_4$-*me ru-qu-ti*
135) *ud-du-sa lit-tas-qar*
136) *i-na pi-i-šú el-li*
137) *liš-šá-kin-ma* ^{d}ALAD *na-ṣi-ru*
138) DINGIR *mu-šal-li-mu im-ma*
139) *ù mu-šá qé-reb-šá liš-tab-ru-ma*
140) *a-a ip-par-ku-ú i-da-a-šá*
141) *qí-bi-tuš-šu mal-ku ba-nu-šá*
142) *ši-bu-ta lil-lik lik-šu-ud*
143) *lit-tu-tu a-na u*$_4$-*me*
144) *da-ru-ti li-bur e-pi-sa*
145) *ina šap-ti-šú el-le-ti*
146) *li-ṣa-a a-ši-ib lìb-bi-šá*
147) *i-na ṭu-ub* UZU *nu-ug lìb-bi*
148) *ù na-mar ka-bat-ti*
149) *qé-reb-šá li-šá-li-la*
150) *liš-ba-a bu-ʾa-a-ri*

mountain sheep colossi of massive mountain stone skillfully made and in the four directions he had (them) hold their (the gates') door bolt(s). He depicted the settlements that he had conquered upon large limestone slabs and surrounded their (the palatial halls') lower courses (with them). He made (them) an object of wonder.

123b–130) He invited the god Aššur, the great lord, and the great gods who dwell in Assyria (to come) inside them (the palace halls), and he offered pure sacrifices before them. He offered them gifts of red *ṣāriru*-gold (and) pure silver as (his) substantial audience gift, and (thus) made their (the gods') moods joyful.

131–150) May the god Aššur, the father of the gods, steadfastly look upon this palace with his holy, radiant face and (135) may he ordain its renovation for future days. May (the following commands) come from (lit.: "be set in") his holy mouth: May the guardian spirit (and) the protective god stay continually in it, day and night, and (140) may they never leave it. At his command, may the ruler who constructed it live long (and) reach extreme old age. May its builder remain in good health forever. May (the following command) issue (145) from his (the god Aššur's) holy lips. May the one who dwells inside it (the palace) rejoice there in physical well-being, merriment, and happiness, (and) may he be fully satisfied with (his) good fortune.

14

Following the king's name, titles, and references to his good treatment of several Babylonian cities and of the Assyrian cities Aššur and Ḫarrān (lines 1–11), the fifth threshold inscription from the palace at Khorsabad records the extent of the king's realm (lines 12–28a). Although the end of this fifth inscription is not fully preserved, the text clearly records the construction of the city of Khorsabad and in particular the erection and decoration of its palace (lines 29a–47).

13 line 117 With regard to ^{d}LAMMA.MEŠ MAḪ.MEŠ (^{d}LAMMA MAḪ.MEŠ on exs. 4 and 6–9), see text no. 2 on-page note to line 479.
13 line 121 Ex. 5 has ŠU.II-*ia* ("that I had conquered" for "that he had conquered").
13 line 124 Exs. 6 and 9 omit GAL.MEŠ (thus, "the gods" rather than "the great gods").
13 line 125 Exs. 4 and 9 have *qer-bi-šá*, "inside it," instead of *qer-bi-šin*, "inside them."
13 line 137 Ex. 7 has ^{d}LAMMA for ^{d}ALAD (or error of modern copyist?).
13 line 144 The reading *li-* in *li-bur* comes from exs. 2, 5, and 6, while ex. 1, the only other exemplar preserved here, has *li*$_x$(LIL)-*bur*, or *lil-bur* if we assume the verb is from *labāru*, "to be/become old." With regard to the understanding of the word (translated here "remain in good health") as coming from *bâru*, see Borger, BAL^2 p. 132 and CAD B p. 126.
13 line 145 Ex. 6 has *a-na* for *ina*.

CATALOGUE

Ex.	Museum Number	Source	Provenance	Dimensions (cm)	Lines Preserved	cpn
1	—	Botta, Monument de Ninive 3 pl. 14	Khorsabad, Palace, Entrance c	—	1–41	n
2	—	Botta, Monument de Ninive 3 pl. 20	Khorsabad, Palace, Entrance δ	—	1–11, 13–25	n
3	—	Botta, Monument de Ninive 4 pl. 181^{c} no. 5	Khorsabad, Palace, Room VIII	—	31, 33–47	n
4	BM 135206 (1970-1-31,10)	Mitchell, BMQ 36 pl. 55d	Probably Khorsabad	34.0×76.5	33–36	c

COMMENTARY

The present whereabouts of exs. 1–3 are not known. It is likely that they were either left in situ or lost in the Tigris disaster in 1855. P.E. Botta states that ex. 3 is one of several "inscriptions détachées" which he collated either from the original or from paper squeezes and that it is a fragment coming from "Salle VIII." Thus, it is not clear if ex. 3 is on a threshold/pavement slab or not. The inscription on the piece, however, appears to fit here. As noted by A. Fuchs (Khorsabad pp. 271–272), it is possible that this exemplar comes from Door P since this is the only doorway in Room VIII whose threshold is not otherwise known and since E. Flandin's detailed drawing of this doorway (Botta, Monument de Ninive 1 pl. 26) indicates that there was an inscription there. No squeezes of the exemplars exist today and if one of ex. 3 once existed, it is no longer preserved with the other squeezes in the Louvre. Exs. 1–3 are edited from the copies published by Botta. H. Winckler's copy of the inscription, which was made from Botta's copies of exs. 1 and 2, provides no independent evidence although it is sometimes mentioned in the list of minor variants. It is clear, however, that at times he restored signs without giving any indication that they were restored. Ex. 4 (formerly in the collection of the Royal Geographical Society, London) has been described as a "limestone relief," but it is more likely a fragment from a threshold.

The line arrangement follows ex. 1 for lines 1–41 and ex. 3 for lines 42–47. The master line for lines 1-41 is a composite from the various exemplars, with preference given to ex. 1 for lines 1–41; lines 42–47 follow ex. 3. The restorations in lines 28–47 are based upon text no. 11 lines 18–41, text no. 12 lines 23–33, and text no. 13 lines 93–122.

BIBLIOGRAPHY

1849 Botta, Monument de Ninive 3 pls. 14 and 20, and 4 pl. 181 no. 5 (exs. 1–3, copy)

1880 Ménant, Manuel pp. 316–322 (ex. 2, variants to text no. 12 ex. 2)

1886 Bezold, Literatur p. 93 §56.13 (study)

1889 Winckler, Sar. 1 pp. X and 158–163; and 2 pl. 40 no. V (exs. 1–2, copy of lines 1–39, edition of lines 1–40a)

1927 Luckenbill, ARAB 2 pp. 48 and 54–55 §§95 and 102 (translation)

1939 Weidner, Reliefs p. 69 n. 126 (ex. 4, transliteration)

1959 Barnett, Geographical Journal 125 p. 198 (ex. 4, edition)

1971–72 Mitchell, BMQ 36 pp. 136 and 145, and pl. 55d (ex. 4, photo, study)

1976 Saporetti, Studi Ciprioti e Rapporti di Scavo 2 pp. 84–85 (lines 14a–15, translation, study)

1986 Renger, CRRA 32 pp. 112–113 (lines 1–11, partial transcription, study)

1987 Heimpel, ZA 77 p. 89 no. 75 (lines 24–26, study)

1994 Fuchs, Khorsabad pp. 271–275 and 362–363 no.2.5.5 (exs. 1–4, edition), and pp. 394–395 (study)

1999 J.M. Russell, Writing on the Wall pp. 108–110 (exs. 1–4, study)

TEXT

1) É.GAL ^{m}LUGAL-GI.NA LUGAL† GAL-*ú* LUGAL *dan-nu*
2) LUGAL *kiš-šá-tim* LUGAL KUR *aš-šur*.KI GÌR.NÍTA
3) KÁ.DINGIR.RA.KI LUGAL KUR EME†.<GI$_{7}$> *ù* URI.KI†
4) *mi*†-*gir* DINGIR.MEŠ ⸢GAL⸣.[MEŠ] *ša*† ZIMBIR†.KI NIBRU.KI
5) KÁ.DINGIR.RA.KI *ù bár-sipa*.KI
6) *za-nin-us*†-*su-un*† *e-tep-pu-*[*šá*] *ša* ⸢BÀD†⸣.AN†.KI
7) ÚRI†.KI UNUG.KI *eridu*.KI ARARMA.KI *kul-*⸢*la*⸣-[*ba*.KI]
8) *ki-sik*.KI URU.*né-med-*⸢^{d}⸣*la-*[*gu*]-*da*† ⸢*áš*⸣-[*kun*]
9) *an-*⸢*du*⸣-*ra-ar*†-*šu-un za-kut* [*bal*]-*til*.KI†
10) ⸢*ù*⸣ [URU].*ḫar-ra-*[*na*] *ša*† *ul-*[*tu*] ⸢*u*$_{4}$†⸣-*me*† *ul-lu-ú-ti*
11) *im-ma-*[*šu*]-⸢*ma*⸣ [*ki-din*]-*nu-*⸢*us*⸣-[*su-un*] *ba-ṭil-ta*† *ú*†-*ter*† *áš*†-*ru-uš-šá*†
12) *i-na e*†-*muq*† DINGIR.MEŠ GAL†.MEŠ EN†.MEŠ-<*ia*> *lu at-a-lak*†-*ma* KUR.[MEŠ]
13) *la ma-gi-ri ḫur-šá-a-ni la kan*†-*šu-ti ú-šak-ni-šá*
14) *a-na* GÌR.II-*ia iš-tu* KUR.*ia-ad-na-na ša*† MURUB$_{4}$ *tam-tim*
15) *ša e-reb* ^{d}UTU-*ši a-di* ⸢*pa*⸣-*aṭ* KUR.*mu-ṣu-ri* ⸢*ù*⸣ KUR.*mu-uš-ki*
16) KUR MAR.TU.KI DAGAL-*tim* KUR.*ḫat-ti a-na si-*⸢*ḫir*⸣-*ti-šá*
17) *nap-ḫa-ar*† *gu-ti-um*.KI KUR.*ma-da-a-a ru-qu-ú-ti*
18) *ša pa-aṭ* KUR.*bi-ik-ni* KUR.*el-li-pi* KUR.*ra-a-ši*
19) *ša i-te-e* KUR.ELAM.MA.KI LÚ.*a-ra-me šá a-aḫ* ÍD.IDIGNA
20) ÍD.*su-rap-pi* ÍD.*uq-né-e gi-mir*† LÚ.*su-ti-i*
21) *ṣa-ab* EDIN *ša* KUR.*ia-ad-bu-ri ma-la ba-šu-ú*
22) *ul-tu* URU.*sa-am-ʾu-ú-na* URU.KÁ-BÀD URU.BÀD-^{d}*te-li-tim*
23) URU.*bu-bé-e* URU.DU$_{6}$-^{d}*ḫum-ba ša mi-ṣir* KUR.ELAM.MA.KI
24) KUR.*kár-dun-ía-áš e-liš u šap-liš si-ḫir-ti* LÚ.*kal-di*
25) *mal*† *ba-šu-ú* KUR.É-^{m}*ia-kin*$_{7}$ *šá* [*ki-šad*] ÍD.*mar-ra-ti*
26) ⸢*a*⸣-*di pa*†-*aṭ* NI.TUK.KI *mit-ḫa-riš*† *lu a-*⸢*bel*⸣-*ma* LÚ.*šu-*⸢*ut*⸣ SAG.[(MEŠ)]-*ia*†
27) LÚ.EN.NAM.MEŠ UGU-*šú-nu áš*†-*tak-kan-ma* ⸢*ni*⸣-[*ir*] *be-lu-ti-ia*
28) *e-mid-su-nu-ti* ⸢*i-na*⸣ *u*$_{4}$-*me-šu-*[*ma i*]-*na ba-ḫu-la-ti*
29) *na-ki-ri ki-šit-ti* ŠU.II-*ia* [*ša* ^{d}]*aš-šur* ^{d}AG†
30) *ù* ^{d}AMAR.[UTU *a-na*] GÌR.II†-*ia ú-*[*šak-ni-šú-ma*

1–4a) Palace of Sargon (II), great king, strong king, king of the world, king of Assyria, governor of Babylon, king of the land of Sumer and Akkad, favorite of the great gods.

4b–11) I continually act[ed] as provider for (the cities) Sippar, Nippur, Babylon, and Borsippa; I [(re)-established] the freedom (from obligations) of (the cities) Dēr, Ur, Uruk, Eridu, Larsa, Kulla[ba], Kissik, (and) Nēmed-La[gu]da. I restored the exemption (from obligations) of (the city) [Bal]til (Aššur) (10) and [the city] Ḫarrā[n], which had fallen into [oblivion] in the distant [pa]st, and [their privile]ged status that had lapsed.

12–28a) By the strength of the great gods, <my> lords, I regularly advanced and made uncompliant land[s] (and) insubmissive mountain regions bow down at my feet. I ruled all together from the land Yadnana (Cyprus), which is in the middle of the Western Sea, (15) as far as the border(s) of Egypt and the land Musku, the wide land Amurru, the land Ḫatti (Syria) in its entirety, all of (the land) Gutium, the distant Medes (who live) on the border of Mount Bikni, the lands Ellipi (and) Rāši on the border of the land Elam, the Arameans who (live) beside the Tigris, (20) Surappu, (and) Uqnû Rivers, all the Sutians, the people of the steppe of the land Yadburu, as many as there are, from the cities Samʾūna, Bāb-dūri, Dūr-Telīte, Bubê, (and) Tīl-Ḫumba which are on the border of the land Elam, the land Karduniaš (Babylonia) from end to end (lit.: "above and below"), all of the Chaldeans, (25) as many as there are, (and) the land Bīt-Yakīn, which is [on the shore] of the sea, as far as the border of Dilmun; I set eunuchs of mine as provincial governors over them and imposed the y[oke] of my lordship upon them.

28b–33a) At that time, using (as laborers) enemy people whom I had captured, [whom] the gods Aššur, Nabû, (30) and Mar[duk] had [made bow down at] my feet, [and] (who) (now) pull my yoke, [in] accordance

14 Ex. 2 has Á for *a-na*; possibly a modern miscopy for *i-na* or *a-na*.
15 Ex. 2 omits *ša*.
19 Ex. 2 has *na-gab* LÚ.*a-ra-me*, "all of the Arameans."

i]-*šu*-⌜*ṭu*⌝
31) *ab-šá-a-ni*† [*ki*]-*i* ⌜*ṭè*⌝-*em*† DINGIR-*ma*† *i*†-[*na* GÌR].II KUR.*mu-uṣ*†-*ri*
32) *e*-⌜*le*⌝-[*nu* NINA.KI *i*]-*na bi*-⌜*bil*⌝ [*lìb*]-⌜*bi*†⌝-*ia*† URU† *e-pu*†-*uš-ma*
33) URU.BÀD-LUGAL-[GIN *az-ku*]-*ra* [*ni-bit*]-⌜*su*⌝ É.GAL.MEŠ

with divine will (and) my [hea]rt's desire, I built a city a[t the foo]t of Mount Muṣri, upst[ream from Nineveh], and [nam]ed it Dūr-Šarru[kīn].

34) ZÚ AM.SI GIŠ.ESI [GIŠ.TÚG] GIŠ.⌜*mu*⌝-*suk-kan-ni* GIŠ.*ere-ni* GIŠ.ŠUR.MÌN
35) GIŠ.*dup*†-*ra-nu* ŠIM.LI *ù* GIŠ.*bu-uṭ-ni* [*a-na mu-šab*] ⌜LUGAL⌝-*ti-ia*
36) *qer-bu-uš-šú ab-ni-ma* GIŠ.[ÙR.MEŠ GIŠ].⌜*ere*⌝-*ni* GAL.MEŠ *e-li-šin*
37) *ú*-[*šat-ri-ṣa* GIŠ.IG.MEŠ GIŠ].ŠUR.MÌN GIŠ.*mu-suk-kan*-⌜*ni*⌝ [*mé-se-er*] URUDU† ⌜*nam*⌝-[*ri*]
38) *ú*-[*rak-kis-ma ú-rat-ta-a né-reb-šin* É] *ap-pa-a-ti tam-šil*
39) É.⌜GAL⌝ [KUR.*ḫat-ti ša i-na li-šá-an* KUR MAR.TU].⌜KI⌝ É† *ḫi-la-ni*
40) *i-šá-as*-⌜*su*⌝-[*šú ú-še-pi-šá mé-eḫ-ret ba-bi-ši*]-*in*†

33b–40) I built inside it (the city) palatial halls using (lit.: "of") elephant ivory, ebony, [boxwood], *musukkannu*-wood, cedar, cypress, *daprānu*-juniper, juniper, and terebinth [to be] my [roy]al [residence] and I [roofed] them with large [ce]dar [beams]. I [bound the doors] of cypress (and) *musukkannu*-wood [with band(s)] of shi[ning] copper [and installed (them) in their entrance(s). (40) I had built in front of th]eir [gates a po]rtico ([*bīt*] *appāti*), a replica of a [Hittite] pal[ace, which is] called a *bīt ḫilāni* [in the language of the land Amurru].

41) [8 UR.MAḪ *tu*]-⌜*ʾa*⌝-*a-me šu-ut* 1 ⌜*šar*$_5$?⌝ [GÉŠ.U 6 UŠ 50.ÀM] ⌜GUN⌝
42) [*mal-tak-ti* URUDU *nam-ri šá ina ši-pir* ^{d}]⌜*nin*⌝-*á-gal*† *ip-pat*-⌜*qu*⌝-[*ma ma-lu-ú nam-ri-ir-ri*]
43) [4 GIŠ.*tim-me* GIŠ.EREN *šu-ta*]-⌜*ḫu*⌝-*ti ša* 1 NINDA.[TA.ÀM *ku-bur-šú-un bi-ib-lat* KUR.*ḫa-ma-ni*]
44) [UGU *pirig-gal-le-e ú*]-⌜*kin*⌝-*ma dáp-pi ku*-⌜*lul*⌝ [KÁ.MEŠ-*šin e-mid* UDU.MEŠ *šad-di* ^{d}LAMMA MAḪ.MEŠ]
45) [*šá* NA$_4$ KUR-*i eš*]-⌜*qí*⌝ *nak-liš* ⌜*ú*⌝-[*še-piš-ma a-na er-bet-ti šá-a-ri*]
46) [*ú-šá-aṣ-bi-ta* SI].GAR-*šin*† *as*†-[*kup-pi* NA$_4$.*pi-i-li* GAL.MEŠ]
47) [*da-ád-me ki-šit-ti qa-ti-ia ṣe-ru-uš-šin*] ⌜*ab*⌝-*šim*-⌜*ma*⌝ [...]
Lacuna

41–47) [Eight tw]in [lion (colossi) of shining copper] that weigh 4,[610 full (lit.: "tested") talen]ts (and) [that] were cast [by the craft of the god N]inagal [and filled with radiance — upon (those) lion colossi I instal]led [four match]ing [cedar columns], whose [diameter(s) are] one *nindanu* [each, the product of Mount Amanus]; and [I positioned] cross-beams (upon them) as a cornice [for their gates]. I [had magnificent mountain sheep colossi of mass]ive [mountain stone] skillfully [made and in the four directions I had (them) hold] their (the gates') [door] bolt(s). [I] depicted [the settlements that I had conquered upon large limestone] s[labs; [...].

(Lacuna)

15

Part of an inscription is found on a stone fragment in the Musée Auguste Grasset, the municipal museum in Varzy (France), that may once have been part of a threshold or pavement slab from the palace at Khorsabad. The fragment is made of gypseous alabaster and was given to the museum in

14 lines 41–47 Exactly how much should be restored at the beginnings and ends of these lines is not certain. The arrangement given here would, however, seem reasonable. Line 41b: Or [... 50].⌜ÀM⌝, with the copy of ex. 1 (the only exemplar with this section) having [...].A*(copy: ZA).<AN>.

14 line 44 Or restore *ur-maḫ-ḫe-e* instead of *pirig-gal-le-e*; see text no. 13 line 115.

14 line 46 Or possibly [... SI].GAR-*šin*† ⌜*as*†⌝-[*mu as-kup-pi* ...], "[...] their resp[ective (lit: "fit[ting") door] bolt(s) ... slabs ...]"; see for example text no. 11 line 39 (variant on ex. 2) and text no. 7 line 164.

1867 by A. Grasset. The inscription likely records the holding of a celebration upon the completion of the building of Dūr-Šarrukīn. The inscription is edited from the published photograph. Restorations are based upon text no. 7 lines 178–79 and cf. text no. 12 lines 39–45.

CATALOGUE

Museum Number	Provenance	Dimensions (cm)	cpn
Musée Auguste Grasset (Varzy) VA 137	Probably Khorsabad	36×34	p

BIBLIOGRAPHY

1994 Lackenbacher in Fontan, Khorsabad p. 162 fig. 7 and pp. 278 and 282 (photo, translation [by Walker], study)

TEXT

Lacuna
1′) [LÚ.EN.NAM.MEŠ KUR]-*ia* LÚ.⸢*ak*⸣-[*li*]
2′) [LÚ.*šá-pi*]-⸢*ri*⸣ LÚ.NUN.[MEŠ]
3′) [LÚ.*šu-ut* SAG].⸢MEŠ⸣ *ù* LÚ.⸢AB⸣.[BA.MEŠ]
4′) [KUR *aš-šur*].⸢KI?⸣ <<*ina*>> *i-na* ⸢*qer*⸣-[*bi* É.GAL-*ia*]
5′) [*ú-šib-ma áš*]-⸢*ta*⸣-*kan ni*-⸢*gu*⸣-[*tú*]
Lacuna

Lacuna
1′–5′) [With ... provincial governors of] my [land], ov[erseers, command]ers, noble[s, eunuch]s, and el[ders of Assyria, I sat down] insi[de my palace and h]eld a fest[ival.
Lacuna

16–21

Stone thresholds from the entrances to six chapels within the palace complex at Khorsabad bear brief inscriptions, each invoking a particular deity and allowing the identification of the deities honored in the respective chapels: Ninurta, Ninšiku (Ea), Sîn, Adad, Ningal, and Šamaš. The first two thresholds were found during V. Place's excavations in 1852, but were left in situ. These two and all the other thresholds were uncovered in the 1930s during excavations conducted by the University of Chicago's Oriental Institute. According to J. Larson (Museum Archivist, Oriental Institute), none of the records from Chicago's excavations indicate that any of these thresholds were given field registration numbers or were removed from the site. Thus, the thresholds were presumably again left in situ. Five of the chapels were entered from Court XXVII and one, that of the goddess Ningal, from Court XXXI. The three larger chapels (those of the deities Sîn, Ningal, and Šamaš) comprised several rooms, while the others (those of the gods Ninurta, Ninšiku, and Adad) appear to have comprised only one or two rooms each. The fully preserved inscriptions have either seven (text no. 20), eight (text nos. 16–17 and 19) or nine (text no. 18) lines. Place thought that the area where he found the first two texts was the harem of the palace and thus these texts have at times been called the Harem Inscriptions.

16

The first of these threshold inscriptions from the religious quarter of the palace at Khorsabad is addressed to the warrior god Ninurta. It has sometimes been called Harem Inscription A.

CATALOGUE

Source	Provenance	Dimensions (cm)	cpn
Oppert, EM 2 pp. 333–338	Khorsabad, Palace, entrance to Room 173 from Court XXVII	—	n

COMMENTARY

This inscription and text no. 17 were originally found by V. Place in 1852 and were thought to have been lost in the Tigris in 1855 while on their way to Basra to be shipped to Europe (see for example Bezold, Literatur p. 93). J. Oppert initially published the inscriptions making use of paper squeezes that had been taken to Paris. Both inscriptions, however, were left in situ and were rediscovered during American excavations at Khorsabad in the early 1930s. The findspot of this threshold is indicated in Loud, Khorsabad 1 fig. 98. The inscription is edited from the copy by T. Jacobsen published in Loud, Khorsabad 1, which indicates that the piece is now somewhat less well preserved than when it was originally found by Place (as indicated by the copy by Oppert). H. Winckler's copy of the text is based on Oppert's copy.

BIBLIOGRAPHY

1859 Oppert, EM 2 pp. 333–338 (copy, edition, study)
1867 Place, Ninive et l'Assyrie 1 p. 129 (provenance)
1874 Ménant, Annales pp. 198–199 (translation)
1878 Oppert, Records of the Past 11 pp. 27–29 (translation)
1886 Bezold, Literatur p. 93 §56.14a (study)
1889 Winckler, Sar. 1 pp. XII and 191–192; and 2 pl. 49 no. 3A (copy, edition)
1927 Luckenbill, ARAB 2 p. 67 §126 (translation)
1936 Loud, Khorsabad 1 pp. 106–108, 128, 131–132 no. 5, and figs. 98 and 113 (photo [inscription not legible]; copy and edition [by Jacobsen], provenance)
1944 Meissner, ZDMG 98 p. 34 (edition)
1953 von Soden, SAHG pp. 281 and 390 no. 24e (translation)
1976 Seux, Hymnes pp. 527 and 529 (translation)
1993 Foster, Before the Muses 2 p. 708 no. IV.2.a.6 (translation)
1994 Fuchs, Khorsabad pp. 283 and 371 no. 3.2.7 (edition)

TEXT

1) ^{d}*nin-*⸢*urta*⸣ EN *a-ba-ri šá šu-tú-qat dan-nu-su*
2) ⸢*a-na*⸣ ^{m}⸢MAN⸣-GIN MAN ⸢ŠÚ⸣ MAN KUR *aš-šur*.KI GÌR.NÍTA KÁ.DINGIR.RA.KI
3) MAN KUR ⸢EME.GI$_{7}$ *ù*⸣ URI.KI ⸢*ba*⸣*-nu-ú ku-mi-ka*
4) *ši-bu-tam šuk-ši-su* liš-ba-a bu-ʾa-a-ri*
5) [*ina*] *qé-reb* ⸢*é*⸣*-sag-*⸢*íl*⸣ *u é-šár-ra ki-in* BALA*-šú*
6) *mur-ni-is-qí-šú šu-te-*⸢*ši-ra*⸣ *šul-li-ma ṣi-in-di-šú*

1–8) O god Ninurta, the one endowed with (lit.: "lord of") power, whose strength is supreme, with regard to S[ar]gon (II), king of the world, king of Assyria, governor of Babylon, king of the land of Su[me]r and Akkad, the one who constructed your cella, make him attain old age. May he be fully satisfied with (his) good fortune. (5) Establish his reign firmly [in]side

3 H. Winckler's copy omits KUR.
4 *-su**: The copy by T. Jacobsen has -ŠU, while those by J. Oppert and H. Winckler have SU.
5 H. Winckler's copy has *é-sag*-DI.
6 H. Winckler's copy omits the *-šú* of *ni-is-qí-šú*.

7) ⸢šu⸣-ut-lim-šú e-mu-⸢qan⸣ [la] ⸢šá⸣-na-an dun-nu ⸢zik⸣-ru-ti

8) ⸢GIŠ⸣.TUKUL.MEŠ-šú šu-ut-bi-ma li-na-ar ga-re-šú

Esagila and Ešarra. Keep his thoroughbred horses in good order (and) his (chariot) teams in good condition. Grant him [un]equaled strength (and) manly might. Mobilize his weapons so that he might strike down his foes.

17

This inscription upon a stone threshold leading into one of the chapels within the palace at Khorsabad indicates that this particular chapel was dedicated to the god Ninšiku (Ea), the god of wisdom and subterranean fresh water. This inscription has sometimes been referred to as Harem Inscription B because V. Place thought that the area in which he found it was the harem of the palace.

CATALOGUE

Source	Provenance	Dimensions (cm)	cpn
Oppert, EM 2 pp. 339–342	Khorsabad, Palace, entrance to Room 192 from Court XXVII	–	n

COMMENTARY

This inscription, like text no. 16, was originally found by V. Place in 1852 and thought to have been lost in the Tigris in 1855. The inscription was initially published by J. Oppert from paper squeezes that had been taken to Paris. The piece, however, was actually left in situ at Khorsabad and was rediscovered during excavations by the Oriental Institute (Chicago) in the early 1930s. The findspot of this particular threshold is indicated in Loud, Khorsabad 1 fig. 98. The threshold appears to have been left in situ by the American archaeologists. The inscription is edited from the copy by T. Jacobsen published in Loud, Khorsabad 1. H. Winckler's copy of the text is based on Oppert's copy.

BIBLIOGRAPHY

1859 Oppert, EM 2 pp. 339–342 (copy, edition, study)
1874 Ménant, Annales pp. 198–199 (translation)
1878 Oppert, Records of the Past 11 pp. 27–30 (translation)
1886 Bezold, Literatur p. 93 §56.14a (study)
1889 Winckler, Sar. 1 pp. XII and 192; and 2 pl. 49 no. 3B (copy, edition)
1927 Luckenbill, ARAB 2 p. 67 §127 (translation)
1936 Loud, Khorsabad 1 pp. 108–109, 128, 132–133 no. 6 and fig. 98 (copy and edition [by Jacobsen], provenance)
1944 Meissner, ZDMG 98 p. 35 (edition)
1953 von Soden, SAHG pp. 279 and 390 no. 24a (translation)
1976 Seux, Hymnes pp. 527–528 (translation)
1983 Galter, Ea/Enki pp. 195–196 (edition)
1993 Foster, Before the Muses 2 p. 706 no. IV.2.a.3 (translation)
1994 Fuchs, Khorsabad pp. 280 and 369 no. 3.2.1 (edition)
2000 Bagg, Assyrische Wasserbauten p. 152 (lines 4b–6a, edition)
2013 Dalley, Hanging Garden p. 90 (translation)

TEXT

1) ^{d}*nin-ši-kù* EN *né-me-qí pa-ti-qu*
2) *kal gim-ri a-na* ^{m}MAN-GIN MAN ŠÚ MAN KUR *aš-šur*.KI
3) GÌR.NÍTA KÁ.DINGIR.RA.KI MAN KUR EME.GI_7 *u* URI.KI
4) *ba-nu-u ku-me-ka nag-bi-ka šu-up-ta-a*
5) *šu-bi-la kùp-pi-šú ma-a-mi ḫi-iṣ-bi u ṭuḫ-di*
6) *šum-ki-ra ta-mir-tuš uz-nu* DAGAL-*tú ḫa-si-su*
7) *pal-ka-a ši-i-mi ši-ma-tuš*
8) *e-piš-tuš šul-li-ma lik-šu-da ni-iz-mat-su*

1–8) O god Ninšiku (Ea), the lord of wisdom who fashions absolutely everything, make your springs open up for Sargon (II), king of the world, king of Assyria, governor of Babylon, king of the land of Sumer and Akkad, the one who constructed your cella. (5) Send forth (water from) his wells (and) provide water in great abundance for his meadowland(s). Determine as his fate wide intelligence (and) broad understanding. Bring his undertaking(s) to completion so that he might attain his desire.

18

This brief inscription invoking the moon god Sîn was found upon a stone threshold leading into the chapel of that god in the palace at Khorsabad. The stone threshold was found during American excavations in the palace at Khorsabad in the early 1930s. The threshold is made of alabaster and was found broken into several pieces. The threshold appears to have been left in situ by the excavators. The inscription is edited from the copy by Jacobsen published in Loud, Khorsabad 1.

CATALOGUE

Source	Provenance	Dimensions (cm)	cpn
Loud, Khorsabad 1 pp. 89 and 130 no. 3, and figs. 100 and 119	Khorsabad, Palace, Entrance Z, which leads from Court XXVII into Room 167	340×360	n

BIBLIOGRAPHY

1933 Frankfort, OIC 16 p. 97 and p. 98 fig. 63 (photo [inscription not legible], provenance)
1936 Loud, Khorsabad 1 pp. 89, 91, 115 and 130 no. 3, and figs. 98, 100 and 119 (photo [inscription not legible]; copy and edition [by Jacobsen]; provenance)
1944 Meissner, ZDMG 98 pp. 34–35 (edition)
1953 von Soden, SAHG pp. 280 and 390 no. 24b (translation)
1976 Seux, Hymnes pp. 527–528 (translation)
1993 Foster, Before the Muses 2 p. 708 no. IV.2.a.7 (translation)
1994 Fuchs, Khorsabad pp. 280 and 369 no. 3.2.2 (edition)

17 lines 5–6 Or "its (the city's) wells ... its meadowland(s)."

TEXT

1) ^{d}EN.ZU DINGIR KÙ KUD-*is* EŠ.BAR *mu-šak-lim*
2) *ṣa-ad-di a-na* ^{m}MAN-GIN MAN ŠÚ MAN KUR *aš-šur*.KI GÌR.NÍTA
3) KÁ.DINGIR.RA.KI MAN KUR EME.GI$_{7}$ *ù* URI.KI *ba-nu-ú*
4) *ku-me-ka ina ku-un lìb-bi-ka ki-niš* IGI.BAR-*su-ma*
5) *bu-un-ni-ka šá me-šá-ri šu-ut-ri-ṣa e-li-šú*
6) *šu-ut-lim-šú* UD.MEŠ DÙG.GA UZU.MEŠ *ru-qu-ti*
7) MU.AN.NA.MEŠ *ḫu-ud lìb-bi ši-i-me ši-ma-tuš*
8) *it-ti* AN-*e u* KI-*tim šu-ri-ik* BALA-*šú*
9) UGU *kib-rat* LÍMMU-*i ki-in* GIŠ.GU.ZA-*šú*

1–9) O god Sîn, the holy god, who renders decisions (and) reveals (ominous) signs, with regard to Sargon (II), king of the world, king of Assyria, governor of Babylon, king of the land of Sumer and Akkad, the one who constructed your cella, duly look at him with your steadfast heart and (5) direct your just countenance upon him. Grant him a long life (lit.: "distant days") of physical well-being. Determine as his fate years of happiness. Make his reign last as long as heaven and netherworld. Establish his throne firmly over the four quarters (of the world).

19

This inscription invoking the storm god Adad was found upon a stone threshold leading into one of the chapels in the palace at Khorsabad and was discovered during American excavations in the palace at Khorsabad in the early 1930s. The threshold was likely left in situ by the excavators. For the findspot of the slab, see Loud, Khorsabad 1 fig. 98. The inscription is edited from the copy by T. Jacobsen published in Loud, Khorsabad 1.

CATALOGUE

Source	Provenance	Dimensions (cm)	cpn
Loud, Khorsabad 1 pp. 122–124 and 130–131 no. 4, and figs. 125–126	Khorsabad, Palace, doorway that leads from Court XXVII into Room 166	–	n

BIBLIOGRAPHY

1933 Frankfort, OIC 16 pp. 101–102 and fig. 66 (photo [inscription not legible], provenance)
1936 Loud, Khorsabad 1 pp. 122–124 and 130–131 no. 4, and figs. 98 and 125–126 (photo [inscription not legible]; copy and edition [by Jacobsen]; provenance)
1944 Meissner, ZDMG 98 pp. 32–33 (edition)
1953 von Soden, SAHG pp. 280–281 and 390 no. 24d (translation)
1976 Seux, Hymnes pp. 527 and 529 (translation)
1993 Foster, Before the Muses 2 p. 705 no. IV.2.a.1 (translation)
1994 Fuchs, Khorsabad pp. 282 and 370 no. 3.2.6 (edition)

18 lines 4–8 These lines are also found in an inscription directed to the god Nabû (see text no. 22 lines 5–11, where we have *ṣe-ru-uš-šu* instead of *e-li-šú*).

TEXT

1) ^{d}IŠKUR GÚ.GAL AN-*e u* KI-*tim mu-nam-me-ru*
2) BÁRA.MEŠ *a-na* ^{m}MAN-GIN MAN ŠÚ MAN KUR *aš-šur*.KI GÌR.NÍTA
3) KÁ.DINGIR.RA.KI MAN KUR EME.GI$_{7}$ *ù* URI.KI *ba-nu-u*
4) *ku-me-ka uk-ki-ip-šú* ŠÈG.MEŠ *ina* AN.MEŠ
5) ILLU.MEŠ *ina nag-bi áš-na-an u piš-šá-tú*
6) *gúr-ri-na ta-mir-tuš ba-ʾu-la-te-e-šú*
7) *ina* ḪÉ.NUN *ù** *ṭuḫ-di šur-bi-ṣa a-bur-riš*
8) *iš-di* GIŠ.GU.ZA-*šú ki-in šul-bi-ra* BALA-*šú*

1–8) O god Adad, the canal inspector of heaven and netherworld, who illuminates the daises, with regard to Sargon (II), king of the world, king of Assyria, governor of Babylon, king of the land of Sumer and Akkad, the one who constructed your cella, bring him at the right times rain from the sky (and) (5) floods from the depths. Pile up grain and oil in his meadowland(s). Have his people dwell (as safely) as in a meadow in great prosperity. Establish the foundation of his throne firmly (and) prolong his reign.

20

American excavations in the palace at Khorsabad in the early 1930s found an inscription that invokes the goddess Ningal, wife of the moon god Sîn, incised upon a stone threshold leading into one the chapels in the palace at Khorsabad. The threshold appears to have been left in situ by the excavators and its inscription is edited from the copy by T. Jacobsen published in Loud, Khorsabad 1.

CATALOGUE

Source	Provenance	Dimensions (cm)	cpn
Loud, Khorsabad 1 pp. 109, 111, 128, and 133 no. 7	Khorsabad, Palace, doorway that leads from Court XXXI into Room 180	–	n

BIBLIOGRAPHY

1936 Loud, Khorsabad 1 pp. 109, 111, 128, and 133 no. 7, and fig. 116 (copy and edition [by Jacobsen]; provenance)
1944 Meissner, ZDMG 98 p. 33 (edition)
1953 von Soden, SAHG pp. 280 and 390 no. 24c (translation)
1976 Seux, Hymnes pp. 527–528 (translation)
1993 Foster, Before the Muses 2 p. 707 no. IV.2.a.5 (translation)
1994 Fuchs, Khorsabad pp. 281 and 369–370 no. 3.2.3 (edition)

TEXT

1) *ka-⸢bit⸣-ti be-le-e-ti ⸢šá⸣-qu-tu* ^{d}*nin-gal*
2) *a-na* ^{m}MAN-GIN MAN ŠÚ MAN KUR *aš-⸢šur⸣*.KI ⸢GÌR.NÍTA⸣ KÁ*.DINGIR.RA.KI

1–7) O most honored of ladies, exalted goddess Ningal, with regard to Sargon (II), king of the world, king of Assyria, governor of Babylon, king of the land of

---

19 line 6 Or "its (the city's) meadowland(s)."
19 line 7 *ù**: Copy has ŠI+KU.
20 line 2 KÁ*: Copy has NAB.

3) MAN KUR ⸢EME.GI$_7$ ù⸣ URI.⸢KI⸣ *ba-nu-*⸢*ú*⸣ *ku-mi-i-ki*
4) *i-na ma-ḫar* ᵈ30 *ḫa-ʾi-ri na-*⸢*ra-me-ka*⸣ *ab-bu-su*
5) *a-mat* MUNUS.⸢SIG$_5$⸣-*šú ti-iz-*⸢*ka*⸣*-ri* ⸢*šá*⸣ [*ku*]-⸢*un*⸣*-ni* BALA-*šú*
6) *ba-laṭ na-piš-ti* UD.MEŠ SÙ.MEŠ *li-*⸢*ši-im*⸣ *ši-ma-tuš*
7) *li-pu-šú a-na ar-kàt* u_4*-me li-be-lu* ⸢*kal*⸣ *da-ad-me*

Sumer and Akkad, the one who constructed your cella, *intercede for* him in the presence of the god Sîn, your beloved husband. (5) Say good thing(s) about him for the [firm] establishment of his reign. May he (Sîn) determine as his fate good health (and) a long life (lit.: "distant days"). May his (Sargon's) descendants rule every inhabited region forever.

21

An inscription dedicated to Šamaš, the sun god, was found upon a limestone threshold near the entrance leading into one of the chapels within the palace at Khorsabad. Unfortunately, the inscription was "so badly weathered as to be undecipherable except for the first line, which fortunately gives us the name of the deity." The threshold was found during excavations in the palace at Khorsabad by the Oriental Institute (Chicago) in the early 1930s and was discovered in Court XXVII, near Door Z′′ leading into Room 172, an anteroom to one of the three larger chapels in the palace (see Loud, Khorsabad 1 pp. 102 and 104, and figs. 98 and 111). The threshold appears to have been left in situ by the excavators. Nothing further is known of the inscription. See also Fuchs, Khorsabad pp. 281 and 370 no. 3.2.4.

CATALOGUE

Source	Provenance	Dimensions (cm)	cpn
Loud, Khorsabad 1 pp. 102 and 104, and figs. 98 and 111	Khorsabad, Palace, Court XXVII, near Entrance Z′′	320 wide	n

22

Numerous copies of an inscription referring to the building of the cella of the god Nabû — a god of wisdom and writing — were found upon thresholds and upon and near steps in the temple of that god at Khorsabad. This is the only independent temple within the citadel area and the largest one discovered at the city.

20 line 4 One expects *nāramiki abbūssu ṣabtī* (or similar).
20 line 5 With regard to the reading [*ku*]-⸢*un*⸣*-ni*, cf. Leichty, RINAP 4 p. 98 no. 43 rev. 15′ and Borger, Asarh. p. 120, commentary to 80-7-19,44 rev. 15.

CATALOGUE

Ex.	Provenance	Lines Preserved	OIP 40	cpn
1	Khorsabad, Nabû temple, on front of the left-hand platform flanking the steps from main cella (Room 21) into the main sanctuary (Room 22)	1–14	A	n
2	Khorsabad, Nabû temple, on the lower five treads of the steps from Room 21 into Room 22	—	B	n
3	Khorsabad, Nabû temple, on front of right-hand platform flanking the steps from Room 21 into Room 22	—	C	n
4	Khorsabad, Nabû temple, on threshold between Room 19 and Room 23	—	D	n
5	Khorsabad, Nabû temple, on top of right-hand platform flanking the steps from Room 23 to Room 24	1–14	E	p
6	Khorsabad, Nabû temple, on top of left-hand platform flanking the steps from Room 23 to Room 24	—	—	n
7	Khorsabad, Nabû temple, on the lower two treads of the steps from Room 23 to Room 24	—	—	n
8	Khorsabad, Nabû temple, on threshold of main entrance between Court II and Room 19	—	—	n
9	Khorsabad, Nabû temple, on threshold of secondary entrance between Court II and Room 19	—	—	n
10	Khorsabad, Nabû temple, see commentary	1–14	—	p

COMMENTARY

For plans showing the findspots of exemplars 1–9, see Loud and Altman, Khorsabad 2 pls. 79 and 83–84. These exemplars were left in situ by the American archaeologists. M. Müller-Karpe provided the author with photos of ex. 10, which were taken by him at the site in 1994; the slab had been exposed by Iraqi archaeologists led by M. Subhi Abdullah. Dr. K. Salim, who kindly provided additional photos of the slab, informs me that the piece was probably found in an "entrance of court 2 (the central court)" and likely "in the southern entrance of the court." Thus it is possible that ex. 10 is to be identified with either ex. 8 or ex. 9.

The inscription is written in a mixture of Assyrian and Babylonian script, with an occasional archaic sign form. The master line and line arrangement follow ex. 1. All exemplars were left in situ and thus none could be collated from the original. Since there are no individual copies or legible photos of exs. 2–4 and 6–9, only the variants for exs. 2–4 noted by Jacobsen in Loud and Altman, Khorsabad 2 that are not simple variant sign forms (e.g., a Babylonian form of LUGAL instead of the Assyrian form) are included in the score.

The inscription on the threshold from Court I into Room 13 is reported to be illegible (Loud and Altman, Khorsabad 2 p. 59), but it may well be a further duplicate of this inscription.

BIBLIOGRAPHY

1938 Loud and Altman, Khorsabad 2 pp. 61–63 and 103–104 no. 1 (ex. 1, copy and edition [by Jacobsen; with variants from exs. 2–5]; exs. 1–9, provenance), and pls. 25C and 26E (exs. 2, 5–7 photo [inscription not legible]) and pl. 27A (ex. 5, photo)

1944 Meissner, ZDMG 98 p. 36 (edition)

1953 von Soden, SAHG pp. 281 and 390 no. 24f (translation)

1976 Seux, Hymnes pp. 527 and 529–530 (translation)

1993 Foster, Before the Muses 2 p. 707 no. IV.2.a.4 (translation)

1994 Fuchs, Khorsabad pp. 281–282 and 370 no. 3.2.5 (exs. 1–9, edition)

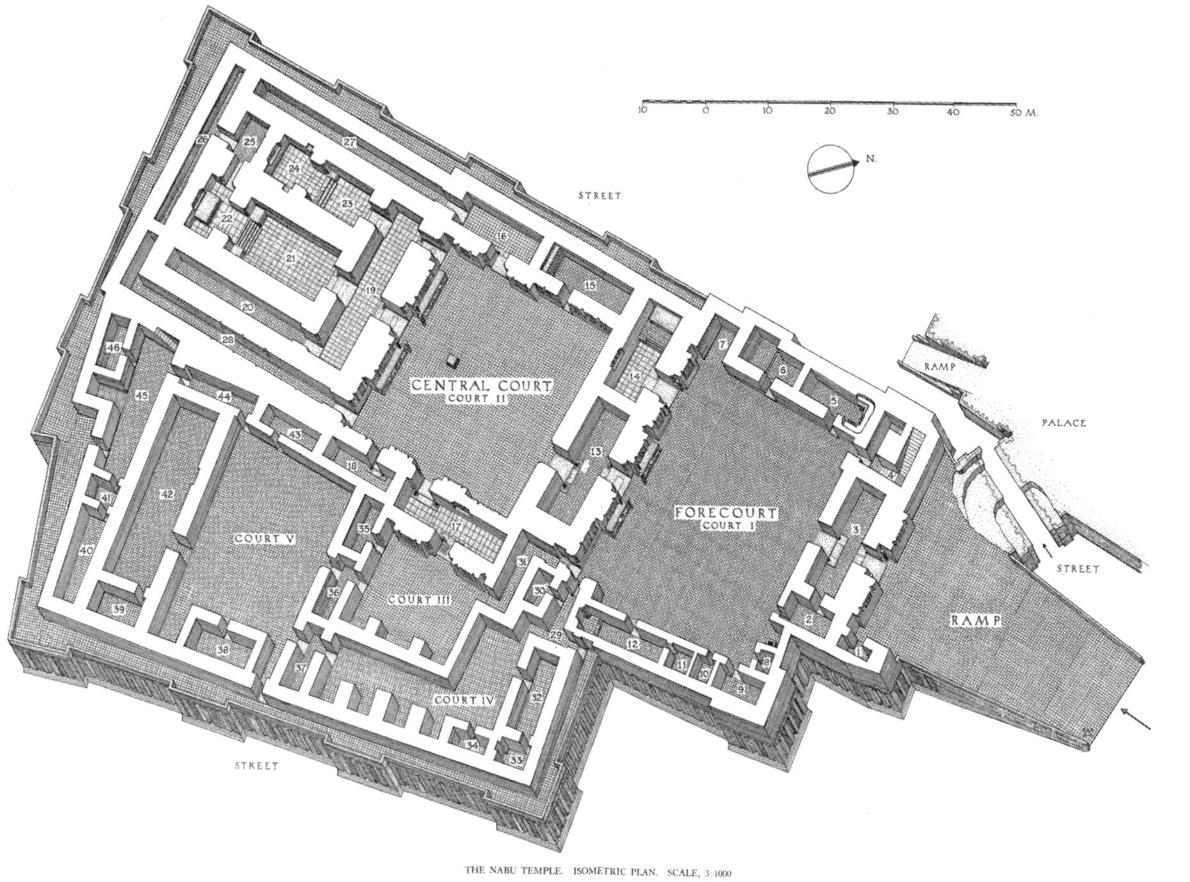

Figure 15. Plan of the Temple of Nabû at Khorsabad. Reprinted from Loud and Altman, Khorsabad 2 pl. 79 courtesy of the Oriental Institute of the University of Chicago.

TEXT

1) ^{d}*na-bi-um* DUB.SAR *gim-ri sa-ni-qu*
2) *mit-ḫur-ti a-na* ^{m}LUGAL-GI-NA LUGAL *kiš-šá-ti*
3) LUGAL KUR *aš-šur*.KI GÌR.NÍTA KÁ.DINGIR.RA.KI LUGAL KUR EME.GI$_7$
4) *ù* URI.KI *ba-nu-ú ku-um-mi-ka*
5) *i-na ku-un lìb-bi-ka ki-niš* IGI.BAR-*su-ma*
6) *bu-ni-ka ša mi-šá-ri šu-ut-ri-ṣa*
7) *ṣe-ru-uš-šu šu-ut-lim-šu* UD.MEŠ
8) DÙG.GA UZU.MEŠ *ru-qu-ti* MU.AN.NA.MEŠ
9) *ḫu-ud lib-bi ši-i-mi ši-ma-tuš*
10) *it-ti* AN-*e ù er-ṣe-tim*
11) *šu-ri-ik* BALA-*šu li-tep-pu-uš*
12) RE.É.UM-*tú ša gi-mir*
13) *ma-ti-tan it-ti áš-ri ù ki-gal-li*
14) *li-ku-na tem-me-en-šu*

1–14) O god Nabû, the scribe of all (the universe), who makes opposing forces agree, with regard to Sargon (II), king of the world, king of Assyria, governor of Babylon, (and) king of the land of Sumer and Akkad, the one who constructed your cella, (5) duly look at him with your steadfast heart and direct your just countenance upon him. Grant him a long life (lit.: "distant days") of physical well-being. Determine as his fate years of happiness. Make his reign last as long (10) as heaven and netherworld. May he continually exercise the shepherdship of all lands. May his foundation be as firm as (this) edifice (lit.: "place") and (its) platform.

---

4 The copy by Jacobsen in Loud and Altman, Khorsabad 2 p. 103 has *ba-nu*-KID, but the transliteration there has *ba-nu-ú*, which is also found on ex. 10.

5–11 These lines are also found in an inscription directed to the god Sîn (see text no. 18 lines 4–8), which has *e-li-šú* instead of *ṣe-ru-uš-šu*).

13 With regard to *ašri u kigalli* "(this) edifice (lit.: "place") and (its) platform," the former term can also stand for "heaven" and the latter for "netherworld." On this matter, see Fuchs, Khorsabad p. 370 n. 611.

14 Or possibly "its (the city's/reign's) foundation" instead of "his foundation"; see Fuchs, Khorsabad p. 370 n. 610.

23–40

A number of epigraphs are found on the stone reliefs from the palace of Sargon II at Khorsabad, sometimes on reliefs that also bear part of the king's Annals (text nos. 1–4 and 6) and sometimes on ones that bear part of his Display Inscription (text no. 7). They have been gathered together here (text nos. 23–40). The epigraphs are presented in order by the room from which they come. For the most part, the editions are based upon P.E. Botta's copies, although on a few occasions E. Flandin's copies have been given precedence. Botta claims to have based his copies of all except text no. 40 upon collations of the originals or squeezes. Squeezes of text nos. 23–30 and 36–37 are preserved in the Louvre and photographs of these have also been utilized.

Text nos. 23–32 and 36–40 are found on slabs which also contained part of Sargon's Annals (see text nos. 1–4 and 6), while text nos. 33–35 are on slabs which also preserved part of Sargon's Display Inscription (see text no. 7 ex. 5).

It has been argued that the reliefs in any one room often depict the events of only one campaign, and in particular that Room II illustrates events of Sargon's sixth regnal year (716), Room V events of his second regnal year (720), Room XIII events of his eighth regnal year (714), and Room XIV events of his seventh regnal year (715). (See in particular the items in the bibliography by M. El-Amin, J.E. Reade, and A. Fuchs.) With regard to epigraphs on Sargon's reliefs and Assyrian reliefs in general, see J.M. Russell, Writing on the Wall pp. 115–122 and Senn.'s Palace pp. 22–31.

Rather than have a detailed bibliography for each individual epigraph, it has been thought preferable to provide one bibliography for the epigraphs as a group, as well as two charts listing the major publications of the epigraphs and the reliefs associated with them. In the latter chart, the first plate number listed for each relief in the columns for Flandin in Botta, Monument de Ninive and Flandin in Albenda, Palace of Sargon shows the relief in small scale and in relation to the other reliefs in the room; any other plates listed show the relief in much larger scale. The plates cited in parentheses in both columns are drawings of the relief with the text omitted (or, in the case of reliefs depicted in small scale, totally illegible). Those without parentheses show both the text and the relief.

SELECTED BIBLIOGRAPHY ON EPIGRAPHS

Text no.	Provenance	Botta, MdN	Winckler, Sar. 2	Luckenbill, ARAB 2	El-Amin, Sumer	Wäfler, AOAT 26	Walker in Albenda	Fuchs, Khorsabad
23	Khorsabad, Palace, Room II, slab 7	4 pl. 180c	pl. 49 no. 2a	§125a	9 p. 51 and fig. 8	p. 269	no. 1	pp. 277, 364
24	Khorsabad, Palace, Room II, slab 14	4 pl. 180c	pl. 49 no. 2b	§125b	9 p. 58 and fig. 13	p. 272	—	pp. 276, 364
25	Khorsabad, Palace, Room II, slab 17	4 pl. 180c	pl. 49 no. 2c	§125c	9 p. 57 and fig. 12	p. 276	—	pp. 276, 364
26	Khorsabad, Palace, Room II, slab 22	4 pl. 180c	pl. 49 no. 2d	§125d	9 p. 55 and fig. 10	p. 269	no. 2	pp. 276, 364
27	Khorsabad, Palace, Room II, slab 28	4 pl. 180c	pl. 49 no. 2e	§125e	9 p. 53 and fig. 9	p. 280	—	pp. 276, 364

28	Khorsabad, Palace, (Room II), Entrance H_1	4 pl. 180c	pl. 49 no. 2o	§125o	9 p. 56 and fig. 11	p. 272	no. 3	pp. 276, 364
29	Khorsabad, Palace, Room V, slab 5	4 pl. 180c	—	—	9 p. 37 and fig. 3	p. 27	no. 4	pp. 277, 364
30	Khorsabad, Palace, Room V, slab 10	4 pl. 180c	pl. 49 no. 2f	§125f	9 p. 39 and fig. 4	p. 27	no. 5	pp. 277, 364
31	Khorsabad, Palace, Room V, slab 15	4 pl. 180c	pl. 49 no. 2g	§125g	9 p. 42 and fig. 5	p. 285	—	pp. 277, 364
32	Khorsabad, Palace, Room V, slab 16	4 pl. 180c	pl. 49 no. 2h	§125h	9 p. 44 and fig. 6	p. 285	—	pp. 277, 364
33	Khorsabad, Palace, Room VIII, slab 12	4 pl. 181c no. 4	—	—	—	pp. 34–35 n. 143	—	pp. 277, 364
34	Khorsabad, Palace, Room VIII, slab 17	4 pl. 181c no. 3	pl. 49 no. 2i	§125i	10 p. 35 and fig. 22	pp. 269–270	—	pp. 278, 364
35	Khorsabad, Palace, Room VIII, slab 25	4 pl. 181c no. 2	pl. 49 no. 2k	§125k	10 p. 27 and fig. 21	p. 133	—	pp. 278, 364
36	Khorsabad, Palace, Room XIII, slab 4	4 pl. 180c	—	—	9 p. 227 and fig. 19	p. 274	no. 6	pp. 278, 364
37	Khorsabad, Palace, Room XIV, slab 2	4 pl. 180c	pl. 49 no. 2l	§125l	9 p. 225 and fig. 17	p. 276	no. 8	pp. 278–279, 364
38	Khorsabad, Palace, Room XIV, slab 10	4 pl. 180c	pl. 49 no. 2n	§125n	9 p. 219 and fig. 16	—	no. 7	pp. 279, 364
39	Khorsabad, Palace, Room XIV, slab 12	4 pl. 180c	pl. 49 no. 2m	§125m	9 p. 216 and fig. 15	p. 272	no. 9	pp. 279, 364
40	Khorsabad	4 pl. 163 (bottom)	pl. 26 no. 55 (bottom)	—	—	—	—	pp. 279, 365

SELECTED BIBLIOGRAPHY ILLUSTRATING THE RELIEFS

Text no.	Provenance	Flandin in Botta, MdN 1–2	Flandin in Albenda	Maniori, Campagne di Sargon
23	Khorsabad, Palace, Room II, slab 7	pl. (52), 55	pl. (110), 112	fig. 5
24	Khorsabad, Palace, Room II, slab 14	pl. (52, 61)	pl. (110, 119)	fig. 6
25	Khorsabad, Palace, Room II, slab 17	pl. (52, 64)	pl. (110, 120)	fig. 8
26	Khorsabad, Palace, Room II, slab 22	pl. (52), 68, 68bis	pl. (110), 125–26	fig. 4
27	Khorsabad, Palace, Room II, slab 28	pl. (52, 70)	pl. (110, 128)	fig. 3
28	Khorsabad, Palace, (Room II), Door H_1	pl. (52), 76	pl. (110), 123	fig. 7
29	Khorsabad, Palace, Room V, slab 5	pl. (85), 89	pl. (92), 95	—
30	Khorsabad, Palace, Room V, slab 10	pl. (85), 93	pl. (92), 98	—
31	Khorsabad, Palace, Room V, slab 15	pl. (85)	pl. (92)	—
32	Khorsabad, Palace, Room V, slab 16	pl. (85)	pl. (92)	—
33	Khorsabad, Palace, Room VIII, slab 12	pl. (116, 118)	pl. (73, 75)	—
34	Khorsabad, Palace, Room VIII, slab 17	pl. (116, 119bis)	pl. (73, 77)	—
35	Khorsabad, Palace, Room VIII, slab 25	pl. (116, 120)	pl. (73, 78)	—
36	Khorsabad, Palace, Room XIII, slab 4	pl. (139), 141	pl. (131), 133	fig. 13
37	Khorsabad, Palace, Room XIV, slab 2	pl. (144), 145	pl. (135), 136	fig. 10
38	Khorsabad, Palace, Room XIV, slab 10	pl. (144), 146	pl. (135), 137	fig. 12
39	Khorsabad, Palace, Room XIV, slab 12	pl. (144), 147	pl. (135), 138	fig. 11
40	Khorsabad, Palace	—	—	—

BIBLIOGRAPHY

1844 Botta, JA 4/3 pp. 94–95 and pls. XXV and XXXI,1 (no. 23, copy, study of relief)
1849 Botta, Monument de Ninive 1–2 pls. 52, 55, 61, 64, 68, 68bis, 70, 76, 85, 89, 93, 116, 118, 119bis, 120, 139, 141, and 144–147 (nos. 23–39, drawing [by Flandin])
1849 Botta, Monument de Ninive 4 pls. 163 bottom, 180, and 181 nos. 2–4 (nos. 23–40, copy)
1874 Ménant, Annales p. 209 (study)
1886 Bezold, Literatur p. 94 §56.14i (study)
1889 Winckler, Sar. 1 pp. 190–191 no. 2 (nos. 23–27, 30–32, 34–35, 37–39, transliteration, partial translation); and 2 pl. 26 no. 55 (no. 40, copy) and pl. 49 no. 2 (nos. 23–28, 30–32, 34–35, 37–39, copy)
1912 Thureau-Dangin, TCL 3 p. XVIII (no. 36, drawing)
1927 Luckenbill, ARAB 2 pp. 66–67 §125a–o (nos. 23–28, 30–32, 34–35, 37–39, translation)
1941 Herzfeld, Iran in the Ancient Near East pp. 197–199 figs. 306–308 (nos. 23, 26, 36, drawing)
1953 El-Amin, Sumer 9 pp. 35–59 and eight pls. following p. 58, and pp. 214–228 and four pls. following p. 228 (nos. 23–32, 36–39, copy, edition, study)
1954 El-Amin, Sumer 10 pp. 23–42 and three pls. following p. 42 (nos. 34–35, copy, edition, study)
1960 Nougayrol, RA 54 pp. 203–207 (no. 36, partial drawing and partial photograph [AO 19892])
1964 Boehmer, Bagh. Mitt. 3 pp. 22–23 and pl. 1 no. 2 and pl. 2 (no. 37, copy, edition)
1966 van Loon, Urartian Art p. 44 (no. 36, drawing)
1966 Tadmor, BiAr 29 p. 90 fig. 9, p. 93 fig. 10, and p. 94 (nos. 29–30, drawing, study)
1975 Wäfler, AOAT 26 pp. 27, 34–35 n. 143, 133, 269–270, 272, 274, 276, 280, and 285, pl. 1 figs. 1–2, and plan 4 (nos. 30, 33, drawing; nos. 23–37, 39, edition, study)
1976 Reade, JNES 35 pp. 95–104 (nos. 23–32, 36–39, translation; study)
1986 Albenda, Palace of Sargon pp. 140–141, 144–150, pls. 95, 98, 112, 123, 125–126, 133, and 136–138, and fig. 90 (nos. 23, 26, 28–30, 36–39, drawing [by Flandin], translation [by Walker], study)
1986 Walker in Albenda, Palace of Sargon pp. 107–112 nos. 1–9 (nos. 23, 26, 28–30, 36–39, edition, study)
1991 Tadmor, Studies Mikasa pp. 421–422 and 425 fig. 2 (no. 37, drawing, study)
1993 Wartke, Urartu p. 56 fig. 17 (no. 36, drawing)
1994 Albenda in Fontan, Khorsabad p. 193 figs. 3d–e and p. 284 (nos. 26, 28, drawing [by Flandin])
1994 Franklin, Tel Aviv 21 p. 267 fig. 5 (no. 29, drawing)
1994 Fuchs, Khorsabad pp. 276–79 and 364–368 no. 3.1 (nos. 23–40, edition, study)
1995 Boehmer, RLA 8/5–6 p. 449 Abb. 5 (no. 36, drawing)
1995 Collon, Ancient Near Eastern Art p. 33 fig. 16 (no. 36, drawing)
1996 Matthiae, I grandi imperi p. 65 (no. 36, drawing)
1999 J.M. Russell, Writing on the Wall pp. 115–122 (nos. 23–40, translation, study)
2001 Reade, RA 95 pp. 73–74 and fig. 7 (no. 37, partial drawing, partial copy)
2002 Guralnick, RA 96 p. 43 and p. 53 pl. 7 (no. 23, copy, translation, study of relief)
2002 Pezzoli-Olgiati, Immagini urbane pp. 77–80 figs. 7–11 (nos. 23, 26–27 37, 39, drawing)
2012 Çilingiroğlu, Biainili-Urartu p. 300 fig. 20.11 (no. 36, drawing)
2012 Curtis, Biainili-Urartu p. 430 fig. 31.03 (no. 36, drawing)
2012 May, Iconoclasm pp. 206 and 225 (no. 38, copy, edition)
2012 Radner, Biainili-Urartu p. 252 fig. 17.06 (no. 36, drawing)
2012 Stronach, Biainili-Urartu p. 312 fig. 21.07 (no. 36, drawing)
2013 Mayer, Assyrien und Urarṭu I p. 64 and fig. 2 and p. 90 fig. 5 (nos. 36–37, drawing of relief, edition)
2014 Maniori, Campagne di Sargon pp. 55–63 D1–D11, p. 158 fig. 3, p. 160 fig. 4, p. 165 fig. 5, p. 167 figs. 6–8, p. 194 fig. 10, p. 196 fig. 11, p. 197 fig. 12, p. 248 fig. 13, and passim (nos. 23–28, 36–39, drawing; nos. 23–28, 34, 36–39, study)
2018 Franke, AoF 45 pp. 157–158 figs. 1a–b (no. 36, drawing)
2018 Zamazalová in Yamada, SAAS 28 p. 186 fig. 1 and p. 189 fig. 2 (nos. 23 and 29, drawing)

23

This epigraph is the first of six found on wall slabs from Room II of the palace at Khorsabad and an adjacent doorway (text nos. 23–28). The reliefs in this room are thought to depict Sargon's campaign to the east in his sixth regnal year (716); see the introduction to text no. 1. The lower register of slab 7 shows Assyrian soldiers attacking a large city and this epigraph is placed within the city. The main inscription on the slab is part of Sargon's Annals (text no. 1 lines 66–78). For bibliography on the epigraph, see the introduction to text nos. 23–40. The transliteration is based on Botta, Monument de Ninive 4 pl. 180c, although earlier copies can be found in Journal Asiatique 4/2 [1843] pls. 25 and 31, 1. (See also in particular El-Amin, Sumer 9 [1953] fig. 8 [following p. 58].) The initial copy of the inscription made by P.E. Botta is found in the Archives of the Institut de France (Botta-Cotta II 2976 folio I sheet 310). A photo of the squeeze of the inscription in the Louvre might suggest that the ḪAR is slightly damaged. E. Flandin's copy of the epigraph (Monument de Ninive 1 pl. 55) appears to be somewhat confused (see Walker in Albenda, Palace of Sargon p. 108). Sargon put down a rebellion in Ḫarḫar, located in western Media, during his sixth regnal year (716) and renamed the city Kār-Šarrukīn (see text no. 1 lines 96b–100, text no. 2 lines 89–95a, and text no. 4 lines 42′b–45′). A rebellion broke out in that area already in the following year (see text no. 1 lines 109b–114a).

CATALOGUE

Source	Provenance	Louvre Squeeze	cpn
Botta, Monument de Ninive 4 pl. 180[c]	Khorsabad, Palace, Room II, slab 7	yes	p

TEXT

1) URU.*ḫar-ḫa-ar*

1) The city Ḫarḫar.

24

This epigraph is placed on slab 14 from Room II of the palace at Khorsabad. The lower register of the slab depicts Assyrian soldiers attacking a city. The main inscription on the slab is part of the king's Annals (text no. 1 lines 157–169). For bibliography on the epigraph, see the introduction to text nos. 23–40. The transliteration is based on Botta, Monument de Ninive 4 pl. 180[c]; a photo of the squeeze in the Louvre would suggest that the URU is partially damaged. (See also in particular El-Amin, Sumer 9 [1953] fig. 13 [following p. 58].) The city of Qindāu, located in the area near Ḫarḫar, was captured in the king's seventh regnal year (715) and renamed Kār-Sîn (see text no. 1 lines 109b–114a).

CATALOGUE

Source	Provenance	Louvre Squeeze	cpn
Botta, Monument de Ninive 4 pl. 180[c]	Khorsabad, Palace, Room II, slab 14	yes	p

TEXT

1) URU.*qí-in-da**-*a*-[(*x*)]-*ú*

1) The city Qindāu.

25

The exact placement of the epigraph on slab 17 from Room II of the palace at Khorsabad is not known, but the lower register of the slab depicts Assyrians attacking a city. The main inscription on the slab is part of the Khorsabad Annals (text no. 1 lines 196–208). For bibliography on the epigraph, see the introduction to text nos. 23–40. The transliteration is based on Botta, Monument de Ninive 4 pl. 180^{c}; a photo of the squeeze in the Louvre would suggest that the URU and KA signs are partially damaged. (See also in particular El-Amin, Sumer 9 [1953] fig. 12 [following p. 58].) Tikrakka is possibly to be identified with the city Šikrakki (see Tadmor, Tigl. III p. 166 note to line 37 for references). For the possible location of that city at Tapeh Sialk in Iran, see most recently Alibaigi and Rezaei, JNES 77 (2018) pp. 15–30.

CATALOGUE

Source	Provenance	Louvre Squeeze	cpn
Botta, Monument de Ninive 4 pl. 180^{c}	Khorsabad, Palace, Room II, slab 17	yes	p

TEXT

1) URU.⸢*ti*$^{?}$⸣-*ik-rak-ka*

1) The city [*T*]ikrakka.

26

The lower register of slab 22 from Room II of the palace at Khorsabad shows Assyrian soldiers attacking a large city. This epigraph is placed on the city wall. The main inscription on the slab is part of the Khorsabad Annals (text no. 1 lines 287–299). For bibliography on the epigraph, see the introduction to text nos. 23–40. The transliteration is based on a photo of the squeeze in the Louvre. (See also in particular El-Amin, Sumer 9 [1953] fig. 10 [following p. 58].) According to P.E. Botta (Monument de Ninive 4 pl. 180^{c}), the KI is fully preserved, but E. Flandin's copy (ibid. 1 pl. 68bis) and the squeeze indicate it is not. The Median city of Kišesim was captured in 716, Sargon's sixth regnal year (see text no. 1 line 93). See also text no. 117, an inscription on a stone stele that records the campaign in that year and that appears to state that it had been erected at Kišesim.

---

24 line 1 -*da**-: H. Winckler's copy (Sar. 2 pl. 49 no. 2b) has a good DA, but the squeeze is unclear. Winckler's copy omits the second to last sign (A).

25 line 1 ⸢*ti*$^{?}$⸣-: H. Winckler's copy has ⸢*u*⸣-. The spacing on the photo of the squeeze would suggest we have the end of the sign, and thus ⸢*ti*⸣- is proposed rather than ⸢*ši*⸣.

CATALOGUE

Source	Provenance	Louvre Squeeze	cpn
Botta, Monument de Ninive 4 pl. 180[c]	Khorsabad, Palace, Room II, slab 22	yes	p

TEXT

1) URU.⸢*ki*⸣-*še-si-im*

1) The city Kišesim.

27

This epigraph was found on slab 28 of Room II, which has a city depicted on the upper register and has Assyrian soldiers attacking a city depicted on the lower register. The main inscription on the slab is part of the Khorsabad Annals (text no. 1 lines 365–377). For bibliography on the epigraph, see the introduction to text nos. 23–40. The transliteration is based on a photo of the squeeze in the Louvre and Botta, Monument de Ninive 4 pl. 180[c]. (See also in particular El-Amin, Sumer 9 [1953] fig. 9 [following p. 58].) The city Ganguḫtu was located in the Zagros area and may be mentioned in text no. 1 line 92 during a campaign in Sargon's sixth regnal year (716).

CATALOGUE

Source	Provenance	Louvre Squeeze	cpn
Botta, Monument de Ninive 4 pl. 180[c]	Khorsabad, Palace, Room II, slab 28	yes	p

TEXT

1) URU.*ga-an-*⸢*gu*⸣*-uḫ-tu*

1) The city Ganguḫtu.

28

This epigraph is found on slab 1 from Door H (between Room II and Room VI) of the palace at Khorsabad. The right side of the lower register shows a structure (fortress?) that may be on fire. The epigraph is placed on the wall of the structure. The main inscription on the slab is part of Sargon's Annals (text no. 1 lines 261–273). For bibliography on the epigraph, see the

27 line 1 The copy by P.E. Botta indicates that the form of the end of the sign GU is anomalous, but H. Winckler's copy (Sar. 2 pl. 49 no. 2e) has a good GU sign. A photo of the squeeze might suggest that the sign is slightly damaged, obscuring the exact formation of the end of the sign.

introduction to text nos. 23–40. The transliteration is based on a photograph of the squeeze in the Louvre; see also E. Flandin's copy in Botta, Monument de Ninive 1 pl. 76. P.E. Botta's copy (ibid. 4 pl. 180^{c}) omits one wedge of the BA sign. (See also in particular El-Amin, Sumer 9 [1953] fig. 11 [following p. 58].) With regard to the city name, see Walker in Albenda, Palace of Sargon p. 109. Bīt-Bagaya is also mentioned in text no. 7 line 64 and is likely to be identified with Bīt-Gabaya, which was located in western Media and was captured in Sargon's seventh regnal year (715) and renamed Kār-Adad or Kār-Ištar (compare text no. 1 lines 113–114 and text no. 7 lines 64–65).

CATALOGUE

Source	Provenance	Louvre Squeeze	cpn
Botta, Monument de Ninive 4 pl. 180^{c}	Khorsabad, Palace, Door H_1	yes	p

TEXT

1) URU.É-*ba-ga-ia*

1) The city Bīt-Bagāya.

29

This epigraph is the first of four found on wall slabs from Room V of the palace at Khorsabad (text nos. 29–32). The reliefs in this room are thought to represent events from Sargon's campaign in his second regnal year (720); see the introduction to text no. 2. The right side of the lower register of slab 5 shows Assyrian soldiers attacking a fortress on a hill and the epigraph is placed next to an individual on the wall of the fortress. The main inscription on the slab is part of the king's Annals (text no. 2 lines 69–85). For bibliography on the epigraph, see the introduction to text nos. 23–40. The transliteration is based on a photo of the squeeze in the Louvre. See also Botta, Monument de Ninive 4 pl. 180^{c}; on E. Flandin's copy (ibid. 1 pl. 89), the URU has a double final vertical wedge. (See also in particular El-Amin, Sumer 9 [1953] fig. 3 [following p. 58].)

Gabbutunu has often been identified with Gibbethon in southern Palestine (see El-Amin, Sumer 9 [1953] p. 37 and Tadmor, JCS 12 [1958] p. 83 n. 243), for which the modern sites Tēl-Malot and Ra's Abū Ḥamīd have been proposed (see Bagg, Rép. Géogr. 7/1 p. 68). G. Schmitt, however, believes Gabbutunu was located in the area of Raphia, modern Rafaḥ in the Gaza strip (ZDPV 105 [1989] pp. 56–69).

CATALOGUE

Source	Provenance	Louvre Squeeze	cpn
Botta, Monument de Ninive 4 pl. 180^{c}	Khorsabad, Palace, Room V, slab 5	yes	p

TEXT

1) URU.*gab-bu-tú-nu*

1) The city Gabbutunu.

30

This reading of the epigraph found on slab 10 from Room V of the palace at Khorsabad is open to question. The lower register of the slab shows Assyrian soldiers attacking a city and the epigraph is placed on the city. The main inscription on the slab is part of the king's Annals (text no. 2 lines 307–323). For bibliography on the epigraph, see the introduction to text nos. 23–40. The transliteration is based on Botta, Monument de Ninive 4 pl. 180^{c} and examination of the squeeze in the Louvre. (See also El-Amin, Sumer 9 [1953] fig. 4 [following p. 58].)

The name of the city has often been read URU.*ʾa-am-qa-*[(*ár/ar*)]*-ru-na*, ʾAmqa(r)rūna, and been identified with Biblical Ekron, modern Tēl Miqne. See, for example, Luckenbill, ARAB 2 p. 66 §125f; El-Amin, Sumer 9 (1953) pp. 37–40 no. 3 and fig. 4; Tadmor, JCS 12 (1958) p. 83 n. 243; Fuchs, Khorsabad p. 421; and Bagg, Rép. Géogr. 7/1 pp. 10–11. C.B.F. Walker (in Albenda, Palace of Sargon p. 110) states "Given the number of attestations of the name Amqarruna in Late Assyrian historical texts there can be no doubt that it is the name to be read here." However, as noted by Walker, P.E. Botta's copy has ṢU for the last sign, not NA; E. Flandin's drawing also indicates a partially damaged ṢU, and not NA. Since the squeeze does not support the reading of the final sign as NA, but would allow ṢU, and since no other royal inscription of Sargon's mentions Ekron, it is tentatively assumed that the name in this epigraph does not refer to Ekron. For the reading with ṢU, see also Naʾaman, Zion 59 (1994) pp. 13–14 [in Hebrew], who connects the first part of the name with the Hebrew word ʿemeq, meaning "valley."

CATALOGUE

Source	Provenance	Louvre Squeeze	cpn
Botta, Monument de Ninive 4 pl. 180^{c}	Khorsabad, Palace, Room V, slab 10	yes	p

Figure 16. Flandin's drawing of the relief on Room V, slabs 10–11, published in Botta, Monument de Ninive 2 pl. 93 (text no. 30) and depicting the conquest of the city Amqa[...]ruṣu.

TEXT

1) URU.ʾ*a-am-qa-*[x]-*ru-ṣu*	1) The city ʾAmqa[...]ruṣu.

31

The exact placement of this epigraph on slab 15 from Room V of the palace at Khorsabad is not known, but the lower register of the slab does show Assyrian soldiers attacking a city and it is possible that the epigraph was located on the walls of that city. The main inscription on the slab is part of the king's Annals (text no. 2 lines 222–238). For bibliography on the epigraph, see the introduction to text nos. 23–40. The transliteration is based on Botta, Monument de Ninive 4 pl. 180^{c}; see also in particular El-Amin, Sumer 9 (1953) fig. 5 (following p. 58). For attempts to locate the city Baʾil-gazara, see El-Amin, Sumer 9 (1953) pp. 41–43 no. 5 (Ghasir); Wäfler, AOAT 26 p. 285

30 line 1 The squeeze would suggest that the AM sign is slightly damaged. C.B.F. Walker (in Albenda, Palace of Sargon p. 110) does not believe that there was a sign between QA and RU, basing this upon the assumption that name of the city was Amqarruna (Ekron) and that the scribe would not have written a reduplicated R in the name; however, as he notes, the final sign must be emended in order to get NA. Based upon the spacing of the signs, we would expect there to be a sign between QA and RU, although, as Walker notes, this is not certain. -*ṣu*: P.E. Botta's copy has -ṢU; E. Flandin's copy (Monument de Ninive 2 pl. 93) has a form that does not fit NA but fits a partially damaged ṢU; and H. Winckler's copy (Sar. 2 pl. 49 no. 2f) has ⸢KUR⸣. The traces on the squeeze are not easily compatible with NA but would fit the beginning of ṢU. (A copy of the traces visible on the squeeze is found in the minor variants section.)

(with further references); and Bagg, Rép. Géogr. 7/1 pp. 41–42 ("im syrisch-palästinischen Raum").

CATALOGUE

Source	Provenance	Louvre Squeeze	cpn
Botta, Monument de Ninive 4 pl. 180[c]	Khorsabad, Palace, Room V, slab 15	no	n

TEXT

1) URU.*ba-il-ga-za-ra*

1) The city Ba'il-gazara.

32

This epigraph is found on slab 16 from Room V of the palace at Khorsabad. It is not known exactly where on the slab the epigraph is placed, but the lower register of the slab does show Assyrian soldiers advancing to the left, attacking a city that is found on the adjoining slab 17 and that is situated on top of a hill. The main inscription on the slab is part of the king's Annals (text no. 2 lines 205–221). For bibliography on the epigraph, see the introduction to text nos. 23–40. The transliteration is based on Botta, Monument de Ninive 4 pl. 180[c]; see also El-Amin, Sumer 9 (1953) fig. 6 (following p. 58). Sinu is possibly to be connected to the cities written Si'annu and Sinnu in other Neo-Assyrian texts and is thought to have been located in northern Syria (see Fuchs, Khorsabad p. 458 and Bagg, Rép. Géogr. 7/1 p. 220).

CATALOGUE

Source	Provenance	Louvre Squeeze	cpn
Botta, Monument de Ninive 4 pl. 180[c]	Khorsabad, Palace, Room V, slab 16	no	n

TEXT

1) URU.*si-nu*

1) The city Sinu.

33

Slab 12 from Room VIII of the palace at Khorsabad has a relief depicting the king receiving the submission of three captives, whom he holds by cords attached to their lower lips, and (apparently) the blinding of one of those captives. This epigraph appears to have been placed above the three captives. The main inscription on the slab is part of the king's Display Inscription (text no. 7 ex. 5) and this slab has line 18–23 of that text. For bibliography on the epigraph, see the introduction to text nos. 23–40. The transliteration is based on Botta, Monument de Ninive 4 pl. 181[c] no. 4. P.E. Botta's copy suggests that there was at least one line after line 4.

CATALOGUE

Source	Provenance	Louvre Squeeze	cpn
Botta, Monument de Ninive 4 pl. 181[c] no. 4	Khorsabad, Palace, Room VIII, slab 12	no	n

TEXT

1) [...] ARAD? [*x*] AN RA [...]
2) [...] E IA *x* [...]
3) [...] KI DÙ? [...]
4) [...] ŠE [...]
5) [...]
Lacuna

1–5) No translation possible.
Lacuna

34

The exact placement of this badly damaged epigraph on slab 17 from Room VIII of the palace at Khorsabad is not known. The slab shows an official? followed by two prisoners; a third prisoner appears on the adjoining slab 18. The main inscription on the slab is part of the king's Display Inscription (text no. 7 ex. 5) and this slab has lines 45–52 of that text. For bibliography on the epigraph, see the introduction to text nos. 23–40. The transliteration is based on Botta, Monument de Ninive 4 pl. 181[c] no. 3; see also in particular El Amin, Sumer 10 (1954) fig. 22 (following p. 42). H. Winckler's copy of the epigraph (Sar. 2 pl. 49 no. 2i) suggests that there was originally a fourth line that is no longer preserved. A somewhat similar passage is found in the Aššur Prism in connection with the campaign in 716 (text no. 63 i′ 16′–17′); see also text no. 117 ii 31–33.

CATALOGUE

Source	Provenance	Louvre Squeeze	cpn
Botta, Monument de Ninive 4 pl. 181^{c} no. 3	Khorsabad, Palace, Room VIII, slab 17	no	n

TEXT

1) [*x*] ŠÚ-ḪU [*x*] GIŠ URU.*pad-*[*di-ri*$^{?}$ (*x*)] NA URU.[...]
2) ^{m}*aš-šur-*ZU* [KUR].*kar**-*al-*[*la-a-a x* (*x*)] IK [...]
3) ŠU.II *ù* GÌR*.II* ⸢*bi-re*⸣*-tú* AN.[BAR] *ad-di-šú-*[*nu-ti*$^{?}$ ...]

1–3) ... of the city *Pad*[*diri*] ... of the city [... (and)] Aššur-*lē*ʾ*i* [of the land] Karal[la ...] I put ir[on] fetters on *th*[*eir*] hands and feet [...]

35

This epigraph is found on slab 25 from Room VIII of the palace at Khorsabad. The slab shows an Assyrian carrying a dead(?) body and the epigraph appears to have been placed above the body. The main inscription on the slab is part of the king's Display Inscription (text no. 7 ex. 5) and this slab has lines 95–106 of that text. For bibliography on the epigraph, see the introduction to text nos. 23–40. The transliteration is based on Botta, Monument de Ninive 4 pl. 181^{c} no. 2; see also in particular El Amin, Sumer 10 (1954) fig. 21 (following p. 42). With regard to Iaū-biʾdī (Ilu-biʾdī) who was captured in Sargon's second regnal year (720), see in particular text no. 7 lines 33–35, text no. 43 line 25, text no. 103 ii 51–56, and text no. 117 ii 4–13, as well as Fuchs and Parpola PNA 2/1 p. 497 sub Iaū-bi'dī and Fuchs, PNA 2/1 p. 526 sub Ilu-bi'dī 1.

CATALOGUE

Source	Provenance	Louvre Squeeze	cpn
Botta, Monument de Ninive 4 pl. 181^{c} no. 2	Khorsabad, Palace, Room VIII, slab 25	no	n

34 line 1 M. El-Amin (Sumer 10 [1954] pp. 29–35 and fig. 22) suggests the following reading: [^{md}]⸢EN-LUGAL⸣-[*ú*]-⸢*ṣur*⸣ URU.⸢*ki*⸣-[*še-si* ^{m}*ki-ba*]-*ba* URU.[*ḫar-ḫar*], i.e., "[B]ēl-šarru-[uṣ]ur of the city K[išēsim, Kiba]ba of the city [Ḫarḫār]."
34 line 2 -ZU*: P.E. Botta's copy has -KI; H. Winckler's copy has -ZU (emended?). *kar**-: Botta's copy omits one vertical wedge; Winckler's copy indicates that the form of the sign is complete. The end of the line is possibly to be restored ... [KUR].*kar**-*al-*[*la-a-a* KÚR.MEŠ] *ek-*[*ṣu-ti*], "... [of the land] Karal[la], fi[erce enemies]," or ... [KUR].*kar**-*al-*[*la-a-a qa-ti*] *ik-*[*šu-ud*], "... [of the land] Karal[la I] con[quered]"; see Fuchs, Khorsabad p. 278. M. El-Amin (Sumer 10 [1954] pp. 34–35 and fig. 22) suggests EN.MEŠ *ek-ṣu-te* for the end of the line.
34 line 3 GÌR*.II*: P.E. Botta's copy has TA; H. Winckler's copy has GÌR.II (emended?), followed by *bi-re-tú*.

TEXT

1)	mdia-<ú>-bi-i'-[di KUR.a-ma]-ta-a-a	1–2) I flayed [the sk]in from Ia<ū>-bi'[dī (Ilu-bi'dī) of the land Hama]th.
2)	[ma]-šak-šú a-[(x)]-⸢ku⸣-[(x)]-⸢uṣ*⸣	

36

Only one wall slab from Room XIII of the palace at Khorsabad, slab 4, is known to have had an epigraph. The lower register of the slab shows soldiers sacking a temple inside a city and this epigraph is placed above the city. The main inscription on the slab is part of the king's Annals (text no. 3 lines 1′–15′). For bibliography on the epigraph, see the introduction to text nos. 23–40. Part of the first sign of the inscription is preserved on AO 19892 (see the photographs in Nougayrol, RA 54 [1960] p. 205; André-Leicknam, Naissance de l'écriture p. 330 no. 275; and Albenda, Palace of Sargon fig. 90) and a squeeze of the inscription made by P.E. Botta is preserved in the Louvre. The transliteration is based on the squeeze and E. Flandin's copy in Botta, Monument de Ninive 2 pl. 141. (See also in particular El-Amin, Sumer 9 [1953] fig. 19 [following p. 228].) Sargon's capture and plunder of the Urarṭian city Muṣaṣir in his eighth year (714) is described in detail in text no. 65. For a study of the temple depicted on the relief, see Franke, AoF 45 (2018) pp. 156–167.

CATALOGUE

Source	Provenance	Louvre Squeeze	cpn
Botta, Monument de Ninive 4 pl. 180c	Khorsabad, Palace, Room XIII, slab 4	yes	p

TEXT

1)	URU.mu-ṣa-ṣir al*-me* [(x x)] KUR-ud	1) I surrounded (and) conquered the city Muṣaṣir.

35 line 1 H. Winckler's copy (Sar. 2 pl. 49 no. 2k) indicates that the -ú- of the personal name is present.

35 line 2 H. Winckler's copy shows the line as being: ma-šak-šú a-[ku]-uṣ. -⸢uṣ*⸣: P.E. Botta's copy has the heads of two slanted wedges (instead of one) before the final vertical.

36 line 1 A photo of the squeeze suggests URU.⸢mu-ṣa-ṣir⸣ x (x) [(x x)] KUR-⸢ud⸣. al*-me*: E. Flandin's copy indicates DU-BAR?-DIŠ-NU and P.E. Botta's copy (Monument de Ninive 4 pl. 180c]) has al-DIŠ-NU. C.B.F. Walker (in Albenda, Palace of Sargon p. 111) suggests that "It seems likely therefore that we should accept Flandin's indication of the spacing as correct, but follow Botta in reading DU as al!; the BAR is likely to be only cracks on the sculpture, as is the slanting wedge which appears to turn ME into DIŠ-NU." The trace(s) on Botta's squeeze are too uncertain at this point to provide any help for the reading. For the reading, see also text no. 39.

Figure 17. Flandin's drawing of the relief on Room XIII, slab 4, published in Botta, Monument de Ninive 2 pl. 141 (text no. 36) and depicting the conquest of the city Muṣaṣir.

37

This epigraph is the first of three found on wall slabs from Room XIV of the palace at Khorsabad. The lower register of slab 2 shows Assyrian soldiers attacking a large city and the epigraph is placed on the city walls. The main inscription on the slab is part of Sargon's Annals (text no. 4 lines 16´–30´). For bibliography on the epigraph, see the introduction to text nos. 23–40. The transliteration is based on E. Flandin's copy in Botta, Monument de Ninive 2 pl. 145. (See also El-Amin, Sumer 9 [1953] fig. 17 [following p. 228].) A photo of the squeeze in the Louvre would suggest that the epigraph had a third line; below the BI of line 2 is the trace of what might be a NA sign and below the TA may be the trace of a sign. Since both P.E. Botta and Flandin saw the original and neither gave any indication that there was a third line, it has been tentatively assumed that the squeeze was done in such a way that some signs from a different inscription found their way onto the squeeze.

The city name at the beginning of line 1 has been read Unši (URU.*un*-⸢*ši*⸣) and Izzar (URU.*iz-za*-⸢*ar*⸣), but M. El-Amin's reading of Pazaši — and its identification with the city Panziš, which was located on the border between Mannea, Zikirtu, and Andia, and which is mentioned in the account of Sargon's eighth campaign (714; text no. 65 lines 76 and 79) — seems more probable (El-Amin, Sumer 9 [1953] pp. 219–225 no. 3 and fig. 17, followed by Walker in Albenda, Palace of Sargon p. 112, and Fuchs, Khorsabad pp. 278–279). Note also Tadmor, Studies Mikasa pp. 421–422 and Mayer, Assyrien und Urarṭu 1 p. 64.

CATALOGUE

Source	Provenance	Louvre Squeeze	cpn
Botta, Monument de Ninive 4 pl. 180^{c}	Khorsabad, Palace, Room XIV, slab 2	yes	(p)

TEXT

1) URU.⸢*pa*?⸣-*za*-⸢*ši* URU⸣.ḪAL.ṢU *šá* KUR.*man-na-a-a*
2) *šá* IGI ⸢*né*⸣-[*re*]-*bi šá* KUR*.*zi-kir-ta-a-a*

1–2) The city *Pazaši*, a fortress of the land Mannea which is (located) in front of the p[a]ss (leading) to the land Zikirtu.

38

A fortified Assyrian camp is depicted on the left side of the lower register of slab 10 from Room XIV of the palace at Khorsabad and this epigraph is placed across the middle of the camp. The main inscription on the slab is part of the king's Annals (text no. 4 lines 31´–45´). For bibliography on the epigraph, see the introduction to text nos. 23–40. The transliteration is based on E. Flandin's copy in Botta, Monument de Ninive 2 pl. 146. The personal name at the end of line has also been read: ^{m}[MAN]-GIN, "[Sar]gon" (see Winckler, Sar. 2 pl. 49 no. 2n) and ^{m}⸢NUMUN-DÙ⸣ [LÚ.*tur-ta-nu*], "Zēra-ib[ni, the *turtānu*]" (see El-Amin, Sumer 9 [1953] pp. 216–219 and fig. 16). The reading given below is based upon a proposal by J.N. Postgate (apud Reade, JNES 35 [1976] p. 99), a reading also accepted by C.B.F. Walker (in Albenda, Palace of Sargon p. 111) and A. Fuchs (Khorsabad p. 279). J.M. Russell (Writing on the Wall p. 116 n. 44) points out that the name Taklāk-ana-Bēl (the eponym for 715) is always written with the sign *tak*, not *tàk*, in the eponym lists; however, one does find [*tà*]*k*- in eponym list A1 v 9 (Millard, SAAS 2

37 line 1 ⸢*pa*?⸣-: E. Flandin's copy and P.E. Botta's copy (Monument de Ninive 2 pl. 145 and 4 pl. 180^{c} respectively) have -IZ; the photo of the squeeze is unclear, but might suggest -⸢PI⸣. H. Winckler's copy (Sar. 2 pl. 49 no. 2l) indicates for the beginning of the line URU ⸢IZ? ḪA? ME GUR⸣ ḪAL.ṢU .... The missing horizontal wedge on Flandin's -ŠI is indicated as being present on Botta's copy and the squeeze would also suggest -⸢ŠI⸣, rather than -ME for the fourth sign.

37 line 2 For the beginning of the line, following the URU, H. Winckler's copy has *ki-bi*, while his transliteration has "Ki-?-bi" (Sar. 1 p. 191 and 2 pl. 49 no. 2l). The photo of the squeeze would suggest ⸢*šá* IGI? *né*⸣-[*re*]-*bi*. KUR*: E. Flandin's copy has ŠE, while P.E. Botta's copy and H. Winckler's copy both have KUR; the squeeze is not clear about the matter.

p. 47). For information on this individual, see Pruzsinszky, PNA 3/2 p. 1304 sub Taklāk-ana-Bēl 1.

CATALOGUE

Source	Provenance	Louvre Squeeze	cpn
Botta, Monument de Ninive 4 pl. 180^c	Khorsabad, Palace, Room XIV, slab 10	no	n

TEXT

1) *uš-ma-nu šá* ⸢m*tàk*⸣-[*lak-a-na*-EN?]	1) Camp of *Tak*[*lāk-ana-Bēl*].

39

The lower register of the relief on slab 12 from Room XIV of the palace at Khorsabad shows Assyrian soldiers attacking a city. This epigraph is placed on the city wall. The main inscription on the slab was not copied by P.E. Botta, but would presumably have been part of the king's Annals (text no. 4). Based upon the number of lines missing between slabs 10 and 12 and in comparison to text no. 1, the text on slab 12 would likely have recorded the campaign in Sargon's seventh regnal year (715). For bibliography on the epigraph, see the introduction to text nos. 23–40. The transliteration is based on Botta's copy in Monument de Ninive 4 pl. 180^c. (See also in particular El-Amin, Sumer 9 [1953] fig. 15 [following p. 228].) According to the Khorsabad Annals, the city Kišešlu was located near Ḫarḫar, was conquered in Sargon's seventh regnal year (715), and was renamed Kār-Nabû (text no. 1 lines 109b–114a).

CATALOGUE

Source	Provenance	Louvre Squeeze	cpn
Botta, Monument de Ninive 4 pl. 180^c	Khorsabad, Palace, Room XIV, slab 12	no	n

38 line 1 P.E. Botta's copy (Monument de Ninive 4 pl. 180^c) has an extra vertical wedge in the UŠ.

TEXT

1) URU.*ki-šeš-lu al-me* KUR*-*ud*	1) I surrounded (and) conquered the city Kišešlu.

40

Two lines were copied by P.E. Botta immediately after a section of Sargon's Annals coming from an unknown room of the palace (Botta, Monument de Ninive 4 pl. 163 and Winckler, Sar. 2 pl. 26 no. 55; see the commentary to text no. 6). J. Renger, however, identified these lines as an epigraph (see Borger, HKL 2 p. 322 sub Winckler, Sargon n55). Neither the original placement of the slab nor anything about what the relief on the slab depicted are known. A. Fuchs suggests that the slab may have come from the throne room of the palace (Khorsabad p. 279). For bibliography on the epigraph, see the introduction to text nos. 23–40. The transliteration is based on Botta's copy.

CATALOGUE

Source	Provenance	Louvre Squeeze	cpn
Botta, Monument de Ninive 4 pl. 163	Khorsabad, Palace	no	n

TEXT

1) E ÁŠ GU RU Ú	1–2) I surrounded (and) conquered ...
2) *al*-me* KUR-*ud*	

41

An inscription on the back of a large number of the stone slabs and a few winged bulls from Khorsabad records the building of that city, and in particular its palace, by Sargon II. The text is less carefully inscribed than those texts found on the front of the slabs and winged bulls and mistakes and abnormal sign forms are often encountered. Since Sargon is not given the titles "governor of Babylon" and "king of the land of Sumer and Akkad," it is likely that the inscription was composed before his defeat of Marduk-apla-iddina II and his assumption of the throne of Babylon in his twelfth year (710). The inscriptions on the front of the pieces often refer to Sargon's

39 line 1 E. Flandin's copy (Botta, Monument de Ninive 2 pl. 147) omits the two vertical wedges of URU, indicates that the KI is partially damaged, omits one of the two final Winkelhaken of ŠEŠ, and indicates that the AL is defective. KUR*: P.E. Botta's copy (Monument de Ninive 4 pl. 180[c]) and Flandin's copy (ibid. 2 pl. 147) have NU, while H. Winckler's copy (Sar. 2 pl. 49 no. 2m) has KUR.
40 line 1 A. Fuchs (Khorsabad p. 279) tentatively suggests that the line might have read originally URU.*áš/ma-gu-ru-ú*, but points out that neither place is attested.
40 line 2 *al**-: P.E. Botta's copy omits one wedge head.

defeat of Marduk-apla-iddina II. Thus, J.M. Russell has suggested that while the reverses of the slabs were inscribed and placed against the palace walls before the ruler's twelfth year, the texts on their fronts were inscribed after the twelfth year (J.M. Russell, Writing on the Wall p. 103). Because museums have generally placed these reliefs against walls, it has not been possible to collate many exemplars of this inscription from the originals. When the Louvre recently rearranged its Near Eastern galleries, photographs of the inscriptions on the backs of the reliefs were made and these have been kindly made available to the author by B. André-Salvini. For a study of this inscription and how it was written, see André-Salvini in Caubet, Khorsabad pp. 15–45, and note also J.M. Russell, Writing on the Wall pp. 101–103 for the general context of the inscription.

CATALOGUE

Ex.	Museum Number	Provenance	Lines Preserved	Botta, MdN	de Longpérier	Louvre Squeeze	Louvre Cast	cpn
1	AO 19862 (Nap. III 2860)	Khorsabad, Palace, Façade n, slab 48	1–28 (on 27)	4 pl. 164	600	no	yes	p
2	—	Khorsabad, Palace, Room II, slab 18	1–28 (on 20)	4 pl. 165	—	no	no	n
3	—	Khorsabad, Palace, Room V, slab 6	1–28 (on 23)	4 pl. 166	—	no	no	n
4	—	Khorsabad, Palace, Façade m, slab 20	1–28 (on 40)	4 pl. 167	—	no	no	n
5	AO 19857 (N 8032; Nap. III 2856)	Khorsabad, Palace, SW side of Entrance k (k, 2)	1–28 (on 28)	4 pl. 168[c]	598	yes	yes	p
6	—	Khorsabad; see commentary	1–28 (on 18)	4 pl. 169	—	no	no	n
7	AO 19887	Khorsabad, Palace, Room X, slab 6	1–28 (on 27)	4 pl. 170	—	no	yes	p
8	—	Khorsabad, Palace, Façade n, slab 37	1–28 (on 22)	4 pl. 171	—	no	no	n
9	—	Khorsabad, Palace, Façade n, slab 10	1–28 (on 30)	4 pl. 172[c]	—	yes	no	p
10	AO 19877	Khorsabad, Palace, Room VIII, slab 19	1–28 (on 17)	4 pl. 173[c]	609	no	yes	p
11	—	Khorsabad, Palace, Façade n, slab 34	1–28 (on 21)	4 pl. 174	—	no	no	n
12	—	Khorsabad, Palace, Façade m, slab 19	1–28 (on 19)	4 pl. 175	—	no	no	n
13	—	Khorsabad, Palace, Façade n, slab 28	1–28 (on 20)	4 pl. 176	—	no	no	n
14	—	Khorsabad, Palace, Room II? (see commentary)	1–28 (on 22)	4 pl. 177[c]	—	yes	no	p
15	—	Khorsabad, Palace, Room VIII, slab 9	1–28 (on 23)	4 pl. 178	—	no	no	n
16	—	Khorsabad, Palace, Façade L, slab 9	1–28 (on 23)	4 pl. 179	—	no	no	n
17	AO 19863 (Nap. III 2862)	Khorsabad, city gate 3, left side of inner entrance	1–28 (on 23)	—	—	no	yes	p
18	A 7369	Khorsabad, Palace, Façade n, 45	1–28 (on 22)	—	—	no	no	p
19	BM 118835A (47-7-2,52)	Khorsabad	14–21	—	—	—	—	c

20	—	Khorsabad; see commentary	12–14	—	—	—	—	n
21	AO 19858 (N 8033; Nap. III 2857)	Khorsabad, Palace, NE side of Entrance k (k, 1)	1–28 (on 20)	—	599	yes	yes	p
22	AO 19865	Khorsabad, Palace, Façade N, slab 25	1–28 (on 21)	—	601	no	yes	p
23	AO 19866	Khorsabad, Palace, possibly Façade m, left of Entrance g	1–15	—	602	no	yes	p
24	AO 19869	Khorsabad, Palace, chamber of detached building, slabs 3–4	nine lines	—	605	no	no	n
25	AO 19870	Khorsabad, Palace, Façade N	9–28	—	604	no	yes	p
26	AO 19871	Khorsabad, Palace, Façade n, slab 13	1–7	—	606	no	yes	p
27	AO 19872	Khorsabad, Palace, Façade m, slab 4	1–18	—	603	no	yes	p
28	AO 19873–AO 19874	Khorsabad, Palace, Façade L, slab 12	1–28 (on 20)	—	607	no	yes	p
29	AO 19876	Khorsabad, Palace, probably Room XI, slab 21	1–28 (on 21)	—	608	no	yes	p
30	AO 19878	Khorsabad, Palace, Façade L, slab 35	1–28 (on 24)	—	610	no	yes	p
31	AO 19879	Khorsabad, Palace, Façade L, slab 34	1–28 (on 29)	—	611	no	yes	p
32	AO 19881	Khorsabad, Palace, Façade L, slab 26	9–28	—	612	no	yes	p
33	AO 19882	Khorsabad, Palace, Façade L, slab 27	8–28	—	613	no	yes	p
34	AO 19883	Khorsabad, Palace, Façade L, slab 31	5–28	—	614	no	yes	p
35	AO 19884	Khorsabad, Palace, Façade L, slab 30	1–25	—	615	no	yes	p
36	AO 19887 (+) A 150547	Khorsabad, Palace, Room X, slab 7	19–28	—	—	no	yes	p
37	AO 19888	Khorsabad, Palace, Façade n, unnumbered slab	26–28	—	—	no	no	p
38	AO 19864	Khorsabad, Place, Façade N, slab 28	1–7	—	—	no	no	c
39	A 7358	Khorsabad, Palace, Façade n, slab 23 (= Court VIII, slab 10)	1–28 (on 25)	—	—	—	—	p
40	A 7359	Khorsabad, Palace, Façade n, slab 15 (= Court VIII, slab 2)	1–28 (on 25)	—	—	—	—	p
41	A 7360	Khorsabad, Palace, Façade n, slab 22 (= Court VIII, slab 9)	1–28 (on 24)	—	—	—	—	n
42	A 7363	Khorsabad, Palace, Room X, slab 2 and part of slab 3	1–28 (on 18)	—	—	—	—	n
43	A 7365	Khorsabad, Palace, Room X, slab 4	12–28	—	—	—	—	p
44	A 7366	Khorsabad, Palace, Façade n, slab 33 (= Court VIII, slab 25)	1–28 (on 21)	—	—	—	—	p

45	A 7367	Khorsabad, Palace, Façade n, slab 35 (= Court VIII, slab 23)	1–28 (on 21)	—	—	—	—	n
46	A 7368	Khorsabad, Palace, Façade n, slab 36 (= Court VIII, slab 24)	1–28 (on 22)	—	—	—	—	p
47	A 11256 (64-L-1, 64-L-2, 64-L-3, and 65-M-1)	Khorsabad, Palace, Room VII (Throne Room), slab 11	1–28 (on 22)	—	—	—	—	p
48	—	Khorsabad; see commentary	14–26, 28	—	—	—	—	n
49	—	Khorsabad; see commentary	19–25	—	—	—	—	n

LIKELY ADDITIONAL EXEMPLARS

Ex.	Museum Number	Provenance
1*	A 7362	Khorsabad, Palace, Room X, slab 5 and part of slab 6
2*	A 11254 (62-J-1, 62-J-2, 62-J-3, 62-J-4, and 62-J-5)	Khorsabad, Palace, Room VII (Throne Room), slab 10
3*	IM 18627	Khorsabad, Palace, Façade n, slab 24
4*	IM 18628	Khorsabad, Palace, Façade n, slab 29?
5*	IM 18631	Khorsabad, Palace, Façade n, slab 31?
6*	IM 60972/2	Khorsabad, Palace, Room VI, slab 15
7*	IM 60972/3	Khorsabad, Palace, Room VI, slab 14
8*	IM 60973	Khorsabad, Palace, Door X (between Rooms VI and XI), lateral wall
9*	IM 60980	Khorsabad, Palace, Room V, unnumbered slab
10*	IM 72126	Khorsabad, Palace, Façade n, slab 32?
11*	IM 72127/1	Khorsabad, Palace; Façade n, slab 16?
12*	IM 72127/2	Khorsabad, Palace; Façade n, slab 17?
13*	IM 72129 (winged bull)	Khorsabad, Gate A of inner city wall

COMMENTARY

Exs. 5, 18, and 21 are found on the backs of winged bull colossi; all the remaining exemplars are from the backs of wall slabs. The provenances given for exs. 1–9 and 11–17 are those stated by P.E. Botta in Monument de Ninive 4. There is some question, however, about the accuracy of the statements for exs. 6 and 14 and thus their identification with pieces in the Louvre; see below.

With regard to exs. 1–17 and 21–37 in the above catalogue, "p" indicates that the exemplar was collated by means of either photographs of the inscription made when the relevant wall slab was moved for relocation in the Louvre, photographs of squeezes of the inscription, photographs of casts of the inscription, examination of casts of the inscription, or (most commonly) by a combination of these methods.

Ex. 1: AO 19862 has been collated from photographs of the original and from casts in the Louvre. The piece is now broken in two and most of line 26 is no longer preserved; in the score Botta's copy has been followed for the missing section.

Exs. 5, 9, 14, and 21: The squeezes of these exemplars have been examined by means of photographs. Regrettably, the squeezes are often damaged or indicate damage to the original in the places where Botta's copies have abnormal sign forms. The squeeze in the Louvre identified as being Botta, Monument de Ninive 3 pl. 51^{c} — part of text no. 9 on k,1 (AO 19858) — is actually of the inscription on the back of k,1 (ex. 21).

Exs. 6 and 14: According to Botta, Monument de Ninive 3 p. III and 4 pls. 169 and 177^{c} (exs. 6 and 14 respectively), the two exemplars of the inscription copied on those plates were found on the backs of Façade L slabs 26 (=AO 19881) and 12 (=AO 19773-19874) respectively. However, Botta's copies do not match the inscriptions actually found on the backs of those two slabs (see also André-Salvini in Caubet, Khorsabad pp. 22 and 29 nn. 14–15). The transliterations for these exemplars are based on Botta's copies.

Ex. 7: AO 19887 is made up of one complete wall slab (Room X, slab 6) and part of an adjoining wall slab (Room X, slab 7). Each is inscribed and each is listed separately above (exs. 7 and 36 respectively). The inscription on the back of Room X, slab 6 was copied and published by Botta as being on slab 8 (Botta, Monument de Ninive 4 pl. 170). Note that Flandin's original drawing misnumbered the reliefs for slabs 6–7 as being on slabs 5–6; see Albenda, Palace of Sargon p. 162. It is not clear to which slab de Longpérier, Notice[3] no. 616 belongs; he seems to indicate that it should be AO 19887, but he says the inscription is on twenty-two lines.

Exs. 8 and 46: Although ex. 8 is said by Botta to come from the back of Façade n, slab 37, and ex. 46 comes from Façade n, slab 36 (= Court VIII, slab 24), comparison of their variants and line arrangement might suggest that they are the same text. The differences noted may simply be the result of miscopying by Botta, but because of these, the two have been kept separate here.

Ex. 10: Botta made a squeeze of the text of Monument de Ninive 4 pl. 173[c], but it is no longer extant. Only the right half of ex. 10 as shown on Botta's copy can be checked by means of casts or photographs of the original. For the provenance of ex. 10, see Albenda, Palace of Sargon p. 160.

Exs. 11 and 44: Although ex. 11 is reported to come from the back of Façade n, slab 34 on Botta, Monument de Ninive 4 pl. 174, and ex. 44 is said to be on the back of Façade n, slab 33 (the front being depicted on Monument de Ninive 1 pl. 30), it is likely that they represent the same exemplar. The line arrangement is the same on both pieces and both have a number of otherwise unique variants (e.g., omitting *šá* ^{d}*é-a* ^{d}*be-let*-DINGIR.MEŠ, "that the god Ea (and) the goddess Bēlet-ilī" in line 14; a ŠI lacking the horizontal wedge in line 27 *a-ši-bu-ut*; and *ana* for *a-na* in line 28). The differences noted between the two may be due to inaccurate copying by Botta. Nevertheless, because of these differences, the two have been kept separate here.

Ex. 18: The inscription on the back of the winged bull colossus A 7369 in the Oriental Institute (Chicago) was collated from photos supplied by J. Renger and by photos of the lower section of the inscription taken by the author. Due to the location of the bull close to the wall of the gallery, it is possible to see only a small part of the inscription clearly.

Ex. 19: C.B.F. Walker kindly supplied a photograph of, and information on, BM 118835A. Since there is a blank space below line 21 on this exemplar, the inscription presumably continued onto the back of another slab or was in a second column.

Ex. 20: According to Botta (JA 4/3 [1844] p. 102 [pl. XXII = Monument de Ninive 1 pl. 12]), the text of ex. 20 is found on the back of Façade L, slab 12 (ex. 14). The copy of ex. 20 (ibid. pl. XXXI no. 2; see also Institut de France Botta-Cotta II 2976 folio I sheet 310), however, cannot be identified with the copy of ex. 14 (Monument de Ninive 4 pl. 177[c]). Thus, either Façade L, slab 12 had the inscription twice, or one of the provenances is incorrect.

Ex. 24: The back of AO 119869 is damaged and smeared with (modern) plaster, making it impossible to read the inscription located there.

Ex. 25: A section running across the middle of slab AO 19870 has been removed at some point. The missing section contained parts of master lines 18–19.

Exs. 32, 34, and 35: The inscriptions on the backs of these exemplars are upside down in relation to the inscriptions and reliefs on the fronts of those slabs. This would indicate that the inscriptions on the backs had been incised off-site, before the slabs were positioned in the palace, and that the material on the fronts was carved after the slabs had been put in place. See also André-Salvini in Caubet, Khorsabad pp. 22–24.

Exs. 39–47: Information on these exemplars and photographs of some of them were kindly supplied by J.A. Brinkman and K. Neumann. Brinkman also provided the author with his own transliterations of exs. 39, 41–43, and 45 and has allowed him to use them here. Only parts of the inscription on ex. 47 are visible on the photos and thus the edition of this exemplar must be considered incomplete and preliminary.

Exs. 48 and 49: These inscriptions were found on stone fragments discovered at Khorsabad by Botta and are edited from copies made by him and preserved in the Institut de France (Botta-Cotta II 2976 folio I sheet 316). He proposes that they come from the same inscription. While this is certainly possible, it has been thought best to edit them separately here. It is possible that they are to be identified with two of the other exemplars about which nothing is known.

Faint illegible traces of additional lines are sometimes visible immediately before the lines indicated in the catalogue. For example, about 8 and 2–3 additional lines are found on exs. 25 and 37 respectively.

In the edition presented below, the arrangement of lines follows ex. 5, but the master line itself is a conflation from several exemplars. The exemplars often exhibit a mixture of sign forms (Babylonian, Assyrian, and archaizing) within the same exemplar and sometimes within the same line.

This inscription is often written very poorly, with numerous signs, and at times words, omitted, or not fully carved, with the lines at times quite slanted, and with numerous mistakes or incorrect sign forms (e.g., KID for É, I-ZA for IA, DIŠ for LIŠ, and ŠÚ for ŠI). Based upon an examination of photographs and/or casts and/or squeezes of the original inscriptions on exs. 1, 5, 7, 9–10, and 14, it is clear that many, but not all, of the abnormal/incorrect sign forms in Botta's copies in Monument de Ninive do not represent what is on the originals. It would be of little value to indicate in the on-page notes every instance when an exemplar omitted a word or had an unimportant difference (e.g, ex. 28 omitting *dan-nu* "strong" in line 1; ex. 3 omitting MAN "king" before KUR *aš-šur*.KI in line 1; and ex. 34 having *a-na* for *i-na* in line 26) and thus these are normally found in the list of minor variants at the back of the book. It would also be of little value to indicate all abnormal sign forms (particularly when many are only known from Botta's copies and cannot be confirmed by examination of the original) or cases of abnormal sign forms in Botta's copies that can be seen to have the correct form from the squeezes or originals; for these, see the scores on Oracc where these are indicated. The casts sometimes show more than is currently preserved on the originals and sometimes the casts and/or squeezes represent only a portion of the inscription copied by Botta.

Several wall slabs (exs. 1*–12*) and at least one winged bull (ex. 13*) preserved in the Oriental Institute (Chicago) or Iraq Museum (Baghdad) have inscriptions on their backs, although this is rarely, if ever, noted in publications. The chart of likely additional exemplars above lists the relevant pieces known to the author to have inscriptions on their backs although it has not been possible to see them or provide information on the individual inscriptions.

The information on the pieces in Chicago (including both exs. 39–47 and exs. 1*–2*) was kindly supplied by J.A. Brinkman. He notes, however, that while this list includes all the major pieces with inscriptions on their backs in the Oriental Institute, it may not include all the small fragments. The list of the pieces in the Iraq Museum (exs. 3*–13*) is also unlikely to be complete and is based upon a quick personal examination of some of the pieces on display in that museum. It has not been possible to examine the pieces in the Oriental Institute or to transliterate those in the Iraq Museum in order to ascertain whether or not the inscriptions found on their backs are duplicates of this text. For general information on these pieces and their findspots, see Albenda, Palace of Sargon pp. 171–180.

BIBLIOGRAPHY

1844 Botta, JA 4/3 p. 102 and pl. XXXI,2 (ex. 20, copy, study)

1849 Botta, Monument de Ninive 4 pls. 164–179 (exs. 1–16, copy)

1850 Botta, Monument de Ninive 5 pp. 183–184 (study)

1854 de Longpérier, Notice[3] nos. 598–615 (exs. 1, 5, 10, 21–35, study)

1865 Ménant, Revers de plaques (ex. 4, copy, edition; exs. 1–3, 5–16, as variants)

1867 Place, Ninive et l'Assyrie 3 pl. 12 (ex. 17, provenance)

1874 Ménant, Annales pp. 196–197 (ex. 4, translation)

1886 Bezold, Literatur pp. 92–93 §55.12 (exs. 1–16, study)

1889 Winckler, Sar. 1 pp. XI, 164–167, and 2 pl. 40 (ex. 5, copy, edition; exs. 1–4, 6–16, as variants)

1918 Pillet, Khorsabad pp. 51 and 95–97 (ex. 17, study)

1924 Pottier, Antiquités assyriennes pp. 69–70 no. 18 (ex. 17, study)

1927 Luckenbill, ARAB 2 pp. 55–56 §§103–105 (translation)

1936 Loud, Khorsabad 1 pp. 42–55 (ex. 18, provenance)

1971 Cagni, Crestomazia pp. 46–51 and 259–260 (ex. 5, edition)

1979 Borger, BAL[2] pp. 59–60, 129–131 and 322 (ex. 5, copy, transliteration; exs. 1–4, 6–16, as variants)

1986 Albenda, Palace of Sargon p. 157 and passim (study) and fig. 9 (ex. 17, partial photo of cast)

1986 Renger, CRRA 32 pp. 112–113 (lines 1–8, partial transcription, study)

1987 Engel, Dämonen pp. 150–151 (lines 22b–23a, edition of exs. 1–16)

1990 Renger, Studies Moran pp. 435–436 (edition)

1990 Wilson and Brinkman, OI Featured Object 8 (ex. 18, translation, provenance)

1994 Fuchs, Khorsabad pp. 54–59 and 300–302 no. 1.3 (exs. 1–17, edition)

1995 André-Salvini in Caubet, Khorsabad pp. 15–45 (translation, study) and figs. 4b, 6–9, 11–12, 16–22 (exs. 5, 17, 21, 28, 30-35, photo; ex. 5, photo of squeeze, copies [by Botta and Winckler])

1999 J.M. Russell, Writing on the Wall pp. 101–103 (study)

TEXT

1) É.GAL ^{m}MAN-GI.NA GAR ^{d}BAD NU.ÈŠ *aš-šur* MAN *dan-nu* MAN ŠÚ MAN KUR *aš-šur*.KI
2) MAN *kib-rat* LÍMMU-*i mi-gir* DINGIR.MEŠ GAL.MEŠ *šá-kin šu-ba-re-e*
3) ZIMBIR.KI NIBRU.KI KÁ.DINGIR.RA.KI *ḫa-a-tin en-šu-te-šú-nu*
4) *e-pir a-ke-e mu-šal-li-mu ḫi-bíl-ti-šú-un ka-ṣir*
5) *ki-din-nu-ut bal-til*.KI *ba-ṭi-il-tu mu-šá-áš-ši-ik tup-šik-ki*
6) BÀD.AN.KI *mu-šap-ši-ḫu* UN.MEŠ-*šú-un an-ḫa-a-ti le-ʾi* DÙ *mal-ki*
7) *šá* UGU URU.*ḫar-ra-na* AN.DÙL-*la-šú it-ru-ṣu-ma ki-i ṣa-ab* ^{d}*a-nim*
8) ^{d}*da-gan iš-ṭu-ru za-kut-su* MAN *šá ul-tu* u$_{4}$-*mi be-lu-ti-šú*
9) *gaba-ra-a-šú la ib-šu-ma i-na qab-li ù ta-ḫa-zi la e-mu-ru*
10) *mu-né-ḫu* KUR.KUR DÙ-*ši-na ki-ma ḫaṣ-bat-ti ú-daq-qi-qu-ma ḫa-am-ma-mi*
11) *šá ar-ba-ʾi id-du-ú ṣer-re-e-ti* LÚ.*šu-ut* SAG.MEŠ-*šú* LÚ.GAR-*nu-ti*
12) UGU-*šú-nu iš-tak-ka-nu-ma bíl-tu ma-da-at-tú ki-i šá áš-šu-ri*
13) *e-mid-su-nu-ti i-na mé-re-ši-ia* DAGAL *ù ḫi-is-sa-at* GEŠTU.II-*ia*
14) *pal-ka-a-ti šá* ^{d}*é-a* ^{d}*be-let*-DINGIR.MEŠ UGU MAN.MEŠ-*ni* AD.MEŠ-*ia*
15) *ú-šá-te-ru ḫa-sis-si i-na bi-bíl lìb-bi-ia i-na* GÌR.II KUR.*mu-uṣ-ri* KUR-*i*
16) *i-na re-bit* NINA.KI URU *e-pu-uš-ma* URU.BÀD-^{m}MAN-GIN MU-*šú ab-bi*
17) *pa-rak-ki ra-áš-du-ti a-na* ^{d}*é-a* ^{d}30 ^{d}UTU ^{d}IŠKUR *ù* ^{d}*nin-urta*
18) *i-na qer-bi-šú nak-liš* ú-šab-ni-ma* É.GAL ZÚ AM.SI GIŠ.ESI GIŠ.TÚG
19) GIŠ.MES.MÁ.KAN.NA GIŠ.*ere*-IGI GIŠ.ŠUR.MÌN

1–2a) Palace of Sargon (II), appointee of the god Enlil, *nešakku*-priest of (the god) Aššur, strong king, king of the world, king of Assyria, king of the four quarters (of the world), favorite of the great gods;

2b–8a) who (re)-established the *šubarrû*-privileges of (the cities) Sippar, Nippur, (and) Babylon, (and) protects the weak among them (lit.: "their weak ones"); who provides food for the destitute (and) made restitution for the wrongful damage suffered by them; who (re)established (5) the privileged status of (the city) Baltil (Aššur) that had lapsed, who abolished corvée duty for (the city) Dēr (and) gave relief to their weary people; (most) capable of all rulers, who extended his protection over the city Ḫarrān and recorded its exemption (from obligations) as if (its people were) people of the gods Anu (and) Dagān;

8b–13a) the king, who since the (first) day of his reign, has had no equal and has met no one who could overpower (him) in war or battle; (10) (who) smashed all (enemy) lands as if (they were) pots and put halters on (all) rebels in the four (quarters of the world); (who) set eunuchs of his as governors over them and imposed upon them (the same) tribute (and) payment(s) as if (they were) Assyrians.

13b–16) With my wide knowledge and broad intelligence that the god Ea (and) the goddess Bēlet-ilī had made greater than those of the kings, my ancestors, (15) (and) in accordance with my heart's desire, I built a city at the foot of Mount Muṣri, a mountain on the *outskirts* of Nineveh, and I named it Dūr-Šarrukīn.

17–18a) I had firmly-founded daises skillfully built inside it for the gods Ea, Sîn, Šamaš, Adad, and Ninurta.

18b–26a) I built a palace using (lit.: "of") elephant ivory, ebony, boxwood, *musukkannu*-wood, cedar, cypress, *daprānu*-juniper, juniper, (and) terebinth (20) to

1 The copy of ex. 2 has the sign MAŠ on a line immediately before the inscription. Ex. 17 has NU.ÈŠ *aš-*⸢*šur*.KI⸣$^{?}$ "*nešakku*-priest of Assyria." NU.ÈŠ normally stands for *nešakku/nēšakku*, for which CAD N/2 p. 190 gives the meaning "(a dignitary)" and CDA p. 251 "(a priest; a dignitary)." CAD N/2 p. 191, however, states: "The royal title NU.ÈŠ ^{d}*Aššur*, attested only for Sargon II, e.g., Lyon, Sar. 25:2 [=text no. 46] represents a scribal conceit, based on the similarity of the two words [*nešakku* and *iššakku*], to render the traditional title *iššak* ^{d}*Aššur*, as can be seen from the writings ÉNSI (PA.TE.SI) ^{d}*Aššur* Lyon, Sar. 27:2 and Winckler, Sammlung 2 1:12 [text nos. 47 and 89, respectively], see Seux, Épithètes [=ERAS] 114." Nevertheless, it has been thought best to translate NU.ÈŠ as "*nešakku*-priest" here.

6 Ex. 42 omits *mu-šap-ši-ḫu*.

7 Exs. 1, 3, 8–16, 27, 29–31, 34–35, and possibly 2 (restored, via spacing) add *ù* after ^{d}*a-nim*, thus "Anu and" rather than "Anu (and)"; *ù* in ex. 27 appears to omit the first horizontal wedge; exs. 17 and 22 add *u* after ^{d}*a-nim*.

12 Ex. 32 Inserts ⸢*u*⸣$^{?}$, "and," after *bíl-tu*, "tribute." The phrase *ki-i šá áš-šu-ri*, "as if (they were) Assyrians," means "comparable to that paid by Assyrians." We might expect the *plene* writing *áš-šu-ri-i*, but the inscriptions of Sargon are consistent in using this writing in this phrase. The *plene* writing only appears in text no. 89 line 3, where it describes the god Enlil (⸢^{d}EN.LÍL⸣ *áš-šu-ru-u*).

14 Exs. 11 and 44 omit *šá* ^{d}*é-a* ^{d}*be-let*-DINGIR.MEŠ, "that the god Ea (and) the goddess Bēlet-ilī." Ex. 22 omits ^{d}*é-a*, "the god Ea."

16 *re-bit* "*outskirts*": See the note to text no. 7 line 23.

18 *-liš**: P.E. Botta's copies and all exemplars examined where the sign is clear have -DIŠ.

19 Exs. 1 and 22 insert *ù** and *u* respectively before GIŠ.*bu-uṭ-ni*, "and terebinth" for "(and) terebinth." The *ù** in ex. 1 omits the horizontal wedge following the first vertical wedge.

GIŠ.*dáp-ra-ni* GIŠ.LI GIŠ.*bu-uṭ-ni*
20) *a-na mu-šab* MAN-*ti-ia ab-ni-ma* É *ḫi-la-an-ni tam-šil* É.GAL KUR.*ḫat-ti*
21) *i-na* KÁ.MEŠ-*šin ap-ti-iq-ma* GIŠ.ÙR.MEŠ GIŠ.*ere*-IGI GIŠ.ŠUR.MÌN *ú-kin*
22) *ṣe-e-ru-šin e-ma-am-mi tam-šil bi-nu-ut* KUR-*i ù tam-tim šá* NA_4 BABBAR-*e*
23) *i-na né-re-bé-ti-ši-na ul-ziz-ma* GIŠ.IG.MEŠ GIŠ.ŠUR.MÌN GIŠ.MES.MÁ.KAN.NA
24) *ú-rat-ta-a* KÁ.MEŠ-*šin* BÀD-*šú ki-ma ki-iṣ-rat* KUR-*i*
25) *ú-šar-šid-ma* UN.MEŠ KUR.KUR *mal* ^{d}UTU *ir-te-ʾu-ú ki-šit-ti*
26) ŠU.II-*ia i-na lìb-bi ú-še-šib* DINGIR.MEŠ GAL.MEŠ *a-ši-bu-ut* AN-*e*
27) KI-*tim ù* DINGIR.MEŠ *a-ši-bu-ut* URU *šá-a-šú e-peš* URU
28) *šul-bur qer-bi-šú iš-ru-ku-in-ni a-na da-riš*

be my royal residence; I fashioned a *bīt ḫilāni*, a replica of a Hittite palace, at their gates and roofed them with beams of cedar (and) cypress. I erected at their entrances animals made of shining stone in the image of creatures of the mountain and sea and installed doors of cypress (and) *musukkannu*-wood in their gates. I made its wall as secure as a mountain massif (25) and settled there people of the lands that I had conquered — as many as the god Šamaš shepherded.

26b–28) The great gods who dwell in heaven (and) netherworld, and the gods who dwell in this city, have granted me the eternal (privilege of) building (this) city (and) growing old in it.

42

A text found on the back of a wall slab from Khorsabad depicting a left-facing winged genie gives a summary of Sargon's conquests. Similar accounts are found on other texts, in particular ones found on palace thresholds (text nos. 10–15; see also text no. 7 lines 16–23 and text no. 8 lines 21–27). The inscription is both unlike and better written than the one found on the backs of other wall slabs from Khorsabad (text no. 41). The inclusion of Chaldea and Bīt-Yakīn "as far as the border of Dilmun" in the area ruled by Sargon (lines 14–17) would suggest that the text was composed after the Babylonian campaigns in king's twelfth and thirteenth regnal years (710–709).

CATALOGUE

Museum Number	Provenance	Dimensions (cm)	cpn
IM 72131?	Khorsabad, Gate A of the inner city wall	—	(c)

COMMENTARY

The museum number is likely IM 72131, but there is some uncertainty about this and it might be IM 72129. It was not possible to ascertain if the matching stone slab (IM 72130) across the entryway from this one has a similar inscription on its reverse or if it even has an inscription there. The edition is based on a photograph and a brief examination of the original.

For photographs showing the discovery of the slab and/or the relief on the front, see Basmachi, Treasures p. 263 fig. 141 and Loud and Altman, Khorsabad 2 pp. 53–54 and pls. 9–10.

41 line 20 Ex. 47 has *e-*⸢*pu*⸣*-*[*uš-ma*] instead of *ab-ni-ma*.

BIBLIOGRAPHY

1986 Albenda, Palace of Sargon p. 180 (study)

2004 Frame, Studies Grayson pp. 101–102 (photo, edition)

TEXT

1) É.GAL ^{m}LUGAL-GI.NA LUGAL GAL-*ú* LUGAL *dan-nu*
2) LUGAL *kiš-šá-ti* LUGAL KUR *aš-šur*.KI GÌR.NÍTA KÁ.DINGIR.RA.KI
3) LUGAL KUR EME.GI$_{7}$ *ù ak-ka-de-e* LUGAL *kib-rat* LÍMMU-*i*
4) *mi-gir* DINGIR.MEŠ GAL.MEŠ LUGAL *ša i-na tu-kul-ti*
5) ^{d}*a-šur* ^{d}AG ^{d}AMAR.UTU *iš-tu* KUR.*ia-ad-na-na*
6) *ša* MURUB$_{4}$ *tam-tim šá-lam* ^{d}UTU-*ši a-di* KUR.*mu-ṣu-ri*
7) *ù* KUR.*mu-us-ki* KUR MAR.TU.KI DAGAL-*tum* KUR.*ḫa-at-ti*
8) *a-na si-ḫir-ti-šá nap-ḫar* KUR.*gu-ti-um*.KI KUR.*ma-da-a-a*
9) *ru-qu-ú-ti ša pa-aṭ* KUR.*bi-ik-ni* KUR.*el-li-pi*
10) KUR.*ra-a-ši ša pa-aṭ* KUR.ELAM.MA.KI *na-gab* LÚ.*a-ri-me*
11) *a-ši-ib a-aḫ* ÍD.IDIGNA ÍD.*su-rap-pi*
12) ÍD.*uq-né-e a-di* URU.*dun-ni*-^{d}*šá-maš*
13) URU.*bu-bé-e* URU.DU$_{6}$-^{d}*ḫum-ba ša mi-ṣir*
14) KUR.ELAM.MA.KI KUR.⸢*kar*⸣-^{d}*du*-⸢*ni*⸣-*áš e-liš* ⸢*ù*⸣ *šap-liš*
15) *gi-mir* KUR.*kal-di ma-la ba-šu-ú* KUR.É-^{m}*ia-ki-ni*
16) *ša* GÚ ÍD.*mar*-⸢*ra*⸣-*ti a-di pa-aṭ* NI.TUK.KI
17) *mit-ḫa-riš i-bí-lu-ma* LÚ.*šu-ut* SAG.MEŠ-*šú*
18) LÚ.EN.NAM.MEŠ UGU-*šú-nu iš-tak*-⸢*ka*⸣-*nu-ú-ma*
19) *ni-ir be-lu-ti-šú e-mì-su-nu-ti*

1–4a) Palace of Sargon, great king, strong king, king of the world, king of Assyria, governor of Babylon, king of the land of Sumer and Akkad, king of the four quarters (of the world), favorite of the great gods;

4b–19) the king who with the support of the gods Aššur, Nabû, (and) Marduk ruled all together from the land Yadnana (Cyprus), which is in the middle of the Western Sea, as far as Egypt and the land Musku, the wide land Amurru, the land Ḫatti (Syria) in its entirety, all of the land Gutium, the distant Medes (who live) on the border of Mount Bikni, the lands Ellipi (and) (10) Rāši on the border of the land Elam, all the Arameans who live beside the Tigris, Surappu, (and) Uqnû Rivers, as far as the cities Dunni-Šamaš, Bubê, (and) Tīl-Ḫumba on the border of the land Elam, the land Karduniaš (Babylonia) from one end to the other (lit.: "above and below"), (15) all of Chaldea, as much as there is (of it), (and) the land Bīt-Yakīn, which is on the shore of the sea, as far as the border of Dilmun; (who) set eunuchs of his as provincial governors over them and imposed the yoke of his lordship upon them.

43

Numerous prismatic clay cylinders from Khorsabad, as well as one from Nineveh, bear an inscription commemorating the construction of the city Dūr-Šarrukīn, and in particular the building of its palace and city wall. Following an introductory section giving the name of the king and his main epithets (lines 1–3), the text describes in summary fashion the major actions and achievements of Sargon's reign (lines 4–38) and then records the building of the city (lines 39–75), concluding with a curse on anyone who "alters the work of my hands, mutilates my features (on a relief), obliterates the reliefs that I have engraved, (or) effaces my own representation(s)" (lines 76–77). The latest events mentioned in the inscription (the deportation of the people of Bīt-Purutaš, lines 23–24) date to the king's ninth regnal year

42 line 19 We would expect *ēmidušunūti*, not *ēmissunūti*, to match *ibīluma* and *ištakkanuma* in lines 17 and 18 respectively.

(713). V. Hurowitz states that this inscription "is marked by an especially high literary level and character" (Exalted House p. 72). The inscription appears in two forms, one that was sixty-seven lines in length (lines 1–33 and 44–77) and an apparently later one that added a further ten lines (lines 34–43). These ten lines dealt with the good things done by the king for the benefit of his land (e.g., resettling abandoned areas, opening up new agricultural land, providing abundant water for irrigation, and attempting to ensure that crops were abundant and food could be purchased cheaply). (With regards to the two versions, see Baruchi-Unna and Cogan, IMSA 9 [2018–2019] p. 47.) The inscription is often referred to as the Khorsabad Cylinder.

Figure 18. A 17587 (text no. 43 ex. 16), a prismatic clay cylinder from the palace at Khorsabad. Courtesy of the Oriental Institute of the University of Chicago.

CATALOGUE

Ex.	Museum Number	Excavation/ Registration No.	Provenance	Dimensions (cm)	Lines Preserved	cpn
1	Louvre —	Nap. III 3156	Khorsabad	20×35	1–77	c
2	Louvre —	Nap. III 3155	Khorsabad	23×40	1–33, 44–77	c
3	BM 22505 (K 1681)	—	Khorsabad	23×12.5	1–33, 44–77	c
4	BM 108775	1914-2-44,1	Khorsabad	22.5×11	1–33, 44–77	c
5	BM 123413 + BM 123422	1932-12-10,356 + 1932-12-10,365	Nineveh, Kuyunjik, Ištar Temple, M.2	9.5×8	6–33, 44–50	c
6	OI —	DŠ 998	Khorsabad	—	1–3, 68–77	c
7	OI —	DŠ 999	Khorsabad, Nabû Temple	—	22–33, 44–61	c
8	OI —	DŠ 1000	Khorsabad, Nabû Temple, Room 33	—	65–77	c

9	OI —	DŠ 1002	As ex. 7	—	1–13, 62–77	c
10	OI —	DŠ 1003	Khorsabad, Nabû Temple, Room 13	6.4×5.6	5–21	c
11	A 17574	DŠ 1264	Khorsabad, Residence K, Room 86	—	1–5, 46–77	c
12	A 17577	DŠ 1267	As ex. 11	—	62–77	c
13	Iraq	DŠ 1288	Khorsabad, Palace F, Room 17	—	1–33, 44–77	n
14	Iraq	DŠ 1289	As ex. 13	—	1–33, 44–77	n
15	Iraq	DŠ 1290	As ex. 13	—	1–33, 44–77	n
16	A 17587	DŠ 1291	As ex. 13	—	1–33, 44–77	c
17	A 17588	DŠ 1292	As ex. 13	—	1–33, 44–77	c
18	A 17589	DŠ 1293	As ex. 13	—	1–33, 44–77	c
19	A 17590	DŠ 1294	As ex. 13	—	1–77	c
20	Iraq	DŠ 1295	As ex. 13	—	1–33, 44–77	n
21	Iraq	DŠ 1298	Khorsabad, Palace F, Room 16	—	—	n
22	Iraq	DŠ 1299	Khorsabad, outside Residence K, northwest of Room 20	—	—	n
23	Iraq	DŠ 1301	Khorsabad, southwest of Sargon's Palace	—	—	n
24	Iraq	DŠ 1302	As ex. 21	—	—	n
25	A 17592	DŠ 1303	As ex. 21	—	19–33, 44–49	c
26	A 17593	DŠ 1304	As ex. 21	—	1–9, 69–77	c
27	OI —	DŠ 32-2	Khorsabad, Sargon's Palace XXVI	—	1–33, 44–54, 58–77	c
28	OI —	DŠ 32-3 + 32-31	As ex. 27 (32-3); Palace F (32-31)	—	1–33, 44–76	c
29	OI —	DŠ 32-4A	Khorsabad	—	3–17	c
30	OI —	DŠ 32-5	Khorsabad, Nabû Temple, Court V	—	1–13, 71–77	c
31	OI —	DŠ 32-6	Khorsabad, Palace F, doorway between Court II and Room 19	—	55–74	c
32	OI —	DŠ 32-12	Khorsabad, Palace F, Room 28	—	5–24	c
33	OI —	DŠ 32-19 (DŠ 470)	Khorsabad Nabû Temple, Room 31	—	60–72	c
34	OI —	DŠ 32-21	Khorsabad, dump	—	16–24	c
35	OI —	DŠ 32-30 DŠ 601)	Khorsabad, Nabû Temple, Court I	—	4–12, 15–40, 55–76	c
36	OI —	DŠ 32-33	As ex. 35	7.8×6.6	22–33, 44–71	c
37	OI —	DŠ 32-34A (DŠ 642)	As ex. 35	—	1–20, 75–77	c
38	OI —	DŠ 32-34B	As ex. 35	—	57–72	c
39	OI —	DŠ 32-35	Khorsabad, Nabû Temple, doorway between Court I and Room 14	—	3–28	c
40	OI —	DŠ 32-36A	As ex. 35	—	18–33, 44–55	c
41	OI —	DŠ 32-36B	As ex. 35	—	3–17	c
42	OI —	DŠ 32-45A	Khorsabad, Nabû Temple, Room 5	—	1–77	c
43	OI —	DŠ 32-45B	As ex. 42	—	1–4, 58–77	c
44	OI —	DŠ 32-46	Khorsabad, southeast of Sargon's Palace	—	51–72	c
45	OI —	DŠ 32-47	As ex. 42	—	1–77	c
46	OI —	DŠ 32-48	Khorsabad, Nabû Temple, Room 4	—	4–23	c

47	OI —	DŠ 32-4W	Khorsabad	—	1–33, 44–77	c
48	OI —	DŠ 32-4X	Khorsabad	—	1–33, 44–77	c
49	OI —	DŠ 32-4Y	Khorsabad	—	1–32, 47–77	c
50	OI —	DŠ 32-4Z	Khorsabad	—	3–8	c
51	IM 24036	—	Khorsabad	—	—	n
52	IM 24037	—	Khorsabad	—	—	n
53	IM 24038	—	Khorsabad	—	—	n
54	IM 24039	—	Khorsabad	23.5×12	—	n
55	UM 38-13-1091	—	Said to be from "Chenchi"	7×6.5	46–62	c
56	FMB 50 (Bodmer Museum, Cologny, Switzerland)	—	—	—	1–14, 67–77	c
57	National Museum of Romanian History (Bucharest) —	—	Khorsabad	22.6×6.3	1–33, 44–77	c
58	IMJ 74.56.251	—	—	23.5×12	1–33, 44–77	c
59	BM 32343	76-11-17,2075	—	7.8×3.5×1.7	60–67	p

COMMENTARY

The longer, and likely later, form of the inscription (including lines 34–43) is only known on a few exemplars (exs. 1, 19, 35, 42, and 45), although some of the exemplars about which little or nothing is known (e.g., exs. 21–23 and 51–54) may also have the longer form, as may some of the exemplars that are very poorly preserved (e.g., exs. 10, 29, and 41). Based on the shape of ex. 49 and its arrangement of signs, this exemplar probably originally had the long form.

When known, complete cylinders have either eight (ex. 58), nine (exs. 1, 3–5, 16, 18–19, 28, 42, 45, 47, 48, and 57) or ten (exs. 2 and 17) faces, each of which has 7–9 lines of inscription (except at times for the final face on each exemplar which often has fewer lines). At the end of the inscription there is often a single or a double line ruling.

During his excavations, V. Place found two cylinders in the wall between Rooms 18 and 20 and fourteen in Façade P and P′ (Ninive et l'Assyrie 1 pp. 61–62 and 111–112); four of these are apparently exs. 1–4 and one ex. 57. (Although ex. 3 has a Kuyunjik number, it was probably found by Place.) One exemplar (ex. 5) was found at Nineveh and one (ex. 55) is reported to come from Chenchi, presumably Tepe Chenchi, which is located near Khorsabad.

A number of the cylinders preserved in the Oriental Institute (especially exs. 6–9, 33, and 42) need to be cleaned and if this is done the reading of several passages on them could be improved. It is unclear from the wording of Loud and Altman, Khorsabad 2 p. 105 no. 49 whether DŠ 1298 and 1302 (exs. 21 and 24) are pieces of the same prism or of different prisms; they have arbitrarily been considered separate exemplars here. Records in the Oriental Institute indicate that the dimensions of DŠ 1298 and 1302 are ".072 dia." and ".067×.125" respectively. Ex. 27 (DŠ 32-2) is made up of about twelve fragments (nine of which are inscribed), all stored in the same box. Only a few of the pieces clearly join and it is possible that not all of the fragments come from the same cylinder. Nevertheless, all the pieces have been attributed to this exemplar. The findspots of the two fragments making up ex. 28 are suspect since they come from buildings approximately 1.3 km apart. Ex. 35 (DŠ 32-30) is made up of about seven fragments, only two of which join; all the fragments have been included in the score; it is not clear that all actually come from the same exemplar although none of the pieces have overlapping text. Ex. 43 (DŠ 32-45B) has about eight small fragments in the same box as the main fragment. Some of these small pieces preserve all or parts of one or more signs; these have not been included in the score for the text.

J.A. Brinkman, who has worked with both the Chicago excavation records and the cylinders, has identified the following pieces listed by G. Loud with the above exemplars: Loud and Altman, Khorsabad 2 p. 105 no. 48 with possibly DŠ 1000 (ex. 8); no. 50 with DŠ 32-12 (ex. 32); no. 52 with probably DŠ 32-46 (ex. 44); no. 53 with DŠ 32-2 and 32-3 (ex. 27 and part of ex. 28); no. 54 with DŠ 32-31, 32-33, 32-34, and 32-36 (exs. 28 [part], 36–38 and 40–41); no. 55 with DŠ 32-35 (ex. 39), no. 56 with possibly DŠ 32-6 (ex. 31), no. 57 with DŠ 32-5 (ex. 30); no. 58 with DŠ 32-48 (ex. 46) and also DŠ 32-32 (an Esarhaddon prism); no. 59 with DŠ 32-45 (exs. 42 and 43); no. 60 with DŠ 32-19 (ex. 33), no. 63 with DŠ 32-21 (ex. 34); and no. 64 with DŠ 32-4A (ex. 29).

Ex. 56 is part of the right end of a prismatic cylinder and preserves parts of four faces. It was kindly collated by S. Borkowski, who notes that the museum number is FMB 50, and not FMB 48 as cited at CDLI P427649.

Ex. 57 was purchased by the Romanian government from a descendant of Place in 1987 (see http://www.sharinghistory.org/database item.php?-id=object;AWE;rm;29;en [accessed July 10, 2017]) and was kindly collated by J. Taylor.

Ex. 58 was purchased by the British Friends of the Israel Museum at auction from Sotheby and Co. on July 9, 1973 and had previously been owned by Mrs. E.L.E. Corsin. The exemplar was kindly collated by A. Baruchi-Unna.

A photo of ex. 59 was kindly supplied to the author by E. Jiménez, who had identified the piece as being a duplicate of Sargon's Khorsabad cylinder.

Regrettably, the copies by E. Norris (1 R pl. 36) and H. Winckler are of limited value since they often do not indicate from which exemplar particular readings come and since they contain numerous errors (often readings coming from different inscriptions). A number of the incorrect readings (sometimes given as variants) are noted in the list of minor variants at the back of this volume. (For the problems with regard to Norris' and Winckler's copies, see also Fuchs, Khorsabad pp. 30–31.) D.G. Lyon's copy (Sar. no. 1) is based on ex. 1 and uses the following abbreviations for variants: P_1 = Nap. III 3156 [ex. 1], P_2 = Nap. III 3155 [ex. 2], L_1 = BM 22505 [ex. 3], and L_2 = BM 108775 [ex. 4]. A. Fuchs (Khorsabad pp. 29–30) uses the same abbreviations (without using subscript for the numbers) and adds the following: L3 = BM 123413 + 123422 [ex. 5], C1 = DŠ 1294 = A 17590 [ex. 19], C2 = DŠ 32-47 [ex. 45], C3 = DŠ 32-45A [ex. 42] and C4 = DŠ 1293 = A 17589 [ex. 18].

The line arrangement is the same on all exemplars. The master line normally follows ex. 1; however, where ex. 1 is either damaged, the only exemplar to have a particular reading (e.g., omission of *ù* in lines 8 and 38; omission of MEŠ following UN in line 30; omission of *-e* after EŠ.BAR in line 57; É for LÍL in ^{d}EN.LÍL in line 58; omission of *-šú* in line 77), or only one of two exemplars with an obviously incorrect or 'unusual' reading (e.g., omission of *-ba-* in line 2; *-ṭí* for *-ṭi* in line 23; *-ú-* for *-saḫ-* in line 76), another exemplar is followed, normally ex. 2 or ex. 19.

BIBLIOGRAPHY

1854 de Longpérier, Notice[3] no. 277 (ex. 2, study)

1855–56 Oppert, Transactions of the Historic Society of Lancashire and Cheshire 8 pp. 105–107 (partial translation)

1856 Oppert, Annales de Philosophie chrétienne 53 pp. 162–163 (lines 1–19, 75–77, translation)

1861 1 R pl. 36 (ex. 3, copy [not always following ex. 3], with variants)

1862 Oppert, Annales de Philosophie chrétienne 65 p. 45 no. 5 and pp. 183–188 (translation)

1862 Oppert, Sargonides p. 3 no. 5 and pp. 35–40 (translation) (identical to the preceding)

1863 Oppert, EM 1 pp. 353–357 (translation)

1867 Place, Ninive et l'Assyrie 1 pp. 61–62 and 111–112 (provenance); and 3 pl. 78 nos 1–2 (exs. 1–2?, héliogravure)

1870 Oppert in Place, Ninive et l'Assyrie 2 pp. 291–303 (ex. 1, copy [in type], edition)

1870 Oppert, Dour-Sarkayan pp. 11–23 (ex. 1, copy, edition) (identical to preceding)

1874 Ménant, Annales pp. 199–204 (exs. 1, 3, translation)

1883 Lyon, Sar. no. 1 (exs. 1–4, copy [based on ex. 1, with variants], edition)

1886 Bezold, Literatur pp. 84–85 §50.1 (exs. 1–4, study)

1886 Strassmaier, AV passim as Sarg. C. and KL.b.2 (partial copy, partial transliteration)

1889 Bezold, Cat. 1 p. 331 (ex. 3, study)

1889 Winckler, Sar. 1 p. XI; and 2 pl. 43 (ex. 1, copy; some variants from exs. 2–3)

1890 Peiser in Schrader, KB 2 pp. 38–51 (exs. 1–4, edition)

1901 Bárta in Harper, Assyrian and Babylonian Literature pp. 59–64 (translation)

1903 Oppert, ZA 17 pp. 66–69 (line 65, study)

1909 Winckler, Textbuch[3] p. 37 (line 19, translation)

1911 Sarsowsky, Urkundenbuch p. 27 (ex. 1, copy of lines 19–26)

1918 Pillet, Khorsabad pp. 83 and 86–88 (exs. 1–4, study)

1922 BM Guide p. 224 nos. 11–12 (exs. 3–4, study)

1926 Ebeling in Gressmann, ATAT[2] pp. 349–350 (lines 19–20, translation)

1926 Schott, Vergleiche p. 100 n. 2 (line 33, study)

1927 Luckenbill, ARAB 2 pp. 60–66 §§116–123 (exs. 1–4, translation)

1933 Frankfort, OIC 16 p. 87 (provenance)

1935 Schott, Vorarbeiten p. 66 n. 1 (line 32, study)

1936 Cameron, Iran p. 155 n. 30 (line 14, study)

1937 Meissner, MAOG 11/1–2 p. 62 (line 55, study)

1938 Loud and Altman, Khorsabad 2 p. 77, p. 98 nos. 75–82, and p. 105 nos. 40–64; and pl. 57 nos. 75–82 (exs. 13–20, photo, provenance; exs. 11–26, study)
1940–41 Contenau, RA 37 pp. 162–163 (line 65, study)
1941–44 Weidner, AfO 14 p. 49 (line 65, study)
1961 Borger, EAK 1 p. 53 n. 3 (line 1, study)
1962 Pillet, Pionnier pl. XXII (exs. 1–2$^{?}$, photo)
1966 Parrot, Trésors no. 186 (ex. 54, photo, study)
1968 Ellis, Foundation Deposits p. 175 no. 14 (lines 57–61, edition)
1968 Lambert and Millard, Cat. p. 23 (ex. 5, study)
1969 Postgate, Royal Grants pp. 117–118 no. 2 (lines 36, 43–52, transliteration)
1976 Basmachi, Treasures p. 245 and fig. 165 (exs. 51–54, photo; exs. 51–53, study)
1977 Briend and Seux, TPOA no. 39B (lines 1–2a and 19–20, translation)
1981 Zaccagnini in Fales, ARIN pp. 289–290 (lines 34–37, edition)
1982 André-Leicknam, Naissance de l'écriture p. 234 no. 180 (ex. 1, photo, partial copy, study)
1983 Calmeyer, AMI 16 pp. 172–173 (lines 12–15, translation)
1983 Khazai, De Sumer à Babylone p. 133 no. 212 (ex. 1, photo, study)
1984 Borger, TUAT 1/4 p. 386 (lines 19–20, translation)
1986 Renger, CRRA 32 pp. 112–113, 120, and 126 (lines 1–6, 17, 26, 29, 53–54, partial transcription, study)
1992 Becking, Fall of Samaria p. 32 (lines 19–20, edition)
1992 Hurowitz, Exalted House pp. 72–74 (study)
1993 Machinist in Raaflaub, Anfänge politischen Denkens p. 95 (lines 72–74, edition)
1994 Fuchs, Khorsabad pp. 29–44 and 289–96 no. 1.1 (exs. 1–5, 18–19, 42, 45, edition), and pp. 386, 388–389, and 396–398 (study)
1994 Lackenbacker in Fontan, Khorsabad p. 163, fig. 8 and p. 282 (ex. 1, photo)
1994 Pongratz-Leisten, Ina Šulmi Īrub p. 210 (lines 66–71, edition)
1996 Mayer, UF 28 p. 471 (line 21, edition, study)
1998 Younger, JBL 117 p. 224 (lines 72–73, translation)
1999 Van De Mieroop, Studies Renger pp. 332 and 336–337 (lines 12–15, 66, edition; lines 34–43, 65–71, translation)
2000 Bagg, Assyrische Wasserbauten pp. 147–149 and 151 (lines 34–37, 44–46, 50–52, 55, edition) and p. 153 n. 272 (line 70, study)
2000 Lanfranchi, Melammu 1 p. 14 (line 21b, edition)
2000 Younger, COS 2 p. 298 no. 2.118H (lines 19–20, translation)
2001 Rollinger, Melammu 2 p. 239 (line 21b, edition)
2002 Pezzoli-Olgiati, Immagini urbane pp. 65–74 (ex. 1, photo; lines 1–11, 34–76, translation; study)
2006 Ponchia, SAAB 15 p. 232 (study)
2007 Cavigneaux, Orientalia NS 76 pp. 169–173 (line 53–54, edition, study)
2008 Cogan, Raging Torrent pp. 97–98 no. 22 (lines 1–2a, 19–20, translation)
2009 Frame, Studies Parpola p. 80 no. a (study)
2012 Worthington, Textual Criticism pp. 185, 236, and 273–275 (study)
2013 Dalley, Hanging Garden p. 89 (line 37, translation)
2014 Maniori, Campagne di Sargon pp. 50–51 g4 and passim (ex. 1, study)
2015 Pongratz-Leisten, Religion and Ideology p. 190 (lines 66–71, translation)
2017 Liverani, Assyria p. 206 (lines 72–74, translation)
2018 Frahm, Last Days pp. 68–70 no. 6 (lines 19–20, 25b, edition, study)
2018–19 Baruchi-Unna and Cogan, IMSA 9 pp. 40–57 (ex. 58, photo, edition, study)
2019 Boyd, JNES 78 pp. 87–111 (lines 72–74, edition, study)
2019 Marchesi, JNES 78 p. 24 (line 26, edition)

TEXT

1) ^{m}LUGAL-GI.NA *šá-ak-nu* ^{d}EN.LÍL NU.ÈŠ *ba-ʾi-it* ^{d}*a-šur ni-šit* IGI.II ^{d}*a-nim ù* ^{d}*da-gan*

2) LUGAL GAL-*ú* LUGAL *dan-nu* LUGAL KIŠ LUGAL KUR *aš-šur*.KI LUGAL *kib-rat ar-ba-ʾi mi-gir* DINGIR.MEŠ GAL.MEŠ

3) RE.É.UM *ke-e-nu ša* ^{d}*a-šur* ^{d}AMAR.UTU LUGAL-*ut la šá-na-an ú-šat-li-mu-šu-ma zi-kir* MU-*šu ú-še-eṣ-ṣu-ú a-na re-še-e-te*

4) *šá-kin šu-ba-re-e* ZIMBIR.KI NIBRU.KI KÁ.DINGIR.RA.KI *ḫa-a-tin en-šu-te-šú-nu mu-šal-li-mu ḫi-bil-ti-šu-un*

5) *ka-ṣir ki-din-nu-tu bal-til*.KI *ba-ṭi-il-tu mu-šá-áš-ši-ik tup-šik-ki* BÀD.AN.KI *mu-šap-ši-ḫu* UN.MEŠ-*šu-un*

6) *le-ʾi* DÙ *mal-ki ša* UGU URU.*ḫar-ra-na* AN.DÙL-*la-šu it-ru-ṣu-ma ki-i ṣa-ab* ^{d}*a-nim u* ^{d}*da-gan iš-ṭu-ru za-kut-su*

7) *zi-ka-ru dan-nu ḫa-lip na-mur-ra-ti ša a-na šum-qut na-ki-ri šu-ut-bu-ú* GIŠ.TUKUL.MEŠ-*šu*

8) LUGAL *ša ul-tu* u_4*-um be-lu-ti-šu mal-ku gaba-ra-a-šu la ib-šu-ma i-na qab-li ù ta-ḫa-zi*

1–2) Sargon (II), appointee of the god Enlil, *nešakku*-priest (and) *desired object* of the god Aššur, chosen of the gods Anu and Dagān, great king, strong king, king of the world, king of Assyria, king of the four quarters (of the world), favorite of the great gods;

3) just shepherd, (one) to whom the gods Aššur (and) Marduk granted a reign without equal and whose reputation (these gods) exalt to the heights;

4–6) who (re)-established the *šubarrû*-privileges of (the cities) Sippar, Nippur, (and) Babylon, protects the weak among them (lit.: "their weak ones"), (and) made restitution for the wrongful damage suffered by them; who (re)-established the privileged status of (the city) Baltil (Aššur) that had lapsed, who abolished corvée duty for (the city) Dēr, (and) who gave relief to their people; (most) capable of all rulers, who extended his protection over the city Ḫarrān and recorded its exemption (from obligations) as if (its people were) people of the gods Anu and Dagān;

7–11) the strong man who is clad in awesome splendor (and) whose weapons are raised to strike down (his) enemies; the king who since the (first) day of his reign has had no ruler who could equal him and has met

la e-mu-ru mu-né-eḫ-ḫu
9) KUR.KUR DÙ-*ši-na ki-ma ḫaṣ-bat-ti ú-daq-qi-qu-ma ḫa-am-ma-mi ša ar-ba-ʾi id-du-ú ṣer-re-e-tu*
10) *ḫur-šá-a-ni bé-ru-ú-ti ša né-reb-šú-nu áš-ṭu la-a mi-na ip-tu-ma e-mu-ru du-ru-ug-šu-un*
11) *ṭu-da-at la aʾ-a-ri pa-áš-qa-a-ti ša a-šar-ši-na šug-lud-du e-ta-at-ti-qu-ma e-te-eb-bi-ru na-gab be-ra-a-ti*

no one who could overpower (him) in war or battle; (who) smashed all (enemy) lands as if (they were) pots and put halters on (all) rebels in the four (quarters of the world); (10) (who) opened up innumerable distant mountainous areas whose pass(es) are difficult and visited their remotest region(s); (who) traversed inaccessible, difficult paths in terrifying location(s) and crossed every *swamp*;

12) *iš-tu* KUR.*ra-a-ši mi-ṣir* KUR.*e-lam-ti* LÚ.*pu-qu-du* LÚ.*da-mu-nu* URU.BÀD-*ku-ri-gal-zi* URU.*ra-pi-qu*
13) *mad-bar* DÙ.A.BI *a-di na-ḫal* KUR.*mu-uṣ-ri* KUR *a-mur-re-e* DAGAL-*tum* KUR.*ḫat-ti a-na si-ḫir-ti-šá i-be-lu*
14) *iš-tu* KUR.*ḫa-áš-mar a-di* KUR.*ṣi-bar pat-ti* KUR.*ma-da-a-a ru-qu-ti ša ṣi-it* ^{d}UTU-*ši* KUR.*nam-ri* KUR.*el-li-pí*
15) KUR.É-*ḫa-am-ban* KUR.*par-su-a* KUR.*ma-an-na-a-a* KUR.*ur-ar-ṭu* KUR.*kas-ku* KUR.*ta-ba-lum a-di* KUR.*mu-us-ki ik-šu-du* GAL-*tum qa-a-su*
16) LÚ.*šu-ut* SAG.MEŠ-*šú šak-nu-ti* UGU-*šú-nu iš-tak-ka-nu-ma bil-tu ma-da-at-tu ki-i ša áš-šu-ri e-mid-su-nu-ti*

12–16) (who) ruled from the land Rāši on the border of the land Elam, the Puqudu (and) Damūnu (tribes), the cities Dūr-Kurigalzu (and) Rapiqu, the entire desert as far as the Brook of Egypt, the wide land Amurru, (and) the land Ḫatti (Syria) in its entirety; (who)se great hand conquered (the area) from the land Ḫašmar to the land Ṣibar — which borders on the distant Medes in the east — the lands Namri, Ellipi, (15) Bīt-Ḫamban, Parsua(š), Mannea, Urarṭu, Kasku, (and) Tabal, as far as the land Musku; (who) set eunuchs of his as governors over them and imposed upon them (the same) tribute (and) payment(s) as if (they were) Assyrians;

17) *eṭ-lu qar-du ša i-na re-bit* BÀD.AN.KI *it-ti* ^{md}*ḫum-ba-ni-ga-áš* LUGAL KUR.*e-lam-ti in-nam-ru-ma iš-ku-nu taḫ-ta-a-šu*
18) *na-si-iḫ* LÚ.KUR.*te-sa-a-a mu-pal-li-ku gu-un-ni-šu šá-lil* KUR.*tu-ʾu-mu-na ša* LÚ.*na-sik-šú-nu i-pi-du-ma ur-ru-ú ma-ḫar* LUGAL KUR.*kal-di*
19) *mu-ri-ib* KUR.É-*ḫu-um-ri-a rap-ši ša i-na* URU.*ra-pi-ḫi* BAD$_5$.BAD$_5$-*ú* KUR.*mu-uṣ-ri* GAR-*nu-ma* ^{m}*ḫa-a-nu-nu* LUGAL URU.*ḫa-zi-te ka-mu-us-su ú-še-ri-ba* URU.*aš-šur*
20) *ka-šid* LÚ.*ta-mu-di* LÚ.*i-ba-di-di* LÚ.*mar-si-i-ma-ni* LÚ.*ḫa-ia-pa-a ša si-it-ta-šú-nu in-né-et-qa-am-ma ú-šar-mu-ú qé-reb* KUR.É-*ḫu-um-ri-a*
21) *le-ʾi tam-ḫa-ri ša i-na* MURUB$_4$ *tam-tim* KUR.*ia-am-na-a-a sa-an-da-niš ki-ma nu-ú-ni i-ba-ru-ma ú-šap-ši-ḫu* KUR.*qu-e ù* URU.*ṣur-ri*

17–21) the valiant man who met Ḫumbanigaš (Ḫumban-nikaš I), king of the land Elam, (in battle) on the *outskirts* of (the city) Dēr and brought about his defeat; who deported the Tešian (king) (and) cut down his elite troops; who plundered the land Tuʾumuna, who(se people) had arrested their sheikh and brought (him) before the king of Chaldea; who made the wide land Bīt-Ḫumria (Israel) tremble, brought about the defeat of Egypt at the city Raphia, and brought Ḫanūnu (Hanno), king of the city Gaza, to the city Aššur in bondage; (20) who conquered the Tamudu, Ibādidi, Marsīmani, (and) Ḫayappa (tribes), whose remnants were transferred here and (whom) I (re)settled in the land Bīt-Ḫumria (Israel); skilled in war, who caught the Ionians in the middle of the sea like fish, as a fowler (does), and pacified the land Que (Cilicia) and the city Tyre;

22) LUGAL *da-pi-nu mu-par-ri-iʾ ar-ma-ḫi* URU.*ši-nu-uḫ-ti mu-nam-mi da-ád-mi-šá ša* ^{m}*ki-ak-ki* LUGAL-*šú-nu ú-la-i-ṭu gi-iš-gi-ni-iš*
23) *mu-né-es-si* KUR.É-*pu-ru-ta-áš ša* ^{m}*am-ba-ri-is*

22–24) the heroic king who cut through the *fruit trees* of the city Šinuḫtu, laid waste its settlements, (and) kept Kiakki, their king, in check as if with a *clamp*; who deported (the people of) the land Bīt-Purutaš, whose

11 *be-ra-a-ti* "*swamp*": See the on-page note to text no. 7 line 15.
13 The "Brook of Egypt" has been identified with Wadi el-Arish in the eastern Sinai Peninsula (e.g., Tadmor, JCS 12 [1958] p. 78 n. 194) or with Nahal Besor, a wadi in southern Palestine (Naʾaman, Tel Aviv 6 [1979] pp. 68–90 and in Liverani, Neo-Assyrian Geography pp. 111–112). See also Bagg, Rép. Géogr. 7/1 p. 291.
14 Exs. 2–4, 10, 16–17, 39, 42, 48, and 58 have URU, "city," instead of KUR, "land," before *ṣi-bar*.
23–24 It is not certain if *idān paglāte*, which is in the dual locative, should be taken by itself, as indicated in the above translation, or with what follows — i.e., "who with (his) powerful arms drove out Mitâ ..."; CAD P p. 11 takes this with the end of line 22 — "had relied on the king(s) of the lands Urarṭu and Musku with (their) powerful forces" — but this is unlikely since new lines tend to begin new ideas in this section of the inscription.

ma-lik-šú-nu da-mi-iq-ti ^{m}LUGAL-GI.NA *im-šu-ma* UGU LUGAL KUR.*ur-ar-ṭi u* KUR.*mu-us-ki it-tak-lu*

24) *i-da-an pag-la-a-te ṭa-rid* ^{m}*mi-ta-a* LUGAL KUR.*mu-us-ki mu-ter ḫal-ṣi* KUR.*qu-e ek-mu-te mu-rap-pi-šu pu-lu-un-ge-šu-un*

25) *qit-ru-du la a-dir tuq-ma-te na-si-iḫ šur-uš* KUR.*a-ma-at-te ša ma-šak* ^{m}*i-lu-bi-i'-di ḫa-am-ma-'i-i iṣ-ru-pu na-ba-si-iš*

26) *na-bi-i'* KUR.*gar-ga-miš* KUR.*ḫa-at-te-e lem-ni ša* ^{m}*pi-si-i-ri da-gíl pa-ni-šú-nu da-bi-ib ṣa-lip-te ik-šu-du* GAL-*tum qa-a-su*

27) *mu-šaḫ-rib* KUR.*ur-ar-ṭi šá-lil* KUR.*mu-ṣa-ṣi-ri ša* ^{m}*ur-sa-a* LUGAL KUR.*ur-ar-ṭi ina pu-luḫ-ti-šu* GAL-*ti ina* GIŠ.TUKUL *ra-ma-ni-šú ú-qa-ta-a na-piš-tuš*

28) *mu-nak-kir šu-bat* URU.*pa-a-pa* URU.*la-lu-uk-ni* URU.*suk-ki-a* URU.*ba-a-la* URU.*a-bi-ti-ik-na ša a-na* KUR.*ka-ak-me-e id-bu-bu na-ba-di-iš*

29) *sa-pi-in* KUR.*an-di-a* KUR.*zi-kir-te ša gi-mir ba-ḫu-la-te-šú-nu as-li-iš ú-ṭa-bi-ḫu-ma kul-lat na-ki-ri is-lu-ḫu i-mat mu-ú-ti*

30) *ma-a-'u ga-mir dun-ni ù a-ba-ri mu-šék-niš* KUR.*ma-da-a-a la kan-šu-te šá-a-giš* UN.MEŠ KUR.*ḫar-ḫar*.KI *mu-šar-bu-ú mi-ṣir* KUR *aš-šur*.KI

31) *mu-pa-ḫir* KUR.*ma-an-na-a-a sa-ap-ḫi mu-ta-qí-in* KUR.*el-li-pí dal-ḫi ša* LUGAL-*ut* KUR.KUR *ki-lal-la-an ú-kin-nu-ma ú-šar-ri-ḫu zi-kir-šu*

32) *da-a-iš* KUR.*ḫab-ḫi ša si-mil-lat* KUR-*e* LÚ.KÚR *ek-ṣi ša* ^{m}*it-ti-i* KUR.*al-lab-ra-a-a ba-ra-a-nu-ú ú-še-eṣ-ṣu-ú* URU-*uš-šu*

33) *mu-ab-bit* KUR.*kar-al-la ša pa-a-ri* ^{md}*a-šur-le-'i* LÚ.EN.URU-*šú-nu il-lu-ri-iš ú-si-mu-ma* ^{m}*a-da-a* KUR.*šur-da-a-a e-mì-du ni-ri aš-šur*

34) LUGAL *it-pe-e-šu muš-ta-bil a-mat* SIG$_5$-*tim a-na šu-šu-ub na-me-e na-du-te ù pe-te-e ki-šub-bé-e za-qáp ṣip-pa-a-te iš-ku-nu ú-zu-un-šu*

35) *ú-ḫu-um-mi zaq-ru-ti ša ul-tu ul-la-a i-na qer-bi-šu-un ur-qi-tu la šu-ṣa-at bil-tu*

king, Ambaris, had forgotten the kindness (shown to him) by Sargon and had put his trust in the king(s) of the lands Urarṭu and Musku; (*the one with*) powerful arms, who drove out Mitâ (Midas), king of the land Musku, brought back (to Assyrian control) the fortress(es) of the land Que (Cilicia) that had been taken away (by the enemy), (and) expanded their borders;

25–26) the brave one, fearless in battle, who eradicated the land Hamath (and) dyed the skin of the rebel Ilu-bi'dī as red as red wool; who plundered the land Carchemish of the evil Ḫittite (king) (and) whose great hand conquered Pisīri(s), *their* subject who (always) spoke treachery;

27–29) who laid waste to the land Urarṭu (and) plundered the city Muṣaṣir; in great fear of whom Ursâ (Rusâ), king of the land Urarṭu, brought an end to his life with his own weapon; who (deported and) settled elsewhere (the people of) the cities Pāpa, Lalluknu, Sukkia, Bāla, (and) Abitikna who had conspired with the land Kakmê *for the purpose of separating (from Assyria)*; who overwhelmed the lands Andia (and) Zikirtu, slaughtered all their people like sheep, and splattered all (his) enemies with deadly venom;

30–33) *the victorious one* who is perfect in strength and power (and) who subjugated the insubmissive Medes; who slaughtered the people of the land Ḫarḫar (and) enlarged the territory of Assyria; who gathered (back together) the scattered land Mannea (and) brought order to the disturbed land Ellipi; who established (his) kingship over both (these) lands and made his name glorious; who trampled down the land Ḫabḫu, (a land) of stepped mountains, a dangerous enemy; who ousted (lit.: "ousts") the rebel Ittî of the land Allabria from his city; who destroyed the land Karalla, dyed the skin of Aššur-lē'i, their city ruler, red like the *illūru*-plant, and imposed the yoke of (the god) Aššur upon Adâ of the land Šurda;

34–37) the wise king who occupies himself with good matters, (who) turned his attention to (re)settling abandoned pasture lands, opening up unused land, (and) planting orchards; (35) (who) conceived the idea of raising crops on high mountain(-slopes) where no

---

24 Exs. 2–3, 5, 17–18, 25, 36, 40, and 47 have *-šú* for *-šu-un*; exs. 16, 19, 35, 42, and 57 *-šu* for *-šu-un*; thus "his/its borders" instead of "their borders."

26 *na-bi-i'*: Cf. *na-pi-i'* in text no. 13 line 23. Exs. 2–3, 7, 16–19, 45, 47–48, and 58 have URU, "city," instead of KUR, "land," before *gar-ga-miš*, "Carchemish." *da-gíl pa-ni-šú-nu*: It is not clear to whom the "their" of "*their* subject" refers (see also text nos. 76 line 17′ and 105 i′ 26′). A. Fuchs (Khorsabad p. 291 n. 48) suggests that it may be an error for "his" and refer to Sargon.

27 Exs. 2–4, 7, 16–19, 42, 48, and 57–58 have URU, "city," for KUR, "land," before *mu-ṣa-ṣi-ri*. With regard to the 'suicide' of Rusâ, see the on-page note to text no. 65 lines 411–413.

30 *ma-a-'u*, "*the victorious one*": The tentative transation follows Marchesi, JNES 78 (2019) pp. 16–17. Exs. 2–4, 16–19, 28, 42, 47–48, and 57–58 omit KUR, "land," before *ḫar-ḫar*.KI; only exs. 1 and 45 have KUR.

31–33 A. Baruchi-Unna and M. Cogan (IMSA 9 [2019–2019] pp. 44 and 47) suggest that an early, unattested draft of this inscription had omitted lines 31–33 ("who gathered (back together) ... the land Šurda"), as well as lines 34–43.

33 Exs. 2–3, 5, 16, 18, 28, 35–36, 40, 42, 47, and 57–58 have ^{d}*a-šur*, "the god Aššur," for *aš-šur*, "(the god) Aššur."

34–43 These lines are omitted on those cylinders with the shorter (likely earlier) version of this inscription; see the catalogue and introduction to this text.

šu-uš-še-e ṣur-ru-uš uš-ta-bil-ma
36) *ki-gal-lum šu-uḫ-ru-ub-tu ša i-na* LUGAL.MEŠ-*ni maḫ-ru-te* GIŠ.APIN *la i-du-ú šèr-ʾi šu-zu-zi-im-ma šul-se-e a-la-la lìb-ba-šú ub-lam-ma*
37) *in-ni ta-mir-ti la ku-up-pi ka-ra-at-tu pe-te-e-ma ki-i gi-piš e-di-i* A.MEŠ *nu-uḫ-ši šu-uš-qí-i e-liš ù šap-liš*
38) LUGAL *pi-it ḫa-si-si le-ʾi i-ni ka-la-ma šin-na-at* ABGAL *ša i-na mil-ki ù né-me-qi ir-bu-ma i-na ta-šim-ti i-še-e-ḫu*
39) *ma-at aš-šur*.KI *ra-pa-áš-tum ti-ʾu-ú-tu neš-bé-e ù bu-luṭ lìb-bi ti-il-le-nu-ú si-mat* LUGAL-*ti su-un-nu-nu ra-ṭi-šu-un*
40) *at-mu-ú re-še-e-te ša i-na su-un-qi ḫu-šaḫ-ḫi e-ṭe-ri-im-ma i-na za-bal* GIŠ.GEŠTIN *a-ku-ú la na-ḫar-šú-še u bi-bil lìb-bi mar-ṣi ba-ṭil-ta la ra-še-e*
41) *áš-šu* Ì.MEŠ *bal-ti a-me-lu-ti mu-pa-ši-iḫ šér-a-ni i-na* KUR-*ia la a-qa-ri-im-ma* ŠE.GIŠ.Ì *ki-i* ^{d}*nisaba i-na* KI.LAM *šá-a-mi*
42) *šu-ur-ru-uḫ nap-ta-ni si-mat* GIŠ.BANŠUR DINGIR *ù* LUGAL *ḫa-a-te-e un-na-te gi-mir* ŠÁM *ga-ni i-ta-te-e-šu šu-zu-zi*
43) *ur-ru ù mu-šu a-na e-peš* URU *šá-a-šu ak-pu-ud si-ma-ak* ^{d}UTU DI.KU$_5$.GAL DINGIR.MEŠ GAL.MEŠ *mu-šak-šid er-nit-ti-ia qer-bu-uš-šu šu-ub-nu-u aq-bi-ma*
44) URU.*ma-ag-ga-nu-ub-ba ša i-na* GÌR.II KUR.*mu-uṣ-ri* KUR-*e i-na* UGU *nam-ba-ʾi ù re-bit* URU.*ni-na-a ki-ma di-im-ti na-du-ú*
45) *ša* 3 ME 50.ÀM *mal-ki la-bi-ru-te ša el-la-mu-u-a be-lu-ut* KUR *aš-šur*.KI *e-pu-šu-ma il-ta-nap-pa-ru ba-ʾu-lat* ^{d}EN.LÍL
46) *a-a-um-ma i-na lìb-bi-šú-nu a-šar-šu ul ú-maš-ši-i-ma šu-šu-ub-šu ul i-de-ma ḫe-re-e* ÍD-*šu ul iz-ku-ur*
47) *i-na mé-re-ši-ia pal-ki ša i-na qí-bit* ^{d}LUGAL ZU.AB EN *né-me-qi ta-šim-ta su-un-nu-nu-ma ma-lu-ú nik-la-a-ti*
48) *ù ḫi-is-sa-at uz-ni-ia pal-ka-a-te ša* UGU LUGAL.MEŠ-*ni* AD.MEŠ-*ia* ^{d}*nin-men-an-na ba-nit* DINGIR.MEŠ *ú-šá-te-ru ḫa-si-si*
49) *a-na šu-šu-ub* URU *šá-a-šú zuq-qú-ur* BÁRA.MAḪ-*ḫi at-ma-an* DINGIR.MEŠ GAL.MEŠ *ù*

vegetation had ever sprouted; (who) was minded to provide with rows of furrows the waste land which had known no plow under previous kings, to have (the plowmen) sing the *alālu*-work song, to open up *for watering place(s)* the springs of a meadowland without wells, and to irrigate all around (lit.: "above and below") with water as abundant as the surge at the (annual) inundation;

38) the king, intelligent (and) skilled in every craft, equal to the sage (Adapa), who grew great in intelligence and wisdom and matured in understanding —

39–43) In order to provide the wide land of Assyria with fully sufficient nourishment, with well-being, (and) with *tillenû* befitting a king, (through) making their canals *flow with water*, (40) (and) to save humanity from famine (and) want, so that the destitute will not collapse at the bringing in of the grape (harvest), that there will be no interruption in what is desired by the sick, that oil — the pride of mankind that makes (tired) muscles relax — does not become expensive in my land, and that sesame might be purchased on the market as (cheaply as) barley, in order to provide lavish meal(s) fit for the table of god and king, to ... *the land*, (and) *to make the fields around it reach* (*their*) *full value*, day and night I planned to build this city. I ordered that a sanctuary be constructed within it for the god Šamaš, the great judge of the great gods, the one who makes me triumph.

44–49) (With regard to) the town Maganubba, which is situated like a tower at the foot of Mount Muṣri, a mountain (rising) above the spring and (on) the *outskirts* of Nineveh, (45) not one of the three hundred and fifty previous rulers who had exercised lordship over Assyria before my time and had governed the subjects of the god Enlil had noted its (the city's) site or come to know how to make it habitable; nor had one ordered the digging of a canal for it. With my broad knowledge that was abundantly provided with understanding and full of cleverness by the command of the divine "King of Deep (*apsû*)" (Ea), the lord of wisdom, and with my broad intelligence that the goddess Ninmenanna, the creator of the gods, had made greater than that of the kings, my ancestors, I planned earnestly day and night how to settle that city (and) how to erect (there) a great shrine — a cella

37 All exemplars that preserved this part of the line (exs. 1, 19, and 45) have *la* following *ta-mir-ti*. The copies by D.G. Lyon (based on ex. 1) and H. Winckler both have ŠU, and CAD K p. 550 reads *tamirtišu*, "of this region," although note the correct reading in CAD T p. 120. With regard to the uncertain meaning of the passage, and the uncertain word *karattu*, see most recently Bagg, Assyrische Wasserbauten pp. 151–154.
38 Ex. 1 omits *ù*, "and" between *mil-ki* "intelligence" and *né-me-qi* "wisdom."
39 The meaning of *tillenû* is not known. A. Fuchs suggests it may refer to a type of beer (Khorsabad p. 292 n. 62).
40 The translation "humanity" for *atmû rēšēti* follows CAD A/2 pp. 498–499; see also CDA p. 302 sub *rēštu(m)*. *na-ḫar-šú-še* "collapse": See Mayer, Orientalia NS 86 (2017) p. 31. *bibil libbi*, "what is desired by": Or following CAD B p. 221 "the voluntary offering of."
42 The meaning of the end of the line remains uncertain. CAD S p. 146 sub *sangāni* reads *sàn-ga-ni*, but notes that the passage is difficult. A. Fuchs (Khorsabad p. 293) translates: "um das ganze ... seiner Grenzen aufzustellen" (or "zu errichten" in n. 74).
44 Maganuba is only mentioned clearly in texts from the reigns of Sargon and Sennacherib; see Bagg, Rép. Géogr. 7/2 pp. 380–381. Ex. 7 omits GÌR.II, "foot" (lit.: "feet").
48 Exs. 3, 16–18, 28, 42, and 48 omit *-an-* in ^{d}*nin-men-an-na*.

É.GAL.MEŠ *šu-bat be-lu-ti-ia ur-ra u mu-šá ak-pu-ud aṣ-rim-ma e-pe-su aq-bi*
50) *ki-ma zi-kir šu-mi-ia ša a-na na-ṣar kit-ti ù mi-šá-ri šu-te-šur la le-ʾi-i la ḫa-bal en-ši im-bu-in-ni* DINGIR.MEŠ GAL.MEŠ
51) *ka-sap* A.ŠÀ.MEŠ URU *šá-a-šú ki-i pi-i ṭup-pa-a-te ša-a-a-ma-nu-te* KÙ.BABBAR *ù* ZABAR.MEŠ *a-na* EN.MEŠ-*šú-nu ú-ter-ma*
52) *áš-šu ri-ga-a-te la šub-ši-i ša ka-sap* A.ŠÀ *la ṣe-bu-ú* A.ŠÀ *mi-ḫir* A.ŠÀ *a-šar pa-nu-šú-nu šak-nu ad-din-šú-nu-ti*

for the great gods — and palatial halls to be my lordly abode; I ordered its construction.
50–52) In accordance with the saying of my name that the great gods had given to me — to protect truth and justice, to guide the powerless, (and) to prevent the harming of the weak — I reimbursed the owners (of the expropriated fields) with silver and bronze, the price for the (expropriated) fields of that town being in accordance with the (original) purchase documents (of those fields); in order that there should be no wrongdoing, I gave to those who did not want (to take) silver for (their) field(s), field(s) corresponding (in value) to (their own) field(s) (and located) wherever they chose.

53) *al-šu ba-ni-i-šu mé-eḫ-ret* PÌRIG ŠU.DU$_{7}$ *a-na* ^{d}*sig*$_{5}$-*ga ù* ^{d}*lugal-dingir-ra da-i-nu-te te-né-še-te ta-li-ma-ni ina te-me-qi ú-šaq-qí-ma*
54) *aḫ-ra-taš u*$_{4}$-*me i-na ṭu-ub lìb-bi ù bu-ʾa-a-ri qer-bu-uš-šu e-re-bi i-na* SUG DIM.GAL KALAM.MA *a-na* ^{d}*ša-uš-ka ra-ši-bat* NINA.KI *at-ta-ši qa-ti*
55) *zík-ri pi-ia ke-e-nu-um ki-i ú-lu* Ì UGU *na-bi* MAḪ.MEŠ EN.MEŠ-*ia ma-aʾ-diš i-ṭí-ib-ma e-peš* URU *ḫe-re-e* ÍD *iq-bu-u-ni*
56) *na-an-nu-uš-šu-un la muš-pe-e-lu at-ta-ki-il-ma ba-ḫu-la-te-ia gap-šá-a-te ad-ke-ma al-lu tup-šik-ku ú-šá-áš-ši*

53–56) Facing east, I raised my two hands in entreaty to the gods Sigga ("Gracious One") and Lugal-dingira ("King of the God(s)"), the judges of humanity, with regard to building it (the new city); to the west, I raised up my hand(s) (in supplication) to the goddess Šauška, *the awe-inspiring one* of Nineveh that in the future I might enter into it (Dūr-Šarrukīn) with happiness and in good health. (55) The just word(s) of my mouth were as pleasing as the finest oil to the august deities, my lords, and they commanded me to build the city (and) to dig a canal (for it). I put my trust in their command that cannot be changed, mustered my numerous people, and had (them) take up the hoe (and) the work basket.

57) *i-na* ITI.*ṣi-i-taš* ITI *bi-in* ^{d}DÀR.GAL KUD-*is* EŠ.BAR-*e mu-šak-lim ṣa-ad-di* ^{d}ŠEŠ.KI AN-*e* KI-*tim qar-rad* DINGIR.MEŠ ^{d}EN.ZU
58) *ša i-na ši-mat* ^{d}*a-nim* ^{d}EN.LÍL *ù* ^{d}*é-a* ^{d}*nin-ši-kù a-na la-ba-an* SIG$_{4}$.MEŠ *e-peš* URU *ù* É ITI ^{d}*kulla na-bu-ú* MU-*šu*
59) *i-na* UD.ÈŠ.ÈŠ *ša* DUMU ^{d}EN *igi-gál-li pal-ke-e* ^{d}AG DUB.SAR *gim-ri mu-ma-ʾe-er kul-lat* DINGIR.MEŠ *ú-šal-bi-na lib-na-as-su*
60) *a-na* ^{d}*kulla* EN *uš-še li-bit-te ù* ^{d}DÍM ŠITIM.GAL-*lum ša* ^{d}EN.LÍL UDU.SISKUR *aq-qí sér-qu as-ru-qu-ma at-ta-ši* ŠU.ÍL.KÁM

57–60) In the month Ṣītaš (III) — the month of the son of the god Daragal, the one who renders decisions (and) reveals (ominous) signs, the divine light of heaven and netherworld, the hero of the gods, the god Sîn — which by the decree of the gods Anu, Enlil, and prince Ea was called the month of the god Kulla, (the month appropriate) for making bricks (and) building citi(es) and house(s), on the day of an *eššešu*-festival for the son of the god Bēl — the exceedingly wise god Nabû, the scribe of all (the universe), who gives orders to all the gods — I had its brickwork made. I offered a sacrifice to the god Kulla, the lord of foundations (and) brickwork, and to the god Mušda, the master builder of the god Enlil. I strewed aromatic offerings, and recited a *šuilakku*-prayer.

---

50 *zi-kir šu-mi-ia*, "saying of my name": Perhaps better "meaning/wording of my name" in this context.
52 With regard to Sargon's providing new fields to the owners of expropriated fields, see also Kataja and Whiting, SAA 12 no. 19, dated to the eponymy of Aššur-bāni (713).
53–54 For the understanding of these lines, see Cavigneaux, Orientalia NS 76 (2007) pp. 169–173. Sigga and Lugal-dingira refer to the gods Šamaš and Adad; see Lambert in RLA 7/1–2 (1987) p. 133. Šauška is the Hurrian name of the goddess Ištar. Ex. 11 has <<*ba-ni*>> *ba-ni-i-šu*. Exs. 2, 4, 17–18, and 48 omit *ù*, "and" between "Sigga" and "Lugal-dingira."
54 *ra-ši-bat*, "*the awe-inspiring one*," might have been an error for *a-ši-bat*, "who dwells in"; see Beckman, JCS 50 (1998) p. 8.
57 Ṣītaš was one name for the third month of the year (May-June). The god Daragal is Enlil.
58 Ex. 11 inserts an unwanted *u*, "and," between ^{d}*a-nim* and ^{d}EN.LÍL.
60 Kulla is the god of bricks (see Lambert, RLA 6/3–4 [1981] p. 305) and Mušda(m) is a builder god (see Krebernik, RLA 8/5–6 [1995] p. 453). Ex. 58 omits the divine determinative before EN.LÍL in both this line and line 68.
61 Gibil is the god of fire. As noted by A. Fuchs (Khorsabad p. 41 line 61 nn. 1 and 2), there is no textual justification to emend *mu-uš-pil/bil am-ba-te* to *mu-ub-bil qar-ba-te* as proposed in CAD Q p. 212. Ex. 3 has *ṣe-ru-uš-šin*, "upon them," for *lib-na-su*, "its brickwork." The copyist may have written the end of line 64 here by mistake; see Fuchs, Khorsabad p. 41 line 61 n. 4.

61) *i-na* ITI.NE.NE.GAR ITI *a-rad* ^{d}GIBIL$_{6}$ *mu-uš-pel am-ba-te ra-ṭu-ub-te mu-kin te-me-en* URU *ù* É *uš-še-e-šú ad-di-ma ú-kin lib-na-su*

61) In the month Abu (V) — the month of the descent (from heaven) of the god Gibil, who *dries out the* moist *field(s)* (and) lays the foundation of citi(es) and house(s) — I laid its foundation and established its brickwork.

62) *pa-rak-ki ra-áš-du-ti ša ki-ma ki-ṣir ge-en-ni šur-šu-du a-na* ^{d}*é-a* ^{d}30 *ù* ^{d}*nin-gal* ^{d}IŠKUR ^{d}UTU ^{d}MAŠ *e-pu-šá qer-bu-uš-šú*

62) I built inside it for the deities Ea, Sîn and Ningal, Adad, Šamaš, (and) Ninurta firmly-founded daises which were made as firm as the mountains.

63) É.GAL ZÚ AM.SI GIŠ.ESI GIŠ.TÚG GIŠ.*mu-suk-kan-ni* GIŠ.EREN GIŠ.ŠUR.MÌN GIŠ.*dáp-ra-ni ù* GIŠ.*bu-uṭ-ni ina qí-bi-ti-šú-nu ṣir-te a-na mu-šab* LUGAL-*ti-ia ab-ni-ma*
64) É *ḫi-la-an-ni ta-an-ši-il* É.GAL KUR.*ḫat-ti mé-eḫ-ret* KÁ.MEŠ-*šin ap-tiq-ma* GIŠ.ÙR.MEŠ GIŠ.EREN GIŠ.ŠUR.MÌN *ú-kin ṣe-ru-uš-šin*

63–64) At their august command, I built a palace using (lit.: "of") elephant ivory, ebony, boxwood, *musukkannu*-wood, cedar, cypress, *daprānu*-juniper, and terebinth to be my royal residence; I fashioned a *bīt-ḫilāni*, a replica of a Hittite palace, in front of their gates and roofed them with beams of cedar (and) cypress.

65) ŠÁR ŠÁR ŠÁR ŠÁR GÉŠ.U GÉŠ.U GÉŠ.U 1 UŠ 3 *qa-ni* 2 KÙŠ *ni-bit* MU-*ia mi-ši-iḫ-ti* BÀD-*šu áš-kun-ma* UGU NA$_{4}$ KUR-*e zaq-ri ú-šar-ši-da te-me-en-šu*
66) *i-na re-e-še ù ar-ka-a-te i-na ṣe-li ki-lal-la-an mé-eḫ-ret* 8 IM.MEŠ 8 KÁ.GAL.MEŠ *ap-te-e-ma*
67) ^{d}UTU *mu-šak-šid er-nit-ti-ia* ^{d}IŠKUR *mu-kil* ḪÉ.GÁL-*li-šu* MU.MEŠ KÁ.GAL ^{d}UTU *ù* KÁ.GAL ^{d}IŠKUR *šá* IGI-*et* IM.KUR.RA *az-ku-ur*
68) ^{d}EN.LÍL *mu-kin iš-di* URU-*ia* ^{d}NIN.LÍL *mu-diš-šá-at ḫi-iṣ-bi zík-ri* KÁ.GAL ^{d}EN.LÍL *ù* ^{d}NIN.LÍL *šá* IGI-*et* IM.SI.SÁ *am-bi*
69) ^{d}*a-nu mu-šal-lim ep-šet qa-ti-ia* ^{d}*iš-tar mu-šam-me-ḫat* UN.MEŠ-*šú ni-bit* KÁ.GAL ^{d}*a-nim ù* ^{d}*iš-tar šá* IGI-*et* IM.MAR.TU *áš-kun*
70) ^{d}*é-a mu-uš-te-šir nag-bi-šu* ^{d}*be-let*-DINGIR.MEŠ *mu-rap-pi-šat ta-lit-ti-šú* MU.MEŠ KÁ.GAL ^{d}*é-a ù* KÁ.GAL ^{d}*be-let*-DINGIR.MEŠ *šá* IGI-*et* IM.U$_{19}$.LU *aq-bi-ma*
71) ^{d}*a-šur mu-lab-bir* BALA.MEŠ LUGAL *e-pi-ši-šu na-ṣir* NUNUZ-*šú* BÀD-*šu* ^{d}*nin-urta mu-kin te-me-en a-du-uš-ši a-na la-bar* UD.MEŠ SÙ.MEŠ *šal-ḫu-ú-šu*

65–71) I made the length of its wall 16,280 cubits, (corresponding to) the rendering of my name, and I made its foundation secure upon (blocks of) massive mountain stone. In front and in back, on both sides, facing the eight winds, I opened eight gates (in the city wall). I named the gate of the god Šamaš and the gate of the god Adad that face the east "The God Šamaš Is the One Who Makes Me Triumph" (and) "The God Adad Is the One Who Maintains Its Prosperity" (respectively). I called the gate(s) of the god Enlil and the goddess Mullissu that face the north "The God Enlil Is the One Who Establishes the Foundation of My City" (and) "The Goddess Mullissu Is the One Who Restores Abundance" (respectively). I made the name(s) of the gate(s) of the god Anu and the goddess Ištar that face the west "The God Anu Is the One Who Makes My Undertakings Successful" (and) "The Goddess Ištar Is the One Who Makes Its People Flourish" (respectively). (70) I pronounced the names of the gate of the god Ea and the gate of the goddess Bēlet-ilī that face the south (to be) "The God Ea Is the One Who Keeps Its Spring(s) in Good Order" (and) "The Goddess Bēlet-Ilī Is the One Who Increases Its (Animals') Offspring" (respectively). Its (city) wall was (called) "The God Aššur Is the One Who Prolongs the Reign of Its Royal Builder (and) Protects His Offspring." Its outer wall was (called) "The God Ninurta Is the One Who Establishes the Foundation of the Wall for (All) Days to Come."

72) *ba-ʾu-lat ar-ba-ʾi* EME *a-ḫi-tu at-mé-e la mit-ḫur-ti a-ši-bu-te* KUR-*e ù* KUR *mal ir-te-ʾu-ú* ZÁLAG DINGIR.MEŠ EN *gim-ri*
73) *ša i-na zi-kir* ^{d}*a-šur* EN-*ia i-na mé-tel ši-bir-ri-ia*

72–74) People from the four (quarters of the world), (speaking) foreign language(s) (and of) diverse speech, those who had dwelt in (both) mountain(s) and (low)land(s), as many as the "Light of the Gods"

64 Ex. 17 omits *ap-tiq-ma*, "I fashioned ... and."
65 With regard to the number and the translation of *nibīt šumiya* as "(corresponding to) the rendering of my name," see the Introduction to the volume, under the section "Name," and the on-page note to text no. 9 lines 79–80.
67 *-mu-kil-* "Maintains": See the on-page note to text no. 9 line 83.
68 Ex. 18 has *zík-ri* <<*zík-ri*>>. See also the on-page note to line 60.
71 *mu-lab-bir* "Who Prolongs," NUNUZ-*šú* "His Offspring," and *a-du-uš-ši* "the Wall": See the on-page notes to text no. 9 lines 90–91.
72 See the note to text no. 9 line 94 with regard to Šamaš being the god referred to with the epithets "the 'Light of the Gods,' the lord of all."
73 *mé-tel*, "power," (CAD M/2 p. 43) or *mé-zez*, "fury" (Fuchs, Khorsabad p. 43). K.L. Younger (JBL 117 [1998] p. 224) translates *pa-a 1-en ú-šá-áš-kin* literally as "I made them of one mouth" and takes this to mean that "the Assyrians instructed some deportees in Assyrian or some common language." For the phrase *pâ ištēn šuškunu* meaning "to make act in concert," see CAD Š/1 p. 141.

áš-lu-la pa-a 1-en ú-šá-áš-kin-ma ú-šar-ma-a qé-reb-šu

74) DUMU.MEŠ KUR *aš-šur*.KI *mu-du-te i-ni ka-la-ma a-na šu-ḫu-uz ṣi-bit-te pa-laḫ* DINGIR *ù* LUGAL LÚ.*ak-li* LÚ.*šá-pi-ri ú-ma-ʾe-er-šú-nu-ti*

(Šamaš), the lord of all, shepherded, whom I had carried off as booty by the power of my staff at the command of the god Aššur, my lord, I made act in concert and (re)settled (them) inside it (Dūr-Šarrukīn). I commissioned native Assyrians, masters of every craft, as overseers (and) commanders to instruct (the settlers) in correct behavior (and how) to revere god and king.

75) DINGIR.MEŠ *a-ši-bu-te* AN-*e* KI-*tim ù* URU *šá-a-šu qí-bi-ti im-gur-ú-ma e-peš* URU *ù šul-bur qer-bi-šú iš-ru-ku-in-ni a-na da-riš*

75) The gods who dwell in heaven (and) netherworld, and in this city, were amenable to my prayer and granted me the eternal (privilege of) building (this) city and growing old in it.

76) *ša ep-šet qa-ti-ia ú-nak-kar-ú-ma bu-un-na-ni-ia ú-saḫ-ḫu-ú ú-ṣu-rat eṣ-ṣi-ru ú-šam-sa-ku si-ma-te-ia ú-pa-šá-ṭu*

77) ^{d}*a-šur* ^{d}UTU ^{d}IŠKUR *ù* DINGIR.MEŠ *a-šib lìb-bi-šú* MU-*šu* NUMUN-*šu i-na* KUR *lil-qu-tu-ma i-na* KI.TA LÚ.KÚR-*šu li-še-ši-bu-šu ka-meš*

76–77) (As for) the one who alters the work of my hands, mutilates my features (on a relief), obliterates the reliefs that I have engraved (lit.: "engrave"), (or) effaces my own representation(s), may the gods Aššur, Šamaš, Adad, and the gods who dwell there remove his name (and) his descendant(s) from the land and make him live in bondage under his enemy.

44–47

During the excavations of V. Place in 1854, several texts inscribed on metal and stone tablets were found inside a stone box with an inscribed lid in the wall between Rooms 17 and 19 of the palace at Khorsabad. The number and material of the tablets found in the coffer has been a matter of confusion for many years. J.A. Brinkman re-examined the problem and showed that five tablets were found: four of metal and one of stone. One of the metal tablets was lost in the boat disaster on the Tigris near Qurna in 1855. The three remaining metal tablets are made of bronze, silver, and gold (text nos. 44–46, respectively). These and the stone (magnesite) tablet (text no. 47) are conserved in the Louvre. The missing tablet was likely made of lead. See Brinkman in Curtis, Bronzeworking Centres pp. 144–150 and 158–159, and note also Bjorkman, OLP 18 (1987) pp. 87–97. The four inscriptions record the construction of the city Dūr-Šarrukīn, and all, in particular text nos. 45–47, have close similarities.

44

The bronze tablet found together with four other metal and stone tablets at Khorsabad (see the introduction to text nos. 44–47) bears a poorly preserved inscription of Sargon II recording the construction of the city of Dūr-Šarrukīn, its sanctuaries, and palace.

CATALOGUE

Museum Number	Registration Number	Provenance	Dimensions (cm)	cpn
AO 21370	Nap. III 2900	Khorsabad, Palace, in the wall between Rooms 17 and 19, inside a stone box with an inscribed lid	19×12×0.5	c

COMMENTARY

The inscription is written in Babylonian script and was collated over a period of several days from the original. The tablet, and in particular its reverse, is in a poor state of preservation and it is unlikely that any scholar would see the traces exactly the same way on different days or that any two scholars would read the traces in exactly the same way. When D.G. Lyon examined the tablet in the nineteenth century he saw some signs or traces of signs that were not visible to the author. Since the tablet may have been in a better state of preservation at that time, these have been indicated in notes to the transliteration although it has not been thought necessary to indicate every case where he copies a perfect sign and the author has put it in half brackets or vice versa. In view of difficulties in reading the inscription, in particular the first half of the reverse (lines 31–47), the number of on-page notes is more numerous than normally the case in this volume.

It has sometimes been stated that this tablet is made of copper, but a chemical analysis of the tablet performed in the 1880s by M. Berthelot has shown that it is made of bronze. With regard to the question of the metal; see Brinkman in Curtis, Bronzeworking Centres pp. 144–150.

Lines 36–39 are similar to text no. 43 lines 63–64 and text no. 46 lines 26–32. Lines 47–60 are similar to text no. 43 lines 65 and 72–77 and text no. 9 lines 79–81, 92–97, and 102–106.

BIBLIOGRAPHY

1867 Place, Ninive et l'Assyrie 1 pp. 62–63 (provenance); and 3 pl. 77 no. 6 (héliogravure of obverse)
1883 Lyon, Sar. no. 3 (copy, edition)
1886 Bezold, Literatur p. 88 §52.3 (study)
1886 Strassmaier, AV passim as TC (partial copy, partial transliteration)
1887 Berthelot, Révue archéologique 9 (3rd series) pp. 10–17 (study)
1889 Winckler, Sar. 1 p. XI; and 2 pl. 42 (copy, study)
1918 Pillet, Khorsabad pp. 84–87 (study)
1924 Pottier, Antiquités assyriennes pp. 125–126 no. 135 (study)
1927 Luckenbill, ARAB 2 pp. 56–57 §§106–109 (translation)
1965 Landsberger, JNES 24 pp. 285–86 (study)
1968 Ellis, Foundation Deposits pp. 101–103 and 194 no. 78 (study, provenance)
1982 André-Leicknam, Naissance de l'écriture pp. 80–81 no. 36 (photo of obverse, study)
1988 Brinkman in Curtis, Bronzeworking Centres pp. 144–150 and 158–159 (study)
1986 Renger, CRRA 32 pp. 112–113 (lines 1–15, partial transcription, study)
1994 Fuchs, Khorsabad pp. 45–48 and 296–298 no. 1.2.1 (edition)
2013 Curtis, Examination of Late Assyrian Metalwork pp. 50–51, 163, and pl. XXII no. 366 (photo, study)
2017 Liverani, Assyria p. 206 (lines 49b–54, translation)

TEXT

Obv.

1) ⸢É$^{?}$⸣.[GAL ^{m}]⸢LUGAL⸣-GI.NA GAR ^{d}EN.LÍL NU.ÈŠ *aš-šur*
2) ⸢LUGAL⸣ [GAL-*ú*] ⸢LUGAL⸣ *dan-nu* LUGAL KIŠ LUGAL KUR *aš-šur*.KI
3) ⸢LUGAL *kib*⸣-[*rat*] ⸢LÍMMU⸣-[*i*] *mi-gir* DINGIR.MEŠ GAL.MEŠ

1–3) Pa[lace of Sa]rgon (II), appointee of the god Enlil, *nešakku*-priest of (the god) Aššur, [great k]in[g], strong [kin]g, king of the world, king of Assyria, king of the four quar[ters] (of the world), favorite of the great gods;

2 D.G. Lyon's copy has ⸢LUGAL⸣ at the beginning of the line.
3 D.G. Lyon's copy has ⸢LUGAL *kib-rat*⸣.

4) ⸢RE.É⸣.[UM *ke-e*]-⸢*nu*⸣ *ša* ^{d}*a-šur u* ^{d}AMAR.UTU
5) [LUGAL-*ut*] ⸢*la šá*⸣-*na-an ú-šat-li-mu-šú-ma*
6) ⸢*zi*⸣-[*kir*] ⸢MU⸣-*šú ú-še-ṣu-u a-na re-še-e-ti*
7) [*šá*]-⸢*kin*? *šu*⸣-*ba-re-e* ZIMBIR.KI NIBRU.KI
8) [KÁ.DINGIR].RA.KI *ḫa-a-tin en-šu-te-šú-nu*
9) [*mu*]-⸢*šal*⸣-*li-mu ḫi-bil-ti-šú-un ka-ṣir*
10) [*ki-din*]-*nu-ut bal-til*.KI *ba-ṭi-il-tu*
11) [*mu*]-*šá-áš-ši**-*ik tup-šik-ki* BÀD.AN.KI
12) [*mu*]-*šap-ši**-*ḫu* UN.MEŠ-*šú-un an-ḫa-a-ti*
13) ⸢*le*⸣-*ʾi* DÙ *mal-ki šá* UGU URU.*ḫar-ra-na* AN.DÙL-*la-šú*
14) ⸢*it*⸣-*ru-ṣu-ma ki-i ṣa-ab* ^{d}*a-nim u* ^{d}*da-gan*

4–6) [jus]t shephe[rd], (one) to whom the gods Aššur and Marduk granted a [reign] without equal and whose re[putat]ion (these gods) exalted to the heights;
7–15a) [who (re)-established] the *šubarrû*-privileges of (the cities) Sippar, Nippur, (and) [Babyl]on, protects the weak among them (lit.: "their weak ones"), (and) [makes] restitution for the wrongful damage suffered by them; who (re)-established (10) [the privileged] status of (the city) Baltil (Aššur) that had lapsed, abolished corvée duty for (the city) Dēr, (and) gave relief to their weary people; (most) capable of all rulers, who extended his protection over the city Ḫarrān and recorded its exemption (from obligations) [as] if (its people were) people of the gods Anu and Dagān;

15) *iš-ṭu-ru za-kut-su-un zi-ka-ru dan-nu*
16) ⸢*la*⸣-*a-biš na-mur-ra-ti ša a-na šum-qut*
17) ⸢*na*⸣-*ki-ri šu-ut-bu-ú* GIŠ.TUKUL.MEŠ-*šú*
18) [LUGAL] *šá ul-tu* u_4-*me be-lu-ti-šú gaba-ra-a-šú*
19) *la ib-šu-ma i-na qab-li ù** *ta-ḫa-zi*
20) ⸢*la*⸣ *e-mu-ru mu-né-ḫu* KUR.KUR DÙ-*ši-na*
21) [*ki*]-*ma ḫaṣ-bat-ti ú-daq-qí-qu-ma ḫa-am-ma-me*
22) ⸢*ša*⸣ LÍMMU-*i id-du-ú ṣer-re-e**-*ti*
23) ⸢LÚ⸣.*šu-ut* SAG.MEŠ-*šú* LÚ.GAR-*nu-ti* UGU-*šú-nu*
24) ⸢*iš*⸣-*tak-ka-nu-ma bil-tú ma-da-at-tú*
25) [*ki*]-⸢*i*⸣ *ša áš-šu-ri e-mid-su-nu-ti*

15b–25) the strong man who is clothed in awesome splendor (and) whose weapons are raised to strike down (his) enemies; [the king], who since the (first) day of his reign has had no equal or met with anybody who could overpower him in war or battle; (20) (who) smashed all (enemy) lands [as] if (they were) pots and put halters on (all) rebels in the four (quarters of the world); (who) regularly set eunuchs of his as governors over them and imposed upon them (the same) tribute (and) payment(s) [as] if (they were) Assyrians.

26) ⸢*i-na*⸣ *bi-bil lìb-bi-ia* GÌR.II KUR.*mu-uṣ*-⸢*ri*⸣
27) KUR-⸢*i*⸣ *ina re-bit* NINA.KI URU DÙ-*ma* URU.BÀD-^{m}MAN-⸢GIN⸣

26–28a) In accordance with my heart's desire, I built a city at the foot of Mount Muṣri, a mountain on the *outskirts* of Nineveh, and named it Dūr-Šarrukīn.

28) ⸢*az*⸣-*ku-ra ni-bit-su pa-rak-ki ra-áš-du*-⸢*ti*⸣
29) ⸢*a*⸣-*na* ^{d}*é-a* ^{d}EN.ZU ^{d}UTU ^{d}IŠKUR *u* ^{d}⸢*nin-urta*⸣
30) ⸢DINGIR⸣.MEŠ ⸢GAL.MEŠ⸣ EN.MEŠ-*ia ina qer-bi-šú ad*-⸢*di*⸣

28b–30) I erected firmly-founded daises for the gods Ea, Sîn, Šamaš, Adad, and Ninurta, the great gods, my lords, inside it.

Rev.

31) [*x x x x x*] *x* [*x*] *x* ⸢ŠÁ LA⸣ *x* [*x* (*x*)]
32) (traces)

31–32) No translation possible.

33) (traces) [É].⸢GAL.MEŠ ZÚ⸣ [AM.SI]
34) [GIŠ].⸢ESI?⸣ [GIŠ.TÚG GIŠ.MES].⸢MÁ.KAN⸣.[NA GIŠ.*ere*-IGI GIŠ.ŠUR.MÌN]
35) ⸢GIŠ?.*dup*?-*ra*?-*ni* ŠIM?.LI GIŠ.*bu*⸣-[*uṭ-ni* ...]
36) [*a-na mu*]-⸢*šab* LUGAL?-*ti-ia ab*⸣-[*ni*]-⸢*ma*? É?⸣ [*ḫi*]-⸢*la*?⸣-[(*an*)-*ni*?]
37) [*tam*]-⸢*šil* É.GAL⸣ KUR.⸢*ḫat*⸣-*ti mé*-[*eḫ-ret*]

33–49a) I bui[lt palatial] halls using (lit.: "of") [elephant] ivory, [ebo]ny, [boxwood, *musu*]*kkan*[*nu*-wood, cedar, cypress], *daprānu*-juniper, juniper, [(and)] te[rebinth (...) to be] my royal [resi]dence. I *then* fashioned a *bīt* [*ḫilāni*, a repli]ca of a Hittite palace, in fr[ont of the]ir gates and [roo]fed them with beams of cedar (and) [cypr]ess. Limestone slabs (40) [...] ... I

4 D.G. Lyons's copy has ⸢RE.E⸣.[UM].
5 D.G. Lyon's copy has [*šar-ru*]-*ut*.
9 D.G. Lyon's copy has ⸢*mu-šal*⸣-*li-mu*.
10 D.G. Lyon's copy has [*ki*]-⸢*din*⸣-*nu-ut*.
11 D.G. Lyon's copy has ⸢*mu*⸣- at the beginning of the line. *ši**: The form of the sign here and elsewhere in the text (including when it is part of Ù) is similar to PI, but can be distinguished from it.
18 D.G. Lyon's copy has ⸢LUGAL⸣.
22 *e**: Sign form slightly abnormal (see copy by D.G. Lyon).
25 D.G. Lyon's copy has ⸢*ki*⸣-*i*.
26 Likely <*ina*> before GÌR.II.
30 D.G. Lyon's copy has all the signs in the line perfectly preserved.
34 A. Fuchs (Khorsabad p. 47) reads [GIŠ].⸢ESI⸣ [GIŠ.TÚG] GIŠ.⸢MES?.MÁ⸣.[KAN.NA GIŠ].⸢*ere*⸣-[IGI] ⸢GIŠ⸣.[ŠUR.MÌN].
35 D.G. Lyon's copy has [*x x* (*x*)]-⸢*ni* GIŠ?.ŠIM?.LI?⸣ [...] *x* [...] and A. Fuchs (Khorsabad p. 47) would suggest [*dáp-ra*]-*ni* ⸢GIŠ.ŠIM.LI GIŠ.*bu-uṭ*⸣-[*ni*].
37 D.G. Lyon's copy has [*tam-šil*] ⸢É⸣.GAL KUR.*ḫat-ti mé*-[*eḫ-ret* KÁ.MEŠ-*šú*]-⸢*un*?⸣. A. Fuchs' transliteration (Khorsabad p. 47) has -[*ši*]-⸢*in*?⸣ at the end of the line.

⸢KÁ.MEŠ-*šin*?⸣
38) ⸢*ap-tiq*?⸣-*ma* GIŠ.⸢ÙR⸣.MEŠ GIŠ.EREN ⸢GIŠ⸣.[ŠUR].⸢MÌN⸣
39) ⸢*ú*⸣-[*kin*] ⸢*ṣe-ru*⸣-*uš-šin* NA$_4$.⸢KUN$_4$⸣.MEŠ *pi*-⸢*i-li*⸣
40) [x x (x)] x x ⸢*ú*⸣-*šal*-⸢*me*?⸣ x x ⸢KU?⸣ ŠI* SIK
41) [x x] x x ⸢TI?⸣ *ú*-⸢*šar-ši*⸣-*da uš-še*-⸢*šin*?⸣
42) [x x x x] x x x x x [x x x] x x
43) [x x x x] x x (x) ⸢MA⸣ (x) ⸢ŠAR? RI?⸣ [x x] x x
44) [x x] x x [x x] ⸢GIŠ⸣.MES.MÁ.KAN.⸢NA NA$_4$?.ZA?.GÌN?⸣
45) [x x (x)] x x *ú-rak*-⸢*kis*⸣-*ma* KI ⸢MA?⸣ [(x)] x [(x)]
46) [x x x x x] (x) ḪI IL LA A [x x x]
47) [ŠÁR ŠÁR ŠÁR ŠÁR GÉŠ.U GÉŠ.U] ⸢GÉŠ⸣.[U 1 UŠ] ⸢3⸣ *qa-ni* 2 KÙŠ *ni*-⸢*bit* MU-*ia*⸣
48) [*mi-ši-iḫ-ti*] ⸢BÀD⸣-*šú áš-kun-ma* ⸢UGU NA$_4$⸣ KUR-*i*
49) [*ú*]-⸢*šar*⸣-[*ši*]-⸢*da*⸣ *te-me-en-šú ba-ʾu-lat* LÍMMU-*i*
50) [*a-ši*]-⸢*bu-te*? KUR⸣-*i u* KUR *mal ir-te-ʾu-u* ZÁLAG DINGIR.MEŠ
51) [EN? *gim*?]-⸢*ri*?⸣ PA x (x) x-*ma ú-šar-ma-a*
52) [*qé-reb*]-⸢*šu* DUMU.MEŠ KUR *aš*⸣-*šur*.KI *mu-du-ut i-ni*
53) [*ka-la*]-⸢*ma a-na*⸣ *šu-ḫu-uz ṣi-bit-te*
54) [*pa-laḫ* DINGIR *u*] ⸢LUGAL⸣ LÚ.*ak-li* LÚ.*šá-pi-ri ú-ma-ʾe*-⸢*er-šú-nu*⸣-*te*
55) [DINGIR.MEŠ *a-ši*]-⸢*bu-ut*⸣ AN-*e* ⸢KI⸣-*tim* ⸢*u* URU⸣ *šá*-⸢*a*⸣-*šú*
56) [*qí-bi-ti*] ⸢*im*?-*gur*?-*ú*⸣-[*ma e*]-⸢*peš* URU *u šul*?⸣-*bur* ⸢*qer*⸣-*bi-šú*
57) [*iš-ru-ku-in*]-⸢*ni a-na da-riš šá ep*⸣-[*šet*] ⸢ŠU.II-*ia ú*⸣-*na-kar*-⸢*ú*⸣-*ma*
58) [*bu-un-na-ni*]-⸢*ia ú-saḫ*⸣-[*ḫu-u ú*?-*ṣu*]-⸢*rat e*⸣-[*ṣe*]-⸢*ru*⸣ *ú-šam-sa-ku-ma*
59) [^{d}*a-šur*] ⸢^{d}?*nin*?-*gal*? ^{d}?⸣[IŠKUR *u* DINGIR.MEŠ] ⸢GAL?⸣.[MEŠ *a*]-⸢*ši-bu*?-*te i*?-*na*? ŠÀ-*šú* MU-*šú*⸣ NUMUN-*šú*

had surround ... [...] ... I made their foundation secure [...] ... [...] ... [...] ... [...] ... [...] ... [...] *musukkannu*-wood, *lapis lazuli* (45) [...] ... I *bound* and ... [...] ... [...]. I made [the length] of its wall [16,28]0 cubits, (corresponding to) the rendering of [m]y [na]me, and [I] made its foundation se[cu]re upon mountain stone.

49b–54) People from the four (quarters of the world), those who [had dw]elt in (both) [mount]ain(s) and (low)land(s), as many as the "Light of the Gods" (Šamaš), [*the lord of al*]*l*, shepherded, ... and I (re)settled (them) [inside] it (Dūr-Šarrukīn). I commissioned native Assyrians, masters of [eve]ry craft, as overseers (and) commanders to instruct (the settlers) in correct behavior (and how) [to revere god and ki]ng.

55–57a) [The gods who dwe]ll in heaven (and) netherworld, and in this city, [*we*]*re* [*ame*]*nable* to [my prayer and granted] me the eternal [(privilege of) bu]ilding (this) city and growing old in it.

57b–60) (As for) the one who alters the wo[rk of] my [hands], mutilates my [features] (on a relief), (or) obliterates [the rel]iefs that I have e[ngrave]d, [may the god Aššur], *the goddess Ningal, the god* [Adad, and th]e gre[at gods who dw]ell there [rem]ove his name (and) his descendant(s) [from the land] and make him live in bondage under his enemy.

---

38 D.G. Lyon's copy has ⸢*ap-tiq*⸣-*ma*.
39 D.G. Lyon's copy has ⸢*ú-kin*⸣. H. Winckler's copy erroneous has NA$_4$.<I>.UDU.MEŠ for NA$_4$.KUN$_4$.MEŠ.
40 H. Winckler's copy has [...] *ú-šal-di-da* [...] ŠI SIK, but the author cannot confirm the -*di-da*.
41 D.G. Lyon's copy has [x x] x [(x)] GIŠ x U before *ú*-⸢*šar-ši*⸣-*da*.
42 D.G. Lyon's copy would suggest [...] ⸢ŠÚ⸣ x ⸢A?⸣ x [x x x (x)] ⸢*i*?-*na*⸣ and A. Fuchs (Khorsabad p. 47) read [x x x x] ŠÚ? AŠ ZU? x x [x x x] *i-na*.
43 D.G. Lyon's copy has [x x x] x x ⸢BE-*ma* ŠAR? RI?⸣ [...] and A. Fuchs (Khorsabad p. 47) read [x x x x] x MA? ŠÚ? SAR? ⸢ḪU?⸣ [x] x x.
44 For the beginning of the line, D.G. Lyon's copy might suggest [x] ⸢DINGIR?⸣ [(x)] ⸢MEŠ⸣ [x x] and A. Fuchs (Khorsabad p. 47) has [x x x] NU? [x x].
45 D.G. Lyon's copy has [x (x)] ⸢ŠE?⸣ [x (x)] for the beginning of the line; A. Fuchs (Khorsabad p. 47 line 45 nn. 1 and 2) suggests that this might possibly be [x] ⸢LI DA⸣.
46 D.G. Lyon's copy has ⸢NI?⸣ after A.
47 With regard to the number, see the on-page note to text no. 9 lines 79–80.
50 D.G. Lyon's copy of the beginning of the lines has [*a-ši*]-⸢*bu-te* KUR⸣-*i*.
51 Based upon text no. 9 line 95 and text no. 43 lines 72–73, one expects *pa-a 1-en ú-šá-áš-kin-ma*, "I made act in concert and," at the beginning of the line. The -⸢*ri*?⸣ could conceivably be read ⸢1-*en*⸣, but the traces following this do not seem to fit *ú-šá-áš-kin* and there would not sufficient room for this reading before MA.
52 D.G. Lyon's copy and A. Fuchs' reading (Khorsabad p. 48) have [*qé-reb-šú*] at the beginning of the line.
56 D.G. Lyon's copy has [*qí-bi-ti*]-⸢*im*? GUR?⸣-*ú*-⸢*ma e-peš*⸣ for the beginning of the line and H. Winckler's copy erroneously has [...]-*ul-bur* towards the end of the line.
58 D.G. Lyon's copy has [*bu-un-na-ni*]-⸢*ia ú-saḫ-ḫu-u e-ṣu-rat e*⸣-[*ṣe*]-⸢*ru*⸣ for the beginning of the line. Note that Lyon thought he saw traces of *e-ṣu-rat*. Although the author could see no clear traces of the first two signs, we would expect *uṣurāt* not *eṣurāt*.
59 D.G. Lyon's copy has [^{d}*a-šur*] ⸢^{d}*nin-gal* ^{d}IŠKUR *u* DINGIR.MEŠ GAL.MEŠ *a-ši-bu-te ina*⸣ ŠÀ-*šú* MU-*šú* NUMUN-*šú* but much of this is now illegible or uncertain and the tablet clearly had *i-na* not *ina* even though the traces are indistinct today.

60) [*ina* KUR *lil*]-⸢*qu*?-*tú*?-*ma*? *i*?-*na* KI⸣.TA LÚ.⸢KÚR⸣-*šú* ⸢*li*?-*še-ši*⸣-*bu-šú ka-meš*

45

An inscription of Sargon II recording the construction of the city of Dūr-Šarrukīn, its sanctuaries, and its palace is found on a silver tablet discovered at Khorsabad in an alabaster coffer together with four other metal and stone tablets (see the introduction to text nos. 44–47). The silver tablet is preserved in the Louvre and weighs 435 grams. Text no. 48 may be a duplicate of this inscription since it preserves parts of lines 11–20 of this text. This inscription and the one on the gold tablet (text no. 46) refer to the gods Ea, Sîn, Šamaš, Adad, and Ninurta being installed on their daises and this may be connected to the statement in the Assyrian Eponym Chronicle that "the gods of the city Dūr-Šarrukīn entered their temples" on the twenty-second day of Tašrītu (VII) in the eponymy of Ša-Aššur-dubbu (707).

CATALOGUE

Museum Number	Registration Number	Provenance	Dimensions (cm)	cpn
AO 21371	Nap. III 2898	Khorsabad, Palace, in the wall between Rooms 17 and 19, inside a stone box with an inscribed lid	11.8×6×0.6	c

BIBLIOGRAPHY

1867 Place, Ninive et l'Assyrie 1 pp. 62–63 (provenance); and 3 pl. 77 nos. 3–4 (héliogravure)
1870 Oppert in Place, Ninive et l'Assyrie 2 pp. 304–306 (copy, edition)
1870 Oppert, Dour-Sarkayan pp. 24–26 (copy, edition) (identical to preceding)
1878 Oppert, Records of the Past 11 pp. 36–39 (translation)
1883 Lyon, Sar. no. 4 (copy, edition)
1886 Bezold, Literatur p. 88 §52.4 (study)
1886 Strassmaier, AV passim as TA (partial copy, partial transliteration)
1887 Berthelot, Révue archéologique 9 (3rd series) pp. 10–17 (study)
1889 Winckler, Sar. 1 p. XI; and 2 pl. 43 (copy, study)
1911 Weissbach, ZDMG 65 p. 683 (study)
1912 Thureau-Dangin, TCL 3 p. 58 n. 2 (lines 28–29, study)
1916 Weissbach, ZDMG 70 pp. 74–75 (study)
1918 Pillet, Khorsabad pp. 84–87 (study)
1924 Pottier, Antiquités assyriennes pp. 125–126 no. 133 (study)
1927 Luckenbill, ARAB 2 pp. 56 and 58 §§106 and 110–111 (translation)
1965 Landsberger, JNES 24 pp. 285–286 (study)
1968 Ellis, Foundation Deposits pp. 101–103, 176 no. 16, and 194 no. 78 (lines 40–44a, edition; study, provenance)
1975 Borger, WAO[2] no. 282 (photo of obverse)
1982 André-Leicknam, Naissance de l'écriture p. 233 no. 179 (photo of reverse, study)
1986 Renger, CRRA 32 pp. 112–113 (lines 1–3, partial transcripton, study)
1988 Brinkman in Curtis, Bronzeworking Centres pp. 144–150 and 158–159 (study)
1990 Renger, Studies Moran pp. 436–437 (edition)
1994 Fuchs, Khorsabad pp. 48–50 and 298–299 no. 1.2.2 (edition)
2013 Curtis, Examination of Late Assyrian Metalwork pp. 50–51, 163, and pl. XXII no. 366 (photo, study)

44 line 60 D.G. Lyon's copy has [*ina* KUR *lil*]-⸢*qu-te-ma i-na*⸣ at the beginning of the line and H. Winckler's copy has [*ina* KUR *lil*]-*qu-te-ma i-na*. Against A. Fuchs' statement that the LÚ is not present (Khorsabad p. 48 line 60 n. 3), the sign is found on the tablet.

TEXT

Obv.

1) ⌜É.GAL⌝ ^{m}LUGAL-GI.⌜NA⌝
2) GAR ^{d}⌜BAD$^{?}$⌝ NU.ÈŠ ^{d}*a*-⌜*šur*⌝
3) ⌜LUGAL⌝ *dan-nu* LUGAL KIŠ LUGAL KUR *aš-šur*
4) ⌜LUGAL⌝ *šá ul-tú ṣi-ta-an*
5) *a-di šil-la-an kib-rat*
6) LÍMMU-*i i-be-lu-u*-⌜*ma*⌝
7) *iš-tak*-⌜*ka*⌝-*nu* LÚ.GAR-*nu*-⌜*ti*⌝
8) *i-na* u_4-*me-šu-ma i-na bi-ib-lat*
9) ŠÀ-*ia i-na re-bit* NINA.⌜KI GÌR⌝.II
10) KUR.*mu-uṣ-ri* KUR-*i* URU DÙ-*ma*
11) URU.BÀD-^{m}LUGAL-GI.NA ⌜*az*⌝-*ku-ra*
12) *ni-bit-su šu-bat* ^{d}*é-a*
13) ^{d}30 ^{d}UTU ^{d}IŠKUR ^{d}MAŠ
14) DINGIR.MEŠ GAL.MEŠ EN.MEŠ-*ia*
15) *i-na qer-bi-šú ad*-(*x*)-⌜*di*⌝
16) *bu-un-na-né-e* DINGIR-*ti-šú-nu*
17) GAL-*ti nak*-⌜*liš*⌝ *ú-še-piš-ma*
18) *ú-šar-ma-a pa-rak* ⌜*da*⌝-*ra-a-te*
19) É.GAL.MEŠ ZÚ AM.SI GIŠ.ESI
20) GIŠ.TÚG GIŠ.*mu-suk-kan*-<*ni*> GIŠ.*ere*-IGI
21) GIŠ.ŠUR.MÌN GIŠ.*dup-ra-ni* GIŠ.⌜ŠIM⌝.LI
22) *u* GIŠ.*bu-uṭ-ni ina qer-bi-šú* DÙ-*ma*
23) *i-na* É *ḫi-la-ni tam-šil* É.GAL
24) KUR.*ḫat-ti us-si-ma* KÁ.MEŠ-⌜*šin*⌝
25) *ú-ma-am* KUR-*i u ti-amti ina a*-⌜*ban*⌝

Rev.

26) ⌜KUR-*i zaq*⌝-*ri ina nik-lat* ^{d}⌜*nin*$^{?}$⌝-[*zadim*$^{?}$]
27) ⌜*ú*⌝-[*še*]-⌜*piš*⌝-*ma i-na qé*-⌜*re*⌝-[*bi*]-*ši-na*
28) ⌜KUR.MEŠ-*niš*⌝ *ú-šar-šid-ma né-reb-ši-na*
29) ^{d}ŠEŠ.KI-*ri-iš ú-šaḫ*-⌜*li*⌝
30) GIŠ.ÙR.MEŠ GIŠ.*ere*-IGI GIŠ.ŠUR.MÌN
31) UGU-*ši**-*na ú-ṣal*-⌜*lil-ma*⌝
32) GIŠ.IG.MEŠ GIŠ.ESI GIŠ.TÚG
33) GIŠ.*mu-suk-kan-ni ina* KÁ.MEŠ-*ši-na*
34) *ú-rat-ti* BÀD.MEŠ-*šú*
35) *dan-nu-ti ki-ma ki-iṣ-rat*
36) *ú-ḫum-me ú-zaq-qir*$_6$*
37) 10 *ina* 1.KÙŠ GAL-*ti ú-ḫab-bir-ma*
38) UGU 3.UŠ.TA.ÀM *ti*-⌜*ib-ki*⌝
39) *gaba*-⌜*dib*⌝-*bi-šú-nu ak-ṣur*
40) *i-na ṭup-pi* KÙ.GI KÙ.BABBAR
41) URUDU AN.NA A.BÁR NA$_4$.ZA.GÌN
42) NA$_4$.GIŠ.NU$_{11}$.GAL *ni-bit*
43) MU-*ia áš-ṭur*-⌜*ma*⌝ *i-na*
44) *uš-še*-⌜*šin*⌝ *ú-kin* NUN ⌜EGIR⌝
45) *an*-⌜*ḫu*⌝-*us-su lu-ud-diš*

1–7) Palace of Sargon (II), appointee of the god *Enlil*, *nešakku*-priest of the god Aššur, strong king, king of the world, king of Assyria; king who ruled the four quarters (of the world), from east to west, and set governors (over them).

8–12a) At that time, in accordance with my heart's desire, I built a city on the *outskirts* of Nineveh, at the foot of Mount Muṣri, and named it Dūr-Šarrukīn.

12b–18) I erected dwelling(s) for the gods Ea, Sîn, Šamaš, Adad, (and) Ninurta, the great gods, my lords, (15) inside it. I had images of their great divine majesties skillfully made and installed (them) on (their) eternal dais(es).

19–44a) I built inside it (the city) palatial halls using (lit.: "of") elephant ivory, ebony, boxwood, *musukkannu*-wood, cedar, cypress, *daprānu*-juniper, juniper, and terebinth. I then enhanced their gates with a *bīt ḫilāni*, a replica of a Hittite palace. (25) Through the art of the god *Nin*[*zadim*], I had animals of the mountain and sea made from (blocks of) massive mountain stone; I made (them) as secure as a mountain inside them (the palatial halls) and made their entrances as bright as the moon. (30) I roofed them with beams of cedar (and) cypress and installed doors of ebony, boxwood, (and) *musukkannu*-wood in their gates. (35) I raised its strong walls like a mountain massif, made (them) ten large cubits thick, and constructed their crenellations on top of one hundred and eighty layers of brick. (40) I wrote my name upon tablets of gold, silver, copper, tin, lead, lapis lazuli, (and) alabaster and placed (them) in their foundations.

44b–48) May a future prince renovate its dilapidated sections, write his own commemorative inscription,

---

2 ^{d}⌜BAD$^{?}$⌝: There does not appear to be sufficient room to read ^{d}EN.LÍL, but the traces do not conform well to BAD.

6 H. Winckler's copy correctly indicates the presence of the penultimate sign (U) that is omitted on the copies by J. Oppert and D.G. Lyon.

26 Ninzadim was a god of craftwork, including stone cutting (see Cavigneaux and Krebernik, RLA 9/7–8 [2001] pp. 471–473 sub Nin-muga, Nin-zed, Ninzadim); the tentative restoration follows Fuchs, Khorsabad p. 50 sub line 26 n. 1.

31 -ŠI*-: The text apparently has -PI-.

36 *qir*$_6$*: Text has TÙM.

46) NA$_4$.NA.RÚ.A-*šú liš-ṭur-*⸢*ma*⸣
47) *it-ti* NA$_4$.NA.RÚ.⸢A-*ia*⸣
48) *liš-kun aš-šur* ⸢ŠÙD⸣-*šú i-šem-me*
49) *mu-nak-kir ep-šet* ŠU.II-*ia*
50) *mu-pa-šiṭ-ṭu si-ma-te-ia aš-šur*
51) EN GAL-*u* MU-*šú* NUMUN-*šú ina* KUR *li-ḫal-liq*

and set (it) with my commemorative inscription. (The god) Aššur will (then) listen to his prayer(s).

49–51) (As for) the one alters the work of my hands (or) effaces my own representation(s), may (the god) Aššur, the great lord, make his name (and) his descendant(s) disappear from the land.

46

An inscription of Sargon II on a gold tablet from Khorsabad records the construction of the city of Dūr-Šarrukīn, its sanctuaries, and its palace. It was found in 1854 during the French excavations of the city together with four other metal and stone tablets (see the introduction to text nos. 44–47). The gold tablet weighs 167 grams.

CATALOGUE

Museum Number	Registration Number	Provenance	Dimensions (cm)	cpn
AO 19933	Nap. III 2897	Khorsabad, Palace, in the wall between Rooms 17 and 19, inside a stone box with an inscribed lid	7×4.2×0.4	c

BIBLIOGRAPHY

1856 Oppert, Annales de Philosophie chrétienne 53 pp. 350–351 (translation)
1856 Oppert, Chronologie pp. 39–40 (translation) (identical to preceding)
1859 Oppert, EM 2 pp. 343–350 (copy, edition, study)
1867 Place, Ninive et l'Assyrie 1 pp. 62–63 (provenance); and 3 pl. 77 nos. 1–2 (héliogravure)
1870 Oppert in Place, Ninive et l'Assyrie 2 pp. 303–304 (copy, edition)
1870 Oppert, Dour-Sarkayan pp. 23–24 (copy, edition) (identical to preceding)
1874 Ménant, Annales p. 198 (translation)
1878 Oppert, Records of the Past 11 pp. 33–35 (translation)
1883 Lyon, Sar. no. 5 (copy, edition)
1886 Bezold, Literatur p. 88 §52.5 study)
1886 Strassmaier, AV passim as TO (partial copy, partial transliteration)
1887 Berthelot, Révue archéologique 9 (3rd series) pp. 10–17 (study)
1889 Winckler, Sar. 1 p. XI; and 2 pl. 44 (copy, study)
1911 Weissbach, ZDMG 65 p. 683 (study)
1916 Weissbach, ZDMG 70 pp. 74–75 (study)
1918 Pillet, Khorsabad pp. 84–87 (study)
1924 Pottier, Antiquités assyriennes pp. 125–126 and pl. XXVIII no. 132 (photo, study)
1927 Luckenbill, ARAB 2 pp. 56 and 58–59 §§106 and 112–113 (translation)
1948 Heidel, JNES 7 p. 100 n. 19 (study)
1965 Landsberger, JNES 24 pp. 285–286 (study)
1968 Ellis, Foundation Deposits pp. 101–103, 176 no. 16, and 194 no. 78 (study, provenance)
1975 Borger, WAO^2 no. 281 (photo of obverse, translation)
1982 André-Leicknam, Naissance de l'écriture p. 233 no. 178 (photo of obverse, study)
1986 Renger, CRRA 32 pp. 112–113 (lines 1–4, partial transcription, study)
1994 Fuchs, Khorsabad pp. 51–52 and 299–300 no. 1.2.3 (edition)
2013 Curtis, Examination of Late Assyrian Metalwork pp. 50–51, 163, and pl. XXII no. 366 (photo, study)

TEXT

Obv.

1) É.GAL ^{m}LUGAL-GI.NA
2) GAR ^{d}EN.LÍL NU.ÈŠ
3) ^{d}*a-šur* LUGAL *dan-nu*
4) LUGAL KIŠ LUGAL KUR *aš-šur*
5) LUGAL *šá ul-tú ṣi-tan*
6) *a-di šil-la-an*
7) *kib-rat* LÍMMU-*i*
8) *i-be-lu-ma iš-tak-ka-nu*

1–9a) Palace of Sargon (II), appointee of the god Enlil, *nešakku*-priest of the god Aššur, strong king, king of the world, king of Assyria; (5) king who ruled the four quarters (of the world), from east to west, and set governors (over them).

9) LÚ.GAR-*nu-ti i-na*
10) *bi-bil* ŠÀ-*ia* GÌR.II
11) KUR.*mu-uṣ-ri* KUR-*i*
12) URU DÙ-*ma* URU.BÀD-MAN-GIN
13) *az-ku-ra ni-bit-su*

9b–13) In accordance with my heart's desire, I built a city at the foot of Mount Muṣri and named it Dūr-Šarrukīn.

14) *šu-bat* ^{d}*é-a* ^{d}30
15) ^{d}UTU ^{d}IŠKUR *u* ^{d}MAŠ
16) *i-na qer-bi-šú ad-di*
17) *bu-un-na-né-e*
18) DINGIR-*ti-šú-nu* GAL-*te*
19) ^{d}*nin-ši-kù ba-an*
20) *mim-ma ú-lid-ma*

Rev.

21) *ir-mu-u pa-rak-ki*

14–21) I erected dwelling(s) for the gods Ea, Sîn, Šamaš, Adad, and Ninurta inside it. The god Ninšiku (Ea), the creator of everything, fashioned images of their great divine majesties and they occupied (their) daises.

22) É.GAL.MEŠ ZÚ AM.SI
23) GIŠ.ESI GIŠ.TÚG GIŠ.MES.MÁ.KAN.<NA>
24) GIŠ.*ere*-IGI GIŠ.ŠUR.MÌN GIŠ.*dáp-ra-ni*
25) GIŠ.LI *u* GIŠ.*bu-uṭ-ni*
26) *i-na qer-bi-šú* DÙ-*ma*
27) É *ḫi-la-an-ni*
28) *tam-šil* É.GAL KUR.*ḫat-ti*
29) *me-eḫ-ret* KÁ.MEŠ-*šin*
30) *ap-tiq-ma* GIŠ.ÙR.MEŠ
31) GIŠ.*ere*-IGI GIŠ.ŠUR.MÌN *ú-kin*
32) *ṣe-ru-uš-šin ina* DUB KÙ.GI
33) KÙ.BABBAR URUDU AN.NA A.BÁR NA$_4$.ZA.GÌN
34) NA$_4$.GIŠ.NU$_{11}$.GAL *ni-bit*
35) MU-*ia áš-ṭur-ma*
36) *ina uš-še-šin ú-kin*

22–36) I built inside it (the city) palatial halls using (lit.: "of") elephant ivory, ebony, boxwood, *musukkannu*-wood, cedar, cypress, *daprānu*-juniper, (25) juniper, and terebinth. I then fashioned a *bīt ḫilāni*, a replica of a Hittite palace, in front of their gates (30) and roofed them with beams of cedar (and) cypress. I wrote my name upon tablet(s) of gold, silver, copper, tin, lead, lapis lazuli, (and) alabaster and placed (them) in their foundations.

37) *mu-nak-kir ep-šet*
38) ŠU.II-*ia mu-pa-šiṭ-ṭu*
39) *si-ma-te-ia aš-šur* EN GAL
40) MU-*šú* NUMUN-*šú ina* KUR *li-ḫal-liq*

37–40) (As for) the one who alters the work of my hands (or) effaces my own representation(s), may (the god) Aššur, the great lord, make his name (and) his descendant(s) disappear from the land.

---

10 Possibly <*ina*> GÌR.II, but the *ina* is also omitted in text no. 44 line 26, text no. 45 line 9, and text no. 47 line 8.

47

A short inscription of Sargon II recording the construction of the city of Dūr-Šarrukīn, its sanctuaries, and its palace is found on a magnesite tablet from that city. The tablet was found in the palace in 1854 together with four metal tablets (see the introduction to text nos. 44–47).

CATALOGUE

Museum Number	Registration Number	Provenance	Dimensions (cm)	cpn
Louvre —	Nap. III 2899	Khorsabad, Palace, in the wall between Rooms 17 and 19, inside a stone box with an inscribed lid	10.2×6.2	c

COMMENTARY

It has often been stated that this tablet is made of antimony, but a chemical analysis of the tablet performed in the nineteenth century by M. Berthelot showed that it is made of magnesite. With regard to the question of the stone, see Brinkman in Curtis, Bronzeworking Centres pp. 144–150. J. Bjorkman (OLP 18 [1987] pp. 91–97) accepts the identification of the type of stone by Berthelot and argues that the tablet of *gišnugalli* (generally translated "alabaster," as in line 20 below) mentioned in these texts is this particular tablet.

The engraver made several of the signs slightly abnormal in form: URU (line 10), SI (line 14), KA (line 15), and KUN (line 24); these signs are marked with * in the transliteration below.

BIBLIOGRAPHY

1859 Oppert, EM 2 p. 350 (line 25, study)
1867 Place, Ninive et l'Assyrie 1 pp. 62–63 (provenance); and 3 pl. 77 no. 5 (héliogravure of obverse)
1870 Oppert in Place, Ninive et l'Assyrie 2 pp. 306–307 (copy, edition)
1870 Oppert, Dour-Sarkayan pp. 26–27 (copy, edition) [identical to preceding]
1878 Oppert, Records of the Past 11 p. 40 (translation)
1883 Lyon, Sar. no. 6 (copy, edition)
1886 Bezold, Literatur p. 89 §52.6 (study)
1886 Strassmaier, AV passim as TAl (partial copy, partial transliteration)
1887 Berthelot, Revue archéologique 9 (3rd series) pp. 10–17 (study)
1889 Winckler, Sar. 1 p. XI; and 2 pl. 43 (copy, study)
1918 Pillet, Khorsabad pp. 84–87 (study)
1924 Pottier, Antiquités assyriennes pp. 125–126 no. 134 (study)
1927 Luckenbill, ARAB 2 pp. 56 and 59 §§106 and 114–115 (translation)
1965 Landsberger, JNES 24 pp. 285–286 (study)
1968 Ellis, Foundation Deposits pp. 101–103, 176 no. 16, and 194 no. 78 (study, provenance)
1986 Renger, CRRA 32 pp. 112–113 (lines 1–3, partial transcription, study)
1988 Brinkman in Curtis, Bronzeworking Centres pp. 144–150 and 158–159 (study)
1994 Fuchs, Khorsabad pp. 52–53 and 300 no. 1.2.4 (edition)
2013 Curtis, Examination of Late Assyrian Metalwork pp. 50–51, 163, and pl. XXII no. 366 (photo, study)

Figure 19. Obverse of Nap. III 2899 (text no. 47 lines 1–15), a magnesite tablet found in the palace at Khorsabad. Photo courtesy of A. Thomas. © Musée du Louvre.

TEXT

Obv.
1) É.GAL ^{m}MAN-GIN
2) GAR ^{d}BAD ÉNSI *aš-šur*
3) MAN KAL MAN ŠÚ MAN KUR AŠ
4) MAN *šá* TA *ṣi-ta-an*
5) *a-di šil-la-an kib-rat* LÍMMU
6) *i-be-lu-ma iš-tak-ka-nu*
7) LÚ.GAR-*nu-te ina* u_4*-me-šú-ma*
8) *ina re-bit* NINA.KI GÌR.II
9) KUR.*mu-uṣ-ri* KUR-*i*
10) URU DÙ-*ma* URU*.BÀD-MAN-GIN
11) MU-*šu ab-bi šu-bat* ^{d}30
12) ^{d}UTU ^{d}IŠKUR ^{d}MAŠ DINGIR.MEŠ GAL.MEŠ
13) *ina qer-bi-šu ad-di*
14) É.GAL.MEŠ ZÚ AM.SI* GIŠ.ESI
15) GIŠ.TÚG GIŠ.*mu-suk-ka**-*ni*
Rev.
16) ⸢GIŠ⸣.*ere*-⸢IGI⸣ GIŠ.ŠUR.MÌN ⸢GIŠ.*dup-ra*⸣-*ni*

1–7a) Palace of Sargon (II), appointee of the god Enlil, vice-regent for (the god) Aššur, strong king, king of the world, king of Assyria; king who ruled the four quarters (of the world), from east to west, and set governors (over them).

7b–11a) At that time, I built a city on the *outskirts* of Nineveh, at the foot of Mount Muṣri, (10) and named it Dūr-Šarrukīn.

11b–13) I erected dwelling(s) for the gods Sîn, Šamaš, Adad, (and) Ninurta, the great gods, inside it.

14–21) I built inside it palatial halls using (lit.: "of") elephant ivory, ebony, (15) boxwood, *musukkannu*-wood, cedar, cypress, (and) *da*[*pr*]*ānu*-juniper. I then wrote my name upon tablet(s) of gold, silver, copper,

16 The copies by J. Oppert, D.G. Lyon, and H. Winckler have *dáp*-, not ⸢*dup*⸣-, but examination of the tablet would suggest the latter reading.

17) *ina* ⸢*qer*⸣-*bi-šu* DÙ-*ma*
18) *ina* DUB KÙ.GI KÙ.BABBAR URUDU
19) AN.NA A.BÁR NA$_{4}$.ZA.GÌN
20) NA$_{4}$.GIŠ.NU$_{11}$.GAL *ni-bit* MU-*ia*
21) SAR-*ma ina* UŠ$_{8}$-*šú ú-kin*
22) NUN EGIR *an-ḫu-su lu-diš*
23) NA$_{4}$.NA.RÚ.A-*šú* SAR-*ma*
24) KI ⸢NA$_{4}$⸣.NA.RÚ.A-*ía liš-kun**
25) *aš-šur* ⸢*ik*$^{?}$⸣-*ri-bi-šú* ŠE.GA

tin, lead, lapis lazuli, (and) alabaster and placed (them) in its foundations.

22–25) May a future prince renovate its dilapidated sections, write his own commemorative inscription, and set (it) with my commemorative inscription. (The god) Aššur will (then) listen to his prayers.

48

A fragment of the left side of a clay tablet found in 1932 bears an inscription of Sargon II that duplicates part of the inscription on the silver tablet from Khorsabad (text no. 45) and records the construction of sanctuaries and the royal palace at Dūr-Šarrukīn. Since it is not certain that the clay tablet originally had the whole inscription found on text no. 45, it is arbitrarily treated separately here. Only one side of this fragment is inscribed; the Neo-Assyrian signs are written clearly and are large in size. The restorations in the transliteration are based upon lines 12–20 of text no. 45. The provenance of the piece is not certain. Although no mention is made in Loud and Altman, Khorsabad 2 pp. 104–105 of any item not coming from Khorsabad, T. Jacobsen indicated on the excavation card for this piece that it may have come from Chenchi instead of Khorsabad.

CATALOGUE

Museum Number	Excavation Number	Provenance	Dimensions (cm)	cpn
OI —	DŠ 32-13	Khorsabad$^{?}$	6.5×7.8×2	c

TEXT

Lacuna
1′) ⸢*az-ku-ra ni*⸣-[*bit-su šu-bat* ^{d}*é-a*]
2′) ^{d}30 ^{d}UTU ^{d}⸢IŠKUR$^{?}$⸣ [^{d}MAŠ DINGIR.MEŠ GAL.MEŠ]
3′) *be-lí-ia i-na* ⸢*qer*⸣-[*bi-šú ad-di*]
4′) *bu-un-na-né-e* ⸢DINGIR⸣-[*ti-šú-nu* GAL-*ti*]
5′) *nak-liš** *ú-še-piš*-⸢*ma*⸣ [*ú-šar-ma-a*]
6′) *pa-rak da-ra-a*-[*te* É.GAL.MEŠ ZÚ AM.SI]
7′) ⸢GIŠ.ESI⸣ GIŠ.TÚG GIŠ.⸢*mu*⸣-[*suk-kan*-<*ni*> GIŠ.*ere*-IGI]
Lacuna

Lacuna
1′–6′a) I named [it Dūr-Šarrukīn. I erected dwelling(s) for the gods Ea], Sîn, Šamaš, A[dad, (and) Ninurta, the great gods], my lords, ins[ide it]. I had images of [their great] divi[ne majesties] skillfully made an[d installed (them) on] (their) etern[al] dais(es).
6′b–7′) [I built inside it (the city) palatial halls using (lit.: "of") elephant ivory], ebony, boxwood, *m*[*usukkann*]*u*-wood, [cedar, cypress, *daprānu*-juniper, juniper, and terebinth].
Lacuna

48 line 1′ The translation assumes that URU.BÀD-^{m}LUGAL-GI.NA was found in the previous line (see text no. 45 line 11).
48 line 5′ -*liš**: The text has DIŠ.
48 line 7′ The translation assumes that following this line was GIŠ.ŠUR.MÌN GIŠ.*dup-ra-ni* GIŠ.ŠIM.LI *u* GIŠ.*bu-uṭ-ni ina qer-bi-šú* DÙ-*ma* (see text no. 45 lines 21–22).

49

This inscription dedicated to the Sebetti ("the divine Seven"), a group of seven beneficent deities, is found upon a large number of stone altars from Khorsabad. Most or all of these altars come from a temple dedicated to the Sebetti. With regard to the Sebetti, see Wiggermann, RLA 12/5–6 (2010) pp. 459–466 sub "Siebengötter."

CATALOGUE

Ex.	Museum Number/ Source	Excavation Number	Provenance	Dimensions (cm)	Lines Preserved	cpn
1	AO 19900 (Nap. III 2871)	—	Khorsabad, 100 paces from the village	Height: 83; diameter: 68	1	c
2	EŞ 4784	—	Khorsabad	Height: 104; diameter: 75	1	n
3	IM —	DŠ 1195	Khorsabad, in the town outside and to the west of citadel gate A	—	1	n
4–14	See commentary	—	Khorsabad, Sebetti temple, antecella	—	1	n
15–16	See commentary	—	Khorsabad, Sebetti temple, courtyard	—	1	n

COMMENTARY

P.E. Botta states that he found two stone altars at Khorsabad (Monument de Ninive 5 p. 171), although he only published the piece that is now in the Louvre (ex. 1). Botta apparently made a squeeze of the inscription on ex. 1, but it is either no longer extant or not kept in the Louvre. The original copy of ex. 1 is currently preserved in the Archives of the Institut de France (Botta-Cotta II 2976, folio I, sheet 325). A.H. Layard (Discoveries p. 131) states that his workmen found at Khorsabad "inscribed altars or tripods, similar to that in the Assyrian collection of the Louvre"; one of these may have been the second altar found by Botta. The present location of these pieces is not known. Ex. 2 was acquired by B. Bey at Basra in 1904 and it entered the museum in Istanbul in 1910. As noted by E. Nassouhi (RA 22 [1925] p. 85), it is possible that this exemplar is the second altar found by Botta. However, a fair portion of the inscription is preserved on ex. 2 while Botta states that only a few cuneiform characters remained on the second altar seen by him (JA 4/2 [1843] pp. 211–212). In addition to ex. 3, the Oriental Institute expedition found another altar at Khorsabad (DŠ 1194, now in the Oriental Institute, Chicago); however, the section of this altar which would have borne the inscription is not preserved (see Loud and Altman, Khorsabad 2 p. 96 and pl. 48 no. 19). As noted by F. Safar (Sumer 13 [1957] pp. 220–221), the two exemplars found by the Oriental Institute excavations may come from the Sebetti temple.

Thirteen exemplars with this text (exs. 4–16) were found in the Sebetti temple as the result of Iraqi excavations prompted by the discovery of three of them during leveling operations for a highway. The bottom part of one further altar, presumably without an inscription, was found in the courtyard of that temple. Although Safar states in the English version of his article that thirteen altars were found in the temple's antecella, only eleven (exs. 4–14) actually come from that room (see Sumer 13 [1957] p. 194 and fig. 1 following p. 196 [Arabic version] against p. 220 [English version]). At least some of these altars were left in situ. All thirteen altars found by the Iraqi excavations are said to have the same inscription, but none of the inscriptions are fully legible from the published photographs. F. Basmachi (Treasures p. 251) states that fourteen were found in the temple, arranged in two rows of seven (thus two altars for each of the seven deities), and that one is IM 67886. In the score, there is no transliteration for exs. 5–16 and what appears for ex. 4 follows the copy published by Safar.

The top of each altar is circular and is placed above a tripod base; the bottom of each of the three corners of the base is in the form of a lion's paw. The inscription is incised around the edge of the circular top of each altar. The master line is a composite made from the various exemplars.

Figure 20. AO 19900 (text no. 49 ex. 1), one of numerous altars found in the temple of the Sebetti at Khorsabad. Photo courtesy of A. Thomas. © Musée du Louvre.

BIBLIOGRAPHY

1843 Botta, JA 4/2 pp. 70–71 and pls. XI–XII (ex. 1, copy, drawing, study)

1849 Botta, Monument de Ninive 2 pl. 157 (drawing); and 4 pl. 181 no. 1 (ex. 1, copy)

1850 Botta, Monument de Ninive 5 p. 171 (ex. 1, study)

1854 de Longpérier, Notice[3] no. 14 (ex. 1, study)

1884 Perrot and Chipiez, Histoire de l'art 2 p. 268 fig. 108 (drawing)

1886 Bezold, Literatur p. 94 §56.14.k (ex. 1, study)
1889 Winckler, Sar. 1 p. 190; and 2 pl. 49 no. 1 (ex. 1, copy, edition)
1924 Pottier, Antiquités assyriennes pp. 92–93 no. 58 and pl. XXXI (ex. 1, photo, translation, study)
1925 Nassouhi, RA 22 pp. 85–90 (ex. 1, edition; ex. 2, photo, copy, edition)
1927 Gressmann, ABAT^{2} p. 127 and pl. CLXXV fig. 439 (ex. 1, drawing)
1927 Luckenbill, ARAB 2 p. 66 §124 (ex. 1, translation)
1938 Loud and Altman, Khorsabad 2 pp. 95–96 no. 18, p. 104 no. 3, and pl. 48 no. 18 (ex. 3, photo, copy and edition [by Jacobsen])
1957 Safar, Sumer 13 pp. 219–221 [English] and pp. 193–196 and figs. 1–4 [Arabic] (exs. 4–16, photo [inscription not legible], copy, translation, provenance)
1969 Pritchard, ANEP^{2} pp. 193 and 319 no. 580 (ex. 2, photo, study)
1976 Basmachi, Treasures p. 251 (study)
1986 Albenda, Palace of Sargon pp. 97, 112–113, 116, and 152, and pls. 2 and 148 (ex. 1, drawings [by Botta and Flandin]; edition [by Walker] exs. 1–3, study)
1994 Fuchs, Khorsabad pp. 284 and 371 no. 3.3 (exs. 1–4, edition)

TEXT

1) *a-na* ^{d}IMIN.BI *qar-rad la šá-na-*⸢*an*⸣ ^{m}LUGAL-GI.NA MAN *kiš-šat* MAN KUR *aš-šur*.KI GÌR.NÍTA KÁ.DINGIR.RA.KI MAN KUR EME.GI$_{7}$ *ù* URI.KI GÁ-*ma* BA-*iš*

1) To the Sebetti, warrior(s) without equa[l], Sargon (II), king of the world, king of Assyria, governor of Babylon, king of the land of Sumer and Akkad, set up and presented (this object).

50

This short brick inscription of Sargon II that simply gives his name with several titles and epithets has been found at numerous sites in addition to Khorsabad: Nimrud, Nineveh, Karamles (ancient Kār-Ninlil/Kār-Mullissi), Tag, and possibly Djigan. The text is sometimes stamped on the brick and sometimes inscribed. On the basis of Sargon's titulary in the text, A. Fuchs (Khorsabad p. 372 and n. 620) suggests that this inscription is to be dated before the king's twelfth year (710).

CATALOGUE

Ex.	Museum Number/ Source	Excavation/ Registration No.	Provenance	Dimensions (cm)	Botta, MdN	Lines Preserved	cpn
1	BM 90238	1979-12,20,144	—	34.5×34.5×12	—	1–3	n
2	BM 90239	48-11-4,27	Nimrud, Central Palace	34.5×34.5×12	—	1–3	n
3	BM 90240	1979-12-20,145	—	34.5×34.5×12	—	1–3	n
4	BM 90241	1979-12-20,146	—	34×33×11	—	1–3	n
5	BM 90819	1979-12-20,368	—	27×26.5×10	—	1–3	n
6	VA 3212	—	Khorsabad	34.8×34.8×12	—	1–3	p
7	N 8078?	—	Khorsabad or Nineveh	33×33×13	4 pl. 183^{c} no. 2	1–3	c
8	N 8076?	—	Khorsabad	30×32×10	4 pl. 183^{c} no. 3	1–3	c
9	Layard, ICC pl. 82 [D.1]	—	Karamles	—	—	1–3	n
10	Thompson, Arch. 79 pl. XLV no. 72	—	Tag	36.2×15.9×12.1	—	1–3$^{?}$	n
11	As ex. 10	—	Tag	As ex. 10	—	1–3$^{?}$	n

49 line 1 With regard to the use of the logogram GÁ for *šakānu* in royal inscriptions, see the note to text no. 2011 line 6.

12	Thompson, AAA 18 p. 100	—	Nineveh, Kuyunjik, SE of the Nabû temple, A 17	33×33×10.5	—	1–3?	n
13	Loud and Altman, Khorsabad 2 pl. 65 top right	—	Khorsabad	—	—	1–3	p
14	Pillet, Pionnier pl. XXIII fig 27 upper row left	—	Probably Khorsabad	—	—	1–3	p
15	As ex. 14 upper row middle	—	As ex. 14	—	—	—	—
16	As ex. 14 lower row left	—	As ex. 14	—	—	—	n
17	As ex. 14 lower row second from left	—	As ex. 14	—	—	—	n
18	As ex. 14 pl. XXIV fig. 28	—	Possibly Djigan	—	—	1–3	p
19	As ex. 14 pl. XXIV fig. 29	—	As ex. 18	—	—	1–3	p
20	Chevalier and Lavédrine in Fontan, Khorsabad p. 204 fig. 7	—	As ex. 14	—	—	1–3	p
21	—	DŠ 35	Khorsabad, city gate 7	33×17×12	—	1–3	n
22	—	DŠ 36	Khorsabad, Palace, Throne Room (Court VII)	23×21×9	—	1–3	n
23	—	DŠ 37	As ex. 21	34×34×11	—	1–3	n
24	—	—	Khorsabad, Palace	33×33×10	—	1–3	p

COMMENTARY

A. Ungnad (VAS 1 p. X) states that the inscription on ex. 6 is stamped and that the area stamped measures 6×15.5 cm. No museum numbers are found on the two bricks with this inscription in the Louvre (exs. 7–8), but museum records indicate that N 8076 and N 8078 bear this inscription and the measurements recorded for these fit the bricks indicated. One brick in the Louvre (ex. 7) is the only one known so far to match the exact text of the brick copied by P.E. Botta as Monument de Ninive 4 pl. 183^{c} no. 2. However, museum records state that N 8078 came from Nineveh while Botta says that the brick he copied came from Khorsabad. Botta's original copy of ex. 8 is found on the Institut de France manuscript 2976 sheet 56.

C.B.F. Walker (CBI p. 117) notes that although the brick published by A.H. Layard in ICC pl. 82 [D] (and listed above as ex. 9) is said to come from Karamles and to have both this inscription and text no. 53 on it (see also Layard, Nineveh 1 p. 52), no brick in the British Museum has both inscriptions and the only brick in the British Museum registered as coming from Karamles has only text no. 53 (ex. 5). Since Layard gives variant forms for two signs in line 2, it is likely that the copy published by him represents more than one brick. This is supported by the fact that on Layard notebook MS A p. 320 (Department of the Middle East, British Museum) there are two copies of this inscription and the label for these says "on bricks from Karamles."

According to Thompson, Arch. 79 (1929) p. 124 and pl. XLV no. 72, two bricks with this inscription (exs. 10–11) were found at Tag, near 'Ain Sefna (Ain Sifni, in the Shekhan district of northern Iraq); they are said to have the inscription on the face of the brick and to measure 14.25"×6.25"×4.75". However, elsewhere he refers to only one brick with this inscription from 'Ain Sefna (ibid. p. 109).

Ex. 13 is edited from the photo in Loud and Altman, Khorsabad 2 pl. 65 (top right) and Oriental Institute photograph 31189.

Exs. 14–20 are depicted on photographs taken by Gabriel Tranchand of items found by V. Place and published by M. Pillet (exs. 14–19) and N. Chevalier and B. Lavédrine (ex. 20). Exs. 14–17 and 20 likely come from Khorsabad, although this is not explicitly stated in the publications. According to Pillet, Pionnier pl. XXIV, exs. 18 and 19 come from Djigan, located about 25 km west of Khorsabad (see also ibid. p. 116), but Place does not refer to having found any bricks of this ruler at Djigan (Place, Ninive et l'Assyrie 2 pp. 150–151). Ex. 16 and ex. 19 may be the same exemplar, but this is not absolutely clear from the published photographs.

Information on exs. 21–23 comes from the excavation field cards for the objects. Ex. 21 is noted as not having been kept; exs. 21 and 23 are each noted as having a "brick-mark" (maker's mark?) in their upper right hand corner. Copies of these cards were kindly supplied by K. Neumann, who informs me that the bricks were likely found in the 1930–31 excavation season.

Ex. 24 was found on the site of the palace by Shatha Almashadany and was handed over to the directorate of Nineveh.

The line arrangement is the same on all exemplars known, except for ex. 24, which has the text on four lines (with the third line of the master text split into two, following MAN ŠÚ). The master line follows ex. 6. As is the practice with RINAP, no score for this brick inscription is given on Oracc, but the minor variants are listed at the back of the book.

Z. Niederreiter (Iraq 70 [2008] pp. 77–78 and 85) notes that the brick with ex. 13 has the impression of a bull stamped on it, the one with ex. 14 has the figure of the head of an arrow (or spearhead) on it, and the one with ex. 20 has a figure in the form of an amulet on it.

Various references are made in the literature to bricks of Sargon II being found at Khorsabad that do not specify which Sargon inscription(s) was present. These are likely to be text nos. 50–55. See for example de Longpérier, Notice[3] p. 44 no. 46 (quite likely text no. 50); Frankfort, OIC 16 pp. 87 and 89 (Palace F); Loud and Altman, Khorsabad 2 p. 14 ("Bricks bearing identical inscriptions [text nos. 50–55] are employed in the construction of every building so far investigated. In the Nabu temple or in any of the several residences near or distant from the palace are therefore encountered innumerable bricks on which is stamped the ubiquitous inscription beginning 'Palace of Sargon ...'"); and Safar, Sumer 13 (1957) p. 220 (Temple of the Sebetti). See also Frankfort, OIC 16 p. 99 fig. 64 and Loud, Khorsabad 1 p. 104 fig. 111 (pavement in front of the chapel of Šamaš in the main palace).

BIBLIOGRAPHY

— Layard, MS A p. 320 (ex. 9 and others, copy)
1844 Botta, JA 4/4 pp. 313–314 (ex. 8, copy, study)
1849 Botta, Monument de Ninive 4 pl. 183 nos. 2–3 (exs. 7–8, copy)
1851 Layard, ICC pl. 82 [D.1] (ex. 9, copy)
1854 de Longpérier, Notice[3] nos. 45 and 47 (exs. 7–8, copy)
1859 Oppert, EM 2 pp. 328–329 (copy, edition, study)
1867 Place, Ninive et l'Assyrie 1 p. 228 (translation)
1874 Ménant, Annales p. 158 (translation)
1883 Descemet, Studi e documenti 4 p. 98 n. 3 (translation)
1886 Bezold, Literatur p. 93 §56.14c and d (exs. 7–9, study)
1889 Winckler, Sar. 1 p. 193; and 2 pl. 49 nos. 7a–b (exs. 7–9, copy, edition)
1907 Lehmann-Haupt, Mat. p. 48 no. 26 and fig. 23 (ex. 6, photo of squeeze, edition)
1907 Ungnad, VAS 1 no. 72 (ex. 6, copy)
1922 BM Guide p. 73 nos. 264–267 (exs. 1–2, 4–5, study)
1927 Luckenbill, ARAB 2 p. 68 §128 (translation)
1929 Thompson, Arch. 79 pp. 109 and 124, and pl. XLV no. 72 (exs. 10–11, copy, edition)
1931 Thompson, AAA 18 p. 100 (ex. 12, study)
1938 Loud and Altman, Khorsabad 2 p. 14 and pl. 65 top right (ex. 13, photo)
1962 Pillet, Pionnier p. 116, pl. XXIII fig. 27 upper row left, upper row middle, lower row left and lower row second from left, and pl. XXIV figs. 28–29 (exs. 14–19, photo [not all fully legible])
1981 Walker, CBI p. 117 no. 167 Sargon II C (exs. 1–5, transliteration)
1994 Chevalier and Lavédrine in Fontan, Khorsabad p. 204 fig. 7 and p. 284 (ex. 20, photo [partially illegible])
1994 Fuchs, Khorsabad pp. 286 and 372 no. 3.5.a (exs. 1–19, edition)
2008 Niederreiter, Iraq 70 pp. 77–78 I.a.10 (ex. 13, edition, study), and p. 85 IV.a.1 and IV.a.2 (ex. 14, translation; ex. 20, edition)
2015 Abdulkareem, Sumer 61 pp. 1–10 (ex. 24, photo, copy, edition, study)

TEXT

1) É.GAL ^{m}MAN-GIN
2) GAR ^{d}BAD NU.ÈŠ *aš-šur*
3) MAN *dan-nu* MAN ŠÚ MAN KUR AŠ

1–3) Palace of Sargon (II), appointee of the god Enlil, *nešakku*-priest of (the god) Aššur, strong king, king of the world, king of Assyria.

51

This short brick inscription of Sargon II has been found at both Khorsabad and Nineveh. The titulary employed for Sargon and the fact that the text records the construction of Dūr-Šarrukīn indicate that the inscription should date to 710 or later.

CATALOGUE

Ex.	Museum Number/ Source	Provenance	Dimensions (cm)	Lines Preserved	cpn
1	N 8075	Nineveh	43×41×7	1–4	c
2	Thompson, Arch. 79 pl. XLVI no. 115	Nineveh, surface	7.6 thick	1–4	n
3	A 25449	Khorsabad	42×40.5×7.8	1–4	c
4	A 39949	As ex. 3	40.8×41×7.3	1–4	p
5	A 169366	As ex. 3	41×41×8	1–4	c
6	A 169367	As ex. 3	40×40×8	1–4	c
7	A 169368	As ex. 3	41×41×8	1–4	c
8	A 169369	As ex. 3	42×42×8	1–4	c

COMMENTARY

The inscription is found on the face of the bricks and is inscribed, not stamped. The present location of ex. 2 is not known and the inscription on ex. 6 is badly worn. Information on the museum numbers and measurements of exs. 5–8 was provided by A. Dix. The master line follows ex. 1. No score is given on Oracc, but the minor variants are listed at the back of the book.

BIBLIOGRAPHY

1854 de Longpérier, Notice[3] no. 44 (ex. 1, study)
1889 Winckler, Sar. 1 p. 194; and 2 pl. 49 no. 8 (ex. 1, copy, edition)
1927 Luckenbill, ARAB 2 p. 68 §129 (ex. 1, translation)
1929 Thompson, Arch. 79 pl. XLVI no. 115 (ex. 2, copy)
1994 Fuchs, Khorsabad pp. 286 and 372 no. 3.5.b (exs. 1–2, edition)

TEXT

1) É.GAL ^{m}MAN-GIN MAN ŠÚ
2) MAN KUR AŠ GÌR.NÍTA KÁ.DINGIR.KI
3) MAN KUR EME.GI$_7$ *u* URI.KI
4) *e-piš* URU.BÀD-^{m}MAN-GIN

1–4) Palace of Sargon (II), king of the world, king of Assyria, governor of Babylon, king of the land of Sumer and Akkad, builder of the city Dūr-Šarrukīn.

52

This five-line brick inscription records the building of the city of Dūr-Šarrukīn and its palace.

CATALOGUE

Ex.	Museum Number/ Source	Excavation Number	Provenance	Dimensions (cm)	Lines Preserved	cpn
1	Loud, Khorsabad 1 p. 129 no. 2	—	Khorsabad, Palace, debris in Throne Room	—	1–5	n
2	AO 7380	—	Khorsabad	40.0×40.0×7.5	1–5	c
3	Institut de France sheet 355	—	Nahrawan	—	1–5	n
4	—	DŠ 34	Khorsabad, Palace, Throne Room (Court VII)	26×31×10	1–5	n

COMMENTARY

It is possible that ex. 1 and ex. 4 are the same brick since both were found by the American excavations in the throne room at Khorsabad and since the differences in the published copy of ex. 1 and the transliteration of ex. 4 on the excavation find card are relatively minor. Information on ex. 4 comes from that card for DŠ 34, kindly supplied by K. Neumann, who informs me that that brick was likely found in the 1930–31 excavation season. A note on that card states that a duplicate of the text was found in 1929 and that that exemplar had *ab-ni* preserved at the end of line 5, in contrast to ex. 4 (and also in contrast to the copy of ex. 1).

Ex. 3 is attested by a copy by P.E. Botta now preserved in the Archives of the Institut de France (Botta-Cotta II 2976 folio I, sheet number 355). A notation with the copy states that the inscription is "Sur le milieu d'une grande brique venant de Nahrawan à 6 heures de Mossul." The copy, if correct, would suggest that several of the sign forms on that exemplar are abnormal. A comparison of ex. 2 with Botta's copy of ex. 3 would suggest that they represent different exemplars.

The line arrangement is the same for all exemplars and the edition is a composite one. There are no variants and no score in given on Oracc.

BIBLIOGRAPHY

1936 Jacobsen in Loud, Khorsabad 1 p. 129 no. 2 (ex. 1, copy, edition)

1944 Meissner, ZDMG 98 p. 30 (ex. 1, edition)

1994 Fuchs, Khorsabad pp. 287 and 372 no. 3.5.d (ex. 1, edition)

TEXT

1) ^{m}LUGAL-GI.NA MAN ŠÚ MAN KUR *aš-šur*.KI
2) *i-na bi-bil* ŠÀ-*ia*$_5$ URU DÙ-*ma*
3) BÀD-^{m}MAN-GI.NA.KI MU-*šú ab-bi*
4) É.GAL *ta-aṣ-ba-ti šá i-na kib-*⌈*rat*⌉

1–5) I, Sargon (II), king of the world, king of Assyria, built a city in accordance with my heart's desire and named it Dūr-Šarrukīn. I built inside it a palace that was according to my wishes (and) that had no equal

4 The word *taṣbâtu* is attested only twice, here and in the Cuthean legend of Narām-Sîn. CAD T pp. 283–284 gives as the meaning of the word "wish (fulfilled), gratification" and translates the passage here as "a palace according to my wishes." AHw p. 1337 tentatively translates the word as "Wunscherfüllungen." See also Jacobsen in Loud, Khorsabad 1 p. 129 n. 2.

5) LÍMMU-*i* NU TUKU <<AŠ>> GABA.RI-*šá qé-reb-šú ab-*⸢*ni*⸣ — in the four quarters (of the world).

53

This five-line Sumerian inscription of Sargon II recording the building of the city of Dūr-Šarrukīn and its palace ("The-Palace-Which-Has-No-Equal") has been found on numerous bricks from Khorsabad, Nineveh, Nimrud, Karamles (ancient Kār-Mullissi), and Tepe Gawra.

CATALOGUE

Ex.	Museum Number/ Source	Excavation/ Registration No.	Provenance	Dimensions (cm)	Lines Preserved	cpn
1	BM 90232	1979-12-20,139	—	34×33.5×11	1–5	n
2	BM 90233	1979-12-20,140	—	32.5×32.5	1–5	n
3	BM 90235	1979-12-20,142	—	19×15×11	1–3	n
4	BM 90236	1979-12-20,143	—	34×33×12	1–5	n
5	BM 90237	48-11-4,36	Karamles	32×32×11	1–5	n
6	BM 90274	1979-12-20,167	—	23.5×15.5×10.5	1–5	n
7	BM 90359	1979-12-20,212	—	19×23×10	1–5	n
8	BM 90361	1979-12-20,213	—	23×14.5×8.5	1–5	n
9	BM 90748	1979-12-20,335	—	13.5×12×11	2–4	n
10	BM 90750 + BM 90803	1979-12-20,336	—	27.5×22.5×11	1–5	n
11	BM Add. MS. 30413 fol. 35	—	—	—	1–5	n
12	Botta, Monument de Ninive 4 pl. 183^c no. 5	—	Khorsabad	—	1–5	n
13	Louvre —	—	Khorsabad	—	1–5	c
14	Louvre —	—	Khorsabad	34×34.0×12	1–5	c
15	Louvre —	—	Khorsabad	32.5×32.5×10.5	1–5	c
16	Louvre —	—	Khorsabad	32.5×32.5×11	1–5	c
17	Louvre —	—	Khorsabad	32.5×33×10.5	1–5	c
18	Lehmann-Haupt, Mat. pp. 48–49 no. 27 and fig. 24	—	Khorsabad	—	1–5	p
19	As ex. 18 p. 49 no. 28 and fig. 25	—	—	—	1–5	p
20	Thompson, Arch. 79 pl. XLVI no. 122	—	Nineveh, Temple of Nabû, XX B 13 (pit)	10.8 thick	1–5	n
21	Thompson, AAA 18 pl. XIX no. 37	—	Nineveh, fields south of Nebi Yunus	—	1–5	n
22	Museo Gregoriano Egizio (Vatican) 15025	—	Khorsabad	35×35	1–5	p
23	Pillet, Pionnier pl. XXIII fig. 27 upper row right	—	Possibly Khorsabad	—	1–5	n

52 line 5 Based on the published information on exs. 1 and 3–4 and on examination of ex. 2, each exemplar appears to have the extraneous wedge after TUK. The name of the palace is "The Palace That Has No Equal"; see text no. 2 line 473, text no. 7 line 159, and the note to text no. 53 line 4.

24	Scott and MacGinnis, Iraq 52 (1990) pl. Xa	—	Nineveh, Nebi Yunus	—	1–5	p
25	As ex. 24 pl. Xb (upper left)	—	As ex. 24	—	1–5	p
26	As ex. 24 pl. Xb (upper right)	—	As ex. 24	—	1–5	p
27	As ex. 24 pl. Xb (lower left)	—	As ex. 24	—	1–5	p
28	UM 37-16-8	G 6-604A	Tepe Gawra, Northeast Base	35×35.5×12	1–5	c
29	Wheaton College Archaeology Museum, Joseph P. Free collection	—	—	—	1–5	n
30	Private collection	—	—	—	1–5	p
31	IM —	ND 2050	Nimrud, found in Burnt Palace room XII, loose	33×33×11	1–5	n
32	—	DŠ 31	Khorsabad, Palace, Throne Room (Court VII)	25×30×10	1–5	n
33	—	DŠ 32	Khorsabad, in city gate 7	24×20×10	2–5	n
34	—	DŠ 33	As ex. 32	27×26×1	1–5	n
35	—	DŠ 40	See commentary	17×21×10	2–4	n
36	BM 92192	N 2003 (London)	Nimrud, North-West Palace	10.6×12.07×8.89	2–4	p

COMMENTARY

Additional information on exs. 1–10 was provided by C.B.F. Walker. The exemplars found in the British Museum (exs. 1–10) are impressed with a stamp measuring 10.2/9.2×22.8/20.6 cm. Walker (CBI p. 118) notes that "George Smith's note-book of his 1873 excavations (Add. MS. 30413 fol. 35) has a copy of a broken duplicate (beginnings of lines 3–5 lost) which is not in the British Museum." This is treated as ex. 11. Walker (CBI p. 117) notes that although the brick published by A.H. Layard as ICC pl. 82 [D] is said to come from Karamles and to have both this inscription and text no. 50 on it, no brick in the British Museum has both inscriptions. The only brick in the British Museum registered as coming from Karamles is BM 90237, which does come from Layard's work in Iraq. It is assumed here that BM 90237 (ex. 5) is the brick copied by Layard. Two copies of this inscription (one damaged and one complete) are found in Layard MS A p. 320 and labeled as being from Karamles.

Ex. 12 is only known from P.E. Botta's copy in Monument de Ninive (4 pl. 183[c] no. 5). A copy by Botta of this inscription is also found in the Archives of the Institut de Fance (Botta-Cotta II 2976, folio I, sheet 315), but it depicts an exemplar less well preserved than ex. 12 and is not taken into consideration here. Exs. 13–17 are reported to be N 8069–73 in the Louvre, but it is not clear which exemplar has which particular museum number.

Ex. 19 is in a museum in Tiflis (Tbilisi) according to C.F. Lehmann-Haupt (Mat. p. 49 no. 28).

It is possible that ex. 23 (known via a photograph taken by G. Tranchard published by M. Pillet) is to be identified with one of the bricks in the Louvre (exs. 13–17). It may come from Khorsabad since it derives from the work of Place.

Exs. 24–27 were found during excavations at Nebi Yunus in 1954, but their exact findspots are not known; see Scott and MacGinnis, Iraq 52 (1990) pp. 65–66. Ex. 28 was collated by J. Novotny.

Ex. 30, which is a private collection, is said to come from Khorsabad (Cogan, Bound for Exile p. 48), but that provenance may simply based upon the fact that the text deals with work at that city.

The Nimrud field catalogue states that ND 2050 (ex. 31), as well as some unregistered duplicate fragments, have a Sumerian inscription of Sargon "recording his building of the Palace at Khorsabad: duplicate of published inscription." This text is the only inscription which fits this description. The field catalogue also states that the brick was baked and had one edge glazed (information courtesy J.N. Postgate).

Information on exs. 32–35 comes from the excavation field cards for the objects. Exs. 32 and 33 are noted as not having been kept, and ex. 35 has "In town office building" in the section for where the brick was found. Copies of these cards were kindly supplied by K. Neumann, who informs me that the bricks were likely discovered during the 1930–31 excavation season. The transliterations on the cards have DIM instead of DÍM in line 5, but this is assumed to be an error here (or a different understanding of which sign is DIM).

According to British Museum records, BM 92182 was found in the North-West Palace at Nimrud, possibly by A.H. Layard. The piece has a glazed rosette (remains of five white petals around a yellow center on a blue background) on one side and the inscription stamped on another side. The piece is currently listed under the numbers BM 92182 and BM 92192 on the British Museum website (August, 2019), with the latter number indicating that the piece may have come from Khorsabad. According to J. Taylor, the correct number for the piece is BM 92182.

The two exemplars from Nimrud (exs. 31 and 36) each have one edge glazed. A copy of a brick with this inscription reportedly discovered at Nimrud (SE corner of the tell?) is found in Layard's notebook MS A p. 322 (Department of the Middle East, British Museum). That copy appears to have been poorly executed and is not taken into consideration here.

The copies of Botta, Layard, A. Amiaud, P. Jensen, H. Winckler, and R. Campbell Thompson indicate that the forms of several signs are somewhat abnormal (variously line 1: GI, LUGAL, KI, and ŠÁR; line 2: GIN; line 3: MU, BÍ, IN, and SA_4; line 4: GAL and TUK; and line 5: TA, MU, UN, and DÍM). These have not been noted as variants. Winckler notes that some exemplars have KU for KI in line 1; however, it is more likely that the signs are simply poorly copied and/or misread. For ex. 22, A. Pohl (RPARA 19 copy and transliteration) has bí-in-na-sa_4-a in line 3, but the photo of the original shows the piece has the expected bí-in-sa_4-a. The transliteration of ex. 29 published in NABU 2010 erroneously omits the masculine determinative at the beginning of the first line (collation courtesy A. Miglio). There are no variants for this inscription and no score is provided on Oracc.

BIBLIOGRAPHY

1849 Botta, Monument de Ninive 4 pl. 183 no. 5 (ex. 12 copy)

1851 Layard, ICC pl. 82 [D.2] (ex. 5, copy)

1854 de Longpérier, Notice[3] nos. 38–42 (exs. 13–17, copy)

1886 Bezold, Literatur pp. 93–94 §56.14d and l (exs. 5 and 12, study)

1887 Amiaud, ZA 2 p. 346 (exs. 13–17, copy, study)

1887 Jensen, ZA 2 pp. 213–214 (ex. 5, copy, edition)

1887 Lehmann, ZA 2 pp. 450–451 no. 2 (exs. 13–17, study)

1889 Winckler, Sar. 1 p. 193; and 2 pl. 49 no. 6 (exs. 12–17, six of exs. 1–10, copy, edition)

1898 Belck and Lehmann, ZA 13 p. 309 (ex. 19, study)

1902 Marucchi, Catalogo Vaticano pp. 338–339 no. 20 (study)

1904 Peiser, OLZ 7 col. 9 and n. 2 (ex. 22, study)

1907 Lehmann-Haupt, Mat. pp. 48–49 nos. 27–28 and figs. 24–25 (exs. 18–19, photo, study)

1922 BM Guide pp. 72–73 nos. 253–258 (exs. 1–6, study)

1927 Luckenbill, ARAB 2 p. 67 §127a (translation)

1929 Thompson, Arch. 79 pl. XLVI no. 122 (ex. 20, copy)

1931 Thompson, AAA 18 pl. XIX no. 37 (ex. 21, copy)

1942–43 Pohl, RPARA 19 pp. 247–251 no. 17 (ex. 22, copy, edition)

1962 Pillet, Pionnier p. 116 and pl. XXIII fig. 27 upper row right (ex. 23, photo [mostly illegible])

1981 Walker, CBI p. 118 no. 168 Sargon II D (exs. 1–11, transliteration)

1985 Behrens, JCS 37 p. 243 no. 77 (ex. 28, study; erroneously cited as UM 32-22-6, which is in fact a brick of Sennacherib [Grayson and Novotny, RINAP 3/2 pp. 135–137 no. 92])

1990 Scott and MacGinnis, Iraq 52 pp. 65–66 and 72–73, and pls. Xa-b (exs. 24, 25 [upper left], 26 [upper right], 27 [lower left], photo, edition)

1994 Fuchs, Khorsabad pp. 286 and 372 no. 3.5.c (exs. 1-27, edition)

1995 Cagni in Dolce and Nota Santi, Dai Palazzi Assiri pp. 290–91 no. 67 and fig. 136 (ex. 22, photo, study)

2010 Miglio, NABU 2010 pp. 104–105 no. 86 (ex. 29, edition)

2013 Cogan, Bound for Exile p. 48 fig. 12 (ex. 30, photo, translation)

TEXT

1) ^{m}MAN-GI.NA lugal ki-šár-ra
2) uru an-dù URU.BÀD-MAN-GIN
3) mu-bi bí-in-sa_4-a
4) é-gal-bi gaba-ri nu-tuku
5) šà-bi-ta mu-un-na-dím

1–5) Sargon (II), king of the world, built a city (and) named it Dūr-Šarrukīn. He constructed inside it its palace that has no equal.

2–3 In view of the *-a* at the end of line 3, we should possibly take these lines as a subordinate clause and translate them as "who built a city (and) named it Dūr-Šarrukīn." The current translation assumes that the scribe had in mind such Akkadian passages as text nos. 52 lines 2b–3 and 54 lines 2–3a.

4 é-gal-bi gaba-ri nu-tuku "its palace that has no equal": Or take this as the name of the palace, as in text no. 2 line 473 and text no. 7 line 159, which have the name written as *é-gal-gaba-ri-nu-tuku-a* ("Palace That Has No Equal"). Cf. also text no. 52 lines 4–5.

54

The building of the city of Dūr-Šarrukīn and the construction of a temple for the gods Sîn and Šamaš are recorded on this inscription of Sargon II. Bricks with this inscription have been found at Khorsabad, Nineveh, and Nimrud; the ones from Nineveh and Nimrud may have been taken there from Khorsabad when Sennacherib moved the capital following the death of Sargon (Scott and MacGinnis, Iraq 52 [1990] p. 65). The inscription may refer to the chapels of Sîn and Šamaš in the royal palace at Khorsabad rather than to an independent temple (see also text nos. 18, 21, and 55).

CATALOGUE

Ex.	Museum Number/ Source	Excavation/ Registration No.	Provenance	Dimensions (cm)	Lines Preserved	cpn
1	BM 90245	1979-12-20,150	—	32.5×32×11	1–5	n
2	BM 90450 + BM 90451	1979-12-20,257	—	22×16×9	1–5	n
3	BM 102464	1907-7-12,2	—	32×32×12	1–5	n
4	Scott and MacGinnis, Iraq 52 (1990) pl. Xb lower row right	—	Nineveh, Nebi Yunus	—	1–5	p
5	Institut de France sheet 315	—	Khorsabad	—	1–5	n
6	IM —	ND 2051	Nimrud, BP XII loose	31×23×10	1–5	n
7	—	DŠ 38	Khorsabad, Palace, Throne Room (Court VII)	27×21×9	1–5	n

COMMENTARY

Exs. 1 and 3 are inscribed on the face, while ex. 2 is stamped on the face with a stamp measuring 10.5×21 cm. Additional information on exs. 1–3 was provided by C.B.F. Walker. H. Winckler states that he made his copy of this inscription from an original in London (Sar. 1 p. 194); Walker (CBI p. 117) identifies this original with BM 90245 (ex. 1).

Ex. 5 is known from a copy by P.E. Botta preserved in the Archives of the Institut de France (Botta-Cotta II 2976, folio I, sheet 315). The copy would suggest that a number of the signs on that exemplar are defective in form.

The unpublished Nimrud field catalogue states that ND 2051 (ex. 6), as well as duplicate fragments, has an Akkadian inscription of Sargon "recording his building of Dur-Sharrukin (Khorsabad) and the temples of the gods Sin and Shamash there: duplicate of published inscription" (information courtesy J.N. Postgate). This inscription is the only text that fits that description.

Ex. 7 was likely found during the Oriental Institute's 1930–31 excavation season and is known from the excavation field card for the piece, a copy of which was kindly supplied by K. Neumann.

Winckler's copy of ex. 1 indicates that the form of 30 in line 3 is abnormal and looks more like GAM; however, Walker does not note this with regard to any of the bricks in the British Museum. A copy of a brick with this inscription reportedly discovered in debris of the Nabû temple is found in L.W. King's notebook "Kuyunjik: Notes on Sculpture & Inscriptions" (Department of the Middle East, British Museum) and has a GAL sign in place of ŠÚ in line 1. The copy, however, has shading over the GAL and thus likely simply indicates that King was unable to read the sign and assumed that it was GAL.

No variants to the inscription are known and no score for this brick inscription is provided on Oracc.

BIBLIOGRAPHY

1889 Winckler, Sar. 1 pp. 194–195; and 2 pl. 49 no. 10 (ex. 1, copy, edition)

1921 Bezold, Studies Lehmann-Haupt p. 116 no. 6 (ex. 1, transliteration)

1922 BM Guide p. 73 nos. 259–260 (exs. 1, 3, study)

1927 Luckenbill, ARAB 2 p. 68 §131 (ex. 1, translation)

1981 Walker, CBI p. 117 no. 166 Sargon II A (exs. 1–3, transliteration)

1990 Scott and MacGinnis, Iraq 52 pp. 65–66, 73 and pl. Xb lower row right (ex. 4, photo, edition)

1994 Fuchs, Khorsabad pp. 287 and 372 no. 3.5.e (exs. 1–4, edition)

TEXT

1) ^{m}MAN-GIN MAN ŠÚ MAN KUR AŠ
2) URU DÙ-*ma* BÀD-MAN-GIN
3) MU-*šú ab-bi šu-bat* ^{d}30
4) ^{d}UTU *ana* TI-*a* GIN BALA-*a*
5) *qé-reb-šú lu ab-ni*

1–5) I, Sargon (II), king of the world, king of Assyria, built a city and named it Dūr-Šarrukīn. For the sake of my life (and for) the firm establishment of my reign, I built inside it an abode for the gods Sîn (and) Šamaš.

55

This brick inscription of Sargon II records the building of a temple to the gods Sîn and Šamaš inside the city Dūr-Šarrukīn. It is found on two bricks, one from Khorsabad and one from Nineveh.

CATALOGUE

Ex.	Museum Number/ Source	Provenance	Dimensions (cm)	Botta, MdN	Lines Preserved	cpn
1	N 8074	Khorsabad	32.5×32.5×11.8	4 pl. 183^{c} no. 4	1–7	c
2	Thompson, Arch. 79 pl. XLV no. 80	Nineveh, Temple of Nabû, XXVIII 12	10.8 thick	—	1–7	n

COMMENTARY

P.E. Botta's copy of ex. 1 indicates that several of the sign forms are abnormal or incorrect, but collation of the exemplar indicated that these signs were either correct or slightly damaged. The line arrangement is the same for both exemplars and the master line is a conflation of the two.

According to Winckler, Sar. 1 p. 194, there is a brick with this inscription in London; however, no such brick was found by C.B.F. Walker in the British Museum.

No score for this brick inscription is given on Oracc, but the variants are listed at the back of the book.

BIBLIOGRAPHY

1849 Botta, Monument de Ninive 4 pl. 183 no. 4 (ex. 1, copy)
1854 de Longpérier, Notice^{3} no. 43 (ex. 1, copy)
1859 Oppert, EM 2 pp. 330–333 (copy, edition, study)
1873 Lenormant, Choix no. 75 (ex. 1, copy)
1874 Ménant, Annales p. 198 (ex. 1, translation)
1886 Bezold, Literatur p. 93 §56.14b (ex. 1, study)
1889 Winckler, Sar. 1 p. 194; and 2 pl. 49 no. 9 (ex. 1, copy, edition)
1927 Luckenbill, ARAB 2 p. 68 §130 (ex. 1, translation)
1929 Thompson, Arch. 79 p. 124 and pl. XLV no. 80 (ex. 2, copy, edition)
1956 Borger, Asarh. p. 120, commentary to 80-7-19,44 rev. 15 (line 5, study)
1994 Fuchs, Khorsabad pp. 287 and 372 no. 3.5.f (exs. 1–2, edition)

TEXT

1) ^{m}MAN-GIN MAN ŠÚ MAN KUR *aš-šur*.KI
2) É ^{d}30 ^{d}UTU EN.MEŠ-*šú*
3) *šá* ŠÀ URU.BÀD-^{m}MAN-GIN
4) TA UŠ$_{8}$-*šú a-di gaba-dib-bi-šú*
5) *ana* TI-*šú* GIN BALA.MEŠ-*šú*
6) SI.SÁ *e-bur* KUR *aš-šur*.KI
7) *šá-lam* KUR *aš-šur* DÙ-*uš*

1–7) Sargon (II), king of the world, king of Assyria, built the temple of the gods Sîn (and) Šamaš, his lords, that is inside the city Dūr-Šarrukīn from its foundations to its crenellations (5) for the sake of his life, the firm establishment of his reign, the success of the harvest of Assyria, (and) the well-being of Assyria.

56

The Khorsabad excavation field card in the Oriental Institute (Chicago) for DŠ 39 records an inscribed brick found in city gate 7. The card has a copy of the cuneiform text on the brick; however, the inscription was either badly written or badly copied and thus the edition given here must be considered tentative. The inscription does not appear to be a duplicate of any other known brick inscription of Sargon II. Information on the brick was kindly supplied by K. Neumann, who states that the brick was probably found during the Oriental Institute's 1930–31 excavation season.

CATALOGUE

Museum Number	Excavation Number	Provenance	Dimensions (cm)	cpn
—	DŠ 39	Khorsabad, city gate 7	36×36×9	n

TEXT

1) É.GAL ^{m}MAN-⸢GIN⸣ [...]
2) MAN KUR <<*x*>> *aš-šur*.KI$^{?}$ [...]
3) *šá*$^{?}$ *qé*$^{?}$*-reb* URU.⸢BÀD$^{?}$-$^{m?}$LUGAL$^{?}$⸣-[GIN$^{?}$ ...]

1–3) Palace of Sargo[n (II), ...], king of Assyria, [...] *that is inside* the city *Dūr*-[*Šar*]*ru*[*kīn* ...]

57

Several fragments of glazed bricks that preserve all or parts of one or more signs have been found at Khorsabad. No complete inscription can be determined and it is likely that they represent parts of more than one inscription.

CATALOGUE

Frgm.	Museum Number	Excavation/ Registration No.	Provenance	Dimensions (cm)	cpn
A	Louvre —	Nap. III 2924	Khorsabad	—	n
B	N 8093	Nap. III 2925	As Frgm. A	—	c
C	N 8091	—	Probably Khorsabad	—	c
D	N 8092	—	As Frgm. C	—	c
E	N 8094	—	As Frgm. C	—	c
F	N 8095	—	As Frgm. C	—	c
G	N 8096	—	As Frgm. C	—	c
H	N 8097	—	As Frgm. C	—	c
I	N 8089	—	As Frgm. C	—	c
J	N 8090	—	As Frgm. C	—	c
K	OI —	DŠ 5	Khorsabad, Palace, NW end of Court VII (Throne Room)	—	n
L	OI —	DŠ 89	Khorsabad, Palace F, trench M	—	n
M	A 11807	DŠ 88a+b	As Frgm. L	24.5×17.5×9	c

COMMENTARY

Pieces of several glazed bricks from Khorsabad with cuneiform characters are known and these have been gathered here. It is unlikely, however, that they come from only one inscription since some bricks have one line of characters in white glaze (Frgms. I–J) while others have two lines of smaller characters in yellow glaze (Frgms. B–H, and possibly A), and since Frgm. K was found in Sargon's palace at Khorsabad, while Frgms. L–M come from Palace F at that site.

Frgms. A–B: These two pieces were found by P.E. Botta (Monument de Ninive 2 pl. 156 nos. 11 [Nap. III 2924] and 9 [Nap. III 2925] respectively). (These are cited as Inv. Nap. 2994 and 2995 in Albenda, Palace of Sargon p. 113.) Each has traces of two lines of characters, those of frgm. A being white on a green background and those of Frgm. B being yellow on a green background.

Frgms. C–H: Each fragment has traces of two lines of yellow characters on a green background. Most or all of Frgms. C–H are likely to be identified with de Longpérier, Notice[3] nos. 61–67.

Frgms. I–J: These fragments have a single line of white characters on a green background and are likely to be identified with de Longpérier, Notice[3] nos. 59–60.

Frgm. K: The fragment was found on February 3, 1931. The signs are reported to be in yellow on a light blue background and the transliteration is based on a copy of the text on the excavation catalogue card for the piece in the Oriental Institute. See also Walker in Albenda, Palace of Sargon p. 113.

Frgm. L: The fragment has traces of a single sign and was found on March 26, 1931. The transliteration is based on a copy of the text on the excavation field card for the piece in the Oriental Institute. See also Walker in Albenda, Palace of Sargon p. 113 n. 37.

Frgm. M: This fragment of a glazed brick has white signs on a blue-green background. The piece was found on March 25, 1931. The transliteration is based on examination of the fragment in 2012 and on a copy of the text on the excavation catalogue card. The fragment no longer preserves the trace of the first sign indicated on the copy.

At least two pieces were given the number DŠ 5 by the Oriental Institute archaeologists at Khorsabad. One is Frgm. K and the other is a nail that has the Oriental Institute number A 7067. Information on Frgm. M and on Frgms. K–L that is not found in Albenda, Palace of Sargon was kindly provided by K. Neumann. C.B.F. Walker (in Albenda, Palace of Sargon p. 113) suggests that the throne room, where Frgm. K was found, may also have been the original location of Frgms. A and B. V. Place refers to having found glazed bricks and glazed inscriptions mixed in the debris at Khorsabad (Ninive et l'Assyrie 1 pp. 89 and 233–234; and 2 p. 86). Frgms. C–J are likely some of these.

With regard to the fragments in the Louvre having two lines, de Longpérier, Notice[3] sub nos. 61–67 noted the presence of two geographical names: Media (KUR.*ma-da-a-a*) and an incomplete name which might be "Amardi de l'Atropatène." The former place may have been found on Frgm. H, where the trace of the sign at the end of the second line could be the beginning of DA (i.e., KUR.*ma*-⸢*da*⸣-[*a-a*]). Possibly the Amatti (Hamath) on Frgm. C is the "Amardi" of de Longpérier.

Since the inscription(s) would have run across several bricks it is assumed in the transliteration below that each fragment (except Frgm. D) was continuing the inscription from a previous brick and that the inscription continued onto another brick. Frgm. D likely preserves the beginning of an inscription since there is some decoration on the brick to the left of the cuneiform signs and since numerous other royal inscriptions of Sargon begin with "Palace of Sargon ..." (e.g., text no. 8).

BIBLIOGRAPHY

1849 Botta, Monument de Ninive 2 pl. 156 nos. 9 and 11 (Frgms. A–B, drawing)

1850 Botta, Monument de Ninive 5 p. 171 (Frgms. A–B, study)

1854 de Longpérier, Notice[3] nos. 59–67 (Frgms. B–J$^{?}$, study)

1986 Albenda, Palace of Sargon pp. 113–114 nos. 11–12, p. 153, and pl. 151 nos. 9 and 11 (Frgms. A–B, drawing; Frgms. A–B, K–L, study [by Walker])

1995 Reade in Caubet, Khorsabad p. 247 fig. 10 (Frgm. B, drawing)

TEXT

Fragment A

1) [...] *x* [(*x*)] *x x* [...]
2) [...] *x* [(*x*)] *x* [...]

Fragment B

1) [...] IM ḪA *x* ⸢ÁŠ$^{?}$⸣ MA [...]
2) [... URU].⸢*ḫar-ḫar**⸣ *mu-si*-[...]

Fragment C

1) [...] ⸢d$^{?}$⸣*a*-⸢*šur* MAN *dan*$^{?}$-*nu*$^{?}$⸣ [...]
2) [...] (*x*) KUR.⸢*a*⸣-*ma-at-ti* [...]

Fragment D

1) É.⸢GAL⸣ ^{m}[LUGAL-GIN ...]
2) *mi-gir* DINGIR.[MEŠ GAL.MEŠ ...]

Fragment E

1) [...]-⸢*ti*⸣-*ia* [...]
2) [...] *x* E SI [...]

Fragment F

1) [...] *i-na qer-bi x* [...]
2) [...] ḪA UGU [...]

Fragment A

Frgm. A 1–2) No translation possible.

Fragment B

Frgm. B 1–2) [...] ... [... the city] Ḫarḫar ... [...]

Fragment C

Frgm. C 1–2) [...] *the god* Aššur, *strong* king [...] land Hamath [...]

Fragment D

Frgm. D 1–2) Palace of [Sargon (II) ...] favorite of the [great] god[s ...]

Fragment E

Frgm. E 1–2) [...] my [...] ... [...]

Fragment F

Frgm. F 1–2) [...] inside [...] upon [...]

Frgm. B line 1 Possibly *im-ḫa*-⸢*ṣu*$^{?}$⸣-*ma*, "they smote and."
Frgm. B line 2 -*ḫar**: Copy by P.E. Botta has -ḪI-PA. Ḫarḫar appears as an epigraph on a wall relief from Room II of Sargon's palace at Khorsabad (text no. 23).

Fragment G

1) [...] *x* ⸢AB?⸣ *x* [...]
2) [...] *x* SI ⸢IḪ⸣ [...]

Fragment G

Frgm. G 1–2) No translation possible.

Fragment H

1) [...] SA A *x* [...]
2) [...] KUR.*ma-x* [...]

Fragment H

Frgm. H 1–2) [...] ... [...] the land Ma... [...]

Fragment I

1) [...] *x* ⸢UŠ?⸣ [...]

Fragment I

Frgm. I 1) No translation possible.

Fragment J

1) [...] ⸢mLUGAL-GIN?⸣ [...]

Fragment J

Frgm. J 1) [...] *Sarg[on* ...]

Fragment K

1) [...] *re-eš* [(...)]
2) [...] *x* ⸢IM/'*u*⸣ [(...)]

Fragment K

Frgm. K 1–2) [...] *head* [...] ... [(...)]

Fragment L

1) [...] ⸢ḪI⸣ [...]

Fragment L

Frgm. L 1) No translation possible.

Fragment M

1) [...] *x* LUGAL *x* [...]

Fragment M

Frgm. M 1) [...] king [...]

58

In an inscription on some clay prisms from the reign of Esarhaddon (Leichty, RINAP 4 pp. 200–201 no. 104 vii 10–12) is the phrase *lumāšē tamšīl šiṭir šumīya ēsiq*, which E. Leichty translates as "I depicted hieroglyphs representing the writing of my name." This passage has been understood by many scholars to refer to figures/symbols that are found upon three clay prisms and one stone monument of Esarhaddon; they are taken to be a cryptographic writing of the royal name Esarhaddon and some of his titles/epithets. Thus, those symbols have been interpreted to be Assyrian hieroglyphs or astroglyphs and to have been possibly influenced by Egyptian hieroglyphs. For possible interpretations of the symbols, see Leichty, RINAP 4 pp. 238–243 no. 115. (For the connection of some of the various figures with particular constellations, see for example Miglus, Studies Hrouda p. 189.) Beginning with C.J. Gadd in 1948 (Ideas of Divine Rule pp. 93–95), a series of figures depicted on glazed brick friezes at Khorsabad have similarly been interpreted to be a cryptographic writing of the name and title(s) of Sargon II. The friezes are found on both sides of some major doorways in the chapels of the deities Sîn, Šamaš, and Ningal within Sargon's palace complex and in the temple of Nabû.

In addition to these glazed brick friezes, there are nineteen fragments of bronze bands/fittings from sanctuaries at Khorsabad that have depictions of various figures (e.g., lions, bulls, fig trees, ploughs, bulls, bull-men, fish-men, and men holding spears) and some of these may have been used to indicate the name and titles of Sargon (see in particular Miglus, Studies Hrouda, pp. 182–183; Finkel and Reade, ZA 86 [1996] pp. 251–253 and 267–268 figs. 3–5;

57 Frgm. M line 1 The trace after LUGAL would fit ⸢KAL⸣ or ⸢*dan*⸣-[*nu*], among various other possibilities.

J.E. Curtis in Curtis and Tallis, Balawat Gates pp. 79–81; Guralnick, CRRAI 51 pp. 389–404; and Niederreiter, Iraq 70 [2008] p. 58 fig. 7 and p. 80 I.d.6–8). L. Morenz (AoF 30 [2003] pp. 24–25) has suggested that the representations on the royal throne of Sargon may also have represented the king's name. The ends of two prisms of Sargon II (text no. 82 and text no. 63) have symbols cut or impressed onto them, but I. Finkel and J.E. Reade suggest that it is "more probable that the ... designs were related to the identities of the gods for whose temples the prisms were made" rather than being "hieroglyphs" (ZA 86 [1996] pp. 246–247 and figs. 7–8 following p. 268). Note also the image of a lion on several vases (text no. 77), a scorpion on a gold bowl and an electrum mirror of the queen Atalia (text no. 2001 exs. 1 and 3), and a dromedary and an omega on the macehead of Sargon's brother Sîn-aḫu-uṣur (text no. 2003).

TEXT A EXEMPLARS

Ex.	Provenance	cpn
1	Khorsabad, palace complex, Court XXVII, façade of the chapel of the god Sîn, m (left of Entrance Z)	n
2	As ex. 1, but right of Entrance Z	n
3	Khorsabad, Palace Complex, Court XXVII, façade of the chapel of the god Šamaš, n (left of Entrance Z′′)	n
4	As ex. 3, but right of Entrance Z′′	n
5	Khorsabad, Nabû temple, Court II, façade to left of entrance to Room 19	n
6	As ex. 5, but right of entrance to Room 19	n

TEXT B EXEMPLARS

Ex.	Provenance	cpn
7	Khorsabad, Palace Complex, Court XXXI, façade of the chapel of the goddess Ningal, left of Entrance L	n
8	As ex. 7, but right of Entrance L	n
9	Khorsabad, Nabû temple, Court I, façade to left of entrance to Room 13	n
10	As ex. 9, but right of entrance to Room 13	n

COMMENTARY

These "inscriptions" are located in pairs, on the façades of platforms that jut out on each side of a major doorway, and are "read" beginning at the doorway and then going either left or right. Thus each inscription of a pair is in effect a mirror image of the other. The condition of the individual reliefs when first found appears to have varied a great deal and for the most part all that we know about these glazed brick reliefs comes from general statements about what was found, a few partial and/or unclear photographs, and, most importantly, the drawings published by V. Place.

It has also been stated that there was a wall painting with similar figures in the cella of the chapel of the god Adad in the palace complex (Room 166; see in particular Place, Ninive et l'Assyrie 1 p. 128 and 3 pl. 25 no. 5, but the information on this is somewhat unclear and Place states that the reconstructed drawing of the figures was based upon the glazed brick panels. Thus, it will not be dealt with here.

Inscription A is made up of seven symbols in the following order: a king (1), a lion (2), a bird (3), a bull (4), a fig tree (5), a plough (6), and a man holding a spear pointed towards the ground (7). Inscription B is a shorter variant of this, omitting the third and fourth symbols (bird and bull). In each case, the first symbol (king) and the last symbol (man holding a spear) are located on opposite sides of a platform, with the remaining symbols on the front of the platform. (The king faces into the chapel, towards the cella, and the man holding a spear faces toward the courtyard.) Thus, if one looked at a platform directly from the front, one would not see the first and last symbols of an "inscription." In addition, as pointed out by A. Zgoll and M. Roaf, the figures on the front of a platform are placed within a frame of rosettes, in effect separating them from what is on the sides. As a result, some scholars (e.g., Reade [1979]; Zgoll and Roaf; and E. Frahm) do not consider the first and last symbols, or perhaps just the last symbol, to be part of the "inscription," although Zgoll and Roaf do take the first symbol, the image of the king, to stand for the king and thus "Sargon." In 1979, J.E. Reade suggested that the man with the spear might represent one of Sargon's earlier namesakes (Larsen, Power and Propaganda p. 342), although he later appears to have changed his mind about this.

J.E. Reade (in Caubet, Khorsabad pp. 234–236) was perhaps the first to offer a real interpretation of these figures/symbol, but more recently, several scholars have proposed various different interpretations. These interpretations seek to identify the symbols with Akkadian words or with the signs of the underlying cuneiform script. In general, scholars think that the lion (2) and bull (4) both stand for "king" (*šarru*), since both animals appear as symbols of royalty and strength in Mesopotamian texts, with the kings sometimes called a wild bull (*rīmu*) or a lion (*labbu*); see in particular Roaf and Zgoll, ZA 91 (2001) pp. 277–280 and Watanabe, Animal Symbolism, particularly pp. 42–68. Note also the presence of the figure of the lion on the Assyrian royal seal and on several objects with inscriptions of Sargon (see for example text no. 77). The view that the lion and the bull have the same meaning might be supported by the the fact that A has a bull before the fig tree while B has a lion before the fig tree; see also Leichty, RINAP 4 no. 115 ex. 1 versus exs. 2–4 for the animal placed before the image of a mountain. There is also a general assumption that the final title is "king of Assyria" ("king of the land of Aššur"). The interpretations (and reasoning for similar interpretations) of the other symbols can vary. For full explanations of the various proposals, see the relevant items listed in the Bibliography.

In the past, the symbols have also been thought to be divine symbols (e.g., the lion for the goddess Ištar and the bull for the god Adad); see for example Unger, RLA 2/4 (1936) p. 252.

For a study of the analysis and conservation of the bricks in the façade of the chapel of the god Sîn, see Whyte, Muros, and Barack in Greene and Griffin, Proceedings OSG 32 pp. 172–189. For a study of Assyrian bricks with high relief from Nineveh that might have a rebus writing for the name Esarhaddon, see Nadali, Iraq 70 (2008) pp. 87–104.

BIBLIOGRAPHY

1867 Place, Ninive et l'Assyrie 1 pp. 115–120, 125–127, and 135 (exs. 1–4, 7–8, study); and 3 pls. 23–24 and 26–31 (exs. 1–2, drawings)

1933 Frankfort, OIC 16 pp. 97–98 and 100 (exs. 1–4, study)

1934 Frankfort, OIC 17 p. 84 (exs. 1–2, study)

1936 Loud, Khorsabad 1 pp. 90–97, 102–104, and 110–112, and figs. 99–100, 104–106, 110, and 115–115 (exs. 1–2, 4, photo; exs. 1–2, 7–8, drawing; exs. 1–4, 7–8, study, provenance)

1938 Loud and Altman, Khorsabad 2 pp. 41–42, 59 and 61, and pls. 17c–e, 21d–e, 83, and 85 (exs. 5–6, 9–10, photo; exs. 5–6, 9–10, drawing; study)

1941–44 Weidner, AfO 14 pp. 48–49 (study)

1948 Gadd, Ideas of Divine Rule pp. 93–95 (study)

1979 Reade, Bagh. Mitt. 10 pp. 45–46 (study)

1988 Nunn, Wandmalerei pp. 175–178 (study) and pls. 142–143 (exs. 1–2, drawing)

1994 Miglus, Studies Hrouda pp. 181–189 (ex. 2, drawing; study)

1995 Reade in Caubet, Khorsabad pp. 234–236 and 248–250 figs. 12–14 (drawings, translation, study)

1996 Finkel and Reade, ZA 86 pp. 247–250 and 266 fig. 1 (drawing, translation, study)

1996 Matthiae, I grandi imperi pp. 87–88 (exs. 1–2, drawing)

1997 Scurlock, NABU 1997 pp. 85–86 no. 92 (study)

2001 Roaf and Zgoll, ZA 91 pp. 267 and 289–90 (ex. 2, drawing; study)

2002 Zgoll and Roaf, Antike Welt 33/1 pp. 8 and 12–15 (ex. 2, drawing, edition; study)

2003 Morenz, AoF 30 pp. 18–27 (study)

2003 Morenz in Morenz and Bosshard-Nepustil, Herrscherpräsentation pp. 203–211, 217–219, and 271 fig. 60 (ex. 2, drawing, translation, study)

2005 Frahm, NABU 2005 pp. 46–50 no. 44, esp. n. 28 (study)

2008 Niederreiter, Iraq 70 pp. 79–80 I.d.1–5 (exs. 1–10, drawing, edition, study)

Figure 21. Drawing of the façade of the chapel of the god Sîn and Entrance Z in the palace of Sargon at Khorsabad, with glazed brick panels on either side of the doorway (text no. 58 exs. 1–2), published in Place, Ninive et l'Assyrie 3 pl. 24.

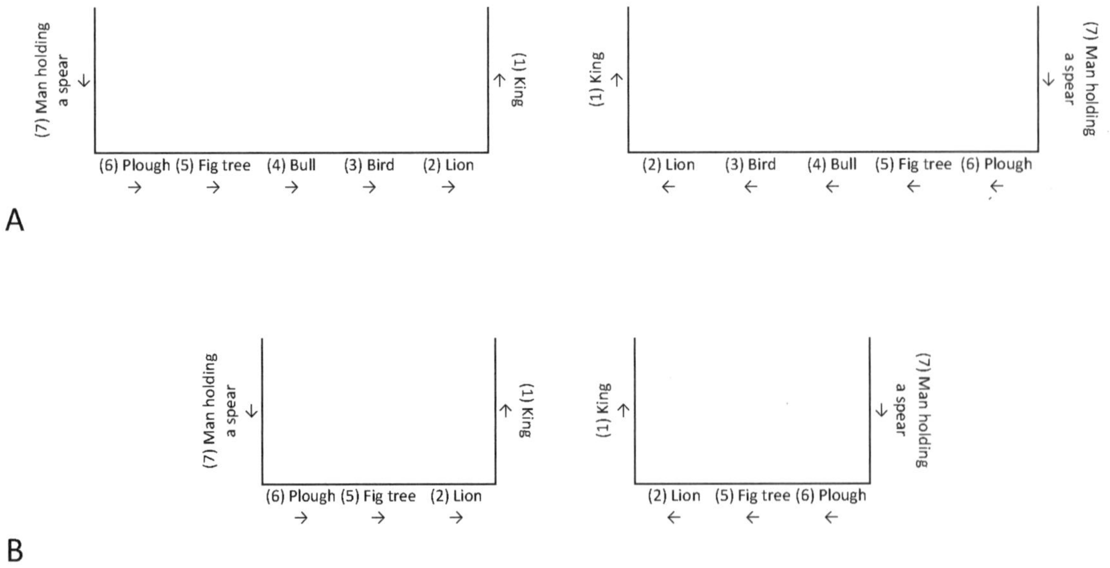

Figure 22. Diagram showing the arrangement of glazed brick figures representing Assyrian "hieroglyphs" (text no. 58). Diagram courtesy of M. Roaf.

TEXT A

(1) King, (2) Lion, (3) Bird, (4) Bull, (5) Fig tree, (6) Plough, (7) Man holding a spear

TEXT B

(1) King, (2) Lion, (5) Fig tree, (6) Plough, (7) Man holding a spear

INTERPRETATIONS AND TRANSLATIONS

Reade (1995) and Finkel and Reade: **A** (1–7) "Sargon, great king, king of the land of Assyria"; (1) "Sargon," (2) "king," (3) "great," (4) "king," (5) "land" (6) "Aššur," (7) determinative for place names.

B (1–2, 5–7) "Sargon, king of the land of Assyria"; (1) "Sargon," (2) "king," (5) "land," (6) "Aššur," (7) determinative for place names.

Zgoll and Roaf: **A** (1) "Sargon." (2–6) "king of totality, king of the land of Aššur"; (2) "king," (3) "totality," (4) "king," (5) "land," (6) "Aššur," (7) uncertain.

B (1) "Sargon." (2, 5–6) "king of the land of Aššur"; (2) "king," (5) "land," (6) "Aššur," (7) uncertain.

Morenz 1: **A** (1–7): "Sargon, great king, king of the land of Assyria"; (1) "Sargon," (2) "king," (3) "great," (4) "king," (5) "land," (6) "Aššur," (7) determinative for place names.

B (1–2, 5–7) "Sargon, king of the land of Assyria"; (1) "Sargon," (2) "king," (5) "land," (6) "Aššur," (7) determinative for place names.

Morenz 2: **A** (1–7): "He praises/reveres (the god ...): Sargon, great king, king of the land of Assyria"; (1) "He praises/reveres (the god ...): Sargon," (2) "king," (3) "great," (4) "king," (5) "land," (6) "Aššur," (7) determinative for place names.

B (1–2, 5–7) "He praises/reveres (the god ...): Sargon, king of the land of Assyria"; (1) "He praises/reveres (the god ...): Sargon," (2) "king," (5) "land," (6) "Aššur," (7) determinative for place names.

Frahm: **A** (2–6) "Sargon, king of the land of Assyria"; (2) *šarru*, (3) *ukīn*, (4) "king," (5) "land," (6) "Aššur."

Zgoll and Reade do not take (1) and (7), in particular (7), as being really part of the inscription; see the commentary.

Morenz His translation actually has "starker König" rather than "great king" even though he is taking the figure for *rabû* (in Morenz and Bosshard-Nepustil, Herrscherpräsentation p. 210 n. 95). He does not exactly indicate how he gets Assyria in the translation for the plough (6), but he does state that his work builds on that of Finkel and Reade, Scurlock, and Zgoll and Roaf (ibid. p. 204).

Frahm does not take (1) and (7) as part of the inscription; see the commentary.

59

Seven fragments of a clay bowl (possibly a *sikkatu*?) were found in the Sîn chapel of the palace at Khorsabad and are preserved in the Oriental Institute (Chicago). According to Oriental Institute records, the pieces were found in December 1932. Three adjoining pieces have this brief inscription.

CATALOGUE

Museum Number	Excavation Number	Provenance	Dimensions (cm)	cpn
OI —	DŠ 32-1 (DŠ 525)	Khorsabad, Palace, Room XXVI of the Sîn chapel	—	c

BIBLIOGRAPHY

1938 Loud and Altman, Khorsabad 2 p. 105 no. 32 (study)

TEXT

1) [... ^m^LUGAL-GI].NA LUGAL GAL-*ú* LUGAL *dan-nu* LUGAL [...]
2) [...] *x x du-ru-uš-še* [...]
3) [...] *ka-la* [(*x*)] DINGIR.MEŠ [...]

1–3) [... Sargo]n, great king, strong king, king [...] foundations [...] ... the gods [...].

60

Three fragments of a clay bowl with a brief inscription in the Oriental Institute (Chicago) were found at Khorsabad. It is possible that these fragments are to be identified with Loud and Altman, Khorsabad 2 p. 105 no. 33, which Oriental Institute records indicate was found outside the northwest wall of the Nabû temple in March 1934 and which bears the field register number DŠ 101. Although the text does not mention Sargon, since it was found at Khorsabad and since Sargon did use the titles "strong king, king of the world," it has been assigned to him here.

CATALOGUE

Museum Number	Excavation Number	Provenance	Dimensions (cm)	cpn
OI —	DŠ 32-24 (DŠ 101?)	Khorsabad	—	c

BIBLIOGRAPHY

1938 Loud and Altman, Khorsabad 2 p. 105 no. 33? (study)

TEXT

1) [...] LUGAL *dan-nu* MAN KIŠ LUGAL ⸢KUR?⸣ [...]
2) [...] *x ki-iṣ-ṣu* [...]
3) [...] DINGIR.MEŠ GAL.MEŠ [...]

1–3) [...] strong king, king of the world, king of [*Assyria* ...] shrine [...] the great gods [...]

61

An eye-stone that likely comes from Khorsabad has a short dedicatory inscription of Sargon to the goddess Ningal.

CATALOGUE

Museum Number	Registration Number	Provenance	Dimensions (cm)	cpn
Louvre —	Nap. III 3400	Possibly Khorsabad	2.3×2.4×1.0	c

COMMENTARY

The eye-stone was acquired by V. Place, and thus may well come from his work at Khorsabad, although this cannot be considered certain. The piece is made of banded agate and is white, with a pink pupil. The eye-stone was originally mounted on a disk of blue glass which measured 3.3×3.2 cm and from which it has now become detached.

H. Winckler erroneously refers to the piece as being a "Siegelabdruck" (Sar. 1 p. 196). The copies published by Place and Winckler (the latter being based on the former) omit the *ana* of line 1 and all of line 4. Examination of the original in the Louvre shows that *ana* and line 4 are faint and written on the white outer part of the eye, in contrast to the rest of the inscription that is written on the pupil.

BIBLIOGRAPHY

1867 Place, Ninive et l'Assyrie 3 pl. 76 no. 31 (copy)
1889 Winckler, Sar. 1 p. 196; and 2 pl. 49 no. 13 (copy, edition [erroneously referred to as being a "Siegelabdruck. Place, Nin. et l'Ass. vol. III, pl. 76, no. 21"])
1918 Pillet, Khorsabad p. 86 no. 18 (study; assignment here not certain)
1923 Delaporte, Louvre 2 p. 180 no. A.825 and pl. 93 fig. 13 (photo, edition)
1924 Pottier, Antiquités assyriennes no. 120 (study)
1927 Luckenbill, ARAB 2 p. 114 §230 (translation)
1969 Lambert, RA 63 pp. 69–70 (study)
1987 Galter, ARRIM 5 pp. 12, 14, and 21 no. 40 (edition, study)
1995 Tallon, Pierres p. 76 no. 119 (study)

TEXT

1) *ana* ᵈ*nin-gal*
2) GAŠAN-*šú* ᵐMAN-GIN
3) MAN KUR AŠ
4) *ana* TI-*šú* BA

1–4) To the goddess Ningal, his lady: Sargon (II), king of Assyria, presented (this object) for the sake of his life.

62

A bronze macehead found at Khorsabad has two one-line inscriptions on it, one ascribing the object to the palace of Sargon — "Palace of Sargon, king of the world, king of Assyria" — and the other stating that it belonged to Sîn-aḫu-uṣur — "(Property) of Sîn-aḫu-uṣur, the grand vizier." Although the former inscription could have been edited here, it has been decided to present the two together at text no. 2003.

63

A fragment of a clay prism found at Aššur in 1910 records parts of the campaigns in 716–713, which are assigned in this text to the ruler's fifth through eighth regnal years (*palûs*), in line with the assignment found in the Nineveh Prism (text no. 82) and, as far as it is preserved, a tablet fragment in the Oriental Institute (text no. 102), and against that found in the Khorsabad Annals (text nos. 1–4) and (apparently) the Najafabad Stele (text no. 117), which assign the events to Sargon's sixth through ninth regnal years. The fragment describes campaigns against Mannea, Karalla, and Urarṭu. The text is commonly known as the Aššur Prism of Sargon II and C.J. Gadd refers to it as prism C (Iraq 16 [1954] p. 175). It is possible that the inscription on this fragment was simply a duplicate of what was on the Nineveh Prism (text no. 82), at least with regard to the section preceding the building report (see Tadmor, JCS 12 [1958] p. 24 n. 20). If this is correct, columns i′, ii′, and iii′ would likely duplicate parts of text no. 82 columns ii (towards the bottom of the column), iii (towards the bottom of the column), and iv–v (end of column iv and start of column v) respectively; see also Fuchs, SAAS 8 pp. 8 and 23–35. However, the two texts only overlap for a few lines: text no. 63 ii′

6′–18′ ≈ text no. 82 iii 1‴–17‴ and text no. 63 iii′ 7′–14′ ≈ text no. 82 v 1–8. The Nineveh Prism was composed in Sargon's eleventh regnal year (711), or possibly the following year (710). Thus, if the two texts are duplicates, the Aššur Prism must also have been composed no earlier than 711.

CATALOGUE

Museum Number	Excavation Number	Photograph Number	Provenance	Dimensions (cm)	cpn
VA 8424	Ass 16587	Ass ph S 4812 and 4816	Aššur, forecourt of the Aššur temple (iC4III)	8.7×11×5.5	c

COMMENTARY

The prism originally had eight columns, of which the fragment preserves the ends of three. The restorations are based for the most part on those proposed by E. Weidner and A. Fuchs.

Assuming that the various prisms of Sargon bore basically the same text, Weidner estimated that each column of the Aššur prism had at least 120–150 lines, perhaps even 150–180 lines, and thus that the eight-sided prisms had originally 960–1,440 lines. He also estimated that the Aššur prism had been originally 32–48 cm high. (See AfO 14 [1941–44] pp. 40–41.)

The building portion of the inscription is not preserved, but the prism was found in the temple of the god Aššur. Since Sargon is known to have carried out work in that temple (see text no. 74 i 25–28 and text no. 84 line 3′), it is possible that the prism was commissioned to commemorate work on that temple. (See Fuchs, SAAS 8 p. 5.) On the bottom end of the prism fragment are found damaged representations of a stylized tree and an animal, possibly a kid. (For photographs of these, see Weidner, AfO 14 [1941–44] p. 48; Finkel and Reade, ZA 86 [1996] fig. 7 following p. 268; Fuchs, SAAS 8 p. ii; and Aššur excavation photograph S 4816.) The goat was an attribute of the god Aššur and thus its appearance on the fragment may support the supposition that the prism was created to commemorate work on the temple of that god. (See Finkel and Reade, ZA 86 [1996] pp. 246–247.) Designs are also found on the bottom of a prism from Nineveh, text no. 82; see the commentary to that text with regard to these representations.

BIBLIOGRAPHY

1941–44 Weidner, AfO 14 pp. 40–53 (copy, edition, study)
1945 Alt, ZDPV 67 pp. 128–138 (ii′ 5′–11′, translation [by Weidner], study)
1956 Albright, BASOR 141 pp. 23–25 (ii′ 8′–11′, edition, study)
1958 Tadmor, JCS 12 pp. 22–40 and 77–100, especially 24–26, 77–78, 88, 90 n. 288, and 92–95 (ii′ 1′–11′, edition; ii′ 12′–16′, transliteration; study)
1958 Wiseman, DOTT p. 62 (ii′ 5′–11′, translation)
1966 Tadmor, BiAr 29 pp. 91–92 (ii′ 1′–11′, translation)
1968 Borger in Galling, Textbuch² p. 62 no. 33 (ii′ 1′–11′, translation)
1969 Oppenheim, ANET³ p. 286 (ii′ 5′–11′, translation)
1971 Weippert, Edom p. 90 (ii′ 18′b–25′, transliteration)
1977 Briend and Seux, TPOA no. 38 (ii′ 8′–11′, translation)
1979 Na'aman, Tel Aviv 6 p. 71 and n. 6 (ii′ 3′–7′, edition, study)
1982 Eph'al, Arabs p. 37 (ii′ 6′–12′, study)
1984 Borger, TUAT 1/4 pp. 382–383 (ii′ 2′–11′, translation)
1986 Pedersén, Archives 2 p. 13 n. 9 (study)
1988 Na'aman and Zadok, JCS 40 p. 38 (i′ 17′, study; ii 3′–7′, translation)
1994 Fuchs, Khorsabad p. 386 (study)
1997 Pedersén, Katalog p. 158 (study)
1998 Fuchs, SAAS 8 pp. 3, 5, 8–12, 23–25, 28–29, 34–36, 54–55, 57–58, 64–65, and pl. 2 (copy, edition, study)
1999–00 Na'aman, AfO 46–47 p. 363 (ii′ 3′–6′, translation, study)
2002 Younger in Chavalas and Younger, Mesopotamia and the Bible p. 312 (ii′ 1′–11′, translation)
2008 Cogan, Raging Torrent pp. 105–107 no. 26 (ii′ 1′–11′, translation, study)
2014 Maniori, Campagne di Sargon pp. 39–40 A8 and passim (study)
2017 Gries, Assur-Tempel p. 289 no. 2718 (study)
2018 Rollinger, Interpreting Herodotus pp. 129–137 (iii′ 9′b–11′a, translation, study)
2018 Rollinger, Studies Neumann pp. 585–609 (iii′ 9′b–11′a, edition, study)

Figure 23. Cols. i′–iii′ of VA 8424 (text no. 63), the Aššur Prism. © Staatliche Museen zu Berlin-Vorderasiatisches Museum. Photo by O.M. Teßmer.

TEXT

The initial column(s) of the prism are not preserved.
Col. i′
Lacuna
1′) [...] *x*
2′) [...]-*ma*
3′) [... *a-na šu-zu*]-⸢*ub*⸣ ZI-*šú*
4′) [*iṣ-ṣu-riš*$^{?}$ *ip-par-šam-ma*$^{?}$ GÌR.II.(MEŠ)-*ia*] *iṣ-bat*
5′) [ANŠE.KUR.RA.MEŠ$^{?}$ *ṣi-in-da-at*$^{?}$ *ni*]-⸢*ri*$^{?}$⸣ GU$_{4}$.NÍTA.MEŠ
6′) [...] ⸢*ni-ṣir*⸣-*te* É.GAL-*šú*
7′) [...] *x x* DA *kàd-ra-a-šú*
8′) [*ú-šá-bi-la*$^{?}$ ^{m}*ul-lu-su-nu*$^{?}$] UGU KUR.*ma-an-na-a-a*
9′) [*áš-kun-ma*$^{?}$ UN.MEŠ$^{?}$ URU.*i*]-*zi-ir-ti ša áš-lu-la*
10′) [*a-na*$^{?}$ *áš-ri-šú-nu*$^{?}$ *ú-ter*]-⸢*ma*$^{?}$⸣ *ma-da-at-tú ki-i ša*
11′) [^{m}*ir-an-zi*$^{?}$ AD-*šú*$^{?}$ *e-mid*]-*su i-na u*$_{4}$-*me-šú-ma* ^{m}*aš-šur*-ZU
12′) [URU.*kar-al-la-a-a*] ^{m}*i-ti-i* URU.*pad-dir-a-a*

The initial column(s) of the prism are not preserved.

Lacuna
i′ 1′–11′a) [... in order to sav]e his life [*he came flying like a bird and*] grasped hold of [my feet. (i′ 5′) *Horses trained to the yoke*], oxen, [...] the treasure of his palace [... *he brought me*] as his gift. [*I set Ullusunu*] over the land Mannea; [*the people of* the city I]zirtu whom I had carried off as booty [*I returned to their* (*former*) *places an*]*d* [I imposed] upon him (the same) payment(s) as [*his father Iranzi* (*had paid*)].

i′ 11′b–22′) At that time, Aššur-lēʾi [of the city Karalla] (and) Ittî of the city Paddiri [*became hostile to*] me. [*He took to*] a high mountain peak. [...] ... he plotted evil.

i′ 3′–4′ For the restorations, see text no. 1 line 88, text no. 7 line 50, and text no. 117 ii 30.
i′ 6′ Based on text no. 1 line 74, A. Fuchs (SAAS 8 p. 24) suggests restoring *it-ti* before *niṣirte* ("[... together with] the treasure ...").
i′ 8′–9′ Cf. text no. 1 lines 88–89.

13′) [*ik-ki-ru*? *it-ti*]-*ia* ŠU.SI ⸢KUR⸣-*i šá-qí-ti*
14′) [*iṣ-bat*? ...] A ṢI *ik-pu-ud* ḪUL-*tú*
15′) [*i-na tu-kul-ti*] ⸢^{d}⸣*a-šur*$_4$ EN-*ia* BAD$_5$.BAD$_5$-*šú am-ḫaṣ*
16′) [^{m}*aš-šur*-ZU URU.*kar*]-*al*-⸢*la-a*⸣-*a* ^{m}*i*-⸢*ti-i* URU⸣.*pad-dir-a-a*
17′) [*ina qé-reb uš-ma-ni-ia ad*]-*di-šú-nu bi-re-tú* AN.BAR
18′) [... *as-su*]-⸢*ḫa*?⸣-*ma a-na qé-reb* KUR *aš-šur*.KI
19′) [*ub-la-áš-šú*]-⸢*nu*?⸣-*ti* URU.⸢*kar*⸣-*al-lu a-di na-gi-i-šú*
20′) [UGU *pi-ḫa-at* KUR].⸢*lul*⸣-*lu-mi-i ú-rad-di-ma*
21′) [*mi-ṣir*? KUR *aš-šur*].⸢KI?⸣ *ú-rap-piš* ⸢^{m}⸣^{d}EN-IBILA-SUM.NA
22′) [...]-*ú-ti* UGU URU.*pad-di-ri áš-kun-ma*

(i′ 15′) [With the support of] the god Aššur, my lord, I inflicted a defeat on him. [In the midst of my camp, I thr]ew [Aššur-lēʾi of the city Kar]alla (and) Ittî of the city Paddiri in iron fetters. [*I removed/deported* ...] and [brought th]em to Assyria. The city Karalla, together with its district, (i′ 20′) I added [to the province of the land L]ullumû and I (thereby) expanded [*the territory of Assyria*]. I appointed Bēl-aplu-iddina [to] the position of [...] over the city Paddiri and

Col. ii′

Lacuna

1′) ⸢*a-di*⸣ x (x) [...]
2′) *ù* US$_5$.⸢UDU⸣.[ḪI.A ...]
3′) *ul-tu qé-reb* ⸢KUR?⸣.[... *as-suḫ-ma*?]
4′) *i-na ma-a-ti* ⸢*ša*⸣ [...]
5′) *ša pat-ti* URU *na-ḫal* ⸢*mu-uṣ*?⸣-[*ri na-gi-i*? *ša*? *a-ḫi*? *tam-tim*?]
6′) *ša šùl-mu* ^{d}UTU-*ši ú-šá*-⸢*aṣ-bit*?⸣ [*i-na* ŠU.II LÚ.*qí-pi-ia*?]
7′) LÚ.*na-si-ku ša* URU.*la-ba-an* [*am-nu-šu-nu-ti*]

Lacuna

ii′ 1′–7′) together with [...] and sheep and [goats ... *I deported*] from *the la*[*nd ... and*] *I sett*[*led* (them) in the land *that/of* [...] (ii′ 5′) on the border of the city of the Brook of Eg[ypt, *a district which is on the shore of the*] Western [*Sea*. I assigned them to the authority of *a qīpu-official of mine*], the sheikh of the city Laban.

8′) ^{m}*ši-il-kan-ni* LUGAL KUR.*mu-uṣ-ri* ⸢*ša a*⸣-[*šar-šú*? *ru-ú-qu*?]
9′) *pu-luḫ-tu me-lam-me ša* ^{d}*a-šur*$_4$ EN-*ia* [*is-ḫu-pu-šu-ma*]
10′) 12 ANŠE.KUR.RA.MEŠ GAL.MEŠ *ša* KUR.*mu-uṣ-ri ša i-na* ⸢*ma*⸣-*a-ti*
11′) *la ib-šú-ú tam-šil-šú-un iš-šá-a ta-mar-tuš*

ii′ 8′–11′) (As for) Šilkanni, king of Egypt, *whose lo*[*cation is far away* (and whom) fear of the brilliance of the god Aššur, my lord, [had overwhelmed], he brought me as his audience gift twelve large horses from Egypt whose like did not exist in (my) land.

12′) *i-na* 6 BALA-*ia* ^{m}*ur-sa-a* KUR.*ur-ar-ṭa-a-a*
13′) *la a-dir ma-mit* DINGIR.MEŠ GAL.MEŠ *a-bi-ku de-en* ^{d}*šà-máš*
14′) ⸢*ša*⸣ *ina a-lak ger-ri-ia maḫ-ri-i a-na* ^{m}*ul-lu-su-ni*
15′) KUR.*ma-an-na-a-a a-na ni-ir* ^{d}*a-šur*$_4$

ii′ 12′–25′) In my sixth regnal year, Ursâ (Rusâ), the Urarṭian — who did not respect the oath (sworn) by the great gods; who overturned the decision of the god Šamaš; whom, during the course of my previous campaign against Ullusunu, the Mannean, (ii′ 15′) I had subjugated to the yoke of the god Aššur, (and)

---

i′ 13′ Or [*ú-šá-an-ki-ir/ú-šam-kir it-ti*]-*ia*, "Aššur-leʾi [of the city Karalla] incited Ittî of the city Paddir [to rebel against] me"; see Fuchs, SAAS 8 p. 24 and n. 23.
i′ 14′ The tenative restoration is based on Tadmor and Yamada, RINAP 1 p. 31 Tiglath-pileser III no. 7 line 2.
i′ 15′ Or [*i-na qí-bit*] ^{d}*a-šur*$_4$, "[At the command of] the god Aššur" (Fuchs, SAAS 8 p. 24).
i′ 16′–22′ For duplicate or similar passages useful for restoration, see in particular text no. 117 ii 31–33. For i′ 16′–17′, cf. text no. 34.
i′ 19′ For the restoration, see text no. 74 v 66.
i′ 21′ For the restoration, cf. text no. 73 line 9.
i′ 22′ A. Fuchs (SAAS 8 p. 25 n. 30) suggests [*a-na* LÚ.*qé-pu*]-*ú-ti* ("I appointed Bēl-aplu-iddina [to the position of *qīpu*-off]icial"); cf. Tadmor and Yamada, RINAP 1 p. 112 Tiglath-pileser no. 44 line 16′ and Naʾaman, NABU 1997 p. 139 no. 150. Fuchs believes that it is hardly likely that Allabria/Paddir was made into a province and thus that the passage should probably not be restored [*a-na* LÚ.EN.NAM]-*ú-ti*.
ii′ 4′–7′ Possibly restore in ii′ 4′ *i-na ma-a-ti* ⸢*ša*⸣ [*a-šar-ša*? *la*? *i-du-ú*? *i-na*? URU? ...], "in a land whose [*location they had never known* (*before*), *in the city* ...]," and at the end of ii′ 6′ a personal name instead of LÚ.*qí-pi-ia*?, "*a qīpu-official of mine*." See Naʾaman, Tel Aviv 6 (1979) p. 71 and n. 6 and AfO 46–47 (1999–2000) p. 363. For the restoration in ii′ 5′, see text no. 1 line 145.
ii′ 6′–11′ For a duplicate passage, see text no. 82 iii 1‴–8‴.
ii′ 8′ For the restoration, see text no. 73 line 8. Šilkanni may be Osorkon IV; see Weidner, AfO 14 (1941–44) pp. 44–46; Kitchen, Third Intermediate Period^{2} pp. 376 and 551–552; and Schwemer, PNA 3/2 pp. 1421–1422 sub Usilkanu 1.
ii′ 12′–18′ The restorations are based upon text no. 82 iii 9‴–16‴.
ii 14′–16′ In the previous campaign it was actually the Mannean Ullusunu who was defeated, not the Urarṭian king Rusâ; see Fuchs, SAAS 8 pp. 57–58 n. 26 with regard to a possible rewording of the passage to deal with this problem.

ú-šak-ni-šú-šú-ma
16′) *e-mid-du-uš ab-*⌈*šá*⌉*-a-nu* 12 URU.ḪAL.ṢU.MEŠ-*šú dan-na-a-ti*
17′) *ša* UGU KUR.*ur-ar-ṭi* KUR.*an-di-a* KUR.*na-ʾi-i-ri*
18′) *a-na ka-a-di na-da-a e-*⌈*kim*⌉*-šú-ma ú-ṣa-ḫir* KUR-*su*
19′) LÚ.*mun-daḫ-ṣe* LÚ.ERIM.MEŠ *šu-lu-ti-šú qé-reb-šin*
20′) *ú-še-rib-ma ú-dan-ni-na rík*?*-si-šin a-na tu-ur gi-mil-*⌈*li*⌉
21′) ^{m}*ul-lu-su-*⌈*ni*⌉ KUR.*ma-an-na-a-a um-ma-na-at* ^{d}*a-šur*$_{4}$
22′) *gap-šá-a-ti ad-ke-e-ma a-na ka-šad* URU.ḪAL.ṢU.MEŠ *ša-ti-na*
23′) *áš-ta-kan pa-ni-ia* URU.ḪAL.ṢU.MEŠ *ša-ti-na* ⌈*ak*⌉*-šu-[ud]*
24′) *áš-lu-la šal-la-si-*⌈*in*⌉ LÚ.ERIM.MEŠ-⌈*ia*⌉ *a-di ša* ^{m}*ul-lu-su-*⌈*ni*?⌉
25′) KUR.*ma-an-na-a-a ú-še-ri-ba qé-reb-*⌈*šin*⌉

upon whom I had imposed (my) yoke — took away from him (Ullusunu) twelve of his strong fortresses that were situated as guard posts on (the border with) the lands Urarṭu, Andia, (and) Naʾiri, and (thus) reduced (the size of) his land. He stationed fighting men inside them as his garrison troops (ii′ 20′) and reinforced their defenses (lit.: "structures"). In order to avenge Ullusunu, the Mannean, I mustered the numerous troops of the god Aššur and set out to conquer these forts. I conque[red] these forts [(and)] carried off booty from them. I stationed inside th[em] my troops, together with those of Ullusunu, the Mannean.

Col. iii′
Lacuna
1′) ⌈4? $^{d?}$⌉[*ṣa*]-⌈*lam*?⌉ [URUDU Ì.DU$_{8}$.GAL-*li ma-ṣar* KÁ.MEŠ-*šu šá* 4 KÙŠ]
2′) *mu-la-šú-nu* ⌈*a*⌉-[*di* KI.TUŠ.MEŠ-*šú-nu* URUDU.ḪI.A *šap-ku*]
3′) 1 *ṣa-lam un-ni-*⌈*ni*⌉ [*man-za-az* LUGAL-*ti ša* ^{md}15-BÀD]
4′) DUMU ^{m}*iš-pu-e-*[*ni* LUGAL KUR.*ur-ar-ṭi* KI.TUŠ-*šú* ZABAR]
5′) *ši-ip-ku* 1 GU$_{4}$ [1 GU$_{4}$.ÁB *a-di* GU$_{4}$.AMAR-*šá ša* ^{md}15-BÀD]
6′) DUMU ^{m}*iš-pu-*[*e-ni* ...]
7′) 1 *ṣa-lam* $^{m⌈}$*ir-gi*⌉*-*[*iš-ti* LUGAL KUR.*ur-ar-ṭi*]
8′) *ša* AGA MUL-⌈*ti*⌉ [DINGIR-*ti ap-ru-ma* ŠU ZAG-*šú ka-ri-bat*]
9′) *a-di* É-*šú* 40+[20 GUN URUDU.ḪI.A KI.LÁ 1 *ṣa-lam* ^{m}*ur-sa-a*]
10′) *it-ti* 2 ⌈ANŠE⌉.[KUR.RA.MEŠ *pét-ḫal-lì-šú* LÚ.GIŠ.GIGIR-*šu a-di* KI.TUŠ-*šú-nu*]
11′) URUDU.ḪI.A *ši-*⌈*ip*⌉*-*[*ku šal-la-tu ka-bit-tu*]
12′) ⌈*áš*⌉*-lu-*⌈*la*⌉ [*a-na* KUR *aš-šur*.KI *ub-la*]

Lacuna
iii′ 1′–2′) 4 *divine* [*stat*]*ue*(*s*) [of copper, the chief doorkeepers, guardians of his (Ḫaldi's) gates, (each of) who]se height [is four cubits], toge[ther with their bases, cast in copper];
iii′ 3′–5′a) 1 statue [(depicting) Ištar-dūrī (Sarduri)], son of Išpue[ni, king of the land Urarṭu], praying [(and) *in a royal pose*, (*together with*) its base], cast [in bronze];
iii′ 5′b–6′) 1 bull [(and) 1 cow, together with her bull calf, dedicated by (lit.: "of") Ištar-dūrī (Sarduri)], son of Išpu[eni, ...];
iii′ 7′–9′a) 1 statue of Irg[išti (Argišti), king of the land Urarṭu, wearing] a crown (decorated) with stars, [(an attribute) of divine rank, and with his right hand in a gesture of blessing], together with its *casing*, [which weighs] six[ty talents of copper];
iii′ 9′b–11′a) [1 statue of Ursâ (Rusâ)] with two [of his cavalry] ho[rses (and) his *groom*, together with their base], ca[st] in copper —
iii′ 11′b–12′) I carried off (all these things) as [substantial] booty [(and) brought (them) to the land of Assyria].

---

ii′ 16′ Note the reference to twenty-two strongholds lost (or given) by Ullusunu to the Urarṭian ruler in text no. 1 line 101, text no. 2 line 96, and text no. 7 line 39, and see also Fuchs, SAAS 8 p. 58 n. 27.
iii′ 1′–14′ For restorations and similar passages, see text no. 65 lines 399–405 and text no. 82 v 1–8.
iii′ 6′ There does not appear to be sufficient room to restore all that is found at this point in text no. 65 line 401: ... ^{m}*iš-pu-e-ni* URUDU.ḪI.<A> É ^{d}*ḫal-di-a a-na e-qi ú-ter-ru-ma iš-*⌈*ṭur*⌉ *ṣe-ru-uš-šú-un*, "... son of Išpueni, (made of) copper (and) belonging to the temple of the god Ḫaldi, (*which Ištar-dūrī*) *had made as* a votive offering and upon which he had inscribed (a record of his action)."
iii′ 7′ E. Weidner's copy has $^{m⌈}$*ur*⌉*-gi-*[...] (read by him ^{I}*ur-gi-*[*iš-ti*], AfO 14 [1941–44] p. 48), while A. Fuchs' copy has $^{m⌈}$*ir-gi*⌉*-*[...] (read by him as ^{I}*Ir-*⌈*gi*⌉*-*[*iš-ti*], SAAS 8 p. 35). The sign is somewhat unclear, but Fuchs' reading IR, as opposed to UR, is followed here; this matches text no. 82 v 1 which has [^{m}]*ir-gi-*⌈*iš-ti*⌉ as opposed to text no. 65 line 402 which has ^{m}*ar-giš-ti*.
iii′ 9′b–11′a See the on-page note to text no. 65 lines 403–404.
iii′ 11′ *ši-*⌈*ip*⌉*-*[*ku*]: Text no. 65 line 403 has *šap-ku* here and both E. Weidner and A. Fuchs read ⌈*šap*⌉*-*[*ku*], although their copies and the original have *ši-x* [...], where *x* would fit the beginning of IB. The beginning of the Babylonian ŠAB can at times look somewhat like ŠI, but this text is written in Neo-Assyrian script. Cf. iii′ 4′b–5′a [ZABAR] *ši-ip-ku*.

13′) ⸢*i*⸣-*na* ⸢8 BALA⸣-[*ia ša i-na a-lak ger-ri-ia maḫ-ri*]
14′) ⸢*ša*⸣ ^m^*aš-šur*⸣-[ZU LUGAL KUR.*kar-al-li* ...]
15′) *x x* [...]
16′) *x* (*x*) [...]
17′) *x* [...]
18′) [...]
The remaining column(s) of the prism are not preserved.

iii′ 13′–14′) In [my] eighth reg[nal year, *that which* in the course of my previous campaign] *against* Aššur-[lēʾi, king of the land Karalla ...]
iii′ 15′–18′) No translation possible.

The remaining column(s) of the prism are not preserved.

64

A fragment of a hollow clay cylinder in the Vorderasiatisches Museum preserves part of an inscription of Sargon II that records the end of the description of his military campaign to Babylon in his twelfth and thirteenth regnal years (710–709), as well as the receipt of gifts from the ruler of Dilmun and from seven rulers on Cyprus (lines 1′–17′), and possibly the beginning of a building report (lines 18′–21′). The inscription may have been composed in 707 (see Frahm, KAL 3 p. 76).

CATALOGUE

Museum Number	Excavation Number	Photograph Number	Provenance	Dimensions (cm)	cpn
VAT 15466	Ass 8800	Ass ph 1972	Aššur, at the western border of the excavation, on the mud brick (cD6V)	7.8×7.3×3.5	c

COMMENTARY

The cylinder fragment was found in the area of the former New Palace at Aššur. Although part of the left edge of the piece is preserved, the beginnings of the lines are no longer preserved. As noted by E. Frahm (KAL 3 p. 76), lines 18′–21′ might be the beginning of a building report. While the mention of the "king of the gods" in line 21′ would make one think of the god Aššur and thus work on the temple of that god, he could also be mentioned in connection with work on other building projects, such as the royal palace. If, as Frahm suggests is possible, the provenance of the fragment points to the location of the building project for which the cylinder was intended, the report might deal with work on the city of Aššur's inner wall or processional street.

The restorations in lines 1′–17′ follow Frahm, KAL 3 p. 75 and are for the most part based on text no. 7 lines 134–149 and similar passages in other texts (e.g., text no. 74 vi 63–80 and vii 7–38; text no. 83 iii′ 1–13; and cf. text no. 103 iv 1–42), although for line 6′, see text no. 74 vi 80. The text has been collated by J. Novotny.

BIBLIOGRAPHY

1997 Pedersén, Katalog p. 207 (study [erroneously assigned to Sennacherib])

2009 Frahm, KAL 3 no. 32 (copy, edition, study)

TEXT

Lacuna

1′) [... DUMU.MEŠ ZIMBIR].⌜KI$^{?}$ NIBRU$^{?}$⌝.KI [KÁ.DINGIR.RA.KI *u bár-sipa*.KI *ša i-na la an-ni-šú-nu i-na qer-bi-šú ka-mu-ú ṣi-bit-ta-šú-nu a-bu-ut-ma ú-kal-lim-šú-nu-ti nu-ru*]

2′) [A.ŠÀ.MEŠ-*šú-nu ša ul-tu u*$_{4}$-*me ul*]-⌜*lu*⌝-*ti i*-⌜*na*⌝ [*i-ši-ti ma-a-ti* LÚ.*su-ti-i e-ki-mu-ú-ma ra-ma-nu-uš-šú-un ú-ter-ru*]

3′) [LÚ.*su-ti-i* ERIM].⌜MEŠ$^{?}$ EDIN *i-na* GIŠ.TUKUL *ú-šam*⌝-[*qit ki-sur-ri-šú-nu ma-šu-ú-ti ša ina di-li-iḫ* KUR *ib-baṭ-lu ú-šad-gi-la pa-nu-uš-šú-un*]

4′) [*ša*] ⌜ÚRI⌝.KI UNUG.KI *eridu*.KI ARARMA.KI *kul-aba*$_{4}$.KI ⌜*ki*⌝-[*sik*.KI URU.*né-med*-^{d}*la-gu-da áš-ku-na an-du-ra-ar-šú-un*]

5′) [*ù* DINGIR].⌜MEŠ⌝-*šú-nu šal-lu-ti a-na ma-ḫa-zi*-[*šú-nu ú-ter-ma sat-tuk-ki-šú-nu ba-aṭ-lu-ú-ti ú-ter áš-ru-uš-šú-un*]

6′) [KUR.É-^{m}]⌜*ia*⌝-*ki*-⌜*ni*⌝ *ú-ter-ma a-na eš-šu*-⌜*ti*⌝ [*aṣ-bat* UN.MEŠ KUR.*kúm-mu-ḫi ki-šit-ti qa-ti-ia qé-reb-šú ú-šar-me-ma ú-še-ši-ba ni-du-us-su*]

7′) [(*x*) KUR *šu*]-*a-tú* ⌜*mal*$^{?}$-*ma*$^{?}$-*liš*$^{?}$ *a-zu-uz-ma*⌝ *i-na* ⌜ŠU⌝.[II] ⌜LÚ⌝.[*šu-ut* SAG-*ia* LÚ.GAR.KUR KÁ.DINGIR.RA.KI *ù* LÚ.*šu-ut* SAG-*ia* LÚ.GAR.KUR LÚ.*gam-bu-li am-nu*]

8′) [*a-na* KÁ.DINGIR].⌜RA⌝.KI *ma-ḫa-zi* ^{d}EN.LÍL.LÁ DINGIR.MEŠ *i-na* [*e-le-eṣ lib-bi nu-um-mur pa-ni ḫa-diš e-ru-um-ma* ŠU.II EN GAL-*i* ^{d}AMAR.UTU *aṣ-bat-ma ú-šal-li-ma ú-ru-uḫ* É *á-ki-ti*]

9′) [1 ME 54] ⌜GUN⌝ 26 MA.NA 10 GÍN KÙ.GI *ḫuš-šu-ú* 1 LIM 8 ⌜ME⌝ 4 ⌜GUN⌝ [20 MA.NA KÙ.BABBAR *eb-bu* URUDU.ḪI.A *par-zil-la ša ni-ba la i-šu-ú*]

10′) [NA$_{4}$.ZÚ] ⌜NA$_{4}$⌝.ZA.GÌN.MEŠ NA$_{4}$.BABBAR.DILI.MEŠ NA$_{4}$.AŠ.GÌ.GÌ.⌜MEŠ⌝ [NA$_{4}$.UGU.AŠ.GÌ.GÌ *di-gi-li* NA$_{4}$.BABBAR.DILI NA$_{4}$.MUŠ.GÍR *a-na mu-'u-de-e* (...)]

11′) [SÍG.*ta-kil-tú*] ⌜SÍG⌝.*ar-ga-man-nu lu-bul-ti bir-me ù* [TÚG.GADA GIŠ.TÚG GIŠ.EREN

Lacuna

1′–5′) [... (As for) the citizens of (the cities) Sippar], N[*ippur*, Babylon, and Borsippa who through no fault of their own had been held captive in it (Dūr-Yakīn), I put an end to their imprisonment and let them see the light (of day). (With regard to) their fields, which long ag]o, whi[le the land was in disorder, the Sutians had taken away and appropriated for their own], I stru[ck down (those) Sutians, the people] of the steppe, with the sword. [I (re)assigned to them (the citizens) their territories, (whose boundaries) had been forgotten (and) fallen into disuse during the troubled period in the land. I (re)-established the freedom (from obligations) of (the cities) U]r, Uruk, Eridu, Larsa, Kullaba, K[issik, (and) Nēmed-Laguda. Moreover, I returned] their [god]s that had been carried off as booty to [their] cult centers [and I restored their regular offerings that had been discontinued].

6′–7′) I restored [the land Bīt-Y]akīn and re[organized (its administration). I settled there people from the land Kummuḫu that I had conquered and I had (them) occupy its (Bīt-Yakīn's) abandoned regions]. I divided up [th]at [land] *into equal parts* and [assigned (them)] to the auth[ority] of a [eunuch of mine, the governor of Babylon, and a(nother) eunuch of mine, the governor of the Gambulu (tribe)].

8′–12′) [Happily], with [a joyful heart (and) a radiant face, I entered Babylo]n, the cult center of the Enlil of the gods (Marduk); [I grasped hold of the hands of the great lord, the god Marduk, and brought (him) safely along the road to the *akītu*-house. (With regard to) 154 talen]ts, 26 minas, (and) 10 shekels of red gold, 1,804 talen[ts (and) 20 minas of pure silver, copper, (and) iron in immeasurable quantities, (10′) obsidian], lapis-lazuli, *banded agate, blue turquoise*, [*green turquoise, ... of banded agate* (and) *muššaru*-stone in large quantities, (...) blue-purple wool], red-purple [woo]l, garments with multi-colored trim and [linen garments, boxwood, cedar, cypress, (and) every kind of aromatic, the products of Mount Amanus, whose

6′ [KUR.É-^{m}]⌜*ia*⌝-*ki*-⌜*ni*⌝ *ú-ter-ma a-na eš-šu*-⌜*ti*⌝ [*aṣ-bat*] "I restored [the land Bīt-Y]akīn and re[organized (its administration)]": Possibly translate instead "I again reorga[nized the land Bīt-Y]akīn"; see also text nos. 74 vi 80 and 113 line 23′, as well as text nos. 86 line 15′ (restored) and 87 line 10′ (restored); note also text nos. 7 line 65 and 74 iv 2. Possibly restore AN.ŠÁR EN-*ia*, "(the god) Aššur, my lord," somewhere at the end of the line, following text no. 74 vi 82 and Frahm, KAL 3 p. 76. E. Frahm tentatively restores *ana* before KUR, and translates "Ich kehrte [*in das Land Bīt*]-Jakin züruck," but this translation assumes a G-stem rather than a D-stem of *târu*.

10′ Several metals may be mentioned at the end of the line, as in text no. 74 vii 10–11.

GIŠ.ŠUR.MÌN *ka-la ri-iq-qí bi-ib-lat* KUR.*ḫa-ma-a-ni ša e-ri-su-un ṭa-a-bu*]

12′) [*a-na* ^{d}EN ^{d}*zar-pa-ni*]-⸢*tum*⸣ ^{d}AG ^{d}*taš-me-tum ù* DINGIR.MEŠ [*a-ši-bu-ut ma-ḫa-zi* KUR *šu-me-ri ù* URI.KI *ul-tu* SAG LUGAL-*ti-ia a-di* MU.3.KÁM *ú-qa-i-šá qí-šá-a-ti*]

13′) [^{m}*ú-pe-e-ri* LUGAL *dil-mun*.KI] ⸢*ša*⸣ *ma-lak* 30 KASKAL.GÍD *ina* MURUB$_4$ *tam-*[*tim ni-pi-iḫ* ^{d}UTU-*ši ki-ma nu-ú-ni šit-ku-nu nar-ba-ṣu da-na-an* ^{d}*aš-šur* ^{d}AG ^{d}AMAR.UTU *iš-me-ma ú-šá-bi-la*$^{?}$ *kàd-ra-a-šú*$^{?}$]

14′) [*ù* 7 LUGAL.MEŠ-*ni ša* KUR].⸢*ia*⸣-*a*ʾ *na-ge-e ša* KUR.*ia-ad-*[*na-na ša ma-lak* 7 u_4-*me i-na* MURUB$_4$ *tam-tim e-reb* ^{d}UTU-*ši šit-ku-nu-ma né-es-sa-at šu-bat-su-un*]

15′) [*ša ul-tu* u_4-*me ru*]-⸢*qu*⸣-*ti a-di* <*i*>-^{d}*nanna i-*⸢*na*⸣ [LUGAL.MEŠ-*ni* AD.MEŠ-*ia ša* KUR *aš-šur*.KI *u* KUR.*kar-*^{d}*du-ni-áš ma-nam-ma la iš-mu-ú zi-kir* KUR-*šú-un*]

16′) [*ep-šet i-na qé-reb* KUR.*kal-di*] ⸢*ù*⸣ KUR.*ḫat-ti* ⸢*e*⸣*-tep-pu-*⸢*šu*⸣ [*i-na* MURUB$_4$ *tam-tim ru-qiš iš-mu-ma lib-bu-šú-un it-ru-ku-ma im-qut-su-nu-ti ḫat-tu*]

17′) [KÙ.GI KÙ.BABBAR *ú-nu-ut* GIŠ.ESI] GIŠ.TÚG *né-*⸢*peš*⸣*-ti* ⸢KUR⸣-[*šú-un a-na qé-reb* KÁ.DINGIR.RA.KI *a-di maḫ-ri-ia ú-bi-lu-nim-ma ú-na-áš-ši-qu* GÌR.II-*ia*]

18′) [... *a-ši-bu*$^{?}$]-*tu bal-til*.KI *a-*⸢*na*⸣ [...]

19′) [...]-*ni i-na qer-bi-*[...]

20′) [...] x x x *iš-ru-*[*ka*$^{?}$ ...]

21′) [... ^{d}*aš-šur*$^{?}$ EN$^{?}$] ⸢GAL$^{?}$⸣ LUGAL DINGIR.⸢MEŠ⸣ [...]

Lacuna

scent(s) are pleasant — from the beginning of my reign until (my) third year, I presented (these things) as gifts to the deities Bēl, Zarpanīt]u, Nabû, Tašmētu, and the (other) gods [who dwell in the cult centers of the land of Sumer and Akkad].

13′) [Upēri, king of Dilmun, wh]o(se) [lair is situated] at a distance of thirty leagues in the middle of the [Eastern] Se[a, like (that of) a fish, heard of the might of the gods Aššur, Nabû, (and) Marduk and *brought me his gift*].

14′–17′) [Moreover, seven kings of the land Y]āʾ, a region of the land Yad[nana (Cyprus) — whose abode(s) are situated far away, at a distance of seven days (journey) in the middle of the Western Sea (15′) (and) the name of whose land, from the dist]ant [past] until now, [none] o[f the kings, my ancestors, neither in Assyria nor in the land Karduniaš (Babylonia), had ever heard — heard from afar, in the middle of the sea, of the deeds] I had been doi[ng in Chaldea] and the land Ḫatti (Syria). [Their hearts then pounded and fear fell upon them. They brought before me in Babylon gold, silver, (and) utensils of ebony] (and) boxwood, product(s) of [their] lan[d, and they kissed my feet].

18′) [... *the inhabitan*]ts of (the city) Baltil (Aššur) to [...]

19′) [...] inside [...]

20′) [...] ... *he gran*[*ted me* ...]

21′) [... *the god Aššur, the*] *great* [*lord*], king of the gods [...]

Lacuna

65

A large, four-column tablet with 430 lines of text was found in a private house in the city of Aššur and records a formal letter, written in the first person, from Sargon II to the god Aššur in which the ruler reports on a campaign conducted against the land Urarṭu and the city Muṣaṣir in the ruler's eighth regnal year (714). According to line 6, the campaign began in the month Duʾūzu (June–July) and a lunar eclipse that is mentioned in line 318 as an omen towards the close of the campaign and immediately before

64 line 12′ MU.3.KÁM, "(my) third year": This should refer to Sargon's third year on the throne of Babylon (707). Or MU.4.KÁM, "(my) fourth year," following text no. 74 vii 19.

64 line 13′ Text no. 74 vii 20 refers to Aḫundāra as king of Dilmun here rather than Upēri; the former may have been the latter's successor. Text no. 7 line 144 has simply 30 KASKAL.GÍD, "(at a distance of) thirty leagues," rather than *ma-lak* 30 KASKAL.GÍD, "at a distance of thirty leagues." As noted by E. Frahm (KAL 3 p. 76), possibly restore at the end of the line *iš-šá-a man-da-tuš*, "brought me his tribute" (following text no. 74 vii 24), or *iš-pu-ra ar-du-tú*, "sent (a message to do) obeisance (to me)" (following text no. 103 iv 27), instead of *ú-šá-bi-la kàd-ra-šu*, "brought me his gift" (following text no. 7 line 145).

64 line 15′ Or *a-di-*^{d}*nanna*, a sandhi-writing; see already Frahm, KAL 3 p. 76.

the attack on Muṣaṣir has been dated to the evening of October 24, 714. This indicates that the campaign lasted at least three or four months. The text was likely composed in 714 or soon thereafter. This text is commonly referred to as Sargon's Eighth Campaign, Sargon's Letter to the God, or Sargon's Letter to Aššur.

The inscription consists of an initial address (lines 1–5), the body of the text (lines 6–425), and a concluding statement/colophon (lines 426–430), which informs us that the tablet had been written by the royal scribe Nabû-šallimšunu, who was the son an earlier royal scribe, Ḫarmakki. The address (lines 1–5, with each line separated by a line ruling) invokes blessings on the god Aššur, the other deities who dwell in his temple Eḫursaggalkurkurra, the deities who dwell in the city Aššur, and the city Aššur itself, as well as all who dwell in it, in particular those living in its palace; and it concludes by stating that all was well with Sargon and his troops. The body of the text is divided by line rulings into fifteen sections. The first five sections (lines 6–166) describe the king assembling his troops, setting out on campaign, and proceeding through the Zagros Mountains, where he received tribute and gifts from vassal rulers and those who wanted to win his friendship and prevent hostile actions being directed against them. In order to help the Mannean ruler Ullusunu, his vassal, he met the forces of Rusâ (written Ursâ in this and numerous other inscriptions of Sargon II) and Mitatti, the rulers of Urarṭu and Zikirtu respectively, in battle on Mount Uauš, which resulted in a major Assyrian victory and the flight of Rusâ. Sargon then decided to break off his campaign to the lands of Andia and Zikirtu and set out for Urarṭu (line 162). Sections six through twelve (lines 167–305) record Sargon's march through Urarṭian territory. For the most part, the natives fled before the Assyrian advance and these sections provide a description of Urarṭu, including its irrigation works. The Assyrians carried out numerous destructive actions as they marched through Urarṭu. The thirteenth section (lines 306–308) simply records the receipt of tribute from Ianzû, the king of the land Na'iri, indicating that Sargon had left Urarṭu and was on his way home. The fourteenth (and longest) section (lines 309–414) describes Sargon's decision to halt his journey back to Assyria as a result of the lunar eclipse mentioned earlier and instead take a small force to attack the city Muṣaṣir, a small state that bordered both Assyria and Urarṭu. Muṣaṣir was also a "holy city," sacred to the god Ḫaldi, a deity highly honored in Urarṭu; the text records that in this city Urarṭian kings were crowned. That city was captured, looted, and destroyed; and a long, detailed list of the booty taken from the palace of king Urzana and from the temple of Ḫaldi is given. The final section (lines 415–425) recapitulates the major achievements of the campaign. The exact route taken by Sargon during the course of this campaign is a matter of intense scholarly debate (see below).

A.L. Oppenheim has argued that texts of this type were "not to be deposited in silence in the sanctuary, but to be actually read to a public that was to react directly to their contents" and that "they replace in content and most probably in form the customary oral report of the king or his representative on the annual campaign to the city and the priesthood of the capital" (JNES 19 [1960] p. 143). With regard to letters of gods in general and this one in particular, see Borger, RLA 3/8 (1971) pp. 575–576; Oppenheim, JNES 19 (1960) pp. 133–147; and Pongratz-Leisten in Hill, Jones, and Morales, Experiencing Power pp. 295–301. For a letter to the god, likely coming from the reign of Shalmaneser IV, see Grayson, RIMA 3 pp. 243–244 A.0.105.3; for one from Esarhaddon, see Leichty, RINAP 4 pp. 79–86 no. 33. Although the text is written in Babylonian dialect, at times Assyrian dialectical features appear (e.g., *lā* for *ul* in line 84, *iqabbûšuni* for *iqabbûšu* in lines 11 and 188, and *iṣbutū* for *iṣbatū* in line 177). The Akkadian text is composed in a very literary style and is at times complicated, with regard to both syntax and content (Vera Chamaza, SAAB 6 [1992] p. 128) and, as V. Hurowitz has noted, many passages could be described as "poeticized prose" (Studies Ephʿal p. 105 n. 8). For these reasons, it is impossible to give a fully acceptable translation that at all times both reflects the Akkadian syntax accurately and does not violate the rules of good English.

CATALOGUE

Museum Number	Source	Excavation Number	Lines Preserved	cpn
AO 5372 +	Thureau-Dangin, TCL 3	—	1–333, 338–430	c
VAT 8634 +	Schroeder, KAH 2 no. 141	Ass 17861d	334–344	c
VAT 8698a +	Weidner, AfO 12 (1937–39) pl. XI no. 1	Ass 17861b	96–104	c
VAT 8698b +	Weidner, AfO 12 (1937–39) pl. XI no. 2	Ass 17861c	251–259	c
VAT 8698c +	Weidner, AfO 12 (1937–39) pl. XI no. 3	Ass 17861g	334–336	c
VAT 8749	Schroeder, KAH 2 no. 141	Ass 17861a	99–109, 207–237, 337–344	c

COMMENTARY

The tablet is made up of one large and several smaller pieces: AO 5372 + VAT 8634 (Ass 17681d) + VAT 8749 (Ass 17681a) + VAT 8698a–c (Ass 17681b,c,g). VAT 8634 and 8749 are shown on the Aššur excavation photograph 5280. AO 5372 was purchased by the Louvre Museum from the antiquities dealer Géjou in 1910. The fragments in the Vorderasiatisches Museum with the excavation number Ass 17681 were found at Aššur in 1910 in the house of the exorcist (hD81, excavation trench). The tablet is one of the largest cuneiform tablets known; the largest piece, AO 5372, measures 37.5×24.5×4 cm. Its four columns (two on the obverse and two on the reverse) have 109 (1–109), 114 (110–223), 110 (224–333), and 97 (334–430) lines respectively. The scribe, Nabû-šallimšunu, has placed a Winkelhaken to the left of the beginning of every tenth line. There are small holes at regular intervals along all four edges of the tablet and in the space between the two columns on each side of the tablet; the right edge, for example, has eleven holes.

There are numerous studies dealing primarily with the geographical and historical aspects of Sargon's eighth campaign. In particular, there has been a great deal of discussion over the route taken by Sargon. Did he encircle Lake Urmia or did he only go up its western side? Did he go around or even reach Lake Van? The first editor of this text, F. Thureau-Dangin (TCL 3), believed that Sargon went up the eastern side of Lake Urmia, continued over to Lake Van, and then went along the northern and western shores of that lake before returning to Assyria via Muṣaṣir. In 1977, however, L. Levine proposed a much shorter route, one that took Sargon around neither Lake Urmia nor Lake Van (Levine in Levine and Young, Mountains and Lowlands pp. 135–151). In a recent publication (Muscarella and Elliyoun, Eighth Campaign of Sargon II [2012]), studies by O.W. Muscarella and S. Kroll came to different conclusions, although both agreed that Sargon did not get close to Lake Van. Muscarella (following work by H.A. Rigg, L.D. Levine, and M. Salvini) believes that Sargon "campaigned solely along Lake Urmia's southern and western shores and adjacent districts before turning back to Assyria" (pp. 5–9, especially p. 8 [article reprinted in Muscarella, Archaeology, Artifacts and Antiquities pp. 523–530]), while Kroll (following work by P. Zimansky, M. Liebig, and J.E. Reade, and making use of an unpublished study by A. Fuchs) believes that Sargon went around Lake Urmia, although not always close to the coast (pp. 11–17). For the latter view, see also Fuchs in Yamada, SAAS 28 pp. 42–47. Recently, however, J. Marriott and K. Radner (JCS 67 [2015] p. 139) have argued that for reasons of food logistics the campaign cannot have gone around Lake Urmia and was more likely in the area southwest of that lake. See in addition the following studies: Bagg, Assyrische Wasserbauten pp. 130–132; Çilingiroğlu, Anadolu Araştırmaları 4–5 (1976–77) pp. 252–271; Danti, Expedition 56/3 (2014) pp. 27–33; Diakonoff and Medvedskaya, BiOr 44 (1987) pp. 388–391; Hipp, Folia Orientalia 24 (1987) pp. 41–46; Jakubiak, IrAnt 39 (2004) pp. 191–202; Kessler in Haas, Urartu pp. 66–72; Kleiss, AMI NF 10 (1977) pp. 137–141; Kroll in Köroğlu and Konyar, Urartu pp. 160–162; Lehmann-Haupt, MVAG 21/3 (1916) pp. 119–151; Levine in Levine and Young, Mountains and Lowlands pp. 135–151; Liebig, ZA 81 (1991) pp. 31–36 and ZA 86 (1996) pp. 207–210; Mayer, MDOG 112 (1980) pp. 13–33; Medvedskaya in Parpola and Whiting, Assyria 1995 pp. 197–206; Muscarella, JFA 13 (1986) pp. 465–475; Reade, Iran 16 (1978) pp. 137–143; Reade in Liverani, Neo-Assyrian Geography pp. 31–42; Rigg, JAOS 62 (1942) pp. 130–138; Salvini, BiOr 46 (1989) p. 399; Salvini in Pecorella and Salvini, Tra lo Zagros, particularly pp. 15–16 and 46–51; van Loon, JNES 34 (1975) pp. 206–207; Vera Chamaza, AMI NF 27 (1994) pp. 91–118 and AMI NF 28 (1995–96) pp. 235–267 (esp. p. 239 fig. 1 and pp. 253–264); Wiessner, AfO 44–45 (1997–98) pp. 146–155; Wright, JNES 2 (1943) pp. 173–186; Zimansky, Ecology and Empire pp. 40–47; and Zimansky, JNES 49 (1990) pp. 1–21. An important unpublished study of the topography and history of the Zagros region by Fuchs was completed in 2004 (Bis hin zum Berg Bikni: Zur Topographie und Geschichte des Zagrosraumes in altorientalischer Zeit [Tübingen University, 2004]).

There are several abrupt digressions within the section dealing with the city Muṣaṣir. K. Kravitz (JNES 62 [2003] pp. 81–95, especially pp. 94–95) has argued that lines 336–342, 347b–348a, and 411–413 were added to the episode of the sack of that city "when it was already essentially completed" and that the additions "shifted the ultimate outcome of the episode from the punitive plundering of the rebellious Muṣaṣirian vassal to the symbolic disempowerment of the Urarṭian king" (ibid. pp. 81 and 94–95).

V. Hurowitz notes that the total number of lines in the text (including the colophon) is the same as the number of Urarṭian settlements that Sargon claims to have captured (line 422) and argues that "Presenting to the god a 430 line text imitated symbolically the tribute Sargon offered from the 430 cities he conquered" (Studies Ephʿal pp. 107–108).

The inscription refers to Rusâ (Ursâ) as being ruler of Urarṭu at the time of this campaign, but there is some discussion over which Rusâ this was, Rusâ son of Erimena or Rusâ son of Sarduri. Thureau-Dangin thought it was Rusâ son of Erimena, but this view was later opposed by C.F. Lehmann-Haupt who argued for Rusâ son of Sarduri. The latter's view has predominated in recent scholarship (e.g., Fuchs, PNA 3/1 pp. 1054–1056 sub Rusâ 1; and Salvini, Biainili-Urartu p. 133). M. Roaf has recently argued that Thureau-Dangin was correct and that the Urarṭian ruler mentioned in this text was Rusâ son of Erimena (Aramazd 5/1 [2010] pp. 66–82; CRRA 54 pp. 771–780; and Biainili-Urartu pp. 187–216).

BIBLIOGRAPHY

1912 Thureau-Dangin, TCL 3 (AO 5372, photo, copy, edition)
1913 Klauber, DLZ 34 cols. 2139–2141 (study)
1913 Pinches, JRAS pp. 581–601 (lines 1–5, 19–21, 25–26, 158–159, 170–173, 426–430 [plus numerous other shorter passages], translation; study)
1913 Ungnad, ZDMG 67 pp. 175–177 (study)
1914 Bezold, ZA 28 pp. 400–406 (study)
1914 Langdon, PSBA 36 pp. 24–34 (study)
1916 Ehelolf, Wortfolgeprinzip pp. 21–22 (lines 112–114, 118–120, transcription; study of various other passages scattered in the book)
1917 Albright, JAOS 36 pp. 226–232 (study)
1919 Scheil, RA 16 p. 203 (lines 117–118, edition)
1922 Meissner, ZA 34 pp. 113–122 (lines 199–232, edition)
1922 Schroeder, KAH 2 no. 141 (VAT 8634+8749, copy)
1923 Jean, Milieu biblique 2 pp. 295–300 (lines 13–29, 110–161, translation)
1924 Jean, Littérature pp. 246–250 (lines 13–29, 110–161, translation)
1927 Luckenbill, ARAB 2 pp. 73–99 §§139–178 (translation)
1932 Tallqvist, StOr 4/3 p. 60 (lines 315–316, study)
1934 König, AO 33/3–4 pp. 55–58 (lines 42–49, translation, study)
1934 Landsberger, ZA 42 pp. 162–163 and 164–165 (lines 223–228, 412, study)
1937–39 Weidner, AfO 12 pp. 144–148 and pl. XI (VAT 8698a–c, copy, edition, provenance; VAT 8634+8749, collations to lines 216–236)
1941 Herzfeld, Iran in the Ancient Near East pp. 195–196 (lines 64b–67, translation)
1947 Böhl, Chrestomathy 1 nos. 12–13 (lines 1–27, 32–36, 92–105, copy)
1947 Kraus, Orientalia NS 16 p. 185 (line 286, study)
1949 Landsberger, JNES 8 p. 285 n. 120 and p. 287 (lines 100, 209, edition; line 101, translation)
1949 Oppenheim, JNES 8 p. 175 (line 386, edition, study)
1951 Laessøe, JCS 5 pp. 21–32 (lines 202–204, 221–222, edition, study)
1953 Bauer, Lesestücke 1 pp. 83–87; and 2 p. 53 no. 12 (lines 1–41, 51–73, 167–187, copy, study)
1954 Preusser, Wohnhäuser p. 58 (VAT 8698a–c, provenance)
1956 Borger, Asarh. p. 43 commentary to lines 57–58 (lines 58, 414, study)
1960 Lambert, BWL p. 290 (line 226, study)
1960 Oppenheim, JNES 19 pp. 133–147 (study)
1961 Parrot, Assyria fig. 364 (AO 5372, photo)
1966 Hirsch, Orientalia NS 35 pp. 413–416 (lines 18–20, transliteration, study)

1966 van Loon, Urartian Art pp 18–19, 85–86, 125–126, and 128–129 (lines 200–212, 358–361, 362–364, 370–377, 378–383, 392–404, translation)
1968 Hunger, Kolophone no. 264 (lines 428–430, edition)
1979 Mayer, UF 11 pp. 571–95 (lines 346–410, edition, study)
1980 Mayer, MDOG 112 pp. 13–33 (study)
1981 Zaccagnini in Fales, ARIN pp. 263–276 (lines 200–232, translation, study)
1982 André-Leicknam, Naissance de l'écriture p. 199 no. 133 (AO 5372, photo of reverse, study)
1982 Salvini in Klengel, Gesellschaft und Kultur pp. 226–227 (lines 337–342, translation, study)
1982 Spieckermann, Juda unter Assur pp. 330–331 (lines 62–63, edition)
1983 Mayer, MDOG 115 pp. 65–132 (edition)
1985 Dalley, Iraq 47 p. 42 (lines 170–173, translation)
1985 Zimansky, Ecology and Empire pp. 43–44 (lines 189–191, 277–279, 280–291, translation)
1986 Pedersén, Archives 2 p. 71 sub N: 477 (provenance)
1990 Younger, Conquest pp. 115–119 (lines 269–305, edition)
1991 Fales, Studies Tadmor pp. 129–147 (study of numerous passages, including edition of lines 15–16, 18–22, 56–57, 124, 129–130, 155–157, 320–321, 324–331)
1992 Vera Chamaza, SAAB 6/2 pp. 109–128 (study)
1993 Wartke, Urartu pp. 48–50 figs. 14–15 (AO 5372, VAT 8634+8749, photo) and pp. 53, 55–56, 62, 151–152, and 165 (lines 96–102, 134–136, 179–180, 336–342, 400–404, and parts of 354–395, translation [following Mayer]; plus translations of numerous other shorter passages scatttered in the book)
1994 Vera Chamaza, AMI NF 27 pp. 91–118, especially pp. 117–118 (study)
1995–96 Vera Chamaza, AMI NF 28 pp. 235–267 (study)
1995 Koch-Westenholz, Mesopotamian Astrology pp. 153–154 (lines 317–319, translation, study)
1995 Kuhrt, Ancient Near East 2 pp. 517–518 and 532 (lines 52–53, 64–72, translation)
1995 Salvini, Urartäer pp. 93–94 and 96–98 (lines 202–220, 337–342, 346–347, 411–413, translation)
1997 Fales and Lanfranchi in Heintz, Oracles pp. 106-107 (lines 317–319, translation, study)
1998 Fuchs, SAAS 8 especially pp. 97–107, 113, 117, and 119 (lines 58–61 and 155 translation; line 95, edition; lines 372–376, translation, study)
1998 Seidl, ZA 88 p. 101 (lines 373, 379, study)
1998 Zimansky, Ancient Ararat pp. 45–51 (study)
1999 Pongratz-Leisten, SAAS 10 p. 10 n. 11, p. 14, p. 25 n. 75, pp. 39, 217–221, and 263 (lines 1–5, 113, 426–430 edition; lines 317–319, translation)
2000 Bagg, Assyrische Wasserbauten p. 109 n. 142, pp. 127–146, p. 160 n. 347, pp. 273, 276–277, and 319–326 no. 26 (lines 10, 30, 190, 200–232, 242–243, edition, study)
2002 Holloway, Aššur is King p. 135 n. 192 (lines 367–368, 405, partial edition)
2002 Vera Chamaza, Omnipotenz pp. 283 and 348–349 nos. 28 and 101 (lines 116–120, 314–368, edition)
2003 Kravitz, JNES 62 pp. 81-95 (lines 336–343, 345–349, and 411–413, edition; 415–425 partial translation; study)
2003 Levine, Eretz-Israel 27 pp. 111*–119* (lines 1–5, transliteration; study)
2005 Foster, Before the Muses[3] pp. 790–813 no. IV.2.c (translation)
2006 Melville in Chavalas, ANE pp. 337–340 no. 128 (lines 1–36, 51–74, 309–322, 346–351, 408–427, translation)
2006 Ponchia, SAAB 15 pp. 242–243 (lines 167–309, partial edition, study)
2007 Aster, JAOS 127 p. 271 (lines 82–83, edition)
2007 Kuhrt, Persian Empire p. 25 no. 2.A.2.iii (lines 38b–51a, partial translation)
2008 Hurowitz, Studies Ephʿal pp. 104–120 (lines 9, 92–95, 112–115, 118–120, 123–124, 148–151, 156–158, 403–404, 411–414, 426–430, edition; study)
2009 Van Buylaere, Studies Parpola p. 299 (lines 100–102, edition)
2010 Barbato, Kaskal 7 p. 177 (lines 15, 28, 135, 286–288, translation, study)
2010 Green, "I Undertook Great Works" pp. 40–46 (lines 200–232, partial edition, study)
2010 Laato, Studies Ellis p. 386 (lines 1–5, translation, study)
2010 Van De Mieroop, Studies Foster pp. 419–421 and 426–429 (lines 92–94, 112–115, 309–310, 403–404, 411–413, edition, study)
2011 Talon, Annales assyriennes 1 pp. 77–103; and 2 pp. 65–97 (copy, edition)
2012 Worthington, Textual Criticism pp. 60, 90, 178, 182, 185–187, 189, 198–199, 210, 215, 225–226, 232–233, 283–286 (study)
2013 Mayer, Assyrien und Urarṭu I (edition, study), especially pp. 78-89 (lines 348–410, study)
2013 Mayer, Assyrien und Urarṭu II pp. 20, 53, 55–56 (lines 336–342, 397–398, 400–401, 403–404, edition)
2013 Pongratz-Leisten in Hill, Jones, and Morales, Experiencing Power pp. 297–302 (lines 1–5, 426–430, translation, study)
2014 Frame, Expedition 56/3 pp. 30–31 (lines 343–349, 405–414, translation)
2014 Gaspa, Contenitori neoassiri passim (edition and study of the lines between 355 and 397 mentioning vessels)
2014 Maniori, Campagne di Sargon p. 55 M and passim (study)
2014 Rollinger, Studies Lanfranchi pp. 614–617 (lines 96–103a, edition, study)
2015 Pongratz-Leisten, Religion and Ideology pp. 298–299, 327, and 329 (lines 1–5, 110–125, 426–430, translation)
2015 Van De Mieroop, Kaskal 12 pp. 292–299 (lines 132–136, 143, 149–151, transcription, translation, study)
2016 Fales, COS 4 pp. 199–215 no. 4.42 (translation)
2016 Van De Mieroop, JAH 4 pp. 19, 23, and 25 (lines 149–151, 411–414, translation, study)
2017 Liverani, Assyria pp. 30–31, 45–46, 80, 122, 146, 205, and 227 (lines 1–2, 4–5, 59, 80–81, 92–93, 124–125, 127–134, 324–332, 367b, 410, 423b, 424b, 426, translation)
2017 May, BiOr 74 p. 497 (lines 132–133, edition)
2018 Rollinger, Interpreting Herodotus pp. 129–137 (line 403, translation, study)
2018 Rollinger, Studies Neumann pp. 585–609 (lines 403–404a, edition, study)
2018 Zamazalová in Yamada, SAAS 28 pp. 191, 203–204, 206 (lines 15b–16a, 96–102, 127–129, 132–133, translation)
2019 Christiansen, Studies Salvini pp. 134–135 (lines 166, 262–263, transliteration, study)

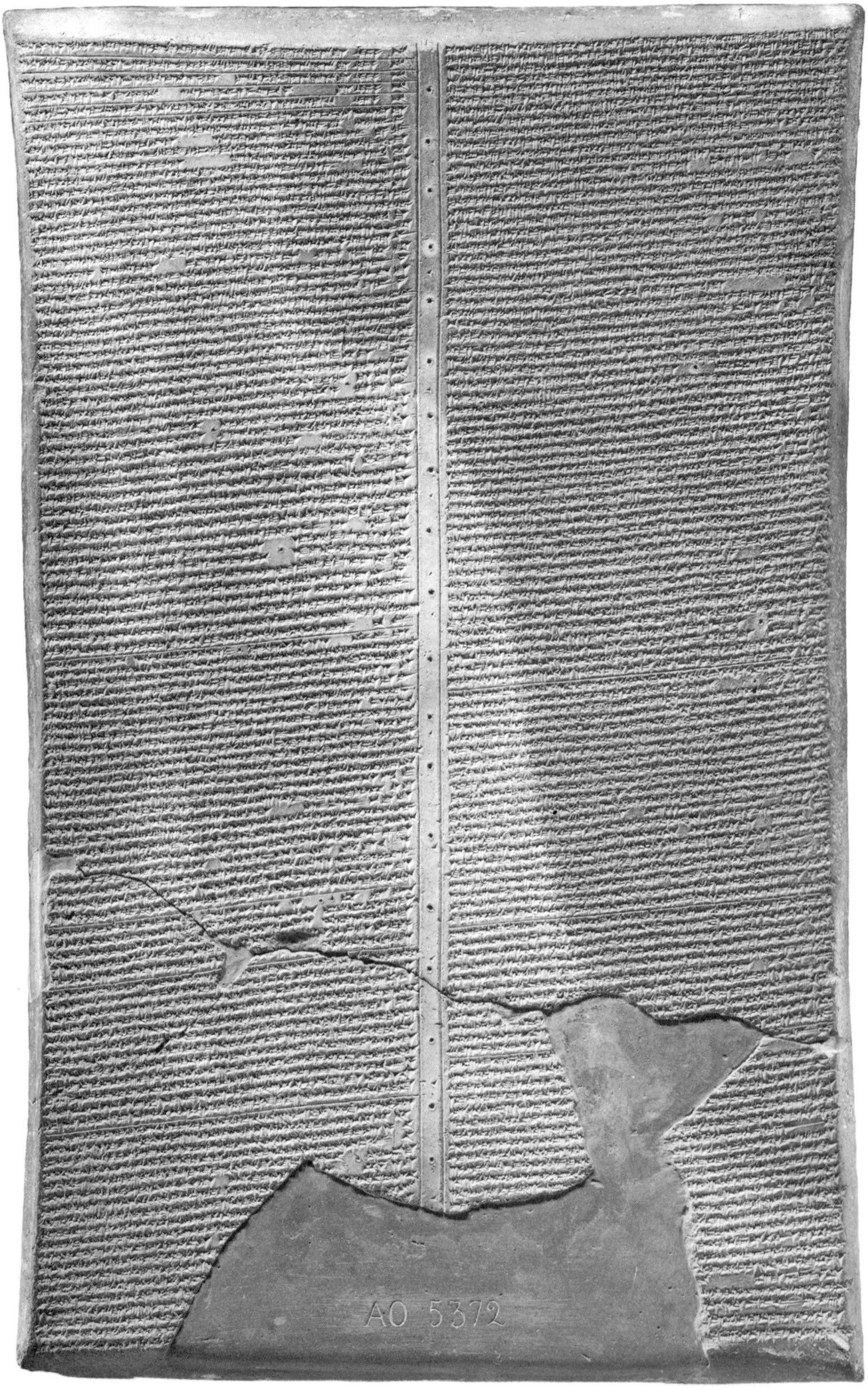

Figure 24. Obverse of AO 5372, Sargon's letter to the god Aššur recording his eighth campaign (714). © Musée du Louvre, dist. RMN - Grand Palais / Raphaël Chipault.

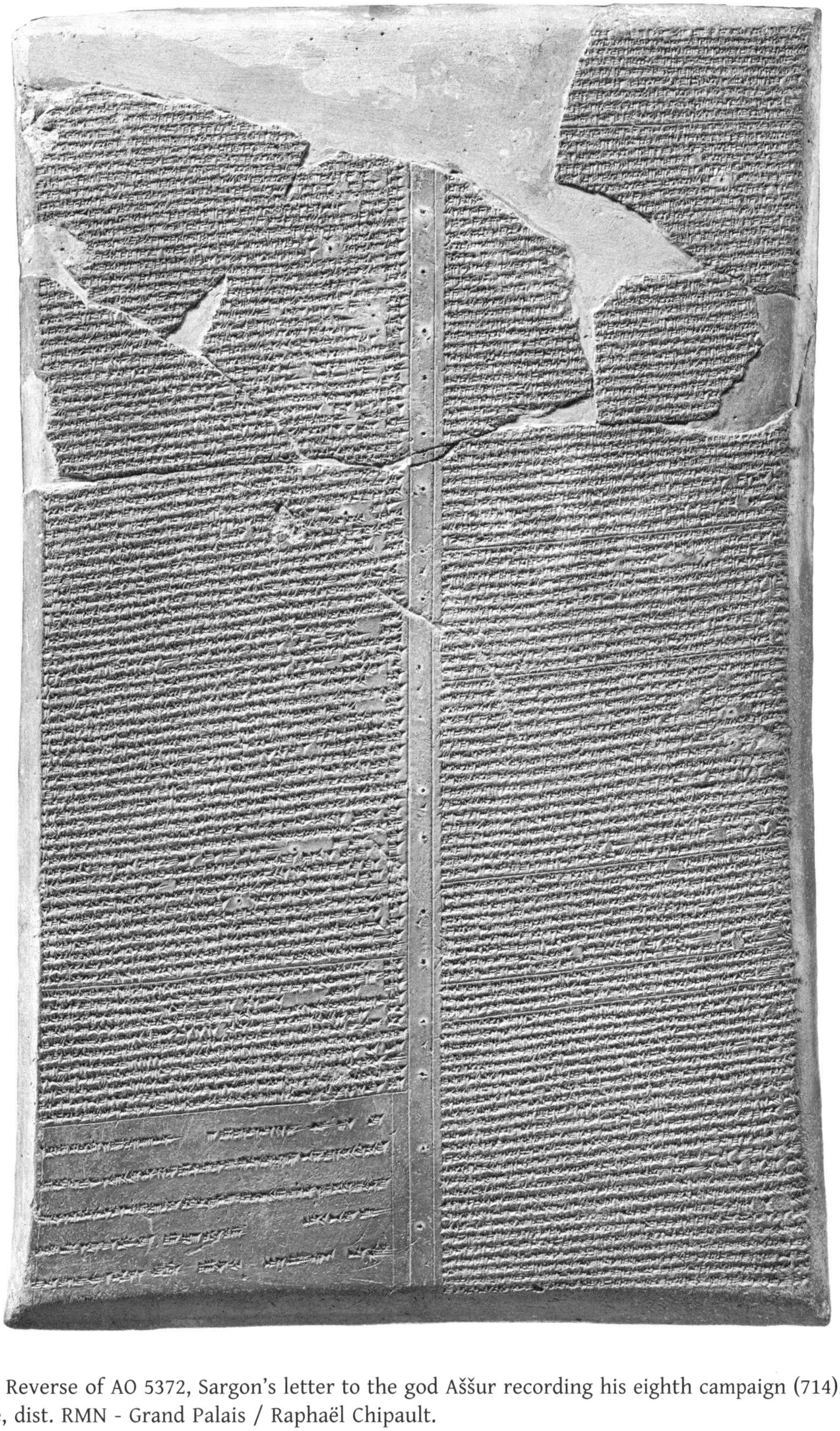

Figure 25. Reverse of AO 5372, Sargon's letter to the god Aššur recording his eighth campaign (714). © Musée du Louvre, dist. RMN - Grand Palais / Raphaël Chipault.

Figure 26. Obverse of VAT 8749 (text no. 65, lines 99–109 and 207–223), Sargon's letter to the god Aššur recording his eighth campaign (714). © Staatliche Museen zu Berlin-Vorderasiatisches Museum. Photo by O.M. Teßmer.

TEXT

1)	*a-na* ^{d}*a-šur a-bu* DINGIR.MEŠ EN GAL-*e a-šib é-ḫur-sag-gal-kur-kur-ra* É.KUR-*šú* GAL-*i a-dan-niš a-dan-niš lu šul-mu*	1) May (all) be extremely well with the god Aššur, father of the gods, the great lord who dwells in Eḫursaggalkurkurra ("House, the Great Mountain of the Lands"), his great temple.
2)	*a-na* DINGIR.MEŠ-*ni* ^{d}NAM.MEŠ ^{d}INANNA.MEŠ *a-ši-bu-ut é-ḫur-sag-gal-kur-kur-ra* É.KUR-*šú-nu* GAL-*i a-dan-niš a-dan-niš lu šul-mu*	2) May (all) be extremely well with the gods (*that issue*) divine decrees (and) with the goddesses, (the deities) who dwell in Eḫursaggalkurkurra, their great temple.
3)	*a-na* DINGIR.MEŠ-*ni* ^{d}NAM.MEŠ ^{d}INANNA.MEŠ *a-ši-bu-ut* URU ^{d}*a-šur*$_{4}$ É.KUR-*šú-nu* GAL-*i a-dan-niš a-dan-niš lu šul-mu*	3) May (all) be extremely well with the gods (*that issue*) divine decrees (and) with the goddesses, (the deities) who dwell in the city Aššur, their great temple.
4)	*a-na* URU *ù* UN.MEŠ-*šú lu šul-mu a-na* É.GAL-*lim a-šib lìb-bi-šá lu šul-mu*	4) May (all) be well with the city and its people! May (all) be well with the palace (and) the one who dwells inside it.
5)	*a-na* ^{m}LUGAL-GI.NA SANGA KÙ ARAD *pa-liḫ* DINGIR-*ti-ka* GAL-*ti ù* KARAŠ-*šu a-dan-niš a-dan-niš šul-mu*	5) (All) is extremely well with Sargon (II) — the holy priest (and) servant who reveres your great divinity — (and) with his (military) camp.
6)	*i-na* ITI.ŠU.GAR.NUMUN.NA *mu-kin ṭè-em ad-na-a-ti* ITI *gaš-ri* IBILA *a-šá-red-di ša* ^{d}EN.LÍL *kaš-kaš* DINGIR.MEŠ ^{d}*nin-urta*	6–12) In the month of Duʾūzu (IV) — (the month) that determines matter(s) for humankind; the month of the mighty one, the eldest son of the god Enlil, the most powerful of the gods, the god Ninurta; (and the month) for which the lord of wisdom, the god Ninšiku (Ea), had inscribed on an ancient tablet the assembly of armies (and) the preparation of a (military) camp — I set out from my royal city Kalḫu and impetuously
7)	*ša a-na pu-uḫ-ḫur um-ma-ni šul-lu-um ka-ra-ši i-na ṭup-pi maḫ-ri iš-ṭu-ru-šu* EN *né-*<*me*>*-qi* ^{d}*nin-ši-kù*	
8)	*ul-tu* URU.*kal-ḫa* URU LUGAL-*ti-ia am-muš-ma* ÍD.*za-ban* AN.TA-*ú i-na kiš-šá-ti-šu šam-riš e-bir*	

4 F. Thureau-Dangin (TCL 3 p. 3), followed by some other scholars (e.g., Fales, COS 4 p. 199), takes *āšib libbiša* to refer to *ēkalli* ("Au palais qui y est situé") while B.R. Foster (Before the Muses^{3} p. 791) treats it separately ("to the palace and the dweller therein"). M. Worthington (Textual Criticism pp. 215–216) argues that an "orthographic–morphological analysis of the manuscript tilts the scales in Foster's favour." If *āšib libbiša* did refer to *ēkalli*, we might expect *āšibat* instead of *āšib* since *ēkallu* is normally considered to be a feminine noun.

9) UD.3.KAM *áš-šu ḫa-ṭa-am pi-i muš-tar-ḫi ka-as pu-rid-di qar-dam-mi a-na* ^{d}EN.LÍL ^{d}NIN.LÍL *pal-ḫiš uš-kin-ma*
10) ÍD.*za-ban* KI.TA-*ú ša né-ber-ta-šú pa-áš-qa-at um-ma-na-at* ^{d}UTU ^{d}AMAR.UTU *pal-gi-iš ú-šá-áš-ḫi-iṭ*
11) *i-na né-re-bi ša* KUR.*kul-la-ar* KUR-*i zaq-ri ša* KUR.*lu-lu-mi-i ša* KUR.*za-mu-a i-qab-bu-šu-ni e-tar-ba*
12) *i-na* KUR.*su-um-bi na-gi-i pi-qit-ti um-ma-ni-ia áš-kun-ma ša* ANŠE.KUR.RA.MEŠ *ù* GIŠ.GIGIR *a-mu-ra mi-na-a-šu-un*
13) *i-na tu-kul-ti-šú-nu* GAL-*ti ša* AN.ŠÁR ^{d}UTU ^{d}AG ^{d}AMAR.UTU *ú-šal-liš-ma a-na qé-reb ḫur-šá-a-ni as-di-ra ta-lu-ku*
14) *a-na* KUR.*zi-kir-te ù* KUR.*an-di-a ša* ^{d}ÙRI.GAL ^{d}IŠKUR *ú-rì-gal-li a-li-kut maḫ-ri-ia ú-šat-ri-ṣa ni-ir-šu-un*
15) *i-na bi-rit* KUR.*ni-kip-pa* KUR.*ú-pa-a* KUR.MEŠ AN.TA.MEŠ *ša gi-mir* GIŠ.MEŠ *ḫi-it-lu-pu-ma qer-bi-šùn e-ši-tùm-ma pit-lu-ḫu né-reb-šú-un*
16) *ki-ma* GIŠ.TIR *ere*-IGI UGU *ta-mir-ti-*<*šu*>*-nu ṣil-lu tar-ṣu-ma a-lik ur-ḫi-šu-nu la im-ma-ru šá-ru-ur* ^{d}UTU-*ši e-tiq-ma*
17) ÍD.*bu-ú-ia* ÍD-*tum bi-ri-šu-nu a-di* 26.ÀM *e-bir-ma um-ma-ni i-na gi-ip-ši-šá la ig-lud-du* A.MEŠ *mi-li*

18) KUR.*si-mir-ri-a* ŠU.SI KUR-*i* GAL-*tu ša ki-ma še-lu-ut šu-kur-ri zaq-pat-ma* UGU *ḫur-šá-a-ni šu-bat* ^{d}*be-let*-DINGIR.MEŠ *šá-qa-at re-e-ši*
19) *ša e-liš re-šá-a-šá šá-ma-mi en-da-ma šap-la-nu šur-šu-šá šuk-šud-du qé-reb a-ra-al-li*
20) *ù ki-ma* EDIN *nu-ú-ni i-di a-na i-di me-te-qa la i-šá-at-ma pa-niš ù ar-kiš šum-ru-ṣu mu-lu-ú-šá*
21) *i-na a-ḫi-šá ḫur-ri na-at-ba-ak* KUR.MEŠ-*e ḫu-du-du-ú-ma a-na i-tap-lu-us ni-ṭil** IGI.II *šit-pu-rat pu-luḫ-tu*
22) *a-na me-le-e* GIŠ.GIGIR *šit-mur* ANŠE.KUR.RA.MEŠ *la ṭa-bat-ma a-na me-te-eq* LÚ.*zu-uk* GÌR.II *šup-šu-qu ma-lak-šá*
23) *i-na pi-it ḫa-sis-si ù šá-dal kar-še ša* ^{d}*é-a ù* ^{d}*be-let*-DINGIR.MEŠ *i-ši-mu-ni-ma a-na sa-pan* KUR *a-a-bi ip-tu-ú pu-rid-di*
24) *ak-kul-li e-re-e dan-nu-ti sag-bu-ú-ia*

crossed the Upper Zab River while it was in full (flood). On the third day, in order to muzzle the mouth of the boastful (and) shackle the legs of the wicked, I reverently prostrated myself before the god Enlil (and) the goddess Mullissu. (10) I then had the troops of the gods Šamaš (and) Marduk leap across the Lower Zab River, whose fording is difficult, as if it were a ditch. I entered the passes of Mount Kullar, a high mountain of the land Lullumû, which is (also) called the land Zamua. I held a review of my army in the district of the land Sumbi and checked the number of horses and chariotry.

13–17) With the great support of the gods Aššur, Šamaš, Nabû, (and) Marduk, I directed the march into the mountains for a third time. I turned the chariot(s) (lit.: "pointed the yoke") of the gods Nergal (and) Adad, (whose) standards go before me, towards the lands Zikirtu and Andia. (15) I advanced in between Mount Nikippa (and) Mount Upâ, high mountains that are thickly covered with all kinds of trees, among which (one becomes completely) confused (as to direction), whose very entry is terrifying, (and) over whose (whole) environs, just as in a cedar forest, a shadow is cast with the result that the one who takes the road through them sees no sunlight. I then crossed the Būya River, the river (which flows) between them, twenty-six times, and (my) army did not fear the floodwaters, despite its (the river's) massive size.

18–30) Mount Simirria is a great mountain peak that points upward like the blade of a spear and who(se) top is higher than the mountains where the goddess Bēlet-ilī dwells. Its summit touches the sky above, and its roots are made to reach down below into the netherworld. (20) Moreover, like the back of a fish, there is no path from (one) side to (the other) side; (thus) ascending it is very difficult both from the front and from the back. Gorges of the outflows of the mountains are deeply cut into its flanks and to the sight of the eye it is shrouded in terror. It is not fit for the ascent of chariotry (or) for allowing horses to show their mettle and its access is very difficult for (even) the passage of foot soldiers. With the intelligence and broad understanding that the god Ea and the goddess Bēlet-ilī decreed for me and (because) they got me moving (lit.: "opened the legs") to overwhelm the land

10 Or, following CAD N/2 p. 145, "whose ford is narrow."
14 ^{d}ÙRI.GAL normally stands for Nergal, but can also stand for Šamaš (see Borger, MZ p. 358). In line 160 we have ^{d}ÙRI.GAL ^{d}IŠKUR *ù* ^{d}*iš-tar be-lí ta-ḫa-zi*, where the three deities are called "the lords of battle." Since Nergal, Adad, and Ištar all had warrior aspects and since Šamaš did not, it seems likely that ^{d}ÙRI.GAL refers to Nergal here.
15 *qer-bi-šùn e-ši-tùm-ma* "among which (one becomes completely) confused (as to direction)": Or *qer-bi-sún e-ši-tùm-ma* "whose midst is confusion" (suggestion courtesy M. Worthington).
18–24 The Akkadian passage is extremely convoluted and a more literal translation would render it as a single sentence.
19 Or emend to *šur-šud-du*, "... are fixed in ...," instead of "... are made to reach ... into ..."; so CAD A/2 p. 226 sub *arallû* a.
20 For the phrase *idi ana idi*, see Hirsch, Orientalia NS 35 (1966) pp. 413–416.
21 *-ṭil*: The text has -AŠ.
24 Limestone is a somewhat soft stone, and thus the idea is that the axes cut through the mountain as if it were butter. The mention of the use of axes to cut through mountains reminds one of the same motif in the Birth Legend of Sargon of Akkad (see Lewis, Sargon Legend p. 26 line 15).

ú-šá-áš-ši-ma pu-lu-uk KUR-*i zaq-ri pi-la-niš*
ú-par-ri-ru-ma ú-ṭi-ib-bu ger-ru
25) *meḫ-ret um-ma-ni-ia aṣ-bat-ma* GIŠ.GIGIR
pet-ḫal-lum ṣa-ab ta-ḫa-zi a-li-kut i-di-ia ki-ma
TI$_8$.MUŠEN.MEŠ *qar-du-ti ṣe*-ru-uš-šá ú-šap-riš*
26) *ṣa-ab ḫup-ši kal-la-pu* EGIR-*šú-nu*
ú-šá-aṣ-bit-ma ANŠE.A.AB.BA.MEŠ ANŠE.MEŠ
bil-ti ki-ma tu-ra-ḫi tar-⌜*bit*⌝ KUR-*i iš-taḫ-ḫi-ṭu*
zuq-ti-šá
27) *um-ma-na-at* ^{d}*a-šur gap-šá-a-ti me-le-šá*
pa-áš-qu-ti ṭa-biš ú-še-li-ma el-en KUR-*i šu-a-tu*
ak-ṣu-ra uš-man-ni
28) KUR.*si-na-ḫul-zi* KUR.*bi-ru-at-ti* KUR.MEŠ
bé-e-ru-te ša ur-qit-su-nu Ú.*kar-šu* ŠIM.GAM.MA
i-ri-šu DÙG.GA
29) ⌜KUR⌝.*tu-ur-ta-ni* KUR.*si-na-bi-ir* KUR.*aḫ-šu-ú-ru*
ù KUR.*su-ú-ia* KUR.MEŠ *se-bet-ti-šú-nu*
nam-ra-ṣi-iš at-ta-bal-kàt
30) ÍD.*rap-pa-a* ÍD.*a-rat-ta-a* ÍD.MEŠ *ti-ib-ki-šu-nu*
i-na mi-li-ši-na i-ki-iš e-ti-iq
31) *a-na* KUR.*su-ri-ka-áš na-gi-i ša* KUR.*man-na-a-a*
ša pat-ti KUR.*kar-al-li ù* KUR.*al-lab-ri-a*
at-ta-rad
32) ^{m}*ul-lu-su-nu* KUR.*ma-an-na-a-a áš-šu a-na*
tu-ur-ri gi-mil-li-šu ša MU.AN.NA-*šam*
la-pa-rak-ku-ú a-lak ger-ri-ia iš-me-ma
33) *šu-ú a-di* LÚ.GAL.MEŠ-*šú ši-i-bi ma-li-ki* NUMUN
É AD-*šú šak-ka-nak-ki ù re-de-e mu-ma-ʾi-ru-ut*
KUR-*šu*
34) *i-na ul-lu-uṣ lìb-bi ù ḫi-du-ut pa-ni ul-tu qé-reb*
KUR-*šú ba-lu li-i-ṭi ḫi-it-mu-ṭi-iš ú-ṣa-am-ma*
35) *ul-tu* URU.*i-zi-ir-ti* URU LUGAL-*ti-šú a-na*
URU.*si-ni-ḫi-ni bir-ti pu-lu-uk* KUR-*šu a-di*
maḫ-ri-ia il-li-ka
36) *ma-da-at-ta-šu* ANŠE.KUR.RA.MEŠ *ṣi-in-da-at*
ni-i-ri a-di til-li-šú-nu GU$_4$.MEŠ *ù* US$_5$.UDU.ḪI.A
ub-lam-ma iš-šiq GÌR.II-*ia*

of (my) enemy, I had my *vanguard* carry strong copper axes; (thus), they cut through high mountain crag(s) as if (they were) limestone and (thereby) improved the path. (25) I took the lead (in front) of my army and made the chariotry, cavalry, (and) battle troops who go at my side, fly over it (the mountain) as if (they were) brave eagles. I had the common soldiers (and) *light infantry* follow behind them; the camels (and) donkeys bearing the baggage leapt up its peaks like ibexes native to the mountains. I had the numerous troops of the god Aššur ascend its difficult slopes in a good order and I (then) set up camp on top of that mountain. (With regard to) Mount Sinaḫulzi (and) Mount Biruatti — remote mountains whose vegetation is the sweet-smelling leek (and) *ṣumlalû*-plant — Mount Turtani, Mount Sinabir, Mount Aḫšūru, and Mount Sūya, I crossed these seven mountains with (great) difficulty. As if (they were) ditches, I crossed the Rappâ (and) the Arattâ Rivers, the rivers flowing off their slopes, when they were in flood.

31–36) I went down to the land Surikaš, a district of the land Mannea, which is on the border of the lands Karalla and Allabria. Because I do not cease avenging him every year, (when) Ullusunu, the Mannean, heard of the advance of my expeditionary force, without (even exchanging) hostages, he (Ullusunu), together with his magnates, elders, counselors, offsprimg of his father's house, governors, and officials, who govern his land, speedily came out from his land with a joyful heart and a happy countenance, and, (35) (traveling) from his royal city Izirtu to the city Siniḫini, a border fortress of his land, he came into my presence. He brought me horses trained to the yoke, together with their trappings, oxen, and sheep and goats, as his tribute and he kissed my feet.

37) *a-na* URU.*la-ta-še-e* BÀD *ša i-na* UGU ÍD-*ti ša*
KUR.*la-a-ru-e-te na-gi-i ša* KUR.*al-*^{la}*lab-ri-a*
aq-ṭe-rib

37–38a) I came to the city Latašê, a fortress that is (situated) on the river of the land Lāruete, a district of the land Allabria. I received horses, oxen, and sheep (and) goats as tribute from Bēl-aplu-iddina of the land Allabria.

38) *ša* ^{m}EN-IBILA-SUM.NA KUR.*al-lab-ri-a-a*
ma-da-ta-šu ANŠE.KUR.RA.MEŠ GU$_4$.MEŠ *ù*
US$_5$.UDU.ḪI.A *am-ḫur a-na* KUR.*par-su-áš*
at-ta-rad
39) LÚ.EN.URU.MEŠ-*ni ša* KUR.*nam-ri*

38b–41) I went down to the land Parsuaš. The city rulers of the lands Namri, Sangibutu, (and) Bīt-Abdadāni, and of the land of the powerful Medes heard of the advance of my expeditionary force; the laying waste of their lands that (had occurred) in my previous

25 *aṣ-bat-ma*, following CAD Ṣ p. 28 and see M/2 p. 51. Or *meḫ-rit um-ma-ni-ia az-ziz-ma*, "I stood facing my army and," following AHw p. 640 sub *meḫretu(m)* 3c. *ṣe**-: The text has AD-.

26 *kal-la-pu*, "*light infantry*": The exact meaning of the term *kallābu/kallāpu* remains uncertain and the translation follows CAD K p. 77 sub *kallābu*. See Postgate, Iraq 62 (2000) pp. 104–105 and Dezsö, Assyrian Army 1/1 p. 60. J. Scurlock (CRRA 52 pp. 724–734) argues that it is "the inactive partners of regular cavalrymen" who later "developed into a corps of lancer cavalry" (ibid. p. 731); and F.M. Fales suggests that it refers to regular Assyrian infantry or unarmored cavalry (Studies Oded pp. 88–93).

29 The text refers to seven mountains, but only six are named in lines 28–29. It is possible that one was omitted or that Mount Simirria was the seventh.

32 *la-pa-rak-ku-ú*: Presumably for *lā apparkkû*; see CAD N/1 p. 280.

KUR.*sa-an-gi-bu-ti* KUR.*É-ab-da-da-ni ù* KUR.*ma-da-a-a dan-nu-ti a-lak ger-ri-ia iš-mu-ma*
40) *šu-uḫ-ru-ub ma-ta-a-ti-šú-nu ša i-na* MU.AN.NA-*ia maḫ-ri-ti i-na uz-ni-šú-nu ib-ši-ma šá-ḫur-ra-tú it-ta-bi-ik* UGU-*šú-un*
41) *ma-da-ta-šú-nu ka-bit-tu ul-tu qé-reb ma-ta-a-ti-šu-nu iš-šu-nim-ma i-na* KUR.*par-su-áš ú-šad-gi-lu pa-ni-ia*

year was (still) in their minds (lit.: "their ears") and deathly quiet overwhelmed them. They brought me their substantial tribute from their lands and handed (it) over to me in the land Parsuaš.

42) *ša* ^{m}*ta-al-ta-a* KUR.*el-li-pa-a-a* ^{m}*uk-sa-tar* ^{m}*du-re-si* ^{m}*sa-tar-e-šú* LÚ.EN.URU.MEŠ-*ni ša* ÍD-*ti*
43) ^{m}*an-zi-i ša* URU.*ḫal-ḫu-bar-ra* ^{m}*pa-a-a-uk-ku ša* URU.*ki-lam-ba-te* ^{m}*ú-zi-i ša* URU.*ma-a-li*
44) ^{m}*ú-a-ki-ir-tu ša* URU.*na-ap-pi* ^{m}*ma-ki-ir-tu ša* URU.É-*sa-ag-bat* ^{m}*ki-ta-ak-ki ša* URU.*ú-ri-an-gi*
45) ^{m}*ma-áš-da-a-a-uk-ku ša* URU.*ki-in-ga-ra-ku* ^{m}*ú-zi-tar ša* URU.*qa-an-ta-a-ú* ^{m}*pa-a-uk-ku ša* URU.É-*kap-si*
46) ^{m}*ḫu-um-bé-e ša* URU.É-*zu-al-za-áš* ^{m}*ú-zu-ma-an-da* <*ša*> URU.*ki-si-la-ḫa* ^{m}*bur-bu-ra-zu ša* URU.É-^{d}15
47) ^{m}*ba-ag-pár*^{ar}*-na ša* URU.*zak-ru-te* ^{m}*da-ri-i ša* KUR.*šá-pár-da* ^{m}*uš-ra-a ša* URU.*ka-an-za-ba-ka-ni*
48) ^{m}*sar-ru-ti ša* URU.*kar-zi-nu-ú* ^{m}*ma-áš-dak-ku ša* URU.*an-dir-pa-ti-a-nu* ^{m}*ak-ku-us-su ša* URU.*ú-si-gur*$^{?}$ ^{m}*bir-ta-tu ša* URU.*ṣi-bur-a-a*
49) ^{m}*za-ar-du-uk-ku ša* URU.*ḫa-ar-zi-a-nu* ^{m}*ma-áš-dak-ku ša* URU.*a-rat-is-ti* ^{m}*sa-tar-pa-nu ša* URU.*ba-ri-ka-nu* ^{m}*kar-ak-ku ša* KUR.*ú-ri-ka-a-a*
50) ANŠE.KUR.RA.MEŠ *pe-tan bir-ki* ANŠE.*pa-re-e ṣar-ḫu-ti* ANŠE.*ud-ri i-lit-ti* KUR-*šu-nu* GU$_4$.MEŠ *ù ṣe-e-ni am-ḫur*

42–50) From Taltâ (Daltâ) of the land Ellipi, U(a)ksatar, Dūrēsi, (and) Satarēšu, the city rulers of the river-(land), Anzî of the city Ḫalḫubarra, Payukku of the city Kilambāti, Uzî of the city Māli, Uakirtu of the city Nappi, Makirtu of the city Bīt-Sagbat, Kitakki of the city Uriangi, (45) Mašdayukku of the city Kingaraku, Uzitar of the city Qantāu, Payukku of the city Bīt-Kapsi, Ḫumbê of the city Bīt-Zualzaš, Uzumanda <of> the city Kisilaḫa, Burburazu of the city Bīt-Ištar, Baga-parna of the city Zakruti, Dārî of the land Šaparda, Ušrâ of the city Kanzabakanu, Sarruti of the city Karzinû, Mašdakku of the city Andirpattianu, Akkussu of the city *Usigur*, Birtātu of the city Ṣibur, Zardukka of the city Ḫarzianu, Mašdakku of the city Aratista, Satarpānu of the city Barikānu, (and) Karakku of the land Uriakku, I received swift horses, fiery mules, Bactrian camels native to their land(s), oxen, and sheep and goats.

---

51) TA KUR.*par-su-áš at-tu-muš a-na* KUR.*mi-is-si na-gi-i ša* KUR.*ma-an-na-a-a aq-ṭe-rib*
52) ^{m}*ul-lu-su-nu a-di* UN.MEŠ KUR-*šu i-na tag-mir-ti lìb-bi ša e-peš ar-du-ti i-na* URU.*si-ir-da-ak-ka bir-ti-šú ú-qa-ʾi ger-ri*
53) *ki-ma* LÚ.*šu-ut* SAG.MEŠ-*ia* LÚ.EN.NAM.MEŠ *ša* KUR *aš-šur*.KI ZÌ.DA.MEŠ GEŠTIN.MEŠ *a-na ta-kul-ti um-ma-ni-ia ka-re-e iš-pu-uk-ma*
54) DUMU-*šú* GAL-*ú it-ti* IGI.SÁ-*e šul-ma-ni ú-šat-li-man-ni-ma a-na kun-ni šar-ru-ti-šú ip-qid-da na-ra-a-šu*
55) ANŠE.KUR.RA.MEŠ GAL.MEŠ LAL-*at ni-i-ri* GU$_4$.MEŠ *ù* US$_5$.UDU.ḪI.A *ma-da-ta-šú*

51–63) Moving on from the land Parsuaš, I came to the land Missi, a district of the land Mannea. With the whole-hearted intention of doing obeisance (to me), Ullusunu, together with the people of his land, waited for my expeditionary force in the city Sirdakka, his fortress. As if (he were one of) my (own) eunuchs, provincial governors of Assyria, he had piled up in heaps flour (and) wine to feed my army; he (then) presented to me his eldest son, with presents (and) gifts, and in order to firmly establish his position as king, he entrusted his *stele* to me. (55) I received from him large horses trained to the yoke, oxen, and sheep and goats as his tribute, and he prostrated

---

47 With regard to the Iranian name Baga-parna, see Eilers, ZDMG 90 (1936) p. 178 n. 1; Fuchs and Schmitt, PNA 1/2 p. 251; and Schmitt, Iranische Personnamen p. 59.
48 URU.*ú-si-gur*$^{?}$: See the copy for *gur*$^{?}$ in the minor variants section. F. Thureau-Dangin suggests possibly URU.*ú-si-is* (TCL 3 p. 10 n. 5); W. Mayer (Assyrien und Urarṭu I p. 100) reads URU.Ú-*si-ib*.
49 For Aratistia (previously read URU.*a-rad-pa-ti*), see also KUR.*a-*⌜*rat*⌝*-is-ta* in text no. 82 vi 28′′ and URU.*a-ra-ti-iš*$^{?}$*-ta* in text no. 117 ii 58.
54 *na-ra-a-šu*, "his *stele*": Quite possibly an error for *kád-ra-a-šu*, "his gift" (suggestion of S. Parpola); cf. text no. 1 lines 368 and 460, and text no. 2 lines 352 and 437.

am-ḫur-šu-ma áš-šú tur-ri gi-mil-li-šu il-bi-na ap-pu
56) GÌR.II KUR.*ka-ak-mi-i* LÚ.KÚR *lem-ni* TA *qé-reb* KUR-*šu pa-ra-si-im-ma ša* ^{m}*ur-sa-a i-na dáb-de-e* EDIN *suḫ-ḫur-ta-šú šá-ka-ni*
57) KUR.*ma-an-na-a-a sap-ḫu a-na áš-ri-šu tur-ri* UGU LÚ.KÚR-*šú i-na li-ti uz-zu-zi-im-ma ma-ṣe-e mal lìb-bi*
58) *šu-ú a-di* LÚ.*ra-ban-ni* LÚ.*šá-kín ṭè-em* KUR-*šú ú-ṣal-lu-ni-ma i-na pa-ni-ia* UGU *er-bé rit-ti-šú-nu ip-taš-ši-lu ki-ma kal-bi*
59) *re-e-ma ar-*<*ši*>*-šu-nu-ti-ma ut-nen-ni-šu-nu al-qe at-mu-šu-nu ša te-nin-ti áš-mé-ma aq-bi-šu-nu a-ḫu-lap*
60) *áš-šu da-na-ni šu-tu-ri ša* ^{d}*a-šur* ^{d}AMAR.UTU *iš-ru-ku-ni-ma* UGU *kul-lat mal-ki ša kiš-šá-ti ú-šar-bu-ú* GIŠ.TUKUL.MEŠ-*ia*
61) *sa-kap* KUR.*ur-ar-ṭi tur-ri mi-iṣ-ri-šu-un* UN.MEŠ KUR.*man-na-a-a dal-pa-a-te šup-šu-ḫi aq-bi-šu-nu-ti-ma ir-ḫi-ṣu lib-bu*
62) *ša* ^{m}*ul-lu-su-nu* LUGAL *be-lí-šu-nu* GIŠ.BANŠUR *tak-bit-ti ma-ḫar-šu ar-ku-su-ma* UGU *ša* ^{m}*ir-an-zi a-bi a-lid-di-šú ú-šaq-qí* GIŠ.GU.ZA-*šú*
63) *šá-a-šu-nu it-ti* UN.MEŠ KUR *aš-šur*.KI *i-na* GIŠ.BANŠUR *ḫi-da-a-ti ú-še-šib-šu-nu-ti-ma ma-ḫar* AN.ŠÁR *ù* DINGIR.MEŠ KUR-*šú-nu ik-ru-bu* LUGAL-*ti*

himself before me in order to return the favors he had received (from me). He, together with the magnates (and) governors of his land, implored me to bar (the people of) the land Kakmê, an evil enemy, from (setting) foot in his land, to bring about the rout of Ursâ (Rusâ) on the battlefield, to restore the scattered land Mannea, to stand in triumph over his enemy, and to achieve whatever (he) wanted; they (Ullusunu and his officials) kept groveling before me on all fours like dogs. I had pity on them and accepted their supplications. I listened to their beseeching words and said to them "So be it" (lit.: "Enough"). (60) Because of the supreme might that the gods Aššur (and) Marduk had granted me and (so) had made my weapons prevail over (those of) all (other) rulers in the world, I promised them to overthrow the land Urarṭu, to restore their (true) boundaries, (and) to bring relief to the troubled people of the land Mannea; and, (as a result) they had confidence (again). I set out a table of honor before Ullusunu, the king, their lord, and (thereby) elevated his rule (lit.: "throne") above that of Iranzi, the father who had begotten him. I had them sit at a festive table with the people of Assyria and they (then) blessed my kingship in the presence of (the god) Aššur and the gods of their own land.

64) ^{m}*zi-i-zi-i ša* URU.*ap-pa-tar* ^{m}*za-la-a-a ša* URU.*ki-it-pat-a-a* LÚ.EN.URU.MEŠ-*ni ša* KUR.*gi-zi-il-bu-un-di na-gi-i*
65) *ša i-na* KUR.MEŠ-*e né-su-ti a-šar ru-uq-te uš-bu-ma i-na šid-*<*di*> KUR.*man-na-a-a ù* KUR.*ma-da-a-a ki-ma giš-ri par-ku*
66) *ù* UN.MEŠ *a-*<*ši*>*-bu-ut* URU.MEŠ-*ni šu-a-tu-nu a-na e-mu-qi ra-ma-ni-šú-nu tak-lu-ma la i-du-ú be-lu-tu*
67) *ša i-na* LUGAL.MEŠ-*ni a-li-kut maḫ-ri-ia a-a-um-ma šu-bat-su-un la e-mu-ru-ma* MU-*šú-nu la iš-mu-ú la im-ḫu-ru bi-lat-su-un*
68) [*i-na*] ⸢*zi*⸣*-kir-šú* GAL-*i ša* ^{d}*a-šur* EN-*ia ša šuk-nu-uš mal-ki ša* KUR.MEŠ-*e ù ma-ḫar* IGI.SÁ-*e-šú-nu iš-ru-ku ši-rik-ti*
69) [*me-te*]*-*⸢*eq ger*⸣*-ri-ia iš-mu-ma pu-luḫ-ti me-lam-me-ia ik-tùm-šu-nu-ti i-na qé-reb* KUR-*šu-nu im-qut-su-nu ḫat-tu*
70) ⸢*ma*⸣*-da-ta-šu-nu* ANŠE.KUR.RA.MEŠ *ṣi-in-da-*<*at*> *ni-i-ri a-na la ma-ni* GU$_{4}$.MEŠ *ù* US$_{5}$.UDU.ḪI.A
71) ⸢TA⸣ URU.*ap-pa-tar ù* URU.*ki-it-pat iš-šu-nim-ma i-na* URU.*zi-ir-di-ak-ka ša* KUR.*man-na-a-a a-di maḫ-*<*ri*>*-ia ub-lu-ni*

64–73) Zīzî of the city Appatar (and) Zalāya of the city of Kitpat — city rulers of the district Gizilbunda, who dwell in remote mountains, far-off place(s), and like a barricade bar (the way) into the region of the lands Mannea and Media — and the people who dwelt in those cities put their trust in their own strength and were not used to being ruled (lit.: "did not know lordship"). None of the kings, my predecessors, had ever seen their abode(s), heard their name(s), (or) received tribute from them. [At] the great command of the god Aššur, my lord — who had granted me as a gift the subjugation of the rulers of the mountain regions and the receipt of presents from them — they heard of the [progr]ess of my expeditionary force and fear of my brilliance overwhelmed them. Fear fell upon them in the midst of their (own) land. (70) From the cities Appatar and Kitpat they brought me as their tribute countless horses trained to the yoke, oxen, and sheep and goats; they brought (these) before me in the city Zirdiakka of the land Mannea. They besought me to spare their lives and they kissed my feet so that (I would) not demolish their (city) walls. Moreover, for the well-being of their land, I appointed a *qīpu*-official over them and assigned them to the authority of a

---

56 KUR.*ka-ak-mi-i*, "land Kakmê": Kakmê/Kakmî is the name of the land Urarṭu in the Mannean language; see Fuchs, Khorsabad pp. 440–441.
65 Borger, BiOr 17 (1960) p. 166a sub 107b suggests <*bi*>*-rit* instead of *šid-*<*di*> (following Bauer, Lesestücke 1 p. 85 sub line 110) and GIŠ.RI (for *talli*) instead of *giš-ri*.
67 "None of the kings .. from them": This is actually a relative clause in the text, beginning with the relative conjunction *ša*.

72) ⸢*áš*⸣-*šu e-ṭer na-piš-ti-šu-un i-ba-lu-ni-ma a-na la na-qar* BÀD.MEŠ-*šú-nu ú-na-áš-ši-qu* GÌR.II-*ia*
73) *ù a-na šá-lam* KUR-*šu-un* LÚ.*qe-e-pu* UGU-*šu-nu ap-qid-ma i-na* ŠU.II LÚ.*šu-ut* SAG.MEŠ-*ia* LÚ.GAR.KUR KUR.*par-su-áš am-nu-šú-nu-ti*

eunuch (lit.: "eunuchs") of mine, the governor of the land Parsuaš.

---

74) TA URU.*zi-ir-di-ak-ka* URU.*bir-ti ša* KUR.*ma-an-na-a-a at-tu-muš*
75) 30 KASKAL.GÍD *qaq-qa-ru i-na bi-rit* KUR.*ma-an-na-a-a* KUR.⸢É⸣-*kap-si ù* KUR.*ma-da-a-*<*a*> *dan-nu-ti šit-mu-riš* al-lik-ma*
76) ⸢*a*⸣-*na* URU.*pa-an-zi-iš bir-ti-šú* GAL-*ti ša* ⸢UGU KUR⸣.*zi-kir-te ù* KUR.*an-di-a a-na ka-a-di na-da-at*
77) ⸢*ša*⸣ *a-na la a-ṣe-e mul-taḫ-ṭi ka-le-e* GÌR.II ⸢LÚ.KÚR⸣ UGU *na-ge-*⸢*e ki-lal-la*⸣-*an rak-sa-tu aq-ṭe-rib*
78) ⸢*ša*⸣ URU.*bir-ti šu-a-ti rik-si-šá ú-dan-nin-ma* ŠE.PAD.MEŠ ⸢Ì$^{?}$⸣.[MEŠ GEŠTIN$^{?}$].⸢MEŠ *ù ú*⸣-[*nu-ut ta*]-*ḫa-zi i-na lìb-bi ú-še-li*

74–78) Moving on from the city Zirdiakka, a fortress of the land Mannea, I marched furiously a distance of thirty leagues between (the territory of) the land Mannea, the land Bīt-Kabsi, and the land of the powerful Medes. I then came to the city Panziš, its strong fortress, which is situated as a guard post on (the border with) the lands Zikirtu and Andia (and) which is fortified against (these) two districts in order to prevent any fugitive getting away (and) to block any incursion by (lit.: "the feet of") the [ene]my. I reinforced the defenses (lit.: "stucture") of that fortress and sent up into it barley, *oil*, [*wine*], and [ba]ttle ge[ar].

---

79) TA URU.*pa-an-zi-iš at-tu-muš* ÍD.*iš-tar-a-ú-ra-a* ⸢ÍD$^{?}$-*tum*$^{?}$⸣ *e-te-bir a-na* KUR.*a-ú-ka-né-e* ⸢*na*⸣-*gi-*⸢*i ša* KUR⸣.*zi-kir-te aq-ṭe-rib*
80) ^{m}*me-ta-at-*<<*ta*>>-*ti* KUR.*zi-kir-ta-a-a ša ni-ir* <^{d}*a-šur*> *iṣ-lu-*⸢*ma*⸣ *še-ṭu-tu* ⸢^{m}*ul*⸣-*lu-su-nu* LUGAL *be-lí-šú il-qu-ú i-mi-šu* ARAD-*su*
81) *a-na* ^{m}*ur-sa-a* KUR.*ur-ar-ṭa-a-a ša ki-i šá-šu-ma ta-šim-tu la i-du-ú né-ra-ri la e-ṭir* ZI-*šú it-ta-kil-ma*
82) UGU KUR.*ú-áš-di-rik-ka* KUR-*i mar-ṣi pal-ḫiš e-li-ma ma-lak ger-ri-ia a-na ru-qe-e-te iṭ-ṭul-ma ir-ru-ṭu* UZU.MEŠ-*šú*
83) *kul-lat* UN.MEŠ KUR-*šú ú-paḫ-ḫir-ma a-na* KUR.MEŠ-*e ru-qu-ú-te nam-ra-ṣi-iš ú-še-li-ma la in-na-mir a-šar-šu-un*
84) *ù šu-ú* URU.*pa-ar-da* URU LUGAL-*ti-šú pa-nu-uš-šu la i-qir-ma bu-še-e* É.GAL-*šú e-zib-ma ú-ṣi ka-ma-ti-iš*
85) ANŠE.KUR.RA.MEŠ-*šú ù ṣa-ab ta-ḫa-*⸢*zi*⸣-*šu ú-zak-ki-ma a-na re-ṣu-ut* ^{m}*ur-sa-a né-ra-ri-šu ú-bíl ki-it-ru*
86) LÚ.ERIM.MEŠ *ti-du-ki-šu ek-du-ti ša i-na né-re-bi ša* KUR.*ú-áš-di-rik-ka a-na ka-a-di uš-bu a-duk-ma*
87) URU.⸢*iš*⸣-*ta-ip-pa* URU.*sak-ta-tu-uš* URU.*na-an-zu* URU.*a-ú-ka-né-e* URU.*ka-a-ba-ni* URU.*gur-ru-su-pa* URU.*ra-ak-si*
88) URU.*gim-da-ak-rik-ka* URU.*ba-ru-nak-ka* URU.*ú-ba-ba-ra* URU.*si-te-ra* URU.*ta-áš-ta-mi* URU.*te-sa-am-mi-a*
89) 12 URU.MEŠ-*šú-nu dan-nu-ti* É BÀD.MEŠ-*ni a-di*

79–90) Moving on from the city Panziš, I crossed the Ištaraurâ River. I came to the land Aukanê, a district of the land Zikirtu. Mitatti of the land Zikirtu — who had thrown off the yoke of <*the god Aššur*>, held Ullusunu, the king, his lord, in contempt, and disregarded his position as vassal — put his trust in Ursâ (Rusâ), the Urarṭian, who like himself had no wisdom, an ally who could not save his life, and, full of fear, he went up onto Mount Uašdirikka, a rugged mountain. Then, (when) he saw from afar the advance of my expeditionary force, his body trembled (in fear). He gathered together all the people of his land and made (them) climb with (great) difficulty up distant mountains; their whereabouts have never been discovered. Moreover, (as for) him, his royal city Parda had no value in his eyes and (so) he abandoned the property of his palace and left town (lit.: "went outside"). (85) He mobilized his horses and his battle troops and brought (*them as*) auxiliary troops to the aid of Ursâ (Rusâ), his ally. I defeated his fierce combat troops who were stationed as a guard post in a pass at Mount Uašdirikka and I conquered all the cities Išta'ippa, Saktatuš, Nanzu, Aukanê, Kābani, Gurrusupa, Raksi, Gimdakrikka, Barunakka, Ubabara, Sitera, Taštami, (and) Tesammia — their twelve strong, walled cities — together with eighty-four settlements in their environs. I destroyed their (city) walls. I set fire to the houses inside them and, as if the Deluge had destroyed (them), I heaped up (their remains) into (ruin) mounds.

---

75 *-riš**: The text has -ŠID.

87–89 As noted by W. Mayer (MDOG 115 [1983] p. 77), although the text refers to a total of twelve cities, thirteen cities are mentioned. F.M. Fales (COS 4 p. 202 n. 35) suggests that if this is not a mistake, Aukanê may not have been included in the count since it could also refer to the entire region.

84 URU.MEŠ-*ni ša se-eḫ-ri-šú-nu gi-mir-tu ak-šu-ud*

90) BÀD.MEŠ-*šú-nu ap-pu-ul* É.MEŠ *qer-bi-šú-nu* ^{d}GIBIL$_{6}$ *ú-šá-aṣ-bit-ma ki-ma ša a-bu-bu ú-ab-bi-tu* DU$_{6}$*-*niš ú-kám-mir*

---

91) TA KUR.*a-ú-ka-né-e at-tu-muš* <*a-na*> KUR.*ú-iš-di-iš na-gi-i ša* KUR.*man-na-a-a ša* ^{m}*ur-sa-a e-ki-mu-uš aq-ṭe-rib*

92) *el-la-mu-u*$_{8}$*-a* ^{m}*ur-sa-a* KUR.*ur-ar-ṭa-a-a la na-ṣir zi-kir* ^{d}*a-šur* ^{d}AMAR.UTU *la pa-li-ḫu ma-mit* EN EN.EN

93) LÚ.*šad-du-u*$_{8}$*-a* NUMUN *né-er-ti ša ta-šim-tu la i-du-u* <*a-na*> *da-ba-ab tuš-ši nu-ul-la-ti ti-iṣ-bu-ra šap-ta-a-šú*

94) *ša* ^{d}UTU DI.KU$_{5}$.GAL DINGIR.MEŠ *zi-kir-šú kab-tu la na-aṣ-ru-ma* MU.AN.NA-*šam a-na la e-ge-e e-te-ti-*<*qu*> GIŠ.ḪUR-*šú*

95) EGIR *ḫi-ṭa-a-te-šú maḫ-ra-a-te gul-lul-tu* GAL-*tu ša ḫe-pe-e* KUR-*šu ù šum-*⸢*qut*⸣ UN.MEŠ-*šú e-pu-uš-ma*

96) *i-na* KUR.*ú-a-uš* KUR-*i* GAL-*i ša it-ti ši-kín* DUNGU *i-na qé-reb* AN-*e* ⸢*um*⸣*-mu-*⸢*da*⸣ *re-šá-a-šu*

97) *ša iš-tu u*$_{4}$*-um ṣa-a-ti* NUMUN *šik-nat* ZI-*tim a-šar-šu la e-ti-qu-*⸢*ma*⸣ *a-lik* ⸢*ur*⸣*-*[*ḫi*] ⸢*la*⸣ *e-mu-ru du-rug-šú*

98) *ù iṣ-ṣur* AN-*e mu-up-par-šu ṣe-ru-uš la i-ba-a*ʾ*-ú-ma a-na šu-uṣ-bu-ub kap-pi* TUR.MEŠ-⸢*šú*$^{?}$⸣ [*la iq*]-⸢*nu*$^{?}$*-nu*⸣ *qin-nam*

99) KUR-*ú zaq-ru ša ki-ma še-él-ti pat-ri zaq-pu-ma ḫur-ri na-at-bak* KUR.MEŠ-*e ru-qu-*[*ú-te x* (*x*)] (*x*)-⸢*ú ṣur-ru-uš-šu*⸣

100) *i-na um-še* GAL.MEŠ *ù dan-na-at* EN.TE.NA *ša qa-áš-tu šu-kud-du* <*i-na*> *še-rim li-lá-a-ti* ⸢*uš*$^{?}$⸣-[*ta*$^{?}$*-ba*$^{?}$*-ru*$^{?}$]-*ú ni-pi-iḫ-šu-un*

101) *šal-gu ur-ru ù mu-šu ṣe-ru-uš-šú kit-mu-ru-ma gi-mir la-a-ni-šu lit-*⸢*bu*$^{?}$⸣*-*[*šu ḫal-pu-ú*$^{?}$] *ù šu-ri-pu*

91–95) Moving on from the land Aukanê, I came <to> the land Uišdiš, a district of the land Mannea that Ursâ (Rusâ) had annexed. Before my time, Ursâ (Rusâ), the Urarṭian — who did not obey the command(s) of the gods Aššur (and) Marduk, who did not revere (any) oath (sworn) by the lord of lords, a mountain dweller (and) a murderer (lit.: "seed of murder"), one who had no wisdom, whose lips were nimble in speaking slanderous (and) malicious things, (and) who did not obey the venerable command(s) of the god Šamaš, the great judge of the gods, but (instead) kept on transgressing against his (Šamaš') design(s) every year without fail — after (all) his previous sins, committed a great crime that (led to) the destruction of his (own) land and the striking down of his (own) people.

96–111) On Mount Uauš — a large mountain, whose peaks reach up into the sky with the cloud(s); whose area no living creature since the distant past had (ever) crossed; whose remote region(s) no [trav]eler had (ever) visited; and over which no winged bird of the sky had ever passed or [bui]lt a nest in order to teach [its] young how to spread (their) wings; a high mountain that points upward like the blade of a dagger; *whose interior* [*is deeply cut up by*] the gorges of the outflows of the dist[ant] mountains; (100) (a mountain) upon which perpetual (lit.: "day and night") snow is piled up in (the seasons of both) extreme heat and severest cold, when the rising of the Bow star (and) Arrow star [*are continually present*] <in> the morning (and) evening (respectively), and whose entire face is co[vered with *frost*] and ice; (and) where the body of the one who crosses its border is blasted by fierce wind and his flesh frostbitten by the

---

90 DU$_{6}$*-: The tablet has DUL-.

92 *el-la-mu-ù*ʾ*-a*, "Before my time": Or "before my arrival" (see CAD E p. 101).

95 Or "commited the great crime of destroying his (Ullusunu's) land and striking down his (Ullusunu's) people." The assumption that it was Rusâ's own land and people that were harmed is based on the translation of F. Thureau-Dangin (TCL 3 p. 17), followed by P. Talon (Annales assyriennes 1 p. 83), F.M. Fales (COS 4 p. 202), and several other scholars; the view that it was Ullusunu's land and people is that of W. Mayer (MDOG 115 p. 77), followed by B.R. Foster (Before the Muses[3] p. 796). With regard to this matter, see Fuchs, SAAS 8 pp. 113–114.

96–147 See Scurlock, Studies Astour pp. 498–503 for a study of the battle tactics used in the battle at Mount Uauš. Note also Grekyan, Aramazd 5/1 (2010) pp. 83–95. Mount Uauš has been identified with Mount Sahand in northwestern Iran by some scholars (see for example Kroll in Muscarella and Elliyoun, Eighth Campaign of Sargon II p. 13).

98 Or DUMU.MEŠ instead of TUR.MEŠ, following CAD Q p. 80 sub *qanānu* a.

99 G. Vera Chamaza (AMI NF 27 [1994] p. 117) suggests ... *ru-qu-*[*u-te ḫu-du-du*] *ṣur-*... (cf. line 21), erroneously omiting the Ú sign before ṢUR. While the trace of the sign copied by O. Schroeder and E. Weidner immediately after the break could be ⸢*du*⸣, and thus allow a reading [... *ḫu-du*]-⸢*du*⸣*-ú*, it is not clear that there is sufficient room for all the proposed restoration. R. Rollinger (Studies Lanfranchi p. 614) restores *ru-qu-*[*u-te šut-tuq*]*-ú* (cf. line 326).

100 The Bow star and the Arrow star are in the constellation Canis Major and the latter star has been identified with Sirius. See Reiner and Pingree, BibMes 2/2 pp. 11–12 and CAD Š/3 p. 228. ⸢*uš*$^{?}$⸣-[*ta*$^{?}$*-ba*$^{?}$*-ru*$^{?}$]-*ú*, [*are continually present*]: The restoration is based on CAD Š/3 p. 229; G. Vera Chamaza (AMI NF 27 [1994] p. 117) suggests instead [*na-pa-ḫu* ...] since the verb *napāḫu* is well attested in connection with stars and heavenly bodies.

101 Following Van Buylaere, Studies Parpola p. 299, possibly restore *šal-gu*, "snow," rather than *ḫal-pu-ú*, "frost"; however, *šalgu* already appears earlier in the line.

102) *e-ti-iq i-te-e-šu i-na ši-biṭ im-ḫul-li zu-⸢mur⸣-šu i-šab-bi-ṭu-ma i-na ⸢da⸣-[na-an e-ri-ia-(a)]-⸢ti⸣ uq-ṭam-mu-ú* UZU.MEŠ-*šú*
103) *um-ma-an-šu ma-a'-du a-di re-ṣe-e-šú id-kam-ma a-⸢na⸣ [tur]-⸢ri?⸣ gi-mil-li ša* [^{m}*me-ta-at-ti* KUR.*zi*]-⸢*kir*⸣-*ta-a-*<*a*> *iš-ku-na pu-ḫur*
104) LÚ.*mun-daḫ-ṣe-šu le-'u-ut ta-ḫa-zi tu-kul-ti um-⸢ma⸣-[ni-šu x (x x)] x x [...-šu]-nu ú-zak-ki-ma*
105) ANŠE.KUR.RA.MEŠ *ru-kub-i-šu-nu pe-tan bir-ki* IZ-x [... *ú-šá*]-*áš-ši-šu-nu-ti* GIŠ.TUKUL.MEŠ
106) ^{m}*me-ta-at-ti* KUR.*zi-kir-ta-a-a ša iš-tu* x [...]-*ti iš-šá-kín re-ṣu-su*
107) *ša* LUGAL.MEŠ-*ni li-mi-ti-šú ša* KUR.MEŠ-*e ka-la-⸢šú⸣-[nu ... i?-tu?]-ram-ma ir-ta-ši né-ra-ra*
108) *a-na gi-piš* ERIM.ḪI.A-*šú ma-a'-di ù kit-ri* [...] *il-qa-a še-ṭu-sún*
109) *ta-nit-ti le-'u-ti ta-ḫa-zi-šú* [...] x KI *šá-nin e-muq-ia*
110) *it-ti-ia a-na mit-ḫu-uṣ tu-šá-ri lìb-ba-šú iḫ-šu-uḫ-ma suḫ-ḫur-ti um-*^{ma}*man* ^{d}EN.LÍL *aš-šur*.KI *i-ka-pid la ta-a-a-ar*
111) *i-na na-kap* KUR-*i šu-a-tu si-dir-tu iš-kun-ma ša taq-ru-ub-ti ù šu-te-lu-up a-na-an-ti iš-pu-ra* LÚ.A *šip-ri*

se[vere cold] — (on this mountain) he (Rusâ) mustered his large army, together with his allies. Then, in order to [ave]nge [Mitatti] of the [land Ziki]rtu, he assembled his fighting men, (men) skilled in battle (and) the mainstay of [his] ar[my (...)]. He mobilized [th]eir [...] and (105) [...] their swift riding horses, [*and had*] them take up (their) weapons. Mitatti of the land Zikirtu who from [...]; aid was provided to him. *From* all the kings of the mountainous regions in his environs [... *he tu*]*rned* and he obtained (military) support. [*He trusted*] in the main force of his large army and the reinforcements [of ... *and*] he held [*my troops*] in contempt. [*Thinking of*] the fame of his (own) abilities in battle [*and believing himself to be*] one who was my equal in strength, (110) his heart wanted to meet me in pitched battle, mercilessly planning the rout of the army of the divine Enlil of Assyria (the god Aššur). He drew up (his) battle line in a pass at that mountain and sent a messenger (challenging me) to combat and to join in battle.

112) *a-na-ku* ^{m}LUGAL-GI.NA LUGAL *kib-rat* LÍMMU-*i re-'i* KUR *aš-šur*.KI *na-ṣir sa-am-ni* ^{d}EN.LÍL ^{d}AMAR.UTU *mu-pi-iq de-en* ^{d}*šá-maš*
113) NUMUN *bal-til*.KI URU *né-me-qi pi-it ḫa-sis-si ša a-mat* DINGIR.MEŠ GAL.MEŠ *pal-ḫiš ú-taq-qu-ma la i-sa-an-ni-qu* GIŠ.ḪUR-*šu-un*
114) LUGAL *ki-i-nu da-bi-ib dam-qa-a-te ša ik-kib-šú a-mat* ⸢*taš*⸣-*ger-ti e-peš* ḪUL-*tim ḫa-ba-lu la uṣ-ṣu-ú i-na pi-i-šu*
115) IGI.GÁL *mal-ki ša kiš-šá-ti ša i-na mil-ki ù ṭè-e-mi ib-ba-nu-ú pa-laḫ* DINGIR.MEŠ *ù* ^{d}*iš-ta-ri ú-kal-lu rit-tu-uš-šú*

112–115) I, Sargon (II), king of the four quarters (of the world), shepherd of Assyria, who keeps oath(s) (sworn) by the gods Enlil (and) Marduk (and) pays attention to the decision of the god Šamaš; the offspring of (the city) Baltil (Aššur), the city of wisdom (and) understanding (lit.: "open with regard to ears"); who reverently pays heed to the words of the great gods and does not question their plan(s); the just king, who (only) speaks benevolently, for whom slander is anathema, (and) from whose mouth (orders) to commit treachery (and) do wrong never come forth; wisest ruler in the world, who was created with intelligence and understanding, (and) who upholds with his hand reverence for the gods and goddesses —

116) *a-na* ^{d}*a-šur* LUGAL *kul-lat* DINGIR.MEŠ *be-el ma-ta-a-te a-lid gim*-ri* LUGAL *gim-rat* DINGIR.MEŠ GAL.MEŠ *la-i-ṭu kib-ra-a-ti*
117) *be-el bal-til*.KI *dan-dan-nu ša i-na uz-za-at*

116–122) To the god Aššur, the king of all the gods, lord of (all) the lands, begetter of everything, king of all the great gods, one who controls (all) regions (of the world); almighty lord of (the city) Baltil (Aššur),

---

105 Possibly *iṣ-⸢ba⸣-[at-ma ...]*, "he sei[zed ...]," following Mayer, Assyrien und Urarṭu I p. 106.
107 [*i?-tu?*]-*ram-ma* "[*he tu*]*rned* and": Or [*iš?-pu?*]-*ram-ma*] "[*he se*]*nt* and."
109 The tentative understanding of this line is based on that of B.R. Foster (Before the Muses[3] p. 796).
111 *na-kap*, "*pass*": The reading follows CAD N/1 p. 156; however, *na-gáb*, "spring" would also be possible.
116 *a-lid gim**(text: BI)-*ri*, "begetter of everything": B.R. Foster (Before the Muses[3] p. 797) translates "begetter of the Mighty One," reading *a-lid gaš-ri*; he takes this to refer to the god Ninurta. Ninurta is called "mighty one" in line 6 of this text. See, however, Fales, COS 4 p. 203 n. 55.
117 The end of the line is obscure and the very tentative translation "*has put the proud to confusion*" assumes that the verb is *ešû* in the Š-stem (a rarely attested form) and that *lalânâte* modifies an unexpressed *nišē*, "people." The basic meanings of *lalânû* are "luxuriant, happy" (*lalânû* A) and "indigent, powerless" (*lalânû* B) according CAD L p. 46, and "flourishing, luxuriant" and "indigent, powerless" according to CDA p. 176 (sub *lalānû*). V. Scheil (RA 16 [1919] p. 203) has ...-*ma uštašila lanâte*, "et a étendu des rets"; W. Mayer (Assyrien und Urarṭu I pp. 108–109) has ...-*ma uš-ta-*<*aḫ*>-*ši-la la-na-a-te*, "... indem er die Gestalten? zerschlägt?"; and B.R. Foster (Before the Muses[3] p. 797) has "pulverizes their bodies." G. Vera Chamaza (AMI NF 27 [1994] p. 117) suggests *uš-ta-*<*aḫ*>-*ši-la la na-a-de*$_{4}$ (i.e., "has crushed the impious") and P. Talon (Annales assyriennes 1 pp. 84–85) suggests *uš-ta-pi!-la la na-a-ṭe*$_{4}$, "qui transforme ceux qui ne sont pas convenables (?)"; however, TE is not normally

te-gim-ti-šu GAL-*ti mal-ki ša kiš-šá-ti e-ṭen*?-*nu-ma uš-ta-ši la-la-na-a-te*
118) *kab-tu qar-ra-du ša i-na giš-par-ri-šú e-piš le-mut-ti la ip-par-šid-du-ma la pa-liḫ ma-miti-šu in-na-sa-ḫu šur-us-su*
119) *a-na la pa-liḫ zik-ri-šu ša a-na e-muq-qí ra-ma-ni-šú tak-lu nàr-bi* DINGIR-*ti-šu mé-e-šu-ma i-da-bu-ba taš-ri-iḫ-tu*
120) *i-na šit-nu-un áš-ga-gi ag-gi-iš ir-ri-ḫu-šu-ma* GIŠ.TUKUL.MEŠ-*šú ú-šab-ba-ru-ma el-lat-su ka-ṣir-tu ú-tar-ru a-na šá-a-ri*
121) *ù a-na na-ṣir šip-ṭí* DINGIR.MEŠ *ša a-na dam-qi de-en* ^{d}UTU *tak-lu-ma ša* ^{d}*a-šur* ^{d}EN.LÍL.LÁ DINGIR.MEŠ *pit-lu-ḫu* DINGIR-*us-su*
122) *ul-mi-šu še-e-ru-ti i-du-uš-šu ú-šal-lak* UGU *a-a-bi ù za-ma-né-e uš-za-a-su i-na* NÍG.È

(the god) who in his great raging anger *crushes* the rulers of the world and *has put the proud to confusion*; the honored one, the hero from whose net the evildoer cannot escape and (with whose net) the one who does not respect an oath (sworn) by him (the god Aššur) is eradicated (lit.: "his root is torn out"); with respect to the one who does not revere his (the god Aššur's) name (and) (instead) trusts in his own strength, disregards the greatness of his (the god Aššur's) divine nature, and talks boastfully, (120) he (the god Aššur) rushes angrily against him in the heat of battle, shatters his weapons, and scatters his well-organized forces to the wind. Moreover, with respect to the one who observes the judgment(s) of the gods, trusts in the fair decision of the god Šamaš, and reveres the divine nature of the god Aššur, the divine Enlil of the gods, he (the god Aššur) has fierce axes go at his side (and) causes him to stand in triumph over (his) enemies and foes —

123) *áš-šu i-te-e* ^{m}*ur-sa-a* KUR.*ur-ar-ṭa-a-a pat-ti* KUR-*šu* DAGAL-*tim la e-ti-qu i-na* EDIN *la aq-qu-ú* ÚŠ.MEŠ *qu-ra-de-e-šú*
124) *i-na qé-reb tam-ḫa-ri si-kip-ta-šu* <*a-na*> *šá-ka-ni ù i-ri-iḫ pi-i-šu* UGU-*šu tu-ur-rim-ma an-na-šu šu-uš-ši-i qa-ti áš-ši-šu*
125) ^{d}*a-šur be-lí at-ma-a-a ša mi-šá-ri iš-mé-ma* UGU-*šu i-ṭi-ib a-na tés-pi-ti-ia kit-ti is-saḫ-ram-ma im-gu-ra tés-li-ti*
126) GIŠ.TUKUL.MEŠ-*šú ez-zu-ti ša i-na a-ṣe-šu-nu iš-tu ṣi-it* ^{d}UTU-*ši a-di e-reb* ^{d}UTU-*ši la ma-gi-ri i-mèš-šu i-du-u*$_{8}$-*a ú-ma-er-ma*

123–126) Because I had never crossed the border of Ursâ (Rusâ), the Urarṭian. (nor) the boundary of his wide land, (and because) I had never spilled the blood of his warriors on the (battle)field, I raised my hand (in prayer to the god Aššur) to bring about his (Rusâ's) overthrow in battle, to turn his insolent utterances against him, and to make (him) bear his punishment. (125) The god Aššur, my lord, listened to my just words and they were pleasing to him. He was inclined (lit.: "turned") to my righteous entreaty and was amenable to my petition. He dispatched at my side his fierce weapons which, whenever they go forth, crush the uncompliant from the east to the west.

127) *um-ma-na-at* ^{d}*a-šur dal-pa-a-ti ša ḫar-ra-an ru-uq-ti il-li-ka-nim-ma šu-nu-ḫa ù mu-uq-qa*
128) KUR.MEŠ-*e bé-e-ru-te ša mu-lu-ú mu-rad-du šup-šu-qu la mi-na e-ta-at-ti-qa-a-ma ik-ki-ra zi-mu-ši-in*
129) *an-ḫu-us-si-in ul ú-šap-ši-iḫ-ma* A.MEŠ *ṣu-mi ul áš-qi uš-man-ni ul áš-kun-ma* BÀD KARAŠ *ul ak-ṣur*
130) LÚ.*qu-ra-di-ia ul ú-ma-ʾe-er la ú-paḫ-ḫi-ra ki-iṣ-ri-ia ša* 15 *u* 2.30 *a-na i-di-ia la* <*ú*>-*te-ram* EGIR-*ú la uq-qi*
131) *ul a-du-ur gi-piš* ERIM.ḪI.A-*šu* ANŠE.KUR.RA.MEŠ-*šú a-še-eṭ-ma a-na* <<*a-na*>> *mu-ʾu-de-e qu-ra-di-šu ša taḫ-lu-up-ti ni-iš* IGI.II *ul ar-ši*

127–131) The exhausted troops of the god Aššur, who had (already) come a long journey and were tired and weary, had (had to) cross innumerable remote mountains that were difficult to ascend (and) descend, and they were (thus) in poor condition (lit.: "their appearance had changed"). (However), I neither allowed them (time) to recover from their fatigue nor gave (them) water to drink for (their) thirst. I neither set up camp nor organized a walled (military) encampment. (130) I did not give orders to my warriors. I did not assemble my (military) contingents. I did not summon (lit.: "return") to my side the right and left wings (of my army); I did not wait for the rear guard. I did not take fright at the main force of his army. I distained his cavalry (lit.: "horses") and did not (even) glance at his numerous armored warriors.

---

attested with the value $de_4/ṭe_4$ during the time of Sargon II (see von Soden and Röllig, Syllabar[3] p. 41). See also F.M. Fales (COS 4 pp. 203–204 and n. 56), who translates "pulverizes the impious," although stating that the passage is difficult. CAD M/1 p. 357 (with the verb *mašālu*) reads *uš-ta-ši-la la-na-a-te* and translates the passage as "... their bodies"; however, it should be noted that no feminine plural form of the noun *lānu* is attested and that *lalânâti* appears in line 265. Could *la-na-a-te* be an error for *ad-na-a-te* (suggestion courtesy J.N. Postgate)?

132–151 For a study of the metaphorical language in this passage, see M. Van De Mieroop, Kaskal 12 (2015) pp. 292–299. *ki-tul-lum*: CAD K p. 476 (followed by CAD P p. 411) tentatively takes *kitullum* here as standing for *idāya* and thus translates it as "(my) side(?)," and this view is tentatively followed here, but AHw p. 495 assumes it refers to a troop formation. M. Worthington (Textual Criticism p. 199) emends the text to

132) *it-ti* GIŠ.GIGIR GÌR.II-*ia e-de-ni-ti ù* ANŠE.KUR.RA.MEŠ *a-li-kut i-di-ia ša a-šar nak-ri ù sa-al-mi la ip-pa-rak-ku-ú ki-tul-lum pe-er-ra* ^{m}30-PAP-PAP (*x x*)
133) *ki-i* GIŠ.*šil-ta-ḫi ez-zi i-na lìb-bi-šu am-qut-ma* BAD$_5$.BAD$_5$-*šú am-ḫa-aṣ-ma ú-saḫ-ḫi-ra ti-ba-a-šu*
134) *di-ik-ta-šu ma-ʾa-at-tu a-du-uk-ma* ADDA.MEŠ *qu-ra-di-šu ki-ma* ŠE.MUNU$_6$ *áš-ṭe-ma sa-pan-ni* KUR-*e ú-mal-li*
135) ÚŠ.MEŠ-*šú-nu ḫur-ri na-at-ba-ki* ÍD-*iš ú-šar-di-ma ṣe-e-ri ki-i-di ba-ma-a-te aṣ-ru-ba il-lu-riš*
136) LÚ.*mun-daḫ-ṣe-šu* ⸢*tu*⸣-*kul-ti um-ma-ni-šu na-áš* GIŠ.PAN *az-ma-re-e pa-an* GÌR.II-*šu ki-ma as-li ú-ṭa-bi-iḫ-ma* SAG.DU.MEŠ-*šú-nu ú-nak-kis*
137) SAG.KAL.MEŠ-*šú ma-li-ki man-za-az pa-ni-šu i-na qé-reb tu-šá-ri* GIŠ.TUKUL.MEŠ-*šú-nu ú-šab-bir-ma a-di* ANŠE.KUR.<RA>.MEŠ-*šú-nu al-qa-šu-nu-ti*
138) 2 ME 60 NUMUN LUGAL-*ti-šú* LÚ.*šu-ut* SAG.MEŠ LÚ.EN.NAM.MEŠ-*šú* LÚ.*šá pet-ḫal-lì-šú i-na* ŠU.II *ú-ṣab-bit-ma ú-šap-ṭi-ra ta-ḫa-zu*
139) *ù šá-a-šu i-na pu-ḫur* KARAŠ-*šu e-sír-šu-ma* ANŠE.KUR.RA.MEŠ LAL-*at ni-ri-šu i-na uṣ-ṣi mul-mul-li ú-šaq-qí-ra šap-lu-uš-šú*
140) *a-na šu-zu-ub* ZI.MEŠ-*šú* GIŠ.GIGIR-*šu e-zib-ma i-na* MUNUS.ANŠE.KUR.RA.MEŠ *ir-kab-ma meḫ-ret um-ma-ni-šu in-na-bit*

132–140) With (only) my personal chariot and the horse(men) that go at my side (and) never leave (me) in either hostile or friendly territory, the *contingent* of Sîn-aḫu-uṣur, I fell upon him (Rusâ) like a fierce arrow, inflicted a defeat on him, and turned back his attack. I inflicted a major defeat upon him; I spread out the corpses of his warriors like malt (spread out for drying) and filled the mountain uplands (with them). (135) I made their blood flow down the gorges (and) gullies like a river and I dyed the steppe, countryside, (and) plains red like the *illūru*-plant. (As for) the fighting men who were the mainstay of his army, (his) bowmen (and) spearmen, I slaughtered (them) at his feet like sheep and cut off their heads. In the midst of the plain I shattered the weapons of his nobles, counselors, (and) courtiers, and I seized them, together with their horses. I captured two hundred and sixty members of his royal family, eunuchs, his provincial governors, (and) his cavalrymen, and I broke up (their) battle order. Moreover, (as for) that (man), I shut him up in the *midst* of his (military) camp and I shot his yoke-trained horses out from under him with *uṣṣu*-arrows (and) *mulmullu*-arrows. In order to save his life, he abandoned his chariot, mounted a mare, and fled in front of his army.

141) ^{m}*me-ta-at-ti* KUR.*zi-kir-ta-a-a a-di* LUGAL.MEŠ-*ni ša li-me-ti-šú pu-ḫur-šu-un ú-šam-qit-ma ú-par-ri-ra ki-iṣ-ri-šu-un*
142) *ša um-ma-na-at* KUR.*ur-ar-ṭi* LÚ.KÚR *lem-ni a-di kit-ri-šu suḫ-ḫur-ta-šu áš-kun-ma i-na qé-reb* KUR.*ú-a-uš* KUR-*i i-né-eʾ ir-tu*
143) ANŠE.KUR.RA.MEŠ-*šu-nu ḫur-ri na-at-bak* KUR-*e im-lu-ma ù šu-nu ki kul-ba-bi i-na pu-uš-qi-šu ú-pat-tu ú-ru-uḫ pa-áš-qa-a-ti*
144) *i-na šit-mur* GIŠ.TUKUL.MEŠ-*ia dan-nu-ti* EGIR-*šu-nu e-li-ma mu-lu-ú ù mu-rad-du ú-mal-la-a* ADDA.MEŠ *muq-tab-li*
145) 6 KASKAL.GÍD *qaq-qa-ru* TA KUR.*ú-a-uš a-di* KUR.*zi-mur* KUR NA$_4$.*aš-pe-e i-na zi-qi-it*

141–147) (As for) Mitatti of the land Zikirtu, together with the kings in his environs, I struck all of them down and broke up their (military) contingents. I brought about the rout of the troops of the land Urarṭu, an evil enemy, together with its auxiliary troops, and on Mount Uauš, he (the enemy) turned tail. Their horses filled the gorges of the outflows of the mountains, while they, like an ant, in desperation opened up narrow paths. I went up after them with my mighty raging weapons, filling both slopes (lit.: "ascent and descent") with the corpses of (their) warriors. (145) I pursued him at arrow point for a distance of six leagues, from Mount Uauš to Mount Zimur, the mountain of jasper. (As for) the remainder of the

ki-tul-lum pe-er-ra-<ni> since *perra* "would be morphologically aberrant on this manuscript" and translates "the *kitullu*, *p.* of Sîn-ah-uṣur." As noted by Worthington, "the *kitullu* and the *perrā<ni>* of Sîn-ah-uṣur could either stand in apposition to the cavalry, or be listed alongside them as separate items." A Sîn-aḫu-uṣur who was a brother of Sargon II is attested in text nos. 2002–2003. Although the copy in the first edition of TCL 3 indicated that there were traces of one or possibly two signs at the end of line 132, these traces were omitted in the second edition of the volume. Collation of the tablet by both T. Kwasman and the author indicates that there are indeed faint traces of possibly two signs there, but also that the signs are rubbed (or erased by the scribe). Kwasman suggests that the scribe may have originally intended to write a title (i.e., ⸢LÚ⸣.*x*) after the personal name or possibly give the name of Sargon's son Sennacherib (i.e., ^{m}30-PAP.PAP-⸢SU$^{?}$-*ba*$^{?}$⸣) rather than that of Sîn-aḫu-uṣur (private communication).

135 The *illūru*-plant may have been the anemone.

140 Two of Tiglath-pileser III's royal inscriptions (Tadmor and Yamada, RINAP 1 p. 85 Tiglath-pileser III no. 35 i 33′ and p. 103 Tiglath-pileser III no. 41 line 20′) refer to the Urarṭian ruler Sarduri fleeing from the Assyrians on a mare. This could suggest that the Assyrians considered it ignoble for a ruler to ride a mare.

143 *ú-pat-tu ú-ru-uḫ* is likely a sandi writing for *ú-pat-tu-ú ú-ru-uḫ* or involves a case of haplography (suggestion M. Worthington).

145 "at arrow point": As noted by F.M. Fales (COS 4 p. 205), the idea is probably that Sargon pursued Rusâ almost within "shooting distance with his bow — for all of six *bērus* (approximately 66km) in the latter's flight."

mul-mul-li ar-du-su
146) *si-ta-at* UN.MEŠ *ša a-na šu-ṣu-ú na-piš-ti ip-par-ši-du li-i-ti* ^{d}*a-šur* EN-*ia a-na da-la-li ú-maš-še-ru-šu-nu-ti*
147) ^{d}IŠKUR *gaš-ru* DUMU ^{d}*a-nim qar-du ri-gim-šu gal-tu* UGU-*šu-nu id-di-ma i-na ur-pat ri-iḫ-ṣi ù* NA$_{4}$ AN-*e ú-qat-ti re-e-ḫa*

people who had fled in order to save (their) lives (and whom) I had let go in order that they might extol the might of the god Aššur, my lord — the powerful god Adad, the valiant son of the god Anu, let loose his terrifying roar against them and finished off those remaining by means of cloudbursts and hailstones.

148) ^{m}*ur-sa-a ma-lik-šu-nu ša i-te-e* ^{d}UTU ^{d}AMAR.UTU *e-ti-qu-ma ša* ^{d}*a-šur* LUGAL DINGIR.MEŠ *la ú-kab-bi-du ma-mit-su*
149) *ri-gim* GIŠ.TUKUL.MEŠ-*ia dan-nu-ti ip-laḫ-ma ki-ma iṣ-ṣur ḫur-ri ša la-pa-an* TI$_{8}$.MUŠEN *ip-par-šid-du it-ru-ku lib-bu-šu*
150) *ki-i ta-bi-ik da-mi* URU.*ṭu-ru-uš-pa-a* URU LUGAL-*ti-šu ú-maš-šir-ma ki-i mun-nab-ti ṣa-a-a-di e-mid-da šá-ḫa-at* KUR-*šú*
151) *ki-ma* MUNUS.*ḫa-riš-ti i-na* GIŠ.NÁ *in-na-di-ma ak-lu ù* A.MEŠ *i-na pi-i-šu ip-ru-us-ma mu-ru-uṣ la* ZI-*e e-mid ra-man-šú*
152) *li-i-ti* ^{d}*a-šur be-lí-ia a-na* u$_{4}$-*mi ṣa-a-ti* UGU KUR.*ur-ar-ṭi áš-kun-ma pul-ḫat-su a-na la ma-še-e e-zi-ba aḫ-ra-taš*
153) *da-na-an kiš-šu-ti-ia šu-tur-tu ù ti-bu-ut* GIŠ.TUKUL.MEŠ-*ia šur-bu-ti ša* <*i-na*> *kib-rat* LÍMMU-*i la im-maḫ-ḫa-ru-ma la i-né-e'-ú ar-*⌜*kiš*⌝
154) *i-na qé-reb tam-ḫa-ri da-ap-ni* UGU KUR.*ur-ar-ṭi ú-šam-ri-ru* UN.MEŠ KUR.*zi-kir-te ù* KUR.*an-di-a as-ḫu-pa i-mat mu-ú-ti*
155) GÌR.II LÚ.KÚR *lem-na* TA *qé-reb* KUR.*man-na-a-a ap-ru-us-ma lìb-bi* ^{m}*ul-lu-su-nu be-lí-šu-nu ú-ṭib-ma a-na* UN.MEŠ-*šú dal-pa-a-te ú-še-ṣi nu-u-*⌜*ru*⌝

148–155) Their ruler Ursâ (Rusâ) — who had transgressed the limits set by the gods Šamaš (and) Marduk and had not honored the oath (sworn) by the god Aššur, the king of the gods — became afraid at the clangor of my mighty weapons and his heart pounded like (that of) a *rock partridge* fleeing before an eagle. (150) He abandoned his royal city Ṭurušpâ as if (he was) one who had committed bloodshed and sought refuge in mountain clefts like (an animal) fleeing from a hunter. He was laid up in bed like a woman in labor; he deprived himself of food and drink and brought upon himself a sickness from which no one ever recovered. I established the might of the god Aššur, my lord, over the land Urarṭu for all time and left behind in him (Rusâ) a terror never to be forgotten in the future. (*By means of*) the might of my supreme power and the onslaught of my exalted weapons — (weapons) that cannot be faced (anywhere) <in> the four quarters (of the world), (that) do not turn back, (and that) I made prevail over the land Urarṭu in heroic battle — I drenched the people of the lands Zikirtu and Andia with deadly venom. I bared the evil enemy from (setting) foot in the land Mannea, pleased the heart of their (the Manneans') lord Ullusunu, and provided light for his troubled people.

156) *a-na-ku* ^{m}LUGAL-GI.NA *na-ṣir kit-ti la e-ti-iq i-te-e* ^{d}*a-šur* ^{d}UTU *šaḫ-tu la mu-up-par-ku-ú pa-liḫ* ^{d}AG ^{d}AMAR.UTU
157) *i-na an-ni-šu-nu ke-e-ni ta-aṣ-mer-ti* ŠÀ-*ia ak-šud-ma* UGU *šar-ḫi mu-ṣa-li-ia az-zi-za i-na li-i-ti*
158) UGU *kul-lat* KUR.MEŠ-*e ka-la-a-šu-*<*nu*> *šaḫ-ra-ar-tu at-bu-uk-ma qu-ú-lu ù di-im-ma-tu e-mid-da* UN.MEŠ *nak-ra-ti*
159) *i-na ḫu-ud lìb-bi ù ri-šá-a-ti it-ti* LÚ.NAR.MEŠ GIŠ.ZÀ.MÍ.MEŠ *ù ta-ba-li a-na qé-reb uš-man-ni-ia e-ru-ub*
160) *a-na* ^{d}ÙRI.GAL ^{d}IŠKUR *ù* ^{d}*iš-tar be-lí ta-ḫa-zi* DINGIR.MEŠ *a-ši-bu-ut* AN-*e* KI-*tim ù* DINGIR.MEŠ *a-ši-bu-ut* KUR *aš-šur*.KI
161) UDU.SÍSKUR.MEŠ-*e taš-ri-iḫ-ti eb-bu-ti aq-qi-ma*

156–161) I, Sargon (II), who protects justice (and) does not transgress against the limits set by the gods Aššur (and) Šamaš, who is always humble, (and) who reveres the gods Nabû (and) Marduk, attained my heart's desire with their (the gods') firm approval and stood in triumph over the proud one who was hostile to me. I poured out deathly silence over all the mountains and (so) inflicted consternation and moaning upon the enemy people. I entered into my camp amidst happiness and rejoicing, accompanied by musicians (playing) lyres and *cymbals*. I offered splendid pure sacrifices to the deities Nergal, Adad, and Ištar, the lords of battle, the gods who dwell in (both) heaven (and) netherworld, and the gods who dwell in Assyria; I stood before them humbly and prayerfully, and I extolled their divine nature.

---

149 *iṣṣūr ḫurri*, "*rock partridge*": Salonen, Vögel pp. 143–146 identifies the *iṣṣūr ḫurri* with Tadorna casarca, a type of ruddy shelduck.
150 *mun-nab-ti ṣa-a-a-di*, "(an animal) fleeing from a hunter": Or possibly "a restless vagrant" following W. Mayer (MDOG 115 [1983] p. 83) and F.M. Fales (COS 4 p. 205).
159 CAD T pp. 177–178 takes *tāpalu* (*tābalu*), which normally means "pair, set of two," to also refer to some type of percussion instrument. CDA p. 398 tentatively suggests they may be castanets and P. Talon (Annales assyriennes 1 p. 87) cymbals; B.R. Foster (Before the Muses[3] p. 799) takes them to be flutes.
160 Nergal: See on-page note to line 14.

i-na la-ban ap-pi ù ut-nen-ni ma-ḫar-šu-un
az-ziz-ma ú-šar-ba-a DINGIR-su-un
162) a-na KUR.an-di-a ù KUR.zi-kir-te a-šar pa-nu-ia šak-nu ger-ri ú-šab-ṭil-ma a-na KUR.ur-ar-ṭi áš-ku-na pa-ni-ia
163) KUR.ú-iš-di-iš na-gu-ú ša KUR.man-na-a-a ša ^{m}ur-sa-a e-ki-mu-ma ra-ma-nu-uš ú-ter-ru
164) URU.MEŠ-šú ma-aʾ-du-ti ša ki-i MUL.MEŠ AN-e mi-i-na la i-šu-ú gi-mir-tu ak-šu-ud
165) BÀD.MEŠ-ni-šu-nu du-un-nu-nu-ti a-di ši-pi-ik uš-ši-šu-nu ḫaṣ-ba-ti-iš ú-daq-qi-iq-ma qaq-qa-riš am-nu
166) qi-ra-a-te-šu-nu ma-aʾ-da-a-ti la-a mi-na ú-pat-ti-ma ŠE.PAD.MEŠ la ni-i-bi um-ma-ni ú-šá-a-kil

162–166) I discontinued my campaign to the lands Andia and Zikirtu, my (original) destination, and I set out for the land Urarṭu. (With regard to) the land Uišdiš, a district of the land Mannea that Ursâ (Rusâ) had annexed and appropriated for his own, I conquered all its numerous cities, which are as innumerable as the stars in the sky. I smashed their very strong (city) walls down to their very foundations as if (they were) pots and I leveled (them) to the ground. I opened up their many, countless granaries and (then) fed my army grain in unlimited quantities.

---

167) TA KUR.ú-iš-di-iš at-tu-muš a-na URU.uš-qa-ia bir-ti GAL-ti re-eš mi-iṣ-ri ša KUR.ur-ar-ṭi aq-ṭe-rib
168) ša i-na né-re-bi ša KUR.za-ra-an-da na-gi-i ki-ma GIŠ.IG ed-lat-ma ka-la-at LÚ.DUMU šip-ri
169) ù i-na KUR.ma-al-la-ú KUR ŠIM.LI pul-uk-kiš a-ṣa-at-ma UGU ta-mir-ti KUR.su-ú-bi šu-⸢tal⸣-bu-šat šá-ru-riš
170) UN.MEŠ a-ši-bu-ut na-gi-i šu-a-tu i-na KUR.ur-ar-ṭi mal ba-šu-ú le-ʾu-ut ANŠE.KUR.RA.MEŠ pet-ḫal-lì la TUKU-ú tam-šil-šu-un
171) mu-re-e mur-ni-is-qi ṣe-eḫ-ḫe-ru-ti i-lit-ti KUR-šu DAGAL-tim ša a-na ki-ṣir LUGAL-ti-šú ú-rab-bu-ú i-ṣab-ba-tu MU.AN.NA-šam
172) a-di a-na KUR.su-ú-bi na-gi-i ša UN.MEŠ KUR.ur-ar-ṭi KUR.man-na-a-a i-qab-bu-šu-ni la il-leq-qu-ma la in-nam-ma-ru li-ti-ik-šú-un
173) ṣe-ru-uš-šu-un ḫal-la la ip-tu-ma a-ṣu-ú se-eḫ-ru ù ta-a-ru si-mat ta-ḫa-zi la kul-lu-mu šup-ṭu-⸢ur⸣ ṣi-mit-tu
174) LÚ.ERIM.MEŠ šu-nu-ti ša bir-ti ù na-gi-i a-bi-ik-ti ^{m}ur-sa-a EN-šú-nu e-mu-ru-ma ki-ma šur-uš kib-ri ÍD ir-bu-ba SUḪUŠ-šú-⸢un⸣
175) a-lik pa-ni-šu-nu mu-du-ut qab-li ša la-pa-an GIŠ.TUKUL.MEŠ ip-par-šid-du i-mat mu-ú-te saḫ-pu-ma iq-ru-bu ṣe-ru-uš-šu-un
176) da-lil ^{d}a-šur be-lí-ia ša i-na pu-ḫur LÚ.mun-daḫ-ṣe-šú-nu mul-taḫ-ṭu la i-se-tu-ma ú-šá-an-nu-šu-nu-ti-ma ik-šud-du mi-tu-ti-⸢iš⸣
177) URU.uš-qa-ia tu-kul-ti KUR-šu a-di se-ḫer URU.MEŠ-ni-šá ḫar-bé-eš ú-še-mu-ú bu-še-e-šú-nu e-zi-bu-ma iṣ-bu-tú a-raḫ la ta-a-ri

167–173) Moving on from the land Uišdiš, I came to the city Ušqaya, a large fortress right on the border of the land Urarṭu, which like a gate acts as a barrier in the pass to the district of Zaranda, holding back messenger(s), and (which) rises up like a rocky pinnacle on Mount Mallāu, a mountain with juniper tree(s), clothed in sun-like splendor over the meadowland(s) of the land Sūbi. (170) The people who dwell in that district have no equal in the whole land Urarṭu with respect to (their) skill with riding horses. Every year they catch the young foals of thoroughbred horses native to his (the king's) wide land, which they rear for his royal (military) contingent. Until they (the young horses) are taken to the district Sūbi — which the people of the land Urarṭu call the land Mannea — and (until) it is observed how they perform, no one attempts to ride them (lit.: "opened the thigh(s) on back of them"), nor are they (the young horses) taught how to advance, turn about, and turn back again — (skills) necessary in battle — (thus) the harness(es) (for them) remain as yet unfastened.

174–177) These people — those of (both) the fortress and the district — saw the defeat of their lord Ursâ (Rusâ) and their legs grew weak, like roots on a riverbank. (When) their leaders — (men) experienced in warfare who had (nevertheless) fled before (my) weapons — came up to them drenched in deadly venom (and) reported to them the glory of the god Aššur, my lord (and) that not (even) a (single) one of all their fighting men had escaped, they became like the dead. They turned the city Ušqaya on which their (lit.: "its/his") land relied, together with its surrounding settlements, into a wasteland. They abandoned their property and took to the road, never to return (lit.: "road of no return").

178) i-na ti-bu-ut GIŠ.TUKUL.MEŠ-ia dan-nu-ti a-na

178–183) With the onslaught of my mighty weapons, I

---

167 Ušqaya has been identified with the Urarṭian fortress of Livar (in the region of Marand) by P. Zimansky (JNES 49 [1990] p. 15; see also S. Kroll in Köroğlu and Konyar, Urartu p. 161).

173 *šup-ṭu-⸢ur⸣ ṣi-mit-tu* "(thus) the harness(es) (for them) remain as yet unfastened": We would expect *šup-ṭu-rat* rather than *šup-ṭu-ur*. CAD P p. 301 translates the passage as (the horses) "had been freed from the harness." Cf. von Soden, OLZ 59 (1964) col. 36 sub S. 199a (*šub-ṭu-lu*!).

bir-ti šu-a-ti e-li-ma bu-še-e-šá šad-lu-ti
áš-lu-lam-ma a-na qé-reb uš-man-ni-ia ú-še-rib
179) BÀD-*šá dan-nu ša tem-men*$_5$*-šu* UGU *ki-ṣir* KUR-*i*
šur-šu-du-ma ù 8 ina 1.KÙŠ *ma-ši-iḫ ku-bur-šu*
180) *ul-tu gaba-dib-bi-šu aṣ-bat-am-ma a-di uš-šu*
zaq-ru-te ak-šud-du iš-te-niš ap-pu-ul-ma
qaq-qa-riš ú-šam-ḫi-ir
181) É.MEŠ *qer-bé-e-šá* ^{d}GIBIL$_6$ *ú-šá-aṣ-bit-ma*
GIŠ.ÙR.MEŠ-*ši-na ši-ḫu-ti di-tal-li-iš ú-še-mi*
182) 1 ME 15 URU.MEŠ-*ni ša li-mi-ti-šá ki-ma ab-ri*
a-qu-ud-ma qu-tur-šu-un ki-ma a-šam-šá-ti
pa-an AN-*e ú-šak-tim*
183) *ki-ma ša a-bu-bu ú-ab-bi-tu qer-bi-sa*
ú-še-piš-ma ki-ma kam-ri áš-pu-ka
URU.MEŠ-*ni-šá áš-bu-ti*
184) URU.*a-ni-áš-ta-ni-a* É *su-gul-la-te-šu i-na mi-ṣir*
KUR.*sa-an-gi-bu-te bi-rit* URU.*uš-qa-ia ù*
URU.*tar-ma-ki-sa ep-šu-u*
185) *a-di* 17 URU.MEŠ-*ni ša li-mi-ti-šú ap-pul-ma*
qaq-qa-riš am-nu GIŠ.ÙR.MEŠ *ta-aṣ-lil-ti-šu-nu*
še-ḫu-ti i-na ^{d}GIBIL$_6$ *aq-mu*
186) BURU$_{14}$.MEŠ-*šu-nu* Ú.*pu-e-šu-nu áš-ru-up*
qi-ra-te na-kam-a-te ú-pat-ti-ma ŠE.PAD.MEŠ *la*
ni-i-bi um-ma-ni ú-šá-a-kil
187) *ki-ma e-ri-bi di-ku-ti bu-ul* KARAŠ-*ia i-na*
ú-šal-li-šú ad-di-ma Ú.ḪI.A *tuk-la-ti-šú*
is-su-ḫu-ma ú-šaḫ-ri-bu A.GÀR-*šú*

went up to that fortress, carried off extensive property as booty and brought (it) into my camp. (With regard to) its strong (city) wall, whose foundation had been made firm on bedrock and whose width was eight cubits, (180) beginning with its crenellations and finishing with its massive foundations, I destroyed (it) all together, making (it) level with the ground. I set fire to the houses inside it and turned their lengthy (roof)-beams into ashes. I set fire to one hundred and fifteen settlements in its environs as if (they were) brushwood pyres and (so) made the smoke from them cover the sky like a dust storm. I had its interior made (to look) as if the Deluge had destroyed (it) and I heaped up its inhabited cities as if (they were) mounds of ruins.

184–187) I destroyed the city Aniaštania — the home of his herds, which had been built on the border of the land Sangibutu, between the cities Ušqaya and Tarmakisa — together with seventeen settlements in its environs, leveling (them) down to the ground. I set fire to their lengthy roof-beams. I burned up their crops (and) their fodder (lit.: "straw"). I opened up (their) granaries (and) storehouses and (then) fed my army grain in unlimited quantities. I let the animals of my (military) camp loose in his meadows like swarming locusts; they pulled up the plants on which he relied and laid waste to his field(s).

---

188) TA URU.*uš-qa-ia at-tu-muš a-na mad-ba-ri*
tu-kul-ti bu-li-šu ša KUR.*sa-an-gi-bu-tu*
i-qab-bu-šu-ni aq-ṭe-rib
189) URU.*tar-ú-i* URU.*tar-ma-ki-sa* É BÀD.MEŠ-*ni*
dan-nu-ti ša i-na KUR.*da-la-a-a ta-mir-ti* É
ŠE.PAD.MEŠ-*šú ma-at-ti ep-šu*
190) BÀD.MEŠ-*ni-šu-nu dun-nu-nu-ma šal-ḫu-šu-nu*
kàṣ-ru ḫi-ri-iṣ-ṣa-ni-šu-nu šup-pu-lu-ma
šu-tas-ḫu-ru li-mi-is-sún
191) *ša i-na qer-bi-šu-nu* ANŠE.KUR.RA.MEŠ
na-kam-ti ki-ṣir LUGAL-*ti-šú i-na ú-re-e*
šu-zu-zu-ú-ma ú-šam-ru-ú MU.AN.NA-*šam*
192) UN.MEŠ *a-ši-bu-tu na-gi-i šu-a-tu ep-šet*
be-lu-ti-ia ša i-na URU.MEŠ-*ni li-me-ti-šu-nu*
e-tep-pu-šu e-mu-ru-ma ir-šu-ú gi-lit-tú
193) URU.MEŠ-*ni-šu-nu ú-maš-še-ru-ma i-na na-ba-li*
a-šar ṣu-ma-mi mad-ba-re-eš in-nab-tu-ma
nap-šá-ta i-še-e'-ú
194) *na-gu-⸢ú šu⸣-a-⸢tu⸣ ḫu-ḫa-riš as-ḫu-up-ma ⸢i-na*
bi⸣-rit URU.MEŠ-*šu-nu dan-nu-ti ú-šak-di-ra*

188–198) Moving on from the city Ušqaya, I came to the steppeland on which his herds rely (for pasture) (and) which is (also) called the land Sangibutu. (With regard to) the cities Tarui (and) Tarmakisa — strong fortresses that had been built in the meadowland(s) of the land Dalāya as (store)houses for his abundant grain, (190) whose (inner) walls had been reinforced, whose outer walls had been (well) joined, whose moats had been made deep and surrounded their (entire) circumference, (and) inside which horses were stationed in teams *as reserves for* his royal (military) contingent and were provided with fodder for the entire year — the people who dwell in that district saw the lordly deeds that I had been doing in the settlements in their environs and became terrified. They abandoned their cities and fled into the desert, an arid land, a waterless region (lit.: "place of thirst"), seeking (to save their) lives. I overwhelmed that district as with a bird trap and waged war in (the area) between their fortified cities. (195) [Beginning]

---

183 *qer-bi-sa* "its interior": Or simply translate "it," assuming that this refers to the fortress rather than its environs (suggestion M. Worthington). *kam-ri* for *kar-mi* (see CAD K p. 218); cf. Borger, BiOr 19 (1962) p. 252b sub S. 157ff.

184 *ep-šu-u* (collation T. Kwasman). The scribe intially wrote *ep-šu-u*, with the signs closer to the preceding line and with the U on the edge of the tablet; he then partially erased the EP and ŠU and redid them somewhat lower on the tablet, thus leaving the U much higher than the new EP and ŠU.

188 The reading *mad-ba-ri*, "steppeland" (as opposed to KUR.*ba-ri*, "land Bari"), follows CAD M/1 p. 12 sub *madbaru* b.

189 Or "which had been built in the land Dalāya, a territory with numerous (store)houses for his grain" (cf. Talon, Annales assyriennes 1 p. 89). ŠE.PAD.MEŠ-*šú ma-at-ti*, "his abundant grain": For the use of MEŠ to mark a sumerogram, as opposed to the plural, see Borger, MZ p. 376 and Worthington, Textual Criticism pp. 284–287.

a-nu-un-tu
195) BÀD.MEŠ-*ni-šu-*⸢*nu*⸣ [*dan*]-⸢*nu-ti ul-tu*⸣ [*gaba-dib-bi-šu-nu aṣ-bat a*]-⸢*di*⸣ *tem-men*$_5$*-ni-šu-nu ak-šu-ud ap-pul-ma qaq-qa-riš ú-šam-ḫi-ir*
196) É.MEŠ *qer-bi-*⸢*šu*⸣*-nu* ^{d}⸢GIBIL$_6$⸣ [*ú-šá-aṣ-bit-ma* GIŠ.ÙR].⸢MEŠ⸣-*ši-na še-ḫu-ú-ti di-tal-li-iš ú-še-mi*
197) BURU$_{14}$-*šu-nu ma-a'-du áš-ru-*⸢*up*⸣ [*qi-ra-te na-kam-a-te ú*]-⸢*pat-ti-ma* ŠE.PAD.MEŠ *la*⸣ *ni-i-bi um-ma-ni ú-šá-a-kil*
198) 30 URU.MEŠ-*ni li-mi-ti-šu-nu* [*ki-ma ab-ri a-qu-ud-ma qu-tur-šu-un ki-ma a-šam-šá-ti*] ⸢*pa*⸣*-an* AN-*e ú-šak-tim*

with [their crenellations (and)] finishing [with] their foundations, I destroyed their [stro]ng (city) walls, making (them) level with the ground. [I set] fire to the houses inside them [and] turned their lengthy [(roof)-beam]s into ashes. I burned up their abundant crop(s), [ope]ned [up (their) granaries (and) storehouses, and] (then) fed my army [grain] in unlimited quantities. [I set fire to] thirty settlements in their environs [as if (they were) brushwood pyres and (so) made the smoke from them] cover the sky [like a dust storm].

---

199) TA URU.*tar-ma-ki-sa at-tu-*⸢*muš*⸣ [...] ⸢*aq*⸣*-ṭe-rib*
200) URU.*ul-ḫu* URU *dan-nu-ti ša i-na* ⸢GÌR⸣.[II KUR.*kiš-pal*? ...] x ⸢SI?⸣ [x]
201) ù UN.MEŠ-*šú ki-ma nu-ú-ni a-na* [*ṣu-um-me-šu-nu*? A.MEŠ? ...] ⸢*i*⸣*-šat-tu-ú la i-šab-bu-*⸢*ú*⸣
202) ^{m}*ur-sa-a* LUGAL *ma-lik-šu-nu i-na bi-ib-*⸢*lat*⸣ [*lìb-bi-šu* ... *mu*]-⸢*še*⸣*-e ma-a-mi ú-šak-lim*
203) *pal-gu ba-bíl* A.MEŠ *šur-du-ti iḫ-*[*re-ma* ... A.MEŠ] ⸢ḪÉ⸣.NUN *ki-ma pu-rat-ti ú-šar-di*
204) *a-tap-pi la mi-i-na ṣur-ru-uš-šá ú-še-ṣa-*⸢*am*⸣*-*[*ma* ...]-*lu-ú ú-šam-ki-ra qar-ba-a-te*
205) A.GÀR-*šú ar-bu ša ul-tu u*$_4$*-um ul-lu-*⸢*ti*⸣ [...] x-*du-ma* GURUN ù GEŠTIN *ki-ma zu-un-ni ú-šá-az-nin*
206) GIŠ.*dul-bu* GIŠ.*šu-rat-ḫu bal-ti* É.GAL-*lì-*[*šú* ...] x *ki-ma* GIŠ.TIR UGU *ta-mir-ti-šú ta-ra-nu ú-šá-áš-ši*
207) ù *i-na qer-bi-ti-šu na-di-ti a-ra-*⸢*aḫ*?⸣-[*ḫi*? ...] x [(x)] ⸢*ri*?⸣*-gim* ^{d}*a-la-la* DÙG.GA *ú-šal-sa-a* UN.MEŠ-*šu*
208) 3 ME ANŠE ŠE.NUMUN.MEŠ *ku-pat* ^{d}*nisaba i-na* ⸢AB⸣.[SÍN.MEŠ?-*šú*] ⸢*ú*⸣*-šaḫ-*[*ni*]*-ib-ma* ŠE.AM *i-na pa-šèr-te uṣ-ṣa-bu te-li-tu*
209) A.ŠÀ A.GÀR-*šú ar-bu-ti saḫ-ḫi-iš ú-še-*⸢*mi*⸣ x [(x x)] x-*ma di-iš pa-an šat-*⸢*ti šam*⸣*-mu ù ri-i-tu la ip-pa-rak-ku-ú ku-ṣu ḫar-pu*

199–212) Moving on from the city Tarmakisa, I came to [...]. Ulḫu, a fortified city that [*is situated*] at the foo[t of Mount *Kišpal* ...]. Moreover, its people drink [water] like fish for [*their thirst* ...], (but) cannot get enough (to quench their thirst). In accordance with [his heart's] desire, Ursâ (Rusâ), the king, their lord, [...] discovered (lit.: "revealed") [a so]urce of water. He d[ug] a canal which could carry off the overflowing water [and ...] he made abundant [water] flow like the Euphrates. He had innumerable irrigation ditches run off from it (the canal) [and ...] ... he had the pasture lands irrigated. (205) His uncultivated field(s) that for a long time had [...] ... and caused fruit and wine to pour forth like rain. He had plane trees (and) *šuratḫu*-trees, the pride of [his] palace, [...], form a canopy over its meadowland(s) like a forest. Moreover, [he *brought back*] *the ara*[*ḫḫu-song*] to his abandoned pasture land(s) [(...) and (...)] caused his people to sing (again) the sweet *alālu*-work song. He caused three hundred homers of seed-field to produce *the choicest* grain in [*its furrows*] (so) abundantly that he increased the yield of grain for disposal. He turned the uncultivated field(s) of his agricultural land into meadows [...] *so that there is* (*always*) new vegetation in the spring (*and so that*) grass and pasturage do not cease in (either) winter (or) summer. (210) He turned it (the meadows) into paddocks for horses and herds (of cattle), and he taught (this) entire *remote* land (the

---

195–198 The restoration of these lines is based on that proposed by Thureau-Dangin, TCL 3 p. 32, which is based on lines 180, 181, 186, and 268 (also 182) respectively.

200–212 For a study of the water-related facilities described in this section and an edition of these lines, see Bagg, Assyrische Wasserbauten pp. 127–146 and 319–326 no. 26. J. Laessøe (JCS 5 [1951] pp. 21–32) proposed that a qanat is described in this section; however, Laessøe's suggestion is no longer accepted by most scholars. See most recently Bagg, Assyrische Wasserbauten pp. 128–130. Furthermore, the restoration KUR.*kiš-pal* in line 200 was proposed by F. Thureau-Dangin and is based upon text no. 1 line 140; W. Mayer (Assyrien und Urarṭu I p. 116) prefers to restore KUR.*kiš-te-er* (see line 212); cf. line 272.

201 The tentative restoration and understanding of this line is based on Schott, Vergleiche p. 97 (who also suggests restoring *da-al-ḫu-ú-ti* after A.MEŠ) and CAD Š/2 p. 252; for other possibilities, see Bagg, Assyrische Wasserbauten p. 322.

204 Laessøe, JCS 5 (1951) p. 32 suggests -[... *i-na* A.MEŠ *ša ú-še*]-*lu-ú*, "[with the water which he had br]ought up ([ra]ised)."

206 GIŠ.*šu-rat-ḫu*, "*šuratḫu*-trees": B.R. Foster (Before the Muses^3 p. 802) suggests they may be walnut trees; see also Mayer, Assyrien and Urarṭu I p. 117.

207 The reading follows CAD A/1 p. 328. B. Meissner (ZA 34 [1922] p. 114, followed by Fales, COS 4 p. 207 n. 85), reads *kīma ili* (i.e., GIM DINGIR), "like a god," but *alāla* is often preceded by the divine determinative and is found after *rigim* in the Erra Epic III 18 (see CAD A/1 p. 328).

209 Cf. the old reading *ma-di-iš pa-an šat-*⸢*ti*⸣; see Bagg, Assyrische Wasserbauten p. 324 for the various ways that that passage has been understood.

210) a-na tar-ba-aṣ ANŠE.KUR.RA.MEŠ ù su-⌜gul?⌝-li ú-ter-šu-ma ANŠE.A.⌜AB⌝.[BA] ⌜gi⌝-mir KUR-šu kut-tum-te ú-šal-mid-ma i-šap-pa-ku er-re-tu
211) É.GAL šu-⌜bat⌝ LUGAL-ti a-na mul-ta-ʾu-ti-šú i-na a-ḫi ÍD-ti ⌜ib?⌝-[ni] GIŠ.ÙR.MEŠ ŠIM.LI ú-ṣal-lil-ši-ma i-ri-sa ú-ṭib
212) URU.sar-du-ri-ḫu-ur-da bir-tu a-na ka-a-di-šú i-na KUR.kiš-te-er [DÙ-ma? (...) KUR....]-⌜ti⌝-na-a-a tu-kul-ti KUR-šu i-na lìb-bi ú-še-rib

use of) cam[el(s)] so that they could (be employed to) construct weir(s). He [built] a palace, a royal abode for his leisure, on the bank of the canal; he roofed it with beams of juniper and (thus) made it smell sweet. [He *had*] the fortress city Sarduriḫurda [*built*] on Mount Kišter to be his guard post [*and*] he stationed there [(...)] people [from the land ...]tina, (men) on whom his land relied.

213) UN.MEŠ na-gi-i šu-a-ti a-mat ma-ru-uš-ti ša i-na pa-an ^{m}ur-sa-[a LUGAL?-šú?-nu?] ⌜ú⌝-šap-ri-ku iš-mu-ma u$_8$-a iq-bu-ú im-ḫa-ṣu šá-pár-šu-un
214) URU.ul-ḫu URU dan-nu-ti-šu-nu a-di URU.sar-du-ri-ḫu-ur-da bir-ti tuk-[la-ti-šú-nu ú]-maš-še-ru-ma a-na šá-ḫat KUR-e pa-áš-qa-te ip-par-šid-du mu-ši-tiš

213–214) (When) the people of this district heard a report about the trouble that I had caused to befall [*their king*] Ursâ (Rusâ), they then cried "Woe!" (and) smote their thigh(s) (in distress). They abandoned their fortified city Ulḫu, as well as the city Sarduriḫurda — a fortress on which which [they] reli[ed] — and they fled by night to narrow mountain clefts.

215) i-na šu-ḫu-uṭ lìb-bi-ia li-mi-it na-gi-i šu-a-ti ki-ma im-ba-⌜ri⌝ [as-ḫu-up]-⌜šu?⌝-ma šid-du ù pu-ú-tu ak-ṣu-ra šu-ri-piš
216) a-na URU.ul-ḫi URU tar-ma-a-te-šú ša ^{m}ur-sa-a e-tel-liš e-ru-⌜ub⌝-[ma a-na qé-reb] ⌜É⌝.GAL-lim šu-bat LUGAL-ti-šú šal-ṭiš at-tal-lak
217) BÀD-šú dan-nu ša i-na NA$_4$ KUR-i zaq-ri ep-šu i-na qul-mi-i AN.[BAR u mar]-⌜ri⌝ AN.BAR ḫaṣ-ba-ti-iš ú-daq-qi-iq-ma qaq-qa-riš am-nu
218) GIŠ.ÙR.MEŠ ŠIM.LI še-ḫu-ti ta-aṣ-lil-ti É.GAL-lì-šú as-⌜suḫ?⌝ [i-na? ka?]-⌜la?⌝-pi ú-maḫ-ḫi-iṣ-ma a-na KUR aš-šur.KI al-qa-a
219) qi-ra-a-te-šú na-kam-a-te ú-pat-ti-ma ŠE.PAD.MEŠ-su ma-at-tu ⌜la⌝ [ni-i]-⌜bi⌝ um-ma-ni ú-šá-kil
220) É GEŠTIN.MEŠ-šú ša ni-ṣir-te e-ru-ub-ma um-ma-nat ^{d}a-šur DAGAL.⌜MEŠ⌝ [ki-ma A].⌜MEŠ⌝ ÍD i-na KUŠ.na-a-de KUŠ.maš-le-e iḫ-bu-ú GEŠTIN DÙG.GA
221) ÍD.ḫi-ri-tu ÍD tuk-la-te-šu a-ru-ur-šá as-kir$_{17}$*(TÙM)-ma A.MEŠ du-[uš]-⌜šu⌝-ti a-na ru-šum-di ú-ter
222) a-da-ap-pi ḫa-li-li si-lit-te ṣur-ri-šá ú-ḫa-ṭi-im-ma šá x [x (x)]-⌜šu?⌝ iš-qi-la-si-na ú-kal-lim ^{d}UTU-šu
223) a-na GIŠ.KIRI$_6$.MEŠ-šú as-ma-a-ti bu-un-na-né-e URU-šú ša GURUN ⌜ù GEŠTIN⌝.MEŠ za-aʾ-na-a-ma ki-ma ti-ik AN-e i-na-⌜tú?⌝-ka
224) LÚ.qu-ra-di-ia ek-du-ti ú?-še?-⌜ri?-ib?⌝-ma (x)

215–232) Furiouly, [I overwhelmed] the region around that district like a fog and *compacted* the length and breadth (of it) like ice. In a lordly manner, I entered the city Ulḫu, the city *where* Ursâ (Rusâ) *went for relaxation*, [and] walked about triumphantly [in] the palace (that had been) his (own) royal abode. With ir[on] axes [and] iron [spad]es, I smashed its strong (city) wall, which had been built with (blocks of) massive mountain stone, as if (it were) a pot, and leveled (it) down to the ground. I *tore* [*out*] the lengthy beams of juniper (that formed) the roof of his palace, *cut* (*them*) *up* [*with pickax*]*es*, and took (them back) to Assyria. I opened up his granaries (and) storehouses and (then) fed my army his abundant grain in u[nlimited quanti]ties. (220) I entered his hidden wine cellars, and the extensive troops of the god Aššur drew sweet wine (to drink) from waterskins (and) leather buckets [as if (it were)] river [water]. I blocked up the outlet of the canal, the canal on which he relied (to provide water), and turned the abu[nda]nt water (supply) into a swamp. I stopped up *the irrigation ditches* (and) *drainage pipes* that forked off from its (the canal's) center, and exposed [...] their pebbles to the sun. *I had* my fierce warriors *e*[*nte*]*r* his well-kept gardens, (which provide) the general impression of his city (and) which were (so) studded with fruit trees and grapevines that they dripped (fruit as abundantly) as a rainfall, and they (the warriors) made the noise of (their) iron pickaxes resound like

210–221 For the most part, the restorations follow those proposed by Meissner, ZA 34 (1922) pp. 116–118.
217 Or i-na qul-mi-i AN.[BAR u pat]-⌜ri⌝ AN.BAR, "With ir[on] axes [and] iron [swor]ds."
221 -kir$_{17}$*-: The tablet has TÙM.
222–223 The exact understanding of these lines is not certain, in particular the meaning of ḫa-li-li; see Bagg, Assyrische Wasserbauten pp. 325–326. For the translation given above, see in particular Laessøe, JCS 5 (1951) pp. 27–28 and CAD S p. 263. Moreover, C. Zaccagnini (in Fales, ARIN p. 267) translates "I exposed (even) the deep(est) of their pebbles to the sun" but does not suggest any Akkadian reading for this translation.
224 ú?-še?-⌜ri?-ib?⌝-ma, "I had ... e[nte]r ... and": The published copy of VA 8749 by O. Schroeder (KAH 2 no. 141) has iš-mu-x, but based upon his collation of the piece in Berlin, E. Weidner read ú!-še!-⌜ri-ib⌝-ma (AfO 12 [1937–39] p. 144 n. 1). Collation indicates that Weidner's reading

ki-ma ^{d}IŠKUR *ú-šá-áš-gi-mu ri-gim ka-la-bi* AN.BAR

225) GURUN-*šú ma-a'-du ša mi-ni-tu la i-šu-*⸢*ú*⸣ *iq-ṭu-pu-ma a-na an-ḫu*$^{?}$*-ti lìb-bi la e-zi-bu da-re-eš šat-ti ṣu-uḫ-ḫu*

226) GIŠ.MEŠ-*šu* GAL.MEŠ *si-mat* É.GAL-*lì-šú ki-ma* ŠE.⸢MUNU$_{6}$⸣ *áš-ṭe-ma* URU *ta-nit-ti-šu ú-ma-si-ik-ma ú-šaṭ-pi-la na-gu-šu*

227) ⸢GIŠ.*gu-up*⸣-*ni šu-a-tu-*<*nu*> *iṣ-ṣa mal ak-šiṭ-ṭu ú-paḫ-ḫir-ma a-na gu-ru-un-ni aq-ru-un-ma i-na* ^{d}GIBIL$_{6}$ *aq-mu*

228) ⸢BURU$_{14}$⸣-*šu-nu ma-a'-du ša ki* ⸢GI⸣ *a-pi ni-*⸢*i*⸣*-ba la i-šu-ú šur-šiš as-suḫ-ma a-na muš-še*$_{20}$*-e te-ṣe-ti la e-zi-ba šu-*⸢*bul*⸣*-tú*

229) A.GÀR-*šu as-mu ša ki-i za-gìn-du-re-e* ⸢*ṣer*⸣*-pa šak-nu-ma i-na di-še ù ḫab-bu-ri šu-ru-šat ta-mir-tu*

230) *i-na* GIŠ.GIGIR *pet-ḫal-lì me-te-eq ki-mar-*⸢*ri*⸣*-ia ki-ma* ^{d}IŠKUR *ar-ḫi-iṣ-ma saḫ-ḫu tu-kul-ti* ANŠE.KUR.<RA>.MEŠ-*šú* ⸢*ki*⸣*-šub-ba-niš um-mi*

231) URU.*sar-du-ri-ḫu-ur-da dan-na-su-nu* GAL-*tu a-di* 57 URU.MEŠ-*ni ša li-mi-ti-šá ša* KUR.*sa-an-gi-bu-tu na-gi-i*

232) *se-ḫer-šu-nu ap-pul-ma qaq-qa-riš am-nu* GIŠ.ÙR.MEŠ *ta-aṣ-lil-ti-šu-nu i-na* ^{d}GIBIL$_{6}$ *aq-mu-ma di-tal-li-iš ú-še-mi*

(the thunder of) the god Adad. (225) They picked a great deal of its fruit, a countless amount, and did not leave (any) for the *weary* heart to smile about in the future. I (cut down and) spread out his large trees, the ornaments of his palace, like malt (spread out for drying); I made his famous city disgusting and its district a subject of revilement. I gathered up those logs — all the trees that I had chopped down —, piled (them) up in heaps, and set them on fire. I tore out by the roots their abundant crops, which are as countless as reeds in a canebrake, and did not leave even a (single) ear of barley to allow the identification of what had been destroyed. (With regard to) his well-kept field(s) that *were spotted with colored flecks* like *polished* lapis lazuli and (*whose*) meadowland(s) were planted with new vegetation and young shoots, (230) like the god Adad, I trampled (it) down with (my) chariotry, (my) cavalry, (and) the passage of my *infantry*, and I turned the meadows that his horses had relied on (for pasture) into wasteland. (With regard to) the city Sardurihurda, their large fortress, together with fifty-seven settlements in the environs of the district Sangibutu, I destroyed all of them, leveling (them) down to the ground. I set fire to their roof-beams and turned (them) into ashes.

---

233) TA URU.*ul-ḫi at-tu-muš a-na a-*⸢*tur*$^{?}$⸣ *un-na-te re-eš* URU.MEŠ-*ni dan-nu-ti ša* KUR.*sa-an-gi-bu-te na-gi-i aq-ṭe-rib*

234) *na-gu-ú áš-bu ṣi-bit* KUR-*šu ša* ⸢*ul*⸣*-tu ul-la-a a-na ru-up-pu-uš* KUR-*šu-nu is-ki-lu* LUGAL *pa-ni a-li-kut maḫ-re-e-šu*

235) ⸢URU.*ḫu*⸣*-ur-nu-ku* URU.*ḫa-ar-da-ni-a* URU.*gi-zu-ar-zu* URU.*šá-áš-zi-is-sa* URU.*ḫu-un-du-ur-na* AN.TA-*ú*

236) ⸢URU⸣.*x* [*x*] *x* ⸢SI/E$^{?}$ URU.*ú*⸣*-at-*⸢*zu*⸣*-un-za* URU.*a-ra-zu* URU.*ša-*^{m}*ṣi-ni-a* URU.*ḫu-un-du-ur-na* KI.TA-*ú*

237) URU.*el-*[... URU....]*-x-nak* URU.*ṣi-it-tu-ar-zu* URU.*zi-ir-ma* URU.*sur-zi-i* URU.*e-li-ia-di-ni-a*

238) URU.*da-*⸢*ag*⸣*-*[... URU....] ⸢URU.*ṣur*⸣*-zi-al-di-ú*

233–246) Moving on from the city Ulḫu, I came to *the village*(s) of the land, *the foremost* of the fortified cities of the district Sangibutu. (This is) an inhabited district seized by his (Rusâ's) land, which long ago earlier king(s), his predecessors, had annexed in order to expand their country. (235) The cities Ḫurnuku, Ḫardania, Gizuarzu, Šašzissa, Upper Ḫundurna, ..., Uatzunza, Arazu, Ša-Ṣinia, Lower Ḫundurna, El[..., ...]nak, Ṣittuarzu, Zirma, Surzî, Eliyadinia, Dag[..., ...], Ṣurzialdiu, Armuna, (and) Kinaštania — twenty-one fortifi[ed] cities [... (*which*)] grew up on the peaks of Mount Arzabia [like] trees that grow in the mountains — (240) are surrounded by very strong walls [... wh]ose crenellations are each one hundred and twenty layers of brick in height, and ... [...] for stationing

---

is possible, but not certain. If *iš-mu-*, one might think of *iš-mu-*⸢*ṭu*⸣*-ma*, thus "my fierce warriors denuded (i.e., stripped off all the fruit in) his well-kept gardens," except that one would not expect *a-na* before GIŠ.KIRI$_{6}$.MEŠ-*šú as-ma-a-ti* in line 223 and the trace at the end of line 224 on VA 8749 fits ⸢RI⸣ better than ⸢TU⸣.

225 The reading *an-ḫu*$^{?}$*-ti* is proposed by Mayer, MDOG 115 (1983) p. 90. The copy has DIŠ-PA and the text ⸢DIŠ$^{?}$-IZ$^{?}$/GUR$^{?}$⸣ for ḪU. Possibly read instead *an-*<<DIŠ>>*-ḫat-ti*.

228 Possibly "(*the place where agricultural*) *work had been suspended*" (see AHw p. 1352) or "(*the site of*) *the destruction* (*of the fields*)" (see CAD M/2 p. 236) instead of "what had been destroyed."

229 *ki-i za-gìn-du-re-e* ⸢*ṣer*⸣*-pa šak-nu-ma*: For the tentative translation "*were spotted with colored flecks* like *polished* lapis lazuli," cf. CAD A/2 p. 337 and Ṣ p. 209. B.R. Foster translates this as "looked like red faience" (Before the Muses^{3} p. 803). A. Bagg translates it as "wie Lapislazuli farbig gesprenkelt (aussah)?" (Assyrische Wasserbauten p. 322); see also ibid. p. 326 for various other proposed translations of this passage. Most recently S. Thavapalan, J. Stenger, and C. Snow (ZA 106 [2016] p. 202) suggest that "the image evoked by the color may be of a flax field in springtime, when the powdery blue blossoms appear to glow in spots against the greenery" and translate the passage as "was overlaid with bright flecks (looking) like turquoise-blue glass."

233 The tentative translation of *a-*⸢*tur*$^{?}$⸣ *un-na-te re-eš* URU.MEŠ-*ni dan-nu-ti* as "*the settlements of the land, the foremost* of the fortified cities" is based on CAD U/W p. 161. M. van Loon (BiOr 44 [1987] p. 259) suggests A.AB.[BA] *un-na-te*, "the sea of the lands," but there does not appear to be sufficient room for this reading and it would not seem to make good sense here.

URU.*ar-mu-na* URU.*ki-in-áš-ta-ni-a*
239) 21 URU.MEŠ-*ni* ⸢*dan-nu*⸣-[*ti* ... *ša*$^{?}$ *ki-ma*] ⸢GIŠ⸣.*gap-ni tar-bit* KUR-*i* UGU ŠU.SI.MEŠ KUR.*ar-za-bi-a a-ṣu-ni*
240) BÀD.MEŠ-*ni dun-nu-nu-*[*ti* (...) *ša* ...] *x* 2 UŠ.TA.ÀM *ti-ib-ki gaba-dib-ú la-ni-šu-nu la-mu-ma*
241) *a-na man-za-az mun-daḫ-*⸢*ṣe*⸣-[(*šu-nu*) ...] *x-ri šu-ṣu-ú a-na e-peš ta-ḫa-zi šu-tal**-*bu-šu pul-ḫa-a-ti*
242) *ḫi-ri-iṣ-ṣi šup-pu-lu-te a-na* ⸢*tu*⸣-[*kul-ti*$^{?}$ ...] ⸢*né*⸣-*reb* KÁ.GAL.MEŠ-*šu-nu ru-uk-ku-sa di-ma-a-ti*
243) ÍD.MEŠ *ba-bi-lat* A.MEŠ *mi-li i-na* (*x*) [...] *x i-na ta-mir-ti-šu-nu la i-šu-ú ba-ṭil-tu*
244) UN.MEŠ-*šu-nu i-na ṭuḫ-di ù meš-*⸢*re*⸣-[*e* ...]-⸢*re*⸣-*di mal ba-šu-ú rit-pu-šu si-kil-tu*
245) É.GAL.MEŠ *rab-ba-a-te šin-na-at x* [...] GIŠ.*né-me-du šu-ut-ru-ṣu si-mat* LUGAL-*ti*
246) GIŠ.ÙR.MEŠ ŠIM.LI *e-ri-šu* DÙG.GA ⸢TA⸣ [...] (*x*)-⸢*ḫa*$^{?}$⸣-*x-ma ša e-*⸢*ri*$^{?}$-*bi*$^{?}$-*ši*$^{?}$-*na*$^{?}$ *ki*⸣-*ma ḫa-šur-ri i-za-qa lìb-bu-uš*
247) UN.MEŠ KUR.*sa-an-gi-bu-te na-gi-i a-*⸢*ši*⸣-[*bu-ut* KUR$^{?}$] ⸢*ù*$^{?}$⸣ *a-ši-bu-ut* URU.MEŠ-*ni šu-a-tu-nu gi-mir-tu*
248) *a-ka-ma ger-ri-ia ša a-na* 1 KASKAL.GÍD.[ÀM (*x*) *x*] *x-tu* UGU KUR.*ur-ar-ṭi a-na paṭ gim-ri-šú šit-ku-*⸢*na-at e-ši*⸣-*tu*
249) *ša ma-ad-gi-li-šu-nu* ⸢*ša*⸣ *na-gu-ú a-na na-*⸢*ak*⸣-[*ri*$^{?}$] ⸢UGU⸣ ŠU.SI.MEŠ KUR-*e di-ma-a-te ru-uk-ku-sa-ma šu-zu-uz-za a-x* [*x* (*x x x*)]
250) *qi-da-at ab-ri ša* GÌR.II *nak-ri ul-lu-*[*x* (*x*)]-*ti-ma di-par še-rim li-lá-a-te e-mu-ru-ma ú-ad-du-*⸢*ú*⸣ [*x x* (*x x*)]
251) *ti-ib a-nun-ti-ia šam-ru ša la iš-šá-*⸢*na*⸣-[*nu*] ⸢*iš*⸣-*ḫu-tu-ma šu-ḫar-ra-tu it-ta-bi-ik-šu-nu-ti-ma* IG-*x*-[(*x x*)]-ZI
252) *a-na bu-ši-i-šu-nu ma-a*'-*di pa-na la iš-šu-*⸢*ú*$^{?}$⸣ BÀD.MEŠ-*šu-nu dan-nu-ti ú-maš-ši-ru-ma e-mid-du šá-*[*ḫa*]-*tu*
253) *ki-ma ur-pat li-lá-a-te šá-pi-ti na-gu-ú šu-a-*⸢*tu*

[(their)] fighting men. They are clothed in terror for the doing of battle. Deep moats [*were dug around them*] for *the su*[*pport ... and*] towers were constructed at the approaches to their gates. The rivers which carry flood-waters in [*abundance* ...] never have any interruption (*in their flow of water*) in their (the cities') meadowland(s). Their people in abundance and wealth [...] ..., as many as there are, have extensive possessions. (245) Great palaces, the equals of [...] chairs befitting a king *were scattered about*. Beams of juniper, the sweet fragrance [...] ... and wafts towards *the one who enters them* (the palaces) like (the fragrance of) *ḫašurru*-cedar.

247–253) All the people of the district of Sangibutu, (both) those dw[elling *in the countryside*] *and* those dwelling in those cities, <*saw*> the cloud of dust (kicked up) by my expeditionary force which [...] for a distance of one league. Confusion was established over the land Urarṭu, to its full extent. Towers had been constructed on the mountain peaks so that they could observe the district (and look out) for the *ene*[*my*]; and [...] had been stationed. (250) They saw the *flames* of the brushwood pyres which (signaled) the approach of the enemy ... the torches (lit) morning (and) evening, and they transmitted (*this information*) [...]. They became afraid of the fierce onslaught of my battle (array) that cannot be withst[ood] (lit.: "equa[led]"); (a state of) stunned numbness spread over them and ... They did not care about their abundant property. They abandoned their strong (city) walls and sought refuge. I covered that district like the dense clouds of evening and overwhelmed all his fortified cities like a turbulent

240 No crenellations or parapets would be 120 layers of brick in height in themselves, but they could well be that many layers of bricks from the ground; see text no. 45 lines 38–39.
241 -*tal**-: The text has -RU-.
243 G. Vera Chamaza (AMI NF 27 [1994] p. 118) suggests the possible restoration *i-na* [*ḫe-en-gal-li*].
246 CAD E p. 280 reads *ša e-ri-*⸢*iš*⸣-*ši-na*, i.e., "the fragrance of which ... wafts through it" instead of *ša ēribišina*, "wafts towards the one who enters them (the palaces)"; however, one would expect *erīssina* rather than *erīššina*. The passage is damaged, but considerations of space might suggest BI rather than IŠ.
247 F. Thureau-Dangin (TCL 3 p. 40) restores *na-gi-i*, "district," after *āš*[*ibūt*, not KUR, "land"; however, as noted by G. Vera Chamaza (AMI NF 27 [1994] p. 118), the copy does not indicate that there is sufficient room for that restoration.
248 KASKAL.GÍD.[ÀM (*x*) *x*] *x-tu*: Or KASKAL.GÍD.[TA.ÀM (*x*)] *x-tu*; however in line 326 we have only KASKAL.GÍD.ÀM. Possibly <*i-mu-ru*> before UGU; see Vera Chamaza, AMI NF 27 (1994) p. 118.
250 B. Landsberger (WO 3/1–2 [1964] p. 75 n. 104) suggests *nak-ri ul-lu-*[*ka-a*]-*ti-ma*, "die heranmarschierenden Feinde."
251 For the end of the line, F. Thureau-Dangin (TCL 3 p. 40) suggested *ik-*⸢*šu*⸣-[*du mi-tu-ti-iš*], and this was followed in CAD Š/1 p. 108, which would give the meaning "they bec[ame as the dead]." Weidner, AfO 12 (1937–39) p. 146 proposed *ig-*⸢*lud*⸣-[*du ta-ḫa*]-*zi*, "th[ey were frightened of (doing) batt]le" (see also AHw p. 274; Mayer, Assyrien und Urarṭu I p. 122; and Foster, Before the Muses[3] p. 804). Collation indicates that there is not sufficient room for either restoration.
253 ILLU "flood": The reading follows CAD M/2 p. 138; cf. CAD E p. 257, which has *a-rib* and takes it to be from the noun *erbu* "locust."

ak⸣*-tùm-ma gi-mir* URU.MEŠ*-šú dan-nu-ti ki-ma* ILLU *mit-ḫur-ti* ⸢*as*?⸣*-ḫu-up*

flood.

254) *i-na bi-rit* KUR*.ar-za-bi-a* KUR*.ir-ti-a* KUR.MEŠ*-e šá-*⸢*qu*⸣*-ti* 12 KASKAL.GÍD *qaq-qa-ru ma-la-ku áš-kun-ma ú-ka-ṣi-*⸢*ra uš*⸣*-man-ni*
255) *i-na šá-ḫa-te nàr-qit lìb-bi-šu-nu qu-ra-di-ia* ⸢*ek*⸣*-du-te ki-ma bi-ib-bi uš-bi-iʾ-ma a-na še-me-e ur-ti-šú-nu la* ⸢*e-zi*⸣*-bu ḫa-a-a-ṭu*
256) *um-ma-na-at* ^{d}*a-šur rap-šá-a-te gi-mir* URU.MEŠ-⸢*ni*⸣*-šu-nu e-ri-biš ú-šak-tim-ma šá-lil-ia er-*⸢*ḫu*?*-ti*⸣ *ú-še-ri-ba ur-ši-šu-un*
257) *bu-šu-ú ma-ak-ku-*⸢*ru ni-ṣir*⸣*-te* ⸢LUGAL?⸣-[*ti*? (*x*) *ub*]*-lu-nim-ma i-šit-ta-šu-nu kit-mur-tu* ⸢*ik-šud*⸣*-du qa-ta-a-a*
258) *ṣa-ab ḫup-ši kal-la-pu* ⸢*na*⸣-[*áš* GIŠ.PAN? *az-ma-re-e*? *a-na*] BÀD.MEŠ*-šu-nu ú-še-li-ma it-ti pa-áš-qi* ⸢*ù*⸣ *a-ṣi-te na-qi-ri ú-šá-aṣ-*⸢*bít*?⸣
259) GIŠ.ÙR.MEŠ ŠIM.LI *ta-*⸢*aṣ*⸣*-lil-ti* É.GAL.MEŠ *ú-*⸢*na*⸣*-si-iḫ-ma* ⸢UN⸣.MEŠ KUR.⸢*man-na*⸣-[*a-a*] ⸢KUR?*.na*?*-ʾi*?*-ri*? *li*?⸣-[*x* (*x*)] ⸢A?⸣ *x* (*x*) *x* ⸢*ú-šal*?⸣*-x* (*x*) [(*x x*)]
260) ⸢*ker*⸣*-ḫe-šu-nu e-lu-ti ša ki-ma* KUR.MEŠ*-e šur-šud***-du a-di tem-men*$_{5}$*-<<ma>>-ni-šu-nu ba-ṣi-*⸢*iš ú*⸣*-x* [...] (*x*) *x*
261) *i-na* É.MEŠ*-šu-nu nak-la-a-te* ^{d}GIBIL$_{6}$ *ú-šá-aṣ-bit-ma qu-tur-šu-nu ú-šat-bi-ma pa-an* AN*-e ki-ma im-ba-ri ú-*⸢*šá*⸣*-aṣ-bit*

254–261) I advanced a distance of twelve leagues between Mount Arzabia (and) Mount Irtia, lofty mountains, and (then) set up camp. (255) I had my fierce warriors pass through their remote recesses like wild sheep and they did not leave any (enemy) spy behind to hear their orders. I had the extensive troops of the god Aššur envelop all their cities like locusts and I had my *aggressive* plundering (troops) enter their private quarters. They [bro]ught me property (and) possessions, *ro*[*yal*] treasure, and my hands took possession of their accumulated riches. I sent common soldiers, *light infantry*, [*bow*]*men*, [(*and*) *spearmen*] up [onto] their (city) walls and I had demolition-men *take up position at the battlements and tower*(*s*). I tore out the palaces' roof-beams of juniper and *caused* the people of the land Manne[a] (and) *the land Naʾiri* ... (260) As if (they were made of) sand, I [*demolished*] to their very foundations their high enclosure walls that had been made as firm as the mountains [(...)]. I set fire to their artfully-built homes and made the smoke from them rise up and cover the sky like a fog.

262) *tab-ka-a-ni* GAL.MEŠ *ša* ŠE.PAD.MEŠ ŠE.GIG.MEŠ *ša i-na u*$_{4}$*-me ma-aʾ-du-ti a-na ba-laṭ* KUR *ù* UN.MEŠ *iš-pu-ku qi-ra-a-te*
263) *nap-ḫar um-ma-ni-ia i-na* ANŠE.KUR.RA.MEŠ ANŠE*.pa-re-e* ANŠE.A.AB.BA ANŠE.MEŠ *ú-šá-az-bil-ma i-na qé-reb uš-man-ni-ia ki-ma* DU$_{6}$.MEŠ *ú-*⸢*šap*⸣*-pik*
264) *a-kal ṭuḫ-di ù neš-bé-e* UN.MEŠ*-ia ú-šá-kil-ma ṣu-ud-de-e tak-bit-ti ša ta-a-a-ar-ti* KUR *aš-šur*.KI *e-pu-šu i-na ḫi-du-ti*
265) GIŠ.KIRI$_{6}$.MEŠ*-šu la-la-a-na-ti ak-šiṭ-ma* GEŠTIN*-šu a-na mu-ʾu-de-e ak-šiṭ-ma ú-šab-ṭi-la mal-ti-su*
266) GIŠ.TIR.MEŠ*-šu rab-ba-a-ti ša ki-ma a-pi ed-lu-ti ḫi-it-lu-pu iṣ-ṣu-ši-in ak-kis-ma ú-nam-ma-a ta-mir-tu-uš*
267) *kul-lat* GIŠ*.gup-ni-šu nak-su-ti ki-ma ḫi-im-ma-at a-šam-šu-ti ú-paḫ-ḫir-ma i-na* ^{d}GIBIL$_{6}$ *aq-mu*
268) 1 ME ⸢46?⸣ URU.MEŠ*-ni ša li-mi-ti-šu-nu ki-ma ab-ri a-qu-ud-ma qu-tur-šu-un ki-ma a-šam-šá-ti pa-an* AN*-e ú-šak-tim*

262–268) I had my whole army carry away on horses, mules, camel(s), (and) donkeys the great stores of barley (and) wheat that they (the enemy) had heaped up in (their) granaries over a long time for the sustenance of (their) land and people, and I heaped up (the grain) inside my camp (so that the piles looked) like (ruin) mounds. I fed my people abundant food until they were completely full (lit.: "food of abundance and satiety") and they joyfully laid up lavish travel provisions for the return journey to Assyria. (265) I chopped down his luxuriant orchards; I chopped down his grapevines in large numbers and (thus) put an end to his (source of) drink. I cut down his great forests, whose trees were as tangled up as impenetrable reed thickets, and I laid waste to his meadowland(s). I gathered up all his felled logs like the flotsam after a dust storm and I set (them) on fire. I set fire to one hundred and *forty six* settlements in their environs as if (they were) brushwood pyres and I made the smoke from them cover the sky like a dust storm.

---

269) TA URU.MEŠ*-ni dan-nu-ti ša* KUR*.sa-an-gi-bu-te*

269–276) Moving on from the fortified cities of the

---

258 *ú-šá-aṣ-*⸢*bít*?⸣ (e.g, CAD N/1 p. 335) or *ú-šá-az-*⸢*ziz*⸣ (e.g, Weidner, AfO 12 [1937–39] p. 146).
260 *šur-šud**(text: BU)*-du*: G. Vera Chamaza (AMI NF 17 [1994] p. 118) prefers to emend BU to ŠU, but BU is closer in form to *šud* than ŠU. Since BU can have a value *šúd* in the Middle Assyrian period (see von Soden and Röllig, Syllabar^{3} p. 40), no emendation may actually be required. For similar forms doubling the final consonant, see for example lines 19 (*šuk-šud-du*) and 100 (*šu-kud-du*).
269 KUR*.ar-ma-ri-<ia>-li-i*: For the emendation, see lines 280 and 290.

at-tu-muš a-na KUR.*ar-ma-ri-<ia>-li-i na-gi-i aq-ṭe-rib*
270) URU.*bu-bu-zi bir-tu* URU.*ḫu-un-du-ur ša* 2 BÀD.MEŠ-*ni la-mu-ú pi-i di-im-ti tu-bal-e ma-ḫi-ri ru-uk-ku-su*
271) URU.*a-a-le-e* URU.*ṣi-ni-iš-pa-la-a* URU.*ṣi-ni-ú-nak* URU.*ar-na* URU.*šar-ni-i*
272) ⸢7⸣ URU.MEŠ-*ni dan-nu-ti a-di* 30 URU.MEŠ-*ni ša li-mi-ti-šu-nu ša i-na* GÌR.II KUR.*ú-bi-an-da* KUR-*e na-du-ú*
273) *se-ḫer-šu-nu ap-pul-ma qaq-qa-riš am-nu* GIŠ.ÙR.MEŠ *ta-aṣ-lil-ti-šu-nu i-na* ^{d}GIBIL$_{6}$ *aq-mu-ma di-tal-li-iš ú-še-mi*
274) *qi-ra-a-te-šu-nu na-kam-a-ti ú-pat-ti-ma* ŠE.PAD.MEŠ-*su-nu ma-ʾa-at-tu ša la ni-i-bi um-ma-ni ú-šá-a-kil*
275) BURU$_{14}$ *tuk-lat* UN.MEŠ-*šú ù* Ú.*pu-e nap-šat bu-li-šu ab-ri-iš a-qu-ud-ma ar-bu-ti-iš ú-šá-li-ka ta-mir-tu-uš*
276) GIŠ.KIRI$_{6}$.MEŠ-*šú-nu a-kis-ma* GIŠ.TIR.MEŠ-*šú-nu ak-šiṭ nap-ḫar* GIŠ.*gup-ni-šu-nu a-na gu-ru-un-ni aq-ru-un-ma i-na* ^{d}GIBIL$_{6}$ *aq-mu*

land Sangibutu, I came to the district of Armariyalî. (With regard to) the cities Bubuzi — a fortress —, Ḫundur — which is surrounded by two (city) walls (*which were*) *constructed at the entrance to the tower by means of a plumb-line* (lit.: "cord of the market") — Ayalê, Ṣinišpalâ, Ṣiniunak, Arna, (and) Šarnî, (a total of) seven fortified cities, together with thirty settlements in their environs, which are situated at the foot of Mount Ubianda, I destroyed all of them, leveling (them) down to the ground. I set fire to their roof-beams and turned (them) into ashes. I opened up their granaries (and) storehouses and (then) fed my army their abundant grain in unlimited quantities. (275) As if (they were) brushwood pyres, I set fire to the crops upon which his people relied (for sustenance) and to the fodder (lit.: "straw") (that maintains) the lives of his herds, and I turned his meadowland(s) into a desolate land. I cut down their orchards and choppped down their forests; I piled all their logs up in heaps and set (them) on fire.

277) *i-na me-taq-*⸢*ti*⸣*-ia a-na* URU.*ar-bu* URU É AD-*šu ša* ^{m}*ur-sa-a ù* URU.*ri-ia-ar* URU-*šú ša* ^{md}15-BÀD *a-lik*
278) 7 URU.MEŠ-*ni ša li-mi-ti-šu-nu ša* ŠEŠ.MEŠ-*šú* NUMUN LUGAL-*ti-šú i-na lìb-bi-šu-nu šu-šu-bu-*⸢*ma*⸣ *dun-nu-nu ma-ṣar-tu*
279) URU.MEŠ-*ni šu-a-*⸢*tu*⸣*-nu ap-pul qaq-qa-riš am-nu* É ^{d}*ḫal-di-a* DINGIR-*šu ab-re-eš a-qu-ud-ma ú-šal-pi-ta sa-a-gi-šu*

277–279) In the course of my march, I went to the city Arbu, Ursâ's (Rusâ's) ancestral city, and to the city Riyar, Ištar-dūrī's (Sarduri's) city. (With regard to) seven settlements in their environs in which his brothers, members of his royal family, had been made to dwell and (whose) garrison(s) had been strengthened, I destroyed these settlements, leveling (them) down to the ground. I set fire to the temple of his god Ḫaldi as if (it was) a brushwood pyre and I desecrated its shrines.

280) TA KUR.*ar-ma-ri-*⸢*ia*⸣*-li-i at-tu-muš* KUR.*ú-i-zu-ku* KUR ŠIM.LI *ša ši-pik-šu* NA$_{4}$.DÚR.MI.NA *at-ta-bal-kàt a-na* KUR.*a-ia-di aq-ṭe-rib*
281) URU.*an-za-li-a* URU.⸢*ku*⸣*-a-ii-*⸢*in*⸣ URU.*qa-al-la-ni-a* URU.*bi-it-a-a* URU.*a-lu-ar-za* URU.*qi-ú-na* URU.*al-*⸢*li*⸣*-i*
282) URU.*ar-zu-gu* URU.⸢*šik*⸣*-ka-nu* URU.*ar-di-ú-nak* URU.*da-ia-zu-na* URU.*ge-e-ta* URU.*ba-a-ni-ú*
283) URU.*bir-ḫi-lu-za* URU.⸢*de*⸣*-e-zi-zu* URU.*di-li-zi-a* URU.*a-ba-in-di* URU.*du-a-in* URU.*ḫa-as-ra-na*
284) URU.*pa-ar-ra* URU.*a-ia-ṣu-un* URU.*a-ni-áš-ta-ni-a* URU.*bal-du-ar-za* URU.*šar-ú-ar-di-i*
285) URU.*šu-ma-at-tar* URU.*šá-al-zi-i* URU.*al-bu-ú-ri* URU.*ṣi-qar-ra* URU.*ú-a-ii-is la-bi-ru*
286) 30 URU.MEŠ-*šú dan-nu-ti ša i-na a-ḫi* A.AB.BA

280–296) Moving on from the land Armariyalî, I crossed Mount Uizuku, a mountain with juniper tree(s) whose base consists of breccia-stone, (and) I came to the land Ayādi. (With regard to) the cities Anzalia, Kuayin, Qallania, Bitāya, Aluarza, Qiuna, Allî, Arzugu, Šikkanu, Ardiunak, Dayazuna, Gēta, Bāniu, Birḫiluza, Dēzizu, Dilizia, Abaindi, Duain, Ḫasrana, Parra, Ayaṣun, Aniaštania, Balduarza, Šaruardî, (285) Šumattar, Šalzî, Albūri, Ṣiqarra, (and) Old Uayis — thirty of its fortified cities which were set up in a straight line in a row along the shore of the roiling sea, on the slopes of the great mountains — the cities Argištiuna (and) Qallania, its strong fortressess, were constructed between them. They (the two fortresses) rise like stars above Mount Arṣidu and Mount Maḫunnia and *their foundations* are visible for two hundred and forty (...) *each way*. His warriors — the best troops in his army, (men)

270 The meaning of the passage *pi-i di-im-ti tu-bal-e ma-ḫi-ri ru-uk-ku-su*, translated "(*which were*) *constructed at the entrance to the tower by means of a plumb-line* (lit.: "cord of the market")," is uncertain (see CAD T p. 445). B.R. Foster (Before the Muses[3] p. 805) tentatively suggests "the entry to its two towers connected with a drawbridge(?) of rope" and is basically followed by F.M. Fales (COS 4 p. 209) who translates "the opening of (each) tower connected with a corresponding drawbridge of rope(?)" The reading *tu-bal-e* follows Borger, BiOr 14 (1957) p. 121 sub S. 201a; cf. CAD Ḫ p. 201.
286 Although the text refers to thirty cities, only twenty-nine are named in lines 281–285.

gal-la-ti ti-bi-ik KUR.MEŠ GAL.MEŠ *sa-ad-ru-ma šu-uṣ-bu-tú ki-ma us-si*

287) URU.*ar-giš-ti-ú-na* URU.*qa-al-la-ni-a bi-ra-ti-šu dan-na-a-te ru-uk-ku-sa bi-ru-uš-*⸢*šu*⸣*-un*

288) *el-en* KUR.*ar-ṣi-du ù* KUR.*maḫ-un-ni-a kak-ka-biš a-ṣa-ma a-na* 4 UŠ.TA.ÀM *in-na-aṭ-ṭa-lu* ⸢SUḪ-*šin*$^{?}$⸣

289) LÚ.*qu-ra-di-šu a-ša-re-tú um-ma-ni-šu le-ʾu-tu ta-ḫa-zi na-áš ka-ba-bi az-ma-ri-i tu-kul-ti* KUR-*šú šu-lu-ú qé-reb-*⸢*šin*⸣

290) *ki-šit-ti* KUR.*ar-ma-ri-ia-li-i na-ge-e i-te-e-šu-nu e-mu-ru-ma it-ru-ra iš-da-a-šu-un*

291) URU.MEŠ-*ni-šu-nu it-ti mar-ši-ti-šu-nu ú-maš-še-ru-ma a-na qé-reb bi-ra-a-ti šu-*⸢*a-ti-na*⸣ *ki-ma iṣ-ṣu-ri* ⸢*ip-par*⸣*-šu*

292) *um-ma-ni ma-ʾa-at-ta-tu a-na* URU.MEŠ-*ni-šu-nu ú-še-li-ma* NÍG.ŠU-*šú-nu a-na mu-ʾu-de-e iš-lu-lu* NÍG.GA-*šu-un*

293) BÀD.MEŠ-*ni-šu-nu dan-nu-ti a-di* 87 URU.MEŠ-*ni ša li-mi-ti-šu-nu ap-pul-ma qaq-qa-riš ú-šak-ši-id*

294) *i-na* É.MEŠ *qer-bi-šu-nu* ^{d}GIBIL$_{6}$ *ú-šá-aṣ-bit-ma* GIŠ.ÙR.MEŠ *ta-aṣ-lil-ti-šu-nu di-tal-li-iš ú-še-mi*

295) *qi-ra-te-šu-nu na-kam-a-te ú-pat-ti-ma* ŠE.PAD.MEŠ *la ni-i-bi um-ma-ni ú-šá-a-kil*

296) GIŠ.KIRI$_{6}$.MEŠ-*šu-nu ak-kis-ma* GIŠ.TIR.MEŠ-*šu-nu ak-šiṭ kul-lat* GIŠ.*gup-ni-šu-nu ú-paḫ-ḫir-ma i-na* ^{d}GIBIL$_{6}$ *aq-mu*

skilled in battle, shield (and) spear bearers, (men) on whom his land relied (to protect it) — had been stationed inside them. (290) They saw the conquest of the land Armariyalî, their neighboring district, and their legs trembled. They abandoned their cities, (along) with their property, and flew like birds into those fortresses. I sent many troops up to their cities and they (Sargon's soldiers) carried off large amounts of property (and) possessions from them as booty. I destroyed their strong fortresses (lit.: "walls"), together with eighty-seven settlements in their environs, causing (them) to be level with the ground. I set fire to the houses inside them and turned their roof-beams into ashes. (295) I opened up their granaries (and) storehouses and fed my army grain in unlimited quantities. I cut down their orchards and chopped down their forests. I gathered up all their logs and set (them) on fire.

---

297) TA KUR.*a-ia-di at-tu-muš* ÍD.*al-lu-ri-a* ÍD.*qa-al-la-ni-a* ÍD.*in-na-a-a* ÍD.MEŠ *e-te-bir*

298) *a-na* URU.*ú-a-ii-is na-gi-i tuk-la-te-šu še-pit mi-iṣ-ri ša* KUR.*ur-ar-ṭi ša pat-ti* KUR.*na-ʾi-ri aq-ṭe-rib*

299) URU.*ú-a-ii-is* URU *dan-nu-ti-šu bir-tu-šu* GAL-*tu ša* UGU *kul-lat bi-ra-a-te-šu dun-nu-na-at-ma nu-uk-ku-lat ep-še-es-sa*

300) LÚ.ERIM.MEŠ *ti-du-ki-šu ek-du-ti* LÚ.*da-a-a-li mu-še-ri-bu ṭè-em* KUR.KUR.MEŠ *li-mi-ti-šú šu-šu-bu qer-bu-uš-šu*

301) LÚ.EN.NAM.MEŠ-*šu a-di ki-iṣ-ri-šu-nu i-na lìb-bi ú-še-li-ma it-ti* BÀD-*šu dan-ni mun-daḫ-ṣi ú-šal-mi*

302) *ša* URU.*bir-ti šu-a-ti ku-tal-la-šá ak-šu-ud*

297–305) Moving on from the land Ayādi, I crossed the Alluria, Qallania, (and) Innāya Rivers. I came to the city Uayis, a district upon which he relied (and located) on the lower border of the land Urarṭu, on the frontier with the land Naʾiri. (With regard to) the city Uayis — his fortified city (and) his great fortress — which had been made stronger and whose construction was more ingenious than all his (other) fortresses, (300) his fierce combat troops (and) the scouts who bring in news about the surrounding lands were garrisoned there. He stationed his provincial governors, together with their (military) contingents, there and he had (his) fighting men man its strong (city) wall. I conquered this fortress from the rear (lit.: "the rear part of this fortress"). I slaughtered his

---

288 The understanding of 4 UŠ.TA.ÀM follows CAD N/2 p. 128; cf. CAD K pp. 44–45 "to a height of 240 (cubits)." F. Thureau-Dangin's translation, followed by such scholars as D.D. Luckenbill and W. Mayer, suggests that that the foundations were visible to a height of 240 cubits. B.R. Foster (Before the Muses^{3} p. 805) translates the passage as indicating that the two fortresses "looked down 240 cubits below." ⸢SUḪ$^{?}$-*šin*$^{?}$⸣: The normal logographic writing for *uššu* is URU$_{4}$, but SUḪ does stand for this word in at least one place in Esarhaddon's royal inscriptions (see Leichty, RINAP 4 p. 206 no. 105 v 31 and Borger, MZ p. 284).

289 *a-ša-re-tú* (CAD A/2 p. 419 sub *ašarittu*) or *a-ša-re-*<*du*>*-ut* (AHw p. 78 sub *ašarēdu(m)* 3).

291 G. Vera Chamaza (AMI NF 27 [1994] p. 118) suggests *ip-par-šu-*<*du*> ("fled" instead of "flew") and forms of the verb *naparšudu* appear several times in this inscription (lines 118, 146, 149, 175, 214, 315, and 333). Nevertheless, the idiom "fly like birds" is well attested in Neo-Assyrian royal inscriptions (see CAD N/I pp. 314–315; cf. this inscription line 25, text no. 1 line 153, and text no. 7 line 50) and thus there seems no compelling reason to accept the emendation.

298 Uayis has been identified with Qalatgah, southwest of Lake Urmia in the Ushnu valley of northwestern Iran, by P. Zimansky (JNES 49 [1990] p. 17; see also Kroll in Köroğlu and Konyar, Urartu pp. 161–162).

LÚ.*qu-ra-di-šu i-na* IGI KÁ.GAL-*šú ki-ma as-li ú-nap-pi-iṣ*
303) ⌜GIŠ⌝.KIRI$_6$.MEŠ-*šú ak-šiṭ-ma* GIŠ.TIR.MEŠ-*šú ak-kis kul-lat* GIŠ.*gup-ni-šu nak-su-ti ú-paḫ-ḫir-ma i-na* ^{d}GIBIL$_6$ *aq-mu*
304) URU.*bar-zu-ri-a-ni* URU.*ú-al-ṭu-qu-ia* URU.*qu-ut-ta* URU.*qi-ip-pa* URU.*a-sa-pa-a*
305) 5 É BÀD.MEŠ-*ni dan-nu-ti a-di* 40 URU.MEŠ-*ni ša li-mi-ti-šu-nu i-na* ^{d}GIBIL$_6$ *aq-mu*

warriors in front of its (city) gate like sheep. I chopped down his orchards and cut down his forests. I gathered up all his felled logs and set (them) on fire. I burned down the cities of Barzuriani, Ualṭuquya, Qutta, Qippa, (and) Asapâ — five strong fortresses — together with forty settlements in their environs.

---

306) *ul-tu* URU.*ú-a-ii-is at-tu-muš a-na na-gi-i ša* ^{m}*ia-an-zu-ú* LUGAL KUR.*na-ʾi-i-ri aq-ṭe-rib*
307) ^{m}*ia-an-zu-ú* LUGAL KUR.*na-ʾi-i-ri* 4 KASKAL.GÍD *qaq-qa-ru* TA URU.*ḫu-bu-uš-ki-a* URU LUGAL-*ti-šú a-na* GABA-*ia il-li-kam-ma iš-šíq* GÌR.II-*ia*
308) *ma-da-ta-šu* ANŠE.KUR.RA.MEŠ LAL-*at ni-i-ri* GU$_4$.MEŠ *ù* US$_5$.UDU.ḪI.A *i-na qé-reb* URU.*ḫu-bu-uš-ki-a* URU-*šú am-ḫur-šu*

306–308) Moving on from the city Uayis, I came to the district of Ianzû, king of the land Naʾiri. Ianzû, king of the land Naʾiri, came from his royal city Ḫubuškia to meet me, a distance of four leagues, and he kissed my feet. Inside his city Ḫubuškia, I received from him as his tribute horses trained to the yoke, oxen, and sheep and goats.

---

309) *i-na ta-a-a-ar-ti-ia* ^{m}*ur-za-na* URU.*mu-ṣa-ṣir-a-a e-piš an-ni ù gil-la-ti e-ti-iq ma-mit* DINGIR.MEŠ *la ka-ni-šu be-lu-ti*
310) *ek-ṣu* LÚ.*šad-da-a-u$_8$-ú ša i-na a-de-e* ^{d}*a-šur* ^{d}UTU ^{d}AG ^{d}AMAR.UTU *iḫ-ṭu-ma ib-bal-ki-tu it-ti-ia*
311) *a-lak maḫ-ri-ia ša ta-a-a-ar-ti ger-ri ú-šab-ṭil-ma it-ti ta-mar-ti-šu ka-bit-te la iš-ši-qa* GÌR.II-*ia*
312) *bíl-tu ma-da-at-tu ta-mar-ta-šu ik-la-ma a-na šá-ʾa-al šul-mi-ia e-de-nu-ú la iš-pu-ra* LÚ.*rak-ba-šu*
313) *i-na šu-ḫu-uṭ lìb-bi-ia kul-lat* GIŠ.GIGIR.MEŠ-*ia* ANŠE.KUR.RA.MEŠ *ma-aʾ-du-ti gi-mir* KARAŠ-*ia ḫar-ra-an* KUR *aš-šur*.KI *ú-šá-aṣ-bit*
314) *i-na tu-kul-ti-šu* GAL-*ti ša* ^{d}*a-šur a-bu* DINGIR.MEŠ *be-el ma-ta-a-ti* LUGAL *kiš-šat* AN-*e* KI-*tim a-lid* <*gim-ri*> EN EN.EN
315) *ša ul-tu u$_4$-um ṣa-a-ti* DINGIR.MEŠ KUR *ù* KUR-*i ša kib-rat* LÍMMU-*i a-na šu-tuq-qu-ri-šu la na-par-šu-di ma-na-ma*
316) *it-ti i-šit-ti-šu-nu kit-mur-ti a-na šu-ru-ub é-ḫur-sag-gal-kur-kur-ra iš-ru-ku-uš* ^{d}EN.LÍL.LÁ DINGIR.MEŠ ^{d}AMAR.UTU
317) *i-na qí-bi-ti ṣir-te ša* ^{d}AG ^{d}AMAR.UTU *ša i-na man-za-az* MUL.MEŠ *ša šu-ut-bé-e* GIŠ.TUKUL.MEŠ-*ia iṣ-ba-tu ta-lu-ku*
318) *ù i-da-at dum-qí ša le-qe-e kiš-šu-ti* ^{d}MÁ.GUR$_8$ EN *a-ge-e a-na šul-pu-ut* KUR.*gu-ti*.KI *ú-šá-ni-ḫa* EN.NUN

309–313) During my return journey, Urzana of the city Muṣaṣir — one who had committed crime(s) and misdeeds, transgressed against the treaty (sworn) by the gods, (and) not submitted to (my) authority — a dangerous (man), a mountain dweller, who had sinned against a treaty (sworn) by the gods Aššur, Nabû, (and) Marduk and revolted against me, had failed to come before me during the return journey of (my) expeditionary force and had not kissed my feet (while bringing) with him a substantial audience gift. He withheld his tribute, payment(s), (and) audience gift and did not send (even) a single mounted messenger of his to inquire about my well-being. Furiously, I had all my chariots, numerous horses, (and) my entire (military) camp take the road to Assyria.

314–322) With the great support of the god Aššur — father of the gods, lord of (all) the lands, king of the totality of heaven (and) netherworld, begetter <of everything>, (and) lord of lords, to whom, in the distant past, the Enlil of the gods, the god Marduk, granted the gods of (all) the (low)land and mountain regions of the four quarters (of the world) in order that they, without any exception, might constantly render honor to him (Aššur) (and) that he might bring (them), with their accumulated riches, into Eḫursaggalkurkurra ("House, the Great Mountain of the Lands") — at the exalted command of the gods Nabû (and) Marduk, who had moved on a path in a station of the stars indicating the mobilization of my weapons, and with a propitious sign for seizing

---

309 Muṣaṣir was likely located in the area of Sidikan; one possible site is Mudjesir (ca. 20 km north of Ruwandiz); see Radner, Biainili-Urartu pp. 245–254 and Danti, Expedition 56/3 (2014) pp. 27–33.

311 Cf. Oppenheim, JNES 19 (1960) p. 135.

314–319 With regard to the divine signs which encouraged/caused Sargon to decide to attack the city Muṣaṣir, see Oppenheim, JNES 19 (1960) pp. 136–138; the lunar eclipse mentioned in line 318 has been dated to the evening of October 24, 714 BC by A. Sachs (ibid. p. 137). See also Koch-Westenholz, Mesopotamian Astrology pp. 153–154. For the addition of *gim-ri* in line 314, see line 116. Magur in line 318 refers to Sîn, the moon god.

319) *i-na an-ni šu-qu-ri ša* ^{d}UTU *qu-ra-di ša* UZU.MEŠ *ti-kil-ti ša a-lak i-di-ia ú-šá-áš-ṭi-ra a-mu-ti*

320) *it-ti 1-et* GIŠ.GIGIR GÌR.II-*ia e-de-ni-ti ù* 1 LIM *pet-ḫal-lì-ia šit-mur-ti ṣa-ab* GIŠ.PAN *ka-ba-bi az-ma-ri-i*

321) LÚ.*qu-ra-di-ia ek-du-ti mu-du-ut ta-ḫa-zi ú-zak-ki-ma ḫar-ra-an* URU.*mu-ṣa-ṣir ur-uḫ m[illegible]r-ṣa-ti aṣ-bat-ma*

322) KUR.*ar-si-ú* KUR-*ú dan-nu ša mu-lu-šu ki-i mé-le-e sim-mil-ti mu-la-a la i-šu-ú um-ma-ni ú-še-li*

power — Magur, lord of the corona, remained eclipsed for more than one watch, portending the defeat of the land of the Gutians — (and moreover) with the valuable approval of the god Šamaš, the warrior, who had trustworthy omens written on a (sacrificed sheep's) liver (indicating that he would) go at my side, (320) I mobilized only my single personal chariot and one thousand of my ferocious cavalry, bowmen, (and) shield (and) spear (bearers), fierce warriors who were experienced in battle. Then, I took the road to the city Muṣaṣir, a rugged path, and I made my troops climb up Mount Arsiu, a mighty mountain that did not have any ascent, (*not even one*) like *that* of a ladder (lit.: "whose ascent has no ascent like the rungs of a ladder").

323) ÍD.*za-ban* AN.TA-*ú ša* UN.MEŠ KUR.*na-ʾi-ri ù* KUR.*ḫab-ḫi* ÍD.*e-la-mu-ni-a i-qab-bu-šu-ni e-te-bir*

324) *i-na bi-rit* KUR.*še-ia-ak* KUR.*ar-di-ik-ši* KUR.*ú-la-a-ia-ú* KUR.*al-lu-ri-ú* KUR.MEŠ-*e e-lu-ti*

325) *ḫur-šá-a-ni šá-qu-ti sim-mil-at* KUR.MEŠ-*e pa-áš-qa-te ša ni-ba ed-ku-ma i-na bi-ri-šú-nu a-na me-te-eq zu-uk* GÌR.II *la* TUKU-*ú da-rag-gu*

326) *na-at-ba-kàt* A.MEŠ *dan-nu-ti i-na lìb-bi-šu-nu šu-ut-tu-qa-a-ma ši-si-it ti-ib-ki-šú-nu a-na* 1 KASKAL.GÍD.ÀM *i-šag-gu-mu ki-ma* ^{d}*ad-di*

327) *kul-lat* GIŠ.MEŠ *ḫi-šiḫ-ti* GURUN* *ù* GEŠTIN.MEŠ *a-pi-iš ḫi-it-lu-pu-ma a-na sa-naq né-re-bi-šu-nu ma-lu-ú pul-ḫa-a-te*

328) *ša* LUGAL *a-a-um-ma a-šar-šu-un la e-ti-qu-ma ù* NUN-*ú a-lik pa-ni-ia la e-mu-ru du-rug-šu-un*

329) GIŠ.*gup-ni-šu-nu* GAL.MEŠ *ú-kap-pi-ir-ma pa-áš-qa-a-te sim-mil-a-te-šú-nu i-na ak-kul-li* ZABAR *lu aḫ-si*

330) *ger-ra qa-at-na me-te-qa su-ú-qa ša zu-uk* GÌR.II *ṣe-la-niš e-ti-qu-ma a-na me-te-eq um-ma-ni-ia i-na bi-ri-šu-nu ú-⸢ṭib⸣*

331) GIŠ.GIGIR GÌR.II-*ia i-na ti-ka-a-ti e-mid-ma ù a-na-ku i-na tar-kub-ti* ANŠE.KUR.RA.MEŠ *meḫ-ret um-ma-ni-ia aṣ-bat-ma*

332) LÚ.*qu-ra-di-ia a-di* ANŠE.KUR.RA.MEŠ *a-li-kut i-di-ia il-tén-nu-ú ú-qa-tin-ma i-na pu-uš-qi-šu-nu ú-še-tiq*

323–332) I crossed the Upper Zab River, which the people of the lands Naʾiri and Ḫabḫu call the Elamunia River. In between Mounts Šeyak, Ardikši, Ulāyû, (and) Alluriu — high mountains, (325) lofty mountain ranges, (and) narrow mountain ledges, which ... and through which there is no pathway for the passage of (even) foot soldiers, (and) in which are carved out gullies made by torrential water — the noise of whose cascades resounds for a distance of one league, just like (the thunder of) the god Adad — (mountains) which are as thickly covered with all kinds of useful trees, fruit trees, and vines as a reed thicket, and the approach to whose passes is fraught with terror, (mountains) whose area no king had ever crossed and whose remote region no prince who preceded me had ever seen — I felled their (the mountains') large tree trunks, and with bronze axes I *hacked* (*a way through*) *the narrow places along* their (mountain) ledges. (330) For the passage of my troops between them (the mountains), I improved the narrow path, a route (so) narrow that foot soldiers could only pass through sideways. I placed my personal chariot on the shoulders (lit.: "necks") (of some of my soldiers) and proceeded at the head of my troops on horseback. I had my warriors, together with the horse(men) who go at my side, form a single narrow file (line) and brought (them) through their (the mountains') defiles.

333) *áš-šu la na-par-šu-di-šu* ⸢LÚ⸣.*šu-ut* SAG.MEŠ-*ia*

333–342) In order that he (Urzana) should not escape,

---

322 KUR-*ú dan-nu ša mu-lu-šu ki-i mé-le-e sim-mil-ti mu-la-a la i-šu-ú* "a mighty mountain that did not have any ascent, (*not even one*) like *that* of a ladder (lit.: "whose ascent has no ascent like the rungs of a ladder")": The tentative translation assumes that climbing up the mountain was even more difficult than it would have been for the Assyrian army, with all its military equipment (weapons, armor, horses, chariots, etc.), to climb up an extraordinarily tall, steep ladder one person after another. Cf. CAD M/2 p. 14. Making use of a figurative meaning of *simmiltu* "referring to a vista of receding ranges of mountains and to mountain ledges" (CAD S p. 274), F.M. Fales (COS 4 p. 211) translates "a mighty mountain, whose climb, like steps in sequential ridges, had no (real) ascent" taking the passage not to indicate that the mountain "was impossible in its ascent, but that to the contrary ... was wearying in its unending sequence of scarcely sloping stepped passages."

325 *ša ni-ba ed-ku-ma* "which ... and": F. Thureau-Dangin (TCL 3 p. 51) translates "qui excluent toute description"; W. Mayer (Assyrien und Urarṭu I p. 129) has *ša ni-ba et-qú-ma*, "mit nicht zählbaren Stufen (hindurch)." B.R. Foster (Before the Muses^{3} p. 807) has "which defy description(?)," reading *ed-lu*$^{!?}$*-ma* for *ed-ku-ma* (see CAD N/2 p. 205) but noting that the passage is obscure (Before the Muses^{3} p. 813). We might expect *ša nība lā īšûma*. "countless and." M. Worthington tentatively suggests that the writing might stand for *ša nība lā ēdâkuma*, "of which I do not know the number" (private communication).

327 GURUN*: The text has DUG.

331 *aṣ-bat-ma* or *az-ziz-ma*; see on-page note to line 25.

LÚ.EN.NAM.MEŠ *a-di ki-iṣ-ri-šu-nu ur-tu*
ú-ma-er-ma ḫi-it-mu-ṭi-iš áš-pur
334) [... *a*]*-ka-ma ger-ri-ia e-*⸢*mur-ma*⸣ [x x (x)] ⸢PI$^{?}$⸣
UB x (x) [...]
335) [...] x x *na-bu-šú-*⸢*ma*$^{?}$⸣ UN.⸢MEŠ⸣ [x x]
⸢*ú*⸣*-dan-ni-nu* [...]
336) [... KUR.*ur*]*-ar-ṭi-ma a-na* URU [x (x)] x
LUGAL*-ti-šu šu-bat* ^{d}*ḫal-*⸢*di*⸣*-*[*a* DINGIR$^{?}$*-šu*$^{?}$ (x)]
337) [... KUR].⸢*ur*⸣*-ar-ṭi a-na paṭ gim-ri-šu ša el*
šá-a-šú i-na šá-ma-mi u qaq-qa-ri la i-du-⸢*ú*⸣ (x)
[x (x)]
338) [x x x (x x)] ⸢*šum*$^{?}$*-šu*$^{?}$⸣ [...] x ⸢*ša*⸣ *ul-la-nu-uš-šu*
GIŠ.GIDRU *ù a-gu-ú la in-na-áš-šu-ú si-mat*
re-⸢*é-ú*$^{?}$⸣*-*[*ti*$^{?}$]
339) [(x)] x x ⸢*mal*⸣*-ku* SIPA UN.MEŠ KUR.⸢*ur-ar*$^{?}$⸣*-*[*ṭi*
...] x *ub-ba-lu-šu-ma a-a-um-ma i-na lìb-bi*
DUMU.MEŠ*-šú ṣa-bi-tu* GIŠ.GU.ZA*-šú*
340) [*a*]*-*⸢*di*⸣ KÙ.GI *ù* KÙ.BABBAR *mim-ma aq-ru*
ni-ṣir-te É.GAL*-lì-šú i-na* URU.*mu-ṣa-ṣir ma-ḫar*
^{d}*ḫal-di-a ú-še-ri-bu-ma i-qi-šu qi-šá-as-su*
341) [GU$_{4}$].⸢MEŠ⸣ *kab-ru-ti* UDU.MEŠ *ma-*⸢*ru*⸣*-ti a-na*
la ma-ni ma-ḫar-šú i-⸢*naq-qu-ú*⸣ *a-na gi-mir*
URU*-šu i-šak-ka-nu ta-*⸢*kul*⸣*-tu*
342) [IGI] ⸢^{d}⸣*ḫal-di-a* DINGIR*-šu* AGA *be-lu-ti*
ip-pi-ru-šu-ma ú-šá-áš-šu-šu GIŠ.GIDRU
⸢LUGAL⸣*-ti* KUR.⸢*ur-ar*⸣*-ṭi ù* UN.MEŠ*-šú i-x-*⸢*ú*⸣
NUMUN*-šu*

I gave orders to my eunuchs, the provincial governors, together with their (military) contingents, and I quickly dispatched (them). [...] he (Urzana) saw [the clo]ud of dust (kicked up) by my expeditionary force and [... (335) ...] ... *him, and* the people strengthened [... the land Ur]arṭu and to the city (that was) his royal [*ab*]*ode* (and) the abode of the god Ḫald[i, *his god, ... throughout* the land U]rarṭu, to its full extent, greater than whom none is known in heaven or (in) netherworld [...] ... [...] without whose permission neither scepter nor crown can be taken up as emblems of *the position of sheph*[*erd*] ... the prince, the shepherd of the people of the land Ura[rṭu ...] they bring him and make (lit.: "made") the one among his sons who was to succeed to his throne (340) enter into the city Muṣaṣir (and) into the presence of the god Ḫaldi, [together] with gold, silver, (and) everything valuable, the treasure of his palace; they present him (with them) as gift(s). They offer before him countless fattened [oxen] (and) fattened sheep (and) give a (ceremonial) banquet for his entire city. [In front of] his god Ḫaldi, they place upon him the crown of lordship and have him take up the royal scepter of the land Urarṭu. Then, his people ... his offspring.

343) ⸢UGU⸣ URU *šu-a-ti ri-gim um-ma-ni-ia gal-tu*
ki-ma ^{d}IŠKUR *ú-šá-áš-gi-im-ma a-ši-bu-*⸢*ut*
lìb$^{?}$⸣*-*[*bi-šá*$^{?}$ ...] x BE ḪA [...] x MI
344) ⸢UN⸣.MEŠ*-šú* LÚ.*ši-i-bu* MUNUS.*ši-ib-tu* UGU
ÙR.MEŠ É.MEŠ*-šu-nu e-lu-ma ṣar-piš i-ba-ku-*[*ú*
...] x
345) *áš-šu e-ṭer na-piš-ti-šu-nu* UGU *er-bi rit-ti-šu-nu*
ip-taš-ši-lu-ma qa-ti-šu-nu x [x x (x)] Ú x x x
(x) [(x)]
346) *áš-šu ša* ^{m}*ur-za-na* LUGAL *ma-lik-šu-nu a-na*
zi-kir ^{d}*a-šur la iš-ḫu-tu-ma ni-ir be-lu-ti-*⸢*ia*⸣
is-lu-ma i-mi-šu ar-du-ti
347) *ša* UN.MEŠ URU *šu-a-ti šá-lal-šu-nu ak-pid-ma*

343–349) I let the terrifying roar of my troops resound [ov]er that city like (the thunder of) the god Adad, and those who dwelt *in*[*side it* ...] ... [...]. His/Its people, (even) old men (and) old women, climbed up onto the roofs of their houses, crying bitterly [...]. (345) In order to save their live(s), they crawled around on all fours and [...] their hands [(...)]. Because King Urzana, their ruler, had not respected the command of the god Aššur, but had (instead) thrown off the yoke of my lordship and disregarded his position as a vassal to me, I planned to carry off the people of that city as booty and I ordered the removal of the god Ḫaldi, (the god) on whom the land Urarṭu relied (for protection).

334 E. Weidner (AfO 12 [1937–39] p. 146) tentatively restored at the beginning of the line [... *a-la*]*-ka-ma* ("[... *the app*]*roach*"). For the restoration [... *a*]*-ka-ma* ("[... the clo]ud of dust"), see line 248 and CAD A/1 p. 259.
335 Instead of *-šú-*⸢*ma*$^{?}$⸣ possibly *-šú-*⸢*pa*⸣ or *-*⸢*di*⸣.
336 Possibly [...] *ar-de-ma* ..., "[...] I led and ..." instead of [... KUR.*ur*]*-ar-ṭi-ma*, "[... the land Ur]arṭu." E. Weidner (AfO 12 [1937–39] p. 146) suggested URU.[*mu-ṣa-ṣir šu*]*-bat* LUGAL*-ti-šu*, "city [of Muṣaṣir], his royal [ab]ode," and he has been followed in this reading by several other scholars (e.g., Mayer, Assyrien und Urarṭu I p. 130), but there is not sufficient room for this restoration although the sign before LUGAL might be *bat*.
337 CAD Q p. 123 translates "[...] (Urartu) apart from which no [...] is known in heaven or on earth"; following Weidner, AfO 12 (1937–39) p. 147, possibly translate instead (somewhat freely) "(in comparison to) which no larger (land) is known."
339 E. Weidner thinks the line may have indicated that the prince of Urarṭu had died (AfO 12 [1937–39] p. 147), while M. Salvini thinks that the passage may have stated something along the lines of "if the prince of Urarṭu comes to Muṣaṣir" (Salvini in Klengel, Gesellschaft und Kultur pp. 226–227). F.M. Fales (COS 4 p. 212) translates "[after his death?], they would bring to him (=Ḫaldi)."
342 Following Weidner, AfO 12 (1937–39) p. 146, the end of the line is normally read UN.MEŠ*-šú i-*⸢*nam*⸣*-*[*bu*]*-*⸢*ú*⸣ MU*-šu*, "his people would ac[laim (lit.: "call")] his name,"; however, both the published copy (Schroeder, KAH 2 no. 141) and collation indicate that there is not sufficient room for the restoration and that the traces after *i-* are not good for the beginning of a Neo-Assyrian NAM sign. In addition, independent collations by G. Frame and J. Marzahn indicate that the penultimate sign is NUMUN, rather than MU.
346–410 See Mayer, UF 11 (1979) pp. 571–595 for a detailed study of the booty taken by Sargon II. The precise meaning of some of the Akkadian terms remains elusive. The words for containers are discussed in Gaspa, Contenitori neoassiri.

ša ^{d}*ḫal-di-a tu-kul-ti* KUR.*ur-ar-ṭi aq-ta-bi šu-ṣa-a-šu*	Triumphantly, I had (him) sit in front of his (city) gate and I carried off as booty his (Urzana's) wife, his sons, his daughters, his people, (and) (other) offspring of his father's house. I counted (them) (along) with 6,110 people, 12 *kūdanu*-mules, 380 donkeys, 525 oxen, (and) 1,235 sheep, and brought (them) inside the wall(s) of my (military) camp.
348) *meḫ-ret* KÁ.GAL-*šu šal-ṭiš ú-še-ši-ib-ma* DAM-*su* DUMU.MEŠ-*šú* DUMU.MUNUS.MEŠ-*šú* UN.MEŠ-*šú* NUMUN ⸢É⸣ AD-*šu áš-lu-la*	
349) ⸢*it*⸣*-ti* 6 LIM 1 ME 10 UN.MEŠ 12 ANŠE.*ku-dini* 3 ME 80 ANŠE.MEŠ 5 ME 25 GU$_4$.MEŠ 1 LIM 2 ME 35 UDU.NÍTA.MEŠ ⸢*am*⸣*-nu-ma a-na* BÀD KARAŠ-*ia ú-še-rib*	
350) [*a-na* URU].⸢*mu*⸣*-ṣa-ṣir šu-bat* ^{d}*ḫal-di-a šal-ṭiš e-ru-ub-ma i-na* É.GAL *mu-šab* ^{m}*ur-za-na e-tel-liš ú-ši-ib*	350–351) I entered triumphantly [into the city M]uṣaṣir, the abode of the god Ḫaldi, and in a lordly manner I occupied the palace, the residence of Urzana. [(With regard to) the] heaped up [*storerooms*] which were overflowing with accumulated riches, I broke open the seals of their treasure caches.
351) [...] ⸢*nak*⸣*-mu-ti ša i-šit-tu kit-mur-tu du-uš-šu-ú ki-in-gi ni-ṣir-te-šu-nu ú-pat-ti-ma*	
352) [34 GUN 18] ⸢MA⸣.NA KÙ.GI 1 ME 67 GUN 2 1/2 MA.NA KÙ.BABBAR URUDU.ḪI.A BABBAR-*ú* AN.NA NA$_4$.GUG NA$_4$.ZA.GÌN NA$_4$.BABBAR.DILI *ni-siq-ti* NA$_4$.MEŠ *a-na mu-ʾu-de-e*	352) [34 talents and 18 m]inas of gold, 167 talents and 2 1/2 minas of silver, shining copper, tin, carnelian, lapis lazuli, *banded agate*, (and other) precious stones in large numbers;
353) [*x* GIŠ.ŠIBIR.MEŠ] ZÚ AM.SI GIŠ.ESI GIŠ.TÚG *a-di* GIŠ.NA$_5$.MEŠ *ša iḫ-zu-ši-na šu-pu-šu* KÙ.GI *ù* KÙ.BABBAR	353) [x (items): staves] of elephant ivory, ebony, (and) boxwood, together with wooden caskets, whose mountings are made of gold and silver;
354) [*x* GIŠ].⸢BANŠUR?⸣.MEŠ ZÚ AM.SI GIŠ.ESI GIŠ.TÚG GAL.MEŠ *si-mat* LUGAL-*ti ša iḫ-zu-ši-na šu-pu-šu* KÙ.GI *ù* KÙ.BABBAR	354) [x (items)]: large [*tab*]*les* of elephant ivory, ebony, (and) boxwood, (*tables*) fit for a king, whose mountings are made of gold and silver;
355) 8 GIŠ.⸢*maḫ-ri-ṣi*⸣ *dan-nu-ti ù* GIŠ.*sa-al-li* Ú *ur-qi* ZÚ AM.SI GIŠ.ESI GIŠ.TÚG *ša iḫ-zu-*<<*ši*>>*-šu-nu* KÙ.GI *ù* KÙ.BABBAR	355) 8 (items): sturdy *maḫraṣu*-objects and vegetable baskets of elephant ivory, ebony, (and) boxwood, whose mountings are of gold and silver;
356) 6 GIŠ.*kan-ni* GIŠ.⸢*kan-kan*⸣*-ni* GIŠ.*táḫ*-KAL GIŠ.GU.ZA.MEŠ GIŠ.GAN BI.LUL ZÚ AM.⸢SI GIŠ⸣.ESI GIŠ.TÚG *ša iḫ-zu-*⸢*šu*⸣*-nu* <<ŠU>> KÙ.GI *ù* KÙ.BABBAR	356) 6 (items): a stand, a potstand, *a folding screen*, chairs, (and) *a cupbearer's* (*pot*)*stand* (made) of elephant ivory, ebony, (and) boxwood, whose mountings are of gold and silver;
357) 6 GÍR.MEŠ KÙ.⸢GI *te?-rin*⸣*-nat* KÙ.GI GÍR.TUR KÙ.GI *ša* ⸢NIM⸣ [KÙ].⸢GI⸣ NA$_4$.*pur-si-it* NA$_4$.GIŠ.NU$_{11}$.GAL *tam-lit* NA$_4$.MEŠ KÙ.GI	357) 6 (items): gold knives *with* gold (*handles in the shape of*) cones, a gold dagger, a [gol]d fly wh[isk], (and) an alabaster offering-bowl inlaid with stones (and) gold;
358) 11 *kap-pi* KÙ.BABBAR ^{m}*ur-sa-*⸢*a a-di*⸣	358) 11 (items): a silver *kappu*-bowl belonging to Ursâ

348 It is not completely clear whom/what Sargon caused to sit at the city gate. K. Kravitz (JNES 62 [2003] p. 87; see also Fales, COS 4 p. 212) believes that it was the statue of the god Ḫaldi, while P. Talon (Annales assyriennes 1 p. 97) takes it to be "son épouse, ses fils et ses filles." B.R. Foster (Before the Muses^{3} p. 808 n. 2) thinks that it was Urzana "because Sargon makes special mention of his efforts to prevent Urzana's flight (line 333)," while noting that "there is no mention of Urzana's fate" in this text. Sargon's Annals from Room II (text no. 1 lines 152–155; see also text no. 7 lines 72–76) state that Urzana had fled like a bird and disappeared when he heard of the approach of Sargon's army and does not mention him among the people (including his wife, sons, and daughters) whom Sargon took away from Muṣaṣir. It would seem more likely that it was the statue of the god Ḫaldi even though that means that the "his," on KÁ.GAL, "(city) gate," and DAM, "wife," do not have the same referent.

352 For the restoration at the beginning of the line, see text no. 1 line 155.

353 For the restoration GIŠ.ŠIBIR.MEŠ (following Thureau-Dangin, TCL 3 p. 52) rather than GIŠ.GU.ZA.MEŠ (e.g., Talon, Annales assyriennes 1 p. 98 and Mayer, Assyrien und Urarṭu I pp. 79 and 132) at the beginning of the line, see text no. 82 iv 16′.

355 For the restoration at the beginning of the line, see text no. 82 iv 21′. W. Mayer (UF 11 [1979] p. 582) suggests that a *maḫraṣu* (see also line 390) may be a wooden serving plate (or similar), while S. Gaspa (Contenitori neoassiri pp. 312–314 and 488) takes it to refer to a support/holder for a vessel.

356 For *kannu* and *kankannu* stands/supports/holders, see Gaspa, Contenitori neoassiri pp. 305–311 and 487–488. For the tentative meaning "folding screen" for GIŠ.*táḫ*-KAL, see Mayer, UF 11 (1979) pp. 582–583 (sub *taḫlīptu*). Or GIŠ.GAN.BI.LUL (see CAD K p. 155). Or *šu-*<*pu-šu*>, "... whose mountings are made of gold and silver"; see text no. 82 iv 25′.

357 With regard to *terinnu* (pl. *terinnātu*) and its meaning here, see Mayer, UF 11 (1979) p. 583.

358 W. Mayer argues that the items translated as "hauberks" (or "breastplates") (*qur-pi-si*) and "arrows" (*šil-ta-ḫi*) were actually types of vessels and spits respectively (UF 11 [1979] pp. 583–584), while S. Gaspa (Contenitori neoassiri p. 222) takes them to refer here to vessels with decoration in the form of armor — "(vasi) ... (dalla decorazione in foggia) di corazza" — and skewers ("*spiedi*") repectively. Their appearance together with spears, bows, and shields in lines 378 and 392 would suggest that they were also some type of weapon or military equipment.

nak-ta-mi-šu ⌜*kap*⌝-[*pi ša*] ⌜KUR⌝.*ta-ba-li* GEŠTU.II.MEŠ KÙ.GI *qur-pi-si* KÙ.BABBAR *šil-ta-ḫi* KÙ.BABBAR *né-eḫ-su* KÙ.GI

(Rusâ), together with its lid, *ka*[*ppu*-bowls from the] land Tabal with lug-handles of gold, *hauberks* with silver (scales), (and) silver *arrows with* gold inlays;

359) 34 *kap-pi* KÙ.BABBAR ŠU.SI.MEŠ *dan-na-*⌜*a-te*⌝ *qa*⌝-*al-la-a-*[*te qa-ta*]-*na-a-te luṭ-ṭi ù su-sa-ni* KÙ.BABBAR

359) 34 (items): silver *kappu*-bowls with deep, shallow, (and) [nar]row fluting (lit.: "fingers"), *luṭṭu*-bowls, and *susānu*-vessels of silver;

360) 54 *kap-pi* KÙ.BABBAR *ṣu-pu-ti* <*a-di*> *nak-te-*⌜*mi*⌝-[*šu-nu*] ⌜GÚ⌝.ZI.MEŠ *ṣip-ra-a-te* U$_4$.SAKAR.MEŠ ḪAR.MEŠ KÙ.BABBAR

360) 54 (items): silver-*plated kappu*-bowls, <together with> [their] lids, cups (*decorated with*) *cone-shaped* ornaments (*and*) crescent-shaped ornaments, (and) silver torcs;

361) 5 *a-za-na-at* KÙ.BABBAR *qa-bu-a-te mu-kar-ri-*⌜*si*⌝ [*nab*]-*li* NÍG.NA.MEŠ KUR.*ta-ba-li ù mu-qa-te-rat* KÙ.BABBAR

361) 5 (items): *azannu-stands* of silver, *qabūtu*-cups, *mukarrisu*-dishes, (*and*) [*nab*]*lu*-vessels, (*altogether forming*) censers from the land Tabal, and silver incense burners;

362) 13 *ki-ú-ri* URUDU *tap-ḫa-a-ni* URUDU *nàr-ma-ka-a-*⌜*te* URUDU⌝ *a-sa-al-la-te* URUDU ÚTUL.MEŠ URUDU *qu-li-a-te* URUDU

362) 13 (items): copper basins, copper cauldrons, copper washbasins, copper *asallu*-bowls, copper *diqāru*-pots, (and) copper *qulliu*-bowls;

363) ⌜24⌝ *kan-ni* URUDU *ki-ú-ri* URUDU *ḫu-ru-pa-a-te* URUDU ⌜*kur-ku*⌝-*ri* URUDU *qu-ul-li* URUDU *na-as-ri* URUDU É *bu-ṣi-ni* URUDU

363) 24 (items): copper stands (*for*) copper basins, copper *ḫuruppu*-bowls, copper *kurkurru*-vessels, copper *qullu-clasps*, copper *nasru-hooks*, (and) copper lamps;

364) [1?] ⌜ME⌝ 20 *ú-de-e* URUDU *dan-nu-*<*ti*> *qa-lu-ti e-piš-ti* KUR-*šú-nu ša ni-bit* MU-*šú-nu a-na šá-ṭa-a-ri la ṭa-a-bu*

364) [1]20 (items): copper objects, (both) heavy (ones and) light (ones), the work of their own land, (objects), the pronunciation of whose name(s) are not easy to write down;

365) [*x*] *ka-nu-nu* AN.BAR *né-se-pí* AN.BAR *na-as-ri* AN.BAR *a-ru-ut-ḫi* AN.BAR É *bu-ṣi-ni* AN.BAR

365) [x] (items): an iron brazier, iron *shovel*(*s*), iron *nasru-hooks*, iron *aruthu*-objects, (and) iron lamps;

366) [1?] ME 30 *lu-bul-ti bir-me* GADA *ta-kil-tu ù* SÍG.MEŠ *lu-bul-ti ta-bar-ri ša* KUR.*ur-ar-ṭi ù* KUR.*ḫab-ḫi*

366a) [1]30 (items): garments with multi-colored trim, linen (garments), (garments of) blue-purple wool and (*plain*) wool, (and) garments of red wool from the lands Urarṭu and Ḫabḫu —

367) ⌜*a*⌝-*di bu-še*$_{20}$-*e* É.GAL-*lì-šú áš-lu-lam-ma ak-mu-ra* NÍG.GA-*šú* LÚ.*šu-ut* SAG.MEŠ-*ia* LÚ.*re-di-ia* <*a*>-*na* É ^{d}*ḫal-di-a áš-pur-ma*

367) I carried off (all these things) as booty, together with the (remaining) property of his palace, and I heaped up his possessions. I sent my eunuchs (and) my officials to the temple of the god Ḫaldi.

368) ⌜^{d}⌝*ḫal-di-a* DINGIR-*šu ù* ^{d}*ba-ag-bar-tu* ^{d}15-*šu a-di* NÍG.GA É.KUR-*šú ma-ʾa-at-ti mal ba-šu-ú*

368) His god Ḫaldi and his goddess Bagbartu, together with the numerous possessions of his temple, as many there were (of them);

369) [x]+⌜4⌝ GUN 3 MA.NA KÙ.GI 1 ME 62 GUN 20 MA.NA 6-*su* LAL KÙ.BABBAR 3 LIM 6 ME GUN ZABAR *ši-bir-tu*

369) [x]+4 talents and 3 minas of gold; 162 talents and 20 minas of silver, less one sixth (of a mina of silver); 3,600 talents of bronze in pieces;

---

359 The translation follows Foster, Before the Muses[3] p. 809. The meaning of "fingers" here is unclear and W. Mayer (UF 11 [1979] p. 574) assumes it means a type of decoration; see also Fuchs, SAAS 8 p. 61 n. 40.

360 Or "*massive kappu*-bowls of silver"; see AHw p. 1112 versus CAD Ṣ pp. 248–249. According to W. Mayer (UF 11 [1979] pp. 574 and 584), *ṣipru* is actually a cone-shaped top for an incense stand and the "crescent-shaped ornaments" are pectorals in the form of a cresent moon. B.R. Foster (Before the Muses[3] p. 809) assumes that the last three items are describing ornamentation on the just-mentioned objects: "(decorated with?) bosses, crescents, and rings of silver."

361 W. Mayer (UF 11 [1979] pp. 575 and 584 and Assyrien und Urarṭu 1 p. 81; see also Fuchs, SAAS 8 p. 61 and n. 44) suggests that the first four items were parts of censers and S. Gaspa (Contenitori neoassiri p. 322) translates them as "Five *pedestals in the shape of* silver *quivers*, cups, dishes, [*nab*]*lu*-vessels (for) incense burners from the country of Tabal" ("Cinque *piedistalli in foggia di faretra* d'argento, coppe, piatti, [vasi *nab*]*lu* (per) bruciaprofumi del paese di Tabal").

364 and 366 The restoration of 1 follows F. Thureau-Dangin and is based on the available spacing.

365 According to W. Mayer (UF 11 [1979] pp. 575 and 585), an *aruthu* may be a type of shovel, while S. Gaspa (Contenitori neoassiri p. 284) translates the term as pliers ("pinze"). B.R. Foster (Before the Muses[3] p. 809) translates the line as "[items]: an iron stove with fire rake, poker, shovel, and lamps of iron." Since there is a MA reference to a set (*iltenniūtu*) of this object (see CAD U p. 272 sub *uruthu*), a translation "tongs," "pliers," or something similar might be appropriate (suggestion courtesy J.N. Postgate).

367 A. Fuchs (SAAS 8 p. 62 n. 52) argues that *rēdû* refers here not to soldiers, but rather to officials (scribes) sent to compile a list of the booty taken.

368 Bagbartu or Bagmastu. See König, RLA 1/5 (1931) p. 391 and Schmitt, AfO 27 (1980) p. 191.

369 6-*su*: See Borger, MZ p. 252 for the meaning one-sixth.

370) [6] ⸢*a*⸣*-ri-at* KÙ.GI *ša i-na at-ma-ni-šú im-nu ù šu-me-lu et-ʾu-la-a-ma iḫ-tal-la-a šá-ru-riš*
371) [*ù*] ⸢SAG⸣.DU *lab-bi na-ad-ru-te ṣur-ru-ši-in a-ṣu-nim-ma* 5 GUN 12 MA.⸢NA⸣ *sa-a-mu ru-uš-šu-ú ti-iṣ-bu-tu* KI.LÁ
372) ⸢1⸣ x (x) x x ⸢*qar*⸣*-ni še-*⸢*la*?*-la*?*-te*⸣ *áš-kut-ti* KÁ.MEŠ*-šú šá* 2 GUN KÙ.GI *sa-ge-*⸢*ru i-na šu-qu*⸣*-ul-ti šap-ku*
373) 1 SAG.KUL KÙ.GI *rit-te a-me-lu-ti ri-kis mu-ter-te ša a-bu-bu mu-up-par-šu* ⸢*šur-bu-ṣu*⸣ *ṣe-ru-uš-*⸢*šu*⸣
374) 1 *sik-kàt* KÙ.GI *ka-la-at sik-ku-ri mu-dan*-ni-na-at ri-kis* É.KUR *na-ṣi-rat bu-še-e nak-mi ù ma-ak-ku-*⸢*ri*⸣
375) 2 *nam-za-qi* KÙ.GI ^{d}LAMMA*-at a-ge-e na-šat* GIŠ*.mit-ṭi ù kip-pa-te ša ši-*ḪAR GÌR.II*-ši-na šuk-bu-sa lab-bi na-ad-ru-te*
376) *er-bet-ta-šu-nu mar-kas ba-a-bi ú-su-um pa-pa-ḫi ša* 2 GUN 12 MA.NA KÙ.⸢GI *šu*⸣*-qul-tu ṣab-tu-ma mu-kil-lu* GIŠ.IG
377) 1 GÍR KÙ.GI GAL*-ú nam-ṣa-ar i-di-šu ša* 26 MA.NA 3*-su* KÙ.GI ⸢*šit*⸣*-ku-nu* KI.LÁ
378) 96 *šu-kur-ri* KÙ.BABBAR *qur-pi-si* KÙ.BABBAR GIŠ.PAN KÙ.BABBAR *šil-ta-ḫi* KÙ.BABBAR *ša* ⸢*né-eḫ*⸣*-sí ù iḫ-zi* KÙ.GI
379) 12 *a-ri-at* KÙ.BABBAR *dan-na-a-te ša* SAG.DU *a-bu-bi* UR.MAḪ *ù* ⸢AM *bu*⸣*-un-nu-ú ni-ip-ḫi-ši-in*
380) 67 *ki-ú-ri* KÙ.BABBAR *kan-ni* KÙ.BABBAR *ka-nu-ni* KÙ.BABBAR *sa-al-li ur-qi* KÙ.BABBAR *ša iḫ-zi ù né-eḫ-si* KÙ.GI
381) 62 *mu-ṣa-ri-ir-te* KÙ.BABBAR *lu-rin-te* KÙ.BABBAR *ú-de-e* KÙ.BABBAR *la mit-ḫa-ru-ti ša né-eḫ-si ù iḫ-zi* KÙ.GI
382) 33 GIŠ.GIGIR.MEŠ KÙ.BABBAR GIŠ.PAN KÙ.BABBAR *iš-pat* KÙ.BABBAR *mit-ṭi* KÙ.BABBAR GIŠ.GIDRU KÙ.BABBAR *ma-an-zi-a-še* KÙ.BABBAR *a-ri-at* KÙ.BABBAR *ṣip-rat* KÙ.BABBAR *pur-ṭi-i* <KÙ.BABBAR> *šu-ri-ni* KÙ.BABBAR

370–371) [6] gold shields which were hung in his sanctuary on the right and left, which shone like the sunlight, [and] from whose centers project the heads of fierce lions, and whose weight was established to be 5 talents and 12 minas of shining red (gold);
372) 1 ... *with* horns ... the locking bar for his doors, which were cast from refined gold 2 talents in weight;
373) 1 gold door bolt (in the shape of) a human hand, a fastening for a double door, upon which a winged Deluge (monster) is (represented) in a recumbent position;
374) 1 gold peg, which held back the door bolt, securing the fastening of the temple, (and) protecting the stored property and possessions;
375) 2 gold keys (in the shape of) divine protectresses (who wear) crowns (and) hold the rod and ring, (and) the *soles* of whose feet tread upon fierce lions
376) — these (last) four (things) comprised the door fastening, one befitting the shrine, whose weight was established to be 2 talents and 12 minas of gold, and which held the door (in place);
377) 1 large gold sword, the sword (the god Ḫaldi wore) at his side, which weighs 26 and 1/3 minas of gold;
378) 96 (items): silver spears, *hauberks* with silver (scales), silver bow(s), (and) silver arrows, with inlays and mountings of gold;
379) 12 heavy silver shields whose *bosses* are decorated with the head(s) of Deluge monster(s), lion(s), and wild bull(s);
380) 67 (items): silver basins, silver stands, silver braziers, (and) silver vegetable baskets, with mountings and inlays of gold;
381) 62 (items): silver *muṣarrirtu*-dishes, silver pomegranates, (and) silver objects of varying sizes, with inlays and mountings of gold;
382) 33 (items): silver chariots, silver bow(s), silver quivers, silver maces, silver scepter(s), silver *manziaše*-objects, silver shields, silver *ṣipru-ornaments*, <silver> *purṭû*-objects, (and) silver standards;

370 The restoration "[6]" is based upon text no. 82 iv 56′.
371 Cf. CAD A/2 p. 269 sub *arītu* 1.a.2′ *kalbē nadrūte*, "raging dogs."
372–376 The exact meaning of the various Akkadian terms used for parts of locking devices for doors are much debated. With regard to devices for locking doors, see most recently P. Ferioli and E. Fiandra in Studies Palmieri pp. 269–287; Fuchs, SAAS 8 pp. 97–107; Leichty, JCS 39 (1987) pp. 190–196; Potts, Mesopotamia 25 (1990) pp. 185–192; and Scurlock, Orientalia NS 57 (1988) pp. 421–433.
374 *-dan*-*: The text has -UN-.
375 GIŠ*.mit-ṭi ù kip-pa-te* "rod and ring": A more literal translation would be "mace and circle." For these symbols of divine order, authority, and power, see Wiggerman, RLA 11/5–6 (2007) pp. 414–421, as well as Slanski in Crawford, Regime Change pp. 37–59 and Abram, Studia Antiqua 10/1 (2011) pp. 15–36. *ši-*ḪAR: Or *ši-kín*. The reading *ši-*ḪAR and the tentative translation "*soles*" follows CAD Š/1 p. 109 sub *šaḫūru* B; see also Kraus, Orientalia NS 16 (1947) p. 199 n. 2.
379 F.M. Fales (COS 4 p. 213 and n. 150) translates "outer bands" instead of "bosses" and refers to how actual Urarṭian shields were decorated. See Seidl, ZA 88 (1998) pp. 100–113 with regard to the Deluge monster (*abūbu*).
380 *ka-nu-ni*, "braziers": B.R. Foster (Before the Muses^{3} pp. 810 and 813) assumes that this is an error for *kankanne*, "pot racks."
381 Or, following S. Gaspa (Contenitori neoassiri p. 198), "silver libation vessels, (decorative elements in the shape of) silver pomegranates" ("vasi per libagione d'argento, (elementi decorativi in foggia di) melagrane d'argento").

383) 3 ME 93 *kap-pi* KÙ.BABBAR *dan-nu-ti qa-al-lu-ti né-peš-ti* KUR *aš-šur*.KI KUR.*ur*-ar-ṭi ù* KUR.*ḫab-ḫi*

383) 393 (items): silver *kappu*-bowls — (both) heavy (ones and) light (ones) — of Assyrian, Urarṭian, and Ḫabḫian workmanship;

384) 2 *qar-na-at* AM GAL.MEŠ *ša iḫ-zu-ši-na ù nik-ka-su-ši-na* <KÙ.BABBAR$^?$> *ù kam-mat* KÙ.GI *šu-tas-ḫu-ra iḫ-zi-ši-in*

384) 2 large wild bull horns whose mountings and platings are <*of silver*> and whose mountings are surrounded by gold rivets;

385) 1 *tim-bu-ut-te* KÙ.GI *ša a-na šul-lu-um par-ṣi ša* ^{d}*ba-ag-bar-ti al-ti* ^{d}*ḫal-di-a šu-tam-lu-ú ni-siq-ti* ⸢NA$_4$⸣.MEŠ

385) 1 gold harp that is covered with precious stones for performing the rites of the goddess Bagbartu, the wife of the god Ḫaldi;

386) 9 *lu-*⸢*ba**⸣*-re-e* <*ta*>*-al-bul-ti* DINGIR-*ti-šu ša ni-ip-ḫi* KÙ.GI *ia-ar* KÙ.GI *ši-pit-su-nu i-na mu-ur-de-e ṣu-ub-bu-tu*

386) 9 garments belonging to his (Ḫaldi's) divine wardrobe, whose seams are edged with gold disks (and) gold rosettes in *open work*;

387) 7-*šú* KUŠ.DA.E*.SIR *ša* MUL.MEŠ KÙ.GI *mul-lu-ma it-ti iš-tuḫ-ḫi* KÙ.BABBAR *ša kip-lu ù iḫ-zi* KÙ.GI

387) 7 *pairs of* leather shoes that are covered with gold stars, (along) with a silver whip (handle) with *kiplu*-decoration and a mounting of gold;

388) 1 GIŠ.NÁ ZÚ *ma-a-a-al-ti* KÙ.BABBAR *tap-šu-uḫ-ti* DINGIR-*ti-ma tam-lit* NA$_4$.MEŠ KÙ.GI

388) 1 ivory bed (*with*) a silver *bed-frame*, the resting place of the deity, inlaid with stones (and) gold;

389) 1 ME 39 GIŠ.ŠIBIR.MEŠ ZÚ GIŠ.BANŠUR.MEŠ ZÚ *sa-al-li ur-qi* ZÚ GÍR ZÚ GÍR.TUR.MEŠ ZÚ GIŠ.ESI *ša iḫ-zu-ši-na* KÙ.GI

389) 139 (items): ivory staves, ivory tables, ivory vegetable baskets, ivory knive(s), (and) daggers of ivory (and) ebony, whose mountings are of gold;

390) 10 GIŠ.BANŠUR.MEŠ GIŠ.TÚG *maḫ-ri-ṣi* GIŠ.TÚG *né-me-di* GIŠ.ESI GIŠ.TÚG *ša iḫ-zu-šu-nu* KÙ.GI *ù* KÙ.BABBAR

390) 10 (items): tables of boxwood, *maḫraṣu*-objects of boxwood, (and) chairs of ebony (and) boxwood, whose mountings are of gold (and) silver;

391) 2 GI.DU$_8$ 14 NA$_4$.MEŠ *sa-ma-ḫu-te ti-iq-ni* DINGIR-*ti šu-ka-ni* ^{d}*ḫal-di-a ù* ^{d}*ba-ag-bar-ti* DAM-*šú*

391) 2 *portable altars* (*with*) 14 *assorted* stones, adornments (fit) for gods, jewelry of the god Ḫaldi and the goddess Bagbartu, his wife;

392) 25 LIM 2 ME 12 *a-ri-at* URUDU *dan-na-a-te qa-al-la-a-te ṣip-rat* URUDU *qur-pi-si* URUDU *ù gul-gul-lat* URUDU

392) 25,212 (items): heavy (and) light copper shields, *cone-shaped helmets* of copper, *hauberks* with copper (scales), and skull-shaped *helmets* of copper;

393) 1 LIM 5 ME 14 *šu-kur-ri* URUDU *dan-nu-ti qa-al-lu-te še-la-at šu-kur-ri* URUDU *dan-na-a-te pur-ṭi-i* URUDU *ku-ta-ḫi* URUDU *a-di* KI.TA.MEŠ-*šú-nu* URUDU

393) 1,514 (items): heavy (and) light copper spears, heavy copper spear-heads, copper *purṭû*-objects, copper *kutāḫu-lances*, together with their copper bases;

394) 3 ME 5 LIM 4 ME 12 GÍR.MEŠ URUDU *dan-nu-ti qa-al-lu-te* GIŠ.PAN.MEŠ URUDU *a-za-na-te* URUDU *ù šil-ta-ḫi* URUDU

394) 305,412 (items): heavy (and) light copper daggers, copper bows, copper *quivers*, and copper arrows;

395) 6 ME 7 *ki-ú-ri* URUDU *dan-nu-ti qa-al-lu-te nàr-ma-ka-a-ti* URUDU *a-sa-la-a-te* URUDU ÚTUL.MEŠ URUDU *qu-li-a-te* URUDU

395) 607 (items): heavy (and) light copper basins, copper washbasins, copper *asallu*-bowls, copper *diqāru*-pots, (and) copper *qulliu*-bowls;

396) 3 *ki-ú-ri* URUDU *dan-nu-ti ša* 50-A.A *i-*<*na*> *mìn-da-at* A.MEŠ *lìb-ba-šú-nu ṣab-tu a-di kan-ni-šu-nu dan-nu-ti* URUDU

396) 3 heavy copper basins that can hold fifty measures of water in them, together with their heavy copper stands;

---

383 *ur*-ar-*: The text has Ú-*ar-*. Urarṭu is mentioned frequently in this text and in every other occasion it begins with *ur-ar-*.
384 CAD Q p. 137 suggests *ni-iḫ*(text: *nik-ka*)*-su-ši-na*, "inlays," instead of "platings"; see also AHw p. 775 sub *neḫsu* II.
386 *-ba*-*: Form has an extraneous vertical wedge.
387 E*: The text has IZ/PA-ŠÁ; the reading KUŠ.DA.E.SIR follows Mayer, MDOG 115 (1983) p. 108.
388 Or, following CAD M/1 p. 117, 1 GIŠ.NÁ <<ZÚ>> *ma-a-a-al-ti* KÙ.BABBAR, "1 silver bed."
390 B.R. Foster (Before the Muses^3 pp. 810–811) translates this line as "10 items: boxwood tables with frames of boxwood, legs of ebony and boxwood, and gold and silver mountings."
391 *sa-ma-ḫu-te*: The translation "assorted" follows CAD S p. 381 sub *summuḫu*; AHw p. 1018 sub *samḫu* (followed by Mayer, UF 11 [1979] p. 578) takes the adjective to mean "miteinander verbunden."
392 See Mayer, UF 11 (1979) pp. 578 and 589 for the understanding of *ṣipru* and *gulgullu* as types of helmets. Text no. 82 iv 5′′ has 20 LIM 5 <ME> ⸢12⸣ here.
393 B. Foster (Before the Muses^3 p. 811) translates *purṭī* as "throw spears(?)" and KI.TA.MEŠ as "storage racks"; however, it seems unlikely that storage racks would be made of copper instead of wood.
396–397 See Gaspa, SAAB 16 (2007) pp. 169–171 and n. 177 and Contenitori neoassiri pp. 85–87 and 179–186 with regard to the *kiūru* and *harû* (*hariu*) vessels. Two large vessels are shown standing in front of the temple of Ḫaldi in the depiction of Sargon's sack of Muṣaṣir from the palace at Khorsabad (see Figure 17).

397) 1 *ḫa-ru-ú* URUDU GAL-*tu ša* 80 *i-na mìn-da-at* A.MEŠ *lìb-ba-šá ṣab-tu a-di kan-ni-šá* GAL-*i* URUDU
398) *ša* LUGAL.MEŠ-*ni ša* KUR.*ur-ar-ṭi a-na e-peš* UDU.SISKUR.MEŠ *ma-ḫar* ^{d}*ḫal-di-a ú-mal-lu-ú* GEŠTIN.MEŠ *ma-qi-te*

397–398) 1 large copper *ḫarû*-vessel that can hold eighty measures of water in it, together with its large copper stand, which the kings of the land Urarṭu used to fill with libation wine for making offerings before the god Ḫaldi;

399) 4 ^{d}*ṣa-lam* URUDU Ì.DU$_{8}$.GAL-*li ma-ṣar* KÁ.MEŠ-*šu ša* 4 KÙŠ *mu-la-a-šú-nu a-di* KI.TUŠ.MEŠ-*šú-nu* URUDU.ḪI.A *šap-ku*

399) 4 divine statue(s) of copper, the chief doorkeepers, guardians of his (Haldi's) gates, (each of) whose height is 4 cubits, together with their bases, cast in copper;

400) 1 *ṣa-lam ut-nen-ni man-za-az* LUGAL-*ti ša* ^{md}15-BÀD DUMU ^{m}*iš-pu-e-ni* LUGAL KUR.*ur-ar-ṭi* KI.TUŠ-*šú* ZABAR *ši-ip-ku*

400) 1 statue (depicting) Ištar-dūrī (Sarduri), son of Išpueni, king of the land Urarṭu, praying (and) *in a royal pose*, (*together with*) its base, cast in bronze;

401) 1 GU$_{4}$ 1 GU$_{4}$.ÁB *a-di* GU$_{4}$.AMAR-*šá ša* ^{m}<^{d}>15-BÀD DUMU ^{m}*iš-pu-e-ni* URUDU.ḪI.<A> É ^{d}*ḫal-di-a a-na e-qi ú-ter-ru-ma iš-⸢tur⸣ ṣe-ru-uš-šú-un*

401) 1 bull (and) 1 cow, together with her bull calf, dedicated by (lit.: "of") Ištar-dūrī (Sarduri), son of Išpueni, (made of) copper (and) belonging to the temple of the god Ḫaldi, (*which Ištar-dūrī*) *had made as* a votive offering and upon which he had inscribed (a record of his action);

402) 1 *ṣa-lam* ^{m}*ar-giš-ti* LUGAL KUR.*ur-ar-ṭi ša* AGA MUL-*ti* DINGIR-*ti ap-ru-ma* ŠU.II 15-*šú ka-ri-bat a-di* É-*šú* 60 GUN URUDU.ḪI.A KI.LÁ

402) 1 statue of Argišti, king of the land Urarṭu, wearing a crown (decorated) with stars, (an attribute) of divine rank, and with his right hand in a gesture of blessing, together with its *casing*, which weighs sixty talents of copper;

403) 1 *ṣa-lam* ^{m}*ur-sa-a it-ti* 2 ANŠE.KUR.RA.MEŠ *pét-ḫal-lì-šú* LÚ.GIŠ.GIGIR-*šú a-di* KI.TUŠ-*šú-nu* URUDU.ḪI.A *šap-ku*
404) *ša taš-ri-iḫ-ti ra-ma-ni-šú ma-a i-na* 2 ANŠE.KUR.<RA>.MEŠ-*ia ù* 1-*en* LÚ.GIŠ.GIGIR-*ia* LUGAL-*ut* KUR.*ur-ar-ṭi ik-šu-du qa-ti ba-rim* EDIN-*šú-un*

403–404) 1 statue of Ursâ (Rusâ) with two of his cavalry horses (and) his *groom*, together with their base, cast in copper, upon which was engraved his own self-praise, namely "With (the help of) my two horses and my one *groom*, I personally obtained the kingship of the land Urarṭu" —

405) *a-di* NÍG.GA-*šú ma-at-ti ša ni-i-ba la i-šu-ú áš-lu-la*
406) *e-zib ú-de-e* KÙ.GI KÙ.BABBAR AN.NA ZABAR AN.BAR ZÚ GIŠ.ESI GIŠ.TÚG *ù gi-mir* GIŠ.ḪI.A *ka-la-a-ma*
407) *ša ul-tú* URU É.GAL-*lim ù* É DINGIR *um*-ma-na-at* ^{d}*a-šur* ^{d}AMAR.UTU *a-na la ma-ni iš-lu-lu-ni*
408) NÍG.ŠU.MEŠ É.GAL-*lì* ^{m}*ur-za-na ù* ^{d}*ḫal-di-a a-di* NÍG.GA-*šú ma-aʾ-di ša* TA *qé-reb* URU.*mu-ṣa-ṣir áš-lu-la*
409) *um-ma-na-te-ia rap-šá-a-te i-na gi-ip-ši-<ši>-na e-mid-ma a-na qé-reb* KUR *aš-šur*.KI *ú-šal-di-id*
410) UN.MEŠ *na-gi-i ša* URU.*mu-ṣa-ṣir it-ti* UN.MEŠ KUR *aš-šur*.KI *am-nu-ma il-ku tup-šik-ku ki-i ša*

405–410) I carried off (all these things) as booty, together with numerous, countless (other) possessions of his, not to mention the objects of gold, silver, tin, bronze, iron, ivory, ebony, boxwood, and every (other) kind of wood that the troops of the gods Aššur (and) Marduk carried off in countless numbers as booty from the city, palace, and temple. I loaded the property of the palace of Urzana and of the god Ḫaldi, together with his (Urzana's) numerous possessions that I had carried off as booty from the city Muṣaṣir, on (the backs of the soldiers of) the main body of my extensive army and I had (them) convey (it) to Assyria. I considered the people of the district of the city Muṣaṣir as people of Assyria and I imposed upon them (the same state) service (and) corvée duty as if

---

399 The wall relief depicting Sargon's sack of Muṣaṣir has a large statue, in a standing position and with one hand raised in a gesture of worship/adoration, on each side of the door of the temple of the god Ḫaldi (see Figure 17).
400 *manzaz šarrūti*, "*in a royal pose*": The phrase has usually been understood to mean "upon a socle (indicating his) royal position"; see CAD M/1 p. 235. F.M. Fales (COS 4 p. 214) translates the beginning of the line as "1 worshipper statue, standing for the king, (gift of) Sarduri ..." and see also Fuchs, SAAS 8 p. 64. Possibly <*a-di*> KI.TUŠ-*šú*, "<together with> its base"; see lines 399 and 403.
401 A cow apparently nursing a calf is depicted in front of the temple of the god Ḫaldi in the the relief of Sargon's sack of Muṣaṣir (see Figure 17).
403–404 For studies of this passage and text no. 63 iii′ 9′b–11′a, see Fuchs, SAAS 8 pp. 108–111 and Rollinger, Studies Neumann pp. 585–609. LÚ.GIŠ.GIGIR stands for *susānu* (see Parpola, SAAB 2 [1988] p. 78 n. 2) and may have been a mounted companion.
407 *um**-: The text has AD-.

áš-šu-ri e-mid-su-nu-te
411) *iš-mé-ma* ^{m}*ur-sa-a qaq-qa-riš ip-pal-si-iḫ na-aḫ-lap-a-te-šú ú-šar-riṭ-ma uš-še-ra i-de-e-šu*
412) *iš-ḫu-uṭ ku-bu-us-su pe-rat-su iḫ-si-ip-ma ú-rep-pi*-is lìb-ba-šu i-na ki-lal-li-šú bu-up-pa-niš is-sa-ḫi-ip*
413) *iz-ziz-ma ṣur-ru-šu iḫ-mu-ṭa ka-bat-tuš i-na pi-i-šu it-taš-ku-nu qu-ub-bé-e mar-ṣu-ú-te*
414) *i-na* KUR.*ur-ar-ṭi a-na paṭ gim-ri-šú si-pit-tu ú-šá-aṣ-riḫ-ma ger-<ra>-nu ša du-ur u*$_4$*-me i-na* KUR.*na-ʾi-ri ú-šá-áš-kín*

(they were) Assyrians.
411–414) Ursâ (Rusâ) heard (of this) and threw himself on the ground. He ripped his garments and bared his arms. He tore off his headdress, pulled out his hair, and beat his chest (lit.: "heart") with both (fists). He lay flat (on the ground), face down. His mood became angry (lit.: "becomes angry") and his temper burned (hot). Woeful lamentations were on his lips. I caused lamentation to be wailed throughout the land Urarṭu, to its full extent, and established perpetual wailing in the land Naʾiri.

---

415) *i-na e-mu-qi ṣi-ra-a-te ša* ^{d}*a-šur* EN-*ia i-na li-i-te da-na-ni ša* ^{d}EN ^{d}AG DINGIR.MEŠ *tik-le-ia*
416) *i-na an-ni ke-e-ni ša* ^{d}UTU DI.KU$_5$.GAL DINGIR.MEŠ *ša ṭu-ú-di ip-tu-ma ṣu-lu-lu iš-ku-nu* UGU *um-ma-ni-ia*
417) *i-na nàr-bi ša* ^{d}U.GUR *dan-dan* DINGIR.MEŠ *a-lik i-di-ia na-ṣir* KARAŠ-*ia*
418) TA KUR.*su-um-bi na-gi-i i-na bi-rit* KUR.*ni-kip-pa* KUR.*ú-pa-a* KUR.MEŠ-*e mar-ṣu-ti a-na* KUR.*ur-ar-ṭa e-tar-ba*
419) *i-na* KUR.*ur-ar-ṭi* KUR.*zi-kir-ti* KUR.*ma-an-na-a-a* KUR.*na-ʾi-i-ri ù* KUR.*mu-ṣa-ṣi-ri*
420) *ki-ma lab-bi na-ad-ri ša pu-luḫ-tu ra-mu-ú e-tel-liš at-tal-lak-ma la a-mu-ra mu-né-eḫ-ḫu*
421) *ša* ^{m}*ur-sa-a* KUR.*ur-ar-ṭa-a-a* ^{m}*me-ta-at-ti* KUR.*zi-kir-ta-a-a i-na* ⸢*da*⸣*-ab-de-e ṣe-e-ri* ERIM.ḪI.A-*šú-nu ma-at-tu ú-šam-qit*
422) 4 ME 30 URU.MEŠ-*ni ša* 7 *na-ge-e ša* ^{m}*ur-sa-a* KUR.*ur-ar-ṭa-a-<a> gi-mir-tu ak-šud-ma ú-šaḫ-rib* KUR-*su*
423) *ša* ^{m}*ur-za-na* URU.*mu-ṣa-ṣir-a-a* ^{d}*ḫal-di-a* DINGIR-*šu* ^{d}*ba-ag-bar-tu* ^{d}*iš-tar-šú a-di bu-še-e* ⸢É.KUR⸣-*šú ma-aʾ-di*
424) *it-ti* 6 LIM 1 ME 10 UN.MEŠ 12 ANŠE.*ku-dini* 3 ME 80 ANŠE.MEŠ 5 ME 25 GU$_4$.MEŠ 1 LIM 2 ME 85 UDU.MEŠ ⸢DAM-*su*⸣ DUMU.MEŠ-*šú* DUMU.MUNUS.MEŠ-*šú áš-lu-la*
425) *i-na né-re-bi ša* KUR.*an-da-ru-ut-ta* KUR-*i mar-ṣi* SAG URU.*ḫi-ip-tú-na at-tu-ṣi-a šal-*⸢*miš*⸣ *a-*⸢*na*⸣ KUR-*ia a-tu-ra*

415–425) Through the superior strength of the god Aššur, my lord, through the power (and) might of the gods Bēl (and) Nabû, my divine helpers, with the firm approval of the god Šamaš, the great judge of the gods, who opened up my path and established (his) protection over my army, (and) through the great power of the god Nergal, mightiest of the gods, who goes at my side (and) protects my (military) camp, I entered into the land Urarṭu, (going) from the district Sumbi, in between Mount Nikippa (and) Mount Upâ, rugged mountains. I marched about through the lands of Urarṭu, Zikirtu, Mannea, Naʾiri, and Muṣaṣir (420) in a lordly manner, like a fierce lion that is endowed with fearsomeness, and I met no one who could overpower (me). On the battlefield, I stuck down the large army of Ursâ (Rusâ), the Urarṭian, (and) of Mitatti of the land Zikirtu. I conquered in all 430 settlements in seven districts belonging to Ursâ (Rusâ), the Urarṭian, and I laid waste to his land. I carried off as booty from Urzana of the city Muṣaṣir, his god Ḫaldi (and) his goddess Bagbartu, together with abundant property from his temple, (along) with 6,110 people, 12 *kūdanu*-mules, 380 donkeys, 525 oxen, 1,285 sheep and goats, his wife, his sons, (and) his daughters. I departed through the pass at Mount Andarutta, a rugged mountain facing the city Ḫiptunu, (and) returned safely to my (own) land.

---

426) 1-*en* LÚ.EN GIŠ.GIGIR 2 LÚ.*ša pet-ḫal-lì* 3

426) One charioteer, two cavalrymen, (and) three *light*

411–413 Text no. 43 line 27 states that Rusâ "brought an end to his life with his own weapon" (*ina* GIŠ.TUKUL *ra-ma-ni-šú ú-qa-ta-a na-piš-tuš*). For a discussion of the death of the Urarṭian king — and the argument that in the aftermath of Sargon's campaign, the Urarṭian ruler Rusâ was assassinated by some of his own nobles — see Roaf, CRRA 54 pp. 771–780. See also Van De Mieroop, Studies Foster pp. 427–430 and Van De Mieroop, JAH 4 (2016) pp. 16–39 on the death of Rusâ. *qaq-qa-riš ip-pal-si-iḫ*: Possibly "squatted on the ground" rather than "threw himself on the ground"; see Hurowitz, Studies Ephʿal p. 119 n. 30.

412 *-pi**(text: SAL?)-: The sign may have been written over an erasure. This would be the only attestation of *rapāsu*, "to beat, thrash" in the D-stem; see CAD R pp. 151–152.

413 Or "stood still" instead of "became angry (lit.: "becomes angry")," taking *izziz* to come from the verb *izuzzu* (preterite tense) rather than *ezēzu* (present tense).

424 Line 349 refers to 1,235 sheep and goats, not 1,285.

425 D.A. Marf (Akkadica 136 [2015] pp. 127–140) has recently argued for the identification of Hiptunu with modern Haudian in the Diana-Ruwanduz valley and Mount Andaruta with Mount Hendrên.

426–430 These five lines are separated from one another by a larger space than is found between the lines in the remainder of the inscription. For a recent study of this 'colophon,' see Hurowitz, Studies Ephʿal pp. 105–110; he prefers to divide the lines into three sentences: line 426,

LÚ.*kal-la-ba-a-ni de-e-ku*
427) LÚ.EME.SAG.MEŠ ^{m}DÙG.GA-IM-^{d}*a-šur* LÚ.AGRIG GAL-*ú i-na* UGU ^{d}*a-šur be-lí-ia ul-te-bi-la*
428) *ṭup-pi* ^{md}AG-*šal-lim-šu-nu* LÚ.DUB.SAR *šar-ri* GAL-*ú* LÚ.GAL.⸢GI⸣.BÙR LÚ.*um-ma-an* ^{m}LUGAL-GI.NA LUGAL KUR *aš-šur*.KI
429) *bu-uk-ru* ^{m}*ḫar-ma-ak-ki* LÚ.DUB.SAR LUGAL BAL.TIL.KI-*ú*
430) *i-na li-i-mi* ^{md}INANNA-BÀD LÚ.GAR.KUR URU.LÍMMU-*ḫa na-ṣu*

infantrymen were killed.
427) Ṭāb-šār-Aššur, the chief treasurer sent *the chief (enemy) informers* to the god Aššur.
428–429) Tablet of Nabû-šallimšunu, the chief royal scribe, chief tablet-writer (and) scholar of Sargon (II) king of Assyria, (and) son of Ḫarmakki, the royal scribe, an Assyrian.

430) (This report) was brought in the eponymy of Ištar-dūrī, the governor of Arrapḫa.

66

A brief inscription of Sargon is found upon some glazed wall plaques for clay cones from Aššur. This is the only royal inscription known that states that Sargon was the son of Tiglath-pileser III. For a letter that might also indicate that Sargon was the son of Tiglath-pileser (Dietrich, SAA 17 no. 46 [=CT 54 no. 109]), see Thomas, Studies Bergerhof pp. 467–470.

CATALOGUE

Ex.	Museum Number	Excavation Number	Photograph Number	Provenance	Dimensions (cm)	Lines Preserved	cpn
1	EŞ 3282	—	Istanbul K 44	Aššur	—	—	(p)
2	VA Ass 2332a–d + VA Ass 2366b	Ass 31	VAN 4027	Aššur, gB5I, East-West trench, close above the floor, at the wall	33×25×6	1	(c)
3	—	Ass 46	—	Aššur, gB5I, East-West trench, room with niches	—	—	n
4	VA Ass 2333a+c–h	—	VAN 4028	Aššur, AP, northeast of the main court	32×23×5.5	1	c
5	VA —	—	—	As ex. 1	Dia. (base): 9.5	1	n

line 427, and lines 428–430, in the latter case taking *ṭuppi* of line 428 as the subject (or object) of the verb at the end of line 430 ("The tablet ... they/was delivered ..."). Line 426: The exact same number of soldiers killed was used in Esarhaddon's "Letter to the God" (see Leichty, RINAP 4 p. 85 no. 33 iv 13′ and cf. Grayson, RIMA 3 p. 244 A.0.105.3 rev. 1′–2′). B.R. Foster feels that this line does not refer to the "actual casualties" suffered during the campaign, but rather to "a memorial ceremony in honor of all soliders lost in the campaign" and thus he translates this line as "(Herewith) one charioteer, two horsemen, and three scouts (of those who) were killed" (Before the Muses^{3} p. 812). See also Luckenbill, ARAB 2 p. 99 n. 1.

65 line 426 LÚ.EN GIŠ.GIGIR: The term means literally "lord/owner of a chariot" and thus may indicate an individual of a higher status than someone who just drove a chariot.

65 line 427 For similar passages, see Grayson, RIMA 3 p. 244 A.0.105.3 rev. 3′–4′ and Leichty, RINAP 4 p. 85 no. 33 iv 11′–12′. The understanding of this line and the interpretation of LÚ.EME.SAG.MEŠ (written *li-šá-a-nu re-še-e-ti* in Leichty, RINAP 4 p. 85 no. 33 iv 11′) are matters of scholarly discussion (e.g., Levine, Eretz-Israel 27 [2003] pp. 114* and 118* n. 18). In particular, some instead consider LÚ.EME.SAG.MEŠ to refer to Ṭāb-šār-Aššur as "a first-class speaker" (see Leichty, RINAP 4 p. 85 note to no. 33 iv 11′) or to refer to the individuals who brought the first reports on the events of the campaign back to Assyria, and some take the verb *ul-te-bi-la* to be first person singular ("I," i.e, Sargon), thus making Ṭāb-šār-Aššur (or the chief informers and Ṭāb-šār-Aššur) the object of the verb. The assumption tentatively followed here that LÚ.EME.SAG.MEŠ refers to individuals who could attest to what happened during the campaign (or perhaps just at Muṣaṣir) follows B. Levine (Eretz-Israel 27 [2003] p. 114* and p. 118* n. 18); see also Fales, COS 4 p. 215 n. 167. With regards to Ṭāb-šār-Aššur, who is known from several Neo-Assyrian letters, see text no. 2005; Parpola, SAA 1 nos. 41–74; and Perroudon, PNA 3/2 pp. 1344–1346 sub Ṭāb-šār-Aššūr 1.

65 line 428 M. Luukko (SAAB 16 [2007] p. 230 n. 17) takes LÚ.GAL.GI.BÙR (LÚ.GAL.GI.U) to be a variant spelling for *rab ṭupšarri*, "chief scribe."

65 line 430 Or "In the eponymy of Ištar-dūrī, the governor of Arrapḫa, they (the bodies) were presented" (see Grayson, RIMA 3 p. 244 A.0.105.3 rev. 5′). See also the on-page note to lines 426–430.

6	VA —	Ass 14?	—	As ex. 1	Dia. (text): 9.4	1	n
7	VA Ass 3512	—	—	As ex. 1	15.2×10.5	1	n
8	VA Ass 3512	—	—	As ex. 1	11×11.4×2.6	1	n

COMMENTARY

According to E. Unger, ex. 1 came from the royal palace at Aššur, but no excavation number or excavation photo number is known for it. Thus, it is edited from the published copy by Unger, with some help from the published photographs. A. Nunn (Knaufplatten p. 107 no. 61) states that EŞ 3282 (ex. 1) is the current museum number for Ass 46 (ex. 3) and that it measures 31×31×3 cm; however, O. Pedersén (Katalog pp. 110 and 215) and F. Pedde and S. Lundström (Palast p. 182 n. 275) treat them separately. The two are kept separate here, but Nunn may be correct in identifying them as one and the same piece. Nunn (Knaufplatten p. 107 no. 62) notes that while the excavation journal says that ex. 2 was found in gB5I, the inventory book indicates it was found in gA5II. Ex. 3 is made up of seven large and several small pieces. Ex. 4 is made up of five joined fragments, as well as several separate pieces with no traces of an inscription. The inscriptions on exs. 1, 2, and 4 are written counter-clockwise around the middle of the plaque (the area in which the peg for the cone was placed). The signs on ex. 4 are quite faint.

All information on exs. 5–8 comes from Nunn (Knaufplatten p. 117 nos. 269–272), who states that the four pieces (like the preceding exemplars) come from glazed square plaques for cones. She considers ex. 5 to have two inscriptions, one above on the molding ("Profilleiste") ([...] MAN GAL MAN *dan-nu* [...]) and one below on the plate itself ([...] KUR *aš-šur* A ^{m}*tukul-ti-*[...]); they are treated here as parts of the same inscription. She also notes that the inscription on ex. 5 is written from the inside out ("von innen nach außen") rather than the normal direction, from the outside in ("von außen nach innen"). Very little of the inscription on exs. 6–8 is preserved and no part of the royal name; thus, their assignment to this inscription is not completely certain.

BIBLIOGRAPHY

1933 Unger, Forschungen und Fortschritte 9 p. 246 (ex. 1, copy, study)
1933 Unger, IAMN 9 pp. 6–7 and 16–17, and pls. I–III (ex. 1, photo, copy, edition)
1933–34 Weidner, AfO 9 p. 79 (ex. 1, copy, transliteration)
1992 Vera Chamaza, SAAB 6 p. 32 (ex. 1, edition)
1993 Thomas, Studies Bergerhof pp. 465–466 (ex. 1, copy, edition)
1997 Pedersén, Katalog pp. 110 and 215–216 (exs. 1–4, study)
2002 Vera Chamaza, Omnipotenz pp. 283–284 no. 29 (edition)
2006 Nunn, Knaufplatten p. 107 nos. 61–62 and 65, and p. 117 nos. 269–272 (exs. 1–4, study; exs. 5-8, transliteration, study)
2008 Pedde and Lundström, Palast p. 182 n. 275 (exs. 1–4, study)

TEXT

1) É.GAL ^{m}MAN-*ú-ki-in* MAN GAL MAN *dan-nu* MAN ŠÚ MAN KUR *aš-šur* A ^{m}*tukul-ti-*A-*é-šár-ra* MAN KUR *aš-šur-ma*

1) Palace of Sargon (II), great king, strong king, king of the world, king of Assyria, son of Tiglath-pileser (III), (who was) also king of Assyria.

67

This inscription is found on several clay cones and one unidentifiable clay object from Aššur. It records the king's work on Eḫursaggalkurkurra, the cella of the temple of the god Aššur and was written in the fifth month of the eponymy of Nasḫur-Bēl (705). For brick inscriptions of Sargon recording work on Eḫursaggalkurkurra, see text nos. 69–70; note also text no. 84 line 3′ and likely text no. 74 i 25–27.

CATALOGUE

Ex.	Museum Number	Excavation Number	Photograph Number	Provenance	Dimensions (cm)	Lines Preserved	cpn
1	A 3647 (Istanbul)	Ass 3327	Ass ph 320	Aššur, iA4II, south of the court of the Aššur temple	11.8×14×2.4	1–9	n
2	A 3364 (Istanbul)	Ass 1742	Ass ph 320	Aššur, iC5I, west of the Parthian gate, in debris, deeper than the pavement	6.8×5.1×2	1–9	n
3	A 3378 (Istanbul)	Ass 2927a	Ass ph 320	Aššur, hE4I, in front of the SE tower of the Aššur temple	15×13.3×2	1–2	n
4	A 3379 (Istanbul)	Ass 2927b	Ass ph 320	As ex. 3	4.7×7.5×1.9	2–9	n
5	A 3380 (Istanbul)	Ass 3000	Ass ph 320	Aššur, hD4II, near the door of the long room	8×9.2×2.1	1–5, 7, 9	n
6	A 3582 (Istanbul)	Ass 16007	Ass ph 4786	Aššur, iB3III, exploratory trench, 80 cm deep	7.3×11.4×1.9	2–9	p
7	A 3598 (Istanbul) + A 3599 (Istanbul) + VA Ass 2071	Ass 17342a + Ass 17342b + Ass 17404	Ass ph 5180, 5852	Aššur, hE, slope (A 3598 and 3599); iB4I, middle, debris on the mud brick terrace (VA Ass 2071)	8×5.5 (A 3598); 7×7.5 (A 3599); 14×10×6 (VA Ass 2071)	4–9	p
8	A 3653 (Istanbul)	Ass 3143	Ass ph 320	Aššur, hD3V, court of the Aššur temple, northeast	3.9×7.9×2	1–4	n
9	—	Ass 4397	—	Aššur, hD3V, court of the Aššur temple, north, debris close above the pavement, under the mud brick collapse	—	—	n
10	VA Ass 2070	Ass 4572	—	Aššur, hD3V, northwest wall of the court of the Aššur temple	6×7×4	5–7	c
11	A 641 (Istanbul)	Ass 17791	Ass ph 5664; Istanbul K 209	Aššur, iA3V, middle, upper debris	4.5×4.5	1–5, 7	p
12	VA 5159	—	—	Aššur	—	1–9	c

COMMENTARY

Assur photo 320 depicts several clay cones with this inscription (supposedly exs. 1–5 and 8), but the inscriptions on them are not legible. According to O. Pedersén (Katalog, pp. 133 and 148) exs. 9 and 11 are fragments of glazed clay cones. Ex. 12 is listed under his category "Other Clay Objects" ("Sonstige Tongegenstände") (ibid. p. 223). The line arrangement follows ex. 1, but the master line is a composite from various exemplars. Ex. 12 has lines 7–8 on one line.

BIBLIOGRAPHY

1904 Andrae, MDOG 25 pp. 31–32 (ex. 2, provenance)
1905 Andrae, MDOG 26 p. 22 (ex. 3 and/or 4, study)
1911 Messerschmidt, KAH 1 nos. 40–42 and 71 (exs. 1–5, copy)
1915 Bezold, HKA pp. 47–48 (exs. 1–5, edition)
1926 Weidner, AfO 3 pp. 1–2 (exs. 1–7, edition)
1926 Weidner, IAK pp. 89–90 n. 13 (lines 3–6, study)
1927 Luckenbill, ARAB p. 112 §§219–223 (exs. 1–5, translation)
1982 Jakob-Rost, FuB 22 p. 146 and p. 175 no. 109 (ex. 7, partial copy [VA Ass 2071])
1984 Donbaz and Grayson, RICCA nos. 136 and 228–235 (exs. 1–8, study; exs. 6, 8, copy; ex. 7 partial copy)
1986 Borger, ZA 76 p. 301 (ex. 7, study)
1988 Deller, JAOS 108 p. 516 (ex. 7, partial transliteration)
1997 Pedersén, Katalog pp. 131–134, 147–148, and 223 (exs. 1–12, study)
1999 Frahm, JCS 51 p. 81 (exs. 1–8, edition)
2006 Nunn, Knaufplatten pp. 73 and 164 nos. 1510–1514 (exs. 6–7, 10–11, study)

TEXT

1) *a-na* ^{d}*aš-šur* AD DINGIR.MEŠ EN GAL-*e* EN-*šú*
2) ^{m}MAN-GIN MAN ŠÚ MAN KUR *aš-šur* GÌR.NÍTA KÁ.DINGIR.RA.KI MAN KUR ⸢EME.GI$_{7}$ *u* URI$^{?}$⸣.[KI]
3) *é-ḫur-sag-gal-kur-kur-ra* É *aš-šur be-lí-šú*
4) É.GAR$_{8}$.MEŠ *na-me-ri si-ḫir-ti* É *gab-bu ina si-i-ri* GIBIL-*iš*
5) *na-me-ri né-bé-ḫi sa-me-tu u sí-ka-a-ti*
6) *šu-ut* NA$_{4}$ *ip-tiq-ma ú-šal-ma-a si-ḫir-*⸢*ti*⸣*-*[*šú*$^{?}$]
7) *a-na* TI ZI.MEŠ-*šu* GÍD UD.MEŠ-*šú* GIN BALA.MEŠ-*šú*
8) *sa-kap* LÚ.KÚR.MEŠ-*šú ina* É *aš-šur* EN-*šú* DÙ-*uš*
9) ITI.NE *lim-mu* ^{m}*na-as-ḫur*-EN LÚ.GAR.KUR URU.*si-na-bu*

1) For the god Aššur, the father of the gods, the great lord, his lord:
2–6) Sargon (II), king of the world, king of Assyria, governor of Babylon, king of the land of Sumer and A[kkad] renovated Eḫursaggalkurkurra ("House, the Great Mountain of the Lands"), the temple of (the god) Aššur, his lord, by plastering the walls of the towers all around the temple. He fashioned towers, friezes, parapets and *glazed sikkatu*-cones, and placed (them) all around [*it* (the temple)].
7–8) He built (these) in the temple of (the god) Aššur, his lord, for the sake of ensuring his good health, prolonging his days, firmly establishing his reign, (and) overthrowing his enemies.
9) Month Abu (V), eponymy of Nasḫur-Bēl, the governor of the city Sinabu.

68

A large number of bricks from the city of Aššur are inscribed with a brief four-line building inscription of Sargon II dedicated to the god Aššur. Many of these bricks were found in or near the temple of that god.

67 line 2 KUR.⸢EME.GI$_{7}$ *u* URI$^{?}$⸣.[KI]: Or KUR.⸢EME.GI$_{7}$ *ù*⸣ [URI.KI]; the traces at the end of ex. 6 are not clear. Ex. 12 has KUR *mu*-⸢GÌR⸣ [...]. These are the only two exemplars preserving anything of the line after the KUR; it must be noted that unlike the other exemplars, it is not clear that ex. 12 is on a clay cone.
67 lines 5–6 Cf. CAD N/2 p. 144 "friezes for the towers and the corners, and clay bosses of glazed brick" and Frahm, JCS 51 (1999) p. 81 "(Für) die Türme ... Friese, *Mauersockel* (sowie) *glasierte sikkatu*-Nagel."
67 line 8 Ex. 2 [*i*]-*na* <É> *aš-šur*, "[i]n <the temple of> Aššur," or [*a*]-*na aš-šur*, "[f]or Aššur."
67 line 9 Or ^{m}*na-as-ḫír*-EN, "Nasḫir-Bēl"; see PNA 2/2 p. 932.

CATALOGUE

Ex.	Museum Number	Excavation Number	Photograph Number	Provenance	Dimensions (cm)	Lines Preserved	cpn
1	—	Ass 1519	Ass ph 223	Aššur, iC4V, north of the prosthesis	34×34×10.5	1–4	p
2	—	Ass 740	Ass ph 158	Aššur, iD5I, trench 2, right above, low wall	16.5×11	1–4	p
3	—	Ass 775	—	Aššur, iD5I, trench 4	10 thick	—	n
4	—	Ass 826	Ass ph 158	Aššur, iA5I, western façade of Temple A	—	1–4	p
5	—	Ass 1521	Ass ph 223	Aššur, iC4V, in debris north of the prosthesis	10 thick	1–4	p
6	—	Ass 1482	Ass ph 223	Aššur, iB4V, north of the NW corner of Temple A	—	1–4	p
7	—	Ass 776	—	As ex. 3	10 thick	—	n
8	VA Ass 3276a	Ass 2794	—	Aššur, hD4II, near the outer wall of the 'cella,' south of the door	23.5×16×11	1–4	n
9	VA Ass 3276b	Ass 3280	—	Aššur, hD8I, court, middle	27.5×20×10.5	1–4	n
10	VA Ass 3276c	—	—	Aššur, Aššur temple	18×22×12	1–3	n
11	VA Ass 3276d	—	—	As ex. 10	31.5×29.5×11.5	1–4	n
12	VA 6914	Ass 2970a	—	Aššur, hE4I, court, in front of the tower of the main façade	33.5×29.5×11	1–4	n
13	VA Ass 3276e	—	—	As ex. 10	32×31×11	1–4	n
14	VA Ass 3276f	—	—	As ex. 10	19×20.5×10.5	1–4	n
15	—	Ass 11944	Ass ph 2748	Aššur, iD4V, built into a late Assyrian ("jungassyrisches") private house wall	—	1–4	p
16	—	Ass 816	—	Aššur, iB5I, temple foundation, from the foundation north of xxx	—	—	n
17	—	Ass 1690	—	Aššur, hB4V, southern side of the ziggurrat	—	—	n
18	EŞ —	Ass 2970b	—	As ex. 12	—	1–4	n
19	—	Ass 3054	—	Aššur, hD3V, Aššur temple, court, NW wall	—	1–4	n
20	EŞ —	Ass 3079	—	Aššur, hD3V, NW wall of the temple court	—	1–4	n
21	—	Ass 3166	—	Aššur, hE4I, court pavement, south of the tower	—	—	n
22	—	Ass 3175	—	Aššur, hE4I, court, southeast, pavement	—	1–4	n
23	—	Ass 3285	—	Aššur, hD4I, court, near the SW façade	—	1–4	n
24	—	Ass 3286a	—	Aššur, iA4II, SE of the court, deep	—	—	n
25	—	Ass 3289	—	Aššur, gE4II, near the NE corner of the great ziggurrat	—	—	n
26	—	Ass 4005	—	Aššur, hC4I, western corner of the court	—	1–4	n
27	—	Ass 4411	—	Aššur, hD3V, temple court, north, debris close above the pavement, under the mud brick collapse	—	1–4	n
28	—	Ass 5577	—	Aššur, eB5V, granary room near the courtyard door	35×35×10.5	1–4	n
29	—	—	Ass ph 999	As ex. 10	—	1–4	p
30	EŞ 6669?	—	RIM 374	As ex. 10	34×27.5×10.5	1–4	p

COMMENTARY

Pedersén, Katalog p. 162 indicates that exs. 3, 4, or 7 may be the brick depicted on Assur photo 999 (ex. 29). According to Messerschmidt, KAH 1 no. 39, these exemplars (at least those that are preserved at the relevant point) have *ana* not *a-na* in line 4; the brick depicted on the photo has ⌜*a*?/DIŠ⌝-*na*. The Vorderasiatisches Museum has a composite excavation copy ("Fundkopie") of exs. 3, 4, and 7; although this copy has been consulted, it has not been used here since it does not record any variants that are not known elsewhere and since it is clear that at least one of the exemplars was not fully preserved (ex. 4, see Assur photo 158). J. Marzahn and L. Jakob-Rost (Ziegeln 1) erroneously give the museum number of ex. 9 as VA Ass 3276h. The provenance of this exemplar is given as hD4I by Marzahn and Jakob-Rost (ibid. p. 131 no. 348); the provenance in the catalogue follows O. Pedersén. The excavation number of ex. 10 is not known; it is erroneously given as Assur 18540 in Marzahn and Jakob-Rost, Ziegeln 1 p. 131 no. 349. There is an excavation copy for Ass 2970 and it is assumed here that it represents both exs. 12 (Ass 2970a) and 18 (Ass 2970b). The measurement of ex. 14 follows Marzahn and Jakob-Rost, Ziegeln 1 p. 133 no. 353. Jakob-Rost and Marzahn, VAS 23 p. 9 no. 124 gives that exemplar the measurements 10.5×16.0 cm and does not take it to be an exemplar of this inscription, but it seems likely that it is. Ex. 28 is edited from an excavation copy. The museum number of ex. 30 is not clear and the brick could be 6676 (information courtesy H. Galter). It is possible that ex. 30 is to be identified with one of the exemplars only known by its excavation number, particularly exs. 18, 20, or 21 that were assigned to the museum in Istanbul.

All exemplars known are inscribed, not stamped. There are no known deviations from the line arrangement given below and the master line follows ex. 1.

Exs. 6 and 27 are glazed. According to Andrae, MDOG 22 p. 37, ex. 2 is also a glazed brick, but neither KAH 1 p. X nor Pedersén, Katalog p. 162 indicates this. Pedersén (ibid. p. 171) indicates that ex. 22 has a glazed rosette on it. Ass 16596 (found in iC4III) is said to be a fragment of a "gestempelt" glazed brick of Sargon II, but nothing more is known about it (idid., p. 194; cf. Gries, Assur-Tempel p. 257 no. 2092).

Haller, Gräber p. 36 refers to a brick of Sargon (II) from the Aššur temple being found in grave 456 (bE5V). This should refer to one of text nos. 68–70; the brick is said to measure 41×41 cm, which might suggest either text no. 69 or text no. 70, rather than text no. 68.

According to the Aššur excavation records, Ass 3144 and Ass 3230A are brick fragments which have four inscribed lines each and which can be assigned to Sargon II. Nothing further is known about the inscriptions on them; they may have this inscription or some other inscription of this ruler. Ass 3144 was found in hE4I, court, southeast, and Ass 3230A was found in hD4I, court, middle. Bricks with this inscription were found with the same map coordinates (exs. 12 and 21–23). See Pedersén, Katalog p. 171 and Gries, Assur-Tempel p. 267 no. 2317.

As is the practice in RINAP, no score for this brick inscription is given on Oracc, but the minor variants are listed at the back of the book.

BIBLIOGRAPHY

1904 Andrae, MDOG 21 p. 30 n. ** (ex. 2, edition)
1904 Andrae, MDOG 22 p. 37 (ex. 2, provanance)
1911 Messerschmidt, KAH 1 no. 39 (exs. 1–7, copy, with variants)
1915 Bezold, HKA p. 47 (exs. 1–7, edition)
1927 Luckenbill, ARAB 2 pp. 112–113 §§219 and 225 (exs. 1–7, translation)
1984 Marzahn and Jakob-Rost, Ziegeln 1 nos. 347–353 (exs. 8–14, study, with variants)
1985 Jakob-Rost and Marzahn, VAS 23 no. 124 (ex. 14, copy)
1997 Pedersén, Katalog pp. 162, 164–165, 169–172, 175, 177, 180, 188, 222, and 224 (exs. 1–29, study)
2017 Gries, Assur-Tempel p. 251 no. 1914, p. 254 no. 2010, p. 264 nos. 2266–2268 and 2270–2271, p. 266 nos. 2296, 2303–2304, and 2310–2311, p. 267 nos. 2320, 2322, and 2326–2327, and p. 268 no. 2345 (exs. 1–3, 5–8, 12, 18–24, 26–27, study)

TEXT

1)	*a-na* ^{d}*a-šur* EN-*šú*	1–4) To the god Aššur, his lord: Sargon (II), king of the world, king of Assyria, king of the land of Sumer and Akkad, built (this structure) for the sake of his life.
2)	^{m}MAN-GIN MAN ŠÚ MAN KUR *aš-šur*.KI	
3)	MAN KUR EME.GI$_7$ *u* URI.KI	
4)	*a-na* TI-*šú* DÙ-*uš*	

69

This inscription from Aššur records the paving of the processional way of the courtyard of Eḫursaggalkurkurra, the cella of the temple of the god Aššur. It is inscribed on a large number of bricks, many of which were found in or near the temple of that god. The next inscription (text no. 70) is a Sumerian version of this Akkadian text.

CATALOGUE

Ex.	Museum Number	Excavation Number	Photograph Number	Provenance	Dimensions (cm)	Lines Preserved	cpn
1	VA 6925	Ass 1800	Ass ph 219; VAN 1404	Aššur, iD5I, from the double pavement of a small room in the SE corner of the eastern plateau	40.5×40.5×7	1–6	p
2	—	Ass 1598a	—	Aššur, iC4V, in the pavement under the prosthesis of temple A, in situ, near the altar, NE corner of the temple	—	1–6	n
3	—	Ass 1598b	—	As ex. 2	—	1–6	n
4	—	Ass 723	Ass ph 158	Aššur, iD5I, right above ("Ganz oben"), trench 2	41×41×7	1–6	p
5	—	Ass 1525	—	Aššur, iC4V, north of the prosthesis	—	—	n
6	—	Ass 1573	Ass ph 195	Aššur, iD4IV, NE corner, eastern plateau	—	1–6	(p)
7	—	Ass 1586	—	Aššur, iC4IV, north of temple A, near the gully, from pavement remains	—	—	n
8	—	Ass 1595	—	Aššur, city area	—	four lines	n
9	—	Ass 1635	—	Aššur, g4, on the ziggurrat	—	—	n
10	VA 6934	Ass 3298	—	Aššur, hE4II, temple court, south	40.5×40×6.5	1–6	n
11	VA Ass 3275a	Ass 9344	Ass ph 1241	Aššur, bE4V, near the northern corner of the outer hook-wall ("Aussenhakenmauer")	21.5×29×7	1–4	p
12	VA Ass 3275b	Ass 20950	Ass ph 6716	Aššur, fC6III (see commentary)	23.5×25×7	1–4	p
13	VA Ass 3275c	—	—	Aššur, Aššur temple	15×16.5×7	3–6	n
14	—	Ass 19168	Ass ph 5825	Aššur, i4/5, eastern plateau	40.5×40.5×8	1–6	p
15	—	Ass 19167	Ass ph 5826	As ex. 14	41×41×7	1–6	p
16	—	Ass 988	—	Aššur, iB5I, above the southern pivot-box, in the anteroom	—	1–6	n
17	—	Ass 1501	—	As ex. 8	—	1–4	n
18	—	Ass 1884	—	Aššur, iD5I, west of the gate-room, in debris	—	—	n
19	—	Ass 2204	—	Aššur, hA4II, near the ziggurrat, NE corner	—	—	n

20	—	Ass 2258	—	Aššur, iD5I, small pavement at the SE corner of the eastern plateau	—	—	n
21	—	Ass 2367	—	Aššur, hA4III, NE corner of the ziggurrat, in the pavement of the later room	—	—	n
22	—	Ass 2381	—	Aššur, h4, at the eastern façade of the ziggurrat	—	—	n
23	—	Ass 2394	—	Aššur, h4, eastern edge	42×42×6.5	three lines	n
24	—	Ass 2798	—	Aššur, hD4II, near the outer wall of the 'cella,' south of the door	—	1–6	n
25	—	Ass 3007	—	Aššur, hE4I, in front of the tower of the main façade	—	—	n
26	—	Ass 3019	—	Aššur, k6, edge of house ("Hausufer")	—	—	n
27	—	Ass 3139	—	Aššur, hD4I, court, near the western wall, pavement, in situ	—	1–6	n
28	—	Ass 3277	—	Aššur, hD4I, court, middle	—	—	n
29	—	Ass 3587	—	Aššur, iA4III, south of the temple court	—	—	n
30	—	Ass 3652	—	Aššur, gC4III, from the yellow gully-debris	—	—	n
31	—	Ass 3687	—	Aššur, hB3V, south, northern edge, under the small rooms	—	—	n
32	—	Ass 3757	—	Aššur, kA3I, wall of (river) bank	—	—	n
33	—	Ass 3772	—	Aššur, k2, wall of (river) bank	—	—	n
34	—	Ass 3773	—	As ex. 33	—	—	n
35	—	Ass 3788	—	Aššur, kA2V	—	—	n
36	—	Ass 3793	—	As ex. 35	—	three lines	n
37	—	Ass 3794	—	Aššur, gC4I, above the *mušlālu* of Esarhaddon	—	—	n
38	—	Ass 3859	—	Aššur, hB4I$^{?}$, north of the "Peripteros"	—	—	n
39	—	Ass 3898	—	Aššur, hC4I, under the mud debris of the northern "Adyton"	41×41	—	n
40	—	Ass 5581	—	Aššur, eC6I, in the debris of the well	—	—	n
41	—	Ass 7289	—	Aššur, dump	—	—	n
42	—	Ass 13366	—	Aššur, eB5V, Anu-Adad temple, court pavement of the late Assyrian house	—	—	n
43	—	Ass 17969	—	Aššur, iC3V, middle, in situ in the remains of the Sargon pavement in front of the NE ramp	41×41×6.5	1–6	n
44	EŞ —	—	RIM 519	As ex. 13	41.5×41.5×7.5	1–6	n
45	EŞ 6677	—	RIM 1258–1259	As ex. 13	—	1–6	p

COMMENTARY

The findspot given above for ex. 1 follows Pedersén, Katalog p. 166; Andrae, AAT p. 91 states that this brick came from iE5I. Ex. 4 has been edited using the excavation photograph and an excavation copy ("Fundkopie") in the Vorderasiatisches Museum. The excavation photograph of ex. 6 has been consulted, but it was not possible to confirm large parts of the text from it. For ex. 10, Marzahn and Jakob-Rost, Ziegeln 1 p. 129 no. 343 gives the Assur number 3298e; the catalogue follows Pedersén, Katalog p. 172. The provenance for ex. 12 is given as "Sin-Šamaš-Tempel; fc 6III" in Marzahn and Jakob-Rost, Ziegeln 1 p. 130 no. 345; for greater details on the findspot, see Pedersén, Katalog p. 203 and p. 49 sub Ass 20948. Exs. 16 and 17 are edited from excavation copies. O. Pedersén (Katalog p. 179) says that Ass 3859 (ex. 38) was found in hB4I, while H. Gries (Assur-Tempel) p. 268) states that it was found in hC4I. Ass 5581 (ex. 40) actually refers to fragments of two bricks (see Pedersén, Katalog p. 180). Ass 3898 refers to several fragments of pavement bricks that have text nos. 69 and 70 (see Pedersén, Katalog p. 175); thus, ex. 39 may represent more than one exemplar. It is not certain that the inscription on ex. 41 is a duplicate of this text; see Pedersén, Katalog p. 183. It is quite possible that the two exemplars seen in Istanbul (exs. 44–45) also appear in the catalogue under their excavation numbers. H. Galter kindly supplied information on exs. 44–45 as well as photographs of them.

All exemplars that have been checked are inscribed, not stamped, and all have the same line arrangement. The master line follows ex. 1.

Bricks recording the construction of the processional way of the Aššur temple (this inscription and text no. 70) were found at that temple (see also Andrae, MDOG 44 [1910] pp. 47–48 and fig. 16, and Haller, Heiligtümer pp. 62–63) and in such other structures as the palace of Ashurnasirpal II (see Preusser, Paläste p. 23 and text no. 70 exs. 2–3), the Sîn-Šamaš temple (see Haller, Heiligtümer p. 89 and ex. 12), and the Anu-Adad temple (see Andrae, AAT pp. 91–93).

No score for this brick inscription is given on Oracc, but the minor variants are listed at the back of the book.

BIBLIOGRAPHY

1904 Andrae, MDOG 25 pp. 23, 28, and 35 (exs. 1–3, 6, provenance, study)

1909 Andrae, AAT pp. 91–92, fig. 90, and pl. XXI (ex. 1, photo, copy, edition; ex. 42, study)

1911 Messerschmidt, KAH 1 no. 37 (exs. 1–9, copy, with variants)

1915 Bezold, HKA p. 46 (exs. 1–9, edition)

1927 Luckenbill, ARAB 2 pp. 112–113 §§219 and 224 (exs. 1–9, translation)

1984 Marzahn and Jakob-Rost, Ziegeln 1 nos. 342–346 (exs. 1, 10–13, study, with variants)

1997 Pedersén, Katalog pp. 161–175, 180, 183, 191, 198, 200–201, 203, and 222 (exs. 1–43, study)

2017 Gries, Assur-Tempel p. 264 no. 2264, p. 265 nos. 2273, 2275, 2278, 2280–2281, and 2289, p. 266 nos. 2294, 2299, and 2309, p. 267 nos. 2316, 2323, and 2328, p. 268 nos. 2339–2341, and p. 274 no. 2465 (exs. 1–7, 10, 18, 24–25, 27–29, 38–39, 43, study)

TEXT

1) *a-na* AN.ŠÁR AD DINGIR.MEŠ *be-lí-šú*
2) ^{m}MAN-GIN LUGAL ŠÚ LUGAL KUR *aš-šur*.KI
3) GÌR.NÍTA KÁ.DINGIR.RA.KI LUGAL KUR EME.GI$_7$ *u* URI.KI
4) *ú-šal-bi-in-ma a-gur-ri ú-tú-ni* KÙ-*tim*
5) *tal-lak-ti ki-sal é-ḫur-sag-gal-kur-kur-ra*
6) GIM *u*$_4$-*me ú-nam-mir*

1–6) To (the god) Aššur, the father of the gods, his lord: Sargon (II), king of the world, king of Assyria, governor of Babylon, king of the land of Sumer and Akkad, had bricks made and made the processional way of the courtyard of Eḫursaggalkurkurra ("House, the Great Mountain of the Lands") shine like daylight with baked bricks from a (ritually) pure kiln.

70

This inscription is a Sumerian version of the previous Akkadian inscription recording the paving of the processional way of the courtyard of Eḫursaggalkurkurra. Most of the exemplars with this inscription were found in the temple of the god Aššur at Aššur.

69 line 2 Exs. 10 and 14 have LUGAL-*ú-kin* for ^{m}MAN-GIN.

CATALOGUE

Ex.	Museum Number	Excavation Number	Photograph Number	Provenance	Dimensions (cm)	Lines Preserved	cpn
1	—	Ass 1801	Ass ph 220	Aššur, iD5I, from the double pavement ("Doppelpflaster") of a small room in the southeast corner of the East plateau	40×40×7	1–6	p
2	—	Ass 82	Ass ph 195	Aššur, gB5I, used as an orthostat	41×41×7	1–6	(p)
3	—	Ass 1500	—	Aššur, Ashurnasirpal palace	—	—	n
4	—	Ass 1582	—	Aššur, iC4IV, north of the prosthesis	—	—	n
5	—	Ass 1598d	—	Aššur, iC4V, in the pavement under the prosthesis of temple A, in situ, near the altar, northeast corner of the temple	—	1–6	n
6	—	Ass 1496	—	Aššur, iC4V south, north of the northeast corner of temple A	—	—	n
7	—	Ass 13367	—	Aššur, eB5V, Anu-Adad temple, court pavement of the late Assyrian house	—	—	n
8	—	Ass 3174	—	Aššur, hE4I, court, southeast, pavement, debris	—	1–6?	n
9	—	—	Bab ph 441	Probably Aššur	—	1–6	p
10	—	Ass 3898	—	Aššur, hC4I, under the mud debris of the northern "Adyton"	41×41	—	n

COMMENTARY

The findspot given above for ex. 1 comes from Pedersén, Katalog p. 166 (see also KAH 1 p. X); Andrae, AAT p. 91 states that this brick came from iE5I. Large portions of the inscription on ex. 2 are not really legible on Ass ph 195. The excavation copies ("Fundkopie") of exs. 2–3 in the Vorderasiatisches Museum have been used, but these are of limited help. It is not certain that the six-line text reported to be on ex. 8 is actually a duplicate of this inscription; see Pedersén, Katalog p. 171. Ex. 9 is only known from a Babylon photo. Since some items depicted on Babylon photographs are known to have come from Aššur, it is likely that this piece did as well. It may even be one of exs. 2–8 or 10. Ass 3898 (ex. 10) refers to several fragments of pavement bricks on which are found text nos. 69 and 70.

A brick found in hE3V and depicted on Ass ph 5216 may have this inscription as well; see Gries, Assur-Tempel p. 264 no. 2262 and pl. 61d.

With regard to the use of bricks with this inscription in structures other than the Aššur temple, see the commentary to text no. 69.

The line arrangement for the text is the same for all exemplars and the master line follows ex. 1. No variants to the inscription are known and no score is presented on Oracc.

BIBLIOGRAPHY

1903 Koldewey, MDOG 20 p. 24 (ex. 2, provenance)
1904 Andrae, MDOG 25 pp. 23, 28, and 35 (exs. 1, 2, 5, study, provenance)
1909 Andrae, AAT pp. 91–92, fig. 91, and pl. XXI (ex. 1, photo, copy, edition; ex. 7, study)
1911 Messerschmidt, KAH 1 no. 38 (exs. 1–5, copy)
1915 Bezold, HKA p. 46 (exs. 1–5, edition)
1927 Luckenbill, ARAB 2 pp. 112–113 §§219 and 224 (exs. 1–5, translation)
1997 Pedersén, Katalog pp. 160, 164–166, 171, 175, and 191 (exs. 1–8, 10, study)
2017 Gries, Assur-Tempel p. 251 no. 1922, p. 265 nos. 2277, 2283, and 2290, and p. 267 no. 2321 (exs. 1, 4–6, 8, study)

TEXT

1) AN.ŠÁR ad-da dingir-didli lugal-a-ni-ir
2) LUGAL-*ú-kin* lugal ki-šár-ra lugal ma-da *aš-šur*.KI-ke$_4$
3) GÌR.NÍTA TIN.TIR.KI lugal ki-in-gi uri.KI-bi
4) sig$_4$ al-ùr-ra udun kù-ga ši-ni-du$_8$-du$_8$
5) gìr-gin kisal é-ḫur-sag-gal-kur-kur-ra
6) u$_4$-gin$_7$ ba-an-zálag

1–6) To (the god) Aššur, the father of the gods, his lord: Sargon (II), king of the world, king of Assyria, governor of Babylon, king of the land of Sumer and Akkad, had baked bricks made from a (ritually) pure kiln (and) made the processional way of the courtyard of Eḫursaggalkurkurra ("House, the Great Mountain of the Lands") shine like daylight.

71

A poorly preserved glazed-brick frieze from the temple of the god Aššur at Aššur has some epigraphs on it that are likely to be attributed to Sargon II and to refer to events connected with that ruler's eighth campaign (714).

CATALOGUE

Museum Number	Excavation Number	Provenance	Dimensions (cm)	cpn
VA Ass 2283–2286	—	Aššur, Aššur temple, façade of one of the ramps leading up from the forecourt platform to the platform on which the temple was situated	80×180	n

COMMENTARY

Only a small portion of the frieze has been published and this depicts a mountainous region, with an individual (king?) in a chariot, accompanied by several other soldiers, and a king enthroned. Several pieces are clearly misplaced and W. Andrae thought that the frieze had been patched together in ancient times with pieces from more than one scene (FKA pp. 11–12). According to an inventory book in the Vorderasiatisches Museum, some of the bricks making up the frieze bear the museum numbers VA Ass 2283–2286 (information courtesy J. Marzahn). The edition is based upon Andrae's published drawing.

Following E. Weidner, we can distinguish five groups of signs on the frieze:

1. *ina bi-rit*, "between"
2. *e-tiq*, "I/He traversed"
3. KUR.*ni*-⸢*kip*⸣-*pi*, "Mount Ni[k]ippa"
4. KUR.*ú-pa-a* KU$_6$-*ub*, "Mount Upâ I/He entered"

5.1. KUR.⸢*si*$^{?}$-*mir*⸣-[*ri-a*], "Mount [S]imir[ria]"

5.2. ⸢KUR⸣.*ú-x* [...], "Mount U[...]," or ⸢KUR⸣-*ú x* [...], "mountain [...]"

In group 1, the *rit* sign is presented upside down. Groups 2 and 3 are on bricks in the same row, but separated by the figure of the individual in a chariot. Group 5 is found on one brick in the upper right corner of the frieze, in the same row as group 1; it has parts of two lines of inscription. Also following Weidner, we tentatively divide these five groups into three epigraphs (groups 1, 3, and 4; group 2; and group 5). This assumes that *e-tiq* (group 2) was at the end of an epigraph to the left of the section preserved here.

The ruler to whom the glazed-brick frieze is to be attributed has been a matter of discussion. Andrae and A. Haller assigned it to Tiglath-pileser I, B. Meissner (DLZ 46 [1925] col. 419) and A. Fridman to Tiglath-pileser III, and Weidner, A. Nunn, and P.R.S. Moorey (Materials p. 317) to Sargon II. The relief has been thought to represent Sargon's eighth campaign. See in particular text no. 65 lines 15 (for groups 1, 3, and 4), 16 (for group 2), 18 (for group 5), and 418 (for groups 1, 3, and 4).

Other fragments of inscribed glazed bricks have been found in this temple, but these are poorly preserved and their assignment to Sargon II is far from certain. A few better preserved fragments were found tumbled down in the court of the Aššur temple or walled up in later buildings (especially in temple A). Weidner gives two examples:

A. Ass 1024+1026: [*šu*]-*lum* NUMUN-*šú šá*-⌜*lam*⌝ [URU-*šú*], "[the well]-being of his offspring, the well-being [of his city]." Ass 1024 was found in iE5I (eastern prosthesis, eastern slope) and Ass 1026 in iC5I (southern prosthesis, under the Parthian building); the pieces were assigned to the museum in Istanbul. The first part of the inscription (up to and including the *šá*) is edited from an excavation copy ("Fundkopie") of Ass 1024 in the Vorderasiatisches Museum; the latter part of the inscription is based on Weidner's edition (AfO 3 [1926] p. 5). See Andrae, MDOG 22 (1904) pp. 13–14 and Pedersén, Katalog p. 163.

B. Ass 5268e, g: ⌜*pít-ḫal*?-*lum*⌝, "horseman." The piece was found in iB4III; it is shown on Ass ph 1763 and 1765 and has been collated from Ass ph 1763. See also Pedersén, Katalog p. 179. It cannot be considered absolutely certain that these two fragmentary texts should be assigned to the time of Sargon II, but it has been thought advisable to include them here.

In addition, Ass 16596 (found in iC4III) is a glazed brick fragment which is reported to have a stamped inscription of Sargon II; see Pedersén, Katalog p. 194. Ass 5269e, s, a fragment of a glazed brick found in iB4III, may also bear an inscription of this ruler; see ibid. p. 179.

With regard to the provenance of the frieze, see in particular Haller, Heiligtümer p. 58 fig. 17 no. 12 and pp. 60–61; see also Andrae, MDOG 43 (1910) pp. 34 and 36–38, and 44 (1910) pp. 45–47. With regard to glazed bricks and glazed-brick friezes in general, see Moorey, Materials and Industries pp. 312 and 315–322. For the glazed-brick friezes from Aššur in the Vorderasiatisches Museum in Berlin, see Fügert and Gries in Fügert and Gries, Glazed Brick Decoration pp. 28–47.

BIBLIOGRAPHY

1923 Andrae, FKA pp. 11–12, figs. 4–5, and pl. 6 (photo [inscription not legible], drawing, provenance, study)
1925 Andrae, Coloured Ceramics pp. 21–23, figs. 4–5, and pl. 6 (photo [inscription not legible], drawing, provenance study)
1925 Unger, RLV 3 p. 195 and pl. 41 (drawing, study)
1926 Weidner, AfO 3 pp. 3–6 (edition, study)
1955 Haller, Heiligtümer pp. 55–62, especially pp. 60–61 no. 12 (provenance)
1963 Yadin, Art of Warfare p. 454 (drawing)
1965 W.S. Smith, Interconnections p. 45 and fig. 71 (drawing, study)
1969 Fridman, RA 63 pp. 172–175 (drawing [Andrae], study)
1980 Mayer, MDOG 112 pp. 21–22 and fig. 2 (drawing, study)
1988 Nunn, Wandmalerei pp. 180–182 and pl. 144 (drawing, study)
1993 Wartke, Urartu pl. 57 (drawing])
1995 Reade in Caubet, Khorsabad p. 248 fig. 11 (drawing)
2013 Mayer, Assyrien und Urarṭu I p. 63 fig. 1 (drawing; epigraph 2, translation)
2014 MacGinnis, Erbil p. 58 (drawing)
2014 Maniori, Campagne di Sargon p. 63 D12–D13 and passim (study)
2017 Gries, Assur-Tempel pp. 105–108 and pls. 210–211 (drawing, edition, study)
2020 Fügert and Gries in Fügert and Gries, Glazed Brick Decoration p. 37 figs. 9–10, p. 40 Fig. 12, and p. 42 Fig. 14 (drawing; epigraphs 1–2, photo)

TEXT

Epigraph 1

1) [...] *e-tiq*

Epigraph 2

1) *ina bi-rit* KUR.*ni*-⌜*kip*⌝-*pi* KUR.*ú-pa-a* KU_4-*ub*

Epigraph 3

1) KUR.⌜*si*?-*mir*⌝-[*ri-a* (...)] ⌜KUR⌝-*ú x* [...]

Epigraph 1

Epigraph 1 1) I/He traversed [...].

Epigraph 2

Epigraph 2 1) I/He entered (the region) between Mount Ni[k]ippa (and) Mount Upâ.

Epigraph 3

Epigraph 3 1) Mount [S]*imir*[*ria* (...)] mountain [...].

72

A fragment of part of the right side of a clay tablet in the Vorderasiatisches Museum (VAT 10716) preserves part of an inscription of Sargon II that appears to refer to Kibaba (city ruler of Ḫarḫar) and Daltâ (king of Ellipi), thus likely to the Assyrian campaign into Iran during Sargon's sixth regnal year (716). The piece has several so-called "firing holes" in it. It is not certain which side is the obverse and which the reverse. Side A has been collated, but the edition basically follows that published by E. Frahm. The inscription on side B is almost completely worn away and the transliteration of it is based solely on the published copy.

CATALOGUE

Museum Number	Excavation Number	Provenance	Dimensions (cm)	cpn
VAT 10716	—	Aššur	6.9×9.6	(c)

BIBLIOGRAPHY

2009 Frahm, KAL 3 no. 31 (copy, edition, study)

TEXT

Side A

Lacuna
1′) [...] *x* (*x*) *x* [*x*]
2′) [...] *x x*
3′) [...] ⸢*am*⸣-*šú-uḫ*
4′) [...]-*su-nu*
5′) [... *i*$^{?}$]-⸢*na*$^{?}$⸣ É ^{d}AMAR.UTU *é-kur-ri-šú-nu a-na da-ra-ti*
6′) [*ul-ziz*$^{?}$ ...] ⸢^{m}*ki*⸣-*ba-ba ša* URU.*ḫar*-⸢*ḫar*⸣
7′) [... ANŠE.KUR].⸢RA$^{?}$⸣.MEŠ ANŠE.*pa-re-e am*-⸢*ḫur*⸣

8′) [... URU$^{?}$.*ḫar*$^{?}$]-⸢*ḫar*⸣ *ú-zu-un-šú-un*
9′) [... ^{m}*da*]-⸢*al*⸣-*ta-a ú-rab-bu-ú e-li-šú*-⸢*un*⸣
10′) [...] *x* ŠÀ-*šú*$^{?}$-⸢*un*$^{?}$⸣

Side A

Lacuna
A 1′–2′) Not sufficiently preserved to allow translation.
A 3′) [...] I measured
A 4′) [...] *them*
A 5′) [... *i*]*n* the temple of Marduk, their temple, for all time
A 6′–7′) [*I erected ... from* (...) K]ibaba of the city Ḫarḫa[r ...] I receiv[ed ... *hors*]*es* (and) mules.

A 8′–9′) [... *the city Ḫarḫ*]*ar* their understanding [...] they elevated [Da]ltâ over the[m].
A 10′) [...] *their* heart

A 4′–6′a Following Frahm, KAL 3 pp. 71 and 73, and based (loosely) on text no. 1 line 95, text no. 7 line 63, text no. 82 iii 17′–21′, and text no. 117 ii 70–71, possibly restore: [(...) *ṣa-lam* LUGAL-*ti-ia* DÙ-*uš-ma ep-še-et* NÍG.È AN.ŠÁR EN-*ia ša* UGU ^{m}*ul-lu*]-*su-nu* / [KUR.*man-na-a-a ... e-te-ep-pu-šu* UGU-*šú áš-ṭur-ma i*]-⸢*na*⸣ É ^{d}AMAR.UTU *é-kur-ri-šú-nu a-na da-ra-ti* / [*ul-ziz* ...], "[(...) I made a royal image of myself and wrote upon it the victorious deeds of Aššur, my lord, that I continually carried out against Ullu]sunu, [the Mannean, ...; I erected (it)] (to stand) forever [i]n the temple of Marduk, their temple [...]."
A 6′b–7′ Cf. text no. 82 iii 22′–25′.
A 8′–9′ Following Frahm, KAL 3 pp. 71 and 74, and partially based upon text no. 1 lines 96–97, possibly restore: [... UN.MEŠ *a-ši-bu-ut* URU.*ḫar*]-⸢*ḫar*⸣ *ú-zu-un-šú-un* / [*ul ib-ši-ma* (...) ^{m}*ki-ba-ba* EN URU-*šú-nu ir-du-du-ma* (...) ^{m}*da*]-⸢*al*⸣-*ta-a ú-rab-bu-ú e-li-šú*-⸢*un*⸣, "[... the people who live in the city Ḫarḫ]ar [possessed no] understanding [... they chased (away) Kibaba, their city lord, and (...)] elevated [Da]ltâ over the[m]."
A 10′–11′ E. Frahm (KAL 3 p. 74) compares this passage to one of Sennacherib's describing the siege of Jerusalem and suggests that it might refer to the inhabitants of Ḫarḫar becoming afraid because of the possible consequences of their anti-Assyrian actions (line 10′; cf. for example *ip-làḫ lìb-ba-šú-un*, Grayson and Novotny, RINAP 3/1 p. 64 no. 4 line 43) and acquiring military aid to oppose an Assyrian attack (line 11′; cf. for example *ir-šu-u til-la-a-te*, Grayson and Novotny, RINAP 3/1 p. 66 no. 4 line 55).

11′) [... ir?]-⸢šu?⸣-ú til-la-a-⸢ti?⸣
12′) [...] x RI BIT SU x [(x)]
13′) [...] x qi-šá-a-[ti?]
14′) [...] ú-mal-[x (x)]
15′) [...]-ia a-tu-[ram?-ma?]
16′) [... ú?]-⸢ṣab⸣-bi-su ak-[x (x)]
17′) [... URU?.kar?-^{m}]⸢LUGAL?⸣-GI.NA x [x x (x x)]
18′) [...] ⸢e⸣-pu-uš-⸢ma?⸣ [x x x]
19′) [...] x [x x x x]
Lacuna

Side B

Lacuna
1′) [...] x [x x x (x)]
2′) [...] x [x] ⸢MEŠ?⸣ [(x)] x [(x)]
3′) [...] x (x) x [x]
4′) [...] ⸢AN?⸣ KAL [x]
5′) [...] ⸢GA? ŠÁ?⸣ [x (x)]
6′) [...] x ⸢PA?⸣ NA x [x (x)]
7′) [...] x [(x)] x
8′) [...] ⸢ú-ter⸣
9′) [...] x x x x x
10′) [...] x x [(x)] x
11′) [...] A [(x)] NA x
12′) [...] x (x) x
13′) [...]
14′) [...]
15′) [...] ⸢KI?⸣ [(x)]
16′) [...] TI [(x)]
17′) [...] x [(x)]
Lacuna

A 11′) [... *they obta*]*ined* reinforcements
A 12′) [...] ...
A 13′) [...] gift[s]
A 14′) [...] *fil*[*led*]
A 15′–19′) [...] my [...] *I ret*[*urned and* ...] *seized it* [... *the city Kār-Šarr*]*ukīn* [...] I built *a*[*nd* ...]
Lacuna

Side B

Lacuna
B 1′–17′) Not sufficiently preserved to allow translation.
Lacuna

73

This text from Kalḫu (modern Nimrud) is generally referred to as the Nimrud Inscription or the Juniper Palace Inscription. It describes Sargon's restoration of the "juniper palace" at Kalḫu, which had originally been built by Ashurnasirpal II (883–859 BC), and his storing in it of gold and silver that had been taken as booty from Pisīri(s), king of Carchemish. It is found on two stone slabs from the North-West Palace. The text includes references to events down to at least the king's fifth regnal year (717) in view of the mention of the conquest of the city of Carchemish in line 10 (see also lines

---

72 line A 12′ As suggested by E. Frahm (KAL 3 p. 74), possibly [...] ⸢uš⸣-tal-pit-su x [(x)], "[...] I destroyed it ..." or [...] x re-bit-su x [(x)], "[...] his/its plaza ..." The end of the line may simply be -su-⸢un⸣, "them/their."
72 line A 14′ Likely a D-stem of the verb *malû*.
72 line A 15′–16′ Following Frahm, KAL 3 pp. 71–72 and 74, possibly restore: [... i-na me-tiq ger-ri]-ia a-tu-[ram-ma] / [a-na URU.ḫar-ḫar (...) URU šu-a-tu ú]-ṣab-bi-su ak-[šud (x x)], "[... in the course of] my [campaign] I ret[urned to Ḫarḫar (...)], seized [that city], (and) co[nquered (it) ...]."
72 line A 17′ Following Frahm, KAL 3 pp. 72 and 74, and based on text no. 1 line 100 and text no. 7 line 63, possibly read: [... URU.kar-^{m}]⸢LUGAL⸣-GI.NA ⸢šu⸣-[um-šú ab-bi/az-kur], "[... I (re)named (it) Kār-Šarr]ukīn," although the writing šu-um-šú here rather than MU-šú would be unusual in Sargon's royal inscriptions.
72 line A 18′ Following Frahm, KAL 3 pp. 72 and 74, and based on text no. 82 iii 2′′ (also largely restored), possibly read: [... É.KUR šu-bat DINGIR.MEŠ GAL.MEŠ eš-šiš] ⸢e⸣-pu-uš-⸢ma⸣ [x x x], "[...] I built [anew the temple, the abode of the great gods, ...]." Cf. also text no. 117 ii 44.

21–22) that took place in that year and thus N. Na᾿aman has argued that the text was composed in late 717 or early 716 (SAAB 8 [1994] pp. 17–20). For the archaeological context of the inscription, see J.M. Russell, Writing on the Wall p. 99.

CATALOGUE

Ex.	Museum Number	Registration Number	Provenance	Dimensions (cm)	Lines Preserved	cpn
1	BM 118923	48-11-4,24	Nimrud, North-West Palace, Room U, Entrance	56×188	1–22	c
2	—	—	As ex. 1	—	1–22	(c)

COMMENTARY

A.H. Layard states that these two gypsum slabs, which bear no sculpted relief, were placed on the palace wall above the standard inscription of Ashurnasirpal II (see ICC pl. 33 and Nineveh 1 p. 389). They may have been placed at the entry to the room in which the booty from Sargon's conquest of Carchemish was stored.

The master line is based on ex. 1, although in a few places a sign on that exemplar is partially damaged/unclear and fully preserved/clear on ex. 2; in these cases, the sign is indicated without any indication of damage in the master line. A squeeze of ex. 2 is preserved in the British Museum and that exemplar was collated by means of an examination of the squeeze. The copy of the inscription published by Layard follows sometimes one exemplar and sometimes the other exemplar, with the divergent reading being cited as a variant; this is contrary to Layard's indication that all his variants were found on one particular exemplar. (According to J.M. Russell, the original Layard hand copy is MS A, pp. 124–126.) Layard made his copies in the early days of the decipherment of cuneiform and a number of signs indicated on his copy as being abnormal or incorrect are in fact correct sign forms (e.g., AK not ENGUR in line 1 and ZI not GI in line 2). H. Winckler's copy was made from Layard's and thus has no independent value; no reference is generally made to divergences between it and Layard's copy below.

BIBLIOGRAPHY

—	Layard MS A pp. 124–126 (copy)
1849	Layard, Nineveh 1 p. 389 (provenance)
1851	Layard, ICC pls. 33–34 nos. 1–2 (copy, with variants)
1862	Oppert, Annales de Philosophie chrétienne 65 p. 45 no. 10 and pp. 182–183 (translation)
1862	Oppert, Sargonides pp. 3 no. 10 and 34–35 (translation) [identical to the preceding]
1874	Ménant, Annales pp. 204–206 (translation)
1886	Bezold, Literatur p. 91 §53.8 (exs. 1–2, study)
1886	Lyon, Manual pp. 9–10 and 68–69 (transliteration, study)
1889	Winckler, Sar. 1 pp. vi and 168–173; and 2 pl. 48 (copy, edition)
1890	Peiser in Schrader, KB 2 pp. 34–39 (edition)
1909	Winckler, Textbuch^3 p. 37 (lines 7–8, edition)
1911	Sarsowsky, Urkundenbuch p. 27 (lines 7–8, copy)
1911	Weissbach, ZDMG 65 p. 634 (lines 21–22, study)
1916	Weissbach, ZDMG 70 p. 70 n. 2 (line 21, study)
1926	Ebeling in Gressmann, ATAT^2 p. 350 (lines 7–8, translation)
1927	Luckenbill, ARAB 2 pp. 71–73 §§136–138 (translation)
1958	Wiseman, DOTT p. 62 (lines 1, 8, translation)
1969	Oppenheim, ANET^3 p. 287 (line 8, translation)
1977	Briend and Seux, TPOA no. 37 (lines 1, 7b–9, translation)
1984	Borger, TUAT 1/4 p. 387 (line 8, translation)
1986	Renger, CRRA 32 pp. 112–113 (lines 1–2, partial transcription, study)
1994	Fuchs, Khorsabad p. 386 (study)
1994	Na'aman, SAAB 8 pp. 17–20 (lines 7–12, study)
1999	J.M. Russell, Writing on the Wall p. 99 (study)
2000	Younger in Hallo, COS 2 pp. 298–299 no. 2.118I (lines 7–12, translation)
2001	J. and D. Oates, Nimrud pp. 56–57 (lines 13–22, partial translation, study)
2008	Cogan, Raging Torrent pp. 100–103 no. 24 (lines 7–12, translation, study)
2018	Frahm, Last Days pp. 66–68 no. 5 (lines 7–8, edition, study)
2019	Marchesi, JNES 78 pp. 21 and 24 (lines 10b, 21–22, edition)

TEXT

1) É.GAL ^{m}LUGAL-GI.NA *šá-ak-nu* ^{d}EN.LÍL NU.ÈŠ ^{d}*a-šur ni-šit* IGI.II ^{d}*a-nim ù* ^{d}EN.LÍL MAN *dan-nu* MAN KIŠ MAN KUR *aš-šur*.KI MAN *kib-rat* LÍMMU-*i mi-gir* DINGIR.MEŠ GAL.MEŠ
2) SIPA *ke-e-nu šá* ^{d}*a-šur* ^{d}AMAR.UTU *ut-tu-šu-ma zi-kir šu-mi-šú ú-še-ṣu-u a-na re-še-e-te*

1–2) Palace of Sargon (II) appointee of the god Enlil, *nešakku*-priest of the god Aššur, chosen of the gods Anu and Enlil, strong king, king of the world, king of Assyria, king of the four quarters (of the world), favorite of the great gods, just shepherd, whom the gods Aššur (and) Marduk choose and whose fame (these gods) exalted to the heights;

3) *zi-ka-ru dan-nu ḫa-lip na-mur-ra-te ša a-na šum-qut na-ki-ri šu-ut-bu-u kak-ku-šu*
4) *eṭ-lu qar-du šá ul-tu* u_4*-um be-lu-ti-šú mal-ku* GABA.RI-*šú la ib-šu-ma mu-né-ḫa šá-ni-na la i-šu-ú*
5) KUR.KUR DÙ-*ši-na* TA *ṣi-it* ^{d}UTU-*ši a-di e-reb* ^{d}UTU-*ši i-be-lu-ma ul-taš-pi-ru ba-ʾu-lat* ^{d}EN.LÍL
6) *mu-ʾa-a-ru* BU.BU.LU *ša e-mu-qa-an ṣi-ra-a-te* ^{d}*nu-dím-mud iš-ru-ku-uš* GIŠ.TUKUL *la maḫ-ri uš-ṭib-bu i-du-uš-šú*

3–6) the strong man who is clad in awesome splendor (and) whose weapons(s) are raised to strike down (his) enemies; the valiant man who since the (first) day of his reign has had no ruler who could equal him and no one who could overpower (or) rival (him); (who) ruled all the lands from the east to the west (lit.: "from the rising of the sun to the setting of the sun") and governed the subjects of the god Enlil; experienced hero, to whom the god Nudimmud (Ea) granted superior strength (and) at whose side (the god) made (his) irresistible weapon beautiful;

7) NUN *na-aʾ-du ša ina re-bit* BÀD.AN.KI *it-ti* ^{md}*ḫum-ba-ni-ga-áš* LUGAL KUR.*e-lam-ti in-nam-ru-ma iš-ku-nu taḫ-ta-šú*
8) *mu-šak-niš* KUR.*ia-ú-du šá a-šar-šú ru-ú-qu na-si-iḫ* KUR.*ḫa-am-ma-te ša* ^{md}*ia-ú-bi-iʾ-di ma-lik-šú-nu ik-šu-du* ŠU.II-*šú*
9) *mu-né-eʾ i-rat* KUR.*ka-ak-mé-e* LÚ.KÚR *lem-ni mu-ta-qi-in* KUR.*man-na-a-a dal-ḫu-ú-te mu-ṭib lib-bi* KUR-*šú mu-rap-piš mi-ṣir* KUR *aš-šur*

7–9) the pious prince who met Ḫumbanigaš (Ḫumban-nikaš I), king of the land Elam, (in battle) on the *outskirts* of (the city) Dēr (and) brought about his defeat; who subjugated the land Judah, whose location is far away; who deported (the people of) the land Hamath (and) who personally captured Iaū-biʾdī (Ilu-biʾdī) their ruler; who repulsed the land Kakmê, the evil enemy; who brought order to the disturbed Manneans; who made the heart of his land happy (and) expanded the territory of Assyria;

10) *mal-ku pit-qu-du šu-uš-kal la-a ma-gi-ri ša* ^{m}*pi-si-ri* LUGAL KUR.*ḫat-ti* ŠU-*su ik-šu-du-ma* UGU URU.*gar-ga-miš* URU-*šú iš-ku-nu* LÚ.UŠ-*šú*
11) *na-si-iḫ* URU.*ši-nu-uḫ-ti ša* ^{m}*ki-ak-ki* LUGAL KUR.*ta-ba-li a-na* URU-*šú aš-šur*.KI *ub-lam-ma* KUR.*mu-us-ki e-mid-du ab-šá-an-šú*
12) *ka-šid* KUR.*man-na-a-a* KUR.*kar-al-lu ù* KUR.*pad-di-ri mu-ter gi-mil-li* KUR-*šú mu-šem-qít* KUR.*ma-da-a-a ru-qu-ú-te a-di* KUR ^{d}UTU-*ši*

10–12) the prudent ruler, snare of the uncompliant, who personally captured Pisīri(s), king of the land Ḫatti (Syria), and set his (own) official over the city Carchemish, his (Pīsīris') city; who deported (the people of) the city Šinuḫtu; who brought Kiakki, king of the land Tabal, to his city Aššur and imposed his yoke upon the land Musku; who conquered the lands Mannea, Karalla, and Paddiri; who avenged his land; who overthrew the distant Medes as far as the rising of the sun.

13) *i-na* u_4*-mi-šu-ma* É.GAL GIŠ.*dup-ra-ni ša* URU.*kal-ḫa ša* ^{m}*aš-šur*-ÙRU-IBILA NUN *a-lik pa-ni-ia i-na pa-na e-pu-šu*
14) *ša* É *šu-a-tu uš-šu-šú ul dun-nu-nu-ú-ma* UGU *du-un-ni qaq-qa-ri ki-ṣir* KUR-*i ul šur-šu-da iš-da-a-šú*
15) *i-na ra-a-di ti-ik* AN-*e an-ḫu-ta la-bi-ru-ta il-lik-ma še-pit-su ip-pa-ṭir-ma ir-mu-ú rik-su-šú*
16) *a-šar-šú ú-ma-si-ma dan-na-su ak-šu-ud* UGU NA_4.*pi-i-li dan-ni tem-mé-en-šú ki-ma ši-pik*

13–18) At that time, (with regard to) the juniper palace in the city Kalḫu that Ashurnasirpal (II), a prince who preceded me had previously built, the foundations of this house had not been made strong and its foundations had not been secured upon firm ground, (on) bedrock. (15) It had become old (and) dilapidated (lit.: "dilapidated (and) old") due to downpours of rain; its footing had dissolved and its bondings given way. I identified its (former) location and reached the bottom of its foundation pit. I

---

6 For the reading BU.BU.LU (*šiteʾû*), see CAD Š/2 p. 355 and CAD M/2 p. 157. The reading *uš-ṭib-bu* follows Borger, BiOr 32 (1975) p. 71 sub S. 53b; CAD Š/1 p. 230 reads *iš-lu-pu* (from *šalāpu*, "to draw from a sheath, to tear out, to pull out, to extricate, rescue"), but the exemplars have a clear UŠ, not IŠ.

8 For a possible campaign of Sargon against Judah ca. 720, see Sweeney, Biblica 75 (1994) pp. 457–470 and Younger, Biblica 77 (1996) pp. 108–110; cf. Hallo in Levine, Jerusalem pp. 36–37.

KUR-*i zaq-ri áš-pu-uk*
17) TA *uš-še-šú a-di gaba-dib-bi-šú ar-ṣip ú-šak-lil* KÁ *zi-i-qi a-na mul-ta-ʾu-ti-ia ina* 2.30 KÁ-*šú ap-ti*
18) *ka-šad* URU.MEŠ-*ni* NÍG.È GIŠ.TUKUL.MEŠ-*ia ša* UGU LÚ.KÚR.MEŠ *áš-ku-nu ina qé-reb-šú e-ṣir-ma a-na bit-re-e lu-le-e ú-mal-li-šú*
19) ^{d}ÙRI.GAL ^{d}IŠKUR *ù* DINGIR.MEŠ *a-ši-bu-ut* URU.*kal-ḫa a-na lìb-bi aq-re-ma* GU$_4$.MAḪ-*ḫi* GAL.MEŠ UDU.NÍTA.MEŠ *ma-ru-ti* KUR.GI.MUŠEN.MEŠ UZ.TUR.MUŠEN.MEŠ
20) MUŠEN.MEŠ AN-*e mut-tap-riš-ú-te ma-ḫar-šu-un aq-qi ni-gu-tú áš-kun-ma ka-bat-ti* UN.MEŠ KUR *aš-šur*.KI *ú-šá-li-iṣ*
21) *i-na u$_4$-me-šu-ma i-na* É *na-kam-te šu-a-ti* 11 GUN 30 MA.NA KÙ.GI 2 LIM 1 ME GUN 24 MA.NA KÙ.BABBAR *ina* GAL-*ti*
22) *ki-šit-ti* ^{m}*pi-si-ri* LUGAL URU.*gar-ga-miš ša* KUR.*ḫat-ti*.KI *ša* GÚ ÍD.*pu-rat-ti ša qa-ti ik-šu-du ina lìb-bi ú-še-rib*

piled up its foundation terrace upon heavy limestone blocks like the base of a high mountain. I completely (re)constructed (it) from its foundations to its crenellations. I opened up an air passage to the left of its door for my pleasure. I depicted inside it (the palace) the conquest of cities, the triumph of my weapons, that I had achieved over the enemy, and I filled it with abundance for the inspection (of the people).

19–20) I invited the god Urigal (Nergal), the god Adad, and the gods who dwell in the city Kalḫu (to come) inside (it) and I offered before them large prize bulls, fattened sheep, geese, ducks, (and) birds that fly in the sky (lit.: "flying birds of the sky"). I held a festival and (thus) made the hearts of the people of Assyria rejoice.

21–22) At that time, I brought into this treasure house 11 talents (and) 30 minas of gold (and) 2,100 talents (and) 24 minas of silver, (measured) by the large (weight), booty (taken) from Pisīri(s), king of the city Carchemish, of the land Ḫatti (Syria), (situated) on the bank on the Euphrates River, that I personally had conquered.

74

A fragmentary inscription of Sargon II is found on pieces of two clay prisms discovered during British excavations at Nimrud. The inscription commemorates the construction of Dūr-Šarrukīn and records various military actions carried out during Sargon's reign. These military actions are not recorded in chronological order. The inscription was probably composed in the king's sixteenth regnal year (706) since it refers to Sargon's fourth year as ruler of Babylonia (vii 19), which would have been 706; see van der Spek, JEOL 25 (1977–78) pp. 65–66 and Naʾaman, NABU 2000 p. 1 no. 1. This text is usually referred to as the Nimrud Prism and C.J. Gadd refers to the two exemplars of the text as prisms D and E (Iraq 16 [1954] p. 175).

CATALOGUE

Ex.	Museum Number	Excavation Number	Provenance	Lines Preserved	Gadd prism	cpn
1	IM 67661	ND 2601 + ND 3401 + ND 3403 + ND 3417	ND 2601: Nimrud, ZT, Room 10; ND 3401, 3403 and 3417: Nimrud, ZT, on pavement of the east corridor	i 4–12, 18–32, ii 1–13, iii 1–14, 36–48, iv 1–58, v 17–76, vi 14–76, vii 7–69, viii 1′–33′	D	(c)
2	IM 67662	ND 3400 + ND 3402 + ND 3408 + ND 3409 + ND 3404	Nimrud, ZT, on pavement of the east corridor	ii 1′–20′, iii 42–57, iv 32–53, v 13–43, vi 13–86, vii 29–85, viii 1′′′–25′′′	E	(c)

COMMENTARY

The fragments were found during British excavations at Nimrud in 1952 and 1953. For a plan showing the provenances of the pieces, see Mallowan, Iraq 16 (1954) pl. XIV. It has been possible to collate only two pieces of the inscription: ND 3403 (ex. 1, iii 1–14 and iv 1–8) and ND 3408 (ex. 2, ii 1′–20′, iii 42–57, and iv 32–53); the remaining pieces could not be located in the Iraq Museum in 1982 and 1998 when the author was working there. Thus, most of the inscription is edited from the published copies, although some use has been made of the photograph of part of ex. 1 published by C.J. Gadd in Iraq 16 (1954) pl. XLIII. Unfortunately, the published copy is mostly a composite of exs. 1 and 2 and it is generally not possible to be certain exactly what is on each exemplar. Lines for which only a composite copy of exs. 1 and 2 exists are iii 42–48, iv 32–53, v 17–42, vi 14–76, and vi 29–69; of these, it has been possible to collate ex. 2 (ND 3408) for iii 42–48 and iv 32–53. Thus, no score for the inscription can be presented on Oracc. Instead, a transliteration of ND 3408 (part of ex. 2) is presented there. It seems that when making his composite copy, Gadd relied mostly on ex. 1. In order to facilitate the use of older scholarship, the line numbering follows that used by Gadd.

Gadd presumably designated the two prisms D and E in order to follow on after fragmentary prisms A and B, which come from Nineveh and are now thought to be parts of the same prism (see text no. 82), and prism C, which also comes from Nineveh (text no. 83).

ND 3404 (Gadd, Iraq 16 [1954] pp. 174-175), found on the pavement of the east corridor of building ZT at Nimrud, is reported to have a totally illegible inscription (parts of two columns of 12–13 lines each) and to measure 4.9×4.5×1.2 cm. Gadd stated that it did not join any of the other Nimrud prism fragments, but according to J. Renger (private communication), A. Cavigneaux has joined it to ex. 2. Nothing is known about what is on the fragment.

For ND 3406, which may well preserve part of col. viii of this inscription and either have been originally part of one these two exemplars or have been part of a third exemplar of this inscription, see text no. 75.

Gadd (Iraq 16 [1954] p. 188) notes the close similarities between this inscription and 81-7-27,3 (text no. 83), a fragment of a prism in the Kuyunjik collection of the British Museum, and suggests that they may be duplicates. Since it is clear that the two are not exact duplicates ca. vii 7–11 and text no. 83 iii′ 1-5, they have been kept separate here.

Col. i: This is found only on ex. 1; the restorations in i 1–13 are based upon text no. 7 lines 1–7 and text no. 8 lines 1–3.

Col. ii: Lines 1–13 are found on ex. 1 and 1′–20′ are found on ex. 2. The edition follows Gadd in assuming that no lines are missing at the beginning of the column and that ex. 2 follows ex. 1. According to Gadd, although "measuring from the preserved top of both prisms, they overlap physically," in view of the content "it seems clear ... that the E fragment [ex. 2] follows the D [ex. 1]" (Iraq 16 [1954] p. 176). The size of the gap between exs. 1 and 2 is not clear.

Col. iii: Lines 1–41 describe Sargon's famous eighth campaign (714) to the land of Urarṭu; for the places mentioned in lines 1 and 12, see for example text no. 1 lines 137 and 139 and text no. 65 lines 168 and 189.

Col. iv: Most of our information on what was in col. iv comes from ex. 1. Only a little of iv 32–53 is found on ex. 2 ("the ends of a certain number of lines," Gadd, Iraq 16 [1954] p. 180). The beginning of the column, iv 1–12, is the end of an account describing an Assyrian victory over Mutallu of Kummuḫu while Sargon was in Babylonia; cf. text no. 2 lines 451–454 and text no. 7 lines 112–117 (particularly 115–117). For iv 13–24, see in particular text no. 1 lines 72–75. The rebellion and defeat of Samaria, which is related in Sargon's accession year in the Khorsabad Annals, is treated in iv 25–49, although the passage here may be a conflation of incidents in the king's accession year and second regnal year (722 and 720); see Gadd, Iraq 16 (1954) p. 181.

Col. v: Gadd states that there are about five lines missing at the beginning of the column in ex. 1 and about twelve in ex. 2 (Iraq 16 [1954] pl. XLVII). He notes that ex. 2 actually has "little of this column, for only a part of the right side of it remains" (ibid. p. 184). With regard to v 13–33, cf. in particular text no. 1 lines 196–204a and text no. 7 lines 30–32. With regard to v 34–40, see text no. 1 lines 125b–126. For v 41–76, cf. text no. 1 lines 204b–216a and text no. 7 lines 78–82.

Col. vi: Gadd states that there are about five lines missing at the beginning of this column in ex. 1 and about twelve in ex. 2 (Iraq 16 [1954] pl. XLVII). He notes that col. vi is the best preserved part of ex. 1 while only the extreme right ends of many of the lines in the lower half of ex. 2 are preserved. He also notes that "Distribution of the matter between lines varies slightly in the two copies, but there are no significant differences" (ibid. p. 187). Gadd (ibid. p. 188) notes that if the prism records matters in the same order as the prism fragment 81-7-27,3 (text no. 83), the first part of the column would have described "the wars against the kings of Ashdod and Meluḫḫa" (i.e., the episode of the rebel Iāmānī of Ashdod who fled to Egypt but was later delivered up to Sargon by the Kushite ruler). For vi 14–80, see in particular text no. 7 lines 121–37, text no. 86 lines 1′–16′, and text no. 113 lines 6′–23′.

Col. vii: According to Gadd (Iraq 16 [1954] pp. 191 and 193), there are about six lines missing at the top of col. vii of ex. 1 and that exemplar has only the first halves of the lines preserved. Gadd notes that ex. 2 begins at line 29, but is neither well-preserved nor clear until ND 3408+3402 joins the exemplar (beginning at line 50). For vii 7–38, see in particular text no. 7 lines 141–49, text no. 83 iii′ 1–13, and text no. 103 iv 8–42.

Col. viii: Gadd (Iraq 16 [1954] p. 197) notes that although the remains of col. viii in exs. 1 and 2 "overlap when the prisms are set side by side it is not possible to discern any connexion between their texts." Gadd does not indicate the number (if any) of lines likely to be missing at the beginning of the prism on ex. 1, but states that ex. 2 comes from near the bottom of the column on that exemplar. Thus, ex. 1 is presented first in the edition (viii 1′–33′) and ex. 2 second (viii 1′′–25′′). The edition indicates that there may be a lacuna between the two sections, but no gap may exist and the two may actually overlap. For a further prism fragment that may well have been part of column viii (ND 3406), see text no. 75.

Since the inscription does not record the events of Sargon's reign in chronological order, the following chart lists the major events recorded in the body of this inscription together with the dates for them (mostly based upon statements in the Khorsabad Annals [text nos. 1–6]).

CONTENTS OF TEXT NO. 74

Text no. 74	Topic	Date
i 1–13+	Introduction	—
i (+)23–28(+)	Work on/for Eḫ[ursaggalkurkurra?]	—
ii 1–13, 1′–20′	Mannea	6th *palû* (716)
iii 1–41	Mannea, Urarṭu, Muṣaṣir	8th *palû* (714)
iii 42–56	Ellipi, Media	9th *palû* (713)
iv 1–12	Kummuḫu	14th *palû* (708)
iv 13–24	Carchemish	5th *palû* (717)
iv 25–41	Samaria	*rēš šarrūti* (722)
iv 42–49	Opening of Egyptian harbor district	*rēš šarrūti* (722)
iv 50–58	Šinuḫtu	4th *palû* (718)
v 13–33	Tabal, Bīt-Purutaš	9th *palû* (713)
v 34–40	Que (Cilicia)	7th *palû* (715)
v 41–76	Melid, Kammanu	10th *palû* (712)
	Gurgum, Marqasa	11th *palû* (711)
vi 14–85	Babylonia	12th and 13th *palûs* (710–709)
vii 7–19	Babylonia	13th–16th *palûs* (709–707?)
vii 20–24a	Dilmun (Aḫundara)	(16th *palû*?) (706?)
vii 24b–44	Yadnana (Cyprus)	(14th *palû*?) (708?)
viii 1′–33′	Uncertain	—
viii 1′′–9′′	Dūr-Šarrukīn	—
viii 10′′–25′′	Uncertain	—

BIBLIOGRAPHY

1953 Wiseman, Iraq 15 pp. 138–139 (provenance)
1954 Gadd, Iraq 16 pp. 173–201 and pls. XLIII–L (ex. 1, photo; exs. 1–2, composite copy, edition)
1956 Borger, Asarh. pp. 52–53 commentary to line 74 (iii 40, study)
1957–58 Borger, AfO 18 p. 116 sub §27 (iii 40, study)
1958 Tadmor, JCS 12 p. 34 (iv 25–49, edition)
1958 Wiseman, DOTT p. 60 (iv 25–41, translation)
1964 Brinkman, Studies Oppenheim p. 44 no. 44.2.20.c.ii (study)
1968 Borger in Galling, Textbuch[2] pp. 60–61 no. 30 (iv 25–49, translation)
1976 Saporetti, Studi Ciprioti e Rapporti di Scavo 2 pp. 84–85 (vii 24b–44, translation, study)
1977 Briend and Seux, TPOA no. 36 (iv 25–41, translation, study)

1979 Elayi and Cavigneaux, OrAnt 18 p. 64 (vii 42–44, edition)
1981 Zaccagnini in Fales, ARIN pp. 276–282 (vii 45–76, translation, study)
1982 Ephʿal, Arabs pp. 38–39 (iv 25–49, study)
1982 Spieckermann, Juda unter Assur pp. 349–350 (iv 25–33a, edition)
1984 Borger, TUAT 1/4 p. 382 (iv 25–49, translation)
1984 Brinkman, Prelude p. 53 n. 248 (vii 46, study)
1985 Dalley, Iraq 47 p. 36 (iv 25–39a, translation, study)
1986 Renger, CRRA 32 pp. 114–18 (iv 13–24, 50–58, v 20–33, 41–76, transcription)
1988 Cogan and Tadmor, II Kings p. 336 no. 6A (iv 25–41, translation)
1990 Na'aman, Biblica 71 pp. 209–210 (iv 25–30, translation, study)
1990 Potts, Arabian Gulf 1 p. 335 no. 8 (vii 20–24a, translation, study)
1991 Hayes and Kuan, Biblica 72 pp. 171–175 (iv 25–28, edition, study)
1992 Becking, Fall of Samaria pp. 28–31 (iv 25–41, edition, study)
1994 Cole, JNES 53 p. 88 (vii 45–68, translation)
1994 Fuchs, Khorsabad p. 387 (study)
1995 Brinkman in Liverani, Neo-Assyrian Geography pp. 26–27 (vii 45–68, translation)
1995 Galil, CBQ 57 pp. 54–55 (iv 25–28, edition)
1995 Malbran-Labat in Caubet, Khorsabad pp. 171–172 and 178 n. 20 (vii 39–44, edition; study [erroneously cited as ND 3411])
1998 Fuchs, SAAS 8 p. 5 (i 24–28, edition)
1998 Na'aman, Orientalia NS 67 pp. 239–240 (vii 24b–44, translation)
1998 Uehlinger, Studies Loretz pp. 742–743 (iv 25–41, translation, study)
1998 Younger, JBL 117 pp. 216–217 (iv 25–41, edition)
1999 Younger, CBQ 61 pp. 469–473 (iv 25–41, edition, study)
2000 Bagg, Assyrische Wasserbauten pp. 143, 162, and 327–328 nos. 27–28 (vi 32–44, vii 57–72, edition)
2000 Na'aman, NABU 2000 p. 1 no. 1 (iii 55–56, iv 21, 31, 33, study)
2000 Younger, COS 2 pp. 295–296 no. 2.118D (iv 25–49, translation)
2001 Na'aman, CRRA 45/1 p. 358 (vii 24–38, study)
2002 Younger in Chavalas and Younger, Mesopotamia and the Bible pp. 291 and 301 (iv 25–41, translation)
2008 Cogan, Raging Torrent pp. 89–93 no. 19 (iv 25–49, translation, study)
2013 Frame in Berlejung and Streck, Arameans, Chaldeans, and Arabs pp. 93–94 (vii 45–76, translation)
2014 Maniori, Campagne di Sargon pp. 46–47 G6–G7 and passim (study)
2018 Frahm, Last Days pp. 71–75 no. 8 (iv 25–41, edition, study)
2019 Aster, JAOS 139 pp. 602–609 (iv 37–41, edition, study)
2019 Edmonds in Dušek and Mynářová, Aramaean Borders p. 45 (vii 45–76, translation)
2019 Marchesi, JNES 78 p. 23 (iv 13–24, edition)

TEXT

Col. i

1) [^{m}LUGAL-GI.NA LUGAL GAL-(*ú*) LUGAL *dan-nu*]
2) [LUGAL *kiš-šá-ti* LUGAL KUR *aš-šur*.KI]
3) [GÌR.NÍTA KÁ.DINGIR.RA.KI LUGAL KUR *šu-me-ri*]
4) ⸢*ù*$^{?}$⸣ [URI.KI] ⸢LUGAL$^{?}$⸣ [*kib-rat* LÍMMU-*i*]
5) ⸢*mi*⸣-*gir* DINGIR.MEŠ GAL.⸢MEŠ⸣ [...]
6) AN.ŠÁR ^{d}*na-bi-um* [^{d}AMAR.UTU]
7) LUGAL-*ut la šá-na-an* ⸢*ú*⸣-[*šat-li-mu-ni-ma*]
8) *zi-kir šu-mì-ia* [*dam-qu*]
9) *ú-še-ṣu-ú* ⸢*a*⸣-[*na re-še-e-ti*]
10) *ša* ZIMBIR.⸢KI NIBRU⸣.KI [KÁ.DINGIR.RA.KI *u* *bár-sipa*.KI]
11) ⸢*za*⸣-*nin*-⸢*us*$^{?}$⸣-[*su-un e-tep-pu-šá*]
12) ⸢*ša*$^{?}$⸣ [ERIM.MEŠ$^{?}$ *ki-din-ni*$^{?}$ *mal*$^{?}$ *ba-šu-ú*$^{?}$]
13) [*ḫi-bil-ta-šú-nu*$^{?}$ *a-rib-ma*$^{?}$ (...)]
14) [...]
15) [...]
16) [...]
17) [...]
18) *x* [...]
19) ⸢Ú$^{?}$⸣ [...]
20) EŠ [...]
21) GIM [...]
22) KUR ⸢RU⸣ *x* [...]
23) *ú-šar-ri-*[*iḫ*$^{?}$ ...]

i 1–5) [Sargon (II), great king, strong king, king of the world, king of Assyria, governor of Babylon, king of the land of Sumer] *and* [Akkad, *ki*]*n*[*g* of the four quarters (of the world)], favorite of the great gods [...].

i 6–9) The gods Aššur, Nabû, (and) [Marduk granted me] a reign without equal [and] exalted my [good] reputation t[o the heights].

i 10–13) [I continually acted] as provider for (the cities) Sippar, Ni[ppur, Babylon, and Borsippa, (and) *I made restitution for the wrongful damage suffered*] by [*the people of privileged status, as many as there were* (*of them*); (...)]

i 14–22) Too poorly preserved to allow translation.

i 23–32) I *made splen*[*did* ...] 177 tale[nts ...] 730 talents

i 5 Possibly restore *a-na-ku*, "(am) I" at the end of the line? Cf. text no. 111 line 1, where the line ends with ⸢*a*$^{?}$⸣-[*x x*], and see the on-page note to text no. 103 ii 4.

24) 1 ME 77 ⸢GUN⸣ [...]
25) 7 ME 30 GUN 22+[(x)] ⸢GÍN⸣ [za-ḫa-lu-ú? eb-bu?]
26) a-na ši-pir é-⸢ḫur⸣-[sag-gal-kur-kur-ra?]
27) ⸢at⸣-man* AN.ŠÁR ⸢ú?⸣-[...]
28) ⸢GIM⸣ UD.DA ⸢ú?⸣-[nam-mir? ...]
29) ⸢i⸣-na 16 ⸢GUN?⸣ [(...) KÙ.GI (...)]
30) ⸢ru⸣-uš-[ši-i ...]
31) ⸢a-šar⸣-[...]
32) x [...]

Lacuna

and 22[(+)] sh[ekels *of pure zaḫalû-silver*] for work on Eḫ[*ursaggalkurkurra*], the sanctuary of (the god) Aššur [... *I made* (*it*) *shine* l]ike daylight [(...)]. With 16 *ta*[*lents* (...)] shin[ing gold (...)] ... [...]

Lacuna

Col. ii

1) [...] (x) [(x)] x
2) [... ^{m}mi-ta-at-ti? KUR.zi]-⸢kir?⸣-ta-a-a
3) [...] x-ma
4) [... KUR....]-⸢na?-ma?⸣-a-a
5) [... KUR.man]-⸢na⸣-a-a
6) [...]-šú-nu-ti
7) [...] ⸢ú⸣-še-šib-šú-nu-ti
8) [...] ⸢KUR⸣.mi-si ⸢KUR⸣.an-di-a
9) [... KUR....] x-ra-a-a
10) [... as?-su?]-ḫa-am-ma
11) [...] ⸢ú⸣-še-ti-iq-ma
12) [man-da-at-tu?] ⸢ka?-bit⸣-ta e-mid
13) [... ^{m}ba-ag-da-at-ti?] KUR.ú-iš-da-a-a

Lacuna

ii 1–13) [...] ... [... *Mitatti* of the land Ziki]rtu [...] and [...] of [the land ...]*namu*, (ii 5) [... of the land Mann]ea [...] them [...] I settled them [... the l]and Missi, the land Andia, [...] of [the land ...] (ii 10) [... *I deport*]*ed* and [...] I *made pass* and [...] I imposed [(*the payment of*) *su*]*bstantial* [*tribute ... Bag-dāti*] of the land Uišdiš

Lacuna

1′) [...] IM x [(x)]
2′) [... šal-la-su]-nu ka-bit-tu
3′) [a-na KUR aš]-⸢šur⸣.KI ú-ra-a
4′) [...] a-na eš-šú-ti ⸢aṣ⸣-bat
5′) [... MU-šú] ⸢ú-nak⸣-kir-ma
6′) [...] URU.kar-⸢AN?⸣-x-RI
7′) [...] x URU.kar-^{m}⸢SUḪUŠ?-GI.NA⸣
8′) [...] ⸢É/Ú⸣ x x x
9′) [...].⸢MEŠ?-ia?⸣ x x ⸢ú?⸣-še-šib
10′) [...] x x ⸢IK?⸣ x ⸢TI?⸣
11′) [...] x x x ⸢AN?⸣
12′) [...] am-nu-šú-⸢nu-ti⸣
13′) [... ú]-še-piš-ma
14′) [...] ⸢AN⸣.ŠÁR be-lí-ia
15′) [...] KUR.man-na-a-a
16′) [...] x x x MA
17′) [...] ul-ziz
18′) [...] x URU.MEŠ
19′) [...] x A A ⸢DA?⸣
20′) [...] x

Lacuna

ii 1′–20′) [...] ... [... th]eir substantial [booty ...] I brought [to Ass]ryia. [...] I reorganized. (ii 5′) [...] I changed [its name] and [...] the city Kār-AN...RI [...] the city Kār-Šarrukīn [...] ... [...] *my* [...]s ... I settled. (ii 10′) [...] ... [...] ... [...] I considered them. [... I] caused to be made and [... (the god) A]ššur, my lord, (ii 15′) [... of] the land Mannea [...] ... [...] I erected. [...] cities [...] ... [...]

Lacuna

i 25–28 The tentative restoration is based on text no. 84 line 3′ and Fuchs, SAAS 8 p. 5.
i 27 -*man**: The copy has -KUR.
ii 9–10 See text no. 1 lines 89–90 and possibly restore [... ^{m}it-ti-i KUR.al]-⸢lab?⸣-ra-a-a [a-di qin-ni-šu as-su]-ḫa-am-ma.
ii 1′–20′ Cf. text no. 1 lines 94–100, text no. 2 lines 86–95, and text no. 4 lines 39′–45′.
ii 6′–7′ During the campaign of 716, Sargon changed the names of the cities Kišesim and Ḫarḫar to Kār-Nergal and Kār-Šarrukīn respectively. Thus, C.J. Gadd (Iraq 16 [1954] p. 177) suggests that what appears to be a SUḪUŠ in ii 7′ might be LUGAL, allowing a reading Kār-Šarrukīn, instead of Kār-Išdu-ukīn. In line 6 possibly URU.kar-⸢^{d}⸣x-RI.
ii 14′–15′ Following Gadd, Iraq 16 (1954) p. 177 and based on text no.1 lines 81–82 and text no. 4 line 24′, possibly [... a-na] ⸢AN⸣.ŠÁR be-lí-ia [a-na tur-ri gi-mil-li] KUR.man-na-a-a.
ii 17′ The passage likely refers to the setting up of a statue of the king or a monumental inscription; see text no. 1 lines 95 and 100, and text no. 2 lines 87 and 93.

Col. iii

1) [...] *x* URU.*tar-ú-i* URU.*tar-*⸢*ma*⸣*-ki-sa*
2) [...] *x* 9 URU.ḪAL.ṢU.MEŠ
3) [...] ⸢*ša li*⸣*-me-ti-ši-na*
4) [...] *x ša* ^{m}*ur-sa-a*
5) [KUR$^{?}$.*ur*$^{?}$*-ar*$^{?}$]-⸢*ṭa*$^{?}$⸣*-a-a ak-šud*^{ud}*-ma*
6) [...] *x áš-lu-la*
7) [...] ⸢URU⸣.ḪAL.ṢU.MEŠ-<<*šá*>>-*ši-na*
8) [...] *aṣ-bat*
9) [... *ina lìb*]-⸢*bi*⸣ *ú-še-li*
10) [...] *ar-*⸢*de*$^{?}$⸣
11) [...] ⸢UB$^{?}$⸣ TÚ
12) [...] ⸢KUR.*za*⸣*-ra-an-da*
13) [...] NI
14) [...] *x*

iii 1–14) [...] the city Tarui, the city Tarmakisa [...] nine fortresses [... i]n their environs [...] of Ursâ (Rusâ)], (iii 5) the [*Urarṭ*]*ian*, I conquered and [...] I plundered. [...] their fortresses [...] I seized. [...] I stationed [the]re. (ii 10) [...] *I led* [...] ... [... the lan]d Zaranda [...]

Lacuna of about 21 lines

36) ⸢*šal-la-tú ka-bit*⸣-[*tú* ...]-⸢*ma*⸣
37) URU *šu-a-tú ap-pu-*⸢*ul*⸣ [*aq-qur ina* IZI *áš*]*-ru-up*
38) UGU KUR.*ur-ar-ṭi* ⸢*a*$^{?}$⸣-[*na paṭ gim*]-⸢*ri*⸣*-šá*
39) *si-pit-tum ú-šab-ši* [^{m}*ur-sa-a*] ⸢*ma*⸣*-lik-šú-nu*
40) *ḫat-tu rama-ni-šú im-qut-*⸢*su*⸣*-ma*
41) *i-na* GÍR.AN.BAR *šib-bi-šú* ZI.[MEŠ-*šú*] ⸢*ú*⸣*-qat-ti*

iii 36–41) [*I took away*] subst[antial] booty and I destroyed, [demolished, (and) bu]rned that city down [with fire]. I caused there to be lamentation throughout the land Urarṭu, t[o] its [fu]ll [extent]. His own fear(s) fell upon their ruler [Ursâ (Rusâ)], and he brought an end to [his] life with the iron dagger from his belt.

---

42) ^{m}*dal-ta-a* KUR.*el-li-*⸢*pa*⸣*-a-a*
43) *ar-du kan-šú šá-di-id* [*ni*]-⸢*ri*⸣*-ia*
44) 5 *na-ge-e-šú ib-bal-*[*ki*]-⸢*tu*⸣*-šú-ma*
45) *man-da-at-ti* AN.ŠÁR *be-lí-ia na-dan šat-ti-šú-nu*
46) *ik-lu-ú na-ge-e šá-šu-nu ḫu-ḫa-riš*
47) *as-ḫu-up* URU.*ḫu-ba-aḫ-na*
48) URU *dan-nu-ti-šú-un a-di* 25 URU.MEŠ ⸢*ù*⸣ *x* [*x x*]-*x-šú-nu*
49) *ša ni-ba la i-*[*šu*]-⸢*ú*⸣
50) ⸢*ak*⸣*-šud*^{ud}*-ma di-ik-*[*ta-šú-nu a*]-⸢*duk*⸣
51) 33 LIM 6 ME UN.MEŠ 11 LIM 6 ⸢ME⸣ [...] *x*
52) ANŠE.KUNGA.MEŠ* ANŠE.MEŠ *šal-*⸢*la*⸣-[*su-nu*]
53) *ka-bit-tu a-na* KUR *aš-*⸢*šur*$^{?}$⸣ *x x* [*ú-ra-a*]

iii 42–53) (As for) Daltâ of the land Ellipi, a submissive subject who pulled my [yo]ke, five of his districts revol[ted] against him and withheld (iii 45) their annual payment of tribute to (the god) Aššur, my lord. I overwhelmed those districts as with a bird trap. I conquered their fortified city Ḫubaḫna, together with 25 settlements and their countless [*villages*], (iii 50) and [I in]flicted a defe[at upon them. I brought] to the land of Assy[ria] 33,600 people, 11,600[(+) ...] mules (and) donkeys as substantial boo[ty from them].

54) *i-na mé-ti-iq* ⸢*ger*$^{?}$⸣-[*ri-ia* ...]
55) *ša* 45 LÚ.EN.URU.MEŠ *ša* KUR.⸢*ma-da*⸣-[*a-a dan-nu-ti*]
56) ⸢8 LIM 6⸣ ME ⸢9 ANŠE.KUR.RA.MEŠ⸣ [...]
57) *x* [...]

iii 54–57) In the course of [my] ca[mpaign ... *I received*] from 45 city rulers of the [powerful] Med[es] 8,609 horses [...]

Lacuna

Col. iv

1) *a-na* KUR *aš-šur*.KI *al-*⸢*qa*⸣-[*a* (...)]
2) *ú-ter-ma* KUR *šu-a-tú a-na eš-*⸢*šú*⸣-[*ti aṣ-bat*]

iv 1–12) I took to Assyria. [(...)] I restored and I re[organized (the administration of)] that land. I

---

iii 1 Text no. 1 line 139 has KUR.É-*sa-an-gi-bu-ti* before the cities Tarui and Tarmakisa and the trace at the beginning of the line could be -⸢*ti*⸣. C.J. Gadd (Iraq 16 [1954] p. 178) notes that there is not sufficient room at the beginning of the line for such a restoration, though he does in fact restore this.
iii 37–39 and 41 The restorations are based on those proposed by C.J. Gadd, but would require more room than Gadd's copy would indicate is available. For line 38, see text no. 65 line 414.
iii 42–53 Compare text no. 7 lines 70b–72a and text no. 2 lines 207b–218a.
iii 48 We would expect *a-di* 25 URU.MEŠ-(*ni*) *šá/ša li-me-ti-šú-nu*, but the traces do not support such a reading.
iii 50 The restoration is based on that proposed by C.J. Gadd, but would require more room than Gadd's copy indicates is available.
iii 52 MEŠ*: The text has ME$^{?}$.
iii 55–56 See also text no. 1 lines 192b–193, which however has 4,609 not 8,609.
iv 2 For the restoration, see ii 4′.

3) UN.MEŠ KUR.É-^{m}ia-ki-ni ⸢ki⸣-[šit-ti ŠU.II-ia]
4) *i-na lìb-bi* ⸢*ú*⸣-[*še-šib*]
5) LÚ.*šu-ut* SAG-*ia* ⸢UGU⸣-[*šú-nu áš-kun*]
6) LÚ.*tur-*⸢*ta-nu* É⸣ [GÙB *aq-bi-šú-ma*]
7) ⸢MI⸣ [ḪI$^{?}$ ...]
8) *x* [...] GIŠ.⸢GIGIR⸣ [...]
9) [... 1] LIM 5 ME ANŠE.[*pét-ḫal-lum*]
10) [*x* ERIM.MEŠ GIŠ].⸢PAN⸣ 10 LIM *na-áš* GIŠ.*ka-ba-*[*bi*]
11) [...] *x i-na lìb-bi-šú-nu ak-ṣur-*⸢*ma*⸣
12) [UGU *ki*]-⸢*ṣir*⸣ LUGAL-*ti-ia ú-rad-di*

[settled] there people of the land Bīt-Yakīn that [I had] c[onquered. (iv 5) I set] a eunuch of mine ov[er them, named him] field marshal of the [left (wing of the army) (lit.: "field marshal of the house [of the left]"), and ...] I conscripted [...] chariot(s) [... 1],500 ca[valry, (iv 10) ...] bow[men], (and) 10,000 shie[ld (*and spear*)] bearers [(...)] from among them and added (them) [to] my royal [(military) contingent].

---

13) [^{m}*pi*]-⸢*si*$^{?}$⸣-*i-ri* URU.*kar-ga-miš-a-a*
14) [*i-na*] ⸢*a*⸣-*de-e* DINGIR.MEŠ GAL.MEŠ *iḫ-ṭi-ma*
15) [*šá-a-šú*] ⸢*ga*⸣-*du* DAM-*šú* DUMU.MEŠ-*šú* DUMU.MUNUS.MEŠ-*šú*
16) [*kim*$^{?}$]-⸢*ti*⸣ NUMUN É AD-*šú*
17) [*i-na* KUR] ⸢*aš*⸣-*šur*.KI *ú-ra-a-šú*
18) [UGU UN].MEŠ *a-ši-bu-ut* URU.*kar-ga-miš*
19) [LÚ.*šu-ut*] SAG-*ia a-na* LÚ.NAM-*ti áš-kun-ma*
20) [(*x*) *it*]-⸢*ti*⸣ UN.MEŠ KUR *aš-šur*.KI *am-nu-šú-nu-ti*
21) [... GIŠ].⸢GIGIR⸣ 5 ME ANŠE.*pét-ḫal-lum*
22) [...] LÚ.*zu-uk* ⸢*še-e*⸣-*pi*
23) [*ina*] ⸢*lìb*⸣-*bi-šú-nu ak-ṣur-ma*
24) [UGU] ⸢*ki*⸣-*ṣir* LUGAL-*ti-ia ú-rad-di*

iv 13–24) [Pis]īri(s) of the city Carchemish sinned [against] the treaty (sworn) by the great gods and (as a result) I brought him [to A]ssyria, together with his wife, his sons, his daughters, [(*his*) *family*], (and) the (other) offspring of his father's house. I set [a eun]uch of mine as governor [over the people] who lived in the city Carchemish and (iv 20) considered them [a]s people of Assyria. I conscripted [from] among them [... chario]t(s), 500 cavalry [... (and) ...] foot soldiers, and I added (them) [to] my royal (military) contingent.

---

25) [LÚ.(URU).*sa*]-*me-ri-na-a-a ša* ⸢*it*⸣-*ti* LUGAL
26) [LÚ.KÚR$^{?}$]-*ia a-na la e-peš* ⸢*ar*⸣-*du-ti*
27) [*ù la na*]-*še-e bil-ti*

iv 25–41) (As for) the people of [(the city) Sa]maria who *had* [*altogeth*]*er come to an agreement* with a king [*hostile to*] me not to do obeisance (to me) [or to

---

iv 6–7 See text no. 2 line 452.
iv 8–11 See text no. 2 lines 453b–454a and text no. 7 lines 116–117 for possible restorations; however, the amount of space available for restoration sometimes appears to be insufficient (e.g., for restoring [20 LIM ERIM.MEŠ GIŠ].⸢PAN⸣ in line 10 and [*u* GIŠ.*az-mar-re*]-⸢*e*⸣ in line 11).
iv 16 Or [*ni-šu*]-⸢*ti*⸣; see for example text no. 7 line 31.
iv 19 C.J. Gadd restores [UGU-*šú-nu* LÚ.*šu-ut*] at the beginning of the line (Iraq 16 [1954] p. 179). Although UGU-*šú-nu* is expected in the passage, the copy would suggest that there is room to restore no more than one or two signs and in similar passages in this inscription the phrase is placed immediately before the verb (e.g., iv 40).
iv 21–22 Text no. 1 line 75 has 50 chariots, 200 cavalry, and 3,000 foot soldiers at this point.
iv 25–28 Following Frahm, Last Days pp. 71–72, possibly [*id-bu*]-⸢*bu*⸣ instead of [*a-ḫa*]-⸢*meš*⸣ at the beginning of line 28, thus "... who [*had spok*]*en* (*and*) *come to an agreement with* a king [*hostile to*] me ..." instead of "... who *had* [*altogeth*]*er come to an agreement* with a king [*hostile to*] me ..."; the trace of the sign before *ig-me-lu* would fit the end of a BU sign as well as the end of a MEŠ. For the restoration in iv 27, see text no. 1 line 68 and text no. 4 line 7′. The understanding of iv 25–28 and in particular the restorations at the beginnings of iv 26 and 28 are much disputed. There have been two basic views of the matter. The first view — tentatively reflected in the edition above, but one which would also work with the alternate reading [*id-bu*]-⸢*bu*⸣ in iv 28 — assumes that the Samarians came to an agreement with a ruler hostile to Sargon not to be subservient to Assyria; see in particular Gadd, Iraq 16 (1954) pp. 179–82 (restoring instead [*na-ki-ri*$^{?}$]-*ia* in iv 26); Tadmor, JCS 12 (1958) p. 34; Hayes and Kuan, Biblica 72 (1991) pp. 171–175; Becking, Fall of Samaria pp. 28–30 (also preferring [*na-ki-ri*]-*ia* in iv 26 and restoring "[to Ashur?] at the beginning of iv 28, i.e., "[or to br]ing tribute [*to Aššur*]"); Briend and Seux, TPOA no. 36; Younger, COS 2 p. 295 (who, like B. Becking, restores "to Aššur" at the beginning of iv 28); and Cogan and Tadmor, II Kings p. 336 no. 6A. Note, however, that the trace at the beginning of line iv 28 as copied by C.J. Gadd would fit the end of a MEŠ sign, but not the end of a ŠUR sign or a KI (i.e., is against a restoration [(*a-na*) ^{d}*aš*]-⸢*šur*⸣ or [(*a-na*) *aš-šur*].⸢KI⸣). The second view assumes that the Samarians had become angry at Sargon's predecessor. This view is based on restoring [*a-lik* IGI]-*ia* or [IGI.DU]-*ia* in iv 26 and reading *ik-me-lu-ma* rather than *ig-me-lu-ma* in iv 28. Thus, "(With regard to) the people of [Sa]maria who had become angry [(...)] with the king, my [predecessor] with the result that they would not do obeisance (to me) [or br]ing tribute (to me)." With regard to the second view, see R. Borger apud Spieckermann, Juda unter Assur pp. 349–350 and n. 93; Dalley, Iraq 47 (1985) p. 36 (also restoring [*ibbalkitū*/*ikpudū*] in iv 28 and translating the passage: "The Samarians, who had [conspired?] against the king my [predecessor] not to endure servitude nor to bring tribute, became angry?"); and Borger, TUAT 1/4 (1984) p. 382. N. Na'aman (Biblica 71 [1990] pp. 209–210) has [*ālik pāni*]-*ia* at the beginning of iv 26 and in iv 28 suggests [ŠÀ-*šu*]-⸢*nu*⸣ *ikmelūma* (i.e., "whose [hearts]? became angry? against/to the king my [predecessor]") or [*lemutt*]*i*? *igmelūma* ("who had repaid? [evil]? to the king my [predecessor]"). G. Galil (CBQ 57/1 [1995] pp. 54–55) reads [LÚ.KÚR]-*ia* at the beginning of iv 26 and [ḪUL]-⸢*tú*⸣ *ig-me-lu-ma* at the beginning of iv 28 and translates "... who renewed [evil] with a king [hostile] to me, not to be (my) servants, [and not to de]liver tribute ...." The most extensive discussion of the matter is found in Hayes and Kuan, Biblica 72 (1991) pp. 171–175. E. Frahm (Last Days pp. 71–72) also suggests the translation "... who [*had spok*]*en* (*and*) *come to an agreement with* a king [*who preceded*] me ... tribute, *had become angry* and offered battle" (translation slightly modified from that of Frahm to match the one given above) if we restore at the beginning of iv 26 [*ālik pāni*]-*ia*. No proposal is entirely free of textual problems.

28) [a-ḫa]-⸢meš$^{?}$⸣ ig-me-lu-ma e-pu-šú ta-ḫa-zu
29) [i]-⸢na⸣ e-mu-uq DINGIR.MEŠ GAL.MEŠ ⸢EN.MEŠ⸣-ia
30) ⸢it⸣-ti-šú-nu am-da-ḫi-[iṣ-ma]
31) [20$^{?}$]+27 LIM 2 ME 80 UN.MEŠ a-di GIŠ.⸢GIGIR⸣.[MEŠ$^{?}$-šú-nu$^{?}$]
32) ù DINGIR.MEŠ ti-ik-le-šú-un šal-la-⸢ti⸣-[iš]
33) am-nu 2 ME GIŠ.GIGIR ki-ṣir ⸢LUGAL⸣-[ti-ia]
34) i-na lìb-bi-šú-nu ak-ṣur-⸢ma⸣
35) si-it-ta-ti-šú-nu
36) i-na qé-reb KUR aš-šur.KI ú-šá-aṣ-bit
37) URU.sa-me-ri-na ú-ter-ma UGU šá pa-ni
38) ú-še-me UN.MEŠ KUR.KUR ki-šit-ti ŠU.II-ia
39) i-na lìb-bi ú-še-rib LÚ.šu-ut SAG-ia
40) LÚ.EN.NAM UGU-šú-nu áš-kun-ma
41) it-ti UN.MEŠ KUR aš-šur.KI am-nu-šú-nu-ti

br]ing tribute (to me) and (who) had offered battle — [with] the strength of the great gods, my l[ord]s, (iv 30) I foug[ht] them [and] counted [as] booty 47,280 people, together with [*their*] chariots and the gods who helped them. I conscripted two hundred chariots from among them into [my] royal (military) contingent and settled (iv 35) the remainder of them in Assyria. I *restored* the city Samaria and *made* (it) greater than before. I brought there people from the lands that I had conquered. I set a eunuch of mine as provincial governor over them and considered them as people of Assyria.

42) UN.MEŠ KUR.mu-ṣur ù LÚ.a-ra-bi
43) šá-lum-mat AN.⸢ŠÁR be⸣-lí-ia ú-šá-as-ḫi-ip-ma
44) ⸢a⸣-na zi-kir šu-mì-ia lib-bu-šú-un
45) ⸢it⸣-ru-ku ir-ma-a i-da-a-šú-un
46) [ka$^{?}$]-⸢a$^{?}$-ri$^{?}$⸣ KUR.mu-ṣur kan-gu ap-te-e-ma
47) [UN$^{?}$].MEŠ KUR aš-šur.KI ù KUR.mu-ṣur
48) [it-ti] ⸢a⸣-ḫa-meš ab-lul-ma
49) [ú-še]-⸢pi⸣-šá ma-ḫi-ru

iv 42–49) I had the awesome radiance of (the god) Ašš[ur], my lord, overwhelm the people of Egypt and the Arabs. At the mention of my name, their hearts (iv 45) pounded (and) their arms grew weak. I opened up *a sealed-off* [*harbor*] *district* of Egypt, mingled [to]gether [*the people*] of Assyria and Egypt, and [allowed (them) to eng]age in trade.

---

50) [^{m}ki-ak]-⸢ki⸣ URU.ši-nu-uḫ-ta-a-a
51) [šá$^{?}$ a-na$^{?}$ ^{m}]⸢mi⸣-ta-a LUGAL KUR.mus-ki
52) [it-tak-lu$^{?}$]-ma ⸢bil$^{?}$-tu$^{?}$⸣ man-da-at-tu
53) [ú-šab-ṭil$^{?}$]-ma [ik]-⸢la⸣-a ta-mar-tuš
54) [šá-a-šú$^{?}$ a-di$^{?}$ UN.MEŠ$^{?}$] URU-šú GIŠ.GIGIR.MEŠ-šú
55) [... DUMU.MUNUS$^{?}$].MEŠ-šú
56) [... am$^{?}$]-⸢nu$^{?}$⸣-šú
57) [...]-šú
58) [...] x

Lacuna

iv 50–58) [Kiakk]i of the city Šinuḫtu, [*who had put his trust in* M]itâ, king of the land Musku, [*stopped* (*his delivery of*)] t[ribut]e (and) payment(s) and [with]held his audience gift. [*I coun*]*ted* him [*as booty, together with the people of*] his city, his chariots, [...], his [*daughter*]s, [...].

Lacuna

---

iv 31 Various exemplars of text no. 7 line 24 have 27,290, 27,280, and apparently 24,280. For the proposal that the number in the Nimrud Prism was 47,280, see Na'aman, NABU 2000 p. 1 no. 1, but note that his reference to the Khorsabad Annals (text no. 1 line 15) in connection with this passage is misleading since the number there is totally restored.

iv 33 Text no. 1 line 15 and text no. 7 line 24 have fifty chariots.

iv 37–38 URU.*sa-me-ri-na ú-ter-ma* UGU *šá pa-ni ú-še-me* "I *restored* the city Samaria and *made* (it) greater than before": The understanding and translation of the two verbs in this passage remains somewhat problematic. S. Dalley (Iraq 47 [1985] p. 36) translates "I repopulated Samaria more than before," assuming that *ú-ter-ma* comes from *atāru* rather than *târu* and reading *ú-še-šib* (from *wašābu*) rather than *ú-še-me* (from *ewû*). For the (slightly restored) duplicate passage in text no. 1 line 16, A. Fuchs (Khorsabad pp. 88 and 314, with n. 225) noted and apparently rejected Dalley's understandings of the two verbs, kept the reading *ú-še-me*, and translated "Samaria wandelte ich um und machte (es) größer als zuvor." S.Z. Aster (JAOS 139 [2019] pp. 594–595, especially nn. 14–15) accepts Dalley's understanding of the latter verb, but not the former, and translates the passage as "I again settled Samaria, more than (it had) previously (been settled)." E. Frahm (Last Days pp. 71–72) also rejects taking the former verb from *atāru* and is uncertain about whether one should read the latter as *ú-še-šib* or *ú-še-me*, although his translation assumes *ú-še-šib*: "I *resettled* Samaria, making it more (*populous*) than before." If the former verb came from *atāru*, we would really expect the writing *ut-tir-ma* (see for example text no. 1 line 71) or *ú-šá-tir-ma*, and so the derivation from the verb *târu* seems much more likely than one from *atāru*, although it is not certain whether *târu* is being used in hendiadys with the following verb (i.e., "I again made the city Samaria greater than before" or "I again settled/populated the city Samaria more than before") or as translated above. I am not aware of the phrase *eli ša pāna* being used with either the verb *wašābu* or *ewû* in any other Neo-Assyrian royal inscription.

iv 46–49 The Khorsabad Annals place the passage about the reopening of trade with Egypt in the account of Sargon's accession year (text no. 1 lines 17b–18a). iv 46: Or ⸢*kar*⸣-*ri*, following Tadmor, JCS 12 (1958) p. 34. Borger, TUAT 1/4 (1984) p. 382 suggests [*ki*]-⸢*sur*⸣-*re* ("[bor]der"), but see text no. 1 line 17 and Fuchs, Khorsabad p. 88 n. 1 to line 17. See also Eph'al, Arabs pp. 101–102 n. 339. It is not known where the *entrepôt*, or port, was located, but both Tell Abu Salima and Ruqeish have been proposed (see Cogan, Raging Torrent p. 92).

iv 51–55 The restorations in lines 51–52 and 54–55 are based on the readings proposed by Renger, CRRA 32 p. 114; for the restoration in iv 53, see text no. 7 line 113.

iv 56 The copy of the trace before ŠÚ resembles ⸢KUR⸣ rather than NU.

Col. v

Lines 1–12 not preserved

13) [...] ⸢*iṣ*⸣-*bat* [*x* (*x*)]
14) [...] ⸢*ad*⸣-*din-šu*-[*ma*]
15) [...] ⸢*re*⸣-*ṣu-us-su*
16) [*ina* GIŠ.GU.ZA (ᵐ*ḫul-li-i*) AD]-*šú ú-še-šib-šu-ma*
17) *x x* (*x*) ÁŠ? *it-ti* KUR.*ḫi-lak-ki*
18) *pa-nu-uš*-⸢*šú*⸣ *ú-šad-gi-il-ma*
19) *ú-taq-qí-na da-li-iḫ-tu* KUR-*su*
20) *ù šu-ú* LÚ.*ḫat-tu-ú*
21) *la na-ṣir kit-te a-na* ᵐ*ur-sa-a*
22) KUR.*ur-ar-ṭa-a-a ù* ᵐ*mì-ta-a*
23) LUGAL KUR.*mus-ki ša e-ke-mi mì-iṣ-ri-ia*
24) *iš-pu-ra* DUMU *šip-ri*
25) ᵐ*am-ri-is* LUGAL KUR.É-*pu-ru-ti-iš*
26) *a-di* NUMUN É AD-*šú* SAG.KAL-*ut ma-ti-šú*
27) *ka-mu-su-nu it-ti* 1 ME GIŠ.GIGIR-*šú*
28) *a-na* KUR *aš-šur*.KI *al-qa-a*
29) KUR.É-*pu-ru*-⸢*ti*⸣-*iš* KUR.*ḫi-lak-ku*
30) *a-bur*-⸢*riš ú*⸣-*šar-bi-iṣ*
31) LÚ.*šu*-⸢*ut*⸣ [SAG]-⸢*ia*⸣ LÚ.EN.NAM
32) UGU-*šú*-⸢*nu*⸣ *áš-kun-ma*
33) *it-ti* UN.MEŠ KUR ⸢*aš*⸣-[*šur*.KI]
⸢*am*⸣-*nu-šú-nu-ti-ma*

Lines 1–12 not preserved

v 13–33) [... he] seized [... I] gave him [and ...] to his aid. I seated him [on the throne of (Ḫullî)], his [father], and entrusted to him ..., (along) with the land Ḫilakku. I then brought order to his disturbed land. (v 20) However, that (man), a Hittite who did not protect justice, sent a messenger to Ursâ (Rusâ), the Urarṭian, and Mitâ, king of the land Musku, about taking away territory of mine. I took in bondage to Assyria (v 25) Amris (Ambaris), king of the land Bīt-Purutaš, together with the offspring of his father's house (and) the nobles of his land, (along) with one hundred of his chariot(s). (v 30) I had the lands Bīt-Purutaš (and) Ḫilakku dwell (as safely) as in a meadow. I set a eun[uch of m]ine as provincial governor over them and considered them as people of A[ssyria].

34) *ša* ᵐ*mi-ta-a* ⸢LUGAL⸣ KUR.*mus-ki*
35) *i-na na-gi-šú rap-ši*
36) *a-di* 2-*šú* [BAD$_5$].⸢BAD$_5$⸣-*šú áš-kun-ma*
37) URU.*ḫa-ru-u*-[*a*] ⸢URU⸣.*uš-na-ni-is*
38) URU.ḪAL.ṢU.[MEŠ] ⸢URU⸣.*qu-e*
39) ⸢*ša ul-tu u*$_4$-*me dan*?⸣-[*niš*?] *e-ki-mu*
40) [*ú*]-⸢*ter*⸣-*ra áš*-[*ru*]-⸢*uš*⸣-*šun*

v 34–40) For a second time, I brought about [the defe]at of Mitâ, king of the land Musku, in his (own) wide district and [I (then) rest]ored to their former st[atu]s the cities Ḫarru[a] (and) Ušnanis, fortress[es of the ci]ty Que, which he had taken away [*by*] *for*[*ce*] in the past.

---

41) [ᵐ*tar*]-*ḫu-na-zi* URU.[*me*]-⸢*lid*⸣-*da-a-a*
42) [ᵐ]⸢*tar*⸣-*ḫu-la-ra* URU.⸢*mar*⸣-*qa-sa-a-a*
43) ⸢*ša*⸣ LUGAL-*su-nu* ⸢*da*⸣-*li-iḫ-tú*
44) *ú-taq-qí-nu-ma*
45) *gi-mir* KUR.MEŠ-*šú-nu rap-šá-a-ti*
46) *ú-šad-gi-la pa-nu-uš-šu-un*
47) *ù šú-nu* LÚ.*ḫat-te*-⸢*e*⸣ *lem-nu-ti*
48) *ep-šet da-mì-iq*-⸢*ti-ia*⸣
49) *lib-ba-šú-un la iḫ*-⸢*su*⸣-*us-ma*
50) *a-na* ᵐ*mi-ta-a* LUGAL ⸢KUR⸣.*mus-ki*
51) *ze-ra-a-ti* KUR *aš-šur*.KI *il-tap-pa-ru*
52) *il-qu-ú še-ṭu-tu*

v 41–50) [(As for) Tar]ḫun-azi of the city [Meli]d (and) [T]arḫu-lara of the city [Ma]rqasa, to whose disturbed kingdom(s) I had brought order and (v 45) the whole of whose extensive lands I had entrusted to them, those (men), evil Hittites, did not remember my good deeds but (rather) sent (messages) hostile to Assyria to Mitâ, king of the land Musku. They held (Assyria/me) in contempt.

53) *i-na ug-gat lìb-bi-ia um-ma-na-at* KUR *aš-šur*.KI
54) *gap-šá-a-ti ad-ke-e-ma*
55) *qé-reb* KUR.*kam-ma-ni* KUR.*gúr-gu-me*
56) *na-ge-e rap-šu-ú-ti*
57) *a-di da-ád-me li-me-ti-šú-un*
58) *im-ba-riš ak-tùm*

v 53–76) Angrily, I mustered the numerous troops of Assyria and, like a fog, overwhelmed extensive districts (v 55) within the lands Kammanu (and) Gurgum, together with settlements in their environs. I brought to Assyria Tarḫun-azi of the land Kammanu (and) (v 60) Tarḫu-lara of the land Gurgum, together

---

v 16 For the restoration, cf. text no. 7 line 30; there seems insufficient room on the copy to include the father's name. Or possibly [*ina* GIŠ.GU.ZA LUGAL-*ti*]-*šú*, "[on] his [royal throne]"; see text no. 1 line 196.

v 17 Text no. 1 line 198, text no. 2 line 230, and text no. 7 line 30 have *bi-in* / [*in*]-*ti**(var. -*tu*), "a daughter of mine" (var. "a daughter (of mine)") before *it-ti* KUR.*ḫi-lak-ki*. Possibly ⸢DUMU.MUNUS-*ia*?⸣.

v 33 C.J. Gadd's copy would not suggest that there is sufficient room for the required restoration in the middle of the line.

v 38 Ex. 2 has KUR.*qu-e*, "land Que."

59) ^{m}*tar-ḫu-na-zi* KUR.*kam-ma-nu-u-a*
60) ^{m}*tar-ḫu-*⸢*la*⸣*-ra* KUR.*gúr-gu-ma-a-a*
61) *a-di* DAM.MEŠ-*šú-nu*
62) DUMU.MEŠ-*šú-nu* DUMU.MUNUS.MEŠ-*šú-nu*
63) KÙ.GI KÙ.BABBAR NÍG.ŠU NÍG.GA
64) *ni-ṣir-ti* É.GAL.MEŠ-*šú-nu*
65) *it-ti šal-lat* KUR.MEŠ-*šú-nu ka-bit-ti*
66) *a-na* KUR *aš-šur*.KI *ub-la-áš-šú-nu-ti*
67) KUR.MEŠ *šá-ši-na a-na eš-šu-ti aṣ-bat*
68) ⸢UN⸣.MEŠ *a-ši-bu-ut* KUR-⸢*ia*⸣
69) ⸢*ni*⸣*-pi-iḫ* ^{d}UTU-*ši*
70) [*ki*]-⸢*šit*⸣*-ti qa-ti-ia*
71) [LÚ].⸢*su*⸣*-ti-i na-áš* GIŠ.PAN
72) [(LÚ).ERIM.MEŠ *e*]-⸢*piš*⸣ *ta-ḫa-zi i-na lìb-bi ú-še-šib*
73) [LÚ.*šu-ut*] SAG-*ia a-na* LÚ.NAM-⸢*ú-ti*⸣
74) [...] UD *áš-tak-kan-*[*ma*]
75) [*ni-ir be-lu-ti*]-⸢*ia*⸣ *e-mid-*⸢*su*⸣-[*nu-ti*]
76) [...] x x [x x (x)]

with their wives, their sons, their daughters, gold, silver, property, (and) possessions, the treasure of their palaces, (v 65) (along) with substantial booty from their lands. I reorganized (the administration of) those lands. I settled there people who had lived in the eastern (part of) my land (v 70) [that] I [had con]quered, [S]utians, bowmen, (and) fighting [men]. I set [a eu]nuch of mine as provincial governor [*over the*]*m* [and] imposed [the yoke of m]y [lordship] upon t[hem ...] ... [...]

Lacuna

Col. vi

Lines 1–12 not preserved

13) [...] x [...]

Lacuna

Lines 1–12 not preserved

vi 13) [...]

---

14) [^{md}AMAR.UTU]-⸢IBILA⸣-SUM.NA ⸢LUGAL KUR.*kal-di*⸣
15) [*ša ki*]-⸢*i*⸣ *la lìb-bi* DINGIR.⸢MEŠ⸣ [*a*]-*na er-ṣe-et*
16) ⸢KUR EME⸣.GI$_{7}$ *ù* URI.KI *ú-ri-dam-ma*
17) LUGAL-*ut* KÁ.DINGIR.RA.KI *pa-nu-uš ú-ter-ru*
18) ^{md}*ḫum-ba-ni-ga-áš* LÚ.ELAM.MA.KI
19) *a-na re-ṣu-ti is-ḫur*
20) UGU ÍD.*mar-ra-ti gu-pu-uš e-de-e*
21) *it-ta-kil-ma ik-la-a ta-mar-tuš*
22) *um-ma-na-at* AN.ŠÁR *gap-šá-a-ti ad-ke-e-ma*
23) ÍD.IDIGNA ÍD.BURANUN.KI *a-di* ÍD.MEŠ
24) TUR.MEŠ *la mi-na e-teb-bi-ra*
25) LÚ.*kal-du a-na paṭ gim-re-e-šú*
26) *a-bu-biš as-ḫu-*⸢*up*⸣
27) *ul-la-nu-u-a* ^{md}AMAR.UTU-IBILA-SUM.NA
28) URU.MEŠ-*šú áš-bu-ti ù* DINGIR.MEŠ
29) *a-šib lib-bi-šú-un ú-paḫ-ḫir-ma*
30) *a-na* URU.BÀD-^{m}*ia-ki-na ú-še-rib-ma*
31) *ú-dan-ni-na ker-ḫe-e-šú*
32) 10 NINDA.TA.ÀM *la-pa-an* BÀD-*šú* GAL-*i ú-né-si-ma*
33) 2 ME *ina* 1.KÙŠ DAGAL *ḫa-ri-*⸢*ṣi*⸣ *iš-kun-ma*
34) 1 1/2 NINDA *ú-šap-pil-ma ik-šu-da* A.MEŠ

vi 14–21) [Marduk-ap]la-iddina (II) (Merodach-Baladan), the k[in]g of Chaldea, [who ag]ainst the will of the gods had come down t[o] the territory of the land of Sumer and Akkad and had appropriated for himself the kingship of Babylon, turned to Ḫumbanigaš (Ḫumban-nikaš I), the Elamite, for aid. He put his trust in the sea (and its) surging waves and withheld his audience gift.

vi 22–42) I mustered the numerous troops of (the god) Aššur and crossed the Tigris (and) Euphrates Rivers, as well as innumerable small streams. Like the Deluge, I overwhelmed (vi 25) the Chaldeans to their (lit.: its) full extent. In the face of my advance (lit.: "before me"), Marduk-apla-iddina gathered together the inhabitants of his cities (lit.: "his inhabited cities") and the gods dwelling in them, and (vi 30) brought (them) into the city Dūr-Yakīn. He strengthened its enclosure walls (and), moving back a distance of ten *nindanu* from in front of its main wall, he made a moat two hundred cubits wide; he made (the moat) one and a half *nindanu* deep and reached ground water. He cut (vi 35) a channel from the Euphrates River, (thereby)

---

v 67–75 According to text no. 1 lines 248–249a, text no. 2 lines 267–273, and text no. 3 lines 1´–6´a, Gurgum was annexed in Sargon's eleventh regnal year (711) during the time of Tarḫu-lara's son Mutallu.

v 74 We expect [UGU-*šú*]-⸢*nu*⸣ at the beginning of the line. The UD could be the end of NA and permit a reading [UGU-*ši*]-⸢*na*⸣, but this would result in a lack of accord with -⸢*su*⸣-[*nu-ti*] in the following line.

v 75 For the restoration (following Gadd, Iraq 16 [1954] p. 185), see for example text no. 7 lines 22–23.

vi 22–62 See Scurlock, Studies Astour pp. 503–505 for a study of the battle tactics used in the battle at Dūr-Yakīn.

vi 25 Ex. 2 has *gim-ri* instead of *gim-re-e-šú*.

vi 32 Text no. 7 line 127 has *áš-la*.TA.ÀM instead of 10 NINDA.TA.ÀM. For the translation "moving back a distance of ten *nindanu* from in front of its main wall," see Powell, JCS 34 (1982) pp. 59–60 and n. 3, which has "All along in front of its main wall he moved back a distance of 10 *nindan* (var.: an *aslu*)." Ten *nindanu* are approximately 60 m (see Powell, RLA 7/5–6 [1989] p. 459).

nag-bi
35) *bu-tuq-tu ul-tu qé-reb* ÍD.BURANUN.KI
36) *ib-tuq-ma ú-šar-da-a ta-mir-tuš*
37) A.GÀR.MEŠ-*šú a-šar mit-ḫu-ṣi*
38) A.MEŠ *im-ki-ir-ma ú-šap-ši-qa né-ber-tú*
39) *šu-ú a-di* LÚ.*re-ṣi-šú*
40) ERIM.MEŠ MÈ-*šú ina bi-rit* ÍD.MEŠ
41) *ki-ma ku-mé-e*.MUŠEN *za-ra-tú* LUGAL-*ti-šú*
42) *iš-kun-ma ú-pa-ḫi-ra ka-ras-su*

making (its water) flow (in)to its meadowland. He flooded its fields, where battles (are fought), and made crossing difficult. Together with his allies (and) (vi 40) his battle troops, he pitched his royal tent in a bend of the river (lit.: "between rivers") like a *crane* and assembled his (military) camp.

43) *i-na qí-bit* AN.ŠÁR ^{d}AG ^{d}AMAR.UTU
44) UGU ÍD.MEŠ-*šú a-ram-mu ú-šak-bi-is-ma*
45) *šá-a-šú ga-du* LÚ.*mun-daḫ-ṣe-šu*
46) GIM TI$_{8}$.MUŠEN *mut-tap-ri-ši a-bar-šú ina še-e-ti*
47) *pag-re nu-bal-li-šú ù* LÚ.*aḫ-la-me-e*
48) *ṣa-ab* EDIN *a-li-kut i-de-e-šú*
49) *ki-ma* ŠE.MUNU$_{6}$ *áš-ṭe-e-ma i-ta-at* URU-*šú ú-mal-li*
50) URU.BÀD-^{m}*ia-ki-ni* É *ni-ṣir-ti-šú*
51) URU.*iq-bi*-^{d}EN URU.*kap-ru*
52) URU.É-^{m}*za-bi-da-a-a* URU.*šá-at*-SUM.NA
53) URU.*za-ra-a-ti* URU.*raq-qa-tu*
54) URU.*e-ku-uš-šú* URU.*ḫur-sag*-GAL$_{5}$.LÁ.MEŠ
55) URU.BÀD-^{d}EN-URU-*ia* URU.BÀD-^{d}EN.LÍL
56) URU.É-^{m}*qí-ib-la-te* URU.*né-med*-^{d}30
57) URU.*li-mi-tum* URU.*mad-a-kal-šá*
58) 15 URU.MEŠ *dan-nu-ti a-di* URU.MEŠ
59) *ša li-me-ti-šú-un ti-la-niš ú-še-me*
60) UN.MEŠ *ṣe-ḫer ra-bi a-ši-bu-ut na-ge-e*
61) *ù* DINGIR.MEŠ *ti-ik-le-šú-un iš-te-niš*
62) *áš-lu-lam-ma la e-zi-ba mul-taḫ-ṭu*

vi 43–62) At the command of the gods Aššur, Nabû, (and) Marduk, I had a causeway constructed (lit.: "trodden down") across his canals and I caught him, together with his fighting men, like a flying eagle in a net. I spread out like malt (spread for drying) the corpses of his vanguard and of the Aḫlamû, the people of the steppe who go at his side, and I filled the surroundings of his city (with them). (vi 50) The city Dūr-Yakīn — his treasure house — (and) the cities Iqbi-Bēl, Kapru, Bīt-Zabidāya, Šāt-iddina, Zarāti, Raqqatu, Ekuššu, Ḫursaggalla, (vi 55) Dūr-Bēl-āliya, Dūr-Enlil, Bīt-Qiblāte, Nēmed-Sîn, Limītu, (and) Mād-akālša, (a total of) fifteen fortified cities, together with the settlements in their environs, I turned into (ruin) mounds. I carried off as booty at the same time (vi 60) (both) the people — young (and) old — who lived in the district and the gods who helped them; I did not allow a (single) person to escape.

63) DUMU.MEŠ ZIMBIR.KI NIBRU.KI KÁ.DINGIR.RA.KI
64) *bár-sipa*.KI *ša i-na la an-ni-šú-nu*
65) *i-na qer-bi-šú-un ka-mu-ú*
66) *ṣi-bit-ta-šú-nu a-bu-ut-ma*
67) *ú-kal-lim-šú-nu-ti nu-ú-ru*
68) [A].ŠÀ.MEŠ-*šú-nu ša ul-tu u$_{4}$-me ul-lu-ti*
69) [*i-na*] ⸢*i*⸣-*ši-ti ma-a-ti* LÚ.*su-ti-i*
70) [*e*?-*ki*]-*mu-ú-ma ra-ma-nu-uš-šú-un ú-ter-ru*
71) [LÚ.*su*]-⸢*ti*⸣-*i ṣa-ab* EDIN *ina* GIŠ.TUKUL *ú-šam-qit*
72) [*ki-sur-ri*]-⸢*šú*⸣-*nu ma-šu-ú-ti*
73) [*ša i-na di*]-⸢*li*⸣-*iḫ ma*-⸢*a*⸣-*ti ib-baṭ-lu*
74) [*ú-šad-gi*]-⸢*la*⸣ *pa-nu-uš-šú-un*
75) [*ša* ÚRI.KI] ⸢UNUG⸣.KI *eridu*.KI ARARMA.KI
76) [*kul-aba$_{4}$*.KI *ki-sik*.KI URU.*né-me*]-⸢*ed*⸣-*la-gu-da*
77) [*áš-ku-na an-du-ra*]-⸢*ar*⸣-*šú-un*
78) [*ù* DINGIR.MEŠ-*šú-nu šal-lu-ú-ti a-na*

vi 63–79) (As for) the citizens of (the cities) Sippar, Nippur, Babylon, (and) Borsippa who through no fault of their own had been held captive in them (the fifteen cities), I put an end to their imprisonment and let them see the light (of day). (With regard to) their [fi]elds, which long ago, while the land was [in] disorder, the Sutians (vi 70) [had taken] away and appropriated for their own, I struck down (those) [Sut]ians, the people of the steppe, with the sword. [I (re)assign]ed to them (the citizens) their [territories], (whose boundaries) had been forgotten (and) fallen into disuse [during the troubled] period in the land. [I (re)-established the freedom (from obligations) (vi 75) of (the cities) Ur, Uru]k, Eridu, Larsa, [Kullaba, Kissik, (and) Nēme]d-Laguda. [Moreover], I returned [their gods that had been carried off as booty to] their [cult centers] and [restor]ed [their regular offerings

vi 45–46 For the differing accounts of what happened to Marduk-apla-iddina, see the Introduction to this volume, under the section "Military Campaigns."
vi 49 See text no. 65 lines 134 and 226; CAD Š/2 p. 343 sub *šeṭû*; and Akdoğan and Fuchs, ZA 99 (2009) p. 83; cf. CAD P p. 541 sub *puṣuddu*.
vi 57 For the reading of the second city name, see Weippert, GGA 224 (1972) p. 157 and Borger, HKL 2 p. 75.
vi 65 *i-na qer-bi-šú-un* "in them": The "them" must refer to the fifteen cities listed in line vi 50–58. In text no. 7 line 135, we find *ina qerbišu*, "in it/there," which just refers to Dūr-Yakīn.
vi 68–80 Restorations are based on text no. 7 lines 135–137 and text no. 113 lines 19′–23′. Based on C.J. Gadd's copy, there would, however, not seem to be sufficient room to restore what is given for the beginning of iv 70.
vi 70 C.J. Gadd's copy has [*x x*]-⸢*ma*⸣ *ra-ma-nu-uš-šú-un ú-ter-ru*, but a note to the copy states that prism E (ex. 2) "suppl. [*i-ki*]-*mu-ú-ma*."

ma-ḫa-zi]-šú-nu ú-ter-ma
79) [sat-tuk-ki-šú-nu ba-aṭ-lu-ú-ti ú-ter áš]-ru-uš-šú-un
80) [KUR.É-^{m}ia-ki-ni ú-ter-ma a-na eš-šu]-⸢ti⸣ aṣ-bat
81) [...] x ⸢E?⸣
82) [... AN].ŠÁR EN-ia
83) [...] ⸢LÚ.šu-ut SAG⸣-ia
84) [...] x ⸢ŠÁ? A⸣ x
85) [...] x x [x (x)]

that had been discontinued].

vi 80–85) [I *restored* the land Bīt-Yakīn and] reorga[nized (its administration) ...] ... [... (the god) Aš]šur, my lord [...] a eunuch of mine [...] ... [...] ... [...]

---

86) [...] x [x (x)]
Lacuna
Col. vii
Lines 1–6 not preserved
7) ⸢NA$_4$⸣.AŠ.GÌ.GÌ [NA$_4$.UGU.AŠ.GÌ.GÌ?]
8) ⸢NA$_4$⸣.di-⸢gi?⸣-[li NA$_4$.BABBAR.DILI? (x x)]
9) ⸢NA$_4$⸣.MUŠ.[GÍR ...]
10) URUDU AN.NA ⸢AN⸣.BAR ⸢A⸣.[BÁR ...]
11) en-qu-ti ÁŠ? [...]
12) SÍG.ta-kil-tum [SÍG.ar-ga-man-nu]
13) lu-bul-ti bir-[me ù (TÚG).GADA]
14) GIŠ.TÚG GIŠ.EREN GIŠ.⸢ŠUR⸣.[MÌN ka-la ri-iq-qí]
15) bi-ib-lat KUR.ḫa-ma-ni ša [e-ri-su-un ṭa-a-bu]
16) a-na ⸢^{d}⸣AMAR.UTU ^{d}zar-pa-⸢ni⸣-[tum ^{d}AG ^{d}taš-me-tum]
17) ù DINGIR.MEŠ a-ši-⸢bu⸣-[ut ma-ḫa-zi]
18) KUR EME.GI$_7$ u URI.KI [ul-tu SAG LUGAL-ti-ia]
19) a-di MU.4.KÁM ú-⸢qa⸣-[i-šá qí-šá-a-ti]
20) ^{m}a-ḫu-un-da-ra LUGAL [dil-mun.KI ša ma-lak 30 KASKAL.GÍD]
21) i-na MURUB$_4$ tam-tim ⸢ni⸣-[pi-iḫ ^{d}UTU-ši]
22) ki-⸢ma nu⸣-ú-ni ⸢šit⸣-[ku-nu nar-ba-ṣu]
23) da-na-an AN.ŠÁR ^{d}⸢AG⸣ [^{d}AMAR.UTU iš-me-ma]
24) iš-šá-a man-da-tuš ⸢ù?⸣ [7 LUGAL.MEŠ]
25) ša KUR.ia-a' na-⸢ge⸣-[e ša KUR.ia-ad-na-na]
26) ša ma-lak 7 u$_4$-me [i-na MURUB$_4$ tam-tim]
27) e-reb ^{d}UTU-ši ⸢šit⸣-[ku-nu-ma]
28) né-sa-at šu-⸢bat⸣-[su-un]
29) ša ul-tu u$_4$-me ru-⸢qu⸣-[ti a-di i-^{d}nanna]
30) i-na LUGAL.MEŠ-ni ⸢AD⸣.[MEŠ-ia]
31) ša KUR aš-šur.KI KUR.kar-^{d}[du-ni-áš]
32) ma-⸢nam⸣-ma ⸢la⸣ iš-mu-u ⸢zi⸣-[kir KUR-šú-un]
33) ep-⸢šet⸣ i-na qé-reb KUR.kal-[di u KUR.ḫat-ti]
34) e-tep-pu-šá i-na MURUB$_4$ tam-tim ⸢ru⸣-[qiš iš-mu-ma]
35) lib-bu-šú-un it-ru-ku im-qut-su-nu-ti ḫat-[tu]
36) KÙ.GI KÙ.BABBAR ú-nu-ut GIŠ.ESI GIŠ.TÚG né-peš-ti KUR-šú-un
37) a-na qé-reb KÁ.DINGIR.RA.KI a-di maḫ-ri-⸢ia⸣

vi 86) [...]
Lacuna

Lines 1–6 not preserved

vii 7–19) *blue turquoise, [green turquoise]*, ... *[of banded agate* (and)] *muš[šaru*-stone ...], (vii 10) copper, tin, iron, l[ead, ...] *skilled* [...], blue-purple wool, [red-purple wool], garments with multi-colo[red trim and linen (garments)], boxwood, cedar, cy[press, (and) every kind of aromatic], (vii 15) the products of Mount Amanus, who[se scent(s) are pleasant — from the beginning of my reign] until (my) fourth year, I pr[esented (these things) as gifts] to the deities Marduk, Zarpan[ītu, Nabû, Tašmētu], and the (other) gods who dwell [in the cult centers] of the land of Sumer and Akkad.

vii 20–24a) Aḫundāra (Ḫundāru), king [of Dilmun, who(se) lair] is s[ituated at a distance of thirty leagues] in the middle of the E[astern] Sea, like (that of) a fish, [heard of] the might of the gods Aššur, Na[bû, (and) Marduk and] brought me his tribute.

vii 24b–38) *Moreover*, [seven kings] (vii 25) of the land Yā', a reg[ion of the land Yadnana (Cyprus)] — who[se] abode(s) are si[tuated] far away, at a distance of seven days (journey) [in the middle of the] Western [Sea], (and) the n[ame of] who[se land], from the dist[ant] past [until now], none (vii 30) of the kings, [my] ance[stors], neither in Assyria nor in the land Kar[duniaš (Babylonia)], had ever heard — [from afar], in the middle of the sea, [heard] of the deeds I had been doing in Chal[dea and the land Ḫatti (Syria)]. (vii 35) Their hearts [then] pounded (and) fe[ar] fell upon them. They brought before me in Babylon gold, silver, (and) utensils of ebony (and) boxwood, product(s) of their land, and they kissed [my] feet.

---

vi 80–85 See for example text no. 64 lines 6′–7′ and text no. 87 lines 10′–11′ for the likely sense of the passage.
vii 19 Text no. 7 line 144 has MU.3.KÁM, "(my) third year."
vii 20 Aḫundāra (see also text no. 116 line 27) is likely a variant of the name Ḫundāru; see Gadd, Iraq 16 (1954) p. 194 and Brinkman, PNA 2/1 p. 479. He was likely the successor of Upēri, who appears in other texts of Sargon (see Baker, PNA 3/2 p. 1390). See also Potts, Arabian Gulf 1 pp. 335–336.
vii 35 C.J. Gadd's copy for the line ends with *im-qut-⸢su⸣ [x x]*, but a note to the copy states that "Line ends *-su-nu-ti ḫat-[tu]*," which presumably means that ex. 2 had that.

38) *ú-bi-lu-nim-ma ú-na-ši-qu* ⸢GÌR.II⸣-[*ia*]
39) *i-na e-mu-uq* DINGIR.MEŠ GAL.MEŠ
40) *ša* UGU *kul-lat na-ki-*[*ri-ia*]
41) *li-i-tu ki-šit-ti qa-ti-*⸢*ia* GAR$^{?}$-*nu*$^{?}$-*ma*$^{?}$⸣
42) *i-na* NA$_4$.NA.RÚ.A *ú-ša-áš-*⸢*ṭir-ma*⸣
43) *i-na qé-reb* KUR.*ia-a' na-ge-*⸢*e*⸣
44) *ša* KUR.*ia-ad-na-na e-zi-ba* ⸢*aḫ-ra-taš*⸣

vii 39–44) I had inscribed upon a stele (the record of) the victorious conquest(s) that *I had personally achieved* over all [my] enem[ies] by the strength of the great gods and I left (it) for all ti[me] in the land Yā', a region of the land Yadnana.

---

45) *i-na* u$_4$-*mi-šú-ma ger-ri ša ul-*⸢*tu ṣa-ti*⸣
46) *a-na a-lak* KÁ.DINGIR.RA.KI *ma-ḫa-zi* ^{d}⸢EN.LÍL DINGIR⸣.[MEŠ]
47) *la pe-tu-ma la na-ṭu-u ú-ru-*[*uḫ-šú-nu*$^{?}$]
48) KUR.*ma-ad-bar ša ul-tu* u$_4$-*me* ⸢*ul*$^{?}$⸣-[*lu-ti*$^{?}$]
49) *i-na qer-bé-e-šú šup-ru-sa-at a-lak-tú*
50) *ḫar-ra-an-šú šup-šu-qat-ma*
51) *la šit-ku-nu da-rag-gu*
52) *ṭu-da-at la a'-a-ri gi-iṣ-ṣu*
53) *da-ad-da-ru ù* GIŠ.TIR.MEŠ
54) *e-li-šun id-nin-ma lab-bu*
55) *ù zi-i-bu i-na qer-bi-ši-in*
56) *e-mi-du-ma i-dak-ku-ku ka-lu-meš*
57) *i-na* KUR.*ma-ad-bar šá-a-tú* LÚ.*a-ra-me*
58) LÚ.*su-ti-i a-ši-bu-ut kuš-ta-ri*
59) *mun-nab-tu sa-ar-ru* DUMU *ḫab-ba-ti*
60) *šu-bat-sún id-du-ma uš-ḫar-ri-ru me-ti-iq-šú*
61) *da-ád-me qer-bi-šú-un*
62) *ša ul-tu* u$_4$-*me ma-a'-du-ti*
63) *il-li-ku na-mu-tu*
64) UGU *ta-mir-ti-šú-un* ⸢*i*⸣-*ku ù ši-ir-'u*
65) *ul ib-ši-ma šá-ta-at qé-e et-tu-ti*
66) A.GÀR.MEŠ-*šú-un ḫab-ṣu-ti e-mu-u ki-šub-bi-iš*
67) *ta-me-ra-ti-šú-un zi-im-ru ṭa-a-bu*
68) *zu-um-ma-a šup-ru-sa* ^{d}*nisaba*
69) GIŠ.TIR.MEŠ *ak-šiṭ-ma gi-iṣ-ṣu da-ad-da-ru*
70) ^{d}GIŠ.BAR-*iš aq-mu* LÚ.*a-ra-me* DUMU *ḫab-ba-ti*
71) *i-na* GIŠ.TUKUL *ú-šam-qit ša* UR.MAḪ.MEŠ
72) *ù* UR.BAR.RA.MEŠ *áš-ku-na* BAD$_5$.BAD$_5$-*šú-un*
73) *i-ta-at ki-*⸢*šub-bé-e maḫ-ru-ti*⸣
74) *x x (x) x* [*x x x (x)*] *x x* ⸢*aṣ*$^{?}$-*bat-ma*⸣
75) ⸢UN.MEŠ KUR.KUR *na-ki*⸣-[*ri ki*]-⸢*šit-ti* ŠU.II-*ia*⸣
76) ⸢*ú-kin*$^{?}$⸣ *x x* [*x (x) qé*]-⸢*reb-šú-un*⸣

vii 45–76) At that time, the ancient roads for going to Babylon, the cult center of the Enlil of the god[s] (Marduk), were not open; [*their*] tra[ck(s)] were not fit (for travel). It was a desert region through which passage had been blocked for a [*long*] time. (vii 50) Journey through it was very difficult and no pathways were laid out. Thorny-plants, thistles, and (brushwood) thickets encroached upon impassable paths. Lions (vii 55) and jackals took cover in them and gamboled about like lambs. Arameans (and) Sutians — tent-dwellers, fugitives, criminals, (and) thieves (lit.: "son(s) of thieves") — (vii 60) had set up their abodes in that desert region and had made passage through it desolate. (With regard to) the settlements there that had long ago turned into wastelands, there were neither irrigation ditches nor furrows on their meadowland; (vii 65) (the area) was covered over with cobwebs. Their rich fields had turned into wasteland. Their meadowlands no longer heard (lit.: "were deprived of") the sweet (harvest) song. Grain had ceased to grow (lit.: "been cut off"). I chopped down the brushwood thickets and (vii 70) set fire to the thorny plants (and) thistles. I struck down the thieving Arameans (lit.: "Arameans, son(s) of thieves") with the sword. I slaughtered (lit.: "brought about their defeat") the lions and wolves. I *occupied* the territory of what had previously been wasteland ... and *established* people from the host[ile] countries that I [had con]quered ... [ins]ide them.

77) ⸢*i-na*⸣ *x x x* [*x x*] *x* ⸢RU$^{?}$ TI$^{?}$⸣
78) ⸢Ú$^{?}$⸣ *x x x* [...]
79) ⸢ÁŠ$^{?}$⸣ *x* ⸢DIŠ NE$^{?}$⸣ [...]
80) ⸢Ú DUL$_6$⸣ *x* [...]
81) ⸢*ú-šá*⸣-*x* [...]
82) ⸢*a*$^{?}$-*na* $^{m?}$KID⸣-*x x* [...]
83) *x x x x* [...]
84) ⸢*i-na*⸣ *x* ⸢A$^{?}$⸣ *x* [...]
85) ⸢GIŠ.MEŠ MU ŠI⸣ [...]

vii 77–85) Not sufficiently preserved to allow translation.

Lacuna

Lacuna

Col. viii

Lacuna

Lacuna

1′) [...] (*x*) *x*

viii 1′–33′) Not sufficiently preserved to allow trans-

---

vii 45 For the end of the line, see Brinkman in Liverani, Neo-Assyrian Geography p. 26 n. 68.

lation.

2′) [...] x ⸢IB$^{?}$ UD$^{?}$ ŠÚ$^{?}$ MA$^{?}$⸣
3′) [...] ⸢NA⸣ x x ⸢TI⸣
4′) [...] x ⸢TI ŠÚ⸣
5′) [...] ⸢ŠI RA⸣
6′) [...] x x x
7′) [...] x ⸢ÍD⸣
8′) [...] (x) x ⸢*maḫ-ru-ti*⸣
9′) [...] ⸢PAP U A⸣
10′) [...] ⸢KIR ŠÚ⸣ x [(x)]
11′) [...] ⸢UL UB⸣ [(x)] x
12′) [...] ⸢LUGAL-GI.NA⸣
13′) [...] (x) x ⸢DINGIR.MEŠ GAL.MEŠ⸣
14′) [...]-⸢*re-e*$^{?}$*-ti*⸣ [(x)] x (x) x [(x)]
15′) [...] ⸢A$^{?}$ GI⸣
16′) [...] x ⸢ṢU MA⸣
17′) [...] x [x (x)] ⸢DAN⸣ [(x)]
18′) [...] x ⸢ḪA⸣ x ⸢*rap-ši*⸣
19′) [...] x ⸢*lìb-bi-ia*⸣ x [x] x
20′) [...] x x x x x
21′) [...] x ⸢*i-na*⸣ x [x] x
22′) [...] x (x) [x] ⸢*na-mu-ta*$^{?}$⸣
23′) [...] ⸢*i-na qer-bi-šá* AḪ$^{?}$⸣ [x (x)] ⸢MA$^{?}$⸣
24′) [...] x [x (x)] ⸢QI/ŠÍK$^{?}$⸣ x x ⸢ŠÁ⸣
25′) [...] x [(x)] x x ⸢DU$^{?}$⸣ x ⸢^{d}*iš-tar*⸣
26′) [...] ⸢BI ŠÚ⸣ [x x] ⸢NA$_4$.ZA.GÌN *eb-bi*⸣
27′) [...] ⸢NIN⸣ x x ⸢ŠU *ù li-pit*$^{?}$ ŠU.II⸣
28′) [...] x ⸢LI EREN$^{?}$ *ú-še-piš*$^{?}$*-ma*⸣
29′) [...] ⸢*maḫ-ri* LA AG⸣ x ⸢MA$^{?}$⸣
30′) [...] x (x) x x
31′) [...] x x
32′) [...] ⸢LI⸣
33′) [...] ⸢LÁ⸣

Lacuna
1″) ⸢*ša* E$^{?}$ TAR$^{?}$ SU⸣ x [...]
2″) *tar-bit* KUR.*ḫa-ma-a-ni* [*e-li-šin*]
3″) *ú-šat-ri-ṣa* [...]
4″) GIŠ.IG.MEŠ GIŠ.ŠUR.MÌN ⸢GIŠ⸣.[*mu-suk-kan-ni*]
5″) *me-sér* URUDU *nam-ri* ⸢LI⸣ [...]
6″) *ú-rak-kis-ma* [*ú-rat-ta-a né-reb-šin*]
7″) GIŠ.KIRI$_6$.MAḪ-*ḫu tam*-⸢*šil*⸣ [KUR.*ḫa-ma-(a)-ni*]
8″) *ša gi-mir* GURUN [KUR-*i qé-reb-šú*$^{?}$]
9″) *ḫur-ru-šú* ⸢*ab*⸣-[*ta-ni i-ta-tuš*]
10″) ^{d}*iš-tar* GAŠAN [...]
11″) *zi-i-bi* x [...]
12″) *ni-iq* ⸢ŠÀ⸣ [...]
13″) *ma-ḫar* (x) [...]
14″) *it-ti* (x) [...]
15″) *ša a-na* [...]

Lacuna
viii 1″–6″) ... I roofed [them with *great cedar beams*] that had grown on Mount Amanus, [...] I bound the doors of cypress (and) [*musukkannu*-wood] with band(s) of shining copper [...] and [installed (the doors) in their entrances].

viii 7″–9″) I [created around it] a botanical garden, a repli[ca of Mount Amanus, in] whi[ch] were gathered every kind of fruit-bearing [mountain] tree.
viii 10″–11″) The goddess Ištar, the lady [...] food offerings [...]
viii 12″–25″) Not sufficiently preserved to allow translation.

---

viii 9′ As noted by C.J. Gadd (Iraq 16 [1954] p. 197), if the U does not actually exist, one might think of reading [... (^{md})*aš-šur*]-PAB-A, "[... Ashur]nasirpal."
viii 12′ C.J. Gadd (Iraq 16 [1954] p. 197) suggests that the line may have the end of the city-name Dūr-Šarrukīn.
viii 26′–28′ These lines seem to refer to the building of some object or structure, possibly for the goddess Ištar (mentioned in viii 25′).
Lacuna after viii 33′ See the commentary for the question of whether or not there is a gap between the section of this column found on ex. 1 (viii 1′–33′) and that found on ex. 2 (viii 1″–25″).
viii 2″–9″ For the restorations, see text no. 7 lines 160–161, text no. 8 lines 28–29 and 36, text no. 9 lines 41–42 and 64–66, text no. 11 lines 25–28, and text no. 13 lines 101–105.

16″) *ù* (*x*) [...]
17″) Ú (*x*) [...]
18″) KÙ.GI (*x*) [...]
19″) SÍG.*x* [...]
20″) SU *x* [...]
21″) TA *x* [...]
22″) *i-nu x* [...]
23″) *ša x* [...]
24″) ⸢NUN⸣ [...]
25″) *x* [...]
Lacuna

Lacuna

75

A fragment of a clay prism found at Nimrud preserves part of a description of the construction of the palace of Sargon II at Dūr-Šarrukīn and quite likely should be considered part of the previous inscription (text no. 74), preserving part of the last column (col. viii) of that inscription.

CATALOGUE

Museum Number	Excavation Number	Provenance	Dimensions (cm)	cpn
—	ND 3406	Nimrud, ZT, on pavement of the east corridor	—	n

COMMENTARY

Since text no. 74 ex. 2 and most of text no. 74 ex. 1 were found in the same place as ND 3406 and since all are prism fragments assignable to Sargon II, it is quite probable that all bear parts of the same inscription, as suggested by C.J. Gadd (e.g., Iraq 16 [1954] p. 173). ND 3406 may in fact have originally been part of either text no. 74 ex. 1 or ex. 2; Gadd (ibid. pp. 196–197) notes that ND 3406 is "not securely attributable to either, though its general appearance is rather more like E [ex. 2]." Gadd attributed ND 3406 to part of col. viii (of text no. 74) "only on the ground of its contents, as containing part of a building-inscription." While acknowledging the probability that the text on this fragment is really part of the previous inscription (text no. 74), the author has preferred to edit it separately since we do not know its exact relationship to the parts of col. viii found on the other two prisms. The inscription is edited from the published copy.

The restorations are based on those proposed by Gadd. Similar passages to lines 6′–9′ are found in several inscriptions of Sargon II (e.g., text no. 12 lines 30–33). For lines 11′–12′ and 18′–19′, see also text no. 2 lines 466–467.

74 viii 23″ As noted by C.J. Gadd (Iraq 16 [1954] p. 197), possibly the beginning of a personal name (*ša* ^{md}[...]).

BIBLIOGRAPHY

1954 Gadd, Iraq 16 pp. 173–175, 196–98, and pl. L (copy, edition, study)

TEXT

Lacuna

1′) [...] É [...]

2′) ⸢ù⸣ *ḫi-⸢bi*?⸣*-[iš*?*-ti*? ...]

3′) ⸢*i*⸣*-na qé-⸢reb*?⸣ [...]

4′) ⸢*ú*⸣*-šá-ʾ-x* [...]

5′) ⸢*ú*⸣*-šar-ma-a x* [...]

6′) É.GAL.MEŠ ZÚ AM.SI ⸢GIŠ⸣.[ESI GIŠ.TÚG]

7′) GIŠ.MES.MÁ.KAN.NA GIŠ.⸢EREN⸣ [GIŠ.ŠUR.MÌN]

8′) GIŠ.*dup-ra-ni* ŠIM.LI ⸢*ù*⸣ [GIŠ.*bu-uṭ-ni*]

9′) [*a*]*-⸢na*⸣ *mu-šab* LUGAL*-ti-ia qer-⸢bu*⸣*-[uš-šu ab-ni-ma*]

10′) [(LÚ).*aš*?]*-šur*.KI*-a-a-ú tar-bit* [...]

11′) [*it*]*-ti te-ne-še-e-ti* [*na-ki-ri*]

12′) [*ki*]*-⸢šit*⸣*-ti qa-ti-ia i-⸢na*⸣ [...]

13′) [x] 90? ⸢Ú⸣ KA ⸢BI?⸣ [...]

14′) [x] x *ma-ḫa-zi* KUR *aš-šur*.⸢KI⸣ [...]

15′) [*i*?]*-na* MU*-ti* DINGIR.MEŠ [...]

16′) [(x)] x A.AB.BA AN x [...]

17′) [(x)] x *mit-ḫa-[riš* ...]

18′) [*ni-ir*] *be-lu-ti-⸢ia*⸣ [*e-mid-su-nu-ti*]

19′) [*i-šu*]*-⸢ṭu*⸣ *ab-šá-a-⸢ni*⸣ [...]

Lacuna

Lacuna

1′–5′) [...] and *pie*[*ces* (*of aromatic woods*) ...] insi[de ...] ... [...] I settled [...]

6′–19′) [I built] insi[de it] palatial halls using (lit.: “of”) elephant ivory, [ebony, boxwood], *musukkannu*-wood, ceda[r, cypress], *daprānu*-juniper, juniper, and [terebinth to] be my royal residence. (10′) [As]syrians, who had grown up [... wi]th [enemy] people [whom] I [had cap]tured, in [...] ... [...] cult centers of Assyria [...] (15′) ... the gods [...] the sea [...] all toget[her ... I imposed the yoke] of m[y] lordship [upon them (and) they (now) pull] my yoke [...]

Lacuna

76

Five fragments of prismatic cylinders appear to have parts of the same inscription of Sargon II, an inscription that is written in Babylonian script and that summarizes a large number of his military actions. The latest actions mentioned — campaigns against Gurgum/Marqasi and Kammanu (lines 24′–27′, heavily restored) — occurred in the ruler's eleventh regnal year (711) and thus the inscription must have been composed no earlier than that year. The two fragments whose provenance is certain (exs. 2 and 5) come from Nimrud and Tell Baradān respectively. The text has sometimes been called the Nimrud Cylinder.

CATALOGUE

Ex.	Museum Number	Excavation Number	Provenance	Dimensions (cm)	Lines Preserved	cpn
1	K 1660	—	Possibly Nineveh, Kuyunjik	8.0×5.5	1–5, 21′–27′	c
2	IM —	ND 3411	Nimrud, ZTW 4; in fill against the southern wall of the room	15.8×7.1	1′–21′, left end 2–3	n
3	MS 2368	—	—	6.2×12.0	8′–27′	c
4	S. Moussaieff collection	—	—	—	12′–27′	p
5	IM 85067	35	Tell Baradān, Room 3, level 3	8.4×4.5	19′–27′	n

COMMENTARY

Ex. 1 comes from the center of a prismatic cylinder that originally had nine faces; it preserves parts of the beginning and end of the inscription. Assuming that the first eight faces had four lines each as on the first face — the penultimate face had four or more lines — and knowing that the final face had three lines, the inscription on this exemplar would have been ca. thirty-five lines in length. The piece is catalogued as part of the Kuyunjik collection in the British Museum; however, some pieces in that collection were actually not found at that site (see J.E. Reade in CRRA 30 p. 213). This raises the possibility that this fragment could have come from Nimrud, just like ex. 2.

Ex. 2 amounts "in bulk to rather more than a quarter of the whole" piece (Gadd, Iraq 16 [1954] p. 198). C.J. Gadd indicates that the fragment preserves parts of six faces of the "originally nine faces" of the cylinder. As it is currently preserved, each face had four lines, except for one that had only three lines (lines 8′–10′ of that exemplar). Thus, this exemplar would likely have had an inscription of approximately thirty-five lines. Gadd proposed that only five lines were missing at the beginning of the inscription (i.e., one complete face of the cylinder and the first line of the next face) and thus treated the first line preserved on that piece as his line 6. He noted that the beginning of the piece must have had an "abridged version" of the text found on the Khorsabad Cylinder of Sargon (text no. 43) since the beginning of the first preserved line (our 1′) is found at the end of line 8 on the Khorsabad text. If exs. 1 and 2 are in fact exemplars of the same inscription, and if the first part of the inscription (1–10′a) essentially duplicates text no. 43 lines 1–17, as seems to be the case from what is preserved on exs. 1 and 2, then the first preserved line on ex. 2 might well have been on the third face of that cylinder rather than the second as assumed by Gadd. He numbers the lines on ex. 2 as 6–25, which in our edition are 1′–21′. Gadd has suggested that the piece "might prove to have been made for 'export' to some temple or structure in the South" (Iraq 16 [1954] p. 199); however, if the inscription originally ended with line 27′ (see below), there would be nothing in it to suggest that the piece was not intended for use in Assyria. R. Borger (HKL 1 p. 140) has suggested that exs. 1 and 2 may have come from the same cylinder, but this cannot be proven. With regards to the findspot of the fragment, ZT 4, see Pedersén, Libraries pp. 147–149.

Ex. 3 originally had eight faces and approximately half of the circumference of the piece is preserved. Parts of nineteen lines on five faces are extant; each face whose full length is known had five lines. Since the last line preserved on the fragment may well have been the last line of the inscription and since it was the second line on that face, this exemplar may have originally had thirty-seven lines.

Based on the published photographs of ex. 4, parts of five faces and fourteen lines of text are preserved; when a face is fully preserved, the number of lines on it varies from three to four, although one face may possibly have five lines. It is not known how many faces this cylinder would have had and thus it is not possible to estimate how many lines of text were originally on it. K. Abraham kindly supplied the author with information on ex. 4 before the article by her and J. Klein was published.

Ex. 5 preserves parts of three faces and eight lines of text, one line on the first face, five lines on the second face (the only fully preserved face) and two on the third face. It is not known how many faces the cylinder originally had and thus it is not possible to estimate how many lines of text this cylinder originally had. The author must thank K. Kessler for providing both a copy of the inscription and information on the piece itself.

While it is not certain that the inscriptions on

the five exemplars were exact duplicates, at those points where the pieces overlap there is nothing to suggest that they were not. It is assumed here that the first half of the inscription (lines 1–10′a) basically duplicated text no. 43 lines 1–17. The end of the inscription (lines 26′–27′) is somewhat uncertain. The inscription on ex. 1 clearly ended with line 27′ since that line is followed by a line ruling and since the next face of the piece preserves the beginning of the inscription. It is uncertain whether or not the inscription on ex. 3 ended at this point since the cylinder is broken immediately following this line (indeed only the top half of most of the signs in line 27′ is preserved) and since there would have been room for two or possibly three more lines on that face of the cylinder. Ex. 4 probably also ended with line 27′ since there are no traces of a line following it, even though there is room for one, and since some of the signs towards the end of that line are spaced widely apart. Some of the signs on the last line of ex. 5 (part of 27′) are also widely spaced, suggesting that they may come from the last line of the inscription on that exemplar. Thus, it seems likely that line 27′ was the last line of the inscription on at least three of the exemplars (exs. 1, 4, and 5).

The line arrangement is based on ex. 1 for lines 1–5, on ex. 2 for lines 1′–14′ (lines 6–19 according to Gadd's line numbering of this exemplar [see above]), and on ex. 3 for lines 15′–27′ (lines 7′–19′ of that exemplar). The reading of lines 1–5 follows ex. 1 and that of lines 1′–7′ follows ex. 2; lines 8′–27′ are a composite of two or more exemplars. Restorations in lines 1–4, 1′–8′, and 12′–14′ are based upon text no. 43 lines 1–4, 8–15, and 19–22 respectively. See also Frame, CUSAS 17 pp. 138–140 for the arrangement of the five exemplars and in particular the line equivalences for lines 8′b–27′.

BIBLIOGRAPHY

1889 Bezold, Cat. 1 p. 326 (ex. 1, partial copy, study)
1894 Winckler, Sammlung 2 p. 4 top (ex. 1, copy)
1953 Wiseman, Iraq 15 pp. 137 and 139 (ex. 2, study, provenance)
1954 Gadd, Iraq 16 pp. 175, 198–201, and pl. LI (ex. 2, copy [by D.J. Wiseman], edition)
1994 Fuchs, Khorsabad pp. 385–386, 388–389, and 396–398 (ex. 1, study)
2001 Rollinger, Melammu 2 p. 239 (line 14′b, edition)
2007 Abraham and Klein, ZA 97 pp. 252–261 (ex. 4, photo, copy, edition)
2009 Frame, Studies Parpola pp. 80–82 nos. b–e and m (exs. 1–5, study)
2011 Frame, CUSAS 17 pp. 138–143 and pl. LII no. 72 (ex. 3, photo, edition; exs. 1–5, study)
2014 Maniori, Campagne di Sargon pp. 51–52 g5–g6 and passim (exs. 1–2, study)
2019 Marchesi, JNES 78 p. 24 (17′a, edition)

TEXT

1) [^{m}LUGAL-GI.NA *šá-ak-nu* ^{d}EN.LÍL NU].⸢ÈŠ⸣ *ba-ʾi-it* AN.ŠÁR *ni-ši-it* IGI.II ^{d}*[a-nim ù* ^{d}*da-gan]*

2) [LUGAL GAL-*ú* LUGAL *dan-nu* LUGAL KIŠ] ⸢LUGAL KUR⸣ ^{d}*aš-šur* ⸢LUGAL⸣ *kib-rat er-bet-*⸢*ti*⸣ [*mi-gir* DINGIR.MEŠ GAL.MEŠ]

3) [RE.É.UM *ke-e-nu ša* ^{d}*a-šur* ^{d}AMAR.UTU LUGAL-*ut la*] ⸢*šá*⸣*-na-an ú-šat-li-[mu-šu-ma zi-kir* MU-*šú ú-še-(eṣ)-ṣu-ú a-na re-še-e-te]*

4) [*šá-kin šu-ba-re-e*] ⸢ZIMBIR⸣.KI NIBRU.KI *u* ⸢KÁ⸣.[DINGIR.RA.KI ...]

5) [...] *x* (*x*) *x* [...]

Lacuna of ca. 4–5 lines

1′) *la* ⸢*i-mu*?⸣*-[ru mu-né-eh-hu* KUR.KUR DÙ-*ši-na ki-ma haṣ-bat-ti ú-daq-qi-qu-ma ha-am-ma-mi ša ar-ba-ʾi]*

2′) *id-du-ú ṣer-re-e-ti* ⸢*hur-sa-a-ni*⸣ *bé-ru-ú-ti šá né-reb-šu-nu* ⸢*áš*⸣*-[ṭu la-a mi-na ip-tu-ma]*

1–3) [Sargon (II), appointee of the god Enlil, *nešak*]*ku*-priest (*and*) *desired object* of (the god) Aššur, chosen of the god[s Anu and Dagān, great king, strong king, king of the world, kin]g of Assyria, king of the four quarters (of the world), [favorite of the great god];

3) [just shepherd, (one) to whom the gods Aššur (and) Marduk] have gran[ted a reign without e]qual [and whose reputation (these gods) exalt/exalted to the heights];

4–5) [who (re)-established the *šubarrû*-privileges of (the cities) Sippa]r, Nippur, and Ba[bylon, ...] ... [...]

Lacuna of ca. 4–5 lines

1′–4′a) [who ...] has me[t with] no [one who could overpower (him) in war or battle; (who) smashed all (enemy) lands as if (they were) pots and] put halters [on (all) rebels in the four (quarters of the world); (who) opened up innumerable] distant mountainous

3 It is not clear that there was actually room in ex. 1 to restore everything indicated in order to completely duplicate text no. 43 line 3.
5 Ex. 1 possibly [... *ba-ṭi*]-⸢*il-ta*⸣ [...]; cf. text no. 43 line 5.
1′ The translation assumes that immediately before this line was *ša ... i-na qab-li ù ta-ha-zi*, based on text no. 43 line 8.

3′) i-mu-ru du-ru-ug-šu-un ṭu-da-a-ti la a᾿-a-ri pa-áš-qa-[a-ti ša a-šar-ši-na šug-lud-du]
4′) i-ta-at-ti-qu-ma* i-te-eb-bi-ru na-gab be-ra-a-ti iš-tu KUR.[ra-a-ši mi-ṣir KUR.e-lam-ti]
5′) LÚ.pu-qu-du LÚ.da-mu-nu URU.BÀD-ku*-ri-gal-zu ù URU.ra-⌜pi⌝-[qu mad-bar DÙ.A.BI]
6′) a-di na-ḫal KUR.mu-uṣ-ri KUR a-mur-ri-i DAGAL-ti KUR.ḫat-ti a-⌜na⌝ [si-ḫir-ti-šá i-be-lu]
7′) iš-tu KUR.ḫa-áš-mar a-di KUR.ṣi-bar pat-ti KUR.ma-da-a-a ru-qu-ú-[ti ša ṣi-it ^{d}UTU-ši]
8′) KUR.nam-ri KUR.el-li-pí KUR.É-ḫa-am-ban KUR.par-su-maš KUR.ma-an-na-a-a KUR.[ur-ar-ṭu KUR.kas-ku KUR.ta-ba-lum]
9′) a-di KUR.mu-uš-ki ik-šu-du GAL-ti ŠU-su LÚ.šu-ut SAG.MEŠ-šú LÚ.GAR.MEŠ-ti UGU-šú-nu iš-tak-ka-nu-ma
10′) bil-ti man-da-at-ti ki-i šá áš-šu-ri e-mid-su-nu-ti eṭ-lu qar-du šá-kin taḫ-de-e ^{md}ḫum-ba-ni-ga-áš
11′) LUGAL KUR.e-lam-ti šá LÚ.te-šá-a-a LÚ.tu-᾿u-na-a-a is-su-ḫu ma-tu-uš-šu mu-ri-ib KUR.É-ḫu-um-ri-a
12′) rap-ši i-na URU.ra-pi-ḫi BAD_5.BAD_5 KUR.mu-uṣ-ri iš-ku-nu-ma ^{m}ḫa-[a-nu-nu LUGAL URU.ḫa-zi-te]
13′) ka-mu-su ú-še-ri-ba URU ^{d}aš-šur ka-šid LÚ.ta-mu-di LÚ.i-ba-di-di ⌜LÚ⌝.[mar-si-i-ma-ni$^{?}$ LÚ.ḫa-ia-pa-a$^{?}$]
14′) šá i-na MURUB$_4$ tam-tim KUR.ia-am-na-a-a sa-an-da-ni-šu i-bar-ru mu-par-ri-i᾿ ⌜ar⌝-[ma-ḫi URU.ši-nu-uḫ-ti (...)]
15′) ù KUR.É-^{m}puru-ta-áš šá ^{m}ki-ak-ki ù ^{m}am-ri-iš ma-li-ki-šú-nu im-nu-ú šal-⌜la⌝-[ti-iš]
16′) ṭa-rid ^{m}mi-ta-a LUGAL KUR.mu-uš-ki mu-ter ḫal-ṣi KUR.qu-e ek-mu-ti mu-rap-pi-šu pu-lu-ug-<ge>-šu
17′) na-bi-i᾿ KUR.a-ma-at-ti ù URU.ga-al-ga-meš šá ^{md}ia-ú-bi-i᾿-di ù ^{m}pi-si-i-ri da-gil pa-ni-šú-nu
18′) ik-šu-du GAL-ti ŠU-su mu-šaḫ-rib KUR.ú-ra-áš-ṭu URU.mu-ṣa-ṣi-ri KUR.an-di-ia u KUR.zi-kir-ti šá ^{m}ru-sa-a-a
19′) KUR.ú-ra-áš-ṭu-a-a ina ra-šub-bat GIŠ.TUKUL.MEŠ-šú mi-tu-ut ŠU.II-šú i-mu-tu mu-šak-niš KUR.ma-da-a-a ru-qu-ú-ti
20′) šá-gi-iš UN.MEŠ URU.ḫar-ḫar mu-paḫ-ḫir KUR.ma-an-na-a-a KUR.el-li-pí sa-ap-ḫu-⌜tu⌝ [...]

areas whose pass(es) are diffi[cult and] visited their remotest region(s); (who) traversed inaccessible, difficult paths [in terrifying location(s)] and crossed every *swamp*;

4′b–10′a) [(who) ruled] from the land [Rāši on the border of the land Elam], the Puqudu (and) Damūnu (tribes), the cities Dūr-Kurigalzu and Rap[iqu, the entire desert] as far as the Brook of Egypt, the wide land Amurru, (and) the land Ḫatti (Syria) in [its entirety]; (who)se great hand conquered (the area) from the land Ḫašmar to the land Ṣibar — which borders on the distant Medes [in the east] — the lands Namri, Ellipi, Bīt-Ḫamban, Parsumaš (Parsuaš), Mannea, [Urarṭu, Kasku, (and) Tabal], as far as the land Musku; (who) set eunuchs of his as governors over them and imposed upon them (the same) tribute (and) payment(s) as if (they were) Assyrians;

10′b–16′) the valiant man who brought about the defeat of Ḫumbanigaš (Ḫumban-nikaš I), king of the land Elam; who deported the Tēša (and) Tu᾿u(mu)na (tribes) to his land; who made the wide land Bīt-Ḫumria (Israel) tremble; (who) brought about the defeat of Egypt at the city Raphia and brought Ḫa[nūnu (Hanno), king of the city Gaza], to the city Aššur in bondage; who conquered the Tamudu, Ibādidi, [*Marsīmani, (and) Ḫayappa* (tribes)]; who caught the Ionians in the middle of the sea as a fowler (does); who cut through the *f*[*ruit trees* of the city Šinuḫtu (...)] (15′) and the land Bīt-Purutaš; who counted their rulers Kiakki and Amriš (Ambariš) [as] boo[ty]; who drove out Mitâ (Midas), king of the land Musku, brought back (to Assyrian control) the fortress(es) of the land Que (Cilicia) that had been taken away (by the enemy), (and) expanded its borders;

17′–25′) who plundered the land Hamath and the city Carchemish; whose great hand conquered Iaūbi᾿dī (Ilu-bi᾿dī) and Pisīri(s), *their* subjects; who laid waste to the land Urarṭu, the city Muṣaṣir, the land Andia, and the land Zikirtu; at the awesome terror of whose weapons Rusâ, the Urarṭian, died by his own hand; who subjugated the distant Medes; (20′) who slaughtered the people of the land Ḫarḫar; who gathered (back together) the scattered (people of) the lands Mannea (and) Ellipi [...]; who (deported

4′ Ex. 2 -*ma**, the copy has -GIŠ.
5′ Ex. 2 *ku**-, the copy has ŠU-.
9′ Ex. 3 omits -*šú* after SAG.MEŠ, thus "eunuchs <of his>."
10′ *taḫdê* for *taḫtê*; the word is preserved only in ex. 3.
15′ It is not clear that ex. 4 has sufficient room to restore all of this line. Ex. 2 omits *ù*, "and," before ^{m}*am-ri-iš*.
16′ *pu-lu-ug-<ge>-šu* is only found on ex. 2.
17′ It is unclear to whom "*their*" in "*their* subjects" refers; see the note to text no. 43 line 26.
20′ C.J. Gadd (Iraq 16 [1954] pp. 200–201) suggests *mu-taq-qí-in*$^{?}$ KUR$^{?}$ *el*$^{?}$*-li*$^{?}$*-pí*$^{?}$ (slightly modified), "who brought order to the land Ellipi" immediately before *munakkir* (start of line 21′) in ex. 1; see text no. 43 line 31.

21′) *mu-nak-kir šu-bat* URU.*pa-a-pa* URU.*lal-lu-uk-nu* URU.*suk-ki-i* URU.*ba-a-la* URU.*a-*⸢*bi-ti-ik-na*⸣ [(...)]
22′) *šá* ^{m}*it-ti-ia* URU.*al-la-ab-ra-a-a ú-še-ṣu-*[*ú* URU-*uš-šu mu*]-⸢*ab*⸣-*bi-it* KUR.*kar-al-la*
23′) *šá pa-a-ri* ^{md}*aš-šur-le-ʾi* LÚ.EN.URU-*šú-nu il-*⸢*lu*?⸣-[*ri-iš ú-si-mu-ma* ^{m}*a*]-⸢*da*⸣-*a*
24′) KUR.*šur-da-a e-mid-du ni-ir* ^{d}*aš-šur mu-la-iṭ* KUR.*kam-ma-ni šá* [^{m}*gu-un-zi-na-nu*]
25′) *ul-tu* URU.*me-li-di* URU LUGAL-*ti-šú ú-še-ṣu-ma* UGU *kul-lat* KUR-*šú i-qí-pu* [LÚ.*šá-ak-nu-ti*?]
26′) *ti-bu gal-tu la a-dir tu-qu-un-tu mu-nak-kir* LUGAL-*ut* ^{m}*tar-ḫu-la-ra* URU.*mar-qa-šá-a-*[*a* (...)]
27′) *šá paṭ* ⸢*gi-mir* URU.*gu-ur-gu-um-me a*⸣-*na mi-ṣir* KUR ^{d}*aš-šur ú-ter-ra* [(...)]

Lacuna

Left end of ex. 2

Left edge
1) [ITI?....]
2) UD.12.KAM
3) SAR

and) settled elsewhere (the people of) the cities Pāpa, Lalluknu, Sukkia, Bāla, (and) Abitikna [(...)]; who made Ittî of the land Allabria leave [his city; who de]stroyed the land Karalla, [dyed] the skin of Aššur-lēʾi, their city-ruler, [red like] the *ill*[*ūru*-plant, and] imposed the yoke of the god Aššur [upon Ad]â of the land Šurda; who kept in check the land Kammanu; who expelled [Gunzinānu] from the city Melid, his (Gunzinānu's) royal city, and appointed [*governors*] over all his land;

26′–27′) terrifying attack(er), fearless in battle, who did away with the kingship of Tarḫu-lara of the city Marqasa [(...)] (and) who made all of the city Gurgum (part of) the territory of Assyria [(...)].

Lacuna

Left end of ex. 2

Left edge 1–3) Written [*in the month* ...], day twelve.

77

A brief label mentioning Sargon is found on a green glass vase and on several stone jars; all exemplars whose provenance is known come from Nimrud. Each exemplar has a depiction of a lion before the inscription. This depiction may be an official mark indicating that the article derived from or belonged to the palace or treasury of the king, Sargon. With regard to the use of the figure of a lion, see Millard, Iraq 27 (1965) p. 15; Curtis and Reade, Art and Empire p. 146; Galter, Journal for Semitics 16/3 (2007) pp. 646–648; and Niederreiter, Iraq 70 [2008] pp. 51–86, esp. pp. 51–59.

---

76 lines 21′–25′ Cf. text no. 8 lines 9–10, text no. 43 lines 28 and 32–33, and text no. 13 lines 23–27.
76 line 24′ With regard to Gunzinānu, cf. text no. 8 lines 9–10 and text no. 13 lines 23–24. K. Abraham and J. Klein (ZA 97 [2007] pp. 256 and 261 prefer to restore Tarḫun-azi, rather than Gunzinānu.
76 line 25′ The published copy of ex. 1 has *kul-lat* KUR.KUR-*šú*, "all his lands," but collation shows that the text has *kul-lat* KUR-*šú*, "all his land."
76 lines 26′–27′ Cf. text no. 13 lines 28–31 and text no. 8 lines 10–11.
76 line 27′ While ex. 1 ends at this point, with this line being followed by a line ruling, ex. 3 may have had one or more additional lines.
76 Left end C.J. Gadd (Iraq 16 [1954] pp. 198–199) notes that "to judge by their position" the two lines preserved on the left end of ex. 2 could have been "preceded by no more than the name of a month" and that the signs of the end are larger and different in form to those found in the main text, "especially in the distinctive Assyrian form of the sign SAR".

CATALOGUE

Ex.	Museum Number	Registration Number	Object	Provenance	Dimensions (cm)	Lines Preserved	cpn
1	BM 90952 (=BM 12084)	N 2070 (London)	glass vase	Nimrud, North-West Palace, Room I	Height: 8.8; dia.: 6.2	1	(p)
2	BM 91460	48-11-4,165	white calcite jar fragment	As ex. 1	Height: 11.7; dia.: 10.0	1	c
3	BM 118443	48-11-4,166	yellowish calcite (or alabaster) jar fragment	As ex. 1	Height: 5.1; dia.: ca. 5.5	1	c
4	BM 91639	N 1561 (London)	alabaster jar	As ex. 1	Height: 17.8; dia. 9.4; rim dia.: 5.8	1	c
5	BM 91595	48-11-4,286	alabaster jar	As ex. 1	Height: 21.5; rim dia.: 7.2	1	c
6	BM 104894	1983-1-1,69	white calcite jar fragment	—	12.9×15.8; dia.: 12.5	1	c
7	VA 970	—	alabaster jar fragment	—	Height: ca. 25; dia.: 41.5	1	c

COMMENTARY

A.H. Layard found numerous fragments of vessels of white alabaster and baked clay below fallen stone slabs in Room I of the North-West Palace at Nimrud. Some of the fragments had cuneiform signs upon them, among which Layard "perceived the name and title of the Khorsabad king" (Layard, Nineveh 1 p. 342). He also found in the room three whole vessels: a glass vessel (ex. 1), an alabaster vessel (ex. 4), and a vessel that was broken by a workman (ex. 5?). Ex. 6 was also likely among the pieces found by Layard in this room at Nimrud. (See Layard, Nineveh 1 pp. 342–343 and Searight, Assyrian Stone Vessels.) Copies of three exemplars of this inscription are found in Layard's notebook MS A on pp. 320 and 322 (British Museum); these copies likely represent exs. 2, and 1 and 4 respectively. The statements as to the type of stone for exs. 2–5 and 7 are based upon museum records and/or published accounts (in particular Searight, Assyrian Stone Vessels).

Ex. 1 is a "squat *alabastron* of pale green cast and cut glass" (Collon, Ancient Near Eastern Art p. 175). D. Barag (Catalogue pp. 53–54 and 61) suggests that the vessel may have been made in Phoenicia or in Assyria by Phoenician artisans; J.E. Curtis (Curtis and Reade, Art and Empire p. 146) notes that the inscription may have been added later. The inscription has been collated from the published photos, but these are not always clear.

Ex. 5 was "found in a box from palace of Nimrud" (British Museum records; Searight, Assyrian Stone Vessels p. 18 no. 52). Ex. 6 preserves only the beginning of the inscription (É.GAL) and it is possible that the remainder of its inscription did not duplicate this one. It is assigned to Sargon in view of the presence of a depiction of a lion immediately to the left of the signs; for a possible origin in Nimrud, see ibid. no. 53. Ex. 7 was purchased by the Vorderasiatisches Museum. Comparing ex. 7 to two vases from Cyprus, F.W. von Bissing suggested that it also came from Cyprus (ZA 46 [1940] p. 153).

BIBLIOGRAPHY

— Layard, MS A pp. 320 and 322 (exs. 1–2, 4?, copy)

1849 Layard, Monuments p. 22 and pl. 97 no. 9 (ex. 5, drawing)

1849 Layard, Nineveh 1 pp. 342–343 (exs. 1, 4, 5, provenance); and 2 p. 421 (ex. 1, study)

1851 Layard, ICC pls. 83E and 84A (exs. 1–2, copy)

1853 Layard, Discoveries pp. 196–197 (exs. 1, 4, 5, drawing, study)

1886 Bezold, Literatur p. 93 §56.14.e–f (exs. 1–2, study)

1889 Winckler, Sar. 1 p. 192; and 2 pl. 49 nos. 4–5 (exs. 1–2, copy, transliteration; ex. 7 study)

1907 Ungnad, VAS 1 no. 73 (ex. 7, copy)

1922 BM Guide pp. 195–196 nos. 204, 210, 219, 221, and p. 237 no. 134 (ex. 1, photo, partial copy, transliteration; exs. 2, 6, study; ex. 3, translation; ex. 5, copy)

1927 Luckenbill, ARAB 2 p. 114 §228 (exs. 1–2, translation; ex. 7, study)

1940 von Bissing, ZA 46 p. 153 no. 6 (ex. 7, edition [by Falkenstein], study)
1966 Forbes, Ancient Technology^{2} 5 p. 132 fig. 22 (ex. 1, photo)
1966 von Saldern in Mallowan, Nimrud 2 p. 626 and fig. 584 (ex. 1, photo, study)
1970 von Saldern in Oppenheim, Glass p. 218 no. 17 (ex. 1, edition, study, additional bibliography)
1985 Barag, Catalogue pp. 25–26, 28, 32, 53–54, and 60–61, and fig. 2, pl. 3, and col. pl. B no. 26 (ex. 1, copy, study; edition [by Sollberger])
1994 Lackenbacher in Fontan, Khorsabad p. 155 fig. 1b and p. 282 (ex. 4, photo)
1995 Collon, Ancient Near Eastern Art pp. 174–175 fig. 139a (ex. 1, photo, translation)
1995 Collon, Studies Boehmer p. 72 and p. 73 fig. 7 (exs. 1, 4, drawing)
1995 Curtis in Curtis and Reade, Art and Empire p. 146 no. 115 (ex. 1, photo [inscription not legible], edition) and p. 148 no. 117 (ex. 4, photo, edition)
2004 Marzahn, Könige am Tigris pp. 107–109 no. 19 (ex. 7, photo, translation)
2008 Mango, Marzahn and Uehlinger, Könige am Tigris p. 197 Kat. 42 (ex. 7, photo, translation, study)
2008 Niederreiter, Iraq 70 pp. 51–86, esp. p. 53 figs. 1a–d, p. 77 nos. La.4–9, and p. 85 (ex. 1–2 and 4–7, edition; exs. 2, 4–6, copy, transliteration; ex. 3, edition)
2008 Searight, Assyrian Stone Vessels pp. 16–19 and figs. 8–9 nos. 51–54 and 57 (exs. 2–6, copy, edition, study)
2018 Tubb in Brereton, Ashurbanipal pp. 124–125 no. 127 (photo, translation)

TEXT

1)	É.GAL ^{m}MAN-GI.NA MAN KUR AŠ	(1) Palace of Sargon (II), king of Assyria.

78

In 1846, A.H. Layard found sixteen bronze weights of varying sizes in the shape of crouching lions under one of the winged bull colossi in Entrance b of the throne room of the North-West Palace at Nimrud. Thirteen of these bear cuneiform inscriptions and these allow the assignment of one to Tiglath-pileser III (Tadmor and Yamada, RINAP 1 pp. 152–153 Tiglath-pileser III no. 63), nine to Shalmaneser V (Tadmor and Yamada, RINAP 1 pp. 171–181 Shalmaneser V nos. 1–9), one to Sennacherib (Grayson and Novotny, RINAP 3/2 no. 211), and two to Sargon II (text nos. 78–79). A third lion weight (BM 91235), which has only the weight written on it in Aramaic (*šqln* 2), might also be assigned to Sargon according to F.M. Fales (Studies Milano pp. 488, 491, and 501–505 no. 14). The largest of the two lion weights of Sargon II has two brief texts, one in Akkadian and one in Aramaic, and both state that the object weighed "one mina of the king."

Major studies dealing with the bronze lion weights from Nimrud by T.C. Mitchell, F.M. Fales, C. Zaccagnini, and L. Peyronel are found in Gyselen, Prix pp. 129–138; Studies Lipiński pp. 33–55 and Studies Milano pp. 483–510; Studies Heltzer pp. 259–265; and Mesopotamia 50 (2015) pp. 93–112 respectively. Note also J. Reade's important study on Assyrian weights and money in SAAB 24 (2018) pp. 125–193. For further bibliography on the lion weights, see de Vogüé, CIS 2/1 p. 2 and Fitzmyer and Kaufman, Aramaic Bibliography 1 p. 37 no. B.2.4. For a photograph of one of the lion weights of Shalmaneser V, see Pritchard, ANEP^{2} p. 36 no. 119.

---

77 line 1 Ex. 5 has ^{m}<MAN>-.

CATALOGUE

Museum Number	Registration Number	Provenance	Dimensions (cm)	cpn
BM 91229	48-11-4,74	Nimrud, North-West Palace, under one of the winged bull colossi in Entrance b of the Throne Room (Chamber B)	9.4×4.5	c

COMMENTARY

The larger and heavier of the two bronze lion weights ascribed to Sargon II weighs 468.388g/468.5g. There is no handle on the back. Published references to this weight have often mixed information about it and BM 91227, a bronze lion weight weighing 480.149g and bearing an inscription of Shalmaneser V (Tadmor and Yamada, RINAP 1 pp. 178–179 Shalmaneser V text no. 7; attributed to Tiglath-pileser III by T.C. Mitchell). The two pieces were kindly weighed for the author several years ago by the staff of the British Museum and he was informed that BM 91229 was the one that weighed 468.388g. In the meantime several publications have continued to state that BM 91229 weighed 480.149g, and so its weight was again checked for the author by J.E. Reade in June 2018, when it was found to weigh 468.5g, a difference of about one tenth of a gram from the earlier weight of 468.388 and a difference that is likely due to different scales being used. In any case, it is clear that BM 91229 is over eleven grams lighter than BM 91227. In the bibliography provided below, it has been thought advisable to cite information on both weights in a few cases since it is not always easy to disentangle the information.

The Akkadian text is found on the back of the lion; line 1 of the Aramaic text is found on the left flank of the lion and line 2 on the base. The edition is for the most part based upon the published copies and the edition by Fales (Studies Lipiński p. 42), although the original has also been examined.

BIBLIOGRAPHY

1853 Layard, Discoveries p. 601 and pl. facing p. 601 nos. 10–11 (copy of Aramaic, study)

1856 Norris, JRAS 16 pp. 217, 219, 221, and pl. facing p. 222 nos. 10–11 (partial copy of Akkadian and Aramaic, study)

1864 Madden, Jewish Coinage p. 262 nos. 10–11 (translation, study)

1884 Aurès, RA 1/1 pp. 11–16 (study)

1884 Ledrain, RA 1/1 pp. 16–17 (study)

1889 de Vogüé, CIS 2/1 p. 9 and pl. I no. 8 (photo of Aramaic inscription line 2, copy, edition)

1891 Müller, WZKM 5 p. 5 (study)

1901 Johns, ADD 2 pp. 260 leo 10 (transliteration, study)

1907 Weissbach, ZDMG 61 p. 401 no. 69 (translation)

1912 Lehmann-Haupt, ZDMG 66 pp. 682–683, 685, 687, 691–692 (study)

1921 Thureau-Dangin, RA 18 p. 139 no. 10 (study)

1975 Segert, Altaramäische Grammatik p. 496 no. 22 (copy of Aramaic)

1984 Braun-Holzinger, Bronzen p. 111 no. 383j (translation of Akkadian, study)

1990 Mitchell in Gyselen, Prix pp. 129–138 nos. 10–11 [inscription under no. 11] (edition, study)

1995 Fales, Studies Lipiński pp. 42–43 no. 9 (copy, edition)

1997 Fales, Économie antique p. 293 no. 9 (translation)

2013 Curtis, Examination of Late Assyrian Metalwork pp. 74–75 and 173 no. 542 (translation, study)

2015 Peyronel, Mesopotamia 50 pp. 94, 97, 99–100, and 102 N10 (translation, study)

2016 Fales, Studies Milano pp. 485, 488, and 500–505 no. 9 (edition, study)

2018 Reade, SAAB 24 p. 136 fig. 7 (left), p. 166, and p. 181 no. B 15 (photo [inscription not legible], partial translation, study)

TEXT

Akkadian Inscription

1) ⸢KUR⸣ ^{m}MAN-GIN ⸢MAN KUR AŠ⸣
2) 1 MA.⸢NA⸣ *ša* MAN

Aramaic Inscription

1) 1
2) *mnḫ mlk*

Akkadian Inscription

Akkadian 1) Palace of Sargon (II), king of Assyria.
Akkadian 2) One mina of the king.

Aramaic Inscription

Aramaic 1) One.
Aramaic 2) Mina of the king.

Akkadian inscription 1 For the use of KUR for *ēkallu*, "palace" or "royal property," see CAD E pp. 52 and 60.

79

The second bronze lion weight from Nimrud that can be assigned to Sargon II also bears both Akkadian and Aramaic texts. The Akkadian one states that the object belonged to the palace of Sargon, while the Aramaic one states that it weighed three shekels.

CATALOGUE

Museum Number	Registration Number	Provenance	Dimensions (cm)	cpn
BM 91234	48-11-4,79	Nimrud, North-West Palace, under one of the winged bull colossi in Entrance b of the Throne Room (Chamber B)	4.1×2.1	n

COMMENTARY

The bronze lion weight has no handle on its back and currently weighs 49 g (52.36 g in Peyronel, Mesopotamia 50 [2015] p. 99 N15). It was found with two rings (now missing) around its neck and with the rings would have weighed ca. 54.6 g (note also Mitchell in Gyselen, Prix p. 135 no. 15; Curtis, apud Fales, Studies Lipiński p. 45 and n. 24; and Curtis, Examination of Late Assyrian Metalwork p. 173 no. 547). In a personal communication (July 15, 2018), J.E. Reade has pointed out to the author that the two rings around the neck of the lion may not originally have been part of this weight and that this had already been noted back in 1864 by the respected numismatist Reginald Stuart Poole: "The weight of the shekel, obtained by including the rings is excessive ... I am therefore of opinion that these rings are smaller weights, originally of flexible metal" (in Madden, Jewish Coinage p. 264 n. 9).

The Akkadian text is found on the back of the lion; line 1 of the Aramaic text is found on the left flank of the lion and line 2 on the base. The presence of a "badly preserved fourth line" in the Akkadian inscription was noted by F.M. Fales (Studies Lipiński p. 46), who suggested a tentative reading of that line (Studies Milano p. 501 no. 13 and n. 54); cf. text no. 78 line 2 of the Akkadian inscription.

BIBLIOGRAPHY

1849 Layard, Monuments p. 22 and pl. 96 nos. 7–8 (drawing)
1853 Layard, Discoveries p. 601 and pl. facing p. 601 no. 15 (copy of Aramaic, study)
1856 Norris, JRAS 16 pp. 216, 222–223, and pl. facing p. 222 no. 15 (copy of Aramaic, study)
1864 Madden, Jewish Coinage pp. 263–264 no. 15 (translation, study)
1884 Aurès, RA 1/1 pp. 11–16 (study)
1889 de Vogüé, CIS 2/1 pp. 12–13 and pl. I no. 13 (photo of Aramaic inscription line 2, copy, edition)
1891 Müller, WZKM 5 p. 5 (study)
1901 Johns, ADD 2 pp. 261–262 leo 15 (transliteration, study)
1907 Weissbach, ZDMG 61 p. 402 no. 74 (translation)
1909 Lehmann-Haupt, ZDMG 63 pp. 724–725 no. 74 (study)
1912 Lehmann-Haupt, ZDMG 66 pp. 691–692 n. 2 (study)
1921 Thureau-Dangin, RA 18 p. 139 no. 15 (study)
1975 Segert, Altaramäische Grammatik p. 496 no. 22 (copy of Aramaic)
1984 Braun-Holzinger, Bronzen p. 112 and pl. 74 no. 383n (drawing, translation of Akkadian, study)
1990 Mitchell in Gyselen, Prix pp. 129–138 no. 15 (edition, study)
1995 Fales, Studies Lipiński pp. 45–46 no. 13 (copy, edition)
1997 Fales, Économie antique p. 293 no. 13 (translation)
2013 Curtis, Examination of Late Assyrian Metalwork pp. 74–75 and 173 no. 547 (translation, study)
2015 Peyronel, Mesopotamia 50 pp. 96–97, 99–101, and 102 N15 (translation, study)
2016 Fales, Studies Milano pp. 485, 488–491, 496, 498, and 500–505 no. 13 (edition, study)
2018 Reade, SAAB 24 pp. 166 and 181 no. B 13 (partial translation, study)

TEXT

Akkadian Inscription

1) É.GAL
2) ^{m}MAN-GIN
3) MAN KUR AŠ
4) ⌜GÍN$^{?}$⌝ [3$^{?}$]

Akkadian Inscription

Akkadian 1–3) Palace of Sargon (II), king of Assyria.

Akkadian 4) [*Three*] *sh*[*ekels*].

Aramaic Inscription

1) 3
2) *šqln* 3

Aramaic Inscription

Aramaic 1) Three.
Aramaic 2) Three shekels.

80

Fragments of sixteen ivory writing boards (ND 3557–3572) and seven wooden writing boards (ND 3575–3581) were found in "Layard's well" of the North-West Palace at Nimrud in 1953. One of the ivory writing boards has an inscription engraved upon its polished outer face recording that Sargon II had had the series of celestial omens Enūma Anu Enlil copied on it and deposited in his palace at Dūr-Šarrukīn.

CATALOGUE

Museum Number	Excavation Number	Provenance	Dimensions (cm)	cpn
IM 56967	ND 3557	Nimrud, North-West Palace, "Layard's well" in Room AB	33.8×15.6×1.4	p

COMMENTARY

The inscription on the piece could be viewed as a colophon to the copy of Enūma Anu Enlil, but it has been included here among Sargon's royal inscriptions since it is incised on the outer surface of the writing board and since it does not refer to one specific tablet of the series. It has been edited both from the published photographs and photographs kindly supplied by J. Renger. A few sections of wax with inscriptions on them were still preserved upon some of the boards and those that are legible have been identified as parts of the series Enūma Anu Enlil.

With regard to Mesopotamian writing boards, see San Nicolò, Orientalia NS 17 (1948) pp. 59–70; Mallowan, Iraq 16 (1954) pp. 98–107 and pls. XXII-XXIII; Howard, Iraq 17 (1955) pp. 14–20; Wiseman, Iraq 17 (1955) pp. 3–13 and pls. I-III; Mallowan, Nimrud 1 pp. 152–163; Pritchard, ANEP^{2} pp. 348 and 376 no. 803; Parpola, JNES 42 (1983) pp. 1–8; Nemet-Nejat, Bagh. Mitt. 31 (2000) pp. 249–258; J.M. Russell, Senn.'s Palace p. 29; Freydank, Studies Haas pp. 103–111; MacGinnis, Iraq 64 (2002) pp. 217–236; and Cammarosano, Weirauch, Maruhn, Jendritzki, and Kohl, Mesopotamia 54 (2019) pp. 121–180.

BIBLIOGRAPHY

1954 Mallowan, Iraq 16 pp. 98–99, and pl. XXIII (photo, translation [by Wiseman], provenance)
1955 Wiseman, Iraq 17 pp. 7–8 and pl. I (photo, copy, edition, study)
1966 Mallowan, Nimrud 1 pp. 152–156 and fig. 93 (photo, translation, provenance)
1976 Basmachi, Treasures pp. 249 and 405, and fig. 186 (photo [reversed])
1992 Fales and Postgate, SAA 7 p. 65 fig. 15 (photo)
2000 Nemet-Nejat, Bagh. Mitt. 31 p. 254 (edition)

TEXT

1) É.GAL ^{m}MAN-GI.NA MAN *kiš-šá-ti*
2) MAN KUR *aš-šur*.KI DIŠ UD AN ^{d}EN.LÍL.LÁ ÉŠ.GÀR
3) *ina* GIŠ.LE.U$_{5}$.UM ZÚ AM.SI *ú-šá-áš-ṭir-ma*
4) *ina qé-reb* É.GAL-*šú ina* ⸢URU⸣.BÀD-MAN-GIN *ú-kin*

1–2a) Palace of Sargon (II), king of the world, king of Assyria.
2b–4) He had the series *Enūma Anu Enlil* written on an elephant ivory writing board and he deposited (it) inside his palace in the city Dūr-Šarrukīn.

81

S. Beverly, who was a member of the University of California, Berkeley, archaeological expedition excavating Nineveh in 1989 and 1990, took some photographs of work being carried out at the eastern end of Nebi Yunus by Iraqi archaeologists and made them available on Flickr, an online image hosting service. Two of the photos taken at Nebi Yunus on June 4, 1990 show a fragment of a stone slab with the image of an Assyrian eunuch and a cuneiform inscription. (The figure on the slab originally had a beard, but the slab had later been re-carved, removing the beard.) The inscription, which is part of a longer annalistic text that would have continued on a series of additional slabs, describes some events from Sargon's first and second regnal years (721 and 720), in particular the defeat and deportation of the Tēša and Tu'umuna (two Aramean tribes in northern Babylonia) and the suppression of a rebellion against Assyria led by Iaū-bi'dī of Hamath. E. Frahm has referred to this text as the Mosul Annals (Last Days p. 77).

CATALOGUE

Source	Provenance	Dimensions (cm)	cpn
Frahm, AoF 40 pp. 42–54	Probably Nineveh, Nebi Yunus	ca. 85 cm high	p

COMMENTARY

As noted by E. Frahm, it is not clear if the piece was actually discovered at Nebi Yunus — either erected there by Sargon or brought there from some other site (e.g., Dūr-Šarrukīn) by a later Assyrian monarch (e.g., Sennacherib) — or if it had been found elsewhere and brought to Nebi Yunus at the instruction of M. Jabr (then director of the Mosul Antiquities Office) to be exhibited to a television crew (AoF 40 [2013] pp. 52–53). (See also J.E. Reade in Studies Postgate p. 433.) It should be noted that some bricks with inscriptions dealing with Khorsabad have been found at Nineveh and some other sites (i.e., they were taken there in antiquity); for example, text no. 53 ex. 24 and text no. 54 ex. 4 were also found at Nebi Yunus. J.E. Reade (private communication, March 30, 2019) has suggested to the author that the slab may have originally been erected in Sargon's Juniper Palace at Kalḫu and been brought by Esarhaddon to Nebi Yunus for reuse along with the paving slab of Ashurnasirpal II published by A. Al-Juboori in Iraq 79 (2017) pp. 15-16.

The inscription runs on either side (but not across) the figure carved on the slab. This might suggest that the slab does not come from Khorsabad since the annals inscriptions from Khorsabad are found on a central band between two registers of reliefs (Frahm, AoF 40 [2013] pp. 45–46). Since Frahm estimates that the slab is about 85 cm high, the figure would thus be much smaller in size than comparable figures from Court VIII at Khorsabad; however, he points out that the slab might well come from some other location in or near Khorsabad. He also raises the possibility that the individual depicted was Sîn-aḫu-uṣur (ibid. pp. 51–53).

The current location of the slab is not known, although it is possible that it was once in the Mosul Museum and is now in the Iraq Museum (ibid. p. 44).

Photographs of the slab and inscription were published by Frahm (ibid. pp. 43–44), and the text has been edited from these photographs, but the edition basically follows that of Frahm. Restorations essentially follow those proposed by Frahm and are in particular based upon material in Sargon's Annals (text no. 1 lines 23b–26), the Aššur Charter (text no. 89 lines 18–23), and the Najafabad Stele (text no. 117 ii 4–7).

BIBLIOGRAPHY

2013 Frahm, AoF 40 pp. 42–54 (photo, edition, study)

2018 Frahm, Last Days pp. 77–78 no. 11 (lines 4–20, edition, study)

TEXT

Continued from one or more unpreserved slabs

1) [...] ⸢*a*⸣-*na* ^{d}AMAR$^{?}$.UTU$^{?}$ EN *x* (*x*) ŠÁ UŠ$^{?}$ *x x x*

2) [... ^{d}AMAR.UTU$^{?}$] ⸢*be*$^{?}$⸣-*lí su-up*-⸢*pi*⸣-*ia iš-mé-e-ma* LÚ.*te-sa-a-a*

3) [LÚ.*tu-ʾu-na-a-a*$^{?}$ ...] *x* UN.MEŠ-*šú-nu a-di mar-ši-ti-šú-nu*

4) [*as-su-ḫa-am-ma*$^{?}$ (...) *i-na* KUR.*ḫa-at-ti ú-še-šib i-na* 2-*i*] BALA-*ia* ^{md}*ia-ú-bi-iʾ-di*

5) [KUR.*a-ma-ta-a-a la* EN GIŠ.GU.ZA *la ši-nin-ti* É.GAL *šá ina* SIPA-*ut*] UN.MEŠ *ši-mat-su la ši-mat*

6) [... *ú*$^{?}$]-*ri*-⸢*dam*$^{?}$⸣-*ma it-ti* LÚ.ERIM.MEŠ *ḫup-ši*

7) [... *na-áš* GIŠ.*ka*]-⸢*ba*⸣-*bu* GIŠ.*az*-⸢*ma*⸣-[*ru*]-*ú ú-maš-šir-ma*

Continued from one or more unpreserved slabs

1–4a) [... *I prayed*] to the god *Marduk*, lord ... [... *Marduk*], my lord, listened to my supplications; the Tēša [(*and*) *the Tuʾu*(*mu*)*na* (*tribes*) ... *I deported* ...] their people, together with their property [*and* (...) I (re)settled (them) in the land Ḫatti (Syria)].

4b–11a) [In] my [second] regnal year, Iaū-biʾdī (Ilu-biʾdī) [of the land Hamath, who had no right to the throne, who was not worthy to (live in) a palace, (and) who] had not been fated [to shepherd] the people, [...] *came down* [...] and with common soldiers, [..., shi]eld (and) spe[a]r [bearers], he abandoned [(...)] and [... i]n the city Qarqar, whi[ch] (is) on the bank [*of the Orontes River*, ... he assembl]ed [*the troops of the wide*

1–4a Cf. text no. 1 lines 20b–23 (first regnal year). Sargon claims to have deported the Tēša and Tuʾumuna in text no. 76 line 11′: *šá* LÚ.*te-šá-a-a* LÚ.*tu-ʾu-na-a-a is-su-ḫu ma-tu-uš-šu*, "who deported the Tēša (and) Tuʾumuna (tribes) to his land." The land Tuʾumuna is mentioned in a passage immediately following one about (the ruler of) the Tēša in text no. 43 line 18. Line 1: This line is partially illegible on the photos because the upper edge of the slab protrudes and casts a shadow over the signs. See also Frahm, AoF 40 (2013) p. 47, who notes that what is read as UŠ might instead be E or KAL.

5 For the restoration, see text no. 89 line 18.

7 Possibly restore ... GIŠ.GIGIR.(MEŠ) ... ANŠE.*pét-ḫal-li*, "... chariots ... cavalry" following text no. 103 ii 57. See also text no. 81 line 7.

8) [... i]-⸢na⸣ URU.*qar-qa-ri* ⸢*ša*⸣ *i-na* GÚ
9) [ÍD.*a-ra-an-te*? ... LÚ.ERIM.MEŠ? KUR MAR.TU.KI? DAGAL-*tim*? *ú-paḫ*]-⸢*ḫir*⸣-*ma ma-mit* DINGIR.MEŠ GAL.MEŠ
10) [... KUR MAR.TU.KI? (DAGAL-*tu*?) *ul-tu*] ⸢SAG⸣.MEŠ-*šá a-di še*-⸢*pi*⸣-*te-šá it-ti-ia*
11) [*uš-bal-kit-ma*? *pa-a*? *e-da*? *ú-šá-áš-kin-ma*? *ik-ṣu-ra*? MÈ? (...) *a*]-*na* KUR *aš-šur*.KI UN.[MEŠ]-*šá* ḪUL-*tu*
12) [*la* DÙG.GA-*tú ú-ba-ʾi-i-ma* (...)] ⸢*il*⸣-*qa-a še-ṭu-ú-tú* ⸢URU.*ár*?⸣-[*pad-da*?]
13) [(URU....) URU.*ṣi-mir-ra*? (URU....) URU.*x*-(*x-x-x*)]-*tu* URU.*di-maš-qu* URU.*sa-mir-i*-⸢*na*⸣
14) [(*ú-paḫ-ḫir-ma*) *a-na*? *i-di-šú*? *ú-ter-ra*? (...)] ⸢DUMU⸣.MEŠ KUR *aš-šur*.KI *ša i-na qé-reb*
15) [KUR.*a-ma-at-ti*? ...] *ba-šu-ú ki-i* 1-*en id-duk-ma*
16) [*na-piš-tú ul e-zib* ...] ⸢*a*?⸣-*na* ^{d}EN.ZU LUGAL DINGIR.MEŠ *be-el* KUR.KUR
17) [...] ⸢*na*⸣-*ki-ri mu-ḫal-liq za-ma-ni* EN-*ia*
18) [(...) ŠU.II-*a-a*? *áš-ši-ma*? *áš-šú*? *ka-šad*?] KUR.*a-ma-at-ti sa-kap*
19) [^{md}*ia-ú-bi-iʾ-di*? ... KUR] MAR.TU.KI ⸢DAGAL⸣-*tim am-ḫur-ma*
20) [...]-*ú áš-šu* UN.MEŠ-*šú*

Contnued on one or more unpreserved slabs

land Amurru] and [*transgressed against*] the oath (sworn) by the great gods [... *He incited the* (*wide*) *land Amurru*, from] its upper end to its lower end, [*to rebel*] against me, [*made them act in unison, and prepared for battle* (...)].

11b–16a) [He (Iaū-biʾdī) sought] evil, [(things that were) not good (...), f]or Assyria (and) its people, [and] held (them) in contempt. [He (*assembled*)] the cities Ar[pad, (...), *Ṣimirra*, ...]tu, Damascus, (and) Samaria, [(*and*) *made* (*them*) *side with him*] (...). He killed [the citi]zens of Assyria who were present in [*the land Hamath* ...] altogether and [left no one alive (...)].

16b–20) [(...) *I raised my hands* (*in supplication*)] to the god Sîn, king of the gods (and) lord of the lands, [... *who vanquishes*] (my) enemies (and) destroys (my) foes, my lord, [*and*] I prayed (to him) [*in order to be able to conquer*] the land Hamath, overthrow [*Iaū-biʾdī*, (*and*) ... the] wide [land] Amurru. [...] Because of his people

Continued on one or more unpreserved slabs

82

This inscription, which is often referred to as the Nineveh Prism or the Broken Prism, is poorly preserved and made up from numerous fragments. Initially, the inscription was thought to be found on two prisms (called prism A and prism B), although exactly which fragments were to be assigned to each was debated. (See for example Winckler, Sar. 2 pls. 44–46 and Gadd, Iraq 16 [1954] pp. 174–175.) The assignment of fragments to the two prisms was based primarily upon their physical preservation and color. In the early 1940s, E.F. Weidner suggested that all the fragments came from one prism (AfO 14 [1941–44] pp. 51–52). Later, H. Tadmor showed that the two main fragments (K 1668a and K 1668b) form an indirect join at one point in what is the fifth column of the inscription and demonstrated that all the pieces

81 line 9 Cf. for example text no. 1 line 24 and text no. 117 ii 6.
81 line 10 Possibly restore *e-tiq*, "he transgressed," or *ul a-du-ur-ma*, "he did not fear and" at the beginning of the line; cf. text no. 1 lines 149–150. Possibly restore KUR.*a-ma-at-ti*, "land Hamath," instead of KUR.MAR.TU.KI (DAGAL-*tu*), "(wide) land Amurru."
81 line 11 For the restoration, see text no. 7 line 34.
81 lines 12–13 For the restoration at the beginning of line 12, see text no. 89 line 19, although there one finds *ú-ba-ʾu-ú-ma* rather than the proposed *ú-ba-ʾi-i-ma*. Lines 12–13: As noted by E. Frahm (AoF 40 [2013] p. 48), no exactly similar list of places is attested in the other texts of Sargon, but one can compare it to text no. 7 line 33, text no. 89 lines 19–20, and possibly text no. 1 line 25. Frahm states: "It might seem tempting to restore ^{URU}*A-ma-at*]-*tu* in line 13, but no other Sargon text mentions the city of Hamath among the rebel cities of 720, suggesting that a representative of the Assyrian crown may have managed to stay in power there."
81 line 14 For the restoration, see text no. 89 line 20.
81 line 15 For the restoration, see text no. 108 Frgm. D line 5′.
81 lines 16–19 For the restoration of line 16a, see text no. 89 line 21. Lines 16b–19: Cf. text no. 89 lines 21b–23 and text no. 108 Frgm. D line 7′.

likely come from only one actual prism. (See Tadmor, JCS 12 [1958] pp. 87–92 and more recently Fuchs, SAAS 8 pp. 3–15.)

It is possible that the inscription originally found on the prism was also inscribed, in all or in part, on a fragment of a prism discovered at Aššur (VA 8424, text no. 63) and on a fragment of a tablet acquired from an antiquities dealer in Mosul (A 16947, text no. 102). All three appear to use the same chronological assignment of events, an assignment at variance with the one used by the Annals of Sargon from Khorsabad (text nos. 1–6) and by the Najafabad stele (text no. 117). Thus, these two pieces were combined with this inscription in the most recent edition of the text (Fuchs, SAAS 8). Since only a small section of the text on the Aššur prism fragment overlaps what is known of the Nineveh Prism (text no. 63 ii′ 6′–18′ ≈ text no. 82 iii 1′′′–17′′′ and text no. 63 iii′ 7′–14′ ≈ text no. 82 v 1–8) and since there is some reason to suspect its text would have had a different building report at the end, it has been kept separate here (text no. 63). The same holds true for A 16947, which has no passage also preserved on the Nineveh Prism; moreover, the tablet from which it comes would not have been large enough to have the whole text found on the Nineveh Prism.

The inscription records events in Sargon's reign in chronological order down until the king's eleventh regnal year (711) — referred to in this inscription as his ninth regnal year (vii 13′) — before returning to events in his tenth regnal year, and thus A. Fuchs has recently referred to this inscription as the Annals of the Year 711 ("Die Annalen des Jahres 711"). It is not impossible, however, that the final, poorly preserved column of the text might have also recorded events of the king's twelfth regnal year (SAAS 8 p. 4), but if so, the account would have been unexpectedly brief. The prism was made to commemorate work on a ziggurrat (see viii 5′′′), likely that of the god Adad at Nineveh, in view of the reference to that god in the concluding formulae (viii 8′′′ and 10′′′). (See also Fuchs, SAAS 8 pp. 4–6.)

The edition of this text is the result of collaborative work between G. Frame and Fuchs, but is in effect based on the one published by Fuchs in SAAS 8. Differences between the edition here and the earlier one in SAAS 8 are mostly modifications to fit the style of the RINAP series and to conform to the manner of translation used for the other inscriptions included in this volume.

CATALOGUE

Museum Number	Published Copy (Winckler or Tadmor)	Published Copy (Fuchs)	Fuchs, SAAS §	Lines Preserved
K 1668a + K 1671	Winckler, Sar. 2 pl. 45 A–F	Fuchs, SAAS 8 pls. 5–6	IV.b–d, V.b–d	iv 1′–66′, v 7′–70′
K 1668b + DT 6	Winckler, Sar. 2 pl. 44 A–F	Fuchs, SAAS 8 pls. 5, 7–8	sub V.b–d, VI.b, VII.b, VIII.b	v 1′–15′, vi 1′–42′, vii 1′′–48′′, viii 1′–19′
K 1669	Winckler, Sar. 2 pl. 45	Fuchs, SAAS 8 pl. 3	III.b	iii 1′–35′
K 1672	Winckler, Sar. 2 pl. 45	Fuchs, SAAS 8 pl. 10	VI.e, VII.e	vi 1′′′′′–10′′′′′, vii 1′′′′′–9′′′′′
K 1673	Winckler, Sar. 2 pl. 46 (right column only)	Fuchs, SAAS 8 pl. 4	II.c,	ii 1′–13′,
			III.c,	iii 1′′–12′′,

K 4818	Winckler, Sar. 2 pl. 46	Fuchs, SAAS 8 pl. 1	I.f, VIII.f	i 1′–2′, viii 1‴–11‴ and lower edge
K 8536	Winckler, Sar. 2 pl. 46 ("unnumeriert")	Fuchs, SAAS 8 pl. 10	VI.d	vi 1⁗–7⁗
Rm 2,92	Tadmor, JCS 12 (1958) p. 97	Fuchs, SAAS 8 pl. 1	I.a, II.a	i 1–12, ii 1–8
Sm 2021 + 82-5-22,8	Winckler, Sar. 2 pl. 45 (only Sm 2021)	Fuchs, SAAS 8 pl. 9	IV.a, V.a	iv 1–20, v 1–11
Sm 2022	Winckler, Sar. 2 pl. 45	Fuchs, SAAS 8 pl. 9	VI.a, VII.a	vi 1′–10′, vii 1′–16′
Sm 2049	Tadmor, JCS 12 (1958) p. 98	Fuchs, SAAS 8 pl. 10	VI.c, VII.c	vi 1‴–11‴, vii 1‴–15‴
Sm 2050	Winckler, Sar. 2 pl. 46 (left column only)	Fuchs, SAAS 8 pl. 10	VII.d, VIII.d	vii 1⁗–6⁗, viii 1″–5″
79-7-8,14	Winckler, Sar. 2 pl. 45	Fuchs, SAAS 8 pl. 4	III.e, IV.e	iii 1‴–16‴, iv 1″–8″

ARRANGEMENT OF FRAGMENTS

Column	Lines Preserved	Fuchs, SAAS §	Museum Number	Subject	Date in Khorsabad Annals (text nos. 1-6)
i	i 1–12	I.a	Rm 2,92 i′ 1–12	Introduction	—
	Lacuna				
	i 1′–2′	I.f	K 4818 ii′ 1′–2′	Uncertain	—
ii	ii 1–8	II.a	Rm 2, 92 ii′ 1–8	Uncertain	—
	Lacuna				
		(II.b/c?)	(see text no. 102)		
	Lacuna				
	ii 1′–13′	II.c	K 1673 i′ 1′–13′	Uncertain	—
	Lacuna				
		(II.d)	(see text no. 63 i′)		
	Lacuna				
iii	Lacuna				
	iii 1′–25′	III.b	K 1669 1′–35′	Media (Kišesim)	Sixth regnal year
	iii 26′–35′			Media (Ḫarḫar)	Sixth regnal year
	Lacuna				
	iii 1″–12″	III.c	K 1673 ii′ 1′–12′	Media (Ḫarḫar)	Sixth regnal year
	Lacuna	(III.e)	(see text no. 63 ii′)		
	iii 1‴–8‴	III.e	79-7-8,14 i′ 1′–17′	Šilkani of Egypt	—
	iii 9‴–17‴			[6th regnal year]: Mannea	Seventh regnal year
	Lacuna			[7th regnal year: Urarṭu]	Eighth regnal year
iv	iv 1–20	IV.a	Sm 2021 + 82-5-22,8 i′ 1–20	Urarṭu	Eighth regnal year
	Lacuna				
	iv 1′–66′	IV.b-d	K 1668a + K 1671 i′ 1′–66′	Muṣaṣir	Eighth regnal year
	Lacuna				
	iv 1″–8″	IV.e	79-7-8,14 ii′ 1′–8′	Muṣaṣir	(Eighth regnal year)
	Lacuna	(IV.f)	(see text no. 63 iii′)		
v	v 1–6	V.a	Sm 2021 + 82-5-22,8 ii′ 1–11	Muṣaṣir	(Eighth regnal year)
	v 7–11			Eighth regnal year: Karalla	Ninth regnal year
	Lacuna	(V.a)	(see text no. 63 iii′)		
	v 1′–59′	V.b-d	K 1668b + DT 6 i′ 1′–15′ (+) K 1668a + K 1671 ii′ 7′–70′	Karalla, Ḫabḫu	Ninth regnal year
	v 60′–70′			Ellipi	
	Lacuna				
vi	Lacuna				

	vi 1′–10′	VI.a	Sm 2022 i′ 1′–10′	Ellipi?	(Ninth regnal year)
	Lacuna				
	vi 1′′–13′′	VI.b	K 1668b + DT 6 ii′ 1′–42′	Ellipi	Ninth regnal year
	vi 14′′–42′′			Media	Ninth regnal year
	Lacuna				
	vi 1′′′	VI.c	Sm 2049 i′ 1′–11′	Uncertain	(Ninth regnal year)
	vi 2′′′–11′′′			Tabal, Bīt-Purutaš	Ninth regnal year
	Lacuna				
	vi 1′′′′–7′′′′	VI.d	K 8536 1′–7′	Tabal, Bīt-Purutaš	Ninth regnal year
	Lacuna				
	vi 1′′′′′–10′′′′′	VI.e	K 1672′ i′ 1′–10′	Tabal, Bīt-Purutaš	(Ninth regnal year)
	Lacuna				
vii	Lacuna				
	vii 1′–12′	VII.a	Sm 2022 ii′ 1′–16′	Tabal, Bīt-Purutaš	(Ninth regnal year)
	vii 13′–16′			Ninth regnal year: Ashdod	Eleventh regnal year
	Lacuna				
	vii 1′′–48′′	VII.b	K 1668b + DT 6 iii′ 1′–48′	Ashdod	Eleventh regnal year
	Lacuna				
	vii 1′′′–15′′′	VII.c	Sm 2049 ii′ 1′–15′	Gurgum	Eleventh regnal year?
	Lacuna				
	vii 1′′′′–6′′′′	VII.d	Sm 2050 i′ 1′–6′	Gurgum	Eleventh regnal year?
	Lacuna				
	vii 1′′′′′–9′′′′′	VII.e	K 1672 ii′ 1′–9′	Melid	Tenth regnal year
	Lacuna				
viii	Lacuna				
	viii 1′–15′	VIII.b	K 1668b + DT 6 iv′ 1′–19′	Melid	Tenth regnal year
	viii 16′–19′			Anatolian metalic resources	Tenth regnal year
	Lacuna				
	viii 1′′–5′′	VIII.d	Sm 2050 ii′ 1′–5′	Uncertain	—
	Lacuna				
	viii i′′′–12′′′	VIII.f	K 4818 i′ 1′–12′	Blessings, curses; colophon	—

COMMENTARY

This eight-sided prism is poorly preserved; in particular, only small sections of columns i, ii, and viii are preserved and the exact placement of some fragments is not certain. Charts indicating the relative positions of the fragments on the various sides of the prism are presented in Fuchs, SAAS 8 pp. 8–9. The exact provenances at Nineveh of the various fragments are not known, but at least some came from excavations in the palace of Sennacherib (G. Smith, Assyrian Discoveries p. 98). The only published photograph of any part of the inscription on the prism is found in Ball, Light p. 185 (K 1668a+); see also now Figure 27.

Based upon what is preserved and what duplicates or is similar to passages in other inscriptions, Fuchs has estimated that each column probably had approximately 200 lines, for a total of 1500–1600 lines. He argues that the prism would have been about 60 cm high and 14.5 cm in diameter. (See Fuchs, SAAS 8 pp. 12–15.)

In the chart "Arrangement of Fragments," the column and line numbers given after the museum numbers are those for that particular fragment, not for the Nineveh Prism inscription as a whole. Thus, for example, the end of col. i of the inscription is found on column ii′ (counting from the left) of K 4818.

Cut into the bottom of K 4818 are representations of two animals striding left. (See Caubet, Khorsabad p. 251 fig. 15; Finkel and Reade, ZA 86 [1996] fig. 8 following p. 268; and Fuchs, SAAS 8 p. ii for photographs; see also Niederreiter, Iraq 70 [2008] pp. 54–55 and fig. 2.) One of the animals is a bull and the other probably is as well. Designs are also found on the bottom of the prism fragment of Sargon II from Aššur (text no. 63). Similar symbols are found on glazed bricks and paintings of Sargon; these symbols have been interpreted by I.L. Finkel and J.E. Reade (ZA 86 [1996] pp. 244–268) as hieroglyphs, standing for particular words. They do not see, however, any cogent link between these and the designs on the ends of the prisms. They suggest that the latter may have been "related to the identities of the gods for whose temples the prisms were made" and note that the bull was an attribute of the god Adad (ibid. p. 247). As noted above, the Nineveh

Prism may have been created to commemorate work on the ziggurrat of the god Adad.

In view of the fact that the inscription is made up from numerous fragments, it has been thought helpful to the user to indicate in the edition the museum number of each fragment as it comes into use, and also the column number on that particular fragment. Thus, immediately before the edition of i 1′–2′ is "(K 4818 ii′)," indicating that these line are found on the second column (from the left) of the fragment K 4818.

BIBLIOGRAPHY

1875 G. Smith, Assyrian Discoveries pp. 288–293 (vi 14′′–37′′, vii 13′′–47′′, translation, retored from texts from Khorsabad)

1884 Delitzsch, Sprache der Kossäer pp. 47–49 (vi 14′′–37′′, transliteration, study)

1886 Bezold, Literatur pp. 90–91 §53.7 (study)

1889 Winckler, Sar. 1 pp. 186–189; and 2 pls. 44–46 (K 1668a+, K 1668b+, K 1669, K 1672, K 1673 ii′, K 4818, K 8536, 79-7-8,14, Sm 2021, Sm 2022, Sm 2050 i′, copy, vii 13′–15′, 1′′–46′′, edition)

1889 Winckler, Untersuchungen pp. 118–119 (vi 14′′–37′′, transliteration)

1897 Rost, MVAG 2/2 pp. 111–115 = 214–218 (vi 14′′–38′′, transliteration)

1898 Winckler, AOF 2/1 pp. 71–73 (vi 1′′′′′–10′′′′′, edition)

1898 Winckler, MVAG 3/1 pp. 53–55 (iii 1′′′–16′′′, vii 37′′b–47′′, edition)

1899 Ball, Light pp. 185–186 (K 1668a+, photo, study)

1908 Olmstead, Western Asia pp. 11–14 and n. 42 (study)

1909 Winckler, Textbuch[3] pp. 41–42 (vii 13′–16′, 1′′–48′′ edition)

1911 Sarsowsky, Urkundenbuch p. 31 (vii 1′′–48′′, copy)

1912 Thureau-Dangin, TCL 3 p. IV n. 1, pp. IV–V n. 9, and pp. 76–81 (iv 1′–67′, v 51′–54′, edition; vi 17′′–34′′, study)

1918 Weissbach, ZDMG 72 p. 164 n. 1 (Sm 2022, K 1668b+, study)

1926 Ebeling in Gressmann, ATAT[2] p. 351 (vii 13′–15′, 1′′–47′′, translation)

1927 Luckenbill, ARAB 2 pp. 104–111 §§190–218 (translation)

1934 König, AO 33/3-4 pp. 55–58 (vi 14′′–37′′, translation, study)

1940 Eilers, ZDMG 94 p. 203 (vi 29′′, study)

1941–44 Weidner, AfO 14 pp. 48–49 and 51–52 (K 4818, study)

1948 Landsberger, Sam'al pp. 73–75 (vi 2′′′′′–10′′′′′, edition)

1954 Gadd, Iraq 16 pp. 174–175 (study)

1957 Borger, BiOr 14 p. 121b sub S. 229b (vii 29′′, study)

1958 Tadmor, JCS 12 pp. 23–24, p. 77 n. 182, pp. 79 and 87–93 with nn. 286, 291, and 300–302, and pp. 97–99 (Rm 2,92 i′, Sm 2049, copy, i 1–12, v 1–11, 7′–17′, vi 1′′′–11′′′, vii 13′–15′, 1′′′–15′′′, edition, iii 1′′′–8′′′, iv 1–14, vi 2–3, 6–7, viii 2′–19′, 1′′–2′′, 4′′?, 2′′′–12′′′, transliteration; study)

1958 Wiseman, DOTT p. 61 (vii 13′–16′, 1′–46′′, translation)

1961 von Soden, OLZ 56 cols. 577–578 (vii 5′, study)

1969 Oppenheim, ANET[3] p. 287 (vii 1′′–46′′, translation)

1969 Weippert, ZDMG Suppl. 1/1 pp. 213–215 (vii 5′, study)

1971 Weippert, Edom pp. 87–111 nos. 10 and 10A (transliteration, study; vii 13′–16′, 1′′–48′′, translation)

1973 Weippert, ZDPV 89 p. 50 (vii 5′, study)

1974 Na'aman, BASOR 214 p. 32 (vii 25′′–32′′ translation, study)

1977 Briend and Seux, TPOA no. 40B (vii 25′′b–41′′, translation)

1979 Na'aman, Tel Aviv 6 p. 71 n. 6 (iii 1′′′–2′′′, study)

1984 Borger, TUAT 1/4 pp. 381–382 (vii 13′–16′, 1′′–48′′, translation)

1987 Kapera, Folia Orientalia 24 pp. 29–39 (vii 13′–15′, 1′′–48′′, translation, study)

1988 Na'aman and Zadok, JCS 40 p. 39 n. 17 (iii 22′–25′, study)

1989 Timm, Moab pp. 334–337 (vii 13′–16′, 25′′b–33′′a, edition, study)

1994 Fuchs, Khorsabad p. 386 (study)

1994 Na'aman, Zion 59 p. 29 (vii 13′–15′, 1′′–47′′, translation [in Hebrew])

1994 Postgate, Studies Hrouda p. 236 (v 56′b–58′, edition)

1998 Fuchs, SAAS 8 (copy, edition, study)

1999 Na'aman, UF 31 pp. 426–427 (vi 3′′′′′–8′′′′′, study)

1999-2000 Na'aman, AfO 46–47 pp. 362–363 (iii 3′, 23′–24′, 1′′′–3′′′, and vi 3′′′′′–8′′′′′, study)

2000 Bagg, Assyrische Wasserbauten p. 144 (vii 35′′b–37′′a, edition)

2001 Holloway, CRRA 45/1 pp. 247–249 (iii 7′–9′, edition, study)

2001 Rollinger, Melammu 2 pp. 245–246 (vii 1′′–47′′, translation)

2002 Holloway, Aššur is King pp. 156–158 nn. 250–251 (iii 6′–9′, edition, study; iii 2′′–4′′, transliteration)

2002 Younger in Chavalas and Younger, Mesopotamia and the Bible pp. 312–314 (iii 1′′′–8′′′, vii 13′–16′, 1′′–48′′, translation)

2005 Vera Chamaza, Rolle Moabs pp. 144–148 nos. 7a–b (vii 13′–15′, 1′′–48′′, edition)

2006 Ponchia, SAAB 15 p. 241 n. 174 (iv 5–6, 10–19, edition)

2007 Aster, JAOS 127 p. 276 (v 12′–14′, edition)

2008 Cogan, Raging Torrent pp. 103–105 no. 25 (vii 13′–16′, 1′′–48′′, translation, study)

2014 Maniori, Campagne di Sargon p. 39 A7 and passim (study)

2017 Liverani, Assyria pp. 206 and 222 (iii 5′b–8′, 6′′b–9′′, translation)

Figure 27. K 1668a + K 1671, parts of columns iv and v of the Nineveh Prism (text no. 82), which records events up until Sargon's ninth regnal year (711). © The Trustees of the British Museum.

TEXT

Col. i

Rm 2,92 i′

1) [...] ⸢LUGAL⸣ GAL-*ú šad-la kar-ši*
2) [...] *x-li an-na-šu*
3) [...]-⸢*ú*⸣ *zi-kir-šu* ⸢*kab*⸣-*tu*
4) [...] *x* GI PI IR ^{d}[*x*]
5) [... *a*]-*šib* AN-*e ne-sú-ú*-⸢*te*⸣
6) [...] KA LIŠ ŠU GI *x*
7) [... ^{d}*nu*]-⸢*dím*⸣-*mud mu-um*-⸢*mu*⸣
8) [...] *x* ŠA NE ME [*x*]
9) [...] KU NA *x* [(*x*)]
10) [...] *x* A *x* [*x*]
11) [...] *x* MA *x* [*x*]
12) [...] *x* [*x x*]

Rm 2,92 i′

i 1–8) [...] great [ki]ng, (one with) broad understanding, [... *I requested*] his [*firm*] approval [*and* ...] his venerable word [...] ... (i 5) [... who dw]ells in the far-off heavens, [...] ... [... the god Nud]immud (Ea), the creator, [...] ...

i 9–12) Too poorly preserved to allow translation.

Lacuna

K 4818 ii′

1′) *x* [...]
2′) *i*-⸢*na*⸣ [...]

Lacuna

K 4818 ii′

i 1′–2′) Too poorly preserved to allow translation.

Col. ii

Rm 2,92 ii′

1) [...]
2) [...]
3) [...]
4) *x* [...]
5) *x* [...]
6) *x* [...]
7) [...]
8) *x* [...]

Rm 2,92 ii′

ii 1–8) Too poorly preserved to allow translation.

Lacuna

K 1673 i′

1′) [...] *x*
2′) [...] *x* ŠÁ
3′) [...] *x-ma*
4′) [...] *x* (*x*) *x*
5′) [...] *x* ⸢ŠÁ?⸣ LA?
6′) [...] *x* [(*x*)] *x*
7′) [...] *x x x*
8′) [...] *x x x*
9′) [...] *x* (*x*) *x x x*
10′) [...] *x x* (*x*) *x x* ŠU

Lacuna

K 1673 i′

ii 1′–13′) Too poorly preserved to allow translation.

---

i 1–12 The beginning of the text appears to be different from the opening sections of all other inscriptions of Sargon II. Furthermore, the first line follows a line ruling and the copy by H. Tadmor (JCS 11 [1957] p. 97) indicates traces of signs from one or two lines above that line ruling; he assumes three lines in this area (ibid. p. 98). The copy by A. Fuchs (SAAS 8 pl. 1) also indicates some marks/damage above the line ruling, but he states "Das Fragment enthält über der ersten Zeile des eigentlichen Textes noch weitere unleserliche Kratzer, die zunächst an Zeichenspuren denken lassen. Nach mehrfacher Prüfung des Originals bin ich zu der Überzeugung gelangt, dass es sicht hierbei wohl doch nur um Risse und Löcher handelt, die Zeichenresten nur ähnlich sehen" (ibid. p. 21). It is most unusual not to have begun the inscription at the very top of the column and one would wonder if there had not originally been something written in this area. However, Sm 2021, which also preserves the top of its columns (iv and v of the master text), seems to indicate that the text does begin a bit lower down from the top of the prism than is usual.

i 2–3 The tentative translation assumes ... *an-na-šu* [*ke-e-na a-šá-al-ma* ...]; see Schroeder, KAH 2 no. 54 line 5. Or possibly ... *an-na-šu* [*ke-e-nu* (*la muš-pe-lu*) *at-ta-kil-ma* ...], "[I trusted in] his [firm (and unalterable)] approval]"; see Leichty, RINAP 4 p. 107 no. 48 line 79.

i 4 Possibly [...] ⸢*ša*?⸣-*ge-pi-ir* DINGIR.[MEŠ], "most majestic of the god[s]"?

i 8 Possibly *ša ne-me*-[*qí*], "of wisd[om]" or *ša ne-me*-[*eq-šú*], "who[se] wisd[om]."

ii 1′–13′ If the inscription of text no. 102 was also found on the Nineveh Prism, it would likely have been slightly before or after this section of K 1673.

11′) [...] x x (x) *x-nu-ti-*⸢*ma*⸣
12′) [...] x x ⸢LA$^{?}$⸣ x x (x) [x]
13′) [...] x x [x x]
Lacuna
Col. iii
Lacuna
K 1669
1′) [x x x (x x)] ⸢LUGAL$^{?}$⸣.MEŠ-*šú* ⸢EN ḪI$^{?}$⸣ x x [...]
2′) [x x x (x x)] NU NÍG.ŠU-*šú* NÍG.GA-*šú a-*⸢*na*⸣ [...]
3′) [*it-ti* x (x)].⸢MEŠ⸣ ANŠE.KUR.RA.MEŠ ANŠE.⸢KUNGA⸣.[MEŠ ...]
4′) [*mim-ma*$^{?}$ *aq-ru*$^{?}$ *ni*]-⸢*ṣir*⸣-*ti* LUGAL-*ti ul-tú* ⸢*qé*⸣-[*reb* URU.*ki-še-si-im*$^{?}$]
5′) [*ú-še-ṣa-am*]-*ma* URU ⸢*šu*⸣-*a-tú a-na eš-šu-*⸢*ti*⸣ [*aṣ-bat*]
6′) [x x x (x)] URU.*kar-*^{d}MAŠ.MAŠ MU-*šú* [*ab-bi* GIŠ.TUKUL.MEŠ *ša*]
7′) [^{d}*a-šur*$_{4}$ ^{d}]EN.ZU ^{d}*šà-máš* ^{d}⸢IŠKUR⸣ ^{d}⸢*iš*⸣-[*tar* EN.MEŠ-*ia a-li-kut*]
8′) [*pa-ni-ia ú-še*]-⸢*piš*⸣-*ma i-na lìb-bi* ⸢*ú-šar*⸣-[*me*]
9′) [UN.MEŠ *ki*]-⸢*šit*⸣-*ti qa-ti-ia i-na lìb-bi* ⸢*ú*⸣-[*še-šib/rib*]
10′) [*it-ti* UN.MEŠ] ⸢KUR⸣ *aš-šur*.KI *am-nu-šu-*⸢*nu*⸣-[*ti*]
11′) [...] x *ša* x x [...]
12′) [...] x [...]
13′) [...] x x x [x] x x x [...]
14′) [URU].⸢*ki*⸣-*lam-ba-a-ti* URU.*ar-ma-an-*⸢*gu*⸣ [...]
15′) [x x] *x-ti* UGU *pi-ḫat* URU.*ki-še-si-*⸢*im*⸣ [*ú-rad-di*]
16′) [LÚ].⸢*šu*⸣-*ut* SAG-*ia a-na* ⸢LÚ.EN.NAM-*ú*⸣-[*ti* UGU-*šu-nu*]
17′) [*áš-kun*] ⸢*ṣa*⸣-*lam* ⸢LUGAL⸣-*ti-ia* ⸢DÙ-*uš*⸣-*ma* [*ep-še-et* NÍG.È]
18′) [^{d}*a*]-⸢*šur*$_{4}$⸣ *be-lí-ia ša i-na qé-*⸢*reb*⸣ [KUR.*man-na-a-a*$^{?}$]
19′) [*ù*$^{?}$ KUR].⸢*ma*⸣-*da-a-a e-*⸢*te-ep*⸣-*pu-*⸢*šu*⸣ [UGU-*šú*]
20′) [*áš*]-⸢*ṭur*⸣-*ma i-na* É ^{d}x x x [EN$^{?}$-*ia*$^{?}$]
21′) [x (x) *a*]-*na* ⸢*da*⸣-*ra-a-ti ul-*[*ziz*]
22′) [*ša*$^{?}$ LÚ.EN].⸢URU⸣.MEŠ-*ni ša* URU.*ki-*⸢*mir*⸣-[*ra*]
23′) [x (x) x] KUR.É-*x-*(*x*)-*x-an-gi-*[(*x-x*) ...]
24′) [x (x) URU].É-⸢*zu*⸣-*al-za-*⸢*áš*⸣ x [...]

Lacuna

Lacuna
K 1669

iii 1′–21′) [...] his/its kings ... [...] his property (and) his possessions *to/for* [... with ...]s, horses, mul[es, ... (and) *everything valuable*], royal [trea]sure, [I brought out] from [*the city Kišesim*] (iii 5′) and [I] re[organized (the administration of)] that city. [I] (re)nam[ed] it Kār-Nergal. [I had the weapons of the deities Aššur], Sîn, Šamaš, Adad, (and) I[štar, my lords, who go before me, m]ade and I in[stalled (them)] there. I [settled/caused to enter] there [people whom] I [had cap]tured (and) (iii 10′) I considered th[em as people of] Assyria. [...] ... [...] ... [...] the cities Kilambāti (and) Armang[u ... (iii 15′) ... I added] to the province of the city Kišesim. [I set a] eunuch of mine as provincial governor [over them]. I ma[de] a ro[yal] image of myself, [inscrib]ed [upon it the victorious deeds of the god Ašš]ur, my lord, that I had [acc]omplished in [*the lands Mannea and*] Media, (iii 20′) and ere[cted (it)] (to stand) forever in the temple of the god ..., [*my lord*].

iii 22′–25′) [(As for) the cit]y [ruler]s of the city Kimi[rra, ...], the land Bīt-...angi[...], Bīt-Zualzaš, (and) [..., I received horse]s (and) mul[es (as their tribute)].

---

ii 13′ The contents of text no. 63 i′ may have been found on the Nineveh Prism, and if so, probably at some point after this section of K 1673.
iii 1′–35′, 1″–12″, and 1‴–8‴ These lines apparently describe events for what the inscription would have referred to as the king's fifth regnal year.
iii 2′–9′ Cf. text no. 117 ii 38–39. Possibly *a-*⸢*na*⸣ [*šal-la-ti am-nu*], "[I counted] as [booty]," or *a-*⸢*na*⸣ [*la ma-ni*], "[countless]."
iii 3′ Na'aman, AfO 46–47 (1999–2000) p. 363 suggests restoring [*it-ti* GU$_{4}$].⸢MEŠ⸣, "[together with oxen]."
iii 4′ The restoration at the beginning of the line is based on such passages as text no. 2 line 493. At the end of the line possibly restore URU-*šú*, "his city," instead of URU.*ki-še-si-im*, "the city Kišesim."
iii 6′–8′ For the restorations, cf. text no. 4 line 40′ and text no. 117 ii 38–39.
iii 11′–15′ Cf. text no. 1 lines 95–96, text no. 2 lines 87–88, and text no. 4 lines 41′–42′? The traces would not support the reading expected in 11′ from text no. 117 ii 40: "The land Bīt-Sagabi, which *is* in the Fortress of the Bab[ylonian(s)]."
iii 17′–21′ These lines describe the creation and installation of a stele, likely the one found at Najafabad (text no. 117 and cf. ibid. ii 70–71 and possibly text no. 72 Side A 4′–6′a).
iii 20′–21′ A. Fuchs (SAAS 8 p. 26 and n. 43) suggests *i-na* É ^{d}⸢*a*$^{?}$-*šur*$_{4}$⸣ (LÁL?.S[AR?]), "in the temple of the god Aššur," but, as noted by E. Frahm (KAL p. 73), such temples are rare outside of the city Aššur. In a possibly similar passage in text no. 72, we have [... *i*$^{?}$]-⸢*na*$^{?}$⸣ É ^{d}AMAR.UTU *é-kur-ri-šú-nu a-na da-ra-ti* / [*ul-ziz*$^{?}$ ...], "[... *i*]*n* the temple of the god Marduk, their temple, for all time [*I erected* ...]" (Side A 5′–6′a).
iii 23′–24′ We might expect KUR.É-*sa-an-gi-*[*bu-ti*] in iii 23′, but the traces do not seem to support this. Possibly (iii 23′) [*ša*] KUR.É-*ma*$^{?}$/*ba*$^{?}$-*al-x-an-gi* (iii 24′) [*ù ša* URU].É-⸢*zu*⸣-*al-za-*⸢*áš* GU$_{4}$⸣.[MEŠ]; see Na'aman, AfO 46–47 (1999–2000) pp. 362–363. In Sargon's eighth campaign (714), the ruler of the city Bīt-Zualzaš was Ḫumbê (text no. 65 line 46).

25′) [ANŠE.KUR.RA].MEŠ ANŠE.*pa*-⸢*re*⸣-[*e* (*ma-da-ta-šú-nu*) *am-ḫur*]

26′) [URU$^{?}$.*ḫa-ar-ḫa-ra*$^{?}$]-*ía* ⸢LÚ$^{?}$⸣.[EN$^{?}$.URU-*šú-nu*$^{?}$ *ir-du-du-ma*$^{?}$]
27′) [^{m}*da-al-ta-a* KUR].*el*-⸢*li*⸣-[*ba-a-a ú-rab-bu-ú*$^{?}$ UGU-*šú-un*$^{?}$]
28′) [...] ⸢ANŠE$^{?}$⸣.KUR.⸢RA⸣.[MEŠ ...]
29′) [...] ⸢US$_5$⸣.UDU.ḪI.A *x x* [...]
30′) [...]-*šu ap-pul* [...]
31′) [...] ⸢E$^{?}$⸣ *x* LA SA [...]
32′) [... ANŠE].KUR.RA.MEŠ [...]
33′) [...] *x a*-⸢*šab*⸣-*šu*-[...]
34′) [...] BÀD-*šú* EŠ [...]
35′) [...] TU ⸢MAḪ⸣ [...]
Lacuna

iii 26′–35′) [*The peo*]*ple* [*of the city Ḫarḫar drove out their city ruler and elevated over them* Daltâ of the land] Ell[ipi. ...] hors[es, ...] sheep and goats, ... [...] (iii 30′) his/its [...] I destroyed [...] ... [... ho]rses [...] ... [...] its (city) wall [...] ... [...]

Lacuna

K 1673 ii′
1″) URU.⸢*kar*-^{m}LUGAL⸣-[GI.NA MU-*šú ab-bi* ...]
2″) É.KUR *šu-bat* ⸢DINGIR⸣.[MEŠ GAL.MEŠ *eš-šiš e-pu-uš*]
3″) DINGIR.MEŠ *a-ši-bu*-⸢*ut*⸣ [URU.*ḫar-ḫa-ar a-na áš-ri-šú-nu ú-ter*]
4″) *ša* ^{d}*a-šur*$_4$ ⸢^{d}⸣[30 ^{d}*šà-máš* ^{d}IŠKUR ^{d}*iš-tar* DINGIR.MEŠ$^{?}$ *a-li-kut*$^{?}$ *pa-ni-ia*$^{?}$]
5″) *x x* NI KÙ.GI ⸢KÙ⸣.[BABBAR ...]
6″) ⸢*na*⸣-*gi-šu-nu ú*-[... UN.MEŠ KUR.KUR *ki-šit-ti*]
7″) ŠU.II-*ia i-na* ŠÀ ⸢*ú*⸣-[*še-šib/rib* LÚ.*šu-ut* SAG-*ia*]
8″) *a-na* LÚ.EN.NAM-⸢*ú*⸣-[*ti* UGU-*šu-nu áš-kun-ma*]
9″) *it-ti* UN.MEŠ KUR ⸢*aš*⸣-[*šur am-nu-šu-nu-ti i-šu-ṭu ab-šá-a-ni*]
10″) ⸢6⸣ *na-ge-e dan-nu*-⸢*ti*⸣ [... ÍD-*tu e-li-tum*]
11″) ⸢*ša*⸣ KUR.*a-ra-zi*-⸢*áš*⸣ [...]
12″) [*x x x* (*x*)] *x x* [...]
Lacuna

K 1673 ii′
iii 1″–12″) [I (re)named it] Kār-Ša[rrukīn ... I built anew] the temple, the abode of the [great] god[s (and) restored] the gods who dwelt [in the city Ḫarḫar to their places]. I [...-*ed* the ...] of the deities Aššur, [Sîn, Šamaš, Adad, (and) Ištar, *the deities who go before me*] (iii 5″) ... (*of*) gold (and) sil[ver ...] of their district. I [settled/caused to enter] there [people from the lands that] I [had conquered. I set a eunuch of mine] as provincial governor [over them and considered them] as people of A[ssyria. They (now) pull my yoke. (iii 10″) Six strong districts [... the upper river(land)] of the land Arazia[š (Aranzêšu) ...] ... [...]

Lacuna

79-7-8,14 i′
1‴) [*ša šùl-mu* ^{d}UTU-*ši ú-šá-aṣ*]-⸢*bit*$^{?}$⸣ *i*-⸢*na*⸣ [ŠU.II]
2‴) [LÚ.*qí-pi-ia*$^{?}$ LÚ.*na-si-ku ša* URU.*la-ba-an*] ⸢*am*⸣-*nu*-⸢*šu*⸣-[*nu-ti*]
3‴) [^{m}*ši-il-kan-ni* LUGAL KUR.*mu*]-*uṣ*-[*ri*]

79-7-8,14 i′
iii 1‴–2‴) [*I settle*]*d* [(them) in ... *which is on the shore of the* Western *Sea*]. I assigned t[hem] to [the authority of *a qīpu-official of mine*, the sheikh of the city Laban]. iii 3‴–8‴) [(As for) Šilkanni, king of E]gy[pt, whose

---

iii 25′ For the restoration, see for example text no. 1 lines 124–125.

iii 26′–27′ The tentative restorations are based upon the sense of text no. 2 line 89 and text no. 4 lines 42′–43′. A writing URU.*ḫa-ar-ḫa-ra-ía* would be otherwise unattested. Possibly *e-ba-ku-ma*, "drove off" (see text no. 117 ii 42) instead of *ir-du-du-ma*, "drove out."

iii 30′ Possibly [URU.MEŠ-*ni ša li-me-ti*]-*šu ap-pul* [*aq-qur ina* IZI *aš-ru-up*], "I destroyed, [demolished, (and) burned down with fire the settlements in] its [environs]."

iii 31′ Possibly *la sa*-[*an-qu* ...]?

iii 32′ Cf. text no. 117 ii 42?

iii 33′ Possibly [... *a*]-⸢*na*⸣ *a-šab šu*-[*bat ne-eḫ-ti*], "[... in order] to dwell [in peace]"?

iii 34′ Possibly *eš*-[*šiš*] plus a form of the verb *epēšu*, or the number 30 [...]. The passage likely has to do with the strengthening of the defences of the city Ḫarḫar; cf. for example vii 24′–25 and text no. 117 ii 42.

iii 1″ For the restoration, see text no. 1 line 100 and text no. 2 line 93; possibly *az-kur* rather than *ab-bi* (see text no. 7 line 63).

iii 2″–4″ The restoration of these lines is based on text no. 117 ii 44. Possibly restore DINGIR.MEŠ GAL.MEŠ EN.MEŠ-*ia*, "the great deities, my lords" at the end of iii 4′ rather than DINGIR.MEŠ *a-li-kut pa-ni-ia*, "the deities who go before me."

iii 5″–9″ For the restorations, cf. iii 10′ and 6′–17′, text no. 1 lines 97–98 and 262, text no. 2 lines 90–91 and 286–287, text no. 3 lines 12′–13′, text no. 4 lines 44′–45′, and text no. 7 lines 62 and 108–9.

iii 10″–11″ For the restoration of this passage and following lines, cf. text no. 1 lines 98–99 and text no. 2 lines 92–93; note also text no. 117 ii 45.

Lacuna after iii 12″ The text at the end of this gap was likely similar to or a duplicate of text no. 63 ii′ 1–5′.

iii 1‴–2‴ N. Na'aman (AfO 46–47 [1999–2000] p. 363) suggests there was a personal name at the end of iii 1‴, possibly Ilu-bi'dī ([... ŠU].⸢II⸣ ^{m}*i-x*-[...]). See Na'aman, Tel Aviv 6 (1979) p. 71 n. 6 for a different restoration of these two lines.

4′′′) [*ša a-šar-šú ru-ú-qu pu-luḫ*]-*tu me-lam-me*
5′′′) [*ša* ^{d}*a-šur*$_{4}$ EN-*ia is*]-*ḫu-pu-šu-ma*
6′′′) [12 ANŠE.KUR.RA.MEŠ GAL.MEŠ *ša*] KUR.*mu-uṣ-ri*
7′′′) [*ša i-na ma-a-ti*] ⸢*la*⸣ *ib-šu-ú*
8′′′) [*tam-šil-šú-un iš-šá-a*] ⸢*ta*⸣-*mar-tuš*

location is far away (and whom) fea]r of the brilliance [of the god Aššur, my lord, had ove]rwhelmed, [he brought me] as his audience gift [twelve large horses from] Egypt [whose like] did not exist [in (my) land].

9′′′) [*i-na* 6 BALA-*ia* ^{m}*ur-sa-a*] ⸢KUR⸣.*ur-ar-ṭa-a-a*
10′′′) [*la a-dir ma-mit* DINGIR.MEŠ GAL.MEŠ *a-bi*]-*ku** *de-en* ^{d}*šà-máš*
11′′′) [*ša ina a-lak ger-ri-ia*] *maḫ-ri-i*
12′′′) [*a-na* ^{m}*ul-lu-su-ni* KUR].⸢*ma*⸣-*an-na-a-a*
13′′′) [*a-na ni-ir* ^{d}*a-šur*$_{4}$] ⸢*ú-šak*⸣-*ni-šu-šu-ma*
14′′′) [*e-mid-du-uš ab*]-*šá-a-nu*
15′′′) [12 URU.ḪAL.ṢU.MEŠ-*šú dan-na-a-ti ša*] ⸢UGU⸣ KUR.*ur-ar-ṭi*
16′′′) [KUR.*an-di-a* KUR.*na-ʾi-i-ri a-na ka*]-⸢*a*⸣-*di na*-⸢*da*⸣-[*a*]
17′′′) [*e-kim-šú-ma ú-ṣa-ḫir* KUR-*su* ...]
Lacuna

iii 9′′′–17′′′) [In my sixth regnal year, Ursâ (Rusâ)], the Urarṭian — [who did not respect the oath (sworn) by the great gods; who over]turned the decision of the god Šamaš; [whom, during the course of my] previous [campaign against Ullusunu], the Mannean, I had subjugated [to the yoke of the god Aššur]; and [upon whom I had imposed (my) y]oke — [took away from him (Ullusunu) twelve of his strong fortresses that] were situated [as guard] posts on (the border with) the lands Urarṭu, [Andia, (and) Naʾiri, and (thus) reduced (the size of) his land. ...]

Lacuna

Col. iv

Sm 2021 + 82-5-22,8 i′

1) [...] A$^{?}$ *x x x x x* [*x*]
2) [...] *x a-na* KUR.*ur-ar*-⸢*ṭi al*$^{?}$-*lik*$^{?}$⸣
3) [...] ^{m}*ur-sa-a* KUR.*ur-ar-ṭa-a-a*
4) [...] *x-su id*-⸢*ka*⸣-*am*-⸢*ma*⸣
5) [UGU KUR].⸢*ú-a-uš*⸣ *šad-di-i e*-⸢*li*$^{?}$⸣
6) [*ša it-ti*] *ši*-⸢*kin* DUNGU⸣ *um*-⸢*mu*⸣-*da** ⸢SAG-*šú*⸣
7) [*um-ma-an*]-⸢*šu*⸣ *ma-aʾ-du a-di* ERIM *re*-[*ṣe-(e)*]-⸢*šu*⸣
8) [*x x (x)*] *x* KÀD$^{?}$ IB ŠÌTA ⸢KUR$^{?}$⸣ [*(x)*] *x* [*x*]
9) [*x x (x)*] *x áš*-⸢*kun*⸣-*ma ú-x x x* [*x*]

iv 1–9) [...] ... [...] *I marched* against the land Urarṭu. [...] Ursâ (Rusâ), the Urarṭian, mustered his [...] and (iv 5) *went up* [onto] Mount Uauš, [who]se su[mmit] reaches (up) [among] the cloud(s). [His] large [army], together with the troops of his all[ies ...] ... [...] I set and I ...

10) [*um-ma*]-*na*-⸢*at*⸣ ^{d}*a-šur*$_{4}$ [*dal*]-⸢*pa*$^{?}$⸣-[*a-ti*]
11) [*ša ḫar*]-⸢*ra-an ru-uq*⸣-*te* ⸢*il*⸣-[*li-ka-nim-ma*]
12) [KUR.MEŠ-*e bé*]-*ru*-⸢*ú*⸣-*ti e*-⸢*te-ti*⸣-[*qa-a-ma*]
13) [*ik-ki-ra zi-mu*]-⸢*šin*⸣ *an-ḫu-us-si-na* ⸢*ul*⸣ [*ú-šap-ši-iḫ-ma*]
14) [A.MEŠ *ṣu-mi*] *ul áš-qí uš-man-nu* ⸢*ul*⸣ [*áš-kun-ma*]
15) [BÀD] ⸢KARAŠ *ul*$^{?}$ *ak*$^{?}$-*ṣur*$^{?}$ LÚ.*qu*⸣-[*ra-di-ia ul ú-ma-ʾe-er*]
16) [*it-ti*] ⸢GIŠ⸣.GIGIR GÌR.II-*ia e*-[*de-ni-ti*]
17) [*ù* ANŠE.KUR].⸢RA$^{?}$⸣.[MEŠ] *a*-⸢*li-kut*⸣ [*i-di-ia*]
18) [*ša a*]-⸢*šar nak*⸣-*ri* [*ù sa-al-me*]
19) [*i-da*]-⸢*a*⸣-*a* ⸢*la*$^{?}$ *ip*$^{?}$⸣-[*par-ku-ú*]
20) [...] *x x* [...]
Lacuna

iv 10–15) [The exh]aus[ted troo]ps of the god Aššur, [who] had (already) co[me a] long [jou]rney, had cro[ssed rem]ote [mountains, and were (thus) in poor condition (lit.: "their appearance had changed"). I] nei[ther allowed them (time) to recover from] their fatigue [n]or gave (them) [water] to drink [for (their) thirst. I] neit[her set up] camp [n]or *organized* [a walled (military) encampment. I did not give any orders to my] w[arriors].

iv 16–20) [With] o[nly] my personal chariot [and the caval]ry that go [at my side (and)] never *l*[*eave*] my [*side* in either] hostile [or friendly territo]ry, [...]

Lacuna

---

iii 10′′′ *-ku**: See the copy in the minor variants section.
iii 11′′′–13′′′ See the on-page note to text no. 63 ii′ 14′–16′.
Lacuna after iii 17′′′ The text at the beginning of this gap was likely similar to or a duplicate of text no. 63 ii′ 18′–25′.
iv 1–20, 1′–66′ and 1′′–8′′, and v 1–6 These lines describe events which the inscription would have assigned to the king's seventh regnal year. The section for that year would have begun in the gap at the end of col. iii.
iv 5–7 Cf. text no. 65 lines 82, 96, and 103.
iv 6 *-da**: See the copy in the minor variants section.
iv 8 Possibly *eb-rat* ⸢KUR⸣-[*i*], literally "staircase step of a mountain"; cf. *ša si-mil-lat* KUR-*e*, text no. 43 line 32.
iv 10–19 For restorations, cf. text no. 65 lines 127–130 and 132.
iv 20 Perhaps see text no. 65 line 133 for restorations.

K 1668a + K 1671 i′

1′) [... LÚ.zu-uk GÌR].⸢II⸣-*ia*
2′) [*ṣa-ab* GIŠ.PAN *ka-ba-bi az-ma-ri-i* LÚ].⸢*qu-ra-di*⸣-*ia*
3′) [*ek-du-ti mu-du-ut ta-ḫa-zi ú-zak-ki-ma*] ⸢*ḫar*⸣-*ra-an*
4′) [URU.*mu-ṣa-ṣir ur-uḫ mar-ṣa-ti it-ti* 1-*et*] ⸢GIŠ⸣.GIGIR GÌR.II-*ia*
5′) [*ù* 1 LIM *pet-ḫal-lì-ia šit-mur-ti*] ⸢*aṣ*⸣-*bat-ma*
6′) [A.ŠÀ DÙG.GA *i-na tar-kub*]-*ti* ANŠE.KUR.RA
7′) [*ù mar-ṣa i-na* GÌR].II ⸢*lu*⸣-*ú ar-de*
8′) [*a-na* URU.*mu-ṣa-ṣir šu-bat* ^{d}*ḫal-di*]-⸢*a*⸣ *šal-ṭiš* ⸢*lu*⸣ *e-ru-ub*
9′) [*i-na* É.GAL *mu-šab* ^{m}*ur-za-na*] ⸢*e*⸣-*tel-liš lu*?-*u ú-šib*
10′) [*ki-in-gi ni-ṣir-te-šu-nu*] *ap-te-e-ma*
11′) [34 GUN 18 MA.NA] KÙ.GI
12′) [1 ME 67 GUN 2 1/2 MA.NA] KÙ.BABBAR
13′) [URUDU.ḪI.A BABBAR-*ú* AN].⸢NA⸣ [NA$_4$.GUG NA$_4$].⸢ZA⸣.GÌN
14′) [NA$_4$.BABBAR.DILI *ni-siq-ti* NA$_4$.MEŠ *a*]-⸢*na*⸣ *ma*-⸢*a*ʾ⸣-[*de*]-⸢*e*?⸣
15′) [*x x x* ZÚ AM.SI] ⸢GIŠ⸣.ESI GIŠ.*tas-ka*-⸢*rin*⸣-[*ni*]
16′) [*x* (*x*)] GIŠ.ŠIBIR.MEŠ ZÚ AM.⸢SI⸣
17′) [GIŠ.ESI GIŠ.TÚG *a*]-*di* GIŠ.NA$_5$.MEŠ-*ši*-⸢*na*⸣
18′) [*ša iḫ-zu-ši-na šu*]-⸢*pu*⸣-*šu* ZABAR ⸢*ù*⸣ KÙ.⸢BABBAR⸣
19′) [*x* GIŠ.BANŠUR.MEŠ] ZÚ AM.⸢SI⸣
20′) [GIŠ.ESI GIŠ].⸢TÚG⸣ *si-mat* LUGAL-*ú-ti*
21′) [8? GIŠ.*maḫ-ri*]-⸢*ṣi dan*⸣-*nu-ti*
22′) [ZÚ AM.SI GIŠ.ESI GIŠ].TÚG GIŠ.*kan-ni* GIŠ.*kán-kán-ni*
23′) [GIŠ.*táḫ*-KAL GIŠ].⸢GU⸣.ZA *ù* GIŠ.⸢GAN?⸣ BI.LUL
24′) [ZÚ AM.SI GIŠ].ESI GIŠ.⸢*tas-ka*⸣-*rin-ni*
25′) [*ša iḫ-zu-šu-nu*] ⸢*šu-pu*?⸣-*šu* ⸢ZABAR?⸣ *ù* KÙ.BABBAR
26′) [6 GÍR.MEŠ] KÙ.GI *te-rin-na-at* KÙ.GI
27′) [GÍR.TUR KÙ.GI] *ša zu-um-bi* KÙ.GI
28′) [NA$_4$.*pur-si-it* NA$_4$].⸢GIŠ⸣.NU$_{11}$.GAL *tam-lit* NA$_4$.MEŠ KÙ.GI
29′) [11 *kap-pi* KÙ.BABBAR] ⸢m⸣*ur-sa-a a-di nak-ta-me-šú-nu*
30′) [*kap-pi ša* KUR].⸢*ta*⸣-*bal* GEŠTU.II.MEŠ KÙ.GI
31′) [*qur-pi-si* KÙ].⸢BABBAR⸣ *šil-ta-ḫi* KÙ.BABBAR *né-eḫ-si* KÙ.GI
32′) [34 *kap-pi* KÙ].⸢BABBAR⸣ ŠU.SI.MEŠ *dan-na-a-ti*
33′) [*qa-al-la-a*]-⸢*te*⸣ *qa-at-ta-na-a-te luṭ-ṭi*

K 1668a + K 1671 i′

iv 1′–7′) [... I mobilized (...)] my [foot soldiers, bowmen, (and) shield (and) spear (bearers)], my [fierce] warriors [who were experienced in battle. [Then, with (only)] my [single] personal chariot (iv 5′) [and one thousand of my ferocious cavalry], I took the road [to the city Muṣaṣir, a difficult path]; I proceeded [over favorable terrain on] horse[back and over difficult (terrain) on foot].

iv 8′–10′) I entered triumphantly [into the city Muṣaṣir, the abode of the god Ḫaldi], (and) in a lordly manner, I occupied [the palace, the residence of Urzana]. I broke open [the seals of their treasure caches].

iv 11′–14′) [(With regard to) 34 talents and 18 minas of] gold, [167 talents and 2 1/2 minas of] silver, [shining copper, t]in, [carnelian], lapis lazuli, [*banded agate*, (and other) precious stones i]n large numbers;

iv 15′) [x (items): ... of elephant ivory], ebony, (and) boxwood;

iv 16′–18′) [x (items)]: staves of elephant ivory, [ebony, (and) boxwood, to]gether with their wooden caskets, [whose mountings are ma]de of bronze and silver;

iv 19′–20′) [x (items): *tables*] of elephant ivory, [ebony, (and) boxwo]od, (*tables*) fit for a king;

iv 21′–25′) [8 (items)]: sturdy [*maḫraṣu*-objects of elephant ivory, ebony], (and) boxwood, a stand, a potstand, [*a folding screen*], a chair, and *a cupbearer's* (*pot*)*stand* [(made) of elephant ivory], ebony, (and) boxwood, [whose mountings] are made of [*br*]*onze* and silver;

iv 26′–28′) [6 (items)]: gold [knives] *with* gold (*handles in the shape of*) cones, [a gold dagger], a gold fly whisk, (and) an alabaster [offering-bowl] inlaid with stones (and) gold;

iv 29′–31′) [11 (items): silver *kappu*-bowls] belonging to Ursâ (Rusâ), together with their lids, [*kappu*-bowls from the land T]abal with lug-handles of gold, [*hauberks* with silv]er (scales), (and) silver *arrows with* gold inlays;

iv 32′–34′a) [34 (items): silv]er [*kappu*-bowls] with deep, [shallow], (and) narrow fluting (lit.: "fingers"),

iv 1′–7′ For restorations, cf. text no. 1 lines 150–152 and text no. 65 lines 320–321 and 331.
iv 8′–67′ For restorations and detailed commentary, cf. text no. 65 lines 350–379.
iv 14′ This line is not found in the list of booty in text no. 65.
iv 18′ Text no. 65 line 353 has KÙ.GI, "gold," instead of ZABAR, "bronze."
iv 22′ Possibly "... stands, potstands ...." In text no. 65 line 356 they must be singular in view of the total number of objects listed there, but the passage in text no. 82 is not an exact copy of that text.
iv 31′ See the on-page note to text no. 65 line 358.

luṭṭu-bowls, [and *susānu*-vessels] of silver;

34′) [*ù su-sa-ni*] ⸢KÙ⸣.BABBAR 55 *kap-pi* KÙ.BABBAR *ṣu-up-pu-te*
35′) [...]-*ma-a-ni* GÚ.ZI.MEŠ
36′) [*ṣip-ra-a-te* U$_4$.SAKAR].MEŠ *ù* ḪAR.MEŠ KÙ.BABBAR

iv 34′b–36′) 55 (items): silver-*plated kappu*-bowls, [*together with* (*their*) *li*]*ds*, cups (*decorated with*) [*cone-shaped* ornaments (*and*) crescent-shaped ornament]s, (and) silver rings;

37′) [5 *a-za-na-at* KÙ].⸢BABBAR⸣ *qa-bu-a-ti* KÙ.BABBAR
38′) [*mu-kar-ri-si*] ⸢*nab-li* NÍG⸣.[NA.MEŠ]
39′) [KUR.*ta-ba-li ù mu-qa-te-rat* KÙ.BABBAR]

iv 37′–39′) [5 (items): *azannu-stands* of sil]ver, *qabūtu*-cups of silver, [*mukarrisu*-dishes], (*and*) *nablu*-vessels, (*altogether forming*) ce[nsers from the land Tabal, and silver incense burners];

40′) [13 *ki-ú-ri* URUDU *tap-ḫa-a-ni* URUDU *nàr-ma*]-⸢*ka-a*⸣-[*te* URUDU]
41′) [*a-sa-al-la-te* URUDU ÚTUL].⸢MEŠ⸣ URUDU

iv 40′–42′a) [13 (items): copper basins, copper cauldrons, copper wa]shbas[ins, copper *asallu*-bowls], copper [*diqāru*-pot]s, [(and) copper *qulliu*-bowls];

42′) [*qu-li-a-te* URUDU 24 *kan-ni*] ⸢URUDU⸣ *ki*-⸢*ùr*⸣ URUDU
43′) [*ḫu-ru-pa-a-te* URUDU *kur-ku-ri*] ⸢URUDU⸣ *qu-ul-li* URUDU
44′) [*na-as-ri* URUDU É *bu-ṣi*]-*in-ni* URUDU

iv 42′b–44′) [24 (items): coppe]r [stands] (*for*) copper basins, [copper *ḫuruppu*-bowls, coppe]r [*kurkurru*-vessels], copper *qullu-clasps*, [copper *nasru-hooks*], (and) copper [lam]ps;

45′) [1$^{?}$ ME 20 *ú-de-e* URUDU *dan-nu*]-⸢*ti*⸣ *qa-al-lu-ti*
46′) [*e-piš-ti* KUR-*šú-nu ša ni*]-*bit* MU-*šú-nu a-na šá-ṭa*-⸢*ri*⸣

iv 45′–47′a) [120 (items): copper objects, (both) heavy (ones and)] light (ones), [the work of their land, (objects), the pronun]ciation of [who]se name(s) [are not easy] to write down;

47′) [*la ṭa-a-bu x ka-nu-nu*] AN.BAR ⸢*ne*⸣-*se-pi* AN.BAR
48′) [*na-as-ri* AN.BAR *a-ru-ut*]-⸢*ḫi*⸣ AN.BAR É ⸢*bu*⸣-*ṣi-in-ni* AN.BAR

iv 47′b–48′) [x (items): an] iron [brazier], iron *shovel*(*s*), [iron *nasru-hooks*], iron [*aruth*]*u*-objects, (and) iron lamps;

49′) [1$^{?}$ ME 30 *lu-bul-ti bir-me*] ⸢TÚG⸣.GADA SÍG.*ta-kil-ti* ⸢*ar-ga*⸣-*man*-⸢*ni*⸣
50′) [*lu-bul-ti ta-bar-ri*] ⸢*ša*⸣ KUR.*ur-ar-ṭi*

iv 49′–51′a) [130 (items): garments with multi-colored trim] (and) linen (garments), (garments of) blue-purple wool (and) red-purple wool, [(and) garments of red wool] from the lands Urarṭu [and Ḫabḫu] —

51′) [*ù* KUR.*ḫab-ḫi a-di*] ⸢*bu*⸣-*še-e* É.GAL-*šu*

iv 51′b–52′a) [I carried off (all these things) as booty, together with] the (remaining) property of his palace, [and I heape]d up his possessions.

52′) [*áš-lu-lam-ma ak*]-⸢*mu*⸣-*ra* NÍG.GA-*šú* LÚ.*šu-ut* SAG-*ia*
53′) [LÚ.*re-di-ia a*]-⸢*na*⸣ É ^{d}*ḫal-di-a áš-pur-ma*

iv 52′b–53′) I sent a eunuch of mine [(and) my officials t]o the temple of the god Ḫaldi.

54′) [^{d}*ḫal-di-a* DINGIR-*šu*] *ù* ^{d}*ba-ag-bar-tú* ^{d}*iš-tar-šú*
55′) [*a-di* NÍG.GA *é*]-⸢*kur*⸣-*ri-šú ma-ʾa*-⸢*at*⸣-*ti ma-la ba-šu-ú*

iv 54′–55′) [His god Ḫaldi] and his goddess Bagbartu, [together with the] numerous [possessions] of his [temp]le, as much as there were (of them):

56′) [x+4 GUN 3] MA.NA KÙ.GI 6 *a-ri-at* KÙ.GI
57′) [1 ME 62] ⸢GUN⸣ 20 MA.NA 6-*su* LAL KÙ.BABBAR

iv 56′–57′) [x+4 talents and 3] minas of gold, 6 gold shields, [162 talen]ts and 20 minas of silver, less one sixth (of a mina of silver);

58′) [1$^{?}$ *áš-kut*]-⸢*ti*⸣ KÁ-*šú ša* 2 GUN KÙ.GI ⸢KI⸣.LÁ
59′) [1 SAG.KUL KÙ.GI] ⸢1 *sik*⸣-*kàt* KÙ.GI 1 *nam-za-qu* KÙ.BABBAR
60′) [^{d}LAMMA-*at a-ge-e*] ⸢*na*⸣-*šá-at* GIŠ.*miṭ-ṭi ù* GIŠ.*kip-pa-ti*
61′) [*er-bet-ta-šu-nu mar*]-⸢*kas*⸣ KÁ *ú-su-um* É *pa-pa-ḫi*
62′) [*ša* 2 GUN 12 MA].⸢NA⸣ KÙ.GI KI.LÁ-*šú-nu*

iv 58′–62′) [1 locking ba]r for its door which weighs 2 talents of gold; [1 gold door bolt]; 1 gold peg; (and) 1 silver key [(in the shape of) a divine protectress (who wears) a crown (and)] holds the rod and ring — [these (last) four (things) comprised the] door [faste]ning, one befitting the shrine, [whose] weight was [2 talents and 12 min]as of gold;

---

iv 34′ Text no. 65 line 360 has 54 not 55.
iv 35′ Text no. 65 line 360 has <*a-di*> *nak-te*-⸢*mi*⸣-[*šu-nu*] ⸢GÚ⸣.ZI.MEŠ.
iv 37′–39′ See the on-page note to text no. 65 line 361.
iv 49′ Text no. 65 line 366 has *ù* SÍG.MEŠ, "and (*plain*) wool," instead of *ar-ga-man-ni*, "(and) red-purple wool."
iv 59′ Text no. 65 line 375 has 2 *nam-za-qi* KÙ.GI, "2 gold keys."
iv 60′ With regard to the "rod and ring," see the note to text no. 65 line 375.

63′) [1 GÍR KÙ.GI GAL-*ú ša* 10]+16 MA.NA 3-*su* KÙ.GI KI.⸢LÁ⸣
64′) [96 *šu-kur-ri* KÙ.BABBAR *qur*]-*pi-is* KÙ.BABBAR GIŠ.PAN [KÙ.BABBAR]
65′) [*šil-ta-ḫi* KÙ.BABBAR *ša né*]-*eḫ-si ù iḫ*-⸢*zi*⸣ [KÙ.GI]
66′) [12 *a-ri-at* KÙ.BABBAR] ⸢*ša*⸣ SAG.⸢DU *a*⸣-[*bu-bi*]
67′) [UR.MAḪ *ù* AM *bu-un-nu-ú ni-ip-ḫi-ši-in*]

Lacuna
79-7-8,14 ii′
1″) ⸢ZÚ⸣ [GÍR ZÚ GÍR.TUR.MEŠ ZÚ GIŠ.ESI *ša iḫ-zu-ši-na* KÙ.GI]
2″) 10 ⸢GIŠ.BANŠUR⸣.[MEŠ GIŠ.TÚG *maḫ-ri-ṣi* GIŠ.TÚG *né-me-di* GIŠ.ESI GIŠ.TÚG]
3″) *ša* ⸢*iḫ*⸣-[*zu-šu-nu* KÙ.GI *ù* KÙ.BABBAR 2 GI.DU$_8$ 14 NA$_4$.MEŠ]
4″) *sa*-⸢*maḫ*⸣-[*ḫu-te šu-ka-ni* ^{d}*ḫal-di-a ù* ^{d}*ba-ag-bar-ti* DAM-*šú*]
5″) 20 LIM 5 <ME> ⸢12⸣ [*a-ri-at* URUDU *dan-na-a-te*]
6″) *qa-al*-⸢*la*⸣-[*a-te ṣip-rat* URUDU *qur-pi-si* URUDU]
7″) *ù* ⸢*gul*⸣-[*gul-lat* URUDU 1 LIM 5 ME 14 *šu-kur-ri* URUDU]
8″) *dan*-⸢*nu*⸣-[*ti qa-al-lu-te* ...]
Lacuna
Col. v
Sm 2021 + 82-5-22,8 ii′
1) 1 *ṣa-lam* [^{m}]*ir-gi*-⸢*iš-ti*⸣ [LUGAL KUR.*ur-ar-ṭi*]
2) *ša* ⸢AGA⸣ MUL-⸢*ti*⸣ DINGIR-⸢*ti*⸣ [*ap-ru-ma*]
3) ŠU ZAG-⸢*šú*⸣ *ka-ri-bat a-di** É-⸢*šú*⸣ [60 GUN URUDU.ḪI.A KI.LÁ]
4) 1 *ṣa-lam* ^{m}⸢*ur*⸣-*sa-a it-ti* 2 ANŠE.⸢KUR⸣.[RA.MEŠ *pét-ḫal-li-šú* LÚ?]
5) ⸢GIŠ.GIGIR⸣-*šu a-di* KI.TUŠ-*šú-nu* URUDU.⸢ḪI⸣.[A *ši-ip-ku* (...)]
6) *šal-la-tu ka-bit-tu áš-lu-la a*-⸢*na*⸣ [KUR *aš-šur ub-la*]

---

7) ⸢*i*⸣-*na* ⸢8⸣ BALA-*ia ša i-na a-lak ger*-⸢*ri*⸣-[*ia maḫ-ri*]
8) [*ša*] ^{m}*aš-šur*-ZU LUGAL KUR.⸢*kar*⸣-*al-li a*-[...]
9) [x (x)] x ŠU x ^{d}*a-šur*$_4$ x x [...]

iv 63′) [1 large gold sword which] weighs [2]6 and 1/3 minas of gold;
iv 64′–65′) [96 (items): silver spears, a *hau*]*berk* with silver (scales), [silver] bow(s), [(and) silver arrows, with in]lays and mountings [of gold];

iv 66′–67′) [12 silver shields whose *bosses* are decorated with] the head(s) of De[luge (monsters), lion(s), and wild bull(s)];
Lacuna
79-7-8,14 ii′
iv 1″) i[vory ..., ivory knive(s), (and) daggers of ivory (and) ebony, whose mountings are of gold];
iv 2″–3″a) 10 (items): t[ables of boxwood, *maḫraṣu*-objects of boxwood, (and) chairs of ebony (and) boxwood], who[se] mo[untings are of gold (and) silver];
iv 3″b–4″) [2 *portable altars (and)* 14] *assor*[*ted* stones, jewelry of the god Ḫaldi and the goddess Bagbartu, his wife];

iv 5″–7″a) 20,*512* (items): [heavy (and)] light [copper shields, *cone-shaped helmets* of copper, *hauberks* with copper (scales)], and sk[ull-shaped *helmets* of copper];
iv 7″b–8″) [1,514 (items)]: hea[vy (and) light copper spears, ...]

Lacuna

Sm 2021 + 82-5-22,8 ii′
v 1–3) 1 statue of Irgišti (Argišti), [king of the land Urarṭu, wearing] a crown (decorated) with stars, (an attribute) of divine rank, [and] with his right hand in a gesture of adoration, together with its *casing*, [which weighs 60 talents of copper];
v 4–5) 1 statue of Ursâ (Rusâ) with two of [his cavalry] hors[es (and)] his chariot[eer], together with their base, [cast in] copper, [(...)] —

v 6) I carried off (all these things) as substantial booty (and) [brought (them)] to [Assyria].

---

v 7–11) In my eighth regnal year, *that which* in the course of [my previous] campaign [against] Aššur-lēʾi, king of the land Karalla, [...] ... the god Aššur ... [...] ... in *servit*[*ude* ...]

Lacuna after iv 67′ The text in this gap was likely similar to or a duplicate of text no. 65 lines 380–389.
iv 1″–8″ For restorations and detailed commentary, cf. text no. 65 lines 389–393.
iv 4″ It is unlikely there was sufficient room to include the *ti-iq-ni* DINGIR-*ti*, "adornments (fit) for gods," found in text no. 65 line 391.
iv 5″ The tentative interpretation of the number assumes that ME was omitted: 20 LIM 5 <ME> 12, which would be at variance with text no. 65 line 392, which has 25 LIM 2 ME 12, "25,212," at this point.
Lacuna after iv 8″ The text in this gap was likely similar to or a duplicate of text no. 63 iii′ 1′–6′ and/or text no. 65 lines 393–401.
v 1–6 For restorations and detailed commentary, cf. text no. 63 iii′ 7′–12′ and text no. 65 lines 402–403.
v 3 *-di**: H. Winckler's copy shows the sign as complete, while A. Fuchs' copy has the sign missing the first vertical wedge.
v 4–5 LÚ.GIŠ.GIGIR-*šú*: Note that the determinative LÚ is at the end of v 4, while the rest of word is at the beginning of v 5; compare text no. 65 line 403 and text no. 63 iii′ 10′ (restored).
v 9 D.D. Luckenbill (ARAB 2 p. 107 §202) translates "not(?) submissive (*pl.*), Assur ..." and thus presumably read here ⸢*la*⸣ *kan-šu-te* ^{d}*a-šur*$_4$. Perhaps *ša* instead of ŠU x.

10) [x (x)] x-iš i-na ARAD-⸢ú?⸣-[ti? ...]
11) [x (x) x] x [...]

Lacuna

K 1668a + K 1671 ii′ (+) K 1668b + DT 6 i′

1′) [...] x
2′) [...] ⸢RU⸣
3′) [...] x MA
4′) [...] x ZA
5′) [...] x A KAL
6′) [...] x-ú
7′) x [x (x)] x IGI x [...] x LA

Lacuna

K 1668a + K 1671 ii′ (+) K 1668b + DT 6 i′

v 1′–7′) Too poorly preserved to allow translation.

8′) *ip-laḫ-ma a-na šu-⸢zu⸣-[ub* ZI-*šú* KUR].⸢*šur*⸣-*da*
9′) KUR-*ú ib-bal-kit a-na* m[*a-da-a* KUR.*šur*]-⸢*da*⸣-*a-a*
10′) *da-bab la kit-ti ša* ⸢*it*⸣-[*ti-ia a-na šum*]-⸢*ku*⸣-*ri*
11′) *iš-pu-ru e-li-tú* m*a-da-*[*a* KUR.*šur*]-⸢*da*⸣-*a-a*
12′) *pu-luḫ-ti mé-lam-me-ia* ⸢*is*⸣-[*ḫup*]-⸢*šu*⸣-*ma*
13′) *šá-a-šu ga-du* LÚ.ERIM.MEŠ-*šú i-na* ⸢GIŠ⸣.[TUKUL x] x-*ma*
14′) 1-*en* ⸢*i*⸣-*na lìb-bi-šú-nu a-na da-lil* dx [(x) *ul*] ⸢*e*⸣-*zib*
15′) m*at-ka-a-a-*⸢DUG⸣ m*at-ka-a-*[*a*]-x
16′) DUMU.MEŠ *nab-nit lìb-bi-šú bal-ṭu-*[*us-su-un*]
17′) *it-ti qaq-qád* m*a-mi-*⸢*taš*⸣-[*ši* AD-*šu-un*?]
18′) ANŠE.KUR.RA.MEŠ NÍG.[GA? ...]
19′) *ki-ma ta-mar-ti* [...] x [...]
20′) *áš-šu* x [x] x x x LA x [...]
21′) ⸢GIŠ?⸣ [x] x KI.⸢TUŠ⸣ *ne-eḫ-tú šu-*[*šu-bu*]
22′) [x] *x-un-né-e* KI KID [...]
23′) [x x]-*la-niš ut-nen-šu áš-ma-a* x [...]
24′) [ḪAR.MEŠ] KÙ.GI *rit-te*$_9$*-e-šu ú-rak-*[*kis-(ma)*]
25′) [x] x x x-*ma za-bíl ku-dúr-ri ša* [x x x]
26′) [x x] x *e-mid-su* ⸢*i*⸣-*na* ŠU.II LÚ.[*šu-ut* SAG-*ia*]
27′) [LÚ].⸢EN.NAM⸣ KUR.⸢*lu*⸣-*lu-mi-i am-*⸢*ta-nu*⸣-[*šu-(nu-ti)*]
28′) [KUR].⸢*kar*?⸣-[*al*]-⸢*li*?⸣ *a-na paṭ gim-ri-šú* ⸢UGU⸣ [*pi-ḫa-at*]
29′) [KUR].*lu-*⸢*lu-mi*⸣-*i ú-*⸢*rad*⸣-[*di*]
30′) *gi-né-e* d*a-šur*$_4$ *a-na du-ur* [*da-ri ú-ki-in*]

v 8′–11′a) He (Amitašši) became afraid and crossed Mount [Š]urda in order to sav[e his life]. Deceit(fully), they sent to [Adâ of the land Šurd]a a mendacious message intended [to make (him) ho]stile t[o me].

v 11′b–30′) Fear of my brilliance ov[erwhelmed] Adâ [of the land Šurd]a and (as a result) [*he put*] him (Amitašši) to [*the sword*], together with his men. He did [not] spare (even) one of them to praise the god ... [... *He brought to me*] alive (v 15′) Atkaya*dug* (and) Atkaya-..., the children of his (Amitašši's) own body, with the (severed) head of Amita[šši, *their father*], (as well as) horses, *pr*[*operty* ...] as (his) audience gift. (v 20′) Because ... [...] ... to allow [to live] in peace ... [...] *like a* [...] I listened to his supplication(s) [...] I pu[t] gold [bracelets] upon his wrists [(and)] (v 25′) ... and I imposed upon him labor duty *of* [...]. I assigned [*them*] to the authority of a [eunuch of mine, the provinc]ial [gove]rnor of the land Lullumû. I a[dded] the [land] *K*[*arall*]*a* to its full extent t[o the province of the land] Lullumû. [I established] regular offerings for the god Aššur fore[ver].

31′) *i-na u*$_4$*-me-šu-ma* UN.MEŠ KUR.*ḫab-ḫi* ⸢*ša*⸣ [*i-na bi-rit*]
32′) KUR.⸢*kar*⸣-*al-li ù* KUR.*nam-ri i-na* [x x x x]
33′) *ḫu-*⸢*ur*?⸣*-ba-ti ša* KUR-*i áš-*⸢*ṭu*?⸣-[*ti*?]
34′) ⸢*ep*⸣-*šet ma-ru-uš-ti ša i-na* KUR.⸢*kar*⸣-[*al-li*]
35′) *e-*⸢*te*⸣-*pu-šu iš-mu-ma* LÚ.DUMU *šip-*⸢*ri*⸣-[*šú-nu*]
36′) *ša e-peš ar-du-ti iš-*⸢*pu-ru*⸣-[*nim-ma*]
37′) *i-na* ŠU.II LÚ.*šu-ut* SAG-*ia* ⸢LÚ⸣.[EN.NAM]
38′) KUR.⸢*lu*⸣-*lu-mi-i am-nu-*⸢*šu*⸣-[*nu-ti*]

v 31′–39′) At that time the people of the land Ḫabḫu — whi[ch is (located) between] the lands Karalla and Namri in [...] *inac*[*cessible*] mountain wilderness — heard of the harsh deeds that I had carried out in the land Kar[alla] and sent [me] a messenger to do obeisance (to me). I assigned t[hem] to the authority of a eunuch of mine, the [provincial governor] of the land Lullumû. [I imposed] the yoke of the god Aššur upon them.

---

v 8′–9′ Or "the [Š]urda mountains."

v 13′ We expect *ušamqitma* or *urassibma* at the end of the line, but there does not appear to be sufficient room for either unless a logographic writing was used instead of a syllabic one (e.g., ⸢ŠUB?⸣-*ma*).

v 18′ NÍG.[GA? ...] "*prop*[*erty* ...]": Or *šá* [...], "of/which [...]."

v 21′ Cf. text no. 2 line 466.

v 22′ Possibly [*nu*]-⸢*du*⸣-*un-né-e*, "dowry"? Possibly *qé-reb*?, "inside," for KI KID?

v 33′ Or possibly *áš-*⸢*bu*⸣-[*ú*], i.e., " wh[o] dwe[ll between] the lands Karalla and Namri in [...] mountain wilderness" rather than "whi[ch is (located) between] the lands Karalla and Namri in [...] *inac*[*cessible*] mountain wilderness."

39′) ⸢*ni*⸣-*ir* ^{d}*a-šur*$_{4}$ ⸢UGU⸣-*šú-nu* ⸢*ú*⸣-[*ki-in*]
40′) *i-na qí-bit* ^{d}*a*-⸢*šur*$_{4}$⸣ EN-*ia* [x x x]
41′) *ša ul-tu u*$_{4}$-*me be*-⸢*lu*⸣-*ti-ia* x [x x x]
42′) *ki-ma a-a-li* ⸢*tu*⸣-*ra-ḫi* Ú ⸢LAM⸣ [x x x]
43′) ⸢*ú*⸣-*šar-ši-šu-nu-ti lib*-⸢*bu*⸣ [LUGAL.MEŠ-*ni*?]
44′) ⸢*ru*⸣-*qu-ti ša a-ḫi tam*-⸢*tim*⸣ [*ù mad-ba-ri*?]
45′) ⸢*ša*⸣ *ṣi-it* ^{d}UTU-*ši maḫ*-x [x x x x]
46′) [x] x x MA ⸢AG⸣ x x [x x x x]

v 40′–46′) At the command of the god Aššur, my lord, [...] who/which since the (first) day of my reign [...] like deer (or) ibexes ... [...] I made them have courage. Distant [*kings*] from the shore of the sea [and *the desert*] of the east ... [...] ... [...]

47′) [^{m}*ul-lu-su-nu*? KUR.*ma-an-na-a-a*? (...)]
48′) ⸢ŠA⸣ x [x x x x] x ⸢*šá*⸣ LUGAL.⸢MEŠ?-*ni*?⸣ [*a-li-kut*]
49′) *maḫ-ri-šu ba-la li-ṭi la* LI x x x x [x]
50′) *i-na zi-kir* ^{d}*a-šur*$_{4}$ *be-lí*-⸢*ia*⸣
51′) *mu-šar-bu-ú* MU-*ia* 6 KASKAL.GÍD *qaq-qa*-[*ru*]
52′) *ul-tu* URU.*i-zi-ir-ti* URU LUGAL-*ti*-⸢*šu*⸣
53′) *šit-mu-riš uṣ-ṣa-am-ma i-na* KUR.*la-a-ru*-⸢*e*⸣-[*te*]
54′) *ša* KUR.*al-lab-ri-a a-di maḫ-ri*-⸢*ia*⸣ *il-li*-⸢*kam*?⸣-[*ma*]
55′) *ma-da-at-ta-šu ka-bit-tu* ⸢ANŠE⸣.KUR.RA.MEŠ GU$_{4}$.⸢NÍTA⸣.[MEŠ]
56′) *ù* US$_{5}$.UDU.ḪI.A *am-ḫur-ma it-ta-šíq* GÌR.II-⸢*ia*⸣
57′) *lu-bul-ti bir-me* GADA *ú-lab-bi*-⸢*su*⸣
58′) ḪAR.MEŠ *tam-le-e tú-li-ma-nu-uš ar-kus*-[*ma*]
59′) *i-na ḫi-du-ut pa-ni i-tur* KUR-*uš*-⸢*šu*⸣

v 47′–59′) [*Ullusunu, the Mannean,* (...)] ... [...] *whose royal prede*[*cessors*] *had never* ... without (even exchanging) hostages, (v 50′) at the command of the god Aššur, my lord, who makes my fame great, impetuously left his royal city Izirtu, a distance of six leagues (away), and came before me in the land Lārue[te], which is (part) of the land Allabria. I received (v 55′) horses, ox[en], and sheep and goats as his substantial tribute, and he kissed my feet. I clothed him in a linen garment with multi-colored trim. I fastened inlaid bracelets on his two wrists, [whereupon] he joyfully returned to his (own) land.

60′) *el-la-mu-u*$_{8}$-*a* ^{m}*dal-ta-a* KUR.*el-li-pa-a*-⸢*a*⸣
61′) ARAD *kan-še šá-di-id ni-ir* ^{d}*a-šur*$_{4}$ *be-lí*-⸢*ia*⸣
62′) *na-še-e bil-ti* ⸢*ù ta*⸣-*mar-ti ša* LUGAL.MEŠ-⸢*ni*⸣
63′) AD.MEŠ-*ia a-li-kut maḫ-ri* ⸢*ug*⸣-*gat* DINGIR.MEŠ GAL.⸢MEŠ⸣
64′) *ša ḫe-pe-e* KUR-*šú ṣu-uḫ-ḫur* UN.MEŠ-[*šú*]
65′) UGU-*šu ib-ši-ma* ⸢UN⸣.MEŠ *in-né-šá-a*-⸢*ma*⸣
66′) *i-da-bu-ba ṣa-lip-tu kul-lat* KUR-*šú mit-ḫa*-⸢*riš*⸣
67′) ⸢*iš*⸣-*nu-nu-šu-ma il-qu-ú še-ṭu-su*
68′) *ù šu-ú* ^{m}*dal-ta-a* LUGAL *ma-lik-šú-nu*
69′) ⸢*ša*⸣-*na-an-šú*-⸢*nu*⸣ *e-dúr-ma*
70′) [*áš-šú*] *gul-lul*-⸢*ti*⸣-[*šu-nu dul-lu*]-⸢*uḫ*⸣ *ù uš-šu*-⸢*uš*⸣

v 60′–70′) Before my time, the anger of the great gods was (directed) against Daltâ of the land Ellipi — a submissive subject who pulled the yoke of the god Aššur, my lord, (and) had brought tribute and audience gift(s) to the kings, my ancestors who had preceded (me) — (an anger which would lead) to the destruction of his land (and) the decimation of [his] people. (v 65′) The people became bewildered and spoke treachery. His entire land was united in defying him; they held him in contempt. Moreover, that (man), Daltâ, the king, their ruler, took fright at their defiance; [he became disturb]ed and distressed [on account of their] crime(s).

Lacuna

Col. vi

Lacuna

Sm 2022 i′

1′) [...] x NU ⸢NI⸣ x [x x x (x)]
2′) [...] x KUR NAB TU [x] x [(x)] ⸢NA⸣
3′) [...] *ma-an-za-at* KUR-⸢*i*⸣ x [(x) x]
4′) [...] x IGI URU.*ul-x-x-x-ti*
5′) [...] (x) x x KUR ⸢TU⸣ x x
6′) [...] x ⸢AB UD? *a*⸣-*ši*-⸢*bu*⸣-*ut*
7′) [...] x ⸢*áš-lu-lam*?-*ma*⸣

Lacuna

Sm 2022 i′

vi 1′–7′) [...] ... [...] ... [...] a mountain rainbow [...] ... the city Ul-...-ti (vi 5′) [...] ... [...] ... inhabitants of [...] I carried off as booty and

---

v 42′ Cf. Tadmor and Yamada, RINAP 1 p. 91 Tiglath-pileser III no. 37 line 20. Possibly *ú*-⸢*lam*⸣-[*mi-id-ma*], "I/he tau[ght and]"?
v 43′ Or possibly *šu-tap*-⸢*pu*⸣, "partner," instead of *lib*-⸢*bu*⸣, "courage."
v 44′–45′ The eastern sea might refer here to that of Lake Urmia or the Caspian Sea instead of the Persian Gulf; see Fuchs, SAAS 8 p. 66 n. 74. For the restoration at the end of v 44′, see text no. 1 line 124.
v 69′ Or ⸢*da*⸣-*na-an-šu*-⸢*nu*⸣, "their strength," instead of ⸢*ša*⸣-*na-an-šu*-⸢*nu*⸣, "their defiance."
v 70′ Or [*i-na*] instead of [*áš-šú*]. The restoration in the middle of the line is that proposed in CAD A/2 p. 424.
vi 2′ Possibly KUR.*nab-tu*- or ⸢*mun*?⸣-*nab-tu*?

8′) [...] *x x x x* [*x x* (*x*)]
9′) [...] *x x* [(*x*)] *x x* (*x*) *x*
10′) [...] *x* [*x*]
Lacuna
K 1668b + DT 6 ii′
1″) [*x x* (*x*)] URU.MEŠ TA ⸢*qé-reb*⸣ [...]
2″) [*ú-še-ṣa-áš*?]-*šu-ma* UN.MEŠ URU.*bu*-[*x* ...]
3″) [URU.*x*-(*x*)]-*x-ba* URU.*a*-⸢*li*⸣-*i-na* URU.*x-x-x-x*
4″) [URU.*x*-(*x*)]-*ta-a*-⸢*a*⸣-*x* URU.*an-da*-⸢*ab*⸣-*x*
5″) [URU.MEŠ]-⸢*ni*⸣ *dan-nu-ti* ⸢*ša*⸣ KUR.*ḫal-di-ni-še*
6″) [*x* (*x*) *x*] *x* GIM *sa-par-ri is-ḫup-šú-nu-ti*
7″) [ÚŠ.MEŠ] ⸢UN⸣.MEŠ-*šú-nu ḫur-ri na-at-bak* KUR-*i*
8″) [*ú-šar*]-*di si-ta-ti-šú-nu ša la-pa-an* GIŠ.TUKUL.MEŠ-*ia*
9″) [*ip-par-ši*]-*du iṣ-ba-tu* KUR-*ú ul-tu qé*-⸢*reb*⸣
10″) [KUR-*i*] ⸢*ú*⸣-*še-ri-dam-ma a-na šal-la*-⸢*ti*⸣ *am-nu-šú-nu*-⸢*te*⸣
11″) [*lìb-bi* ^{m}]⸢*da*⸣-*al-ta-a* ⸢*ma*⸣-*li-ki-šu-nu ú-ṭib-ma*
12″) [UN.MEŠ KUR].*el*-⸢*li*⸣-*pí a-na paṭ gim-ri-šá*
13″) [*ú-še*]-⸢*ši*⸣-*ba šu-bat né-eḫ-ti*

vi 8′–10′) Too poorly preserved to allow translation.

Lacuna
K 1668b + DT 6 ii′
vi 1″–10″) [(*With regard to*) ...] cities, [*I brought*] him/it [*out*] from inside [...]; like a net, [...] overwhelmed the people of the cities Bu[..., ...]ba, Alīna, ..., [...]tāya-..., (and) Andab..., (vi 5″) fortified [cities] of the land Ḫaldiniše. [I made the blood] of their people [fl]ow down the gorges of the outflows of the mountains. I brought down from the [mountains] the remainder of them who had [fle]d from my weapons (and) had taken to the hills, and I counted them as booty.

vi 11″–13″) (Thus), I made [the heart of D]altâ, their ruler, happy and [allowed the people of the land] Ellipi, to its full extent, [to l]ive in peace.

14″) [^{m}]*x-pa*-⸢*ar*⸣-*nu-a* URU.*si-ik-ri-is-a-a*
15″) ^{m}⸢*šu/ku*⸣-*tir-na ša* URU.*x*-[(*x*)]-⸢*sa-na*⸣-*a*
16″) ^{m}⸢*up*⸣-*pa-am*-⸢*ma*⸣-*a ša* URU.⸢*ḫa*⸣-[*x*]-*ta*-⸢KA?/SAR?⸣-*na*
17″) ^{m}*ma-áš-da-ku ša* URU.*a-ma-ak-ki*
18″) ^{m}*iš-te-su-ku* ⸢*ša*⸣ URU.*iš-te-up-pu*
19″) ^{m}*ú-ar-za-an* ⸢*ša*⸣ KUR.*ú-qu-ut-ti*
20″) ^{m}*áš-pa-ba-ra* ⸢*ša*⸣ KUR.*ka-ak-kam*
21″) ^{m}*sa-tar-e-šu* ^{m}⸢*pa*?⸣-*ru-ra-su*
22″) LÚ.EN.URU.MEŠ *ša* KUR.É-*ba-a-ri*
23″) KUR.É-*bar-ba-ri na*-⸢*gi-i*⸣ *dan-nu-ti*
24″) ^{m}*sa-tar-pa-nu ša* ⸢KUR⸣.*up-pu*-⸢*ri*⸣-*a*
25″) ^{m}*pa-ar-ku*-⸢*ku*⸣ *ša* KUR.*an-dir-pat-ti-a-nu*
26″) ^{m}*a-ri-ia ša* KUR.⸢*bu*⸣-*uš-tu*-⸢*us*⸣
27″) ^{m}*uš-ra-a ša* KUR.⸢*kan-za-ab-ka*⸣-*nu*
28″) ^{m}*ma*-⸢*áš*⸣-*tuk-ku ša* KUR.*a*-⸢*rat*⸣-*is-ta*
29″) ^{m}*za-ar-duk*-⸢*ka*⸣ *ša* KUR.⸢*ḫa*⸣-*ar-zi-a-nu*
30″) ^{m}*iš-te*-⸢*su*?⸣-*ku* ^{m}*a-ú-a-ri-is*-⸢*ar-nu*⸣
31″) LÚ.EN.URU.MEŠ *ša* KUR.⸢*ka*⸣-*i-ta-nu*
32″) ^{m}*ar-ba-ku ša* KUR.*ar-na-si-a*
33″) [^{m}]⸢*sar*⸣-*ru-ti* ⸢*ša* URU.*kar*⸣-*zi-nu-ú*
34″) [^{m}*sa*]-⸢*tar-pa*⸣-*nu ša* ⸢KUR⸣.*ba-ri-ka-a-nu*
35″) [^{m}...] ⸢*ša* KUR⸣.*za-za-ak-nu*
36″) [^{m}... *ša*] ⸢KUR⸣.*qar-ka-si-a*
37″) [^{m}... KUR].⸢*pa*⸣-*ar-ta-ka-nu*

vi 14″) ...-parnua of the city Sikris,
vi 15″) Šutirna/Kutirna of the city ...-sanâ,
vi 16″) Uppammâ of the city Ḫa-...ta*KA*na,
vi 17″) Mašdakku of the city Amakki,
vi 18″) Ištesukka of the city Ište'uppu,
vi 19″) Uarzan of the land Uqutti,
vi 20″) Ašpa-bara of the land Kakkam,
vi 21″–23″) Satarēšu (and) *Parurasu*, city rulers of the large districts of Bīt-Bāri (and) Bīt-Barbari,
vi 24″) Satarpānu of the land Uppuria,
vi 25″) Parkuku (Partukku) of the land Andirpattianu,
vi 26″) Aria of the land Buštu[s],
vi 27″) Ušrâ of the land Ka[nz]abkanu,
vi 28″) Maštukku of the land A[ra]tista,
vi 29″) Zardukka of the land Ḫarzianu,
vi 30″–31″) Ište*su*ku (Ištesukka) (and) Auarisarnu, city rulers of the land Kaitanu,
vi 32″) Arbaku of the land Arnasia,
vi 33″) Sarruti of the city Karzinû,
vi 34″) [Sata]rpānu of the [lan]d Barikānu,
vi 35″) [...] of [the lan]d Zazaknu,
vi 36″) [... of the lan]d Qarkasia,
vi 37″) [...] Partakanu;

---

vi 2″ The tentative restoration is based on text no. 7 line 81. Or [*as-suḫ*]-*šu-ma*, "[I removed] him and" (see text no. 8 line 10).
vi 4″ Possibly URU.*an-da*-⸢*ap-pa*⸣?
vi 6″ There does not appear to be sufficient room at the beginning of the line to restore the expected subject of the verb "overwhelmed," namely "the fear of the god Aššur, my lord" (see for example vii 41′′).
vi 7″–8″ The restorations are based on text no. 65 line 135.
vi 11″ The restoration is based on text no. 1 line 183 and text no. 2 line 218.
vi 14″–37″ Cf. a similar list of rulers in text no. 65 lines 42–49. Possibly [^{m}]⸢*ta*⸣-*pa*-⸢*ar*⸣-*nu-a* or [^{m}]⸢*iš*⸣-*pa*-⸢*ar*⸣-*nu-a* in vi 14″.
vi 21″ Based on text no. 65 line 42, which mentions a ^{m}*du-re-si* immediately before a ^{m}*sa-tar-e-šú*, we might expect ^{m}*du-ru-ra-su* here.
vi 30″–31″ Cf. text no. 117 ii 62 ^{m}*iš-te-su-uk*-⸢*ka*?⸣ [(*šá*)] ⸢URU?⸣.*ka*-⸢*ia-ta*⸣-*ni*.
vi 34″ For the restoration at the beginning of the line, see text no. 65 line 49 and text no. 117 ii 61.
vi 36″ In the sixth regnal year of Sargon II, the ruler of Qarkasia was Šummušrâ, according to text no. 117 ii 69.

38″) [...].⸢RA?⸣.MEŠ *šá-qu-u-ti*
39″) [...]-*nu ša bi-bil*
40″) [...] ⸢ANŠE⸣.NUN.MEŠ
41″) [...] *x* ⸢*am*⸣-*ḫur-ma*
42″) [...]-E

vi 38″–42″) [...] high [...] of the bringing of [... m]ules [...] I received and [...]

Lacuna

Sm 2049 i′

1‴) [...] *x*-⸢*ia*⸣

vi 1‴) [...] my [...]

2‴) [*a-di a-na-ku* ... KUR].*el-li*-⸢*pí*⸣
3‴) [...] ⸢URU⸣.*šá-par*-⸢*da*⸣
4‴) [... KUR].⸢*uq*⸣-*qu-ti*
5‴) [...] ⸢*ka*⸣-*bit-tú* ⸢GUN⸣
6‴) [NUN? *a-lik? pa-ni-ia*?] ⸢*a*⸣-*na* ^{m}*ḫul-li-i*
7‴) [LUGAL? KUR?.É-*pu-ru-ta-áš*?] ⸢*i*⸣-*gu-ug-šu*-⸢*ma*⸣
8‴) [... *sa-pa*]-⸢*aḫ*⸣ KUR-*šú*
9‴) [*šu-ú a-di kim-ti-šu a-na qé*]-⸢*reb*⸣ KUR *aš-šur*.KI
10‴) [*ú-raš-šu-nu-ti im-ta-ni ki-i ṣa*]-⸢*ab*⸣ *ḫup-ši*
11‴) [(*x x x*) ^{m}*ḫul-li-i*? *a-na áš-ri-šu*] ⸢*ú*⸣-*ter*-⸢*ma*⸣

vi 2‴–5‴) [While I *was in the process of defeating* ... the land] Ellipi [... the ci]ty Šaparda, [... (and) the land U]qquti [(and) *receiving*] substantial tribute, (*the following happened in the west*):
vi 6‴–11‴) [*My princely predecessor*] had become angry with Ḫullî, [*king of the land Bīt-Purutaš*], and [... *had commanded* the dissolut]ion of his land. [He brought him (Ḫullî), together with his family, to] Assyria [(and) had considered (them) (there) as if (they were) membe]rs of the lower class. [(...)] I restored [*Ḫullî* to his position] and

Lacuna

K 8536

1′′′′) [...] *x x x x* [*x*] *x* [...]
2′′′′) [...]-⸢*ni*⸣-*šu-ma a-na qé-reb* ⸢KUR⸣.[...]
3′′′′) [*ša e-ke-me*] ⸢KUR⸣.*qu-e ù šá-lal* ⸢KUR⸣-[*ia*? ...]
4′′′′) [... LÚ].⸢SUKKAL⸣-*šú a-na* ^{m}⸢*ur*⸣-[*sa-a* LUGAL? KUR?.*ur-ar-ṭi*?]
5′′′′) [...] ⸢AZ⸣ *ši-pìr-tú ur*-⸢*ri*⸣-[*ḫa* ...]
6′′′′) [...] ⸢KIN⸣ BA *x x* [...]
7′′′′) [...] *x x* [...]

vi 1′′′′–5′′′′) [...] ... [...]ed him and in the land [... in order to take away (from me) the l]and Que (Cilicia) and plunder [*my*] la[nd ... *he sent*] his [vi]zier to U[rsâ (Rusâ), *king of the land Urarṭu*, (vi 5′′′′) ...] he sent a message qui[ckly ...]
vi 6′′′′–7′′′′) Too poorly preserved to allow translation.

Lacuna

K 1672 i′

1′′′′′) [...] *x x* [...]
2′′′′′) [...] ⸢*ša*?⸣ KUR.⸢*ta-bal*⸣
3′′′′′) [...] ⸢LÚ⸣.*šu-ut* SAG.MEŠ-*ia*
4′′′′′) [LÚ.EN.NAM.(MEŠ?)] ⸢URU⸣.*sa-am-al-la*
5′′′′′) [URU.*ar-pad-da*? KUR].⸢*ḫa*⸣-*am-ma-tu* URU.*di-maš-qu*
6′′′′′) [...] ⸢*a*⸣-*di* ANŠE.*pét-ḫal-li-ia*
7′′′′′) [*ša*? ...] *x i-na qé-reb* KUR.*ḫa-ma-at-ti*
8′′′′′) [...] *uš-zi*-⸢*zu*⸣
9′′′′′) [*um-ma-na-at* ^{d}*a*]-⸢*šur*$_{4}$⸣ *gap-šá*-⸢*a*⸣-[*ti*]
10′′′′′) [... KUR?].⸢*ta*?-*bal*?⸣ [*x x x*]

vi 1′′′′′–10′′′′′) [...] ... [... o]*f* the land Tab[al ...] eunuchs of mine, [*the provincial governor(s)* of the ci]ty Sam'al, (vi 5′′′′′) [*the city Arpad*, the city H]amath, the city Damascus, [...] together with my cavalry, [*which*] *I* had stationed [...] in the land Hamath [...] the numerous [troops of the god Aššu]r [... *the land T*]*abal* [...]

Lacuna

Col. vii

Lacuna

---

vi 39″–40″ Possibly ... *bi-bil* [*lìb-bi-ia* ...], thus "[my heart's] desire."

vi 2‴–5‴ For the restoration and understanding of the passage cf. text no. 1 lines 444b–451a and text no. 7 lines 149–150.

vi 6‴ The restoration is based on text no. 1 lines 194. Or possibly restore ^{d}*a-šur*$_{4}$, "the god Aššur," as subject of the verb?

vi 7‴ Or possibly restore [LUGAL KUR.*ta-bal*], "[king of the land Tabal]"; cf. text no. 1 line 194 and text no. 2 line 226.

vi 8‴ For the restoration, cf. v 63–65 and text no. 4 line 27′.

vi 9‴–11‴ The restorations and understanding of the passage are based on text no. 1 line 195, text no. 2 line 227, and text no. 89 line 33.

vi 3′′′′ The restoration is made on the lines of text no. 1 line 200, text no. 2 line 232, text no. 7 line 31, and text no. 74 v 20–24.

vi 3′′′′′–8′′′′′ N. Na'aman suggests restoring the passage to read: "my eunuchs, [the governors] of the cities of Sam'al, [of Ṣubat??], of Hamath, of Damascus, [of Ḫatarikka??], with my cavalry [which m]y [commanders] stationed in the lands Hamath [and Ḫatarikka??]" (UF 31 [1999] pp. 426–427 and AfO 46–47 [1999–2000] p. 363). The passage cited by him (Fales and Postgate, SAA 11 no. 1 rev. i 12′) is not sufficient reason to restore Ṣubat (Ṣupāt) in vi 5′′′′′ instead of Arpad. The restorations would mean that most of the governors who are about to go and fight in the north (Tabal) would have come from central or southern Syria. Cf. Landsberger, Sam'al p. 73 with regard to the restorations in vi 4′′′′′–5′′′′′.

Sm 2022 ii′

1′) [...] x [...]
2′) [x (x) ŠU u] ⌜GÌR⌝.II bi-[re-tú AN.BAR]
3′) ⌜id-du⌝-u$^{?}$-⌜šú⌝-nu-ti-⌜ma⌝ [...]
4′) ⌜šal⌝-la-⌜ti⌝-iš x [...]
5′) ^{m}kur-ti-i KUR.a-tu-na-a-a ša ⌜UGU ^{m}⌝[mi-ta-a]
6′) ⌜KUR⌝.mu-us-ka-a-a it-tak-[lu]
7′) ki-šit-ti ^{m}am-ri-is ù šá-lal [UN.MEŠ-šú]
8′) e-⌜mur⌝-ma lìb-ba-šú ik-kud a-⌜na⌝ [na-še-e]
9′) ta-mar-ti ⌜a⌝-na ni-ir ^{d}a-[šur$_{4}$ šá-da-di]
10′) LÚ.DUMU šip-ri-šú-nu ša a-mat [MUNUS.SIG$_{5}$ na-šu-ú]
11′) ⌜a⌝-na KUR.sik-ri-is ša KUR.ma-⌜da⌝-[a-a]
12′) a-di maḫ-ri-ia ub-lam-ma ⌜ú⌝-[šá-li-iṣ lìb-bi]

Sm 2022 ii′

vii 1′–4′) [...] they put [iron] fe[tters] on their [hands and] feet and [...] as booty [...].

vii 5′–12′) (When) Kurtî of the land Atunna, who had put his tru[st] in [Mitâ] of the land Musku, saw the capture of Amris (Ambaris) and the carrying off [of his people], his heart pounded. His (lit.: "their") messenger, bearing the [happy] news, brought to me in the land Sikris — which is (situated) in the land Med[ia] — (a message indicating his willingness) to [bring (me)] an audience gift (and) [pull] the yoke of the god A[ššur]; he (thus) [made my heart rejoice].

13′) ⌜i⌝-na 9 BALA-ia a-na [URU.as-du-di ša a-ḫi]
14′) [ti]-⌜amti⌝ GAL-ti ⌜a-lik⌝ [...]
15′) [(x) URU].as-du-di [...]
16′) [...] x [...]

vii 13′–16′) In my ninth regnal year I marched to [the city Ashdod which is (situated) on the shore of the] great [s]ea. [... the city] Ashdod [...]

Lacuna

Lacuna

K 1668b + DT 6 iii′

1″) áš-šu [ḪUL-tu e-pu-šu ...]
2″) iš-tu ⌜URU.as⌝-[du-di ú-še-ṣa-áš-šum-ma]
3″) ^{m}a-ḫi-me-ti [...]
4″) a-ḫu ta-lim-šú ⌜UGU⌝ [UN.MEŠ$^{?}$ URU.as-du-di$^{?}$]
5″) ⌜ú⌝-rab-⌜bi⌝-ma ú-[še-šib-šu i-na GIŠ.GU.ZA AD$^{?}$-šu]
6″) bil-tu ma-da-at-⌜tu⌝ [za-bíl ku-dúr-ri a-lik KASKAL]
7″) ki-⌜i⌝ ša ⌜LUGAL⌝.MEŠ-ni [AD.MEŠ-ia e-mid-du]

K 1668b + DT 6 iii′

vii 1″–8″a) Because of [the evil he (Azuri) had done ... I brought him out] from the city A[shdod], elevated Aḫī-Mīti [...], his *favorite* brother, o[ver *the people of the city Ashdod*], (vii 5″) and [set him on the throne of his *father*]. I established for him (the same) tribute, payment(s), [labor duty, (and) military service] as the kings, [my ancestors, had imposed].

8″) UGU-šú áš-kun ⌜ù$^{?}$⌝ [šu-nu LÚ.ḫat-ti-i]
9″) lem-nu-ti i-na IGI x [...]
10″) ⌜a⌝-na la na-še$_{20}$-e ⌜bil⌝-ti [ŠÀ-šú-nu]
11″) kit-pu-da le-mut-tu [a-na UGU]
12″) ma-li-ki-šú-nu si-ḫu ⌜bar⌝-[tu e-pu-šu-ma]
13″) ⌜ki⌝-i ta-bik da-me ul-⌜tú⌝ [qé-reb URU.as-du-di]

vii 8″b–33″a) *However*, [those] evil [Hittites] with/in ... [...] plotted evil [in their heart(s)] (so as) to no longer (have to) bring tribute (to me). [They made] an insurrection (and) up[rising against] their ruler, [and] drove him out [of the city Ashdod] as if he was one who had committed bloodshed. ... [... They made] king over

---

vii 1′ The section before what is found in vi 2′–3′ might have referred to something along the lines of "Am(ba)ris, king of the land Bīt-Purutaš, together with the (other) offspring of his father's house (and) the nobles of his land"; see text no. 1 line 201, text no. 2 line 233, and text no. 74 v 25–26, and cf. text no. 7 line 31.
vii 2′ The restoration is based on text no. 8 line 14.
vii 4′ The traces do not support reading ⌜im⌝-[nu-šu-nu-ti] and we would not expect ⌜am⌝-[nu-šu-nu-ti] since the passage is in the third person plural.
vii 7′–12′ For restoration and understanding of these lines, compare text no. 1 lines 451–456, text no. 2 lines 431–435, and text no. 7 lines 152–153.
vii 9′–10′ H. Winckler's copy appears to show the šur$_{4}$ of line 9′ and the MUNUS of line 10′ to be completely or partially preserved; collation indicates that there appears to be a new break at this spot on the fragment.
vii 14′ G. Vera Chamaza (Rolle Moabs p. 146) reads the line as [ti-a]-mat GAL-ti šá ⌜e⌝-[rib ^{d}UTU-ši x x x x x x x x], but collation indicates that the copy by A. Fuchs is correct — i.e., -⌜amti⌝(⌜GÉME⌝) not -mat —, no šá after -ti, and a- not ⌜e⌝-.
vii 1″ The restoration is based on text no. 1 line 251, text no. 3 line 7′, and text no. 7 line 92.
vii 2″ For the restoration, cf. text no. 7 line 81. G. Vera Chamaza (Rolle Moabs p. 145) reads iš-tu ⌜LUGAL⌝-[ti-šú UGU KUR-šú ú-nak-kir], "[I did away] with [his] ru[lership over his land]," based on text no. 7 line 93, but the traces fit iš-tu ⌜URU.as⌝-[du-di] better.
vii 4″ G. Vera Chamaza (Rolle Moabs p. 145) restores just ⌜UGU⌝-[šú-nu], "ov[er them]," at the end of the line based on text no. 3 line 8′ and text no. 7 line 94, but we would expect several more signs in the line.
vii 5″ Or restore ŠEŠ-šu, "his brother," instead of AD-šu, "his father." G. Vera Chamaza (Rolle Moabs pp. 145 and 148) reads ú-⌜rab-bi⌝ šu-ú [a-na ni-ri-ia iš-du-ud], "I raised. He [pulled my yoke]"; however the fourth sign is MA, not ŠU.
vii 6″–7″ For the restorations, see text no. 105 ii′ 9–12 and note v 25′–26′ of this text. For line 7″ G. Vera Chamaza (Rolle Moabs p. 145) reads ki-ma ša LUGAL.MEŠ-ni [maḫ-ru-ti AD.MEŠ-ni], "like the [previous] kings, [(my) ancestors]"; however, the second sign is clearly I, not MA.
vii 8″ For the restorations of the line, cf. text no. 1 lines 198–199 and 253, text no. 3 line 8′, and text no. 7 lines 94–95, and see Fuchs, SAAS 8 p. 45 n. 140.
vii 12″ Or restore ú-šab-šu-ma instead of i-pu-šu-ma; see Grayson, RIMA 3 p. 188 A.0.103.1 iv 40.
vii 13″ Or restore ul-⌜tú⌝ [qé-reb/lìb-bi URU-šu], "out [of his city]."

14″) ⸢*ú*⸣-*še-ṣu-šu i-x x* [...]
15″) ^{m}⸢*ia*⸣-*ma-ni* ⸢LÚ⸣.ERIM.⸢MEŠ *ḫup*⸣-[*ši la* EN GIŠ.GU.ZA]
16″) *a-na* ⸢LUGAL-*ti*⸣ UGU-*šú-nu* ⸢*iš*⸣-[*ku-nu i-na* GIŠ.GU.ZA]
17″) *be-lí-šu ú-še-ši*-⸢*bu*⸣-[*šu* ...]
18″) URU-*šú-nu* MA?/GAL? *x* [...]
19″) *ša mit*-⸢*ḫu*⸣-[*ṣi* ...]
20″) *x* [*x* (*x*)] *x* [...]
21″) [*x x* (*x*)] *x x x* [...]
22″) [(*x*)] *x* ḪI *x* Ú BAD ⸢ḪAR⸣ [...]
23″) [*i*]-⸢*na*⸣ *li-me-ti-šú ḫi-ri-ṣa*-⸢*ni*?⸣-[*šu*?-(*nu*?) ...]
24″) 20 ⸢*i*⸣-*na* 1.KÙŠ *a-na šu-pa*-⸢*li*⸣ [...]
25″) *ik-šud-du* A.MEŠ *nag-bi a-na* ⸢LUGAL⸣.[MEŠ-*ni*]
26″) *ša* ⸢KUR⸣.*pi-liš-te* KUR.*ia-ú-di* KUR.*ú*-⸢*du*⸣-[*me*?]
27″) ⸢KUR.*ma*⸣-*a-bi a-ši-bu-ut tam-tim na-áš bil*-⸢*ti*⸣ [*u*]
28″) ⸢*ta*⸣-*mar-ti ša* ^{d}*a-šur*$_{4}$ *be-lí*-⸢*ia*⸣
29″) *da-bab sa-ar-ra-a-ti at-me-e nu-ul-la-a-te*
30″) *ša it-ti-ia a-na šum-ku-ri* <*iš-pu-ru*> UGU ^{m}*pi-ir-ʾu-u*
31″) ⸢LUGAL⸣ KUR.*mu-uṣ-ri mal-ku la mu-še-zi-bi-šú-nu*
32″) *šul-man-na-šú-nu iš-šu-ú-ma e-ter-ri-šu-uš*
33″) ⸢*ki-it*⸣-*ra a-na-ku* ^{m}LUGAL-GI.NA NUN *ke-e-nu*
34″) *pa-li-iḫ ma-mit* ^{d}*šà-máš* ^{d}AMAR.UTU *na-ṣi-ru*
35″) *zik-ri* ^{d}*a-šur*$_{4}$ ÍD.IDIGNA ÍD.BURANUN.KI
36″) *i-na* ILLU *kiš-šá-ti e-du-ú* IGI *šat-ti* ⸢ERIM?.ḪI?.A?⸣
37″) *na-pa-liš ú-še-tiq* ⸢*ù šu*⸣-*ú* ^{m}*ia-ma-ni*
38″) ⸢LUGAL⸣-*šú-nu ša* ⸢*i*⸣-*na* ⸢*e-muq ra-man*⸣-*i*-⸢*šu*⸣
39″) ⸢*it*⸣-*tak-lu-ma ul* ⸢*ik*⸣-[*nu*]-⸢*šu a-na*⸣ *be-lu-ti*
40″) [*a*]-*lik ger-ri-ia a*-⸢*na*⸣ [*ru*]-⸢*qa*⸣-*a-ti iš-me-ma*
41″) [*na*]-⸢*mur*⸣-*rat* ^{d}[*a-šur*$_{4}$ EN]-*ia is-ḫup-šu-ma*
42″) [*x x*] *x x* [*x ki-ma šur-še*] ⸢*ša*⸣ *kib-ri* ÍD
43″) [*ir-bu-ba* SUḪUŠ-*šú* ...] *x x šup-li* A.MEŠ
44″) [*ru-qu-*(*ú*)*-ti ki-ma* KU$_{6}$.MEŠ] ⸢*iṣ*⸣-*ba-tú pa-še*-⸢*ru*⸣

them (vii 15″) Iāmānī, a member of the low[er class who had no right to the throne], (and) they sat [him on the throne] of his lord. [...] their city ... [...] of batt[le ...] (vii 20″) ... [...] ... [...] ... [... in] its environs [*its/their*] moats [... *they dug*] twenty cubits deep [*until*] (vii 25″) they reached groundwater. <They sent> mendacious messages (and) malicious words to the ki[ngs] of the lands Philistia, Judah, Ed[om], (and) Moab, (as well as to) those who live on the sea(coast), (all) those who brought tribute [and] audience gift(s) to the god Aššur, my lord, (vii 30″) in order to make (them) hostile to me. They took gift(s) to Pir'û (Pharaoh), king of Egypt, a ruler who could not save them, and they repeatedly asked him for (military) aid.

vii 33″b–48″) I, Sargon, the just prince, who reveres oath(s) (sworn) by the gods Šamaš (and) Marduk (and) who obeys (vii 35″) the commands of the god Aššur, had (my) troops cross the Tigris (and) Euphrates Rivers at the height of (their) flooding, (namely) at the spring inundation, (as easily) as if (they were) dry land. Moreover, that (man) Iāmānī, their king, who had put his trust in his own strength and had not su[bmitted] to any(one else's) rule, (vii 40″) heard from [af]ar of [the app]roach of my expeditionary force. Then, the [aw]esome splendor of the god [Aššur], my [lord], overwhelmed him and ... [his legs grew weak, like roots] on a river bank. [...] ... [Like fish, th]ey chose the depths of [far-off] waters (for their) hiding place.

---

vii 15″ One does not expect MEŠ after LÚ.ERIM if it refers to Iāmānī. For the restoration of the end of the line, cf. text no. 7 lines 33 and 95, text no. 1 line 254, and text no. 3 line 9′.
vii 16″–17″ For the restorations, cf. text no. 1 lines 252–253, text no. 3 line 8′, and text no. 7 line 39.
vii 19″ The word *mitḫuṣi* appears in text no. 2 line 380.
vii 22″ Or *mit-ḫur-*[*ti/tu*]?
vii 23″ Cf. text no. 65 line 190 for the tentative reading of the end of the line. At the end of the line, G. Vera Chamaza (Rolle Moabs p. 145) reads *ḫi-ri-ṣa* [*iḫ-ru-u*], "[they dug] a moat."
vii 24″ At the end of the line, G. Vera Chamaza (Rolle Moabs p. 145) restores [*iḫ-ru-u adi*], "[they dug until]."
vii 26″ At the end of the line, G. Vera Chamaza (Rolle Moabs p. 145) reads KUR.*ú*-[*du-me* KUR.É-*am-ma-na-a u*]," Ed[om, Ammon, and]," but there is not sufficient room to restore more than one sign after -⸢*du*⸣.
vii 30″ The verb *iš-pu-ru* appears to have been omitted after *šum-ki-ri*; cf. v 10′–11′.
vii 36″ The height of flooding of the Tigris is in April and that of the Euphrates in May (Redman, Rise of Civilization p. 35).
vii 38″ For the end of the line, G. Vera Chamaza (Rolle Moabs p. 146) reads *i-na e-*[*mu-qi-šú*], "in [his] str[ength]," but collation does not support this reading.
vii 40″ We would expect [*a*]-*lak* rather than [*a*]-*lik*; see text no. 7 line 101 and note the variant *a-lik* in ex. 5.
vii 42″–43″ The restorations are based on text no. 65 line 174.
vii 44″ Cf. Novotny and Jeffers, RINAP 5/1 p. 246 no. 11 v 20 (*ki-ma* KU$_{6}$.MEŠ *iṣ-bat šu-pul* A.MEŠ *ru-qu-u-ti*) and text no. 6 line 6′a (*ú*†*-šá-aṣ-bi-ta pa-ši-ru*).

45″) [...] *x ru-qa-a-ti*
46″) [...] ⸢UN⸣ *in-na-bit*
47″) [... URU].⸢*as*⸣*-du-di*
48″) [...] *x* AZ *x* [*x*]

(vii 45″) [...] far [...] he fled [... the city A]shdod [...] ...

Lacuna

Sm 2049 ii′

1‴) [*x x x*] *uz-*⸢*ni*$^{?}$⸣ [...]
2‴) [*iz/uš*$^{?}$]*-*⸢*zi*⸣*-zu-ma x* [...]
3‴) ⸢*ri*⸣*-ig-me ma-*⸢*li*⸣*-*[*li*$^{?}$ ...]
4‴) [*x*]*-ma ti-ik-le-*[*šú*$^{?}$*-*(*nu*$^{?}$) ...]
5‴) ⸢*a*⸣*-na* URU.*za-i-ni* ⸢URU⸣ [*dan-nu-ti*$^{?}$ *šá*$^{?}$ KUR.*gúr-gu-me*$^{?}$]
6‴) ⸢*e*⸣*-ru-ub-ma x* [... ^{m}*tar-ḫu-la-ra*$^{?}$]
7‴) ⸢*i*⸣*-gu-*⸢*ug*⸣*-ma* ^{m}*mut-*[*tal-lum* ...]
8‴) *x a-na a-lik bé-*⸢*e*⸣*-x* [...]
9‴) [*i*]*-da-at* LUGAL*-te* Á [...]
10‴) [^{m}]⸢*qu*$^{?}$⸣*-maš-ši* DUMU AD*-šú šá x* [...]
11‴) [*x*] ⸢RU⸣ UB BU Ú ⸢RA⸣ [...]
12‴) *ú-ma-ʾe-ru-ma a-*⸢*li*$^{?}$⸣ / ⸢*tu*$^{?}$⸣*-*[...]
13‴) ⸢*šit*⸣*-mu-ru* UR NÍG ⸢AN$^{?}$/TI$^{?}$⸣ *x* [...]
14‴) ⸢*ma*⸣*-la ba-šu-ú mal-ma-*⸢*liš*⸣ [*i-zu-zu-ma* ...]
15‴) *x* (*x*) *x* ⸢^{m}*tar*⸣*-ḫu-la-ra x* [...]

Lacuna

Sm 2049 ii′

vii 1‴–15‴) [...] *of understanding* [... *they st*]*ood* and [...] the sound of a *fl*[*ute ... his/their*] helper(s) [...] (vi 5‴) into the city Zaʾini, a [*fortified*] cit[*y of the land Gurgum*], he entered and [... *Tarḫu-lara*] became angry and Mut[allu ...] to one who goes ... [... si]gns of kingship [... (vii 10‴) Q]umašši, son of his father, who [...] ... [...] they sent and ... [...] ferocious ... [...] as many as there were, [they divided up] into equal par[ts and ...] ... Tarhu-lara [...]

Lacuna

Sm 2050 i′

1⁗) [...] *x* [*x* (*x*)]
2⁗) [...] ⸢*be*⸣*-lut*-su*
3⁗) [...] ⸢*ger*⸣*-ru*
4⁗) [... KUR].*gúr-gu-me*
5⁗) [...] ŠU
6⁗) [...] *x*

Lacuna

Sm 2050 i′

vii 1⁗–4⁗) [...] his rule [... ca]mpaign [... the land] Gurgum [...]

vii 5⁗–6⁗) Too poorly preserved to allow translation.

Lacuna

K 1672 ii′

1′′′′′) *x* [...]
2′′′′′) KUR.*x* [...]
3′′′′′) *ki-ma* ⸢*ur*$^{?}$⸣*-*[*pa-ti*$^{?}$ *ak-tùm*$^{?}$ *ú-nam-ma-a*$^{?}$]
4′′′′′) *ta-*⸢*mir-tuš*⸣ [...]
5′′′′′) *ri-*⸢*gim*⸣ GIŠ.⸢TUKUL⸣.[MEŠ*-ia* ...]
6′′′′′) *e-du-ru-*[*ma ip-tu-ú* KÁ*-šu-un* ...]
7′′′′′) *uṣ-ṣu-*[*nim-ma ú-na-áš-ši-qu* GÌR.II*-ia* URU.*me-lid-du*]
8′′′′′) URU LUGAL*-*⸢*ti*⸣*-*[*šu a-di na-gi-i ša li-me-ti-šu*]

Lacuna

K 1672 ii′

vii 1′′′′′–9′′′′′) [...] the land [... *I covered*] like a *c*[*loud. I laid waste to* its] meadowland(s) [...] (vii 5′′′′′) the noise of [my] weap[ons ...] took fright [and opened their gate ...]. They came out [and kissed my feet. I gave his] royal city [Melid, together with its surrounding district], to the king [of the land Kummuḫu ...]

---

vii 45″–48″ G. Vera Chamaza (Rolle Moabs p. 146) restores these lines as [... *a-na*] *ru-qa-a-ti* / [*a-na* KUR.*mu-uṣ*]*-*⸢*ri*⸣ *in-na-bit* / [*ù la in-na-mir a-šar-šú* URU].*as-du-di* / [URU.*gi-im-tu ù* URU].*as-*⸢*du*⸣*-*[*di-im-mu*], "[...] he fled [(...)] far off, [to Egyp]t; [his (present) whereabouts have not been discovered. The cities] Ashdod, [Gath, (and)] Ashd[od-Yam]," based on text no. 7 lines 103–104. The traces before *in-na-bit* in line 46″, however, would not fit the end of a RI, while they are fully consistent with UN, and the traces after the AZ in 48″ are not particularly good for ⸢DU⸣, although such a reading can not be excluded.

vii 5‴ Instead of ⸢URU⸣ [*dan-nu-ti*], "[fortified] city," other possible restorations include ⸢URU⸣ [LUGAL*-ti*], "[royal] city," and ⸢URU⸣.[ḪAL.ṢU], "fo[rtress]."

vii 10‴ Assuming that there was a name at the beginning of the line, other possible readings include [^{m}]⸢*qu*⸣*-bar-ši*, [^{m}]⸢*bi*⸣*-maš-ši*, and [^{m}]⸢*bi*⸣*-bar-ši*.

vii 11‴ Possibly [*šu*]*-*⸢*ru*⸣*-up-pu-ú*, "[ch]ills"? Cf. Novotny and Jeffers, RINAP 5/1 p. 132 no. 6 ix 7′.

vii 13‴ Possibly *ur-ša-an*, "hero"?

vii 14‴ For the restoration, cf. for example text no. 7 line 118 and text no. 8 line 19.

vii 2⁗ *-lut*-*: The copy has -E-U-.

vii 2′′′′′ Possibly KUR.⸢*ḫat*⸣*-*[*ti*], "land Ḫat[ti]," or KUR*-*⸢*ú*$^{?}$/*i*$^{?}$⸣ "mountain."

vii 3′′′′′ For the tentative restorations, see text no. 1 line 211 and text no. 65 line 266. Or possibly *ar-bu-ti-iš ú-šá-li-ka*, "I turned into a desolate land," instead of *ú-nam-ma-a*, "I laid waste to"; see text no. 65 line 275.

vii 6′′′′′–9′′′′′ For restorations, cf. text no. 1 lines 211 and 220–221.

9′′′′′) [*a*]-*na* ⸢LUGAL⸣ [KUR.*kúm-mu-ḫi ad-di-in* ...]

Lacuna

Lacuna

Col. viii

Lacuna

Lacuna

K 1668b + DT 6 iv′

1′) *x* [...]
2′) URU.*x* [...]
3′) ⸢URU⸣.*x* [...]
4′) UGU ⸢*ša*?⸣ [*maḫ-ri*? ...]
5′) MU-*šú*-⸢*nu*⸣ [... UN.MEŠ *ki-šit-ti* ŠU.II-*ia*]
6′) *i-na* ⸢*lib*⸣-[*bi ú-še-rib il-ku tup-šik-ku*]
7′) *ki-i* ⸢*ša*⸣ [^{m}*gu-un-zi-na-nu e-mid-su-nu-ti*]
8′) URU.*lu*-⸢*uḫ*⸣-[*su* URU.*pur-ṭir* URU.*an-mu-ur-ru*]
9′) ⸢URU.*ki*?⸣-[*a*?-*ka*? URU.*an-du-ar-sa-li-a*]
10′) ⸢UGU⸣ KUR.[*ur-ar-ṭi ú-dan-ni-na* EN.NUN]
11′) URU.*ú*-[*si* URU.*ú-si-an* URU.*ú-ar-gi-in pa-a-ṭi*]
12′) KUR.*mu-us*-[*ki ad-di-ma ša la mu-ṣe-e aṣ-ba-ta*]
13′) KÁ.MEŠ-⸢*šú*⸣ [URU.*el-li-bir* URU.*ši-in-da-ra-ra*]
14′) ⸢UGU⸣ UN.⸢MEŠ⸣ [KUR.*ka-as-ku ar-ku-us* (*x x x*)]
15′) *áš-šu la x* [...]

K 1668b + DT 6 iv′

viii 1′–15′) [...] the city [...] the city [...] *more th*[*an previously* ...] (viii 5′) their name(s) [... I had people whom I had captured enter] th[ere. I imposed upon them (the same state) service (and) corvée duty] as (there had been in the time) of [Gunzinānu. I strengthened the garrison(s of)] the cities Lu[ḫsu, Purṭir, Anmurru], *K*[*iaka*, (and) Anduarsalia] (viii 10′) against the land [Urarṭu. I erected] the cities U[si, Usian, (and) Uargin on the border] of the land Mus[ku and seized] the entrance ways (to that land) (lit.: "its gates") [so that nothing (more) could come out (from that land to Assyria). I constructed the cities Ellibir (and) Šindarara] against the people [of the land Kasku]. In order not [...]

16′) *i-na* u_4-[*me-šu-ma ka-tim-ti* KUR.MEŠ-*e ša* KUR.*ḫat-ti ip-pe-te*]
17′) *i-na* [u_4-*me*? BALA-*ia*? ...]
18′) GÚ [...]
19′) IŠ *x* [...]

Lacuna

Sm 2050 ii′

1′′) ⸢MA⸣ [...]
2′′) NI [...]
3′′) *x* [...]
4′′) NU [...]
5′′) *x* [...]

Lacuna

K 4818 i′

1′′′) [...] (*x*) [...]
2′′′) [...] NA *x* [...]
3′′′) [...] *x* ⸢IA⸣ NI [...]
4′′′) [...] *x a-na* ⸢*ar*⸣-[*kàt* u_4-*me* NUN]
5′′′) [*ar-ku-ú e*]-⸢*nu*⸣-*ma* É *ziq*-⸢*qur*⸣-[*ra-tu ši-i*]
6′′′) [*i-lab-bi-ru-ma*] ⸢*e*⸣-*na*-⸢*ḫu*⸣ *an-ḫu-us*-⸢*sa*⸣ [*lu-ud-diš*]
7′′′) [MU.SAR-*a-a u*] ⸢MU⸣.SAR-*e* LUGAL.MEŠ AD.MEŠ-⸢*ia*⸣ *a-na* ⸢KI-*šú*⸣-[*un*]
8′′′) [*lu-ter* ^{d}*a*]-⸢*šur*$_4$⸣ ^{d}IŠKUR *ik-ri-bi*-⸢*šu*⸣ *i-šem-mu-ú*
9′′′) [*ša ep-šet* ŠU.II]-*ia iš-tú* ⸢*áš-ri*⸣-*šú* ⸢*ú*⸣-*nak-ka*-⸢*ru*⸣
10′′′) [^{d}*a-šur*$_4$ ^{d}]⸢IŠKUR⸣ DINGIR.MEŠ GAL.⸢MEŠ⸣ *ez-zi-iš*
11′′′) [*li-ru-ru-šu-ma* MU-*šú*] ⸢NUMUN⸣-*šú* ⸢*i*⸣-*na* KUR ⸢*li*⸣-*ḫal-li-qu*

viii 16′–17′) At [that] ti[me, (everything) that was hidden in the mountains of the land Ḫatti was revealed (*to me*)]. *Du*[*ring my reign* ...]

viii 18′–19′) Too poorly preserved to allow translation.

Lacuna

Sm 2050 ii′

viii 1′′–5′′) Too poorly preserved to allow translation.

Lacuna

K 4818 i′

viii 1′′′–4′′′a) Too poorly preserved to allow translation.

viii 4′′′b–8′′′) In [days to come, wh]en [this] ziggu[rrat becomes old and] dilapidated, [may a future prince renovate] its dilapidated sections. [May he return my inscribed object and (any) insc]ribed object(s) of the kings, my ancestors, to the[ir] place(s). The gods [Aššš]ur (and) Adad will (then) listen to his prayers.

viii 9′′′–11′′′) [(As for) the one who] removes [the work of] my [hands] from its (current) location, may the gods Aššur (and) A]dad, the great gods, [curse him] angrily [and] make [his name (and)] his [des]cendant(s) disappear from the land.

Lower edge

12′′′) [...] ^{m}⸢LUGAL⸣-GI.NA LUGAL KUR *aš-šur*.KI

Lower edge

viii 12′′′) [... (*of*)] Sargon, king of Assyria.

---

viii 5′–17′ For restorations, cf. text no. 1 lines 214–223 and text no. 2 lines 256–260.

viii 15′ Tadmor, JCS 12 (1958) p. 91 n. 300 suggests *áš-šu la n*[*a-pa-ar-ka-a* ..... *ad-di-in*], referring to text no. 1 lines 220–221.

viii 4′′′–11′′′ For restorations, cf. text no. 8 lines 82–87 and such other places as Grayson, RIMA 1 p. 274 A.0.78.23 lines 119–120, text no. 43 line 76, text no. 103 iv 64–69, and text no. 117 ii 75.

viii 6′′′ Or [*ú-šal-ba-ru-ma*]; see for example Grayson, RIMA 1 p. 186 A.0.77.1 line 159 and CAD L p. 16.

viii 9′′′ Or [*ša šiṭ-ri* MU]-*ia*, "my [inscribed name]"; see text no. 103 ii 64.

83

A fragment of a prism preserves parts of three columns of an inscription of Sargon II. While only a few signs are preserved for the first column, the other two columns have passages dealing with Sargon's involvement with Iāmānī of Ashdod in his eleventh regnal year (711; ii′ 1–11) and the Chaldean ruler Marduk-apla-iddina in the following years (ii′ 12–15), as well as Sargon's dedication of various valuable commodities to the gods of Babylonia (iii′ 1–13′). According to C.J. Gadd (Iraq 16 [1954] p. 188), this fragment "has a remarkable similarity to the Nimrud prisms in width of columns, style of writing, disposition of text, and general appearance, so great that it might be a duplicate, and in all these respects it is equally unlike the Kuyunjik fragments, to which there can be no question of its belonging." Some pieces in the Kuyunjik collection were not actually found at Nineveh (see Reade, CRRA 30 p. 213) and thus it is not impossible that the fragment came from Nimrud. Gadd (Iraq 16 [1954] p. 188) notes: "What its actual provenance may have been there is no means of ascertaining." Thus, it is not impossible that this piece should be treated with text no. 74; however, it is also clear that they are not exact duplicates (see commentary to text no. 74). This inscription is sometimes referred to as prism C.

CATALOGUE

Museum Number	Registration Number	Photograph Number	Provenance	Dimensions (cm)	cpn
—	81-7-27,3	BM 56568–9	Probably Nineveh, Kuyunjik	8.5×7.5×6.0	c

COMMENTARY

This prism fragment in the Kuyunjik collection of the British Museum is part of the top of what was probably an eight-sided prism. C. Bezold assigned the fragment to Sennacherib (Cat. 4 p. 1795), but E. Weidner recognized that it actually belongs to Sargon II (AfO 14 [1941–44] p. 49).

As noted by Weidner, col. ii′ 1–11 likely deal with Sargon's involvement with Ashdod and the extradition of Iāmānī from Egypt by the Nubian ruler of that land, Šapataka' (Shebitko). Iāmānī had fled from Assyrian forces in 711 and was extradited at some point in or before 706. See text no. 7 lines 90–112 (especially 107–109 and 111–112), text no. 8 lines 11–14 (especially 14), and text no. 116 lines 19–21 (especially 21).

For ii′ 12–15, see text no. 74 vi 14–17 and text no. 113 line 6′.

For iii 1′–12′, see text no. 2 lines 364–368, text no. 7 lines 141–144, text no. 103 iv 6–22, text no. 74 vii 7–19, and text no. 113 line 26′.

BIBLIOGRAPHY

1896 Bezold, Cat. 4 p. 1795 (study)
1941–44 Weidner, AfO 14 pp. 49–51 (copy [erroneously labeled 81-7-23,3], edition)
1945 Alt, ZDPV 67 pp. 138–146 (ii′ 1–11, translation [by Weidner], study)
1954 Gadd, Iraq 16 pp. 174 and 188 (study)
1958 Tadmor, JCS 12 p. 25 n. 26 and p. 80 (study)
1994 Fuchs, Khorsabad p. 387 (study)
1999 Frame, Orientalia NS 68 p. 53 n. 25 (ii′ 1–5, edition)
2014 Maniori, Campagne di Sargon p. 47 G8 and passim (study)

TEXT

Col. i′

1) [...] *x* UB
2) [...] *x-šú-nu*
3) [...]-⸢*li*?⸣-*šú*
4) [...] *x x*

i′ 1–4) Not sufficiently preserved to allow translation.

Lacuna

Col. ii′

1) ⸢*pu-ul*⸣-*ḫi me*-⸢*lam*⸣-*me ša* ⸢AN⸣.ŠÁR
2) ^{d}AG ^{d}AMAR.UTU EN.MEŠ-*ia is-ḫu*-⸢*pu*⸣-*šú-ma*
3) ŠU.II *u* GÌR.II *bi-re*-⸢*tú*⸣ AN.BAR *id-di-šú-ma*
4) *a-na qé-reb* KUR *aš-šur*.KI *a-di maḫ-ri-ia*
5) *ú-še-bi-la-áš-šú ka-meš*
6) URU.MEŠ *šá-a-šú-nu a-na eš-šú-ti aṣ-bat*
7) UN.MEŠ KUR.⸢KUR⸣ *ki-šit-ti qa-ti-ia*
8) *ša qé-reb* ⸢KUR⸣-*i ṣi-it* ^{d}UTU-*ši*
9) *i-na lìb-bi ú-še-šib*
10) LÚ.*šu-ut* SAG-⸢*ia*⸣ LÚ.EN.NAM UGU-*šú-nu* *áš-kun-ma*
11) *ni-ir be-lu-ti-ia e-mid-su-nu-ti*

Lacuna

ii′ 1–11) Fear of the brilliance of the gods Aššur, Nabû, (and) Marduk, my lords, overwhelmed him (the king of Meluḫḫa) and he put iron fetters on his (Iāmānī's) hands and feet. (ii′ 5) He then had him brought in bondage to Assyria, into my presence. I reorganized (the administration of) those cities. I settled there people from the lands in the eastern mountains that I had conquered. (ii′ 10) I set a eunuch of mine as provincial governor over them and imposed the yoke of my lordship upon them.

---

12) ^{md}AMAR.UTU-IBILA-SUM.NA LUGAL KUR.*kal-di*
13) *ša ki-i la lìb-bi* DINGIR.MEŠ *a-na er*-⸢*ṣe*?-*et*?⸣
14) KUR EME.GI$_{7}$ ⸢*ù* URI⸣.KI *ú*-⸢*ri*⸣-[*dam-ma*]
15) LUGAL-*ut* ⸢KÁ⸣.[DINGIR.RA.KI *pa-nu-uš ú-ter-ru*]

Lacuna

ii′ 12–15) Marduk-apla-iddina (II) (Merodach-Baladan), king of Chaldea, who against the will of the gods had c[ome down] to the territory of the land of Sumer and [Ak]kad [and had appropriated for himself] the kingship of Ba[bylon]

Lacuna

Col. iii′

1) [1 ME 54] ⸢GUN⸣ 26 [MA.NA 10 GÍN KÙ.GI *ḫuš-šu-ú*]
2) 1 LIM 6 ME 4 ⸢GUN⸣ [20 MA.NA KÙ.BABBAR *eb-bu* URUDU? AN.BAR?]
3) NA$_{4}$.ZÚ.⸢MEŠ⸣ NA$_{4}$.[ZA.GÌN NA$_{4}$.BABBAR.DILI? (...)]
4) NA$_{4}$.AŠ*.GÌ.GÌ.MEŠ NA$_{4}$.[UGU.AŠ.GÌ.GÌ? (...)]
5) NA$_{4}$.MUŠ.GÍR.MEŠ [*a-na mu-ʾu-de-e*]
6) SÍG.*ta-kil-tum* ⸢SÍG⸣.[*ar-ga-man-nu*]
7) *lu-bul-ti bir*-⸢*me*⸣ [*ù* (TÚG).GADA]
8) GIŠ.TÚG GIŠ.EREN ⸢GIŠ⸣.[ŠUR.MÌN *ka-la ri-iq-qí*]
9) *bi-ib-lat* KUR.*ḫa-ma-a-ni* [*ša e-ri-su-un ṭa-a-bu*]
10) *a-na* ^{d}AMAR.UTU ^{d}*zar*-⸢*pa*⸣-[*ni-tum* ^{d}AG

iii′ 1–13) [(With regard to) 154] talents, 26 [minas, (and) 10 shekels of red gold], 1,604 talen[ts (and) 20 minas of pure silver, *copper, iron*], obsidian, [lapis-lazuli, *banded agate,* (...)] *blue turquoise,* [*green turquoise* (...)], (iii′ 5) (and) *muššaru*-stone [in large quantities], blue-purple wool, [red-purple wool], garments with multicolored [trim and linen (garments)], boxwood, cedar, [cypress, (and) every kind of aromatic], the products of Mount Amanus, [whose scent(s) are pleasant — *from the beginning of my reign until* (*my*) *third year,* I presented (these things) as gifts] (iii′ 10) to the deities Marduk, Zarp[anītu, Nabû, Tašmētu], and the (other)

---

ii′ 6 As noted by E. Weidner (AfO 14 [1941–44] p. 50), "those cities" likely refers to the cities Ashdod, Gimtu (Gath), and Asdudimmu (Ashdod-Yam); see text no. 1 lines 258–259, text no. 2 lines 282–283, text no. 3 line 10′, and text no. 7 line 104.
iii′ 1 The restoration follows text no. 7 line 141; text no. 103 iv 6 has 6-*su* rather than 10 GÍN.
iii′ 2 Text no. 103 iv 6 has 8 ME rather than 6 ME.
iii′ 4 AŠ*: The copy has BE.

ᵈ*taš-me-tum*]	
11) *ù* DINGIR.MEŠ *a-ši-*[*bu-ut ma-ḫa-zi*]	gods who dwe[ll in the cult centers of] the land of Sumer and Akkad.
12) ⸢KUR⸣ EME.GI$_7$ *ù* URI.[KI *ul-tu*? SAG? LUGAL-*ti-ia*?]	
13) [*x*] *x x x* [(...) *ú-qa-i-šá qí-šá-a-ti*]	
Lacuna	Lacuna

84–88

The five fragmentary cylinder texts presented here all certainly or probably come from Nineveh. They may actually represent only one or two different inscriptions, but it has been thought best to present them separately. Text nos. 84 and 85 overlap, as do text nos. 86 and 87, and W.G. Lambert and A.R. Millard (Cat. p. 13) have suggested that text no. 84 may come from the same cylinder as text no. 86. If text nos. 84–87 represent one inscription, text nos. 84 and 85 would be placed before text nos. 86 and 87. Following the account of the campaign against Mutallu of Kummuḫu (707) at the end of text no. 84 would likely have been the description of one or more other campaigns, concluding with the beginning of the campaign against Marduk-apla-iddina II, the campaign recorded at the start of text nos. 86 and 87. It must be noted, however, that although text nos. 84 and 85 overlap, the former is a barrel cylinder fragment (as are text nos. 86 and 87) while the latter a fragment of a prismatic cylinder. Text no. 88 preserves part of what is likely the introductory section of an inscription, with epithets and participial forms, rather than finite verbal forms as in the other texts. Like text no. 85, text no. 88 is found on a fragment of a prismatic cylinder.

84

This fragmentary inscription is found upon a barrel cylinder from Nineveh. After mentioning work on temples at Aššur and Ḫarrān, it records the building of the city Dūr-Šarrukīn and its palace. The text then goes on to describe various military actions, including victories over Elam, Mannea, Urarṭu, Hamath, and Kummuḫu, the latter of which took place during Sargon's fourteenth regnal year (708). Since the text refers to the king's fifteenth regnal year (707) in line 7′ and also to the installation of various gods inside Dūr-Šarrukīn (line 9′), which the Assyrian Eponym Chronicle records for that year, this text must have been composed no earlier than 707.

---

83 iii′ 13 The translation assumes *a-di* MU.3.KÁM at the beginning of the line, following text no. 7 line 144 and cf. text no. 103 iv 21 (*a-di* 3 MU.MEŠ); text no. 74 vii 19 has *a-di* MU.4.KÁM.

CATALOGUE

Museum Number	Registration Number	Provenance	Dimensions (cm)	cpn
BM 122614 + BM 122615	Th 1930-5-8,3 + Th 1930-5-8,4	Nineveh, palace of Ashurnasirpal II, Square C at depths of 15 and 11 feet below datum (C, 15' and C, 11')	8.5×17	c

COMMENTARY

BM 122614 + 122615 is part of a solid barrel cylinder. The inscription is written in Neo-Assyrian script. Collation of the inscription revealed a number of inaccuracies in R. Campbell Thompson's copy, in particular: ⸢*ša*⸣ instead of his ⸢*am-ḫur*⸣ in line 7′; the presence of several signs at the end of line 12′ omitted by Campbell Thompson; his addition of *ma* after *ú-še-šib* in line 20′; and -⸢*tu*⸣ instead of his *-tum a-* in line 21′.

With regard to restorations, for lines 1′–2′, see text no. 7 lines 5–7 and 10–12. For lines 7′b–10′, see text no. 7 lines 23, 154–56, and 158–59. For the end of line 7′, see text no. 111 line 10 and for the end of line 9′, see text no. 45 line 18 and text no. 111 line 12. For line 11′a, see text no. 14 lines 28-29. For lines 12′–20′, see text no. 103 ii 22–65; see also text no. 8 lines 6–7 for lines 12′–13′ and text no. 105 ii′ 5 for line 20′. For lines 21′–26′, see text no. 7 lines 74, 85–86, and 112–117.

BIBLIOGRAPHY

1940 Thompson, Iraq 7 pp. 86–89 and 112–113 figs. 1–2 no. 1 (copy, edition)

1968 Lambert and Millard, Cat. p. 13 (study)

1994 Fuchs, Khorsabad p. 386 (study)

1998 Fuchs, SAAS 8 p. 5 (lines 3′–4′, partial transliteration)

2009 Frame, Studies Parpola pp. 75–76 and 81 no. g (lines 3′–7′, transliteration; study)

2014 Maniori, Campagne di Sargon p. 52 g7 and passim (study)

2018 Frahm, Last Days pp. 79–80 no. 14 (lines 18′–20′, edition, study, combined with text nos. 103 and 105)

TEXT

Lacuna

1′) [*ša* ZIMBIR.KI NIBRU.KI KÁ.DINGIR.RA.KI *ù bár-sipa*.KI *za-nin-us-su-un e-tep*]-⸢*pu-šá*⸣ <*ša*> ⸢LÚ.ERIM⸣.MEŠ *ki-din-ni* ⸢*mal*⸣ [*ba-šu-ú ḫi-bil-ta-šú-nu a-rib-ma*]

2′) [*za-kut bal-til*.KI *ù* URU.*ḫar-ra-ni šá ul-tu* u_4*-me ma-a'-du-ti*] ⸢*im*⸣*-ma-šu-ma ki-din-nu-us-su-*⸢*un ba*⸣-[*ṭil-ta ú-ter áš-ru-uš-šá*]

3′) [...] *za-ḫa-lu-ú eb-bu a-na ši-pir é-ḫur-sag-gal-kur-kur-ra at-man* ^{d}*aš-šur* x [...]

4′) [...] x SU Ú TAR ⸢DA$^{?!}$⸣ ^{d}*šar-rat*-NINA.KI *ù* ^{d}*be-let*-URU.LÍMMU-DINGIR *ši-pir* x [...]

5′) [...] x *ṣi-*⸢*in*⸣*-di bu-ru-mi* [...]

6′) [...] x [x] 7 1/2 MA.NA KÙ.BABBAR *eb-bu a-na ši-pir é-ḫúl-ḫúl maš-tak* ^{d}30 *a-šib*

Lacuna

1′–2′) [I continually ac]ted [as provider for (the cities) Sippar, Nippur, Babylon, and Borsippa (and) I made restitution for the wrongful damage suffered by] the people of privileged status, as many [as there were (of them); I restored the exemption (from obligations) of (the city) Baltil (Aššur) and the city Ḫarrān, which] had fallen into oblivion [in the distant past], and their privileged status that had la[psed].

3′–7′) [...] (with) pure *zaḫalû*-silver for the work on Eḫursaggalkurkurra ("House, the Great Mountain of the Lands"), the sanctuary of the god Aššur [...] ... the goddesses Queen of Nineveh and Lady of Arbela, the work [...] (5′) *the arrangement* of the firmament (of the heavens) [...] seven and a half minas of pure silver for the work of Eḫulḫul ("House which Gives

2′ Possibly restore *ru-qu-ú-ti* or *ul-lu-ú-ti* instead of *ma-a'-du-ti*; see text no. 8 line 5, text no. 14 line 10, and text no. 103 ii 19.

3′ For clay cone and brick inscriptions of Sargon II recording his work on Eḫursaggalkurkurra, see text nos. 67–69. See text no. 74 i 25–28 for possible restorations.

5′ There is a large gap without any writing after *bu-ru-mi* and before the left end of the cylinder fragment.

URU.*ḫar-ra-*⸢*an*⸣ [...]

7′) [... MA].NA KÙ.BABBAR *eb-bu ni-siq-ti* NA$_4$.MEŠ *la ni-bi ša ul-tu* SAG LUGAL-*ti-*⸢*ia*⸣ *a-di* MU.15.KÁM *a-na* DINGIR.MEŠ *a-ši-*⸢*bu*⸣*-[ut* ...]

8′) [*i-na* GÌR.II KUR.*mu-uṣ-ri* KUR-*i e-le]-*⸢*na*?⸣ URU.NINA.KI ⸢*i*⸣*-na* ⸢*bi*⸣*-bil lib-bi-ia* URU ⸢DÙ-*uš*⸣*-ma* URU.BÀD-^{m}LUGAL-GI.NA *az-ku-*⸢*ra*⸣ [*ni-bit-su*]

9′) [^{d}*é-a* ^{d}30 ^{d}UTU ^{d}AG ^{d}IŠKUR ^{d}*nin-urta ù ḫi-ra]-*⸢*ti*⸣*-šú-nu* GAL.MEŠ ⸢*i*⸣*-na qé-*⸢*reb*⸣ *é-ḫur-sag-gal-kur-kur-ra ú-šá-a'-lid-ma i-na qer-bi-šu ú-*⸢*šar-ma-a pa*⸣*-[rak da-ra-(a)-ti*]

10′) [É.GAL.MEŠ ZÚ AM.SI GIŠ.ESI GIŠ.TÚG GIŠ.*mu-šuk-ka-ni*] ⸢GIŠ.EREN⸣ GIŠ.ŠUR.MÌN GIŠ.⸢*dup*⸣*-ra-ni* ŠIM.LI *ù* GIŠ.*bu-uṭ-ni a-na mu-šab* LUGAL-*ti-ia qer-*⸢*bu-uš-šu*⸣ *ab-*⸢*ni*⸣*-[ma*]

11′) [... *ba-ḫu-la]-*⸢*ti*⸣ *na-ki-ri ki-šit-ti qa-ti-ia i-na qer-bi-šu par-ga-niš ú-šar-bi-iṣ-ma it-ti* ⸢*ma*⸣*-[ḫa]-*⸢*zi* KUR *aš-šur*⸣.KI *am-nu-*⸢*šu*⸣

12′) [(...) *i-na tukul-ti* DINGIR.MEŠ GAL.MEŠ (*lu*) *at-tal-lak-ma* UN].MEŠ ÍD.*mar-ra-ti* AN.TA *a-di* ⸢ÍD⸣.*mar-ra-ti* KI.TA *ki-i iš-te*$_9$-<*en*> *a-bel-ma* KUR.MEŠ *la ma-gi-*⸢*ri ḫur*⸣*-[šá]-*⸢*a*⸣*-ni la kan-šu-ti ú-šak-ni-šá* ⸢*še*?*-pu*?⸣*-[u*$_8$*-a*]

13′) [*ú-par-ri-ir el-lat* ^{md}*ḫum-ba-ni-ga-áš* LÚ.ELAM.MA.KI] ⸢*ú*⸣*-ab-bit* KUR.*kar-al-lu* KUR.*šur-*⸢*da*⸣ KUR.*ki-ši-si-im* URU.*ḫar-ḫar šá* KUR.*ma-da-a-a a-di pa-aṭ* KUR.*bi-ik-ni* ⸢*u*?⸣ KUR.*el-li-pi la e-zi-ba pér-ḫi-šú-*⸢*un*⸣

14′) [UN.MEŠ KUR.*ḫat-ti ki-šit-ti* ŠU.II-*ia qé-reb-šun ú]-*⸢*še*⸣*-ši-ba* LÚ.*šu-ut* SAG.MEŠ-*ia* LÚ.EN *pa-ḫa-a-ti* UGU-*šú-nu áš-tak-kan-ma ú-*⸢*šal*⸣*-di-da ab-šá-a-ni*

15′) [*ú-šak-niš* KUR.*man-na-a-a* KUR.*an-di-a* KUR.*zi-kir-tu* ^{m}*ur]-za-na* LUGAL URU.*mu-ṣa-ṣi-ri a-di* UN.MEŠ KUR-*šú* ^{d}*ḫal-di-a* ^{d}*ba-ag-bar-*⸢*tu*⸣ DINGIR.⸢MEŠ-*šú*⸣ *a-na šal-la-ti am-nu-šu*

16′) [KUR.*ur-ar-ṭu a-na paṭ gim-ri-šá ú-šá-áš-šá-a nag-la-ba* (x) x]*-at-te ù ṣur-ri ù* UN.MEŠ *a-šib lìb-bi-šá* ⸢*a*⸣*-[na ar]-*⸢*kàt*?⸣ *u*$_4$*-me e-mì-da si-pit-tu ù ṣer-ḫa*

17′) [*di-ik-ti* ^{m}*ur-sa-a* KUR.*ur-ar-ṭa-a-a i-na* KUR].⸢*ú*⸣*-a-uš* KUR-*i mar-ṣi áš-kun-ma ta-ḫa-zi dan-nu e-*⸢*du-ur*⸣*-[ma ina* ŠU.II] ⸢*rama*⸣*-ni-šu ina* GÍR.AN.BAR *šib-bi-šú na-piš-ta-šú ú-qat-ti*

18′) [KUR.*a-ma-at-tu a-na paṭ gim-ri-šá a-bu-biš as-pu-un* ^{md}*ia]-*⸢*ú*⸣*-bi-i'-di* LUGAL-*šú-nu a-di* ⸢*kim*⸣*-ti-šu mun-*⸢*daḫ*⸣*-[ṣe-šú šal-lat* KUR]-⸢*šú*⸣ *ka-mu-us-su a-na* KUR *aš-šur*.KI *ub-*⸢*la*⸣

19′) [3 ME GIŠ.GIGIR.MEŠ 6 ME ANŠE.*pét-ḫal-lum*

Joy"), the abode of the god Sîn who dwells in the city Ḫarrān [... mi]nas of pure silver (and) countless precious stones *which* from the beginning of my reign until (my) fifteenth year to/for the gods who dwe[ll ...].

8′–11′) In accordance with my heart's desire, I built a city [at the foot of Mount Muṣri, a mountain upstre]am from the city Nineveh, and named [it] Dūr-Šarrukīn. I had [the gods Ea, Sîn, Šamaš, Nabû, Adad, Ninurta, and] their great [spous]es created inside Eḫursaggalkurkurra and I installed (them) inside it (Dūr-Šarrukīn) on (their) [eternal] d[ais(es)]. (10′) I built inside it [palatial halls using (lit.: "of") elephant ivory, ebony, boxwood, *musukkannu*-wood, ce]dar, cypress, *daprānu*-juniper, juniper, and terebinth to be my royal residence [and ...] I had enemy [people] whom I had captured dwell inside it (as safely) as in meadowland and I considered i[t] as (one of) the cul[tic center]s of Assyria.

12′–17′) [(...) With the support of the great gods, I advanced and] ruled [the people] (from) the Upper Sea to the Lower Sea as if (they were) one (people). I made uncompliant lands (and) insubmissive mountain regions bow down at [my] feet. [I dispersed the forces of Ḫumbanigaš (Ḫumban-nikaš I), the Elamite]. I destroyed the lands Karalla, Šurda, (and) Kišesim (and) the city Ḫarḫar; I did not leave any offspring of the land Media as far as the border of Mount Bikni *and* the land Ellipi. [I] settled [in their midst people of the land Ḫatti (Syria) that I had conquered]. I set eunuchs of mine as provincial governors over them and had (them) pull my yoke. (15′) [I subjugated the lands Mannea, Andia, (and) Zikirtu]. I counted as booty [Ur]zana, king of the city Muṣaṣir, together with the people of his land (and) his deities Ḫaldi (and) Bagbartu. [I had (the people of) the land Urarṭu, to its full extent, wield razor(s)], ... and flint blades (in order to slash themselves in mourning), and I imposed for the future lamenation and dirge (singing) upon the people who lived there. I brought about [the defeat of Ursâ (Rusâ), the Urarṭian, at Mount] Uauš, a rugged mountain. He then took fri[ght] at (engaging in) fierce battle with me [and by] his own [hands], he brought an end to his life with the iron dagger from his belt.

18′–20′) [Like the Deluge, I overwhelmed the land Hamath to its full extent]. I brought their king [Ia]ū-bi'dī (Ilu-bi'dī) to Assyria in bondage, together with his family, [his] figh[ting men, (and) the booty of] his [land]. I conscripted from among them (a contingent

11′ Or restore *tenēšēti* instead of *baḫulāti*; see text no. 8 line 27 and text no. 2 line 467. For the end of the line, see text no. 111 line 14.
16′ R. Campbell Thompson (Iraq 7 [1940] p. 87 and n. 14) suggests [... *pa*]*-at-te* and translates "tinder (??)," though acknowledging that he has no philological support for this. He was presumably connecting [*pa*]*-at-te* with *pēmtu/pēntu*, meaning "charcoal."
19′ Or restore [2 ME ...], "[200 ...]," instead of [3 ME ...], "[300 ...]"; see text no. 105 ii′ 1.

na-áš GIŠ.ka-ba-bi GIŠ].⸢az⸣-ma-re-e ina lìb-bi-šú-nu ⸢ak⸣-ṣur-⸢ma⸣ [(x x x)] ⸢UGU⸣ ki-ṣir LUGAL-ti-ia ú-rad-⸢di⸣

20′) [6 LIM 3 ME LÚ.aš-šur-a-a EN ḫi-iṭ-ṭi (...) ina] ⸢qé⸣-reb KUR.ḫa-ma-ti ú-še-šib LÚ.šu-ut ⸢SAG⸣-[ia LÚ].⸢EN⸣.NAM UGU-šú-nu áš-kun-ma bil-tu man-da-at-tu ú-kin UGU-šú-un

21′) [^{m}mut-tal-lum LÚ.kúm-mu-ḫa-a-a UGU ^{m}ar-giš-ti LUGAL KUR.ur-ar-ṭi it-ta-kil-ma] ⸢bil⸣-tu man-da-at-⸢tu⸣ na-⸢dan⸣ [MU.AN].⸢NA$^{?}$⸣-šu ú-šab-ṭil-ma ik-la-a ta-mar-tuš

22′) [i-na ug-gat lib-bi-ia it-ti GIŠ.GIGIR GÌR.II-ia ù ANŠE.pét-ḫal-li-ia] ⸢ša$^{?}$⸣ a-šar sa-al-me i-na qé-reb KUR [x x Á].⸢II⸣-a-a la ip-par-ku-ú ḫi-it-mu-ṭiš [(x x)] ⸢a$^{?}$⸣-lik-⸢ma$^{?}$⸣ [(x)]

23′) [a-ka-mu$^{?}$ ger-ri-ia$^{?}$ e-mur-ma$^{?}$ ...] ⸢e$^{?}$⸣-zib-ma ⸢e$^{?}$-den$^{?}$⸣-nu-⸢uš$^{?}$⸣-[šú$^{?}$ ip]-⸢par⸣-šid-ma la in-na-mir [a]-⸢šar⸣-[šú]

24′) [... NÍG.ŠU NÍG].GA ni-ṣir-ti É.GAL-šú it-ti UN.MEŠ [KUR-šú áš-lu-lam-ma]

25′) [... ina lìb-bi] ⸢ú⸣-še-šib LÚ.šu-ut SAG-ia ⸢LÚ.EN⸣.[NAM UGU-šú-nu]

26′) [áš-kun ... i-na] ⸢lib⸣-bi-šú-nu ak-ṣur-⸢ma⸣ [ú-šad-gi-la$^{?}$ pa-nu-uš-šú$^{?}$]

27′) [...] x x MU ⸢É⸣ [...]

Lacuna

of) [300 chariots, 600 cavalry, (and) shield (and)] spear [bearers], and [(...)] I added (them) to my royal contingent. I settled [6,300 Assyrian criminal(s) (...) in] the land Hamath. I set a eun[uch of mine as] provincial [gov]ernor over them and I imposed upon them (the delivery of) tribute (and) payment(s).

21′–27′) [Mutallu of the land Kummuḫu put his trust in Argišti, king of the land Urarṭu], stopped his [annual] delivery of tribute (and) payment(s), and withheld his audience gift. [Angrily], I quickly advanced [with (only) my personal chariot and my cavalry wh]o never leave my [side] (even) in friendly territory in the land [... *He saw the cloud of dust (kicked up) by my expeditionary force*], abandoned [...], and [fl]ed away *by* [*him*]*self*; [his where]abouts have never been discovered. [(...) I carried off as booty ... (his) property (and) posse]ssions, the treasure of his palace, (along) with the people [of his land and ...] I settled [there ... I set] a eunuch of mine as [provincial] gove[rnor over them (25′) ...] I conscripted [... from am]ong them and [*I made (them) subject to him (the new governor)* ...] ... [...]

Lacuna

85

A fragment of a clay prismatic cylinder in the Kuyunjik collection of the British Museum preserves part of the description of the construction of the city of Dūr-Šarrukīn. The first part of the text is poorly preserved but lines 3′–11′ duplicate parts of text no. 84 lines 7′–15′ and it is possible that this fragment should be treated as a duplicate of that inscription.

CATALOGUE

Museum Number	Registration Number	Provenance	Dimensions (cm)	cpn
BM 98518	Th 1905-4-9,24	Probably Nineveh, Kuyunjik possibly the Nabû temple	3.2×4.1×0.6	c

84 line 22′ Cf. *ša a-šar nak-ri ù sa-al-mi la ip-pa-rak-ku-ú* (text no. 65 line 132) and *ša a-šar sal-me* ⸢Á⸣.II-*a-a la ip-par-ku-ú* (text no. 7 line 85).
84 line 26′ The restoration at the end of the line follows text no. 7 line 117. Another possible restoration is UGU *ki-ṣir* LUGAL-*ti-ia ú-rad-di*, "I added (them) to my royal contingent"; see text no. 74 iv 12.

COMMENTARY

The piece is merely a thin flake from a clay prismatic cylinder with an inscription in Neo-Assyrian script. Lines 1′–3′ are on one face of the cylinder and 4′–10′ on the adjoining face. Since it is unclear how much is missing on either side of the flake, only minimal restoration has been done in the transliteration.

BIBLIOGRAPHY

1914 King, Cat. p. 52 no. 438 (study)
2003 Renger, Studies Wilcke p. 235 n. 38 (study)
2009 Frame, Studies Parpola pp. 81–82 no. i (study)

TEXT

Lacuna
1′) [...] *x* [...]
2′) [...] *x x x* [...]
3′) [...] ⸢SAG LUGAL⸣-[*ti-ia* ...]
4′) [... URU.BÀD-^{m}LUGAL]-⸢GI⸣.NA ⸢*az*⸣-[*ku-ra* ...]
5′) [...] ⸢*ú*⸣-*šá*-⸢*lid*⸣-*ma* ⸢*i-na*⸣ [...]
6′) [...] ⸢GIŠ⸣.*bu-uṭ-ni a-na* ⸢*mu*⸣-[*šab* ...]
7′) [...] (*x*) *par*-(*x*)-*ga-niš ú*-⸢*šar-bi*⸣-[*iṣ-ma* ...]
8′) [...] ⸢*ki*⸣-*i iš-tén a*-⸢*bel*⸣-*ma* KUR.MEŠ [...]
9′) [... KUR.*ma-da*]-*a-a a-di pa-aṭ* KUR.*bi-ik*-[*ni* ...]
10′) [... *áš-tak*]-⸢*kan*$^{?}$-*ma*⸣ *ú-šal*-⸢*di*⸣-[*da* ...]
11′) [...] ⸢DINGIR.MEŠ⸣-*šú* ⸢*a*$^{?}$⸣-[*na* ...]
Lacuna

Lacuna
1′–2′) Not sufficiently preserved to allow translation.

3′) [... from] the beginning of [my] rei[gn ...]
4′–7′) [In accordance with my heart's desire, I built a city at the foot of Mount Muṣri, a mountain upstream from the city Nineveh, and] n[amed it Dūr-Šarru]kīn. I had [the gods Ea, Sîn, Šamaš, Nabû, Adad, Ninurta, and their great spouses] created [inside Eḫursaggalkurkurra] and [I installed (them)] in[side it (Dūr-Šarrukīn) on (their) eternal dais(es). I built inside it palatial halls using (lit.: "of") elephant ivory, ebony, boxwood, *musukkannu*-wood, cedar, cypress, *daprānu*-juniper, juniper, and] terebinth to be [my royal] resi[dence and ...] I had [enemy people whom I had captured] dw[ell inside it] (as safely) as in meadowland [and I considered it as (one of) the cultic centers of Assyria].
8′–11′) [(...) With the support of the great gods, I advanced and] ruled [the people (from) the Upper Sea to the Lower Sea as] if (they were) one (people). [I made uncompliant] land[s (and) insubmissive mountain regions bow down at my feet. I dispersed the forces of Ḫumbanigaš (Ḫumban-nikaš I), the Elamite. I destroyed the lands Karalla, Šurda, (and) Kišesim (and) the city Ḫarḫar; I did not leave any offspring of the land Med]ia as far as the border of Mount Bik[ni *and* the land Ellipi. I settled in their midst people of the land Ḫatti (Syria) that I had conquered. I set eunuchs of mine as provincial governors over them] and had (them) pu[ll my yoke. I subjugated the lands Mannea, Andia, (and) Zikirtu. I counted] *a*[*s* booty Urzana, king of the city Muṣaṣir, together with the people of his land (and)] his deities [Ḫaldi (and) Bagbartu].
Lacuna

86

A large fragment of a barrel cylinder in the Kuyunjik collection of the British Museum preserves part of an account written in Neo-Assyrian script that describes Sargon's defeat of Marduk-apla-iddina II (Merodach-Baladan) at Dūr-Yakīn (709) and his entry into Babylon, an account which is for the most part a duplicate of that found on the Nimrud Prism (text no. 74 vi 23–83) and a Malatya cylinder (text no. 113 lines 8′–26′). The mention of deporting people from Kummuḫu to Bīt-Yakīn (line 15′) would suggest that the text was composed no earlier than 708, when the Assyrian Eponym Chronicle states that that city was captured. The inscription partially overlaps text no. 87, another fragment of a barrel cylinder from Nineveh. Although it is quite possible that the two pieces are duplicates of the same inscription, it has been thought useful to present them separately in view of their fragmentary state.

CATALOGUE

Museum Number	Registration Number	Provenance	Dimensions (cm)	cpn
BM 98528	Th 1905-4-9,34	Probably Nineveh, Kuyunjik, possibly the Nabû temple	8.3×5.7×3.2	c

COMMENTARY

The text is written in the Neo-Assyrian script. It is suggested in Lambert and Millard, Cat. p. 13 that BM 122614 + 122615 (text no. 84) may come from the same cylinder as BM 98528. With regard to the restorations used in the translation, in addition to text no. 87, note:

Lines 1′–6′: See text no. 74 vi 22–42 and text no. 113 lines 8′–12′; cf. text no. 7 lines 126–129.

Lines 7′–9′: See text no. 74 vi 43–62 and text no. 113 lines 13′–17′. Based upon the spacing, this text abbreviated text no. 74 vi 50–58 and text no. 113 lines 15′–16′, which list the fifteen cities destroyed by Sargon.

Lines 10′–14′: See text no. 74 vi 63–79 and text no. 113 lines 18′–22′; note also text no. 7 lines 134–137.

Lines 15′–16′: See text no. 2 lines 424 and 426, text no. 7 lines 139–140, text no. 64 lines 6′–7′, text no. 87 lines 10′–11′, and text no. 113 lines 23′–24′; cf. text no. 74 vi 80–85.

Lines 17′–18′: See text no. 7 lines 140–142, text no. 103 iv 1–9, and text no. 113 lines 25′–26′.

Since it is not clear how much space is missing at the beginning and end of each line, restorations have been kept to a minimum in the transliteration.

BIBLIOGRAPHY

1914 King, Cat. p. 53 no. 447 (study)
2003 Renger, Studies Wilcke p. 235 n. 38 (study)
2009 Frame, Studies Parpola p. 81 no. f (study)

TEXT

Lacuna

1′) [...] *x x* [...]

2′) [... ÍD].MEŠ TUR.MEŠ *la* [*mi-na* ...]

3′) [...] ⸢*ú*⸣-*paḫ-ḫir-ma a*-⸢*na*⸣ [...]

4′) [...] ⸢*iš*⸣-*kun-ma* 1 1/2 NINDA *ú*-[*šap-pil-ma* ...]

5′) [... *ta-mir*]-⸢*tuš*?⸣ A.GÀR.MEŠ-*šú a-šar mit-ḫu*-⸢*ṣi*⸣ [...]

6′) [... *ki*]-⸢*ma*⸣ MUŠEN.*ku-mé-e za-ra-tu* LUGAL-⸢*ti*⸣-[*šú* ...]

Lacuna

1′–6′) [I mustered the numerous troops of (the god) Aššur and crossed the Tigris (and) Euphrates Rivers, as well as in]numerable small [stream]s. [Like the Deluge, I overwhelmed the Chaldeans to their (lit.: its) full extent. In the face of my advance (lit.: "before me"), Marduk-apla-iddina (II) (Merodach-Baladan)] gathered together [the inhabitants of his cities (lit.: "his inhabited cities") and the gods dwelling in them], and [brought (them) in]t[o the city Dūr-Yakīn. He strengthened its enclosure walls (and), moving back a distance of ten *nindanu* from in front of its main wall], he made [a moat two hundred cubits wide]; he [made (the moat)] one and a half *nindanu* [deep and reached ground water. He cut a channel from the Euphrates River, (thereby) making (its water) flow (in)to it]s [meadowland. He flooded] its fields, where battles (are fought), [and made crossing difficult. Together with his allies (and) his battle troops, he pitched his] royal tent [in a bend of the river (lit.: "between rivers") lik]e a *crane* [and assembled his (military) camp].

7′) [... *ú*]-⸢*šak*⸣-*bi-is-ma šá-a-šú ga-du* LÚ.*mun*-⸢*daḫ*?⸣-[*ṣe-šu* ...]

8′) [... *i-de-e*]-*šu ki-ma* ŠE.MUNU$_6$ *áš-ṭe-e-ma i-ta*-⸢*at*⸣ [...]

9′) [...] ⸢*li*⸣-*mi-ti-šú-un ti-la-niš ú-še-me* UN.MEŠ *ṣe-ḫer* ⸢*ra*⸣-[*bi* ...]

7′–9′) [At the command of the gods Aššur, Nabû, (and) Marduk, I had a causeway] constructed (lit.: "trodden down") [across his canals] and [I caught] him, together with [his] fight[ing men, like a flying eagle in a net]. I spread out like malt (spread for drying) [the corpses of his vanguard and of the Aḫlamû, the people of the steppe who go at] his [side], and [I filled] the surroundi[ngs of his city (with them). ... together with the settlements in] their [en]virons, I turned into (ruin) mounds. [I carried off as booty at the same time (both)] the people — young (and) o[ld — who lived in the district and the gods who helped them; I did not allow a (single) person to escape].

10′) [...] ⸢*la*⸣ *an-ni-šú-nu i-na qer-bi-šú-un ka-mu-ú ṣi-bit-ta-šú*-⸢*nu*⸣ [...]

11′) [...] ⸢LÚ⸣.*su-ti-i e-ki-mu-ú-ma ra-ma-nu-uš-šú-un* [...]

12′) [...] *ma*-⸢*šu-ú*⸣-*ti ša ina di-li-iḫ ma-a-ti ib-baṭ-lu ú*-⸢*ter*⸣ [...]

13′) [...] URU.*né-med*-^{d}*la-gu-da áš-ku-na an-du-ra-ar*-[*šú-un* ...]

14′) [... *sat*]-⸢*tuk*⸣-*ki-šú-nu ba-aṭ-lu-ti ú-ter* [...]

10′–14′) [(As for) the citizens of (the cities) Sippar, Nippur, Babylon, (and) Borsippa who through n]o fault of their own had been held captive in them, [I put an end to] their imprisonment [and let them see the light (of day). (With regard to) their fields, which long ago, while the land was in disorder], the Sutians had taken away and [appropriated] for their own — [I struck down (those) Sutians, the people of the steppe, with the sword]. I restored [to their former status their territories, (whose boundaries)] had been forgotten (and) fallen into disuse during the troubled period in the land. I (re)-established the freedom (from obligations) [of (the cities) Ur, Uruk, Eridu, Larsa, Kullab, Kissik, (and)] Nēmed-Laguda. [Moreover, I returned their gods that had been carried off as booty

---

9′ It is quite possible that there is not sufficient room to allow the restoration given in the translation for the end of the line, which is based on text no. 74 vi 60–62 and text no. 113 line 17′.

12′ *ú*-⸢*ter*⸣: See text no. 87 line 9′ and the on-page note to that line.

15′) [... UN.MEŠ KUR].⸢*kúm*⸣-*mu-ḫi ki-šit-ti qa-ti-ia qé-reb-šú ú-šar-me-*[*ma*? ...]
16′) [...] ⸢KÁ?.DINGIR?.RA.KI⸣ *ù* LÚ.*šu-ut* SAG-*ia* LÚ.[GAR.KUR ...]

17′) [... *e*]-⸢*ru*⸣-*um-ma* ŠU.II EN ⸢GAL⸣-[*i* ...]
18′) [...] ⸢URUDU.ḪI.A⸣ [...]

Lacuna

to their cult centers and] I rest[ored] their [regular] offerings that had been discontinued.

15′–16′) [I restored the land Bīt-Yakīn and reorganized (its administration)]. I settled there [people from the land K]ummuḫu that I had conquered [and I had (them) occupy its (Bīt-Yakīn's) abandoned regions. I divided up that land into equal parts and assigned (them) to the authority of a eunuch of mine, the governor of B]abylon, and a(nother) eunuch of mine, the [governor of the Gambulu (tribe)].

17′–18′) [Happily, with a joyful heart (and) a radiant face, I] entered [Babylon, the cult center of the Enlil of the gods (Marduk); I grasped hold of] the hands of the gre[at] lord, [the god Marduk, and brought (him) safely along the road to the *akītu*-house. (With regard to) 154 talents, 26 minas, (and) 10 shekels of red gold, 1,604 talents (and) 20 minas of pure silver], copper [(and) iron in immeasurable quantities ...]

Lacuna

87

W.G. Lambert and A.R. Millard identified this fragment of a barrel cylinder in the Kuyunjik collection of the British Museum as having an inscription of Sargon II (Lambert and Millard, Cat. p. 24). It preserves part of Sargon's account describing his defeat of Merodach-Baladan II at Dūr-Yakīn (709) and his triumphal entry into Babylon. The inscription partially overlaps text no. 86, which is also a fragment of a barrel cylinder from Nineveh. Although the two pieces may be duplicates of the same inscription, it has been thought best to present them separately.

CATALOGUE

Museum Number	Registration Number	Provenance	Dimensions (cm)	cpn
BM 123416	1932-12-10,359	Nineveh, Kuyunjik, palace of Ashurnasirpal II, Square C, 25 feet below the datum level	5.5×7.1	c

COMMENTARY

The piece comes from the right end of the barrel cylinder. With regard to the restorations used in the translation:

Lines 3′–4′: See text no. 74 vi 47–49 and 62, text no. 86 lines 8′–9′, and text no. 113 lines 14′ and 16′–17′.

Lines 5′–9′: See text no. 2 lines 416–421, text no. 7 lines 135–137, text no. 74 vi 63–79, text no. 86 lines 10′–14′, and text no. 113 lines 18′–22′.

Lines 10′–11′: See text no. 7 lines 139–140, text no. 64 lines 6′–7′, text no. 86 lines 15′–16′, and text no. 113 lines 23′–24′; note also text no. 74 vi 80–85.

Lines 12′–16′: See text no. 7 lines 140–144, text no. 74 vii 7–19, text no. 86 lines 17′–18′, text no. 103

iv 1–22, and text no. 113 lines 25′–26′.

Lines 17′–21′: See text no. 7 lines 145–149, text no. 74 vii 20–38 (Aḫundara instead of Upēri), and text no. 103 iv 23–42.

Where the parallel texts diverge, preference has generally been given in the restoration to text nos. 7 and 86.

BIBLIOGRAPHY

1968 Lambert and Millard, Cat. p. 24 (study)

2009 Frame, Studies Parpola p. 81 no. h (study)

TEXT

Lacuna

1′) [...] *x x* [(*x*)]

2′) [...] *x* ⸢LI I?⸣ *x* [(*x*)]

3′) [... *i-ta-at* URU-*šú*] ⸢*ú*⸣-*mal*-⸢*li*⸣

4′) [... *la e-zi*]-⸢*ba*⸣ *mul-taḫ-ṭu*

5′) [DUMU.MEŠ ZIMBIR.KI NIBRU.KI KÁ.DINGIR.RA.KI *u bár-sipa*.KI *ša i-na la an-ni-šú-nu i-na qer-bi-šú-un ka-mu-ú ṣi-bit-ta-šú-nu a-bu-ut-ma ú-kal-lim*]-⸢*šú*⸣-*nu-ti nu-ru*

6′) [A.ŠÀ.MEŠ-*šú-nu ša ul-tu* u$_{4}$-*me ul-lu-ti i-na i-ši-ti ma-a-ti* LÚ.*su-ti-i e-ki-mu-ú-ma ra-ma-nu-uš-šú-un*] *ú*-⸢*ter*⸣-*ru*

7′) [LÚ.*su-ti-i* ERIM.MEŠ EDIN *i-na* GIŠ.TUKUL *ú-šam-qit ki-sur-ri-šú-nu ma-šu-ú-ti ša ina di-li-iḫ* KUR *ib-baṭ-lu ú*]-⸢*ter*?⸣ *áš-ru-uš-šú-un*

8′) [*ša* ÚRI.KI UNUG.KI *eridu*.KI ARARMA.KI *kul-aba*$_{4}$.KI *ki-sik*.KI URU.*né-med*-^{d}*la-gu-da áš-ku-na an*]-⸢*du*⸣-*ra-ar-šú-un*

9′) [*ù* DINGIR.MEŠ-*šú-nu šal-lu-ti a-na ma-ḫa-zi-šú-nu ú-ter-ma sat-tuk-ki-šú-nu ba-aṭ-lu-ú-ti ú-ter*] *áš-ru-uš-šú-un*

10′) [KUR.É-^{m}*ia-ki-ni ú-ter-ma a-na eš-šu-ti aṣ-bat* UN.MEŠ KUR.*kúm-mu-ḫi ki-šit-ti qa-ti-ia qé-reb-šú ú-šar-me-ma ú-še*]-⸢*ši*⸣-*ba ni*-⸢*du*⸣-*us-su*

11′) [KUR *šu-a-tu mal-ma-liš a-zu-uz-ma ina* ŠU.II LÚ.*šu-ut* SAG-*ia* LÚ.GAR.KUR KÁ.DINGIR.RA.KI *ù* LÚ.*šu-ut* SAG-*ia*] LÚ.GAR.KUR LÚ.*gam*-⸢*bu*⸣-*li am-nu*

12′) [*a-na* KÁ.DINGIR.RA.KI *ma-ḫa-zi* ^{d}EN.LÍL.LÁ DINGIR.MEŠ *i-na e-le-eṣ lib-bi nu-um-mur pa-ni ḫa-diš e-ru-um-ma* ŠU.II EN GAL-*i* ^{d}AMAR.UTU *aṣ-bat*]-⸢*ma*⸣ *ú-šal-li-ma ú*-⸢*ru*⸣-*uḫ* É *á-ki-te*

13′) [1 ME 54 GUN 26 MA.NA 10 GÍN KÙ.GI *ḫuš-šu-ú* 1 LIM 6 ME 4 GUN 20 MA.NA KÙ.BABBAR *eb-bu* URUDU.ḪI.A *par-zil-la ša*] ⸢*ni*⸣-*ba la i-šu-ú*

14′) [NA$_{4}$.ZÚ NA$_{4}$.ZA.GÌN NA$_{4}$.BABBAR.DILI NA$_{4}$.AŠ.GÌ.GÌ NA$_{4}$.UGU.AŠ.GÌ.GÌ *di-gi-li*

Lacuna

1′–2′) Too poorly preserved to allow translation.

3′–4′) [...] I filled [the surroundings of his city (with them). ... I did not allo]w a (single) person to escape.

5′–9′) [(As for) the citizens of (the cities) Sippar, Nippur, Babylon, (and) Borsippa who through no fault of their own had been held captive in them, I put an end to their imprisonment and let t]hem [see] the light (of day). [(With regard to) their fields, which long ago, while the land was in disorder, the Sutians had taken away and] appropriated [for their own — I struck down (those) Sutians, the people of the steppe, with the sword. *I restor*]*ed* to their former status [their territories, (whose boundaries) had been forgotten (and) fallen into disuse during the troubled period in the land. I (re)-established the fr]eedom (from obligations) [of (the cities) Ur, Uruk, Eridu, Larsa, Kullaba, Kissik, (and) Nēmed-Laguda. Moreover, I returned their gods that had been carried off as booty to their cult centers and I rest]ored [their regular offerings that had been discontinued].

10′–11′) [I restored the land Bīt-Yakīn and reorganized (its administration). I settled there people from the land Kummuḫu that I had conquered and I had] (them) occupy its (Bīt-Yakīn's) abandoned regions. [I divided up that land into equal parts and] assigned (them) [to the authority of a eunuch of mine, the governor of Babylon, and a(nother) eunuch of mine], the governor of the Gambulu (tribe).

12′–16′) [Happily, with a joyful heart (and) a radiant face, I entered Babylon, the cult center of the Enlil of the gods (Marduk); I grasped hold of the hands of the great lord, the god Marduk], and brought (him) safely along the road to the *akītu*-house. [(With regard to) 154 talents, 26 minas, (and) 10 shekels of red gold, 1,604 talents (and) 20 minas of pure silver, copper (and) iron in] immeasurable quantities, [obsidian, lapis-lazuli, *banded agate, blue turquoise, green turquoise, ... of banded*

7′ The restoration of the line follows text no. 2 line 419.

9′ [... *ú-ter*] *áš-ru-uš-šú-un*, "[... I rest]ored": For the restoration *ú-ter*, see text no. 86 line 14′. Text no. 7 line 136 has instead *ú-šad-gi-la pa-nu-uš-šú-un*, "I (re)assigned to them (the citizens)"; see also text no. 74 vi 74.

NA$_4$.BABBAR.DILI NA$_4$.MUŠ.GÍR *a-na*] *mu-ʾu-de-e*
15′) [SÍG.*ta-kil-tú* SÍG.*ar-ga-man-nu lu-bul-ti bir-me* *ù* TÚG.GADA GIŠ.TÚG GIŠ.EREN GIŠ.ŠUR.MÌN *ka-la ri-iq-qí bi-ib-lat* KUR.*ḫa-ma-a-ni*] ⸢*ša*⸣ *e-ri-su-un ṭa-a-bu*
16′) [*a-na* ^{d}EN ^{d}*zar-pa-ni-tum* ^{d}AG ^{d}*taš-me-tum ù* DINGIR.MEŠ *a-ši-bu-ut ma-ḫa-zi* KUR *šu-me-ri ù* URI.KI *ul-tu* SAG LUGAL-*ti-ia a-di* MU.3].⸢KAM⸣ *ú-qa-i-šá a-na qí-šá-a-ti*

agate (and) *muššaru*-stone in] large quantities, [blue-purple wool, red-purple wool, garments with multi-colored trim and linen garments, boxwood, cedar, cypress, (and) every kind of aromatic, the products of Mount Amanus, wh]ose scent(s) are pleasant — [from the beginning of my reign until (my) third year], I presented (these things) as gifts [to the deities Bēl, Zarpanītu, Nabû, Tašmētu, and the (other) gods who dwell in the cult centers of the land of Sumer and Akkad].

17′) [^{m}*ú-pe-e-ri* LUGAL *dil-mun*.KI *ša* 30 KASKAL.GÍD *ina* MURUB$_4$ *tam-tim ni-pi-iḫ* ^{d}UTU-*ši ki-ma nu-ú-ni šit-ku-nu nar-ba-ṣu da-na-an* ^{d}*aš-šur* ^{d}AG] ⸢^{d}⸣AMAR.UTU *iš-me-ma iš-šá-a ta-mar-tuš*

17′) [Upēri, king of Dilmun, who(se) lair is situated (at a distance of) thirty leagues in the middle of the Eastern Sea, like (that of) a fish], heard [of the might of the gods Aššur, Nabû, (and)] Marduk and brought me his audience gift.

18′) [*ù* 7 LUGAL.MEŠ-*ni ša* KUR.*ia-aʾ na-gi-i ša* KUR.*ia-ad-na-na ša ma-lak* 7 *u*$_4$-*me i-na* MURUB$_4$ *tam-tim e-reb* ^{d}UTU-*ši šit-ku-nu-ma né-es*]-⸢*sa*⸣-*at šu-bat-su-un*
19′) [*ša ul-tu u*$_4$-*me ru-qu-ti a-di i-*^{d}*nanna a-na* LUGAL.MEŠ-*ni* AD.MEŠ-*ia ša* KUR *aš-šur*.KI *u* KUR.*kar-*^{d}*du-ni-áš ma-nam-ma la iš*]-⸢*mu*⸣-*ú zi-kir* KUR-*šú-un*
20′) [*ep-šet i-na qé-reb* KUR.*kal-di u* KUR.*ḫat-ti e-tep-pu-šu i-na* MURUB$_4$ *tam-tim ru-qiš iš-mu-ma lib-bu-šú-un it-ru-ku-ma im-qut-su-nu*]-⸢*ti*⸣ *ḫat-tum*
21′) [KÙ.GI KÙ.BABBAR *ú-nu-ut* GIŠ.ESI GIŠ.TÚG *né-peš-ti* KUR-*šú-un a-na qé-reb* KÁ.DINGIR.RA.KI *a-di maḫ-ri-ia ú-bi-lu-nim-ma ú-na-áš-ši*]-⸢*qu*?⸣ GÌR.II-*ia*

18′–21′) [Moreover, seven kings of the land Yāʾ, a region of the land Yadnana (Cyprus) — who]se abode(s) [are situated far] away, [at a distance of seven days (journey) in the middle of the Western Sea (and)] the name of [who]se land, [from the distant past until now, none of the kings, my ancestors, neither in Assyria nor in the land Karduniaš (Babylonia), had ever hea]rd — [heard from afar, in the middle of the sea, of the deeds I had been doing in Chaldea and the land Ḫatti (Syria). Their hearts then pounded and] fear [fell upon the]m. [They brought before me in Babylon gold, silver, (and) utensils of ebony (and) boxwood, product(s) of their land, and they kisse]d my feet.

22′) [...] *x* ⸢IN?⸣
23′) [...] *x*
Lacuna

22′–23′) Not sufficiently preserved to allow translation.
Lacuna

88

A fragment from the left end of a prismatic clay cylinder in the Kuyunjik collection of the British Museum preserves some of the epithets of Sargon, including reference to his laying waste to the land Urarṭu (cf. in particular text no. 13 lines 13–31).

---

87 line 16′ Text no. 74 vii 19 has MU.4.KÁM.
87 lines 22′–23′ At this point text no. 74 vii 39–44 and text no. 103 iv 43–57 each records the creation of a stele; text no. 7 lines 149–153 describe actions of the governor of Que against Mitâ (Midas) of the land of Musku.

CATALOGUE

Museum Number	Registration Number	Photograph Number	Provenance	Dimensions (cm)	cpn
BM 98724	Th 1905-4-9,230	BM 56538, 56583-4	Probably Nineveh, Kuyunjik, possible the Nabû temple	5.7×3.8×3.0	c

COMMENTARY

The fragment preserves part of two faces of a prism-like cylinder with an inscription written in Neo-Assyrian script. Lines 1′–5′ are on the first face of the fragment and lines 6′–10′ are on the second face.

Lines 2′–4′ are restored based on such passages as text no. 9 lines 6b–7, text no. 13 lines 6–8a, text no. 41 lines 4b–8a, text no. 43 lines 4b and 6, and text no. 44 lines 9–15a. Restorations in lines 5′–10′ are based on text no. 13 lines 13b–29a (cf. text no. 9 lines 12b–15a).

BIBLIOGRAPHY

1914 King, Cat. p. 67 no. 632 (study)
2003 Renger, Studies Wilcke p. 235 n. 38 (study)
2009 Frame, Studies Parpola p. 82 no. j (study)

TEXT

Lacuna

1′) *a-na* (*x*) [...]

2′) *mu-šal-*⸢*li*⸣*-*[*mu ḫi-bíl-ti-šú-un ... mu-šá-áš-šík tup-šik-ki* BÀD.AN.KI]

3′) ÚRI.⸢KI⸣ [*eridu*.KI ARARMA.KI *kul-la-ba*.KI *ki-sik*.KI *né-med-*^{d}*la-gu-da*.KI ...]

4′) *le-*ʾ*i* DÙ *mal-*⸢*ki šá*$^{?}$⸣ [UGU$^{?}$ URU.*ḫar-ra-na*$^{?}$ AN.DÙL-*la-šu*$^{?}$ *it-ru-ṣu-ma*$^{?}$ *ki-i*$^{?}$ *ṣa-ab*$^{?}$ ^{d}*a-nim*$^{?}$ *u*$^{?}$ ^{d}*da-gan*$^{?}$ *iš-ṭu-ru*$^{?}$ *za-kut-su*$^{?}$]

5′) *eṭ-lu qar-du šá-kin* ⸢*taḫ*⸣*-*[*te-e* ^{md}*ḫum-ba-ni-ga-áš* LÚ.ELAM.MA.KI-*i mu-ab-bit* KUR.*kar-al-la*]

6′) KUR.*šur-da* URU.*ki-še-si* URU.*ḫar-*[*ḫar* KUR.*ma-da-a-a* KUR.*el-li-pi e-mid-du ni-ir* ^{d}*aš-šur*]

7′) *mu-šaḫ-rib* KUR.*ur-ar-*⸢*ṭi*⸣ [*šá-lil* URU.*mu-ṣa-ṣir šá-giš* KUR.*an-di-a* KUR.*zi-kir-tu mu-šap-ši-ḫu* KUR.*man-na-a-a*]

8′) *mu-ri-ib mal-ki* ⸢KUR⸣.[*a-ma-at-ti* URU.*gar-ga-miš* KUR.*kúm-mu-ḫi na-pi-i*ʾ KUR.*kam-ma-ni ša* ^{m}*gu-un-zi-na-nu*]

9′) *iš-tu* ⸢*qé*⸣*-*[*reb* URU.*me-lid-di* URU LUGAL-*ti-šú is-su-ḫu-ma* UGU *gi-mir* KUR.MEŠ-*šú-nu iš-tak-ka-nu* LÚ.*šá-ak-nu-ti*]

10′) ⸢*mu-nak*⸣*-*[*kir* LUGAL-*ut* ^{m}*tar-ḫu-la-ra* LÚ.URU.*mar-qa-sa-a-a* ...]

Lacuna

Lacuna

1′) to/for [...]

2′–3′) who makes restit[ution for the wrongful damage suffered by them; ...; who abolished corvée duty for (the cities) Dēr], Ur, [Eridu, Larsa, Kullab, Kissik, (and) Nēmed-Laguda (...)];

4′) (most) capable of all rulers, w[ho *extended his protection over the city Ḫarrān and recorded its exemption (from obligations) as if (its people were) people of the gods Anu and Dagān*];

5′–10′) the valiant man who brought about the d[efeat of Ḫumbanigaš (Ḫumban-nikaš I), the Elamite; who destroyed the land Karalla], the land Šurda, the city Kišesim, the city Ḫar[ḫar, the land Media, (and) the land Ellipi, (and) imposed the yoke of the god Aššur upon (them)]; who laid waste to the land Urarṭu, [plundered the city Muṣaṣir, slaughtered the lands Andia (and) Zikirtu, (and) pacified the land Mannea]; who made the rulers of the la[nd Hamath, the city Carchemish, and the land Kummuḫu] tremble (and) [plundered the land Kammanu; who deported Gunzinānu] from [the city Melid, his (Gunzinānu's) royal city, and set officials over all of their lands]; who did aw[ay with the kingship of Tarḫu-lara of the city Marqasa ...];

Lacuna

89

The so-called Aššur Charter is one of the earliest of Sargon's royal inscriptions, mentioning events only up to 720 BCE. It describes the historical circumstances connected with Sargon's succession to the Assyrian throne and his actions with regard to the city of Hamath in his "second regnal year" (720). The text commemorates the restoration of privileges for the city of Aššur, which is called *āl kidinni*, "city of privileged-status," and the dedication of a silver object to the god Aššur. The inscription is found on a clay tablet in the British Museum's Kuyunjik collection and was presumably either copied from the inscription on the silver object (see lines 40b–43) or a model for the inscription to be engraved on that object. H. Tadmor believes that this text "is superior to all other Annalistic sources of Sargon as to historical reliability and exactness of dating" (JCS 12 [1958] p. 32).

CATALOGUE

Museum Number	Provenance	Dimensions (cm)	cpn
K 1349	Probably Nineveh, Kuyunjik	11.8×6.8×2.3	c

COMMENTARY

The scribe appears to have utilized every way that he knew to write the word Aššur. The name appears as ^{d}*a-šur* (line 1, god), *a-šur* (line 28, city), ^{d}*a-šur*$_4$ (e.g., lines 12 and 30, country and god), *aš-šur* (line 14, country), and AN.ŠÁR (e.g., line 19, god); see also *bal-til*.KI for the city (e.g., line 29). Most restorations follow those proposed by H.W.F. Saggs.

BIBLIOGRAPHY

1894 Winckler, Sammlung 2 p. 1 (copy)
1897 Winckler, AOF 1/5 pp. 401–406 (lines 13–43, edition)
1927 Luckenbill, ARAB 2 pp. 69–71 §§132–135 (translation)
1938 Tallqvist, Götterepitheta p. 188 (lines 3–4, study)
1958 Tadmor, JCS 12 pp. 31-32 and n. 78 (line 16, edition; study)
1969 Postgate, Royal Grants p. 12 no. 5 (lines 38–40, edition)
1974 Postgate, Taxation p. 79 no. 1.35 and p. 132 no. 1.4.2 (lines 31, 33, 38–40, edition)
1975 Garelli in Finet, Opposition p. 208 (lines 29b–35, edition)
1975 Saggs, Iraq 37 pp. 11–20 (copy, edition)
1977 Briend and Seux, TPOA no. 33 (lines 1a, 12b–27, translation)
1984 Borger, TUAT 1/4 p. 387 (lines 16–28a, translation)
1992 Becking, Fall of Samaria pp. 34–35 (lines 17b–28a, edition)
1992 Vera Chamaza, SAAB 6 pp. 21–33 (lines 4–15, 27–43, edition)
1994 Frahm, NABU 1994 p. 50 no. 56 (line 8, study)
1994 Fuchs, Khorsabad p. 386 (study)
1995 Mayer, Politik und Kriegskunst pp. 319–320 (lines 30–35, edition)
1998 Mayer, Studies Loretz pp. 546–547 (lines 12b–15, 30–35, edition)
2000 Younger, COS 2 p. 295 no. 2.118C (lines 16–28a, translation)
2005 Vera Chamaza, Rolle Moabs pp. 79–80 n. 557 (lines 16–22, edition)
2008 Cogan, Raging Torrent pp. 96–97 no. 21 (lines 16–28a, translation, study)
2014 Maniori, Campagne di Sargon p. 41 A11 and passim (study)
2018 Frahm, Last Days pp. 59–61 no. 1 (lines 16–28a, edition, study)

Figure 28. Obverse of K 1349 (text no. 89), the Aššur Charter. © The Trustees of the British Museum.

TEXT

Obv.

1) [*a-na*] ^{d}*a-*⸢*šur* KUR-*i*⸣ GAL-*e* LUGAL KIŠ ^{d}NUN.GAL *u* ^{d}*a-nun-na-ki* [*x x x x x x x x x* (*x x*)]

2) [*x x*] ⸢TA$^{?}$⸣ *x x-ti šá mì-lik-šú a-pa-a šu-tuq-qu i-kaš-*[*ša-du*$^{?}$ *x x x x x x* (*x x*)]

3) ⸢^{d}EN.LÍL⸣ *áš-šu-ru-u ša e-la šá-šú šip-*⸢*ṭu la*⸣ *i-gam-ma-ru* GIŠ *x kit*$^{?}$*-riš i*$^{?}$*/mu*$^{?}$ *x* [*x x x x x x x* (*x x*)]

4) *la uš-ta-en-nu-ú eš-ret* EŠ.BAR *la uš-tam-sa-ku* DINGIR *ma-nam-ma kab-tu šá x* [*x x x x x x* (*x x*)]

5) AN-*ú* KI-*tum ul-ta-nap-šá-qu-ma* KUR.MEŠ *ù* A.AB.BA *i-ḫi-il-*⸢*lu*⸣ LUGAL ⸢LUGAL.LUGAL⸣ [(*x x x x*) *šá ma-mit-su*$^{?}$]

6) *la ip-par-ra-ṣu-ma i-du i-ti-šú la in-net-ti-qu a-gu-ú ez-zu šu-ga-*⸢*ri*$^{?}$⸣*-*[*u*$^{?}$ *x x x x x* (*x x*)]

7) *mu-sa-ḫi-ip kul-lat la ma-gi-ri mu-let-ti šak-ṣi* u_4*-mu na-an-du-ru šá a-na la na-*⸢*a*’$^{?}$⸣*-*[*di*$^{?}$ *x x x* (*x x*)]

8) *muš-te-en-ni* GIŠ.ḪUR-*i-šú i-kan-na-ku za-mar* DINGIR *raš-bu šá ina pa-rak* LUGAL-*ti-šú ina* ⸢GIŠ.GU.ZA⸣-[*šú*$^{?}$ *x x x* (*x*)]

1–12a) [To] the god Ašš[ur], the great mou[ntain], king of all the Igīgū gods and Anunnakū gods, [...] ... whose command ... *rea*[*ches* ...]; the Assyrian Enlil without whom judgment cannot be rendered, ... [...] sanctuaries be altered, (or) decisions be canceled *by* any other god; the important one who [...] (5) heaven (and) netherworld are constantly put in difficulty, lands and sea(s) tremble; the king of king[s, (...) *the one by whom*] no [*oath* (*sworn*)] is broken and the flood-tide, (who)se limits cannot be transgressed, the fierce deluge, *the sickle* [*sword*, ...] who overwhelms all the uncompliant (and) crushes the *wild*; the furious storm, who for the *imp*[*ious* ...] *seals* quickly the one who changes his design(s); the awesome god who *from* his royal dais, *from* [*his*] throne [...] plunders every land; lordly one, lord of lords; one clothed in awesome splendor who defeats the wicked, tramples on [all enemies], (10) (and) *overwhelms* foes; the judicious one who loves humankind, (but) whose anger is great; the fe[roc]ious one, [...] who dwe[lls] in Eḫursaggalkurkurra ("House, the Great Mountain of the Lands") — the mighty shrine, primordial reflection (lit.: "design") of the

2 Possibly for *appa ikaššadu*, "triumphs" (see CAD A/2 p. 187)?

5 The tentative restoration at the end of the line follows AHw p. 832.

7 The understanding of the end of the line basically follows H.W.F. Saggs (Iraq 37 [1975] pp. 12 and 17), who reads *šá a-na la na-*[*a*$^{?}$*-di*$^{?}$ *x x x*], but collation shows that there may be a trace of a slanted wedge head after NA, suggesting A’ rather than NA. G. Vera Chamaza (SAAB 6 [1992] pp. 22 and 24) reads *šá a-na la na-*[*sa-ki* ...] and translates "who for those who [do not cast themselves in front of him$^{?}$ ...]."

9) *i-šal-la-lu ma-ti-tan e-tel* EN EN.EN *la-biš na-mur-ra-ti sa-kip rag-gi da-iš [kul-lat* (LÚ).KÚR.MEŠ]

10) *mu-ṭib ge-e-ri muš-ta-lu ra-aʾ-im te-ne-še-e-ti šá nu-ug-gat-su ra-bat-ma* ⌜*šam-ru*⌝ [*x x*]

11) ⌜*a-šib*⌝ *é-ḫur-sag-gal-*⌜*kur-kur-ra*⌝ *ki-iṣ-ṣi pu-un-gu-li* GIŠ.ḪUR *ad-na-a-ti reš-ti-tum* EN *bal-til*.[KI]

whole world — the lord of (the city) Baltil (Aššur) — the city of privileged status, the dynastic seat (and) oldest inhabited settlement — the prince, his lord:

12) URU *ki-di-ni šu-bat pa-le-e qu-du-um da-ád-me* NUN-*e* EN-*šú* ^{m}LUGAL-GI.NA ÉNSI KUR ^{d}*a-*⌜*šur*$_4$⌝

13) ⌜SIPA⌝ *ke-e-nu na-du-*⌜*šu*$^?$⌝ ^{d}EN.LÍL ^{d}AMAR.UTU ARAD-*ka šá a-na ud-du-uš šip-ri* É.KUR *šuk-lul ki-du-de-*[*e*]

14) *nu-mur ma-ḫa-zi i-na nap-ḫar ṣal-mat* SAG.DU *ki-niš* IGI.BAR-*ni-ma ul-la-a re-ši-ia* KUR *aš-šur a-na* ⌜*pe*⌝-[(*e*)-*li*]

15) *ù šá-pa-ri ina* ŠU.II-*ia ú-mal-li* ⌜UGU⌝ *kib-ra-a-ti* LÍMMU-*i ú-šam-ri-ra* GIŠ.TUKUL.MEŠ-[*ia*]

12b–15) Sargon (II), vice-regent of the land of the god Ašš[ur], just shepherd, *offspring* of the gods Enlil (and) Marduk, your servant; me, upon whom, among all the black-headed people, he (the god Aššur) duly looked to renovate the structure of the temple, to make the ritual performances perfect, (and) to make the cult centers brilliant. He then exalted me (and) handed over to me the ru[lership] and governance of Assyria. He made [my] weapons prevail over the four quarters (of the world).

16) *i-na* 2-*e* BALA-*ia šá ina* GIŠ.GU.ZA LUGAL-*ti ú-ši-bu-ma a-ge-e be-lu-ti an-na-*[*ap-ru-*(*ma*)]

16–17a) In my second regnal year, having ascended the royal throne and been [crowned] with the crown of lordship, I dispersed the forces of Ḫumba(n)igaš (Ḫumban-nikaš I), king of the land Elam (and) brought about his defeat.

17) ⌜ILLAT ^{md}⌝*ḫu-*⌜*um*⌝*-ba-i-*⌜*ga*⌝*-áš* MAN KUR.*e-lam-ti ú-par-ri-ra áš-ku-na* BAD$_5$.BAD$_5$-*šú* $^{m⌜d⌝}$[*ia-ú-bi-iʾ-di*]

18) ⌜LÚ.*ḫa-ma-ta*⌝*-a-a la* EN GIŠ.GU.ZA *la ši-nin-ti* É.GAL *šá ina* SIPA-*ut* UN.MEŠ *ši-mat-*⌜*su*$^?$⌝ [*la ši-mat ú-ri-dam-ma*$^?$]

19) *a-na* ⌜AN.ŠÁR⌝ KUR-*šú* UN.MEŠ-*šú* ⌜ḪUL-*tu*⌝ *la* ⌜DÙG.GA⌝-*tú ú-ba-ʾu-ú-ma il-qa-a ši-*⌜*ṭu*⌝-[*ti* URU.*ṣi-mir-ra*$^?$ URU.*di-maš-qa*$^?$]

20) ⌜URU⌝.*ar-pa-*⌜*da* URU.*sa*⌝*-me-ri-*⌜*na*⌝ *ú-*⌜*paḫ-ḫir-ma*⌝ *a-na i-di-šú ú-ter-*⌜*ra*⌝ [*x x x x x x x x x* (*x*)]

21) [*x*] *x x x* ⌜GIM$^?$ 1$^?$-*en*$^?$ *id-duk-ma*⌝ *na-piš-*⌜*tú ul e-zib*⌝ [*x x x x x x x x x x x* (*x x x*)]

17b–21a) [Iaū-biʾdī (Ilu-biʾdī)] of Hamath — who had no right to the throne, who was not worthy to (live in) a palace, (and) who [had not been] fate[d] to shepherd the people — [*came down*], sought evil, (things that were) not good, for (the god) Aššur, his land, (and) his people, and held (them) in cont[empt]. He assembled the cities [*Ṣimirra, Damascus*], Arpad, (and) Samaria and made (them) side with him. [...] ... he killed (them) *altogether* and le[ft] no one alive.

Bottom

22) [*x x*] *x x x x* ⌜DI-*ma*⌝ *áš-šú ka-šad* KUR.*ḫa-ma-*⌜*ti*⌝ [*sa-kap*$^?$ ^{md}*ia-ú-bi-iʾ-di*$^?$ *x x x x*

21b–25a) [...] ... and I prayed (to the god Aššur) in order to (be able to) conquer the land Hamath, [*overthrow Iaū-biʾdī (and)* ... the] wide [land Amu]rru. Aššur, the [*great*] god, then [... *li*]*stened* [*to my prayer*] and accepted my supplication. [*I mustered my vast*]

9 For the restoration *kullat nakirī*, see for example Grayson, RIMA 2 p. 275 A.0.101.23 line 4.

10 *mu-ṭib* (following CAD M/2 p. 284) or *mu-dip* (see Saggs, Iraq 37 [1975] p. 17).

13 The reading *na-du-*⌜*šu*$^?$⌝ ("*offspring* of") follows H.W.F. Saggs (Iraq 37 [1975] pp. 14 and 18; see also Vera Chamaza, SAAB 6 [1992] pp. 22 and 24); cf. CAD N/1 p. 104. W. Mayer (Studies Loretz p. 546) reads *na-ṭù* <*a*>-⌜*na*⌝, "geeignet für$^?$."

14 For the reading ⌜*pe*⌝-[(*e*)-*li*], cf. Grayson, RIMA 2 p. 226 A.0.101.2 line 25.

17 Or $^{m⌜}$DINGIR⌝-[*bi-iʾ-di*], "Ilu-[biʾdī], although the spacing might suggest the longer reading.

18 The restoration is based on text no. 81 lines 5–6; although H.W.F. Saggs's copy might not suggest that there was sufficient room for this restoration, collation of the original would suggest there was (see also the photo at CDLI P393884).

19 For the possible restoration, cf. text no. 81 lines 12–13 and text no. 7 line 33.

20–21 Based on text no. 81 lines 14–15, E. Frahm (Last Days p. 59) suggests restoring *mārē aššur ša ina māt ḫamati* at the end of the line 20 and reading [*ba*$^?$]-⌜*šu*$^?$*-ú*$^?$⌝ at the beginning of line 21, thus "He killed [the citizens of Assyria *who we*]*re* [*in the land Hamath* (...)]" (Frahm's translation slightly modified). It is not clear if there would be sufficient room for the former restoration, but the restoration would be a logical one. For the tentative reading ⌜GIM$^?$ 1$^?$-*en*$^?$⌝, "*altogether*," see text no. 81 line 15 and Frahm, AoF 40 (2013) p. 48.

22 For the beginning of the line, H. Winckler's edition would suggest [... *a-na aššur*] *qa-ti áš-ši-ma*, "I raised (my) hands (in prayer) [to the god Aššur] and" (AOF 1/5 p. 403). H.W.F. Saggs (Iraq 37 [1975] pp. 14 and 18) has [*x x*] ⌜*x x x x x x áš*⌝*-š*[*i*]*-*⌜*ma*⌝ (slightly modified) and states that the traces "may conceal some form of *qātī* (or *qātē*^{II}*-ia*) *ana* ^{d}*aššur*" but that "*qa-ti* (following Winckler) is not the preferred reading." While Winckler's reading would make good sense, collation also indicates that, with regard to *áš-ši-ma*, the traces of the first sign are not necessarily compatible with ÁŠ and that the second sign is more likely DI than ŠI. For the tentative restoration *sa-kap* ^{md}*ia-ú-bi-iʾ-di*, "to overthrow Iaū-biʾdī," see text no. 108 Frgm. D line 7′ and text no. 81 line 18.

(*x x*)]
23) [(*x*) KUR *a*]-⸢*mur-re*⸣-*e* ⸢DAGAL⸣-*ti* ⸢*am-ḫur-ma*⸣ AN.⸢ŠÁR DINGIR⸣ [GAL? *x x x x x x x x x x* (*x x*)]

Rev.

24) [*ik-ri-bi-ia*?] ⸢*iš*?⸣-*me*-⸢*ma*⸣ *il-qa-a su-pi-ia* ⸢*um*⸣-[*ma-na-ti-ia*? DAGAL-*ti*? *x x x* (*x x*) *ad-ke-ma*?]
25) [KASKAL KUR *a*]-⸢*mur*⸣-*re-e ú-šá-aṣ-bit* KUR.*ḫa*-[(*am*)-*ma-tu* ...]
26) [*x x* (*x*)] *x* ⸢*mu*⸣-*ṣa-at šá*-⸢*lam*⸣-*du ta-nit*-⸢*ti*⸣ [...]
27) [UN.MEŠ? KUR *a*]-⸢*mur-re*⸣-*e a-na* GÌR.II-*ia ú-šak-ni*-[*iš* ...]
28) ⸢*a-na* URU⸣-*ia* URU.*a-šur ub-la*-⸢*ma*⸣ *áš-šú šá zík-ri* ⸢*pi*⸣-[(*i*)-*ia*? *iš*]-⸢*mu*⸣-[(*u*)-*ma*? ...]
29) *il-li-ku re-ṣu-ti bal-til*.KI URU ⸢*ki-di*⸣-*ni* ⸢BALA.MEŠ? *la*⸣-*bi*-⸢*ru-tu*?⸣ [...]
30) *ma-ḫa-zu ṣi-i-ru šá* ᵈ*a*-⸢*šur*₄⸣ EN-*šú a-na kib-ra-a-te is-su-qa-šú mar-ka*-⸢*as*⸣ [LUGAL-*ti*? *x x x*]
31) *ša šá-nin-šú la i-šu-u šá ul-tu* ⸢*ul-la il*⸣-*ku* ⸢*tup*⸣-*šik-ku la i-du-u* UN.MEŠ-*šú* ᵐ⸢ᵈ⸣[SILIM-*ma-nu*-MAŠ]
32) *la pa-liḫ* ⸢LUGAL⸣ *gim-ri a-na* URU *šu-a-tú* ŠU-*su a-na* ḪUL-*ti ú-bil-ma iš*-⸢*ta*⸣-[*kan x x x* (*x*)]
33) UN.MEŠ-*šú il-ku tup-šik-ku mar*-⸢*ṣi-iš iš*?-*kun*?⸣ *im-ta-ni* ERIM.MEŠ *ḫup-šiš* ⸢*i*?⸣-[*nu-mi-šu*? *x x x* (*x*)]
34) ᵈEN.LÍL DINGIR.MEŠ *ina ug-gat* ŠÀ-*šú* BALA-⸢*šú*⸣ *iš-kip*? *ia*⸣-*a*-⸢*ti*⸣ ᵐ⸢LUGAL-GI⸣.NA MAN *x* (*x*) ÍA *x* [*x x x x x x* (*x*)]
35) *ul-la-a* SAG-*ia* GIŠ.GIDRU GIŠ.GU.ZA AGA *ú-šat-me-ḫa-an*-⸢*ni*⸣ [...] *x x* [*x x x x x x* (*x*)]
36) *áš-šú šur-šud*ᵘᵈ *kar-ri kun-ni* BALA-*ia za-ku*-⸢*su-nu*⸣ [...]
37) *qé-reb é-šár-ra i-tal-lu-ki ma-ḫar-šú áš-šú ba-laṭ* ⸢ŠÀ⸣-[*ia*? ...]
38) *šá* DUMU.MEŠ URU *šu-nu-ti za-ku-su-nu*

tr[*oops* (...) *and*] (25) had (them) take [the road to the land Am]urru.

25b–29) The land Ha[math ...] corpses were spread wide (lit.: "the/a corpse was spread out"). Fame [...] I made [*the people of* the land Am]urru bow [down] at my feet. I brought [...] to my city Aššur, and, because [they (the people of the city Aššur) *li*]*st*[*ened to my*] comma[nd *and* ...] came to my aid, [*I showed favor to*] (the city) Baltil (Aššur), the city of privileged-status *since ancient dynasties.*

30–40a) (With regards to this) august cult center (the city Aššur) that the god Aššur, his lord, had selected to be the (central) link [*of kingship* ...] for the (four) quarters (of the world), (the city) which has no rival (and) whose people have not known (state) service (or) corvée duty since the distant past, [Shalmaneser (V)], who did not revere the king of all (the world), raised his hand against that city with evil intent and esta[blished ...]. *He imposed oppressively* (state) service (and) corvée-duty upon its people (and) treated (them) as if (they were of the) lower class. *At* [*that time*, ...] the Enlil of the gods angrily *overthrew* his reign. (As for) me, Sargon, the ... king [...], (35) he exalted me (and) had me take hold of scepter, throne, (and) crown. [...] In order to make (my) throne secure, to firmly establish my reign, [*to restore*] their exemption (from obligations), [...] so that (I) might walk about in his presence in Ešarra, (and) in order that [*I be*] well of he[art ...] I planned the exemption (from obligations) of those citizens of the city. [(...)] I exempted them [from (*state*) *service, corvée duty*], the levy of the land,

24 Or ⸢*um*⸣-[*ma-na-at*? *aššur gapšāti*? *adkēma*?], "[*I mustered the vast*] *t*[*roops of Aššur and*]," following E. Frahm (Last Days p. 59).

26 E. Frahm (Last Days p. 60) says "*mu-ṣa-at* is apparently a feminine singular stative derived from *wuṣṣû/muṣṣû* 'to spread out,' even though one would rather have expected plural forms here" and translates the beginning of the line as "[...] ... spead out was the corpse."

27 Possibly restore *gi-mir*, "all," instead of UN.MEŠ, "people" at the beginning of the line. At the end of the line would be a statement of who or what was taken back to Assyria, for which cf. text no. 106 ii 11′. Likely based on text no. 117 ii 11, E. Frahm (Last Days p. 59) suggests restoring *Iaū-bi'dī /šâšu adi kimtišu (mundaḫṣēšu)*?, thus "Iaū-bi'dī (or: him), together with his *family* (*and his fighting men*)" (Frahm's edition slightly modified).

33 G. Vera Chamaza (SAAB 6 [1992] pp. 23 and 25) reads [UŠ]-⸢*ma*⸣, "[he] impo[sed] ... and" rather than ⸢*iš*?-*kun*?⸣, "*He imposed*," but there is a trace of the first sign and it would fit the end of IŠ better than UŠ. Collation also shows that there is sufficient room to read *iš-kun* (against Vera Chamaza).

34 ⸢*iš-kip*?⸣: The tentative translation "*overthrew*" follows H.W.F. Saggs (Iraq 37 [1975] pp. 14–15) and G. Vera Chamaza (SAAB 6 [1992] pp. 23 and 25) and assumes that the verb is from *sakāpu* (see CAD S p. 71 sub *sakāpu* 1.d.2′). For the end of the line, Saggs (Iraq 37 [1975] pp. 14–15 and 20) reads MAN ⸢*ka*⸣-*ía*-⸢*nu*⸣ [...] and translates "the legitimate king," but the traces do not fit KA and *kay(y)ānu* means "normal, plain, permanent, constant, regular" (CAD K p. 40). Relying in part on H. Winckler's copy, Vera Chamaza (SAAB 6 [1992] pp. 23 and 25) reads MAN [KUR *aš-šur*] *šá*-[*i-im* ...] and translates the passage "[appointed] me, Sargon, as king [of Assyria]." However, the traces do not fit well with KUR *aš-šur*; the sign is ÍA, not ŠÁ; and we would not expect *šá-'-im* to stand for "appointed" in this context.

36–38 The exact sense of the passage is not clear. H.W.F. Saggs (Iraq 37 [1975] pp. 16–17 and 20) prefers to take the ends of line 36 and line 37 as being what Sargon planned to do and translates the passage "In order to give a sure foundation to the throne-base, to make my dynasty firm, I conceived a desire to bring about the freedom of those citizens, *to restore* their freedom (from taxes), to *permit them* to walk about within Ešarra before Him, for the sake of *their* heart's life." In the break at the end of line 36, Saggs (Iraq 37 [1975] p. 16) reads [*tu*?-*ur*?-*ri*? ...] and G. Vera Chamaza (SAAB 6 [1992] p. 23) [*šá-ka-ni* ...], i.e., "[to restore/(re)-establish ...]."

37 Following H.W.F. Saggs (Iraq 37 [1975] pp. 17 and 20), possibly ⸢ŠÀ⸣-[(*bi*)-*šu-nu* ...], "[*they be*] ... of he[art ...]."

uš-ta-bil ⌜*ka*⌝*-bat-*[*ti* (...) *i-na il-ki*? *tup-šik-ki*?]
39) *di-ku-ut* KUR *ši-si-ti* ⌜LÚ⌝.NÍMGIR *ina mì-ik-si ka-a-*⌜*ri*⌝ [*né-bé-ri*? ...]
40) É.KUR.MEŠ *gab-bu šá* KUR *aš-šur ú-zak-ki-šú-nu-ti* AN.ŠÁR *be-*⌜*lí*⌝ x [...]
41) *ú-še-piš-ma ḫa-aṣ-bu* KÙ.BABBAR ⌜*ša*⌝ 20 ⌜MA⌝.NA É ŠUM ⌜KU? TA⌝ x [...]
42) UGU-*šú áš-ṭur-ma ú-kín ma-*⌜*ḫar*⌝*-šú šá šip-ru šá-a-tu iš-*⌜*tu*?⌝ [...]
43) [*ú*?]-⌜*saḫ*?⌝*-ḫu-u ši-ma-a-te* AN.ŠÁR EN GAL-*u ez-zi-iš*$_{6}$ *li-*[*ik-kil-me-šu*? (...)]

(and) the proclamation of the herald, from quay [(*and*) *ferry*] dues [...] all the temples of Assyria.

40b–42a) (The god) Aššur, my lord, [...] I had [...] made and a silver *ḫaṣbu*-pot (weighing) twenty minas ... [...] I inscribed upon it and placed it before him.

42b–43) (As for) the one who [*removes*] that object (lit.: "work") *fro*[*m its* (*current*) *location* (...)] (*or*) *mutilates* (*its*) *represention*(*s*), may (the god) Aššur, the great lord, [*glare at him*] angrily [(...)].

90

A clay tablet from Nineveh preserves a short dedicatory inscription of Sargon II to the goddess Anunītu. This text was likely either a copy of an inscription on an object or a draft to be engraved on an object. The inscription is written in pseudo-archaic script and seems to be complete, although only one face of the tablet is preserved. There appear to be fingernail impressions on the left side of the tablet.

CATALOGUE

Museum Number	Registration Number	Provenance	Dimensions (cm)	cpn
BM 134553	1932-12-12,548	Nineveh, Kuyunjik, Ištar Temple, Square OO	2.2×4.9×1.4	c

BIBLIOGRAPHY

1968 Lambert and Millard, Cat. p. 77 (study)

TEXT

1) *a-na* ^{d}*a-nu-ni-tum*
2) GAŠAN-*šú* ^{m}MAN-GIN
3) *ana* TI-*šú* BA-*ìš*

1–3) To the goddess Anunītu, his lady: Sargon (II) presented (this) for the sake of his life.

89 line 43 H.W.F. Saggs (Iraq 37 [1975] pp. 16–17 and 20) reads ⌜*mu*!?⌝*-šim*!? *ši-ma-a-te*, "*the One who fixes* the fates," and assumes this describes Aššur, who is mentioned immediately following. However, a divine name is not generally preceded by an epithet and, as noted by Saggs, the tablet has ḪU-U, not ŠIM. G. Vera Chamaza (SAAB 6 [1992] pp. 23 and 25) reads [*mu-saḫ*]*-ḫu-u ši-ma-a-te* ... *li-*[*iš-i-im-šú*], takes the first word with the preceding and the second word with the following, and translates "[w]hoever [takes away] this work [from its place and] vio[lates it], for him, may the god Aššur determine a fate of death." However, one would prefer a finite verb in the subjunctive to follow the *ša* of line 42. The traces before ḪU would fit well with a SAḪ sign and there may actually be the trace of the top of a vertical wedge for the first sign of the line (thus ⌜*ú*?*-saḫ*?⌝*-ḫu-u*). The tentative translation "*representation*(*s*)" assumes that *ši-ma-a-te* stands for *simāte*. The phrase DN + *ezziš* + a precative of the verb *nekelmû* is common in royal inscriptions (see CAD N/2 pp. 152–153).

91

A clay tablet fragment in the Kuyunjik collection of the British Museum bears a "very fragmentary, poetic description of the campaign of 710 (and 709?)" against Merodach-Baladan and "the complete document must have given a detailed description comparable to that of the annals" (Brinkman, Studies Oppenheim pp. 44–45).

CATALOGUE

Museum Number	Provenance	Dimensions (cm)	cpn
K 4471	Probably Nineveh, Kuyunjik	6.8×5.4×2.4	c

COMMENTARY

The inscription on the fragment does not appear to be a duplicate of any other inscription of Sargon II. In editing this text, H. Tadmor compares lines 2′, 3′, 8′, and 9′ to text no. 1 lines 269, 263, 273–274, and 267 respectively, line 5′ to text no. 65 line 266, line 10′ to text no. 74 vi 38 and vii 50, and line 12′ to text no. 73 line 16. (Tadmor's citation of line numbering does not take into account our line 1′.) In addition, for lines 3′–4′ and 11′, cf. for example text no. 7 lines 122 and 128, and text no. 74 vi 20–21 and 34; for line 4′, cf. text no. 1 line 110.

BIBLIOGRAPHY

1891 Bezold, Cat. 2 p. 635 (study)
1894 Winckler, Sammlung 2 p. 4 bottom (copy [cited as K 4470])
1958 Tadmor, JCS 12 pp. 99–100 (photo, edition)
1964 Brinkman, Studies Oppenheim pp. 44–45 no. 44.2.20.c.vi (study)

TEXT

Lacuna	Lacuna
1′) [...] *x x* [...]	1′) [...] ... [...].
2′) [... BALA].MEŠ-*šú* GIŠ.GIDRU GIŠ.⸢GU⸣.[ZA LUGAL-*ti-šu x x*] NUMUN UR *x* [...]	2′) [... *to change/remove*] his [reign], scepter, (and) [his royal] thr[one ...] ... [...]
3′) [...] ⸢GÚ⸣ ÍD.*mar-ra-ti* [*x x x x x*] *la i-šá-*[*a* ...]	3′) [... s]hore of the sea [...] did not have [...]
4′) [...] ⸢BU?⸣ RI *a-na i-di-šú* ⸢*ú*⸣-[*ter*?-(*x*)]-⸢*šu*?⸣ [(*x*)] *it-ta-*[*kil* ...]	4′) [...] ... he [*made hi*]*m* side with him; he put his [trust ...]
5′) [...] *x-šú-nu mu-tum ḫi-it-*⸢*lu-pu*⸣*-ma i-rat* [...]	5′) [...] their [...] clothed in death and the breast [...]
6′) [...] *x gi-mir* LÚ.*kal-di lem-ni x* [...]	6′) [...] all the evil Chaldeans [...]
7′) [...] *x ú-rap-pi-*⸢*iš*⸣ [...]	7′) [...] he extended [...]
8′) [... *ḫal-ṣa*?]-⸢*ni*⸣*-šú ú-dan-nin mar-ṣi-iš ú-šá-x* [...]	8′) [...] he strengthened his [*fortress*]*es*. He had [...] with (great) difficulty [...]
9′) [... *ša* (...) *lem-ni*?]*-iš i-be-lu-ma be-lut* KUR *ù* ⸢UN?⸣.[MEŠ ...]	9′) [... who (...)] ruled [*evil*]*ly* [(...)] and [...] the lordship of the land and *p*[*eople* ...]

9′ Possibly "[... who] ruled [*evil*]*ly* [for twelve years] and [exercised] rulership over the land and *p*[*eople* ...]"; cf. text no. 1 lines 267–268, text no. 2 lines 295–296, text no. 7 line 124, and Tadmor, JCS 12 (1958) p. 100.

10′) [...] *ger-ri šup-šu-qa-ma* NI [...]
11′) [...] *x-ti* A.MEŠ *ir-tu-šú* A *x* [...]

12′) [... *ki-ma*?] ⸢*šu*?*-pu-uk*⸣ KUR-*i dan-ni* [...]
13′) [...] *x x* ERIM.ḪI.A *x* [...]
Lacuna

10′) [...] the roads are very difficult and [...]
11′) [...] he fixed [*its foundations in the dep*]*th of* the water [...]
12′) [... *as*] the base of a mighty mountain [...]
13′) [...] ... soldiers [...]
Lacuna

92

An inscription found on numerous fragments of clay cones from Nineveh records the king's restoration of the temple of the god Nabû (referred to as the temple of the gods Nabû and Marduk), which had been restored seventy-five years earlier, in the time of Adad-nārārī III (810–783). (For a brick inscription of Adad-nārārī III recording work on the temple of Nabû at Nineveh, see Grayson, RIMA 3 pp. 219–220 A.0.104.14.) Brick inscriptions of Sargon II also record work on this temple (see text nos. 95–96 and possibly no. 97). For the history of the temple, see Menzel, Tempel pp. 119–120 and P 12.

CATALOGUE

Ex.	Museum Number	Registration Number	Provenance	Dimensions (cm)	Publication reference	Lines Preserved	cpn
1	—	56-9-9,171	Nineveh	13.0×9.3	Winckler, Sar. 2 pl. 49 no. 15	1–9	c
2	—	81-2-4,182	As ex. 1	9.8×8.0	Winckler, Sar. 2 pl. 49 no. 14	1–7	c
3	BM 121136	1929-10-12,145	Nineveh, Nabû temple XXIV.9	7.0×7.2	Arch. 79 no. 122D	6–9	c
4	BM 121133	1929-10-12,142	Nineveh, Nabû temple XIV.8	10.0×6.8	Arch. 79 no. 122F	2/3, 4, 6–8	c
5	BM 121134	1929-10-12,143	Nineveh, Nabû temple XXVI.8	5.8×9.9	Arch. 79 no. 122O	4–9	c
6	—	—	Nineveh, Ištar temple A.6	—	AAA 19 no. 102	5–8	n
7	BM 128357	1932-12-10,614	Nineveh, SH I.5	8.8×7.6	AAA 19 no. 110	2?–9	c
8	BM 139287	1932-12-10,741	Nineveh, SH I.3	2.9×5	AAA 19 no. 111	8?–9	c
9	BM 123449	1932-12-10,392	Nineveh, Ashurnasirpal's palace C.18	7.5×8.7	AAA 19 no. 132	4?–9	c
10	BM 139291	1932-12-10,745	Nineveh, Ištar temple MM.10?	2.1×3.8	AAA 19 no. 145	4–6	c
11	BM 123485	1932-12-10,428	Nineveh, Ashurnasirpal's palace C.14	3.2×4.4	AAA 19 no. 152	8–9	c
12	BM 123457	1932-12-10,400	Nineveh, Ashurnasirpal's palace F.16 & C.14	9.5×11	AAA 19 no. 155	1–8	c
13	BM 128363	1932-12-10,620	Nineveh, said to come from the flats below Kuyunjik	4.6×8.1	AAA 19 no. 156	3?–8	c
14	BM 128400	1932-12-10,657	As ex. 1	4×5.7	AAA 19 no. 158	3–7	c
15	BM 123448	1932-12-10,391	Nineveh, Ashurnasirpal's palace C.15	8×8.4	AAA 19 no. 159	3–9	c
16	BM 134510	1932-12-12,505	Nineveh, SH II	4.7×3.6	AAA 19 no. 160	6–9	c
17	BM 128352	1932-12-10,609	Nineveh, SH II.3	8.1×9.2	AAA 19 no. 162	2–4, 6, 8–9	c
18	BM 123451	1932-12-10,394	Nineveh, Ištar temple, Square Q.1	6.7×9.3	AAA 19 no. 166	6–9	c
19	BM 128354	1932-12-10,611	Nineveh, Ištar temple, Square NN.0	5.5×8.5	AAA 19 no. 167	6–9	c

91 line 10′ Or ⸢IR⸣ [...] instead of NI [...].

20	BM 123529	1932-12-10,472	Nineveh, Ištar temple, Square M.0	3.8×4.2	AAA 19 no. 226	4?–5, 7–9	c
21	BM 128164	1929-10-12,820	Nineveh, Wall III, NE, on stone base	7.3×3.8	—	6?-9	c
22	BM 128199	1929-10-12,855	Nineveh, Ashurnasirpal's palace C.16.V	5.6×3.9	—	4, 6–9?	c
23	BM 128200	1929-10-12,856	Nineveh, Ashurnasirpal's palace D.6	5×4.2	—	3–6	c
24	BM 128207	1929-10-12,863	Nineveh, Ashurnasirpal's palace D.2	4.7×2.8	—	6–8	c
25	BM 128209	1929-10-12,865	Nineveh, Ashurnasirpal's palace X? A.6	3.5×4.1	—	5–8	c
26	K 22184	—	As ex. 1	5.3×4.9	—	2–4	c
27	K 22192	—	As ex. 1	6.3×3	—	6–7	c
28	BM 98851	1905-4-9,357	As ex. 1	10.5×10.8	—	2–4, 6–9	c
29	BM 98852	1905-4-9,358	As ex. 1	7×7	—	3?, 5–9	c
30	BM 98853	1905-4-9,359	As ex. 1	7.5×7.3	—	6–8	c

COMMENTARY

The text presented here is made up from numerous tiny fragments and it is possible some actually come from a different original inscription, rather than preserve simple variants to this one. Nevertheless, it has been thought advisable to treat them all here, rather than deal with them separately or argue about the validity of the inclusion of individual pieces. The line arrangement follows ex. 1, but the master line is composed from numerous exemplars. Although the text of lines 4–9 is reasonably certain, that of lines 1–3 is not. There may well have been major divergences among the pieces preserving parts of these three lines (i.e., the name, titles, and epithets of Sargon). R. Campbell Thompson's edition of these lines is as follows:

1. ^{m}*Šar-gi-na šar kiššati šar* ^{mâtu}*Aš-šur*^{ki} *šakin* ^{ilu}*Bêl nišak* ^{ilu}*A-šur*

2. *ri'u [kînu ša* ^{ilu}*A-šur]* ^{ilu}*Marduk [ut-tu-šu ?] ... uš šarru ...-a-ti u(?) ..*

3. *ša a-na šarru-ti ib-bu-u-šu ilâni*^{pl} *rabûti*^{pl} *a-na-ku-ma*

However, it is not possible to find some of his readings on the exemplars known. In particular, in line 1, no exemplar has KIŠ/ŠÚ for Campbell Thompson's *kiššati* or a GAR for his *šakin*, and in line 3, no exemplar has LUGAL-*ti* or MAN-*ti* (for his *šarru-ti*) following *a-na*, although ex. 26 (not known to Campbell Thompson) has *i-na x* [...], where *x* could conceivably be the beginning of LUGAL.

It is worth noting that the copy of ex. 1 by G. Smith in 3 R (used by H. Winckler as the basis for his copy) omits several signs and traces of signs (e.g., *a-šur* in line 1 and ⸢*ul*⸣ in line 6) and incorrectly copies several others (e.g., TI not KI, and LA not MA, in line 7).

BIBLIOGRAPHY

1870 3 R pl. 3 no. 12 (ex. 1, copy)

1874 Ménant, Annales p. 211 (ex. 1, translation, combined with text no. 95 exs. 1–3)

1886 Bezold, Literatur pp. 93–94 §56.14h (ex. 1, study)

1889 Winckler, Sar. 1 p. 196; and 2 pl. 49 nos. 14–15 (exs. 1–2, copy; study)

1896 Bezold, Cat. 4 pp. 1694 and 1769 (exs. 1–2, study)

1914 King, Cat. p. 75 nos. 757–759 (exs. 28–30, study)

1922 BM Guide p. 183 no. 24 (ex. 1, study)

1927 Luckenbill, ARAB 2 p. 113 §227 (exs. 1–2, translation)

1929 Thompson, Arch. 79 pp. 133–134 and pls. XLVII and LII nos. 122D, 122F, and 122O (exs. 3–5, copy; exs. 1–5, edition)

1931–32 Weidner, AfO 7 p. 280 (line 4, study)

1932 Thompson, AAA 19 pp. 103–104 and pls. LXXIII–LXXVI and LXXIX nos. 102, 110–111, 132, 145, 152, 155–156, 158–160, 162, 166–167, and 226 (exs. 6–20, copy; exs. 1–9, 11–20, edition)

1956 Borger, Asarh. p. 7 commentary to Ass. B line 45 (ex. 29, study)

1967 Seux, ERAS p. 175 (line 3, study)

1968 Lambert and Millard, Cat. pp. 12, 26–27, 29, 32, 52, 54–55, 63, 66, and 74 (exs. 3–5, 7, 9, 11–25, study)

1984 Frame, ARRIM 2 pp. 10–11 and 14–16 (exs. 3–20, study)

1992 Lambert, Cat. p. 72 (exs. 26–27, study)

TEXT

1) ^{m}LUGAL-GI.NA ⸢LUGAL$^{?}$⸣ [...] *x* NU.ÈŠ ^{d}*a-šur*
2) SIPA [*ke-e-nu*$^{?}$ ...] ⸢UŠ$^{?}$⸣ MAN [...] GÌR.NÍTA ^{d}AG *ù* ^{d}AMAR.UTU
3) *ša a-na x* [...]-⸢*e*⸣-*ti* ⸢*ù*$^{?}$⸣ [...] *x*-⸢*a*/*e*$^{?}$⸣-*ti ib-bu-ú-šú* DINGIR.MEŠ GAL.MEŠ *a-na-ku-ma*
4) É ^{d}AG ^{d}AMAR.UTU *šá ina tar-ṣi* KÁ.GAL GIBIL-*ti ma-ḫi-rat* IM.SI.SÁ *i-na pa-na ep-šú e-na-aḫ-ma*
5) ^{md}IŠKUR-*né-ra-ri* DUMU ^{md}UTU-*ši*-^{d}IŠKUR LUGAL KUR *aš-šur*.KI [(...) NUN$^{?}$ *a*]-*lik pa-ni-ia e-pu-uš*
6) *ša* É *šá-a-tu šur-šú-šú ul dun-nu-nu-ma* SUḪUŠ-*su ki-i ki-ṣir* KUR-*i ul re-ti* 75.ÀM MU.AN.NA.MEŠ *im-la-a-ma an-ḫu-ta ù la-bi-ru-ta il-lik-ma*
7) *áš-šú* NU KÚR KI.TUŠ-*šú i-na ṭe-eḫ* É ^{d}INANNA *ša* URU.NINA.KI *e-pe-šú pi-i* ^{d}⸢AG$^{?}$⸣ [(...)] ⸢*be*⸣-*lí-ia a-šal-ma an-nu-um ke-nu-um ša* NU KÚR KI.TUŠ-*šú i-na ma-kal-ti* LÚ.ḪAL-*ti i-pu-la-an-ni-ma*
8) É ^{d}AG *ù* ^{d}AMAR.UTU EN.MEŠ-*ia i-na ṭe-eḫ* É ^{d}INANNA *ša* URU.NINA.KI *e-pu-šu ul-tu uš-še-e-šú a-di gaba-dib-bi-šú ar-ṣi-ip ú-šak-lil ù* DUG.*sí-ka*$_{4}$*-a-ti áš-kun*
9) *a-na* TI.LA-*ia šùl-mu* NUMUN-*ia sà-kap* LÚ.KÚR.MEŠ-*ia* SI.SÁ BURU$_{14}$ KUR *aš-šur*.KI *šùl*-⸢*mu*⸣ KUR *aš-šur*.KI [(...)] *e-pu-uš*

1–3) Sargon (II), *k*[*ing* ...], *nešakku*-priest of the god Aššur, [*just*] shepherd [...] king [...], governor (appointed) by the gods Nabû and Marduk, whom [(...)] the great gods appointed to [...] ... *and* [...] ..., I —

4–8) The temple of the gods Nabû (and) Marduk that had previously been built opposite the new gate facing north, became dilapidated and Adad-nārārī (III), son of Šamšī-Adad (V), king of Assyria [(...), *a prince* who pr]eceded me, (re)built (it). The foundations of this temple were not made strong and its foundation wall was not fixed like bedrock. Seventy-five years elapsed and it became old and dilapidated (lit.: "dilapidated and old"). In order not to change its location (and) to build (it) beside the temple of the goddess Ištar of Nineveh, I requested the *command* of the god *Na*[*bû* (...)], my lord, and by means of the diviner's bowl he answered me with (his) firm approval not to change its location. Then, from its foundations to its crenellations, I completely (re)constructed the temple of the gods Nabû and Marduk, my lords, (that) had been built beside the temple of the goddess Ištar of Nineveh, and I set my clay *sikkatu*-cones (in place).

9) For the sake of my life, the well-being of my offspring, the overthrow of my enemies, the success of the harvest of Assyria, (and) the well-being of Assyria [(...)] I (re)built (this temple).

1–2 Exs. 2, 17, and 28 have [...] *x* KUR *aš-šur*.KI GÌR.NÍTA ^{d}⸢EN/AG$^{?}$⸣ [...] ("[...] Assyria, viceroy for the god B[ēl/N[abû ...]"), [...] ⸢KUR⸣ *aš-šur*.KI GÌR.NÍTA ^{d}EN *u* ^{d}AMAR.UTU ("[...] Assyria, viceroy for the gods Bēl and Marduk"), and [...] ⸢SIPA*⸣(?; text: [...]x-IB) KUR *aš-šur*.KI GÌR.NÍTA ^{d}MUATI *ù* ^{d}AMAR.UTU ("[... *she*]*pherd* of Assyria, viceroy for the gods Nabû and Marduk") respectively. This may represent all of master line 2 and possibly the end of master line 1.

2 The exact placement of ⸢UŠ$^{?}$⸣ MAN [...], which is found only on ex. 12, is not certain.

3 Ex. 26 has *i-na* for *a-na*. For the fourth sign of the line, see the copies from exs. 1 and 26 in the minor variants section. Ex. 29 has [...] (*x*) TI ⸢SI SA$^{?}$ KU⸣ UN *x* [...]. Moreover, it is not clear if [...]-⸢*e*⸣-*ti* ⸢*ù*$^{?}$⸣ [...] should go here or in line 2. This reading is based upon ex. 7, where the traces of the Ù are ⸢ŠI⸣ [...]; ex. 14 has [...]-*ti* ⸢ŠI⸣ [...]. As for [...] *x*-⸢*a*/*e*$^{?}$⸣-*ti*, it comes from ex. 1, where the *x* is simply the head of a vertical wedge. Ex. 23 has [...]-⸢*a*$^{?}$/*e*$^{?}$⸣-*ti*.

4 Ex. 4 inserts *u*, "and," after ^{d}AG, "Nabû." Ex. 17 has GIŠ for *ma-ḫi-rat*. Exs. 17 and 28 insert *šá* and *ša* respectively before *i-na*; ex. 26 replaces *i-na* with ⸢*ša*⸣.

6 For the translation of this line, cf. text no. 73 line 14. Ex. 4 has *lu-u* for the first *ul*, thus "The foundation of this temple was indeed made strong ..."

7 Or less likely ... *an-nu-um ki-nu-um ša* NU KÚR KI.TUŠ-⸢*šú*⸣ [...] *x-šú*, "firm approval not to change its site [*or* ...] its [...]."

8 Thompson, AAA 19 (1932) p. 103 has *e-pu-uš*, "I built," after *arṣip ušaklil u*, "I completely (re)constructed ... and," but no known exemplar appears to have this.

9 For a similar passage, see for example Grayson and Novotny, RINAP 3/2 p. 300 no. 214 line 2. Or less likely ... *sà-kap* LÚ.KÚR.MEŠ-[*ia* ...]-*ia* SI.SÁ BURU$_{14}$ ..., "... the overthrow of [my] enemies, [the ...] of my [...], the success of the harvest ..." *šùl*-⸢*mu*⸣: Or SILIM.⸢MU⸣ following CAD Š/1 p. 207.

93

This fragmentary inscription of Sargon II is found on a "marble" fragment from Nineveh. The present location of the piece is not known and the inscription is edited from the published copy by R. Campbell Thompson. Compare in particular text nos. 96–97, which were found on bricks from the temple of Nabû at Nineveh; this inscription might have been a duplicate of text no. 96. Limestone paving slabs with an inscription recording Sargon's work on the temple of Nabû and Marduk have been found at Nineveh (see the commentary to text no. 95).

CATALOGUE

Source	Provenance	Dimensions (cm)	cpn
Thompson, Arch. 79 pl. XLII no. 41	Nineveh	22.9×15.9×7.3	n

BIBLIOGRAPHY

1929 Thompson, Arch. 79 p. 120 and pl. XLII no. 41 (copy)

TEXT

1) ^{m}MAN-GIN [...]
2) É ^{d}[...]
3) *ana* TI-*šú* [...]
Lacuna

1–3) Sargon (II), [*strong king, king of the world, king of Assyria, (completely) built*] the temple of the deity [...] for the sake of his life [(...)]
Lacuna

94

This fragmentary inscription is found on a "marble" fragment from Nineveh. R. Campbell Thompson refers to it as a "Large Inscription." The present location of the piece is not known and the inscription is edited from the published copy. Compare in particular the beginning of text nos. 95–98 (bricks from the temple of Nabû at Nineveh) and text no. 93 (a "marble" fragment from Nineveh). It is likely that nothing is missing before line 1′.

CATALOGUE

Source	Provenance	Dimensions (cm)	cpn
Thompson, Arch. 79 pl. XLII no. 28	Nineveh	16.5×17.8×11.4	n

BIBLIOGRAPHY

1929 Thompson, Arch. 79 pl. XLII no. 28 (copy)

TEXT

Lacuna
1′) mMAN-[GIN ...]
Lacuna

Lacuna
1′) Sar[gon (II) ...]
Lacuna

95

This inscription recording the construction of the temple of the god Nabû (here referred to as the temple of the gods Nabû and Marduk) is found on bricks and limestone pavement slabs from Nineveh.

CATALOGUE

Ex.	Museum Number	Registration Number	Photograph Number	Object	Provenance	Dimensions (cm)	Lines Preserved	cpn
1	BM 90242	1979-12-20,147	—	brick	Nineveh	44×43	1–7	n
2	BM 90243	1979-12-20,148	—	brick	As ex. 1	44×44×8.5	1–7	n
3	BM 90244	1979-12-20,149	—	brick	As ex. 1	43.5×40.5×8.5	1–7	n
4	BM 121150	1929-10-12,159	BM 56548; Thompson 1927–28 no. 76	stone slab	As ex. 1	45.7×55.9×6.4	1–7	c
5	BCM 226’78	—	Thompson 1927–28 no. 77	stone slab	As ex. 1	78×53×8	4–7	p
6	—	—	Thompson 1927–28 no. 80	stone slab	As ex. 1	—	1–7	p

COMMENTARY

H.C. Rawlinson (1 R pl. 6) states that the bricks with this inscription seen by him were from the "Eastern edge of the mound at Koyunjik." Additional information on the bricks in the British Museum (exs. 1–3) comes from C.B.F. Walker; all these are inscribed on the face.

The line arrangement follows ex. 1; exs. 4, 5 (as far as it is preserved), and 6, as well as R. Campbell Thompson's copy in Arch. 79, have the inscription on nine lines (splitting lines 2 and 6 into two lines each).

Campbell Thompson (Arch. 79 [1929] p. 124) states that he found this inscription in the Nabû temple at Nineveh on "limestone slabs in his [Sargon's] pavement (XXVI–XXVII) and NE. doorway : with duplicates from about twenty-eight bricks"; see also Thompson and Hutchinson, CEN pp. 74–75. Three stone slabs are known from photographs from Campbell Thompson's excavations at Nineveh in 1927–28: photo nos. 76 (ex. 4), 77 (ex. 5), and 80 (ex. 6). The photos are stored in the Department of the Middle East in the British Museum. Ex. 5 was found "S.E. side of Temple" and is marked M.41 (information courtesy P. Watson). The present location of none of the bricks found by Campbell Thompson is known and these are not included in the catalogue. Campbell Thompson states that their findspots are: IV, 5; V, 7; V, 7; VIII, 7; XI, B, 8; XIII, 3; XVI, 10; XVII, 9; XVIII, C, 12; XVIII, C, 13, below pavement; XIX, 1; ?XXI, 10; XXII, 9; XXII, 10; XXIII, B, 10; XXVI, 9; XXVII, 12; XXVIII, 12; XXVIII, 12; XLII, 10; LXV, 9; LXVI, 11; LXVII, depth uncertain; LXVIII, 8; LXXIV, 5; LXXVII, 6; XC, 2; and XCII, B, 14. Variant readings to this inscription known only from Campbell Thompson's comments (see Arch. 79 [1929] pl. XLV no. 69) are noted with the indication "Thompson."

A copy of this inscription is found in Layard MS C second p. 58 (Department of the Middle East, British Museum) and supposedly comes from a brick discovered at Kuyunjik. The inscription is said to be "very indistinct in parts" and the copy diverges from our inscription at several points (e.g., ^{d}MAŠ not ^{d}BAD in line 1 and BE DU not NU.ÈŠ in line 2). Since it is not clear if these divergences are errors of the modern copyist or actual variants, they have not been noted here. A copy of lines 1, 3, and 4 of this inscription, with a gap where line 2 would have been and with the notation "3 more lines" after our line 4, is found in L.W. King's notebook "Kuyunjik: Notes on Sculpture & Inscriptions" (Department of the Middle East, British Museum). It is stated to come from a brick from the Nabû temple. In as far as it is preserved, the inscription duplicates our master line. It is possible that one or both of the bricks copied by A.H. Layard and King is to be found among exs. 1–3.

No score for this brick inscription is given on Oracc, but the minor variants are listed at the back of the book.

BIBLIOGRAPHY

1861 1 R pl. 6 no. 7 (ex. 1–3, copy)
1863 Oppert, EM 1 p. 303 (translation)
1874 Ménant, Annales p. 211 (exs. 1–3, translation, combined with text no. 92 ex. 1])
1886 Bezold, Literatur p. 93 §56.14g (exs. 1–3, study)
1889 Winckler, Sar. 1 p. 195; and 2 pl. 49 no. 11 (exs. 1–3, copy, edition)
1910 Pinches, Outline p. 61 no. 2 (exs. 1–3, copy, transliteration)
1922 BM Guide p. 73 nos. 261–263 (exs. 1–3, study)
1927 Luckenbill, ARAB 2 p. 113 §226 (exs. 1–3, translation)
1929 Thompson, Arch. 79 pl. XLII no. 29 (ex. 5, copy), and p. 124 and pl. XLV no. 69 (exs. 4, 6, additional exs., copy, edition)
1929 Thompson and Hutchinson, CEN pp. 74–75 (translation, provenance)
1979 George, Iraq 41 p. 123 no. 64 (ex. 5, study)
1981 Walker, CBI pp. 118–119 no. 169 Sargon II F (exs. 1–3, transliteration)
1984 Frame, ARRIM 2 pp. 6 and 9 (study)

TEXT

1) ^{m}LUGAL-GI.NA *šá-ak-ni* ^{d}BAD
2) NU.ÈŠ *aš-šur* GÌR.NÍTA ^{d}AG *u* ^{d}AMAR.UTU
3) É ^{d}AG *u* ^{d}AMAR.UTU EN.MEŠ-*šú*
4) *ul-tu* UŠ$_{8}$-*šú a-di gaba-dib-bi-šú*
5) *a-na* TI.LA-*šú šùl-mu* NUMUN-*šú*
6) *sà-kap* LÚ.KÚR.MEŠ-*šú* SI.SÁ BURU$_{14}$ *šá* KUR *aš-šur*.KI
7) *šá-lam* KUR *aš-šur*.KI DÙ-*uš*

1–7) Sargon (II), appointee of the god Enlil, *nešakku*-priest of (the god) Aššur, governor (appointed) by the gods Nabû and Marduk, built the temple of the gods Nabû and Marduk, his lords, from its foundations to its crenellations for the sake of his life, the well-being of his offspring, the overthrow of this enemies, the success of the harvest of Assyria, (and) the well-being of Assyria.

3 Exs. 4 and 6 have the rare writing ^{d}KU for ^{d}AMAR.UTU; see Borger, MZ p. 425.

96

A second inscription recording the construction of the temple of the god Nabû is found on bricks from the well and latrine of the Nabû temple at Nineveh.

CATALOGUE

Ex.	Museum Number	Registration Number	Provenance	Dimensions (cm)	Lines Preserved	cpn
1	BM 137468	1929-10-12,179	Nineveh, Kuyunjik, well	33×5×13	1–5	n
2	BCM 336'79	—	Nineveh, Kuyunjik, well, D 9	32×11×13	1–5	n

COMMENTARY

Exs. 1–2 are inscribed along the edge. Additional information on them comes from C.B.F. Walker.

R. Campbell Thompson (Arch. 79 [1929] p. 124) states that bricks with this inscription come from the well and latrine of the Nabû temple; elsewhere (ibid. pl. XLV) he says that exemplars come from the well and from the following findspots: XX, C, 20; LXXVII, 5; LXIX, 7; and XXVI, 8. None of these four findspots appears to be near the latrine, which is located near areas LVIII and LIX (see Thompson and Hutchinson, Archaeologia 79 [1929] pl. LXIII). The present location of none of these bricks is known and they are not included in the catalogue, although variants from them are noted with the comment "Thompson." The bricks found by Campbell Thompson in the well presumably include exs. 1–2.

A copy of this inscription reportedly discovered on bricks in the well of the Nabû temple is found in L.W. King's notebook "Kuyunjik: Notes on Sculpture & Inscriptions" (Department of the Middle East, British Museum). The copy has a misbegotten GÍD and a BALA rather than a TI in line 3. Since the BALA and TI signs are quite similar and since the BALA sign is copied in pencil while almost all of the rest of the inscription is copied in pen, it is likely that King misread the sign.

It is possible that text no. 93 should be treated as a duplicate of this inscription. As is the practice in RINAP, no score for this brick inscription is given on Oracc, but the minor variants are listed at the back of the book.

BIBLIOGRAPHY

1929 Thompson, Arch. 79 p. 124 and pl. XLV no. 70 (copy, edition)

1929 Thompson and Hutchinson, CEN p. 69 (translation)

1981 Walker, CBI p. 119 no. 170 Sargon II G (exs. 1–2, transliteration)

1984 Frame, ARRIM 2 p. 9 (study)

TEXT

1) ^{m}MAN-GIN MAN KAL MAN ŠÚ MAN KUR AŠ
2) É EN ^{d}MUATI ŠÀ URU.NINA.KI
3) *ana* TI ZI.MEŠ-*šú* GÍD TI-*šú*
4) TA UŠ$_{8}$-*šú* EN *gaba-dib-bi-šú*
5) DÙ-*uš ú-šak-lil*

1–5) Sargon (II), strong king, king of the world, king of Assyria, completely built the temple of the lord, the god Nabû, (located) inside the city of Nineveh from its foundations to its crenellations for the sake of ensuring his good health (and) and prolonging his life.

2 É EN ^{d}MUATI "temple of the lord, the god Nabû": Or possibly É <^{d}>EN ^{d}MUATI "temple of <the god> Bēl (and) the god Nabû"? Cf. text no. 95 line 3 É ^{d}AG *u* ^{d}AMAR.UTU, "temple of the gods Nabû and Marduk."

3 The copy by R. Campbell Thompson (Arch. 79 [1929] pl. XLV) has ZI.MEŠ-*šú*, while Walker, CBI p. 119 has NAM.MEŠ-*šú*. The signs ZI and NAM are very similar and the former reading is used here since in similar places TI (or TI.LA or TIN) is followed by ZI (or ZI.MEŠ), not by NAM (or NAM.MEŠ).

4 Omission of -*šú*, "its," after *gaba-dib-bi*, "crenellations" on the brick from LXIX, 7 (Thompson).

97

This fragmentary inscription from Nineveh should possibly be treated as a variant of the preceding inscription with the only variation being in the arrangement of words and lines, but since this is not certain, it has been kept separate here. The current location of the brick fragment is not known and the inscription is edited from the published copy. Text no. 93, found on a stone fragment, may also be a duplicate of this inscription.

CATALOGUE

Source	Provenance	Dimensions (cm)	cpn
Thompson, Arch. 79 p. 124 and pl. XLV no. 71	Nineveh, Kuyunjik, Nabû temple, XXIV, pit, 1 foot below the pavement	–	n

BIBLIOGRAPHY

1929 Thompson, Arch. 79 p. 124 and pl. XLV no. 71 (copy, study)

TEXT

1) ^{m}MAN-GIN [...]
2) É ^{d}[...]
3) *a-na* ⸢TI$^{?}$⸣ [...]
4) ŠÀ URU.[...]
5) DÙ-⸢*uš*⸣ [...]

1–5) Sargon (II), [*strong king, king of the world, king of Assyria, completely*] built the temple of the god [*Nabû* ...] inside the city [*Nineveh* ...] for the sake of *ensuring* [*his good health* (*and*) *prolonging his days*].

98

This fragmentary inscription of Sargon II is found on a brick from the Nabû temple at Nineveh. The present location of the piece is not known and the inscription is edited from the published copy.

CATALOGUE

Source	Provenance	Dimensions (cm)	cpn
Thompson, Arch. 79 p. 124 and pl. XLV no. 74	Nineveh, Kuyunjik, Nabû temple, XXXII 6	11.4 thick	n

BIBLIOGRAPHY

1929 Thompson, Arch. 79 p. 124 and pl. XLV no. 74 (copy, transliteration)

TEXT

1) mMAN-GIN MAN [...]
2) URU *x x* [...]
3) *mu-šab* [...]
4) d[...]
5) *x* [...]
Lacuna

1–5) Sargon (II), king [*of the world, king of Assyria* ...] a city ... [...] residence [...] the deity [...].

Lacuna

99

Two copper coverings for door jambs from the Nabû temple at Nineveh bear a short dedicatory inscription to the god Nabû.

CATALOGUE

Ex.	Museum Number	Provenance	Dimensions (cm)	Lines Preserved	cpn
1	EŞ 7848	Nineveh, Kuyunjik, Nabû temple	–	1–3?	n
2	EŞ 7849	As ex. 1	–	1–3?	n

COMMENTARY

The two copper coverings come from the upper part of two door jambs from the temple of Nabû at Nineveh ("deux couvertures en cuivre de la partie supérieure des deux jambages de la porte"). According to E. Nassouhi, who published the pieces, one is in fragmentary condition, while the other is better preserved and has a lower diameter of 30 cm. Nassouhi states that both pieces have the same size, form, and inscription and that the less well preserved exemplar has below the logogram for Nabû (dAG of line 1) the emblem of the Sebetti gods, seven stars marked by embossed dots.

It was not possible to examine the two objects and thus, since it is not known exactly what is on which exemplar, no score of the inscription is provided on Oracc.

BIBLIOGRAPHY

1927 Nassouhi, MAOG 3/1–2 p. 17 no. 4 and p. 18 no. VIII (exs. 1–2, photo of one exemplar [inscription not legible], composite copy, edition)

TEXT

1) *a-na* dAG EN-*šú*
2) mMAN-GIN MAN KUR AŠ
3) *a-na* TI-*šú* BA-*ìš*

1–3) To the god Nabû, his lord: Sargon (II), king of Assyria, presented (this object) for the sake of his life.

100

An eye-stone in the J. Rosen collection bears a short dedicatory inscription of Sargon to the goddess the Lady of Nineveh. The piece was purchased on the antiquities market and thus its original provenance it not known. It is placed with the inscriptions from Nineveh solely because it is dedicated to the Lady of Nineveh.

CATALOGUE

Source	Provenance	Dimensions (cm)	cpn
Galter, ARRIM 5 pp. 12, 14, and 21 no. 42	—	3.5×1.3	n

COMMENTARY

H. Galter (ARRIM 5 [1987] p. 12) states that the stone is possibly sardonyx, while U. Kasten states that it is agate (information courtesy of W.W. Hallo). The edition presented below is taken from the publication by Galter and has been confirmed by Hallo.

The writing SUM-⸢*ìš*⸣ in line 3 is unusual and is presumably intended to stand for a form of the verb *qâšu*, although one would expect BA-*ìš*.

BIBLIOGRAPHY

1987 Galter, ARRIM 5 pp. 12, 14, and 21 no. 42 (edition, study)

TEXT

1) ⸢a⸣-na GAŠAN-URU.*ni-na*.KI
2) ⸢GAŠAN⸣-*šú* ᵐLUGAL-GI.NA
3) ⸢a⸣-na TI-*šú* SUM-⸢*iš*⸣

1–3) To the Lady of Nineveh, his lady: Sargon (II), presented (this object) for the sake of his life.

101

A tiny clay fragment in the Kuyunjik collection of the British Museum may bear an inscription recording the end of Sargon's first campaign (721) and the beginning of his second campaign (720); cf. text no. 1 lines 23–24. The piece was identified by W.G. Lambert (see Lambert, Cat. p. 69).

CATALOGUE

Museum Number	Provenance	Dimensions (cm)	cpn
K 22030	Probably Nineveh, Kuyunjik	1.7×1.4	c

TEXT

Lacuna
1′) [...] *x x* [...]
2′) [...] ⸢*ú*⸣-*še-šib*-⸢*šu*⸣-[*nu-ti* ...]

3′) [...] ⸢KUR⸣ *aš-šur* E LA ⸢A?⸣ [...]
4′) [... URU].⸢*qar*⸣-*qar* [...]
5′) [...] *x* [...]
Lacuna

Lacuna
1′–2′) [...] ... [...] I settled th[em ...]

3′–5′) [...] Assyria ... [... the city Q]arqar [...]

Lacuna

102

A fragment of one side of a clay tablet in the collection of the Oriental Institute, Chicago, preserves part of the end of an account of Sargon's conquest of Carchemish and the beginning of an account of the campaign against the Mannean Ullusunu. The inscription assigns these campaigns to Sargon's fourth and fifth regnal years respectively. It thus follows the numbering of the Aššur Prism (text no. 63) and the Nineveh Prism (text no. 82), rather than that of the Khorsabad Annals (text nos. 1 and 2) and the Najafabad Stele (text no. 117), which assign these to Sargon's fifth and sixth regnal years (717 and 716) respectively. For the dating of these campaigns, see the introduction to the present volume and Tadmor, JCS 12 (1958) pp. 23 and 94–95. H. Tadmor (ibid. p. 22) has suggested that the fragment "seems to be the only known specimen of Sargon's Annals on a clay-tablet." It is not impossible that the text originally on the tablet duplicated all or part what was on the Aššur and Nineveh prisms for these campaigns and all three were treated in A. Fuchs' recent edition (SAAS 8). Since no part of the text of this fragment overlaps any part of those prisms that is actually preserved and since this tablet is unlikely to have contained the whole text originally on either prism, it is treated separately from those texts here.

CATALOGUE

Museum Number	Provenance	Dimensions (cm)	cpn
A 16947	—	4.8×5.1×1.3	c

COMMENTARY

The provenance of the fragment is not known. H. Tadmor reports that the piece "was acquired in 1928 by the late Prof. Chiera from a local dealer in Mosul" (JCS 12 [1958] p. 22 n. 2). The piece may have come from the neighboring site of Nineveh, although this remains mere speculation. The inscription has been collated from the original and the restorations, for the most part, follow those proposed by H. Tadmor and A. Fuchs.

As noted in the introduction, the text on this fragment may be a duplicate of at least part of what was originally on the Nineveh and Aššur prisms. It would presumably have been found around the middle of the second column of the Nineveh prism (text no. 82 ii) and at some point above the first preserved column of the Assur prism (text no. 63 i′).

BIBLIOGRAPHY

1958 Tadmor, JCS 12 pp. 22–23, 26, and 100 (copy, edition, study)
1994 Fuchs, Khorsabad p. 386 (study)
1998 Fuchs, SAAS 8 pp. 3, 6, 8, 10, 22–23, 53–54, and pl. 1 (copy, edition, study)
2014 Maniori, Campagne di Sargon p. 40 A9 and passim (study)
2019 Marchesi, JNES 78 pp. 21–22 (lines 1′–14′, edition)

TEXT

Lacuna
1′) *x x x* [...]
2′) *a-mat* ⸢ḪUL⸣-[*ti ik-pu-ud*$^{?}$ *pa-a*$^{?}$ *e-da*$^{?}$]
3′) *ú-šá-áš-*[*kin-ma ik-ṣu-ra*$^{?}$ MÈ$^{?}$]
4′) *ia-a-ti* ⸢^{m}⸣[LUGAL-GI.NA ...]
5′) *da-ba-ab* [*sa-ar-ra-a-ti*$^{?}$]
6′) *at-me-e te-ke-e-ti* [*id-bu-ub-ma*]
7′) *ú-šá-aṣ-ri-iḫ* [*ka-bat-ti*$^{?}$]
8′) *šá-a-šu ga-du* [*qin-ni-šú*]
9′) DAM*-*su* DUMU.MEŠ-*šú* ⸢DUMU⸣.[MUNUS.MEŠ-*šú*]

Lacuna
1′) ... [...]
2′–3′) [*He plotted*] evil. He made (them) [*act in unison and he prepared for battle*].
4′–7′) [He spo]ke [*deceitfully*], words complaining about me, [Sargon ... and] *I became enr*[*aged*].
8′–14′) I threw him, together with [his family], his *wife*, his sons, (and) [his] d[aughters], in iron fetters, [and] I brought t[hem] to Assyria. I se[t] a eunuch [of

2′–3′ The restorations are based upon text no. 7 line 34 and text no. 63 i′ 14′.
5′ For the restoration, see text no. 82 vii 29′′ (K 1668b+).
6′ For *tēkītu/tēqītu*, see SAD 2 p. 81. For the restoration, see text no. 1 line 101 and text no. 7 line 38.
7′ Or *ú-šá-aṣ-ri-iḫ* [MÈ ...], "*He made preparations* [for battle ...]": see Tadmor, JCS 12 (1958) p. 22 and pp. 22–23 n. 7 and text no. 7 line 127.
8′–10′ Cf. text no. 1 line 73 and text no. 4 line 15′.
9′ DAM-: The text has SAL-LA-.

10′) *bi-re-tu* AN.BAR *ad-di-šu-[nu-ti-ma]*	mine] as provincial governor over the citizens of that city (and) [made (the city)] (part of) the territory of Assyria.
11′) *a-na qé-reb* KUR *aš-šur*.KI *ub-la-áš-[šú-nu-ti]*	
12′) UGU DUMU.MEŠ URU *šá-tu-nu* LÚ.*šu-ut* ⸢SAG⸣-*[ia]*	
13′) *a-na* LÚ.NAM-*ú-ti áš*-⸢*kun*⸣	
14′) *a-na mi-ṣir* KUR *aš-šur*.KI *[ú-ter-ra]*	
15′) *i-na* 5 BALA-*ia* ^{m}⸢*ul-lu*⸣-*[su-nu (x x)]*	15′) In my fifth regnal year, Ullu[sunu (...)]
Lacuna	Lacuna

103

A stone stele found in the vicinity of the modern city of Larnaca (ancient Kition) on the southern coast of Cyprus has a relief depicting Sargon II and an inscription of that ruler mentioning a number of military achievements, including victories over Urarṭu and Hamath, as well as his joyful entry into Babylon in 710. The inscription also describes the submission of rulers of the land Yāʾ and the erection of a stele in the land Adnana (Cyprus). The erection of (presumably) this stele is also mentioned in text no. 74 vii 39–44. Since the text refers to the king's third year (as ruler of Babylonia) (iv 21), the text must date to 707 or later. This inscription is often referred to as the Cyprus Stele, the Larnaca Stele, or the Kition Stele.

The discovery of this stele on Cyprus, the statement in it and several other inscriptions that seven kings of "the land of Yāʾ, a region of the land of Adnana (or Yadnana), situated in the middle of the Western Sea," had brought gifts to Sargon in Babylon when they had heard of his actions in the lands of Chaldea and Ḫatti (iv 28–42), statements in some other inscriptions that Sargon had subdued those kings (e.g., text no. 9 lines 27–29), and a possible understanding of passages in Sargon's Annals from Rooms II and V (text no. 1 lines 456b–467a and text no. 2 lines 436b–441a), have allowed some scholars to argue that Sargon sent soldiers to Cyprus to help Silṭa, the king of Tyre, put down a rebellion there by some of the latter's vassals and that the seven kings had sent their gifts to Sargon at some point following that event (see in particular Naʾaman, Orientalia 67 [1998] pp. 239–247 and CRRA 45/1 pp. 357–363). Since the passages in Sargon's Annals are poorly preserved, Sargon's exact actions vis-à-vis Silṭa and Cyprus remain uncertain. Whether or not a body of Assyrian troops ever went to Cyprus, it is quite reasonable to assume that some Cypriot rulers had sent gifts to Sargon in order to win his friendship since Assyria controlled Phoenicia, a major trading partner for Cyprus and the ancestral home of some of the people living there, and that Sargon had at some point sent an envoy, likely accompanied by a military escort or bodyguards, to Cyprus. There is no need to assume that Assyrian troops carried out actual military actions on Cyprus — whether in support of Silṭa or not — or that Assyria annexed any city located on Cyprus. Naʾaman's claim that "Sargon conquered Cyprus about 707 B.C.E." (CRRA 45/1 p. 357) cannot be accepted without serious reservations.

An important study by Radner on the erection and purpose of this stele — the only Assyrian artifact discovered up to now on Cyprus — is found in Rollinger, Interkulturalität pp. 429–449; B.N. Porter presents a study of the audiences for the stele in Studies Fales, pp. 669–675.

102 line 14′ For the restoration, see for example text no. 1 lines 103 and 163, text no. 2 lines 98 and 191–192, and text no. 8 lines 11 and 26.

CATALOGUE

Museum Number	Provenance	Dimensions (cm)	cpn
VA 968	Cyprus, southern part of ancient Kition	209×68.5×32–33	c

COMMENTARY

The exact date of discovery and provenance of the stele are matters of scholarly discussion. Local workmen apparently discovered it in 1845 (sometimes said to be 1844) near Larnaca on Cyprus. Most publications state that it was found in ruins to the west of the harbor of ancient Kition, thus at the site of Bamboula (see for example Yon in Caubet, Khorsabad pp. 161–168; and Radner in Rollinger, Interkulturalität pp. 429–430), but, following a thorough study of the early reports about its discovery, R. Merrillees has recently argued that it "was found in the southern part of ancient Kition, possibly on or near a mound in the south-western corner of the wall encircling the city" (Studies Hermary p. 378). It is also uncertain where the stele was originally erected; see iv 52–53 and the on-page notes to those lines. (With regard to where Assyrian steles were set up in general, see Frame, Subartu 18 pp. 61–63.)

The stele is in the Vorderasiatisches Museum, having been purchased in 1846. It is now 32–33 cm thick, but an additional ca. 13 cm had been cut away from the back of the stele, likely in order to lighten it for shipment to Berlin; thus, the cuneiform signs of the inscription that were at the end of right side (col. ii) and beginning of left side (col. iv) are now missing, as well as anything written on the back face (col. iii). The line arrangement assumes that the inscription began on the front of the stele (col. i) and carried on to the right (col. ii), back (col. iii, missing), and left (col. iv) sides respectively. Since col. ii ends at a textually logical point and col. iv begins at a textually logical point, it is not impossible that the back of the stele had not been inscribed and that this encouraged someone to remove it to lighten the weight of the object. Thus, what is given here as col. iv may really have been col. iii. However, based on other Neo-Assyrian steles, we would certainly expect the back to have been inscribed and we would also expect an account of the Assyrian campaign against Marduk-apla-iddina II (Merodach-Baladan) of Babylonia to precede the account of Sargon's joyful entry into Babylon, which is found at the start of the left side (col. iv) of the stele. The inscription was collated from the original, with some additional collations provided by J. Marzahn. Squeezes of col. iv preserved in the British Museum were also examined. Col. i is badly worn and the traces of the inscription are in places obscured by the relief. Thus, at times the copy published by Ungnad is the basis for the transliteration.

The stele is said to be made of black basalt (or gabbro), a stone that can be found on Cyprus in the Troodos massif. However, citing two scholars who have worked on the petrographic analysis of materials from Cyprus (C. Elliott and C. Xenophontoa), Merrillees states that "no block of vesicular basalt the size of the Sargon stele could have been mined in Cyprus, whereas, for example, volcanic deposits in north Syria were evidently suited for the purpose" (Studies Hermary p. 378). He thus hypothesizes that the stele was quarried and carved on the mainland and then sent by boat to Cyprus, although noting that a scientific analysis of the stone of the stele needs to be made.

The relief on the front of the stele depicts the king facing right, holding a mace in his left hand, and raising his right hand. Eight symbols representing various deities are carved in front of the face of the king: a horned crown (Aššur), a crescent moon (Sîn), a star (Ištar), lightning bolts (Adad), a spade (Marduk), a stylus (Nabû), seven circles (the Sebetti), and a winged sun disk (Šamaš). These same deities are invoked at the beginning of the inscription.

The text is written in Babylonian dialect using a mixture of Assyrian sign forms and archaizing Babylonian sign forms. Several passages similar to parts of i 1–25 may be found in Grayson, RIMA 2 pp. 12–13 A.0.87.1 i 1–16, text no. 116 lines 1–10, and text no. 117 i 1–19. For ii 22–65, see text no. 84 lines 12′–20′. For iv 1–42, see text no. 7 lines 140–149 and for iv 11–42, see text no. 74 vii 7–38 (with some significant divergences); see also text no. 86 lines 17′–18′ and text no. 87 lines 15′–21′.

BIBLIOGRAPHY

1846 Ross, Hellenika pp. 69–70 and pl. I (drawing of relief, study)
1854 de Longpérier, Notice^{3} no. 617 (study)
1870 3 R pl. 11 (ii, iv, copy)
1871 G. Smith, ZÄS 9 pp. 68–72 (ii, iv, edition)
1874 Ménant, Annales pp. 206–208 (ii, iv, translation)
1878 Schrader, Keilinschriften und Geschichtsforschung pp. 244–246 (study)
1880 Ménant, Manuel pp. 323–327 (ii 1–21, copy, edition)
1881 Delitzsch, Wo lag das Paradies p. 178 (iv 23–25, transcription, translation, study)
1882 Schrader, Sargonsstele (ii, iv, photo; i, copy; edition, study, provenance)
1886 Bezold, Literatur p. 91 §53.9 (study)
1889 Winckler, Sar. 1 pp. 174–185; and 2 pls. 46–47 (copy; ii, iv, edition)
1893 von Luschan, Ausgrabungen in Sendschirli 1 pp. 20–21, Abb. 5 (drawing, study)
1907 Ungnad, VAS 1 no. 71 (copy; i 1–28, transliteration)
1908 Olmstead, Western Asia pp. 10–11 n. 41 (study)
1911 Zimmern, ZA 25 pp. 196–199 (study)
1912 Thureau-Dangin, TCL 3 p. 21 n. 3 (i 2, study)
1915 Meissner, AO 15 p. 125 and fig. 213 (photo of relief)
1920 Meissner, BuA 1 pl. 36 (photo of relief)
1926 Ebeling in Gressman, ATAT^{2} p. 350 (ii 51–65, translation)
1927 Gressman, ABAT^{2} p. 45 and pl. LIX fig. 135 (photo of relief)
1927 Luckenbill, ARAB 2 pp. 100–103 §§179–189 (translation)
1936 Gadd, Stones p. 214 (study)
1938 Tallqvist, Götterepitheta p. 73 (i 8–9, study)
1945–46 J. Lewy, HUCA 19 pp. 466–467 (iv 32–33, study)
1956 Borger, Asarh. p. 87 commentary to rev. 3 and p. 109 commentary to iv 18f (iv 45–46, 74, study)
1965 Genge, Stelen pp. 15–17, 119–123, 160–162, and 268–272 (edition)
1969 Oppenheim, ANET^{3} p. 284 (ii 51–65, iv 28–42, translation)
1971 Nicolaou, Cypriot Inscribed Stones p. 10 and pl. 3 (photo of front and sides; iv 36–53, translation)
1972 Levine, Stelae p. 53 (study)
1973 Katzenstein, Tyre pp. 239–241 (study)
1976 Saporetti, Studi Ciprioti e Rapporti di Scavo 2 pp. 84–85 (iv 28–53, translation, study)
1979 Elayi and Cavigneaux, OrAnt 18 p. 64 (iv 52–53, edition)
1982 Börker-Klähn, Bildstelen no. 175 (drawing of relief, study)
1982 Spieckermann, Juda unter Assur p. 317 (ii 61–65, edition)
1984 Borger, TUAT 1/4 pp. 385–386 (ii 51–65, translation)
1990 Pomponio, Formule p. 43 no. 46 (iv 63–74, translation)
1990 Potts, Arabian Gulf 1 p. 335 no. 7 (iv 23–27, translation)
1993 Wartke, Urartu pl. 22 (photo of relief)
1994 Fuchs, Khorsabad p. 386 (study)
1994 Reyes, Archaic Cyprus pp. 50–56 and pl. 2 (photo of relief; iv 28–53, translation [by S. Dalley]; study)
1994 Yon in Vandenabeele and Laffineur, Cypriote Stone Sculpture pp. 91–96 and pl. XXIVa–b (photo, drawing, study)
1995 Malbran-Labat in Caubet, Khorsabad pp. 169–179 (iv 28–74, translation; study)
1995 Yon in Caubet, Khorsabad pp. 161–168 (photo of relief, study, provenance)
1996 Tadmor, Eretz-Israel 25 pp. 286–289 (iv 43–57, translation; iv 52–53, study) [in Hebrew]
1999 Frame, Orientalia 68 pp. 41–48 (study)
1999 Tadmor, CRRA 44/1 p. 57 (iv 28–42, translation)
2001 Na'aman, CRRA 45/1 pp. 358 and 361–363 (iv 28–42, translation [composite]; iv 43–57, translation)
2004 Hawkins, Studies Grayson p. 161 ii 51–56 (edition)
2004 Lipiński, Itineraria Phoenicia pp. 29, 46, and 50–53 (study)
2004 Malbran-Labat in Yon, Kition dans les textes pp. 345–354 (photo, edition, study)
2006 Frame, Subartu 18 pp. 53–55 (drawing, study)
2008 Cogan, Raging Torrent pp. 98–100 no. 23 (ii 51–65, translation, study)
2008 J.S. Smith in Sagona, Beyond the Homeland pp. 267–270 (study)
2009 Anthonioz, L'eau pp. 137–139 (iv 23–39a, translation; study)
2010 Radner in Rollinger, Interkulturalität pp. 429–449 (photo; iv 23–42, 57–74 translation; study)
2012 Porter, Studies Fales pp. 669–675 (study)
2014 Galter, CRRA 52 pp. 334 and 336–337 (study)
2014 Maniori, Campagne di Sargon pp. 52–53 g8 and passim (study)
2014 Marzahn, Assyria to Iberia p. 187 no. 74 (photo of relief; iv 43–57, translation; study)
2016 Merrillees, Studies Hermary pp. 349–386 (study)
2016 Van De Mieroop, JAH 4 p. 21 (ii 42–50, translation)
2017 Liverani, Assyria pp. 97 and 205 (ii 23–27, iv 43–57, translation)
2018 Frahm, Last Days pp. 79–80 no. 13 (ii 51–65, edition, study [combined with text nos. 84 and 105])
2018 Kiely in Brereton, Ashurbanipal pp. 138 and. 140–141 no. 148 (photo; ii 1–3 and iv 28–42, translation)

TEXT

Col. i

1) ^{d}*aš-šur* ⸢EN GAL-*ú*⸣ [LUGAL$^{?}$ KIŠ$^{?}$] ^{d}*í-*⸢*gì-gì u* ^{d}⸣A.NUN.NA
2) *a-lid gim-ri* [AD$^{?}$ DINGIR$^{?}$].MEŠ ⸢EN*⸣ KUR.KUR
3) ^{d}30 ⸢ŠEŠ$^{?}$⸣.[KI$^{?}$-*ri*$^{?}$ ...] ⸢*e-tel*⸣ AN-*e ù* KI-*tim*
4) *mu-*[*ḫi*$^{?}$*-iṭ*$^{?}$] *ṣa-*⸢*al*$^{?}$*-pat*$^{?}$⸣ *na-*⸢*ki*$^{?}$*-ru*$^{?}$⸣

i 1–23) The god Aššur, the great lord, [*king of all*] the Igīgū gods and Anunnakū gods, begetter of everything, [*father of the god*]s, lord of the lands; the god Sîn, *lig*[*ht* ...] lord of heaven and netherworld, who [*espies*] *the treachery of the enemy*, (i 5) who renders [...] decisions

---

i 2 For the restoration, see for example text no. 7 lines 124, 167, and 187. Or possibly [LUGAL DINGIR.MEŠ GAL].MEŠ, "[king of the great god]s"; according to J. Marzahn (personal communication), there is room for the longer restoration. ⸢EN*⸣: The copy has ⸢^{d}EN⸣.
i 3 Or possibly ⸢LUGAL⸣ [UB.MEŠ ...], "king [of (all) the regions (of the world) ...]" (Genge, Stelen p. 15).
i 4 For the tentative restoration, see Genge, Stelen p. 15 and cf. Grayson, RIMA 2 p. 12 A.0.87.1 i 7–8.

5) KUD-*is* [(*x*)] *x* [*x* (*x*)] ⸢EŠ.BAR-*e* KI$^{?}$⸣-[*tim mu*$^{?}$]-⸢*ḫal*$^{?}$-*liq*$^{?}$⸣ [*na*$^{?}$]-*ki*$^{?}$-⸢*ru*⸣
6) ^{d}UTU [DI$^{?}$.KU$_5$$^{?}$] ⸢GAL$^{?}$-*ú*$^{?}$⸣ [*x*] *x* [*x x* (*x*)] ⸢RU⸣
7) *mu*-[*x x* (*x*)] ⸢ŠÁ⸣ [(*x*)] *x* [(*x*)] ⸢*ṣa-al-pat*⸣ [(*x*)] *lem-ni*
8) *ù* [*x x*] *a-a-bi mu*-⸢*še-eb*⸣-[*ru ṣe*]-*ni*
9) ^{d}IŠKUR ⸢NUN$^{?}$ GAL⸣ [(*x*)] *ur*-⸢*šá*⸣-[*nu gú-gal*]-*lu*
10) *ra-ḫi-iṣ kib*-⸢*rat*⸣ *x x* E *mu*-⸢*sa*⸣-[*an-bi*]-*i*ʾ
11) *ta*-⸢*ma-a*⸣-*ti* ^{d}⸢AMAR⸣.[UTU] EN *x* [*x x*] BI
12) *e-pir kiš-šat* UN.MEŠ [*x*] *x x* [...]
13) *x x x x* ⸢KIR$^{?}$⸣ [...]
14) *šá-ri-ku* ⸢*šam*⸣-[*mi*$^{?}$ ...]
15) ^{d}AG IBILA [*gít-ma-lu*$^{?}$ (*x x*)] ⸢KUR$^{?}$⸣ [*x* (*x x x*)]
16) [(*x*)] *x x* [(*x x*)]
17) [(*x x*) *x* KUR$^{?}$].⸢MEŠ⸣ *zaq-ru-te*
18) (*x*) ⸢*na-si*$^{?}$-*iḫ*$^{?}$ *la*⸣ *ma-gi-ri*
19) (*x*) *x* (*x*) *x* IB ⸢*šur*⸣-*uš za-ma-ni*
20) ^{d}⸢*iš*⸣-*tar* ⸢*šar*$^{?}$-*ra*$^{?}$-*at*$^{?}$⸣ *a-nun-ti*
21) (*x*) ⸢KA$^{?}$⸣ *x* ⸢TA⸣ *x* ⸢RU$^{?}$ SA$^{?}$⸣ A ḪI *x* ⸢*tar*⸣-*gi*$_4$-*gi*$_4$
22) ^{d}⸢IMIN⸣.BI ⸢*a-li-kut ma-ḫar* DINGIR⸣.MEŠ *ša a-šar šá-áš-mi*
23) *i-di* ⸢LUGAL⸣ *mi*-⸢*ig*$^{?}$⸣-*ri*-⸢*šú-nu*⸣ *i-za*-⸢*zu*⸣-*ma i*-⸢*šak-ka*⸣-*nu* NÍG.⸢È⸣-[(*šú*)]
24) DINGIR.MEŠ GAL.MEŠ *mut-tab-bi-lu*-⸢*ut* AN-*e ù*⸣ KI-*tim*
25) *ša ti-bu-šu*-⸢*nu tu-qu-un-tú*⸣ *ù šá*-⸢*áš*⸣-*mu*
26) ⸢*na*⸣-*šu-ú* ⸢*e*⸣-*ni na-bu*-⸢*ú*⸣ *šu-um* LUGAL
27) *ša ina e-peš* KA-⸢*šú-nu el*$^{?}$-*li*⸣ KUR ⸢UGU⸣ KUR
28) *i-šak-ka-nu-ma ú-šar-bu-ú* [UGU] *mal-ki*

Col. ii
1) ^{m}LUGAL-GI.NA MAN GAL-*ú* [MAN *dan-nu*]
2) LUGAL ŠÚ MAN KUR *aš-šur*.KI GÌR.NÍTA ⸢KÁ⸣.[DINGIR.RA.KI]
3) MAN KUR EME.GI$_7$ *u* URI.KI MAN *kib*-⸢*rat*⸣ [LÍMMU-*i*]
4) *mi-gir* DINGIR.MEŠ GAL.MEŠ *a-x* [*x x*]

for the *ea*[*rth*] (and) *destroys* [*the en*]*emy*; the god Šamaš, [*the*] *gr*[*eat judge* ...], who [...] the treachery of the evil and ... of the foe, (and) exp[oses the vil]lain; the god Adad, the great *prince*, her[o, canal inspect]or, (i 10) who devastates regions ... (and) makes the seas h[ea]ve; the god Mar[duk], the lord [...], who provides all people with food, [...] ... [...], (and) grants *pl*[*ants* ...]; (i 15) the god Nabû, the [*perfect*] heir, [...] ... [...] high [*mountain*]s, *who rem*[*oves*] the uncompliant (and) ... the roots of the enemy; (i 20) the goddess Ištar, *queen* of battle, ... evil-doers; (and) the Sebetti, who go before the gods, stand at the side of the king, their favorite, in the place of battle, and [bri]ng about (his) victory;

i 24–28) Great gods, managers of heaven and netherworld, whose attack means battle and strife, who appoint (rulers) (lit.: "raise the eyes") (and) name king(s), (and) by whose *holy* command they place (one) land over (another) land and make (its ruler) greater [than] (other) rulers.

ii 1–4) Sargon (II), great king, [strong king], king of the world, king of Assyria, governor of B[abylon], king of the land of Sumer and Akkad, king of the [four] quarters (of the world), favorite of the great gods, ... [...].

---

i 6 Following Genge, Stelen p. 15, Malbran-Labat in Yon, Kition dans les textes p. 345 reads, ^{d}UTU [DI.KU$_5$$^{?}$ GAL-*ú*$^{?}$ *ša*$^{?}$ AN-*e*$^{?}$ DINGIR-*u*$^{?}$] ⸢*ga*⸣-*aš-ru*, "Šamaš, [*le grande juge céleste, le dieu*] puissant."

i 7 Following Genge, Stelen p. 15, Malbran-Labat in Yon, Kition dans les textes p. 345 reads, *mu*-⸢*ḫi*⸣-[*i-ṭu*$^{?}$ *šá*$^{?}$ *ṣa-al-pat*$^{?}$] *lem-ni*, "celui qui *per*[*ce à jour les perfidies*] du méchant."

i 10–11 Cf. Grayson, RIMA 2 p. 12 A.0.87.1 i 9–10 *ra-ḫi-iṣ kib-rat* KÚR.MEŠ KUR.MEŠ AB.MEŠ-*ti*, "who storms over hostile regions, mountains, (and) seas."

i 13 Genge, Stelen p. 15 (partially followed by Malbran-Labat in Yon, Kition dans les textes p. 346) tentatively suggests *mu-šar-bu-u* LUGAL-*ti-ia*, "the one who makes great my kingship," based on Leichty, RINAP 4 p. 182 no. 98 line 8.

i 14 The tentative restoration follows CAD Š/2 p. 45. Perhaps instead ⸢Ú⸣.[ḪI.A.(MEŠ) ...]; see text no. 65 line 187 and text no. 2 line 406.

i 15 For *aplu gitmālu*, see text no. 116 line 4. Or IBILA [*ke-e-nu*]; see Tallqvist, Götterepitheta p. 30. Genge, Stelen pp. 16 and 161 tentatively suggests IBILA [SAG *šá é-sag-íl*], "[eldest] offspring [of Esagila]".

i 16–19 The lines are quite short and the suggestion that another god may have been mentioned between Nabû (i 15) and Ištar (i 20) (Frame, Orientalia 68 [1999] p. 42) seems unlikely.

i 17 Possibly [*mu-lat-ti* KUR].⸢MEŠ⸣ *zaq-ru-te*, "[who splits/crushes the] high [mountain]s"; see 4 R pl. 26 no. 3:40 and cf. Genge, Stelen p.16 and Malbran-Labat in Yon, Kition dans les textes p. 346.

i 19 Possibly ⸢*ša/šá-li*⸣-*ip* ⸢*šur*⸣-*uš za-ma-ni*, "who tears out the roots of the enemy" (Genge, Stelen p. 16).

i 20 Cf. *mu-šak-ṣi*-⸢*rat*$^{?}$⸣ *a*-⸢*nun*$^{?}$-*ti*$^{?}$⸣, "*who makes (men) ready for battle*" in text no. 116 line 7.

i 21 H. Genge (Stelen p. 16) tentatively suggests *sa-pi-nat tar-gi*$_4$-*gi*$_4$, "who overthrows evil-doers."

i 22–23 See text no. 116 line 8.

ii 4 The traces do not seem to fit *a*-⸢*na*⸣-[*ku*], "I." Following H. Winckler (Sar. 1 p. 174), possibly *a*-⸢*li*⸣-[*kut maḫ-ri-ia*], "who g[o before me]," but while the traces after A could fit the beginning of a LI sign, it is not clear that there would be sufficient room for the full restoration proposed. H. Genge (Stelen p. 17) suggests *za*-[*nin é-sag-íl*], thus "one who pro[vides for Esagila]," but the first sign is clearly A not ZA and the following traces would not fit the beginning of NIN.

5) ^{d}*aš-šur* ^{d}AG ^{d}[AMAR.UTU]
6) LUGAL-*ut la šá-na-an ú-šat-*⌜*li*⌝-[*mu-ni-ma*]
7) *zi-kir* MU-*ia* [SIG$_5$]
8) *ú-še-ṣu-ú a-na* ⌜*re*⌝-[*še-e-ti*]
9) *ša* ZIMBIR.KI NIBRU.KI ⌜KÁ⌝.[DINGIR.RA.KI]
10) ⌜*za*⌝-*nin-us-su-un e*-[*tep-pu-šá*]
11) *ša* ERIM.MEŠ *ki-din-ni mal* ⌜*ba*⌝-[*šu-ú*]
12) *ḫi-bil-*⌜*ta*⌝*-šú-nu* ⌜*a*⌝-[*rib-ma*]
13) *ú-šá-áš-ši-ik tup-šik-ki* ⌜BÀD⌝.[AN.KI]
14) ŠEŠ.UNUG.KI UNUG.KI *eri*-[*du*$_{10}$.KI]
15) *la-ar-sa*.KI *kul*-[*aba*$_4$.KI]
16) *ki-sik*.KI URU.*né-med*-^{d}⌜*la*⌝-[*gu-da*]
17) *ú-šap-ši-ḫa* UN.⌜MEŠ⌝-[*šú-un*]
18) ⌜*za*⌝-*ku-ut bal-til*.KI *u* URU.[*ḫar-ra-na*]
19) *ša ul-tu* UD.MEŠ *ru*-[*qu-(ú)-ti*]
20) *im-ma-šú-ma ki-din-nu-su-un* [*ba-ṭil-ta*]
21) *ú-ter áš-ru*-[*uš-šá*]
22) *ina tukul-ti* DINGIR.MEŠ GAL.MEŠ *lu at*-[*tal-lak-ma*]
23) UN.MEŠ ÍD.*mar-ra-ti* ⌜*e*⌝-[*li-ti*]
24) *a-di* ÍD.*mar-ra-ti* ⌜*šap*⌝-[*li-ti*]
25) *ki-*⌜*i*⌝ *iš-tén a-*⌜*bel*⌝-[*ma*]
26) *ul-*⌜*tu* KUR⌝.*mu-uṣ-ri a-di* KUR.[*mu-uš-ki*]
27) *ú-šak-ni-šá še-pu-u*$_8$-*a* ⌜*ú*⌝-[*par-ri-ir*]
28) *el-lat* ^{md}*ḫum-ba-ni-ga-áš* LÚ.[ELAM.MA.KI]
29) *ú-ab-*⌜*bit*⌝ KUR.*kar-al-la* KUR.[*šur-da*]
30) URU.*ki-še-si-im* ⌜URU⌝.[*ḫar-ḫar*]
31) KUR.*ma-da-a-a* KUR.*el*-[*li-pi*]
32) *la e-zi-bu pe-re*-[*ʾi-šú-nu*]
33) ⌜UN⌝.MEŠ KUR.*ḫat-ti ki-šit-*⌜*ti*⌝ [ŠU.II-*ia*]
34) ⌜*qé*⌝-*reb-šun ú-še-ši-ba* LÚ.⌜*šu*⌝-[*ut* SAG.MEŠ-*ia*]
35) ⌜*a*⌝-*na* LÚ.NAM-*ú-ti* UGU-*šú-nu* ⌜*áš*⌝-[*kun-ma*]
36) *ú-šal-di-da ab*-[*šá-a-ni*]
37) *ú-šak-niš* KUR.*man-na*-[*a-a*]
38) ⌜KUR⌝.*an-di-a* KUR.*zi-*⌜*kir*⌝-[*tu*]
39) [^{m}]*ur-za-na* MAN URU.*mu-ṣa-ṣir a-di* [UN.MEŠ KUR-*šú*]
40) ^{d}⌜*ḫal*⌝-*di-a* ^{d}*ba-ag-bar-*⌜*tu*⌝ [DINGIR.MEŠ-*šú*]
41) *a-na šal-la-ti* ⌜*am*?⌝-[*nu-šu*]
42) [KUR].*ur-ar-ṭu a-na paṭ* [*gim-ri-šá*]
43) [*ú*]-*šá-áš-šá-a nag-la-ba* [...]
44) [UN].MEŠ ⌜*a*⌝-*šib* ŠÀ-*šú a-na ár*-[*kát u*$_4$-*me*]
45) [*e-mì*]-⌜*da*⌝ *si-pit-tu u* [*ṣer-ḫa*]
46) [*di*]-⌜*ik*?⌝-*ti* ^{m}*ur-sa-a* KUR.[*ur-ar-ṭa-a-a*]
47) [*ina*] ⌜KUR⌝.*ú-a-uš* KUR-*i mar-ṣi* [*áš-kun-ma*]
48) ⌜*ta*⌝-*ḫa-zi dan-nu e-*⌜*du*⌝-[*ur-ma*]
49) *ina* ŠU.II *rama-ni-šú ina* GÍR.AN.BAR [*šib-bi-šú*]

ii 5–8) The gods Aššur, Nabû, (and) [Marduk] gra[nted me] a reign without equal [and] exalted my [good] reputation to the h[eights].

ii 9–21) I [continually acted] as provider for (the cities) Sippar, Nippur, (and) B[abylon] (and) I [made restitution] for the wrongful damage suffered by the people of privileged status, as many as [there were (of them)]; I abolished corvée duty for (the cities) D[ēr], Ur, Uruk, Eri[du], (ii 15) Larsa, Kul[laba], Kissik, (and) Nēmed-L[aguda] (and) gave relief to [their] people. I restor[ed] the exemption (from obligations) of (the city) Baltil (Aššur) and the city [Ḫarrān], which had fallen into oblivion in the dis[tant] past, and their privileged status [that had lapsed].

ii 22–50) With the support of the great gods, I ad[vanced and] ru[led] the people (from) the Up[per] Sea to the Lo[wer] Sea as if (they were) one (people). From Egypt to the land [Musku], I made (them) bow down at my feet. I [dispersed] the forces of Ḫumbanigaš (Ḫumban-nikaš I), the [Elamite]. I destroyed the land Karalla, the land [Šurda], (ii 30) the city Kišesim, the city [Ḫarḫar], the land Media, (and) the land El[lipi]; I did not spare any of [their] offspring. I settled in their midst people from the land Ḫatti (Syria) that [I] had conquered. (ii 35) I [set] e[unuchs of mine] as provincial governors over them [and] had (them) pull [my] y[oke]. I subjugated the lands Mannea, Andia, (and) Zik[irtu]. I [counted] as booty Urzana, king of the city Muṣaṣir, together with [the people of his land (ii 40) (and) his deities] Ḫaldi (and) Bagbartu. [I] had (the people of) [the land] Urarṭu, to [its full] extent, wield razor(s) [...]. (ii 45) [I imp]osed for the fu[ture] lamentation and [dirge (singing) upon the people] who lived there. [I brought about the defe]at of Ursâ (Rusâ), the [Urarṭian, at Mou]nt Uauš, a rugged mountain. He to[ok fright at] (engaging in) fierce battle with me [and] by his own hands, [he brought an end to] his life with the iron dagger [from his belt].

---

ii 18 For the restoration, see text no. 7 line 10 and text no. 8 line 5.

ii 36 F. Malbran-Labat (in Yon, Kition dans les textes p. 347) suggests *ab*-[*šá-an* ^{d}*aš-šur*?], "le j[oug *d'Aššur*]."

ii 39 For the restoration, see text no. 84 line 15′. Or, following F. Malbran-Labat (in Yon, Kition dans les textes p. 347), possibly *a-di* [*kim-ti-šú*], i.e., "together with [his family]." There may not be sufficient room at the end of the line to restore either of the proposed readings.

ii 43 With regard to the use of the razor, see the note to text no. 1 line 369. Text no. 84 line 16′ has here [...]-*at-te ù ṣur-ri*, "[...] ... and flint blades." Possibly restore [*ú-ša-aṣ-riḫ*], "[(and) utter cries (of mourning)]"; see Malbran-Labat in Yon, Kition dans les textes p. 347.

ii 44 F. Malbran-Labat (in Yon, Kition dans les textes p. 347) suggests *a-na ár*-[*ni-šú-nu*?], i.e., "for [*their*] *cri*[*mes*]," instead of *a-na ár*-[*kát u*$_4$-*me*], "for the fu[ture]."

ii 46 There appear to be fewer traces of the sign before TI than copied by A. Ungnad (VAS 1 no. 71); collation would suggest that they could be the end of IG.

50) *na-piš-ta-šú ú-[qat-ti]*
51) KUR.*a-ma-at-tu a-na* ⸢*pat gim*⸣-[*ri-šá*]
52) *a-bu-biš as*-⸢*pu*⸣-[*un*]
53) ⸢^{m}⸣^{d}*ia-ú-bi-iʾ-di* ⸢LUGAL⸣-[*šú-nu*]
54) *a-di kim-ti-šú* LÚ.*mun-dah-*⸢*ṣe*⸣-[*šú*]
55) *šal-lat* KUR-*šú ka-mu-*⸢*us*⸣-[*su-(nu)*]
56) *a-na* KUR *aš-šur*.KI ⸢*ub*⸣-[*la*]
57) 3 ME GIŠ.GIGIR.MEŠ 6 ME ANŠE.*pét-*[*hal-lum*]
58) *na-áš* GIŠ.*ka-ba-bi* GIŠ.*az-ma-*[*re-e*]
59) *i-na lìb-bi-šú-nu ak-*[*ṣur-ma*]
60) UGU *ki-ṣir* MAN-*ti-ia ú-*[*rad-di*]
61) ⸢6⸣ LIM 3 ME LÚ.*aš-šur-a-a* EN ⸢*hi*⸣-[*iṭ-ṭi*]
62) *ina qé-reb* KUR.*ha-am-ma-ti ú-*[*še-šib-ma*]
63) LÚ.*šu-ut* SAG-*ia* LÚ.⸢EN⸣.[NAM]
64) UGU-*šú-nu áš-kun-ma bíl-tu* ⸢*ma*⸣-[*da-(at)-tu*]
65) *ú-kin* UGU-*šú-*[*nu*]

ii 51–65) Like the Deluge, I overwhe[lmed] the land Hamath to [its] fu[ll] extent. I [brought their] ki[ng] Iaū-biʾdī (Ilu-biʾdī) to Assyria in bondage, together with his family, [his] fighting men, (ii 55) (and) the booty of his land. I cons[cripted] from among them 300 chariots, 600 cav[alry], (and) shield (and) spe[ar] bearers, and] I [added] (them) to my royal contingent. I [settled] 6,300 Assyrian cri[minals] in the land Hamath; I set a eunuch of mine as [provincial] gov[ernor] over them and imposed upon th[em] (the delivery of) tribute (and) pa[yment(s)].

Col. iii
Missing or not preserved.

Missing or not preserved.

Col. iv
1) [*a-na* KÁ.DINGIR].RA.KI *ma-haz* ^{d}EN.LÍL DINGIR.MEŠ
2) [*i-na e*]-⸢*le*⸣-*eṣ lìb-bi ù nu-mur pa-ni*
3) [*ha-diš*] *e-ru-um-ma*
4) [ŠU.II EN] ⸢GAL⸣-*e* ^{d}AMAR.UTU *aṣ-bat-ma*
5) [*ú-šal*]-⸢*li*⸣-*ma ú-ru-uh* É *á-ki-ti*
6) [1 ME 54] ⸢GUN⸣ 26 MA.NA 6-*su* KÙ.GI
7) [*huš-šu-ú*] 1 LIM 8 ME 4 GUN 20 MA.NA
8) [KÙ.BABBAR *eb-bu*] *bi-lat* URUDU.HI.A *par-zil-li*
9) [*ša la*] ⸢*i*⸣-*šu-ú ni-ba-šú-un*
10) [NA$_4$.ZÚ] ⸢NA$_4$⸣.ZA.GÌN NA$_4$.BABBAR.DILI NA$_4$.MUŠ.GÍR
11) [NA$_4$.AŠ.GÌ.GÌ] ⸢NA$_4$⸣.UGU.AŠ.GÌ.GÌ *di-gíl* NA$_4$.BABBAR.DILI
12) [NA$_4$.MUŠ].⸢GÍR⸣ *ša ni-ba la i-šu-ú*
13) [SÍG.*ta*]-⸢*kil*?⸣-*tu* SÍG.*ar-ga-ma-nu*
14) [*lu-bul-ti*] *bir-me ù* GADA
15) [GIŠ.*tas-ka*]-⸢*rin*⸣-*nu* GIŠ.*ere-nu* GIŠ.ŠUR.MÌN
16) [*ka-la*] ⸢*ri*⸣-*iq-qi bi-ib-lat* KUR.*ha-ma-ni*
17) [*ša e*]-⸢*ri*⸣-*su-un ṭa-a-bu*
18) [*a-na* ^{d}]EN *u* ^{d}NUMUN-DÙ-*ti* ^{d}AG
19) [^{d}*taš-me*]-⸢*tum*⸣ *ù* DINGIR.MEŠ *a-ši-bu-ut*
20) [*ma-ha-zi*] KUR EME.GI$_7$ *u* URI.KI
21) [*ul-tu* SAG] MAN-*ti-ia a-di* 3 MU.MEŠ
22) [*ú-qa*]-⸢*i*⸣-*šá qí-šá-a-ti*

iv 1–22) [Happily, with a jo]yful heart and a radiant face, I entered [Babyl]on, the cult center of the Enlil of the gods (Marduk); I grasped hold of [the hands of the gre]at [lord], the god Marduk, and (iv 5) [brought] (him) safely along the road to the *akītu*-house. [(With regard to) 154] talents, 26 and 1/6 minas of [red] gold, 1,804 talents (and) 20 minas [of pure silver], (*donkey*) *loads* of copper (and) iron [in im]measurable quantities, (iv 10) [obsidian], lapis-lazuli, *banded agate*, *muššaru*-stone, [*blue turquoise*], *green turquoise*, ... *of banded agate* [(and) *mušša*]*ru*-[stone] in immeasurable quantities, [blue-pur]ple [wool], red-purple wool, [garments] with multi-colored trim and linen (garments), (iv 15) [boxw]ood, cedar, cypress, [(and) every kind of] aromatic, the products of Mount Amanus, [who]se [sce]nt(s) are pleasant — [from the beginning] of my reign until (my) third year, [I pres]ented (these items) as gifts [to the] deities Bēl and Zarpanītu, Nabû, [Tašmēt]u, and the (other) gods who dwell in [the cult centers] of the land of Sumer and Akkad.

23) [^{m}*ú-pe-e*]-⸢*ri*⸣ LUGAL *dil-mun*.KI *šá ma-lak* 30 KASKAL.GÍD
24) [*ina* MURUB$_4$ *tam*]-⸢*tim*⸣ *ša ni-pi-ih* ^{d}UTU-*ši*
25) [GIM KU$_6$ *šit*]-*ku-nu nar-ba-ṣu*

iv 23–27) [Upēr]i, king of Dilmun, who(se) lair is [sit]uated at a distance of thirty leagues [in the middle of the] Eastern [Se]a, [like that of a fish, heard of the might] of the gods Aššur, Nabû, (and) Marduk and sent

ii 51 The name Hamath is written in a variety of ways in the texts of Sargon; see Parpola, Toponyms pp. 14 and 146–147. In this text, we find Amattu (KUR.*a-ma-at-tu*) here and Hammati (KUR.*ha-am-ma-ti*) in ii 62.
ii 56 Or ⸢*al*⸣-[*qa-a*]; see text no. 74 v 28.
iii The back of the stele (col. iii) may have contained (among other things) a description of Sargon's campaign against Mutallu of Kummuhu (which follows after the account about Ilu-biʾdī/Iaū-biʾdī in text no. 84, a cylinder that was composed close to the time of the Cyprus Stele) and of Sargon's defeat of Merodach-Baladan, which would logically precede what is found in col. iv (see Frame, Subartu 18 pp. 54–55 n. 11).
iv 6 See Fuchs, SAAS 8 p. 33 n. 80 with regard to the reading 6-*su*, which has often been thought to be an error for 6 GÍN. Text no. 7 line 141 has 10 GÍN.

26) *[da-na-an]* ^{d}*aš-šur* ^{d}AG ^{d}AMAR.UTU
27) *[iš-me]-⸢ma⸣ iš-pu-ra ar-du-tú*

(a message to do) obeisance (to me).

28) *[(u)* 7 LUGAL.MEŠ*]-ni ša* KUR.*ia-a' na-gi-i*
29) *[ša* KUR.*ad]-⸢na⸣-na ša ma-lak* 7 *u*$_4$*-mi*
30) *[i-na* MURUB$_4$*] tam-tim e-reb* ^{d}UTU*-ši*
31) *[šit-ku-nu]-ma né-sa-at šu-bat-⸢sún⸣*
32) *[ša ul-tu]* ⸢UD⸣.MEŠ SÙ.MEŠ *ṣi-bit* KUR *aš-⸢šur⸣*
33) *[...]-na ina* MAN.MEŠ*-ni* AD.MEŠ*-⸢ia⸣*
34) *[a-li-kut] maḫ-ri ma-am-man*
35) *[la iš]-⸢mu⸣-ú zi-kir* KUR*-šú-un*
36) *[ep-šet ina] ⸢qé⸣-reb* KUR.*kal-di u* KUR.*ḫat-ti*
37) *[e-tep-pu]-šú i-na* MURUB$_4$ *tam-tim*
38) *[ru-qiš iš]-mu-ma lib-bu-šú-un it-ru-ku*
39) *[ḫat-tu*$^{?}$ *ik]-⸢šu*$^{?}$*⸣-da-šú-un* KÙ.GI KÙ.BABBAR
40) *[ú-nu-ut* GIŠ].ESI GIŠ.TÚG *ni-ṣir-ti* KUR*-šú-un*
41) *[a-na qé-reb]* ⸢KÁ⸣.DINGIR.RA.KI *a-di maḫ-ri-ía*
42) *[ú-bi-lu-nim-ma] ú-na-ši-qu* GÌR.II*-ia*

iv 28–42) [(Moreover), seven king]s of the land Yā', a region [of the land Adn]ana (Cyprus) — whose abode(s) [are situated] far away, at a distance of seven days (journey) (iv 30) [in the middle] of the Western Sea, (and) the name of whose land, [from] the distant past, *when* Assyria *was taken over,* [*until now*], none of the kings, my ancestors, [who prec]eded (me), (iv 35) [had ever hea]rd — [he]ard [from afar], in the middle of the sea, [of the deeds I had been do]ing in Chaldea and the land Ḫatti. Their hearts then pounded (and) [*fear sei*]*zed* them. [They brought] before me [in] Babylon gold, silver, (and) [utensils of] ebony (and) boxwood, the treasure of their land, [and] they kissed my feet.

43) *[i-na u*$_4$*-me-šú]-ma* NA$_4$.NA.RÚ.A *ú-še-piš-ma*
44) *[ṣa-lam* DINGIR].MEŠ GAL.MEŠ EN.MEŠ*-ia*
45) *[e-si-qa*$^{?}$*] qé-reb-šú ṣa-lam* MAN*-ti-ia*
46) *[mu-te/ter-ri*$^{?}$*]-⸢iš*$^{?}$*⸣* TI.LA*-ia ma-ḫar-šú-un ul-ziz*
47) *[zi-kir*$^{?}$ UN$^{?}$].⸢MEŠ$^{?}$⸣ *ša iš-tu ṣi-it* ^{d}UTU*-ši*
48) *[a-di e-reb]* ^{d}UTU*-ši ina tukul-ti* ^{d}*aš-šur*
49) [^{d}AG] ⸢^{d}⸣AMAR.UTU DINGIR.MEŠ *tik-le-ia*
50) *[a-na ni]-⸢ir⸣ be-lu-ti-ia ú-šak-ni-šú*
51) *[áš-ṭu*$^{?}$*]-⸢ra⸣ ṣe-ru-uš-šú*
52) *[i-na*$^{?}$ ZAG$^{?}$ KUR$^{?}$].*ba-il-*ḪAR*-ri* KUR*-i*

iv 43–57) [At that time], I had a stele made and [I *engraved*] upon it [image(s) of the] great [god]s, my lords. I had an image of myself as king stand before them (the gods) [*constantly implor*]*ing* (*them for the sake*) of my life. [I *inscrib*]*ed* upon it [*the name(s) of the people*] whom, from the east [to the we]st, (iv 50) I had subjugated [to the yok]e of my lordship with the support of the gods Aššur, [Nabû], (and) Marduk, my divine helpers. I had (it) erected [*beside/facing Mount*] *Ba'il-ḪARri*, a mountain [(*that towers*) *abo*]*ve* the

iv 32–34 Text no. 7 lines 146–147 have *ša ul-tu u*$_4$*-me ru-qu-ti a-di i-*^{d}*nanna a-na**(var. *i-na*) LUGAL.MEŠ*-ni* AD.MEŠ*-ia ša* KUR *aš-šur*.KI *u* KUR *kar-*^{d}*du-ni-áš ma-nam-ma*, "from the distant past until now, none of the kings, my ancestors, neither in Assyria nor in Karduniaš ..." There would appear to be insufficient room at the beginning of iv 33 to restore *[a-di i-na-an]-na* or [EN *i-na-an]-na*. J. Lewy (HUCA 19 [1945–46] pp. 466–467) restores *[i-na pa]-na* at the beginning of iv 33 and translates this and the preceding line as "since the distant days of the seizing of Assyria [aforeti]me," understanding "the seizing of Assyria" to refer to "the occupation of Assyria by Sargon's ancestors and their people." S. Dalley (in Reyes, Archaic Cyprus p. 51) translates "[since] far-off days [they had not paid?] the tax (*ṣibtu*) of Assyria, for none of the kings, my fathers [who preceded] me ...."

iv 39 The parallel passage in text no. 7 line 148 has at this point *im-qut-su-nu-ti ḫat-tu* (see also text no. 74 vii 35). The proposed restoration goes back to Smith, ZÄS 9 (1871) p. 71. To my knowledge, no other text uses *kašādu* with *ḫattu* and it is possibly for this reason that S. Dalley (in Reyes, Archaic Cyprus p. 51) restores instead "their [trib]ute".

iv 43–57 Compare the description of the setting up of this stele "in the land Yā', a region of the land Yadnana," in text no. 74 vii 39–44. iv 43–46: A.T. Reyes (Archaic Cyprus p. 54) argues that the passage indicates "that the stele was set up facing a rock relief" (i.e., the royal image was on the stele and the images of the gods were on the rock relief). It seems more likely, however, that the passage describes only the stele, which has on it a depiction of the king standing in an attitude of prayer before symbols of several gods.

iv 44–45 For the tentative restorations, see Streck, Asb. p. 270 iv 2 and the on-page note to text no. 117 ii 70. In iv 45, possibly restore *[e-ṣi-ir]* or (following Malbran-Labat in Yon, Kition dans les textes p. 348) *[ab-ta-ni]* instead of *[e-si-qa]*. Or restore *[ta-nit-ti* DINGIR].MEŠ and *[ú-šá-áš-ṭir-(ma)]*, "[I had inscribed] ... [the praise of the] great [god]s"; cf. Leichty, RINAP 4 p. 186 no. 98 rev. 50 and 52.

iv 45–46 Malbran-Labat in Yon, Kition dans les textes p. 348 suggests *ṣa-lam* MAN*-ti-ia* / *[šur-ba-a a]-⸢na*$^{?}$*⸣* TI.LA*-ia*, i.e., "for the sake of my life a [*great*] image of myself as king."

iv 47 Possibly restore [KUR].⸢MEŠ⸣, "[of the land]s," instead of [UN].⸢MEŠ⸣, "[of the people]." In Yon, Kition dans les textes p. 348, F. Malbran-Labat tentatively reads for the beginning of the line [KUR.MEŠ$^{?}$ DÙ*-ši*]-⸢*na*$^{?}$⸣, i.e., "[*all thei*]*r* [*lands*]," but it is not clear that there would be room for all this and the traces at the beginning of the line would fit the end of MEŠ, but not NA.

iv 52–53 The proper restoration and understanding of these lines stating where the stele was to be set up is uncertain and a matter of extensive scholarly discussion. For the tentative restorations used here, see in particular Tadmor, Eretz-Israel 25 (1996) pp. 287–288 and Radner in Rollinger, Interkulturalität in der Alten Welt pp. 432–433. For the beginning of line 52, possibly simply [*i-na* KUR], [*a-na* KUR], [*ina* UGU KUR], or [*e-li* KUR], "[at/on Mount]," in which case the stele had either never reached its intended destination, or had been removed from it and taken to Kition, or never actually been intended to be placed there. H. Tadmor (Eretz-Israel 25 [1996] pp. 286–288) discusses parallels to, and the possible meaning of, the name Ba'il/Ba'al-ḫarri/ḫurri — West Semitic *bl hr* — and suggests that the stele was originally erected on a mountain peak, possibly in the mountain range around Mount Stavrovouni, about 20 km east of Larnaca. S. Dalley has suggested that in iv 52 one should translate *ḫur-ri* KUR*-i* as "mines," and from this A.T. Reyes has suggested that the stele was set up in a place associated with the mines of Cyprus, presumably copper mines; see Reyes, Archaic Cyprus p. 54. For iv 53, possibly translate instead "[(*that is situated*) *at the he*]*ad of* the land of Adnana," i.e., on a promontory. See also Na'aman, Orientalia NS 67 [1998] p. 240 "[at the t]op (*i-na* [*re*]*-eš*) of the land of Adnana." C. Saporetti (Studi Ciprioti e Rapporti di Scavo, 2nd fascicle p. 85 and n. 16) reads iv 52–53 as [*ašar*] *ba'il ḫurri māti* / [*nišē*] *Adnana ulziz*, "[Dove$^{?}$] è larga$^{?}$ l'apertura del paese [delle genti$^{?}$] del paese Adnana (l')ho eretta." Lipiński (Itineraria Phoenicia pp. 51–52) would restore these lines to read: "[in the House of the] Baal of Mount Hor [and the god]s of (I)adnana", [*ina* É ^{d}]*ba-il ḫur-ri* KUR*-i* [*u* DINGIR].⸢MEŠ⸣ KUR *ad-na-na*; he assumes

53) [(*ša*) *i-na*$^{?}$ *re*$^{?}$]-*eš* KUR.*ad-na-na ul-ziz*
54) [*ta-nit-ti*$^{?}$] DINGIR.MEŠ GAL.MEŠ EN.MEŠ-*ía*
55) [*ša*$^{?}$ *ina*$^{?}$ *an-ni*$^{?}$]-*šú-un ke-ni at-tal-la-ku-ma*
56) [*šá-ni-na*$^{?}$] *la i-šu-ú*
57) [*a-na* LUGAL.MEŠ]-⸢*ni*⸣ DUMU.MEŠ-*ia ṣa-ti-iš e-zib*

land Adnana (Cyprus]). I left [for] future [king]s, my descendants, [*the praises* of] the great gods, my lords, [*with wh*]*ose* firm [*approval*] I act and have no [*equal*].

58) [*i-na ár*]-*kát* u_4-*me* NUN EGIR-*ú*
59) [NA$_4$.NA.RÚ].A-*a li-mur-ma lil-ta-si*
60) [*zik-ri*$^{?}$] ⸢DINGIR⸣.MEŠ GAL.MEŠ *lit-ta-id-ma*
61) [Ì.GIŠ] *lip-šu-uš ni-qa-a liq-qí*
62) [*la*] ⸢*ú*⸣-*nak-kar a-šar-šú*

iv 58–62) [In fu]ture days, may a later prince look at my [stel]e and read (it). May he praise [*the names*] of the great gods, anoint (the stele) [with oil], (and) offer a sacrifice. [May] he [not] change its location.

63) [*mu-nak*]-*kir* NA$_4$.NA.RÚ.A-*ia*
64) [*mu-pa*]-⸢*šiṭ*$^{?}$⸣ *šiṭ-ri* MU-*ia*
65) [DINGIR.MEŠ] ⸢GAL⸣.MEŠ *ma-la ina* NA$_4$.NA.RÚ.A
66) [*an-né-e*] ⸢MU⸣-*šú-nu na-bu-u ù* DINGIR.MEŠ
67) [*a-ši-bu*]-*ut qé-reb tam-tim* DAGAL-*tim*
68) [*ag-giš*$^{?}$] ⸢*li*⸣-*ru-ru-šu-ma* MU-*šú* NUMUN-*šú*
69) [*i-na*] ⸢KUR⸣ *li-ḫal-li-qu*
70) [*a-a ir-šu-šu*] *re-e-mu ina sun-qi ḫu-šaḫ-ḫi*
71) [*bu-bu-ti*] *li-pit* ^{d}*èr-ra*
72) [*li-ṣa-(aḫ)*]-*ḫi-ru* UN.MEŠ-*šú*
73) [*i-na* KI.TA] ⸢LÚ⸣.KÚR-*šú ka-miš li-še*-⸢*ši*⸣-*bu-šú-ma*
74) [*a-na ni-ṭil*] IGI.II-*šú* KUR-*su liš-tap-par*

iv 63–74) [(As for) the one who alt]ers my stele (or) [*erase*]s my inscribed name, may the [great god]s — as many as are mentioned by name on [this] stele — and the gods [who live] in the middle of the wide sea curse him [*angrily*] and make his name (and) his descendant(s) disappear [from] the land. (iv 70) [May they not have] pity (on him). [May they red]uce his people through famine, want, [hunger], (and) plague. May they make him live in bondage [under] his enemy and may (his enemy) govern his land [in the sight] of his (own) eyes.

104

Three fragments found at Ashdod in 1963 come from one or more stone steles that are likely to be assigned to Sargon II in view of textual parallels on at least one of those fragments with passages in other inscriptions of that ruler. H. Tadmor has suggested that the fragments may have been parts of a stele erected soon after the capture of Ashdod by Sargon in 711 that had been deliberately broken when Hezekiah rebelled against Assyria in 705 (ʿAtiqot, English Series 9–10 [1971] pp. 192–194).

---

the stele was erected in a shrine on the acropolis of Kition (i.e., Bamboula) and near the ancient harbor. It has also been suggested this might refer to a mountain in Phoenicia; see also Bagg, Rép. Géogr. 7/1 pp. 111–112 sub *Ḫurri*. As K. Radner has noted, "there are no parallels for a temple that would be described as the shrine of an unspecified number of gods; in the Mesopotamian view, a temple has one owner and is identified by his or her name (although it can of course house additional deities)" (Radner in Rollinger, Interkulturalität in der Alten Welt p. 433 n. 22). R. Merrillees (Studies Hermary pp. 378–379) has argued that "it seems highly unlikely that the stele was ever physically erected on or near a mountain in Cyprus" and suggested that the stele was set up near one of Kition's city gates where it could be seen by passers-by and that it was found "presumably in or not far from its original position." Certainly, steles were most often set up in cities (normally either in or near temples or at city gates), and not in the countryside, where rock reliefs were the more common Assyrian monuments. .

103 iv 54–55 The tentative restorations are based upon H. Tadmor's understanding of the passage (Eretz-Israel 25 [1996] p. 287); see also Grayson and Novotny, RINAP 3/2 p. 308 no. 222 lines 8–9 and p. 313 no. 223 lines 3–4. Possibly restore instead in line 55 something along the lines of [*ša ina tukul-ti*]-*šú-un* or [*ša ina zík-ri pi*]-*šú-un*, i.e., "[with the support of] the great gods" or "[at the command of] the great gods"(cf. Winckler, Sar. 1 p. 182 and Luckenbill, ARAB 2 p. 103 §188).

103 iv 60 [*zik-ri*$^{?}$] "[*the names*]": For the restoration, see Leichty, RINAP 4 p. 186 no. 98 rev. 57. Possibly restore instead [*ep-šet*], "[the deeds]," based on text no. 117 ii 73. *lit-ta-id-ma*: Rather than translating this as "May he praise" and taking *litta''id* from the verb *nâdu* (following CAD N/1 p. 104), we could translate it as "May he pay attention to," taking it from the verb *na'ādu* (see AHw p. 693). (See also text nos. 105 ii′ 14 and 106 iii 12′.)

103 iv 64 With regard to the restoration, see also text no. 106 iii 15′.

103 iv 73 The restoration KI.TA instead of *pa-an*/IGI, "before," follows text no. 9 line 106, text no. 43 line 77, and text no. 44 line 60.

CATALOGUE

Frgm.	Museum Number	Excavation Number	Provenance	Dimensions (cm)	cpn
A	IAA 63-962 (IAA lot no. 3841)	Ashdod 1161/63	Ashdod Area A	10×13.8	p
B	IAA 63-1053	—	Ashdod	22×23×17	p
C	IAA 63-931 (IAA lot no. 3841)	Ashdod 1638/1	As ex. 1	11.9×11.4	p

COMMENTARY

Three inscribed fragments of black basalt were found during the second season of Israeli excavations at Ashdod (1963) and these are stored in the Israel Museum, Jerusalem. The inscription is edited from the published photographs, with further collations made by J.G. Westenholz, who also provided the information on the museum and field numbers.

H. Tadmor, Z. Kapera, and several other scholars refer to these pieces as fragments 1–3, which correspond to our A–C. W. Horowitz and T. Oshima (Canaan pp. 40–41 and 208) cite our Frgms. A, B, and C as Ashdod 2, 4, and 3 respectively. They state that Frgms. A and C (their Ashdod 2 and 3) "are written in the same script with lines of identical height, but with different indentations at the left edge. Thus they could be from different steles or from two different parts of the same stele." They also say that Frgm. B (their Ashdod 4) "is written in a different hand altogether" and point out that it was found in a different area of the site. Thus, they believe that the three fragments "come from at least two separate originals."

Frgms. A and C preserve parts of two adjoining faces of a stele, referred to below as the left and right faces. Frgm. B preserves part of only one face of the stele; since there is a blank space immediately above the first line of the inscription on this piece, it is assumed that this is the first line that was on that face of the stele.

Due to a lack of clarity in the published records, the exact findspots of the individual pieces are not clear. Westenholz informs me that Frgm. A may be the piece found reused in a Hellenistic wall (Area A locus 45) since it is covered with a patina and its back is worked. This would then suggest that Frgm. C is the piece found in Area A in debris of Stratum 3 in square H/3 near locus 32. (See Dothan, ʿAtiqot, English Series 9–10 [1971] p. 40 and pl. XCVI.) Frgm. B would then be the piece found in the Byzantine dump in Area G (see Swauger, ʿAtiqot, English Series 9–10 [1971] p. 150, which, however, refers to two fragments being found there).

Tadmor (ʿAtiqot, English Series 9–10 [1971] p. 195) points out that the palaeography of the Ashdod, Acharneh (Asharné), and Cyprus inscriptions (text nos. 104, 106, and 103 respectively) are identical and very similar to the inscriptions from Samaria and Carchemish (text nos. 1009 and 1010). Tadmor suggests that the left sides of Frgms. A and C refer to Azuri's rebellion at Ashdod and the tentative restorations generally follow those proposed by Tadmor. Certainly, the phrase *dābib ṣalipti*, which may appear in Frgm. C left face line 2′ (largely restored), is used to refer to the people of Ashdod in text no. 7 line 95. Since, however, the same phrase is used to refer to Mutallu of Kummuḫu in text no. 7 lines 112–113, the mere presence of this phrase would not prove that the passage has to describe the rebellion at Ashdod. Questioning Tadmor's assignment of the left sides of Frgms. A and C to the episode about the rebellion at Ashdod, Kapera (Folia Orientalia 17 [1976] pp. 94–99) assigns the left side of Frgm. C to the episode of Mutallu of Kummuḫu. The restorations in Frgm. B (including the alternative restorations given in the on-page notes) also follow those suggested by Tadmor in his study of this text.

BIBLIOGRAPHY

1963 Freedman, BiAr 26 p. 138 (study)
1964 Dothan, IEJ 14 p. 87 (provenance)
1964 Freedman, Presbyterian Life 17/6 pp. 10–13 (photo, discovery)
1966 Tadmor, BiAr 29 p. 95 fig. 11 (photo)
1967 Dothan, Archaeology 20 p. 184 (study)
1967 Tadmor, Eretz-Israel 8 pp. 75* [English] and 241–245, and pl. following p. 245 [Hebrew] (photo, edition, study)
1968 Borger in Galling, Textbuch[2] p. 61 no. 31.1 (study)
1970 Tadmor, AfO 23 p. 191 (Frgm. B, Frgm. C left side 2′–4′, transliteration)
1971 Dothan, ʿAtiqot, English Series 9–10 p. 40 (provenance)

1971 Swauger, ʿAtiqot, English Series 9–10 p. 150 (provenance)
1971 Tadmor, ʿAtiqot, English Series 9–10 pp. 192–197 and pls. XCVI–XCVII (photo, edition, study)
1972 Levine, Stelae p. 53 (study)
1973 Hestrin, Inscriptions Reveal[2] no. 47 (photo, study)
1976 Kapera, Folia Orientalia 17 pp. 87–99 (transliteration, study, provenance)
1982 Börker-Klähn, Bildstelen no. 174 (study)
1988 Cogan and Tadmor, II Kings third plate following p. 228 (photo)
1990 Stern, Archaeology of the Land of the Bible 2 p. 15 (photo)
1993 Dothan in Stern, New Encyclopedia 1 p. 100 (photo)
1994 Fuchs, Khorsabad pp. 386 and 392–393 (study)
2002 Horowitz, Oshima and Sanders, JAOS 122 p. 755 Ashdod 2–4 (study)
2006 Frame, Subartu 18 p. 51 (study)
2006 Horowitz and Oshima, Canaan pp. 40-41 and 208 Ashdod 2–4 (copy, edition)
2007 Shanks, Biblical Archaeology Review 33/1 58 (Frgm B, photo, copy)
2008 Cogan, Raging Torrent pp. 232–233 no. 2 (photo, study)
2014 Galter, CRRA 52 pp. 334 and 336–337 (study)
2014 Maniori, Campagne di Sargon pp. 53–54 g10 and passim (study)

TEXT

Fragment A

Left side

Lacuna

1′) [...]-⸢*tim*⸣

2′) [...] SIG$_5$

3′) [*it-ti-ia*$^?$ *ú-šam*$^?$]-*ki-ru*

4′) [ERIM.ḪI.A$^?$ KUR *aš-šur*$^?$] ⸢DAGAL⸣-*tim*

Lacuna

Right side

Lacuna

1′) ⸢*in*⸣-[...]

2′) SAL [...]

3′) *šá* ⸢KUR$^?$⸣ [...]

4′) ⸢*ša*⸣ [...]

Lacuna

Fragment B

1) [*ú-par-ri-ir el-lat*] ^{md}*ḫum-ba-ni-*[*ga-áš* LÚ.ELAM.MA.KI-(*i*)]

2) [*ú-ab-bit* KUR.*kar*]-⸢*al*⸣-*lu* KUR.*šur*-⸢*da*⸣ [URU.*ki-še-si-im*]

3) [URU.*ḫar-ḫa-ar* KUR].⸢*ma*⸣-*da-a-a* ⸢KUR⸣.[*el-li-pi*]

4) [*e-mì-du ni-ir* ^{d}]⸢*aš*⸣-*šur ú-*[*šak-niš* KUR.*man-na-a-a*$^?$]

5) [...] *x* [...]

Lacuna

Fragment C

Left side

Lacuna

1′) [...] *x-ú*

2′) [... *da-bi-ib*$^?$ *ṣa*$^?$]-⸢*lip*⸣-*ti*

Fragment A

Left side

Lacuna

Frgm. A left 1′–4′) [... *they made ... ho*]*stile* [*to me. The extens*]*ive* [*troops of Assyria*]

Lacuna

Right side

Lacuna

Frgm. A right 1′–4′) Not sufficiently preserved to allow translation.

Lacuna

Fragment B

Frgm. B 1–5) [I dispersed the forces of] Ḫumbani[gaš (Ḫumban-nikaš I), the Elamite. I destroyed the land of Kar]alla, the land Šurda, [the city Kišesim, the city Ḫarḫar, the land] Media, (and) the la[nd Ellipi, (and) I imposed the yoke of the god] Aššur [(upon them)]. I [subjugated *the land Mannea, ...*]

Lacuna

Fragment C

Left sides

Lacuna

Frgm. C left 1′–5′) [... *who (always) speaks tre*]*achery* [...] he repeatedly sent [... *he withheld*] his [au]dience gift

---

Frgm. A Right side line 1′ ⸢*in*⸣: Or ⸢LUGAL⸣, following Horowitz and Oshima, Canaan p. 41.

Frgm. B line 1 The restoration at the beginning of the line is based on text no. 8 line 7, text no. 103 ii 27–28, and text no. 116 line 16. One might restore instead [*aškun dabdê*], "[I brought about the defeat]"; cf. in a similar position text no. 9 line 12 *šá-kin taḫ-te-e* and text no. 13 line 14 *šá-kin* BAD$_5$.BAD$_5$-*e*.

Frgm. B line 4 The restoration at the beginning of the line is based on text no. 8 line 8 and that of the end of the line is based on text no. 103 line 37. One might restore instead *ú-*[*šaḫ-rib* KUR.*ur-ar-ṭu*], "I [laid waste to the land Urarṭu]"; see text no. 8 line 8 and cf. text no. 9 line 15 and text no. 13 lines 18–19 (participial form of verb).

Frgm. C Left side line 1′ Assuming that the left side of Frgm. C is related to text no. 7 lines 112–113, the episode of Mutallu of Kummuḫu, this line might end [... LÚ.*ḫat*]-⸢*tu*⸣-*ú*, "[... Hitt]ite" (see Kapera, Folia Orientalia 17 [1976] pp. 96–99, which has [... *pa*]-⸢*tu*⸣-*ú*). For a copy of the traces before *ú*, see the minor variants section (collation by J.G. Westenholz).

3′) [...] ⸢*iš*⸣-*tap-par*	[...]
4′) [... *ik-la-a*?] ⸢*ta*⸣-*mar-tuš*	
5′) [...] *x* ⸢DU?⸣	
Lacuna	Lacuna
Right side	Right side
Lacuna	Lacuna
1′) *x* [...]	Frgm. C right 1′–5′) Not sufficiently preserved to allow translation.
2′) AN [...]	
3′) AŠ *x* [...]	
4′) *a*-⸢*na*?⸣ [...]	
5′) ⸢*ša*⸣ [...]	
Lacuna	Lacuna

105

A fragment of stone stele in the Bible Lands Museum (Jerusalem) preserves part of an inscription of Sargon II that describes the events of his second year (720), including the settlement of Assyrians in Hamath (ii′ 1–12). Mention is also made of events that occurred much later in the king's reign, including the submission of the seven kings of Yāʾ (i′ 24′–25′a, mostly restored), which took place in or around 708. J.D. Hawkins, the initial publisher of the text, suggests that it was erected in 708 within the territory of Hamath (Studies Grayson pp. 162–164). The stele has been at times referred to as the Beirut Stele, the Borowski Stele, and the Hamath (or Hama) Stele.

CATALOGUE

Museum Number	Provenance	Dimensions (cm)	cpn
BLMJ 1115	—	58×35.6	p

COMMENTARY

This fragmentary stone stele appeared on the antiquities market in Beirut and thus its original provenance is not known. W.G. Lambert (in Muscarella, Ladders p. 125) suggests that the stele "belongs to a type which was set up locally to commemorate events in the district. So presumably this one commemorates the settlement of Syria and Palestine in 720 B.C. and was set up somewhere in the region on the successful completion of the campaign." J.D. Hawkins suggests that it may have come from the territory of Hamath (Studies Grayson p. 162), possibly from Sheizar, which is located on the Orontes between Acharneh and Hama (CAH[2] 3/1 p. 417 n. 368).

Parts of two faces of the stele are preserved. There is an area without inscription above col. ii′; thus, col. i′ starts higher up on the stele than col. ii′. The inscription is edited from a copy of the inscription made by Hawkins and from photographs of the object provided by J.G. Westenholz (with supplementary collations by Westenholz).

The restorations in col. i′ follow Hawkins and are based upon text no. 43 lines 10–17 and 23–24 for i′ 2′–18′, text no. 13 lines 23–26, 28–31, and 41–45 for i′ 19′–20′a, 21′–22′a, and 24′–25′a, and text no. 43 line 26 for i′ 25′b–26′.

BIBLIOGRAPHY

1975 Finet, Opposition pp. 12–13 and n. 48 (ii′ 5–12, edition; study [by Nougayrol])
1975 Garelli in Finet, Opposition p. 207–208 (ii′ 5–12, translation)
1981 Lambert in Muscarella, Ladders p. 125 no. 83 (photo,; col. ii′, edition, study)
1994 Fuchs, Khorsabad p. 387 (study)
2000 Younger, COS 2 p. 294 no. 2.118B (col. ii′, translation)
2004 Hawkins, Studies Grayson pp. 151–164 (photo, copy, edition, study)
2006 Frame, Subartu 18 p. 51 (study)
2008 Cogan, Raging Torrent p. 99 (ii′ 5–12, translation)
2014 Galter, CRRA 52 pp. 334 and 336–337 (study)
2014 Maniori, Campagne di Sargon p. 53 g9 and passim (study)
2017 Liverani, Assyria p. 183 (i′ 11′–13′, translation)
2018 Frahm, Last Days pp. 79–80 no. 15 (ii′ 1–12, edition; study, combined with text nos. 84 and 103)

TEXT

Col. i′

Lacuna

1′) [...] *x*

2′) [... *ḫur-šá-a-ni bé-ru-ú-ti ša né-reb-šú-nu*] *áš-ṭu*

3′) [*la-a mi-na ip-tu-ma e-mu-ru du-ru-ug-šu-un ṭu-da-at la a*ʾ*-a-ri pa-áš*]-⸢*qa*?⸣-*ti*

4′) [*ša a-šar-ši-na šug-lud-du e-ta-at-ti-qu-ma e-te-eb*]-⸢*bi*?⸣-*ru*

5′) [*na-gab be-ra-a-ti iš-tu* KUR.*ra-a-ši mi-ṣir* KUR.*e*]-⸢*lam*?⸣-*ti*

6′) [LÚ.*pu-qu-du* LÚ.*da-mu-nu* URU.BÀD-*ku-ri-gal-zi* URU.*ra*]-⸢*pi*?⸣-*qi*

7′) [*mad-bar* DÙ.A.BI *a-di na-ḫal* KUR.*mu-uṣ-ri* KUR *a-mur-re-e ra-pa*]-⸢*áš*⸣-*tu*

8′) [KUR.*ḫat-ti a-na si-ḫir-ti-šá i-be-lu iš-tu* KUR.*ḫa-áš*]-*mar*

9′) [*a-di* KUR.*ṣi-bar pat-ti* KUR.*ma-da-a-a ru-qu-ti ša ṣi-it* ^{d}]⸢UTU⸣-*ši*

10′) [KUR.*nam-ri* KUR.*el-li-pí* KUR.É-*ḫa-am-ban* KUR.*par-su-a* KUR.*ma-an-na*]-*a-a*

11′) [KUR.*ur-ar-ṭu* KUR.*kas-ku* KUR.*ta-ba-lum a-di* KUR.*mu-us-ki ik-šu-du* GAL]-⸢*tu*⸣ ŠU-*su*

12′) [LÚ.*šu-ut* SAG.MEŠ-*šú šak-nu-ti* UGU-*šú-nu iš-tak-ka*]-⸢*nu*⸣-*ma*

13′) [*bil-tu ma-da-at-tu ki-i ša áš-šu-ri e-mid-su*]-⸢*nu*⸣-*ti*

14′) [*eṭ-lu qar-du ša i-na re-bit* BÀD.AN.KI *it-ti* ^{md}*ḫum-ba-ni-ga-áš* LUGAL KUR.*e-lam-ti in*]-⸢*nam*⸣-*ru-ma*

15′) [*iš-ku-nu taḫ-ta-a-šu* (...) *mu-né-es-si* KUR.É-*pu-ru-ta-áš ša* ^{m}*am-ba-ri*]-⸢*is*⸣ *ma-lik-šú-nu*

16′) [*da-mi-iq-ti* ^{m}LUGAL-GI.NA *im-šu-ma* UGU LUGAL KUR.*ur-ar-ṭi u* KUR.*mu-us-ki*] ⸢*it*⸣-*tak-lu*

17′) [*i-da-an pag-la-a-te ṭa-rid* ^{m}*mi-ta-a* LUGAL KUR.*mu*]-*us-ki*

18′) [*mu-ter ḫal-ṣi* KUR.*qu-e ek-mu-te mu-rap-pi-šu pu-lu*]-⸢*un*⸣-*ge-šú*

19′) [*na-pi-i*ʾ KUR.*kam-ma-ni ša* ^{m}*gu-un-zi-na-nu ul-tu qé*]-⸢*reb*?⸣ URU.*me-lid*

Lacuna

i′ 1′–5′a) [... who ... opened up innumerable distant mountainous areas whose pass(es)] are difficult [and visited their remotest region(s); who traversed inaccessible, diffic]ult [paths in terrifying location(s) (and) cross]ed [every *swamp*];

i′ 5′b–13) [(who) ruled from the land Rāši on the border of the land El]am, [the Puqudu (and) Damūnu (tribes), the cities Dūr-Kurigalzu (and) Rāp]iqu, [the entire desert as far as the Brook of Egypt, the wid]e [land Amurru, (and) the land Ḫatti (Syria) in its entirety; who]se [grea]t hand [conquered (the area) from the land Ḫaš]mar [to the land Ṣibar — which borders on the distant Medes in the ea]st — [(i′ 10′) the lands Namri, Ellipi, Bīt-Ḫamban, Parsua(š), Mann]ea, [Urarṭu, Kasku, (and) Tabal, as far as the land Musku; who se]t [eunuchs of his as governors over them] and [imposed upon th]em [(the same) tribute (and) payment(s) as if (they were) Assyrians];

i′ 14′–18′) [the valiant man who m]et [Ḫumbanigaš (Ḫumban-nikaš I), king of the land Elam, (in battle) on the *outskirts* of (the city) Dēr] and [brought about his defeat; (...) who deported (the people of) the land Bīt-Purutaš, who]se king, [Ambari]s, [had forgotten the kindness (shown to him) by Sargon and] put his trust [in the king(s) of the lands Urarṭu and Musku; (*the one with*) powerful arms, who drove out Mitâ (Midas), king of the land M]usku, [brought back (to Assyrian control) the fortress(es) of the land Que (Cilicia) that had been taken away (by the enemy), (and) expanded] its [bord]ers;

i′ 19′–25′a) [who plundered the land Kammanu, deported Gunzinānu from] the city Melid, [his (Gun-

20′) [URU LUGAL-*ti-šú is-su-ḫu-ma* ...] ⸢*e*⸣-*sír*
21′) [*mu-nak-kir* LUGAL-*ut* ^{m}*tar-ḫu-la-ra* LÚ.URU.*mar-qa-sa-a-a ša paṭ gi-mir* KUR].*gúr-gu-um-me*
22′) [*a-na mi-ṣir* KUR *aš-šur*.KI *ú-ter-ru* ... ^{m}*ia-ma-ni* URU.*as*]-⸢*du*⸣-*da-a-a*
23′) [...] BU MA
24′) [*mu-šak-niš* 7 LUGAL.MEŠ-*ni ša* KUR.*ia-a*ʾ *na-ge-e ša* KUR.*ia-ad-na-na ša*] ⸢*ma*⸣-*lak* 7 u_4-*me*
25′) [*i-na* MURUB$_4$ *tam-tim šit-ku-na-at šu-bat-su-un na-bi-i*ʾ KUR.*gar-ga-miš* KUR.*ḫa-at-te*]-*e lem-ni*
26′) [*ša* ^{m}*pi-si-i-ri da-gíl pa-ni-šú-nu da-bi-ib ṣa-lip-te ik-šu-du*] ⸢GAL-*tu*⸣ [ŠU]-*su*
27′) [...] *x*
Lacuna

zinānu's) royal city, and ...] ...; [who did away with the kingship of Tarḫu-lara of the city Marqasa (and) made all of the land] Gurgum [(part of) the territory of Assyria; ... Iāmānī of the city Ash]dod [...] ...; [who subjugated seven kings of the land Yāʾ — a region of the land Yadnana (Cyprus) — whose abode is situated at a di]stance of seven days (journey) [in the middle of the sea];

i′ 25′b–27′) [who plundered the land Carchemish of the] evil [Ḫitti]te (king) (and) [who]se great [hand conquered Pisīri(s), *their* subject who (always) spoke treachery; ...]

Lacuna

Col. ii′
1) 2 ME GIŠ.GIGIR.MEŠ 6 ME ANŠE.*pét-ḫal-lum*
2) GIŠ.*ka-ba-bu* GIŠ.*az-ma-ru-ú*
3) *i-na lìb-bi-šú-nu ak-ṣur-ma*
4) *ina* UGU *ki-ṣir* MAN-*ti*-⸢*ia*⸣ *ú-rad-di*
5) 6 LIM 3 ME LÚ.*aš-šur-a-a* EN *ḫi-iṭ-ṭi*
6) *gíl-la-su-nu a-mes-ma*
7) *re-e-ma ar-ši-šú-nu-ti-ma*
8) *ina qé-reb* KUR.*ḫa-mat-ti ú-še-šib-šú-nu-ti*
9) GUN *ma-da-tu za-bal ku-du-u-ri*
10) *a-lak* KASKAL *ki-i šá* MAN.MEŠ AD.MEŠ-*ía*
11) *a-na* ^{m}*ir-ḫu-le-na* KUR.*a-ma-ta-a-a*
12) *e-mid-du e-mid-su-nu-ti*
13) NUN EGIR-*ú ep-šet* AN.⸢ŠÁR⸣
14) *dam-qa-a-ti lit-ta-*ʾ*i-id-ma*
15) *aḫ-ra-taš* ⸢*pul*⸣-*ḫat-su*
16) *li-šal-mi-da ar-ku-ti*
17) UN.⸢MEŠ⸣ KUR.*ḫat-ti ù* KUR.*a-ri-me*
18) *a-ši-*⸢*bu*⸣-*tu* KUR.É-^{m}*a-gu-si*
19) ⸢*ù*⸣ KUR.*un-qi a-na paṭ* ⸢*gim*⸣-*ri* [(*x*)]
20) [...] *x* [(*x*)] ⸢A⸣ *x x* [*x* (*x*)]
Lacuna

ii′ 1–12) I conscripted from among them 200 chariots, 600 cavalry, (and) shield (and) spear (bearers), and I added (them) to my royal (military) contingent. I disregarded the crime(s) of (ii′ 5) 6,300 guilty Assyrians, had pity upon them, and settled them in the land Hamath. I imposed on them (the same) tribute, payment(s), labor duty, (and) (ii′ 10) military service as the kings, my ancestors, had imposed on Irḫulena of the land Hamath.

ii′ 13–16) May (every) future ruler praise the good deeds of (the god) Aššur and have (people) in the future learn to revere him (the god Aššur)!

ii′ 17–20) The people of the lands Ḫatti and Aram who dwell in the lands Bīt-Agūsi and Unqi, to (their) full extent [...] ...

Lacuna

106

A fragment of a basalt stele that was discovered near the bridge crossing the Orontes River at Acharneh (Asharné) bears part of an inscription of Sargon II which appears to describe a victory over the ruler of Hamath. Sargon is known to have conquered Hamath in his second regnal year (720). Thus, this is likely one of the earliest of Sargon's royal inscriptions. For the possibility that Acharneh is to be identified with the third and second millennium city Tunip, see Klengel, Studies Lipiński p. 128, and Goren,

105 i′ 26′ With regard to whom the "*their*" in "*their* subject" refers, see the note to text no. 43 line 26.
105 ii′ 1 Text no. 103 ii 57 has 300 chariots.
105 ii′ 11 Irḫulena, king of Hamath, was part of the coalition opposing Shalmaneser III at Qarqar in 853. See for example Grayson, RIMA 3 pp. 23–24 A.0.102.2 ii 89–102; Hawkins in RLA 5/3–4 (1977) p. 162; and Van Buylaere, PNA 2/1 p. 564.

Finkelstein, and Na'aman, Inscribed in Clay pp. 116–121. N. Na'aman (NABU 1999 pp. 89–90 no. 89) also suggests that Acharneh might be identified with the first millennium city Qarqar; however, Qarqar is normally thought to be modern Tell Qarqūr (see Bagg, Rép. Géogr. 7/1 pp. 194–195).

CATALOGUE

Museum Number	Provenance	Dimensions (cm)	cpn
M 10890	Acharneh	77×43×36	p

COMMENTARY

The inscription was found in 1924 by Commandant Maignan near the Acharneh bridge on the Orontes. It was M 10890 in the Aleppo Museum, but was later moved to the museum in Hama. The piece is inscribed on three sides (ii–iv), with the fourth side (i) being entirely damaged. Following F. Thureau-Dangin, it is assumed here that the totally damaged side had the beginning of the inscription; however, it is conceivable that the inscription did not begin on that side, but rather on our col. iv (i.e., iv > i, i > ii; ii> iii, and iii > iv). The inscription was kindly collated for the author by K. Radner.

BIBLIOGRAPHY

1924 Thureau-Dangin, CRAIB p. 168 (study)
1933 Thureau-Dangin, RA 30 pp. 53–56 and 104, and pl. I (photo, edition; ii 13′–14′, study)
1972 Levine, Stelae p. 57 (study)
1982 Börker-Klähn, Bildstelen no. 177 (study)
1994 Fuchs, Khorsabad p. 386 (study)
2006 Frame, Subartu 18 pp. 49–68 (photo, edition, study)
2014 Galter, CRRA 52 pp. 333 and 336–337 (study)
2018 Frahm, Last Days pp. 62–63 no. 2 (ii 1′–12′, iii 1′–9′, edition, study)

TEXT

Col. i	
Not preserved	Not preserved
Col. ii	
Lacuna	Lacuna
1′) [...] *x x x* [...]	ii 1′) [...] ... [...]
2′) [...] *a-na* A.⸢MEŠ⸣ [*x* (*x*)]	ii 2′) [...] for water [...]
3′) [...]-*šú ú-qí-ru-*⸢*ma*⸣	ii 3′) [...] *they made* his/its [...] *scarce*
4′) [...] ⸢*i*⸣*-te-e* URU-*šu*	ii 4′) [...] the neighborhood of his city
5′) [... *a*]-⸢*na*⸣ *šit-mur* ANŠE.KUR.RA.⸢MEŠ⸣	ii 5′) [... fo]r horses to show their mettle
6′) [...]-*ti* LÚ.*e-qa-x*	ii 6′) [...] ...
7′) [... *di-ik-ta*$^{?}$]-⸢*šú*⸣-*nu ma-at-*⸢*tu*⸣	ii 7′) [... a] major [*defeat* on th]em
8′) [... *is*]-⸢*ki*⸣-*ru* ÍD	ii 8′) [(...) they blo]cked up the river [*with their corpses*].
9′) [... *di*$^{?}$-*tal*$^{?}$]-⸢*li*⸣-*iš iq-mu-ú-*⸢*ma*⸣	ii 9′–12′) They burned [...], (*turning them*) *into* [*ash*]*es*, established [*devastation* in the land] Hamath, a[nd ...]. They brought him (Ilu/Iaū-bi'dī), together with [his]
10′) [*x x* (*x*) *i-na* KUR].*a-ma-at-te iš-ku-nu-*⸢*ma*$^{?}$⸣	
11′) [...] *x šá-a-šú ga-du kim-ti-*[*šú*]	

ii 3′ F. Thureau-Dangin suggests that the Orontes River may have been diverted in order to make water scarce for the enemy.
ii 6′ The traces of the final sign suggest MA, ⸢Ú⸣, or possibly some other sign that can begin with three horizontal wedges, one on top of the other (e.g., IA or I).
ii 9′ The tentative restoration (following F. Thureau-Dangin) is based upon such passages as *aqmūma ditalliš ušēmi*, "I burned down and turned into ashes"; see for example text no. 65 line 232.

12′) [a-na qé]-⸢reb⸣ URU-ia aš-šur.KI ⸢ub-lu⸣-[ni]
13′) [...] i-da-a-a i-⸢tap-pa-lu⸣
14′) [...] ⸢er⸣-nit-ti ak-šu-du x [(x)]
15′) [... am-ṣu?]-⸢ú⸣ ma-la lìb-bi-⸢ia⸣
16′) [a-na ^{d}aš-šur] ⸢EN⸣-ia ak-ru-ub-⸢ma⸣
17′) [...] x ṣi-bit GU$_4$.MEŠ u ṣe-(x)-e-[ni]
18′) [...] x ú-kin sat-tuk-ku-⸢uš⸣-[šú]
19′) [...-šu]-⸢nu⸣ ú-nak-ki-ir-[ma]
20′) [(...)] šap-tuš-šu-⸢un?⸣

family, [int]o my city Aššur.
ii 13′–18′) [*Because the god Aššur who goes*] at my side cont[inually an]swered [...] I obtained victory [... *I was able to achieve*] whatever I wanted. I blessed [the god Aššur], my lord. [I *imposed upon him* ...] the *ṣibtu*-tax on oxen and sheep and g[oats (...) *and*] established as [his] regular offerings.
ii 19′) [(...)] I altered [the]ir [... and]
ii 20′) [(...)] on *their* lips.

Col. iii
Lacuna

Lacuna

1′) [...] x [...]
2′) [...]-ni-ia [...]
3′) [šá ina tukul]-ti ^{d}aš-šur ⸢EN⸣-[ia ...]
4′) [at-ta]-la-ku ù mim-mu-ú [ina? KUR?.ḫa?-am?-ma?-te?]
5′) [e-tep]-pu-šú áš-ṭu-ra ⸢ṣe⸣-[ru-uš-šú-(un)]
6′) [1-en] ⸢ina⸣ KUR.ḫa-am-ma-te 1-en ina [...]
7′) [1-en] ⸢i⸣-na ⸢URU⸣.ḫa-ta-⸢ri⸣-[ka (...)]
8′) [1-en] ⸢ina⸣ URU.KUR-ʾu-a 1-en ina [...]
9′) [ul?-ziz?] a-lik ar-ki RU RI x [...]
10′) [NUN] EGIR-ú NA$_4$.NA.RÚ.[A-a li-mur-ma]
11′) [ši]-⸢ṭir⸣ MU-ia lil-ta-⸢si⸣ [zik-ri? ^{d}aš-šur?]
12′) [lit]-⸢ta⸣-ʾi-id-ma Ì.[GIŠ lip-šu-uš]
13′) [UDU].⸢SISKUR⸣ liq-qí ^{d}⸢aš⸣-šur [...]

iii 1′) [...]
iii 2′) [...] my [...]
iii 3′–9′a) [that I (had carried out while) a]cting [with the suppo]rt of the god Aššur, [my] lo[rd, ...], and everything [that I had] done [*in the land Hamath*], I inscribed u[pon it/them. *I erected*] one (stele)] in the land Hamath, one in [...], [one] in the city Ḫatar[ikka (...)], [one] in the city KURʾua, (and) one in [...]
iii 9′b) One who comes after ... [...]
iii 10′–13′) May a future [prince look at my] stel[e and] read my [inscr]ibed name. [May he (then) pr]aise [*the name of the god Aššur*, anoint (this stele) with] oi[l], (and) offer [a sac]rifice. The god Aššur [*will (then) listen to his prayers*].

14′) [mu]-nak-⸢kir⸣ [NA$_4$.NA.RÚ.A-ia]
15′) [mu-pa]-šiṭ ⸢ši-ṭir⸣ [MU-ia (...)]
16′) [...] x [...]

iii 14′–16′) [(As for) the one who] alte[rs my stele, (or) er]ases [my] inscr[ibed name ...]

Lacuna

Lacuna

Col. iv
Lacuna

Lacuna

1′) [...] x [...]
2′) [...] BU IZ [...]
3′) [...] KID E [...]
4′) [...] e-peš [...]
5′) [...] x x DU x [...]

iv 1′–5′) Too poorly preserved to allow translation.

Remainder not inscribed

Remainder not inscribed

---

ii 13′–14′ [...] *i-da-a-a i-⸢tap-pa-lu⸣* "[... *who goes*] at my side cont[inually an]swered": Or "[...] *cont[inually st]ood in for me*"; see Novotny and Jeffers, RINAP 5/1 p. 305 no. 23 line 79 (partially restored); Bauer, Asb. p. 49 obv. 13′ (81-7-27,70); and von Weiher, SpTU 2 p. 141 no. 31 rev. 4 (W 22669/3). Citing a passage in an inscription of Ashurbanipal as a parallel (Novotny and Jeffers, RINAP 5/1 p. 232 no. 11 i 38), F. Thureau-Dangin proposed restoring *ke-mu-u-a* at the beginning of ii 14′ ("in my stead").

iii 4′ For the tentative restoration, cf. text no. 117 ii 71. Possibly restore Amurru instead of Hamath at the end of the line; see also Frahm, Last Days p. 62.

iii 10′–15′ For the tentative restoration, cf. text no. 103 iv 58–64, text no. 117 ii 72–73, and Leichty, RINAP 4 p. 186 no. 98 rev. 57. With regard to the translation of iii 11′–12′, see the on-page note to text no. 103 iv 60.

iv 5′ The remainder of this side of the fragment is not inscribed and thus this appears to be the last line of the text.

107

A stone fragment from Til-Barsip (modern Tell Ahmar), located on the Euphrates River about 20 km south of Carchemish, bears part of an inscription of Sargon II. Although the ruler's name is not mentioned in the section preserved, it may be assigned to Sargon II because of textual parallels in other inscriptions of this ruler.

CATALOGUE

Museum Number	Provenance	Dimensions (cm)	cpn
M 9944	Tell Ahmar, at a depth of more than a meter, in a late wall, not far from (and to the east of) the western cemetery	40×97×15	p

COMMENTARY

According to F. Thureau-Dangin, the fragment is part of a bull that would have originally been placed at an entranceway. The piece has been set up in the courtyard of the Aleppo Museum. The inscription is poorly preserved and it is edited from the published photograph, with collations by H. Galter. It is not clear how much is missing at the beginning and end of each line and thus restorations in the transliteration have been kept to a minimum.

Lines 1′–6′ are restored from such similar passages as text no. 7 lines 4–7 and 10–12, text no. 8 lines 2–3 and 5, and text no. 84 lines 1′–2′.

BIBLIOGRAPHY

1936 Thureau-Dangin, Til Barsib p. 159 no. 10 and pl. XV no. 3 (photo, study)

1973 Farber and Kessler, RA 67 pp. 163–164 (transliteration, study)

1998 Fuchs, SAAS 8 p. 5 (lines 7′–8′, transliteration)

2004 Galter in Hutter, Offizielle Religion p. 180 (lines 7′–8′, edition, study)

2006 Frame, Subartu 18 p. 53 (study)

TEXT

Lacuna

1′) [... *šá*]-⸢*na*$^{?}$⸣-[*an* ...]

2′) [...] ⸢*dam-qu ú*$^{?}$*-še-ṣu*$^{?}$⸣*-u a*-⸢*na*⸣ [...]

3′) [...] ⸢NIBRU⸣.KI ⸢KÁ$^{?}$.DINGIR$^{?}$ *bár-sipa*$^{?}$ *za-nin*$^{?}$*-us-su*⸣-[*un* ...]

4′) [...] (*x*) *mal ba-šú-u ḫi-bil-ta*-[*šú-nu* ...]

5′) [...] ⸢URU⸣.KASKAL *šá ul-tú* ⸢*u*$_4$⸣*-me* ⸢*ul-lu*⸣*-ti* ⸢*im*⸣-[*ma-šu-ma* ...]

6′) [... *ba-ṭi*]-⸢*il*$^{?}$⸣*-ta ú-ter áš*-[*ru-uš-šá* ...]

7′) [...] ⸢É$^{?}$ ^{d}⸣IŠKUR *ša qé-reb* ⸢URU⸣.[...]

8′) [...] *x* ^{m}⸢*aš-šur*-PAP$^{?}$⸣-A ⸢NUN⸣ *a*-⸢*lik*⸣ *pa*-[*ni-ia* ...]

9′) [...] (traces) [...]

Lacuna

Lacuna

1′–2′a) [... granted me a reign without eq]ua[l and] exalted [my] good [reputation] t[o the heights].

2′b–6′a) [I continually acted] as provider [for (the cities) Sippar, Nippu]r, *Babylon*, (and) Borsippa [(and) I made restitution for] the wrongful damage [suffered by the people of privileged status], as many as there were (of them). I [then] restor[ed the exemption (from obligations) of (the city) Baltil (Aššur) and] the city Ḫarrān, which had f[allen into oblivion] in the distant past, [and their privileged position that had laps]ed.

6′b–9′) [...] *temple* of the god Adad that [...] inside the city [...] *Ashurnasirpal*, a prince who preced[ed me ...] ... [...]

Lacuna

108

Five fragments of a basalt stele found at Tell Tayinat in the Amuq Valley of Turkey's Hatay province likely come from one and the same stele. Tell Tayinat (ancient Kullania) was the capital of the Neo-Assyrian province of Unqi following that area's conquest by Tiglath-pileser III in 738. Frgm. D mentions Qarqar, Samaria, and Hamath, and thus likely refers to Sargon II's defeat of a coalition of Syrian kingdoms in his second regnal year (720). The fragment may well preserve the beginning of the name of the leader of the rebellious coalition, Iaū-bi'dī (Ilu-biʾdī), the ruler of Hamath. Frgm. E also appears to duplicate a section of Sargon's Beirut Stele (text no. 105) dealing with the settling of deportees in Hamath.

CATALOGUE

Frgm.	Museum Number	Excavation Number	Provenance	Dimensions (cm)	cpn
A	Hatay Archaeological Museum —	—	Reportedly found on the surface of the mound of Tell Tayinat	41×21.5	p
B	A 27862	T-3516	Tell Tayinat, possibly in rectilinear debris of the southern wall of Area V	36.5×37.5×26.5	p
C	A 60934	T-2464	Tell Tayinat, surface of Courtyard VIII	8.75×11.55×5.15	p
D	A 27863	—	Tell Tayinat	22.3×24.5×10.5	p
E	A 60933	Possibly T-2209	Tell Tayinat, possibly surface of Trench 11	13.35×11.55×6.45	p

COMMENTARY

Frgm. A is known as the "Taşar Stone," from the name of the owner of the farmstead where it was discovered in 2006 by one of the people working on the excavations at Tell Tayinat. It was being used as a door step in a building, which likely explains the abraded state of the inscription. It had apparently been brought for use there at some point after 1980 and before 2002, when the owner took possession of the farm. In 2009, the piece was taken to the Hatay Arkeoloji Müzesi. The University of Chicago's Syrian-Hittite Expedition (1935–38) discovered Frgms. B–E during excavations at Tell Tayinat and the pieces are now conserved in the Oriental Institute of the University of Chicago. For detailed information on their provenance, see Lauinger and Batiuk, ZA 105 (2015) pp. 57–59 (information partially provided by H. Snow). The existence of Frgms. B–E has previously been mentioned by G.F. Swift (Pottery of the 'Amuq p. 183) and J.A. Brinkman (JCS 29 [1977] p. 62). Only Frgm. B preserves parts of two inscribed faces, the front, Face i, and left side, Face iv, of the stele; what would be Faces ii and iii, the right side and back of the stele, are not preserved on this fragment. J. Lauinger kindly provided the author with photos of Frgms. A–D and information on the discovery of the Frgm. A was provided by S. Batiuk.

Elements of the relief on the front of the stele are preserved on Frgm. A and Face i of Frgm. B. As noted by Lauinger and S. Batiuk (ZA 105 [2015] pp. 60–61), Frgm. A was likely situated higher on the stele than Frgm. B, and thus closer to the beginning of the inscription. The order in which the fragments are numbered is based on the assumed order of the text, with Frgm. A and Face i of Frgm. B preserving parts of the invocation of deities at the beginning of the text, Frgms. C–E preserving parts of the historical report, and Frgm. B Face iv preserving part of the curse at the end of the text. In view of the fact that none of the fragments join any other fragment, each fragment has been treated separately in the edition presented here. In general, the restorations follow those proposed by Lauinger and Batiuk.

Lauinger and Batiuk (ZA 105 [2015] pp. 66–67) suggest that the "most likely possibility seems to us to be that the report of Hamath's destruction is the main historical event described in the text."

BIBLIOGRAPHY

2015 Lauinger and Batiuk, ZA 105 pp. 54–68 (photo, edition, study)

2018 Frahm, Last Days pp. 63–64 no. 3 (Frgm. D lines 1′–10′, edition, study)

TEXT

Fragment A

Too poorly preserved to allow transliteration.

Fragment B, Face i

Lacuna
1′) [*x x* (*x x*)] IB [...]
2′) [*a*]-⌜*li*⌝-*kut* [... ^{d}*iš-tar*$^{?}$]
3′) *x-ka-a-at* [...]
4′) *sa-a-ḫi-ru* [... ^{d}IMIN.BI]
5′) *a-li-kut* [*ma-ḫar* DINGIR.MEŠ *ša a-šar šá-áš-mi*]
6′) *i-di* [LUGAL *mi-ig-ri-šú-nu i-za-zu-ma*]
7′) *i-šak-ka-nu li*-[(*i*)-*tu* DINGIR.MEŠ GAL.MEŠ *mut-tab-bi-lu-ut*]
8′) AN-*e* KI-*tim ša* [*ti-bi-šu-nu tu-qu-un-tú ù šá-áš-mu*]
9′) *na-šu-ú e-ni* [*na-bu-ú šu-um* LUGAL]
10′) *ša i-na e*-⌜*peš*⌝ [KA-*šú-nu el-li* KUR UGU KUR]
11′) ⌜*i*⌝-*šak-ka-nu*-⌜*ma*⌝ [*ú-šar-bu-ú* UGU *mal-ki*]
Lacuna

Fragment C

Lacuna
1′) [...] *x* [...]
2′) [*za-ku-ut bal-til*.KI *u*] URU.⌜*ḫar*⌝-[*ra-na ša ul-tu* UD.MEŠ *ru-qu*-(*ú*)-*ti*]
3′) [*im-ma-šú-ma*] *ki-din*-⌜*nu*⌝-[*su-un ba-ṭil-ta ú-ter áš-ru-uš-šá*]
4′) [...] (blank) [...]
Lacuna

Fragment D

Lacuna
1′) [...] *x* [...]

Fragment A

Too poorly preserved to allow translation.

Fragment B, Face i

Lacuna

Frgm. B i 1′–7′a) [... DNs, who g]o [...; *the goddess Ištar*], ... [...; DN], who encircles [...; the Sebetti], who go [before the gods, stand] at the side [of the king, their favorite, in the place of battle, and] bring about (his) vic[tory];

Frgm. B i 7′b–11′) [Great gods, managers] of heaven (and) netherworld, who[se attack means battle and strife], who appoint (rulers) (lit.: "raise the eyes") [(and) name king(s)], (and) by who[se holy command] they place [(one) land over (another) land] an[d make (its ruler) greater than (other) rulers].

Lacuna

Fragment C

Lacuna

Frgm. C 1′–3′) [... I restored the exemption (from obligations) of (the city) Baltil (Aššur) and] the city Ḫ[arrān, which had fallen into oblivion in the distant past, and their] privileged sta[tus that had lapsed].

Frgm. C 4′) [...]
Lacuna

Fragment D

Lacuna

Frgm. D 1′–10′) [...] He (Iaū-bi'dī) [assembled ... at the

Frgm. A The fragment comes from the left side of the front of the stele and traces of eleven lines are preserved; however, "the inscription is so worn as to be illegible even if individual signs can be discerned here and there (e.g., EN [line 4], URU.*aš-šur* [line 7] and perhaps SIG$_5$ [line 9])" (Lauinger and Batiuk, ZA 105 [2015] p. 60). It is possible that the end of the preserved portion of line 4′ has URU.MEŠ *šá* KUR DÙ-*šú-nu*, that the seventh line begins with *x pa-da-a* URU.*aš-šur x*.MEŠ (where the first indeterminate sign does not appear to be LA), and that the ninth line has *ina na-ge-e* after the tentative SIG$_5$; however, we do not expect to find some of these words/phrases in the introductory section of the inscription where various deities are normally invoked and, as noted in the commentary, Fragment A comes from the beginning of the inscription. Compare for example text no. 103 i 1–28, text no. 116 lines 1–10, and text no. 117 i 1–19a.

Frgm. B, Face i 1′–11′ For the restorations, cf. text no. 103 i 19–28 and text no. 116 lines 1–10.

Frgm. B, Face i 10′ *ša i-na e*-⌜*peš*⌝ [KA-*šú-nu el-li*] "by who[se holy command]": Possibly translate instead "who in order to carry o[ut their holy command]" (cf. Novotny and Jeffers, RINAP 5/1 p. 231 no. 11 i 13).

Frgm. C lines 2′–3′ The restorations are based on text no. 103 ii 18–21. The line breaks are conjectural and some of what is restored at the end of line 3′ may have been on line 4′. For line 3′ J. Lauinger and S. Batiuk (ZA 105 [2015] p. 65) read [... GN]^{ki} *māt*(KUR) [GN ...], but the second sign appears to be DIN rather than KUR; compare the KUR in Frgm. D line 5′ (see the photos on ibid. p. 59).

Frgm. D The exact amount of space missing at the beginnings and ends of the lines is uncertain, as are the line breaks in the restorations.

2′) [... *ina* URU].⸢*qar*⸣-*qa-ri* ⸢*ú*⸣-[*paḫ-ḫir-ma* (...)]
3′) [(...) *uš-bal-kit*? *it*]-*ti-ia* URU.⸢*ar*⸣-[*pad-da* URU.*ṣi-mir-ra* (...)]
4′) [(...) URU.*di-maš-qa* (...) URU].⸢*sa*⸣-*mi-ri-i*-⸢*na*⸣ [...]
5′) [... *ina qé*]-⸢*reb*⸣ KUR.*a-ma-te* É/KIT x [...]
6′) [...] x ᵈ*aš-šur* MAN DINGIR.⸢MEŠ⸣ [(...) *áš-šú*? (...)]
7′) [(...) *ka-šad* KUR.*a-ma*]-⸢*te sa*⸣-*kap* ᵐᵈ⸢*ia*?⸣-[*ú-bi-i*ʾ-*di*? ...]
8′) [(...) KUR *a-mur-re-e*? (DAGAL-*ti*) *am-ḫur*? *ú*]-⸢*ma*⸣-ʾ*e-er-ma* x [...]
9′) [...] ⸢*a-duk-ma*⸣ [...]
10′) [...] x [...]

Lacuna

city Q]arqar and [*incited* (*it/them*) *to rebel* aga]inst me. The cit[ies] A[rpad, Ṣimirra, (...), Damascus, (...), (and) S]amaria [... (5′) ... i]n the land Hamath, *the house* [... *I prayed to*] the god Aššur, the king of the gods, [*in order to* (*be able to*) (...) conquer the land Hama]th, overthrow *I*[*aū-bi*ʾ*dī* (*and*) ... the (wide) land Amurru. I] commanded and [...] I killed an[d ...]

Lacuna

Fragment E

Lacuna

1′) [x] x [...]
2′) *ina qé*-⸢*reb*⸣ [KUR.*ḫa-mat-ti ú-še-šib-šú-nu-ti* GUN *ma-da-tu*]
3′) *za-bal* [*ku-du-u-ri a-lak* KASKAL *ki-i ša* MAN.MEŠ AD.MEŠ-*ia*]
4′) *a-na* ⸢ᵐ⸣[*ir-ḫu-le-na* KUR.*a-ma-ta-a-a e-mid-du*]

Lacuna

Fragment E

Lacuna

Frgm. E 1′–4′) [... I settled them] in [the land Hamath. I imposed on them (the same) tribute, payment(s)], labor [duty, (and) military service as the kings, my ancestors, had imposed] on [Irḫulena of the land Hamath]

Lacuna

Fragment B, Face iv

Lacuna

1′) [*mu-nak-kir*?] *ep-še*-⸢*te*⸣-[*ia* SIG$_5$?]
2′) [*mu-pa-šiṭ*] *ši-ṭir* [MU-*ia*]
3′) [DINGIR.MEŠ] GAL.<MEŠ> *ma*-[*la*]
4′) [x x (x)] *ina* NA$_4$.NA.RÚ.[A]
5′) [*an-né-e* MU-*šú-nu*] *na*-⸢*bu*⸣-[*u*]
6′) [*li-ru-ru-šu-ma*] MU-[*šú* NUMUN-*šú*]

Lacuna

Fragment B, Face iv

Lacuna

Frgm. B iv 1′–6′) [(*As for*) *the one who alters* my *good*] deeds [(or) erases my] inscribed [name, may the] great [gods] — as ma[ny ... as] are ment[ioned by name] on [this] stel[e — curse him and make his] name [(and) his descendant(s) disappear from the land]

Lacuna

Frgm. D lines 2′–9′ For the restorations, cf. in particular text no. 81 lines 8–20 and text no. 89 lines 19–26; see also Frahm, Last Days pp. 63–64. Possibly restore *a-na i-di-šú ú-ter-ra*, "he brought to his side" at the end of line 4′ (also Frahm, ibid. p. 64). E. Frahm (ibid. pp. 63–64) tentatively reads [*mārē aššur ša ina qé*]-⸢*reb*⸣ at the beginning of line 5′, [... *bašû kī ištēn*] at the end of line 5′, and [*iddūk qātī aš-ši*]-⸢*ma*⸣ at the beginning of line 6′, thus "[He killed the citizens of Assyria who were i]n the land Hamath ... [... altogether. I raised my hands a]nd" (Frahm's translation slightly modified), and this would make good sense, but must remain uncertain. He also tentatively suggests restoring EN *ḫi-iṭ-ṭi* in line 9′ before *adūk* based on text no. 7 line 35, thus "I killed [the criminal(s)]" (ibid. p. 64).

Frgm. D line 7′ ⸢*sa*⸣-*kap*, "overthrow": The reading of the signs as *sa-kap* is certain even although the first sign is slightly damaged with only two (instead of three) vertical wedges being clear and the second sign has one more angled wedge head than is expected.

Frgm. E lines 2′–4′ The passage deals with the settling of 6,300 Assyrian criminals in Hamath. The restoration is based on text no. 105 ii′ 8–12 and assumes that the beginning of the following line began with *e-mid-su-nu-ti*. As noted by J. Lauinger and S. Batiuk (ZA 105 [2015] p. 65), in view of Fragment D line 5′, we should perhaps restore KUR.*a-ma-te* in line 2′, rather than KUR.*ḫa-mat-ti*.

Frgm. B Face iv 1′–6′ For the restorations, cf. text no. 103 iv 63–68 and text no. 106 iii 14′–15′. We would expect SIG$_5$.MEŠ rather than just SIG$_5$, but there does not appear to be room to allow this. The translation assumes that the following line had *i-na* KUR *li-ḫal-li-qu*, following text no. 103 iv 69.

109

Three fragmentary prismatic clay cylinders with an inscription of Sargon were found in 2015 during excavations at Carchemish by a Turkish-Italian expedition led by N. Marchetti. The text describes the conquest of Carchemish, the settlement of Assyrians there, the building activities carried out there by Sargon, and the expansion of irrigation in the area of that city. According to text no. 73, after Sargon's conquest of Carchemish in his fifth regnal year (717), booty taken from Pisīri(s), the king of Carchemish, was sent to Kalḫu and stored in the juniper palace there. A short colophon on the right end of ex. 1 states that the piece came from (or belonged to) the "Palace of Sargo[n]." Information on the text was kindly provided to the author by G. Marchesi before its recent publication in JNES.

CATALOGUE

Ex.	Excavation Number	Provenance	Dimensions (cm)	Lines Preserved	cpn
1	KH.15.O.221	Carchemish; palace complex, in layer of fill (F.5859), in a well (P.5345) cut into bedrock	8.8×13.2×3.9	5′–38′; colophon 1–2	p
2	KH.15.O.300	Carchemish; palace complex, near the well (P.5345), embedded in a floor of beaten earth (L.5896) that dated to the Neo-Babylonian phase of the complex	4×5×2.6	1′–13′	p
3	KH.15.O.355	Carchemish; palace complex, in a layer of fill (F.6309), in a well (P.5345) cut into bedrock	3.8×5.3×2.7	14′–20′, 29′–44′	p

COMMENTARY

The three fragments are preserved in the Gaziantepe Archaeological Museum. Ex. 1 originally had a diameter of ca. 8.5 cm and 12 faces. Each of the preserved faces has six lines and thus the text would have likely had 67–72 lines (with the final face having at least one line). Marchesi suggests that the lines on ex. 1 were at least as long as those on the Khorsabad cylinder Nap. III 3156 (text no. 43 ex. 1) and that "the longest lines of text preserved [on KH 15.O.221] are only preserved for about two-thirds of their original length" (JNES 78 [2019] p. 7).

Marchesi (JNES 78 [2019] pp. 11 and 18) argues that the apparent reference in line 13′ to people of Carchemish being deported to some place on the border of the land Kammanu almost certainly refers to a location in the state of Bīt-Purutaš, which was conquered by Sargon in 713. He thus states that this inscription must have been composed after that date. He further notes that the description of the war with Carchemish in this text is more similar to that in the Khorsabad Annals (text no. 1 lines 72–76a and text no. 4 lines 13′–18′a), which he dates to 707, than to that in A 16947 (text no. 102), which he dates to 711, and so he suggests that the Carchemish cylinder inscription is likely to date closer to the time of the former than that of the latter (ibid. pp. 11 and 21–23).

The description of the construction work at Carchemish, the planting of trees in its environs, and the celebrations following the completion of the work are often similar to passages in other texts of Sargon dealing with the city Dūr-Šarrukīn (see also Marchesi, JNES 78 [2019] pp. 11–17).

The restorations follow those proposed by Marchesi, with only a few minor modifications. The master lines are based on ex. 1 for lines 10′–32′, ex. 2 for lines 1′–5′, and ex. 3 for lines 38′–44′. Lines 6′–9′ are a combination of exs. 1 and 2 and lines 33′–37′ are a combination of exs. 1 and 3. The published photos are occasionally not completely clear and as a result the edition must rely at times on that of Marchesi.

BIBLIOGRAPHY

2019 Marchesi, JNES 78 pp. 1–24 (exs. 1–3, photo, edition, study; ex. 3, copy)

TEXT

Lacuna

1′) [*ma-a-ʾu ga-mir dun-ni ù a-ba-ri mu-šék-niš* KUR.*ma-da-a-a la kan-šu-te šá-a-giš* UN.MEŠ KUR.*ḫar-ḫar*.KI *mu-šar-bu-ú*] ⌜*mi-ṣir*⌝ KUR *aš-šur*.⌜KI⌝

2′) [*mu-pa-ḫir* KUR.*ma-an-na-a-a sa-ap-ḫi mu-ta-qí-in* KUR.*el-li-pí dal-ḫi ša* LUGAL-*ut* KUR.KUR *ki-lal-la-an ú-kin-nu-ma ú-šar*]-*ri-ḫu zi-kir-šú*

3′) [... *ina* u$_{4}$-*um be-lu-ti-ia mal-ku gaba-ra-a-a ul*] *ib-ši*-⌜*ma*⌝

4′) [*ina e-peš* MURUB$_{4}$ *u* MÈ *ul a-mu-ra mu-né-ḫu* ^{m}*pi-si-i-ri* URU.*gar-ga-miš-a-a i-na a-de-e* DINGIR.MEŠ GAL.MEŠ *iḫ-ṭi-ma a-na* ^{m}*mi-ta-a* LUGAL KUR.*mu-us-ki*] ⌜*ina*⌝ DÙG.GA *iš-tap-par-ma*

5′) [*il-qa-a še-ṭu-tu a-na* ^{d}*aš-šur be-lí-ia qa-a-ti áš-ši-ma šá-a-šú ga-a-du qin-ni-šú ka-mu-su-nu ú-še-ṣa-šú-nu-ti-ma*] ^{d}*a-šur ú-šab-ri*

6′) [KÙ.GI KÙ.BABBAR *it-ti* NÍG.ŠU É.GAL-*šú ù* URU.*gar-ga-miš-a-a* EN *ḫi-iṭ-ṭi ša it-ti-šu it-ti* NÍG.GA-*šú-nu áš-lu-lam-*(*ma*)] *a-na qé-reb* KUR *aš-šur*.KI *ú-ra-a*

7′) [50 GIŠ.GIGIR 2 ME ANŠE.*pét-ḫal-lum* 3 LIM LÚ.*zu-uk* GÌR.II *i-na lìb-bi-šú-nu ak-ṣur-ma* (*i-na*) UGU *ki-ṣir šar-ru*/LUGAL]-*ti-ia ú-rad-di*

8′) [(...) UN.MEŠ KUR *aš-šur*.KI *i-na qé-reb* URU.*gar-ga-miš ú-še-šib-ma ana* ...]-⌜*ti*⌝ *ú-šar-ḫi-su-nu-ti lib-bu*

9′) [... BÀD-*šú eš-šiš ú*]-*šab-ni-ma* UGU *šá maḫ-ri ú-zaq-qir*

10′) [... UN.MEŠ? *ša*? URU.*gar-ga-miš*? *ul-tu*] ⌜MURUB$_{4}$⌝ URU *ú-še-rid-ma ku-tal-la-šú ú-šá-aṣ-bit*

11′) [... *su*?]-⌜*un*⌝-*na-bu a-na dun-nun* EN.NUN *ina lìb-bi ú-še-rib*

12′) [... *mé*]-⌜*eḫ*⌝-*ret* ÍD.BURANUN.KI *ap-te-ma ú-ṭib ṣur-ra-šú-un*

Lacuna

1′–2′) [*the victorious one* who is perfect in strength and power (and) who subjugated the insubmissive Medes; who slaughtered the people of the land Ḫarḫar (and) enlarged] the territory of Assyria; [who gathered (back together) the scattered land Mannea (and) brought order to the disturbed land Ellipi; who established (his) kingship over both (these) lands and made] his name [glo]rious;

3′–7′) [... Since the (first) day of my reign], there has been [no ruler who could equal me] and [I have met no one who could overpower (me) in war or battle. Pisīri(s) of the city Carchemish sinned against the treaty (sworn) by the great gods and] repeatedly wrote in a friendly manner [to Mitâ (Midas), king of the land Musku], and (5′) [held me in contempt. I raised my hand(s) (in supplication) to the god Aššur, my lord, brought him (Pisīris), together wit his family, out (of their city) in bondage, and] showed (them) to the god Aššur. [I carried off as booty gold (and) silver, (along) with the property of his palace and the guilty people of the city Carchemish who (had sided) with him, as well as their possessions, (and)] brought (them) to Assyria. [I conscripted fifty chariot(s), two hundred cavalry, (and) three thousand foot soldiers from among them and] added (them) [to] my [royal (military) contingent].

8′–16a′) [(...) I settled people of Assyria in the city Carchemish and ...] made them confident. [... I] had [its (city) wall] built [anew] and raised (it) higher than before. (10′) [...] I brought [(...) *the people of the city Carchemish*] down [fro]m the city and *settled* (*them*) *behind it* (*the city wall*). [...] I had [(...) *a* (*military*) co]*ntingent* enter there in order to strengthen (its) garrison. [...] I opened [... fac]ing the Euphrates River and made their heart(s) happy. [... *I deported* (*people of Carchemish and*)] (re)settled (them) [in ..., a d]istant [place] on the border of the land Kammanu. [...] I settled in its neighborhood [... (*people*) *who pull* the

---

1′–2′ For the restorations, see text no. 43 lines 30–31.
3′–4′a For the restorations, see text no. 7 line 13.
4′b–8′ The restorations are based on text no. 1 lines 72–76 and text no. 4 lines 13′–18′.
10′ The exact meaning of the passage is not clear. G. Marchesi translates it as "[... (people of Karkemish)] I brought down [from the cen]ter of the city and made (them) occupy its rear part" and takes it to refer to "a forced relocation of the inhabitants of Karkemish to the Outer Town. The Citadel and the Inner Town were presumably reserved for the newly settled-Assyrians," although noting that "[n]o other example of this kind of displacement of people from one area of a city to another is known" (JNES 78 [2019] pp. 5 and 17–18).
11′ [*su*?]-⌜*un*⌝-*na-bu* "[*a* (*military*) *co*]*ntingent*": The tentative restoration and understanding of this word, which would be a hapax legomenon, follows Marchesi, JNES 78 (2019) p. 18.

13′) [... *as-su-ḫa-am-ma*$^{?}$ *ina ... a-šar*] ⌜*ru*⌝-*uq-te mi-ṣir* KUR.*kám-a-ni ú-še-šib*
14′) [... *šá-di-id*$^{?}$ *ni*]-*ir* ^{d}*a-šur* EN-*ia ú-šar-ma-a li-me-e-su*
15′) [... LÚ.*a*]-*ri-me* KUR.*ṣur-ri* KUR.*mu-uṣ-ri* KUR.*ta-ba-li u* KUR.*mus-ki*
16′) [... *áš-pu-uk-ma* NA$_4$].⌜*pi*⌝-*i-lu dan-nu ki-ma ši-pik* KUR-*i ú-šar-šid*
17′) [... *ina* ITI].⌜SIG$_4$⌝.GA ITI *mit-ga-ri ú-kin uš-še-šá*
18′) [... É *ḫi-la-(a)-ni ta-an/am-ši-il* É].⌜GAL⌝ KUR.*ḫat-ti mé-eḫ-rat* KÁ.MEŠ-*šá ad-di*
19′) [... GIŠ.IG.MEŠ (...) *me*]-*ser* ZABAR *ú-rak-kis-ma ina* KÁ.MEŠ-*ši-na ú-rat-ti*
20′) [...] ⌜A⌝.MEŠ *a-tap-pi ḫi-bi-ib* ÍD *la-a i-ma-ak-ki-ir ta-mir-tuš*
21′) [... A.GÀR.MEŠ$^{?}$ *ḫab-ṣu-ti*$^{?}$ *šá*$^{?}$ *na-gi*]-⌜*i*$^{?}$⌝ *šum-ku-ri na-mu-ù*ʾ*-eš šu-ud-du-u e-mu-u mad-ba-riš*
22′) [(...) *ina zi-ik-ri-šú* GAL-*i šá* ^{d}*aš-šur* EN-*ia šá a-na šu-šu-ub na-me-e na-du-te ù pe-te-e ki-šub*]-⌜*bé*⌝-*e za-qáp ṣip-pa-te iš-ru-ku ši-rik-ti*
23′) [...] *gi-it-pu-šú ina* A.GÀR.MEŠ-*šú na*-⌜*di-u*⌝-*te ú-šaḫ-bi-ba* A.⌜MEŠ⌝
24′) [...] x *ú-kin a-ke-e ina ṣu-um-me-e la na-ḫar-šu-še ú-šaḫ-li-la a-tap-piš*
25′) [...] *ina* ⌜*ta-mir-ti*⌝ URU.*gar-ga-miš am-šú-ḫa ši-qi-i-tú ina ta-mir-ti-šú la-la-ni-te ú-šaḫ-ni-ba ni-sa-a-ba*
26′) [...] x-*ru-ú-te* ŠE.IM *ina la mì-in-di ina qer-bé-ti-šú áš-pu-ka qi-ra-a-te*
27′) [... *gi-mir* GURUN] *ad-na-a-te* GIŠ.GEŠTIN *si-mat* LUGAL-*u-ti* GIŠ.EREN GIŠ.ŠUR.MÌN GIŠ.LI *si-ḫir-tuš az-qup-ma* UGU *i-riš* GIŠ.TIR GIŠ.EREN *i-riš* URU *ú-ṭib*
28′) [...] ⌜GIŠ⌝.GEŠTIN *u* ŠIM.ḪI.A *iš-qu-ma ba-*ʾ*u-lat lìb-bi-šú qur-ru bu-luṭ lìb-bi in-da-na-ḫa-ra nu-um-mu-ru zi-mu-šun*
29′) [... *ana* ...] ⌜*u*⌝ *ru-up-pu-uš ta-lit-ti su-gul-lat* GU$_4$.MEŠ *u ṣe-e-ni saḫ-ḫu ap-te-ma ú-šam-ki-ra* A.MEŠ DÙG.GA.MEŠ
30′) [...] ⌜*ba*⌝-ʾ*u-lat* ŠÀ-*šú a-bur-riš ú-šar-bi-ṣu-ma* GIŠ.KIRI$_6$.MEŠ-*šú-nu in-ba iz-za-a*ʾ*-na-ma* ⌜*iḫ-nu-ba ta-mir-tuš*⌝
31′) [...] x EN.MEŠ-*ia* ^{d}*kar-ḫu-ḫu* ^{d}*gu*-KÁ *a-ši-bu-ut*

yo]ke of the god Aššur, my lord. [... the A]rameans, the lands Tyre, Egypt, Tabal, and Musku [...]

16b′–19′) [... I heaped up and] made the heavy [li]mestone (blocks) as secure as the base of a mountain. [... In the month Sim]anu, an auspicious month, I established its foundations. [...] I erected [a *bīt-ḫilāni*, a replica of a] Hittite [pal]ace, in front of its gates. [...] I bound [(...) the doors (...) with ba]nd(s) of copper and installed (them) in their gates.

20′–30′) "[... *I caused*] the water of the irrigation ditches (and) *the murmur of the current* [*to stop*], (saying) "Let him (Pisiris) not irrigate its (Carchemish's) meadowland(s)" [... *The rich fields*] *of the irrigation* [*distri*]*ct became* a wasteland (and) turned into desert. [(...) At the great command of the god Aššur, my lord, who] granted me as a gift [the (re)settling of abandoned pasture lands, opening up of unused la]nd, (and) planting of orchards [...] *massive* [...] I caused water to murmur through its abandoned fields. [...] I established. *I made (it) gurgle* like an irrigation ditch so that the destitute will not collapse on account of thirst. (25′) [...] I measured the irrigation canal in the environs of the city Carchemish. I made grain grow abundantly in its lush meadowland. [...] ... I piled up grain in immeasurable (quantities) in the granaries in its environs. [...] I planted around it [(...) every type of fruit tree from] all over the world, grapevine(s) fit for royalty, cedar, cypress, (and) juniper, and I made the smell of the city sweeter than the smell of a cedar forest. [...] the grapevine(s) and aromatic plants grew high and the people inside it (Carchemish) continually receive *an invitation to* well-being. Their faces are (thus) radiant (with joy). [...] I opened up the meadows [in order to ...] and to increase the (number of) offspring of the herds of cattle and sheep (and) goats, and I provided fresh water for irrigation. [...] they had [the p]eople inside it dwell (as safely) as in a meadow; their orchards are covered all over with fruit and its meadowland(s) flourished.

31′–34′) [...] I invited [...], my lords, (and) the deities

15′ G. Marchesi (JNES 78 [2019] pp. 11 and 19) suggests that the passage may refer to various peoples and places sending tribute to Sargon.
19′ Cf. text no. 8 line 36.
20′ The exact meaning of the line and the word *ḫi-bi-ib* in particular are uncertain. The tentative translation is based on that proposed by G. Marchesi (JNES 78 [2019] pp. 5 and 19). He takes *ḫibību* as the Assyrian form of *ḫabību* (following a suggestion of W.R. Mayer) and suggests that the person speaking may be Sargon or some deity. With regard to the understanding of *ḫi-bi-ib*, note the appearance of the verb *ḫabābu* in line 23′ (*ušaḫbiba*).
21′ The tentative restoration follows Marchesi, JNES 79 (2019) pp. 4 and 19 and is based on text no. 74 vii 66.
22′ The tentative restoration follows Marchesi, JNES 79 (2019) pp. 4 and 19 and is based on text no. 43 line 34 and text no. 65 line 68.
23′ As noted by G. Marchesi (JNES 79 [2019] p. 20), both *gitpušu* (presumably at Gt form of *gapāšu*) and *nadiʾūti* (presumably for *nadûti*, from the adjective *nadû*) would be hapax legomena.
24′ See Mayer, Orientalia NS 86 (2017) p. 13 and cf. text no. 43 line 40.
27′ For the restoration, see Grayson and Novotny, RINAP 3/1 Sennacherib text no. 17 viii 20.
28′ *qur-ru* "*an invitation to*": See Mayer, Orientalia NS 86 (2017) p. 32.
31′–32′ Cf. text no. 73 lines 19–20. Karḫuḫa and Kubāba are the city god and goddess of Carchemish respectively.

URU.*gar-ga-miš ina qé-reb* É.GAL-*ia aq-re*
32′) [...]-*ti* UDU.NÍTA.<MEŠ> *ú-re-e mi-it-ru-te* KUR.GI.MEŠ UZ.TUR.MUŠEN.MEŠ MUŠEN.MEŠ AN-*e mut-tap-ri-šú-te ma-ḫar-šú-nu aq-*⸢*qí*⸣
33′) [... *man-da-at-tu*$^{?}$ *ka-bit-tu*$^{?}$ *ša*$^{?}$ KUR.MEŠ$^{?}$ *ki-šit-ti*$^{?}$ ŠU.II-*ia*$^{?}$ *e-liš*] ⸢*u*⸣ *šap-liš ina tukul-ti* ^{d}*a-šur* EN-*ia ina qé-reb* URU.*gar-ga-miš am-ḫur*
34′) [... É].⸢GAL⸣ ^{m}*pi-si-ri áš-lu-la ina nu-um-mur pa-ni a-qis-su-nu-ti*

35′) [... *ina li-i-ti u*] ⸢*ki*⸣-*šit-ti* ŠU.II *ra-biš uš-zi-*⸢*za*⸣-*ni*
36′) [...] x *na-ki-ru* [... *maḫ*$^{?}$]-⸢*ri*$^{?}$⸣ *aš-šur e-ris-su-*⸢*nu-ti*⸣
37′) [...] ⸢*ú*⸣-*še-*⸢*rib-ma*⸣ *ik-ru-bu* ⸢LUGAL$^{?}$⸣-[(*ú*)-*ti*$^{?}$]
38′) [...] ⸢*mu*⸣-*ḫad-du-u* ⸢*ka*⸣-*bat-ti* DINGIR-*ti-šú-*⸢*nu*⸣ [...]
39′) [...]-*pa-*⸢*ti*⸣ *ina* BUR-x [...]
40′) [...] (x x) *ú*-[...]
41′) [...] x-*ma ina* GÚ *šá* x [...]
42′) [...]-ŠID *bit-re-e* ⸢*lu*$^{?}$⸣ x [...]
43′) [...] x KI LUGAL-*šu-nu* x [...]
44′) [...] x x [...]
Lacuna

Colophon ex. 1

45′) É.GAL
46′) ^{m}LUGAL-GI.[NA]
Lacuna

Karḫuḫa (and) Kubāba, who dwell in the city Carchemish, (to come) into my palace. [...] I offered before them [(...)] strong rams from the (fattening) shed, geese, ducks, (and) birds that fly in the sky (lit. "flying birds of the sky"). [...] I received in Carchemish [... *substantial tribute from the lands that I had conquered*, from one end] to the other (lit.: "[above] and below"), with the support of the god Aššur, my lord. [(...)] I carried off as booty [... of the pal]ace of Pisīri(s), (and) with a radiant face, I presented (them) to them (the gods).
35′–44′) [...] he (the god Aššur?) allowed me to stand in grandiose manner [(...) in triumph and] conquest. [...] *enemy* [... *befo*]*re* (the god) Aššur, I/he asked them [...] I/he caused to enter and they blessed [*my*] *k*[*ingship* ... w]ho makes thei[r] divine majesties happy [...] ... in ... [... (40′)...] ... [...] and on the *bank/neck* of ... [...] ... superb ... [...] ... their king [...] ... [...]

Lacuna

Colophon ex. 1

45′–46′) Palace of Sargo[n]

Lacuna

110

A brief proprietary inscription of Sargon II is found inscribed on several bricks from Carchemish and one from the nearby site of Tell Amarna (about 8 km south of Jerablus). The conquest and plunder of Carchemish in Sargon's fifth regnal year (717) and the deportation of its royal family is mentioned in several of Sargon's royal inscriptions (see especially text no. 1 lines 72–76, text no. 73 lines 21–22, text no. 74 iv 13–24, text no. 102, and text no. 117 ii 20–22a). See text no. 1010 for a stone fragment from Carchemish with an inscription possibly to be assigned to this ruler.

109 line 33′ The tentative restoration is based on Marchesi, JNES 78 (2019) pp. 6 and 21.

CATALOGUE

Ex.	Museum Number	Excavation/ Registration No.	Provenance	Dimensions (cm)	Lines Preserved	cpn
1	BM 90702 face	H.80.12	Carchemish	15×16×12.5	1–2	n
2	BM 90702 side	H.80.12	As ex. 1	As ex. 1	1–2	n
3	—	AM 1463	Tell Amarna (Syria), pit on the southern border of area N, in locus 4	ca. 23.0×9.5	1–2	p
4	—	KH.14.O.256 side A	As ex. 1	—	1–2	n
5	—	KH.14.O.256 side B	As ex. 1	—	1–2	n
6	—	KH.14.O.636	As ex. 1	—	1–2	p
7	—	KH.14.O.845 face	As ex. 1	—	1–2	p
8	—	KH.14.O.845 side A	As ex. 1	—	1–2	n
9	—	KH.14.O.845 side B	As ex. 1	—	1–2	n
10	—	KH.14.O.974	As ex. 1	—	1–2	p
11	—	KH.16.O.215	As ex. 1	—	1–2	n

COMMENTARY

Exs. 1–2 come from the excavations of P. Henderson at Carchemish in 1879. According to C.B.F. Walker, BM 90702 is part of a half brick and is stamped on the face and along the side (stamp 6.2×7.0 cm). The edition for these exemplars follows that of Walker and has not been collated. Ex. 3 is a fragment of a baked brick and was found in a pit (i.e., out of its original context) on May 7, 1996. Ö. Tunca suggests that it may have been taken from Carchemish after the Neo-Assyrian period for reuse during the Hellenistic or Roman-Byzantine period (Bagh. Mitt. 37 [2006] pp. 180–181). G. Marchesi kindly provided information (including transliterations) on exs. 4–11 and photos of exs. 6, 7, and 10; these unpublished exemplars from Carchemish are cited here through the courtesy of N. Marchetti, director of the Turco-Italian Archaeological Expedition to Karkemish.

According to L. Woolley and R.D. Barnett (Carchemish 3 pp. 211 and 265), a brick was found at Carchemish with an inscription saying "Palace of Sargon King of Nations, King of Assyria" (see ibid. p. 171 for possibly a different brick). Barnett also refers to a brick being found on the surface by Boscawen with a similar inscription (ibid. p. 265). According to Walker (CBI p. 119), "A typescript report entitled 'Report on the excavations at Carchemish 1911' by R.C. Thompson and T.E. Lawrence (now preserved in the Department of Western Asiatic Antiquities, British Museum) refers (p. 51) to the discovery of 'an Assyrian brick inscribed in cuneiform 'Palace of Sargon, king of multitudes, king of Assyria'; and one of the field note-books of the Carchemish excavations has a note in Thompson's hand, 'Assyrian inscribed brick of Sargon 350 × 165 × 120 high. Another found near it 350 × 165 × 110'. The field note-books do not contain any copy, transliteration, or translation of these bricks." The current locations of these bricks are not known and it is not clear whether or not they had a different inscription to the one presented here, although the translation in Woolley and Barnett, Carchemish 3 pp. 211 and 265 would suggest KUR.MEŠ or KUR.KUR (*mātāti*, "lands") instead of ŠÚ (*kiššati*, "world") in line 2. The translation "multitudes" for ŠÚ is, however, attested in various other publications of the time (e.g., Thompson, Arch. 79 [1929] p. 124 and pl. XLV no. 70 line 1).

No minor variants are attested for this inscription and, as is the practice in RINAP, no score for this brick inscription is given on Oracc.

BIBLIOGRAPHY

1952 Woolley and Barnett, Carchemish 3 pp. 211 and 265 (translation, study)

1981 Walker, CBI p. 119 no. 171 Sargon II X (ex. 1, transliteration, study)

2006 Tunca, Bagh. Mitt. 37 pp. 179–184 (ex. 3, photo, copy, edition)

2015 Marchetti, Current World Archaeology 70 p. 24 (photo)

2019 Marchesi, JNES 78 pp. 15–16 n. 15 (translation, study)

TEXT

1)	É.GAL ^{m}MAN-GIN	1–2) Palace of Sargon (II), king of the world, king of Assyria.
2)	MAN ŠÚ MAN KUR AŠ	

111–114

Four fragments of clay barrel cylinders bearing inscriptions of Sargon II were either certainly or likely found at Arslantepe (ancient Melid), near modern Malatya: text nos. 111–114. Text nos. 111 and 113–114 must come from different cylinders and it is clear that the inscription on text no. 111 is different to those on text nos. 113 and 114. It is possible that text nos. 113 and 114 are both duplicates of the same inscription, but since the line arrangement would differ in at least two places — text no. 113 lines 13´–17´ and 18´–22´ are each on five lines, rather than on four lines as on text no. 114 (lines 2´–5´ and 6´–9´ respectively) — and since only a little of text no. 114 is preserved, it has been thought best to keep them all separate here. Text nos. 111 and 112 were once physically joined together, but that was a false join since their inscriptions clearly deal with different topics where they were attached. It is not impossible, however, that the two fragments came from the same cylinder, but since this cannot be considered certain, they have also been kept separate here.

During the 1938 season of excavations at Arslantepe, L. Delaporte found two cylinder fragments with inscriptions of this ruler under the pavement of the Assyrian palace. The pieces were sent to the Ankara museum, but their inscriptions were not published at the time, although they were said to agree exactly with the text of Sargon's Annals (Landsberger, Samʾal p. 81 n. 213). It seems probable that one of these pieces was text no. 112 since at least part of the inscription on that piece does appear to duplicate part of Sargon's Annals. The other was likely text no. 111 or text no. 114, even though these are not duplicates of the Annals. Records in the Ankara Museum state that text no. 111 (AnAr 21717/323) was found at Arslantepe. While the provenance of text no. 114 (AnAr 21718/324) is not noted in the museum inventory, the piece is numbered and listed immediately following text no. 111; thus, it is quite possible that it also came from Arslantepe. (See Frame, Studies Parpola pp. 65–66; and Akdoğan and Fuchs, ZA 99 [2009] p. 85.) Since text nos. 111 and 112 were once physically joined together — albeit erroneously — it is not impossible that they were considered by B. Landsberger to be one piece and that his two cylinder fragments were text nos. 111+112 and text no. 114; however, in view of Landsberger's great expertise with cuneiform texts, it would seem unlikely that he would have accepted the join of text nos. 111 and 112. Text no. 113 was found at Arslantepe during excavations in 1968.

Sargon's conquest of and relations with Melid are mentioned in several other inscriptions of his (e.g., text no. 1 lines 204–210, text no. 2 lines 236–238 and 443, text no. 7 lines 78–80, text no. 8 lines 9–10 and 22, text no. 13 lines 24–26, and text no. 74 v 41–76). For an overview of this ruler's involvement with Melid, see Frame, Studies Parpola pp. 66–68.

---

110 line 1 ^{m}MAN: Ö. Tunca's edition of ex. 3 has simply MAN, while his copy shows the heads of two vertical wedges. As noted by G. Marchesi (private communication), the published photo of ex. 3 would suggest $^{m⌜}$MAN$^{⌝}$.

111

The first cylinder fragment from Arslantepe is part of the right end of a clay barrel cylinder. Its inscription mentions the creation/building of sacred objects/temples at Nineveh and Kalḫu (lines 5–10), the building of the city Dūr-Šarrukīn (lines 11–14), military campaigns to the east and northeast and the deportation of people from there to the west and northwest (lines 15–33), and, after a long gap, the end of an account describing the defeat of Marduk-apla-iddina II (lines 1′-9′) and possibly the annexation of an area to Assyria (lines 10′–12′). Line 10 of the inscription refers to the ruler's fourteenth year (708), but the text should have been composed no earlier than his fifteenth year (707) because it refers to the installation of the gods of Dūr-Šarrukīn in their shrines (line 12), which took place in the eponymy of Ša-Aššur-dubbu (707).

CATALOGUE

Museum Number	Provenance	Dimensions (cm)	cpn
Malatya Archaeological Museum 1997	Arslantepe	10.8×9.5	(c)

COMMENTARY

The cylinder fragment was transferred to the Malatya Archaeological Museum in 1970 from the Museum of Anatolian Civilizations in Ankara, where it had the inventory number 21717/323. The inventory in Ankara states that the piece was found at Arslantepe. (See Akdoğan and Fuchs, ZA 99 [2009] p. 84, and Frame, Studies Parpola p. 68.)

Parts of forty-seven lines are preserved, thirty-three from the beginning of the inscription and fourteen from the end of the inscription. The original inscription would have been over twice as long and each line would have been about five times as long as is currently preserved. The original has not been examined and the edition is based on the examination of a cast of the fragment that was kindly supplied by M. Frangipane and photographs of the original that were kindly made available by J. Renger.

Lines 1–4 are restored based upon text no. 103 ii 1–12 and 18–21; cf. text no. 74 i 1–11 and text no. 7 lines 1–7. Lines 10b–14 are restored based upon text no. 84 lines 7′a–11′; cf. also text no. 7 lines 154–156 and 158–159 and text no. 13 lines 94–101. Lines 1′–9′ are restored based upon such passages as text no. 74 vi 27–62 and text no. 86 lines 2′–9′. For lines 1′–9′, see also text no. 113 lines 9′–17′ and for lines 4′–9′ see also text no. 114 lines 1′–5′.

BIBLIOGRAPHY

1939 Delaporte, RHA 5/34 p. 54 (study)
1940 Delaporte, Malatya p. 9 (study)
1941 Kalaç, Sumeroloji Araştırmaları pp. 990–991 and 1011 (study)
1948 Landsberger, Sam'al p. 81 n. 213 (study)
2004 Frame in Frangipane, Alle origini pp. 175–177 (photo, translation, study)
2004 Frangipane, Alle origini pp. 172 and 201 no. 183 (photo, study)
2009 Akdoğan and Fuchs, ZA 99 pp. 84–85 (study)
2009 Frame, Studies Parpola pp. 65–79 (copy, edition, study)
2014 Maniori, Campagne di Sargon pp. 47–48 G10 and passim (study)

TEXT

1) [^{m}LUGAL-GI.NA MAN GAL-*ú* MAN *dan-nu* LUGAL ŠÚ MAN KUR *aš-šur*.KI GÌR.NÍTA KÁ.DINGIR.RA.KI MAN KUR EME.GI$_{7}$ *u* URI.KI MAN *kib-rat* LÍMMU-*i mi-gir*] DINGIR.MEŠ GAL.MEŠ ⸢*a*?⸣-[x x]

2) [^{d}*aš-šur* ^{d}AG ^{d}AMAR.UTU (DINGIR.MEŠ *ti-ik-le-ia*) LUGAL-*ut la šá-na-an ú-šat-li-mu-in-ni-ma zi-kir* MU-*ia dam-qu ú-še*]-*ṣu-ú a-na* ⸢*re*⸣-[*še-(e)-ti*]

3) [*ša* ZIMBIR.KI NIBRU.KI KÁ.DINGIR.RA.KI (*ù bár-sipa*.KI) *za-nin-us-su-un e-tep-pu-šá ša* ERIM.MEŠ *ki-din-ni mal ba-šu-ú*] *ḫi-bil-ta-šú*-⸢*nu*⸣ [*a-rib-ma*]

4) [*za-ku-ut bal-til*.KI *u* URU.*ḫar-ra-na ša ul-tu* UD.MEŠ *ru-qu-(ú)-ti im-ma-šú-ma ki-din-nu-us-su-un ba-ṭil-ta ú*]-*ter áš*-⸢*ru*?⸣-[*uš-šá*]

5) [...]-*zi-i* TAB? x [x x (x)]

6) [...] x UD.DA ^{d}ŠEŠ.KI-⸢*ri*⸣ [x (x)]

7) [... *qé*]-*reb* NINA.KI *u* URU.*kal-ḫa* x [x x (x)]

8) [...]-⸢*ši*⸣-*in* KÙ.MEŠ *ab-šim-ma* [x x (x)]

9) [...] x *ab-ni-ma ú-šá-an-biṭ* ⸢^{d}?⸣[UTU?-*niš*?]

10) [... *ša*? *ul-tu* SAG LUGAL-*ti-ia a*]-⸢*di*⸣ MU.14.KÁM *a-na* DINGIR.MEŠ *a-ši-bu*-⸢*ut*⸣ [x x]

11) [(...) *i-na* GÌR.II KUR.*mu-uṣ-ri* KUR-*i e-le-na* URU.NINA.KI *i-na bi-bil lib-bi-ia* URU DÙ-*uš-ma* URU.BÀD-^{m}]LUGAL-GI.NA *az-ku-ra ni-bit*-⸢*su*⸣

12) [^{d}*é-a* ^{d}30 ^{d}UTU ^{d}AG ^{d}IŠKUR ^{d}*nin-urta ù ḫi-ra-ti-šú-nu* GAL.MEŠ *i-na qé-reb é-ḫur-sag-gal-kur-kur-ra ú-šá-aʾ-lid-ma i-na qé*]-⸢*reb*⸣-*šú ú-šar-ma-a pa-rak da-ra-a-ti*

13) [É.GAL.MEŠ ZÚ AM.SI GIŠ.ESI GIŠ.TÚG GIŠ.*mu-šuk-ka-ni* GIŠ.EREN GIŠ.ŠUR.MÌN GIŠ.*dup-ra-ni* ŠIM.LI *ù* GIŠ.*bu-uṭ-ni a-na mu-šab* LUGAL-*ti-ia*] ⸢*qer-bu*⸣-*uš-šu ab-ni-ma*

14) [... *ba-ḫu-la-ti na-ki-ri ki-šit-ti qa-ti-ia i-na qer-bi-šu par-ga-niš ú-šar-bi-iṣ-ma*] *it*-⸢*ti ma*⸣-*ḫa-zi* KUR *aš-šur*.KI *am-nu-šú*

15) [*i-na tukul-ti* DINGIR.MEŠ GAL.MEŠ (*lu*) *at-tal-lak-ma* UN.MEŠ ÍD.*mar-ra-ti* AN.TA *a-di* ÍD.*mar-ra-ti* KI.TA *ki-i iš-te*$_{9}$*-en a-bel-ma* KUR.MEŠ *la ma-gi-ri*] ⸢*ḫur*⸣-*šá-a-ni la kan-šu-ti ú-šak-ni-šá še-pu-u-a*

16) [...] x-*ti iš-ku-nu pa-ni-šu-un*

17) [... *aš*]-⸢*kun*?⸣-*ma* ÚŠ.MEŠ-*šú-nu ḫur-ri na-at-bak* KUR-*i ú-šar-di*

18) [... *qé*]-*reb* KUR.*ḫa-at-ti ú-še-šib*

1) [Sargon (II), great king, strong king, king of the world, king of Assyria, governor of Babylon, king of the land of Sumer and Akkad, king of the four quarters (of the world), favorite] of the great gods, [...] —

2) [The gods Aššur, Nabû, (and) Marduk, (the gods, my helpers), granted me a reign without equal and exa]lted [my good reputation] to the h[eights].

3–4) [I continually acted as provider for (the cities) Sippar, Nippur, Babylon), (and Borsippa). I made restitution for] the wrongful damage [suffered by the people of privileged status as many as there were (of them); I] resto[red the exemption (from obligations) of (the city) Baltil (Aššur) and the city Ḫarrān, which had fallen into oblivion in the distant past, and their privileged status that had lapsed].

5–10) [...] ... [...] ... [*like*] the light of the moon [... i]n (the city) Nineveh and the city Kalḫu [...] I created [th]eir holy [...] and [...] I built and made shine [*like the sun ... that* from the beginning of my reign unt]il (my) fourteenth year to/for the gods who dwell [...]

11–14) [In accordance with my heart's desire, I built a city at the foot of Mount Muṣri, a mountain upstream from the city Nineveh, and] I named it [Dūr]-Šarrukīn. [I had the gods Ea, Sîn, Šamaš, Nabû, Adad, Ninurta, and their great spouses created inside Eḫursaggalkurkurra ("House, the Great Mountain of the Lands") and] I installed (them) [insi]de it on (their) eternal dais(es). I built inside it [palatial halls using (lit.: "of") elephant ivory, ebony, boxwood, *musukkannu*-wood, cedar, cypress, *daprānu*-juniper, juniper, and terebinth to be my royal residence] and [... I had enemy people whom I had captured dwell inside it (as safely) as in meadowland and] I considered it a[s (one of) the cu]lt centers of Assyria.

15–33) [With the support of the great gods, I advanced and ruled the people from the Upper Sea to the Lower Sea as if (they were) one (people).] I made [uncompliant lands (and)] insubmissive [mou]ntain regions bow down at my feet. [...] they set out [... *I establ*]*ished* and I made their blood flow down the gorges of the outflows of the mountains [...] I settled [i]n the land Ḫatti (Syria). [...] *of* a rugged mountain he sought refuge. (20) [...] ... and he grasped hold of

1 Possibly ⸢*a*⸣-[*na-ku*], "(am) I" at the end of the line? See Frame, Studies Parpola p. 75 and the on-page note to text no. 103 ii 4.
5–10a These lines may duplicate in part, or deal with similar matters as, text no. 84 lines 3′–7′a. See Frame, Studies Parpola pp. 75–76.
6 Cf. perhaps text no. 45 lines 28–29.
9 Or perhaps ⸢*zi*⸣-[*mu-šú*]; see CAD N/1 p. 23 sub *nabāṭu* 4.a.
15 With regard to the restoration, cf. for example text no. 84 line 12′, as well as text no. 8 line 6, text no. 14 lines 12–14, and text no. 103 ii 22–27.
18 and 21 Cf. text no. 1 lines 66–68 and 76–78, text no. 4 lines 3′–6′ and 18′–20′, text no. 7 line 57, and text no. 43 line 28 with regard to the settling of Manneans in the west.

19) [...]-*ri* KUR-*i mar-ṣi šá-ḫa-ta e-mid*
20) [...] *x-ú-ma* ⸢*iṣ-ba*⸣-*ta še-pi-ia*
21) [...] ⸢*as*⸣-*suḫ-šú-nu-ti i-na qé-reb* KUR.*ḫat-ti ú-še-šib*
22) [...] *x-ik-ma* UN.MEŠ KUR.*man-na-a-a pu-luḫ-tú e-mid*
23) [...] *x-ma qé-reb* KUR.*a-ma-at-ti ú-še-šib*
24) [...].⸢MEŠ⸣-*šú-nu ka-bit-tu a-na* KUR *aš-šur*.KI *ub-la*
25) [...] *áš-kun-ma ni-ir be-lu-ti-ia e-mid*-⸢*su*⸣-*nu-ti*
26) [...] *x-a ak-šud*^{ud}
27) [...] ⸢*ap*⸣-*pu-ul aq-qur i-na* IZI *áš-ru*-⸢*up*⸣
28) [...]-⸢*ia*$^?$⸣ *na-dan šat-ti-šú-nu ik-lu*-⸢*ú*⸣
29) [...] *x* ⸢*i*$^?$-*ku*$^?$⸣-*ú* ⸢*ak-šu*⸣-*ud-ma di-ik-ta-šú-nu a*-⸢*duk*⸣
30) [...] *a-na* KUR *aš-šur*.KI *al-qa*-⸢*a*⸣
31) [...]-*áš* ^{m}*a-da-a* KUR.*šur-da-a-a e-mì-da* ⸢*ni-ir* $^{d?}$⸣[*aš-šur*$^?$]
32) [... URU.*ḫu-bu*]-⸢*uš*⸣-*ki-a* URU ⸢LUGAL⸣-*ti-šú* [*x x* (*x*)]
33) [...] *x x x x x x x* [*x x x*]

Lacuna

1′) [*ul-la-nu-u-a* ^{md}AMAR.UTU-IBILA-SUM.NA URU.MEŠ-*šú áš-bu-ti ù* DINGIR.MEŠ *a-šib lib-bi-šú-un ú-paḫ-ḫir-ma a-na* URU.BÀD-^{m}*ia-ki-na ú-še-rib-ma ú-dan-ni-na ker-ḫe*]-⸢*e*⸣-[*šú*]
2′) [10 NINDA.TA.ÀM *la-pa-an* BÀD-*šú* GAL-*e ú-né-es-si-ma* 2 ME *ina* 1.KÙŠ DAGAL *ḫa-ri-ṣi iš-kun-ma* 1 1/2 NINDA *ú-šap-pil-ma ik-šu-da* A.MEŠ *nag*]-*bi*
3′) [*bu-tuq-tu ul-tu qé-reb* ÍD.BURANUN.KI *ib-tuq-ma ú-šar-da-a ta-mir-tuš* A.GÀR.MEŠ-*šú a-šar mit-ḫu-ṣi* A.MEŠ *im-ki-ir-ma ú-šap-ši-qa né*]-⸢*ber*⸣-*tu*
4′) [*šu-ú a-di* LÚ.*re-ṣi-šú* ERIM.MEŠ MÈ-*šú i-na bi-rit* ÍD.MEŠ *ki-ma ku-mé-e*.MUŠEN *za-ra-tú* LUGAL-*ti-šú iš-kun-ma ú-pa-ḫi-ra ka-ras*]-*su*
5′) [*i-na qí-bit* AN.ŠÁR ^{d}AG ^{d}AMAR.UTU UGU ÍD.MEŠ-*šú a-ram-mu ú-šak-bi-is-ma šá-a-šú ga-du* LÚ.*mun-daḫ-ṣe-šu* GIM TI$_8$.MUŠEN *mut-tap-ri-ši a-bar-šú i*]-⸢*na*$^?$⸣ *še-e-ti*
6′) [*pag-re* LÚ.*nu-bal-le-e-šú ù* LÚ.*aḫ-la-me-e ṣa-ab* EDIN *a-li-kut i-de-e-šú ki-ma* ŠE.MUNU$_6$ *áš-ṭe-e-ma i-ta-at* URU-*šú ú*]-⸢*mal*⸣-*li*
7′) [URU.BÀD-^{m}*ia-ki-ni* É *ni-ṣir-ti-šú* URU.*iq-bi*-^{d}EN URU.*kap-ru* URU.É-^{m}*za-bi-da-a-a* URU.*šá-at*-SUM.NA URU.*za-ra-a-ti* URU.*raq-qa-tu* URU.*e-ku-uš-šú* URU.*ḫur*]-⸢*sag*⸣-GAL$_5$.LÁ.MEŠ
8′) [URU.BÀD-^{d}EN-URU-*ia* URU.BÀD-^{d}EN.LÍL URU.É-^{m}*qí-ib-la-te* URU.*né-med*-^{d}30 URU.*li-mi-tum* URU.*mad-a-kal-šá* 15 URU.MEŠ *dan-nu-ti a-di* URU.MEŠ *ša*] ⸢*li-me-te-šú*⸣-[*un*]

my feet. [... I] deported them (and) settled (them) in the land Ḫatti. [...] ... and I imposed fear upon the people of the land Mannea. [...] and I settled (them) in the land Hamath. [...] I brought their substantial [*tribute*] to Assyria. (25) [...] I established and imposed on them the yoke of my lordship. [...] I conquered. [...] I destroyed, demolished, (and) burned down with fire. [...] they withheld their annual (tribute) payment(s). [...] ... I conquered and inflic[ted] a defeat on them. (30) [...] I took to Assyria. [...] upon Adâ of the land Šurda, I imposed the yoke of *the god* [*Aššur. ... Ianzû, king of the land Na'iri, ...* Hub]uškia, his royal city [...] ... [...]

Lacuna

1′–4′) [In the face of my advance (lit.: "before me"), Marduk-apla-iddina (II) (Merodach-Baladan) gathered together the inhabitants of his cities (lit.: "his inhabited cities") and the gods dwelling in them and brought (them) into the city Dūr-Yakīn. He then strengthened its enclosure wall]s [(and), moving back a distance of ten *nindanu* from the front of its main wall, he made a moat two hundred cubits wide. He made (it) one and a half *nindanu* deep and reached gro]und [water. He cut a channel from the Euphrates River, (thereby) making (its water) flow (in)to its meadowland. He flooded its fields, where battles (are fought), and made cros]sing [difficult. Together with his allies (and) his battle troops, he pitched his royal tent in a bend of the river (lit.: "between rivers") like a *crane* and assembled] his [(military) camp].

5′–9′) [At the command of the gods Aššur, Nabû, (and) Marduk I had a causeway constructed (lit.: "trodden down") across his canals and I caught him, together with his fighting men, like a flying eagle i]n a net. [I spread out like malt (spread for drying) the corpses of his vanguard and of the Aḫlamû, the people of the steppe who go at his side and I fi]lled [the surroundings of his city (with them). The city Dūr-Yakīn — his treasure house — (and) the cities Iqbi-Bēl, Kapru, Bit-Zabidāya, Šāt-iddina, Zarāti, Raqqatu, Ekuššu, Ḫursa]ggalla, [Dūr-Bēl-āliya, Dūr-Enlil, Bīt-Qiblāte, Nēmed-Sîn, Limītu, (and) Mād-akālša, (a total of) fifteen fortified cities, together with the settlements in] th[eir e]nvirons, I turned into (ruin) [mo]unds. [I carried off as booty at the same

19–20 Possibly a reference to the submission of Ullusunu, the Mannean ruler, in 714. Cf. text no. 7 lines 40–41 and 50.
22 Possibly [... *e*]-⸢*ti*$^?$⸣-*iq-ma*, "[... I cr]ossed and," or some other form of the verb *etēqu* at the beginning of the line.

⸢*ti*⸣*-la-niš ú-še-me*
9′) [UN.MEŠ *ṣe-ḫer ra-bi a-ši-bu-ut na-ge-e ù* DINGIR.MEŠ *ti-ik-le-šú-un iš-te-niš áš-lu-lam-ma la e-zi*]-⸢*ba*⸣ *mul-taḫ-ṭu*
10′) [...] ⸢BU?⸣ *šá be-lut-si-in*
11′) [...] *x* UGU KUR-*ia ú*-⸢*rad?-dè?*⸣
12′) [...] ⸢KUR⸣ IB ṢA [*x x*]
13′) [...] ⸢d⸣AMAR.UTU *ik-ri-bi-šú* [*i-še-mu-u?*]
14′) [...] ⸢*a*⸣*-a ir-šu-šu* ⸢*re*⸣-[*e-mu*]

time (both) the people — young (and) old — who lived in the district and the gods who helped them; I did not all]ow a (single) person to escape.

10′–12′) [...] *whose* lordship [...] *I added* to my land [...] ... [...].

13′–14′) [... (*and*)] the god Marduk [will (then) listen to] his prayers. [...] may they not have p[ity] on him!

112

In 2017, J. Renger kindly sent the author some photos of various royal inscriptions of Sargon II that were in his possession and that had been used by him during his work on Sargon's royal inscriptions. Among them were photos of two fragments of a clay barrel cylinder that had been joined together. He had received the photos, which had been taken by A. Palmieri in the Malatya Archaeological Museum, from A. Archi around 1974. The larger of the two fragments has been edited here as text no. 111 and likely comes from L. Delaporte's excavations at Arslantepe in 1938. That fragment was once in the Archaeological Museum in Ankara, but was moved to the Malatya Museum in 1970. While the other fragment also preserves a text of Sargon II, a study of the inscriptions on the two pieces clearly shows that the two pieces do not join where they were fixed on the photo. This false join must have been recognized at some point since the two pieces are no longer attached. The current museum number of the smaller piece is not known to the author and recent searches for it in the museum have not located it. Since both pieces are only fragments, it is not impossible that the two come from the same cylinder, although based on what is known of the two pieces, it does not appear that they preserve parts of the same line at any point. The smaller piece is edited here, but it must be noted that due to the fragmentary state of the piece, the photos are not always clear, that the beginning and end of the text are for the most part illegible, and that the edition presented must be considered only preliminary. Unlike the inscriptions on the other cylinder fragments from Malatya, the text on this piece, for the most part, duplicates sections from Sargon's Annals dealing with Ambaris of Tabal/Bīt-Purutaš during Sargon's ninth campaign (713).

---

111 line 11′ Possibly [... *a*/*i*]-⸢*na*⸣ at the beginning of the line.
111 lines 13′–14′ [*i-še-mu-u?*]: Or [*i-šem-me*], in which case only Marduk would be subject of the verb. There does not appear to be sufficient room to restore *i-še-mu-ú* at the end of line 13′, but we would expect a form in the plural in view of the plural *ir-šu-šu* in line 14′.

CATALOGUE

Museum Number	Provenance	Dimensions (cm)	cpn
Malatya Archaeological Museum —	Probably Arslantepe	—	(p)

COMMENTARY

As noted earlier (introduction to text nos. 111–114), B. Landsberger (Sam'al p. 81 n. 213) stated that two cylinder fragments found by L. Delaporte at Arslantepe in 1938 and located at that time in the Ankara museum agreed exactly with the text of Sargon's Annals. However, none of the cylinder fragments previously thought to come from Malatya duplicate passages from the Annals, although they might at times deal with similar topics. The present piece, however, as far as one can tell, does agree for the most part with the text of the Annals from Room II (text no. 1), This would suggest that the current piece and possibly the fragment to which it was once (erroneously) joined (text no. 111) were one or both of the pieces that Landsberger saw.

On the photos of this fragment and text no. 111, line 11′ of text no. 111 (which deals with the founding of the city Dūr-Šarrukīn) was joined as a continuation of line 8′ of the present fragment (which deals with the appointment of governors over the land Bīt-Purutaš, following the defeat of its ruler Ambaris). Lines 5′–11′ of the present fragment may be compared to, and restored from, text no. 1 lines 198, 200, 202, 204, 125–126, 207, and 208 respectively (cf. text no. 2 lines 230, 232, and 235). Note that line 9′ matches parts of lines 125–126 of text no. 1, which come from the report of the Annals seventh campaign, unlike the remainder of the text which comes from the report of the ninth campaign. Since it is not clear how much is missing at the beginning and end of each line, restorations have been kept to a minimum in the transliteration.

BIBLIOGRAPHY

1939 Delaporte, RHA 5/34 p. 54 (study)
1940 Delaporte, Malatya p. 9 (study)
1941 Kalaç, Sumeroloji Araştırmaları pp. 990–991 and 1011 (study)
1948 Landsberger, Sam'al p. 81 n. 213 (study)

TEXT

Lacuna
1′) [...] (traces) [...]
2′) [...] (traces) [...]
3′) [...] (x) x x ⸢UN?.MEŠ? É? AD?⸣-*šú* x [...]
4′) [...] x x *ina* ⸢*qé*⸣-*reb* KUR ⸢*aš-šur*⸣.KI x [...]
5′) [...] KUR? (x) x x x x ⸢*it*⸣-*ti* KUR.*ḫi-lak-ki* x x (x) [...]
6′) [...] (x) x x x KUR.*mu*-⸢*us*⸣-*ki ša e*-⸢*ke*⸣-*mu mi*-[*ṣir-ia* ...]
7′) [...] *it-ti* 1 ME GIŠ.GIGIR-*šú a-na* KUR [*aš-šur*.KI ...]
8′) [... LÚ.EN].⸢NAM UGU⸣-*šú-nu áš*-⸢*kun-ma*⸣ *it-ti* UN.MEŠ [...]
9′) [... URU.*ḫa*]-⸢*ar?-ru*⸣-*a* URU.⸢*uš*⸣-*na-ni-is* URU.ḪAL.ṢU.MEŠ KUR.*qu-e šá* ⸢*ul*⸣-[*tu* ...]

Lacuna
1′–2′) No translation possible.
3′) [...] ... *people of the house of his father* [...]
4′) [...] ... in Assyria [...]
5′) [...] ... with the land Ḫilakku ... [...]
6′) [... that (man) (Ambaris) ... wrote to ...] *Mitâ, king* of the land Musku, about taking away terr[itory of mine ...]
7′) [... I brought in bondage] to [Assyria Ambaris ...], with one hundred of his chariot(s) [...]
8′) [...] I set [a eunuch of mine as provincial govern]or over them and [considered them] as people [of Assyria ...]
9′) [... I (then) restored to their former status the cities Ḫa]rrua (and) Ušnanis, fortresses of the land Que (Cilicia) that [he had annexed by force] i[n the distant

10′) [...] (*x*) *x x x x x x* KUR.MEŠ-*šú-nu rap-šá-a-te* [...]
11′) [...] ⸢LUGAL⸣ KUR.*mu-us-ki ze-ra-a-tú* ⸢KUR⸣ [*aš-šur*.KI ...]
12′) [...] (traces) [...]
13′) [...] (traces) [...]
14′) [...] (traces) [...]
Lacuna

past ...]
10′) [...] ... [to (whom) I handed over] *lordship* of their wide lands [...]
11′) [... he repeatedly sent to Mitâ, kin]g of the land Musku, (messages) hostile to [Assyria. ...]
12′–14′) No translation possible.

Lacuna

113

Lines 1′–5′ of this fragment from the left side of a clay barrel cylinder found at Arslantepe in 1968 and currently stored in the Malatya Archaeological Museum describe the episode of Iāmānī of Ashdod and lines 6′–27′ summarize Sargon's campaigns against Marduk-apla-iddina II (Merodach-Baladan) (710–709), and in particular the capture of the latter's stronghold Dūr-Yakīn, which took place in Sargon's thirteenth regnal year (709). The inscription duplicates parts of the Nimrud prism (text no. 74) and two cylinder fragments from Niniveh (text nos. 86–87), as well as parts of two other cylinders from Arslantepe (text nos. 111 and 114).

CATALOGUE

Museum Number	Provenance	Dimensions (cm)	cpn
Malatya Archaeological Museum 855 (registration date 14.IX.1968)	Arslantepe, north of the mound	8.7×7.0×3.3	(c)

COMMENTARY

The inscription was collated from a cast of the piece kindly loaned to the author by M. Frangipane in January 2004.

The mention of the king of Meluḫḫa and the fear of the brilliance of the gods Aššur, Nabû, and Marduk (line 4′) suggests that lines 1′–5′ describe the incident of Iāmānī, who usurped the throne of Ashdod, fled at the approach of Sargon's forces, took refuge in Meluḫḫa, and was later handed over to Assyria by the king of Meluḫha out of fear of the power of those three gods and of the Assyrian king (see text no. 7 lines 95–112 and text no. 8 lines 11–14).

For restorations in lines 6′–23′, see for example text no. 1 lines 404–408, text no. 2 lines 375–383, text no. 7 lines 126–129, 134–137, and 140–142; text no. 74 vi 14–80; text no. 86 lines 1′–18′; and text no. 87 lines 3′–14′. For lines 9′–17′, see also text no. 111 lines 1′–9′, and for lines 12′–27′, see also text no. 114 lines 1′–13′.

BIBLIOGRAPHY

1975 Castellino in Pecorella, Malatya 3 pp. 69–73 and pl. LXVIII (photo, copy, edition, study)

1999 Na'aman, NABU 1999 p. 64 no. 65 (line 4′, study)

2004 Frame in Frangipane, Alle origini pp. 176–177 (photo, translation)

2009 Frame, Studies Parpola pp. 79–80 (study)

2014 Maniori, Campagne di Sargon p. 47 G9 and passim (study)

TEXT

Lacuna

1′) [...] *x x x x x* [...]

2′) [... ^{m}*ia-ma-ni* MAN]-⸢*šú* GIŠ⸣.TUKUL.MEŠ-*ia e-du-ur-ma gi*-⸢*piš*⸣ [...]

3′) [...] ⸢IM⸣ NÍG.ŠU NÍG.GA *ni-ṣir-ti* É.GAL-*šú šal-la-su* x [...]

4′) [^{m}*šá-pa-ta-ku*]-⸢*u*'⸣ LUGAL KUR.*me-luḫ-ḫa pu-ul-ḫi me-lam-me šá* ^{d}*aš-šur* ^{d}AG ^{d}AMAR.UTU ⸢EN.MEŠ⸣-[*ia* ...]

5′) [*x x*]-⸢*šu*$^{?}$-*nu*⸣ *a-na eš-šu-ti aṣ-bat* UN.MEŠ KUR.KUR *šá qé-reb* KUR-*i ṣi*-⸢*it*⸣ ^{d}UTU-*ši* KUR.*ti-šu*$^{?}$-[*x* ...]

6′) [^{md}]⸢AMAR.UTU⸣-IBILA-SUM.NA LUGAL KUR.*kal-di šá ki-i la lìb-bi* DINGIR.MEŠ [*a-na er-ṣe-et* KUR EME.GI$_7$ *ù* URI.KI *ú-ri-dam-ma* LUGAL-*ut* KÁ.DINGIR.RA.KI *pa-nu-uš ú-ter-ru*]

7′) [^{m}]⸢^{d}⸣*ḫum-ba-ni-ga-áš* LÚ.ELAM.MA.KI *a-na re-ṣu-ti is-ḫur* ⸢UGU⸣ [ÍD.*mar-ra-ti gu-pu-uš e-de-e it-ta-kil-ma ik-la-a ta-mar-tuš*]

8′) ⸢*um*⸣-*ma-na-at* KUR *aš-šur*.KI *gap-šá*-⸢*a*⸣-*ti ad-ke-e-ma* ÍD.⸢IDIGNA⸣ [ÍD.BURANUN.KI *a-di* ÍD.MEŠ TUR.MEŠ *la mi-na e-teb-bi-ra* LÚ.*kal-du a-na paṭ gim-re-e-šú a-bu-biš as-ḫu-up*]

9′) ⸢*ul*⸣-*la-nu-ú-a* ^{md}AMAR.UTU-⸢IBILA-SUM.NA⸣ URU.MEŠ-*šú áš-bu-ti ù* DINGIR.MEŠ [*a-šib lib-bi-šú-un ú-paḫ-ḫir-ma a-na* URU.BÀD-^{m}*ia-ki-na ú-še-rib-ma ú-dan-ni-na ker-ḫe-e-šú*]

10′) *áš-la*.TA.ÀM *la-pa-an* ⸢BÀD-*šú* GAL⸣-*e ú-né*-⸢*es*⸣-*si-ma* [2 ME *ina* 1.KÙŠ DAGAL *ḫa-ri-ṣi iš-kun-ma* 1 1/2 NINDA *ú-šap-pil-ma ik-šu-da* A.MEŠ *nag-bi*]

11′) *bu-tuq-tu ul-tu qé-reb* ÍD.⸢BURANUN⸣.KI *ib-tuq-ma ú-šar-da-a ta*-⸢*mir*⸣-[*tuš* A.GÀR.MEŠ-*šú a-šar mit-ḫu-ṣi* A.MEŠ *im-ki-ir-ma ú-šap-ši-qa né-ber-tú*]

12′) *šu-ú a-di* LÚ.*re-ṣe-e-šú* ⸢LÚ⸣.ERIM.⸢MEŠ MÈ-*šú*⸣ *i-na* [*bi-rit* ÍD.MEŠ *ki-ma ku-mé-e*.MUŠEN *za-ra-tú* LUGAL-*ti-šú iš-kun-ma ú-pa-ḫi-ra ka-ras-su*]

Lacuna

1′–5′) [...] ... [... Iāmānī, i]ts [king], took fright at my weapons; the main force [*of my army* ...] property (and) possessions, the treasure of his palace, booty of his, [...]. Fear of the brilliance of the gods Aššur, Nabû, (and) Marduk, [my] lords, [overwhelmed Šapataku]' (Shebitko), king of the land Meluḫḫa [*and* ...] their [...] I reorganized. People of the lands which are (located) in the mountain region to the east, the land Tišu[...]

6′–7′) [Mar]duk-apla-iddina (II) (Merodach-Baladan), king of Chaldea, who against the will of the gods [had come down to the territory of the land of Sumer and Akkad and appropriated for himself the kingship of Babylon], turned to Ḫumbanigaš (Ḫumban-nikaš I), the Elamite, for aid. [He put his trust] i[n the sea (and its) surging waves and withheld his audience gift].

8′–12′) I mustered the numerous troops of Assyria and [crossed] the Tigris [(and) the Euphrates] River[s, as well as innumerable small streams. Like the Deluge, I overwhelmed the Chaldeans to their (lit.: its) full extent]. In the face of my advance (lit.: "before me"), Marduk-apla-iddina [gathered together] the inhabitants of his cities (lit.: "his inhabited cities") and the gods [dwelling in them and brought (them) into the city Dūr-Yakīn. He then strengthened its enclosure walls] (10′) (and), moving back a distance of one measuring rope from in front of its [ma]in wall, [he made a moat two hundred cubits wide; he made (the moat) one and a half *nindanu* deep and reached ground water]. He cut a channel from the Euphrates River, (thereby) making (its water) flow (in)to [its] meadow[land. He flooded its fields, where battles (are fought), and made crossing difficult]. Together with his allies (and) his battle troops, he [pitched his royal tent] in [a bend of the river (lit.: "between rivers") like a *crane* and assembled his (military) camp].

2′–4′ The restorations at the beginning of the lines are based upon text no. 116 lines 19–20. The -*šú* after É.GAL is omitted on the published copy but clear on the cast.

5′ Possibly *šat-ti-šu*$^{?}$ [...] instead of KUR-*ti-šu*$^{?}$-[...]?

9′ -⸢IBILA⸣-: against the published copy that has simply -DUMU-.

10′ -⸢*es*⸣-*si*-: against the published copy that has -KU-PA-.

13′) *i-na qí-bit* ^{d}*aš-šur* ^{d}⸢AG⸣ ^{d}AMAR.UTU UGU ÍD.MEŠ-*šú a-ram-mu ú-šak-*⸢*bi*⸣-[*is-ma šá-a-šú ga-du* LÚ.*mun-daḫ-ṣe-šu* GIM TI$_{8}$.MUŠEN *mut-tap-ri-ši a-bar-šú ina še-e-ti*]

14′) *pag-re* LÚ.*nu-bal-*⸢*le*⸣*-e-šú* ⸢*ù*⸣ LÚ.*aḫ-la-mi-i* ⸢*ṣa*⸣-[*ab* EDIN *a-li-kut i-de-e-šú ki-ma* ŠE.MUNU$_{6}$ *áš-ṭe-e-ma i-ta-at* URU-*šú ú-mal-li*]

15′) URU.BÀD-^{m}*ia-ki-ni* É *ni-ṣir-ti-šú* URU.⸢*iq-bi*-^{d}EN⸣ URU.*kap-ru* [URU.É-^{m}*za-bi-da-a-a* URU.*šá-at*-SUM.NA URU.*za-ra-a-ti* URU.*raq-qa-tu* URU.*e-ku-uš-šú* URU.*ḫur-sag*-GAL$_{5}$.LÁ.MEŠ]

16′) URU.BÀD-^{d}EN-⸢URU⸣-*ia* URU.BÀD-^{d}EN.LÍL URU.É-^{m}*qí-ib-la-te* URU.[*né-med*-^{d}30 URU.*li-mi-tum* URU.*mad-a-kal-šá* 15 URU.MEŠ *dan-nu-ti a-di* URU.MEŠ *ša li-me-ti-šú-un ti-la-niš ú-še-me*]

17′) UN.MEŠ *ṣe-ḫer ra-bi a-ši-bu-ut na-ge-e* [*ù* DINGIR.MEŠ *ti-ik-le-šú-un iš-te-niš áš-lu-lam-ma la e-zi-ba mul-taḫ-ṭu*]

18′) DUMU.MEŠ ZIMBIR.KI NIBRU.KI ⸢KÁ⸣.DINGIR.RA.KI *bár-*⸢*sipa*⸣.[KI *ša i-na la an-ni-šú-nu i-na qer-bi-šú-un ka-mu-ú ṣi-bit-ta-šú-nu a-bu-ut-ma ú-kal-lim-šú-nu-ti nu-ú-ru*]

19′) A.ŠÀ.MEŠ-*šú-nu šá ul-tu u$_{4}$-me ul-lu-ti* [*i-na i-ši-ti ma-a-ti* LÚ.*su-ti-i e-ki-mu-ú-ma ra-ma-nu-uš-šú-un ú-ter-ru*]

20′) LÚ.*su-ti-i ṣa-ab* EDIN *i-na* GIŠ.TUKUL *ú-šam-*⸢*qit*⸣ [*ki-sur-ri-šú-nu ma-šu-ú-ti ša i-na di-li-iḫ ma-a-ti ib-baṭ-lu ú-šad-gi-la pa-nu-uš-šú-un*]

21′) ⸢*ša*⸣ ÚRI.KI UNUG.KI *eridu*.KI ARARMA.KI [*kul-aba$_{4}$*.KI *ki-sik*.KI URU.*né-me-ed-la-gu-da áš-ku-na an-du-ra-ar-šú-un*]

22′) ⸢*ù*⸣ DINGIR.MEŠ-*šú-nu šal-lu-ú-ti a-na ma-ḫa-a-*⸢*zi*⸣-[*šú-nu ú-ter-ma sat-tuk-ki-šú-nu ba-aṭ-lu-ú-ti ú-ter áš-ru-uš-šú-un*]

23′) [KUR].⸢É⸣-^{m}*ia-ki-ni ú-ter-ma a-na eš-*⸢*šu*⸣-[*ti aṣ-bat* UN.MEŠ KUR.*kúm-mu-ḫi ki-šit-ti qa-ti-ia qé-reb-šú ú-šar-me-ma ú-še-ši-ba ni-du-us-su*]

24′) [KUR] ⸢*šu*⸣*-a-tum ma-al-ma-liš a-zu-uz-*⸢*ma*⸣ [*ina* ŠU.II LÚ.*šu-ut* SAG-*ia* LÚ.GAR.KUR KÁ.DINGIR.RA.KI *ù* LÚ.*šu-ut* SAG-*ia* LÚ.GAR.KUR LÚ.*gam-bu-li am-nu*]

25′) [*a*]-⸢*na*⸣ KÁ.DINGIR.RA.KI *ma-ḫa-zu* ⸢^{d}EN⸣.[LÍL.LÁ DINGIR.MEŠ *i-na e-le-eṣ lib-bi nu-um-mur pa-ni ḫa-diš e-ru-um-ma* ŠU.II EN GAL-*i* ^{d}AMAR.UTU *aṣ-bat-ma ú-šal-li-ma ú-ru-uḫ* É *á-ki-ti*]

26′) [1 ME] ⸢54 GUN⸣ 26 MA.[NA 10 GÍN KÙ.GI

13′–17′) At the command of the gods Aššur, Nabû, (and) Marduk I had a causeway constru[cted] (lit.: "trodden [down]") across his canals [and I caught him, together with his fighting men, like a flying eagle in a net. I spread out like malt (spread for drying)] the corpses of his vanguard and of the Aḫlamû, the p[eople of the steppe who go at his side, and I filled the surroundings of his city (with them)]. (15′) The city Dūr-Yakīn — his treasure house — (and) the cities Iqbi-Bēl, Kapru, [Bīt-Zabidāya, Šāt-iddina, Zarāti, Raqqatu, Ekuššu, Ḫursaggalla], Dūr-Bēl-āliya, Dūr-Enlil, Bīt-Qiblāte, [Nēmed-Sîn, Limītu, (and) Mād-akālša, (a total of) fifteen fortified cities, together with the settlements in their environs, I turned into (ruin) mounds. I carried off as booty at the same time] (both) the people — young (and) old — who lived in the district [and the gods who helped them; I did not allow a (single) person to escape].

18′–22′) (As for) the citizens of (the cities) Sippar, Nippur, Babylon, (and) Borsippa [who through no fault of their own had been held captive in them (the fifteen cities), I put an end to their imprisonment and let them see the light (of day)]. (With regard to) their fields, which long ago, [while the land was in disorder, the Sutians had taken away and appropriated for their own] — (20′) I struck down (those) Sutians, the people of the steppe, with the sword. [I (re)assigned to them (the citizens) their territories, (whose boundaries) had been forgotten (and) fallen into disuse during the troubled period in the land. I (re)-established the freedom (from obligations) o]f (the cities) Ur, Uruk, Eridu, Larsa, [Kullaba, Kissik, (and) Nēmed-Laguda]. Moreover, [I returned] their gods that had been carried off as booty to [their] cult centers [and I restored their regular offerings that had been discontinued].

23′–24′) I restored [the land] Bīt-Yakīn and re[organized (its administration). I settled there people of the land of Kummuḫu that I had conquered and I had (them) occupy its (Bīt-Yakīn's) abandoned regions]. I divided up [t]hat [land] into equal parts and [assigned (them) to the authority of a eunuch of mine, the governor of Babylon, and a(nother) eunuch of mine, the governor of the Gambulu (tribe)].

25′–27′) [Happily, with a joyful heart (and) a radiant face, I entered] Babylon, the cult center of the En[lil of the gods (Marduk); I grasped hold of the hands of the great lord, the god Marduk, and brought (him) safely along the road to the *akītu*-house. (With regard to)

14′ *-mi-*: against the published copy that suggests a Babylonian LUM sign.
16′ -^{m}*ki-*: masculine determinative omitted on the published copy.
20′ *ú-šad-gi-la pa-nu-uš-šú-un*: Or restore *ú-ter áš-ru-uš-šú-un* (see text no. 86 line 14′ and text no. 87 line 9′).
23′–24′ For the restoration of the lines, see for example text no. 7 lines 139–140, text no. 86 lines 15′–16′, and text no. 87 lines 10′–11′.
24′ The published copy has [x] *a-na-ku* and *a-su-uz-ma*, but the cast shows [KUR] ⸢*šu*⸣*-a-tum* and *a-zu-uz-*⸢*ma*⸣.

ḫuš-šu-ú 1 LIM 6 ME 4 GUN 20 MA.NA KÙ.BABBAR *eb-bu* URUDU.ḪI.A *par-zil-la ša ni-ba la i-šu-ú*]
27′) [NA$_4$.ZÚ] ⸢NA$_4$⸣.ZA.GÌN ⸢NA$_4$⸣.[BABBAR.DILI ...]
Lacuna

15]4 talents, 26 mi[nas, (and) 10 shekels of red gold, 1,604 talents (and) 20 minas of pure silver, copper, (and) iron in immeasurable quantities, obsidian], lapis-lazuli, [*banded agate*, ...]
Lacuna

114

This clay barrel cylinder fragment in the Museum of Anatolian Civilizations (Ankara) was likely found by L. Delaporte at Arslantepe in 1938 (see the introduction to text nos. 111-114). The inscription preserves the end of an account describing the capture of Marduk-apla-iddina II's tribal stronghold of Dūr-Yakīn in Sargon's thirteenth regnal year (709) and the reorganization of the administration of Bīt-Yakīn (lines 1′-11′), as well the beginning of an account recording Sargon's triumphal entry into Babylon in the preceding year (lines 12′-13′). The inscription is similar to passages in several other texts, including the Khorsabad Display Inscription and the Nimrud Prism (text nos. 7 and 74), as well as in two other Malatya texts (text nos. 111 and 113).

CATALOGUE

Museum Number	Provenance	Dimensions (cm)	cpn
AnAr 21718/324	Probably Arslantepe	7.4×3.0×3.0	(p)

COMMENTARY

The provenance of the piece is not recorded in the museum inventory, but the immediately preceding piece (see text no. 111) is stated to come from Arslantepe (Malatya). The inscription is written in Neo-Assyrian script and, according to R. Akdoğan and A. Fuchs, in no place is more than at most one third of a line preserved (ZA 99 [2009] p. 83). Although the published photograph has been examined, the transliteration basically follows that of Akdoğan and Fuchs (ZA 99 [2009] p. 82).

Since it is not known where the line breaks would have occurred in the text, only minimal restorations are given in the transliteration even though the translation is restored in full. For the restorations in lines 1′–5′, see in particular text no. 111 lines 4′–9′, and for the restorations in lines 1′–13′, see text no. 113 lines 12′–26′. For line 1′, see also text no. 74 vi 39–42; cf. text no. 7 line 129. For lines 2′–5′, cf. text no. 74 vi 43–62. For lines 6′–9′, cf. text no. 7 lines 134–137 and text no. 74 vi 63–79. For 10′–11′, cf. text no. 7 lines 137–140 and text no. 74 vi 80–85. For lines 12′–13′, see text no. 7 lines 140–142.

BIBLIOGRAPHY

1939 Delaporte, RHA 5/34 p. 54 (study)
1940 Delaporte, Malatya p. 9 (study)
1941 Kalaç, Sumeroloji Araştırmaları pp. 990–991 and 1011 (study)
1948 Landsberger, Sam'al p. 81 n. 213 (study)
2009 Akdoğan and Fuchs, ZA 99 pp. 82–86 (photo, transliteration, study)
2009 Frame, Studies Parpola pp. 65–66 (study)

TEXT

Lacuna

1′) [... *ki-ma ku-mé*]-⸢*e*.MUŠEN⸣ [*za-ra-tú*] ⸢LUGAL$^{?}$⸣-*ti-šú iš*-⸢*kun*⸣-[*ma* ...]

2′) [... *šá-a-šú ga*]-⸢*du*⸣ LÚ.*mun*-[*daḫ-ṣe-šu* ...]

3′) [... *i-de-e*]-*šu* ⸢*ki*⸣-[*ma*] ⸢ŠE.MUNU$_6$⸣ [*áš*]-*ṭe-e*-⸢*ma*⸣ [...]

4′) [... URU].*šá-at*-SUM.NA URU.*za-ra-a-te* URU.*raq-qa-tum* URU.⸢*e*⸣-[*ku-uš-šú* ...]

5′) [... *a-di*] ⸢URU⸣.MEŠ *ša li-me*-⸢*ti*⸣-*šú-un ti-la-niš* ⸢*ú*⸣-[*še-me* ...]

Lacuna

1′) [Together with his allies (and) his battle troops], he pitc[hed] his [*roy*]*al* [tent in a bend of the river (lit.: "between rivers") like a *cran*]*e* [and assembled his military camp].

2′–5′) [At the command of the gods Aššur, Nabû, (and) Marduk, I had a causeway constructed (lit.: "trodden down") across his canals and I caught him, toge]ther with [his] fig[hting men, like a flying eagle in a net. I spr]ead out l[ike m]alt (spread for drying) [the corpses of his vanguard and of the Aḫlamû, the people of the steppe who go at] his [side], an[d I filled the surroundings of his city (with them). The city Dūr-Yakīn — his treasure house — (and) the cities Iqbi-Bēl, Kapru, Bīt-Zabidāya], Šāt-iddina, Zarāti, Raqqatu, E[kuššu, Ḫursaggalla, Dūr-Bēl-āliya, Dūr-Enlil, Bīt-Qiblāte, Nēmed-Sîn, Limītu, (and) Mād-akālša, (a total of) fifteen fortified cities, together with the se]ttlements in their environs, I [turned] into (ruin) mounds. [I carried off as booty at the same time (both) the people — young (and) old — who lived in the district and the gods who helped them; I did not allow a (single) person to escape].

6′) [... ZIMBIR].⸢KI⸣ NIBRU.KI ⸢KÁ⸣.[DINGIR].⸢RA⸣.KI *bár-sipa*.KI *ša* [*i-na la an-ni-šú-nu* ...]

7′) [... *i-na i-ši*]-⸢*ti*⸣ *ma-a-ti* LÚ.*su-ti-i e-ki*-⸢*mu*⸣-[*ú-ma* ...]

8′) [... *ša i-na di*]-⸢*li*⸣-*iḫ-ti* KUR *ib-baṭ-lu ú-šad-gil pa-nu*-⸢*uš*⸣-[*šú-un* ...]

9′) [... DINGIR.MEŠ-*šú-nu šal-lu-ti*] ⸢*a*⸣-*na ma-ḫa-zi-šú-nu ú-ter-ma sat-tuk*-[*ki-šú-nu* ...]

6′–9′) [(As for) the citizens of (the cities) Sippar], Nippur, B[abylo]n, (and) Borsippa who [through no fault of their own had been held captive in them (the fifteen cities), I put an end to their imprisonment and let them see the light (of day). (With regard to) their fields, which long ago, while] the land [was in disord]er, the Sutians had taken aw[ay and appropriated for their own, I struck down (those) Sutians, the people of the steppe, with the sword]. I (re)assigned to t[hem (the citizens) their territories, (whose boundaries) had been forgotten (and)] fallen into disuse [during the troub]led period in the land. [I (re)-established the freedom (from obligations) of (the cities) Ur, Uruk, Eridu, Larsa, Kullab, Kissik, (and) Nēmed-Laguda. Moreover], I returned [their gods that had been carried off as booty] to their cult centers and [I restored their] regular offeri[ngs that had been discontinued].

10′) [... UN.MEŠ KUR].⸢*kúm*⸣-*mu-ḫi ki-šit-ti qa-ti-ia qé*-[*reb-šú ú-šar-me* ...]

11′) [... LÚ.*šu-ut* SAG-*ia* LÚ].GAR KUR KÁ.DINGIR.RA.KI *ù* LÚ.⸢*šu*⸣-[*ut* SAG-*ia* ...]

10′–11′) [*I restored the land Bīt-Yakīn and reorganized (its administration).* I settled] th[ere people from the land Ku]mmuḫu that I had conquered, [*and I had (them) occupy its (Bīt-Yakīn's) abandoned regions. I divided*

12′) [... *nu-um*]-⸢*mur pa-ni*⸣ *ḫa-diš e-ru-um-ma* [...]
13′) [...] *par-zil-lu ša ni-ba* ⸢*la*⸣ [*i-šu-ú* ...]
14′) [...] *x x x* [...]

Lacuna

up that land into equal parts and assigned (them) to the authority of a eunuch of mine, the] governor of Babylon, and a(nother) e[unuch of mine, the governor of the Gambulu (tribe)].

12′–14′) Happily, [with a joyful heart (and) a radian]t face, I entered [Babylon, the cult center of the Enlil of the gods (Marduk); I grasped hold of the hands of the great lord, the god Marduk, and brought (him) safely along the road to the *akītu*-house. (With regard to) 154 talents, 26 minas, (and) 10 shekels of red gold, 1,604 talents (and) 20 minas of pure silver, copper], (and) iron in im[measurable] quantities, [...].

Lacuna

115

In 2015, a workman gave a fragment of the front side of a stone stele to a group of Iranian archaeologists excavating at Qal'eh-i Imam, near Lake Zeribor, under the direction of Dr. Hassan Karimian. The poorly preserved inscription can probably be assigned to Sargon II and likely deals with his military actions in the Zagros Mountains. Information on the piece was kindly supplied to the author by K. Radner and M. Masoumian before their publication of the text.

CATALOGUE

Museum Number	Provenance	Dimensions (cm)	cpn
Archaeological Museum of Sanadaj	Qal'eh-i Imam, drystone wall	30×22×12.5	p

COMMENTARY

The greenschist fragment was found in secondary context, within a drystone wall of the village Barqaleh located at Qal'eh-i Imam. It is conserved in the Archaeological Museum of Sanandaj. As noted by Radner and Masoumian, the inscription is likely to be assigned to Sargon II because of the use of a (partially preserved) phrase in line 4′ that is otherwise only attested in the inscriptions of this ruler: *ardu kanše/kanšu šādid nīriya/nīr aššur* (*bēliya*); see text no. 7 lines 36, 70, and 117, text no. 74 iii 43, and text no. 82 v 61′. In the latter texts, the phrase is regularly used to describe Daltâ of the land Ellipi, who appears already in the time of Tiglath-pileser III and who likely died in 708 or 707, although it is used once (text no. 7 line 36) for the Mannean ruler Iranzi, who is mentioned in the Khorsabad Annals in connection with Sargon's third campaign (719). In addition, the city Ḫarḫar, which is mentioned in line 5′, appears frequently in inscriptions of Sargon II, although most often with the determinative URU rather than KUR. Sargon renamed the city Kār-Šarrukīn and made it the capital of a new province during his campaign of 716 (see, for example, text no. 1 lines 96b–100).

BIBLIOGRAPHY

2020 Radner and Masoumian, ZA 120 pp. 84–93 (photo, copy, edition, study)

TEXT

Lacuna
1′) [...] *x* [...]
2′) [...] (*x x*) *x* [...]
3′) [...] *x x x* [...]
4′) [... *ar*]-⸢*di*⸣ *kan-še* ⸢*ša-di*⸣-[*id ni-ri-ia*$^{?}$ ...]
5′) [... LUGAL$^{?}$ KUR$^{?}$.*el*$^{?}$-*li*$^{?}$]-⸢*pí*⸣ KUR.⸢*ḫar-ḫar*⸣ [...]
6′) [...] *x* KUR [...]
Lacuna

Lacuna
1′–3′) No translation possible.

4′–6′) [... a] submissive [subje]ct who pul[led *my yoke ... king of the land Ellip*]*i*, the land Ḫarḫ[ar ...] land [...]

Lacuna

116

The Tang-i Var rock relief (or Urāmānāt relief) is carved on the flanks of the Kūh-i Zīnānah in the Tang-i Var pass in Iranian Kurdistan, about 50 km southwest of Sanandaj and 85 km northwest of Kermanshah. The relief is found in a niche cut into the cliff face about 40 m above ground level and depicts an Assyrian ruler in a standard pose. A badly worn cuneiform inscription runs across the relief. The inscription records a campaign to the land of Karalla (lines 37–44) and also refers to Sargon's defeat of the Babylonian ruler Marduk-apla-iddina II (Merodach-Baladan) which occurred in 710–709. Since the Assyrian Eponym Chronicle mentions Karalla (albeit in damaged context) in its entry for 706 (see Millard, SAAS 2 p. 48 B4 rev. 21′ and p. 60), it is likely that there was a campaign to Karalla in that year, and that the relief and inscription of Sargon at Tang-i Var were made during or shortly after that campaign. This is the only known account of the campaign in Sargon's sixteenth regnal year, a campaign that was not led by the Assyrian king. It was the third time that the Assyrians had had to campaign in Karalla, the two previous campaigns taking place in the king's sixth and ninth regnal years (716 and 713 respectively). The inscription provides a useful chronological link with Egypt's twenty-fifth dynasty since it states that the ruler who sent the fugitive Iāmānī of Ashdod back to Sargon was Šapataku' (Shebitko). Šapataku' is called the king of the land Meluḫḫa (i.e., Nubia) in line 20 of this text.

115 line 4′ The restoration is based on text no. 7 lines 36 and 117, and text no. 74 iii 43. Possibly instead ⸢*ša-di*⸣-[*id ni-ir* ^{d}*aš-šur* ...], "who pul[led the yoke of the god Aššur" (following text no. 7 line 70) or ⸢*ša-di*⸣-[*id ni-ir* ^{d}*a-šur*$_{4}$ *be-lí-ia* ...], "who pul[led the yoke of the god Aššur, my lord, ...]" (following text no. 82 v 61′).

115 line 5′ The tentative restoration is that proposed by Radner and Masoumian, who also suggest as an alternate reading [... *i-na lib*]-⸢*bi*⸣ KUR.*ḫar*-⸢*ḫar*⸣ [...], "[... insid]e the land Ḫarḫ[ar ...]."

CATALOGUE

Source	Provenance	Dimensions (cm)	cpn
Frame, Orientalia NS 68 pp. 31–57 and pls. I-XVIII	Kūh-i Zīnānah, in the Tang-i Var pass	–	p

COMMENTARY

The inscription was originally edited by the author from photographic materials of the original made by F. Vallat in 1971 (Frame, Orientalia NS 68 [1999] pp. 31–57 and pls. I-XVIII). Subsequently, through the intermediary actions of H. Arfaei and W. Nahm, A.A. Sarfarāz kindly provided the author with photographs of the squeezes made by him at the site in the late 1960s. In 2009, Z. Deylamipout of the Ingenieurbüro Gilan (Berlin) made laser scans of the relief for the Iranian Cultural Heritage and Tourism Organization and graciously gave the author copies of these important materials for use in revising the edition of the inscription for this volume.

The inscription is badly damaged and some sections are inevitably better represented on the photographic materials, squeezes, and laser scans than other sections. Parts of the text cannot be read and the reading of other parts is problematic. In particular the first section of the inscription (invocations of various deities [lines 1–10]) and the last three sections of the inscription (description of the campaign to Karalla [lines 37–44], description of the creation of the monument [lines 45–1′], and concluding formulae [lines 2′–6′]) are the least legible; the second section (name and titles of Sargon II [lines 11–12]) and third section (description of the major accomplishments of Sargon II [lines 13–36]) are the most legible.

The relief depicts the Assyrian king facing right, with his right hand raised and his left hand holding an object (likely a mace or scepter). Symbols of various deities are depicted at the top of the relief, in front of the king's face. The only symbol that is clearly visible is a series of circles that represent the Pleiades, the divine Seven (Sebetti), although there also appears to be traces of a winged disk, the symbol of the god Šamaš, and possibly of the symbols of Marduk (spade) and Nabû (tablet and stylus).

For photographs of the relief and a fuller study of the inscription, including a discussion of its date and of the image depicted on the relief, see Frame, Orientalia NS 68 (1999) pp. 31–57 and pls. I-XVIII.

Lines 1–10 are likely to have had some passages similar to ones found in text no. 103 i 1–28, text no. 108 Fragment B i 1′–11′, text no. 117 i 1–18, and Grayson, RIMA 2 pp. 12–13 A.0.87.1 i 1–18 and pp. 32–33 A.0.87.2 lines 1–8.

For passages similar to lines 13–15, see in particular text no. 8 lines 2–3 and 5 and text no. 103 ii 5–12 and 18–21.

For a passage similar to lines 16–18, see in particular text no. 8 lines 7–10 and note such texts as text no. 13 lines 14–27.

For Sargon's dealings with Ashdod (lines 19–21), see in particular text no. 1 lines 249–262, text no. 3 lines 10′–13′, text no. 7 lines 90–112, text no. 8 lines 11–14, text no. 82 vii 13′–16′ and 1′′–48′′, and text no. 83 ii′ 1-11.

For lines 22–24, see in particular text no. 8 lines 16–18 and note such texts as text no. 13 lines 35–45.

For lines 25–27, see in particular text no. 7 lines 121–122 and 144–45, text no. 8 lines 18–21, and text no. 13 lines 45–58; note also such texts as text no. 9 lines 30–36.

Lines 28–36 are basically duplicated by text no. 7 lines 16–23 (with the only major divergence being for line 33) and text no. 13 lines 59–89 (except that Sargon is treated in the first person, rather than the third person). Note also such texts as text no. 10 lines 5–23.

BIBLIOGRAPHY

1968–69 Sarfarāz, Majallah-i Barrasīhā-i Tārīkhī 3/5 pp. 13–20 and fourteen plates (photo, drawings, partial copy, study)
1969 Anonymous, Iran 7 p. 186 (provenance)
1977 Reade, IrAnt 12 p. 44 (study)
1982 Börker-Klähn, Bildstelen no. 248 (study)
1983 Vanden Berghe, Reliefs rupestres de l'Irān pp. 22, 32, and 156 (study, provenance)
1995 Curtis in Curtis, Later Mesopotamia and Iran p. 20 and pl. VI (photo [inscription not legible])
1995 Reade in Liverani, Neo-Assyrian Geography p. 39 (study)
1999 Frame, Orientalia NS 68 pp. 31–57 and pls. I–XVIII (photo, edition, study)
1999 Redford, Orientalia NS 68 pp. 58–60 (study)
2000 Younger, COS 2 pp. 299-300 no. 2.118J (lines 11–26a, translation)
2001 Kahn, Orientalia NS 70 pp. 1–18 (lines 19–21, translation; study)
2001 Rollinger, Melammu 2 p. 247 (lines 19–21, translation)
2006 Frame, Subartu 18 pp. 56–58 (photo, study)
2008 Cogan, Raging Torrent p. 87 (lines 19–21, translation)
2012 Alibaigi, Shanbehzadeh and Alibaigi, IrAnt 47 pp. 30–31 and 35 pl. 2a (drawing [by Sarfaraz], study)
2013 Frame, Persian Gulf Conference 3 pp. 433–435, 437–441, and 444–445 (photo, study)
2014 Maniori, Campagne di Sargon p. 54 g11 and passim (study)
2019 Marchesi, JNES pp. 23–24 (line 18, edition)

TEXT

1) [(x)] ⸢^{d}⸣*aš*-⸢*šur* EN⸣ GAL-[*ú*$^{?}$] MAN ⸢KIŠ$^{?}$ $^{d?}$⸣*í-gì-gì* (traces)
2) [x (x)] x GA$^{?}$ x x x x [(x)] x LU (traces)
3) [^{d}]⸢MES$^{?}$⸣ EN TIL ⸢*e*$^{?}$-*pir*$^{?}$ *kiš*$^{?}$-*šat*$^{?}$ UN$^{?}$⸣.MEŠ ⸢*mu*$^{?}$⸣-*bal-liṭ* (traces)
4) [^{d}MUATI$^{?}$] A *gít-ma-lu* x (x) x BI x [(x)] x KUR.⸢MEŠ⸣ [...] (traces)
5) [^{d}]⸢30⸣ *e-tel* AN-*e u* ⸢KI$^{?}$⸣ (traces)
6) [^{d}UTU] ⸢DI⸣.KU$_{5}$.GAL AN-⸢*e u* KI-*tim*⸣ (traces)
7) ⸢^{d}⸣[*iš*]-*tar mu-šak-ṣi*-⸢*rat*$^{?}$⸣ *a*-⸢*nun*$^{?}$-*ti*$^{?}$⸣ (traces)
8) ⸢$^{d?}$⸣x x ⸢*a*$^{?}$-*li*⸣-*kut ma-ḫar* DINGIR.⸢MEŠ⸣ *šá a*-⸢*šar*⸣ x [(x) x] x x x (x) ⸢RI$^{?}$⸣ x [x x x x x x (x)]-*ma i*-⸢*šak-ka*$^{?}$-*nu*$^{?}$ *li*$^{?}$-*i-ta*⸣ [(x x)]

1–8) The god Aššur, the great lord, king *of a*[*ll the*] Igīgū *gods* [*and Anunnakū gods* ...] ... [...; the god *Mardu*]*k*, lord of all, *who provides* [*all*] *people with food* (and) *revives the dying* [...; the god *Nabû*], perfect heir, ... lands [...; (5) the god S]în, lord of heaven and netherworld [...; the god Šamaš], great judge of heaven and netherworld [...]; the goddess [Iš]tar, *who makes* (*men*) *ready for battle* [...]; *the Sebetti*, who go before the gods, [*stand*] *at the side of the king*, [*their favorite*], in the place *of battle*, and bring about (his) victory;

9) ⸢DINGIR.MEŠ$^{?}$ GAL.MEŠ⸣ *mut-tab-bi*-⸢*lu-ut* AN-*e* *ù*$^{?}$⸣ [KI]-⸢*tim*$^{?}$⸣ *šá ti-bu-šú-nu* (x) [(x x) *tu-qu*]-⸢*un-tu ù*$^{?}$⸣ [*šá*$^{?}$]-⸢*áš*⸣-[(x)]-⸢*mu*$^{?}$⸣ [(x)]
10) *na-šú-u* ⸢*e-ni*⸣ *na-bu-u šu*-⸢*um* MAN *ša*$^{?}$⸣ [*ina*$^{?}$ *e*]-⸢*peš*$^{?}$⸣ *pi-i-šú-nu* ⸢KÙ KUR$^{?}$⸣ [(x x x x x)] ⸢UGU KUR *i-šak-ka*$^{?}$⸣-[*nu-ma*] ⸢*ú-šar-bu*⸣-x [(x x)]

9–10) Great gods, managers of heaven *and* [nether-wo]rld, whose attack means [con]flict *and* [*st*]*rife*, who appoint (rulers) (lit.: "raise the eyes") (and) name *king*(s), (and) [by who]se holy command they *pla*[*ce*] (*one*) *land* [(...)] over (another) land [and] make (its ruler) greater [(than other rulers)]:

11) ^{m}MAN-GIN MAN GAL MAN *dan-nu* MAN ŠÚ MAN ⸢KUR *aš-šur*.KI$^{?}$ GÌR$^{?}$.NÍTA⸣ KÁ.DINGIR.⸢RA.KI⸣ MAN ⸢KUR⸣ [*šu-me-ri u ak*]-*ka-de*-⸢*e*$^{?}$ *mi*$^{?}$⸣-*gir* ⸢DINGIR.MEŠ GAL.MEŠ⸣ [(...)]
12) *ur-šá-a*-⸢*nu gít*⸣-*ma-lu* ⸢*zi*⸣-*ka*-⸢*ru*⸣ x x [(x) NUN$^{?}$] ⸢*na*⸣-*a'-du eṭ*-⸢*lu*⸣ *tab*-⸢*ra-a*$^{?}$-*ti*$^{?}$ ŠÁ$^{?}$ KI$^{?}$⸣ [(x x x)] ⸢RE.É.UM⸣ x (x) x x.⸢MEŠ⸣ x x (x) x [(...)]

11–12) Sargon (II), great king, strong king, king of the world, king of Assyria, governor of Babylon, king of the land [of Sumer and Ak]kad, favorite of the great gods, perfect hero, ... man, pious [*prince*], admirable man, ... shepherd ...

13) ^{d}*aš-šur* ⸢^{d}MUATI ^{d}⸣MES DINGIR.MEŠ *ti*-⸢*ik-le*⸣-[(*ia*)] ⸢MAN⸣-[(*ut*) *la*] ⸢*šá*⸣-*na-an* *ú-šat*-⸢*li-mu*$^{?}$-*in*$^{?}$⸣-[*ni*]-*ma* ⸢*zi*$^{?}$⸣-[*kir*] ⸢MU⸣-*ia* ⸢*dam-qu ú*$^{?}$-*še*$^{?}$-*ṣu*$^{?}$-*u*$^{?}$⸣ (x) x ⸢*re-še-ti*⸣ [(x x x)]

13) The gods Aššur, Nabû, (and) Marduk, the gods, [(my)] helpers, granted [me] a reign [without] equal and *exalted* my good reputation *to* the heights.

14) *šá* ⸢ZIMBIR.KI NIBRU$^{?}$.KI⸣ KÁ.DINGIR.RA.⸢KI$^{?}$⸣ [*za*]-⸢*nin*⸣-[*us*]-⸢*su*⸣-*un e*-⸢*tep*$^{?}$⸣-[*pu*]-*šá* ⸢*šá* ERIM⸣.[MEŠ *ki-din-ni*] ⸢*ma*$^{?}$-*la ba-šu*$^{?}$-*u*$^{?}$⸣ (x)

14–15) I co[ntinually ac]ted [as pro]vi[der] for (the cities) Sippar, Ni[ppur], (and) Babylon, (and) I made restitution for the wrongful damage suffered by the

---

3 The translation "*who revives the dying*" assumes a reading *mu-bal-liṭ mi-(i)-ti* or *mu-bal-liṭ* (LÚ).ÚŠ.

10 See the note to text no. 108 Fragment B, Face i 10′. We expect *ú-šar-bu-ú* UGU *mal-ki* at the end of the line; see text no. 103 line 28.

12 One might expect *dan-nu* after *zikaru* based on such passages as text nos. 9 line 11, 43 line 7, and 44 lines 15–16; however, all the cases of *zikaru dannu* in the inscriptions of Sargon are followed by *ḫālip/lābiš namurrati/namurrate*, "who is clad/clothed in awesome splendor."

ḫi-⸢*bíl-ta*?⸣-[*šú-nu*] ⸢*a-rib-ma*⸣ (x) [(x)]

people [of privileged status], as many as there were (of them); I re[sto]red the exemption (from obligations) of

15) *za-kut bal-*[*til*.KI] ⸢*ba*⸣-*ṭil-ta a-na* ⸢*áš-ri*⸣-[*šá*] ⸢*ú*?-*ter*⸣ URU.KASKAL *a-na* ⸢UD?.MEŠ⸣ *x x x* ⸢KÁ⸣ *x* [(*x*) *te*?]-*ne-*⸢*še-ti*⸣ *x* [(*x*)] *x* ⸢*az-qu-pa ki-din*?-*nu*⸣ [(*x*)]

(the city) Bal[til (Aššur) that had been l]apsed. (*With regard to*) the city Ḫarrān, for *future days* ... I set up *a kidinnu-symbol* (*indicating their privileged status*) *in the gat*[*e of the pe*]*ople*.

16) ⸢*ú-par-ri-ir il*?-*lat*⸣ ^{md}*ḫum-ba-ni-*⸢*ga-áš* (*x*) ELAM?.MA?⸣.KI-*i ú-ab-bit* ⸢KUR.*kar*?⸣-[*al*]-⸢*lu* KUR.*šur-da* URU.*ki*⸣-[*še-si*]-*im* URU.⸢*ḫar-ḫar*⸣ [KUR.*ma*]-⸢*da-a-a* KUR.*el-li-pi*⸣ [(*x*)]

17) *ú-šaḫ-*⸢*rib* KUR.*ur-ar*⸣-*ṭu áš-lul* URU.[(*x x*) *mu-ṣa*]-⸢*ṣir*?⸣ <<MAN?>> KUR.*man-na-a-a áš-giš* ⸢KUR.*an-di*?-*a*? KUR?⸣.[*zi-kir-tú*? (*x x*) *gi*]-*mir* ⸢*da-ád-me*?⸣-[*šú*]-⸢*nu*⸣ *ú-*⸢*še*?-*šib*?⸣ (*x x*) ⸢MEŠ?⸣ [(*x x*)]

18) *a-na-ar mal-*⸢*ki* KUR.*a-ma*⸣-*at-ti* URU.*gar-ga-*[*miš* URU.*kúm-mu*]-⸢*ḫi*⸣ KUR.*kam-ma-nu* UGU KUR.MEŠ-*šú-*⸢*nu*?⸣ *x* [*x x* (*x*) *x x*] ⸢*áš-tak-ka*?⸣-[*na*] ⸢LÚ?.*šá*?-*ak*?-*nu*?-*ti*?⸣ [(*x x x*)]

16–18) I dispersed the forces of Ḫumbanigaš (Ḫumban-nikaš I), the Elamite. I destroyed the land K[aral]la, the land Šurda, the city Ki[šes]im, the city Ḫarḫar, [the land Me]dia, (and) the land Ellipi. I laid waste to the land Urarṭu, plundered the city [Muṣaṣi]r (and) the land Mannea, slaughtered the lands *Andia* [(*and*) *Zikirtu*, (*and*)] *allowed* [(...) a]ll [th]eir settlements *to dwell* .... I struck down the rulers of the land Hamath, the city Carche[mish, the city Kummu]ḫu, (and) the land Kammanu; over *their* lands [...] I se[t] *officials*.

19) *áš-lul* URU.⸢*as*⸣-*du-du* ^{m}*ia-ma-ni* MAN-*šú* ⸢GIŠ⸣.[TUKUL].⸢MEŠ-*ía e*⸣-*du-ur-ma e-*⸢*zib*⸣ URU-*uš-šú a-*⸢*na*⸣ *pa-*⸢*aṭ* KUR?.*me-luḫ*?⸣-[(*x*)]-⸢*ḫa in-na-bit-ma šar-ra-qiš*⸣ *ú-*⸢*šib*⸣ [(*x x x*)]

20) ^{m}*šá-pa-ta-ku-*⸢*u*ʾ MAN⸣ KUR.*me-luḫ-ḫa da-na-*[*an* (^{d})]⸢*aš-šur* $^{d?}$MUATI? ^{d}⸣MES *šá* UGU *kul-lat* ⸢KUR.MEŠ *áš-tak*?⸣-[*ka*?-*nu*?] (*x*) *iš-ma-*⸢*a*⸣ (*x*) [(*x*)] ⸢NI? SA? ḪA? IŠ⸣ [(*x x x*)]

21) *il-lu-ur-tú u* ⸢*ṣi*⸣-*iṣ-*⸢*ṣu*⸣ *ú-šat-me-ḫa x* [*x* (*x*) *x*] *x* [(*x*)] *x* DU *x* (*x*) *x* (*x*) [*x* (*x*) *x x a*]-*di maḫ-*(*x*)-*ri-ia* ⸢*ú-še*⸣-[*bi*]-⸢*la*?-*áš-šú ka-meš*⸣ (*x*) [(*x*)]

19–21) I plundered the city Ashdod. Iāmānī, its king, took fright at my [weapon]s and abandoned his city. He fled to the border of the *land* Meluḫḫa and lived (there) stealthfully (lit.: "like a thief"). Šapataku' (Shebitko), king of the land Meluḫḫa, heard of the mig[ht] of the gods Aššur, *Nabû*, (and) Marduk that *I had esta*[*blished*] over all lands, ... He put (Iāmānī) in handcuffs and manacles ... [...] he had him [brou]ght in bondage [in]to my presence.

22) *gi-mir* KUR.*ta-*⸢*ba-lum*⸣ KUR.*kas-ku* KUR.*ḫi-*⸢*lak-ku*?⸣ [*x* (*x*)] *x* [*x x*] *x x šá* ^{m}*mi-*⸢*ta-a*⸣ MAN ⸢KUR.*mu*?⸣-*us-ki* ⸢*da*?⸣-*ád-me-šú* ⸢*e*?⸣-*x-x-*(*x*)-⸢*ma*? *ú-ṣa-ḫi-ir* KUR-*su*?⸣ [(*x x*)]

23) *ina* URU.*ra-pi-ḫi pa-*⸢*an*⸣ *um-ma-na-*⸢*ti*⸣ [*x*] *x x* (*x*) *x-ma* MAN URU.*ḫa-zi-ti šá* ⸢*a-na*?⸣ [*ni*]-⸢*ri*⸣-*ia la ik-nu-šú šal-*⸢*la*?-*ti*?-*iš*⸣ *am-*⸢*nu-šú*⸣ [(*x x x*)]

24) *ú-šak-niš* 7 MAN.⸢MEŠ-*ni*⸣ *šá* KUR.*ia-*⸢*a*ʾ *na-gi-i šá* KUR?.*ia*?⸣-*ad-na-na šá ma-lak x* [*x* (*x*) *ina qa*]-⸢*bal tam-tim e-reb* ^{d}UTU-*ši šit-ku-na-at šu-bat-sún*⸣ [(*x x*)]

22–24) [*I deported* (*the people of*)] all the lands Tabal, Kasku, (and) Ḫilakku; *I took away* settlements *belonging to* Mitâ (Midas), king of the land Musku, *and* reduced (the size of) *his* land. At the city Raphia *I defeated the vanguard* of the army *of Egypt* and counted as booty the king of the city Gaza who had not submitted to my [yo]ke. I subjugated seven kings of the land Yā', a region of the *l*[*and*] Yadnana (Cyprus) — whose abode is situated at a distance of ... [in the mid]dle of the Western Sea.

25) *u* ^{md}MES-A-⸢SUM.NA MAN KUR.*kal-di a-šib ki-*⸢*šad* ÍD.*mar-ra*⸣-*ti šá ki-i la lìb-*⸢*bi*?⸣

25–26) Moreover, My great *hand* defeated Marduk-apla-iddina (II) (Merodach-Baladan), king of Chaldea,

---

15 Possibly ⸢KÁ.GAL?⸣ [*te*?]-*ne-še-*⸢*ti*⸣? For the second half of the line, compare *a-na* u_4-*me ṣa-a-te ina* KÁ-*šú-nu az-qu-up ki-din-nu* (Leichty, RINAP 4 p. 124 no. 57 iii 13–15). Possibly *a-na* ⸢^{d}30⸣, "to/for the god Sîn," after URU.KASKAL?

16 Possibly ⸢KUR?.ELAM?.MA?⸣.KI-*i*. For the end of this line, text no. 8 lines 7–8 have ... KUR.*ma-da-a-a a-di pa-aṭ* [KUR.*bi-ik-ni*] ⸢KUR⸣.*el-li-pi e-mi-du ni-ir* ^{d}*aš-šur*.

19 Cf. text no. 8 lines 11–12.

20 Some scholars have questioned the presence of the masculine determinative at the beginning of the line. It can be seen clearly on the laser scans and on enlarged prints of some of photos published in Orientalia NS 68 [1999] (in particular pl. IV), although it is just to the left and off the photo on pl. XI. For an attempt to find a different reading of the name and to dismiss the identification of the person here with the Nubian ruler Shebitko, in connection with a view to locating Meluḫḫa in Arabia and not in the Sudan, see Michaux-Colombot in Tavernier, Topography and Toponymy pp. 159–163.

22 Possibly a form of the verb *ekēmu* before *uṣaḫḫir* (cf. text no. 7 lines 44 and 52).

24 We expect ... *ma-lak* 7 u_4-*me i-na qa-bal* ... based on text no. 8 lines 17–18 (and other texts), but the traces after *ma-lak* do not seem to fit 7 u_4-*me*. Possibly *ma-lak* ⸢30⸣ [KASKAL.GÍD *i-na qa*]-*bal* ... (cf. text no. 7 line 144 and text no. 8 line 20).

[DINGIR.MEŠ] ⸢MAN-*ut* KÁ.DINGIR.RA.KI *e*⸣-[*pu*$^{?}$]-⸢*šú*$^{?}$ *ik-šú-da* GAL-*tú qa-a*$^{?}$-*ti*$^{?}$⸣ (*x x*)

who dwelt on the shore of the sea (and) who *ex*[*erc*]*ised* kingship over Babylon against the wil[l of the gods].

26) *ù gi-mir* KUR.É-^{m}*ia-ki-ni* ⸢NA$^{?}$⸣ *x* (*x*) *x x* ⸢DA$^{?}$⸣ [(*x x*)] *x x* LI$^{?}$ *a-na x* (*x*) [*x* (*x*) *x*] ⸢AD$^{?}$ RI$^{?}$ TU/LI$^{?}$ PAD$^{?}$⸣/ŠÁ (*x*) BE (*x*) [(*x*) *x x x x x*] *x x*-⸢*uš-šú-nu*$^{?}$⸣ (*x x*)

Moreover, all the land Bīt-Yakīn ... [...] ...

27) ^{m}*a-ḫu-un-da-ri* MAN *dil*-⸢*mun*⸣.KI *šá* ⸢*ma-lak*⸣ *x x* (*x*) ⸢KASKAL.GÍD$^{?}$⸣ [*x x*] *x x x x* [*x x x x*] *x* ⸢*nar-ba-ṣu*$^{?}$⸣ *da*-⸢*na*⸣-[*an be-lu*]-⸢*ti*$^{?}$-*ia iš-me-ma iš*⸣-*šá-a ta*-[*mar-tuš*]

27) Aḫundāra (Ḫundāru), king of Dilmun, who(se) lair [*is situated*] at a distance of ... *leagues* [*in the middle*] *of the sea like that of a fish*, heard of my [lord]ly mig[ht] and brought me [his] aud[ience gift].

28) ⸢*ina*⸣ *li-i-ti u* ⸢*da*⸣-*na-ni šá* DINGIR.⸢MEŠ⸣ GAL.MEŠ EN$^{?}$.MEŠ$^{?}$-*ía*$^{?}$ [*šá* GIŠ.TUKUL.MEŠ-*ia ú-šat-bu-ma ú-ra*]-⸢*as*$^{?}$⸣-*si-bu na*-[*gab* (*x x*) *ga*]-⸢*re*$^{?}$⸣-[*ia* (*x*)]

29) ⸢*iš-tu*$^{?}$ KUR.*ia*⸣-*ad-na-na šá qa-bal* ⸢*tam-tim*$^{?}$⸣ [*šá-lam* ^{d}UTU-*ši a-di pa-aṭ* KUR.*mu-ṣu*]-⸢*ri*⸣ [(*u*) KUR].⸢*mu*$^{?}$⸣-*us*-⸢*ki*⸣ [KUR MAR.TU.KI DAGAL-*tum*] ⸢KUR$^{?}$.*ḫat*$^{?}$⸣-[*ti* (...)]

30) ⸢*nap*⸣-*ḫa-ar* ⸢KUR$^{?}$.*gu*$^{?}$⸣-*ti-um*.KI KUR.*ma-da-a-a* ⸢*ru-qu-u*$^{?}$⸣-*x* (*x*) [*x x x x x* (*x x*) KUR.*el*]-⸢*li*$^{?}$⸣-*pi* KUR.*ra-a-ši ina* ⸢*i*⸣-*te-e* [KUR.ELAM.MA.KI (...)]

31) ⸢*šá*⸣ *a-aḫ* ⸢ÍD⸣.IDIGNA ⸢LÚ⸣.*i-tu*-⸢'*u* LÚ.*ru*⸣-[*bu-'u* LÚ.*ḫa-ṭal*]-⸢*lum*⸣ LÚ.⸢*lab*⸣-*du-du* LÚ.*ḫa-am-ra-nu* LÚ.⸢*ú-bu-lum*⸣ [LÚ.*ru-'u*]-*x*-⸢*a* LÚ.*li*⸣-[*i'-ta-a-a*]

32) ⸢*šá a-aḫ* ÍD⸣.*su-rap*-⸢*pi* ÍD.*uq-ni*⸣-*i* ⸢LÚ.*gam*⸣-[*bu-lu*] ⸢LÚ⸣.*ḫi*-⸢*in*⸣-*da-ru* LÚ.⸢*pu*⸣-*qu-du* LÚ.*su-te-e* ERIM.MEŠ ⸢EDIN *šá* KUR.*ia*$^{?}$⸣-*ad-bu-ri* ⸢*ma-la*⸣ [*ba-šú-u*]

33) ⸢*ul-tu*⸣ URU.*sa-am-ú-na a*-⸢*di*⸣ URU.*bu-bé*-⸢*e* URU.DU$_6$⸣-^{d*}*ḫum-ba* (text: TI? for DINGIR) *x x x* (*x x x x*) *šá mì-ṣir* ⸢ELAM.<<AN$^{?}$>>.MA.⸢KI⸣ (...)

34) ⸢KUR.*kár*$^{?}$⸣-*dun-ía-áš e-liš* ⸢*u*$^{?}$ *šap-liš* KUR⸣.É-^{m}*e*-⸢*muk-ka-ni* KUR$^{?}$.É-^{m}*da*⸣-*ku-ri* (*x x x x x*) KUR.É-^{m}*a-šil-a-ni* KUR.É-^{m}*sa-'a*-⸢*al-lu*⸣ (...)

35) ⸢*si-ḫir*⸣-*ti* KUR.*kal-di ma-la* ⸢*ba*⸣-*šú-u* KUR.⸢É-^{m}*ia*⸣-[*ki*]-⸢*in*⸣ *šá ki-šad* ÍD.*mar-ra*-⸢*ti*⸣ [(*x*)] *a-di pa-aṭ* (*x*) NI.⸢TUK.KI⸣ (...)

36) ⸢*mit-ḫa-riš*⸣ *lu a-bél-ma* LÚ.*šu-ut* ⸢SAG.MEŠ⸣-*ia* [(*x*)] ⸢LÚ$^{?}$⸣.EN.NAM.MEŠ UGU-*šú-nu* ⸢*áš*$^{?}$⸣-[*tak*]-⸢*kan*$^{?}$⸣-*ma ni-ir be-lu-ti*-⸢*ía*⸣ (*x*) *e-mid-su*$^{?}$-*nu*$^{?}$-*ti*⸣ (*x*)

28–36) With the power and might (granted me) by the great gods, *my lords*, [who mobilized up my weapons, I cut] down al[l my fo]es. I ruled all together from the land Yadnana (Cyprus), which is in the middle of the [Western] Sea, [as far as the border(s) of Egyp]t [(and) the land M]usk[u, the wide land Amurru], the *land Ḫ*[*atti* (Syria) (in its entirety)], (30) all of the land Gutium, the distant Medes [(*who live*) *on the border of Mount Bikni*, the land El]lipi, (and) the land Rāši on the border [of the land Elam], those who (live) beside the Tigris River — the Itu'u, Ru[bu'u, Ḫaṭal]lu, Labdudu, Ḫamrānu, Ubulu, [Ru']u'a, (and) Li[ʾta'u] (tribes) — those who (live) beside the Surappu (and) the Uqnû Rivers — the Gam[bulu], Ḫindaru, (and) Puqudu (tribes) — the Sutians, people of the steppe of the land Yadburu, as many as [there are], from the city Samʾūna as far as the cities Bubê (and) Tīl-Ḫumba, ... which are on the border of Elam, Karduniaš (Babylonia) from one end to the other (lit.: "above and below"), the lands Bīt-Amukāni, Bīt-Dakkūri, (...) Bīt-Šilāni, (and) Bīt-Saʾalli, (35) all of Chaldea, as much as there is (of it), (and) the land Bīt-Ya[k]īn, which is on the shore of the sea as far as the border of Dilmun. I *s*[*e*]*t* eunuchs of mine as provincial governors over them and I imposed the yoke of my lordship *upon them*.

37) ⸢*ina u*$_4$⸣-*me-šú-ma te-ne-še-ti* KUR.⸢*kar*⸣-*al-li* ⸢LUGAL/LÚ⸣ *x* (*x*) *x* ⸢ÁŠ$^{?}$⸣ *šá a-na*$^{?}$ *šá-a-ṭu* ⸢*sèr*⸣-[*de-e la*] *kan-šú-ma la i-du-u pa-laḫ be-lu*-⸢*ti*⸣ (...)

38) ⸢UGU *ḫur*⸣-*šá-a-ni zaq-ru-ti it-tak*-⸢*lu*⸣-*ma x x* [*x*] (*x*) ⸢*šu-ut* SAG$^{?}$⸣-(*x*)-*ia* LÚ.GAR.KUR *x* [*x x* (*x*)] *x gi-mir* KUR.NAR-*bi-tum/i it*-⸢*bu*$^{?}$-*ú*$^{?}$ LAK$^{?}$⸣ *x x* (...)

37–44) At that time the people of the land Karalla ... who had [not] submitted to pull (any ruler's) chariot [pole] and did not know how to respect (any) authority, put their trust in the high mountains and (...) *rose up against* (...) a *eunuch* of mine, the governor [...] all the land NARbitu ... they established and *prepared for battle*. ... they became enraged like lions and cut down the people of *their land*. (40)

26 Cf. text no. 8 lines 19–20, text no. 9 lines 32–34, and text no. 13 lines 49–54. Possibly ⸢*at*$^{?}$-*tal*$^{?}$-*ka*$^{?}$⸣ for ⸢AD$^{?}$ RI$^{?}$ TU/LI$^{?}$⸣.

27 For Aḫundāra, see the commentary to text no. 74 vii 20.

29 Possibly restore *a-na si-ḫir-ti-šá* at the end of the line, following text no. 7 line 17 and text no. 13 line 66.

30 The translation assumes that the text originally had ... *ru-qu-*(*ú*)*-ti šá/ša pa-aṭ* KUR.*bi-ik-ni* KUR.*el-li-pi* ...; this reading is based on text no. 7 lines 17–18 and text no. 13 lines 68–69.

37 See text no. 1 line 255 and text no. 3 line 9′ for the reading of the end of the line.

38 Cf. text no. 2 line 443 for the first part of the line.

39) ⸢BU$^{?}$⸣ x x iš-ku-nu-ma ik-⸢ṣu-ru ta$^{?}$-ḫa$^{?}$-zu$^{?}$⸣ x [(x)] x GE E E$^{?}$ x la-ab-⸢bi-iš$^{?}$ iš⸣-še-gu-ma ú-⸢ra$^{?}$-si-bu⸣ (x) UN.MEŠ ⸢KUR$^{?}$-šú$^{?}$-nu$^{?}$⸣ (x) (...)

40) ⸢ANŠE⸣.KUR.RA.MEŠ ANŠE.KUNGA.⸢MEŠ⸣ ANŠE.⸢MEŠ$^{?}$ GU$_4{}^{?}$.MEŠ⸣ x [(x)] x x ⸢E$^{?}$ TI maḫ⸣-ri-⸢šú$^{?}$⸣-nu ra-ma-⸢nu$^{?}$-uš$^{?}$-šú$^{?}$⸣-un ú-ter-ru-ma UL IM$^{?}$ (x) x x (x) (...)

41) ⸢ṭu$^{?}$-da$^{?}$-at$^{?}$⸣ KUR-šú$^{?}$ uš-ḫa-ri-⸢ru-ma Ú$^{?}$⸣ x ⸢ṢU$^{?}$⸣ x x (x) x ⸢a-lak$^{?}$⸣ ger-ri ka-⸢a-a⸣-an iḫ-ta-⸢nab-ba$^{?}$⸣-tu ip-ru-su (x) ⸢da-rag$^{?}$-gu$^{?}$⸣ (...)

42) ⸢LÚ.UKU⸣.UŠ.MEŠ-ia la a-⸢dir$^{?}$⸣ x-⸢uq$^{?}$⸣-ma-ti ⸢ú$^{?}$⸣-ma-⸢ʾe$^{?}$⸣-[ra$^{?}$] ṣe-ru-uš-šú-un x x x x [x (x) ú$^{?}$]-⸢ma$^{?}$-še-ru⸣-ma a-na šá-ḫat KUR.MEŠ ⸢mar-ṣu⸣-te a-⸢ra-niš⸣ (...)

43) ⸢IR/NI$^{?}$⸣ x x (x) x-⸢šú-nu⸣ (x) x x ⸢iš-ku-nu⸣ x x ⸢TA$^{?}$⸣ [x (x)] (x) x muq-tab-li-šú-nu ⸢ki$^{?}$-i$^{?}$⸣ [x x x x] BU TI ú-⸢mal$^{?}$-lu$^{?}$⸣-u qé-reb ḫur-šá-a-ni (...)

44) ⸢si$^{?}$-ta$^{?}$-ti$^{?}$-šú-nu⸣ x x IS$^{?}$ x QI$^{?}$ x x x x [x (x) x] (x) A PI KUR-i x x [x x x x x] x-ma im-nu-u šal-la-ti-⸢iš⸣ (...)

Horses, mules, donkeys, (and) *oxen ... their presence* they appropriated *for themselves* and ... They made *the paths through his* land desolate and ... they were constantly, repeatedly robbing caravans while they were en route. They blocked *the pathways. I sen[t]* my soldiers, *who were fearless in battle*, against them. [*Th*]*ey* (the enemy) *abandoned* ... and ... to the clefts of rugged mountains like eagles, (...) their ... they established ... They (the Assyrian soldiers) *filled* the mountains *with the corpse*(s) of their warriors *as* (*with*) [...] ... *The remainder* of them ... mountain ... [...] and they (the Assyrians) counted (them) as booty.

45) ⸢NA$_4$.NA.RÚ.A ú⸣-še-piš-ma ṣa-lam DINGIR.MEŠ ⸢GAL.MEŠ$^{?}$⸣ [x x (x)] (x) x x x x x x (x) [x mu]-⸢sa$^{?}$-pu$^{?}$⸣-u DINGIR-ti-šú-un GAL-ti ma-⸢ḫar⸣-šú-⸢un⸣ ul-⸢ziz$^{?}$⸣ (x) [(x x)]

46) ⸢li-ta-at ^{d}aš-šur a$^{?}$⸣-bu (x) DINGIR.⸢MEŠ⸣ EN x [(x)] ⸢EN$^{?}$⸣ (x) [x (x)] x ⸢kul$^{?}$-lat$^{?}$⸣ x (x) [x x x x (x x) ú-šá]-áš-ṭi-ra ṣe-ru-⸢uš-šu$^{?}$⸣ (x x)

45–46) I had a commemorative monument made and *engraved upon it* image(s) of the great gods, [*my lords*]. I had *an image of myself as king* stand before them [*pr*]*aying to* their great divine majesties. The victories of the god Aššur, *father* of the gods, lord [...] *lord* [...] *all* [... I had] inscribed upon it.

Possible traces of a line

Gap

Possible traces of a line

1′) (traces) [...] ⸢DINGIR$^{?}$.MEŠ$^{?}$⸣ ul-ziz-ma a-na MAN.MEŠ-ni DUMU.MEŠ-ía e-zib ṣa-ti-iš (x x)

2′) (traces) [...] x I$^{?}$ x x x [x] x a-na$^{?}$ x A$^{?}$ (x) ŠAK$^{?}$ ⸢a$^{?}$-šar$^{?}$⸣ la a-ri$^{?}$ x x (x) RA$^{?}$ x

3′) x x x x (x) x x x Ú x x [...] x x SA [...]

4′) x x x x LI$^{?}$ ⸢QI$^{?}$⸣ x IŠ$^{?}$ TE$^{?}$ x x [...] x [...]

5′) x x x MEŠ$^{?}$ x x x x x IA [...]

6′) im-ma-ru Ì.GIŠ lip-šú-uš x x x (x) [...]

Possible traces of a line

Gap

Possible traces of a line

1′) ... [... *of*] *the gods* I erected and left for future kings, my descendants.

2′–6′) ... [...] ... *place where one does not go* ... [...] ... [...] ... [...] ... [... who] sees [...], may he anoint (it) with oil. ... [...]

---

39 Possibly ⸢pu$^{?}$-uḫ$^{?}$-ru$^{?}$⸣ iš-ku-nu-ma, "They arranged *a gathering* (*of their forces*) and."

40 For the reading ra-ma-⸢nu$^{?}$-uš$^{?}$-šú$^{?}$⸣-un ú-ter-ru-ma, cf. text no. 2 line 418 and text no. 7 line 136.

41 Cf. text no. 74 vii 51–52 and 60. Cf. text no. 1 lines 381–382 (a-lak ger-⸢ri⸣ DUMU KÁ.DINGIR.RA.⸢KI iḫ⸣-ta-nab-ba-tu ka-a-a-nu, "constantly, repeatedly robbing caravan(s) of the citizen(s) of Babylon while they were en route") and text no. 2 lines 361–362 (mostly restored).

42 *la a-⸢dir$^{?}$⸣ x-⸢uq$^{?}$⸣-ma-ti*: The traces do not fit well for an expected *a-dir tu-uq-ma-ti*, with the third sign in particular unlike TU; cf. text no. 43 line 25 *a-dir tuq-ma-te*. For ⸢ú$^{?}$⸣-ma-⸢ʾe$^{?}$⸣-[ra$^{?}$] ṣe-ru-uš-šú-un, cf. text no. 2 line 447. The reading [ú$^{?}$]-⸢ma$^{?}$-še-ru⸣-ma is based on text no. 65 line 214.

43 The translation assumes some form and writing of the nouns *pagru* or *šalamtu*, "corpse," before *muq-tab-li-šú-nu*. Text no. 65 line 144 has ADDA.MEŠ *muq-tab-li*, but the traces immediately before *muq* in this text do not fit either MEŠ or ÚŠ, although they might allow ⸢pag$^{?}$⸣-ri$^{?}$.

45 Cf. text no. 103 iv 43–46, text no. 117 ii 70, Streck, Asb. p. 270 iv 2–3, and Leichty, RINAP 4 p. 136 no. 60 line 28′.

117

A badly damaged stele of dark grey limestone with a relief and inscription of Sargon II was found at the village Najafabad (less correctly Najafehabad) in the Assadabad valley about 15 kilometers to the northeast of the Kangavar valley in western Iran. The inscription describes events in Sargon's second through sixth regnal years (720–716), but the account of the campaign into the central Zagros region, in particular against the Medes, in his sixth regnal year (716) is the most detailed. The inscription on the stele appears to state that it was erected in the city of Kišesim (written URU.*ki*-⌈*sa*?-*si*⌉, ii 71). It is likely that the inscription on the stele was composed during, or shortly after, the campaign. This text has often been referred to as the Najafehabad Stele and the edition of this text is the result of collaborative work between G. Frame and A. Fuchs.

CATALOGUE

Museum Number	Provenance	Dimensions (cm)	cpn
National Museum of Iran, Historical Department 5544/21110	Najafabad	165×65×70	(c)

COMMENTARY

The village of Najafabad is built on the slope of a mound and a local inhabitant claims to have found the stele while excavating a foundation for an addition to his house. Its existence was reported to L.D. Levine and T.C. Young, who were conducting a preliminary season of excavations at Godin Tepe in 1965. They examamined the piece and informed the Iranian authorities of its existence. Levine argues that Najafabad was not the original site of the stele, and that it may have been moved there from one of the other mounds in the area, possibly Godin Tepe (Stelae p. 25).

The inscription begins on the lower portion of the front surface, initially just flanking the figure of the king, and then running across it. The right side of the stele appears never to have been inscribed. On the back of the stele, the lines run across the back and continue on across the left side. The inscription is poorly preserved; in particular column i (face) and the end of column ii (the parts of the lines found on the left side) are badly worn and/or damaged. The inscription appears to have been made by an inexperienced scribe since numerous signs are slightly abnormal in form or have fewer or more wedges than expected. For example, AR in ii 48 has five vertical wedges instead of four and MU in ii 70 is AŠ+KUR not AŠ+ŠE. These abnormal sign forms have not normally been noted below.

Latex squeezes of the front, back, and a small part of the bottom of left side of the stele (ROM 965.274.1. 1–4), as well as unpublished photographs of the back of the stele, are preserved in the Royal Ontario Museum; these have been collated by G. Frame. The squeezes had been made in the National Museum of Iran when the stele was moved there soon after it was seen by L.D. Levine and T.C. Young. While the stele is currently on display inside the National Museum of Iran in Tehran, it had unfortunately been on display in the open air for many years and thus the inscription has been badly weathered and is no longer as clear as when first found. Thus, although both Frame and A. Fuchs have examined the original stele in Tehran, the edition is for the most part based on Frame's examination of the squeezes in the Royal Ontario Museum. The signs on the left side (i.e., the ends of the lines beginning on the back of the stele) are frequently unclear on the relevant squeeze. Additional photos of the stele, including three of the left side, have been kindly provided by S. Razmjou and A.M. Arfaee of the National Museum of Iran.

Unfortunately, since it is very badly worn, most of the left side remains illegible. The edition of most of the left side has had to be based in large part upon the published copy. The approximate point at which the squeeze of the back (col. ii) ends is indicated in the copy by a bullet (•), but this must be taken as only a rough indication. The photographs of the left side suggest that there are traces of many more signs in lines 1–61 than are indicated in the edition, but they are so faint or unclear as to make it best to omit them. In sum, numerous uncertainties in the reading of the text remain.

On the front of the stele (col. i), the first eighteen lines are split in half by the figure of the ruler, while beginning with line 19, the lines run all the way across the stele. Before i 19 there are eighteen lines to the left of the figure, but only seventeen to the right of it. It is assumed in the edition below that line 16 appears only to the left of the column and was not carried on over to the right side when the scribe realized that he was going to have trouble with the line alignment once he began to run the lines across the figure. None of line 16 is preserved, but its existence is clearly indicated by line rulings. Thus, what is given as the right side of i 2–16 on the published copy is the right side i 1–15 in the present edition.

The relief on the front of the stele depicts the king facing left, holding a mace in his left hand, and raising his right hand. Symbols of several deities are carved in front of the head of the king. Three of the symbols have been identified by Levine as being a crescent, a horned disk, and a winged sun disk (Levine, Stelae p. 27), with the first and third representing the moon god Sîn and the sun god Šamaš, who are also mentioned in i 7 and 9 of the text. The horned crown probably stands for the god Aššur, who is likely mentioned in one or both of i 1 and 4.

With regard to the restoration of i 1–14, see in particular text no. 103 i 1–23 and text no. 116 lines 1–8; for i 15–19a, see in particular, Grayson, RIMA 2 p. 13 A.0.87.1 i 15–19 and p. 33 A.0.87.2 lines 7–8, text no. 103 i 24–28, and cf. text no. 116 lines 9–10; for i 19–23, see in particular text no. 43 lines 1–3 and text no. 76 lines 1–2; for i 24–27, see in particular text no. 43 lines 4–5; and for i 29–32, see text no. 73 lines 3–5.

For a brief study of the extent of the campaign in 716 as described in this text, see Zadok, NABU 2000 p. 9 no. 5. S. Alibaigi, I. Rezaei, and S.I. Beheshti (ZA 107 [2017 pp. 261–273) discuss the finding of the stele (suggesting that it was likely erected originally at Najafabad) and the stele's stone (concluding that it is local limestone), and argue that the stele was erected in the land of Urattus, the last place mentioned in the course of the campaign (KUR.*ú-ra-ta-as*, ii 68). In a recent article, S. Alibaigi and J. MacGinnis (ZOrA 11 [2018] pp. 198–211, especially p. 202) argue that the place the stele was erected, URU.*ki-⌜sa?-si⌝* (ii 71), cannot refer to the city Kišesim since the episode dealing with that city is much earlier in the text and since there the place is written URU.*ki-še-si-im* (ii 39). They proceed to suggest that the place mentioned in ii 71 was instead the capital city of Urattus, the last place to which Sargon campaigned in the text, and that the land Urattus included Mount Alvand and the city located at Najafabad. However, it must be pointed out that the spelling of personal and place names is not always consistent in Neo-Assyrian royal inscriptions, that there is the well-attested š/s interchange in Assyrian texts (written /š/ standing for /s/ and written /s/ for /š/ — this text being written in Babylonian dialect but using Assyrian sign-forms), and that this particular text, as noted earlier, seems to have been written by an inexperienced scribe. Moreover, it is known from other texts that Sargon erected a stele/image/weapon in Kišesim during the campaign of 716 (text no. 1 lines 93–95, text no. 2 lines 86–87a [mostly restored], and text no. 82 iii 1′–21′; see also text no. 7 lines 59–60) and it would seem unwise to postulate another stele being erected during the same campaign in a different place with such a similar name. Finally, there is no particular reason that the stele had to be erected at the final place mentioned in the campaign report (or the one furthest from the Assyrian heartland) as opposed to being erected in perhaps the most important place captured and annexed during the campaign.

BIBLIOGRAPHY

1967 Young, Iran 5 p. 140 and pl. I (photo, study)

1967 Smith and Young, Archaeology 20 pp. 63–64 (photo, study)

1969 Levine, Historical Geography pp. 193–214 (edition)

1971 Levine, Expedition 13/3–4 p. 43 (photo)

1972 Levine, Stelae pp. 25–50, 60–62, 66–75 figs. 3–12, and 82–86 pls. VII–XI (photo, copy, edition, study)

1973 Calmeyer, Reliefbronzen pp. 228–229 (study)

1974 Levine, Iran 12 pp. 106 and 118 (study)

1974 Levine, Geographical Studies pp. 106 and 118 (study)

1975 Borger, HKL 2 p. 185 sub Lie, Sargon annals Z. 279 Anm. 7 (ii 27, 43, study)

1982 Börker-Klähn, Bildstelen no. 173 (drawing of relief, study

1986 Renger, CRRA 32 pp. 114–115 (ii 17–22, partial transcription, study)

1994 Fuchs, Khorsabad p. 386 (study)
1995 Reade in Liverani, Neo-Assyrian Geography p. 39 and pl. I following p. 42 (ii 66–73, partial photo, study)
1998 Fuchs, SAAS 8 p. 27 nn. 52 and 56, and p. 115 (ii 22–23, edition, study; ii 42, 44, study)
1999 Frame, Orientalia 68 pp. 41–50 (lines ii 31–32, edition; study)
2000 Zadok, NABU 2000 p. 9 no. 5 (study)
2001 Holloway, CRRA 45/1 pp. 247–249 (ii 39, edition, study)
2002 Holloway, Aššur is King pp. 157–159 nn. 251–252 (ii 39, 44, edition, study)
2003 Lanfranchi, Continuity of Empire p. 82 n. 16 (ii 70, study)
2003 Radner, Continuity of Empire p. 120 (ii 70, study)
2006 Frame, Subartu 18 pp. 55–57 and 60 (photo and drawing of front of stele; ii 70–73, translation; study)
2007 Kuhrt, Persian Empire pp. 24–25 no. 2.A.2.i (ii 46b–71a, translation)
2011 Gopnik and Rothman, On the High Road pp. 291–295 (photo of obverse; ii 41b–73a, partial translation; study)
2012 Alibaigi, Shanbehzadeh and Alibaigi, IrAnt 47 pp. 30 and 34 (photo of obverse, study)
2013 Frahm, AoF 40 p. 47 (ii 5, study)
2013 Frame, Persian Gulf Conference 3 pp. 433–443 (photo; ii 70–71, translation; study)
2014 Galter, CRRA 52 pp. 333–334 and 336–337 (study)
2014 Maniori, Campagne di Sargon pp. 40–41 A10 and passim (study)
2018 Alibaigi and MacGinnis, ZOrA 11 pp. 198–211 (photo, study)
2018 Frahm, Last Days pp. 64–66 no. 4 (ii 4–13a, edition, study)
2019 Marchesi, JNES 78 p. 21 (ii 20–22, edition)

TEXT

Col. i

1) ⸢$^{d?}$*a*$^{?}$⸣-*x* (*x*) *x* ⸢GAL$^{?}$⸣-*u* LUGAL KIŠ ^{d}[NUN.GAL$^{?}$ *u*$^{?}$]
2) *x x x x x x* EN ⸢KUR$^{?}$.KUR$^{?}$⸣ [...]
3) ⸢AN$^{?}$⸣ *x x* (*x*) *x* BU *x* [...]
4) ⸢AN$^{?}$.ŠÁR$^{?}$⸣ *x x x* E *x* [...]
5) ^{d}AMAR.⸢UTU EN TIL *e-pir*$^{?}$⸣ *kiš*-⸢*šat*⸣ [UN.MEŠ$^{?}$]
6) ⸢*šá*$^{?}$⸣-*ri-ku* DA$^{?}$ *x* [*x*]
7) ^{d}⸢30 *e*$^{?}$⸣-*tel*$^{?}$ AN-*e* ⸢*ù*$^{?}$⸣ [KI-*tim*]
8) ⸢*šá*$^{?}$-*qu*⸣-*ú* ^{d}⸢ŠEŠ$^{?}$⸣.KI$^{?}$ [DINGIR.MEŠ$^{?}$]
9) ⸢^{d}⸣UTU *x x* ⸢*nam*$^{?}$-*ru*⸣ KUL/MU$^{?}$ ŠÁ [...]
10) [*x*] *x* ⸢ŠÁ⸣ [(*x*)] ⸢BI$^{?}$⸣ *za-ma-*[*ni* ...]
11) [*x* (*x*)] *x x* (*x*) *x* MA ŠÈG$^{?}$ [...]
12) [...] ⸢ŠÁ⸣ AŠ *x* [...]
13) [...] ⸢NU$^{?}$⸣ MA (*x*) [...]
14) [...] *x* ÁŠ [...]

i 1–14) *The god Aššur, great lord*, king of all the [*Igīgū*] god[s *and*] *Anunnakū gods*, lord *of the lan*[*ds*] ... [...], *Aššur* ... [...]; (i 5) the god Marduk, lord of all, *who provides* all [*people*] *with food* (and) grants [...]; the god Sîn, *lord* of heaven *and* [netherworld], exalted one, *divine li*[*gh*]*t* [*of the gods*]; the god Šamaš, *bright* ... [...] (i 10) ... the fo[e ...] ... [...] ... [...] ... [...] ... [...]

15) [DINGIR.MEŠ GAL].⸢MEŠ⸣ *mu-*[*ut-tab-bi-lu-ut*]
16) [AN-*e ù* KI-*tim*]
17) [*šá ti-bu-šú*]-*nu* (*x*) GIŠ.LÁ *u* [*šá-áš-mu*]
18) [*na-bu-ú*$^{?}$] ⸢*šu*$^{?}$-*um*$^{?}$⸣ (*x*) ^{m}MAN-GI.⸢NA LUGAL⸣ [...]

i 15–19a) [Great god]s, ma[nagers of heaven and netherworld, who]se [attack means] battle and [strife, *who nam*]*ed* Sargon (II), ki[ng ...] ... [*in accordance with*] *your heart's desire*:

19) [...] *x* BI (*x*) [(*x*)] ⸢*bi*$^{?}$⸣-*ib-lat* ⸢*lìb*⸣-*bi*-⸢*ku*$^{?}$-*un*$^{?}$⸣ ^{m}MAN-GI.NA *šá-*[*ak-ni* ^{d}EN.LÍL]
20) [(*x x*) NU.ÈŠ] ⸢*ba-'i-it*⸣ AN.ŠÁR *ni-šit e*-⸢*ni*$^{?}$⸣ ^{d}⸢*a-nim*⸣ [(*u*)] ^{d}[*da-gan* (*x x*)]
21) [MAN GAL-(*u*) MAN KAL-(*nu*)] MAN ⸢KIŠ MAN⸣ KUR *aš-šur*.⸢KI⸣ (*x x*) ⸢MAN⸣ *kib*-⸢*rat ar*⸣-[*ba-'i* (*x x*)]

i 19b–22a) Sargon (II), app[ointee of the god Enlil, (...) *nešakku*-priest (*and*)] *desired object* of (the god) Aššur, *chosen* of the gods Anu [(and) Dagān, (...) great king, strong king], king of the [world], king of Assyria, king of the f[our] quarters (of the world), [(...) favorite of the] great [god]s;

22) [*mi-gir* DINGIR.MEŠ] ⸢GAL.MEŠ$^{?}$ RE⸣.É.*x* ⸢*ke*$^{?}$⸣-*e-nu ša* AN.ŠÁR *u* ⸢^{d}⸣[AMAR.UTU]
23) [LUGAL-*ut la šá*]-*na-*[*an*] ⸢*ú-šat*⸣-*li*-⸢*mu-šu*⸣-*ma zi-kir*-⸢*šu ú*⸣-[*še-*(*eṣ*)-*ṣu-ú*]

i 22b–24a) just shepherd, (one) to whom the gods Aššur and [Marduk] granted [a reign without eq]ua[l] and whose reputation (these gods) [exalt/exalted to the heights];

24) [*a-na re-še-e*]-⸢*te*⸣ *šá*-⸢*ki*⸣-*in* ⸢*šu-ba*$^{?}$⸣-*re-e* ⸢ZIMBIR⸣.KI [NIBRU.KI]
25) [KÁ.DINGIR.RA.KI *mu*]-⸢*šal*⸣-*li*-⸢*mu*⸣

i 24b–34) who (re)-established the *šubarrû*-privileges of (the cities) Sippar, [Nippur, (and) Babylon, (and) made resti]tution for the wrongful damage suffered

i 6 Possibly *ša*-⸢*am*⸣-[*mi*]; see text no. 103 i 14.
i 13–14 Cf. text no. 103 i 22–23 and text no. 116 line 8. Possibly [^{d}IMIN.BI *a-li*]-⸢*kut*$^{?}$⸣ *ma-*[*ḫar* DINGIR.MEŠ] / [*šá a-šar*] ⸢*šá*$^{?}$⸣-*áš-*[*mi* ...]?
i 19 Possibly simply [...] *x bi-ib-lat* at the beginning of the line.

Figure 29. Obverse of National Museum of Tehran 5544/21110 (text no. 117), a stone stele found at Najafabad, Iran, that commemorates Sargon's sixth campaign (716). © Royal Ontario Museum.

ḫi-bil-ti-šu-un ˹šá-ki-in˺ x [...]
26) [...] (x) x IK? x ^{d}˹EN˺.LÍL (x) ŠU x (x) x A x (x) x [...]
27) [mu-šá-áš-ši-ik] tup-šik-[ki] ˹BÀD˺.AN.KI x [(x x) x]-šu-˹nu˺ mu-˹šap?˺-[ši-ḫu UN.MEŠ-šu-un?]
28) [...] ˹URU˺.KASKAL x x x ˹UN˺.MEŠ-šu x x (x) ˹ú?˺-še-[...]
29) [...] ZA [x (x)] MA? x x x (x) šá a-˹na? šum˺-qut? (x) [...]
30) [šá ul-tu u$_4$?]-me [be-lu]-˹ti?-šú? mal?˺-[ku?] ˹gaba?-ra-a?-šú˺ la ib-šu-[ma? ...]
31) [...] x [...] ˹$^{d?}$šam?˺-ši a-di šá-la-˹am˺ [^{d}šam-ši ...]
32) [...] (x) ˹ba˺-ʾu-lat x [...]
33) [...] x [...] x A (x) MA x [...]
34) [...] TU? x [...]

by them; who (re)-established [...] ... the god Enlil ... [... who abolished] corvée duty for (the city) Dēr ... who [*gave relief to their people* ...] the city Ḫarrān ... his people ... [...] ... *to strike down* [... (i 30) *who from the* (*first*) *da*]*y of his* [*reign*] has had no *rul*[*er*] *who could equal him* [... from ea]st to we[st ...] the subjects [*of the god Enlil* ...] ... [...] ... [...]

Col. ii
1) [...] (traces) [...]
2) [(x x)] x x x x LU x x NU? KID/Ú? x x x x x x x x (x x') [...]
3) (x x) x x x x x SA x x x ˹KI?˺ x ḪI ˹IM? MA/ŠU?˺ x x x x x x' [...]

ii 1–3) Too poorly preserved to allow translation.

4) (x x) x x [^{m}]˹ia˺-ú-bi-iʾ-di ˹LÚ˺.KUR.˹ḫa˺-am-ma-ta-a-˹a˺ x x x x x (x') [...]
5) [(x)] (x x) x x x x x x x x x x ˹GIŠ?.az?-ma-ru?-ú ú?-maš?˺-x x x (x') [...]
6) (x) x A x (x) x x TI? x (x) NU LÚ.˹ERIM˺.MEŠ ˹ú˺-pa-˹ḫir˺-ma ma-mit ˹DINGIR.MEŠ GAL.MEŠ˺ (x') [...]
7) (x) x DI x ˹ú-ter?˺-ma ˹a-na˺ e-mu-qi-šú it-ta-˹kil˺ um-ma-na-at AN.˹ŠÁR˺ gap-˹šá˺-[a-ti ad-ke-e-ma? ...]
8) x (x) ˹I? DI?˺ GI IB ˹ŠU?˺ x (x) x it-ba-a GIŠ.˹GIGIR˺ pet-ḫal-lu ANŠE.˹KUR.MEŠ˺ ina URU.AB-x'-[x-x ...]
9) [(x)] ˹MA?˺ BU? x (x) RI? ÁŠ ˹DI?˺ x x (x) x-šú-nu ÍD na-ba-lu ˹na˺-ba-si-iš ˹aṣ-ru˺-up A x x' [...]
10) (x) ˹ID? É/DAN? URU? UD/ŠÚ?˺ x (x) ˹UN˺/A? ˹TU/LI?˺ (x) x x ˹KAN?˺ ina GIŠ.a-ši-bi ˹dan˺-ni ˹BÀD-šú kar?˺-pa-ti-˹iš ú˺-pa-˹ri'˺-[ir-ma? ... URU.qar-qa-ru?]
11) [(ina)] ˹^{d}GIBIL$_6$˺ aq-mu šá-a-˹šú a˺-di ˹kim-ti˺-šú LÚ.mun-daḫ-ṣe-šú a-˹na URU-ia? aš˺-šur.KI ub-la ina IGI ˹KÁ˺.GAL' [(...) ma-šak-šú? a-ku-uṣ? (...)]

ii 4–13a) ... Iaū-biʾdī (Ilu-biʾdī) of the land Hamath ... [...] (ii 5) ... *spears he abandoned* [...] ... he assembled (his) troops and [*transgressed against*] the oath (sworn) by the great gods [...] *he brought* (*them*) *to his side* and put his trust in his (own) forces. [*I mustered*] the numer[ous] troops of (the god) Aššur [*and* ...] ... he/they rose up. Chariotry, cavalry, (*and*) horses in the city AB[...] ... their ... I dyed (both) the river (Orontes) (and) the dry land as red as red wool ... [...] (ii 10) ... with a mighty battering ram I smas[hed] his (city) wall like a pot [*and ... the city Qarqar*] I burned down [with] fire. I took him, together with his family (and) his fighting men, to my city Aššur. [*I flayed the skin from him*] in front of the (city) gate [...] ... I set eunuchs of mine as provincial governors over them. The [*people of the*] land Hamath [...] ...

ii 5 The passage is likely to be similar to text no. 81 line 7: [... na-áš GIŠ.ka]-˹ba˺-bu GIŠ.az-˹ma˺-[ru]-ú ú-maš-šir-ma, "[..., shi]eld (and) spe[a]r [bearers], he abandoned [(...)] and."
ii 6 Cf. text no. 81 line 9.
ii 7 The translation "*he brought* (*them*) *to his side* and" assumes a reading a-na i-di-šú ú-ter-ma; see text no. 89 line 20.
ii 8 Possibly gi-ip-˹šu?˺, "massed" (i.e., a massed body of troops). For URU AB x [...], E. Frahm (Last Days p. 65) suggests reading URU.ab-tam-[ma-ku ...] and identifying it with a city of Hamath that is mentioned in an inscription of Shalmaneser III (Grayson, RIMA 3 p. 76 A.0.102.16 line 75′).
ii 9 While one expects "with their blood," "with the blood of their warriors," or something similar, the traces do not seem to favor any obvious reading. "I dyed (both) the river (Orontes) (and) the dry land as red as red wool" or "I dyed the Nabalu River (ÍD.na-ba-lu) as red as red wool."
ii 10 For the reading of middle of the line, see text no. 1 lines 63–64; for the tentative restoration "city Qarqar" at the end of the line, see text no. 7 line 35.
ii 11 ma-šak-šú? a-ku-uṣ?, "*I flayed the skin from him*." The restoration is based on text no. 7 line 35; as noted by E. Frahm (Last Days p. 65), the a-ku-uṣ may be at the beginning of line 12. Otherwise, the passage may refer to the slaughtering of the enemy in front of the city gate (see text no. 65 line 302 and cf. ii 28).

12) (*x*) *x x x* ⌈*šu*⌉-*ut* LÚ.⌈SAG.MEŠ⌉-*ia a-na* LÚ.EN.NAM-⌈*ú*⌉-*ti* UGU-*šú-nu áš-kun* KUR.*ḫa-am-ma-*⌈*ta*$^{\bullet}$⌉-[*a-a*$^{?}$ ...]

13) (*x x*) *x* ⌈ID$^{?}$ KU/KI⌉ *x* (*x*) *ina* ⌈3⌉ BALA-*ia* URU.*šu-un-*⌈*da*$^{?}$-*ḫu*$^{?}$⌉-*ul* URU.*du-ur-du-*⌈*uk*$^{?}$⌉-*ka* URU.MEŠ *dan-nu-ti* É ⌈BÀD$^{?\bullet}$⌉.[MEŠ ...]

14) ⌈*i*$^{?}$-*mi*$^{?}$-*šú*$^{?}$ *ar*⌉-(*x*)-⌈*du*⌉-*ú-tu šá* ^{m}*ir-an-zi* KUR.*man-*⌈*na*⌉-*a-a* LÚ.EN-*šú-nu il-qu-u še-ṭu-us-su* A *x*$^{\bullet}$ [...]

15) ⌈*meḫ*$^{?}$-*ret*$^{?}$⌉ *um-*⌈*ma-na*⌉-*at* AN.ŠÁR ⌈*aṣ*⌉-*bat-ma* ⌈*a*⌉-*na ka-šad* URU.⌈MEŠ⌉ *šu-a-tu-nu a-na* KUR.*man-na-a-a a-lik di-ik-ta-šú ma-*⌈*at*$^{\bullet}$⌉-[*tu a-duk* ...]

16) IZ/TÚ$^{?}$ *x x* ⌈Ú/DAN$^{?}$ PI$^{?}$⌉ *x* MA *x x x x* (*x*) *x* NU *x* ḪI RU$^{?}$ BÀD *ki-i* NA_4 AN-*e ú-šá-za-nin* UN.MEŠ *a-di mar-ši-*⌈*ti*$^{\bullet}$⌉-[*šú-nu* ...]

ii 13b–16) In my third regnal year, the cities *Šundaḫul* (and) Durdukka, strong, *w*[*alled*] cities [...] *disregarded* (their) position as vassal to Iranzi, the Mannean, their lord, (and) held him in contempt [...] *I took the lead* (*in front*) *of* the troops of Aššur and I marched to the land Mannea in order to conquer those cities. [I inflicted] a ma[jor] defeat upon it [...] ... I caused to pour forth like hailstones. [*I carried off as booty*] the people, together with [their] property [...].

17) ⌈*ina* 4 BALA-*ia*⌉ *a-na* KUR.⌈*ta-ba-li al*$^{?}$-*lik*⌉ URU.*ši-nu-uḫ-tú* URU *dan-nu-ti-šú šá* ^{m}*ki-ak-ki* KUR-*ud šá-a-šú ga-*⌈*di kim*⌉-[*ti*$^{\bullet}$-*šú* ...]

18) ⌈KUŠ⌉ AM.⌈SI⌉ ZÚ AM.SI GIŠ.⌈ESI⌉ GIŠ.TÚG *lu-*⌈*bul*⌉-*ti bir-me* TÚG.GADA GIŠ.*til-li ú-nu-ut ta-*⌈*ḫa-zi* IZ$^{?}$ KI$^{?}$⌉ *x* NU$^{?\bullet}$ [...]

19) *ṣe-ni-šú-nu su-gúl-lat* ANŠE.⌈KUR.MEŠ⌉ ANŠE.MEŠ *a-*⌈*na la ma-ni*⌉ *áš-lu-la ma-da-at-tu ša* MAN.MEŠ-*ni ša* KUR.⌈*ta-ba-li*$^{\bullet}$⌉ [*am-ḫur*$^{?}$ ...]

ii 17–19) In my fourth regnal year, I marched to the land Tabal. I conquered the city Šinuḫtu, Kiakki's fortified city. That (individual), together with [his] fam[ily, ...] elephant hides, elephant ivory, ebony, boxwood, garments with multi-colored trim (and) linen garments, equipment, battle gear ... [...], their sheep and goats, herds of horses, (and) donkeys, I carried off as booty in countless numbers. [*I received*] tribute from the kings of the land of Tabal [...].

20) *ina* 5 BALA-*ia* URU.*kar-ga-*⌈*miš*⌉ *ša* GÚ ÍD.*pu-rat-ti ak-šu-ud* ^{m}*pi-si-i-ri* MAN-*šú a-di* ^{m}*šem-tar-ru* Ú$^{\bullet}$ [...]

21) *it-ti* NÍG.GA É.GAL-*šú mim-*⌈*ma*⌉ *x x* ⌈*ni-ṣir*⌉-*ti šar-ru-ti-šú áš-lu-lam-ma a-na* URU-*ia aš-šur*.KI *ub-la* UN.MEŠ URU.*kar*$^{\bullet}$-[*ga-miš* ... *bíl-tu*$^{?}$ *ma-da-at-tú*$^{?}$]

ii 20–22a) In my fifth regnal year, I conquered the city Carchemish which is (located) on the bank of the Euphrates River. Pisīri(s), its king, together with Šemtarru [...] (along) with the possessions of his palace, every *valuable* object, his royal treasure, I carried off as booty and brought to my city Aššur. I imposed upon the people of the city Car[chemish ... (*the same*) *tribute* (*and*) *payment*(*s*)] as if (it were part of) Assyria. [*I presented*] to the gods Aššur (and) *Marduk*, ... gods [(...)] the gold (and) silver that I had personally seized at the city Carchemish [(...)].

22) *ki-i* KUR ⌈*aš-šur*⌉.KI *e-mid-su-*⌈*nu* KÙ⌉.GI KÙ.BABBAR *ša* URU.*kar**-*ga-miš qa-ti ik-*⌈*šu*⌉-*du a-na* AN.ŠÁR ^{d}⌈AMAR$^{?}$.UTU A$^{?}$⌉ *x* DINGIR.⌈MEŠ$^{?\bullet}$⌉ [... *ina* 6 BALA-*ia* ^{m}*ul-lu-su-nu*$^{?}$ KUR.*man-na-a-a*$^{?}$ (...)]

ii 22b–25) [In my sixth regnal year], the wrath of Aššur was directed against [*Ullusunu, the Mannean*, (...)] (ordaining) the dissolution of the land Mannea, the destruction of (his) people, (*and*) *the demolition* of his (city) wall. [*He* (*Ullusunu*)] then [*put his trust*] *in* Rusâ

---

ii 12 The traces at the beginning of the line do not fit either *ú-še-rib* or *ú-še-šib*, which are often found before the statement about the appointment of new governors (e.g., text no. 1 line 98 and text no. 7 line 32). For a possible translation "a eunuch of mine as provincial governor" instead of "eunuchs of mine as provincial governors," taking the sign sequence SAG.MEŠ as "a late echo of the dual-based Middle Assyrian term for eunuch, *ša-rēšēn*," see Frahm, Last Days p. 66, who also compares the passage to text no. 84 line 20′ and text no. 103 ii 63.
ii 13–16 Cf. text no. 1 lines 58–64.
ii 14 For the tentative reading *imīšū*, "disregarded," see text no. 65 lines 80 and 346 and text no. 7 line 73.
ii 15 ⌈*aṣ*⌉-*bat-ma*: Or ⌈*az*⌉-*ziz-ma*; see the note to text no. 65 line 25.
ii 17 The published copy has *a-lik*, but the squeeze suggests that AL is more likely than A.
ii 19 Or possibly *ma-da-at-tu ša* MAN.MEŠ-*ni ša* KUR.⌈*ta-ba-li*$^{\bullet}$⌉ [UGU *ša pa-na ut-tir-ma* UGU-*šú áš-kun* (...)], "[I imposed upon him] (the payment of) tribute that [was higher than] kings of the land Tabal [(had paid) previously (...)]," following, Renger, CRRA 32 p. 114 and based on text no. 1 line 71 and text no. 4 line 12′.
ii 20 ^{m}*šem-tar-ru*: The name was originally read ^{m}*bi-iš-tar-ru*, but see Groß, PNA 3/2 p. 1256. The PNA only mentions the occurrence of this name in this text, but see also ND 2084 line 2 ^{m}*šem-tar-i* (Parker, Iraq 23 [1961] p. 18 and pl. IX).
ii 21 One expects *mim-ma aq-ru* (see for example text no. 65 line 340), but the traces would not seem to support this reading. With regard to the tentative restoration at the end of line 21, compare for example text no. 41 lines 12–13.
ii 22–23 For the tentative restorations at the end of lines 22 and 23, see text no. 1 lines 84–85 and text no. 4 lines 27′–28′. Line 22: *kar**-: The squeeze has ŠE-A-.

23) *šib-sa-at* AN.ŠÁR *šá sa-paḫ* KUR.*man-na-a-*⸢*a*⸣ *u* <<*u*>> *ḫul-lu-uq* UN.MEŠ ⸢*na?-qar*⸣ BÀD-*šú* UGU-*šú ib-ši-ma a-*<*na*> m?*ru-sa-*⸢*a*⸣ URU.[*x* (*x*)] *x*˙ [(...) *it-ta-kil?* m*aš-šur-*ZU? KUR.*kar-al-la-a-a?* m*it-ti-i?* KUR.*al-lab-ra-a-a?*]

24) *it-ti-ia* ⸢*ú*⸣*-šá-bal-kit-ma pa-a e-*⸢*da ú*⸣*-šá-*⸢*áš*⸣*-kín ni-ir* AN.ŠÁR *iṣ-li-ma x* [*x x* (*x*)] ⸢ŠÁ/ŠUR?⸣ KI *il-qe ma-da-ta-šú ik-la-*⸢*ma*˙⸣ [... (*šá*) (...)]

25) ⸢*e*⸣*-te-qu ni-is-su kab-tu la* ⸢*ip-la-ḫu*⸣*-ma in-šu-ú ma-mit-*⸢*su*⸣ [*x* (*x*)] ⸢*a*⸣*-ma-ti šu-a-ti* U BAL UD UL *x* TAR MA KU? (*x*˙) [...]

of the city [...]. He caused [*Aššur-lē'i of the land Karalla* (*and*) *Ittî of the land Allabria*] to rebel against me and made (them) act in unison. He threw off the yoke of (the god) Aššur and took [...] ... He withheld his tribute and [... (*who*) (...)] transgressed, did not respect his mighty oath, and forgot his sworn agreement ... [...]

26) ⸢*lib*⸣*-ba ar-ḫu-uṣ-ma e-*⸢*te-li*⸣*-iṣ* ⸢*ka*⸣*-bat-ti um-ma-na-at* ⸢AN?⸣.[ŠÁR?] ⸢*rap?*⸣*-šá-a-ti ad-ke-e-ma a-na* KUR.*man-na-a-a a-*⸢*lik*˙⸣ [...]

27) ⸢Ú?⸣ *x* ⸢ŠAR?⸣ MA *x* GÍD DA KA MA ⸢TI?⸣ *x* ⸢ŠU⸣ A *x x* ME *x a-di* 2 KASKAL.GÍD u_{4}*-me* ⸢*la šá*⸣*-qe-e* BÀD-*šú ki-ma kar-pat pa-ḫa-ri ú-*⸢*pa*˙⸣*-*[*ri-ir-*(*ma*) ...]

28) ⸢*ina qa?*⸣*-ti ú-ṣab-bit* UN.MEŠ-*šú a-di* ⸢*mar-ši*⸣*-ti-šú-nu ina?* ⸢IGI?⸣ KÁ?.GAL?-*šú? ki-ma mi-nu-ut ṣe-e-ni am-nu* URU.*i-zi-ir-tu* URU *dan*˙-[*nu-ti-šú* ...]

29) [*x* (*x*)] *x* MA? ⸢KAR?⸣ *qu-tur* ⸢*na-aq-mu-te*⸣ URU.*i-zi-ir-tú e-mu-ru-ma* ⸢*i-ma?*⸣*-'u-ú mar-tu ur-du-nim-ma ú-na-šá-*⸢*qu?*˙⸣ [GÌR.II.MEŠ-*ia?* ...]

30) [*a*]-⸢*na*⸣ (*x*) *šu-zu-ub* ZI.MEŠ-*šú* ⸢GÌR.II⸣.MEŠ-*ia iṣ-bat* ANŠE.KUR.MEŠ GU_{4}.MEŠ *ṣe-e-ni ma-da-ta-šú am-ḫur* (*x*˙) [...]

31) *x* (*x*) *x* ⸢m⸣*aš-šur-*ZU URU.*kar-al-la-a-*⸢*a e-piš lem*⸣*-né-e-ti šá-a-šú ga-di* LÚ.ERIM.MEŠ-*šú ina qé-reb uš-ma-ni-ia ad-di-šú-nu bi-re-*⸢*e?*⸣*-tú*˙ [AN.BAR? ...]

32) [*as*]-⸢*su*⸣*-uḫ-ma a-na* ⸢URU⸣*-ia* KUR *aš-šur* ⸢*ú*⸣*-bil* URU.*kar-al-la a-di* KUR.*na-gi-šú* UGU *pi-*⸢*ḫa*⸣*-at* URU.*lu-lu-me ú-*⸢*rad*⸣*-di* A (*x*˙) [... mdEN-IBILA-SUM.NA (...)]

ii 26–33a) I became confident and my mood became jo[yf]ul. I mustered the [exte]nsive troops of (the god) Aš[*šur*] and ma[rched] to the land Mannea. [...] ... be[fore] the day had proceeded two double-hours, I [had smashed] his (city) wall as if (it were) a potter's vessel [(and) ...] I personally captured. *In front of his* (*city*) *gate* I considered his people, together with their property, as if (they were) a number of sheep and goats. [His] for[tified] city Izirtu [...] ... they saw the smoke of the conflagration of the city Izirtu and vomited gall. They came down to kis[s *my feet* ... (ii 30) In] order to save his life he grasped hold of my feet. I received horses, oxen, (and) sheep and goats as his tribute. [...] *I captured* Aššur-lē'i of the city Karalla, an evil-doer. In the midst of my camp, I threw him, together with his soldiers, in [*iron*] fetters. [... I re]moved and brought to my city Aššur (lit.: "Assyria"). I added the city Karalla, together with its district, to the province of the city Lullumû. [...] I elevated [Bēl-aplu-iddina (...)] over the city Paddiri. I imposed upon him more (state) service (and) corvée duty than before.

33) ⸢UGU URU⸣.*pad-dir ú-rab-bi-*⸢*šú?*⸣ *il-ku tup-šik-ku* UGU *šá maḫ-ri e-mid-su* TA URU.*pad-dir at***-tu-muš a-na* ⸢URU?⸣.*ni-*⸢*iq?-qar*⸣ *x*˙ [...]

34) ⸢URU.*ki*⸣*-na-aḫ-ri? šá* URU.*šur-ga-di-a* ⸢URU⸣.MEŠ-*ni dan-*⸢*nu*⸣*-ti* KUR.*gu-ti-i la ba-*⸢*bil*⸣ *šip-ri šá* u_{4}*-me-šam-ma a-ṣi-it* UN.⸢MEŠ˙⸣ [...]

ii 33b–35a) Moving on from the city Paddir(i), [*I came*] to the city *Niqqar* [...] the city Kinaḫri, of the city Šurgadia, fortified [citi]es of the land of the Gutians, those who do no work, *who* daily [...] *the expeditionary force of the people* [...] I carried off as booty [(...)] their people, together with their property, their horses, their oxen, (and) their sheep and goats. Šēp-šarri ... the city ruler [...].

35) UN.⸢MEŠ⸣*-šú-nu a-di mar-ši-ti-šú-nu* ⸢ANŠE.KUR⸣.MEŠ-*šú-nu* GU_{4}.⸢MEŠ-*šú*⸣*-nu ṣe-ni-šú-nu áš-lu-la* mGÌR.II-MAN MAN KA LU? LI LÚ.EN.URU (*x*˙) [... TA? ... *at-tu-muš?*]

ii 35b–38a) [*Moving on from* ...], I came to the city Ḫundir. Bēl-*šarru*-uṣur of the city Kišesim spoke mendaciously to the city rulers of [his] en[virons ...] He brought before me in the city Ḫundir as his tribute

ii 23 One expects KUR.*ur-ar-ṭa-a-a* or KUR.TILLA-*a-a*, "the Urarṭian," after Rusâ. Parpola, Toponyms pp. 370–373 lists only one case (a Babylonian chronicle) when Urarṭu is preceded by URU rather than KUR, but note also Grayson, RIMA 3 p. 20 A.0.102.2 ii 48.
ii 28 The end of the line likely mentioned the burning of city (cf. text no. 1 lines 86–87 and text no. 7 lines 41–42).
ii 32 For the restoration at the end of ii 32, see text no. 63 col. i′ 21′.
ii 33 *at**-: The squeeze has MA-.
ii 34 For Šēp-šarri, the ruler of Šurgadia, see also text no. 1 lines 92–93, text no. 4 line 38′, and text no. 7 line 58.

36) ⸢*a*⸣-*na* URU.*ḫu*$^{?}$-*un-dir aq-ṭé-rib* ^{m}EN-*x*-⸢*ú*⸣-*ṣur* URU.*ki-še-sa-a*-⸢*a*$^{?}$⸣ *da-ba-ab la kit-ti id-bu-ub a*-⸢*na*⸣ LÚ.EN.⸢URU$^{?}$⸣.MEŠ-*ni šá li**-[*me-ti-šú* ...]

37) ⸢*ma-da*⸣-*ta-šú* ANŠE.KUR.MEŠ GU$_{4}$.MEŠ *ṣe-e-ni a-na* URU.*ḫu-un*-⸢*dír*⸣ *a-di maḫ-ri-ia il-qa-a ina qé-reb uš-ma*-⸢*ni-ia am*$^{?}$-*ḫur*$^{?}$-*šú*$^{?}$-*nu*$^{?}$-*ti*$^{?*}$⸣ [...]

38) [*a*]-⸢*na šal*$^{?}$⸣-*la-ti am-nu* ANŠE.KUR.MEŠ LAL*-*at** *ni-i-ri* NÍG.ŠU-*šú* NÍG.GA-⸢*šú*⸣ KÙ.GI KÙ.BABBAR *lu-bul-ti bir-me* TÚG.GADA GIŠ.*til-li a-nu-ut ta-ḫa-zi x** [(...) *a-na*$^{?}$ KUR *aš-šur*.KI$^{?}$ *ú-ra-a*$^{?}$ (...) GIŠ.TUKUL.MEŠ$^{?}$ *ša*$^{?}$ AN.ŠÁR ^{d}30 ^{d}UTU]

39) ⸢^{d}IŠKUR⸣ ^{d}*iš-tar* EN.MEŠ-*ia a-li-kut pa-ni-ia ú*-⸢*še-piš-ma*⸣ *ina* ⸢*qer*⸣-*bi-šú ú-šar-me* UN.MEŠ URU.*ki-še-si-im* KUR.*na-gi-šu a-bur*-⸢*riš*$^{?*}$⸣ [*ú-šar-bi-iṣ-ma* ...]

40) ⸢LÚ.*šu*⸣-*ut* SAG-*ia a-na* LÚ.EN.NAM-*ú-ti* ⸢UGU⸣-[*šú-nu*] *áš-kun* KUR.É-*sa-ga-bi šá qé-reb dan-ni-ti ša* DUMU KÁ*.[DINGIR.RA.KI ...]

41) ⸢*il*⸣-[*ku*] ⸢*tup*⸣-*šik-ku za-bal ku-du-ri ša* AN.ŠÁR ⸢EN⸣-*ia e*-⸢*mid-su*⸣-*nu ina* ⸢*u*$_{4}$-*me*⸣-*šú-ma* URU.*ḫar-ḫa-ar-a-a kan-šu-tu* AN.ŠÁR *za-bil tup-šik-ki x* (*x x**) [...]

42) [^{m}*ki-ba*]-⸢*ba*⸣ LÚ.EN.URU-*šú-nu e-ba-ku-ma* ANŠE.KUR.⸢MEŠ⸣ *ni-dan* MU.AN.NA *ma-da-ta-šú-nu ik-lu-ú* BÀD-*šú-nu ú-dan-ni*-⸢*nu*⸣-*ma e-ter*-⸢*ri*$^{?*}$⸣-[*šu*$^{?}$ *ki-it-ra*$^{?}$ ...]

43) [*x* (*x*)] *x x u*$_{4}$-*me la šá-qe-e* BAD$_{5}$.⸢BAD$_{5}$⸣-*šú-un am-ḫa-aṣ di-ik-ta-šú-nu ma-at-tu a-duk* LÚ.⸢*mun*⸣-*daḫ-ṣe-šú-nu a-na tim-me ú-še*-⸢*li*⸣ [...]

44) ⸢*ar*$^{?}$-*ṣip*$^{?}$⸣ *ú-šak-lil* É.KUR-*šú eš-šiš e-pu*-⸢*uš*⸣ DINGIR.MEŠ-*šú a-na áš-ri-šú-nu ú-ti-ir šá* AN.ŠÁR ^{d}30 ^{d}UTU ^{d}IŠKUR ^{d}*iš-tar* DINGIR.MEŠ* [*a-li-kut*$^{?}$ *pa-ni-ia*$^{?}$ ...]

45) *x* KUR *x*.MEŠ *a-na la mi-ni ina qé-re-ti-šú at-bu-uk* ÍD-⸢*tu*⸣ *e-lit-tu šá* KUR.*a*-⸢*ra*⸣-*zi-šú* ÍD-*tu šap-lit-tu šá* É-^{m}*ra-ma-ti*-⸢*ia*⸣ *x** [... *ku-du-ri*$^{?}$]

46) ⸢*ki-i šá áš*⸣-*šu-ri ú-šá-za-bil-šú-nu* TA URU.*ḫar-ḫar at-tu-muš* ÍD A.MEŠ *ka-ṣu-ti e-te-bir a-na* URU.*zak-ru-ti aq*-⸢*ṭé-rib*⸣ (*x*) ⸢ŠA$^{?}$⸣ *x*

horses, oxen (and), sheep and goats. *I received them* inside my camp. [...] I counted (them) [as] booty.

ii 38b–41a) [*I brought to Assyria*] horses trained to the yoke, property, possessions, gold, silver, garments with multi-colored trim, linen garments, equipment, (and) battle gear [(...)] I had [*the weapons of* the deities Aššur, Sîn, Šamaš], Adad, (and) Ištar, my lords, who go before me, made [and] I installed (them) there. [I had] the people of the city Kišesim (*and*) its district [dwell (as safely) as in] a meado[w and ...] (ii 40) I set a eunuch of mine as provincial governor over [them]. [I ...] the land Bīt-Sagabi (Bīt-Sagbat), which *is* in the Fortress of the Bab[yonian(s) ...] I imposed upon them (state) ser[vice], corvée duty, (and) labor duty for (the god) Aššur, my lord.

ii 41b–46a) At that time, the people of the city Ḫarḫar who are submissive to Aššur (and) perform labor service [...] They drove off [Kibab]a, their city ruler, and withheld the horses (which were) to be given yearly as their tribute. They strengthened their (city) wall and *repeatedly as*[*ked for (military) aid* ...] *before* the day had proceeded [x *double-hours*] I brought about their defeat; I inflicted a major defeat on them. I impaled their fighting men on stakes [...] I completely [(*re*)*con*]*str*[*ucted*]. I built its temple anew (and) restored its gods to their places. [*I ...-ed* the ...] of the deities Aššur, Sîn, Šamaš, Adad, (and) Ištar, the deities [*who go before me.* (...)] I poured out innumerable *offerings* at its festival. The upper river(land) of the land Arazišu (Aranzêšu), the lower river(land) of Bīt-Ramatua [...] I had them perform [(...) *labor duty*] as if (they were) Assyrians.

ii 46b) Moving on from the city Ḫarḫar, I crossed a river with cold water (and) came to the city Zakruti. ... [...]

---

ii 36 For the reading Bēl-šarru-uṣur, see for example text no. 1 line 93 and text no. 7 line 59.

ii 38 LAL*-*at**: The squeeze has ME-ṢI. For the tentative restoration at the end of line 38, cf. text no. 1 line 94, text no. 4 lines 39′–40′, text no. 82 iii 6′–7′, and the present text ii 44.

ii 40 For the Fortress of the Babylonian(s), see Tadmor, Tiglath-pileser III pp. 72–73, commentary to Ann. 15 line 11. H. Tadmor states that similar references in the inscriptions of Tiglath-Pileser III "point to the existence of Babylonian colonies in western Media" and that their origin "should be sought in the late Kassite period."

ii 42 For the restoration Kibaba, see text no. 7 line 61. *ni-dan* MU.AN.NA "(which were) to be given yearly": Although the orignal publisher of the stele, L.D. Levine, read *er-bet* MU.AN.NA and translated the passage as "for four years" (Stelae pp. 40–41 and 71), the squeeze clearly indicates that the stele had *ni-dan* rather than *er-bet*; the form *ni-dan* is, however, unexpected. For the tentative reading *e-ter*-⸢*ri*$^{?}$⸣-[*šu*$^{?}$ *ki-it-ra*$^{?}$ ...], "*repeatedly as*[*ked for* (*military*) *aid* ...]," cf. text no. 82 vii 32′′b–33′′a *e-ter-ri-šu-uš* ⸢*ki-it*⸣-*ra*. The end of the line might have referred to Daltâ of the land of Ellipi (see text no. 1 lines 96–97).

ii 43 At the beginning of the line one expects *a-di x* KASKAL.GÍD *u*$_{4}$-*me la šá-qe-e*, "Before the day had proceeded x double-hours" (see ii 27), but the trace before *u*$_{4}$-*me* does not fit the end of KASKAL.GÍD. The trace looks like: [...] LIŠ or the end of the DA sign.

ii 45 One expects SÍSKUR.MEŠ (or UDU.SISKUR.MEŠ) at the beginning of the line, but the traces do not seem to favor this reading. É ^{m} has five vertical wedges, with the last two apparently connected to the first three by a horizontal line. With regards to "the upper river(land)" and "the lower river(land)," see the on-page note to text no. 1 line 98. For further possible restorations at the end of the line, cf. text no. 1 lines 98–99.

(x) ⌈TU/LI?⌉ [(x)] x x' [...]

47) ⌈TA⌉ URU.*zak-ru-ti at-tu-muš a-na* URU.*ku-ur-ab-li aq-ṭé-rib ma-da-at-tú ša* m*da-i-ku ša* URU.*šá-pár-da-a-a šá* mUŠ-⌈AN/TI?⌉ x x (x) x x x (x) ⌈*šá*?⌉ x x x (x') [... *am-ḫur* ...]

48) [(x)] x KUR x x BA? A KUR.*i-gal-i* KUR.*si-ik-ri-is* KUR.É-*ú-ar-gi* KUR.*na-ge-e ru-qu-ú-te šá* MAN.MEŠ-*ni a-li-ku-ti pa-ni-*⌈*ia zi?-kir?-šú-nu*⌉ x ⌈MU?⌉ x x x (x) [x x x] (x') [...]

49) [*pul*]-⌈*ḫi me-lam-me*⌉ *ik-tùm-šu-nu-ti-ma* URU.MEŠ-*ni-šú-nu ú-maš-še-ru* UN.MEŠ-*šú-nu mar-ši-su-nu ú-paḫ-ḫi-ru-ma* KUR.*ab-ra-ú* x [x (x)] ⌈*a-na tuk-la-ti?-šú?-nu*?⌉ x x' [...]

50) [x x x] x x ⌈*ina* GIŠ⌉.TUKUL.MEŠ *ú-šam-qit-ma si-ta-te-šú-nu* UN.MEŠ ANŠE.KUR.MEŠ ANŠE.KUNGA.MEŠ GU$_4$.MEŠ UDU.MEŠ ANŠE.MEŠ *áš-lu*-la* x [x] x x x ⌈*a-na* KI⌉ [x] (x) x (x') [...]

51) [...] ⌈*ap*⌉-*pul* ⌈*aq*⌉-*qur ina* IZI GÍBIL TA KUR.*si-ik-ri-is at-tu-muš a-na* KUR.*a-ru-us-sa aq-ṭé-rib na-gu-ú šá-a-šú a-*⌈*di*?⌉ x (x) x ⌈NE?⌉ x' [...]

52) (x) x x x [x x x] AB? QA? ÍD.*pa-at-ta-us* ÍD-*tu e-*⌈*te*⌉*-bir a-na* KUR.*ú-ku-ta aq-ṭé-rib* UN.MEŠ KUR.*na-gi-*⌈*i*⌉ *šu-a-*⌈*ti*?⌉ x x x x x (x x') [...]

53) *ki-ma di-*⌈*pa*⌉*-ri a-qu-du-ma* ŠE *e-bur-šú-nu a-na mu-ʾu-de-e um-ma-na-ti-ia ú-šá-a-kil* ⌈LÚ⌉.*qu-ra-di-ia a-na šá-lal* x x ⌈KA?⌉ x [x x] x' [...]

54) (x) *iš-lu-lu-ni* TA KUR.*ú-ku-ta at-tu-muš* KUR.*a-ru-sa-ka* KUR-*ú dan-nu pi-is-nu-uq-qiš at-ta-ab-bal-kat** KUR.*an-za-ak-*⌈*né*⌉ (x) ⌈*aq-ṭé-rib*⌉ x [x] x (x x') [...]

55) ⌈QI?⌉ MU/QAB? ⌈LI⌉ *kak?-ka-biš ú-šá-ṣa-ri-iḫ* m*ka-ra-ak-ka* KUR.*ú-ri-ia-ka-a-a qu-tur na?-aq-mu-ut* URU.MEŠ *šá* KUR.*an-za-*⌈*ak-né?-e*⌉ x x x (x) x x x x x x x (x') [...]

56) TA KUR.*an-za-ak-né-e at-tu-muš ina né-re-bi šá* KUR.*ú-pur-ia ina bi-rit* KUR.*pa-at-ta-áš-šu-un* KUR.*da-ru-ú-e* ⌈KUR⌉.MEŠ-*e šá-qu-ti* ⌈*e-tar?-ba*⌉ *ina* GÌR.II⌉ KUR.⌈*ú-a-ab*?⌉*-x-*⌈*šu*?⌉*-x* ⌈KUR?.?⌉-[*e? ak-ṣu-ra? uš-man-ni?* (...)]

57) ANŠE.*pét-ḫal-lum* LÚ.ERIM.MEŠ GIŠ.PAN *a-na ḫu-bu-ut* EDIN *a-na* URU.MEŠ-*ni šá* URU.*bu-us-tu-us ši-li-pu* ⌈*ú*⌉*-ma-áʾ-er* LÚ.*ṣa-ab* EDIN x ⌈NU?⌉ x ⌈DU? ŠU⌉ x MA ⌈Ú?⌉ x x ⌈MEŠ?⌉ [x (x)] x' [... *ma-da-at-tú? šá?* ...]

58) *šá* KUR.*ú-pur-ia šá* m*ma-áš-dàk-ka šá* KUR.*a-ra-ti-iš?-ta am-ḫur* m*ra-zi-iš-tu šá*

ii 47–51a) Moving on from the city Zakruti, I came to the city Kurabli. [I received] as tribute from Daīku of the city Šaparda (*and*) from UŠ... [... *Moving on from the city Kurabli*, ...] the land of ..., the land Igali, the land Sikris, (and) the land Bīt-Uargi, distant regions whose *name(s)* the kings who preceded me *had never heard*, [... Fe]ar of (my) brilliance overwhelmed them and they abandoned their cities. They gathered their people (and) their property and [...] the land Abrau ... *for their support* [...] I struck down with the sword and carried off the remainder of them as booty, (namely) people, horses, mules, oxen, sheep, (and) donkeys. ... to/for ... [...] I destroyed, demolished, (and) burned down with fire.

ii 51b) Moving on from the land Sikris, I came to the land Arussa. That region, *together with* ... [...]

ii 52–54a) ... I crossed the Pattaus River (and) came to the land Ukuta. The people of *th*[*at*] region ... [... *who/which*] I set on fire like a torch, I fed my troops their grain crop in large quantities. My warriors in order to plunder ... [...] they carried off as booty.

ii 54b–55) Moving on from the land Ukuta, I crossed over Mount Arusaka, a mighty mountain, *with great difficulty* (and) came to the land Anzaknê ... [...] ... *I made flare up like a star.* Karakku of the land Uriakku *saw* the smoke of the conflagration of the cities of the land Anzaknê ... [...].

ii 56–59a) Moving on from the land Anzaknê, I entered the pass of the land Uppuria in between Mount Pattaššun (and) Mount Darūe, high mountains. [*I set up camp*] at the foot of Mount Uab...šu.... [(...)] I sent [(...)] cavalry (and) bowmen ...ly against the settlements of the city Bustus in order to take booty from the steppe. The soldiers of the steppe ... [...] I received [*as tribute from* ...] of the land Uppuria (and) from Mašdakku of the land Aratišta. Razištu of the land Bustus (and) Ušrâ of the land Kan[za]bkanu [*came before me*] in the land Uppuria [*and kissed my feet.* (...)] Razidatu (Razištu), the city ruler of the city Bustus, spoke mendaciously,

ii 50 *-lu*-*: The squeeze has -IB-.
ii 52 ÍD.*pa-at-ta-us*: Not ÍD.*pa-at-tu-us* as in the copy in Levine, Stelae p. 72.
ii 54 *-kat**: The squeeze has -AŠ. Based on the writings in lines ii 55 and 56, we would expect KUR.*an-za-ak-*⌈*né*⌉*-e* before *aqṭerib*; however, there does not appear to be room for the *-e* and it is not clear that there is actually a trace of a sign between the -⌈*né*⌉ and the *aq-*.
ii 56 The reading RU in ⌈*e-ru?-ba*⌉ is particularly uncertain. For the restoration at the end of the line, cf. text no. 65 line 27.
ii 57 *ši-li-pu* "...ly": See the note to text no. 1 line 447.
ii 58 Text no. 65 line 49 has URU.*a-rat-is-ti* and text no. 82 vi 28′′ has KUR.*a-*⌈*rat*⌉*-is-ta*. The translation assumes a restoration *a-di maḫ-ri-ia il-li-ku-nim-ma ú-na-aš-ši-qu* GÌR.II-*ia* at the end of the line.

KUR.*bu-us-tu-us* ^{m}⸢*uš*⸣-*ra-a šá*
KUR.*ka-an-*[*za*]-⸢*ab-ka-ni a*⸣-*na* KUR.*ú-pur-*⸢*ia*$^{?}$⸣
(*x*) *x*• [...]

abandoned his land, and fled far away. I destroyed his cities, [*leveling* (*them*) *down to*] *the ground* [(...)].

59) ^{m}*ra-zi-da-tu* LÚ.EN.URU *šá* URU.*bu**-⸢*us*⸣-*tu-us* *da-ba-ab la kit-ti id-bu-*⸢*ub*⸣-*ma* KUR-*su* *u-maš-še-er-ma ru-ú-qiš* ⸢*in*$^{?}$-*na-a-bit* URU⸣.MEŠ-*šú ap-*⸢*púl-ma qaq*$^{?}$-*qa*$^{?}$-*riš*$^{?!}$⸣ [... TA KUR.*ú-pur-ia at-tu-muš*]

ii 59b–60a) [Moving on from the land Uppuria], I came to the land Datumbu. I received horses as tribute from Ušrâ of the city Ka(n)zabkanu.

60) *a-na* KUR.*da-tu-um-bu aq-ṭé-rib ma-da-at-tu šá* ^{m}*uš-ra-a ša* URU.*ka-za-ba-ka-ni* ANŠE.KUR.MEŠ *am-ḫur* TA KUR*.*da-tu-um-bu at-tu-*⸢*muš a-na* URU.*kar*⸣-*zi-nu* ⸢*aq-ṭé-rib ma-da-at-tu ša*$^{?!}$⸣ [...]

ii 60b–61a) Moving [on] from the land Datumbu, I came to the city Karzinû. I received [(...)] horses as tribute from [...]. Moving on from the city Karzinû, I came to the land Birnakan. [I received ... *as tribute*] from Satarpānu of the city Barikānu, from Uppa[...] of the city ..., from ... [...].

61) ANŠE.KUR.MEŠ *am-ḫur** TA URU.*kar-zi-nu* *at-tu-muš a-na* KUR.*bir-na*$^{?}$-*ka-an aq-ṭé-rib ša* ^{m}*sa-tar-ba-nu šá* URU.*ba**-*ri-ka-nu šá* ^{m}*up-pa-*[*x-x*] ⸢*šá* URU⸣.*x* ⸢KI$^{?}$⸣ *x* ⸢TI$^{?}$⸣ *x x* ⸢LA⸣ *x* ⸢*šá*⸣ *x x* (*x*•) [... *am-ḫur* TA KUR.*bir-na*$^{?}$-*ka-an*]

ii 61b–62a) Moving on [from the land Birnakan], I came to the land Sakâ. [I received] (...) *horses* ... as tribute from Zardukka of the city Ḫarzianu, from Ištesukk[a of the ci]ty Kayatani, (*and*) from *Kir...-ni of the city* ... [(...)].

62) ⸢*at*⸣-*tu-muš a-na* KUR.*sa-ka-a aq-ṭé-rib* *ma-da-at-tu šá* ^{m}⸢*za*⸣-*ar-du-ka-a šá* URU.*ḫa-ar-zi-a-ni* ⸢*šá*⸣ ^{m}*iš-te-su-uk-*⸢*ka*$^{?}$⸣ [(*šá*)] ⸢URU$^{?}$⸣.*ka-*⸢*ia-ta*⸣-*ni* ⸢*šá* ^{m}*ki-ir*$^{?}$⸣-*x*-[(*x*)]-*ni x x*• *x x* *x* ⸢ANŠE$^{?}$⸣.KUR.MEŠ *x x x x x x x x* [... *am-ḫur* (...) TA KUR.*sa-ka-a*]

ii 62b–63) Moving on [from the land Sakâ], I crossed the Darūe River (and) came to the land Rāmanda. Šitaqupa, the city ruler of the city [...] ... *from* the cities ... [...]

63) *at-tu-muš* ÍD.*da-ru-e* ÍD-*tu e-te-bir a-na* KUR.*ra-ma-an-da aq-ṭé-rib* ^{m}*ši-ta-qu-pa* LÚ.EN.URU *šá* ⸢URU⸣.[*x x* (*x*)] *x x x x x x x x x x* *x x x*• *x x x* TA$^{?}$ URU.MEŠ *x x x x x x x x* [...]

64) TA KUR.*ra-ma-an-da at-tu-muš a-na* KUR.*ir-ni-sa aq-ṭé-rib ma-da-at-tu šá* ^{m}*ši-dir-áš-šu-ra-a šá* KUR.*ir-ni-sa šá* ^{m}*ba-*⸢*at*$^{?}$⸣-[(*x*)]-⸢*ti*$^{?}$-*gur*$^{?}$ *šá* URU.ḪU$^{?}$⸣-*x x x x x*• *x* *x x x x x x x a-*⸢*na*$^{?}$ KUR$^{?}$⸣.*x x x* ⸢DU$^{?}$⸣ *x x x* [...]

ii 64–68a) Moving on from the land Rāmanda, I came to the land Irnisa. I received [...] as tribute from Šidiraššurâ of the land Irnisa (*and*) from *Battigur* of the city *Ḫu... to/for the land* ... [...]. Uardatti of the city Ṣibar who had neither stretched out his hand to (any of) the previous kings (of Assyria) (*nor*) *inquired about* their health ... [...] district of the land Ayalaya ... *of* the (military) camp which *covered the sky* for a distance of one league, the river Na... large horses *trained to the yoke* ... [... *At the command of the god* ...], who makes (me) triumph, and of the god *Nergal, my protection*, the tireless one, fit for battle, [*he* (Uardatti) *came to me*], to the land Irnisa, in order to save his land (and) allow (his) *people* to live in peace ... [...] he grasped hold of my f[eet] and submitted (himself) to the yoke of (the god) Aššur, my lord.

65) ⸢*am-ḫur*⸣ ^{m}*ú-ar-da-at-*⸢*ti*⸣ [(*x*)] ⸢URU.*ṣi*⸣-*bar-a-*⸢*a*⸣ *šá a-na* MAN.MEŠ-*ni maḫ-ru-ti* ŠU-*su la it-ru-ṣu* *nap-šá-*⸢*ti-šu*⸣-*un la i-*⸢ŠU$^{?}$⸣ *x x x*• *x x x x x x x x* *x x x* NA$^{?}$ *x x x x x x* [...]

66) ⸢*na*⸣-*ge-e šá* KUR.*a-a-la-*⸢*ia*⸣ ŠU UD/PI ⸢GI$^{?}$/MÁŠ$^{?}$ E$^{?}$⸣ BA AḪ KARAŠ ⸢*šá a*⸣-*na* 1 KASKAL.GÍD.ÀM *pa-an* AN-*e ṣab-tu* ÍD.*na-x-ku/*⸢*lu* IM$^{?}$⸣ *x x* (*x*) *x* ⸢MU$^{?}$⸣ *x* MU UR$^{?}$ *x* ANŠE.KUR.MEŠ GAL.MEŠ *ṣi*$^{?!}$-⸢*in*$^{?}$-*da*$^{?}$-*at*$^{?}$⸣ *ni-*⸢*i*$^{?}$-*ri*$^{?}$⸣ *x x x* ⸢*šá*$^{?}$⸣ *x* [...]

67) [(*x*)] ⸢*mu*⸣-*šak-ši-du er-nit-ti* ⸢*ù*$^{?}$⸣ *ša* ^{d}U.GUR$^{?}$ *ki*$^{?}$-*din-ia la-ni-ḫi si-mat ta-ḫa-zi* KUR-*su* [(*x*)] *a-na šu-zu-*⸢*ub*$^{?}$⸣ (*x*) *x* MEŠ (*x*) *né-ḫi-iš* ⸢*ana*$^{?}$⸣

---

ii 59 Razidatu is the same person as Razištu in ii 58; see Baker and Schmitt, PNA 3/1 pp. 1036–1037. *bu**-: The squeeze has KUR-AŠ-. A writing *in-na-a-bit* for *innabit* would be unique and thus questionable.
ii 60 KUR*: The squeeze has ŠE.
ii 61 *-ḫur**: The squeeze has -ḪI-MA. *ba**-: The squeeze has ZU-. For the reading Barikānu, rather than Zurikanu, see text no. 82 vi 34′′ and text no. 65 line 49.
ii 62 Text no. 82 vi 29′′ mentions ^{m}*za-ar-duk-*⸢*ka*⸣ *ša* KUR.⸢*ḫa*⸣-*ar-zi-a-nu* and vi 30′′–31′′ mention ^{m}*iš-te-*⸢*su*$^{?}$⸣-*ku* ^{m}*a-ú-a-ri-is-*⸢*ar-nu*⸣ LÚ.EN.URU.MEŠ *ša* URU.⸢*ka*⸣-*i-ta-nu*. For the end of the line, one might think of ⸢ANŠE$^{?}$⸣.KUR.MEŠ ⸢*ma*$^{?}$-*da*$^{?}$-*ta*$^{?}$-*šú*$^{?}$-*nu*$^{?}$ *am*$^{?}$-*ḫur*$^{?}$⸣ *x x* [...].
ii 63 For a connection of Rāmanda with modern Rāmend, see Zadok, NABU 2000 p. 9 no. 5. With regard to Šitaqupa, cf. ^{m}*šá-ta-qu-pi šá* URU.⸢*ú*$^{?}$⸣-*pa-ri-a* in Tadmor and Yamada, RINAP 1 p. 86 Tiglath-pileser III no. 35 ii 35′.
ii 67 One might expect something like *a-di maḫ-ri-ia* after KUR *ir-ni-*⸢*sa*⸣, but the traces do not seem to favor this.

šu-šu-bi? ⌜*a*⌝-*na* KUR.*ir-ni*-⌜*sa*⌝ *x x*˙ (*x*) *x x* ⌜IA?⌝ *x* [...]

68) ⌜GÌR?⌝.[II]-⌜*ia*⌝ *iṣ-bạt-ma a-na aš-šur* EN-*ia* *ik-nu-šá a-na*? *ni-i-ri* ⌜TA⌝ URU.*ir-ni-sa* *at-tu-muš a-na*? KUR.*ú-ra-ta-as aq*-⌜*ṭé-rib* *ma-da-tu šá*⌝ ^{m}*a-za-ma-da* ⌜*šá*⌝ URU.⌜*ú*⌝-*x-x*-(*x*)-*a*˙-⌜*ta*? *šá*?⌝ ^{m}TAK?-*x-x* [...]

69) ⌜*ša*? URU?.*ḫa*?⌝-*gab-ta-a šá* ^{m}*bur-bu-a-su*? *šá* KUR.*ú-rat-is*-⌜*ta*?⌝ ^{m}*šum-mu-uš-ra-a šá* (*x*) URU.*qar-ka-si-a* [(*šá*)] ⌜^{m}*bur*?-*bu-a*⌝-*zu šá* URU.*gi-in-ki-ir šá* ⌜^{m}⌝*bu*?-*x-x-bar*?-⌜*ta*?⌝-*nu šá* KUR˙.*ru-ur*?-*x x* [... ANŠE?.KUR?.MEŠ?]

ii 68b–70a) Moving on from the city Irnisa, I came to the land Uratas. I received [(...) *horses*] trained to the yoke as tribute from Azamada of the city U..., *from TAK*... [..., from ...] of the city Ḫagabtâ (Ecbatana), from Burbuasu of the land Uratis*ta*, (from) Šummušrâ of the city Qarkasia, [(from)] *Burbuazu* of the city Ginkir, (*and*) from *Bu...bartanu* of the land Rur[... (...)].

70) ⌜*ṣi*⌝-<*in*>-⌜*da*⌝-*at ni-ri am-ḫur ina* *u*$_4$-*me-šú-ma* NA$_4$.NA.RÚ.A DÙ-*ma ṣa-lam* DINGIR.MEŠ GAL.MEŠ EN.MEŠ-*ia mu**-⌜*šak-ši*?-*du er-nit*⌝-*ti-ia* *šá x* NI MA LI KI ŠU UM *šá x x x* ⌜NU⌝ (*x*) ⌜NI⌝ *x x*˙ [... *e-si-qa*? (...)]

71) *ep-še-et* NÍG.È AN.ŠÁR *ki-šit-ti* ŠU.II-*ia šá* UGU *kib-rat* LÍMMU-*i* ⌜*áš*⌝-*ku-nu* (*x*) *mim-mu-u ina* URU.*ki-x-x* ⌜*e-pu-uš*?⌝ UGU-*šú* ⌜*áš-ṭur ina*⌝ URU.*ki*-⌜*sa*?-*si*⌝ *ša* ŠU.II ⌜*ik-šu-da*⌝ *a-na mu-x*˙ [... *ul*?-*ziz*? (...)]

ii 70b–72a) At that time, I had a stele made and [*I engraved upon it*] image(s) of the great gods, my lords, who make me triumph ... [...]. I inscribed upon it [(...)] the victorious deeds of (the god) Aššur, my conquests that I made over the four quarters (of the world), (*and*) everything *that I had done* in the city *Kišesim*. [*I erected* (*it*)] for all time in the city *Kišesim* that I had personally con[quered], for ... [...].

72) *aḫ-ra-taš* NUN EGIR-⌜*ú*⌝ *šá* AN.ŠÁR MAN *kiš-šat* ^{d}*í-gì-gì* ⌜*i-na-bu*?⌝-*ma a*-⌜*na*⌝ *be*-⌜*lu*⌝-*ti* KUR (*x*) *aš-šur*.KI *i-zak*-⌜*ka-ru* MU⌝-*šú* NA$_4$.NA.RÚ.A *šu-a-tú* ⌜*lil-ta*⌝-(*x*)-*si*-(*x*)-⌜*ma* Ì.GIŠ? *lip**-*šu*˙⌝-[*uš* (...)]

ii 72b–73a) May a future prince — (one) whom (the god) Aššur, king of all the Igīgū gods, will summon and nominate for the lordship of Assyria — read this stele and ano[int (it)] with o[il. (...)] May he offer a sacrifice. May he praise the good deeds of (the god) Aššur and have future generations learn to revere him (Aššur).

73) UDU.SISKUR *liq-qí ep-še-et* AN.ŠÁR SIG$_5$.MEŠ *lit-ta-id-ma pul-ḫat-su* (*x*) *li*-⌜*šal*⌝-*mì-da* *ár-ku*-⌜*u*?⌝-*ti šá* NA$_4$.NA.RÚ.A ⌜UR$_5$-*tú*⌝ *x x* ⌜LI?⌝ MUT TU ⌜IA⌝ UB? ⌜RU?⌝ *šu-bat*-⌜*su*˙ *ú-nak*?-*kar*?-*ú*⌝ *x x x x x* MA *x* [(...)]

74) *pa-az-re-eš i-nak-ki-mu-ni ù* ÍD.⌜MEŠ⌝ *i-šal-lu-ma* ⌜*i*⌝-[*tam*?-*me*?-*ru*?] *ep-re-eš ina*? ^{d}GIBIL$_6$? *i-qam-mu-u-ma x* GÚ? BU UL (*x*) *x* *i-šak-ka-nu-ma ú**-*saḫ-ḫu-ú**-*ma x*˙ *x x x* MU? *x x x* [...]

75) DINGIR.MEŠ GAL.MEŠ *a*-⌜*ši*⌝-*bu-ti* AN-*e* KI-*ti* *ag-gi-iš li*-⌜*ru-ru-šú* MU⌝-*šú* NUMUN-*šú ina* KUR [(*x*)] *li-ḫal-li*-⌜*qu*˙⌝

ii 73b–75) (As for) the one who ... *this* stele, ... *changes* its resting place ... [...], secretly stores (it) away, or throws (it) *into* a river (lit.: "rivers"), or [*buries*] (it) in the ground, (or) destroys (it) by fire, or places (it) ..., or mutilates (it), or ... [...], may the great gods who dwell in heaven (and) netherworld curse him angrily. May they make his name (and) his descendant(s) disappear from the land.

---

ii 69 Ḫagabtâ can be identified with Ecbatana, modern Hamadan (A. Fuchs). For the city of Qarkasia, see also text no. 82 vi 36′′. It is not clear if Burburazu, the Median ruler of Bīt-Ištar appearing in Sargon's eighth campaign in 714 (text no. 65 line 46), should be identified with either Burbuasu of Uratista or Burbuazu of Ginkir; see Schmitt, Iranische Personnamen pp. 71–72.

ii 70 *mu**-: The squeeze has AŠ-KUR-. Or restore *e-ṣi-ir* instead of *e-si-qa*; see text no. 103 iv 45 and the on-page note to that line.

ii 71 Sargon is known to have erected a monument depicting himself at Kišesim during this campaign (see text no. 1 lines 93–95, text no. 2 lines 86–87a, text no. 7 lines 59–60, and text no. 82 iii 1′–21′). The writing URU.*ki-sa-si* for Kišesim is also found in Luukko, SAA 19 no. 91 line 12. Too little is preserved of the two signs following the first URU.*ki*- in the line to propose any reading for that city, but we might assume that the same place was indicated.

ii 72–73 With regard to the reading of these lines, see text no. 103 iv 58–62, text no. 105 ii′ 13–16, and text no. 106 iii 10′–13′. *lip**-: The copy has ŠU-PA-. Possibly ⌜*le*⌝-*mut-tu*, "evil," in line 73.

ii 74 Cf. Grayson, RIMA 2 p. 30 A.0.87.1 viii 68. *ú**-: See the copy in the minor variants section. -*ḫu-ú**-: The stele appears to have -U$_5$- (see the copy in the minor variants section), but this is surely an error for -*ḫu-ú*-.

118

A small, barrel-shaped bead found at Persepolis has a short dedicatory inscription of Sargon to the goddess Aya. The objects with this inscription and with text nos. 119–122 were probably taken to Persepolis as booty, either directly or indirectly from Assyria following its destruction by the Babylonians and Medes towards the end of the seventh century.

CATALOGUE

Museum Number	Excavation Number	Photograph Number	Provenance	Dimensions (cm)	cpn
—	PT4 548a	Persepolis field negative Ps-320	Persepolis, Room 33 of the Treasury (SE corner, in refuse 1–1.5 [m] above floor)	2.6×1.3	p

COMMENTARY

This small bead was found in 1936 by the Oriental Institute excavations at Persepolis and was allotted to the Iranian Antiquity Service. It is made of onyx that is bluish white and brown in color; the piece is pierced lengthwise. (For information on the other items found in Room 33, see Schmidt, Persepolis 1 pp. 174–175.) The edition is based upon the published photograph and an unpublished copy of the inscription made by D.E. McCown (kindly supplied by J. Larson of the Oriental Institute).

The inscription should not be attributed to Sargon I of Assyria, who reigned in the Old Assyrian period, since that earlier ruler is only attested in contemporary texts with the title "vice-regent of the god Aššur" (ÉNSI ᵈ*a-šùr*), not "king of Assyria"; see Grayson, RIMA 1 pp. 45–46 A.0.35.1 and A.0.35.2001. Moreover, the other votive objects found in the Treasury at Persepolis with this bead all come from the middle of the first millennium BC, in particular, from the reigns of Esarhaddon, Ashurbanipal, and Nebuchadnezzar II; see Schmidt, Persepolis p. 56.

BIBLIOGRAPHY

1957 Schmidt, Persepolis 2 pp. 56–57 and 145, and pl. 25 no. 1 (photo of impression, edition [by Cameron], study)

1989 Galter, NABU 1989 p. 41 no. 63 sub no. 84 (study)

TEXT

1) *ana* ᵈ*a-a*
2) GAŠAN-*šú* ᵐMAN-GIN
3) MAN KUR AŠ
4) *ana* TI-*šú* BA*

1–4) To the goddess Aya, his lady: Sargon (II), king of Assyria, presented (this object) for the sake of his life.

4 BA*: The published edition has BA[!]-*eš*[?]. The sign/signs are not legible on the published photograph, but the unpublished copy by D.E. McCown has simply BA, with what appear to be two vertical wedges at the end of the sign, rather than one. The copy also indicates that the ŠÚ of line 2 has two vertical wedges. Could the engraver's tool have slipped in both places?

119

A fragment of an eye-stone found at Persepolis has a short dedicatory inscription to the god Šamaš that is probably to be assigned to Sargon.

CATALOGUE

Museum Number	Excavation Number	Photograph Number	Provenance	Dimensions (cm)	cpn
—	PT6 233	Persepolis field negative Ps-324	Persepolis, Room 53 of the Treasury (East end, refuse)	2×2.1×0.8	n

COMMENTARY

This fragment of an oval-shaped eye-stone was found in 1938 by the Oriental Institute excavations at Persepolis and was allotted to the Iranian Antiquity Service. (For information on other items found in Room 53, see Schmidt, Persepolis 1 p. 181.) The piece is made of bluish-green turquoise and has a highly polished convex top, a beveled side, and a groove in the base. The inscription is written on the beveled side and the bottom, and is edited from the published copy. The text is said to be "rather carelessly written." Text no. 120 may be a duplicate of this inscription. (Information on the dimensions of this piece was kindly supplied by J. Larson.)

BIBLIOGRAPHY

1957 Schmidt, Persepolis 2 pp. 56–58 and 154, and pl. 25 no. 5 (copy, edition [by Cameron])

1989 Galter, NABU 1989 p. 41 no. 63 sub no. 86 (study [erroneously referred to as PT4 233])

TEXT

1) [*ana* ᵈ]UTU EN-*šú*
2) [ᵐ]⸢LUGAL⸣-GIN?
3) ⸢LUGAL⸣ ŠÁR BA

1–3) [To the god] Šamaš, his lord: [*Sa*]*rgon* (II), [kin]g of the world, presented (this object).

120

A fragment of an eye-stone found at Persepolis has a short dedicatory inscription to the god Šamaš that is probably to be assigned to Sargon.

119 line 2 The transliteration by G. Cameron (Schmidt, Persepolis 2 p. 58) indicates that the GIN is clear, but the published copy indicates that the sign has more wedges than are found with a normal GIN sign.

CATALOGUE

Museum Number	Excavation Number	Photograph Number	Provenance	Dimensions (cm)	cpn
—	PT4 495	—	Persepolis, Room 33 of the Treasury (NE corner, floor)	3.2×1.8×1	n

COMMENTARY

This eye-stone fragment was found by the Oriental Institute excavations at Persepolis and was allotted to the Iranian Antiquity Service. It is made of onyx, has a polished top with a gray center and a white margin, and is pierced laterally. The inscription is edited from an unpublished copy made by D.E. McCown that was kindly made available to the author by J. Larson of the Oriental Institute. The restorations in lines 3–4 assume that the inscription is identical with text no. 119, but the two texts have been arbitrarily kept separate here.

BIBLIOGRAPHY

1957 Schmidt, Persepolis 2 pp. 56–58 and 145 (edition [by McCown])

1989 Galter, NABU 1989 p. 41 no. 63 sub no. 85 (study)

TEXT

1) *ana* ᵈUTU EN-*šú*
2) [ᵐ]⌜LUGAL-GIN⌝
3) [LUGAL ŠÁR]
4) [BA]

1–4) To the god Šamaš, his lord: Sa[rg]on (II), [king of the world, presented (this object)].

121

A fragment of an eye-stone found at Persepolis has a short dedicatory inscription of Sargon.

CATALOGUE

Museum Number	Excavation Number	Photograph Number	Provenance	Dimensions (cm)	cpn
—	PT4 1170	—	Persepolis, the area of Room 33 of the Treasure (refuse)	Dia.: 3	n

COMMENTARY

This eye-stone fragment was found in 1936 by the Oriental Institute excavations at Persepolis and was allotted to the Iranian Antiquity Service. It is made of chalcedony; the top has a gray center (chipped off) and a white margin. The piece is inscribed on the bottom. The edition presented below is based upon an unpublished copy of the inscription made by D.E. McCown (kindly supplied by J. Larson) and G. Cameron's understanding of the text. The unpublished copy would suggest that there is room to restore little if anything at the beginning of the line and one wonders if instead of restoring *šá* at the beginning of the line (and assuming that the inscription is basically a duplicate of text no. 122), we should assume that a whole line is missing and restore a dedication to a deity, i.e., "[To DN, (his lord/lady)], Sargon dedicated (this object)."

BIBLIOGRAPHY

1957 Schmidt, Persepolis 2 pp. 56–58 and 149 (edition [by Cameron])

1989 Galter, NABU 1989 p. 41 no. 63 sub no. 87 (study)

TEXT

1) [(m)]MAN-GIN BA-*iš*

1) Sargon (II) presented (this object).

122

Two eye-stone fragments found at Persepolis have what may be short dedicatory inscriptions of Sargon duplicating text no. 121.

CATALOGUE

Ex.	Museum Number	Excavation Number	Provenance	Object	Dimensions (cm)	Lines Preserved	cpn
1	—	PT4 1169	Persepolis, the area of Room 33 of the Treasury	fragment of a pink and white calcite eyestone	Height: 0.7; dia: 2.8	1	n
2	—	PT4 1172	As ex. 1	fragment of a grey and white onyx eyestone	Height: 0.6; dia.: 2.5	1	n

121 line 1 G.G. Cameron (in Schmidt, Persepolis 2 p. 58) restored *ša* at the beginning of the line and translated the text as "[which] Sargon presented"; however, we would then expect the verb to be in the subjunctive (i.e., *iqīšu* rather than *iqīš*).

COMMENTARY

The two eye-stone fragments were found by the Oriental Institute excavations at Persepolis in 1936 and were allotted to the Iranian Antiquity Service. The objects are each inscribed on the bottom. Both exemplars were transliterated from unpublished copies made by D.E. McCown that were kindly supplied to the author by J. Larson (Oriental Institute). The edition is based on ex. 2; ex. 1 has only *šá* LUGAL-[...]. Following G. Cameron, the edition assumes that the inscription is basically a duplicate of text no. 121, but they have been arbitrarily kept separate here.

BIBLIOGRAPHY

1957 Schmidt, Persepolis 2 pp. 58 n. 87 and 149 (exs. 1–2, study)

1989 Galter, NABU 1989 p. 41 no. 63 sub nos. 88–89 (exs. 1–2, study)

TEXT

1) *šá* LUGAL-⸢GIN?⸣ [BA-*šu*?]

1) That which *Sarg[on* (*II*) *presented*].

123

Text nos. 123 and 124 are brick inscriptions that deal with the restoration of Babylon's city walls for the god Marduk during the time of Sargon II. The first, written in Akkadian, is found on at least twenty exemplars from Babylon and Kish. In addition to recording work on Imgur-Enlil ("The God Enlil Showed Favor") and Nēmet-Enlil ("Bulwark of the God Enlil") — the inner and outer city walls respectively — the inscription mentions work on the quay-wall of Babylon. Sargon is given the traditional titles "governor (GÌR.NÍTA) of Babylon" and/or "king of the land of Sumer and Akkad" in this and several other Babylonian inscriptions (text nos. 124–127).

CATALOGUE

Ex.	Museum Number	Excavation/ Registration No.	Photograph Number	Provenance	Dimensions (cm)	Lines Preserved	cpn
1	EŞ —	—	—	Kish, trench to SE corner of ziggurrat	9×34.2×12	1–25	c
2	Ash 1924.640	—	—	Kish	11.5×4.9×5	7–14	c
3	Ash 1932.652	—	—	As ex. 2	6.5×8.2×8.5	14, 17, 19–20, 22–23, 25	c
4	Ash 1932.977	—	—	As ex. 2	10×9.5×7.5	1–5, 7–8,10	c
5	BM 90599 + BM 90629	81-7-1,3406	—	—	18.5×9×7	19–25	n
6	—	—	—	As ex. 2	35×9.5	1–25	p
7	—	BE 30680	Bab ph 869	Babylon, NW corner of southern palace, Sargon's wall	30	1–25	n
8	—	BE 30681	Bab ph 868	As ex. 7	30	1–25	n
9	—	BE 30682	—	As ex. 7	30	1–25?	n

10	—	BE 30683	Bab ph 867	As ex. 7	—	1–25	p
11	—	BE 30684	Bab ph 868	As ex. 7	30	1–25	n
12	—	BE 30698	Bab ph 868	As ex. 7	—	1–25	n
13	—	BE 30700	—	As ex. 7	30	1–25?	n
14	—	BE 30706	Bab ph 868	As ex. 7	—	1–25	n
15	—	BE 30707	Bab ph 869	As ex. 7	—	1–25	n
16	YBC 13510	BE 30708	Bab ph 867	As ex. 7	30.5×7.5×2.8–3.9	1–25	c
17	—	BE 30709	Bab ph 869	As ex. 7	30	1–25	p
18	—	BE 30710	Bab ph 868	As ex. 7	30	1–25	n
19	—	BE 31080	—	As ex. 7	—	19–25	n
20	—	BE 32062	—	As ex. 7	—	1–25?	n

COMMENTARY

According to M. Gibson (Iraq 34 [1972] p. 120), the bricks found at Kish with this inscription may have been brought there from Babylon for reuse in the Neo-Babylonian temple. In every case where information is available, the inscription appears in contemporary Babylonian script. The text is inscribed (not stamped) on the edge of each brick, with the number and arrangement of lines varying greatly among the exemplars. While some bricks have the inscription written down the edge (exs. 1–2, 7, 13, 15–17, and 19) in 24–28 lines, others have it written across the edge, in either one (exs. 8–12, 14, 18, and 20) or more columns (exs. 3–6) of 5–7 lines each. The line arrangement and the master line are based on ex. 1, with help from ex. 10 in lines 9–12.

H. de Genouillac's excavations at Ḳish in 1912 discovered exs. 1 and 6. Since ex. 6 was both catalogued among pieces in Paris (Kich 2 p. 29 P.208) and given a reference number indicating that it was in Istanbul (Kich 2 pl. 1 O.5), it is not known whether this exemplar was sent to Paris or to Istanbul. The Oxford-Field Museum, Chicago, expedition to Kish 1923–1933 discovered exs. 2–4, and ex. 5 was found during H. Rassam's excavations in Babylonia (probably at Babylon, according to Walker, CBI p. 65).

Excavations conducted by the Deutsche Orient-Gesellschaft discovered exs. 7–20 at Babylon. The inscriptions on several are known only from excavation photographs and no details are available on several exemplars. Two Babylon photos (nos. 868 and 869) show five and four exemplars respectively. Excavation records give the excavation numbers of four pieces for each photo, but do not indicate which bricks shown have which excavation numbers. The variants from all but two of these nine bricks are cited by the photo number followed by A, B, C, etc. (e.g., 689D), with A indicating the brick on the photo which is separated from the others by the ruler. It is possible to be reasonably certain about the identification of two bricks on photo 689 — nos. B and C, exs. 17 and 7 respectively — and they are cited by exemplar number. Not all the bricks are in good condition and many of the inscriptions are difficult to read, particularly from photographs. Thus, readings must often be considered tentative. The minor variants are listed at the back of the book, but no score for this brick inscription is given on Oracc.

BIBLIOGRAPHY

1913 de Genouillac, RA 10 pp. 83–87 (ex. 1, copy, edition [translation by Thureau-Dangin]; variants from ex. 6)

1924 de Genouillac, Kich 1 pp. 18 and 45, and pl. 2 no. O.4 (ex. 1, copy, study, provenance)

1924–25 Unger, AfK 2 p. 21 no. 2 (ex. 10, study)

1925 de Genouillac, Kich 2 p. 29 no. P.208, pl. XXII no. 2, and pl. 1 no. O.5 (ex. 6, photo, copy, study)

1925 Koldewey, WEB[4] pp. 135–136 and fig. 86 (ex. 10, photo, translation [by Delitzsch])

1930 Unger in Wetzel, Stadtmauern p. 79 (exs. 7–20, study)

1930 Wetzel, Stadtmauern pp. 64–65 and pl. 12 (exs. 7–20, provenance)

1981 Walker, CBI pp. 64–65 no. 76 Sargon II O (exs. 2–5, transliteration)

1987 Beckman, ARRIM 5 pp. 2–3 no. 3 (ex. 16, copy, edition)

1988 Beckman, ARRIM 6 p. 2 (ex. 16, study)

1992 George, Topographical Texts pp. 344–345 (lines 10–20, edition)

1995 Frame, RIMB 2 pp. 143–145 no. B.6.22.1 (exs. 1–20, edition)

TEXT

1) *ana* ^{d}AMAR.UTU EN GAL-*i*
2) DINGIR *reme-ni-i*
3) *a-šib é-sag-gíl* EN TIN.TIR.KI UMUN-*šú*
4) LUGAL-GIN LUGAL *dan-nu*
5) LUGAL KUR *aš-šur*.KI LUGAL ŠÚ
6) GÌR.NÍTA TIN.TIR.KI
7) LUGAL KUR *šu-me-ru u* URI.KI
8) *za-nin é-sag-íl*
9) *ù é-zi-da*
10) *ana* DÙ-*eš* BÀD *im-gur*-^{d}EN.LÍL
11) GEŠTU-*šú* GÁL-*ma ú-šal-bi-in-ma*
12) *a-gur-ru ki-ru* KÙ-*tim*
13) *ina kup-ru ù* ESIR
14) *ina* GÚ ÍD.*pu-rat-ti*
15) *ina qé-reb an-za-nun-ze-e*
16) KAR *ib-ni-ma*
17) BÀD *im-gur*-^{d}50
18) *ù* BÀD *né-met*-^{d}50
19) *ki-ma ši-pik* KUR-*i*
20) *ú-šar-šid ṣe-ru-uš-šú*
21) *šip-ri šá-a-šú* ^{d}AMAR.UTU EN GAL-*ú*
22) *lip-pa-lis-ma a-na* LUGAL-GIN
23) NUN *za-nin-šú liš-ruk* TIN
24) *ki-ma te-me-en* TIN.TIR.KI
25) *li-ku-nu* BALA.MEŠ-*šú*

1–3) For the god Marduk, great lord, compassionate god who dwells in Esagila, lord of Babylon, his lord:

4–11a) Sargon (II), strong king, king of Assyria, king of the world, governor of Babylon, king of the land of Sumer and Akkad, the one who provides for Esagila and Ezida, thought of (re)building the (city) wall Imgur-Enlil.

11b–20) He then had bricks made and constructed a quay-wall of baked bricks from a (ritually) pure kiln, (laid) in (both) refined and crude bitumen, along the bank of the Euphrates River, (15) in deep water. He then made the (city) wall Imgur-Enlil and the (city) wall Nēmet-Enlil as secure upon it as the base of a mountain.

21–25) May the god Marduk, great lord, look upon this work of mine (with pleasure) and may he grant (a long) life to Sargon, the prince who provides for him. May his reign be as firm as the foundation of Babylon.

124

A Sumerian inscription written on four bricks found at Babylon also describes the restoration of Babylon's inner and outer city walls — Imgur-Enlil and Nēmet-Enlil, respectively — for Marduk, the patron deity of the city, by Sargon II.

123 line 14 Exs. 10, 16, and 868D insert *i-te-e* KÁ.GAL ^{d}15 after *ina*, "beside the gate of the goddess Ištar, on the bank of the Euphrates River" for "along the bank of the Euphrates River." Exs. 7, 17, 868E, 869A, and 869D are all damaged but likely have the same insertion; they have ⸢*i-te-e* KÁ.GAL⸣ [...], [*x x*]-*e* KÁ.GAL ^{d}15, ⸢*i*?⸣-*te*-⸢*e*⸣ [...], *i*-⸢*te*⸣-[*e*] KÁ.GAL ^{d}⸢15⸣, and ⸢*i*?⸣-*te-e* ⸢KÁ⸣.GAL *x x* respectively.

CATALOGUE

Ex.	Museum Number	Excavation Number	Photograph Number	Provenance	Dimensions (cm)	Lines Preserved	cpn
1	—	BE 38583	Bab ph 2007, 2305	Babylon, Merkes g_1 26 +5.00 m	—	10–18	p
2	—	BE 41861	Bab ph 2194, 2305, 2330	Babylon, in debris in the bridge gate; Sachn y 40 +2.80 m	—	2–7	p
3	—	BE 42335 + BE 42417	Bab ph 2305, 2320, 3458	Babylon, Sachn aa 40, ca. -1.50 m	—	1–14	p
4	EŞ —	BE 58377	Bab ph 3458	Babylon, southeast corner of inner city wall in debris at edge of mud-brick outer wall	—	1–14, 16–18	p

COMMENTARY

The excavations of the Deutsche Orient-Gesellschaft at Babylon discovered all of the exemplars. The inscription, written in Babylonian script, is inscribed (not stamped) down the edge of each brick. The edition of lines 1–2 and 8 is a conflation of exs. 3 and 4; lines 3–7 and 9–10 follow ex. 3; and lines 11–18 follow ex. 1. Ex. 4 may omit line 15 or have had it on the same line as 14 (the end of which is not preserved). No other variants are attested and no score for this brick inscription is presented on Oracc.

BIBLIOGRAPHY

1930 Unger in Wetzel, Stadtmauern p. 79 (exs. 1–4, study, provenance)
1930 Wetzel, Stadtmauern pp. 61 and 65, and pls. 37–38 and 51 (exs. 1–4, provenance)
1995 Frame, RIMB 2 pp. 145–146 no. B.6.22.2 (exs. 1–4, edition)

TEXT

1) x x x (x) [x]
2) ù-mu-un ⸢gal⸣
3) lugal-a-ni-ir
4) LUGAL-GI.NA
5) lugal ma-da
6) *aš-šur*.KI-ke$_4$
7) lugal ki-šár-ra
8) GÌR.NÍTA
9) KÁ.DINGIR.RA.KI
10) lugal ki-in-gi
11) uri.KI-ke$_4$
12) bàd *im-gur-*^{d}EN.LÍL
13) bàd *né-met-*^{d}EN.LÍL
14) nam-tìl-la-a-ni-šè
15) gibil-bi
16) ù-mu-un-na-dím
17) u$_4$-gin$_7$
18) ba-an-zálag

1–18) For *the god Marduk*, the gr[eat] lord, his lord: Sargon (II), king of the land of Assyria, king of the world, governor of Babylon, (10) king of Sumer (and) Akkad, constructed anew the (city) wall Imgur-Enlil (and) the (city) wall Nēmet-Enlil for the sake of his life (and) made (them) shine like daylight.

125

Two Akkadian inscriptions and two Sumerian inscriptions commemorate Sargon's work on the Eanna temple of the goddess Ištar at Uruk (text nos. 125–128). This clay cylinder has an Akkadian inscription that is modeled upon one of Marduk-apla-iddina II (Frame, RIMB 2 pp. 136–138 no. B.6.21.1) and may have been intended to replace it. The cylinder has a colophon stating that it had been copied and collated from another exemplar.

CATALOGUE

Museum Number	Provenance	Dimensions (cm)	cpn
YBC 2181	Possibly Uruk	13.2×6.5	c

COMMENTARY

This barrel cylinder was given to the Yale Babylonian Collection in New Haven by Dr. and Mrs. J.B. Nies, likely in 1912 or 1913 when the collection was being first formed. The inscription is reported to have been discovered at Uruk by local diggers, is composed using contemporary Babylonian script, and is presented in two columns of 40 and 41 lines respectively. Line rulings are found after every two or three lines and there is one before the colophon.

One may note the use of *-mu* and *-mi* for the enclitic particle *-ma* in lines i 19, 20, 22 and 38, and ii 3, 23 and 34; the vowel used is the same as the one immediately preceding the enclitic particle. See also Röllig, ZA 56 (1964) p. 231.

BIBLIOGRAPHY

1915 Clay, YOS 1 no. 38 (photo, copy, edition)
1930 Jordan, UVB 1 p. 8 (study)
1933 von Soden, OLZ 36 col. 424 (i 3, study)
1953 Gadd, Iraq 15 pp. 125–132 (study)
1954 Follet, Biblica 35 pp. 413–428 (partial transliteration, study)
1995 Frame, RIMB 2 pp. 146–149 no. B.6.22.3 (edition)
1998 Borger, BiOr 55 p. 846 sub S. 136ff. and S. 146ff. (study)
2009 Frame, Studies Parpola p. 82 no. 1 (study)
2010 Novotny, Studies Ellis p. 463 no. 5.19 (study)
2012 Worthington, Textual Criticism p. 219 (study)

TEXT

Col. i

1) [*a-na*] ⸢^{d}INANNA⸣ *be-let* KUR.KUR *ti-iz-qar-ti* DINGIR.MEŠ
2) [*qa-rit-ti*$^{?}$] *i-la-a-ti*
3) [*x x x* (*x x*)] ⸢*a*⸣-*bu-bu ez-zu šug-lu-tu*
4) [*x x x* (*x x*)] *x za-a'-na-át*
5) [*x x x* (*x x*)] QAR TI *šag-ga-pur-tu*
6) [*x x x* (*x x*)] *pul-ḫa-a-ti*
7) [*x x x* (*x x*)] *x* Ú ŠAT *bu-ru-mu*
8) [*x x x* (*x x*)] ⸢AḪ$^{?}$⸣ ZU-*šu-un* ⸢ŠI$^{?}$ DA$^{?}$ AT$^{?}$⸣

i 1–13) [For] the goddess Ištar, mistress of the lands, (most) eminent of the gods, [(*most*) *valiant*] of the goddesses, [...] fierce, terrifying deluge, [(...) who] is endowed with [...] (i 5) [...] ... majestic, [...] awe, [...] ... the firmament (of the heavens), [...] ... [...] humble, (i 10) [... *who give*]*s* judgment and decision, [...] purification rites, [...] which is inside Uruk, [the great lady], his lady:

---

i 2 The restoration is based upon 5 R pl. 33 i 9–10 (*qa-rit-ti i-la-a-ti*) and cf. Leichty, RINAP 4 p. 271 no. 133 line 1 (*qa-rit-ti* DINGIR.MEŠ).
i 5 Possibly [... *tiz*]-*qar-ti*, "[emi]nent."

9) [*x x x x* (*x*)] *šá aš-rum*
10) [*x x* (*x*) *ga-mi*]-⸢*ra*?⸣-*át šip-ṭu u* EŠ.BAR
11) [*x x x* (*x x*)] *šu-luḫ-ḫu*
12) [*x x x x* (*x*)] *x* KÙ *šá qé-reb* UNUG.KI
13) [GAŠAN GAL]-⸢*tum*⸣ GAŠAN-*i-šu*
14) [LUGAL-GI.NA LUGAL (KUR) *aš*]-⸢*šur*⸣ LUGAL ŠÚ GÌR.NÍTA KÁ.DINGIR.MEŠ.KI
15) [LUGAL (KUR) *šu-me*]-⸢*ru*⸣ *u* URI.KI NUN *za-a-nin-šá*

i 14–15) [Sargon (II), king of Assy]ria, king of the world, governor of Babylon, [king of (the land of) Sume]r and Akkad, prince who provides for her,

16) [*a-na* TI? ZI].⸢ME?⸣-*šú* GÍD.DA u_4*-me-šú la-bar* BALA-*šú*
17) [*x x x*] *x-šú sa-kap* LÚ.KÚR-*i-šu*

i 16–17) [For the sake of ensuring] his [*good health*], prolonging his days, lengthening his reign, [...ing] his [...], (and) overthrowing his enemy,

18) [*é-an*]-⸢*na*⸣ *šá* ^{d}*šul-gi* LUGAL *maḫ-ru*
19) ⸢*ú-še*⸣*-pi-šu-mu il-li-ku la-ba-riš*
20) É *šu-a-tum* <*šá*> É.GAR$_8$.MEŠ-*šú i-qu-pú-mu*
21) *up-ta-aṭ-ṭi-ru rik-su-ú-*$šu_{14}$
22) *sa-mit-su us-sar-ri-ḫu-ú-mu*
23) ⸢*iḫ*⸣-*ḫar**-*mi-mu tem-mé-en-šú*
24) *ina lìb-bi* LUGAL.MEŠ *a-lik maḫ-ru*
25) *la ib-bal-ki-tu* DÙ-*eš šip-ri-šu*

i 18–25) [(With regard to) Ean]na, which Šulgi, a previous king, had had built and which had become old, (i 20) (with regard to) this temple, whose walls had buckled, whose bondings had disintegrated, <who>se parapet had become ruined, whose foundation had collapsed, (and) whose (re)construction had not occurred to (any of) the kings, (his) predecessors —

26) *i-nu-šú* LUGAL-*ú-kin* LUGAL KUR *aš-šur* LUGAL KIŠ
27) GÌR.NÍTA TIN.TIR.KI *ni-bit* ^{d}*asar-ri*
28) EN GAL-*ú* ^{d}AMAR.UTU GEŠTU.II *ṣir-ti iš-ruk-šum-ma*
29) ⸢*ú*⸣-*rap-pi-iš ḫa-si-is-su*

i 26–29) At that time, the great lord, the god Marduk, granted excellent judgment to Sargon (II), king of Assyria, king of the world, governor of Babylon, one who was chosen by the god Asari, and increased his intelligence.

30) [*ana*] ⸢*ud*⸣-*du-šu ma-ḫa-zu u eš-re-e-ti*
31) *kal* DINGIR.MEŠ *na-du-tu šá* KUR URI.KI GEŠTU.II-*šú* GÁL-⸢*ši*⸣-*ma*
32) *áš-rat é-an-na šu-bat* ^{d}INANNA GAŠAN KUR.KUR GAŠAN-*i-šú*
33) *iš-te-ʾe-e-ma*
34) É.GAR$_8$ *é-an-na ki-da-a-nu*
35) *šá ki-sal-li šap-li-i*
36) *sa-mit-su is-suḫ-ma* ZÁLAG-*ir te-mé-en-šú*

i 30–36) He (Sargon) directed his attention [to] renovating the abandoned cult centers and sanctuaries of all the gods of the land Akkad. He was assiduous toward the sanctuaries of Eanna, the abode of the goddess Ištar, mistress of the lands, his lady. (With regard to) the outer wall of Eanna in the lower courtyard, he tore down its parapet and laid bare its foundation.

37) UŠ$_8$.MEŠ-*šú ina te-me-qí ik-ri-bu*
38) *ù la-ba-a-nu ap-pi id-di-i-mi*
39) *tem-mé-en-šú ina i-rat ki-gal-la*
40) *ú-šar-ši-id šá-du-ú-ú-a-iš*

Col. ii

1) *ina ši-pir* ^{d}*kulla* LÚ.ŠITIM.GAL-*la*
2) *ù* UM.ME.A ⸢*mu*⸣-*de-e šip-ri*
3) *ina* SIG$_4$.ḪI.A KÙ-*tim* SAG.ME-*šú ul-li-mi*
4) *ú-šak-li-il ši-pi-ir-šú*
5) UGU *šá pa-an ú-šá-tir-ma*
6) *uš-te-ši-ra ú-ṣu-ra-a-ti*

i 37–ii 6) With entreaties, prayers, and expressions of humility he (Sargon) laid its foundations (anew) and he made its foundation as secure as a mountain on the breast of the netherworld. (ii 1) With the craft of the god Kulla, the master builder, and (with the help of) craftsmen who know (their) trade, he raised its top with (ritually) pure bricks and completed its construction. He made (it) superior to what had been there before and carried out the plans correctly.

7) *ana šat-ti šip-ru šá-a-šú* ^{d}INANNA GAŠAN KUR.KUR

ii 7–15) On account of this, may the goddess Ištar, mistress of the lands, look upon this work happily and

---

i 10 Or [... *na-di*]-⸢*na*⸣-*át* instead of [... *ga-mi*]-⸢*ra*⸣-*át*.
i 13 [GAŠAN GAL]-⸢*tu*⸣: Clay (YOS 1 p. 51) and RIMB 2 restore *be-el-ti* instead of GAŠAN, but the spacing might suggest that the latter reading is preferable.
i 23 *ḫar**: Text has *tam*.
ii 1 Kulla was the god of bricks (see Lambert, RLA 6/3–4 [1981] p. 305) and his "craft" could refer either to the skill of that god or to (new) brickwork. Similar passages appear frequently in inscriptions of Esarhaddon and Ashurbanipal (e.g., Leichty, RINAP 4 p. 262 no. 128 line 16 and Frame, RIMB 2 p. 198 B.6.32.1 line 21).
ii 7 The translation "On account of this" assumes that *ana šat-ti* stands for *ana šâti*.

8) ḪÚL-*iš lip-pa-lis-ma*
9) *a-na* LUGAL-GI.NA LUGAL KUR *aš-šur*.KI
10) LUGAL ŠÁR GÌR.NÍTA KÁ.DINGIR.RA.KI
11) LUGAL *za-a-nin-šá liš-ruk* TI.LA
12) *ma-ḫar* ^{d}AMAR.UTU LUGAL DINGIR.MEŠ
13) MUNUS.SIG$_{5}$-*šú lit-tas-qar*
14) *ina šá-áš-mu ù ta-ḫa-zu*
15) *lil-lik re-ṣu-ú-šu*

may she bestow a (long) life on Sargon, king of Assyria, (ii 10) king of the world, governor of Babylon, the king who provides for her. May she say good thing(s) about him before the god Marduk, king of the gods. May she go (with him) as his helper in strife and battle.

16) GIŠ.TUKUL.MEŠ ⸢*lem*⸣-*nu-ti-šú li-šab-bir-ma*
17) *li-im-ṣa-a ma-la lìb-bu-uš*
18) *gi-mir ma-al-ku la kan-šú*-<<*nu*>>-*ti-šú*
19) *li-šak-ni-šá še-pu-uš-šu*
20) *ina qí-bit* ^{d}INANNA *na-ram-ti* EN DINGIR.MEŠ
21) *li-iṣ-ṣi-ib bu-ʾa-a-ru*
22) TIN UD.MEŠ GÍD.DA.MEŠ *ṭu-ub lìb-bu*
23) *na-mar ka-bat-ti liš-šá-rik-šum-mu*
24) *li-ri-ik pa-lu-ú-šu*$_{14}$
25) SUḪUŠ GIŠ.GU.ZA-*šú ana u*$_{4}$-*mi ṣa-a-ti*
26) *li-šar-šid-ma li-ma-ʾe-er*
27) *kib-ra-a-ti*

ii 16–27) May he shatter the weapons of his enemies and may he achieve whatever he wants. May he make all the rulers who are not submissive to him bow down at his feet. (ii 20) By the command of the goddess Ištar, beloved of the lord of the gods, may he increase (his) good fortune. May long life, happiness, and gladness be bestowed on him and may his reign be long. May he make the foundation of his throne secure for future days and may he govern (all) regions (of the world).

28) *šá* ERIM.MEŠ UBARA *šu-bar-e* DINGIR.MEŠ GAL.MEŠ
29) *ma-al-ku-ut-su-nu li-tep-pu-uš*
30) *šá šu-ba-re-e šu-nu-ú-tu ina* BALA-*šú*
31) *a-a ib-ba-ši e-šit-su-un*
32) *e-gi-it-su-nu li-šat-bil-ma*
33) *li-pa-as-si-is ḫi-ṭi*$_{5}$-*it-su*-⸢*un*⸣
34) *saḫ*$_{4}$-*maš-tum lu-ú ik-kib-šu-nu-mu*
35) *li-šá-li-iṣ kab-ta-at-su-un*
36) *ki-ma* ⸢*tem*?-*mé*⸣-*na* UNUG.KI
37) *ù é-an-na*
38) *li-ku-ú-na iš-da-šu-un*

ii 28–38) May he constantly exercise the rule over the people who are of privileged status (and have) *šubarrû*-privileges (granted) by the great gods. (ii 30) During his reign may those ones with *šubarrû*-privileges not become disordered. May he take away their negligence and erase their sin. Let turmoil be anathema to them (ii 35) (and) may he make their heart(s) rejoice. Like the foundations of Uruk and Eanna, may their foundations be firm.

Colophon

39) GABA.RI MU.SAR-*e*
40) *šu-bul-tì* É.GAL KUR *aš-šur*.KI
41) *šá-ṭir-ma* IGI.KÁR

Colophon

ii 39–41) Copy of the inscription, dispatch *to/of* the palace of Assyria; written and collated.

126

A large number of bricks found at Uruk are stamped with an Akkadian inscription recording that fact that Sargon had reconstructed parts of the Eanna temple. It is worthy of note that the king's name is preceded by the divine determinative in line 1; see also text nos. 127 line 6 and 128 line 4. However, M. Karlsson argues that "the overwhelming absence of divine determinatives" before the names of Assyrian rulers (unless a ruler's name commenced with the name of a deity) indicates that they "did *not* claim divine status in their royal inscriptions" (NABU 2020/1 pp. 33–36 no. 16).

---

125 ii 16 and 19 The goddess Ištar may be the subject of the verbs "shatter" and "make bow down" rather than the king.
125 ii 32 *li-šat-bil-ma* "May he take away": The reading follows AHw p. 190 and cf. Lambert, BWL p. 50 line 60. R. Borger (BiOr 55 [1998] p. 845 sub S. 146ff., following Gadd, Iraq 15 [1953] p. 130 n. 1) read *li-maṭ-ṭi*$_{5}$-*ma*, "May he decrease"; however, in view of *iddīmi* and *ullīmi*, instead of *iddīma* and *ullīma*, in i 38 and ii 3 respectively, we would have expected *imaṭṭīmi*, not *imaṭṭīma* (suggestion courtesy M. Worthington).

CATALOGUE

Ex.	Museum Number	Excavation Number	Provenance	Dimensions (cm)	Lines Preserved	FuB 27	cpn
1	VA 14664m, edge	W 1635a	Uruk, Od XVI 4, debris	7.5×17×17	1–8	31A	n
2	—	W 1831a	Uruk, Oc XVI 3, highest debris	34×18×7	1–8	—	n
3	VA 14664a	W 1831b	As ex. 2	18×25×8	1–8	20	n
4	—	W 2589	Uruk, Qb XIV 2	34×18×7	1–12	—	n
5	VA 14664b	W 2703	Uruk, Oc XVI 2, at the door's pivot box in Room 39 of Sargon's enclosure	18×34.5×8	1–12	21	n
6	—	W 2704	Uruk, Od XVI 4, Room 43	34×18×7	1–12	—	n
7	VA 14664c	W 2705	Uruk, city area	7×20×21.5	5–12	22	n
8	VA 14664d	W 3200a	Uruk, Oc XVI 2, Per. Room 2 in the door's pivot box	18×34.5×8.5	1–12	23	n
9	VA 14664e	W 5753	Uruk, Eanna, SE enclosure wall	17.5×35×8.5	1–12	24	n
10	VA 14664f	W 6420a	As ex. 7	18×35×8	1–12	25	n
11	VA 14664g	W 6420b/c	As ex. 7	18×35×8.5	1–12	26	n
12	VA 14664h	W 13393	Uruk, Oe XVI 4	18×34×8	1–12	27	n
13	VA 14664i	—	Uruk	17×34.5×8.5	1–12	28	n
14	VA 14664k	—	As ex. 13	18×26.5×8.5	1–12	29	n
15	VA 14664l	—	As ex. 13	18×21.5×7.5	1–8	30	n
16	—	—	Uruk, G 22 b1 (from surface survey)	—	—	—	n

COMMENTARY

German excavations at Uruk discovered all the exemplars of this inscription. The provenances given for exs. 1 and 8 come from the excavation's registry of finds rather than from the statements in UVB 1 (see Marzahn, FuB 27 [1989] pp. 60–61 and 64 nn. 17 and 21). Findspots for exs. 1, 5, and 8 are marked on pl. 3 of UVB 1 and these would suggest that ex. 1 was found in Od XVI 3 (as stated in UVB 1) and that ex. 5 was found in Ob XVI 1 rather than Oc XVI 2. The registry refers to three exemplars with the excavation number W 6420 (W6420a–c). Ex. 10 is W 6420a and ex. 11 is either W 6420b or c (the letter is no longer recognizable); one of exs. 13–15 may be the third brick originally given this excavation number. (See Marzahn, FuB 27 [1989] p. 64 n. 19.)

The inscription is stamped on an edge of exs. 1 and 7 and on the face of exs. 2–6 and 8–15. Ex. 1 also has text no. 127 stamped on its face. The text appears in three columns, with each column having four lines. The edition is based upon the published composite copy and J. Marzahn's work in FuB 27. No variants are attested and no score for this brick inscription is presented on Oracc.

BIBLIOGRAPHY

1930 Jordan, UVB 1 pp. 6–7 (provenance)

1930 Schott, UVB 1 p. 56 and pl. 28 no. 20 (exs. 1–8, composite copy, edition, provenance)

1989 Marzahn, FuB 27 pp. 59–61 no. X, nos. 20–31A (transliteration; exs. 1, 3, 5, 7–15, study)

1991 Kessler in Finkbeiner, AUWE 4 p. 183 no. 26 (ex. 16, study)

1995 Frame, RIMB 2 pp. 149–150 no. B.6.22.4 (exs. 1–16, edition)

TEXT

1) ^{d}LUGAL-*ú-kin*
2) LUGAL GAL-*ú*
3) LUGAL *kiš-šat*
4) LUGAL TIN.TIR.KI
5) LUGAL KUR *šu-me-rú u* URI.KI
6) *mu-er-rú* KUR ^{d}*aš-šur*
7) *u gi-mir* MAR.TU-*i*
8) *ker-ḫu ki-da-a-nu*
9) KISAL *é-an-na*
10) KÁ *qá-tan*
11) *u* KÁ *ki-i-nu*
12) *ú-še-pi-iš*

1–12) Sargon (II), great king, king of the world, king of Babylon, (5) king of the land of Sumer and Akkad, commander of Assyria and of all Amurru, had the outer enclosure wall, the courtyard of Eanna, (10) the narrow gate, and the regular gate built.

127

A number of bricks discovered during excavations at Uruk are stamped with a Sumerian inscription that records Sargon's paving of the processional way of the Eanna temple for the goddess Inanna (Ištar).

CATALOGUE

Ex.	Museum Number	Excavation Number	Photograph Number	Provenance	Dimensions (cm)	Lines Preserved	FuB 27	cpn
1	EŞ —	W 2	Warka ph 8	Uruk, Eanna area, surface	34.5×34.5×7.5	1–14	—	p
2	VA 14664m, face	W 1635a	Warka ph 824	Uruk, Od XVI 4, debris	7.5×17×17	1–6	31B	p
3	VA 14663a	W 1635c	Warka ph 823	As ex. 2	34×33.5×8	1–14	32	c
4	VA 14663b	W 1635d	Warka ph 823	As ex. 2	34.5×34×8	1–14	33	c
5	—	W 1635e	Warka ph 824	As ex. 2	33×33×7.5	1–14	—	p
6	VA 14663c	W 4663	Warka ph 821	Uruk, ziggurrat, north	22.5×29.5×8	1–9	34	p
7	VA 14663d	W 11747	—	Uruk, Oe XVI 4, 5 m NW of the door in the SW wall of temple III, from debris under pavement of Cyrus	22.5×20×7.5	1–9	35	n
8	VA 14663e	W 13182	—	Uruk	34.5×24×8	1–14	36	c

COMMENTARY

The Deutsche Orient-Gesellschaft excavations at Uruk discovered all the exemplars of this inscription. Numerous bricks with this inscription and measuring 34×34×7 cm were found within Eanna at one spot north of the ziggurrat (see Jordan, Uruk-Warka p. 48). The provenances given for exs. 2–5 come from the excavation's registry of finds rather than from the statements in UVB 1 (see Marzahn, FuB 27 [1989] pp. 61–62 and 64 n. 21). With regard to the findspot of ex. 2, see the commentary to text no. 126. The inscription is found stamped on the face of the brick. Ex. 2 also has text no. 126 stamped on one edge. No variants are attested for this inscription and no score for this brick inscription is provided on Oracc.

The last sign in line 8, a*, is composed of three vertical wedges, one next to the other. The reading of line 14 is problematic. Although the published copies and the transliteration by J. Marzahn suggest ki-bi bí-in-túm ("he brought to its place," i.e., "he restored"), in comparison with other inscriptions, including brick inscriptions of Sargon from Babylon (text no. 124) and Aššur (text no. 70) and one of Esarhaddon's brick inscriptions from Babylon (Leichty, RINAP 4 pp. 267–269 no. 131 and Frame, RIMB 2 p. 180 B.6.31.13, Akkadian), we might expect u_4-gin_7 bí-in-zálag ("made shine like daylight"). Based upon all the originals and photos examined, u_4, gin_7, and zálag appear to be as good or better than ki, bi, and túm respectively; in particular, the second sign appears to have a vertical wedge at the end (see also the copy in UVB 1). The final sign is more elongated than the first one and this might suggest túm rather than zálag, but the two vertical wedges appear to be angled, narrowing toward the left.

BIBLIOGRAPHY

1913 Jordan, MDOG 51 pp. 52–53 (ex. 1?, study [by Delitzsch])

1928 Jordan, Uruk-Warka pp. 42–43, 48, and 50–51 no. 6, and pl. 105c–d (ex. 1, photo, copy, edition [by Schroeder], provenance)

1930 Schott, UVB 1 pp. 55–56 and pl. 28 no. 19 (exs. 1–6, composite copy, edition, provenance)

1989 Marzahn, FuB 27 pp. 61–62 no. XI, nos. 32–36 and 31B (transliteration; exs. 2–4, 6–8, study)

1995 Frame, RIMB 2 pp. 150–151 no. B.6.22.5 (exs. 1–8, edition)

TEXT

1) ᵈinanna
2) nin unu.KI-ga-ta
3) dúr mar é-an-na
4) gašan maḫ bùlug-gá
5) nin-a-ni-ir
6) ᵈLUGAL-GI.NA
7) lugal ki-šár-ra
8) GÌR.NÍTA KÁ.DINGIR.RA.KI-a*
9) lugal ki-in-gi uri.KI
10) sipa ma-da *aš-šur*.KI-ke_4
11) sig_4 al-ùr-ra
12) ù-me-ni-dù-dù
13) gìr-gin é-an-na
14) u_4?-gin_7? bí-in-zálag?

1–14) For the goddess Inanna, lady of Uruk, who dwells in Eanna, the august, supreme lady, (5) his lady: Sargon (II), king of the world, governor of Babylon, king of Sumer (and) Akkad, (10) shepherd of the land of Assyria, had baked bricks made (and) *made* the processional way of Eanna *shine like daylight*.

128

Two bricks found at Uruk by the expedition sponsored by the Deutsche Orient-Gesellschaft are stamped with a Sumerian inscription that describes Sargon's reconstruction of the Eanna temple for the goddess Inanna (Ištar). The edition presented below is based upon the copy and information published by J. Marzahn in FuB 27. No score is provided on Oracc for this brick inscription.

CATALOGUE

Ex.	Museum Number	Excavation Number	Provenance	Dimensions (cm)	Lines Preserved	FuB 27	cpn
1	VA 14663f	W 5452	Uruk, Qd XVI, between highest pavements	34.5×35.5×8	1–12	37	n
2	VA 14663g	—	—	34.5×34.5×8	1–7	38	n

BIBLIOGRAPHY

1989 Marzahn, FuB 27 pp. 62–63 no. XII and nos. 37–38 (transliteration; ex. 1, copy; exs. 1–2, study)

1995 Frame, RIMB 2 pp. 151–152 no. B.6.22.6 (exs. 1–2, edition)

TEXT

1) nin ^{d}⸢inanna⸣
2) nin ⸢kur-kur-ra⸣
3) nin-a-ni-ir
4) ^{d}LUGAL-*ú-kin*
5) lugal ⸢kalag$^{?}$⸣-ga
6) lugal KÁ.DINGIR.RA.⸢KI⸣
7) lugal ki-šár-⸢ra⸣
8) ⸢lugal$^{?}$⸣ [x x x]
9) ⸢lugal$^{?}$⸣ [x x] x
10) ⸢é-an-na⸣
11) ⸢é ki-ág-gá-ni⸣
12) ⸢mu-un-na-dím⸣

1–12) For the lady, the goddess Inanna, mistress of the lands, his lady: Sargon (II), (5) s[*tron*]g king, king of Babylon, king of the world, *king* [...], *king* [...], (re)constructed (10) Eanna, her beloved temple.

129

A fragment of a clay cylinder from Tell Haddad (ancient Mê-Turnat) in the Hamrin area bears an inscription of Sargon II that is almost a total duplicate of the cylinder inscription found at Khorsabad (text no. 43). The line arrangment of this text, however, differs from that of the latter text. Unfortunately, the portion of the text that mentions the structure being rebuilt is not preserved. Since the fragment was found near the temple of Nergal (Ešaḫula), the inscription may have referred to work on that structure. For an axe head dedicated by one of Sargon's eunuchs to the god of that temple, see text no. 2008 and note also text no. 2009.

128 line 5 J. Marzahn notes that the traces of the sign after lugal could be those of either unu or kala. Since no other inscription from this period accords a ruler the title "king of Uruk" while several use the epithet "strong king" (e.g., Frame, RIMB 2 p. 222 B.6.32.16 line 6), the latter restoration is preferred here.

CATALOGUE

Museum Number	Provenance	Dimensions (cm)	cpn
IM —	Tell Haddad, in the area of housing outside the temple of Nergal (near the north corner of Area 3, next to the north-east section, in Level 1), in fill about 150 cm below the surface	10.9×4.6–6.5	n

COMMENTARY

Neither the excavation number nor the museum number of this fragment of the right end of an eight-sided cylinder is known. Parts of the first two faces are preserved, as is a small portion of the last (eighth) face. The text is in Neo-Babylonian script and is edited from the published copy.

The restoration of lines 1–21 is based upon text no. 43 lines 1–17 and 19; for lines 8–21 see also text no. 76 lines 3′–13′.

BIBLIOGRAPHY

1994 Al-Rawi, Iraq 56 pp. 37–38 no. 3 and p. 36 fig. 4 (copy, transliteration)

2009 Frame, Studies Parpola p. 82 no. k (study)

TEXT

1) [^{m}LUGAL-GI.NA *šá-ak-nu* ^{d}EN.LÍL NU.ÈŠ *ba-ʾi-it* ^{d}*a-šur ni-šit* IGI.II] ⸢^{d}⸣*a-nim u* ^{d}*da-gan*

2) [LUGAL GAL-*ú* LUGAL *dan-nu* LUGAL KIŠ LUGAL KUR *aš-šur*.KI LUGAL *kib-rat ar-ba-ʾi mi-gir*] DINGIR.MEŠ GAL.MEŠ

3) [RE.É.UM *ke-e-nu ša* ^{d}*a-šur* ^{d}AMAR.UTU LUGAL-*ut la šá-na-an ú-šat-li-mu-šu-ma*] ⸢*zi*⸣-*kir* MU-*šú** *ú-še-ṣu-ú a-na re-še-e-ti*

4) [*šá-kin šu-ba-re-e* ZIMBIR.KI NIBRU.KI KÁ.DINGIR.RA.KI *ḫa-a-tin en-šu-te-šú-nu mu-šal*]-⸢*li*⸣-*mu ḫi-bil-ti-šu-un*

5) [*ka-ṣir ki-din-nu-tu bal-til*.KI *ba-ṭi-il-tu mu-šá-áš-ši-ik tup-šik-ki* BÀD.AN.KI] ⸢*mu*⸣-*šap-ši-ḫu* UN.MEŠ-*šu-un*

6) [*le-ʾi* DÙ *mal-ki ša* UGU URU.*ḫar-ra-na* AN.DÙL-*la-šu it-ru-ṣu*]-*ma ki-i ṣa-ab* ^{d}*a-nim* ⸢*ù*⸣

7) [^{d}*da-gan iš-ṭu-ru za-kut-su zi-ka-ru dan-nu ḫa-lip na-mur-ra-ti ša*] *a-na šum-qu-ti* KUR *na-ki-ri*

8) [*šu-ut-bu-ú* GIŠ.TUKUL.MEŠ-*šu* LUGAL *ša ul-tu* u_4-*um be-lu-ti-šu mal-ku gaba-ra-a-šu*] *la ib-šu-ú i-na qab**-*la*

1–2) [Sargon (II), appointee of the god Enlil, *nešakku*-priest (and) *desired object* of the god Aššur, chosen of] the gods Anu and Dagān, [great king, strong king, king of the world, king of Assyria, king of the four quarters (of the world), favorite of] the great gods;

3) [just shepherd, (one) to whom the gods Aššur (and) Marduk granted a reign without equal and] whose reputation (these gods) exalted to the heights;

4–8a) [who (re)-established the *šubarrû*-privileges of (the cities) Sippar, Nippur, (and) Babylon, protects the weak among them (lit.: "their weak ones"), (and) made rest]itution for the wrongful damage suffered by them; [who (re)-established the privileged status of (the city) Baltil (Aššur) that had lapsed, who abolished corvée duty for (the city) Dēr, (and who)] gave relief to their people; [(most) capable of all rulers, who extended his protection over the city Ḫarrān] and [recorded its exemption (from obligations)] as if (its people were) people of the gods Anu and [Dagān; the strong man who is clad in awesome splendor (and) whose weapons are raised] to strike down the land of (his) enemies;

8b–12a) [the king who since the (first) day of his reign] has had no [ruler who could equal him (and) has met no one who could overpower (him)] in war [(or)

---

3 -*šú**: The copy has -LAL.
7 Text no. 43 line 7 just has *a-na šum-qut na-ki-ri*, "to strike down (his) enemies"; see also text no. 1 line 5.
8 *qab**-: The copy has ZI-.

9) [(ù) *ta-ḫa-zi la e-mu-ru mu-né-eḫ-ḫu* KUR.KUR DÙ-*ši-na ki-ma ḫaṣ-bat-ti ú-daq*]-⸢*qi*?⸣-*qu-ma ḫa*-⸢*am*⸣-*ma-ʾi šá* ar*-ba-ʾi*
10) [*id-du-ú ṣer-re-e-tu ḫur-šá-a-ni bé-ru-ú-ti ša né-reb-šú-nu áš*]-*ṭu la mi-na ip-tu-ma i-mu-ru**
11) [*du-ru-ug-šu-un ṭu-da-at la aʾ-a-ri pa-áš-qa-a-ti ša*] ⸢*a*⸣-*šar-ši-na šug-lu-tú i-ta-at-ti-qu-ma*
12) [*e-te-eb-bi-ru na-gab be-ra-a-ti iš-tu* KUR.*ra-a-ši mi*]-⸢*ṣir*⸣ KUR*.*e-lam-ti* LÚ.*pu-qu-du* LÚ.*da-mu-nu*
13) [URU.BÀD-*ku-ri-gal-zi* URU.*ra-pi-qu mad-bar* DÙ.A.BI] *a-di na-ḫal* KUR.*mu-uṣ-ri* KUR *a-mur-ri-i* DAGAL-*ti*
14) [KUR.*ḫat-ti a-na si-ḫir-ti-šá i-be-lu iš-tu* KUR.*ḫa-áš-mar a-di*] ⸢URU.*ṣi*⸣-*bar pat-ti* KUR.*ma-da-a-a ru-qu-ú-ti*
15) [*ša ṣi-it* ^{d}UTU-*ši* KUR.*nam-ri* KUR.*el-li-pí* KUR.É-*ḫa-am-ban* KUR].⸢*par*⸣-*su-maš* KUR.*ma-an-na-a-a* KUR.*ú-ra-áš-ṭu*
16) [KUR.*kas-ku* KUR.*ta-ba-lum a-di* KUR.*mu-us-ki ik-šu-du* GAL-*tum qa-as*]-⸢*su*⸣
17) [LÚ.*šu-ut* SAG.MEŠ-*šú šak-nu-ti* UGU-*šú-nu iš-tak-ka-nu-ma bil-tu ma-da*]-⸢*at*⸣-*ti*
18) [*ki-i ša áš-šu-ri e-mid-su-nu-ti eṭ-lu qar-du ša i-na re-bit* BÀD.AN.KI *it-ti* ^{md}*ḫum-ba-ni*]-⸢*ga*⸣-*áš*
19) [LUGAL KUR.*e-lam-ti in-nam-ru-ma iš-ku-nu taḫ-ta-a-šu* (...) *mu*]-*ri-ib* KUR.É-*ḫu-um-ri*
20) [*rap-ši ša i-na* URU.*ra-pi-ḫi* BAD$_{5}$.BAD$_{5}$-*ú* KUR.*mu-uṣ-ri* GAR-*nu-ma* ^{m}*ḫa-a-nu-nu* LUGAL URU.*ḫa-zi-te ka-mu-us*]-⸢*su*⸣ *ú-še-ri*-⸢*bu*⸣
21) [URU.*aš-šur* ...]
Lacuna of ca. 75 lines
1′) [... *ana mi*]-⸢*ṣir*⸣ KUR ^{d}*aš-šur ú-ter-ra*

battle; (who) sma]shed [all (enemy) lands as if (they were) pots] and (10) [put halters on] (all) rebels in the four (quarters of the world); (who) opened up innumerable [distant mountainous areas whose pass(es) are diff]icult and visited their [remotest region(s); (who)] traversed [inaccessible, difficult paths in] terrifying location(s) and [crossed every *swamp*];

12b–18a) [(who) ruled from the land Rāši on the bord]er of the land Elam, the Puqudu (and) Damūnu (tribes), [the cities Dūr-Kurigalzu (and) Rapiqu, the entire desert] as far as the Brook of Egypt, the wide land Amurru, [(and) the land Ḫatti (Syria) in its entirety]; (who)se [great hand conquered (the area) from the land Ḫašmar to the cit]y Ṣibar — which borders on the distant Medes (15) [in the east — the lands Namri, Ellipi, Bīt-Ḫamban, Pa]rsumaš, Mannea, Urarṭu, [Kasku, (and) Tabal, as far as the land Musku; (who) set eunuchs of his as governors over them and imposed upon them (the same) tribute (and) payme]nt(s) [as if (they were) Assyrians];

18b–21) [the valiant man who met Ḫumbanig]aš (Ḫumban-nikaš I), [king of the land Elam, (in battle) on the *outskirts* of (the city) Dēr and brought about his defeat; (...); who made] the [wide] land Bīt-Ḫumri (Israel) tremble, [brought about the defeat of Egypt at the city Raphia, and] brought [Ḫanūnu (Hanno), king of the city Gaza, to the city Aššur in bondag]e; [...]

Lacuna of ca. 75 lines
1′) [...] I made [(part of) the territ]ory of Assyria.

130

The Louvre obtained this small barrel-shaped cylinder or bead in 1889 from M. Barré de Lancy, who had acquired it in the region of Mosul. The piece is made of brown agate, with light bands, and is pierced lengthwise. It has a short dedicatory inscription of Sargon to the goddess Damkina.

129 line 9 *šá**: The copy has ZA. *ar**-: The copy has ŠU-ḪU-.
129 line 10 -*ru**: The copy has -U-MA.
129 line 12 KUR*: The copy has ŠE.
129 line 19 This inscription appears to omit all or most of text no. 43 line 18: *na-si-iḫ* LÚ.KUR.*te-sa-a-a mu-pal-li-ku gu-un-ni-šu šá-lil* KUR.*tu-ʾu-mu-na ša* LÚ.*na-sik-šú-nu i-pi-du-ma ur-ru-ú ma-ḫar* LUGAL KUR.*kal-di*, "who deported the Tešian (king) (and) cut down his elite troops; who plundered the land Tuʾumuna, who(se people) had arrested their sheikh and brought (him) before the king of Chaldea."

CATALOGUE

Museum Number	Provenance	Dimensions (cm)	cpn
AO 1936	—	3.8×1.6	c

BIBLIOGRAPHY

1923 Delaporte, Louvre 2 p. 180 no. A.826 and pl. 93 fig. 15 (photo, edition)
1924 Pottier, Antiquités assyriennes p. 120 no. 119 (study)
1987 Galter, ARRIM 5 pp. 12, 14, and 21 no. 41 (edition, study)
1995 Tallon, Pierres pp. 73 and 76 no. 120 (photo, study)

TEXT

1) *ana* ^{d}*dam-ki-na*
2) GAŠAN-*šú* ^{m}MAN-GIN
3) MAN KUR AŠ
4) *ana* TI-*šú* BA

1–4) To the goddess Damkina, his lady: Sargon (II), king of Assyria, presented (this object) for the sake of his life.

1001

An "historical(?) tablet" was found in Room 166 (the chapel of Adad) of Sargon's palace at Khorsabad (Loud and Altman, Khorsabad 2 p. 104 no. 18). Nothing further is known about the inscription, but it is placed here since most historical inscriptions from Khorsabad come from the reign of Sargon II.

CATALOGUE

Source	Provenance	Dimensions (cm)	cpn
Loud and Altman, Khorsabad 2 p. 104 no. 18	Khorsabad, Palace, Room 166	–	n

1002

A sealing published by P.E. Botta together with his finds from Khorsabad depicts a man killing a lion; see Botta, Monument de Ninive 2 pl. 164 no. 2; Albenda, Palace of Sargon p. 114 no. 14 (entry by C.B.F. Walker) and pl. 152; and Figure 30. The image appears have a cuneiform inscription around it and to be from a royal stamp seal similar to other royal Assyrian seals; see Sachs, Iraq 15 (1953) pp. 167–170 and pls. XVIII–XIX; and Millard, Iraq 27 (1965) pp. 12–16 and pl. I. According to Walker, "One could think of restoring the visible signs at the top as *šar*$_4$ KUR *aš-šur*, 'king of Assyria', but this could be completely wrong." Since the piece presumably comes from Khorsabad, the inscription might have mentioned Sargon and is thus presented here. The current location of the sealing is not known. Cf. the sealing Sm 2297 (see Figure 1 in the Introduction to this volume), as well as the seal depicted on Botta, Monument de Ninive 2 pl. 154 no. 2 and listed in Albenda, Palace of Sargon p. 114 no. 14.

CATALOGUE

Source	Provenance	Dimensions (cm)	cpn
Botta, Monument de Ninive 2 pl. 164 no. 2	possibly Khorsabad	–	n

Figure 30. Drawing of a clay sealing published in Botta, Monument de Ninive 2 pl. 164 no. 2 (text no. 1002).

1003

A fragment of a clay cone from Aššur bears an inscription that may come from the time of Sargon II. The initial publisher of the inscription assigned it to Ashurnasirpal II, but the text mentions Akkadî in line 2′ and that does not appear in the inscriptions of Ashurnasirpal II. Ḫašmar (line 3′) appears only in inscriptions of that king and Sargon II (see Bagg, Rép. Géogr. 7/2-1 p. 219), and thus the text is tentatively assigned here to Sargon. It should be noted that Ḫanigalbat (line 4′) does not appear in any other inscription of Sargon II, while it does appear in early Neo-Assyrian royal inscriptions and in one inscription of Esarhaddon (ibid., p. 206).

CATALOGUE

Museum Number	Excavation Number	Photograph Number	Provenance	Dimensions (cm)	cpn
VA Ass 2066	Ass 23090	Ass ph S 7028	Aššur, city area	4.5×9.6×1.3	c

BIBLIOGRAPHY

1982 Jakob-Rost, FuB 22 pp. 141 and 159 no. 41 (copy, study)
1991 Grayson, RIMA 2 pp. 339–340 commentary to A.0.101.67 (study)
1997 Pedersén, Katalog p. 152 (study)

TEXT

Lacuna
1′) [... GAR] ⸢^{d}⸣BAD ⸢SANGA⸣ [^{d}*aš-šur* ...]
2′) [...] *x* AN *ša* KUR *ak-ka-*⸢*di*⸣*-*[*i* ...]
3′) [...] ⸢NI$^{?}$⸣ KUR.*za-mu-a* KUR.*ḫa-áš-*[*mar* ...]
4′) [... KUR.*ḫa*]*-*⸢*ni*⸣*-gal-bat-i* DAGAL *x* [...]
Lacuna

Lacuna
1′–4′) [... appointee of] the god Enlil, priest [of the god Aššur ...] ... of the land Akkad [...] the land Zamua, the land Ḫaš[mar, ...] the wide [land Ḫan]igalbat [...]
Lacuna

1004

A fragment of a clay cone found at Aššur may bear an inscription from the time of Sargon II. L. Jakob-Rost, the initial publisher of the inscription, tentatively assigned it to Sargon II, but R. Borger has stated that it should more probably be assigned to Shalmaneser III (ZA 76 [1986] p. 301). Very little of the inscription is preserved and it does not appear to duplicate exactly the known inscriptions of either ruler. Note that like text no. 67 (an inscription also on clay cones from Aššur), this cone originally bore the date on which it was composed. O. Pedersén's and A. Nunn's recent works follow Jakob-Rost's tentative assignment of the text and thus, arbitrarily, this inscription is presented with those of Sargon. The fragment was found with several other clay cone fragments; for further details on the provenance compare Nunn, Knaufplatten p. 73 and p. 164. Line 3′ of the inscription is indented.

CATALOGUE

Museum Number	Excavation Number	Photograph Number	Provenance	Dimensions (cm)	cpn
VA Ass 2049	Ass 10112Ah	Ass ph 1554	Aššur, bA5IV, on the outside face, corner inner wall	7.5×4×0.7–1.0	c

BIBLIOGRAPHY

1913 Andrae, Festungswerke pp. 11 and 118 (study)
1982 Jakob-Rost, FuB 22 pp. 146 and 175 no. 110 (copy, study)
1986 Borger, ZA 76 p. 301 (study)
1997 Pedersén, Katalog p. 140 (study)
2006 Nunn, Knaufplatten pp. 73 and 164 no. 1515 (study)

TEXT

Lacuna
1′) *x* MU *x* [...]
2′) *li-mu* ^{m}[...]
3′) LÚ.[...]

Lacuna
1′) ... [...]
2′–3′) Eponymy of [...], the [...].

1005

A fragment of a baked brick, or perhaps more likely a clay plaque, from Aššur in the Vorderasiatisches Museum in Berlin bears a fragmentary inscription — [...] ⸢KUR⸣ *aš-šur*.⸢KI?⸣ [...] — that A. Nunn has tentatively assigned to Sargon II (Knaufplatten p. 117 no. 273). The inscription was collated by F. Weiershäuser. If the piece comes from a plaque it might be a duplicate of text no. 66.

CATALOGUE

Museum Number	Excavation Number	Provenance	Dimensions (cm)	cpn
VA Ass 4194	Ass 6471c?	Aššur, city area	5.8×4.5×2.2	c

1006

Two fragments of a prismatic cylinder from Nimrud preserved in the British Museum have an inscription that is arbitrarily presented here. It might be assigned to Sargon II because another prismatic cylinder inscription of his is known from that city (text no. 76).

CATALOGUE

Museum Number	Excavation Number	Provenance	Dimensions (cm)	cpn
BM —	ND 2075a+b	Nimrud	—	c

COMMENTARY

ND 2075a, which is comprised of three joined fragments, is part of the left end of the cylinder and ND 2075b, which is composed to two joined fragments, is part of the central section. The cylinder would likely have had ten faces originally, but parts of only five inscribed faces, and traces of two others, are preserved. Unfortunately, neither the beginning nor the end of the inscription is preserved. The faces are not of the same width. The first and second inscribed faces have four lines each, while the third, fourth, and fifth have three lines each. There is an uninscribed margin ca. 1.7–1.8 cm wide to the left of the inscription.

The text is written in Neo-Babylonian script and has been collated both from the original fragments and from photographs. Photographs of ND 2075a were kindly supplied to the author by G. Van Buylaere and photos of ND 2075b by M. Touillon-Ricci.

TEXT

	Lacuna	Lacuna
1′)	*x* [...]	1′–3′) Not sufficiently preserved to allow translation.
2′)	NI$^{?}$ [...] / *x* [...]	
3′)	ŠI *x* [...]	
4′)	*a-na x* [...]	4′) to/for [...]
5′)	*i-li-iṣ-⸢ma⸣* [...]	5′) he rejoiced an[d ...]
6′)	UGU *ku-ru-ma-ti* [*x x x x x x* (*x x*)] *x* ⸢BU$^{?}$ ŠÚ⸣ *x* [...]	6′) over the food allocation [...] ... [...]
7′)	*iḫ-du lìb-ba-⸢šú⸣* [*x x x x* (*x*)] *im-mir-⸢ma⸣* [...]	7′) he was happy [... *his face*] shone an[d ...]
8′)	E MI$^{?}$ DI PA *x* [*x x x x* (*x*)] *ik-ru-ba* ⸢IA⸣ [...]	8′) ... [...] he prayed [...]
9′)	*ba-laṭ* ZI-*tim* [*x x x x* (*x*)] ⸢*ku*⸣-*un-nu* BALA-*e* ⸢MI/UL⸣ [...]	9′) to ensure (my) good health [...] to firmly establish (my) reign [...]
10′)	*i-da-a-a a-⸢la⸣-*[*ku x x x* (*x*)] ⸢*i*$^{?}$⸣-*zu-zi ina li-⸢i-ti*$^{?}$⸣ [...]	10′) to g[o] at my side [... to st]and in *trium*[*ph* ...]
11′)	*mu-ud-di-iš* ⸢É$^{?}$⸣ [*x x x x* (*x*)] *x x* NIN *x x* [...]	11′) one who renovates [*this*] *temple* [...] ... [...]
12′)	*šá a-na kul-lu-me* [*x x* (*x*)] ⸢KI$^{?}$⸣ *i-šak-ka-⸢nu*$^{?}$/*na*$^{?}$⸣ [...]	12′) who to show [...] he/th[ey] will establ[ish ...]
13′)	*dan-nu šu*-BU-[*x x* (*x*)]-BU-UB *a-a-bi* AN *x* [...]	13′) strong ... [...] ... enemy ... [...]
14′)	*lil-li-ik-ma* [(*x*) $u_4^{?}$]-*um ga-ru-šú i-na* ID *x* [...]	14′) may he go and [*wh*]*en* his foes in ... [...]
15′)	*lik-mi-*[(*ma*)] *um-man-šú šá* E *x* [...]	15′) may he bind [(*and*)] his army that ... [...]
16′)	*ú-ša-ab-ba-⸢ru⸣* [...]	16′) he/th[ey] will shatter [...]
17′)	NI *x x* IA [...]	17′) ... [...]
	Lacuna	Lacuna

8′ ⸢IA⸣ or *i-⸢a/za⸣*.

1007

A fragmentary inscription on a limestone block found by R. Campbell Thompson at Nineveh and currently in the British Museum was tentatively assigned to Sennacherib by Campbell Thompson and to Sargon or Sennacherib by R. Borger (HKL 1 p. 536; and 3 pp. 26–27) and E. Frahm (Sanherib p. 143 no. 5 and NABU 2000 p. 77 no. 66). The inscription refers to an *akītu*-house and, as noted by Frahm, Ashurbanipal explicitly states that Sargon had built the *akītu*-house of Ištar at Nineveh (Novotny and Jeffers, RINAP 5/1 p. 220 no. 10 v 33–42). The inscription is thus tentatively assigned to Sargon II even though his name is not mentioned in what is preserved of the text. (For two stone fragments found at Nineveh that mention Sargon, see text nos. 93 and 94.)

CATALOGUE

Museum Number	Photograph Number	Provenance	Dimensions (cm)	cpn
BM —	Thompson 81	Nineveh, between the Ištar and Nabû temples	—	c

BIBLIOGRAPHY

1929 Thompson, Arch. 79 p. 120 and pl. XLII no. 43 (copy, study)
1997 Frahm, Sanherib p. 143 no. 5 (study)
2000 Frahm, NABU 2000 pp. 75–79 no. 66, esp. p. 77 and p. 78 n. 23 (transliteration, study)
2005 Reade, Iraq 67 p. 380 (study)

TEXT

Lacuna
1′) [...] *la iš*-[*šak*$^?$-*nu*$^?$]-⸢*ma*$^?$⸣
2′) [... *a-na* (...)] GIN BALA-*šú* É *á-ki-it*
3′) [... NA$_4$$^?$.NA$^?$].⸢RÚ$^?$.A$^?$⸣ *iš-ku-un*
4′) [...] *x* KU *ú-še-piš*

Lacuna
1′–4′) [... *had*] not [*been*] *es*[*tablished*] *a*[*nd* ... in order (...)] to firmly establish his reign, an *akītu*-house [...] he placed [(...) *a st*]*ele*. [...] he had [(...) a ...] ... made.

1008

A.H. Layard mentions a pair of lions made of coarse limestone that were found in Sennacherib's palace at Nineveh and that had a "nearly illegible" inscription. H. Galter et al. (ARRIM 4 [1986] p. 31 no. 12) suggests that the copy of a "fragment on part of [a] yellow bull at entrance" among Layard's papers in the British Museum might represent this text. E. Frahm (Sanherib pp. 122–123) raises the possibility that the yellow bull may not come from Nineveh and that the text copied by Layard may actually duplicate part of a description of the building of Sargon's palace at Khorsabad that is found on several bulls discovered at Khorsabad (text no. 9 lines 71–78). Unfortunately,

(1) the reading of a large number of the signs in lines 1′–6′ is not at all clear, (2) there are problems with regard to the space for the restorations in those lines, and (3) the traces of lines 7′–8′ do not seem to fit that inscription of Sargon. Since the present location of the piece is not known and the inscription could not be collated, the edition is based on Layard's copy and Frahm's suggested transliteration. Without examination of the original, it is not possible to determine with any degree of certainty if this inscription actually duplicates all or part of Sargon's bull inscription from Khorsabad or if it should even be attributed to this ruler.

CATALOGUE

Source	Provenance	Dimensions (cm)	cpn
Layard MS C p. 58 recto	Nineveh, Palace of Sennacherib, Court XIX, Door a	–	n

BIBLIOGRAPHY

–	Layard, MS C p. 58 recto (copy)
1853	Layard, Discoveries p. 230 (provenance)
1986	Galter et al., ARRIM 4 p. 31 no. 12 (study)
1997	Frahm, Sanherib pp. 122–123 and pl. 5 (copy [by Layard], transliteration, study)

TEXT

Lacuna
1′) [... *ip?-pat?*]-*qu*-[*ma?* ...]
2′) [... GIŠ?].*ere*-⸢IGI*⸣ [...]
3′) [... *ur?*]-*maḫ**-*ḫe**-*e** [...]
4′) [... UDU.MEŠ? *šad?*]-*di** dLAMMA* [MAḪ.MEŠ? ...]
5′) [...] *ap*-⸢*tiq*⸣-*ma a*-[*na?* ...]
6′) [...] *ki**-*šit-ti* ŠU*.II*-⸢*ia?*⸣ [...]
7′) [...] SI IS *x* ḪI *x* [...]
8′) [...] *a-na* DA ṢI [...]
Lacuna

Lacuna
1′–6′) [... *were cas*]*t* [*and* ...] *ced*[*ar* ... *l*]*ion colossi* [... *moun*]*tain* [*sheep as august*] *protective spirit*[*s* ...] I fashioned and *t*[*o* ...] *that I had conquered* [...]

7′–8′) [...] ... [...] to ... [...]

Lacuna

2′ -⸢IGI*⸣: A.H. Layard's copy has AŠ [...] for ⸢IGI⸣ [...].
3′ A.H. Layard's copy for this line has [...] GIM IM [...].
4′ A.H. Layard's copy for this line has [...] KAB/ḪÚB dKID [...].
6′ A.H. Layard's copy for this line has [...] U LU *šit-ti* ⸢KUR APIN?⸣ [...], where the LU is in the Babylonian form of that sign.
7′ As noted by E. Frahm (Sanherib p. 123), the traces copied by A.H. Layard would seem unlikely to fit *ú-šá-as-ḫi-ra* of text no. 9 line 79.
8′ As noted by E. Frahm (Sanherib p. 123), a reading *a-na da-ṣi*, "in order to treat unjustly," might be possible here.

1009

A tiny limestone fragment with part of a cuneiform inscription was found at Samaria and is currently preserved in the Rockefeller Museum in Jerusalem. Since the inscription is written on stone, it is likely to have been a royal inscription. As noted by C.J. Gadd, the script shows a mixture of Assyrian and Babylonian forms, suggesting that it comes from the time of one of the Neo-Assyrian kings of the ninth through seventh centuries. It is edited with the inscriptions of Sargon II because many inhabitants of Samaria were deported during his reign. Thus, Sargon may well have left an inscribed stele at Samaria, just as he did as Ashdod (text no. 104). There is, however, nothing in the inscription that suggests its assignment to Sargon II in particular. The inscription is edited from the published photograph.

CATALOGUE

Museum Number	Excavation Number	Provenance	Dimensions (cm)	cpn
IAA 33.3725	D 1430	Samaria, built into a modern field wall in Dn	24×19.5×11.5	p

BIBLIOGRAPHY

1942 Crowfoot, Samaria-Sebaste 1 p. 15 (provenance)
1957 Gadd in Crowfoot, Samaria-Sebaste 3 p. 35 and pl. IV nos. 2–3 (photo, copy, study)
1968 Borger in Galling, Textbuch[2] p. 61 no. 31.5.a (study)
1972 Levine, Stelae p. 56 (study)
1973 Hestrin, Inscriptions Reveal[2] no. 46 (photo, study)
1982 Börker-Klähn, Bildstelen no. 179 (study)
1988 Cogan and Tadmor II Kings second plate following p. 228 (photo)
1990 Stern, Archaeology of the Land of the Bible 2 p. 15 (photo)
1992 Becking, Fall of Samaria p. 114 no. 4 (study)
1993 Avigad in Stern, New Encyclopedia 4 p. 1306 (photo)
2002 Horowitz, Oshima and Sanders, JAOS 122 p. 759 Samaria 4 (study)
2006 Frame, Subartu 18 p. 53 (study)
2006 Horowitz and Oshima, Canaan pp. 19, 115, and 217 Samaria 4 (copy, edition)
2008 Cogan, Raging Torrent pp. 231–233 no. 1 (photo, study)

TEXT

Lacuna
1′) [...] (*x*) *x* [...]
2′) [...] *x* ME ⸢UZ?⸣ [...]
3′) [...] (*x*) *u*$_4$*-me* ÁŠ *x* [...]
4′) [...] *x* ⸢*ba*?⸣*-nu-u x* [...]
5′) [...] ⸢BURU$_5$⸣.ḪI.A ⸢BI?⸣ [...]
6′) [...] ÁŠ ME ṬU *x* [...]

Lacuna
1′–2′) Too poorly preserved to allow translation.
3′) [...] days ... [...]
4′) [...] *creator* [...]
5′) [...] locusts [...]
6′–8′) Too poorly preserved to allow translation

2′ Possibly ⸢*u*$_4$⸣*-me*, "days," following Horowitz and Oshima, Canaan p. 115.
4′ C.J. Gadd (in Crowfoot, Samaria-Sebaste 3 p. 35) suggests that what is preserved might be the end of a place name *-ba?-nu-u*.⸢KI⸣, while W. Horowitz and T. Oshima (Canaan p. 115) read [...] ⸢*ib*⸣*-ba-nu u x* [...], "[... w]ere built and . [...]"
5′ Locusts are mentioned at least three times in Sargon's inscriptions (text no. 1 line 86 and text no. 65 lines 187 and 256), but in no case does the context fit the passage here.
6′ W. Horowitz and T. Oshima (Canaan p. 115) read [...] *áš-me-ṭu x* [...], "[...] dust-storm . [...]," and suggest that if the traces of the last sign are those of A the end of the line might be restored *a*[*šamšūtu*]. However, the former word only appears once in all of cuneiform literature, in the lexical series MALKU, where *áš-me-tú* is given as a synonym of *ašamšūtu* (see CAD A/2 p. 450 and AHw p. 82). The use of the ṬU sign here rather than *-tu* or *-tú* makes the identification of the word in this line with the *áš-me-tú* of MALKU uncertain. Possibly *šip-ṭu*, "judgement" or "threat," instead of ME ṬU.

7′) [...] MA SI *x* [...]
8′) [...] *x x* [...]
Lacuna

Lacuna

1010

A basalt stone fragment with a cuneiform inscription was found at Carchemish in the early part of the last century during excavations by a British Museum expedition. The fragment is a corner fragment of a stone object, "perhaps an obelisk" (i.e., stele) in the view of the original publisher of the piece. The inscription on it is presented with those of Sargon II since cylinder and brick inscriptions of Sargon II have also been found at Carchemish (text nos. 109–110), while inscriptions of no other Neo-Assyrian ruler have been found at this site. Sargon is also known to have left inscribed steles in various locations in the western part of his realm. According to H. Tadmor, the palaeography of the inscriptions on this fragment and text no. 1009 (from Samaria) is "very similar" to that of the Cyprus, Ashdod, and Tell Acharneh steles of Sargon (text nos. 103, 104, and 106 respectively) ('Atiqot, English Series 9-10 [1971] p. 195).

CATALOGUE

Source	Provenance	Dimensions (cm)	cpn
Barnett in Woolley and Barnett, Carchemish 3 pl. A.33 m–m*	Carchemish	—	n

COMMENTARY

Neither the exact provenance of the fragment nor its current location is known. R.D. Barnett states that the originals of the cuneiform inscriptions from Carchemish published by him "are lost" and that he made use of squeezes in his work (Woolley and Barnett, Carchemish 3 p. 279 n. 3). The fact that the one fully preserved side is relatively narrow and that the lines of text run from that side onto the adjoining side raises questions about the idea that the fragment comes from a stele since this would be an almost unique arrangement. (The inscription on the back of the Najafabad stele [text no. 117] also runs over onto the adjoining side.) The inscription is edited from the published copy, with some help from the published photo and a scan of the original photo kindly supplied by N. Marchetti. A squeeze of the inscription is preserved in the British Museum, but it was not available for collation.

In a recent publication, G. Marchesi refers to a "very fragmentary" stele with "a non-standard inscription of Sargon that has no phraseological parallels in other texts of the Sargonid corpus" that will be published by him and Marchetti (JNES 78 [2019] p. 11 n. 9). He has kindly informed me that this object is made up of four fragments that do not join and that two of the fragments were found by the British Museum excavations and two by the recent Turkish-Italian excavations led by N. Marchetti; one of the four pieces is the one edited here.

Although the asseverative particle *lū* does occasionally appear in Sargon's royal inscriptions (e.g., text nos. 8 line 6, 14 line 12, and in particular 82 iv 7′, 8′, and 9′), the fact that it occurs in three successive lines (lines 2′, 3′, and 4′), is noteworthy.

1009 line 7′ W. Horowitz and T. Oshima (Canaan p. 115) read [...] *ma-si-*⌜*na*?⌝ [...], "[...] *thei*[*r*?] *land* [...]."

BIBLIOGRAPHY

1952 Barnett in Woolley and Barnett, Carchemish 3 pp. 265 and 279–280 and pl. A.33 m–m* (photo, copy, edition)

1982 Börker-Klähn, Bildstelen no. 178 (study)

1983 Winter, AnSt 33 p. 194 n. 89 (study)

2006 Frame, Subartu 18 p. 53 (study)

TEXT

Lacuna

1′) *x x x* [(*x*)] *x* [...]

2′) *lu-ú e-sir-šú ma-da-ta-šú* KÙ.BABBAR ˹KÙ$^{?}$˺.[GI$^{?}$ ...]

3′) LAL*-*at* GIŠ.*ni-ri lu am-ḫur* DUMU.MUNUS-˹*su*$^{?}$˺ [...]

4′) *lu a-qur-ma* NU *mu-sa-pu-u* DINGIR$^{?}$-*ti* ˹KI$^{?}$˺ [...]

5′) *ana še-me-e qí-bit pi-šú ana mit-gu-ri*$^{?}$ [...]

6′) ḪÉ.NUN *ṭuḫ-du ḫi-iṣ-ba* ḪÉ.˹GÁL˺ [...]

7′) *ana še-x* (*x*) [*x x*] *x x* (*x*) [...]

Lacuna

Lacuna

1′) ... [...]

2′–6′) I shut him up. I received as his tribute silver, g[*old*, ...], (and horses) trained to the yoke. [*I carried off*] h[*is*] daughter [(...)] I demolished [...] and [*I erected* (...)] an image (*of myself*) praying *to* (*his*) divine *majesty* [...] to obey (lit.: "hear") his (the god's) command, to *be in agreement* [...] plenty, abundance, affluence, weal[th ...]

7′) ... [...] ... [...]

Lacuna

2′ ˹KÙ$^{?}$˺.[GI$^{?}$], "*g*[*old*]": Since gold is normally mentioned before silver in Neo-Assyrian royal inscriptions, the restoration is uncertain.

3′ LAL*-: According to the photo, the text has ME-.

4′ NU *mu-sa-pu-u* DINGIR$^{?}$-*ti*, "an image (*of myself*) praying *to* (*his*) divine *majesty*": Cf. Leichty, RINAP 4 p. 136 no. 60 line 28′ *ṣa-lam* LUGAL-*ti-ia mu-sa-pu-u* DINGIR-*ti-šú-un* (see also CAD S p. 394). R.D. Barnett suggested reading NU.MU.SA-*pu-u-rat-ti*.KI, "the city of Almat-puratti" (lit.: "widow of the Euphrates"), although noting that no city with this name is otherwise attested (Woolley and Barnett, Carchemish 3 p. 280). We would also expect URU before the city name and NU.MU.SU instead of NU.MU.SA. Assuming that the passage does mean "widow of the Euphrates," I. Winter suggested that it "could conceivably refer to Carchemish after its conquest" (AnSt 33 [1984] p. 194 n. 89). J. Penuela and D.J. Wiseman suggested KUR.*mu-ṣa-ṣir* ..., "the land of Musasir ...," a suggestion which Barnett describes as "most plausible ... The ambiguity is due to faults of copying" (Woolley and Barnett, Carchemish 3 p. 280 n. 1). The photograph is not clear enough to confirm a reading KUR for the copy's NU and, according to S. Parpola (Toponyms p. 250), Muṣaṣir is always written with ṢA, not SA. (The one instance given by Parpola of a writing with SA — KUR M(U)-SA-ṢI-RA (WO 2 230.178) — is a typographical error; the text in question [Grayson, RIMA 3 p. 70 A.0.102.14 line 178] has ṢA.)

5′ R.D. Barnett suggested *ana mit*$^{?}$*-gu*$^{?}$*-ur*$^{?}$ for the end of the line (Woolley and Barnett, Carchemish 3 p. 280). While the copy allows reading *ana mit-gu-*, the traces of the final sign copied do not fit UR, but might allow RI. Cf. Grayson and Novotny, RINAP 3/2 p. 354 no. 1016 rev. 2′.

2001

In 1989, Iraqi excavations of a tomb chamber below Room 49 of the North-West Palace at Nimrud (Tomb II) uncovered the bodies of two women and numerous precious items, including four inscribed gold bowls, one inscribed jar apparently of rock crystal, and an electrum mirror. Inscriptions on them refer to three Assyrian royal wives: Yabâ, the wife of Tiglath-pileser III; Bānītu (or possibly Banītu), the wife of Shalmaneser V; and Atalia, the wife of Sargon II. Since only two bodies were found in the grave, their identities has been a matter of some discussion, with one suggestion being that they are Yabâ and Atalia (with the latter being buried with property inherited from Bānītu; Kamil in Damerji, Gräber p. 13), another suggestion being that they are Bānītu and Atalia (George, Minerva 1/1 [1990] p. 31), and the most recent suggestion being that Yabâ and Bānītu were one and the same person, so that the grave then holds Yabâ (=Bānītu) and Atalia (Dalley, New Light on Nimrud pp. 171–175). As pointed out by A.R. George, although the name Bānītu is a good Assyrian name, that of Atalia and possibly that of Yabâ are Northwest Semitic, suggesting that these two "were thus probably of Syrian or Levantine birth, entering the Assyrian harem as a result of diplomatic marriages or as spoils of the many western campaigns undertaken by the Assyrian armies of this period" (Minerva 1/1 [1990] p. 31). S. Dalley has proposed that Yabâ and Atalia were both princesses from Jerusalem (e.g., SAAB 12 [1998] pp. 83–98) and (as already mentioned) that Yabâ and Banītu were actually one and the same person since Yabâ means "beautiful" in Hebrew and Banītu is the Akkadian equivalent (New Light on Nimrud pp. 171–175). The evidence adduced by Dalley to support a Judean ancestry, while intriguing, is open to other interpretations. E. Frahm, for example, has tentatively suggested that Atalia might have been of Israelite background, although noting that "the uncertainties in identifying Atalyā's true background are so substantial that it seems preferable to abstain from further speculation" (Last Days p. 81; see also Frahm in Sennacherib at the Gates of Jerusalem pp. 186–189). For a linguistic discussion of the name Atalia suggesting that it might be of Arabian derivation, see Zadok, Studies Ephʿal pp. 327–329. See also Kertai, AoF 40 (2013) pp. 114–116 with regard to the three queens and note Tadmor and Yamada, RINAP 1 p. 164.

A short proprietary inscription of Atalia's is written on a gold bowl, a jar of (apparently) rock crystal, and an electrum mirror found in the tomb chamber.

CATALOGUE

Ex.	Museum Number	Excavation Number	Provenance	Object	Dimensions (cm)	Lines Preserved	cpn
1	IM 105695	ND 1989/4	Nimrud, North-West Palace, Tomb II	gold bowl	Rim: 20.4; height: 12	1	n
2	IM 124999	ND 1989/66	As ex. 1	rock crystal jar	Rim: 10; depth: 8	1	n

3	IM 115468	ND 1989/194	As ex. 1	electrum mirror	Rim: 14; thickness: 0.3; length of handle: 16	1	n

COMMENTARY

The gold bowl (ex. 1) was found resting on the breast of one of the two bodies found in the tomb and it has been suggested that Atalia was buried in this tomb (Damerji, Gräber p. 8). The inscriptions on exs. 1–2 are found on the outer surface of the vessels, running in one line around each vessel's neck; the one on ex. 3 is in two lines (with the second line beginning after MUNUS.É.GAL) and is found on the handle of the mirror. It has not been possible to collate the exemplars and the inscription is edited from the published copies.

A drawing of a scorpion is found on the neck of ex. 1 (just before the the beginning of the inscription) and on the handle of ex. 3 (at the end of the inscription). With regard to the scorpion on Neo-Assyrian artifacts as a marker of the property of the queen, see most recently Galter, Journal for Semitics 16/3 (2007) pp. 646–671; Niederreiter, Iraq 70 (2008) pp. 51–86, esp. 59–62; and Radner, Studies Fales pp. 690–693. A bronze duck weight (ND 1898/158) with brief inscriptions in Akkadian and Aramaic stating that it weighed one-sixth of a mina and with the depiction of a scorpion on it was also found in Tomb II and F.N.H. Al-Rawi has argued that it also belonged to Atalia (see New Light on Nimrud pp. 126–130 no. 7 and Hussein, Nimrud: The Queens' Tombs pp. 22–23).

BIBLIOGRAPHY

1990 George, Minerva 1/1 pp. 29 and 31 (exs. 1–2, translation, provenance)
1990 Harrak, BCSMS 20 pp. 7 and 9 (ex. 1, translation, provenance)
1991 Damerji, Studies Mikasa pp. 11, 13, 14 fig. 2 right end, and 15 fig. 3 left end (ex. 2?, photo; ex. 3, photo [inscription not legible]; study)
1998 Dalley, SAAB 12 pp. 93–94 (translation, study)
1998 Damerji, Jahrbuch des Römisch-Germanischen Zentralmuseums Mainz 54/1 pp. 6–8, pp. 16–17 text 5, and p. 18 nos. 5–7, and fig. 23, fig. 24 top right, and fig. 32.1 (exs. 1–2, photo; copy, edition, study, provenance)
1999 Damerji, Gräber pp. 6–8, 38 and 46, and figs. 24 (top right) and 32 (top) (exs . 1–2, photo, study, provenance)
1999 Kamil in Damerji, Gräber pp. 13 and 16–18 nos. 5–7 (exs. 1–3, copy, edition)
2000 Hussein and Suleiman, Nimrud pp. 104, 106 and 111, and Pic. 38, 41, and 58 (ex. 1, photo [label states IM 105595]; exs. 2–3, photo; exs. 1–3, study)
2001 J. and D. Oates, Nimrud pp. 83 and 221, and pls. 8a and 8b (exs. 1–2, photo; exs. 1, 3, translation, study)
2002 Achenbach, Biblische Notizen 113 pp. 29–38, esp. 30 (edition, study)
2002 Younger, VT 52/2 pp. 207–218, esp. 216–218 (translation, study)
2004 Dalley, JSOT 28 pp. 395–396 (study)
2007 Galter, Journal for Semitics 16/3 pp. 648–650 (exs. 1, 3, edition, study)
2008 Al-Rawi, New Light on Nimrud pp. 137–138 nos. 21 and 23–24 (exs. 1–3, copy, edition, study)
2008 Collon, New Light on Nimrud pp. 117–118, fig. 14u top right (ex. 2, photo; exs. 1–2, study) and pl. IVa top left (ex. 1, photo)
2008 Dalley, New Light on Nimrud pp. 171–175 (study)
2008 Niederreiter, Iraq 70 p. 82 II.a.2 and 3 (exs. 1 and 3, edition, study)
2016 Hussein, Nimrud: Queens' Tombs pp. 14, 16, 23, 70, 86, and 105, and pls. 32, 40d, 42a, and 43c (exs. 1–3, photo, study, provenance; ex. 1, translation)

TEXT

1) *šá* ^f^*a-ta-li-a* MUNUS.É.GAL *šá* ^m^MAN-GIN MAN KUR AŠ

1) (Property) of Atalia, queen of Sargon (II), king of Assyria.

---

1 Ex. 3 has ^f^*a-tal-ia-a* for ^f^*a-ta-li-ia-a*. S. Parpola (SAAB 2/2 [1988] pp. 73–76) argues that the reading of MUNUS.É.GAL is *issi ekalli* > *sēgallu*; cf. the discussion in Borger, MZ pp. 346–348. The translation of this term, which literally means "palace woman," as "queen" is a matter of some scholarly discussion; it is translated as "queen" in Tadmor and Yamada, RINAP 1 pp. 164–167 Tiglath-pileser III nos. 2003–2005 and pp. 187–188 Shalmaneser V nos. 2001–2002 and as "wife" in Leichty, RINAP 4 pp. 313–323 nos. 2001–2009.

2002

An inscription of Sîn-aḫu-uṣur, a brother of Sargon II, is found upon three stone pavement slabs from doorways in Residence L (or Palace L) in the citadel at Khorsabad; he is also the owner of an bronze macehead (text no. 2003). Residence L was the second largest building in the citadel, exceeded in size only by Sargon's palace. The inscription on the paving slabs identifies the residence as belonging to the grand vizier (*sukkalmaḫḫu*) Sîn-aḫu-uṣur. A Sîn-aḫu-uṣur is mentioned in the eighth campaign of Sargon II (text no. 65 line 132) and it is quite likely that that individual is to be identified with the king's brother.

CATALOGUE

Ex.	Museum Number	Excavation Number	Photograph Number	Provenance	OIP 40	Dimensions (cm)	Lines Preserved	cpn
1	IM 60976	DŠ 1315	OI ph 24578	Khorsabad, Residence L, doorway between Rooms 119 and 116	p. 104 no. 2C; pl. 36A	ca. 10×7 m	1–7	c
2	A 17597	DŠ 1314	OI ph 29634, 31081	Khorsabad, Residence L, doorway between Room 116 and Court 117	p. 104 no. 2B; pls. 36B and 66	ca. 2×3 m	1–7	p
3	—	DŠ 1313	OI ph 24576	Khorsabad, Residence L, doorway between Forecourt 144 and Room 119	p. 104 no. 2A; pl. 36C	—	1–7	p

COMMENTARY

The findspots of the exemplars are indicated on Loud and Altman, Khorsabad 2 pl. 72. Ex. 3 was left in situ and, according to the excavator, its inscription is "barely legible" (Khorsabad 2 p. 70). Thus, the transliteration for this exemplar presented in the score and made from a published photo is at times tentative. Each inscription is on seven lines and written across the middle of the slab. "The areas above and below the inscription are entirely filled with the usual daisy-like rosettes, each in its individual square" (Khorsabad 2 p. 48). The line arrangement and master line are based upon ex. 1.

In their translations of this inscription, T. Jacobsen (in Loud and Altman, Khorsabad 2 p. 104) and B. Meissner (ZDMG 98 [1944] p. 38) assume that the subject of the verbs in lines 4–6 ("completely constructed," "invited," and "offered") is Sîn-aḫu-uṣur, while A. Fuchs assumes it is Sargon. The latter view is supported by passages similar to lines 4b–6a on other paving stones from Khorsabad that clearly refer to Sargon (text no. 12 lines 34–37 and text no. 13 lines 123–126).

For information on Sîn-aḫu-uṣur, see Mattila, PNA 3/1 p. 1128 sub Sīn-aḫu-uṣur 1; Niederreiter, RA 99 (2005) pp. 57–76; and May, BiOr 74 (2017) pp. 491–528. For 707 or 706 as the suggested date of this inscription, see May, Iconoclasm p. 199 n. 41.

BIBLIOGRAPHY

1936 Frankfort, OIC 20 pp. 101 and 103 fig. 81 (ex. 1, photo)
1938 Loud and Altman, Khorsabad 2 pp. 48, 70, 96 nos. 11–13, and 104 no. 2, and pls. 36A–C and 66 (exs. 1–3, photo, edition [by Jacobsen], provenance; ex. 1, copy)
1944 Meissner, ZDMG 98 pp. 37–38 (ex. 1, edition)
1976 Basmachi, Treasures p. 239 (ex. 1, study)
1994 Fuchs, Khorsabad pp. 285 and 371 no. 3.4 (exs. 1–3, edition)
2008 Niederreiter, Iraq 70 p. 64 and n. 45 (study)
2011–12 May, SAAB 19 p. 162 (edition)
2012 May, Iconoclasm pp. 199–202 (edition, study)
2017 May, BiOr 74 pp. 498–499 (edition)

TEXT

1) ^{md}EN.ZU-ŠEŠ-*ú-ṣur* LÚ.SUKKAL.MAḪ *ta-lim* ^{m}MAN-GIN MAN *kiš-šat*
2) MAN KUR *aš-šur*.KI GÌR.NÍTA KÁ.DINGIR.RA.KI MAN KUR EME.GI$_7$ *u* URI.KI
3) ⸢*mi*⸣*-gir* DINGIR.MEŠ GAL.MEŠ É *šá-a-šú* TA UŠ$_8$*-šú* EN *gaba-dib-bi-šú*
4) *ir-ṣi-ip ú-šak-lil* DINGIR.MEŠ GAL.MEŠ *a-ši-bu-ut*
5) KUR *aš-šur*.KI *ù* URU *šá-a-šú ina qer-bi-šú iq-re-ma* UDU.SISKUR.MEŠ
6) KÙ.MEŠ *ma-ḫar-šú-un iq-qí ina ku-un lìb-bi-šú-nu* KÙ ^{m}MAN-GIN
7) *ik-tar-ra-bu-ma šá* ^{md}30-PAP-PAP ŠEŠ *ta-lim-me-šú iq-bu-u šá ṭa-bu-uš*

1–7) Sîn-aḫu-uṣur, grand vizier (and) *favorite (brother)* of Sargon (II), king of the world, king of Assyria, governor of Babylon, king of the land of Sumer and Akkad, favorite of the great gods, completely constructed this house from its foundations to its crenellations. (5) He invited the great gods who dwell in Assyria and in this city (to come) inside it, and he offered before them pure sacrifices. In their steadfast, pure hearts they continually blessed Sargon and spoke that which is good concerning Sîn-aḫu-uṣur, his *favorite* brother.

2003

During his excavations at Khorsabad, V. Place found a bronze macehead that had the heads of four lions on its top (see Figure 31 below). The object has two one-line inscriptions engraved on it; the top one connects the object to the palace of Sargon and the lower one states that it belonged to Sîn-aḫu-uṣur, the grand vizier (*sukkallu rabû*). Sîn-aḫu-uṣur was the brother of Sargon II and the occupant of Residence L at Khorsabad; see text no. 2002, where he is given the title *sukkalmaḫḫu* and said to be Sargon's *favorite brother* (*ta-lim* ^{m}MAN-GIN). The first inscription (inscription A below) could have been presented earlier with those of Sargon from Khorsabad and is in fact cited there as text no. 62; however, it has been thought best to edit both inscriptions on the macehead here.

2002 line 1 This text provides the only attestation of the title *sukkalmaḫḫu* in the Neo-Assyrian period. Since Sîn-aḫu-uṣur is also called *sukkallu rabû* in text no. 2003, H. Baker has suggested that the two titles were interchangeable (PNA 4/1 p. 135). Lines 1 and 7: A. Bartelmus argues that *talīmu*, which is tentatively translated here as *favorite (brother)* and *favorite*, was "the official designation of the highest possible rank among the king's relatives, but obviously of lower position than the king himself" (SAAB 16 [2007] pp. 287–302, esp. p. 299), while N. May suggests that Neo-Assyrian scribes gave it the meaning "'somewhat special' brother" when referring to Assyrian royal siblings (SAAB 19 [2011–12] pp. 153–174, esp. p. 168).

2002 line 7 The line arrangement is different to the master line in ex. 3, with the last line of the exemplar beginning with ⸢GAL$^{?}$ LU$^{?}$ *ša* ^{md}⸣EN.ZU-ŠEŠ-⸢*ú-ṣur*⸣ and the end of the previous line of the exemplar appearing to end with ⸢*ik-tar*$^{?}$⸣*-x-*⸢*bu-ma*⸣. The identification of the first two signs as GAL and LU seems fairly clear, but their meaning in the context (*qal-lu*, "slave"?) is not.

CATALOGUE

Museum Number	Registration Number	Provenance	Dimensions (cm)	cpn
AO 21368	Nap. III 3102	Khorsabad, Palace, corner of Room 18	8.3×3.6	c

COMMENTARY

This macehead was found together with fifty-three other bronze maceheads in one of the corners of Room 18 of Sargon's palace (Place, Ninive et l'Assyrie 1 p. 65; Niederreiter, RA 99 [2005] pp. 57–58). The inscriptions run around the macehead, with the two lines on different bands of the object; inscription A is on the upper band and inscription B on the lower band. Just before the beginning of inscription B a dromedary and an omega-like symbol are incised on the macehead. These are also found on two stamp seal impressions from Kalḫu, which has led Niederreiter to identify Sîn-aḫu-uṣur as the owner of the seal that made those impressions (Iraq 70 [2008] pp. 62–65 and RA 99 [2005] pp. 66–69). N. May (SAAB 19 [2011–12] pp. 168–170) has argued that the dromedary and omega are "Assyrian hieroglyphs," with omega standing for *aḫu*, "brother," and dromedary for *talīmu* (with regard to the meaning of this word, see the on-page note to text no. 2002 line 1). For another opinion about their interpretation, see Niederreiter, Iraq 70 [2008] pp. 62–65.

BIBLIOGRAPHY

1867 Place, Ninive et l'Assyrie 1 pp. 65–66; and 3 pl. 74 no. 11 (drawing, provenance)
1884 Perrot and Chipiez, Histoire de l'art 2 p. 726 fig. 385 (drawing)
1918 Pillet, Khorsabad p. 86 no. 13 (study?)
1924 Pottier, Antiquités assyriennes p. 138 no. 156 (study)
1951 Cocquerillat, RA 45 p. 23 no. 28 (study)
1969 Calmeyer, Datierbare Bronzen p. 94 no. 45o (study)
1988 Albenda, BASOR 271 p. 17 fig. 25 (photo)
1988 Curtis, Bronzeworking Centres p. 87 (study)
2005 Niederreiter, RA 99 pp. 57–61 (copy, edition, study)
2008 Niederreiter, Iraq 70 pp. 62–65 and 85 III.a.1 (edition, study)
2011–12 May, SAAB 19 pp. 168–170 (drawing, edition, study)
2012 May, Iconoclasm pp. 201–202 (edition)
2014 Niederreiter, CRRA 52 pp. 582, 588, 593–595, 597, and 600 Kh2 (drawing, copy, translation, study)
2015 May, SAAB 21 p. 90 (edition)
2017 May, BiOr 74 pp. 497–498 (drawing, edition)

TEXT

Inscription A

1) É.GAL ^{m}MAN-GIN MAN ŠÚ MAN AŠ

Inscription B

1) *šá* ^{m}30-PAP-PAP SUKKAL GAL-*u*

Inscription A

Inscription A 1) Palace of Sargon, king of the world, king of Assyria.

Inscription B

Inscription B 1) (Property) of Sîn-aḫu-uṣur, the grand vizier.

Figure 31. AO 21368 (text nos. 62 and 2003), a bronze macehead found in the palace at Khorsabad with inscriptions of Sargon and his brother Sîn-aḫu-uṣur. Photo courtesy of A. Thomas. © Musée du Louvre.

2004

A stamp seal impression found at Khorsabad in 1929 bears a brief Aramaic inscription of one of Sargon's eunuchs, Pān-Aššur-lāmur. It is not known if he is to be identified with the homonymous author of two poorly preserved letters to Sargon II (Parpola, SAA 1 nos. 156 and 157 [=Harper, ABL no. 1064 and CT 53 no. 525]). Although the inscription is in the Aramaic script and language, it has been thought useful to include the text in this volume.

CATALOGUE

Museum Number	Excavation Number	Photograph Number	Provenance	Dimensions (cm)	cpn
A 7036	DŠ 51	OI P.17194 (negative N.9916)	Khorsabad, Palace, Room 12	2.0×1.5	n

COMMENTARY

The seal impression was found in 1929. Information on the museum, excavation, and photograph numbers and on the measurements was kindly supplied by J. Larson. The edition presented below follows that of S. Kaufman (JAOS 104 [1984] p. 94), who examined the original seal impression in the Oriental Institute (Chicago). The transliteration of the inscription by P. Bordreuil (in Caubet, Khorsabad p. 261) restores "y" at the end of the second line, rather than at the beginning of the third line, but in his commentary (ibid. p. 264), Bordreuil appears to refer to restoring it at the beginning of the last line (referred to as "ligne 4"). K. Watanabe, K. Åkerman, and most others do not restore "y" in their editions (see bibliography below).

BIBLIOGRAPHY

1932 Sprengling, AJSL 49/1 pp. 53–55 (photo, study)
1962 Greenfield, JAOS 82 p. 297 (edition)
1971 Vattioni, Augustinianum 11/1 p. 61 no. 123 (transliteration, study)
1982 Tadmor, CRRA 25 pp. 450 and 461–462 n. 23 (edition [with collations by Kaufman])
1983 Kaufman in Sokoloff, Arameans pp. 53–54 (edition)
1983 Millard, Iraq 45 pp. 103–104 (study)
1984 Kaufman, JAOS 104 p. 94 (edition)
1986 Fales, Epigraphs pp. 138–139 and cf. pp. 132–134 (edition)
1989 Kaufman, JAOS 109 p. 97 n. 1 (edition)
1990 Fadhil, Bagh. Mitt. 21 p. 481 (edition)
1992 Fitzmyer and Kaufman, Aramaic Bibliography 1 pp. 184–185 no. 216SI (study)
1992 Herbordt, SAAS 1 p. 170 and pl. 27 no. 3 Ḫorsābād 1 (photo, edition, study)
1992 Watanabe, Bagh. Mitt. 23 p. 366 no. 4.1.8 (edition)
1993 Watanabe, Orient 29 pp. 116–117 and 134 no. 6.7 (photo, edition)
1995 Bordreuil in Caubet, Khorsabad pp. 261–269 (photo, edition, study, provenance; museum no. cited erroneously as A 7038)
2002 Åkerman, PNA 3/1 p. 984 sub Pān-Aššūr-lāmur 4 (edition)

TEXT

1) *⸢l⸣pn'sr*
2) *[l]mr srs z*
3) *[y] srgn*

1–3) (Property) of Pān-Aššur-[lā]mur, eunuch o[f] Sargon (II).

2005

A corner fragment of an alabaster coffer found at Aššur records a dedication to the god Adad by Ṭāb-šār-Aššur, the treasurer (*masennu*). Ṭāb-šār-Aššur served as eponym in 717 and is mentioned in text no. 65 line 427, as well as in several letters (see in particular, Parpola, SAA 1 nos. 41–74 and Perroudon, PNA 3/2 pp. 1344–1346 sub Ṭāb-šār-Aššūr 1).

CATALOGUE

Museum Number	Excavation Number	Photograph Number	Provenance	Dimensions (cm)	cpn
VA Ass 4512	Ass 14703	Ass 4181; VAN 1237a	Aššur, gC9I (investigation trench 9I)	10.0×16.0×8.0	c

BIBLIOGRAPHY

1918 Kinscherf, Inschriftbruchstücke no. 82 (copy, edition, study)
1997 Pedersén, Katalog p. 22 (study)
2001 Schwemer, Wettergottgestalten pp. 607–608 (edition)
2011 Perroudon, PNA 3/2 pp. 1344–1346, esp. p. 1345 sub Ṭāb-šār-Aššūr 1.b (study)

TEXT

1) *a**-*na* ^{d}IŠKUR ⸢GÚ.GAL⸣ [AN-*e* (*u*)]
2) KI-*tim* NUN *x* [*x* (*x*)]
3) ^{m}DÙG-IM-*aš-šur* LÚ.⸢AGRIG⸣
4) *ana* TI ZI.MEŠ-*šú* ⸢BA⸣-[*ìš*]

1–4) To the god Adad, the canal inspec[tor of heaven (and)] netherworld, prince [...]: Ṭāb-šār-Aššur, the trea[surer], pre[sented (this)] for the sake of ensuring his good health.

2006

A clay sealing that was discovered at Nimrud (ancient Kalḫu) in 1956 and is preserved in the Metropolitan Museum of Art in New York bears impressions of a stamp seal and a cylinder seal. The cylinder seal impression has a short inscription of Aššur-bāni, a governor of Kalḫu who served as eponym in 713 and who wrote several letters to the king and one to the vizier (see Whiting, PNA 1/1 pp. 158–159 sub Aššūr-bāni 5 and Parpola, SAA 1 nos. 111–123). The inscription has been collated from the published photos.

CATALOGUE

Museum Number	Excavation Number	Provenance	Dimensions (cm)	cpn
MMA 57.27.22	ND 5486	Nimrud, in an ash deposit on the floor of Room 11 (an oil storeroom) of the Ninurta temple	4.29×7.01×10.8	p

2005 line 1 *a**: The text has DIŠ. Or read *ana* <<*na*>> .
2005 line 2 Perhaps ⸢*bé*⸣-[*lí-šú*] or ⸢EN?⸣-[*šú*], "[his] l[ord]," at the end of the line; D. Schwemer (Wettergottgestalten p. 607 n. 4906) suggests possibly ⸢*dan*⸣-[*ni*], ⸢*ez*⸣-[*zi*], ⸢*gaš*⸣-[*ri*], or ⸢*ṣi*⸣-[*ri*], "mi[ghty]," "fi[erce]," or "po[werful]."
2005 line 3 If D. Schwemer is correct that there is not sufficient room to restore LÚ.⸢AGRIG⸣ [GAL-*u*/*ú*] (Wettergottgestalten p. 608 n. 4907), the inscription was presumably composed before Ṭāb-šār-Aššur was promoted to chief treasurer.
2005 line 4 The restoration follows text no. 2010 line 5.

BIBLIOGRAPHY

1957 Mallowan, Iraq 19 p. 20 (study, provenance)
1962 Parker, Iraq 24 pp. 26 and 31, and pl. XII fig. 4 (photo, transliteration, study)
1966 Mallowan, Nimrud 1 p. 91 (provenance)
1985 Deller, Bagh. Mitt. 16 p. 330 (edition)
1992 Herbordt, SAAS 1 pp. 203–204 Nimrūd 128–129 and pl. 21 no. 5 (photo, edition, study)
1992 Watanabe, Bagh. Mitt. 23 p. 367 no. 4.2.2 (edition; cited erroneously as ND 5484)
1993 Watanabe, Orient 29 pp. 113 and 133 no. 5.4 (photo, edition; cited erroneously as ND 5484)
1998 Whiting, PNA 1/1 p. 158 sub Aššūr-bāni 5 (transliteration)
2008 Niederreiter, Iraq 70 pp. 67–68 and fig. 13 (photo, edition, study)

TEXT

1) NA$_4$.KIŠIB ^{m}*aš-šur-ba-ni*
2) LÚ.GAR.KUR URU.*kal-ḫu*

1–2) Seal of Aššur-bāni, governor of the city Kalḫu.

2007

A cylinder seal of agate bears a short inscription of Nabû-uṣalla, the governor of the city Tamnūnu and eunuch of Sargon. As noted by W.G. Lambert and C.E. Watanabe, it is likely that the owner of the seal is to be identified with one or more individuals by this name who either sent, or are mentioned in, a few letters of the period (Parpola, SAA 1 nos. 177 and 237; Lanfranchi and Parpola, SAA 5 no. 104; Luukko, SAA 19 no. 183; see Luppert-Barnard, PNA 2/2 p. 900 sub Nabû-uṣalla 2 and 3).

CATALOGUE

Source	Provenance	Dimensions (cm)	cpn
Watanabe, Bagh. Mitt. 23 (1992) pp. 357–369 and pls. 70–71	—	4.83×2.32	p

COMMENTARY

The cylinder seal is in a private collection in Japan but was on display in the Ancient Orient Museum (Tokyo) from July 20 until September 1, 1991 with the exhibition number II-1-19. The inscription is incised so that when impressed it appears in mirror writing. The inscription was collated from the published photograph.

2006 line 1 B. Parker, K. Deller, S. Herbordt, and K. Watanabe read the final sign of the personal name as *-an*, but, as noted by R. Whiting, and confirmed by a collation by I. Spar, it is in fact *-ni*.

BIBLIOGRAPHY

1991 Matsushima in Ishida, Insho-no-sekai p. 17 (photo, translation [in Japanese])
1991 Lambert, NABU 1991 pp. 58–59 no. 86 (edition)
1992 Watanabe, Bagh. Mitt. 23 pp. 357–369 and pls. 70–71 (photo, copy, edition, study)
1993 Watanabe, Orient 29 pp. 113–114 and 133 no. 5.5 (copy, edition)
2001 Luppert-Barnard, PNA 2/2 p. 900 sub Nabû-uṣalla 2 (study)
2015 Niederreiter, SAAB 21 pp. 128 and 147–148 no. D (photo, edition)

TEXT

1) NA_4.KIŠIB [md]MUATI-*ú-ṣal-la*
2) LÚ.GAR.KUR* URU.*tam-nu-na*
3) LÚ.SAG *šá* [m]MAN-GI.NA
4) MAN KUR [d]*aš-šur*

1–4) Seal of Nabû-uṣalla, governor of the city Tamnūnu (and) eunuch of Sargon (II), king of Assyria.

2008

A broken stone axe head from Tell Haddad (ancient Mê-Turnat) bears an inscription of an individual who was one of Sargon's eunuchs and who was also likely governor of Na'iri. The inscription records the dedication of the axe head to the god Nergal of the temple Ešaḫula. A brick inscription from the time of Ashurbanipal deals with work on this temple (Frame, RIMB 2 p. 229 B.6.32.22). A fragment of a clay cylinder with an inscription of Sargon II was also found at Tell Haddad (text no. 129) and note also text no. 2009.

CATALOGUE

Museum Number	Excavation Number	Provenance	Dimensions (cm)	cpn
IM 95520	Haddad 581	Tell Haddad, Neo-Assyrian temple (area 3, level 1)	9×6.4×1.7	p

COMMENTARY

According to E. Valtz, this fragmentary stone axe head is made of "bluish marble" and is trapezoidal in shape and triangular in section. Lines 1–8 are found on the upper surface of the object and line 9 on the trailing edge. The edition is based upon the published photograph and copy, with help from F.N.H. Al-Rawi's edition that also made use of a paper squeeze of the inscription. Restorations are based on those proposed by Al-Rawi; as noted by him, for lines 5 and 6, see Leichty, RINAP 4 p. 20 no. 1 iv 38 and cf. King, BBSt no. 36 iv 15–19 respectively.

The first published reference to this inscription assigned it to the Assyrian king Shalmaneser III (Mancini, Land Between Two Rivers p. 418) and thus this inscription was originally to appear in Grayson, RIMA 3. The edition was removed from that volume before publication (see ibid. p. 155 A.0.102.98).

2007 line 2 KUR*: The text has MAN. For the writing of the place name Tamnūnu (as URU.*tam-nu-na* or URU.*tama-nu-na*) and a possible location east of the Tigris opposite Eski Mosul, see Bagg, Rép. Géogr. 7/2-2 pp. 585–587.

BIBLIOGRAPHY

1985 Valtz, Land Between Two Rivers pp. 320 and 418 no. 211 (photo, study [erroneously given the number IM 95920])

1994 Al-Rawi, Iraq 56 pp. 35–37 no. 2 and fig. 3 no. 2 (copy, edition)

TEXT

1) [*ana* ^{d}U.GUR] SAG DINGIR.DINGIR *la a-dir* GIŠ.TUKUL *šá-aš-me*
2) [... *kaš*]*-kaš* DINGIR.DINGIR *la* ŠU ḪUL.ME
3) [*a-šib é-šà*]-⸢*ḫúl*⸣ *šá qé-reb* URU.*me-tur*$_{7}$*-ni* EN GAL EN-*šú*

4) [^{m}... GAR$^{?}$] ⸢KUR⸣.*na-i-ri* LÚ.SAG ^{m}MAN-GIN MAN KUR AŠ
5) [*ina tak-kas* NA$_{4}$.ZA].⸢GÌN⸣ *ḫi-ip* KUR-*šú ina ši*-pir*
6) [^{d}*nin-zadim u* ^{d}*nin-kur*]*-ra* ⸢DÙ⸣-*ma ana* TIN ZI.ME-*šú*
7) [GÍD.(DA$^{?}$) UD.MEŠ-*šú*$^{?}$] DÙG ŠÀ-*šú* KUR ḪUL.ME-*šú*
8) [NU/*la* GÁL-*e*] TU.RA *la ga-me-lu*
9) [*ù šu*]*-lu-uṣ* ŠÀ-*šú* GIN

1–3) [For the god Nergal], foremost of the gods, who does not fear (any) battle weapon, [... most pow]erful of the gods, who does not pardon those who are evil, [who dwells in Ešaḫ]ul ("House of the Happy Heart") that is inside the city Mēturna (Mê-Turnat), the great lord, his lord:

4–9) [PN, *governor* of the l]and Na'iri (and) eunuch of Sargon (II), king of Assyria, made (this object) by the craft [of the gods Ninzadim and Ninku]ra [out of a block of lapis-l]azuli hewn from its mountain (quarry) and he set (it) up for the sake of ensuring his good health, [*prolonging his days*], his happiness, capturing his enemies, [the absence] of relentless illness, [and m]aking his heart joyful.

2009

A small clay barrel cylinder found on the surface of Tell Baradān in 1977 and now in the Iraq Museum describes the construction of the wall of the city Sirara (a literary rendering for Mê-turnat), apparently by Nabû-bēlu-ka''in, the governor of the city Arrapḫa, and following the wishes of Sargon.

CATALOGUE

Museum Number	Provenance	Dimensions (cm)	cpn
IM —	Tell Baradān, surface	—	n

2008 line 5 *ši**: The sign appears to be U-AŠ.

COMMENTARY

Tell Baradān is located in the Diyala region about 500 meters from Tell Haddad. Ancient Mê-Turnat is either Tell Haddad or Tell Baradān, or possibly both since they are located close to each other. No information on the exact provenance of the piece, its excavation number, or its current museum number is known. The edition of the piece is based upon the copy and edition published by Kessler in AfO 50 (2003–04) pp. 105–110.

For Neo-Assyrian references to Mê-Turnat and its location, see Bagg, Rép. Géogr. 7/2-2 pp. 426–427, and note also p. 534 sub Sirara 2.

K. Kessler has argued that this inscription is more likely one of the governor of Arrapḫa Nabû-bēlu-ka''in (mentioned in line 15′) than that of Sargon because of the Babylonian and, in places, Elamite, character of the text, as well as because of the various scribal errors and graphic peculiarities (AfO 50 [2003–04] p. 107); however, as noted by Kessler, the construction of the city wall appears to have been in accordance with the will of Sargon (lines 14′–15′a). Nabû-bēlu-ka''in is known to have been an important Assyrian official active in the Diyala region and to have been governor of Kār-Šarrukīn (formerly known as Ḫarḫar, which Sargon had renamed) in western Iran before becoming governor of Arrapḫa around 710 or 709. (For information on Nabû-bēlu-ka''in, see Mattila, PNA 2/2 pp. 815–817 sub Nabû-bēlu-ka''in 1 and Postgate and Mattila, Studies Grayson pp. 251–253, esp. n. 50.)

BIBLIOGRAPHY

2003–04 Kessler, AfO 50 pp. 105–110 (copy, edition, study)

TEXT

Lacuna

1′) *e*-⸢*nu*$^{?}$⸣-[*ma*$^{?}$ ...]

2′) *pa-ti-iq* ⸢*nab*$^{?}$⸣-[*ni-ti*$^{?}$ ...]

3′) DINGIR *muš-ta-lum šá la* ⸢*i*⸣-[*nen-nu-ú qí-bi-su*]

4′) ^{d}AMAR.UTU *ti-iz-qa-ru šá qí-bi-su* [...]

5′) *še-mu-ú tés-li-ti pa-ri-is* EŠ.BAR *ṣa-bi-ti* [*x x* (*x x x*)]

6′) *na-din is-qu* NIDBA.MEŠ *a-na* DINGIR.MEŠ *šu-ut* [AN-*e u* KI-*tim*]

7′) *ma-lik ṣal-mat* SAG.DU *mu-ki*-⸢*in*⸣ GIDRU LÚ.MEŠ [*x x* (*x x x*)]

8′) *kar-áš nik-la-a-ti a-ḫi-iz rid-di šá*-⸢*qu*⸣-*ú* [DINGIR.MEŠ$^{?}$]

9′) *ina* AN-*e u* KI-*tim šup-lu-ḫa-at* EN-*lu-ú-su* ⸢*šur*⸣-*ba-ti* [*x x* (*x x x*)]

10′) IGI.GÁL *it-peš ma-lik* ^{d}*í-gì-gì* DINGIR *réme-nu-ú šá nap-lu-su* [*x x* (*x x x*)]

11′) LUGAL-GI.NA LUGAL KUR *aš-šur*.KI LUGAL ŠÚ NUN-*ú ti-ri-iṣ* [ŠU.(II)-*šú*]

12′) *sùk-ka-lu*$^{?}$ *mut*-^{in}*nin-nu-ú pa*-[*líḫ*] DINGIR-*ú-ti-šú ṣir-ti* GÌR.NÍTA ^{d}EN.LÍL ⸢LUGAL⸣ [*x x* (*x x x*)]

13′) NUN-*ú pa-líḫ-šú* BÀD ⸢*sírara*⸣.KI *šá ul*-<*tú*> *u*$_{4}$-*me pa-ni ep-šu-mu* IL$^{?}$-*šú x* [*x x* (*x x x*)]

14′) *a-na e-peš* BÀD *šu-a-ti šá* LUGAL-GI.NA LUGAL

Lacuna

1′–16′) *Wh*[*en* ...] the one who fashions *li*[*ving creatures* ...], the judicious god who[se command] cannot [be altered], the emminent god Marduk, whose command [...], (5′) who hears petition(s), renders decisions, (and) takes [...], who gives share(s) of the (food) offerings to the gods of [heaven and netherworld], the ruler of the black-headed people, who assigns the scepter of men, [...] (who has) a cunning mind, circumspect, high(est) [*among the gods*], (who)se supreme lordship induces awe in heaven and netherworld, [...] (10′) the wise, intelligent one, counselor of the Igīgū gods, the merciful god, whom to look [...], Sargon, king of Assyria, king of the world, the prince, [his (Marduk's)] prot[égé], the pious vizier who rev[eres] his (Marduk's) divine majesty, the governor (appointed) by the god Enlil, the king [...], the prince who reveres him, the (city) wall of Sirara, which had been built from earlier days *and* ... [...] in order to build this wall that Sargon, king of Assyria, king of the world, *had desired* [...], Nabû-bēlu-ka''in, the governor of the city Arrapḫa [...] *t*[*o* ...]

12′ Note the unusual gloss *in* preceding the sign *nin* in *mutninnû/mutnennû*.

13′ Bricks with an inscription of Ashurbanipal were found at Tell Haddad stating that the king had enlarged part of the temple Ešaḫula for the god Nergal, "the lord of Sirara" (Frame, RIMB 2 p. 229 B.6.32.22). For the use of *-mu* for the enclitic particle *-ma*, see the commentary to text no. 125.

KUR *aš-šur*.KI LUGAL ŠÚ ŠÀ-*šú* [...]
15′) *ú*-⌜*ba*?-*lam*? mdMUATI-EN-GI.NA LÚ⌝.GAR KUR URU.*ár-rap-ḫe* x [...]
16′) ⌜*a-na*?⌝ [...]
Lacuna

Lacuna

2010

A stele found at Til-Barsip (modern Tell Ahmar) bears a votive inscription of Aššur-dūr-pāniya, governor of Kār-Shalmaneser, dedicated to the goddess Ištar of Arbela. Til-Barsip had been renamed Kār-Shalmaneser by Shalmaneser III (Grayson, RIMA 3 p. 19 A.0.102.2 ii 34–35). An official by the name of Aššur-dūr-pāniya is attested in several letters (see Parker, PNA 1/1 p. 180 sub Aššūr-dūr-pāniya 1). For the assignment of this inscription to that individual in the reign of Sargon II, see Radner, Bagh. Mitt. 37 (2006) pp. 188–192.

CATALOGUE

Museum Number	Provenance	Dimensions (cm)	cpn
AO 11503	Tell Ahmar, in secondary usage (in a later wall, northeast of the western cemetery, ca. 1 m in depth)	121×82×30	c

COMMENTARY

The stele is made of reddish limestone and was found during the French excavations at Tell Ahmar led by F. Thureau-Dangin. The stele, which is now in the Louvre and said to join AO 16083, has a relief on it depicting the goddess standing on the back of a lion. The inscription is written in Neo-Assyrian script across the upper part of the front of the stele. The edition presented here is based on that published by K. Radner, who examined the original in 2005.

BIBLIOGRAPHY

1936 Thureau-Dangin and Dunand, Til-Barsib pp. 156-157 no. 4 and pl. XIV no. 1 (photo, copy, edition)
1969 Pritchard, ANEP² pp. 177 and 312 no. 522 (photo)
1961 Parrot, Assyria p. 76 fig. 85 (photo)
1982 Börker-Klähn, Bildstelen no. 252 (drawing, study)
1991 Dezsö and Curtis, Iraq 53 pp. 107-108 and pl. 15 (photo of front of stele, transliteration, study)
1976 Seidl, RLA 5/1-2 p. 88 and fig. 3 on page before p. 87 (drawing of image, study of image)
2001 Green and Hausleiter, Studies Haas pp. 156-160 and 168 Abb. 8 no. 9 (photo, study)
2006 Radner, Bagh. Mitt. 37 pp. 185-195 (drawing of relief, edition, study)
2018 Tubb in Brereton, Ashurbanipal p. 134 no. 144 (photo)
2019 Thomas in Blanchard, Royaumes oubliés p. 421 no. 271 (photo, translation, study)

TEXT

1) *ana* ^{d}15 *a-ši-bat* URU.LÍMMU-DINGIR
2) GAŠAN-*šú* ^{m}*aš-šur*-⸢BÀD⸣-IGI-*a* ⸢LÚ.GAR⸣-*nu*
3) ⸢*šá*⸣ URU.*kar*-⸢^{md}SILIM-*ma*⸣-
4) -*nu*-MAŠ *ana* TI ZI.ME-*šú*
5) ⸢BA⸣-*ìš*

1–5) To the goddess Ištar who dwells in the city Arbela, his lady: Aššur-dūr-pāniya, the governor of the city Kār-Shalmaneser, presented (this stele) for the sake of ensuring his good health.

2011

An inscribed basalt stele was found in 2003 at Turlu Höyük (Turkey), ca. 30 km northwest of Carchemish. Over a quarter of the stele (the lower part) is no longer preserved. The stele has the image of a bearded individual carved on it. Since the figure has a horned headdress, is holding a bundle of three lightning bolts in his right hand, and is standing on a (partially preserved) bull, the figure has been identified as the storm god. The back of the stele bears a six-line votive inscription of one Bēl-iddin, who is given no title. The initial publishers of the text suggested that Bēl-iddin is a previously unknown Assyrian prince or high official. While he might be one of the "independent" Assyrian officials and governors from the period ca. 850–740, they thought that he more likely comes from the time of Sargon since (1) we do not know if the area where the stele was found was under Assyrian control in the earlier period, (2) Bēl-iddin does not bear a title, and thus we do not know what authority/function he had there, and (3) the expanded dedicatory formula including GÁ-*ma* is first attested in the time of Sargon II. Thus, although the exact date of the inscription remains uncertain and the position that Bēl-iddin held is unknown, the inscription is tentatively presented here. The inscription is edited from the published photo and copy.

CATALOGUE

Museum Number	Provenance	Dimensions (cm)	cpn
Archaeological Museum of Gaziantep —	Turlu Höyük	105×52×23.5	p

BIBLIOGRAPHY

2006 Balcıoğlu and Mayer, Orientalia NS 75 pp. 177–181 and pls. XII–XIII (photo, copy, edition, study)

TEXT

1) *a-na* dIŠKUR GÚ.GAL
2) AN-*e u* KI-*tim*
3) EN GAL-*u* EN-*šú*
4) mEN-AŠ *ana ba-laṭ*
5) ZI.MEŠ-*šú* NU *an-na-a*
6) GÁ-*ma* BA-*iš*

1–6) To the god Adad, the canal inspector of heaven and netherworld, the great lord, his lord: Bēl-iddin set up and presented this stele for the sake of ensuring his good health.

6 As noted by B. Balcıoğlu and W. Mayer (Orientalia NS 75 [2006] p. 180), GÁ is used for the verb *šakānu* in royal votive inscriptions from the Sargonid period in texts of Sargon II (text no. 49 line 1), Sennacherib's wife Zakūtu/Naqi'a (Leichty, RINAP 4 p. 319 no. 2005 line 8), and a wife of Ashurbanipal (Johns, ADD no. 644 line 8), as well as in a text on a fragment of a circular disk of banded agate, whose date is unknown (Gurney in Kraabel, Journal of Jewish Studies 30 [1979] pp. 56–58).

Minor Variants and Comments

Text No. 7

1.4 omits ^{m} in ^{m}LUGAL-GI.NA. 1.3 GAL-ú for GAL. 1.4–5 ⌜LUGAL⌝ for the first MAN. 1.5 ⌜LUGAL⌝ for the second MAN. 2.5 LUGAL for MAN. 2.5 Botta's copy omits KUR without any indication of damage; but the squeeze suggests [KUR]. 2.3 EME.GI$_{7}$ for šu-me-ri. 3.5 Botta's copy erroneously omits MEŠ after GAL; this was likely miscopied one line lower, after la. 4.4 LUGAL-ú-tu for šar-⌜ru⌝-ut. 4.5 Botta's copy has a MEŠ after la, but this was likely an error since the MEŠ after GAL in the previous line has been erroneously omitted by Botta. 4.3–4 ú-šat-li-mu-in-ni-[ma] for ú-šat-li-mu-ni-ma. 6.3–4 bár-sípa.KI and bár-⌜sípa⌝.[KI] respectively for bár-sipa.KI. 7.1 omits šú in ḫi-bil-ta-šú-nu. 8.4–5 ⌜ÚRI*⌝(copy: ⌜ŠEŠ†⌝.MURUB$_{4}$).KI and ⌜ÚRI*(copy: ŠEŠ.⌜MURUB$_{4}$⌝).KI⌝ respectively for ÚRI.KI. 8.4 UNUG*(copy: MURUB$_{4}$).⌜KI⌝ for UNUG.KI. 9.5 ARARMA*(copy and squeeze: UD.MURUB$_{4}$).KI for ARAMA.KI. 9 kul-aba$_{4}$.KI: ex. 1 omits KI; and exs. 4–5 have kul-⌜aba$_{4}$*⌝(copy: ⌜MURUB$_{4}$⌝).KI and kul-aba$_{4}$*(copy and squeeze: MURUB$_{4}$).KI resepctivley.

10.4–5 ša for šá. 12.4–5 i-na for ina. 12.4–5 ŠÀ-šú-nu for lìb-bi-šú-nu. 13.4–5 i-[na] and i-na resepctively for the first ina. 13.1 Winckler's copy omits ma in ib-ši-ma. 13.4–5 i-na for the second ina. 13.4 MURUB$_{4}$*(copy: UNUG) for MURUB$_{4}$. 13.3–5 ù for u. 13.4–5 mu-né-eḫ-ḫu for mu-né-ḫu. 14.5 [ḫa]-am-ma-a-mi for ḫa-am-ma-mi. 14.4 ša for šá. 15.4–5 ú-pat-ti-i-ma and ú†-pat-ti-⌜i⌝-[ma] respectively for ú-pa-ti-ma. 16.3–5 ù for u. 16 da-na-ni: ex. 3 has ⌜da⌝-na-a-ni; and exs. 4–5 have da-na-a-ni. 16.3–4 ša for šá. 16 MURUB$_{4}$: exs. 3–4 have qa-bal; and ex. 5 has [qa]-⌜bal⌝. 17.3–4 omit ú in ru-qu-ú-ti. 18.4 šá for the first ša. 18 KUR.el-li-pí: ex. 3 has KUR.el-li-pi; ex. 4 has KUR.[el]-⌜li⌝-pi; and ex. 5 has [KUR].el†-li-pi. 18.5 ša for šá. 18.5 ÍD.IDIGNA*(copy: BAR-GÚ) for ÍD.IDIGNA. 19.3–4 [LÚ].⌜li⌝-i'-it-ta-a-a and LÚ.li-i'-it-ta-[a-a] respectively for LÚ.li-i'-ta-a-a. 19.4–5 LÚ.gam-bu†-lum and [LÚ.gam-bu]-⌜lum†⌝ respectively for LÚ.gam-bu-lu.

21.4–5 ⌜ù†⌝ and ù respectively for u. 21.4–5 KUR.É-^{m}da-ku-ri and [KUR].É-da†-ku-ri respectively for KUR.É-^{m}dak-ku-ri. 21.3 omits ^{m} in KUR.É-^{m}sa-'a-al-la. 21.5 u in ba-šu-u not on Botta's copy but visible on squeeze. 23.4 ša for šá. 23.4–5 i-na for ina. 23.4–5 taḫ-ta-a-šú and ⌜taḫ⌝-ta-a-šú respectively for taḫ-ta-šú. 24.4–5 i-na and i-⌜na⌝ respectively for ina. 24 si-it-tu-ti: ex. 3 has si-it-tu-te; ex. 4 has ⌜si⌝-[it-tu]-⌜te⌝; and ex. 5 has si-⌜it⌝-tu-te. 24.4–5 maḫ-ri-i for maḫ-re-e. 25.3–5 LUGAL for MAN. 25.3, 5 URU.⌜ḫa⌝-zi-te and URU.[ḫa]-zi-te respectively for URU.ḫa-zi-ti. 25.3, 5 ⌜LÚ.tur-ta⌝-nu and [LÚ.tur$^{?}$]-ta-nu respectively for LÚ.tar-tan-nu. 27 ma-da-at-tu: ex. 3 has mad-da-⌜at-tum⌝; ex. 4 has mad-da-[at-tum$^{?}$]; and ex. 5 has mad-[da]-at-tum. 27.5 LUGAL for MAN. 27.3, likely 5 (via spacing) omit a in ^{m}it-'a-am-a-ra. 28.5 ik-lu-u for ik-lu-ú. 28 am-nu-šu: exs. 3, 5 have am-nu-šú; and ex. 4 has ⌜am⌝-nu-šú. 29 MAN-ti-šú: exs. 3, 5 have LUGAL-ti-šú; and ex. 4 has ⌜LUGAL*⌝(copy: AD [)-[ti-šú]. 29 ANŠE.pa-re-e: exs. 3, 5 have ANŠE.KUNGA.MEŠ; and ex. 4 has ANŠE.⌜KUNGA⌝.MEŠ. 29.3, possibly 4 (via spacing), 5 omit at in man-da-at-ti-šú. 29.4 adds an extraneous AŠ sign before maḫ-ri-ti.

30 ša is based on exs. 3 and 5. Winckler's copy has šá; this is presumably based on the squeeze of ex. 1, which appears to have ⌜šá⌝. 30.3, 5 mì-ṣir for mi-ṣir. 30.3, 5 ú-rap†-pi-šá and ú-⌜rap⌝-pi-šá respectively for ú-rap-piš. 31.3–4 KUR.ur-ar-ṭa-a-a and KUR.ur-ar-ṭa-⌜a⌝-[a] respectively for KUR.URI-a-a. 31.1 spacing would suggest this exemplar had u not ù. 31.3–4 LUGAL and ⌜LUGAL*⌝(copy:] MA [) respectively for MAN. 31.3 ša for šá. 31.3–4 KIN for šip-ri. 31.3–4 ni-šu-tim and ⌜ni⌝-šu-tim respectively for ni-šu-ti. 32.3 al-qa-áš-šu for al-qa-áš-šú. 32.3 omits ut in LÚ.šu-ut. 32.3–4 bíl-tu for GUN. 32.3 man-da-at-tú for ma-da-at-tu. 32.3 ⌜UGU†⌝-šú-un for e-li-šú-un. 33.3 ERIM.MEŠ for ṣa-ab. 33.3 URU.di-maš-qu for URU.di-maš-qa. 33.3 URU.sa-mir-i-na for URU.sa-me-ri-na. 34.3–4 [ta-ḫa]-⌜zu⌝ and ⌜ta⌝-ḫa-zu*(copy: SU) respectively for MÈ. 34.3 ^{d}aš-šur for ^{d}a-šur. 34.3–4 ad-ke-e-ma and ad-⌜ke-e⌝-ma*(copy: GIŠ) respectively for ad-ke-ma. 34.3–4 i-na for ina. 35.3 adds ni after URU.MEŠ. 35.3 omits u in su-lum-mu-u. 35.3–4 add MEŠ after GIŠ.GIGIR. 35 lum of ANŠE.pét-ḫal-lum follows ex. 3. Botta's copy of ex. 1 has ANŠE.pét-AN, possibly for ANŠE.pét-ḫal-⌜lim⌝/⌜lum⌝; Winckler's copy has simply ANŠE.pét-ḫal and the squeeze has ANŠE.pét-[x]. 36.3 ina for i-na. 36.3–4 <lìb>-bi and [lìb]-bi respectively for ŠÀ. 36.3–4 i-na and i-[na] respectively for ina. 36.3 u$_{4}$-mi for u$_{4}$-me. 36.3–4 ar-du and ar*(copy: ŠÚ-RI)-du respectively for ARAD. 38.3 ù for u. 38.3–4 i-[na] and i-na respectively for ina. 38.3–4 EN-šú-nu for EN-šu-nu. 39.3 omits ma in it-ta-kil-ma (via spacing).

40.3 [gap-šá]-a-te for gap-šá-a-ti. 40.1 omits lu in ^{m}ul-lu-su-nu. 40.5 [KUR].ma-⌜na⌝-[a-a] for KUR.man-na-a-a. 41.3 i-na for ina. 41.3 URU.ar†-me-et-ta for URU.ar-me-et. 42.3 ša for šá. 42.3 KUR.ú-a-a-uš for KUR.ú-a-uš. 42.5 KUR$^{?}$-e for KUR-i. 42.3 <2> ME in Monument de Ninive copy; 2 ME in Institut de France copy. 42.3 LUGAL-⌜ti⌝-[šú] for MAN-ti-šú. 43.3 ina ŠU.II for i-na qa-ti. 43.3 adds ni after URU.MEŠ. 43.3 ina for i-na. 44.3 ša for šá. 44.3 na-⌜gi⌝-i in Monument de Ninive copy; na-gi*(copy: RAD)-i in Institut de France copy. 46.3 e-du-ur-ma for e-dúr-ma. 47.5 adds ni after URU.MEŠ. 47.3 šal-lat†-su-un for šal-la-su-un. 48.3 ⌜šal⌝-la-su†-nu for šal-lat-su-nu. 49.3 omits the final a in KUR.ú-iš-di-iš-a-a. 49.5 ki-[im-ti-šú] for kim-ti-šú.

50.3, 5 add i-na before qé-reb. 51 Wincker's copy has ḫi-it-ti-šu for ḫi-ṭa-ti-šu; no exemplar known has this reading. 51.3 ḫi-ṭa-ti-šú for ḫi-ṭa-ti-šu. 52.3 [x]+12: Monument de Ninive has [x]+2, while the Institut de France copy has [x]+12. 52.3 a-di 2*(copy: 1) in Monument de Ninive, but 2 in Institut de France copy. 52.3 ad-din-šu-ma for ad-din-šú-ma. 52.3, 5 da-li-iḫ-tum and da-⌜li⌝-iḫ-tum respectively for da-li-iḫ-tu. 53.5 omits i in li-i-ti. 53 be-lí-ia: ex. 3 has EN-⌜ia⌝; ex. 4 has EN-[ia]; and ex. 5 has EN-ia. 53.3, 5 UGU-šú for UGU-šu. 54.3, 5 LUGAL for MAN. 54.3 i-na for ina. 55.3, 5 ^{m}aš-šur-ZU for ^{md}aš-šur-le-'i. 55 Winckler's copy of ex. 1 omits la and ex. 3 omits the final a in KUR.al-la-ab-ra-a-a. 56.3, 5 omit ^{d} in ^{md}aš-šur-ZU. 56.3, 5 qin-ni-šu for qin-ni-šú. 57 Or URU.zu-uk-ki-a for URU.su-uk-ki-a: ex. 1 has URU.su-uk-ki-a, while exs. 3, 5 have URU.su*(copy: ZU)-uk-ki-a and URU.su*(copy: ZU)-uk-ki-⌜a⌝ respectively. 57.5 adds an extraneous ŠÚ sign after URU.pa-ap-pa. 57.3–5 i-na for ina. 57.5 ù*(copy: ŠÚ-LU) for u. 58 The Journal Asiatique and Institut de France copies of ex. 3 have ⌜ša$^{?}$⌝ for šá, but there are no traces of the sign on the Monument de Ninive copy; ex. 5 has ša. 58.5 omits KUR.ni in KUR.ni-ik-sa-am-ma. 58 ak-šu-ud: ex. 2 has ak†-šud*(copy: MUŠ); ex. 3 has ak*(copy: KI)-šud; ex. 4 has [ak]-⌜šud⌝; and ex. 5 has ak-⌜šud⌝. 58.3, 5 šu-a-tu-nu for šú-a-tú-nu. 59 ^{m}EN-LUGAL-ú-ṣur: ex. 2 has ^{d}EN-⌜LUGAL⌝-[ú]-⌜ṣur⌝; ex. 3 has ^{md}EN*(copy: ḪU)-LUGAL-ú-ṣur*(copy: BI); and ex. 5 has ^{md*}(copy: E)EN-LUGAL†-ú-ṣur. 59.5

⸢*ú*⸣*-raš-šu* for *ú-raš-šú*.

60.3 DÙ-*uš-ma* for [*e*]-⸢*pu*⸣-*uš-ma* of ex. 1. Possibly instead ⸢DÙ⸣-*uš-ma* for ex. 1, but the spacing of the copy suggests [*e*]-⸢*pu*⸣-*uš-ma* is more likely. **60**.3, 5 *i-na* for *ina*. **60**.3 *pi-ḫa-ti*†*-šú* for *pi-ḫa-ti-šu*. **61**.2 *šá* for *ša*. **61**.2 URU.*ḫar**(copy: ÁŠ)-*ḫar**(copy: ŠA) for URU.*ḫar-ḫa-ar*. **61**.3–4 *am-nu-šú* for *am-nu-šu*. **62**.3 *šu-a-tú* for *šu-a-tu*. **62**.3–4 *i-na* for *ina*. **62**.3–4 *lìb-bi* for ŠÀ. **63**.4 URU.*kar*-^{m}LUGAL-GI.[NA] for URU.*kar*-^{m}MAN-GI.NA. **63**.4 *pa-ṭi-šú* for *pa-ṭi-šu*. **64**.4 *ak-šud-ma* for *ak-šu-ud-ma*. **64** URU.É-^{m}*ba-ga-ia*: Winckler's copy of ex. 1 omits ^{m}; and ex. 4 has URU.⸢É⸣-^{m}*ba-ga-a-a*. **64**.4 *ak-šud*^{ud} for *ak-šu-ud*. **66**.4 *ma-ṣar*†*-tú* for *ma-ṣar-tu*. **66**.2, 4 ⸢*na*⸣*-gi-i* and *na-gi-i* respectively for *na-ge-e*. **66**.5 adds an extraneous AŠ sign before *akšudma*. **66**.4–5 *ak-šud-ma* for *ak-šu-ud-ma*. **67**.5 ⸢URU⸣.*e-riš**(copy: ḪU)*-ta-na* or ⸢URU⸣.*e-ri**(copy: ḪU)-<*iš*>*-ta-na* for URU.*e-ri-iš-ta-na*. **68**.5 adds an extraneous AŠ sign before *a-di*. **68**.4 omits *ni* in URU.MEŠ-*ni*. **68**.2 omits *me* in *li-me-ti-šú*. **68**.3–4 [*ak*]-⸢*šud*⸣[(^{ud})] and *ak-šud*^{ud} respectively for KUR-*ud*.

70.3–4 *ina* for *i-na*. **70**.3–4 *ša* for *šá*. **70**.4 *pa-ṭi-šú* for *pa-ṭi-šu*. **71**.4 *šá-a-tu-nu* for *šu-a-tu-nu*. **73**.4 *i-mé-e-šu* for *i-mi-šu*. **73**.3–4 *ina* for *i-na*; the Monument de Ninive copy of ex. 3 does not have the *ina* but it is found on the Institut de France copy. **73** *tùm*† in *ak-tùm*†*-ma*: exs. 1 and 3–4 omit the Winkelhaken at the upper right of the sign, i.e, ÁB×KÁR-DIŠ; the sign not preserved on exs. 2 and 5. **74**.4 KUR-*šú* for KUR-*šu*. **74**.5 According to Winckler, this exemplar has *a-na* after *ipparšidma*, but Botta's copy does not support this. **74**.3–4 URU.*mu-ṣa-ṣir* for URU.*mu-ṣa-ṣi-ri*. **76** ^{d}*ba-ag-bar-tum*: ex. 3 has ^{d}*ba-ag*†*-bar-tu*; ex. 4 has ^{d}*ba-ag-*⸢*bar*⸣*-tu*; and ex. 5 has [^{d}*ba*]-⸢*ag*?⸣-[*bar*]*-tu*. **76**.3 DINGIR.⸢MEŠ-*šu*⸣ for DINGIR.MEŠ-*šú*. **76**.5 omits ^{m} in ^{m}*ur-sa-a*. **77**.4 DINGIR-*šú* for DINGIR-*šu*. **77**.4–5 ⸢*rama*⸣-[*ni-šú*] and *rama*†-<*ni*>-*šú* respectively for *ra-ma-ni-šú*. **78** Winckler's copy of ex. 1 has *ki-ḫul-lu-ú* <*ú*>*-šab-ši* (haplography by Winckler?); Botta's copy of ex. 4 has *ki-ḫul-lu* [x] ⸢*šab*†⸣-[*ši*] but the squeeze has *ki-ḫul-*⸢*lu-ú*⸣ <*ú*>-⸢*šab*⸣-[*ši*]. **78**.5 omits MEŠ in UN.MEŠ. **78**.5 *a-*⸢*šib*⸣ for *a-ši-ib*. **78**.4 ŠÀ-*šá* for *lìb-bi-šá*. **79**.5 URU.⸢*mé*⸣-[*lid-da-a-a*] for URU.*me-lid-da-a-a*. **79**.4–5 *i-bu-uk-*⸢*ma*⸣ and *i**(copy: AD)*-bu-*⸢*uk**⸣(copy:] UD)*-ma* respectively for *e-bu-uk-ma*. **79**.4–5 *i-na* and *i-*[*na*] respectively for *ina*. **79**.4 *lib**(copy: UD-A)*-bi-ia**(copy: I) for ŠÀ-*ia*.

80.4–5 *mal* for *ma-la*. **80**.4–5 *ba-šu-u* and *ba-šú-u* respectively for *ba-šu-ú*. **81**.1 URU.DU$_6$*-ga-rim-me*: Botta's copy adds an extraneous DIŠ sign between *ga* and *rim*, but it is not present on the squeeze. **81**.4 *am-nu-šú* for *am-nu-šu*. **82**.4 ⸢ERIM⸣.MEŠ (so squeeze) for *ṣa-ab*. **82**.4 KUR.*kam-ma-an* for KUR.*kam-ma-nu*. **82**.1 The reading of *šú* in *si-ḫir-ti-šú* is based on ex. 4. Botta's copy of ex. 1 has ⸢*šu*†⸣, while Winckler's copy has *šu*. The squeeze appears to support Botta's copy with the sign ending with the tops of two vertical wedges next to one another. **82**.5 omits *ma* in *ú-šá-aṣ-bit-ma*. **83**.4 ⸢*i*⸣*-na* for *ina*. **84**.4–5 omit *as* in *ú-ra-as-si-bu-šu-ma*. **84**.4 *ina* for the second *i-na*. **84**.4 *lib-bi-ia**(copy: AD) for *lìb-bi-*⸢*ia*⸣. **85**.4 adds MEŠ after GIŠ.GIGIR. **85**.4–5 *ù* for *u*. **85**.4–5 ANŠE.*pét-ḫal-lum* and ⸢ANŠE*⸣(copy: DU).[*pét-ḫal*]-⸢*lum**⸣(copy: SAL []) respectively for ANŠE.*pét-ḫal-lì-ia*. **85**.4 *sa-al-me* for *sal-me*. **85**.4 *i-da-a-a* for ⸢Á⸣.II*-a-a*. **86**.4 ^{m}*mut-tal-lum* for ^{m}*mut-tal-lu*. **86** KUR.É-^{m}*pa-'a-al-la*: ex. 1 has KUR.É-[(^{m})]*pa-'a-al-la*; ex. 4 has É-^{m}*pa-'a-al-*⸢*la*⸣; and ex. 5 has ⸢KUR.É†⸣-^{m}*pa-*[*'a-al-la*]. **87**.4 Copy suggests *šú* was omitted in *am-nu-šú*, but squeeze suggests possibly [*šú*].

93.4 Winckler's copy indicates that this exemplar has KUR-*šú*, but the text is not preserved at this point for this exemplar. **96**.5 *ša* for *šá*. **96**.5 *šá-šu-nu-ma* for *šá-a-šú-nu-ma*. **96**.5 ⸢*pa*⸣-[(x)-*la*]-⸢*aḫ*⸣ for *pa-laḫ*. **99**.5 *ša* for *šá*.

101 ⸢*al*⸣*-lik-ma*: ex. 1 has ⸢*al**⸣(copy: *al*†; squeeze: ⸢*al*⸣)*-lik-ma*; and ex. 5 has ⸢*al**⸣(copy: DU; squeeze: ⸢*al*⸣)*-lik-*<*ma*>. **101**.5 *a-lik* for *a-lak**(copy: KID) of ex. 1. **109**.1 Botta's copy omits ⸢*ina*⸣, but the beginning of *ina* is visible on the squeeze.

110.4 Botta's copy has [...] KU [..] approximately where ex. 1 has [...] SU [...]. **113**.5 ^{m*}(copy: GIŠ; squeeze: DIŠ)*ar-giš-tu* for ^{m}*ar-giš-ti*. **113**.4–5 [*mu-še-zi*]*-bi-šu* and [*mu*]*-še-zi-bi-*<<AŠ>>*-šu* respectively for *mu-še-zi-bi-šú*. **113**.4–5 *bil-tum* for *bil-tu*. **113**.5 *man-da-at-tu* for *man-da-at-tú*. **113**.5 ŠÀ-*ia* for *lib-bi-ia*. **114**.4–5 ANŠE.*pét-ḫal-lì-ia* and ANŠE.*pét-ḫal-lì-*⸢*ia*⸣ respectively for ANŠE.*pít-ḫal-li-ia*. **114**.4–5 *ša* for *šá*. **114**.5 *šu-a-tú* for *šú-a-tu*. **115** The number 62 is written with six Winkelhaken and two vertical wedges. **115**.5 [*ak*]*-šu-ud* for *ak-šud*. **115**.1 Winckler's copy for this exemplar has NÍG.GA and *áš-lu-lam-ma* both fully preserved. **115**.4 *šu-a-tu* for *šú-a-tú*. **116**.4 The copy would suggest that there was only room for one sign between SAG-*ia* and UGU. **116**.4 LÚ.⸢ERIM*⸣(copy: UD; squeeze: ⸢ERIM⸣).MEŠ for ERIM.MEŠ. **117**.1 Botta's copy of *u* GIŠ†.⸢*az*†⸣ in *u* GIŠ.⸢*az*⸣*-ma-re-e* has the sign UL followed by two parallel horizontal wedges leading into a small damaged area, while Winckler's copy has UL *iz*; see Fuchs, Khorsabad p. 224. **117**.4 u_4*-mi* for u_4*-me*. **117** KUR.⸢*el*⸣*-li-pi*†: Botta's copy for *pi*† in ex. 1 has QA, thus likely ⸢*pi*⸣. **118**.4 *ip-pu-šu* for *ip-pu-šú*. **119**.4 *e-ṭé-er* for *e-ṭe-er*.

120.4 [*te*]*-me-qí* for *te-me-qi*. **120**.4 *gi-mil-li-šu* for *gi-mil-li-šú*. **120**.4 [*e-la*]*-mé-e* for *e-la-mi**(copy: LÍMMU)*-i* of ex. 1. **121**.4 ⸢URU⸣.*mar-ú-bi-iš-tu* for URU.*mar-ú-bi-iš-ti*. **121**.4 *da-li-iḫ-tum* for *da-li-iḫ-tú*. **121**.4 ⸢*pa**⸣(†; squeeze: ⸢PA⸣)*-nu-uš-šu* for *pa-nu-uš-šú*. **122**.4 ⸢*e*⸣*-bu-uk-ma* for *i-bu-uk-ma*. **123**.4 *re-eṣ-ṣu-ti* for *re-ṣu-ti*. **123**.4 ERIM.MEŠ for *ṣa-ab*. **124**.4 ŠÀ for *lìb-bi*. **124**.4 *ina* for *i-na*. **125**.4 [^{m}]⸢^{d}⸣AMAR.UTU-IBILA*(copy: RA-UŠ; squeeze: DUMU-⸢UŠ⸣)-SUM.NA for ^{md}MES-A-SUM.NA. **125**.4 *ḫa-*⸢*at*⸣-[*tu/tú*] for *ḫat-tu*. **125**.4 *im-qu-su-ma* for *im-qut-su-ma*. **126**.4 *áš-bu-tu* for *aš-bu-te*. **126**.4 1-*en* for *iš-tén*. **126**.1 Winckler's copy has *pu-qu-du* fully preserved.

131.1 Winckler's copy indicates LUGAL-*ti*-<*šú*>, with space left for the *šú*, but no indication of damage. **134**.1 Wincker's copy omits ^{d} in ^{d}GIŠ.BAR. **137**.4 omits *ú* in *ba-aṭ-lu-ú-ti*. **137**.4 KUR.É-^{m}*ia-ki-ni* for KUR.É-^{m}*ia-kin*$_7$. **138**.4 *ù* for *u*. **138**.4 KUR.*ḫa-at-ti* for KUR.*ḫat-ti*. **139**.4 *ik-šud-da* for *ik-šu-da*. **139**.4 *i-na* for *ina*. **139**.4 ^{md}MUATI-SIG$_5$-DINGIR.MEŠ for ^{md}AG-SIG$_5$-DINGIR.MEŠ. **139**.4 ELAM.MA.KI for KUR.ELAM.MA.KI-*i*. **139**.4 URU.*bir-tu* for URU.*bir-tú*.

140.4 *ma-a-tú* for KUR. **140**.4 *i-na* for *ina*. **140**.4 [*ma*]*-ḫa-zu* for *ma-ḫa-zi*. **140**.4 *lìb-bi* for *lib-bi*. **142**.1 Winckler's copy omits NA$_4$.AŠ.GÌ.GÌ. **143**.4 omits *a* in KUR.*ḫa-ma-a-ni*. **143**.4 EME.GI$_7$ for ⸢*šu*†⸣*-me-ri* of ex. 1. **144**.4 NI.TUK.KI for *dil-mun*.KI. **144**.1 Winckler's copy omits ^{d} in ^{d}UTU-*ši*. **145**.4 *kàd-ra-šú* for *kàd-ra-šu*. **145**.4 omits *ni* in LUGAL.MEŠ-*ni*. **146**.4 ⸢*ina*⸣ for *i-na*. **146**.4 UD.MEŠ for u_4*-me*. **147**.4 *i-na* for *a-na*. **147**.4 omits *ni* in LUGAL.MEŠ-*ni*. **148**.4 *ina* for *i-na*. **149**.1 Winckler's copy omits KUR after *dáb-de-e*.

151.4 *na-gi-šu* for *na-gi-šú*. **154**.4 URU.[NINA.(KI)] for NINA.KI. **155**.3–4 ⸢*i*⸣*-li-*⸢*im**⸣(copy: PA; squeeze: ⸢IM⸣)*-ma* and *i-li-im-ma* respectively for DINGIR-*ma*. **155**.3 *bi-bíl* for *bi-bil*. **155**.3 ŠÀ-x for *lib-bi-ia*. **155**.5 [URU.BÀD-^{m}MAN]-GI.NA for URU.BÀD-^{m}MAN-GIN. **157**.4 ⸢URU*⸣(copy: GIŠ; squeeze: ⸢URU⸣).⸢BÀD*⸣ (copy: LI; squeeze: ⸢BÀD⸣)-^{m}LUGAL-GI.[NA] for URU.BÀD-^{m}MAN-GIN; according to Winckler, the NA is fully preserved. **157**.1 Both Botta's and Winckler's copies have AN for ÈŠ in LÚ.NU.ÈŠ.MEŠ. **158**.1 Both Botta's and Winckler's copies have ŠEN for BA in AN.GUB.BA.MEŠ; and Winckler's copy omits MEŠ. **158**.4 *ma-ḫar-šú-un**(copy: MA-ZA) for *ma-ḫar-šu-un*. **159**.5 ŠIM.⸢LI⸣ for GIŠ.LI.

160.1 Botta's and Winckler's copies have DU?/UŠ?-NU-*šin* and DU-NU-*šin* respectively for *uš-ši-šin*; for the correct reading, see Borger, BiOr 19 (1962) p. 253 sub CAD D p. 185b. No other exemplar preserves the *uš*, but *ši* is preserved on ex. 4. **160**.4–5 GIŠ.⸢*ere*⸣*-ni* and [GIŠ].*ere-*⸢*ni*⸣ respectively for GIŠ.*ere*-IGI. **161** *me-se-er*: exs. 3, 5, have *mé-se-er*; and ex. 4 has ⸢*mé*?⸣*-se-er*. **161**.3–4 [KUR.*ḫa*]*-at-ti* and KUR.*ḫa-*[*at-ti*] respectively for KUR.*ḫat-ti*. **161** *li-šá-an*: exs. 3 has *li-šá-a-ni*; ex. 4 has ⸢*li*†⸣*-šá-a-ni*; and ex. 5 has *li-šá-ni*. **162**.4 *ḫi-la-a-ni* for *ḫi-la-an-ni*. **162**.3 omits *ret* in *mé-eḫ-ret*. **162**.3–4 omit TA in 50.TA.ÀM. **163**.3–4 *nam**(copy: IG)*-ri-ir-ri* and *nam-*⸢*ri-ir-ri**⸣(copy:] ḪA) respectively for *nam-ri-ri*. **163**.3–4 omit GIŠ in GIŠ.*tim-me*. **163**.3 GIŠ.*ere-ni* for GIŠ.*ere*-IGI. **163**.5 [*ku*]*-bur-šu-*[*un*] for *ku-bur-šú-un*. **163**.3 *pirig-gal-le-e* for

PIRIG.GAL-*e*. **164**.3 KÁ-*ši-in**(copy: ŠE-NI) for KÁ.MEŠ-*šin*. **164**.1 Both Botta's and Winckler's copies have ḪU for *ša*. **164**.3–4 SI.[GAR-*ši*]-*in* and [SI.GAR]-*ši-in* respectively for SI.GAR-*šin*. **165**.3–4 *ṣe-ru-uš-šin* and *ṣe*-⸢*ru*⸣-*uš-šin* respectively for *ṣe-ru-uš*-⸢*ši*⸣-*in*. **165**.4 ⸢*ab*⸣-*šim*†-<*ma*> for *ab-šim-ma*. **165**.3–4 *a-sur-ru*-[*šin*] and *a-sur-ru-šin* respectively for *a-sur-ši-in*. **165**.1 Both Botta's and Winckler's copies have UN for *tan* in *ma-ti-tan*. **167**.3–4 *ru-uš-ši-i* for *ru-uš-še*$_{20}$-*e*. **168**.3 *ta**(copy: KID)-*mar-tú* for *ta-mar-tu*. **168**.3–4 *ú-šam-ḫir-šú-nu-ti-ma* for *ú-šam-ḫir-šu-nu-ti-ma*. **169**.1 Winckler's copy omits *u*. **169**.3–4 *šá* for *ša*.

170.1 *re-še**(copy and squeeze: KUR)-*et* for *re-še-et*. **170**.3 KUR.MEŠ for KUR.KUR.MEŠ. **171**.4 ŠU-⸢*ia*†⸣ for ŠU.II-*ia*. **176**.1 adds an extraneous sign before *ù* in Botta's copy; not present on Winckler's copy. **176**.4–5 *u* for *ù*. **176**.3 *a-ši-bu-ut* for *a-ši-bu-ti*. **178**.1 Winckler's copy omits the sign between LÚ and *pa* in LÚ.EN$^{?}$ *pa-ḫa-ti*. **179**.3 *i-na* for *ina*.

186.4 Both Botta's and Winckler's copies have NA for *tu* in *i-tu-ut*. **188** UD†: Only found on ex. 4, where Botta's copy omits the final vertical wedge; possibly ⸢UD⸣, but this cannot be confirmed from the squeeze.

194.4 Botta's copy has *lìb-bi* ŠÚ [x (x)] ⸢*ka*⸣-*bat-ti*, where ŠÚ could be the first part of *ù* (thus ⸢*ù*⸣), while Winckler's copy has *lib-bi-šú na*-[*mar*] ⸢*ka*⸣-*bat-ti*. The squeeze supports ⸢*ù*⸣ rather than *na*.

Text No. 9

1.8, 14, 18 omit *ú* in GAL-*ú*. **1**.8 MAN for LUGAL (last three occurrences in line, not preserved for first two occurrences). **1** *aš-šur*.KI: ex. 1 has ^{d}*a-šur*.KI; and exs. 10, 22 have ^{d}*aš-šur*.KI. **2**.16 MAN for LUGAL. **2**.5 omits KUR. **2**.22 *šu-me-ri* for EME.GI$_{7}$. **2** *ù*: exs. 12, 14, 22 have *u*; ex. 6 has *u*/⸢*ù*⸣; and ex. 10 has (x) where this might be ⸢*u*⸣. **2** URI.KI: exs. 5, 8, 22 have *ak-ka-de-e*; and ex. 18 has *ak*-<*ka*>-*de-e*. **3** ^{d}*aš-šur*: ex. 14 omits ^{d}; and ex. 10 has ^{d}*a-šur*. **3** LUGAL-*ut*: ex. 5 has [*šar*]-*ru-ut*; exs. 6, 8 have *šar-ru-ut*, ex. 12 has LUGAL-*tu*; ex. 20 has *šar*-[*ru*]-*ut*; and ex. 18 has ⸢*šar*$^{?}$⸣-[*ru-ut*]. **4**.10, 14 *ú-šat-li-mu-šú-ma* for *ú-šat-li-mu-šu-ma*. **4** *šu-mì-šu*: ex. 8 has *šu-mì-šú*; and exs. 10, 14, 22 have MU-*šú*. **4**.10 *ú-še-ṣu-u* for *ú-še-ṣu-ú*. **5**.12 *šá-ki-in* for *šá-kin*. **6**.22 *mu-šá-áš-ši*†-*ik* for *mu-šá-áš-šík*. **7**.6 URU.*kul-la-ba* for *kul-la-ba*.KI. **7**.8 ⸢*ki*†-*is-sik*⸣.KI for *ki-sik*.KI. **8**.12 UN.MEŠ-*šu-un* for UN.MEŠ-*šú-un*. **8**.14 *ki-din-nu-ti* for *ki-din-nu-ut*. **9**.8 *šá* for *ša*. **9**.20 *ḫar-ra-na*.KI for URU.*ḫar-ra-na*. **9**.8, 16, 18 omit *ú* in *it-ru-ṣu-ú-ma*.

10.10, 14, 16 *u* for *ù*. **10**.10, 22 *za-kut-sún* for *za-kut-su-un*. **11**.16 *šum-qu*-[*ut*] for *šum-qut*. **12** *šu-ut-bu-u*: ex. 5 has *šu*-[*ut*]-*bu-ú*; and exs. 6, 12, 16, 18, 22 have *šu-ut-bu-ú*. **12**.12, 14 GIŠ.TUKUL.MEŠ-*šu* for GIŠ.TUKUL.MEŠ-*šú*. **12**.20 *šá-ki*-⸢*in*⸣ for *šá-kin*. **12**.5 squeeze has ^{md}[*ḫum-ba-ni*]-⸢*ga*⸣-*áš*, not <^{m}>^{d}[...]-⸢*ga*⸣-*áš* of copy. **13** LÚ.ELAM.MA.KI: ex. 5 has LÚ.⸢ELAM⸣.MA.⸢KI-*i*⸣; ex. 6 has LÚ.[ELAM.MA].KI-*i*; exs. 8, 20 have LÚ.ELAM.MA.KI-*i*, and ex. 18 has LÚ.ELAM.MA.[KI]-*i*. **13**.12, 14 KUR.*ma-na-a-a* for KUR.*man-na-a-a*. **14** KUR.*zi-kir-tú*: exs. 8, 16, 18, 20 have KUR.*zi-kir-tu*; and ex. 22 has KUR.*zi-kir*-⸢*tu*⸣. **15**.10, 22 *e-mi-du* for *e-mid-du*. **15**.8, 12, 14, 18 add ^{d} before *aš-šur*. **15** URU.*mu-ṣa-ṣir*: exs. 10, 20 have URU.*mu-ṣa-ṣi-ri*; and ex. 22 has URU.*mu*-[*ṣa-ṣi*]-⸢*ri*⸣. **15**.6, 8, 16, 18, 20, 22 *ša* for *šá*. **16** exs. 5 has [KUR].*ú-ra-ar-ṭa-a-a*; ex. 8 has KUR.⸢*ú-ra*⸣-*ar-ṭa-a-a*, and exs. 18, 20 have KUR.*ú-ra-ar-ṭa-a-a*. **16**.5, 12 *pu-luḫ-ti-šu* for *pu-luḫ-ti-šú*. **16**.14 adds MEŠ after GIŠ.TUKUL. **17**.12 *ra-ma-ni-šu* for *ra-ma-ni-šú*. **17**.6 *ša-lil* for *šá-lil*. **18**.5 KUR.⸢*a*⸣-*ma-at*-⸢*te*⸣ for KUR.*a-ma-at-ti*. **18** KUR.*kúm-mu-ḫi*: ex. 10 has URU.*ku-um-mu-ḫi*; ex. 20 has URU.*kúm*-⸢*mu*⸣-[*ḫi*]; and ex. 16 has [URU$^{?}$].*ku-um-mu-ḫi*. **18**.10, 16 URU.*as-du-di* and URU.*as-du-di**(copy: KI) respectively for URU.*as-du-du*. **18** LÚ.*ḫa-at-te-e*: ex. 8 omits LÚ; and ex. 22 has LÚ.*ḫa-at**(copy: I)-*te*$_{9}$-*e*. **19**.4, 10, 14, 18, 22 *šá* for *ša*. **19**.1 omits UGU. **19**.22 KUR.MEŠ-⸢*šú*⸣/⸢*šu*⸣-*nu* for KUR.MEŠ-*šú-nu*.

20.6 Botta's copy has SAG†.MEŠ-[x] ⸢LÚ⸣.NAM-*ú-ti*, where there would not be room to restore *a-na* as well as *šú* in SAG.MEŠ-*šú*. **20**.10, 12 LÚ.NAM-*ti* and LÚ.EN.NAM-*ú-ti* respectively for LÚ.NAM-*ú-ti*. **20**.12 *iš-tak-kan-nu-ú-ma* for *iš-tak-ka-nu-ma*. **20**.5, 10, 18 omit KI in *aš-šur*.KI. **21**.8, 10 *im-nu-šú-nu-ti* for *im-nu-šu-nu-ti*. **21**.12 omits *la* in *ka-la*. **21**.1, 4, 18, and possibly 5 (based on spacing) omit ^{m} in KUR.É-^{m}*ḫu-um-ri-a*. **22** KUR.*ta-ba-lu*: ex. 4 has [KUR].⸢*ta*⸣-*ba*-⸢*li*⸣, exs. 6, 10, 12, 14 have KUR.*ta-ba-li*; ex. 16 has [KUR].⸢*ta*⸣-*ba-li*; and ex. 22 has KUR.*ta-ba*-⸢*li*⸣. **22**.10, 20 *šá* for *ša*. **22**.10, 16, 20, 22 *i-na* for *ina*. **23** KUR.*mu-uṣ-ri*: ex. 4 has KUR.[*mu*]-*ṣu-ri*; ex. 5 has KUR.*mu-ṣu-ri**(copy: EN); exs. 6, 12 have KUR.*mu-ṣu-ri*; ex. 8 has KUR.*mu-ṣu*-⸢*ri*⸣; ex. 18 has KUR.⸢*mu*⸣-*ṣu*†-[*ri*]; and ex. 22 has KUR*(copy: ŠE).*mu**(copy: ŠE)-*ṣu-ri*. **23**.4, 10 omit *a* in ^{m}*ha-a-nu-nu*. **23**.10 MAN for LUGAL. **23**.1, 10 (against copy by Botta) *im-nu-u* for *im-nu-ú*. **24**.10 URU.*ši-nu-uḫ-te* for URU.*ši-nu-uḫ-ti*. **24**.1 ^{m}*mì-ta-a* for ^{m}*mi-ta-a*. **25**.4, 16 *šá* for the first *ša*. **25** *nu-ú-ni*: exs. 10, 22 have *nu-u-ni*; ex. 14 has KU$_{6}$.MEŠ; and ex. 16 has KU$_{6}$. **26** KUR.*kam-ma-nu-u-a*: ex. 1 has KUR.*kam-ma-nu-u-a-a*; ex. 5 has KUR.*kam-ma-nu-ú-a*; and ex.14 omits *u*. **26**.10 adds an extraneous *la* between *gu* and *ma* of KUR.*gúr-gu-ma-a-a*. **27**.20 *šá* for *ša*. **27**.10, 14 KUR.KUR.MEŠ-*šú-nu* for KUR.MEŠ-*šú-nu*. **27**.5 omits KI in *aš-šur*.KI. **27**.5 *ú*-⸢*ter*⸣-*ru* for *ú-ter-ra*. **28**.1 omits *ni* in LUGAL.MEŠ-*ni*. **28**.10, 16 *šá* for the first *ša*. **28**.10, 14 *šá* for the second *ša*. **28**.10 *šá* for the third *ša*. **28** 7 *u*$_{4}$-*me*: Botta's copy of ex. 6 has 4 *u*$_{4}$-*me* while squeeze suggests ⸢7 *u*$_{4}$⸣-*me*. **28**.12, 14, 18 *ina* for *i-na*. **28**.4, 6, 10, 12, 14, 16, 18, 20, 22 *tam-tim* for *tam-ti*. **29**.18 *šá* for *ša*. **29**.16 *šit-ku-nu* for *šit-ku-nat* (error of modern copyist?). **29**.10 The *ka* of *ka-šid* is slightly abnormal in Botta's copy, but the original is fine. **29**.14 KUR.*a-ra-ši* for KUR.*ra-a-ši*. **29**.10 KUR.*pu-qu-du* for LÚ.*pu-qud-du*.

30.10 URU.*la-ḫi-ra* for URU.*la-ḫi-ri*. **30**.4–6, 12, 14, 18, 20 *ša* for *šá*. **30** *ab-šá-an-šu*: exs. 4–5, 10 have *ab-šá-an-šú*; and ex. 6 has *ab**(copy: ⸢DU⸣)-*šá-an*-⸢*šú*⸣. **30**.12, 14 *šá-ki-in* and *ša-kin* respectively for *šá-kin*. **30**.5 BAD$_{5}$.BAD$_{5}$ for *dáb-de-e*. **30**.10 Botta's copy indicates *dáb*†-*de*†-*e* (basically the first two signs are run together) but collation indicates that there is nothing wrong with the signs. **30** ^{md}AMAR.UTU-IBILA-SUM.NA: Lyon's copy of ex. 1 omits ^{d}, but Botta's copy and the original have it present; ex. 6 has ^{md}[AMAR].UTU-A-SUM.NA; ex. 10 has ^{md}ŠÚ-A-SUM.NA as per the squeeze though ^{m} is omitted on Botta's copy; and ex. 20 has ^{md}AMAR.UTU-A-SUM.NA. **31**.10 Despite Botta's copy the *bu* and *lem* in *a-a-bu lem-nu* are written correctly. **31**.10, 16 *šá* for *ša*. **31**.10 omits *i* in *ki-i*. **31**.10 Bezold, Literatur p. 87 indicates that the *la* is missing, but it is in fact present. **31**.10 ŠÀ for *lìb-bi*. **31** *šar-ru-ut*: ex. 6 has LUGAL†-*tu*†; and exs. 10, 16 have LUGAL-*ut*. **31** *e-pu-šu-ma*: ex. 6 has ⸢*e*⸣-*pu-uš-ma*; ex. 10 has DÙ-*uš-ma*; and ex. 16 has [x (x)]-*uš*†-*ma*. **31**.4, 14 *tak-šú-du* and *tak-šu-da* respectively for *tak-šu-du*. **32** GAL-*tú*: ex. 1 has GAL-*tum*; exs. 6, 12, 18, 20 have GAL-*tu*; and ex. 8 has [*ra*]-*bi*-[x]. **32**.10, 14, 16 ŠU.II-*su* for *qa-as-su*. **32**.10, 14, 16 *šu-ru-uš* for *šur-uš*. **32** URU.BÀD-^{m}*ia-ki-in-ni*: ex. 5 omits ^{m}; and exs. 5, 10, 14, 16 omit *in*. **33**.4, 14 *tuk-la-ti-šu* for *tuk-la-ti-šú*. **33**.1 *ša**: The sign has one extraneous wedge. **33**.10 *šá* for *ša*. **34**.6, 10, 12, 14 *tam-tim* for *tam-ti*. **34**.8 ^{m}*ú-pe-e-ri* for ^{m}*ú-pe-ri*. **34**.8 MAN for LUGAL. **34**.20 NI.TUK.KI for *dil-mun*.KI. **35**.10, 16 *šá* for *ša*. **35**.18 *ina* for *i-na*. **35** *šá*: ex. 4 has ⸢*ša*$^{?}$⸣; and exs. 5–6, 8, 12, 14, 18, 20 have *ša*. **35** *nu-ú-ni*: exs. 6, 10, 12 have *nu-u-ni*; and ex. 14 omits *ú*. **36**.1 *ta-mar-tuš*: The scribe appears to have written two horizontal wedges at the end of the *mar* sign, and then effaced the lower one. **36**.5–6, 10, 12, 14, 20 *it-pe-šú* for *it-pe-šu*. **37** *muš-ta-bíl*: ex. 8 has *muš*†-*ta**(copy: IA)-*bíl*; and ex. 20 has *muš-ta-bíl*. **37** *da-mì-iq-ti*: ex. 12 omits *iq*; and ex. 10 has MUNUS.SIG$_{5}$. **37**.10 *šá* for *ša*. **37**.8 *šu-šú-ub* for *šu-šu-ub*. **38**.18 *u* for *ù*. **38**.1 *qi-šub-bé-e* for *ki-šub-bé-e*. **38**.18 *ṣip-pa-a-te* for *ṣip-pa-a-ti*. **39** *ú-zu-un-šu*: ex. 6 has *ú-zu-un-šú*; ex. 10 has *us-su-un-šú*; and ex. 20 has *ú-zu**(copy: SI)-⸢*un-šú*$^{?}$⸣. **39**.14 *u*$_{4}$-*me-šú-ma* for *u*$_{4}$-*me-šu-ma*. **39**.5–6, 12, 14, 18, 20 *ša* for *šá*; ex. 1 *šá**: The scribe appears to have written BUR, and then effaced the three initial horizontal wedges.

40.6, 10, 20 KUR-*i* for KUR-*e*. **40** *ni-na-a*.KI: ex. 6 has NINA*(copy: AB×ZA).KI; exs. 8, 10, 12, 20 have NINA.KI; and ex. 18 has NINA*(copy: AB×ZA).⸢KI⸣. Bezold, Literatur p. 87 indicates that ex. 10 omits the KI, though it is found on Botta's copy.

40.10, 12 DÙ-*uš-ma* and DÙ-*ma* respectively for *e-pu-uš-ma*. **40**.10 Bezold, Literatur p. 87 indicates that the form of the URU before BÀD has an extra vertical wedge, but this is not the case. **40** URU.BÀD-^{m}MAN-GIN: Lyon's copy of ex. 1 omits ^{m}, but Botta's copy and the original have it present; ex. 5 has [URU.BÀD-^{m}]LUGAL-GI.NA; ex. 8 has URU.BÀD-^{m}MAN-GI.NA; and exs. 10, 14, 18 have URU.BÀD-^{m}LUGAL-GI.NA. **41** GIŠ.KIRI$_6$.MAḪ-*ḫu*: ex. 5 omits *ḫu*; and for ex. 10, Bezold, Literatur p. 87 indicates PA rather than the GIŠ of Botta's copy, but the following sign simply runs right into the GIŠ. **41** *ša*: ex. 1 has *šá*; and ex. 10 omits it. **42**.10 KUR.*ḫa-at-ti* for KUR.*ḫat-ti*. **42**.6, 10, 18 KUR-*i* for KUR-*e*. **42**.12 DÙ-*šu-un* for DÙ-*šú-un*. **42** *ḫu-ur-ru-šu*: ex. 5 has *ḫu-ur*†*-ru-šú*; exs. 6, 10 have *ḫu-ur-ru-šú-ma*; exs. 12, 14 have *ḫu-ru-šu-ma*; and ex. 18 has *ḫu-ur-*⸢*ru*⸣*-šú*. **43**.10 *šá* for the first *ša*. **43**.6 *la-bi-ru-ú-ti* for *la-bi-ru-ti*. **43**.10, 18 *šá* for the second *ša*. **43**.31 omits *u* in *el-la-mu-u-a*. **43**.6 *be-lu-tu* for *be-lu-ut*. **44**.1, 10 *e-pu-uš-šu-ma* and *e-pu-uš-ma* respectively for *e-pu-šu-ma*. **45**.10 ŠÀ-*šú-nu* for *lìb-bi-šú-nu*. **45**.13 *a-šar-šu* for *a-šar-šú*. **45**.18 *ú-mas-si-ma* for *ú-maš-ši-ma*. **45**.8, 18 *šu-šu-*⸢*ub*⸣*-šu* and *šu-šú-*⸢*ub*⸣*-šú* respectively for *šu-šu-ub-šú*. **46**.8, 10 ÍD-šu*(copy: MA) and ÍD-*šu* respectively for ÍD-*šú*. **46** *ṣip-pa-te-šú*: ex. 6 has *ṣip-pa-a-ti-šú*; ex. 8 has *ṣip-pa-te-šu*; exs. 10, 13, 20 have *ṣip-pa-ti-šú*; and ex. 14 has *ṣip-*⸢*pa*⸣*-ti-šú*. **46**.1 omits *na* in *a-na*. **47**.8 *šá-a-ši* for *šá-a-šú*, which is possibly modern copyist error of ŠI for ŠÚ. **47** *zuq-qú-ur*: The *qú* of ex. 10 omits the top horizontal. **48**.23 omits *ia* in *be-lu-ti-ia*. **48** *mu-šu*: exs. 5, 10, 14 have *mu-šú*; and ex. 8 has *mu-ši*, which is possibly modern copyist error of ŠI for ŠÚ. **48**.10 aṣ-rim*(text: KU)-ma for *aṣ-rim-ma*. **49**.6, 13, 15 *še-me-e* for *še-mé-e*. **49**.13, 15 *u*$_4$*-me* for *u*$_4$*-mu*.

50.15 *ina* for *i-na*. **51**.10 Despite Botta's copy, the *al* in GIŠ.*al-lu* is fine. **51** *ú-šat-ri-ik-ma*: The squeeze of ex. 5 indicates ⸢*šat*⸣, not <*šat*> of Botta's copy. **52** *li-bit-tu*: exs. 13, 15 have *li-bit-tú*; ex. 19 has ⸢li⸣-bit-ti*(copy: MEŠ$^{?}$); and for ex. 10, as in Botta's copy, the *tu* has a slightly anomalous form, omitting one horizontal wedge. **52** *a-ra-aḫ*: Bezold, Literatur p. 87 indicates *a-i+na-aḫ* for ex. 10, but the *ra* is fine. **53**.15 *šá* for *ša*; and for ex. 10, the sign šá* (as in Botta's copy) omits the top wedge. **53** SAG.DU: ex. 5 omits SAG; exs. 6, 13 have *qaq-qa-di*; ex. 9 has qaq*(copy: BA)-qa-di; and ex. 19 has *qaq-*[*qa-di*]. **54**.7 *i-na* for *a-na*. **54**.10 *ri-mi-ti-ši-na* for *ri-mì-ti-ši-na*. Botta's copy has *ri-mi-ti-šú-na*, but this is not correct. **54**.15, 19 *i-pat-ta-qa* and *ú-*[*pat*]*-ti-*⸢*qa*⸣ respectively for *i-pat-ti-qa*. **56**.3, 9 ⸢*pe*⸣*-el-šu* and *pe-el-šu* respectively for *pe-el-šú*. **56** *uš-še-e-šú*: ex. 3 has *uš-še-e-šu*; ex. 5 has ⸢*uš*⸣*-še-*[*e*]*-šu*; and ex. 15 omits *e*. **57**.25 *pa-rak-ku* for *pa-rak-ki*. **58**.7, 11, 25 *šá* for *ša*. **58**.9 *šur-šú-du* for *šur-šu-du*. **59** ^{d}30: exs. 3, 7, 9, 13, 15, 19 have ^{d}EN.ZU; ex. 5 has ^{d}EN.[ZU]; and ex. 21 has ^{d}EN.⸢ZU⸣. **59** ^{d}MAŠ: exs. 3, 25, 27 have ^{d}*nin-urta*; and ex. 19 has ^{d}*(copy: LA)nin-⸢urta⸣.

60 *qer-bu-uš-šu*: ex. 3 has *qer-bu-*⸢*uš-šú*⸣; and exs. 7, 15, 25, 27 have *qer-bu-uš-šú*. **60**.11 omits MEŠ in É.GALMEŠ. **61** GIŠ.*mu-suk-kan-ni*: ex. 5 has [GIŠ.MES.MÁ].⸢KAN.NA$^{?}$⸣; exs. 7, 13, 15, 27 have GIŠ.MES.MÁ.KAN.NA; and in ex. 25, *suk* is missing one interior vertical wedge. **61**.11, 25 GIŠ.*ere-ni* for GIŠ.*ere*-IGI. **61**.15, 25 GIŠ.*dáp-ra-ni* for GIŠ.*dup-ra-ni*. **62** GIŠ.ŠIM.LI: exs. 3, 5, 7, 9, 11, 13, 21, 27 omit GIŠ; the squeeze indicates (with Botta's copy and against Pohl's copy [RPARA 19]) that ex. 11 omits GIŠ; and ex. 25 omits ŠIM. **62** *u*: ex. 3 has ⸢*ù*⸣; and exs. 9, 13, 19, 21, 25 have *ù*. **62**.1 GIŠ.*bu-uṭ-nu* for GIŠ.*bu-uṭ-ni*. **62**.27 *a-na* for *i-na*. **62**.3 *qí-bi-ti-šu-nu* for *qí-bi-ti-šú-nu*. **63** *šar-ru-ti-ia*: exs. 11, 25 have LUGAL-*ti-ia*; ex. 15 has MAN-*ti-ia*; ex. 23 has ⸢LUGAL-*ti-ia*⸣; and ex. 27 has ⸢MAN-*ti-ia*⸣. **64** GIŠ.ÙR.MEŠ: exs. 15, 21 have GIŠ.*gu-šu-re*; and ex. 19 has [GIŠ.*gu*]-⸢*šu*⸣*-re*. **64** GIŠ.*ere*-IGI: ex. 3 has <GIŠ>.⸢*ere-ni*⸣; exs. 11, 23, 25 have GIŠ.*ere-ni*; and ex. 19 has <GIŠ>.⸢*ere*-IGI⸣. **65**.21 omits *ni* in GIŠ.*mu-suk-kan-ni*. **65**.13, 15, 27 *me-ser* for *mé-se-er*. **65**.19 ⸢*nam-ra*$^{?}$⸣ [(x x)] for *nam-ri*. **66**.25 The *ta* in *ú-rat-ta-a* is missing one horizontal wedge. **67**.25 omits *pa* in *ap-pa-a-ti*. **67**.15 KUR.*ḫat-te* for KUR.*ḫat-ti*. **67** *ša*: ex. 3 has ⸢*šá*$^{?}$⸣; and exs. 11, 25 have *šá*. **67**.1, 25 *ina* for *i-na*. **67**.11, 23, 25 EME for *li-šá-an*. **68**.7 omits KI in MAR.TU.KI. **68** *ḫi-la-ni*: exs. 4, 7, 9, 11, 13, 21, 25, 27 have *ḫi-la-an-ni*; ex. 5 has *ḫi-la-an-*⸢*ni*⸣; ex. 15 has ⸢*ḫi*⸣*-la-a-ni*; and ex. 19 has ḫi*(copy: ŠÚ)-la-an-ni. **68**.7, 11, 15, 25, 27 *i-šá-as-šú* for *i-šá-as-šu*. **69**.5 *mé-eḫ-*⸢*ret*⸣, not *mé-eḫ-*<*ret*> of copy. **69** KÁ.MEŠ-*ši-in*: ex. 3 has KÁ.MEŠ-⸢*šin*⸣; ex. 7 has KÁ.MEŠ-*šin*; ex. 19 omits *ši*; and ex. 25 has *ba-bi-ši-in*.

70.3, 5, 7, 9, 13, 19, 25, 27, and probably 21 (restored via spacing) add MEŠ after UR.MAḪ; Winckler's copy has UR.MAḪ-*ḫe*, but no known exemplar has this reading. **70** *tu-ʾa-a-me*: exs. 2, 11 have *tú-ʾa-a-me*; and ex. 3 omits *ʾa*. **70**.2 The GÚ portion of GUN omits the two initial small vertical wedges (as on Botta's copy). **71**.25 *šá* for *ša*. **71**.2 omits *i-na*. **71**.2 omits *á* in ^{d}*nin-á-gal*. **71** *ip-pat-qu-ma*: exs. 7, 27 have *ip-pat-qu-ú-ma*; and ex. 19 has *ip-pat-qu-*[(*ú*)]*-ma*. **72**.5 (against Botta copy), 25 *mal-lu-u* for *ma-lu-ú*. **72**.7, 11, 13, 15, 25, 27 add GIŠ before *tim-me*. **72**.11, 26 GIŠ.*ere-ni* for GIŠ.*ere*-IGI. **72** *šu-ta-ḫu-te*: in ex. 2, the Winkelhaken of *ḫu* has not been cut out fully but is nonetheless visible on the original; ex. 4 has *šu-ta-*⸢*ḫu*⸣*-ti*; exs. 7, 9, 11, 13, 19, 21, 25, 27 have *šu-ta-ḫu-ti*; and ex. 15 has *šu-ta-ḫu-*⸢*ti*⸣. **72**.15, 27 *šá* for *ša*. **72**.2 omits TA in NINDA.TA.ÀM. **73** *ku-bur-šu-nu*: ex. 5 has *ku-*⸢*bur*⸣*-šú-un*; exs. 7, 11, 21, 27 have *ku-bur-šú-un*; and ex. 15 has *ku-bur-šú-nu*. **74**.3, 7, 9, 27 add GIŠ before *dáp-pi*. **74** *ba-bi-ši-in*: ex. 3 has *ba-bi-šin*; ex. 5 has ⸢KÁ⸣.MEŠ-*šin*; ex. 7 has KÁ.MEŠ-*šin*; exs. 11, 15, 25, 27 have KÁ.MEŠ-*ši-in*; and ex. 23 has ⸢KÁ.MEŠ⸣-*ši-in*. **75**.2 adds an extraneous *u* (an erasure?) between *šad* and *di* of *šad-di*. **75** *šá*: exs. 3–4, 7, 13, 15, 21, 25, 27 have *ša*; and exs. 5, 19 have ⸢*ša*⸣. **75**.11, 25 add MEŠ after NA$_4$. **75** KUR-*i*: ex. 9 omits KUR; and ex. 27 has KUR-*e*. **76**.25 The *tiq* in *ap-tiq-ma* has only one vertical wedge at the beginning of the sign. **77** SI.GAR-*ši-in*: ex. 3 has SI.GAR-⸢*šin*$^{?}$⸣; ex. 5 has SI.GAR-⸢*šin*⸣; and exs. 9, 15, 25, 27 have SI.GAR-*šin*. **77** NA$_4$.*pi-li*: ex. 3 has NA$_4$.⸢*pi*⸣-[(*i*)]-⸢*li*⸣; and exs. 11, 25 have NA$_4$.*pe-el*. **78** *qa-ti-ia*: ex. 9 has ŠU-*ia*; ex. 23 has ŠU.II-⸢*ia*⸣; and exs. 25, 27 have ŠU.II-*ia*. **78** *ṣe-ru-uš-šin*: Botta's copy of ex. 5 has *ṣe-ru-uš-*<<ŠÚ>>*-šin* and the squeeze suggests *ṣe-ru-uš-*(x)*-šin*; exs. 15, 27 have *ṣe-ru-uš-ši-in*; and in ex. 25, the *ṣe* omits one horizontal wedge. **78**.25 *a-sur-ri-šin* for *a-sur-ru-ši-in*. **79**.9 omits *a* in *a-na*. **79**.9 omits U in GÉŠ.U. **79**.5 Botta's copy has <1> UŠ*(copy: MAL), while the squeeze indicates 1 ⸢UŠ⸣.

80 *mi-še-eḫ-ti*: ex. 21 omits *ti*; and ex. 25 has [*mi*]*-ši-iḫ-ti*. **80**.3 adds an extraneous MEŠ after *mi-še-eḫ-ti*. **80**.3, 15 BÀD-*šu* for BÀD-*šú*. **80** *e-li*: exs. 5, 25 have UGU; and exs. 7, 27 have *i-li*. **81**.27 *ú-šar-še-da* for *ú-šar-ši-da*. **81** *te-em-me-en-šú*: ex. 3 has ⸢*te-em-me-en*$^{?}$⸣*-šu*; ex. 7 omits *em*; exs. 9, 13, 15, 27 have *te-em-me-en-šu*; and ex. 19 has *te-em-me-*⸢*en*⸣*-šu*. **81**.3 <<12>> after *i-na*. **81** *ù*: exs. 2, 13, 15 omit it; ex. 9 has *u*; and ex. 11 has [*u*]/<*ù*>. **81**.5, 7, 9, 11, 13, 15, 19, 21, 23 omit *a* in *ar-ka-a-ti*. **82**.4 *me-*⸢*eḫ*⸣*-*[*ret*] for *mé-eḫ-ret*. **82** *ap-te-e-ma*: ex. 13 has *ap-te*$_9$*-e-ma*; and exs. 15, 21 omit *e*. **83**.19 ^{d}*šá-maš* for ^{d}UTU. **84**.11, 25 *šá* for *ša*. **85**.15, 25 *mu-di-ša-at* and *mu-diš-šá-*⸢*at*⸣ respectively for *mu-di-šá-at*. **85**.5, 7, 11, 13, 15, 19, 23, 25, 27 ^{d}EN.LÍL for ^{d}BAD. **86**.9 *u* for *ù*. **86**.11, 15, 23, 25, 27 *šá* for *ša*. **86** ^{d}*a-nu*: ex. 7 has ^{d}a*(copy: ZA)-num; and exs. 13, 15, 21, 25, 27 have ^{d}*a-num*. **87** *qa-ti-ia*: ex. 5 has ŠU.⸢II-*ia*⸣; and exs. 7, 11, 13, 15, 25 have ŠU.II-*ia*. **88** *ù*: exs. 5, 11, 19, 23 have *u*; and ex. 9 (via spacing) has ⸢*u*$^{?}$⸣. **88**.5, 19 ^{d}INANNA for ^{d}*iš-tar*. **88**.11, 15, 21, 23, 25 *šá* for *ša*. **88** IM.MAR.TU: in ex. 2, the MAR sign was originally written as copied by Botta, but the extra horizontal wedge at the end of the sign was then erased, resulting in a correct form; and ex. 19 adds an extraneous KUR sign between IM and MAR. **88**.21 muš-te-šir*(copy and squeeze: SAL) for *muš-te-šir*. **88**.19 ⸢*nag*⸣*-bi-šu* for *nag-bi-šú*. **89**.11, 21 *u* for *ù*. **89** *šá*: exs. 3, 21 have ⸢*ša*⸣; exs. 5, 7, 13, 15, 17, 19, 23 have *ša*; and ex. 9 has ša*(copy: UŠ).

90 IM.U$_{18}$.LU: ex. 3 has IM.⸢U$_{19}$.LU⸣; exs. 5, 11, 15, 17, 27 have IM.U$_{19}$.LU; ex. 7 has IM.U$_{19}$.[LU]; and ex. 19 has IM.U$_{19}$*(copy: LA).⸢LU⸣. **90** *pa-le-e*: exs. 11, 23 have BALA-*e*; and exs. 13, 15, 28 have BALA.MEŠ. **90** *e-pi-ši-šu*: ex. 5 has *e-pi-ši-*⸢*šu*⸣/⸢*šú*⸣; ex. 7 has *e-pi-*⸢*ši*⸣*-šú*; exs. 13, 15, 27–28 have *e-pi-ši-šú*; and ex. 25 has *e-pi-ši-*⸢*šú*⸣. **91** *um-ma-ni-šu*: ex. 3 has *um-ma-ni-*⸢*šú*⸣; ex. 7 has [ERIM].ḪI.A*(copy: ZA)-šú; exs. 11, 15, 23, 27–28 have ERIM.ḪI.A-*šú*; ex. 13 has *um-ma-ni-šú*; and ex. 21 has [*um-ma*]*-ni-šú*. **91** BÀD-*šú*: ex. 5 has ⸢BÀD-*šú*⸣/⸢*šu*⸣, though Winckler's copy omits the

⸢*šú*⸣/⸢*šu*⸣; and exs. 9, 27 have BÀD-*šu*. **91**.25 *te-em-me-en* for *te-me-en*. **91** *a-li-šu*: exs. 3, 5, 9, 19 have *a-li-šú*; exs. 11, 15, 23, 25, 28 have URU-*šú*, and exs. 13, 27 have URU-*šu*. **92**.7 omits *la* in *la-bar* (though possibly [*la*]-*bar*). **92**.7, 15, 27, 28 u_4-*me* for UD.MEŠ. **92** *ru-qu-ú-ti*: exs. 1, 17 omit *ú*; and ex. 5 has SÙ.MEŠ. **92** *šal-ḫu-šú*: exs. 3, 7 have *šal-ḫu-ú-šu*; ex. 4 has [*šal*]-*ḫu-ú-šu*; exs. 5, 9, 11, 17, 21, 23, 25, 27 have *šal-ḫu-ú-šú*; and ex. 19 has *šal-*⸢*ḫu*⸣*-ú-šu*. **92** *li-šá-nu*: exs. 5, 11, 13, 15, 23, 25, 27–28 have EME; ex. 7 has ⸢EME⸣; and ex. 17 has EME*(copy: NAG). **93**.5, 11, 15, 17, 28 *a-ḫi-tú* for *a-ḫi-tu*. **93** *a-ši-bu-ut*: ex. 7 has [*a-ši*]-⸢*bu*⸣*-ti*; exs. 13, 15, 28 have *a-ši-bu-ti*; and ex. 27 has *a-ši-bu-tu*. **93**.4–5 *u* for *ù*. **93**.17 KUR for *ma-a-ti*. **93** *ma-la*: exs. 11, 13, 23, 27–28 have *mal*; and for ex. 15, Botta's copy, which has *mal*, is correct, while Pohl's copy, which indicates *mà-*⸢*la*⸣, is erroneous. **93**.2 *ir-te-ʾu-u*, with *u* omitted on Botta's copy. **94**.15, 28 *gi-im-ri* for *gim-ri*. **94**.4, 11, 23 *šá* for *ša*. **94** *zi-kir*: ex. 7 has *zik-*⸢*ri*⸣; exs. 11, 13, 15, 27–28 have *zik-ri*; and ex. 17 has [*zik*]-⸢*ri*⸣. **94** *ina*: exs. 3, 5, 7, 11, 13, 15, 25, 27–28 have *i-na*; ex. 17 has ⸢*i-na*⸣; ex. 19 has ⸢*i*?*-na*?⸣; and ex. 23 has ⸢*i*⸣*-na*. **94**.3, 9, 17 *mé-tel* for *me-tel*. **95** *aš-šur*.KI: The copy for ex. 21 has <*aš*>-*šur*.KI, but the squeeze has *aš-šur*.⸢KI⸣; and ex. 28 omits KI. **96**.2 The *uz* in *šu-ḫu-uz* has five slanted wedges at the beginning (2+3) rather than four. **96**.5 *ṣi-bit-te* for *ṣi-bit-ti*. **96**.13 adds MEŠ after DINGIR. **97**.3, 9, 13 *ú-ma-ʾe-er-šu-nu-ti* for *ú-ma-ʾe-er-šú-nu-ti*. **97** *ul-tu*: ex. 5 has *ul-*⸢*tú*⸣; and exs. 7, 11, 13, 15, 28 have *ul-tú*. **97** *ši-pìr*: exs. 7, 11, 13, 15, 25, 27–28 have *ši-ip-ri*; and ex. 23 has ⸢*ši-ip-ri*⸣. **98**.28 *ú-qat-tú-ú* for *ú-qat-tu-ú*. **99**.11, 13, 15, 27–28 omit *e* in *aq-re-e-ma*. **99**.2 omits *ta* in *ta-šil-ta-ši-na*. **99**.15 The *kun* in *áš-kun* is perfectly correct (with Botta's copy and against Pohl's copy). **99**.5, 11, 15, 23, 28 *šá* for *ša*. **99** first ^{d}UTU-*ši*: exs. 13, 15 have ^{d}*šam-ši*; and ex. 28 has ^{d}*šam-*<*ši*>. **99**.2 The *ù* is ŠÚ-LU. **99** ^{d}UTU-*ši*: exs. 13, 15, 28 have ^{d}*šam-ši*; and ex. 19 omits ^{d}.

100.13 *ša-ti-na* for *šá-ti-na*. **100**.2 There are the ends of two horizontal wedges at the end of *mar* in *ta-mar-ta-šú-nu*, rather than one. **100**.4 possibly [*ta-mar-ta*]-*šu*-[*nu*], but placement not certain. **100** *ka-bit-tú*: ex. 3 has [*ka*]-⸢*bit-tu*⸣; ex. 4 has [*ka-bit*]-⸢*tu*⸣; exs. 5, 19 have *ka-bit-*⸢*tu*⸣; exs. 7, 13, 27 have *ka-bit-tu*; and ex. 9 has ⸢*ka*⸣*(copy:] ḪU)-*bit-tu*. **101** *šá-a-šu*: Winckler's copy omits *a*; exs. 3, 11, 15, 19, 21, 27–28 have *šá-a-šú*, and ex. 23 has [*šá*]-⸢*a*⸣*-šú*. **101**.5 [*qa*]-*ti*-[*ia*] for ŠU.II-*ia*. **101** *li-im-ma-ḫi-ir-ma*: ex. 3 has ⸢*lim*⸣*-ma-*[*ḫi*]*-ir-*[*ma*]; ex. 7 has [*lim*]*-ma-ḫi-ir-*<*ma*> ; exs. 9, 21 omit the final *ma*; ex. 11 has *lim-ma-ḫi-ir-*⸢*ma*⸣; exs. 13, 15, 25, 28 have *lim-ma-ḫi-ir-ma*; ex. 19 has *lim-ma-ḫi-ir-*<*ma*>; ex. 23 has *lim-*⸢*ma*⸣*-*[*ḫi-ir-ma*]; and ex. 27 has *lim-*<<*im*>>*-ma-ḫi-ir-*<*ma*>. **101** *pa-nu-uš-šú-un*: ex. 5 has ⸢*pa*⸣*-nu-uš-šu-un*; ex. 9 has [*pa-nu*]*-uš-šu-un*; and ex. 25 has *pa-nu-uš-šu-un*. **102**.13, 15, 28 *a-ši-ib* for *a-šab*. **102**.19 omits *iṣ* in *ki-iṣ-ṣi-šú-un*. **102**.19 *u* for *ù*. **102** *kun-nu*: exs. 3, 5, 19 have GIN; ex. 7 has ⸢*ku*⸣*-un*; and exs. 11, 13, 15, 27–28 have *ku-un*. **102**.25 *pa-li-ia* for BALA.MEŠ-*ia*. **102**.19, 21 *liq-bu-u* for *liq-bu-ú*. **102**.11 *du-ur* for *du-rí*. **103**.11, 15, 21, 23, 28 *šá* for *ša*. **103** *qa-ti-ia*: exs. 3, 28 have ŠU.II-*ia*; ex. 19 has ŠU.II-⸢*ia*⸣; and ex. 23 has ⸢ŠU⸣.II-⸢*ia*⸣. **103** *ú-nak-ka-ru-ma*: exs. 13, 27 have *ú-nak-ka-ru-ú-ma*; and ex. 19 has *ú-nak-ka-ru-*[(*ú*)]*-*⸢*ma*⸣. **103**.28 The final *ú* in *ú-saḫ-ḫu-ú* is in the form KID. **104**.5 Against Botta's copy this exemplar has *ú-šam-sa-*[*ku*]*-ma*. **104**.3 *si-ma-*⸢*te-ia*⸣ for *si-ma-ti-ia*. **104**.2 The *ú* in *ú-pa-áš-šá-ṭu* is in the form KID. **104** ^{d}30: ex. 5 has ⸢^{d}⸣[EN].⸢ZU⸣; ex. 9 has ^{d}EN†.[ZU]; and ex. 19 has ^{d}EN.ZU. **104**.5 ⸢^{d}*šá*⸣*-maš* for ^{d}UTU. **105**.11 *u* for *ù*. **105**.3 Botta's copy has *a*-KU-*bi-šú* with wide spaces between the signs and no indication of damage; the passage is not clear on the squeeze, but might be *a-*[*ši*]*-*⸢*ib*?⸣ [(x)] x-⸢*bi*⸣*-šú*. **105**.21 *lib-bi-šu* for *lib-bi-šú*. **105**.13 MU-*šu* for MU-*šú*. **105**.9 NUMUN-*šu**(copy: MA) for NUMUN-*šú*. **105**.2 *ina* for *i-na*. **105**.27 *ma-a-ti* for KUR. **105** *lil-qu-tú-ma*: ex. 5 has [*lil*]-⸢*qu*?*-tu-ma*⸣, ex. 7 has ⸢*lil*⸣*-qu-tu-ú-ma*; exs. 9, 19 have *lil-qu-tu-ma*; ex. 13 has *lil-qu-tu-ú-ma*; ex. 21 has ⸢*lil-qu-tu*⸣*-ma*; ex. 23 has ⸢*lil-qu*⸣*-tu-*⸢*ma*⸣; and ex. 27 has *lil-qu-tú-ú-ma*. **106** *i-na*: ex. 3 has ⸢*ina*⸣; ex. 19 has *ina**(copy: ḪAL); and ex. 21 has *ina*. **106**.13, 15, 28 LÚ.KÚR-*šu* for LÚ.KÚR-*šú*. **106**.2, 21 *li-še-ši-bu-šú* for *li-še-ši-bu-uš*.

Text No. 10

1.3 AŠ for É.GAL; possibly [É].⸢GAL⸣ or ⸢É⸣.[GAL] but the Monument de Ninive copy would not support this. **1**.2 ^{m}MAN-GI.NA for ^{m}LUGAL-GI.NA. **1**.3 GAL-*ú* for GAL-*u*. **2**.2 MAN for LUGAL. **2**.3 <LUGAL *kiš*>-*šá-ti* in Monument de Ninive copy, but IdF copy suggests [LUGAL/MAN *kiš*]-*šá-ti*. **2**.2–3 *kiš-šá-ti* and <*kiš*>-*šá-ti* respectively for *kiš-šá-tim*. **3**.2. MAN for LUGAL. **3**.3 ^{d}*a-šur* for *aš-šur*.KI. **3**.1 omits RA in KÁ.DINGIR.RA.KI. **4**.2 MAN for LUGAL. **4**.3 Possibly insufficient room to restore KUR as well as LUGAL (or MAN) at start of line. **4**.2 EME†.GI_7 for *šu-me-ri*. **4**.2–3 *ak-ka-de-e* for URI.KI. **5**.2 *šá* for *ša*. **5**.2 *ina* for *i-na*. **5**.3 omits *tu* in *tu-kul-ti*. **6**.2 ^{d}*na-bi-um* for ^{d}AG. **6**.2 ^{d}AMAR*(copy: BI).<UTU> for ^{d}AMAR.UTU. **7**.2 KUR.*ia*†*-ad-na-na* in Monument de Ninive copy but KUR.*ia-ad-na-na* in JA and IdF copies. **8**.2 omits *mu* in KUR.*mu-ṣu-ri*. **8**.2 KUR.*mu-us**(copy: ŠUD)-[(x)]-*ki* for KUR.*mu-uš-ki*. **9**.3 *a-mur-re-e* for MAR.TU.KI. **9**.2 *ra**(copy: DUMU)-*pa-áš-ti*† for DAGAL-*tim*. **9**.3–4 *a-na* and ⸢*a*⸣-x respectively for *ana*. **9**.3 *si-ḫi-ir-ti-šá* for *si-ḫir-ti-šá*.

10.2–3 *nap*†*-ḫa*†*-ar*† and [*nap-ḫa*]*-ar**(copy: ḪUL) respectively for *nap-ḫar*. **10** *ru-qu-te*: ex. 2 has *ru**(copy: ŠÀ)-*qu-ú**(copy: KID)-*ti* in Monument de Ninive copy, though IdF copy has *ru-qu-ú-ti*; ex. 3 has *ru-qu-ú-ti*; and ex. 4 has ⸢*ru-qu*⸣*-ú-ti*. **11**.2 adds an exraneous sign between *pa* and *aṭ* of *pa-aṭ*. **11**.2–3 KUR.*el*†*-li*†*-pi*† and [KUR].⸢*el*⸣*-li-pi* respectively for KUR.*el-li-pí*. **11**.3–4 KUR.*ra-a-ši* for KUR.*ra-a-še*. **12**.2 LÚ†.*a-ra-me* for LÚ.*a-ri-me*. **13**.2–3 *a-ši-ib* for *a-šib*. **13**.3 ÍD.*su-rap-pu**(copy: ŠE) for ÍD.*su-rap-pi*. **16**.2 *ša* for *šá*. **16**.4 KUR.ELAM.<MA>.⸢KI⸣ for ELAM.MA.KI. **17**.3–4 [KUR].⸢*kár*†⸣-^{d}*du-ni-áš* and KUR.*kár-dun-iá-*<*áš*> respectively for KUR.*kár-dun-iá-áš*. **17**.2 *e-*<*liš*> *ù šap-*<*liš*>, but the JA and IdF copies both have *e-*<*liš*> *ù šap-liš*†. **18**.3–4 KUR.É-^{m}*ia-ki-ni* for KUR.É-^{m}*ia*-GIN. **18**.3–4 *ki-šad**(copy: TAR) <<TAB>> and *ki-šad* respectively for GÚ. **19**.3–4 ÍD.*mar-ra*†*-a-ti* and ⸢ÍD⸣.*mar-ra-a-ti* respectively for ÍD.*mar-ra-te*.

20 *i-be-lu-ma*: ex. 2 has *i-bí**(copy: AM-DIŠ)-*lu-ma*; ex. 3 has *i-bí-*⸢*lu*⸣*-ú-ma*; and ex. 4 has *i-bí-*⸢*lu-ú*⸣*-ma*. **20**.2–3 SAG.MEŠ-⸢*šu*†⸣ and SAG.MEŠ-*šu* respectively for SAG.MEŠ-*šú*. **22**.2–4 omit *ú* in *iš-tak-ka-nu-ú-ma*. **23**.4 ⸢*be-lu*⸣*-ti-šú* for *be-lu-ti-šu*. **23**.2–3 *e*†*-mid-*<*su*>*-nu-*⸢*ti*⸣ and *e-mid-su*†*-nu**(copy: AŠ)-*ú-ti* respectively for *e-mid-su-nu-ti*.

Text No. 11

1.2 LUGAL for first MAN. **2**.2 *šu-me-ri* for ⸢EME⸣.GI_7. **2**.2 *ak-ka-de-e* for URI.KI. **3**.2 ^{d}AMAR.UTU for ^{d}MES. **5**.2 <^{d}>*šam-ši* for ^{d}UTU-*ši*. **5**.1 Monument de Ninive copy has *pa-aṭ**(copy: MA), but the JA and IdF copies have *pa-aṭ*. **8**.1 Monument de Ninive copy has KUR.*ma-da-a**(copy: ŠÁ)-*a*, but the JA and IdF copies have KUR.*ma-da-a*†*-a*. **8**.2 *ša* for *šá*. **9**.2 KUR.⸢*ra*⸣*-a-ši* for KUR.*ra-a-še*. **9**.2 *ša* for *šá*.

12.1–2 have DUL† and DUL for DU_6 respectively. **12**.2 *šá* for *ša*. **13**.2 *u* for *ù*. **15**.1 Botta's copies indicate the first sign in the line is not preserved, but Winckler's copy, which is based on this exemplar, has *ša*; ex. 2 has *šá*. **15**.2 *ki-šad* for GÚ. **15**.2 ÍD.*mar-ra-ti* for ÍD.*mar-ra-te*. **19**.2 omits *i* in *i-na*

20.2 URU.NINA for NINA.⸢KI⸣. **23**.2 omits GIŠ in GIŠ.ŠIM.LI. **26**.2 GIŠ.MES.MÁ.KAN.NA for GIŠ.*mu-suk-kan-ni*. **28**.2 *né-reb-ši-in* for *né-reb-*⸢*šin*⸣. **29**.2 omits *a* in *ḫi-la-a-ni*.

30.1 omits *še* in *ú-še-pi-šá*. **30**.2 ⸢*ba*⸣*-bi-šin*, while ex. 1 has KÁ.⸢MEŠ⸣-[(*šin*)]. **31**.2 *tu-ʾá-*⸢*a*⸣*-me* for *tu-ʾa-a-me*. **32**.2 *ša* for *šá*. **34**.2 *šu-ta-ḫu-ti* for *šu-ta-ḫu-te*†. **36**.1 Monument de Ninive copy has *ú-kin*†*-ma*, while the IdF copy has *ú-kin-ma*. **37**.2 *ba-bi-šin* for KÁ.MEŠ-*šin*. **38**.2 *ša* for *šá*. **38**.2 omits *ti* in *er-bet-ti*. **39**.2 SI.GAR-*ši-in* for SI.GAR-*šin*.

41.1–2 *qa-ti-*⸢*šu**⸣(copy: MA [) and ŠU.II-*šu* respectively for *qa-ti-šu*; Winckler's copy made for ex. 1 has *qa-ti*. **41**.1–2 ⸢*ṣe*†⸣*-ru*†*-*[*uš*]*-*⸢*šin*⸣ and *ṣe**(copy: AD)-*ru*†*-uš-šin* respectively for *ṣe*†*-ru*†*-uš-šin*; Winckler's copy made for ex. 1 has *ṣe-ru-uš-šin*. **42**.1 Monument de Ninive copy has *ra*†, while the IdF copy has *ra* for *tab*†*-ra-a-ti.* **43**.1 Winckler's copy made for ex. 1 has *te-ne-še-ti*, not the *da-*⸢*ád*⸣*-me**(copy: DIŠ) of Botta's copies. In addition to omitting a gap between the third and fourth vertical wedges (taken here to be the end of ÁD and the beginning of ME), Botta's copies may have omitted an indication of damage in the space following the fourth vertical wedge and thus ex. 1 may have had *da-*⸢*ád-me*⸣ not *da-*⸢*ád*⸣*-me**(copy: DIŠ). **43**.2 *ša* for *šá*. **43**.2 *ul**(copy: AMAR)*-tu* for *iš-tu*; Winckler's copy made for ex. 1 has *ul-tu*, with *iš-tu* as a variant. **44**.2 *i**(copy: MA)*-na* for *ina*. **45**.2 *i-*[*na*] for *ina*. **45**.1 omits *pir* in ⸢*ši-pir*⸣.

Text No. 12

1.2–3 ^{m}LUGAL-GIN for ^{m}LUGAL-GI.NA. **1**.2 MAN*(copy: MEŠ) for LUGAL. **1** *kiš-šá-ti*: ex. 2 has ŠÚ; and exs. 3–4 have *kiš-šá-tim*. **2**.3, 5 adds ^{d} before *aš-šur*.KI. **2**.2 omits RA in KÁ.DINGIR.RA.KI. **3**.2 MAN for LUGAL. **3**.4–5 *šu-me-ri* and *šu**(copy: MA)*-me-ri* respectively for EME.GI$_{7}$. **3**.2–3 URI*(copy: ŠU-ŠÁ-ŠÁ).KI and URI.KI respectively for *ak-ka-di-i*. **4**.2 *šá* for *ša*. **4**.3 *ina* for *i-na*. **6**.2 *qa-bal* for MURUB$_{4}$. **6**.3–5 omit second *ša*. **6**.3 *ša-lam* for *šá-lam*. **8**.3, 5 KUR.*mu-us-ki* for KUR.*mu-uš-ki*. **9**.2, 4 KUR.<*ḫa*>*-at**(copy: I)-⸢*ti*⸣ and KUR.*ḫa-at-ti* respectively for KUR.*ḫat-ti*. **9**.2 *ana*$^{?}$ for *ana*.

10.5 *nap**(copy: AB)*-ḫa**(copy: ZA)*-ar* for *nap-ḫar*. **10**.4 omits *um* in *gu-ti-um*.KI. **11**.3, 5 *ša* for *šá*. **11**.4–5 KUR.*el-li-pi* for KUR.*el-li-pí*. **12**.2 *šá* for *ša*. **13** LÚ.*a-ri-me*: ex. 2 has LÚ.⸢*a*⸣*-ra-me*; ex. 4 has LÚ.*a-*⸢*ra*⸣*-*[*me*]; and ex. 5 has LÚ.*a-ra/ri**(copy: É)*-mi**(copy: I). **13**.2 *a-šib* for *a-ši-ib*. **13**.2 *a-ḫi* for *a-aḫ*. **14** ÍD.*su-rap-pi*: The variant ÍD.*su-rap-pe-e* in Winckler, Sar. pl. 38 is a misunderstanding of Botta, Monument de Ninive 3 pl. 10 (=ex. 3) line 9 in which *pi*†/*pí*† is followed by ÍD† for ÍD.*uq-né-e*; and ex. 5 has ÍD.[*su*]*-rap**(copy: LUGAL)*-pu*. **15**.2 omits ^{d} in URU.DU$_{6}$-^{d}*ḫum-ba*. **16**.3–4 *ša* for *šá*. **18**.5 KUR.É-^{m}*ia-ki-ni* for KUR.É-^{m}*ia*-GIN. **18**.2 *šá* for *ša*. **18** *ki-šá-di*: ex. 2 has GÚ; and exs. 3, 5 have *ki-šad*. **19**.2 ÍD.*mar-ra-te* for ÍD.*mar-ra-ti*.

20.2, 5 [*a*]*-bíl-ma* and *a-bil-ma* respectively for *a-be-el-ma*. **20** SAG.MEŠ-*ia*: ex. 2 has SAG.MEŠ-*iá*; and exs. 4–5 omit MEŠ. **22**.2–3 omit *tak* and *ma* respectively in *áš-tak-kan-ma*. **23**.2, 4–5 *i-na* for first *ina*. **23** *u*$_{4}$*-me-šú-ma*: ex. 3 has *u*$_{4}$*-me-šu-ma*; and ex. 5 omits *ma*. **23**.3, 5 *i-na* for second *ina*. **23**.3, 5 ⸢*ba*⸣*-*[*ḫu-la*]*-ti* and *ba-ḫu-*⸢*la*†⸣*-ti* respectively for *ba-ḫu-la-te*. **24**.3–5 *ša* for *šá*. **24** ^{d}*aš-šur*: ex. 3 omits ^{d}; and ex. 4 has ^{d}*a-šur*. **25** *ú-šak-ni-šú-ma*: exs. 3–4 have *ú-šak-ni-šu-ma*; and ex. 5 has *ú-*[*šak-ni*]*-šu-ma*. **26**.3, 5 omit *a* in *ab-šá-a-ni*. **26** Winckler, Sar. pl. 38 no. III (based upon ex. 1) has *ki*, not *ki-i*. **27**.3–4 *i-na* for *ina*. **27** Winckler, Sar. pl. 38 no. III (based upon ex. 1) has *e-le-nu*, not *e-le-en*. **28**.4–5 *i-na* for *ina*. **28**.3, 5 *bi-bíl*†/*bil*† and *bi-bil* respectively for *bi-bíl*. **28**.3 *e-*⸢*pu*⸣*-uš-*⸢*ma*⸣ for DÙ-*uš-ma*. **29**.3–4 URU.BÀD-^{m}LUGAL-GIN and URU.⸢BÀD⸣-^{m}⸢LUGAL⸣-GI.NA*(copy: UD) respectively for URU.BÀD-^{m}MAN-GIN.

31.5 [GIŠ].⸢MES†⸣.MÁ.GAN.NA for GIŠ.*mu-suk-kan-ni*. **31**.3, 5 GIŠ.EREN† and GIŠ.⸢EREN⸣ respectively for GIŠ.*ere-ni*. **31**.3–5 GIŠ.*dup-ra-ni* for GIŠ.*dáp-ra-ni*. **32**.2, 4 omit GIŠ in GIŠ.ŠIM.LI. **32**.3, 5 *u* for *ù*. **33**.2, 5 MAN-⸢*ti*⸣*-ia**(copy:] MA-A) and *šar-ru**(copy: MAL)*-ti-ia* respectively for LUGAL-*ti-ia*. **34**.5 *ù**(copy: ŠÚ-MAL) for *ù*. **34**.5 DINGIR*(copy: AŠ-ŠUR).MEŠ for DINGIR.MEŠ. **34**.3 *a-ši-bu-tu* for *a-ši-bu-ut*. **35**.4–5 *i-*[*na*] and *i-na* respectively for *ina*. **35** *qer-bi-ši-in*: ex. 1 omits *bi*; and exs. 2, 5 have *qer-bi-šin*. **35**.4–5 omit *e* in *aq-re-e-ma*. **36**.3, 5 *ma-ḫar-šu-un* and *ma-ḫar-*<*šú*>*-*⸢*un*⸣ respectively for *ma-ḫar-šú-un*. **37** first *ša*: ex. 1 omits it; and ex. 2 has *šá*. **37**.2 *šá* for second *ša*. **38**.5 *ik**(copy: ḪU)*-nu-šú-ma* for *ik-nu-šu-ma*. **39**.2, 5 *nap-šat-su-*[(x x)]*-un* and *nap-šat-su-*[(x)]*-un* respectively for *nap-šat-sún*. **39**.2, 5 KUR-*ia* for *ma-ti-ia*.

40.2 omits *šá* in LÚ.*šá-pi-ri*. **41**.3 *šá-tam-mi* for *šá-tam-me*. **42**.2–3 *ta-mar-ta-šú-nu* for *ta-mar-ta-šu-nu*. **43** *ka-bit-tu*: ex. 2 has *ka-bit-tú*; and ex. 3 adds an extraneous DIŠ sign between *ka* and *bit*. **44**.5 *ina* for *i-na*. **45**.2–3 omit *na* in *áš-ta-kan-na*. **45**.3 *ni-gu-tu* for *ni-gu-tú*.

Text No. 13

1 ^{m}LUGAL-GI.NA: exs. 1, 9 omit ^{m}; and ex. 3 has ^{m}LUGAL-⸢GIN⸣. **1**.2, 5 ⸢MAN⸣ and MAN respectively for second LUGAL. **2** first LUGAL: ex. 3 has ⸢MAN⸣; and exs. 5, 7 have MAN. **2**.3, 5 MAN for second LUGAL. **2**.9 *kiš-šá-tim* for *kiš-šá-ti*. **2**.2–3, 5, 8 MAN for third LUGAL. **2**.4, 6, 9 add ^{d} before *aš-šur*.KI. **2**.5 omits *aš* in *aš-šur*.KI. **3**.3, 5 MAN for LUGAL. **3**.5, 7–8 KUR *šu-me-ri* for EME.GI$_{7}$. **4**.9 *u* for *ù*. **4**.2, 9 URI*(copy: ŠÁ-ŠÁ).⸢KI†⸣ and URI.KI respectively for *ak-ka-de-e*. **6** *mu-šá-áš-šík*: ex. 4 has *mu-*[*šá-áš*]*-šik*; ex. 7 has *mu-šá-áš-šik*; and ex. 9 has *mu-šá-áš-ši-ik*. **6** ÚRI.KI: exs. 2–3 have LÚ for ŠEŠ (as part of ÚRI); and MURUB$_{4}$ for UNUG (as part of ÚRI) in all clear cases except ex. 4. **7** MURUB$_{4}$ for UNUG in all clear cases except ex. 4. **7** MURUB$_{4}$ for UNUG (as part of ARARMA) in all clear cases. **7** *kul-aba*$_{4}$.KI: MURUB$_{4}$ for *aba*$_{4}$ in all clear cases except ex. 4; and ex. 7 has *kul-la-ba*.KI. **7**.5 *ki-is-sik*.KI for *ki-sik*.KI. **8** URU.*né-med-*^{d}*la-gu-da*: ex. 2 has URU.*né-med*†-^{d}*la**(copy: MA)*-gu**(copy: SAL)*-da**(copy: AN); ex. 6 has <URU>.*né-med-*^{d}*la-gu-da*.KI; and ex. 8 has URU.*né-med-*^{d}*la-gu-du*. **9** *ki-din-nu-ut*: ex. 4 has *ki-din-nu-tu**(copy: KUR-MA); and exs. 6, 8–9 have *ki-din-nu-tu*.

10.9 URU.*ḫar-ra-an* for URU.*ḫar-ra-na*. **12**.3 ERIM.MEŠ for *ṣa-ab*. **12**.7 adds an extraneous DIŠ sign after ^{d}*a-nim*. **12**.4 *u* for *ù*. **13**.5 adds an extraneous AŠ sign between *ṭu* and *ru* of *iš-ṭu-ru*. **13**.4–5, 7 *za-kut-su-un* for *za-kut-sún*. **13**.2, 4 *eṭ-lum* and *eṭ-*⸢*lum*⸣ respectively for *eṭ-lu*. **14**.2 omits BAD$_{5}$-*e* in BAD$_{5}$.BAD$_{5}$-*e*. **15** LÚ.ELAM.MA.KI-*i*: ex. 3 has LÚ.ELAM.MA.KI-*i*†/*e*†; and exs. 6, 8 omit *i*. **16**.1, 7 KUR.*kar-al-lu* for KUR.*kar-al-la*. **16**.3 URU.*ki-še-si*† (or less likely URU.*ki-še-su*†) for URU.*ki-še-su*. **17** URU.*ḫar-ḫar*: ex. 3 has URU.*ḫar-ḫa-ar*; ex. 4 has URU†.*ḫar-ḫa-*⸢*ar*⸣; and ex. 6 has URU.*ḫar-ḫa**(copy: A-U)*-ar*. **17**.5 omits final *a* in KUR.*ma-da-a-a*. **17**.2–3, 6 *el-li-pí* for KUR.*el-li-pi*. **18**.4, 6, 9 *e-me-du* for *e-mid-du*. **18**.6 omits *aš* in ^{d}*aš-šur*. **19**.3 KUR.TILLA for KUR.*ur-ar-ṭi*. **19**.7 URU.*mu-ṣa-ṣi-ru* for URU.*mu-ṣa-ṣir*.

20.6–7, 9 *ša-giš* for *šá-giš*. **20**.5 ⸢KUR⸣.*zi-*⸢*kir*†*-tú*$^{?}$⸣ for KUR.*zi-kir-tu*. **21**.7, 9 KUR.*ma-na-a-a* for KUR.*man-na-a-a*. **23** *na-pi-iʾ*: exs. 2, 9 have *na-pí-iʾ*; ex. 3 has *na-pí-iʾ**(copy: AN); ex. 4 has *na-pí-*[*iʾ*]; and ex. 6 has *na-pi**(copy: ŠI)*-iʾ*. **23**.7 KUR.*kam-ma-nu* for KUR.*kam-ma-ni*. **24**.3–5 *šá* for *ša*. **24**.9 ^{m}*gu-un**(copy: KID)*-zi-na-ni* for ^{m}*gu-un-zi-na-nu*. **24**.1 adds an extraneous *ša* before *ul-tu*. **24**.2–3, 7 TA for *ul-tu*. **25**.3 omits *reb* in *qé-reb*. **25**.1–2 LUGAL-*ti-šu* for LUGAL-*ti-šú*. **26** KUR.MEŠ-*šú-nu*: ex. 3 has KUR†.KUR-*šú-nu*; ex. 4 has KUR.MEŠ-*šu-nu*; and ex. 6 has KUR.MEŠ-*šu-*[*nu*]. **27**.7 LÚ.GAR-*nu-ti* for LÚ.*šá-ak-nu-ti*. **28** LUGAL-*ut*: exs. 1, 6 have LUGAL-*tu*; ex. 7 has LUGAL-*ú-tu*; and ex. 9 has LUGAL-<*tu/ut*>. **28**.2 omits ^{m} in ^{m}*tar-ḫu-la-ra*. **29**.2 omits LÚ in LÚ.URU.*mar-qa-sa-a-a*. **29**.3–4 *šá* for *ša*.

30.3 omits KI in *aš-šur*.KI. **31** *ú-ter-ru*: ex. 3 omits *ru*; and ex. 9 has *ú-ter-ra*. **31**.4, 6 *ka-a-šid* for *ka-šid*. **31** URU.*sa-mir-i-na*: exs. 3–4, 6, 9 have URU.*sa-me-ri-na*; and ex. 7 has URU.*sa-me-ri**(copy: UR)*-na*. **32**.3 *gi-*⸢*mi*$^{?}$⸣*-*[(x)]*-ir* for *gi-mir*. **32** KUR.É-^{m}*ḫu-um-ri-a*: ex. 1 omits ^{m}; and ex. 5 has KUR.É-^{m}*ḫum-ri**(copy: UR-ŠÚ)*-a*. **33**.9 *ša-lil* for *šá-lil*. **33**.7 URU.*as-du-ú-di* for URU.*as-du-di*. **34**.3, 5 *šá* for the first *ša*. **34**.5 KUR.*ia-*⸢*am*⸣*-na-a**(copy: MIN)-<*a*> for KUR.*ia-am-na-a-a*. **34**.4–5 *šá* for the second *ša*. **34**.2 *tam-ti* for *tam-tim*. **35**.9 *nu-u-ni* for *nu-ú-ni*. **35**.4, 6 omit *a* in *i-ba-a-ru*. **36**.3, 9 KUR.*kas-ku* and KUR.*ka-as*†*-ki* respectively for KUR.*ka-as-ku*. **36** KUR.*ta-ba-li*: ex. 1 has KUR.*ta-ba-a-li*; ex. 3 has KUR.*ta-*⸢*bal*⸣*-*[*li/la*]; ex. 6 has KUR.*ta-bal-la*; and ex. 7 has KUR.*ta-bal-li*. **37**.1, 7 KUR.*ḫi-lak-ku* for KUR.*ḫi-lak-ki*. **37**.6 does not appear to have sufficient room to restore [*ù* KUR.*ḫi-lak-ku*] at the beginning of the line. **37** ^{m}*mi-ta-a*: ex. 3 has ^{m}*mì-ta-a*; and ex. 6 omits ^{m}. **38**.3–5 MAN for LUGAL. **38**.4, 6, 9 KUR.*mu-uš-ki* for KUR.*mu-us-ki*. **38**.3 *šá* for *ša*. **38** *ina*: ex. 5 has ⸢*i*⸣*-na*†; and exs. 7–8 have *i-na*. **38**.4, 6 omit *ḫi* in KUR.*ra-pi-ḫi*. **39**.8 omits *e* in BAD$_{5}$.BAD$_{5}$-*e*. **39**.7 KUR.*mu-uṣ-ri* for KUR.*mu-ṣu-ri*.

40.3, 5 MAN for LUGAL. **40**.7, 9 URU.*ḫa**(copy: ZA)*-a-zi-ti* and URU.*ḫa-a-zi-ti* respectively for URU.*ḫa-zi-ti*. **41**.3 *im-nu-u* for *im-nu-ú*. **41**.5 omits *niš* in *mu-šak-niš*. **42**.4 omits *ni* in

LUGAL.MEŠ-*ni*. **42**.3 *šá* for *ša*. **42**.8 *na-gi-i* for *na-ge-e*. **43**.3 *šá* for both *ša*. **44**.2–4, 6 *ina* for *i-na*. **44**.8 *qa-bal* for MURUB$_4$. **44**.9 *šit-ku-nat* for *šit-ku-na-at*. **45** *šu-bat-su-un*: ex. 3 has *šu-bat*-x*(copy: ŠÚ-IZ), possibly for *šu-bat-sún* or *šu-bat-šú-un*$^?$; and exs. 5, 7–9 have *šu-bat-sún*. **45**.6–7 ^{md}[AMAR].⸢UTU⸣-A*(copy: MIN)-SUM.NA and ^{md}AMAR.UTU-A-SUM.NA respectively for ^{md}AMAR.UTU-IBILA-SUM.NA. **46**.3–4 MAN for LUGAL. **46**.5 does not appear to have sufficient room to restore [LUGAL KUR.*kal-di*] at the beginning of the line. **46**.2 *a-ši-[ib]* for *a-šib*. **46**.6, 9 *ki-šad* for GÚ. **46**.4 ÍD.*mar-ra-te* for ÍD.*mar-ra-ti*. **47**.3, 5 *šá* for *ša*. **47**.6 ŠÀ for *lìb-bi*. **47**.1, 7 LUGAL-*tu* and LUGAL-*tum*† respectively for LUGAL-*ut*. **48** *e-pu-uš-ma*: ex. 1 has *e-pu-šu*; ex. 4 has *e-pu*-<*šu*/*uš*>-*ma* or possibly simply *e-pu-šu**(copy: MA); ex. 5 has *e-pu-šu*-[(*ma*)]; and ex. 8 has *e-pu-šu-ma*. **49** GAL-*tu*: ex. 3 has ⸢GAL-*tum*$^?$⸣; exs. 4–6 have GAL-*tum*; and ex. 8 has GAL*(copy: MA)-*tum*. **49**.1 ŠU.II-*su* for *qa-as-su*. **49**.1 KUR-*šu* for KUR-*šú*.

50.3, 7 [DAGAL]-*ti* and DAGAL-*ti* respectively for DAGAL-*tim*. **50**.4, 6–7, 9 omit *ú* in *i-zu-zu-ú-ma*. **51**.4 *ina* for *i-na*. **52**.5 omits RA in KÁ.DINGIR.RA.KI. **52**.5 omits *ù*. **52**.8 SAG-*šu* for SAG-*šú*. **53**.5 does not appear to have sufficient room to restore [LÚ.GAR.KUR KUR.*gam-bu-li*] at the beginning of the line. **53**.5–7, 9 *im-nu-ú-ma* for *im-nu-ma*. **54**.1 *e-mi-du* for *e-mid-du*. **54**.1 *ni-ru-uš-šu* for *ni-ru-uš-šú*. **54** ^{m}*ú-pe-e-ri*: exs. 5, 7–8 omit *e*; and ex. 9 omits ^{m}. **55** *dil-mun*.KI: ex. 6 has NI.<TUK>.KI; ex. 7 has NI.TUK†.KI; and ex. 9 omits KI. **56**.2, 4, 7, 9 *ina* for *i-na*. **56**.7 *tam-ti* for *tam-tim*. **57**.1 *nar**(copy: MA-TAB)-*ba-a-ṣu* for *nar-ba-ṣu*. **58**.8 *be-lu-ti-šu* for *be-lu-ti-šú*. **59**.3–4 *ina* for *i-na*.

60.2–4, 6 *šá* for *ša*. **61**.4 EN*(copy: NA).MEŠ-[(x)]-*šu* for EN.MEŠ-*šú*. **61**.3, 6 ⸢*šá*$^?$⸣ and *šá* respectively for *ša*. **61**.7–8 *ú-šat-bu-ú-ma* for *ú-šat-bu-ma*. **62** *ú-ra-si-bu*: exs. 2, 6–7 have *ú-ra-si-ba*; ex. 3 has *ú*-⸢*ra*⸣-*si*-⸢*ba*$^?$⸣; ex. 8 has *ú-ra-si-bu-ma*; and ex. 9 has *ú-ra*†-[*si*]-*ba*. **62** *ga-re-e-šu*: ex. 4 omits *e*; ex. 6 has *ga-re-e-šú*; ex. 7 has *ga-re*-<*e*>-*šú*; and ex. 9 has [*ga*]-*re*-<*e*>-*šú*. **63**.3 *iš*-<*tu*>, or possibly TA†, for *iš-tu*. **63**.2–3, 5–6 *šá* for *ša*. **63**.8 *qa-bal* for MURUB$_4$. **63** *tam-tim*: ex. 3 has [*tam*]-*ti*; and exs. 6–7 have *tam-ti*. **64**.7 ^{d}UTU-*šú* (or miscopied *šú* for *ši*) for ^{d}UTU-*ši*. **65**.3, 6 KUR.*mu-uš-ki* for KUR.*mu-us-ki*. **65**.8 omits KI in MAR.TU.KI. **65** DAGAL-*tu*: ex. 2 has DAGAL-*tum*; ex. 3 has DAGAL†-⸢*tim*$^?$⸣; and exs. 6–7 have DAGAL-*tim*. **66**.3 *nap-ḫar**(copy: ḪI×MA) for *nap-ḫa-ar*. **68**.7–8 *ru-qu-ú-ti* for *ru-qu-ti*. **68**.3 *šá* for *ša*. **69**.3, 6 KUR.*el-li-pí* for KUR.*el-li-pi*. **69** KUR.*ra-a-ši*: ex. 3 has KUR.*ra-a-še*; and exs. 7–8 have KUR.*ra-a-šú* (possibly copyist error for *ši*).

70.3 has ḪI [x x (x)] following KUR.ELAM.MA.KI and before *šá*. **70**.3, 6 *šá* for *ša*. **70**.7 *a-ḫi* for *a-aḫ*. **73**.9 LÚ.*ḫa-am-ra-a-nu* for LÚ.*ḫa-am-ra-nu*. **73**.2, 6 LÚ.*ú*-⸢*bu*⸣-*lu* and LÚ.*ú-bu-lu* respectively for LÚ.*ú-bu-lum*. **74**.5–6 LÚ.*ru*-⸢*ʾu*⸣-*u*$_8$-⸢*a*⸣ and LÚ.*ru-u*$_8$†-*a* respectively for LÚ.*ru-ʾu-ú-a*. **74**.1 Winckler's copy omits *iʾ* of *li-iʾ-ta-a-a*. **75**.7 ⸢ÍD⸣.*su-ra*-[(*ap*)-*pi*] for ÍD.*su-rap-pi*. **76**.2 LÚ.*gam-bu**(copy: KUR)-⸢*lu*⸣ for LÚ.*gam-bu-lum*. **77**.7 does not appear to have sufficient room to restore all this line. **77**.2, 4 LÚ.*pu-qud-du* for LÚ.*pu-qu-du*. **77**.9 LÚ.*su-te*$_9$-*e* for LÚ.*su-te-e*. **78**.9 *mal* for *ma-la*. **78**.3 [*ba*]-*šú-ú* for *ba-šu-ú*. **79**.5, 6 *ul**(copy: AMAR)-*tú* and *ul-tú* respectively for *ul-tu*. **79**.3, 6 omits *ʾu* and *ú* respectively in KUR.*sa-am-ʾu-ú-na*.

80.2, 5–6, 9 copies have DUL for DU$_6$ in URU.DU$_6$-^{d}*ḫum-ba*; only ex. 1 has DU$_6$. **81**.2 *šá* for *ša*. **82** KUR.É-^{m}*a-muk-ka-ni*: ex. 1 has KUR.É-^{m}*a-muk-ka-a-ni*; ex. 4 has KUR.[É-(^{m})*a*]-*mu*-[*ka*-(*a*)-*ni*]; and exs. 5–6 omit ^{m}. **83** KUR.É-^{m}*da-ku-ri*: ex. 2 has KUR.É-[^{m}]*dak-ku*-⸢*ri*†⸣; ex. 6 has ⸢KUR⸣.É-[^{m}]*dak-ku-ri*; and ex. 9 has KUR.É-^{m}*dak-ku**(copy: KI)-⸢*ri*⸣. **83**.2 omits ^{m} in KUR.É-^{m}*šil-a-ni*. **85** *ma-la*: exs. 3–4 have *mal*; and ex. 7 has ⸢*mal*$^?$⸣. **85** KUR.É-^{m}*ia-ki-ni*: ex. 1 has KUR.É-^{m}*ia*-GIN; ex. 2 has [KUR].É-^{m}*ia-ki-in-ni*; ex. 3 has [KUR.É-^{m}]⸢*ia*⸣-GIN; and ex. 4 adds an extraneous AŠ sign between ^{m} and *ia*. **86**.6 *šá* for *ša*. **86**.6 x (x) for *ki-šad*; possibly ⸢*ki*†-*šad*⸣ or ⸢GÚ†⸣. **86**.7 *dil-mun*.KI for NI.TUK.KI. **87**.9 *i-bí-lu**(copy: KU)-*ú-ma* for *i-bí-lu-ma*. **87**.4 omits *šu* in LÚ.*šu-ut*. **87** SAG.MEŠ-*šú*: exs. 5, 8 omit MEŠ; and ex. 6 has SAG.⸢MEŠ⸣-*šu*. **88**.9 omits MEŠ in LÚ.EN.NAM.MEŠ. **88**.9 UGU-*šu-nu* for UGU-*šú-nu*. **88**.9 *iš-tak-ka-nu-ú-ma* for *iš-tak-ka-nu-ma*. **89** *e-mid-su-nu-ti*: ex. 5 omits *mid*; and ex. 8 has *e-mid-su-nu-te*.

90 *u*$_4$-*me-šu-ma*: ex. 3 has [*u*$_4$]-⸢*mi**⸣(copy: BI)-*šú-ma*; ex. 4 has *u*$_4$-<*me*>-*šú-ma*; and ex. 6 has *u*$_4$-*me-šú*†-*ma*. **90**.4, 6 *ina* for *i-na*. **90**.3–4, 8 *ba-ḫu-la-te* for *ba-ḫu-la-ti*. **91**.6 adds an extraneous sign after *na-ki-ri*. **91**.4 ŠU.<II>-*šu* for ŠU.II-*šú*. **91**.5 omits *aš* in ^{d}*aš-šur*. **92**.8 ^{d}MES for ^{d}AMAR.UTU. **92**.5 *ti*-[*ik*]-⸢*li*⸣-*šu* for *ti-ik-li-šú*. **93** *is-qu-uš-šú*: exs. 4, 6 have *iš-qu-uš-šú*; and ex. 7 has *iš-qu-uš-šin*. **93**.7 *ṭè-e-me* for *ṭè-em*. **94**.4, 6, 8 *ina* for *i-na*. **94** *e-le-nu*: exs. 2, 6 have *e-le-na*; and ex. 5 omits *nu*. **95** URU.NINA: ex. 2 has NINA*(copy: NAB×ZA).KI; ex. 4 has NINA.KI*(copy: ŠU); exs. 6, 9 have NINA.KI; and ex. 7 has URU.NINA.KI. **95**.2, 4 *ina* for *i-na*. **95** *lìb-bi-šú*: ex. 1 has *lib-bi-šu*; ex. 2 has [...] BE; ex. 3 has [*lìb*]-*bi*-⸢*ia*⸣; and ex. 4 has ⸢*lìb*⸣-*bi-ia*. **96**.3, 9 URU.BÀD-^{m}MAN*(copy: 30)-⸢GIN*⸣(copy:] ME) and URU.BÀD-^{m}MAN-GIN*(copy: IŠ) respectively for URU.BÀD-^{m}LUGAL-GI.NA. **97**.1, 5 *iz-ku-ru* and ⸢*iz-ku*⸣-*ru* respectively for *iz-ku-ra*. **97**.3, 9 omit MEŠ in É.GAL.MEŠ. **97**.1 adds an extraneous sign after AM.SI. **98**.5 GIŠ.SA-ḪU-*ni* for GIŠ.*mu-suk-kan-ni* (likely modern copyist error). **98**.3 [GIŠ].*ere*-⸢*ni*⸣ for GIŠ.EREN. **99** GIŠ.*dup-ra-nu*: ex. 3 has GIŠ.*dáp-ra*†-*a*-⸢*ni*⸣; exs. 4, 7 have GIŠ.*dup-ra-ni*; and ex. 6 has GIŠ*(copy: QA).*dáp-ra-ni**(copy: IR). **99**.4, 6, 8 add GIŠ before ŠIM.LI. **99**.4 *u* for *ù*.

100 LUGAL-*ti-šú*: ex. 3 has MAN-*ti-šú*; and exs. 7–8 have LUGAL-*ti-šu*. **100**.4, 7, 9 *qer-bu-uš-šú* for *qer-bu-uš-šu*. **101**.3 GIŠ.*ere-ni* for GIŠ.EREN. **102**.4 *ú**(copy: KID)-<*šat*>-*ri-ṣa* for *ú-šat-ri-ṣa*. **103**.3 GIŠ*(copy: MA).MES.⸢MÁ⸣.[KAN.NA] for GIŠ.*mu-suk-kan-ni*. **103**.5–6 GIŠ.*mu-suk-ka*†-*ni* and GIŠ.*mu-suk**(copy: ŠÀ)-*ka**(copy: IŠ)-*ni* respectively for GIŠ.*mu-suk-kan-ni*. **103** *mé-se-er*: ex. 3 has *me*-[*se-er*]; and exs. 4, 7, 9 have *me-se-er*. **105**.8 *né-reb-ši-in*† for *né-reb-šin*. **106**.4 omits *ti* in KUR.*ḫat-ti*. **106**.4, 9 *ina* for *i-na*. **106**.1, 8 omit KI in MAR.TU.KI. **107**.2, 4, 6 omit *a* in *ḫi-la-a-ni*. **107**.4, 8 *i-šá-as-su-šu* for *i-šá-as-su-šú*. **108** *ba-bi-ši-in*: exs. 2, 6, 9 have KÁ.MEŠ-*šin*; ex. 4 has *ba-bi-šin*; and ex. 7 has KÁ.MEŠ-*ši-in*. **108**.4–5, 7, 9 add MEŠ after UR.MAḪ. **109**.8 *tu-ʾa-a-mi* for *tu-ʾa-a-me*. **109**.1 *šar*$_5$ for ŠÁR. **109**.6 omits U in GÉŠ.U. **109**.8 8 UŠ for 6 UŠ. **109** 50.ÀM: ex. 2 has 40.⸢ÀM⸣; ex. 4 has 40.ÀM; ex. 5 has [...]+40.ÀM*(copy: DIŠ-AN); ex. 7 has 50.TA.ÀM; and ex. 9 has 60.TA.ÀM.

110.8 *mal-tak-tú* for *mal-tak-ti*. **111**.2, 4, 6, 9 *ina* for *i-na*. **112**.7 *ip-pat-qu-ú-ma* for *ip-pat-qu-ma*. **112** *nam-ri-ri*: exs. 4, 7–8 have *nam-ri-ir-ri*; and ex. 9 has *nam-ri-ir**(copy: NI)-*ri*. **113**.2, 6 omit GIŠ in GIŠ.*tim-me*. **113**.1, 7 GIŠ.*ere*-IGI and GIŠ.*ere-ni* respectively for GIŠ.EREN. **113**.1 Winckler's copy has TAR for *ḫu* in *šu-ta-ḫu-ti*. **114**.5, 9 omit 1. **114** *ku-bur-šú-un*: ex. 5 has ⸢*ku*⸣-*bur-šu-un*†; and exs. 7–8 have *ku-bur-šu-un*. **115**.5 *ú-kin**(copy: LU)-<*ma*> for *ú-kin-ma*. **116**.4 adds GIŠ before *dáp-pi*. **116** KÁ.MEŠ-*ši-in*: exs. 2, 4, 6–7 have KÁ.MEŠ-*šin*; ex. 5 has *ba*-[*bi-ši*]-⸢*in*⸣; ex. 8 has *ba-bi-ši-in*; and ex. 9 has *ba-bi-ši**(copy: ŠÚ)-*in*. **117**.6 *šad-de-e* for *šad-di*. **117**.4, 6–9 omit MEŠ in ^{d}LAMMA.MEŠ. **118**.8 *šá* for *ša*. **118**.6 KUR-*i*/*e**(copy: DÙ) for KUR-*i*. **118** *nak-liš*: ex. 4 has [*nak*]-*li-iš*; and ex. 5 omits *liš*. **119**.5 *ú-šá-aṣ-bi-ti* for *ú-šá-aṣ-bi-ta*.

120.7 SI.GAR-*šin* for SI.GAR-*ši-in*. **120**.8–9 NA$_4$.*pe-el* and NA$_4$†.*pi-i-li* respectively for NA$_4$.*pi-li*. **120**.6 [GAL].ME for GAL.MEŠ. **121**.7 ŠU.II.MEŠ-*šú* for ŠU.II-*šú*. **121** *ṣe-ru-uš-šin*: ex. 4 omits *ru*; and ex. 7 has *ṣe-e-ru-uš-šin*. **122** *a-sur-ru-šin*: ex. 2 has [*a-sur-ru-ši*]-*in*; exs. 5, 8–9 have *a-sur-ru-ši-in*; and ex. 6 has *a-sur-ru-ši**(copy: ME)-*in*. **124** *a-ši-bu-ut*: ex. 1 has *a-ši-bu-ti*; ex. 4 has *aš-bu-ut* (modern copyist error?); and ex. 7 has *a-ši**(copy: ŠÚ)-*bu-tu*. **125** *aš-šur*.KI: ex. 4 copy has ^{d}[x x] ⸢*qer*⸣-*bi-šá*, which likely was *aš*-⸢*šur*†⸣.[KI *ina*] ⸢*qer*⸣-*bi-šá*; exs. 7, 9 have ^{d}*aš-šur*.KI; and ex. 8 has ^{d}*a-šur*.KI. **125**.3, possibly 4 (restored via spacing) *ina* and [*ina*] respectively for *i-na*. **125** *qer-bi-šin*: ex. 4 has ⸢*qer*⸣-*bi-šá*; ex. 5 has *qer*†-*bi-ši-in*; and ex. 9 has *qer-bi-šá*. **126**.1 Winckler's copy omits SISKUR in UDU.SISKUR.MEŠ. **126**.6 *ma-ḫar-šu-un* for *ma-ḫar-šú-un*. **127**.8 *ru-uš-ši-i* for *ru-uš-še*$_{20}$-*e*. **127** *ṣar-pi*: ex. 3 has *ṣar**(copy: SUK)-*pu**(copy: ŠE-NU); ex. 4 has ⸢*ṣar*⸣-*pu*; and exs. 5, 8–9 have *ṣar-pu*. **128**.7, 9 *eb-bu* for *eb-bi*. **128**.4 *ta-mar-tú* for *ta-mar-tu*. **129** *ú-šam-ḫi-ir-šú-nu-ti-ma*: ex. 1 has *ú-šam**(copy: É)-*ḫi-ir-šu-nu-ti-ma*; ex. 3 has *ú-šam*-⸢*ḫir*⸣-*šú*-[*nu-ti-ma*]; ex. 5 has *ú-šam*-

ḫir-šú-nu-ti-ma; and ex. 7 has *ú-šam-ḫi-ir-šu-nu-ti-⸢ma†⸣*.

130 *nu-pa-ar-šú-un*: ex. 5 has *nu-⸢pa⸣-ar-šu-un*; and ex. 8 adds an extraneous ZA sign between *ar* and *šú*. **131**.3 ^{d}*a-šur*† for ^{d}*aš-šur*. **131**.3 *a-bu**(copy: KUR) for AD. **132**.2 has [...] DINGIR.[(x)].MEŠ for this line; this may be a modern dittography, based upon the previous line, which has exactly the same thing. **132**.3, 6, 8 *ina* for *i-na*. **132** *bu-ni-šú*: ex. 1 has *bu-un-ni-šú*; ex. 3 has [*bu*]-*un*†-*ni*-[*šú*]; and exs. 6–7 have *bu-ni-šu*. **133**.1 *el-lu-ti* for KÙ.MEŠ. **133** *lip-pa-lis-ma*: ex. 3 has [*lip*]-*pa-li*-⸢*is*⸣-[*ma*]; and ex. 6 omits *lis*. **136**.4–5 *ina* for *i-na*. **136** *pi-i-šú*: ex. 1 has *pi-i-šu*; ex. 3 has [*pi-i*]-*šu*; and ex. 6 has *pi**(copy: UD)-*i-šu*. **136**.4, 6–9 KÙ for *el-li*. **137**.3, 7 ⸢*li**⸣(copy: BU[)-[*iš*?-*šá-kin-ma*] and *liš-šá-kín-ma* respectively for *liš-šá-kin-ma*. **139**.4 omits *ù*. **139** *mu-šá*: ex. 3 has [*mu*]-*šu*; ex. 5 has *mu*-<*šá*/*šu*>; and ex. 7 has *mu-šu*. **139**.1, 7 *liš-tab-ru-ú-ma* and [*liš-tab-ru*]-⸢*ú*⸣-*ma**(copy: IZ) respectively for *liš-tab-ru-ma*.

141.2–3 *qí-bi-tuš-šú* and [*qí*]-⸢*bi*⸣-*tuš-šú* respectively for *qí-bi-tuš-šu*. **141** *ba-nu-šá*: ex. 2 has *ba-nu-ú*-[(x)]-*šá*; and exs. 5–6 have *ba-nu-ú-šá*. **143**.3 [*lit*]-*tu*-[(x)]-*tú* for *lit-tu-tu*. **144**.3, 9 *da**(copy: AŠ-ŠUR)-*ru-ú-ti* and ⸢*da*†⸣-*ru-ú**(copy: NUN)-[*ti*] respectively for *da-ru-ti*. **145**.1 *i-na* for *ina*. **145** *el-le-ti*: exs. 2, 6 have *el-le-tim*; ex. 4 has [*el*]-⸢*le*⸣-*tim*†; and ex. 5 has *el**(copy: MÁ)-*le-tim*†. **146**.3 adds an extraneous *ta* between *li* and *ṣa* of *li-ṣa-a*. **146** *a-ši-ib*: ex. 2 has [*a*]-*ši*-<*ib*> or [*a*]-*šib**(copy: ŠI); and ex. 6 has *a-šib*. **146**.1, 3 *lìb-bi-šá* and *lìb-bi**(copy: NI IR)-x-[x-(x)]-*šá* respectively for *lib-bi-šá*. **147**.2–3 *ina* for *i-na*. **147**.4, 6 add MEŠ after UZU. **147**.1 *lib-bi* for *lìb-bi*.

Text No. 14

2.1 Winckler, Sar. 2 pl. 40 erroneously has *kiš-šá-ti* for *kiš-šá-tim*. **3**.1 Winckler, Sar. 2 pl. 40 erroneously has GI$_7$ present. **3**.2 [*ak-ka-de*]-*e* for URI.KI†. **6**.1 Winckler, Sar. 2 pl. 40 has *e-tep-pu-ša* ⸢*šá*⸣ PA+KI [x]. **8**.1 Winckler, Sar. 2 pl. 40 erroneously omits URU. **9**.2 [*an-du-ra*]-⸢*ar*⸣-*šú-un* for *an*-⸢*du*⸣-*ra-ar*†-*šu-un*.

10.1 for *ul*-[*tu*] ⸢*u*$_4$⸣-*me*, Botta's copy has *ul*-[x] AN. Winckler, Sar. 2 pl. 40 has *ul-tu* UD.MEŠ. **10**.2 [*ul*]-*lu-ti* for *ul-lu-ú-ti*. **11** *áš*†-*ru-uš-šá*†: ex. 1 omits *šá*; and ex. 2 has [*áš*]-*ru**(copy: KI)-*uš-šá**(copy: ZA). **13**.2 *kan**(copy: I)-*šú-te* for *kan*†-*šu-ti*. **14**.2 GÌR.II-*iá* for GÌR.II-*ia*. **14**.2 *ul-tu* for *iš-tu*. **14**.2 *šá* for *ša*. **15**.2 *u* for ⸢*ù*⸣. **15** *mu-uš-ki* from ex. 2; copy of ex. 1 has *mu*-[x] x; Winckler, Sar. 2 pl. 40 has *mu-us*(var. *uš*)-*ki*. **17**.2 *nap-ḫar* for *nap-ḫa-ar*†. **17**.2 omits *ú* in *ru-qu-ú-ti*. **18**.2 *šá* for *ša*. **18**.2 KUR*(copy: ŠE).*el*†-*li-pí* for KUR.*el-li-pi*. **19**.2 *šá* for *ša*. **19** Winckler, Sar. 2 pl. 40 has *a-šib* for *šá*.

20.2 LÚ.*su-te-e* for LÚ.*su-ti-i*. **21**.2 *šá* for *ša*. **22**.2 [^{d}*te*]-*li-ti* for ^{d}*te-li-tim*. **23**.2 *šá* for *ša*. **24**.2 *ù* for *u*. **31**.1 copy has [x] AM DINGIR IA? MA [which presumably stands for ⸢*ṭè*⸣-*em* DINGIR-*ma i*-[or ⸢*ṭè*⸣-*em* DINGIR-<<*ia*>>-*ma* [. **35**.4 [GIŠ.*dup-ra*]-⸢*ni*⸣ for GIŠ.*dup-ra-nu*. **38**.3 ⸢*ap*⸣-*pa-a-te* for *ap-pa-a-ti*.

Text No. 22

4.5 *ba-nu-u* for *ba-nu-ú*. **7**.5 *še-ru-uš-šú* for *ṣe-ru-uš-šu*. **9**.5 *lìb-bi* for *lib-bi*.

Text No. 30

1 Copy of the traces on the squeeze for *ṣu* in URU.*ʾa-am-qa*-[x]-*ru-ṣu*: 

Text No. 41

1 ^{m}MAN-GI.NA: exs. 1, 6, 9, 13, 15, 17, 21–22, 40, 42 have ^{m}MAN-GIN; and exs. 7, 11, 44 have ^{m}LUGAL-GI.NA. **1** GAR: exs. 11, 44 have *šá-ak-ni*; and ex. 42 has GAR-*nu*. **1**.11, 44 ^{d}†EN.<LÍL> and ^{d}EN.LÍL respectively for ^{d}BAD. **1**.6 omits NU in NU.ÈŠ. **1**.28 omits first MAN. **1**.7 LUGAL† for first and second MAN. **1**.3 omits third MAN. **1**.2, 17 omit KI in *aš-šur*.KI. **2** *šá-kin*: exs. 1, 3, 8, 10, 13–15, 26–27, 29–30, 44, 46 have *šá-ki-in*; ex. 11 has *šá**(copy: A)-*ki-in*; and ex. 45 has *šá*-⸢*ki*⸣-*in*. **2** *šu-ba-re-e*: ex. 7 has *šú-ba-re-e*; ex. 15 omits *e*; and the *šu* in ex. 17 omits the final vertical wedge. **3**.6 ZIMBIR*(copy: <UD>.KIB.NUN).KI for ZIMBIR.KI. **3**.46 The EN sign (as part of NIBRU) has two horizontal wedges. **3** *ḫa-a-tin*: ex. 2 omits *a*; and ex. 22 adds an extraneous *ti* between *a* and *tin*. **3** *en-šu-te-šú-nu*: exs. 1, 11, 45 have *en-šu-ti-šú-nu*; ex. 2 has [*en-šu-ti-šú*]-⸢*un*⸣; exs. 3, 6 have *en-šu-te-šú-un*; ex. 8 has *en-šu-te-šu-nu*; ex. 9 has *en-šú-te-šú-nu*; ex. 10 has *en-šu-ti*-<*šú*>-*nu*; ex. 14 has [*en*]-*šu-ti*-<*šú*>-*nu*; exs. 29, 31 have *en-šu-ti-šu-un*; ex. 35 has *en*-⸢*šu*⸣-*ti-šú-nu*; and ex. 42 has ⸢*en*⸣-*šu*-⸢*ti*⸣-[*šú-nu*]. **4**.7 omits *a* in *a-ke-e*. **4**.1 The *li* in *mu-šal-li-mu* appears to omit the final vertical wedge. **4** *ḫi-bíl-ti-šú-un*: The *bíl* in ex. 1 has two superimposed vertical wedges rather than one vertical wedge at end; ex. 2 has *ḫi-bíl-tú-šu-un*; ex. 3 omits *šú*; exs. 8, 13, 44, 46 have *ḫi-bíl-ti-šu-un*; ex. 11 has *ḫi-bíl*-<*ti*>-*šu-un*; the *bil* in ex. 15 may be an error of modern copyist for *bíl*; ex. 16 omits *ti*; ex. 22 has *ḫi-bíl-te-šú**(text: NU)-*un*; ex. 26 has [*ḫi-bíl*]-⸢*ti*⸣-*šú-nu*; exs. 27, 38 have *ḫi-bíl-ti-šú-nu*; the *ti* in ex. 28 appears to omit the vertical wedge; ex. 29 has *ḫi-bíl-ti-šu-nu*; ex. 31 has *ḫi*-⸢*bíl*⸣-*ti-šú*-⸢*nu*?⸣; and ex. 42 has *ḫi-bíl-ti-šu*-⸢*un*⸣. **4**.5 *ka-ṣi-ir* for *ka-ṣir*. **5** *ki-din-nu-ut*: ex. 1 has *ki-din-nu-tu*; exs. 6, 9, 11, 28, 44–45 have *ki-din-nu-ti*; exs. 8, 46 have *ki-din-nu-te*; ex. 10 has *ki**(copy: KU)-*din*†-*nu-ti*; and ex. 22 has *ki-din*-x*(erased UD?)-*nu-ut*. **5** *ba-ṭi-il-tu*: ex. 1 has *ba*-<*ṭi*>-*il-tú*; exs. 3–4, 6–7, 10–11, 14, 17–18, 29, 31, 44, 46 have *ba-ṭi-il-tú*; ex. 8 has *ba-ṭi*-⸢*il*†⸣-*tú*; the *il* in ex. 22 omits vertical wedges at end of sign; ex. 23 has [*ba-ṭi*]-⸢*il*⸣-*tú*; ex. 27 has *ba*-⸢*ṭi-il*⸣-*tú*; and ex. 45 has ⸢*ba-ṭi-il*⸣-*tú*. **5** *mu-šá-áš-ši-ik*: ex. 1 omits *ši*; ex. 6 omits *áš*; and ex. 17 has *mu-šá-áš-ši**(text: ŠÚ)-*ik*. **5**.12 omits *ki* in *tup-šik-ki*. **6** BÀD.AN.KI: ex. 6 adds an extraneous RA between AN and KI; ex. 12 adds URU before it; and AN in ex. 27 has two superimposed vertical wedges instead of one vertical wedge. **6**.44 *mu-šap-ši-ik**(two angled wedges added later?) for *mu-šap-ši-ḫu*. **6** UN.MEŠ-*šú-un*: exs. 1–2 omit *un*; exs. 6, 17 omit *šú*; exs. 8, 10, 13, 15, 29, 46 have UN.MEŠ-*šu-un*; ex. 31 has UN.II.⸢MEŠ⸣-*šu-un*; ex. 41 adds an extraneous *nu* between *šú* and *un*; and ex. 42 has UN.⸢MEŠ-*šun*⸣. **6**.27 The *a* in *an-ḫa-a-ti* is simply two vertical wedges next to one another. **6**.17 *le-ʾu-ú* for *le-ʾi*. **6**.22 *mal**(text: NI)-*ki* for *mal-ki*. **7** URU.*ḫar-ra-na*: exs. 1, 8 omit *ra*; ex. 9 has <URU>.*ḫar-ra-an*; ex. 11 has URU.*ḫar**(copy: ḪI-AN)-<*ra*>-*na*; ex. 12 has URU.KASKAL-*ni*; ex. 27 has <URU>.*ḫar-ra-ni*; and ex. 35 has URU.KASKAL. **7** AN.DÙL-*la-šú*: The ⸢*šú*⸣ in ex. 1 appears to have two vertical wedges; ex. 3 has AN.DÙL-*la-a-šú*; and ex. 13 has AN.DÙL-*la-šu*. **7** *it-ru-ṣu-ma*: exs. 10, 44 have *it-ru-ṣu-ú-ma*; and ex. 11 has *it-ru-ṣu**(copy: NIN)-*ú-ma*. **7**.9 omits *i* in *ki-i*. **8** *iš-ṭu-ru*: ex. 27 has *iš-ṭu-ra*; and ex. 35 adds an extraneous *ru*? between *ṭu* and *ru*. **8** *za-kut-su*: ex. 27 has *za-ku-su*; the *su* in ex. 35 only has one vertical wedge; and ex. 45 has *za-kut-su-un*. **8**.1, 7 LUGAL for MAN. **8** *ul-tu*: ex. 6 has *ul**(copy: AMAR)-<*tu*>; exs. 8, 46 have TA; ex. 10 has *ul**(text: TI)-<*tu*>; and ex. 40 has ⸢*ul*⸣-<*tu*>. **8**.5 *be-lu-ti-šu* for *be-lu-ti-šú*. **9** *gaba-ra-a-šú*: exs. 5, 7–8, 13, 46 have *gaba-ra-a-šu*; and exs. 9, 28 omit *a*. **9**.22 *la* <<AŠ>> *ib-šu-ma* (the AŠ connects the preceding and following signs). **9** *ib-šu-ma*: exs. 1, 8, 11, 29–31, 45–46 have *ib-šu-ú-ma*; ex. 2 has ⸢*ib*†⸣-<<ŠÚ>>-*šu-ma*; exs. 6, 12, 27, 34, 39 have *ib-šú-ma*; ex. 9 has *ib-šú*-<*ma*>; ex. 10 has *ib-šú*-⸢*ú*⸣-<<x>>-*ma*; exs. 13, 15, 28 have *ib-šú-ú-ma*; ex. 42 has *ib-šu-u*-<*ma*>; and ex. 44 has *ib*-⸢*šu*⸣-*ú-ma*. **9**.6, 18, 27, 40 *ina* for *i-na*. **9** *ù*: exs. 6, 9, 16–18, 22 have *u*; exs. 8, 40 omit it, and ex. 35 has ⸢*ú*?⸣. **9** *ta-ḫa-zi*: exs. 2, 9–11, 29, 34, 39, 41, 44–46 have *ta-ḫa-a-zi*; ex. 8 has *ta-ḫa-a-zi**(copy: GI); and the *ta* in ex. 18 has only two vertical wedges, not three. **9**.15 inserts *u* after *ta-ḫa-zi*.

10.17 DÙ-*ši**(text: ŠÚ)-*na* for DÙ-*ši-na*. **10** *ḫaṣ-bat-ti*: ex. 1 has *ḫa-ṣa-ba-ti*; ex. 4 omits *bat*; ex. 11 has *ḫaṣ-bat-te**(copy: ŠE); and ex. 44 has *ḫaṣ-bat-te*. **10** *ú-daq-qi-qu-ma*: ex. 7 has *ú-dàq*-<*qi*>-*qu-ma*; ex. 9 has *ú-daq*†/*dàq*†-<*qi-qu*>-*ma*; exs. 10, 15, 29–30 have *ú*-

daq-qi-qu-ú-ma; ex. 12 has *ú-da*†*-qi-qu-ma*; ex. 13 has *ú-daq-qi-qu-*⸢*ú*⸣*-ma*; exs. 17, 42 omit *qi*; the *daq* in ex. 22 appears be three superimposed horizontal wedges with the middle one shorter than the other two; ex. 27 has *ú-dàq-qi-qu-ma*; and ex. 28 has *u-daq-qi-qu-ma*. **10** *ḫa-am-ma-mi*: exs. 3, 6, 8, 15, 29, 31, 34, 40, 46 have *ḫa-ma-am-mi*; ex. 9 has [*ḫa*]-⸢*ma*⸣*-am-mi*; exs. 10–11, 44 have ⸢*ḫa*⸣*-ma-am-mi*; ex. 13 has *ḫa-ma-am-*⸢*mi*⸣; ex. 30 has *ḫa-ma-am-*⸢*mi*$^{?!}$⸣; and ex. 42 omits *am*. **11**.23 *ar**(text: ŠÚ-RI)*-ba-ʾi* for *ar-ba-ʾi*. **11**.1, 8, 12, 16, 23, 25, 33, 35 *id-du-u* for *id-du-ú*. **11** *ṣer-re-e-ti*: exs. 1, 11, 17, 27, 30, 44 have *ṣer-re-e-tú*; ex. 10 has *ṣer-re-<e>-tú*; ex. 13 has ⸢*ṣer*⸣*-re-*⸢*e*⸣*-tu*; exs. 14, 29 have *ṣer-re-e-*⸢*tú*⸣; ex. 15 has *ṣer-re-e-tu*; ex. 25 has ⸢*ṣer-re-e*⸣*-tú*; and ex. 45 has *ṣer-re-e-te*. **11**.9–10 omit *ut* and *šu-ut* respectively in LÚ.*šu-ut*. **11**.27 omits *šú* in SAG.MEŠ-*šú*. **11**.41 adds an extraneous *šú* after SAG.MEŠ-*šú*. **11** LÚ.GAR-*nu-ti*: ex. 2 has LÚ.GAR-*nu*.MEŠ; ex. 7 has LÚ.GAR-*nu-*⸢*te*⸣; and ex. 40 has LÚ.GAR-*nu-tú*. **12** UGU-*šú-nu*: ex. 1 has UGU-*šu-nu*; ex. 10 UGU-*šú-nu**(text: TAR?); ex. 13 has ⸢UGU-*šu*⸣*-nu*, ex. 25 has ⸢UGU-*šu-nu*⸣, and ex. 30 has UGU-*šu*$^{?}$-⸢*nu*$^{?}$⸣. **12** *iš-tak-ka-nu-ma*: The *iš* in exs. 5, 21 omits the final vertical wedge; ex. 9 omits *ka*; and ex. 10 omits *tak-ka*. **12** *bíl-tu*: exs. 1, 9, 11, 13–14, 27, 29, 31, 44–45 have *bíl-tú*; ex. 8 has *bíl-tú**(copy: QA); and ex. 17 has ⸢*bíl*⸣*-tú*. **12** *ma-da-at-tú*: exs. 3–4, 12, 15–16, 18, 21–22, 31, 39 have *ma-da-at-tu*; ex. 17 omits *at*; ex. 32 has *ma-da-<at>-tu*; ex. 34 has *ma-da-at-*⸢*tu*⸣; exs. 35, 42 have ⸢*ma-da-at*$^{?}$*-tu*$^{?}$⸣; ex. 40 has ⸢*ma*⸣*-da-at-tu*; and ex. 41 has *ma-*[*da*]-⸢*at*⸣*-tu*. **12**.4 *áš-šú-ri* for *áš-šu-ri*. **13** *e-mid-su-nu-ti*: ex. 2 omits *ti*; ex. 32 omits *su*; ex. 34 has *e-mid-su-nu**(text: TAR$^{?}$)*-ti*; and ex. 39 omits *nu*. **13**.9, 20, 22, 28, 40 *ina* for *i-na*. **13** *mé-re-ši-ia*: ex. 1 has *me-re-ši-ia*; ex. 39 has *mé-re-ši-ia**(text: ṢI); and ex. 45 has *mé-re-ši-i-ia*. **13**.12 adds an extraneous sign after *mé-re-ši-ia*. **13** *ù*: ex. 5 omits it; exs. 6, 9, 22 have *u*; and ex. 40 has [*<ù>/u*]. **13**.42 *ḫi-is-<<sa>>-sat* for *ḫi-is-sa-at*. **13** *ḫi-is-sa-at* GEŠTU.II-*ia*: ex. 14 omits *at* GEŠTU.II-*ia*; and ex. 17 has *ḫi-is-sa-at-tú* ⸢GEŠTU⸣.II-*ia*, or possibly *ḫi-is-sa-at* ⸢GEŠTU.GEŠTU⸣.II-*ia*. **13** GEŠTU.II-*ia*: exs. 15, 30 have GEŠTU.II.MEŠ-*ia*; and ex. 22 adds an extraneous sign between II and *ia*. **14** *pal-ka-a-ti*: ex. 3 has *pal*†*-ka-<a>-ti**(copy: BE); exs. 8, 13, 46 have *pal-ka-a-te*; and ex. 19 has [*pal-ka-a*]-⸢*te*⸣. **14**.29 ^{d}*é**(text: KID)*-a* for ^{d}*é-a*. **14**.28 omits ^{d} in ^{d}*be-let*-DINGIR.MEŠ. **14**.27 UGU*(text: KA) for UGU. **14** MAN.MEŠ-*ni*: exs. 5, 12, 23, 27, 34, 43 omit *ni*; and ex. 7 has LUGAL.MEŠ-*ni*. **15**.9, 18, 40, 42 *ina* for the first *i-na*. **15**.10, 14 ŠÀ-*ia* for *lìb-bi-ia*. **15** second *i-na*: exs. 1, 5–6, 17–18, 22, 28, 40 have *ina*; and ex. 13 has *a-na*. **15**.10, likely 31 omit GÌR.II. **15** KUR.*mu-uṣ-ri*: exs. 5, 41, 44 omit KUR; and ex. 11 has <KUR>.*mu**(copy: ŠE)*-uṣ-ri*. **16** *i-na*: ex. 3 has *a-na*; exs. 7, 9, 13, 28, 39, 42 have *ina*; exs. 12, 19 omit *i* (haplography with *i* of KUR-*i* immediately before it); ex. 22 possibly has [*ina*]; and ex. 40 has ⸢*ina*⸣. **16**.12, 31, 34 add URU before NINA.KI. **16** *e-pu-uš-ma*: exs. 1, 9, 12–13, 15–16, 18, 22, 29, 31, 34 have DÙ-*ma*; and ex. 42 has DÙ-⸢*ma*⸣. **16** URU.BÀD-^{m}MAN-GIN: The vertical wedge of ^{m} in ex. 1 runs into an extraneous Winkelhaken; exs. 5–6, 16, 22, 30, 41 omit ^{m}; ex. 7 has URU.BÀD-^{m}LUGAL-GI.NA; ex. 8 has URU.BÀD-^{m}MAN-GI.NA; ex. 10 omits URU; ex. 19 has [URU].⸢BÀD⸣-^{m}MAN-GI.NA; ex. 25 has URU.BÀD-^{m}<MAN>-⸢GI⸣.NA; ex. 28 has [URU].⸢BÀD$^{?!}$⸣-<^{m}>MAN-GI.⸢NA⸣; ex. 45 has URU.⸢BÀD⸣-<^{m}>MAN-GI.NA; and ex. 46 has URU.BÀD-^{m}MAN-⸢GI⸣.[NA]. **16** MU-*šú*: ex. 13 has ⸢MU⸣*-šu*; ex. 28 omits *šú*; and ex. 45 has MU-*šu*. **17**.4 *pa-a-rak-ki* for *pa-rak-ki*. **17** *ra-áš-du-ti*: exs. 2–3, 8–9, 13, 29, 39, 41, 46 have *ra-áš-du-ú-ti*; ex. 22 has ⸢*ra-áš*⸣*-du-te*; ex. 25 has [*ra-áš*]*-du-ú-ti*; ex. 30 has *ra-*⸢*áš*⸣*-du-ú-<ti>*; ex. 43 has [*ra-áš-du*]*-u-*⸢*ti*⸣; and ex. 46 has *ra-áš-du-*⸢*ú*⸣*-ti*. **17**.22 omits *na* in *a-na*. **17**.2 ^{d}*šá-maš* for ^{d}UTU. **17** *ù*: exs. 6, 42 omit it; and exs. 7, 12, 17–18, 22 have *u*. **17** ^{d}*nin-urta*: exs. 1, 6, 9, 17–18, 22, 29, 40, 43 have ^{d}MAŠ; ex. 7 adds an extraneous AŠ sign between *nin* and *urta*; ex. 16 has ^{d}MAŠ*(copy: ŠI); and ex. 44 has ^{d}*nin-urta**(text: UR). **18** *i-na*: ex. 6 omits it; exs. 9, 17–18, 21–22, 29 have *ina*; and exs. 40, 42 have ⸢*ina*⸣. **18** *qer-bi-šú*: exs. 1, 3, 8, 11, 13, 15, 44–45 have *qer-bé-e-šú*; ex. 25 has *qer-*⸢*bé-e*⸣*-šu*; and ex. 46 has *qer-*⸢*bé*⸣*-e-šú*. **18**.6, 11 omit *liš* in *nak-liš*. **18** *ú-šab-ni-ma*: ex. 6 has *ú-šab-<<ab>>-ni-ma*, with *ú* at the end of one line and the remainder at the beginning of the next line; and ex. 40 has [*ú*]-⸢*šá*$^{?!}$⸣*-ab-ni-ma*. **18**.13 omits AM in AM.SI. **19** GIŠ.MES.MÁ.KAN.NA: Photos of ex. 10 indicate GIŠ.MES.MÁ*.KAN.x, where the lower horizontal of the MÁ is longer than the upper horizontal (with Botta copy); Botta's copy has IZ for the final sign; ex. 14 has GIŠ.*mu-suk-kan-na*; ex. 42 has ⸢GIŠ⸣.*mu-suk-*⸢*kan*⸣*-*[*na*]; and ex. 43 adds an extraneous DIŠ sign between KAN and NA. **19**.1 The IGI in GIŠ.*ere*-IGI omits the final horizontal wedge. **19** GIŠ.*dáp-ra-ni*: ex. 5 has GIŠ.*dáp-ra-a-ni*; ex. 10 has GIŠ.*dáp-ra-a-*⸢*ni*⸣; ex. 28 has GIŠ.*dáp-ra-a-nu*; and ex. 47 has ⸢GIŠ⸣.*dáp-*⸢*ra*⸣*-*[*a*]*-*⸢*ni*⸣ (via spacing). **19**.1 ŠIM.LI for GIŠ.LI. **19** GIŠ.*bu-uṭ-ni*: ex. 1 has GIŠ.*bu-ṭu-ni*; exs. 2, 5, 10, 43 have GIŠ.*bu-uṭ-nu*; ex. 6 has GIŠ.*bu-uṭ**(copy: ŠE)*-nu*; and ex. 25 has [GIŠ.*bu-uṭ*]-⸢*nu*⸣.

20.11 omits *šab* in *mu-šab*. **20** MAN-*ti-ia*: exs. 7, 44 have LUGAL-*ti-ia*; and ex. 11 has LUGAL*(copy: IN)*-ti-ia*; ex. 17 has MAN-*ti-ia**(text: I-ZA); and ex. 19 omits it. **20**.17 The *ab* in *ab-ni-ma* omits the final vertical wedge. **20** É Various exemplars have KID. **20**.43 omits *an* in *ḫi-la-an-ni*. **20** É.GAL: ex. 5 omits GAL; and ex. 39 has ⸢É⸣.GAL*(text: MA). **20**.25 omits *ti* in KUR.*ḫat-ti*. **21**.6, 9, 18, 22, 40, 42 *ina* for *i-na*. **21** KÁ.MEŠ-*šin*: ex. 1 has KÁ.MEŠ-*šú-un*; and the KÁ sign in ex. 25 appears to have a single vertical wedge at the end, followed by a Winkelhaken. **21**.15 omits GIŠ in GIŠ.ÙR.MEŠ. **21** GIŠ.*ere*-IGI: The first horizontal wedge of *ere* in ex. 17 is more similar to a Winkelhaken; and ex. 45 has GIŠ.*ere*-IGI*(text: MAŠ). **22** *ṣe-e-ru-šin*: exs. 1, 15, 29 have *ṣe-e-ru-uš-šin*; exs. 2, 11, 44 have *ṣe-<e>-ru-uš-šin*; exs. 3, 17–18, 22, 25, 42–43 omit *e*; ex. 8 has *ṣe-e-ru-uš**(copy: MAL)*-šin*; ex. 14 has ⸢*ṣer**⸣(copy: BU[)-[*uš*$^{?}$*-šin*$^{?}$⸣]; ex. 31 has ⸢*ṣe-<e>-ru*⸣*-uš-šin*; ex. 45 has *ṣe-e-*⸢*ru-uš*$^{?}$*-šin**⸣; and ex. 47 has ⸢*ṣe-<e>-ru-uš-šin*⸣. **22** *e-ma-am-mi*: ex. 6 omits *ma*; exs. 8, 39, 46 omit *am*; exs. 12, 16, 22, 35, 42 omit *mi*; and ex. 34 has *e-am-ma-mi*. **22** *bi-nu-ut*: ex. 7 follows the master line (i.e., not *bi-nu-<ut>* of Botta's copy); and exs. 9, 11, 13, 15, 44 have *bi-nu-ti*; . **22**.22 adds an extraneous DIŠ sign after KUR-*i*. **22** *ù*: exs. 6, 16, 22, 33–34, 42, 47 have *u*; and ex. 31 has ⸢*ú*$^{?!}$⸣. **22** *tam-tim*: exs. 3, 10–13, 15–16, 25, 29, 31, 33–34, 44–45, 47 have *tam-di*; ex. 5 omits it; and ex. 22 has KI-*tim*. **22**.5, 17–18 add MEŠ after NA_4. **23**.6, 9, 18, 21, 34, 40–42 *ina* for *i-na*. **23** *né-re-bé-ti-ši-na*: exs. 2–3, 42, 44 omit *ti*; exs. 4, 7, 18 have *né-re-biti*(É)*-ši-na*; ex. 9 has *né-re-bé-ti* at the end of one line and [*ši*]-⸢*na*⸣ at the beginning of next; ex. 10 has *né-re-be-ti-ši-na*; ex. 11 has *né-re-bé-<ti>-ši**(copy: ŠÚ)*-na*; ex. 17 has *<né>-re-biti*(É)*-ši-na*; ex. 21 has *né-re-bit*(É)*-ti-ši-na*; ex. 36 has *<né>-re-bit*(É)*-ti-ši-na*; ex. 39 has *<né>-*⸢*re*⸣*-biti*(É)*-ši-na*; and ex. 41 has *<né>-re-*[*biti*(É)*-ši-na*] (restored via spacing). **23**.44 omits *ma* in *ul-ziz-ma*, which is also likely in ex. 11 where the copy has ⸢*ul*⸣-[x]. **23**.12 omits MÌN in GIŠ.ŠUR.MÌN. **23** GIŠ.MES.MÁ.KAN.NA: exs. 1, 29 have GIŠ.*mu-suk-kan-ni*; ex. 8 has [GIŠ.*mu*$^{?}$*-suk*$^{?}$]-⸢*kan*⸣*-ni*; ex. 25 has GIŠ.*mu-suk**(text: omits upper horizontal wedge)*-kan**(text: I, Babylonian form)*-ni*; ex. 28 has GIŠ.MES.MÁ.KAN-*ni*; ex. 33 omits MES; and ex. 42 has ⸢GIŠ.*mu*⸣*-suk-kan-ni*. **24** *ú-rat-ta-a*: The *rat* in ex. 25 has three vertical wedges; and ex. 43 has *u-rat-ta-a*. **24** KÁ.MEŠ-*šin*: ex. 1 has KÁ.MEŠ-*šú-un*; ex. 9 omits MEŠ; the KÁ in ex. 28 appears to begin with three horizontal wedges. **24**.22 [BÀD]-⸢*šu*⸣ (x) for BÀD-*šú*. **24** *ki-ma*: The *ma* in ex. 22 omits the final vertical wedge; and ex. 43 omits *ki*. **24**.1 omits *ki* in *ki-iṣ-rat*. **24**.25 The KUR in KUR-*i* appears to have only two wedges. **25**.15 adds an extraneous IZ sign after *ú-šar-šid-ma*. **25** ^{d}UTU: exs. 1, 3 have ^{d}*šá-maš*; and ex. 12 has ⸢^{d}*šá*⸣-⸢*maš*⸣. **25** *ir-te-ʾu-ú*: ex. 8 has *ir-ti-ʾu**(copy: MAN-AN)*-ú*; ex. 22 omits *ú*; the *ú* in ex. 41 is at the start of the following line; and exs. 42–43 have *ir-te-ʾu-u*. **25** *ki-šit-ti*: The *ki* in ex. 25 appears to be KU; and ex. 28 has *ki-ši-ti*. **26** ŠU.II-*ia*: exs. 10, 30, 32 have ŠU.II.MEŠ-*ia*; ex. 14 has ⸢ŠU⸣.II.MEŠ-<*ia*>; ex. 28 omits ŠU.II; copy from ex. 34 ŠU.II*: 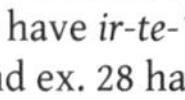 ;

ex. 41 has ŠU.II*(text: DIŠ-U)*-ia*; and ex. 42 has ŠU.II.⸢MEŠ⸣*-ia*. **26** *i-na*: exs. 6, 7, 13, 18, 22, 25, 31, 42, 44 have *ina*; ex. 11 omits it; ex. 34 has *a-na*; and ex. 46 has ⸢*ina*⸣. **26**.7, 34 ŠÀ for *lìb-bi*. **26**.13 adds an extraneous DIŠ sign after *lìb-bi*. **26**.10 *ú-še-šib**(copy: ŠI) or *ú-še-ši-<ib>*. **26**.15, 17 omit MEŠ in GAL.MEŠ. **26** *a-ši-bu-ut*: ex.

5 has a-šib; ex. 6 omits bu; ex. 10 has a-[ši]-bu-te; ex. 11 has a-ši*(copy: ŠÚ)-bu-ti; exs. 15, 25, 45 have a-ši-bu-te; and ex. 44 has a-ši-bu-ti. **26**.22 The e in AN-e has an extraneous vertical wedge head at the end of the sign. **27** ù: exs. 5, 45 omit it; and exs. 6, 42 have u. **27** a-ši-bu-ut: ex. 2 has a*(copy: MIN)-ši*(copy: ŠÚ)-bu-ti†; ex. 6 has a-ši-<bu>-ut*(copy: IZ); ex. 11 has a-ši*(copy: ŠÚ)-bu-ut; ex. 28 has [a-ši]-⸢bu⸣-ti; ex. 44 has a-ši*(no horizontal)-bu-ut; and ex. 45 has a-[ši-bu]-te. **27** šá-a-šú: exs. 2, 16 omit a; exs. 4, 34 have šá-a-šu; and ex. 10 has šá-a-ši. **27**.41 e*(text: GIŠ)-peš for e-peš. **28** qer-bi-šú: 1, 21, 25, 44 have qer-bé-e-šú; exs. 7, 36 have qer-bi-šu; ex. 11 has qer-bé-e-<šú>; ex. 29 has ⸢qer⸣-bé-e-šú; ex. 31 has qer-⸢be$^{?}$⸣-e-šú; and ex. 45 has ⸢qer-bé-e-šú$^{?}$⸣. **28** iš-ru-ku-in-ni: ex. 8 adds an extraneous u between in and ni; ex. 15 omits ni; and the iš in ex. 21 omits the final vertical. **28** a-na: exs. 11, 44 have ana; and ex. 18 has ina.

Text No. 43

1.17 šá-ak*(over erasure)-nu <<u$^{?}$>> ^{d}EN.LÍL NU.ÈŠ*(over erasure) ba*(over erasure)-ʾi-it. **1** The copies by Norris (1 R pl. 36), Lyon (Sar. no. 1) and Winckler (Sar. 2 pl. 43) all have NA-ʾi-it, but in all preserved cases the sign is BA not NA. **1**.43 ⸢u$^{?}$⸣ for ù. **2** KIŠ: exs. 3, 16, 57–58 have kiš-šá-ti; ex. 47 has ⸢kiš-šá-ti⸣; and 1 R pl. 36 has kiš-šat but no known exemplar has this. **2**.1, 47 omit ba in ar-ba-ʾi. **3** No exemplar has num for nu in ke-e-nu despite the copy in 1 R pl. 36 and Lyon, Sar. no. 1. **3** 1 R pl. 36 has ^{d}AG between ^{d}a-šur and ^{d}AMAR.UTU, but no known exemplar has this. **3** ú-šat-li-mu-šu-ma: ex. 4 has [ú-šat-li-mu]-šú-ma; and exs. 17, 58 have ú-šat-li-mu-šú-ma. **3** MU-šu: exs. 2, 4, 16–18, 30, 47, 56, 58 have MU-šú; exs. 3, 26 have ⸢MU⸣-šú, ex. 37 has [MU]-šú, and ex. 42 has ⸢MU-šú$^{?}$⸣. **3** ú-še-eṣ-ṣu-ú: ex. 19 has ú-še-eṣ-ṣu-u; and ex. 37 omits eṣ. **3**.19 omits e in re-še-e-te. **4**.1 The copy of kin in šá-kin by Lyon (Sar. no. 1) indicates an additional horizontal wedge at the beginning of the sign. **5**.2–4, 17–18, 39, 48, 58 ki-din-nu-ut for ki-din-nu-tu. **5**.17 mu-šá-áš*(text: MA)-ši-ik for mu-šá-áš-ši-ik. **6**.2–4, 48, 58 AN.DÙL-la-šú for AN.DÙL-la-šu. **6**.2 it-ru-ṣu-ú-ma for it-ru-ṣu-ma. **6** u: exs. 2–3, 16–19, 45–46, 56, 58 have ù; and exs. 4, 26, 42, 47 have ⸢ù⸣. **7** na-mur-ra-ti: exs. 2–4, 16–17, 58 have na-mur-ra-a-te; ex. 18 has [na]-⸢mur⸣-ra-a-te; ex. 42 has ⸢na-mur-ra-a-te⸣; ex. 47 has [na-mur]-⸢ra-a-te⸣; ex. 48 has na-⸢mur-ra⸣-a-te; and ex. 57 has na-mur-ra-te. **7** GIŠ.TUKUL.MEŠ-šu: exs. 2–4, 17–18, 26, 56, 58 have GIŠ.TUKUL.MEŠ-šú; ex. 5 has [GIŠ.TUKUL.MEŠ]-šú; and ex. 32 has GIŠ.TUKUL.MEŠ-⸢šú⸣. **8** be-lu-ti-šu: exs. 2–3, 16–17, 19, 42 have be-lu-ti-šú; ex. 4 has be-⸢lu⸣-ti-šú; ex. 18 has [be-lu-ti]-⸢šú⸣; ex. 47 has be-⸢lu-ti⸣-šú; and ex. 48 has ⸢be-lu⸣-[ti]-šú. **8** gab-ra-a-šu: exs. 2, 4, 16–18, 48 have gab-ra-a-šú; exs. 3, 47, 58 have gab-ri-a-šú; ex. 42 has ⸢gab-ra⸣-a-šú; and ex. 57 has gab-ri-a-šu. **8**.2, 4, 17–18 la-a for the first la. **8**.1 omits ù. **9**.41 adds MEŠ after KUR.KUR. **9** ṣer-re-e-tu: exs. 2, 4, 16–18, 56–58 have ṣer-re-e-te; exs. 3, 47 have ⸢ṣer⸣-re-e-te; ex. 5 has [...] x-te; ex. 28 has ⸢ṣer⸣-[re]-e-te; ex. 37 has ⸢ṣer-re⸣-e-⸢te$^{?}$⸣; ex. 42 has ṣer-re-e-te$^{?}$; and 1 R pl. 36 gives the variant tú for tu, but no known exemplar has this.

10 ḫur-šá-a-ni: exs. 3, 41 have ḫur-sa-a-ni; and ex. 27 omits a. **10** bé-ru-ú-ti: exs. 2–4, 16–17, 39, 58 have bé-ru-ú-te; and ex. 18 has bé-ru-ú-⸢te⸣. **10**.5 [du-ru-ug]-⸢šú$^{?}$⸣-un for du-ru-ug-šu-un. **11** pa-áš-qa-a-ti: exs. 2–3, 16–17, 42, 48, 57–58 have pa-áš-qa-a-te; exs. 4, 39 have pa-áš-qa-a-⸢te⸣; ex. 29 has [pa-áš-qa]-⸢a-te⸣; and ex. 47 has ⸢pa⸣-áš-qa-a-te. **11** e-ta-at-ti-qu-ma: exs. 2, 17 have e-ta-at-te-qu-ma; ex. 4 has e-⸢ta-at-te⸣-qu-⸢ma⸣; ex. 18 has e-⸢ta⸣-[at]-te-qu-ma; and ex. 56 has [e]-⸢ta⸣-at-te-qu-ma. **11** be-ra-a-ti: 1 R pl. 36 has bi-ra-a-te, but no known exemplar has bi for be; exs. 2–4, 16–18, 47, 56–58 have be-ra-a-te; ex. 5 has [be]-⸢ra⸣-a-te; ex. 28 has [be]-ra-a-te; and ex. 42 has be-⸢ra⸣-a-⸢te⸣. **12** KUR.e-lam-ti: exs. 2–3, 16–17, 42, 47–48, 57–58 have KUR.e-lam-te; ex. 4 has KUR.e-⸢lam-te⸣; ex. 18 has ⸢KUR.e-lam-te⸣; and ex. 29 has [KUR].⸢e-lam-te⸣. **12**.19 URU.ra-pi-i-qu for URU.ra-pi-qu. **13** 1 R pl. 36 has na-ḫal TAR, but no known exemplars has TAR after na-ḫal. **13** a-mur-re-e: exs. 2, 17–18, 42, 45 have a-mur-ri-i; and ex. 4 has a-⸢mur⸣-[ri]-⸢i⸣. **13** si-ḫir-ti-šá: exs. 3, 16, 19, 28, 46, 57–58 have si-ḫi-ir-ti-šá; and ex. 56 has ⸢si⸣-ḫi-ir-ti-šá. **14**.2–4, 10, 16–17, 39, 42, 48, 58 URU instead of KUR before ṣi-bar. **14** ru-qu-ti: exs. 2–3, 17–18, 58 have ru-qu-ú-te; exs. 16, 19, 42, 57 have ru-qu-ú-ti; ex. 46 has [ru]-⸢qu⸣-ú-te; ex. 47 has ru-⸢qu-ú⸣-ti; and ex. 48 has ru-qu-⸢ú⸣-[te/ti]. **15** qa-a-su: exs. 2–3, 5, 17–18, 37, 47, 58 have ŠU-su; ex. 4 has ŠU-⸢su⸣; exs. 16, 57 have qa-as-su; and ex. 32 has ŠU-[su]. **16** šak-nu-ti: exs. 2–4, 10, 16–19, 39, 42, 48, 57 have LÚ.GAR-nu-ti; and ex. 47 has LÚ.⸢GAR⸣-nu-ti. **16** ma-da-at-tu: ex. 58 omits at; and 1 R pl. 36 has te for tu, but all known exemplars have tu. **16**.2 (contra Fuchs), 17–18, 45 šá for ša. **17**.19 ina for i-na. **17** KUR.e-lam-ti: exs. 2–3, 16–18, 42, 46, 58 have KUR.e-lam-te; exs. 4, 47 have KUR.e-⸢lam⸣-te; ex. 34 has ⸢KUR⸣.e-⸢lam-te⸣; and ex. 57 has ⸢KUR⸣.e-lam-te. **17** taḫ-ta-a-šu: exs. 2–3, 17, 19, 58 have taḫ-ta-a-šú; ex. 4 has ⸢taḫ⸣-ta-a-šú; ex. 5 has ⸢taḫ-ta⸣-a-šú; ex. 37 has ⸢taḫ-ta-a⸣-šú; and 1 R pl. 36 has taḫ-ta-šú, but no known exemplar omits the a. **18**.42 omits KUR in LÚ.KUR.te-sa-a-a. **18** gu-un-ni-šu: ex. 2 has gu-un-ni-šú; exs. 17, 39, 48 have gu-un-né-e-šú; ex. 18 has gu-un-né-⸢e⸣-šú; and ex. 47 has ⸢gu-un-ni-šú⸣. **18**.45 It is unclear if one should read ⸢šá⸣-[lil] or ⸢šá⸣-<lil> since the LIL would be right at the join of two fragments. **18** KUR.tu-ʾu-mu-na: exs. 2–4, 16, 19, 27, 39, 42, 47, 57–58 add LÚ before it; exs. 17, 48 have LÚ.KUR.tú-ʾu-mu-na; and ex. 18 has ⸢LÚ⸣.KUR.tú-ʾu-mu-⸢na⸣. **18** LÚ.na-sik-šú-nu: ex. 2 adds KUR after LÚ; exs. 16, 57 have LÚ.na-sik-šu-nu; ex. 34 has ⸢LÚ.na-sik-šu$^{?}$-nu$^{?}$⸣; ex. 47 has LÚ.na-sik-šu-⸢nu⸣; and ex. 42 has ⸢LÚ.na-sik-šu⸣-[nu]. **18** 1 R pl. 36 apparently has a variant without ma on i-pi-du-ma, but all known exemplars have it. **18** ma-ḫar: the ma in ex. 3 has four horizontal wedges; and ex. 47 omits it. **19** rap-ši: 1 R pl. 36 has an abnormal rap but no known exemplar has this form. **19**.2, 17 URU.ḫa-zi-ti for URU.ḫa-zi-te. **19**.4 ú-še-⸢rib⸣ for ú-še-ri-ba.

20.16 omits i in LÚ.mar-si-i-ma-ni. **20** 1 R pl. 36 has a variant ši for šú in si-it-ta-šú-nu, but no known exemplar has this. **20** in-né-et-qa-am-ma: 1 R pl. 36 has LUGAL for in, but no known exemplar clearly has this; and ex. 45 omits am. **20** ú-šar-mu-ú: exs. 2, 25, 45 have ú-šar-mu-u; and ex. 42 has ú-⸢šar⸣-mu-u. **21**.57 sa-an-da-niš*(text: KUR) for sa-an-da-niš. **21** i-ba-ru-ma: exs. 2, 16–17, 47, 57 have i-ba-ru-ú-ma; ex. 28 has [...] (x)-⸢ú⸣-ma; ex. 34 has i-ba-⸢ru-ú-ma⸣; ex. 35 has ⸢i$^{?}$-ba⸣-ru-ú-[ma]; and ex. 42 has ⸢i-ba-ru-ú-ma⸣. **22** URU.ši-nu-uḫ-te: exs. 2–3, 16–17, 39, 42, 48, 57–58 have URU.ši-nu-uḫ-te; ex. 4 has URU.ši-nu-⸢uḫ-te⸣; and ex. 47 has ⸢URU⸣.[ši]-⸢nu⸣-uḫ-te. **23** ^{m}am-ba-ri-is: exs. 2, 4, 17–18, 39, 48 have ^{m}am-ba-ri-is-si; and the ba in ex. 3 is slightly abnormal in form. **23** da-mi-iq-ti: exs. 2–3, 17, 48 have da-mi-iq-te; ex. 4 has da-⸢mi⸣-iq-te; and ex. 18 has ⸢da⸣-mi-iq-te. **23**.2, 4, 17–18, 48 ^{m}MAN-GIN for ^{m}LUGAL-GI.NA. **23**.18 im-šú-ma for im-šu-ma. **23**.1, 45 KUR.ur-ar-⸢ṭí⸣ and KUR.ur-ar-ṭí respectively for KUR.ur-ar-ṭi. **23** u: ex. 2 omits it; exs. 3, 16–18, 25, 35, 42, 47, 58 have ù; and exs. 4, 32 have ⸢ù⸣. **24** ek-mu-te: exs. 2–3, 16–18, 28, 57–58 have ek-mu-ú-te; ex. 4 has ek-mu-⸢ú-te⸣; ex. 35 has ek-mu-⸢ú-te⸣; ex. 42 has ek-⸢mu⸣-ú-⸢te⸣; and ex. 47 has ek-mu-⸢ú⸣-te. **24** mu-rap-pi-šú: exs. 2–4, 16–17, 58 have mu-rap-pi-šú; ex. 25 has [mu-rap]-⸢pi⸣-šú; ex. 35 has mu-⸢rap⸣-[pi]-⸢šú⸣; ex. 42 has ⸢mu⸣-rap-pi-šú; and ex. 47 has ⸢mu-rap⸣-pi-šú. **24** pu-lu-un-ge-šu-un: exs. 2–3, 17–18, 25 have pu-lu-un-ge-e-šú; ex. 5 has ⸢pu⸣-lu-un-ge-e-šú; exs. 16, 35, 42, 57 have pu-lu-un-ge-e-šu; ex. 19 has ⸢pu⸣-lu-un-ge-e-šu; ex. 36 has [pu-lu-un]-⸢ge⸣-e-⸢šú⸣; ex. 40 has ⸢pu⸣-lu-un-ge-e-⸢šú⸣; ex. 47 has pu-lu-un-⸢ge-e-šú⸣; and ex. 58 has pu-lu-un-ge-e-šú-un. **25**.3, 58 tuq-ma-ti for tuq-ma-te. **25** ^{m}i-lu-bi-iʾ-di: exs. 2–3, 16, 28, 57–58 have ^{m}i-lu-ú-bi-iʾ-di; ex. 47 has ^{m}i-⸢lu-ú⸣-bi-iʾ-di; and 1 R pl. 36 has ^{m}i-ib-ú-bi-iʾ-di, but no known exemplar has ib for lu. **26** na-bi-iʾ: exs. 2–3, 16–18, 48, 57–58 have na-a-bi-iʾ; and ex. 49 has na-a-bi-x. **26**.2–3, 7, 16–19, 45, 47–48, 58 URU instead of KUR before gar-ga-miš. **26** ^{m}pi-si-i-ri: exs. 2, 17, 48 have ^{m}pi-i-is-si-ri; exs. 3, 19, 45 have ^{m}pi-i-si-i-ri; ex. 4 has ^{m}pi-i-is-⸢si⸣-ri; ex. 18 has ⸢^{m}⸣pi-i-is-si-ri; ex. 42 has ^{m}pi-i-si-⸢ri⸣; ex. 47 has ^{m}pi-i-⸢si⸣-i-ri; and ex. 58 has ^{m}pi-i-si-i-⸢ri⸣. **26**.18, 25 ṣa-lip-ti and ⸢ṣa⸣-lip-ti respectively for ṣa-lip-te. **26** qa-a-su: exs. 2–3, 5, 16–18, 35–36, 42, 57 have ŠU-su; exs. 4, 25 have ⸢ŠU-su⸣; and exs. 40, 47 have ⸢ŠU⸣-su. **27**.2–4, 7, 16–19, 42, 48, 57–58 URU for KUR before mu-ṣa-ṣi-ri. **27**.16 has NI for sa in ^{m}u-sa-a. **27**.2

⸢*ša*⸣ for LUGAL. **27** KUR.*ur-ar-ṭi*: 1 R pl. 36 has a variant of LÚ for KUR, but no known exemplar has this; and ex. 45 has KUR.*ur-ar-ṭí*. **27.19**, 42, 45 *i-na* for the first *ina*. **27** *pu-luḫ-ti-šu*: exs. 2, 4, 16–19, 42, 45, 47, 57 have *pu-luḫ-ti-šú*; exs. 3, 58 have *pu-luḫ-te-šú*; ex. 28 has [*pu*]-⸢*luḫ*⸣-*ti-šú*; and ex. 48 has ⸢*pu*⸣-*luḫ-ti*-⸢*šú*⸣. **27** GAL-*ti*: exs. 3, 16, 28, 47, 57 have GAL-*te*; and ex. 19 has *ra-bi-ti*. **27.25** adds an extraneous *ma*$^{?}$ between *ma* and *ni* of *ra-ma-ni-šú*. **27** *ú-qa-ta-a*: exs. 2–3, 5, 16–17, 35–36, 42, 57 have *ú-qat-ta-a*; ex. 4 has ⸢*ú*⸣-*qat-ta-a*; ex. 18 has *ú-qat-ta*-⸢*a*⸣; and ex. 47 has *ú-qat*-⸢*ta-a*⸣. **28** 1 R pl. 36 appears to put IŠ as a variant for URU in URU.*suk-ki-a*, but it may instead be the last sign in the line, which the copy would otherwise omit. **28** KUR.*ka-ak-me-e*: exs. 2–3, 16, 18, 57–58 have KUR.*ka-ak-mi-i*; ex. 4 has KUR.*ka*-⸢*ak*⸣-*mi*-⸢*i*⸣; ex. 17 has KUR.*ka-ak-mi*-⸢*i*⸣; ex. 25 has [KUR.*ka-ak*]-⸢*mi*⸣-*i*; ex. 28 has KUR.*ka-ak-mi*-[*i*]; ex. 42 has ⸢KUR⸣.[*ka*]-⸢*ak*⸣-*mi-i*; and ex. 47 has KUR.⸢*ak*⸣-*ka-mi*-[*i*]. **28** 1 R pl. 36 may omit *iš* in *na-ba-di-iš* at the end of the line, but see the earlier note for this line. **29** 1 R pl. 36 has the variant IL for *ba* in *ba-ḫu-la-te-šú-nu*, but no known exemplar has this variant. **29** *ú-ṭa-bi-ḫu-ma*: ex. 3 has *ú-ṭa-ab-bi-ḫu-ma**, in which the *ma* has four horizontal wedges; exs. 16, 57 have *ú-ṭa-ab-bi-ḫu-ma*; ex. 19 has *ú-ṭa-ab*-⸢*bi*⸣-*ḫu-ma*; ex. 28 has [*ú-ṭa*]-⸢*ab*⸣-*bi-ḫu-ma*; ex. 42 has *ú*-⸢*ṭa*⸣-*ab-bi-ḫu-ma*; and ex. 47 has *ú-ṭa-ab-bi*-⸢*ḫu-ma*⸣. **29** *mu-ú-ti*: exs. 2–3, 17–18, 25, 40, 45, 58 have *mu-ú-te*; ex. 4 has *mu*-⸢*ú-te*⸣; and ex. 5 has *mu*-⸢*ú*⸣-*te*.

30.2, 4, 17–18, 48 *la-a* for *la*. **30.1** omits MEŠ in UN.MEŠ. **30.2**–4, 16–19, 28, 42, 47–48, 57–58 omit KUR in KUR.*ḫar-ḫar*.KI. **30.40** *mi-iṣ-ri* for *mi-ṣir*. **30.17** omits KI in *aš-šur*.KI. **31.7** <<⸢*mu*⸣-*ta*-⸢ḪI$^{?}$⸣>> ⸢*mu-ta*$^{?}$-*qí*$^{?}$-*in*$^{?}$⸣. **31.3**, 58 KUR.*el-li-pi* for KUR.*el-li-pí*. **31** *zi-kir-šu*: exs. 5, 17, 25, 40 have *zi-kir-šú*; and ex. 47 has ⸢*zi-kir-šú*⸣. **32** 1 R pl. 36 has DA rather than the first *ša*, but no exemplar has this. **32** KUR-*e*: exs. 2–3, 16–18, 28, 47–48, 57–58 have KUR-*i*; and exs. 7, 45 have KUR-⸢*i*⸣. **32.5** Fuchs, Khorsabad p. 37 indicates that ex. 5 omits the *a* in *ba-ra-a-nu-ú*, but this is not the case. **32.2**, 17–18 omit *eṣ* in *ú-še-eṣ-ṣu-ú*. **32.5**, 17, 25, 40 URU-*uš-šú* for URU-*uš-šu*. **33.3** omits *a* in ^{m}*a-da-a*. **33** *aš-šur*: exs. 2–3, 16, 18, 28, 35–36, 42, 57–58 have ^{d}*a-šur*; ex. 5 has ⸢^{d}*a-šur*⸣; ex. 40 has ^{d}*a*-⸢*šur*⸣; and ex. 47 has ⸢^{d}*a-šur*⸣. **34.45** ⸢*it*⸣-*pe-e-šú* for *it-pe-e-šu*. **34.19** adds an extraneous *ša* after SIG$_5$-*tim*. **34.42**, 45 x-⸢*du-ú*⸣-*te* and *na-du-ú-te* respectively for *na-du-te*. **34.19**, 45 *ú*-⸢*zu-un*⸣-*šú* and *ú-zu-un-šú* respectively for *ú-zu-un-šú*. **35.19** *zaq-ru-ú-ti* for *zaq-ru-ti*. **35.42** ⸢*ur*⸣-*qí*-⸢*tu*⸣ for *ur-qi-tu*. **36.19** omits *im* in *šu-zu-zi-im-ma*. **37** The copies by Lyon and Winckler have ŠU for *la*. **38** The ME of ABGAL sometimes looks more like LAL or LIŠ than ME. **38.1** omits *ù*. **39.45** *ra-pa-áš-tu* for *ra-pa-áš-tum*. **39.42** omits *li* in *ti-il-li-nu-ú*.

40 The copies by Lyon and Winckler have *ḫa-bal* for *za-bal*, but no known exemplar has *ḫa*. **40.19**, 42 *na*-⸢*ḫar*⸣-*šu-še* and *na*-⸢*ḫar*⸣-NA-*še* respectively for *na-ḫar-šú-še*. **41.19**, 45 *a-me-lu-te* for *a-me-lu-ti*. **42** *i-ta-te-e-šu*: exs. 19, 45 have *i-ta-te-e-šú*; and ex. 42 has [...] x-⸢*e*⸣-*šú*. **43.19** *šá-a-šú* for *šá-a-šu*. **43.19**, 42 *qer-bu-uš-šú* for *qer-bu-uš-šu*. **44.7** omits GÌR.II. **44** KUR-*e*: exs. 2, 4, 16–18, 28, 42, 48, 57–58 have KUR-*i*; ex. 3 has KUR*-*i*, in which the KUR looks more like ŠE; ex. 45 has KUR-⸢*i*⸣; and ex. 47 has ⸢KUR⸣-*i*. **44.2**–3, 5, 18, 58 *di-im-te* for *di-im-ti*. **44.19** *na-du-u* for *na-du-ú*. **45** *la-bi-ru-te*: exs. 2–3, 16–18, 47, 57–58 have *la-bi-ru-ú-te*; ex. 7 has *la-bi*-⸢*ru-ú-te*⸣; ex. 42 has [*la*]-⸢*bi*$^{?}$⸣-*ru-ú-te*; and ex. 48 has *la-bi-ru-ú*-⸢*te*⸣. **45** *el-la-mu-u-a*: exs. 16, 57 have *el-la-mu-ú-a*; and ex. 28 has x x x-⸢*ú-a*⸣. **45** 1 R pl. 36 has the variant QA for KUR, but no known exemplar has this. **46.2**, 17–18, 48 *a-šar-šú* for *a-šar-šu*. **46.3** has an erased DIŠ sign after *ú-maš-ši-i-ma*. **46** *šu-šu-ub-šu*: exs. 2–3, 16–18, 47–48, 57–58 have *šu-šu-ub-šú*; and exs. 4, 28, 42 have ⸢*šu*⸣-*šu*-⸢*ub*⸣-*šú*. **46** ÍD-*šu*: exs. 2, 18 have ⸢ÍD⸣-*šú*; exs. 3, 16–17, 57–58 have ÍD-*šú*; ex. 5 has x-*šú*; and ex. 25 has ⸢ÍD-*šú*$^{?}$⸣. **46** *iz-ku-ur*: ex. 5 has ⸢*iz*⸣-*kur*; and exs. 17–18, 25 have *iz-kur*. **47** 1 R pl. 36 has ZU.AD for ZU.AB, but no known exemplar has this. **47** 1 R pl. 36 has *né-me-qí* for *né-me-qi*, but no known exemplar has this. **47** *su-un-nu-nu-ma*: ex. 2, 16–18, 57–58 have *su-un-nu-nu-ú-ma*; ex. 3 has *su*$^{?}$-*un-nu-nu-ú-ma*; ex. 28 has ⸢*su*$^{?}$⸣-*un*-[*nu*]-*nu-ú-ma*; 1 R pl. 36 has *zu* for *su* and Winckler gives this as a variant for ex. 3, but no exemplar clearly has this although the reading of the sign in exs. 3, 28, 42 is uncertain. **47** *nik-la-a-ti*: exs. 2–3, 36, 58 have *nik-la-a-te*; ex. 5 has traces-⸢*la*⸣-*a-te*; exs. 25, 28 have ⸢*nik*⸣-*la-a-te*; and ex. 47 has [*nik-la*]-*a*-⸢*te*⸣. **48.3**, 16–18, 28, 42, 48 omit *an* in ^{d}*nin-men-an-na*. **49** *šá-a-šú*: exs. 7, 19 have *šá-a*-⸢*šu*⸣; exs. 16, 28, 45, 57 have *šá-a-šu*; ex. 42 has [*šá-a*]-⸢*šu*⸣; and ex. 47 has ⸢*šá*⸣-*a-šu*. **49.2** BÁRA-*ma-ḫi* for BÁRA.MAḪ-*ḫi*. **49.17**–18, 48 *be-lu-te-ia* for *be-lu-ti-ia*. **49** 1 R pl. 36 has *ur*-ṢI (not *ur*-ZI as given in Fuchs, Khorsabad p. 39) with the variant URU for ṢI, but no known exemplar has either ṢI or URU. **49.16** *ù* for *u*. **49** *e-pe-su*: exs. 2–3, 16–18, 28, 36, 57–58 have *e-pe-es-su*; ex. 42 has ⸢*e-pe-es*⸣-*su*; ex. 47 has [*e-pe*]-⸢*es*⸣-*su*; and ex. 11 has *e-pe*-x-*su*, where the sign for x appears as: 

50 *kit-ti*: exs. 2, 16–18, 57 have *kit-te*; ex. 4 has [...] x-⸢*te*⸣; and exs. 47–48 have ⸢*kit-te*⸣. **50** 1 R pl. 36 has *mi-šá-ri-šú*, but no known exemplar adds *šú* after *mi-šá-ri*. **50.17** The sign form for *la* is anomalous, similar to TU$^{?}$. **50.45** *en-še* for *en-ši*. **51** *šá-a-šú*: exs. 2, 16, 28, 47, 57–58 have *šá-a-šu*; ex. 7 has *šá*-⸢*a*⸣-*šu*; and ex. 42 has [*šá*]-⸢*a*⸣-*šu*. **51** *ša-a-a-ma-nu-te*: exs. 2 (contra Fuchs), 57 have *šá-a-a-ma-nu-te*; exs. 3, 11, 16–18 have *šá-a-a-ma-nu-ti*; ex. 4 has ⸢*šá*⸣-*a-a-ma-nu*-⸢*te*⸣; ex. 42 has *šá-a-a-ma*-⸢*nu-te*⸣; and ex. 58 has *ša-a-a-ma-nu-ti*. **51.19** The *a* in *ṭup-pa-a-te* has an extraneous wedge. **51.2**–3, 16–18, 28, 58 omit MEŠ in ZABAR.MEŠ. **52** *ri-ga-a-te*: exs. 2, 7, 55 omit *a*; exs. 3, 11, 58 have *ri-ig-ga*-<*a*>-*ti*; exs. 16–18, 28, 57 have *ri-ig-ga*-<*a*>-*te*; ex. 47 has *ri-ig-ga*-[(*a*)-*ti*/*te*]; and ex. 48 has *ri-ig-ga*-<*a*>-⸢*te*⸣. **52** *pa-nu-šú-nu*: exs. 3, 11, 58 have *pa-nu-šu-nu*; and ex. 40 has ⸢*pa-nu-šu*⸣-*nu*. **52** 1 R pl. 36 omits *šak-nu*, but no known exemplar does this. **52.3**, 11, 58 *ad-din-šu-nu-ti* for *ad-din-šú-nu-ti*. **53.11** <<*ba-ni*>> *ba-ni-i-šu*. **53.7** omits *i* in *ba-ni-i-šu*. **53** PÌRIG: The sign in ex. 2 is NÍNDA×ŠE.A$^{?}$.AN$^{?}$; and the sign in ex. 58 is NÍNDA*×UD-EŠ, in which the NÍNDA sign lacks the Winkelhaken. **53.2**, 4, 17–18, 48 omit *ù*. **53** *te-né-še-te*: exs. 2–3, 11, 16–18, 57–58 have <*te*>-*né-še-e-te*; ex. 4 has <*te*>-*né-še*-⸢*e-te*⸣; ex. 28 has [<*te*>$^{?}$-*né-še*]-⸢*e*⸣-*ti*; and ex. 42 has <*te*>-⸢*né-še-e*⸣-[*te*/*ti*]. **53.2**–3, 11, 16–18, 28, 36, 47, 58 *te-me-qí* for *te-me-qi*. **53.11** *u-šaq-qí*-⸢*ma*⸣ for *ú-šaq-qí-ma*. **54** u$_4$-*me*: exs. 2–3, 11, 16–18, 47, 55 have u$_4$-*mi*; ex. 7 has ⸢u$_4$-*mi*⸣; exs. 19, 45 have UD.MEŠ; ex. 28 has [u$_4$]-⸢*mi*⸣; and ex. 48 has u$_4$-⸢*mi*⸣. **54** *qer-bu-uš-šu*: exs. 3, 11, 16, 18–19, 44, 48 have *qer-bu-uš-šú*; ex. 4 has ⸢*qer-bu*⸣-*uš-šú*; ex. 28 has ⸢*qer*⸣-*bu-uš-šú*; ex. 42 has *qer*-⸢*bu-uš-šú*⸣; and ex. 58 has *qer-bu-uš**-*šú*, in which the *uš* omits the Winkelhaken and final vertical wedge **54.19** Fuchs, Khorsabad p. 40 indicates that this exemplar omits *a-na*, but this is not the case. 54 *qa-ti*: exs. 2, 11, 18 have *qa-a-te*; exs. 3, 58 have *qa-a-ti*; exs. 4, 17 have *qa-te*; and ex. 47 has ⸢*qa-a-ti*⸣. **55** *pi-ia*: ex. 2 has *pi-i-ia*; ex. 7 has ⸢*pi*$^{?}$-*i*$^{?}$-*ia*⸣; and ex. 55 has ⸢*pi-i*⸣-*ia*. **55.7**, 19 omit *um* in *ke-e-nu-um*. **55** *ú-lu*: ex. 2–3, 11, 16–19, 44–45, 58 have *ú-lu-ú*; exs. 4, 28, 42 have ⸢*ú-lu-ú*⸣; ex. 35 has [*ú*]-⸢*lu-ú*⸣; and ex. 48 has *ú*-⸢*lu*⸣-*ú*. **55.3** The *ma* in *ma-a'-diš* has four horizontal wedges. **55** *iq-bu-u-ni*: exs. 2–3, 16, 58 have *iq-bu-ú-ni*; ex. 4 has ⸢*iq*⸣-*bu-ú-ni*; ex. 28 has ⸢*iq*⸣-*bu-ú*-⸢*ni*⸣; ex. 36 has *iq-bu-ú*-⸢*ni*⸣; and ex. 45 omits *u*. **56.11** omits *šu* in *na-an-nu-uš-šu-un*. **56** *muš-pe-e-lu*: exs. 2–3, 11, 16–18, 28, 55, 57–58 have *muš-pe-e-lum*; ex. 4 has ⸢*muš*⸣-*pe*-⸢*e-lum*⸣; ex. 35 has [*muš-pe*]-⸢*e*⸣-*lum*; ex. 42 has [*muš-pe*]-⸢*e-lum*⸣; ex. 44 has [*muš*]-⸢*pe*⸣-*e-lum*; and ex. 48 has x-⸢*pe-e*$^{?}$⸣-*lum*. **56** *gap-šá-a-te*: exs. 2, 17–18, 48 have *gap-šá-a-ti*; and ex. 4 has ⸢*gap-šá*⸣-*a-ti*. **56** *ad-ke-ma*: exs. 3, 11, 16, 57–58 have *ad-ke-e-ma*; and ex. 45 has ⸢*ad-ke*⸣-*e*-⸢*ma*⸣. **56.3**–4 Lyon states that these exemplars have *ki* for *ku* in *tup-šik-ku*, but both have *ku*. **57.47** omits *ṣi* in ITI.*ṣi-i-taš*. **57.1** omits *e* in EŠ.BAR-*e*. **58.11** inserts an extraneous *u* after ^{d}*a-nim*. **58.1** ^{d}EN.LÍL*(text: É) for ^{d}EN.LÍL. **58.17** *na-bu-u* for *na-bu-ú*. **58.2**–4, 11, 17, 58 MU-*šú* for MU-*šu*. **59.58** The second ÈŠ in UD.ÈŠ.ÈŠ omits one of the horizontal wedges in the first pair of horizontal wedges. **59** *pal-ke-e*: exs. 2–3, 11, 16–18, 42, 48, 58 have *pal-ki-i*; ex. 4 has ⸢*pal*⸣-*ki-i*; ex. 35 has ⸢*pal-ki-i*⸣; ex. 44 has ⸢*pal*⸣-*ki-i*; and ex. 47 has *pal*-⸢*ki-i*⸣. **59.58** The *gim* in *gim-ri* omits Winkelhaken. **59.19** omits *as* in *lib-na-as-su*.

60 *as-ru-qu-ma*: exs. 2, 16–18, 58 have *as-ru-uq-ma*; ex. 3 has

⌜*as*⌝-*ru*-⌜*uq*⌝-*ma*; ex. 4 has *as-ru*-⌜*uq-ma*⌝; and ex. 42 has ⌜*as*⌝-*ru-uq*-[*ma*]. **60** ŠU.ÍL.KÁM: exs. 2–3, 11, 16–18, 28, 36, 42–43, 57–58 insert LÁ between ÍL and KÁM; ex. 4 has ŠU.⌜ÍL⌝.x.x ; and and ex. 31 has ŠU.[ÍL].⌜LÁ$^{?}$⌝.[KÁM]. **61** *mu-uš-pel*: exs. 2, 4, 11, 16–18, 42, 47–48, 57–58 have *mu-uš-pé-él*; ex. 3 has *mu-uš-pé*-⌜*él*⌝; and ex. 44 has [*mu-uš*]-⌜*pé*⌝-*él*. **61**.57 omits *te-me-en*. **61**.19 omits *e* in *uš-še-e-šu*. **61** *lib-na-su*: exs. 2, 11, 16–17, 42, 57–58 have *lib-na-as-su*; ex. 4 has *lib*-⌜*na-as*$^{?}$-*su*$^{?}$⌝; ex. 18 has *lib-na*-⌜*as*⌝-*su*; ex. 31 has ⌜*lib-na-as-su*⌝; ex. 36 has *lib-na-as*-[*su*]; and ex. 43 has *lib-na*-⌜*as*$^{?}$⌝-*su*. **62** *ra-áš-du-ti*: 1 R pl. 36 has the variant BU$^{?}$ for *du* in *ra-áš-du-ti*; no known exemplar has this variant, but cf. text no. 9 line 57; exs. 2–4, 17–18 have *ra-áš-du-ú-te*; exs. 11, 16, 45, 57–58 have *ra-áš-du-ú-ti*; ex. 28 has [*ra*]-⌜*áš*⌝-*du-ú-ti*; ex. 35 has [*ra*]-*áš-du*-⌜*ú-ti*$^{?}$⌝; ex. 47 has ⌜*ra*⌝-[*áš-du*]-⌜*ú*⌝-*ti*; and ex. 48 has *ra-áš**-*du-ú-te*, in which the *áš* is MA. **62**.3 The *ma* in *ki-ma* has four horizontal wedges. **62** 1 R pl. 36 appears to have a variant omitting the *en* in *ge-en-ni*, but no known exemplar omits this sign. **62**.4, 17–18, 48 *ge-né-e* for *ge-en-ni*. **62**.4, 17–18, 48 *šur-šú-du* for *šur-šu-du*. **62**.11 omits *ù*. **62** *qer-bu-uš-šú*: exs. 2–4, 16 have *qer-bu-uš-šu*; and ex. 19 has *qer*-⌜*bu*⌝-*uš-šu*. **63**.59 has [...]-⌜*ra*⌝-*nu* for GIŠ.*dáp-ra-ni*. **63**.38 The GIŠ in GIŠ.*bu-uṭ-ni* is MA. **63** *ina*: exs. 2–4, 11, 16–18, 27, 33, 59 have *i-na*; ex. 38 has *i*-⌜*na*⌝; ex. 42 has *i*-[*na*]; and ex. 47 has ⌜*i-na*⌝. **63** *qí-bi-ti-šú-nu*: exs. 11, 16, 18, 57 have *qí-bi-te-šú-nu*; ex. 27 has *qí-bi-te*-⌜*šú*⌝-[*nu*]; and ex. 47 has ⌜*qí-bi-te-šú-nu*⌝. **63**.2 *ṣir-ti* for *ṣir-te*. **64** *ta-an-ši-il*: exs. 2, 4, 17–18, 48 have *ta*$_{5}$-*an-ši-il*, Fuchs, Khorsabad p. 42 suggests that the writing UD-AN-*ši-il* is "eine Mischung zwischen *ta-an-ši-il* und *tam-ši-il*"; and ex. 19 omits *ši*. **64**.11 *mé-eḫ-rat* for *mé-eḫ-ret*. **64** 1 R pl. 36 has KÁ.MEŠ-*su*, but no known exemplar has this. **64**.17 omits *ap-tiq-ma*. **65**.4 1 <<U>> UŠ. **65** *mi-ši-iḫ-ti*: exs. 2, 4, 11, 16–18, 27, 47–48, 57–58 have *mi-ši-iḫ-te*; ex. 38 has [*mi*]-*ši-iḫ-te*; ex. 44 has [*mi*]-⌜*ši*⌝-*iḫ-te*; and ex. 59 has [*mi*]-*ši*-⌜*iḫ*⌝-*te*. **65** BÀD-*šu*: exs. 2–3, 16–18, 27, 38, 44, 47–48, 57–58, 59 have BÀD-*šú*; exs. 4, 11 have ⌜BÀD⌝-*šú*; and ex. 33 has ⌜BÀD$^{?}$-*šú*⌝. **65** KUR-*e*: exs. 2–4, 16–18, 27, 57–58 have KUR-*i*; ex. 11 adds an extraneous *u* between KUR and *i*; exs. 31, 45 have ⌜KUR-*i*⌝; ex. 36 has [KUR]-*i*; and ex. 47 has KUR-⌜*i*⌝. **65** *te-me-en-šu*: exs. 2–3, 12, 19, 57 have *te-me-en-šú*; and ex. 4 has ⌜*te*⌝-*me-en-šú*. **66**.2–4, 11, 16–18, 48, 58 omit *a* in *ar-ka-a-te*. **67** ḪÉ.GÁL-*li-šu*: exs. 2–3, 17, 48 have ḪÉ.GÁL-*li-šú*; and ex. 4 has ⌜ḪÉ⌝.GÁL-*li-šú*. **67** *šá*: exs. 2–4, 11, 16–17, 27, 57–58 have *ša*; exs. 8, 12 have ⌜*ša*$^{?}$⌝; and exs. 18, 31, 36, 42, 47 have ⌜*ša*⌝. **67** *az-ku-ur*: exs. 2–3, 11, 17, 58 have *az-kur*; and exs. 4, 12, 18, 28, 31 have ⌜*az*⌝-*kur*. **68**.58 omits ^{d} in the first ^{d}EN.LÍL. **68**.3 Erased ḪI after *mu-diš-šá-at*. **68**.18 *zík-ri* <<*zík-ri*>>. **68** *šá*: exs. 2–4, 16–17, 27, 31, 47, 57–58 have *ša*; and exs. 8–9, 12, 36, 42 have ⌜*ša*⌝. **69**.16, 47, 57–58 ^{d}*a-nu-um* for ^{d}*a-nu*. **69**.58 The *šet* in *ep-šet* has four vertical wedges. **69**.19 ⌜UN⌝.MEŠ-*šu* for UN.MEŠ-*šú*. **69** *šá*: exs. 2–3, 16–17, 27, 31, 47, 58 have *ša*; and exs. 4, 8, 36 have ⌜*ša*⌝.

70 *mu-uš-te-šir*: exs. 2, 4, 17–19, 45, 48, 57–58 have *muš-te-šir*; ex. 47 has *muš*-⌜*te*⌝-*šir*; and ex. 49 has *muš*-(x) [...]. **70**.2 (contra Fuchs), 4, 17–18, 48 *nag-bi-šú* for *nag-bi-šu*. **70** *ta-lit-ti-šú*: ex. 19 has *ta-lit-ti*-⌜*šu*⌝; and contra Fuchs, ex. 2 has *šú*. **70** *šá*: exs. 2–3, 11–12, 16–17, 36, 47, 56, 58 have *ša*; and exs. 4, 9, 27, 31, 42 have ⌜*ša*⌝. **70** IM.U$_{19}$.LU: exs. 2, 16, 31, 36, 42 have IM.U$_{18}$.LU; ex. 4 has IM.U$_{18}$.⌜LU⌝; ex. 9 has ⌜IM.U$_{18}$/U$_{19}$.LU⌝; ex. 12 has ⌜IM⌝.U$_{18}$.⌜LU⌝; exs. 19, 56 have IM.⌜U$_{18}$/U$_{19}$⌝.LU; ex. 26 has [IM].U$_{18}$.LU; and ex. 47 has IM.⌜U$_{18}$⌝.LU. **71**.2 adds MEŠ after LUGAL. **71** *e-pi-ši-šu*: exs. 2–4, 11, 16–18, 48 have *e-pi-ši-šú*; and ex. 47 has ⌜*e*⌝-*pi-ši-šú*. **71** BÀD-*šu*: exs. 2–4, 16–18, 47–48, 58 have BÀD-*šú*; exs. 8, 11, 19, 27 have ⌜BÀD⌝-*šú*; and exs. 38, 42 have ⌜BÀD-*šú*⌝. **71**.11, 19 ^{d}MAŠ for ^{d}*nin-urta*. **71** *šal-ḫu-ú-šu*: exs. 4, 56–58 have *šal-ḫu-ú-šú*; ex. 12 has *šal-ḫu*-⌜*ú-šú*⌝; exs. 17, 19, 26, 45 have *šal-ḫu-u-šú*; and ex. 18 has [*šal*]-⌜*ḫu*⌝-*ú-šú*. **72**.4, 18, 48 *mit-ḫur-te* for *mit-ḫur-ti*. **72** *a-ši-bu-te*: exs. 2–4, 16–18, 47, 57 have *a-ši-bu-ut*; ex. 8 has *a*-⌜*ši-bu*$^{?}$⌝-*ut*; and ex. 42 has ⌜*a-ši-bu-ut*⌝. **72** KUR-*e*: exs. 2–4, 11, 16–18, 27, 57–58 have KUR-*i*; ex. 38 has ⌜KUR-*i*⌝; ex. 42 has KUR-⌜*i*⌝; and ex. 47 has KUR*-*i*, in which the KUR appears to have four Winkelhaken. **72**.4 UD for ZÁLAG. **73**.11 omits 1 in 1-*en*. **73**.11 omits *ma* in *ú-šar-ma-a*. **73** *qé-reb-šu*: exs. 2–4, 17, 26, 56–58 have *qé-reb-šú*; ex. 9 has *qé-reb*-⌜*šú*⌝; ex. 18 has [*qé*]-⌜*reb-šú*⌝; and ex. 31 has ⌜*qé-reb*⌝-*šú*. **74**.2–4, 11, 16–18, 48, 57 *mu-du-ut* for *mu-du-te*. **74** *ṣi-bit-te*: exs. 3, 58 have *ṣi-bit-ti*; and ex. 30 has [*ṣi*]-⌜*bit*⌝-*ti*. **74** *ù*: exs. 2–3, 8, 11, 17–18, 30, 42 have *u*; and ex. 4 has [*u*] (restored via spacing). **74** *ú-ma-ʾe-er-šú-nu-ti*: exs. 2–3 have *ú-ma-ʾe-er-šu-nu-ti*; ex. 9 has *ú-ma-ʾe*-⌜*er-šu*⌝-x (x) [(x)]; ex. 45 has *ú-ma-ʾe*-⌜*er*⌝-*šú-nu*-⌜*te/tú*⌝; and ex. 58 has *ú-ma-ʾe-er-šu-nu-te*. **75** *a-ši-bu-te*: exs. 2–3, 16–18, 27, 47–48, 58 have *a-ši-bu-ut*; ex. 4 has *a-ši-bu*-⌜*ut/te*⌝; and ex. 35 has [*a*]-*ši-bu-ut*. **75**.2–4, 11, 17–18, 48 *šá-a-šú* for *šá-a-šu*. **75**.42 omits *ú* in *im-gur-ú-ma*. **75** *qer-bi-šú*: ex. 2 (contra Fuchs) has *qer-be-e-šú*; exs. 3, 8, 16–17, 26, 30, 42, 47, 56–57 have *qer-bé-e-šú*; ex. 4 has [*qer-bé/be*]-*e-šú*; ex. 9 has ⌜*qer-bé*⌝-*e-šú*; ex. 11 has *qer-bé-e*-⌜*šú*$^{?}$⌝; ex. 12 has ⌜*qer-bé-e-šú*⌝; ex. 19 has *qer-bé-e-šu*; ex. 45 has ⌜*qer*⌝-*bi-šu*; and ex. 58 has ⌜*qer*⌝-*be-e-šu*. **76** *ú-nak-kar-ú-ma*: ex. 2 adds an extraneous *ru* between *kar* and *ú*; and ex. 11 has *ú-nak-kar-u-ma*. **76**.48 *ú-nak-kar-ú-ma* <<*ú-ma*>>. **76** *ú-saḫ-ḫu-ú*: The *saḫ* in exs. 1, 45 is Ú; ex. 2 has *ú-saḫ-ḫu-u*; and ex. 18 has *ú*-⌜*saḫ*⌝-*ḫu-u*. **76** *ú-ṣu-rat*: exs. 2, 16–17 have *iṣ-ṣu-rat*; and ex. 11 omits *ú*. **76** *eṣ-ṣi-ru*: exs. 2–3, 8, 16–17, 30, 42, 47, 58 have *e-ṣi-ru*; ex. 11 has *e-ṣi*-⌜*ru*⌝; and ex. 18 has *e*-⌜*ṣi-ru*⌝. **76**.2–3 (both contra Fuchs), 4, 9, 12, 16–17, 26, 42, 47, 56–57 add *ma* after *ú-šam-sa-ku*. **76** *si-ma-te-ia*: exs. 3, 58 have *si-ma-ti-ia*; and contra Fuchs, ex. 2 has *te*. **76** *ú-pa-šá-ṭu*: exs. 2–3, 9, 16–17, 43, 58 have *ú-pa-áš-šá-ṭu*; exs. 4, 26 have *ú-pa-áš-šá*-⌜*ṭu*⌝; ex. 18 has ⌜*ú*⌝-*pa-áš-šá-ṭu*; ex. 37 has *ú-pa-áš*-⌜*šá-ṭu*⌝; ex. 42 has *ú-pa*-[*áš*]-*šá-ṭu*; ex. 47 has ⌜*ú*⌝-*pa*-⌜*áš*⌝-*šá*-⌜*ṭu*⌝; and ex. 56 has *ú-pa*-⌜*áš-šá*⌝-*ṭu*. **77** *lìb-bi-šú*: ex. 1 omits *šú*; and exs. 19, 45 have *lìb-bi-šu*. **77** MU-*šu*: exs. 2–4, 11, 16–17, 47–48, 57–58 have MU-*šú*; and ex. 18 has [MU]-⌜*šú*⌝. **77** NUMUN-*šu*: exs. 2–4, 11, 16–17, 47–48, 57–58 have NUMUN-*šú*; ex. 18 has ⌜NUMUN-*šú*⌝; ex. 30 has ⌜NUMUN⌝-*šú*; and ex. 42 has [NUMUN]-*šú*. **77** LÚ.KÚR-*šu*: exs. 2–4, 16–17, 26, 42, 56–58 have LÚ.KÚR-*šú*; exs. 9, 18 have ⌜LÚ⌝.KÚR-*šú*; and exs. 30, 47 have ⌜LÚ.KÚR-*šú*⌝. **77** *li-še-ši-bu-šu*: exs. 3–4, 9, 16–17, 26 have *li-še-ši-bu-šú*; and ex. 37 has [*li-še-ši-bu*]-⌜*šú*⌝.

Text No. 49

1.4 omits *an* in *šá-na-an*. 1.4 LUGAL for all three MAN. 1.4 KIŠ for *kiš-šat*. 1.4 EME.GI$_{7}$*(copy: KI) for EME.GI$_{7}$. 1 BA-*ìš*: The copy of ex. 2 published by Nassouhi has BA, not BA-*ìš*, but his transliteration has *aqi-ìš* (i.e., BA-*ìš*) so it is not clear if this exemplar omits *ìš* or not; and the BA in ex. 4 is anomalous.

Text No. 50

1 ^{m}MAN-GIN: ex. 5 has ^{m}LUGAL-GI.NA; ex. 16 has ⌜^{m}MAN⌝-GI.NA; and ex. 19 has ^{m}MAN-GI.NA. 2.15, 17 NU*(photo: PAP).ÈŠ and NU*(photo: PAP).⌜ÈŠ⌝ respectively for NU.ÈŠ. 2 *aš-šur*: ex. 5 has ^{d}*a-šur*; exs. 7, 15 have AŠ; and the copy of ex. 8 by Botta has AN for *aš-šur*, but the brick has *aš*-⌜*šur*⌝. 3 *dan-nu*: exs. 7, 14, 18 have KALAG; and the copy of ex. 8 by Botta has E-BE, but the brick has ⌜*dan*⌝-*nu*, where the NU is written like BE. 3.5, 16, 19 KIŠ for ŠÚ. 3 AŠ: The copy of ex. 8 by Botta has AN for *aš-šur*, but the brick has *aš*-⌜*šur*⌝; ex. 24 has *aš-šur* and exs. 16, 19 have *aš-šur* (x), with x possibly being ⌜KI⌝.

Text No. 51

2.5 KÁ.DINGIR.RA.KI for KÁ.DINGIR.KI. 3.2 URI.KI*(copy: DI) for URI.KI.

Text No. 55

3.2 omits ^{m} in URU.BÀD-^{m}MAN-GIN. 5.2 [*a*]-*na* for *ana*. 6 The copy by Lenormant has BURU$_{14}$ *šá* for *e-bur*. Neither ex. 1 nor ex. 2 has this reading; it may come from text no. 95 line 6. 7.2 adds KI after *aš-šur*.

Text No. 65

48 Copy of *gur*? in URU.*ú-si-gur*?: 

Text No. 67

3.6 EN-*šu* for *be-lí-šú*. **5**.6–7 [*sa*]-⸢*me*⸣-*ti* and *sa*-(x)-⸢*me-tu**⸣(text: ⸢AD⸣[) respectively for *sa-me-tu*. **6**.1 ⸢*ip-tiq*⸣-*ma**(copy: IZ) for *ip-tiq-ma*. **6**.6 omits *a* in *ú-šal-ma-a*. **7**.7 TI.LA for TI. **7** ZI.MEŠ-*šu*: ex. 4 has ⸢ZI⸣.MEŠ-*šú*; ex. 5 has ZI.MEŠ-*šú*; ex. 11 has [ZI.MEŠ]-⸢*šú*⸣; and ex. 12 has ⸢ZI.MEŠ⸣-*šú*. **7**.2, 7 [GÍD].⸢DA⸣ and GÍD (x) respectively for GÍD. **7**.7 UD.MEŠ-⸢*šu*?⸣ for UD.MEŠ-*šú*.

Text No. 68

1 ^{d}*a-šur*: exs. 2, 4, 12, 18, 29 have ^{d}*aš-šur*; ex. 5 has ⸢^{d}⸣*aš-šur*; ex. 6 has ^{d}⸢*aš*⸣-[*šur*]; ex. 13 has ^{d}⸢*aš*⸣-*šur*; ex. 14 has ^{d}*aš*-⸢*šur**⸣, in which the *šur** of the published copy suggests ⸢ŠUK⸣, but the ŠUR in these texts often is similar to ŠUK; ex. 15 has ^{d}AN-⸢*šur*?⸣; and ex. 29 has ^{d}⸢*aš-šur*⸣. **1**.10 [*be*]-*lí-šu* for EN-*šú*. **2** *aš-šur*.KI: exs. 2–3, 5, 7, 9–12, 18, 28, 29, possibly 30 omit KI; exs. 5, 9, 12, 18 have AŠ; ex. 15 has AN x [(x)]; and ex. 29 has ⸢AŠ⸣. **3**.11 omits KI in URI.KI. **4** *a-na*: exs. 3–4, 7 have *ana*; ex. 15 has [(x)] x; and ex. 29 has ⸢*a*?/DIŠ⸣-*na*.

Text No. 69

2 ^{m}MAN-GIN: exs. 6, 15 have LUGAL-GI.NA; and ex. 44 has ⸢LUGAL?-GI?.NA?⸣. **2**.12, 15 MAN for the first LUGAL. **2**.4, 12, 14–15, 45 MAN for the second LUGAL. **2**.12 AŠ KUR (x) [...] for KUR *aš-šur*.KI. **3**.4, 13–15, 45 MAN for LUGAL. **3** *u*: ex. 11 has ⸢*ù*?⸣; and exs. 14, 45 omit it. **4**.15 *a-gúr-ri* for *a-gur-ri*. **4**.10, 15 *ú-tu-ni* and UDUN respectively for *ú-tú-ni*. **5**.45 omits *ra* in *é-ḫur-sag-gal-kur-kur-ra*.

Text No. 73

1.2 omits KI in *as-šur*.KI. **4**.2 *ša* for *šá*. **7**.2 *šá* for *ša*. **8**.2 *šá* for *ša*. **9**.2 adds KI after *aš-šur*.

Text No. 74

iii 44.2 *na-ge-šú* for *na-ge-e-šú*. **iii 44**.2 *ib*-⸢*bal*⸣-[*ki*]-⸢*tu*⸣-*šu-ma* for *ib-bal*-[*ki*]-⸢*tu*⸣-*šú-ma*.

iv 35.2 *si*-⸢*ta*⸣-*te-šú-nu* for *si-it-ta-ti-šú-nu*. **iv 42**.2 KUR.*mu-ṣu-ri* for KUR.*mu-ṣur*. **iv 43**.2 EN-*ia* for ⸢*be*⸣-*lí-ia*. **iv 46**.2 KUR.*mu-ṣu-ri* for KUR.*mu-ṣur*.

v 23.2 KUR.*mu-us-ki* for KUR.*mus-ki*.

v 34.2 KUR.*mu-us-ki* for KUR.*mus-ki*.

vi 56.2 URU.É-^{m}*ki-ib-la-a-te* for URU.É-^{m}*ki-ib-la-te*.

Text No. 76

8′.3 omits *am* in KUR.É-*ḫa-am-ban*. **8′**.3 KUR.*par*-⸢*šu*⸣-*maš* for KUR.*par-su-maš*. **13′**.3 *ka-mu-us-su* for *ka-mu-su*. **14′**.3–4 *sa-an-da-ni-šú* and [*sa-an*]-⸢*da*⸣-*ni-šú* respectively for *sa-an-da-ni-šu*. **14′**.3–4 *i-ba*-[*ru*] and *i-ba-ru* respectively for *i-bar-ru*. **15′**.3 omits ^{m} in KUR.É-^{m}*puru-ta-áš*. **15′**.3 *ša* for *šá*. **15′**.3 ^{m} in ^{m}*ki-ak-ki* written over an erasure. **17′**.3 *ša* for *šá*. **17′**.4 omits ^{d} in ^{md}*ia-ú-bi-iʾ-di*. **18′**.4 ŠU.II-*su* for ŠU-*su*. **19′**.4–5 Copies have ŠU for TUKUL in GIŠ.TUKUL.MEŠ-*šú*, and the copy of ex. 4 also has A for *šú*.

20′.4 Copy has ŠU for *ma* in KUR.*ma-an-na-a-a*. **21′**.5 The *suk* in URU.*suk-ki-i* is slightly abnormal in form. **24′**.4–5 [KUR.*šur*]-*da-a-a* and KUR.*šur-da-a-a* respectively for KUR.*šur-da-a*. **25′**.4 [...] x-*di** for URU.*me-li-di*; the copy has [...] x-KI, which was read as [...]-⸢*lid*?⸣-*di* by Abraham and Klein. **25′**.4–5 *ú-še-ṣu-ú* and *ú-še-ṣu*-⸢*ú*⸣ respectively for *ú-še-ṣu-ma*. **25′**.4 ⸢UGU?⸣ for UGU; the sign following *ú-še-ṣu-ú* is uncertain; Abraham and Klein read *ú-še-ṣu*-⸢*šú*⸣ x [...] but from the copy ⸢UGU⸣ seems more likely. **25′**.5 Copy has KUR for *kul* in *kul-lat*. **26′**.5 [*tu-qu-un*]-⸢*tu*⸣/⸢*tú*⸣ for *tu-qu-un-tu*. **26′**.1 LUGAL-*u-ut* for LUGAL-*ut*. **26′**.5 LÚ.*mar-qa*-⸢*sa*?⸣-[*a-a*] for URU.*mar-qa-šá-a*-[*a*].

Text No. 77

1.2, 7 ^{m}MAN-GI.NA for ^{m}MAN-GIN. **1**.2, 7 *aš-šur* for AŠ.

Text No. 82

iii 10‴ Copy of *ku** in [*a-bi*]-*ku**: 

iv 6 Copy of *da** in *um*-⸢*mu*⸣-*da**: 

Text No. 92

1.1 ^{m}MAN-(x) [...] for ^{m}LUGAL-GI.NA. **1**.12 *aš-šur* for ^{d}*a-šur*. **2**.17 *u* for *ù*. **2**.4 has traces of four signs that could go here or in line 3. **3** Copies of the fourth sign of line 3 in exs. 1 and 26 respectively:  and . **3**.28 *šá* for *ša*. **4**.14 ⸢*ša*⸣ for *šá*. **4**.14 *i-na* for *ina*. **4**.26 ⸢GIBIL⸣-*te*: Thompson (AAA 19 [1932] p. 103) reads *es-še-ti*, but no known exemplar has this reading. **5**.2, 7 ^{m}10-ERIM.TAḪ and ^{m}10-⸢ERIM⸣.TAḪ respectively for ^{md}IŠKUR-*né-ra-ri*. **5**.6, 25 omit *ši* in ^{md}UTU-*ši*-^{d}IŠKUR. **5**.12, 15 DÙ-*uš* and ⸢DÙ?⸣-*uš* respectively for *e-pu-uš*. **6**.7 *ki*-⸢*ma*?⸣ for *ki-i*. **6** KUR-*i*: exs. 14, 30 have KUR-*e*; the copy of ex. 14 has [...]-⸢*ṣir*?⸣ KUR-*e*, but all that is currently preserved is [...]-⸢*e*⸣. **6**.13–14 [*ri*]-*i-ti* and *re-e-ti* respectively for *ri-ti*. **6** 75.ÀM: ex. 3 has ⸢72?⸣.ÀM; ex. 14 has 71+[...]; and ex. 28 has [...]+⸢75⸣.ÀM. **6**.17 *im*-⸢*la*?-*ma*?⸣ for *im-la-a-ma*. **6**.29 ⸢*la*⸣-*be-ru-ta* for *la-bi-ru-ta*. **7**.7 *šub*-[*ta-šú*] for the first KI.TUŠ-*šú*. **7**.4 ⸢^{d}⸣*iš-tar* for ^{d}INANNA. **7**.4 *šá* for the first *ša*. **7**.24 ⸢*e*⸣-*pe-šu* for *e-pe-šú*. **7**.18 omits *a* in *a-šal-ma*. **7**.30 omits *nu* in *ke-nu-um*. **7**.30 omits NU. **7** *i-pu-la-an-ni-ma*: ex. 3 has ⸢*e*⸣-*pu-la-an-ni-ma*; ex. 15 has [*i*/*e*]-⸢*pu*⸣-*lu-an-ni-ma*; and ex. 28 has *e-pu-la-an-ni-ma*. **8**.3 ^{d}MUATI for ^{d}AG. **8**.29 ^{d}15 for ^{d}INANNA. **8** Thompson (AAA 19 [1932] p. 103) indicates URU.*ni-na-a*, but no known exemplar has this. **8**.4 ⸢UŠ$_{8}$⸣-*šú* for *uš-še-e-šú*. **8**.24 ⸢*uš*⸣-*še-e-šu* for *uš-še-e-šú*. **8**.12 omits *dib* in *gaba-dib-bi-šú*. **9**.11 ⸢SILIM⸣ for the first *šùl-mu*. **9**.21, 28 NUMUN.MEŠ-*ia* for NUMUN-*ia*. **9**.5 *sa-kap* for *sà-kap*. **9**.5 omits MEŠ in LÚ.KÚR.MEŠ-*ia*. **9**.16 BURU$_{14}$ is slightly anomalous. **9**.18 [...] KI *aš-šur* for BURU$_{14}$ *as-šur*.KI. **9**.29 *šá*-[*lam*] for *šùl-mu*.

Text No. 95

1.4, 6 ^{m}MAN-GI.NA for ^{m}LUGAL-GI-NA. **1**.4, 6 GAR for *šá-ak-ni*. **2**.4, 6 ^{d}*a-šur* for *aš-šur*. **2**.4, 6 ^{d}MUATI for ^{d}AG. **2** *ù* for *u* (Thompson). **2** Omission of ^{d} in ^{d}AMAR.UTU on exemplar from LXVI, 11 (Thompson). **2**.6 Photo suggests ^{d}AMAR.ŠÚ for ^{d}AMAR.UTU. **3**.4, 6 ^{d}MUATI for ^{d}AG. **3** Omission of *šú* in EN.MEŠ-*šú* (Thompson). **4** *ul-tu*: ex. 4 has [TA] (via spacing); ex. 6 has TA; and *ul-tú* (Thompson). **4**.1–3 Walker, CBI p. 118 indicates that these have APIN-*šu* not APIN-*šú*; this is likely a misprint since the copy in 1 R has APIN-*šú* and since elsewhere in the inscription *šú* rather than *šu* is used. **5**.4, 6 omit LA-*šú* and LA respectively in TI.LA-*šú*. **6**.1 and Thompson omit LÚ in LÚ.KÚR.MEŠ-*šú*. **6**.4, 6 *e-bur* for BURU$_{14}$ *šá*. **6** *aš-šur*.KI: ex. 2 and Thompson omit KI; ex. 4 omits *aš*; and ex. 5 has ^{d}*a*-⸢*šur*⸣.[KI]. **7** Addition of ^{d} before *aš-šur* (Thompson). **7**.2 omits KI in *aš-šur*.KI. **7** DÙ-*uš*: exs. 2–3, Thompson have *e-pu-uš*; ex. 4 has DÙ KI; ex. 5 has DÙ-[*uš*/*e*]; and ex. 6 has DÙ-*e*.

Text No. 96

5 *u-šak-lil* for *ú-šak-lil* (brick from LXIX, 7 [Thompson]).

Text No. 104

Frgm. C 1′ Copy of the traces before *ú* in [...] x-*ú*: 

Text No. 109

31′.3 [URU.*gar-ga-m*]*ìš* for URU.*gar-ga-miš*. **31′**.3 *ana* for *ina*. **32′**.3 *mut-tap-*⸢*ri*⸣*-šu-*⸢*te*⸣ for *mut-tap-ri-šú-te*. **32′**.3 IGI-*šú-nu* for *ma-ḫar-šú-nu*. **33′**.3 URU.*gar-ga-mìš* for URU.*gar-ga-miš*.

Text No. 117

ii 74 Copies of *ú** and *ḫu-ú** in *ú*-saḫ-ḫu-ú*-ma* respectively:
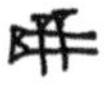 and 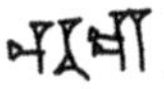.

Text No. 123

1 *ana*: ex. 16 omits it; and ex. 17 has ⸢*a*$^{?}$*-na*$^{?}$⸣. **1**.16 omits *i* in GAL-*i*. **2**.16, 868E *reme-nu-u* and *re-*[*me*]-⸢*ni-i*⸣ respectively for *reme-ni-i*. **3**.17 *é-sag-*⸢*íl*$^{?}$⸣ for *é-sag-gíl*. **3**.16–17 KÁ.DÙG.⸢KI⸣ and ⸢KÁ.DINGIR⸣.RA.KI respectively for TIN.TIR.KI. **3** UMUN-*šú*: exs. 10, 16, 868E have EN-*šú*; ex. 17 has ⸢EN$^{?}$⸣-[*šú*]; and 869A has ⸢*be*⸣*-lí-šú*. **4**.10 LUGAL-⸢GIN⸣ squeezed in between lines, below *šú* ⸢LUGAL *dan*⸣. **5**.868D omits KI in *aš-šur*.KI. **5–6**.7 traces after *aš-šur* and before start of line 7 unreadable; likely part omitted. **6**.17, 868D *šak-*⸢*ka-nak-ka*⸣ and ⸢*šak-ka-nak-ka*⸣ respectively for GÌR.NÍTA. **6**.10, 16 KÁ.DINGIR.RA.KI and KÁ.DINGIR.RA.⸢KI⸣ respectively for TIN.TIR.KI. **7** *šu-me-ru*: ex. 4 has ⸢*šu-me-ri*⸣; exs. 6, 10, 17, 868E have *šu-me-ri*; ex. 7 has ⸢EME$^{?}$.GI$_7$$^{?}$⸣; ex. 16 has ⸢*šu*⸣*-me-ri*; and 869A has ⸢EME⸣.GI$_7$; only ex. 1 clearly has *šu-me-ru*. **7**.6 *ù* for *u*. **8** *é-sag-íl*: ex. 2 has [*é*]-⸢*sag*⸣*-gíl*; exs. 6, 16–17 have *é-sag-gíl*; and ex. 7 has ⸢*é*⸣*-sag-*⸢*gíl*⸣. **9**.6–7, 10, 16–17 *u* for *ù*.

10.869A ⸢*a-na*⸣ for *ana*. **10** DÙ-*eš*: ex. 7 has *e-peš*; exs. 10, 16 have *e-pe-šú* (against *e-*BE*-šú* of published copy of ex. 16); exs. 17, 869A have *e-pe-ši*; 868C has *e-*⸢*pe*⸣-x; 868E has ⸢*e*⸣*-pe-*[*šú/ši*]; and 868E has *e*-x-x. **10**.7, 10, 16, 17, 869D omit BÀD. **10** *im-gur-*^{d}*en-líl*: ex. 2 has ⸢*im*⸣*-gur-*^{d}50; and exs. 7, 16 have *im-gur-*^{d}⸢50⸣. **11** GEŠTU-*šú*: exs. 6, 10, 16, 868D have *ú-zu-un-šú*; and ex. 17 has ⸢*ú*⸣*-zu-un-šú*. **11** GÁL-*ma*: ex. 2 has ⸢*ib*⸣*-ši-ma*; exs. 6, 10, 16, 868D have *ib-ši-ma*; ex. 7 has ⸢*ib-ši-ma*⸣; and ex. 17 has *ib-ši*$^{?}$*-ma*. **12** *a-gur-ru*: exs. 2, 868D, 869D have *a-gur-ri*; ex. 6 has *a-gur-*⸢*ri*⸣; and ex. 17 has [*a*]-⸢*gur*⸣*-ri*. **12** *ki-ru*: ex. 6 has ⸢*ki-ri*⸣; ex. 7 has ⸢GIR$_4$⸣; exs. 10, likely 868C have GIR$_4$; and exs. 16–17, 868D, 869D have *ki-ri*. **12**.17 ⸢*el*$^{?}$*-li*$^{?}$*-ti*$^{?}$⸣ for KÙ-*tim*. **13**.869A *i-na* for *ina*. **13** *kup-ru*: exs. 6, 16, 868C–E, 869D have *kup-ri*; ex. 7 has ⸢*kup-ri*⸣; and ex. 17 has [*kup*]-*ri*. **13**.7, 10, 16–17, 868C–E, 869D *u* for *ù*. **13** ESIR: exs. 10, 16, 868C have *it-te-e*; ex. 17 has *it*$^{?}$*-te-*⸢*e*⸣; and 868D has *it*$^{?}$*-te-e*$^{?}$. **14**.869A *i-na* for *ina*. **16**.869A *ka-a-*⸢*ru*$^{?}$⸣ for KAR. **16**.6, 16 ⸢DÙ$^{?}$*-ma*$^{?}$⸣ and *ib-*⸢*ni/nu*⸣*-ma* respectively for *ib-ni-ma*. **17**.7, 10, 16–17, 868D–E omit BÀD. **17** *im-gur-*^{d}50: ex. 3 has *im-gur-*^{d}EN.⸢LÍL⸣; ex. 17 has ⸢*im*$^{?}$*-gur*$^{?}$⸣-^{d}EN.LÍL; and 868D–E have *im-gur-*^{d}EN-LÍL. **18**.6 omits *ù*. **18**.7, 10, 16, 868D–E, 869A *u* for *ù*. **18**.7, 10, 16–17, 868D–E omit BÀD. **18** *né-met-*^{d}50: ex. 7 has ⸢*né-met*⸣*-ti-*^{d}50; ex. 10 has *né-met-ti-*^{d}50; ex. 16 has *né-met-tú-*^{d}50; ex. 17 has ⸢*né*⸣*-met-ti-*^{d}EN.LÍL; and 868D–E have *né-met-ti-*^{d}EN.LÍL. **19** *ki-ma*: ex. 7 has ⸢GIM⸣; exs. 10, 868E have GIM; and ex. 17 has ⸢GIM$^{?}$⸣.

21.5 *šá-a-ši* for *šá-a-šú*. **21** GAL-*ú*: ex. 16 has GAL-*u* (*u* omitted on published copy, but present); and exs. 7, 868E omit *ú*. **22**.7, 10, 16, 868C, 868E IGI.BAR-*ma* for *li-pa-lis-ma*. **22**.6, 10, 16, 868C–E, 869A *ana* for *a-na*. **22**.5 LUGAL-*ú-kin* for LUGAL-GIN. **23** TIN: exs. 5, 16 have *ba-la-ṭu*; exs. 17, 868D have *ba-la-ṭi*; and 868E has ⸢TI⸣.LA. **24**.7, 10, 868E GIM for *ki-ma*. **24** TIN.TIR.KI: ex. 10 has KÁ.DIŠ.KI; ex. 16 has URU.DÙG.⸢KI⸣; ex. 17 has [KÁ].⸢DINGIR⸣.RA.KI; and 868D has URU.⸢DÙG⸣.KI. **25**.10 GIN-*un* for *li-ku-nu*. **25**.17, 868D BALA.ME-*šú* for BALA.MEŠ-*šú*.

Text No. 2001

1.2 *aš-šur*.KI for AŠ.

Text No. 2002

1.3 ⸢LUGAL-GI.NA⸣ for MAN-GIN. **1**.3 KIŠ for *kiš-šat*. **2**.2 *ù* for *u*. **2**.3 [*ak*]-⸢*ka*⸣*-de-e* for URI.KI. **3**.2–3 *iš-tu* and ⸢*iš-tu*⸣ respectively for TA. **3**.3 ...-⸢*šu*$^{?}$⸣ for *gaba-dib-bi-šú*. **5**.2 has traces of two smallish signs (or one long sign) between *aš-šur* and *šá-a-šú*; possibly *u* ⸢URU⸣. **6**.3 ⸢*el-lu*$^{?}$*-ti*$^{?}$⸣ for KÙ.MEŠ. **6**.3 ⸢*i-na*⸣ for *ina*. **6**.3 ⸢*el-li*⸣ for KÙ. **7**.1 The ^{d} in ^{md}30-PAP-PAP omits the vertical wedge. **7**.3 [*iq-bu*]-⸢*ú*⸣ for *iq-bu-u*.

Index of Museum Numbers

Aleppo, National Museum

Ankara, Museum of Anatolian Civilizations

Baghdad, Iraq Museum

Berlin, Vorderasiatisches Museum

No.	RINAP 2
VA 14664d	126.8
VA 14664e	126.9
VA 14664f	126.10
VA 14664g	126.11
VA 14664h	126.12
VA 14664i	126.13
VA 14664k	126.14
VA 14664l	126.15
VA 14664m	126.1; 127.2
VA 15466	64
VA —	66.5
VA —	66.6
VA Ass 2049	1004
VA Ass 2066	1003
VA Ass 2070	67.10
VA Ass 2071+	67.7
VA Ass 2283–2286	71
VA Ass 2332a-d+	66.2
VA Ass 2333a+c–h	66.4
VA Ass 2366b+	66.2
VA Ass 3275a	69.11
VA Ass 3275b	69.12
VA Ass 3275c	69.13
VA Ass 3276a	68.8
VA Ass 3276b	68.9
VA Ass 3276c	68.10
VA Ass 3276d	68.11
VA Ass 3276e	68.13
VA Ass 3276f	68.14
VA Ass 3276h	68 commentary
VA Ass 3512	66.7–8
VA Ass 4194	1005
VA Ass 4512	2005
VA Ass 2332a-d+	66.2
VAT 8634+	65
VAT 8698a+	65
VAT 8698b+	65
VAT 8698c+	65
VAT 8749+	65
VAT 8634+	65
VAT 10716	72
VAT 15466	64

Birmingham, The City of Birmingham Museums and Art Gallery

No.	RINAP 2
BCM 226'78	95.5
BCM 336'79	96.2

Bucharest, National Museum of Romanian History

No.	RINAP 2
—	43.57

Chicago, Oriental Institute

No.	RINAP 2
A 7036	2004
A 7358	41.39
A 7359	41.40
A 7360	41.41
A 7362	7.1 §5; 41.1*
A 7363	7.1; 41.42
A 7365	7.1 §4; 41.43
A 7366	41.44
A 7367	41.45
A 7368	41.46
A 7369	9.23; 41.18
A 11807	57 Frgm. M
A 11254	7.4 §10; 41.2*
A 11255	7.4 §§12–13
A 11256	7.4 §11; 41.47
A 11258	5 §1′
A 16947	102
A 17574	43.11
A 17577	43.12
A 17587	43.16
A 17588	43.17
A 17589	43.18
A 17590	43.19
A 17592	43.25
A 17593	43.26
A 17597	2002.2
A 25449	51.3
A 27862	108.B
A 27863	108.D
A 39949	51.4
A 58101(+)	7.4 §1
A 58116(+)	7.4 §1
A 60933	108.E
A 60934	108.C
A 150519(+)	7.1 §2
A 150547(+)	7.1 §7, 41.36
A 169366	51.5
A 169367	51.6
A 169368	51.7
A 169369	51.8
62-J-1-5	41.2*
64-L-1-3	41.47
65-M-1+	41.47
OI unregistered 4(+)	7.1 §2
OI unregistered 5(+)	7.1 §7
OI unregistered 9	7.1 §9
—	43.6–10
—	43.27–50
—	48
—	57 Frgms. K and L
—	59–60

Cologny, Bodmer Museum

No.	RINAP 2
FMB 50	43.56

Florence, Archbishop's Palace

No.	RINAP 2
—	9.29
—	9.30

Gaziantep, Archaeological Museum

No.	RINAP 2
—	2011

Geneva, Musée d'Art et d'Histoire

No.	RINAP 2
MAH O.22	9.31

Genoa, Museo di Archeologia

No.	RINAP 2
532+	9.15

Hatay, Archaeological Museum

No.	RINAP 2
—+	108.A

Istanbul, Archeological Museum

No.	RINAP 2	No.	RINAP 2	No.	RINAP 2
A 641	67.11	A 3647	67.1	EŞ 7848	99.1
A 3364	67.2	A 3653	67.8	EŞ 7849	99.2
A 3378	67.3			EŞ —	68.18
A 3379	67.4	EŞ 3282	66.1	EŞ —	68.20
A 3380	67.5	EŞ 4784	49.2	EŞ —	69.44
A 3582	67.6	EŞ 6676?	68 commentary	EŞ —	124.4
A 3598+	67.7	EŞ 6677	69.45	EŞ —	123.1
A 3599+	67.9	EŞ 6669?	68.30	EŞ —	127.1

Jerusalem, Bible Lands Museum

No.	RINAP 2
BLMJ 1115	105

Jerusalem, Convent of Les Dames de Sion

No.	RINAP 2
—(+)	9.15

Jerusalem, Israel Museum

No.	RINAP 2
IAA 63-962	104.A
IAA 63-931	104.C
IAA 63-1053	104.B
IMJ 74.56.251	43.58

Jerusalem, Rockefeller Archeological Museum

No.	RINAP 2
IAA 33.3725	1009

Leiden, Liagre Bohl Collection

No.	RINAP 2
LB 1309(+)	9.15

London, British Museum

No.	RINAP 2
BM 12084	77.1
BM 22466(+)	7.4 §5
BM 22505	43.3
BM 32343	43.59
BM 90232	53.1
BM 90233	53.2
BM 90235	53.3
BM 90236	53.4
BM 90237	53.5
BM 90238	50.1
BM 90239	50.2
BM 90240	50.3
BM 90241	50.4
BM 90242	95.1
BM 90243	95.2
BM 90244	95.3
BM 90245	54.1
BM 90274	53.6
BM 90359	53.7
BM 90361	53.8
BM 90450+	54.2
BM 90451+	54.2
BM 90599+	123.5
BM 90629+	123.5
BM 90702	110.1–2
BM 90748	53.9
BM 90750+	53.10
BM 90803+	53.10
BM 90819	50.5
BM 90952	77.1
BM 91229	78
BM 91234	79
BM 91460	77.2
BM 91595	77.5
BM 91639	77.4
BM 92192	53.36
BM 98518	85
BM 98528	86
BM 98724	88
BM 98851	92.28
BM 98852	92.29
BM 98853	92.30

Malatya, Archaeological Museum

No.	RINAP 2
Malatya 855	113
Malatya 1997	111
—	112

Moussaieff Collection

No.	RINAP 2
—	76.4

New Haven, Yale Babylonian Collection

No.	RINAP 2
YBC 2181	125
YBC 13510	123.16

New York, Metropolitan Museum of Art

No.	RINAP 2
MMA 57.27.22	2006

Oslo, Schøyen Collection

No.	RINAP 2
MS 2368	76.3

Oxford, Ashmolean Museum

No.	RINAP 2
Ash 1924.640	123.2
Ash 1932.652	123.3
Ash 1932.977	123.4

Paris, Louvre

No.	RINAP 2	No.	RINAP 2	No.	RINAP 2
AO 1936	130	AO 11503	2010	AO 19859	9.27
AO 5372+	65	AO 19856	9.1, 41.5	AO 19862	41.1
AO 7380	52.2	AO 19857	9.1; 41.5	AO 19863	41.17
AO 7382	Botta's squeezes	AO 19858	9.2; 41.21	AO 19864	41.38

No.	RINAP 2	No.	RINAP 2	No.	RINAP 2
AO 19865	41.22	AO 21370	44	Nap. III 2856	9.1, 41.5
AO 19866	41.23	AO 21371	45	Nap. III 2857	9.2, 41.21
AO 19869	41.24	AO 23012	9.28	Nap. III 2858	9.27
AO 19870	41.25			Nap. III 2860	41.1
AO 19871	41.26	N 8032	9.1, 41.5	Nap. III 2862	41.17
AO 19872	41.27	N 8033	9.2, 41.21	Nap. III 2871	49.1
AO 19873–19874	41.28	N 8069–8073	53 commentary	Nap. III 2884	3 §1′
AO 19876	41.29	N 8074	55.1	Nap. III 2897	46
AO 19877	41.10	N 8075	51.1	Nap. III 2898	45
AO 19878	41.30	N 8076?	50.8	Nap. III 2899	47
AO 19879	41.31	N 8078?	50.7	Nap. III 2900	44
AO 19881	41.32	N 8089	57 Frgm. I	Nap. III 2924	57 Frgm. A
AO 19882	41.33	N 8090	57 Frgm. J	Nap. III 2925	57 Frgm. B
AO 19883	41.34	N 8091	57 Frgm. C	Nap. III 3102	2003
AO 19884	41.35	N 8092	57 Frgm. D	Nap. III 3155	43.2
AO 19887(+)	7.1 §§6–7; 41.7, 36	N 8093	57 Frgm. B	Nap. III 3156	43.1
AO 19888	41.37	N 8094	57 Frgm. E	Nap. III 3400	61
AO 19892	3 §1′	N 8095	57 Frgm. F		
AO 19900	49.1	N 8096	57 Frgm. G	—	53.13–17
AO 19933	46	N 8097	57 Frgm. H		
AO 21368	62, 2003				

Philadelphia, University of Pennsylvania Museum of Archaeology and Anthropology

No.	RINAP 2
UM 32-22-6	see UM 37-16-8
UM 37-16-8	53.28
UM 38-13-1091	43.55

Private Collections

No.	RINAP 2
—	53.30
—	2007

Rosen Collection

No.	RINAP 2
—	100

Sanandaj, Archaeological Museum

No.	RINAP 2
—	115

St. Petersburg, Hermitage

No.	RINAP 2
Erm 3946+	9.10
Erm 3947+	9.10
Erm 3948+	9.15
Erm 3949+	9.14

Tehran, National Museum of Iran, Historical Department

No.	RINAP 2
5544/21110	117

Tiflis Museum

No.	RINAP 2
—	53.19

Toronto, Royal Ontario Museum

No.	RINAP 2
ROM 965.274.1.1–4	117 (squeezes)

Turin, Museo delle Antichità Egizie

No.	RINAP 2
P.2054	9.26
P.2055	7.1 §15

Varzy, Musée Auguste Grasset de Varzy

No.	RINAP 2
VA 137	15

Vatican, Museo Gregoriano Egizio

No.	RINAP 2
15025	53.22
15027	9.11
15028+	9.15

Wheaton, Wheaton College Archaeology Museum

Index of Excavation Numbers

Ashdod

No.	RINAP 2
1161/63	104.A
1638/1	104.C
—	104.B

Aššur

No.	RINAP 2
Ass 14?	66.6
Ass 31	66.2
Ass 46	66.3
Ass 82	70.2
Ass 723	69.4
Ass 740	68.2
Ass 775	68.3
Ass 776	68.7
Ass 816	68.16
Ass 826	68.4
Ass 988	69.16
Ass 1024+	71 commentary
Ass 1026+	71 commentary
Ass 1482	68.6
Ass 1496	70.6
Ass 1500	70.3
Ass 1501	69.17
Ass 1519	68.1
Ass 1521	68.5
Ass 1525	69.5
Ass 1573	69.6
Ass 1582	70.4
Ass 1586	69.7
Ass 1595	69.8
Ass 1598a	69.2
Ass 1598b	69.3
Ass 1598d	70.5
Ass 1635	69.9
Ass 1690	68.17
Ass 1742	67.2
Ass 1800	69.1
Ass 1801	70.1
Ass 1884	69.18
Ass 2204	69.19
Ass 2258	69.20
Ass 2367	69.21
Ass 2381	69.22
Ass 2394	69.23
Ass 2794	68.8
Ass 2798	69.24
Ass 2927a	67.3
Ass 2927b	67.4
Ass 2970a	68.12
Ass 2970b	68.18
Ass 3000	67.5
Ass 3007	69.25
Ass 3019	69.26
Ass 3054	68.19
Ass 3079	68.20
Ass 3139	69.27
Ass 3143	67.8
Ass 3166	68.21
Ass 3174	70.8
Ass 3175	68.22
Ass 3277	69.28
Ass 3280	68.9
Ass 3285	68.23
Ass 3286a	68.24
Ass 3289	68.25
Ass 3298	69.10
Ass 3327	67.1
Ass 3587	69.29
Ass 3652	69.30
Ass 3687	69.31
Ass 3757	69.32
Ass 3772	69.33
Ass 3773	69.34
Ass 3788	69.35
Ass 3793	69.36
Ass 3794	69.37
Ass 3859	69.38
Ass 3898	69.39; 70.10
Ass 4005	68.26
Ass 4397	67.9
Ass 4411	68.27
Ass 4572	67.10
Ass 5268e, g	71 commentary
Ass 5577	68.28
Ass 5581	69.40
Ass 6471c?	1005
Ass 7289	69.41
Ass 8800	64
Ass 9344	69.11
Ass 10112Ah	1004
Ass 11944	68.15
Ass 13366	69.42
Ass 13367	70.7
Ass 14703	2005
Ass 16007	67.6
Ass 16587	63
Ass 17342a+	67.7
Ass 17342b+	67.7
Ass 17404+	67.7
Ass 17791	67.11
Ass 17861a+	65
Ass 17861b+	65
Ass 17861c+	65
Ass 17861d+	65
Ass 17861g+	65
Ass 17791	67.11
Ass 17969	69.43
Ass 18540	68 commentary
Ass 19167	69.15
Ass 19168	69.14
Ass 20950	69.12
Ass 23090	1003

Babylon

No.	RINAP 2
BE 30680	123.7
BE 30681	123.8
BE 30682	123.9
BE 30683	123.10
BE 30684	123.11
BE 30698	123.12
BE 30700	123.13
BE 30706	123.14
BE 30707	123.15
BE 30708	123.16
BE 30709	123.17
BE 30710	123.18
BE 31080	123.19
BE 32062	123.20
BE 38583	124.1
BE 41861	124.2
BE 42335+	124.3
BE 42417+	124.3
BE 58377	124.4

Carchemish

No.	RINAP 2
H.80.12	110.1–2
KH.14.O.256	110.4–5
KH.14.O.636	110.6
KH.14.O.845	110.7–9
KH.14.O.974	110.10
KH.15.O.221	109.1
KH.15.O.300	10910
KH.15.O.355	109.3
KH.16.O.215	110.11
—	1010

Khorsabad

No.	RINAP 2
DŠ 5	57 Frgm. K
DŠ 31	53.32
DŠ 32	53.33
DŠ 33	53.34
DŠ 34	52.4
DŠ 35	50.21
DŠ 36	50.22
DŠ 37	50.23
DŠ 38	54.7
DŠ 39	56
DŠ 40	53.35
DŠ 51	2004
DŠ 88a+b	57 Frgm. M
DŠ 89	57 Frgm. L
DŠ 101	60?
DŠ 470	43.33
DŠ 525	59
DŠ 601	43.35
DŠ 642	43.37
DŠ 998	43.6
DŠ 999	43.7
DŠ 1000	43.8
DŠ 1002	43.9
DŠ 1003	43.10
DŠ 1194	49 commentary
DŠ 1195	49.3
DŠ 1264	43.11
DŠ 1267	43.12
DŠ 1288	43.13
DŠ 1289	43.14
DŠ 1290	43.15
DŠ 1291	43.16
DŠ 1292	43.17
DŠ 1293	43.18
DŠ 1294	43.19
DŠ 1295	43.20
DŠ 1298	43.21
DŠ 1299	43.22
DŠ 1301	43.23
DŠ 1302	43.24
DŠ 1303	43.25
DŠ 1304	43.26
DŠ 1313	2002.3
DŠ 1314	2002.2
DŠ 1315	2002.1
DŠ 1995	49.3
DŠ 32-1	59
DŠ 32-2	43.27
DŠ 32-3+	43.28
DŠ 32-4A	43.29
DŠ 32-4W	43.47
DŠ 32-4X	43.48
DŠ 32-4Y	43.49
DŠ 32-4Z	43.50
DŠ 32-5	43.30
DŠ 32-6	43.31
DŠ 32-12	43.32
DŠ 32-13	48
DŠ 32-19	43.33
DŠ 32-21	43.34
DŠ 32-24	60
DŠ 32-30	43.35
DŠ 32-31+	43.28
DŠ 32-33	43.36
DŠ 32-34A	43.37
DŠ 32-34B	43.38
DŠ 32-35	43.39
DŠ 32-36A	43.40
DŠ 32-36B	43.41
DŠ 32-45A	43.42
DŠ 32-45B	43.43
DŠ 32-46	43.44
DŠ 32-47	43.45
DŠ 32-48	43.46
DŠ —	1001

Nimrud

No.	RINAP 2
ND 2050	53.31
ND 2051	54.6
ND 2075a+b	1006
ND 2601+	74.1
ND 3400+	74.2
ND 3401+	74.1
ND 3402+	74.2
ND 3403+	74.1
ND 3404	74.2
ND 3406	75
ND 3408+	74.2
ND 3409+	74.2

Persepolis

Samaria

Tell Amarna (Syria)

Tell Baradān

Tell Haddad

Tell Tayinat

Uruk/Warka

No.	RINAP 2	No.	RINAP 2	No.	RINAP 2
W 2	127.1	W 2589	126.4	W 5753	126.9
W 1635a	126.1; 127.2	W 2703	126.5	W 6420a	126.10
W 1635c	127.3	W 2704	126.6	W 6420b/c	126.11
W 1635d	127.4	W 2705	126.7	W 11747	127.7
W 1635e	127.5	W 3200a	126.8	W 13182	127.8
W 1831a	126.2	W 4663	127.6	W 13393	126.12
W 1831b	126.3	W 5452	128.1	—	126.13–16

Index of Names

Personal Names

Abi-ḫatâ: **1** 325; **2** 329; **3** 47′.
Adâ: **43** 33; **76** 23′; **82** v 9′, 11′; **111** 31.
Adad-nārārī III: **92** 5.
Aḫḫē-iddina: **1** 291; **2** 315; **3** 35′.
Aḫī-Mīti: **1** 252; **2** 276; **3** 8′; **7** 94; **82** vii 3″.
Aḫundāra: See Ḫundāru.
Akkussu: **65** 48.
Ambaris: **1** 194, 201; **2** 226, 233; **7** 29, 31; **43** 23; **74** v 25; **76** 15′; **82** vii 7′; **105** i′ 15′.
Amitašši: **1** 167, 169; **2** 198, 202; **82** v 17′.
Amma...: **2** 314; **3** 35′.
Anda-il: **1** 298.
Anzî: **65** 43.
Arbaku: **82** vi 32″.
Argišti I: **63** iii′ 7′; **65** 402; **82** v 1.
Argišti II: **7** 113; **84** 21′.
Aria: **82** vi 26″.
Ashurnasirpal II (Aššur-nāṣir-apli): **73** 13; **107** 8′.
Asi'ān: **1** 290.
Ašpa-bara (Median ruler of Kakkam): **82** vi 20″.
Ašpa-bara (king of Ellipi): **2** 457, 460; **7** 118, 119, 121.
Aššur-bāni: **2006** 1.
Aššur-dūr-pāniya: **2010** 2.
Aššur-lē'i: **1** 84, 90, 167; **2** 198; **4** 28′; **7** 55, 56; **34** 2; **43** 33; **63** i′ 11′, 16′, iii′ 14′; **76** 23′; **82** v 8; **117** ii 23, 31.
Aššur-nāṣir-apli: See Ashurnasirpal II.
Atalia: **2001** 1.
AtkayaDUG: **82** v 15′.
Atkaya...: **82** v 15′.
Auarisarnu (Awarisarnu): **82** vi 30″.
Aya-lūnu: **1** 352; **2** 341.
Aya-rimmu: **2** 341.
Aya-Sammu: **2** 315; **3** 35′.
Azâ: **1** 80, 81, 82; **2** 72, 73, 74, 75; **4** 22′, 24′, 25′, 26′; **7** 37, 38.
Azamada: **117** ii 68.
Azuktu: **1** 181; **2** 209, 216.
Azūri: **1** 249; **2** 273; **3** 6′; **7** 90.
Bābilê: **1** 298.
Baga-parna: **65** 47.
Bag-dāti: **1** 79, 83; **4** 20′, 25′; **7** 49; **74** ii 13.
Battigur: **117** ii 64.
Ba-...: **2** 314; **3** 34′.
Bēl-āli: **2** 342.
Bēl-aplu-iddina: **1** 192; **2** 225; **63** i′ 21′; **65** 38; **117** ii 32.
Bēl-iddin: **2011** 4.
Bel-šarru-uṣur: **1** 93; **4** 39′; **7** 59; **117** ii 36.
Birtātu: **65** 48.
Burbuasu (Median ruler of Uratista): **117** ii 69.
Burbuazu (Median ruler of Ginkir): **117** ii 69.
Burburazu (Median ruler of Bīt-Ištar): **65** 46.
Bu...bartanu: **117** ii 69.
Daīku: **117** ii 47.
Daiṣṣānu: **1** 352; **2** 341.
Daltâ: **1** 97, 183, 192; **2** 89, 218, 224, 455; **4** 43′; **7** 70, 117; **65** 42; **72** A 9′; **74** iii 42; **82** iii 27′, v 60′, 68′, vi 11″.
Dārî: **65** 47.
Dayukku: **1** 102, 103; **2** 96, 98; **7** 49.
Dīnāya: **1** 297.
Dūrēsi: **65** 42.
Gunzinānu: **1** 205, 215; **2** 237; **7** 83; **8** 9; **9** 26; **13** 24; **76** 24′; **82** viii 7′; **88** 8′; **105** i′ 19′.
Ḫamadānu: See Ḫamdanu.
Ḫamdanu: **1** 293; **2** 314; **3** 34′.
Ḫanūnu: **1** 56; **7** 25, 26; **8** 16; **9** 23; **13** 40; **43** 19; **76** 12′; **129** 20.
Ḫarmakki: **65** 429.
Ḫaukānu: **1** 323; **2** 328; **3** 46′.
Ḫazā-il: **1** 292; **2** 314; **3** 34′.
Ḫullî: **1** 195, 196, 197; **2** 227, 228, 229; **7** 30; **74** v 16; **82** vi 6‴, 11‴.
Ḫumbanigaš I (Ḫumban-nikaš, Ummanigaš): **1** 265; **2** 291; **3** 15′; **7** 23, 123; **8** 7; **9** 12; **13** 14; **43** 17; **73** 7; **74** vi 18; **76** 10′; **84** 13′; **88** 5′; **89** obv. 17; **103** ii 28; **104** Frgm. B 1; **105** i′ 14′; **113** 7′; **116** 16; **129** 18.
Ḫumbê: **65** 46.
Ḫundāru: **74** vii 20; **116** 27.
Ḫuninu: **1** 326; **2** 329; **3** 47′.
Iādi (Iadī'): **1** 288.
Iāmānī: **1** 254; **2** 278; **3** 8′; **7** 95, 101; **8** 11; **82** vii 15″, 37″; **105** i′ 22′; **113** 2′; **116** 19.
Iannuqu: **1** 289, 321; **2** 327; **3** 45′.
Ianzû: **1** 104, 147; **2** 99; **7** 54; **65** 306, 307.
Iašyanu: **1** 293.
Iaū-bi'dī: See Ilu-bi'dī.
Ibnāya: **1** 297.
Ilu-bi'dī (also Iaū-bi'dī): **1** 23; **7** 33; **35** 1; **43** 25; **73** 8; **76** 17′; **81** 4, 19; **84** 18′; **89** obv. 17, bottom 22; **103** ii 53; **108** Frgm. D 7′; **117** ii 4.
Iranzi: **1** 58; **7** 36; **63** i′ 11′; **65** 62; **117** ii 14.
Irḫulena: **105** ii′ 11; **108** Frgm. E 4′.
Išpa-bara: See Ašpa-bara (king of Ellipi).
Išpueni: **63** iii′ 4′, 6′; **65** 400, 401.
Ištar-dūrī (Sarduri I, king of Urarṭu): **1** 144; **63** iii′ 3′, 5′; **65** 277, 400, 401.
Ištar-dūrī (governor of Arrapḫa): **65** 430.

Geographic, Ethnic, and Tribal Names

Divine, Planet, and Star Names

Gate, Palace, Temple, and Wall Names

Concordances of Annals Line Numbers

Concordance 1: RINAP 2 Text 1 (Annals Room II) Line Numbers to Botta, Winckler and Fuchs Line Numbers

[Note: Since Fuchs in Khorsabad marks out where a line of text ends, even if not preserved, the line equivalents are more precise for his column. Generally for Winckler the line equivalents only match what is actually preserved in the version in room II.]

RINAP 2 text 1 (Annals Room II) line nos.	Botta, Monument de Ninive 4 plate, slab, and line nos.	Winckler, Sar. line no.	Fuchs, Khorsabad line no.
1	79 top line —/12; II,2:1	—/12	—/12
2	79 top line 1; II,2:2	1	1
3	79 top line —/13; II,2:3	—/13	—/13
4	79 top line 2; II,2:4	2	2
5	79 top line 3; II,2:5	2–3	3
6	79 top line 4; II,2:6	4	4
7	79 top line 5; II,2:7	5	5
8	79 top line 6; II,2:8	6	6
9	79 top line 7; II,2:9	7	7
10	79 top line 8; II,2:10	8–9	8
11	79 top line 9; II,2:11	9–10	9
12	79 top line 10; II,2:12	10	10
13	79 top line 11; II,2:13	11	11
14	70 II,3:1	14	14
15	70 II,3:2	15	15
16	70 II,3:3	16–17	16
17	70 II,3:4	17	17
18	70 II,3:5	18	18
19	70 II,3:6	19	19
20	70 II,3:7	20	20
21	70 II,3:8	21	21
22	70 II,3:9	22	22
23	70 II,3:10	23	23
24	70 II,3:11	24	24
25	70 II,3:12	25	25
26	70 II,3:13	26	26
27–39 not preserved	— II,4:1–13	—	—
40–52 not preserved	— II,5:1–13	—	—
53	71 II,6:1	27	53
54	71 II,6:2	28	54
55	71 II,6:3	29	55

RINAP 2 text 1 (Annals Room II) line nos.	Botta, Monument de Ninive 4 plate, slab, and line nos.	Winckler, Sar. line no.	Fuchs, Khorsabad line no.
56	71 II,6:4	30	56
57	71 II,6:5	31	57
58	71 II,6:6	32	58
59	71 II,6:7	33	59
60	71 II,6:8	34	60
61	71 II,6:9	35	61
62	71 II,6:10	36	62
63	71 II,6:11	37	63
64	71 II,6:12	38	64
65	71 II,6:13	39	65
66	72 II,7:1	40	66
67	72 II,7:2	41	67
68	72 II,7:3	42	68
69	72 II,7:4	43	69
70	72 II,7:5	44	70
71	72 II,7:6	45	71
72	72 II,7:7	46	72
73	72 II,7:8	47	73
74	72 II,7:9	48	74
75	72 II,7:10	49	75
76	72 II,7:11	50	76
77	72 II,7:12	51	77
78	72 II,7:13	52	78
79	73 II,8:1	53	79
80	73 II,8:2	54	80
81	73 II,8:3	55	81
82	73 II,8:4	56	82
83	73 II,8:5	57	83
84	73 II,8:6	58	84
85	73 II,8:7	59	85
86	73 II,8:8	60	86
87	73 II,8:9	61	87
88	73 II,8:10	62	88
89	73 II,8:11	63	89
90	73 II,8:12	64	90
91	73 II,8:13	65	91
92	74 II,9:1	66	92
93	74 II,9:2	67	93
94	74 II,9:3	68	94
95	74 II,9:4	69	95
96	74 II,9:5	70	96
97	74 II,9:6	71	97
98	74 II,9:7	72	98
99	74 II,9:8	73	99
100	74 II,9:9	74	100
101	74 II,9:10	75	101
102	74 II,9:11	76	102
103	74 II,9:12	77	103
104	74 II,9:13	78	104
105	74bis II,10:1	79	105
106	74bis II,10:2	80	106
107	74bis II,10:3	81	107
108	74bis II,10:4	82	108
109	74bis II,10:5	83	109
110	74bis II,10:6	84	110
111	74bis II,10:7	85	111
112	74bis II,10:8	86	112
113	74bis II,10:9	87	113
114	74bis II,10:10	88	114
115	74bis II,10:11	89	115
116	74bis II,10:12	90	116
117	74bis II,10:13	91	117
118	75 II,11:1	92	118
119	75 II,11:2	93	119
120	75 II,11:3	94	120
121	75 II,11:4	95	121

RINAP 2 text 1 (Annals Room II) line nos.	Botta, Monument de Ninive 4 plate, slab, and line nos.	Winckler, Sar. line no.	Fuchs, Khorsabad line no.
122	75 II,11:5	96	122
123	75 II,11:6	97	123
124	75 II,11:7	98	124
125	75 II,11:8	99	125
126	75 II,11:9	100	126
127	75 II,11:10	101	127
128	75 II,11:11	102	128
129	75 II,11:12	103	129
130	75 II,11:13	104	130
131	76 II,12:1	105	131
132	76 II,12:2	106	132
133	76 II,12:3	107	133
134	76 II,12:4	108	134
135	76 II,12:5	109	135
136	76 II,12:6	110	136
137	76 II,12:7	111	137
138	76 II,12:8	112	138
139	76 II,12:9	113	139
140	76 II,12:10	114	140
141	76 II,12:11	115	141
142	76 II,12:12	116	142
143	76 II,12:13	117	143
144	77 II,13:1	118	144
145	77 II,13:2	119	145
146	77 II,13:3	120	146
147	77 II,13:4	121	147
148	77 II,13:5	122	148
149	77 II,13:6	123	149
150	77 II,13:7	124	150
151	77 II,13:8	125	151
152	77 II,13:9	126	152
153	77 II,13:10	127	153
154	77 II,13:11	128	154
155	77 II,13:12	129	155
156	77 II,13:13	130	156
157	78 II,14:1	131	157
158	78 II,14:2	132	158
159	78 II,14:3	133	159
160	78 II,14:4	134	160
161	78 II,14:5	135	161
162	78 II,14:6	136	162
163	78 II,14:7	137	163
164	78 II,14:8	138	164
165	78 II,14:9	139	165
166	78 II,14:10	140	166
167	78 II,14:11	141	167
168	78 II,14:12	142	168
169	78 II,14:13	143	169
170	79 bottom II,14:1	(144)	170
171	79 bottom II,14:2	(145)	171
172	79 bottom II,14:3	(146)	172
173	79 bottom II,14:4	(147)	(173)
174	79 bottom II,14:5	(148)	(174)
175	79 bottom II,14:6	(149)	(175)
176	79 bottom II,14:7	(150)	(176)
177	79 bottom II,14:8	(151)	177
178	79 bottom II,14:9	(152)	178
179	79 bottom II,14:10	(153)	179
180	79 bottom II,14:11	(154)	180
181	79 bottom II,14:12	(155)	181
182	79 bottom II,14:13	(156)	182
183	80 II,16:1	157	183
184	80 II,16:2	158	184
185	80 II,16:3	159	185
186	80 II,16:4	160	186
187	80 II,16:5	161	187

RINAP 2 text 1 (Annals Room II) line nos.	Botta, Monument de Ninive 3–4 plate, slab, and line nos.	Winckler, Sar. line no.	Fuchs, Khorsabad line no.
188	80 II,16:6	162	188
189	80 II,16:7	163	189
190	80 II,16:8	164	190
191	80 II,16:9	165	191
192	80 II,16:10	166	192
193	80 II,16:11	167	193
194	80 II,16:12	168	194
195	80 II,16:13	169	195
196	81 II,17:1	170	196
197	81 II,17:2	171	197
198	81 II,17:3	172–173	198
199	81 II,17:4	173	199
200	81 II,17:5	174–175	200
201	81 II,17:6	175–176	201
202	81 II,17:7	176	202
203	81 II,17:8	177	203
204	81 II,17:9	178–179	204
205	81 II,17:10	179	205
206	81 II,17:11	180	206
207	81 II,17:12	181	207
208	81 II,17:13	182	208
209	82 II,18:1	183	209
210	82 II,18:2	184	210
211	82 II,18:3	185	211
212	82 II,18:4	186	212
213	82 II,18:5	187	213
214	82 II,18:6	188	214
215	82 II,18:7	189	215
216	82 II,18:8	190	216
217	82 II,18:9	191	217
218	82 II,18:10	192	218
219	82 II,18:11	193	219
220	82 II,18:12	194	220
221	82 II,18:13	195	221
222	83 II,19:1	196	222
223	83 II,19:2	197	223
224	83 II,19:3	198	224
225	83 II,19:4	199	225
226	83 II,19:5	200	226
227	83 II,19:6	201	227
228	83 II,19:7	202	228
229	83 II,19:8	203	229
230	83 II,19:9	204	230
231	83 II,19:10	205	231
232	83 II,19:11	206	232
233	83 II,19:12	207	233
234	83 II,19:13	208	234
235–247 not preserved	– II,20:1–13	—	—
248	84 II,21:1	214	240
249	84 II,21:2	215	241
250	84 II,21:3	216	242
251	84 II,21:4	217	243
252	84 II,21:5	218	244
253	84 II,21:6	219	245
254	84 II,21:7	220	246
255	84 II,21:8	221	247
256	84 II,21:9	222	248
257	84 II,21:10	223	249
258	84 II,21:11	224	250
259	84 II,21:12	225	251
260	84 II,21:13	226	252
261	65 H_1:1	227	253
262	65 H_1:2	227–228	254
263	65 H_1:3	228	255
264	65 H_1:4	229–230	256
265	65 H_1:5	230–231	257

RINAP 2 text 1 (Annals Room II) line nos.	Botta, Monument de Ninive 3–4 plate, slab, and line nos.	Winckler, Sar. line no.	Fuchs, Khorsabad line no.
266	65 H_1:6	231, 233–234	258
267	65 H_1:7	235–236	259
268	65 H_1:8	236–238	260
269	65 H_1:9	238–239	261
270	65 H_1:10	240–241	262
271	65 H_1:11	241–243	263
272	65 H_1:12	243–244	264
273	65 H_1:13	245–246	265
274	65bis H_2:1	246–247; p. 40 n. 4	266
275	65bis H_2:2	p. 40 n. 4; 248	267
276	65bis H_2:3	249	268
277	65bis H_2:4	249–250	269
278	65bis H_2:5	250–251	270
279	65bis H_2:6	251–252	271
280	65bis H_2:7	253	272
281	65bis H_2:8	256	273
282	65bis H_2:9	256; p. 42 n. 9	274
283	65bis H_2:10	258; p. 42 n. 9	275
284	65bis H_2:11	258–259; p. 42 n. 9	276
285	65bis H_2:12	260–261; p. 44 n.1	277–279
286	65bis H_2:13	p. 44 n. 1	279, 279a
287	85 II,22:1	—	279b
288	85 II,22:2	—	279c
289	85 II,22:3	—	279d
290	85 II,22:4	—	279e
291	85 II,22:5	—	279f
292	85 II,22:6	—	279g
293	85 II,22:7	—	279h
294	85 II,22:8	—	279i
295	85 II,22:9	—	279j
296	85 II,22:10	—	279k
297	85 II,22:11	—	279l
298	85 II,22:12	—	279m
299	85 II,22:13	—	279n
300–312 not preserved	— II,23:1-13	—	—
313	92 top II,24:1	—	—
314	92 top II,24:2	—	—
315	92 top II,24:3	—	—
316	92 top II,24:4	—	—
317	92 top II,24:5	266	283
318	92 top II,24:6	266	283
319	92 top II,24:7	266	283
320	92 top II,24:8	266–267	283–284
321	92 top II,24:9	267	284
322	92 top II,24:10	267–268	284–285
323	92 top II,24:11	268	285
324	92 top II,24:12	268–269	285–286
325	92 top II,24:13	269	286
326	86 II,25:1	269	286
327	86 II,25:2	p. 44 n. 3	286a
328	86 II,25:3	p. 44 n. 3	286b
329	86 II,25:4	p. 44 n. 3	286c
330	86 II,25:5	p. 44 n. 3	288
331	86 II,25:6	p. 44 n. 3; p. 46 n. 1	288, 288a
332	86 II,25:7	p. 46 n. 1	288b
333	86 II,25:8	p. 46 n. 1	288c, 288–289
334	86 II,25:9	p. 46 n. 1	289
335	86 II,25:10	p. 46 n. 1	289
336	86 II,25:11	p. 46 n. 1	290
337	86 II,25:12	p. 46 n. 1; 273	290
338	86 II,25:13	273	290
339	92 bottom line 4 ('II,26:4'); II,26:1	274	291
340	92 bottom line 5 ('II,26:5'); II,26:2	274	291
341	92 bottom line ?; II,26:3	—	—
342	92 bottom line ?; II,26:4	—	—
343	92 bottom line ?; II,26:5	—	—

RINAP 2 text 1 (Annals Room II) line nos.	Botta, Monument de Ninive 4 plate, slab and line nos.	Winckler, Sar. line no.	Fuchs, Khorsabad line no.
344	92 bottom line ?; II,26:6	—	—
345	92 bottom line ?; II,26:7	—	—
346	92 bottom line ?; II,26:8	—	—
347	92 bottom line ?; II,26:9	—	—
348	92 bottom line ?; II,26:10	—	—
349	92 bottom line ?; II,26:11	—	—
350	92 bottom line 2 ('II,26:2'); II,26:12	280	297
351	92 bottom line 3 ('II,26:3'); II,26:13	280	297
352	92 bottom lines 8b, 9a ('II,26:8b, 9a'); II,27:1	281	298
353	92 bottom lines 9b, 10a ('II,26:9b, 10a'); II,27:2	282	299
354	92 bottom lines 10b, 11a ('II,26:10b, 11a'); II,27:3	283	300
355	92 bottom lines 11b, 12a ('II,26:11a, 12b'); II,27:4	283–284	301
356	92 bottom line ?; II,27:5	—	—
357	92 bottom line ?; II,27:6	—	—
358	92 bottom line ?; II,27:7	—	—
359	92 bottom line ?; II,27:8	—	—
360	92 bottom line ?; II,27:9	—	—
361	92 bottom line ?; II,27:10	—	—
362	92 bottom line ?; II,27:11	—	—
363	92 bottom line ?; II,27:12	—	—
364	92 bottom line ?; II,27:13	—	—
365	87 II,28:1	290	307
366	87 II,28:2	291	307, 307a
367	87 II,28:3	292	307b, 308
368	87 II,28:4	293	309
369	87 II,28:5	294	309–310
370	87 II,28:6	295	310–311
371	87 II,28:7	296	311
372	87 II,28:8	297	312
373	87 II,28:9	298	312–313
374	87 II,28:10	299	313–314
375	87 II,28:11	300	314
376	87 II,28:12	301	314–315
377	87 II,28:13	302	315–316
378	88 II,29:1	303–304	316–317
379	88 II,29:2	304	317–318
380	88 II,29:3	305	318
381	88 II,29:4	306	318–319
382	88 II,29:5	307	319
383	88 II,29:6	308	319–320
384	88 II,29:7	309	320
385	88 II,29:8	310	321
386	88 II,29:9	311	321, 321a
387	88 II,29:10	312	321b
388	88 II,29:11	313	321c
389	88 II,29:12	314	321d
390	88 II,29:13	—	321e
391–403 not preserved	— II,30:1–13	—	—
404	89 II,31:1	319–321	331–333
405	89 II,31:2	321–323	333–335
406	89 II,31:3	323–325	335–337
407	89 II,31:4	325–327	337–339
408	89 II,31:5	327–329	339–341
409	89 II,31:6	329–331	342–343
410	89 II,31:7	331–333	343–345
411	89 II,31:8	333–335	345–347
412	89 II,31:9	336–337	347–349
413	89 II,31:10	338	349–350
414	89 II,31:11	339	350–351
415	89 II,31:12	340	351
416	89 II,31:13	—	351 n. 3
417–429 not preserved	— II,32:1–13	—	—

RINAP 2 text 1 (Annals Room II) line nos.	Botta, Monument de Ninive 4 plate, slab, and line nos.	Winckler, Sar. line no.	Fuchs, Khorsabad line no.
430–442 not preserved	— II,33:1–13	—	—
443	90 II,34:1	370	384
444	90 II,34:2	371	384–385
445	90 II,34:3	372	386, 386a
446	90 II,34:4	373	386b
447	90 II,34:5	374	386c, 386–387
448	90 II,34:6	375	387
449	90 II,34:7	376	387a
450	90 II,34:8	377	387b
451	90 II,34:9	378	388–389
452	90 II,34:10	379	389–390
453	90 II,34:11	380	390–391, 391a
454	90 II,34:12	381	391a, 391–392
455	90 II,34:13	382	392
456	91 II,35:1a	383	392–393
457	91 II,35:2a, 1b	383	393
458	91 II,35:3a, 2b	383–384	393–394
459	91 II,35:4a, 3b	384	394
460	91 II,35:5a, 4b	384–385	394–395
461	91 II,35:6a, 5b	385	395
462	91 II,35:7a, 6b	386	395, 395a
463	91 II,35:8a, 7b	386	395a
464	91 II,35:9a, 8b	387	397
465	91 II,35:10a, 9b	387–388	397–398
466	91 II,35:11a, 10b	388	398
467	91 II,35:12a, 11b	388–389	398–399
468	91 II,35:13	389	399
469–481 not preserved	— II,1:1–13	—	—

Concordance 2: RINAP 2 Text 2 (Annals Room V) Line Numbers to Botta, Winckler and Fuchs Line Numbers

[Note: Since Fuchs in Khorsabad marks out where a line of text ends, even if not preserved, the line equivalents are more precise for his column. Generally for Winckler the line equivalents only match what is actually preserved in the version in room V.]

RINAP 2 text 2 (Annals Room V) line nos.	Botta, Monument de Ninive 4 plate, slab, and line nos.	Winckler, Sar. line no.	Fuchs, Khorsabad line no.
1–17 not preserved	— V,25:1–17	—	—
18–34 not preserved	— V,24:1–17	—	—
35–51 not preserved	— V,23:1–17	—	—
52–68 not preserved	— V,'22A':17	—	—
69	118 top V,22:1 (Botta V,16)	51	77
70	118 top V,22:2	52	78
71	118 top V,22:3	53	79
72	118 top V,22:4	54	80
73	118 top V,22:5	55	81–82
74	118 top V,22:6	56	82–83
75	118 top V,22:7	57	83, 83a–b
76	118 top V,22:8	58	83b, 84
77	118 top V,22:9	—	85; see p. 98 line 85 n. 1
78	118 top V,22:10	—	see p. 98 line 85 n. 1
79	118 top V,22:11	—	see p. 98 line 85 n. 1
80	118 top V,22:12	—	see p. 98 line 85 n. 1
81	118 top V,22:13	—	see p. 98 line 85 n. 1
82	118 top V,22:14	—	see p. 98 line 85 n. 1
83	118 top V,22:15	—	see p. 98 line 85 n. 1
84	118 top V,22:16	—	see p. 98 line 85 n. 1
85	118 top V,22:17	—	see p. 98 line 85 n. 1; 94
86	119 V,21:1 (Botta V,17)	68	94, 94a
87	119 V,21:2	68–69	94a, 95
88	119 V,21:3	69–70	95–96

RINAP 2 text 2 (Annals Room V) line nos.	Botta, Monument de Ninive 4 plate, slab, and line nos.	Winckler, Sar. line no.	Fuchs, Khorsabad line no.
89	119 V,21:4	70–71	96, 96a
90	119 V,21:5	71–72	96a, 97–98
91	119 V,21:6	72	98
92	119 V,21:7	73	99, 99a
93	119 V,21:8	73–74	99a, 100
94	119 V,21:9	74	100
95	119 V,21:10	74–75	100–101
96	119 V,21:11	75–76	101–102
97	119 V,21:12	76–77	102–103
98	119 V,21:13	77–78	103–104
99	119 V,21:14	78	104
100	119 V,21:15	79	105–106
101	119 V,21:16	80	106–107
102	119 V,21:17	—	107
103–119 not preserved	— V,20:1–17	—	—
120–136 not preserved	— V,19B:1–17	—	—
137–153 not preserved	— V,19A:1–17	—	—
154–170 not preserved	— V,19:1–17	—	—
171–187 not preserved	— V,18:1–17	—	—
188	120 V,17:1a, 2b (Botta V,18)	—	161
189	120 V,17:2a, 3b	(135), 136	161–162
190	120 V,17:3a, 4b	136	162
191	120 V,17:4a, 5b	137	163
192	120 V,17:5a, 6b	137–138	163–164
193	120 V,17:6a, 7b	138	164
194	120 V,17:7a, 8b	139	165
195	120 V,17:8a, 9b	139	165
196	120 V,17:9a, 10b	140	166
197	120 V,17:10a, 11b	140	166
198	120 V,17:11a, 12b	141	167
199	120 V,17:12a, 13b	141	167
200	120 V,17:13a, 14b	141–142	167–168
201	120 V,17:14a, 15b	142	168
202	120 V,17:15a, 16b	142–143	168, 168a
203	120 V,17:16a, 17b	—	168b
204	120 V,17:17a	—	168c
205	116 bottom V,16:1 (Botta V,14)	—	168c/d, 170
206	116 bottom V,16:2	—	171
207	116 bottom V,16:3	—	172
208	116 bottom V,16:4	—	173
209	116 bottom V,16:5	—	174
210	116 bottom V,16:6	—	175
211	116 bottom V,16:7	—	176
212	116 bottom V,16:8	—	177
213	116 bottom V,16:9	—	178
214	116 bottom V,16:10	—	179
215	116 bottom V,16:11	—	180
216	116 bottom V,16:12	—	181
217	116 bottom V,16:13	157	182–183
218	116 bottom V,16:14	157–158	183–184
219	116 bottom V,16:15	158–159	184–185
220	116 bottom V,16:16	159–160	—
221	116 bottom V,16:17	161–162	—
222	117 V,15:1	162–163	189
223	117 V,15:2	163–164	189–190
224	117 V,15:3	164–166	190–192
225	117 V,15:4	166–167	192–193
226	117 V,15:5	167–168	193–194
227	117 V,15:6	(168–169)	194–195
228	117 V,15:7	170	195–196
229	117 V,15:8	170–171	196–197
230	117 V,15:9	172–173	198
231	117 V,15:10	173–174	199–200
232	117 V,15:11	174–175	200–201
233	117 V,15:12	175–176	201–202
234	117 V,15:13	176–177	202–203

RINAP 2 text 2 (Annals Room V) line nos.	Botta, Monument de Ninive 4 plate, slab, and line nos.	Winckler, Sar. line no.	Fuchs, Khorsabad line no.
235	117 V,15:14	177–178	203–204
236	117 V,15:15	178–179	204–205
237	117 V,15:16	179–180	205–206
238	117 V,15:17	180	206
239–255 not preserved	— V,14:1–17	—	—
256	115 bottom V,13:1	192–193	218–219
257	115 bottom V,13:2	193–194	219–220
258	115 bottom V,13:3	194–195	220, 220a
259	115 bottom V,13:4	195–196	220a, 222
260	115 bottom V,13:5	196–197	222–223
261	115 bottom V,13:6	198–199	223–225
262	115 bottom V,13:7	200–201	226–227
263	115 bottom V,13:8	202–203	227–229
264	115 bottom V,13:9	203–204	229–230
265	115 bottom V,13:10	205–206	231–232
266	115 bottom V,13:11	206–207	232–233
267	115 bottom V,13:12	(208), 209	234–235
268	115 bottom V,13:13	210	235–236
269	115 bottom V,13:14	211	236–237
270	115 bottom V,13:15	212	237–238
271	115 bottom V,13:16	212–213	238–239
272	115 bottom V,13:17	213–214	239–240
273	115 top V,12:1	214–215	240–241
274	115 top V,12:2	215–216	241–242
275	115 top V,12:3	216–217	242–243
276	115 top V,12:4	217–218	243–244
277	115 top V,12:5	218–219	244–245
278	115 top V,12:6	220	246
279	115 top V,12:7	220?–221?	246–247
280	—; V,12:8	221–222	247–248
281	—; V,12:9	223	248–249
282	115 top line 8 ('V,12:8'); V,12:10	224	249–250
283	115 top line 9 ('V,12:9'); V,12:11	225	250–251
284	115 top line 10 ('V,12:10'); V,12:12	226	252–253
285	115 top line 11 ('V,12:11'); V,12:13	227	253
286	115 top line 12 ('V,12:12'); V,12:14	227	253–254
287	115 top line 13 ('V,12:13'); V,12:15	227–228	254–255
288	115 top line 14 ('V,12:14'); V,12:16	228	255, 255a–b
289	115 top line 15 ('V,12:15'); V,12:17	229	255b, 256
290	114 V,11:1	230	256–257
291	114 V,11:2	231	257–258
292	114 V,11:3	232	258
293	114 V,11:4	233	258
294	114 V,11:5	234	258
295	114 V,11:6	235	259
296	114 V,11:7	236	259–260
297	114 V,11:8	237	260
298	114 V,11:9	238	260–261
299	114 V,11:10	239	261
300	114 V,11:11	240	262
301	114 V,11:12	241	262–263
302	114 V,11:13	242	263
303	114 V,11:14	243	263–264
304	114 V,11:15	244	264
305	114 V,11:16	245	265
306	114 V,11:17	246	265–266
307	113 V,10:1	247	266, 266a
308	113 V,10:2	248	266b, 267
309	113 V,10:3	249	268–269
310	113 V,10:4	250	269–270
311	113 V,10:5	251	270–271
312	113 V,10:6	252	271a, 271
313	113 V,10:7	253	272
314	113 V,10:8	254	272a
315	113 V,10:9	255	272b
316	113 V,10:10	256	272c

RINAP 2 text 2 (Annals Room V) line nos.	Botta, Monument de Ninive 3–4 plate, slab, and line nos.	Winckler, Sar. line no.	Fuchs, Khorsabad line no.
317	113 V,10:11	257	272d
318	113 V,10:12	258	272e, 275, 276
319	113 V,10:13	259	276
320	113 V,10:14	260–261	277
321	113 V,10:15	261	278
322	113 V,10:16	262	279
323	113 V,10:17	263	280
324	66 top O_1:1	264	281
325	66 top O_1:2	265	282
326	66 top O_1:3	266	283
327	66 top O_1:4	267	284
328	66 top O_1:5	268	285
329	66 top O_1:6	269	286
330	66 top O_1:7	270	287
331	66 top O_1:8	271	288
332	66 top O_1:9	272	289
333	66 top O_1:10	273	290
334	66 top O_1:11	274	291
335	66 top O_1:12	275	292
336	66 top O_1:13	276	293
337	66 top O_1:14	277	294
338	66 top O_1:15	278	295
339	66 top O_1:16	279	296
340	66 top O_1:17	280	297
341	66 bottom O_2:1	281	298
342	66 bottom O_2:2	282	299
343	66 bottom O_2:3	283	300
344	66 bottom O_2:4	284	301
345	66 bottom O_2:5	285	302
346	66 bottom O_2:6	286	303
347	66 bottom O_2:7	287	304
348	66 bottom O_2:8	288	305
349	66 bottom O_2:9	289	306
350	66 bottom O_2:10	290–291	307
351	66 bottom O_2:11	291–292	308
352	66 bottom O_2:12	293–294	309
353	66 bottom O_2:13	294–295	310
354	66 bottom O_2:14	295–296	311
355	66 bottom O_2:15	297–298	312
356	66 bottom O_2:16	298–299	313
357	66 bottom O_2:17	299–300	314
358	112 V,9:1	301–302	315
359	112 V,9:2	302–303	316
360	112 V,9:3	303–304	317
361	112 V,9:4	304–306	318
362	112 V,9:5	306–308	319
363	112 V,9:6	308–309	320
364	112 V,9:7	310–311	321
365	112 V,9:8	—	322
366	112 V,9:9	—	323
367	112 V,9:10	—	324
368	112 V,9:11	313–314, 311	325
369	112 V,9:12	312	326
370	112 V,9:13	315	327
371	112 V,9:14	316	328
372	112 V,9:15	317	329
373	112 V,9:16	318	330
374	112 V,9:17	319	331
375	111 V,8:1	320	332
376	111 V,8:2	321	333
377	111 V,8:3	322	334
378	111 V,8:4	323	335
379	111 V,8:5	324	336
380	111 V,8:6	325	337
381	111 V,8:7	326	338
382	111 V,8:8	327	339

RINAP 2 text 2 (Annals Room V) line nos.	Botta, Monument de Ninive 4 plate, slab, and line nos.	Winckler, Sar. line no.	Fuchs, Khorsabad line no.
383	111 V,8:9	328	340
384	111 V,8:10	329	341
385	111 V,8:11	330	342
386	111 V,8:12	331	343
387	111 V,8:13	332	344
388	111 V,8:14	333	345
389	111 V,8:15	334	346
390	111 V,8:16	335–336	347
391	111 V,8:17	336–337	348
392	110 V,7:1; 116 top line 1	337–338	349–350
393	110 V,7:2; 116 top line 2	338–339	350–351
394	110 V,7:3; 116 top line 3	339–340	351
395	110 V,7:4: 116 top line 4	340–341	352
396	110 V,7:5; 116 top line 5	342	353
397	110 V,7:6; 116 top line 6	343	353–354
398	110 V,7:7; 116 top line 7	344	355
399	110 V,7:8; 116 top line 8	345	356–357
400	110 V,7:9; 116 top line 9	346	357
401	110 V,7:10; 116 top line 10	347	358
402	110 V,7:11; 116 top line 11	348	359
403	110 V,7:12; 116 top line 12	349	360
404	110 V,7:13; 116 top line 13	—	361
405	110 V,7:14; 116 top line 14	—	362
406	110 V,7:15; 116 top line 15	—	363
407	110 V,7:16; 116 top line 16	—	364
408	110 V,7:17; 116 top line 17	—	365
409	109 V,6:1	—	366
410	109 V,6:2	—	367
411	109 V,6:3	—	368
412	109 V,6:4	—	369
413	109 V,6:5	—	370
414	109 V,6:6	—	371
415	109 V,6:7	358	372
416	109 V,6:8	359	373
417	109 V,6:9	360	374
418	109 V,6:10	361	375
419	109 V,6:11	362	376
420	109 V,6:12	363	377
421	109 V,6:13	364	378
422	109 V,6:14	365	379
423	109 V,6:15	366	380
424	109 V,6:16	367	381
425	109 V,6:17	368	382
426	108 V,5:1	369	383
427	108 V,5:2	370–371	384
428	108 V,5:3	371–372	385
429	108 V,5:4	372–373	386
430	108 V,5:5	374–375	387
431	108 V,5:6	377–378; p. 62 n. 4	388
432	108 V,5:7	378–379; p. 62 n. 5	389
433	108 V,5:8	379–380	390
434	108 V,5:9	380–`381	391
435	108 V,5:10	382	392
436	108 V,5:11	383	393
437	108 V,5:12	384	394
438	108 V,5:13	385	395
439	108 V,5:14	386	396
440	108 V,5:15	387	397
441	108 V,5:16	388	398
442	108 V,5:17	389	399
443	107 V,4:1	390	400
444	107 V,4:2	391	401
445	107 V,4:3	392	402
446	107 V,4:4	393	403
447	107 V,4:5	394	404
448	107 V,4:6	395–396	405

RINAP 2 text 2 (Annals Room V) line nos.	Botta, Monument de Ninive 4 plate, slab, and line nos.	Winckler, Sar. line no.	Fuchs, Khorsabad line no.
449	107 V,4:7	396	406
450	107 V,4:8	397	407
451	107 V,4:9	398–399	408
452	107 V,4:10	399	409
453	107 V,4:11	400–401	410
454	107 V,4:12	401	411
455	107 V,4:13	402	412
456	107 V,4:14	403–404	413
457	107 V,4:15	404	414
458	107 V,4:16	405	415
459	107 V,4:17	406	416
460	106 V,3:1	407–408	417–418
461	106 V,3:2	408	418
462	106 V,3:3	409	419
463	106 V,3:4	410	420
464	106 V,3:5	411	421
465	106 V,3:6	411–412	422
466	106 V,3:7	413	423
467	106 V,3:8	414	424
468	106 V,3:9	415	425
469	106 V,3:10	416	426
470	106 V,3:11	417	427
471	106 V,3:12	418	428
472	106 V,3:13	419	429
473	106 V,3:14	420	430
474	106 V,3:15	421–422	431
475	106 V,3:16	422	432
476	106 V,3:17	423	433
477	105 V,2:1	424	434
478	105 V,2:2	425	435
479	105 V,2:3	426	436
480	105 V,2:4	427	437
481	105 V,2:5	428	438
482	105 V,2:6	429	439
483	105 V,2:7	430	440
484	105 V,2:8	431	441
485	105 V,2:9	432	442
486	105 V,2:10	433	443
487	105 V,2:11	434	444
488	105 V,2:12	435	445
489	105 V,2:13	436	446
490	105 V,2:14	437	447
491	105 V,2:15	438	448
492	105 V,2:16	439	449
493	105 V,2:17	440–441	450
494	118 bottom V,1:1	441–442	451
495	118 bottom V,1:2	442–443	452
496	118 bottom V,1:3	443–444	453
497	118 bottom V,1:4	445–446	454
498	118 bottom V,1:5	446–447	455
499	118 bottom V,1:6	448–449	456
500	118 bottom V,1:7	449–450	457
501	118 bottom V,1:8	450–451	458
502	118 bottom V,1:9	451–452	459
503	118 bottom V,1:10	452?–453?	460
504	118 bottom V,1:11	453–454	461
505	118 bottom V,1:12	454–455	462
506	118 bottom V,1:13	455–456	463
507	118 bottom V,1:14	456–457	464
508	118 bottom V,1:15	457–458	465
509	118 bottom V,1:16	458–459	466
510	118 bottom V,1:17	459–460	467

Concordances 3–6: RINAP 2 Texts 3–6 (Annals Room XIII, Room XIV, Throne Room and Unknown Room) Line Numbers to Botta, Winckler and Fuchs Line Numbers

[Note: Since Winckler may be using a different version of the annals (generally the one from room II or room V) as the master for a line, the line equivalents given here do not at times give the same basic text as the version in the room under consideration.]

Concordance 3: RINAP 2 Text 3 (Annals Room XIII) Line Numbers to Botta, Winckler and Fuchs Line Numbers

RINAP 2 text 3 (Annals Room XIII) line nos.	Botta, Monument de Ninive 4 plate, slab, and line nos.	Winckler, Sar. line no.	Fuchs, Khorsabad line no.
1′	155 XIII,4:1	209	235
2′	155 XIII,4:2	210	236
3′	155 XIII,4:3	211	237
4′	155 XIII,4:4	212	238
5′	155 XIII,4:5	213	239
6′	155 XIII,4:6	214–216	240–242
7′	155 XIII,4:7	216–218	242–244
8′	155 XIII,4:8	218–220	244–246
9′	155 XIII,4:9	220–222	246–248
10′	155 XIII,4:10	223–225	249–251
11′	155 XIII,4:11	225–227	251–253
12′	155 XIII,4:12	227	253–254
13′	155 XIII,4:13	228	254–255, 255a
14′	155 XIII,4:14	229–230	255b, 256–257
15′	155 XIII,4:15	230–232	257–258
16′–30′ not preserved	— XIII,5:1–15	—	—
31′	156 XIII,6:1	—	269 n. 1
32′	156 XIII,6:2	250–251	269–271
33′	156 XIII,6:3	251–253	271, 271a, 271–272
34′	156 XIII,6:4	253–254	272, 272a
35′	156 XIII,6:5	254–256	272a–c
36′	156 XIII,6:6	256–257	272c–d
37′	156 XIII,6:7	257–258	272d–e, 275
38′	156 XIII,6:8	258–260	276–277
39′	156 XIII,6:9	260–261	277–278
40′	156 XIII,6:10	261–263	278–280
41′	156 XIII,6:11	263–264	280–281
42′	156 XIII,6:12	264–265	281–282
43′	156 XIII,6:13	265–266	282–283
44′	156 XIII,6:14	266–267	283–284
45′	156 XIII,6:15	267–268	284–285
46′	157 XIII,7:1	268	285
47′	157 XIII,7:2	269	286
48′	157 XIII,7:3	269–270	286–287
49′	157 XIII,7:4	270	287
50′	157 XIII,7:5	271	288
51′	157 XIII,7:6	271–272	288–289
52′	157 XIII,7:7	272	289
53′	157 XIII,7:8	273	290
54′	157 XIII,7:9	273–274	290–291
55′	157 XIII,7:10	274–275	291–292
56′	157 XIII,7:11	275	292
57′	157 XIII,7:12	275–276	292–293
58′	157 XIII,7:13	276–277	293–294
59′	157 XIII,7:14	277–278	294–295
60′	157 XIII,7:15	278	295

Concordance 4: RINAP 2 Text 4 (Annals Room XIV) Line Numbers to Botta, Winckler and Fuchs Line Numbers

RINAP 2 text 4 (Annals Room XIV) line nos.	Botta, Monument de Ninive 4 plate, slab, and line nos.	Winckler, Sar. line no.	Fuchs, Khorsabad line no.
1′	158 XIV,1:1	37–38	63–64
2′	158 XIV,1:2	38–39	64–65
3′	158 XIV,1:3	40	66
4′	158 XIV,1:4	40–41	66–67
5′	158 XIV,1:5	41	67
6′	158 XIV,1:6	41–42	67–68
7′	158 XIV,1:7	42	68
8′	158 XIV,1:8	42–43	68–69
9′	158 XIV,1:9	43, p. 10 n. 1	69, 69a
10′	158 XIV,1:10	p. 10 n. 1	69b, 70
11′	158 XIV,1:11	44–45	70–71
12′	158 XIV,1:12	45	71
13′	158 XIV,1:13	46	72
14′	158 XIV,1:14	46, p. 10 n. 5	72, 72a
15′	158 XIV,1:15	47, p. 10 n. 6	72b
16′	159 top XIV,2:1	48	72c, 74
17′	159 top XIV,2:2	48–49	74–75
18′	159 top XIV,2:3	49–50	75–76
19′	159 top XIV,2:4	50–52	76–78
20′	159 top XIV,2:5	52–53	78–79
21′	159 top XIV,2:6	53	79
22′	159 top XIV,2:7	53–54	79–80
23′	159 top XIV,2:8	54–55	80–81
24′	159 top XIV,2:9	55–56	81–82
25′	159 top XIV,2:10	56–57	82–83
26′	159 top XIV,2:11	57	83, 83a
27′	159 top XIV,2:12	57–58	83b, 84
28′	159 top XIV,2:13	58–59	84–85
29′	159 top XIV,2:14	59, p. 12 n. 9	85
30′	159 top XIV,2:15	p. 12 n. 9	85a
31′	162 XIV,10:1	—	85b
32′	162 XIV,10:2	60	85c, 86–87
33′	162 XIV,10:3	61	87
34′	162 XIV,10:4	62	88–89
35′	162 XIV,10:5	63	89–90
36′	162 XIV,10:6	64	90–91
37′	162 XIV,10:7	65–66	91–92
38′	162 XIV,10:8	66–67	92–93
39′	162 XIV,10:9	67–68	93–94
40′	162 XIV,10:10	68–69	94, 94a
41′	162 XIV,10:11	69	95
42′	162 XIV,10:12	70	96
43′	162 XIV,10:13	71	96a, 97
44′	162 XIV,10:14	71–72	97–98
45′	162 XIV,10:15	72–73	98–99

Concordance 5: RINAP 2 Text 5 (Annals Throne Room) Line Numbers to Botta, Winckler and Fuchs Line Numbers

RINAP 2 text 5 (Annals Throne Room) line nos.	Botta, Monument de Ninive plate, slab, and line nos.	Winckler, Sar. line no.	Fuchs, Khorsabad line no.
1′	—	—	—
2′	—	315	326–327
3′	—	315–316	327–328

Concordance 6: RINAP 2 Text 6 (Annals Unknown Room) Line Numbers to Botta, Winckler and Fuchs Line Numbers

RINAP 2 text 6 (Annals Unknown Room) line nos.	Botta, Monument de Ninive 4 plate, slab, and line nos.	Winckler, Sar. line no.	Fuchs, Khorsabad line no.
1′	163 ?,?:1	329–332	342–344
2′	163 ?,?:2	332–335	344–347
3′	163 ?,?:3	336–338	347–349
4′	163 ?,?:4	338–339	350
5′	163 ?,?:5	339–340	351
6′	163 ?,?:6	340–341	352
7′	163 ?,?:7	342	353
8′	163 ?,?:8	343–344	354–355
9′	163 ?,?:9	344–346	355–357
10′	163 ?,?:10	347	357–358
11′	163 ?,?:11	348	358–359, 359a
12′	163 ?,?:12	—	359a
13′	163 ?,?:13	—	359b
14′	163 ?,?:14	—	359c

Concordance 7: Fuchs, Khorsabad Annals Line Numbers to RINAP 2 Text Nos. 1–6 Line Numbers

[Note: Fuchs' line numbers are given in numerical order, even though in his volume this is not always the case for the ordering for additional/supplementary lines. E.g., here lines 83a and 83b follow lines 83, while in his book they are placed in between two lines 84 (pp. 97–98), and here line 220a follows 220, while in his book it is placed after line 221 (p. 128).]

Fuchs, Khorsabad Annals line nos.	RINAP 2 Texts 1–6 line nos.
1	1:2
2	1:4
3	1:5
4	1:6
5	1:7
6	1:8
7	1:9
8	1:10
9	1:11
10	1:12
11	1:13
12	1:1?
13	1:3?
14	1:14
15	1:15
16	1:16
17	1:17
18	1:18
19	1:19
20	1:20
21	1:21
22	1:22
23	1:23
24	1:24
25	1:25
26	1:26
27–52 not preserved	27–52 not preserved
53	1:53
54	1:54
55	1:55
56	1:56
57	1:57
58	1:58
59	1:59
60	1:60
61	1:61
62	1:62
63	1:63, 4:1′
64	1:64, 4:1′–2′
65	1:65, 4:2′
66	1:66, 4:3′–4′
67	1:67, 4:4′–6′
68	1:68, 4:6′–8′
69	1:69, 4:8′–9′
69a	4:9′
69b	4:10′
70	1:70, 4:10′–11′
71	1:71, 4:11′–12′
72	1:72, 4:13′–14′
72a	4:14′
72b	4:15′
72c	4:16′
73	1:73
74	1:74, 4:16′–17′
75	1:75, 4:17′–18′
76	1:76, 4:18′–19′
77	1:77, 2:69, 4:19′
78	1:78, 2:70, 4:19′–20′
79	1:79, 2:71, 4:20′–22′
80	1:80, 2:72, 4:22′–23′
81	1:81, 2:73, 4:23′–24′
82	1:82, 2:73–74, 4:24′–25′
83	1:83, 2:74–75, 4:25′–26′
83a	2:75, 4:26′
83b	2:75–76, 4:27′
84	1:84, 2:76, 4:27′–28′
85	1:85, 2:77(+), 4:28′–29′
85a	4:30′
85b	4:31′
85c	4:32′

Fuchs, Khorsabad Annals line nos.	RINAP 2 Texts 1–6 line nos.
86	1:86, 4:32′
87	1:87, 4:32′–33′
88	1:88, 4:34′
89	1:89, 4:34′–35′
90	1:90, 4:35′–36′
91	1:91, 4:36′–37′
92	1:92, 4:37′–38′
93	1:93, 4:38′–39′
94	1:94, 2:85–86, 4:39′–40′
94a	2:86–87, 4:40′
95	1:95, 2:87–88, 4:41′
96	1:96, 2:88–89, 4:42′
96a	2:89–90, 4:43′
97	1:97, 2:90, 4:43′–44′
98	1:98, 2:90–91, 4:44′–45′
99	1:99, 2:92, 4:45′
99a	2:92–93
100	1:100, 2:93–95
101	1:101, 2:95–96
102	1:102, 2:96–97
103	1:103, 2:97–98
104	1:104, 2:98–99
105	1:105, 2:100
106	1:106, 2:100–101
107	1:107, 2:101–102
108	1:108
109	1:109
110	1:110
111	1:111
112	1:112
113	1:113
114	1:114
115	1:115
116	1:116
117	1:117
118	1:118
119	1:119
120	1:120
121	1:121
122	1:122
123	1:123
124	1:124
125	1:125
126	1:126
127	1:127
128	1:128
129	1:129
130	1:130
131	1:131
132	1:132
133	1:133
134	1:134
135	1:135
136	1:136
137	1:137
138	1:138
139	1:139
140	1:140
141	1:141
142	1:142
143	1:143
144	1:144
145	1:145
146	1:146
147	1:147
148	1:148

Fuchs, Khorsabad Annals line nos.	RINAP 2 Texts 1–6 line nos.
149	1:149
150	1:150
151	1:151
152	1:152
153	1:153
154	1:154
155	1:155
156	1:156
157	1:157
158	1:158
159	1:159
160	1:160
161	1:161, 2:188–189
162	1:162, 2:189–190
163	1:163, 2:191–192
164	1:164, 2:192–193
165	1:165, 2:194–195
166	1:166, 2:196–197
167	1:167, 2:198–200
168	1:168, 2:200–202
168a	2:202
168b	2:203
168c	2:204
168c/d	2:205
169	1:169
170	1:170, 2:205
171	1:171, 2:206
172	1:172, 2:207
173	1:173, 2:208
174	1:174, 2:209
175	1:175, 2:210
176	1:176, 2:211
177	1:177, 2:212
178	1:178, 2:213
179	1:179, 2:214
180	1:180, 2:215
181	1:181, 2:216
182	1:182, 2:217
183	1:183, 2:217–218
184	1:184, 2:218–219
185	1:185, 2:219
186	1:186, (2:220)
187	1:187, (2:221)
188	1:188, 2:221–222
189	1:189, 2:222–223
190	1:190, 2:223–224
191	1:191, 2:224
192	1:192, 2:224–225
193	1:193, 2:225–226
194	1:194, 2:226–227
195	1:195, 2:227–228
196	1:196, 2:228–229
197	1:197, 2:229
198	1:198, 2:230
199	1:199, 2:231
200	1:200, 2:231–232
201	1:201, 2:232–233
202	1:202, 2:233–234
203	1:203, 2:234–235
204	1:204, 2:235–236
205	1:205, 2:236–237
206	1:206, 2:237–238
207	1:207
208	1:208
209	1:209
210	1:210

Fuchs, Khorsabad Annals line nos.	RINAP 2 Texts 1–6 line nos.
211	1:211
212	1:212
213	1:213
214	1:214
215	1:215
216	1:216
217	1:217
218	1:218, 2:256
219	1:219, 2:256–257
220	1:220, 2:257–258
220a	2:258–259
221	1:221
222	1:222, 2:259–260
223	1:223, 2:260–261
224	1:224, 2:261
225	1:225, 2:261
226	1:226, 2:262
227	1:227, 2:262–263
228	1:228, 2:263
229	1:229, 2:263–264
230	1:230, 2:264
231	1:231, 2:265
232	1:232, 2:265–266
233	1:233, 2:266
234	1:234, 2:267
235	2:267–268, 3:1′
236	2:268–269, 3:2′
237	2:269–270, 3:3′
238	2:270–271, 3:4′
239	2:271–272, 3:5′
240	1:248, 2:272–273, 3:6′
241	1:249, 2:273–274, 3:6′
242	1,250, 2:274–275, 3:6′–7′
243	1:251, 2:275–276, 3:7′
244	1:252, 2:276–277, 3:7′–8′
245	1:253, 2:277, 3:8′
246	1:254, 2:278–279, 3:8′–9′
247	1:255, 2:279–280, 3:9′
248	1:256, 2:280–281, 3:9′
249	1;257, 2:281–282, 3:10′
250	1:258, 2:282, 3:10′
251	1:259, 2:283, 3:10′–11′
252	1:260, 2:284, 3:11′
253	1:261, 2:285–286, 3:11′–12′
254	1:262, 2:286–287, 3:12′–13′
255	1:263, 2:287–288, 3:13′
255a	2:288, 3:13′
255b	2:288–289, 3:14′
256	1:264, 2:289–290, 3:14′
257	1:265, 2:290–291, 3:14′–15′
258	1:266, 2:291–294, 3:15′
259	1:267, 2:295–296
260	1:268, 2:296–298
261	1:269, 2:298–299
262	1:270, 2:300–301
263	1:271, 2:301–303
264	1:272, 2:303–304
265	1:273, 2:305–306
266	1:274, 2:306–307
266a	2:307
266b	2:308
267	1:275, 2:308
268	1:276, 2:309
269	1:277, 2:309–310, 3:31′–32′
270	1:278, 2:310–311, 3:32′
271	1:279, 2:311–312, 3:32′–33′
271a	2:312, 3:33′
272	1:280, 2:313, 3:33′–34′
272a	2:314, 3:34′–35′
272b	2:315, 3:35′
272c	2:316, 3:35′–36′
272d	2:317, 3:36′–37′
272e	2:318, 3:37′
273	1:281
274	1:282
275	1:283, 2:318; (3:37′)
276	1:284, 2:318–319, 3:38′
277	1:285, 2:320, 3:38′–39′
278	1:285, 2:321, 3:39′–40′
279	1:285–286, 2:322, 3:40′
279a	1:286
279b	1:287
279c	1:288
279d	1:289
279e	1:290
279f	1:291
279g	1:292
279h	1:293
279i	1:294
279j	1:295
279k	1:296
279l	1:297
279m	1:298
279n	1:299
280	2:323, 3:40′–41′
281	2:324, 3:41′–42′
282	2:325, 3:42′–43′
283	1:317–320, 2:326, 3:43′–44′
284	1:320–322, 2:327, 3:44′–45′
285	1:322–324, 2:328, 3:45′–46′
286	1:324–326, 2:329, 3:47′–48′
286a	1:327
286b	1:328
286c	1:329
287	2:330, 3:48′–49′
288	1:330–331 and 333, 2:331, 3:50′–51′
288a	1:331
288b	1:332
288c	1:333
289	1:333–335, 2:332, 3:51′–52′
290	1:336–338, 2:333, 3:53′–54′
291	1:339–340, 2:334, 3:54′–55′
292	2:335, 3:55′–57′
293	2:336, 3:57′–58′
294	2:337, 3:58′–59′
295	2:338, 3:59′–60′
296	2:339
297	1:350–351, 2:340
298	1:352, 2:341
299	1:353, 2:342
300	1:354, 2:343
301	1:355, 2:344
302	2:345
303	2:346
304	2:347
305	2:348
306	2:349
307	1:365–366, 2:350
307a	1:366
307b	1:367
308	1:367, 2:351
309	1:368–369, 2:352

Fuchs, Khorsabad Annals line nos.	RINAP 2 Texts 1–6 line nos.
310	1:369–370, 2:353
311	1:370–371, 2:354
312	1:372–373, 2:355
313	1:373–374, 2:356
314	1:374–376, 2:357
315	1:376–377, 2:358
316	1:377–378, 2:359
317	1:378–379, 2:360
318	1:379–381, 2:361
319	1:381–383, 2:362
320	1:383–384, 2:363
321	1:385–386, 2:364
321a	1:386
321b	1:387
321c	1:388
321d	1:389
321e	1:390
322	2:365
323	2:366
324	2:367
325	2:368
326	2:369, 5:2′
327	2:370, 5:2′–3′
328	2:371, 5:3′
329	2:372
330	2:373
331	1:403–404, 2:374
332	1:404, 2:375
333	1:404–405, 2:376
334	1:405, 2:377
335	1:405–406, 2:378
336	1:406, 2:379
337	1:406–407, 2:380
338	1:407, 2:381
339	1:407–408, 2:382
340	1:408, 2:383
341	1:408, 2:384
342	1:409, 2:385, 6:1′
343	1:409–410, 2:386, 6:1′
344	1:410, 2:387, 6:1′–2′
345	1:410–411, 2:388, 6:2′
346	1:411, 2:389, 6:2′
347	1:411–412, 2:390. 6:2′–3′
348	1:412, 2:391, 6:3′
349	1:412–413, 2:392, 6:3′
350	1:413–414, 2:392–393, 6:4′
351	1:414–415, 2:393–394, 6:5′
352	1:416?, 2:395, 6:6′
353	2:396–397, 6:7′
354	2:397, 6:8′
355	2:398, 6:8′–9′
356	2:399; (6:9′)
357	2:399–400, 6:9′–10′
358	2:401, 6:10′–11′
359	2:402, 6:11′
359a	6:11′–12′
359b	6:13′
359c	6:14′
360	2:403
361	2:404
362	2:405
363	2:406
364	2:407
365	2:408
366	2:409
367	2:410
368	2:411
369	2:412
370	2:413
371	2:414
372	2:415
373	2:416
374	2:417
375	2:418
376	2:419
377	2:420
378	2:421
379	2:422
380	2:423
381	2:424
382	2:425
383	2:426
384	1:443–444, 2:427
385	1:444–445, 2:428
386	1:445–447, 2:429
386a	1:445
386b	1:446
386c	1:447
387	1:447–448, 2:430
387a	1:449
387b	1:450
388	1:451, 2:431
389	1:451–452, 2:432
390	1:452–453, 2:433
391	1:453–454, 2:434
391a	1:453–454
392	1:454–456, 2:435
393	1:456–458, 2:436
394	1:458–460, 2:437
395	1:460–462, 2:438
395a	1:462–463
396	2:439
397	1:464–465, 2:440
398	1:466–467, 2:441
399	1:467–468, 2:442
400	2:443
401	2:444
402	2:445
403	2:446
404	2:447
405	2:448
406	2:449
407	2:450
408	2:451
409	2:452
410	2:453
411	2:454
412	2:455
413	2:456
414	2:457
415	2:458
416	2:459
417	2:460
418	2:460–461
419	2:462
420	2:463
421	2:464
422	2:465
423	2:466
424	2:467
425	2:468
426	2:469

Fuchs, Khorsabad Annals line nos.	RINAP 2 Texts 1–6 line nos.
427	2:470
428	2:471
429	2:472
430	2:473
431	2:474
432	2:475
433	2:476
434	2:477
435	2:478
436	2:479
437	2:480
438	2:481
439	2:482
440	2:483
441	2:484
442	2:485
443	2:486
444	2:487
445	2:488
446	2:489
447	2:490
448	2:491
449	2:492
450	2:493
451	2:494
452	2:495
453	2:496
454	2:497
455	2:498
456	2:499
457	2:500
458	2:501
459	2:502
460	2:503
461	2:504
462	2:505
463	2:506
464	2:507
465	2:508
466	2:509
467	2:510

Concordance 8: Lie, Sar. Line Numbers to RINAP 2 Texts 1–7 Line Numbers

[Note: Only the longer passages cited in notes are included here.]

Lie, Sar.	RINAP 2 text and line nos.
lines 1–468	1:1–468
p. 10 n. 8	4:9′–10′
p. 11 n. 14	4:15′–16′
p. 14 nn. 2–3	4:26′–27′
p. 15 n. 6	4:29′–30′
pp. 38–39 lines 1–5	3:1′–5′
p. 32 n. 4	2:226–227
p. 44 n. 7	2:312, 3:33′
p. 45 n. 9	3:34′–41′
pp. 48–49 lines 1–6	2:324–329
p. 49 n. 5	3:47′–54′
pp. 50–53 lines 10–17	2:333–340
pp. 53–55 lines 1–9	2:341–349
p. 54 nn. 5–6	2:351–352
pp. 58–59 lines 13–17	2:370–374
pp. 62–65 lines 5–17	2:396–406
p. 62 n. 3	6:8′
p. 63 nn. 5–6	6:9′–14′
pp. 64–65 lines 6–17	2:414–425
pp. 66–67 lines 1–2	2:426–427
p. 68 n. 4	2:433; 7:152
p. 69 n. 7	2:435–436
p. 69 nn. 9–10	2:438–439
pp. 70–73 lines 1–17	2:443–459
p. 73 n. 9	7:119
pp. 74–77 lines 1–17	2:460–476
p. 76 n. 5	7:157–158
pp. 76–81 lines 1–17	2:477–493
pp. 80–83 lines 1–17	2:494–510

Concordance 9: Winckler, Sar. Annals Line Numbers to RINAP 2 Text Nos. 1–6 and 8 Line Numbers

[Note: Since Winckler used at times the text from one room as the main exemplar and at other times a different room, the line equations are sometimes very loose in view of variations in the text between the rooms. At times it is not clear if Winckler actually used a text cited in the right-hand column in making his edition. In addition to omitting certain lines on slabs that he otherwise used (e.g., RINAP text 1 lines 453–454 on II,34 [Winckler copy no. 25] would fit his lines 380–381), Winckler's list on p. IX omits various slabs used in RINAP (text 1 sections 23, 25, 27 and 28; text 2 sections 16, 17, 20 and 21; text 4 sections 2′ and 3′; and of course text 5, which was discovered after his time).]

[Note: Contra Winckler, Sar. 1 p. IX, his copy of II,19 (Botta, Monument de Ninive 4 pl. 83^{c}) is his no. 16, not no. 24, and his copy of V,1 (Botta, Monument de Ninive 4 pl. 118^{c} bottom) is his no. 52, not no. 58.]

[Note: For his lines 436–462, Winckler used text no. 8 (Display Inscription from room XIV) lines 68–87.]

[Note: In this file I have added information on several extra slabs and lines not used by Winckler in his edition.]

Winckler, Sar. Annals line nos.	RINAP 2 texts 1–6 line nos.
1	1:2
2	1:4–5
3	1:5
4	1:6
5	1:7
6	1:8
7	1:9
8	1:10
9	1:10–11
10	1:11–12
11	1:13
12	1:1?
13	1:3?
14	1:14
15	1:15
16	1:16
17	1:16–17
18	1:18
19	1:19
20	1:20
21	1:21
22	1:22
23	1:23
24	1:24
25	1:25
26	1:26
27	1:53
28	1:54
29	1:55
30	1:56
31	1:57
32	1:58
33	1:59
34	1:60
35	1:61
36	1:62
37	1:63, 4:1′
38	1:64, 4:1′–2′
39	1:65, 4:2′
40	1:66, 4:3′–4′
41	1:67, 4:4′–6′
42	1:68, 4:6′–8′
43	1:69, 4:8′–9′
44	1:70, 4:9′–11′
45	1:71, 4:11′–12′
46	1:72, 4:13′–14′
47	1:73, 4:14′–15′
48	1:74, 4:15?′–17′
49	1:75, 4:17′–18′
50	1:76, 4:18′–19′
51	1:77, 2:69, 4:19′
52	1:78, 2:70, 4:19′–20′
53	1:79, 2:71, 4:20′–22′
54	1:80, 2:72, 4:22′–23′
55	1:81, 2:73, 4:23′–24′
56	1:82, 2:273?–74, 4:24′–25′
57	1:83, 2:75, 4:25′–27′
58	1:84, 2:76, 4:27′–28′
59	1:85, 4:28′–29′
60	1:86, 4:32′
61	1:87, 4:33′
62	1:88, 2:80?, 4:34′
63	1:89, 4:35′
64	1:90, 4:36′
65	1:91, 4:36′?–37′?
66	1:92, 4:37′–38′

Winckler, Sar. Annals line nos.	RINAP 2 texts 1–6 line nos.
67	1:93, 4:38′–39′
68	1:94, 2:86–87, 4:39′–40′
69	1:95, 2:87–88, 4:40′–41′
70	1:96, 2:88–89, 4:42′
71	1:97, 2:89–90, 4:43′–44′
72	1:98, 2:90–91, 4:44′–45′
73	1:99, 2:92–93, 4:45′
74	1:100, 2:93–95
75	1:101, 2:95–96
76	1:102, 2:96–97
77	1:103, 2:97–98
78	1:104, 2:98–99
79	1:105, 2:100
80	1:106, 2:100–101
81	1:107, 2:101–102
82	1:108
83	1:109
84	1:110
85	1:111
86	1:112
87	1:113
88	1:114
89	1:115
90	1:116
91	1:117
92	1:118
93	1:119
94	1:120
95	1:121
96	1:122
97	1:123
98	1:124
99	1:125
100	1:126
101	1:127
102	1:128
103	1:129
104	1:130
105	1:131
106	1:132
107	1:133
108	1:134
109	1:135
110	1:136
111	1:137
112	1:138
113	1:139
114	1:140
115	1:141
116	1:142
117	1:143
118	1:144
119	1:145
120	1:146
121	1:147
122	1:148
123	1:149
124	1:150
125	1:151
126	1:152
127	1:153
128	1:154
129	1:155
130	1:156
131	1:157
132	1:158

Winckler, Sar. Annals line nos.	RINAP 2 texts 1–6 line nos.
133	1:159
134	1:160
135	1:161, 2:188–189
136	1:162, 2:189–190
137	1:163, 2:191–192
138	1:164, 2:192–193
139	1:165, 2:194–195
140	1:166, 2:196–197
141	1:167, 2:198–200
142	1:168, 2:200–202
143	1:169, 2:202–203?
144–156	1:170–182, 2:203–217
157	1:182?–183, 2:217–218
158	1:184, 2:218–219
159	1:185, 2:219–220
160	1:186, 2:220
161	1:187, 2:221
162	1:188, 2:221–222
163	1:189, 2:222–223
164	1:190, 2:223–224
165	1:191, 2:224
166	1:192, 2:224–225
167	1:193, 2:225–226
168	1:194, 2:226–227
169	1:195, 2:227–228?
170	1:196, 2:228–229
171	1:197, 2:229
172	1:198, 2:230
173	1:198–199, 2:230–231
174	1:200, 2:231–232
175	1:200–201, 2:232–233
176	1:201–202, 2:233–234
177	1:203, 2:234–235
178	1:204–205, 2:235–236
179	1:205, 2:236–237
180	1:206, 2:237–238
181	1:207
182	1:208
183	1:209
184	1:210
185	1:211
186	1:212
187	1:213
188	1:214
189	1:215
190	1:216
191	1:217
192	1:218, 2:256
193	1:219, 2:256–257
194	1:220, 2:257–258
195	1:221, 2:258–259?
196	1:222, 2:259–260
197	1:223, 2:260
198	1:224, 2:261
199	1:225, 2:261
200	1:226, 2:262
201	1:227, 2:262
202	1:228, 2:263
203	1:229, 2:263–264
204	1:230, 2:264
205	1:231, 2:265
206	1:232, 2:265–266
207	1:233, 2:266
208	1:234, 2:267
209	2:267–268, 3:1′
210	2:268?, 3:2′

Winckler, Sar. Annals line nos.	RINAP 2 texts 1–6 line nos.
211	2:269–270?, 3:3′
212	2:270–271, 3:4′
213	2:271–272, 3:5′
214	1:248, 2:272–273, 3:6′
215	1:249, 2:273–274, 3:6′
216	1:250, 2:274–275, 3:6′–7′
217	1:251, 2:275–276, 3:7′
218	1:252, 2:276–277, 3:7′–8′
219	1:253, 2:277, 3:8′
220	1:254, 2:278–279, 3:8′–9′
221	1:255, 2:279–280, 3:9′
222	1:256, 2:280–281?, 3:9′
223	1:257, 2:281, 3:10′
224	1:258, 2:282, 3:10′
225	1:259, 2:283, 3:10′–11′
226	1:260, 2:284, 3:11′
227	1:261–262, 2:285–287, 3:11′–12′
228	1:262–263, 2:287–288, 3:13′
229	1:264, 2:289, 3:14′
230	1:264–265, 2:290, 3:14′–15′
231	1:265–266, 2:291, 3:15′
232	2:292, 3:15′
233	1:266, 2:293
234	1:266, 2:294
235	1:267, 2:295
236	1:267–268, 2:296
237	1:268, 2:297
238	1:268–269, 2:298
239	1:269, 2:299
240	1:270, 2:300
241	1:270–271, 2:301
242	1:271, 2:302
243	1:271–272, 2:303
244	1:272, 2:304
245	1:273, 2:305
246	1:273–274, 2:306
247	1:274, 2:307
248	1:274–275, 2:308
249	1:276–277, 2:309
250	1:277–278, 2:310
251	1:278–279, 2:311; 3:32′–33′
252	1:279, 2:312, 3:33′
253	1:280, 2:313, 3:33′–34′
254	2:314, 3:34′–35′
255	2:315, 3:35′
256	1:281–282, 2:316, 3:35′–36′
257	2:317, 3:36′–37′
258	1:283–284, 2:318, 3:37′–38′
259	1:284, 2:319, 3:38′
260	1:285, 2:320, 3:38′–39′
261	1:285, 2:320–321, 3:39′–40′
262	2:322, 3:40′
263	2:323, 3:40′–41′
264	2:324, 3:41′–42′
265	2:325, 3:42′–43′
266	1:317–320, 2:326, 3:43′–44′
267	1:320–322, 2:327, 3:44′–45′
268	1:322–324, 2:328, 3:45′–46′
269	1:324–327, 2:329, 3:47′–48′
270	1:328–329, 2:330, 3:48′–49′
271	1:330–333, 2:331, 3:50′–51′
272	1:333–335, 2:332, 3:51′–52′
273	1:336–339, 2:333, 3:53′–54′
274	1:339–340, 2:334, 3:54′–55′
275	2:335, 3:55′–57′
276	2:336, 3:57′–58′

Winckler, Sar. Annals line nos.	RINAP 2 texts 1–6 line nos.	Winckler, Sar. Annals line nos.	RINAP 2 texts 1–6 line nos.
277	2:337, 3:58′–59′	343	2:397, 6:8′
278	2:338, 3:59′–60′	344	2:398, 6:8′–9′
279	2:339	345	2:399, 6:9?
280	1:350–351, 2:340	346	2:400, 6:9′
281	1:352, 2:341	347	2:401, 6:10′
282	1:353, 2:342	348	2:402, 6:11′
283	1:354–355, 2:343	349	2:403
284	1:355, 2:344	350–357 damaged	see 2:404–414
285	2:345	358	2:415
286	2:346	359	2:416
287	2:347	360	2:417
288	2:348	361	2:418
289	2:349	362	2:419
290	1:365, 2:350	363	2:420
291	1:366, 2:350–351	364	2:421
292	1:367, 2:351	365	2:422
293	1:368, 2:352	366	2:423
294	1:369, 2:352–353	367	2:424
295	1:370, 2:353–354	368	2:425
296	1:371, 2:354	369	2:426
297	1:372, 2:355	370	1:443, 2:427
298	1:373, 2:355–356	371	1:444, 2:427–428
299	1:374, 2:356–357	372	1:445, 2:428–429
300	1:375, 2:357	373	1:446, 2:429
301	1:376, 2:358	374	1:447, 2:429? –430?
302	1:377, 2:358–359	375	1:448, 2:430
303	1:378, 2:359–360	376	1:449
304	1:378–379, 2:360–361	377	1:450, 2:431?
305	1:380, 2:361	378	1:451, 2:431–432
306	1:381, 2:361–362	379	1:452, 2:432–433
307	1:382, 2:362	380	1:453, 2:433–434
308	1:383, 2:362–363	381	1:454, 2:434
309	1:384, 2:363	382	1:455, 2:435
310	1:385, 2:364	383	1:456–458, 2:436
311	1:386, 2:364 and 368	384	1:458–460?, 2:437
312	1:387, 2:369	385	1:460–461, 2:438
313	1:388, 2:368	386	1:462–463, 2:439
314	1:389, 2:368	387	1:464–465, 2:440
315	2:370, 5:2′–3′	388	1:465–467, 2:441
316	2:371, 5:3′	389	1:467–468, 2:442
317	2:372	390	2:443
318	2:373	391	2:444
319	1:404, 2:374	392	2:445
320	1:404, 2:375	393	2:446
321	1:404–405, 2:376	394	2:447
322	1:405, 2:377	395	2:448
323	1:405–406, 2:378	396	2:448–449
324	1:406, 2:379	397	2:450
325	1:406–407, 2:380	398	2:451
326	1:407, 2:381	399	2:451–452
327	1:407–408, 2:382	400	2:453
328	1:408, 2:383	401	2:454–454
329	1:408–409. 2:384, 6:1′	402	2:455
330	1:409, 2:385, 6:1′	403	2:456
331	1:409–410, 2:386, 6:1′	404	2:456–457
332	1:410, 2:387, 6:1′–2′	405	2:458
333	1:410–411, 2:388, 6:2′	406	2:459
334	1:411, 2:389, 6:2′	407	2:460
335	1:411, 2:390, 6:2′	408	2:460–461
336	1:412, 2:390–391, 6:3′	409	2:462
337	1:412, 2:391–392, 6:3′	410	2:463
338	1:413, 2:392–393, 6:3′–4′	411	2:464–465
339	1:414, 2:393–394, 6:4′–5′	412	2:465
340	1:414–415, 2:394–395, 6:5′–6′	413	2:466
341	1:416, 2:395, 6:6′	414	2:467
342	2:396, 6:7′	415	2:468

Winckler, Sar. Annals line nos.	RINAP 2 texts 1–6 line nos.
416	2:469
417	2:470
418	2:471
419	2:472
420	2:473
421	2:474
422	2:474–475
423	2:476
424	2:477
425	2:478
426	2:479
427	2:480
428	2:481
429	2:482
430	2:483
431	2:484
432	2:485
433	2:486
434	2:487
435	2:488
436	2:489
437	2:490, 8:59
438	2:491, 8:60–63

Winckler, Sar. Annals line nos.	RINAP 2 texts 1–6 line nos.
439	2:492, 8:63–65
440	2:493, 8:65–68
441	2:493–494, 8:68
442	2:494–495, 8:69
443	2:495–496, 8:70
444	2:496, 8:71
445	2:497, 8:72
446	2:497–498, 8:73
447	2:498, 8:74
448	2:499, 8:75
449	2:499–500, 8:76
450	2:500–501, 8:77
451	2:501–502, 8:78
452	2:502–503?, 8:79
453	2:503–504, 8:80
454	2:504–505, 8:81
455	2:505–506, 8:82
456	2:506–507, 8:83
457	2:507–508, 8:84
458	2:508-509, 8:85
459	2:509–510, 8:86
460	2:510, 8:87

Concordances of Selected Publications

Börker-Klähn, Bildstelen

No.	RINAP 2	No.	RINAP 2	No.	RINAP 2
173	117	177	106	248	116
174	104	178	1010	252	2010
175	103	179	1009		

Borger, TUAT 1/4

P.	RINAP 2	P.	RINAP 2	P.	RINAP 2
378–381	1–2	383–385	7	386	43
381–382	82	385	8	387	73
382	74	385–386	103	387	89
382–383	63	386	13		

Botta, Monument de Ninive 3–4

Pl.	RINAP 2	Pl.	RINAP 2	Pl.	RINAP 2
1	10.2	29^{c}	9.6	57^{c}	9.19
2	11.1	30^{c}	9.7	58^{c}	9.20
3	10.3	31^{c}	9.7	59^{c}	9.20
4	13.2	32^{c}	9.8	60^{c}	9.21
5^{c}	11.2	33^{c}	9.8	61^{c}	9.21
6	13.3	34^{c}	9.9	62	9.22
7:1-4	13.4	35^{c}	9.9	63	7.3
8	12.2	36^{c}	9.10	64	7.3
9	12.1	37^{c}	9.10	65^{c}	1 §21
10	12.3	38^{c}	9.11	65$^{bis\ c}$	1 §22
11:1-4	13.5	39^{c}	9.11	66^{c} top	2 §20
12 1-4	13.6	40^{c}	9.12	66^{c} bottom	2 §21
13	10.1	41^{c}	9.12	67^{c}	8 §5
14	14.1	42^{c}	9.13	68^{c}	8 §6
15	12.4	43^{c}	9.13	69 left	7.2
16:1-4	13.1	44^{c}	9.14	69 right	7.2
17	13.7	45^{c}	9.14	70^{c}	1 §2
18:1-4	13.8	46^{c}	9.15	71^{c}	1 §5
19:1-4	13.9	47^{c}	9.15	72^{c}	1 §6
20	14.2	48^{c}	9.1	73^{c}	1 §7
21	12.5	49^{c}	9.1	74^{c}	1 §8
22^{c}	9.3	50^{c}	9.2	74$^{bis\ c}$	1 §9
23^{c}	9.3	51^{c}	9.2	75^{c}	1 §10
24^{c}	9.4	52	9.16	76^{c}	1 §11
25^{c}	9.4	53	9.17	77^{c}	1 §12
26^{c}	9.5	54^{c}	9.18	78^{c}	1 §13
27^{c}	9.5	55^{c}	9.18	79 top	1 §1
28^{c}	9.6	56^{c}	9.19	79^{c} bottom	1 §14

Pl.	RINAP 2
80^{c}	1 §15
81^{c}	1 §16
82^{c}	1 §17
83^{c}	1 §18
84^{c}	1 §20
85^{c}	1 §23
86^{c}	1 §26
87^{c}	1 §29
88^{c}	1 §30
89^{c}	1 §32
90^{c}	1 §35
91	1 §36
92 top	1 §25
92 bottom	1 §27–28
93	7.3
94	7.3
95	7.3
96	7.3
97^{c}	7.3
98^{c}	7.3
99^{c}	7.3
100^{c}	7.3
101^{c}	7.3
102	7.3
103^{c}	7.3
104^{c}	7.3
105^{c}	2 §29
106^{c}	2 §28
107^{c}	2 §27
108^{c}	2 §26
109^{c}	2 §25
110^{c}	2 §24
111^{c}	2 §23
112^{c}	2 §22
113^{c}	2 §19
114^{c}	2 §18
115^{c} top	2 §17
115^{c} bottom	2 §16
116 top	2 §24
116 bottom	2 §13
117^{c}	2 §14
118^{c} top	2 §5
118^{c} bottom	2 §30
119^{c}	2 §6

Pl.	RINAP 2
120	2 §12
121^{c}	7.4
122^{c}	7.4
123^{c}	7.4
124^{c}	7.4
125^{c}	7.4
126^{c}	7.4
127^{c}	7.4
128^{c}	7.4
129^{c}	7.4
130^{c}	7.4
131^{c}	7.4
132^{c}	7.4
133 top	7.5
133 bottom	7.5
134^{c} top	7.5
134^{c} bottom	7.5
135 top	7.5
135 bottom	7.5
136^{c}	7.5
137^{c}	7.5
138^{c} top	7.5
138^{c} bottom	7.5
139^{c}	7.5
140^{c}	7.5
141^{c}	7.5
142^{c} top	7.5
142^{c} bottom	7.5
143^{c} top	7.5
143^{c} bottom	7.5
144^{c}	7.1
145^{c} top	7.1
145^{c} bottom	7.1
146^{c} top	7.1
146^{c} bottom	7.1
147^{c}	7.1
148^{c}	7.1
149^{c}	7.1
150^{c}	7.1
151^{c} top	7.1
151^{c} bottom	7.1
152^{c} top	7.1
152^{c} bottom	7.1
153^{c}	7.1

Pl.	RINAP 2
154^{c}	7.1
155^{c}	3 §1′
156^{c}	3 §3′
157^{c}	3 §4′
158^{c}	4 §1′
159^{c} top	4 §2′
159^{c} bottom	8 §1
160^{c} top	8 §2
160^{c} bottom	8 §3
161	8 §4
162	4 §3′
163	6 §1′, 40
164	41.1
165	41.2
166	41.3
167	41.4
168^{c}	41.5
169	41.6
170	41.7
171	41.8
172^{c}	41.9
173^{c}	41.10
174	41.11
175	41.12
176	41.13
177^{c}	41.14
178	41.15
179	41.16
180^{c}	23–32, 36–39
181^{c}.1	49.1
181^{c}.2	35
181^{c}.3	34
181^{c}.4	33
181^{c}.5	14.3
182^{c}.1	Asb.
182^{c}.2	Senn.
182^{c}.3	Senn.
182^{c}.4	Senn.
183^{c}.1	Senn.
183^{c}.2	50.7
183^{c}.3	50.8
183^{c}.4	55.1
183^{c}.5	53.12

Cogan, Bound for Exile

P.	RINAP 2
48 fig. 12	53.30

Cogan, Raging Torrent

P.	No.	RINAP 2
82–89	18	7
89–93	19	74
93–96	20	1–3
96–97	21	89
97–98	22	43
98–100	23	103
100–103	24	73
103–105	25	82
105–107	26	63
231–233	1	1009
232–233	2	104

Donbaz and Grayson, RICCA

No.	RINAP 2	No.	RINAP 2	No.	RINAP 2
136	67.7	230	67.4	233	67.6
228	67.2	231	67.5	234	67.7
229	67.3	232	67.1	235	67.8

Fales, COS 4

P.	No.	RINAP 2
199–215	4.42	65

Fales, Studies Lipiński

P.	No.	RINAP 2
42–43	9	78
45–46	13	79

Frahm, KAL 3

No.	RINAP 2
31	72
32	64

Frame, RIMB 2

P.	No.	RINAP 2	P.	No.	RINAP 2
143–145	B.6.22.1	123	149–150	B.6.22.4	126
145–146	B.6.22.2	124	150–151	B.6.22.5	127
146–149	B.6.22.3	125	151–152	B.6.22.6	128

Fuchs, Khorsabad

No.	P.	RINAP 2	No.	P.	RINAP 2
1.1	29–44 and 289–296	43	2.5.1	249–251 and 356	10
1.2.1	45–48 and 296–298	44	2.5.2	251–254 and 356–357	11
1.2.2	48–50 and 298–299	45	2.5.3	254–259 and 358	12
1.2.3	51–52 and 299–300	46	2.5.4	259–271 and 359–362	13
1.2.4	52–53 and 300	47	2.5.5	271–275 and 362–363	14
1.3	54–59 and 300–302	41	3.1	276–279 and 364–368	23–40
2.1	60–74 and 303–307	9	3.2.1	280 and 369	17
2.2	75–81 and 307–312	8	3.2.2	280 and 369	18
2.3	82–188 and 313–342	1–6	3.2.3	281 and 369–370	20
2.4	189–248 and 343–355	7	3.2.4	281 and 370	21

No.	P.	RINAP 2	No.	P.	RINAP 2
3.2.5	281–282 and 370	22	3.5b	286 and 372	51
3.2.6	282 and 370	19	3.5c	286 and 372	53
3.2.7	283 and 371	16	3.5d	287 and 372	52
3.3	284 and 371	49	3.5e	287 and 372	54
3.4	285 and 371	2002	3.5f	287 and 372	55
3.5a	286 and 372	50			

Jacobsen in Loud, Khorsabad 1 pp. 129–133

P.	No.	RINAP 2	P.	No.	RINAP 2
129	1	5	131–132	5	16
129	2	52	132–133	6	17
130	3	18	133	7	20
130–131	4	19			

Jacobsen in Loud and Altman, Khorsabad 2 pp. 103–105

P.	No.	RINAP 2	P.	No.	RINAP 2
103–104	1	22	104	18	1001
104	2	2002	105	32	59
104	3	49.3	105	33	60?
104	4	10.4	105	40–64	43
104	5	11 commentary			

Jakob-Rost and Marzahn, VAS 23

No.	RINAP 2
124	68.14

Layard, ICC

Pl.	RINAP 2	Pl.	RINAP 2	Pl.	RINAP 2
33–34	73.1–2	82 [D.2]	53.5	84A	77.2
82 [D.1]	50.9	83E	77.1		

Luckenbill, ARAB 2

P.	RINAP 2	P.	RINAP 2	P.	RINAP 2
2–25 §§3–51	1–3	48 and 50–51 §§95, 98	12	56, 58–59 §§106, 112–113	46
25–39 §§52–75	7	48 and 51–54 §§95, 99–101	13	56, 59 §§106, 114–115	47
39–45 §§76–90	8	48 and 54–55 §§95, 102	14	60–66 §§116–123	43
45–47 §§91–94	9	55–56 §§103–105	41	66 §124	49
48 §§95–96	10	56–57 §§106–109	44	66 §125a	23
48–50 and §§95, 97	11	56, 58 §§ 106, 110–111	45	66 §125b	24

P.	RINAP 2	P.	RINAP 2	P.	RINAP 2
66 §125c	25	67 §125o	28	100–103 §§179–189	103
66 §125d	26	67 §126	16	104–111 §§190–218	82
66 §125e	27	67 §127	17	112 §§219–223	67
66 §125f	30	67 §127a	53	112–113 §§219, 224	69–70
66 §125g	31	68 §128	50	112–113 §§219, 225	68
67 §125h	32	68 §129	51	113 §226	95
67 §125i	34	68 §130	55	113 §227	92
67 §125k	35	68 §131	54	114 §228	77
67 §125l	37	69–71 §§132–135	89	114 §229	SAA 11 no. 49
67 §125m	39	71–73 §§136–138	73		
67 §125n	38	73–99 §§139–178	65	114 §230	61

Lyon, Sar.

No.	P.	RINAP 2	No.	P.	RINAP 2
1	X–XII, 1–12, 30–39, 58–79	43	4	XIII, 23–24, 50–53, 82	45
2	XII, 13–19, 40–47, 79–81	9	5	XIII, 25–26, 54–57, 82	46
3	XII–XIII, 20–22, 48–51	44	6	XIII, 27, 56–57	47

Maniori, Campagne di Sargon

No.	RINAP 2	No.	RINAP 2	No.	RINAP 2
A1	1	D3	28	G9	113
A2	2	D4	25	G10	111
A3	3	D5	24	g1	8
A4	4	D6	23	g2	9
A5	5	D7	37	g3	13
A6	6	D8	39	g4	43
A7	82	D9	38	g5–6	76.1–2
A8	63	D10	36	g7	84
A9	102	D11	34	g8	103
A10	117	D12–13	71	g9	105
A11	89	G1–5	7.1–5	g10	104
D1	27	G6–7	74	g11	116
D2	26	G8	83	M	65

Marzahn and Rost, Ziegelen 1

No.	RINAP 2	No.	RINAP 2	No.	RINAP 2
342	69.1	346	69.13	350	68.11
343	69.10	347	68.8	351	68.12
344	69.11	348	68.9	352	68.13
345	69.12	349	68.10	353	68.14

Messerschmidt, KAH 1

No.	RINAP 2	No.	RINAP 2	No.	RINAP 2
37	69.1–9	40	67.2	71	67.1
38	70.1–5	41	67.3–4		
39	68.1–7	42	67.5		

Mitchell in Gyselen, Prix

P.	No.	RINAP 2
129–138	10–11	78
129–138	15	79

Oppenheim, ANET[3]

P.	RINAP 2	P.	RINAP 2	P.	RINAP 2
284	13	284–286	7	287	73
284	103	285	8	287	82
284–286	1	286	63		

Place, Ninive et l'Assyrie

Vol. and P./Pl.	RINAP 2	Vol. and P./Pl.	RINAP 2	Vol. and P./Pl.	RINAP 2
2 pp. 283–291	9	2 pp. 309–319	1–4, 8	3 pl. 77 no. 5	47
2 pp. 291–303	43	3 pl. 74 no. 11	62, 2003	3 pl. 77 no. 6	44
2 pp. 303–304	46	3 pl. 76 no. 31	61	3 pl. 78 nos. 1–2	43
2 pp. 304–306	45	3 pl. 77 nos. 1–2	46		
2 pp. 306–307	47	3 pl. 77 nos. 3–4	45		

1 R

Pl.	RINAP 2
6 no. 7	95.1–3
36	43.3

3 R

Pl.	RINAP 2
3 no. 12	92.1
11	103

Schroeder, KAH 2

No.	RINAP 2
141	65

Thompson, AAA 18 (1931)

P./Pl.	No.	RINAP 2
Pl. XIX	37	53.21
P. 100	—	50.12

Thompson, AAA 19 (1932)

Pl.	No.	RINAP 2	Pl.	No.	RINAP 2
LXXIII	102	92.6	LXXVI	158	92.14
LXXIII	110	92.7	LXXVI	159	92.15
LXXIII	111	92.8	LXXVI	160	92.16
LXXIV	132	92.9	LXXVI	162	92.17
LXXV	145	92.10	LXXVI	166	92.18
LXXV	152	92.11	LXXVI	167	92.19
LXXVI	155	92.12	LXXIX	226	92.20
LXXVI	156	92.13			

Thompson, Arch. 79 (1929)

Pl.	No.	RINAP 2	Pl.	No.	RINAP 2
XLII	28	94	XLV	74	98
XLII	29	95.5	XLV	80	55.2
XLII	41	93	XLVI	115	51.2
XLII	43	1007	XLVI	122	53.20
XLV	69	95.4, 6	XLVII	122D	92.3
XLV	70	96	XLVII	122F	92.4
XLV	71	97	LII	122O	92.5
XLV	72	50.10			

Ungnad, VAS 1

No.	RINAP 2	No.	RINAP 2	No.	RINAP 2
71	103	72	50.6	73	77.7

Vera Chamaza, Omnipotenz

No.	RINAP 2	No.	RINAP 2	No.	RINAP 2
11–13	1	29	67	116a	7
28	65	101	65	116b	2

Walker, CBI

P.	No.	RINAP 2
64–65	76 (Sargon II O)	123.2–5
117	166 (Sargon II A)	54.1–3
117	167 (Sargon II C)	50.1–5
118	168 (Sargon II D)	53.1–11
118–119	169 (Sargon II F)	95.1–3
119	170 (Sargon II G)	96.1–2
119	171 (Sargon II X)	110.1

Winckler, Sar.

[Note: Those texts that are mentioned in the Introduction of volume 1 of Winckler, Sar., and have copies in volume 2, but are not edited, are listed first, via the page and reference number to them in the Introduction to volume 1. For the other texts the page number and reference number in the Introduction are not given as the main reference in the concordance below. Two further texts neither mentioned in the Introduction nor edited in volume 1, but with copies in volume 2, are listed at the end of the chart.]

Concordance A:

P., Pl., and No.	RINAP 2
pp. X–XI no. 6 and pls. 41–42	9
p. XI no. 8 and pl. 43	43
p. XI no. 9 and pls. 42–44	44–47
pp. 2–79 and pls. 1–28 nos. 1–52, 55, 58–60; pp. VII–IX no. 3	1–4, 6
pp. 76–79 (lines 441–460)	8
pp. 80–95 and pls. 25–27, 29 nos. 53–54, 56–57, 61–62	8
pp. 96–135 and pls. 30–36 nos. 63–78; p. X no. 4	7
pp. 136–139 and pl. 37 no. I; p. X no. 5	10
pp. 138–143 and pl. 37 no. II; p. X no. 5	11
pp. 142–147 and pls. 37–38 no. III; p. X no. 5	12
pp. 146–157 and pls. 38–40 no. IIII; p. X no. 5	13
pp. 158–163 and pl. 40 no. V; p. X no. 5	14
pp. 164–167 and pl. 40; p. XI no. 7	41
pp. 168–173 and pl. 48; p. VI no. 1	73
pp. 174–185 and pls. 46–47; pp. VI–VII no. 2	103
pp. 186–189 and pls. 44–46; pp. XI–XII no. 10	82
p. 190 and pl. 49 no. 1	49
p. 190 and pl. 49 no. 2.a	23
p. 190 and pl. 49 no. 2.b	24
p. 190 and pl. 49 no. 2.c	25
p. 190 and pl. 49 no. 2.d	26
p. 190 and pl. 49 no. 2.e	27
p. 190 and pl. 49 no. 2.f	30
p. 190 and pl. 49 no. 2.g	31
p. 190 and pl. 49 no. 2.h	32
pp. 190–191 and pl. 49 no. 2.i	34
p. 191 and pl. 49 no. 2.k	35
p. 191 and pl. 49 no. 2.l	37
p. 191 and pl. 49 no. 2.m	39
p. 191 and pl. 49 no. 2.n	38
pp. 190–191 and pl. 49 no. 2.o	28
pp. 191–192 and pl. 49 no. 3A; p. XII no. 11	16
p. 192 and pl. 49 no. 3B; p. XII no. 11	17
p. 192 and pl. 49 no. 4	77
p. 192 and pl. 49 no. 5	77
p. 193 and pl. 49 no. 6	53
p. 193 and pl. 49 nos. 7a–b	50
p. 194 and pl. 49 no. 8	51
p. 194 and pl. 49 no. 9	55
pp. 194–195 and pl. 49 no. 10	54
p. 195 and pl. 49 no. 11	95
p. 196 and pl. 49 no.12	SAA 11 no. 49
p. 196 and pl. 49 no. 13	61
p. 196 and pl. 49 nos. 14–15	92
pl. 26 no. 55 bottom two lines	40
pl. 49 no. 2.o	28

Concordance B:

[Note: This concordance only includes those text copies in Winckler's volume 2 that are found on wall slabs. Those that Winckler indicates were collated from squeezes are indicated with ^{c} after his copy number. Those that were not collated have not been used in the present volume; however, the equivalent text and section here is cited within square brackets.]

Pl. and No.	RINAP 2
pl. 1 no. 1	[1 §1]
pl. 1 no. 2^{c}	1 §2
pl. 2 no. 3^{c}	1 §5
pl. 2 no. 5	[1 §7]
pl. 3 no. 4^{c}	1 §6
pl. 3 no. 6^{c}	1 §8
pl. 4 no. 7^{c}	1 §9
pl. 4 no. 8^{c}	1 §10
pl. 5 no. 9	[1 §11]
pl. 5 no. 10^{c}	1 §12
pl. 6 no. 11^{c}	1 §13
pl. 6 no. 12^{c}	1 §14
pl. 7 no. 13^{c}	1 §15
pl. 7 no. 14^{c}	1 §16
pl. 8 no. 15^{c}	1 §17
pl. 8 no. 16^{c}	1 §18
pl. 9 no. 17^{c}	1 §20
pl. 9 no. 18^{c}	1 §23
pl. 9 no. 19	[1 §25]
pl. 10 no. 20^{c}	1 §26
pl. 10 no. 21	[1 §27, 28]
pl. 10 no. 22^{c}	1 §29
pl. 11 no. 23^{c}	1 §30
pl. 11 no. 24^{c}	1 §32
pl. 12 no. 25^{c}	1 §35
pl. 12 no. 26	[1 §36]
pl. 13 no. 27^{c}	3 §1′
pl. 13 no. 28^{c}	3 §3′
pl. 14 no. 29^{c}	3 §4′
pl. 14 no. 30^{c}	1 §21

Pl. and No.	RINAP 2	Pl. and No.	RINAP 2	Pl. and No.	RINAP 2
pl. 15 no. 31[c]	1 §22	pl. 22 no. 47[c]	2 §25	pl. 30 no. 63[c]	7.1 §1
pl. 15 no. 32[c]	2 §20	pl. 23 no. 48[c]	2 §26	pl. 30 no. 64[c]	7.1 §2
pl. 16 no. 33[c]	2 §21	pl. 23 no. 49[c]	2 §27	pl. 31 no. 65[c]	7.1 §3
pl. 16 no. 34[c]	2 §5	pl. 24 no. 50[c]	2 §28	pl. 31 no. 66[c]	7.1 §4
pl. 17 no. 35[c]	2 §6	pl. 24 no. 51[c]	2 §29	pl. 32 no. 67[c]	7.1 §5
pl. 17 no. 36	[2 §12]	pl. 25 no. 52	[2 §30]	pl. 32 no. 68[c]	7.1 §6
pl. 18 no. 37	[2 §13]	pl. 25 no. 53[c]	8 §5	pl. 33 no. 69[c]	7.1 §7
pl. 18 no. 38	[2 §14]	pl. 25 no. 54[c]	8 §6	pl. 33 no. 70[c]	7.1 §8
pl. 19 no. 39[c]	2 §16	pl. 26 no. 55	[6 §1′]	pl. 33 no. 71[c]	7.1 §9
pl. 19 no. 40[c]	2 §17	pl. 26 no. 56[c]	8 §1	pl. 34 no. 72[c]	7.1 §10
pl. 19 no. 41[c]	2 §18	pl. 27 no. 57[c]	8 §2	pl. 34 no. 73[c]	7.1 §11
pl. 20 no. 42[c]	2 §19	pl. 27 no. 58[c]	4 §1′	pl. 35 no. 74[c]	7.1 §12
pl. 20 no. 43[c]	2 §22	pl. 28 no. 59[c]	4 §2′	pl. 35 no. 75[c]	7.1 §13
pl. 21 no. 44[c]	2 §23	pl. 28 no. 60	[4 §3′]	pl. 36 no. 76[c]	7.1 §14
pl. 21 no. 45[c]	2 §24	pl. 29 no. 61	[8 §3]	pl. 36 no. 77[c]	7.1 §15
pl. 22 no. 46[c]	2 §24	pl. 29 no. 62	[8 §4]	pl. 36 no. 78[c]	7.4 §13

Younger, COS 2

P.	No.	RINAP 2	P.	No.	RINAP 2
293–294	2.118A	1–4	297	2.118F	8
294	2.118B	105	298	2.118G	13
295	2.118C	89	298	2.118H	43
295–296	2.118D	74	298–299	2.118I	73
296–297	2.118E	7	299–300	2.118J	116